# THE COLD CASE BILLY THE KID MEGAHOAX

**THE PLOT TO STEAL BILLY THE KID'S IDENTITY AND TO DEFAME SHERIFF PAT GARRETT AS A MURDERER**

**BY GALE COOPER**

GELCOUR BOOKS

COVER AND BOOK DESIGN BY GALE COOPER

## OTHER BILLY THE KID BOOKS
## BY GALE COOPER

### THE HISTORY

*BILLY AND PAULITA: THE SAGA OF BILLY THE KID, PAULITA MAXWELL, AND THE SANTA FE RING*

*BILLY THE KID'S WRITINGS, WORDS, AND WIT*

*THE LOST PARDON OF BILLY THE KID: AN ANALYSIS FACTORING IN THE SANTA FE RING, GOVERNOR LEW WALLACE'S DILEMMA, AND A TERRITORY IN REBELLION*

*THE SANTA FE RING VERSUS BILLY THE KID: THE MAKING OF AN AMERICAN MONSTER*

*THE CORONER'S JURY REPORT OF BILLY THE KID: THE INQUEST THAT SEALED THE FAME OF BILLY BONNEY AND PAT GARRETT*

### THE HOAXES

*CRACKING THE BILLY THE KID CASE HOAX: THE STRANGE PLOT TO EXHUME BILLY THE KID, CONVICT SHERIFF PAT GARRETT OF MURDER, AND BECOME PRESIDENT OF THE UNITED STATES*

*CRACKING THE BILLY THE KID IMPOSTER HOAX OF BRUSHY BILL ROBERTS*

*BILLY THE KID'S PRETENDER JOHN MILLER*

*THE BILLY THE KID'S BAD BUCKS HOAX: FAKING BILLY BONNEY AS A WILLIAM BROCKWAY GANG COUNTERFEITER*

*BLANDINA SEGALE, THE NUN WHO RODE ON BILLY THE KID: SLEUTHING A FOISTED FRONTIER FABLE*

**For the real Billy Bonney,
whose enemies named him
the outlaw Billy the Kid**

"["Brushy Bill"] Robert's claim [to be Billy the Kid] is a 'slur on the character of my father and on every pioneer in New Mexico at that time' ... I have never capitalized on being Pat Garrett's son," Oscar Garrett said. "I just want to see the record kept straight."

- OSCAR GARRETT, SON OF PAT GARRETT. *Albuquerque Journal.* " 'Billy the Kid' Bubble Bursts as Gov. Mabry Rejects Oldster's Claim." December 1, 1950

**And in memory of
random man, William Hudspeth;
dug from his grave, and torn apart
for no reason, by rampaging,
unpunished "Brushy Bill" and
"Billy the Kid Case" hoaxers**

COPYRIGHT © 2019 Gale Cooper
All Rights Reserved.

FIRST EDITION

*Reproductions, excerpts, or transmittals
of the author's original text or art in this book
are prohibited in any form whatsoever
without written permission of the author.
Infringers will be prosecuted
to the fullest extent of the law.*

ISBN: 978-1-949626-14-8 HARDCOVER
ISBN: 978-1-949626-15-5 PAPERBACK
LCCN: 2019932556

GELCOUR BOOKS
ALBUQUERQUE, NEW MEXICO

ORDERING THIS BOOK:
Amazon.com, BarnesandNoble.com, bookstores

WEBSITE:
GaleCooperBillytheKidBooks.com

YOUTUBE CHANNEL:
Gale Cooper's Real Billy the Kid

Printed in the United States of America
on acid free paper

# CONTENTS

PREFACE ..................................................................................... ix
AUTHOR'S FOREWORD ............................................................ xx
METHODOLOGY ...................................................................... xxii
ACKNOWLEDGMENTS ........................................................... xxii

## PART I:
## HOAXES HIJACKING HISTORY

### CHAPTER 1:
### HOAXING HISTORY

OVERVIEW ................................................................................... 3

### CHAPTER 2:
### THE HOAXES' IMPASSABLE HURDLES

THE CORONER'S JURY REPORT .................................................. 7
STATUTE OF LIMITATIONS FOR MURDER ................................ 16

### CHAPTER 3:
### MORE HISTORICAL HURDLES

A MOUNTAIN OF RECORDS ....................................................... 17
ANTIQUATED SOURCES FOR HOAXING ................................... 18
KEY FIGURES AND OFFICIAL DOCUMENTS ............................ 20
PUBLIC IGNORANCE AS SALVATION ........................................ 30

### CHAPTER 4:
### HISTORY OF BILLY BONNEY

REAL HISTORY ........................................................................... 31
BILLY BONNEY'S CHAMPIONS ................................................... 50

### CHAPTER 5:
### REAL BILLY BONNEY IN HIS OWN WORDS

SPEAKING THROUGH TIME ....................................................... 57
AFFIDAVIT AND DEPUTIZING .................................................... 58
DEPOSITION TO FRANK WARNER ANGEL .............................. 59
"REGULATOR MANIFESTO" ....................................................... 64
HOYT BILL OF SALE ................................................................... 65
LETTER OF MARCH 13, 1879 TO LEW WALLACE ..................... 66
LETTER OF MARCH 20, 1879 TO "SQUIRE" WILSON ................ 67

LETTER OF MARCH 20, 1879 TO LEW WALLACE ................... 67
THE LEW WALLACE INTERVIEW ........................................ 68
THE "BILLIE" LETTER TO LEW WALLACE ........................... 71
LOST GRAND JURY TESTIMONY ......................................... 72
TESTIMONY AGAINST N.A.M. DUDLEY ............................... 73
LETTER OF DECEMBER 12, 1880 TO LEW WALLACE ........... 77
SANTA FE JAIL LETTER: JANUARY 1, 1881 ........................ 79
SANTA FE JAIL LETTER: MARCH 2, 1881 ............................ 80
SANTA FE JAIL LETTER: MARCH 4, 1881 ............................ 80
SANTA FE JAIL LETTER: MARCH 27, 1881 .......................... 81
LETTER TO ATTORNEY EDGAR CAYPLESS ...................... 82
NEWSPAPER INTERVIEWS ................................................ 83
CONCLUSION .................................................................... 88

# PART II:
# THE "BRUSHY BILL" ROBERTS BILLY THE KID IMPOSTER HOAX

## CHAPTER 1:
## CREATORS OF THE "BRUSHY BILL" IMPOSTER HOAX

THE "BRUSHY BILL" HOAX ................................................. 91
THE "BRUSHY BILL" HOAX TRIUMVIRATE .......................... 92
CREATING THE HOOK AND THE BOOK ............................ 100

## CHAPTER 2:
## "BRUSHY BILL'S" BEGINNING AS BILLY

A PASSEL OF PRETENDERS ............................................. 101
BETTING ON "BRUSHY" ................................................... 103
MORRISON'S RESEARCH ................................................. 104

## CHAPTER 3:
## THE BILLY THE KID PARDON PRIZE

PRIMED FOR THE PARDON PRIZE .................................... 115
PARDON REJECTED BASED ON NO BILLY THE KID
    TO PARDON .................................................................. 116
"BRUSHY'S" PRESS .......................................................... 118
HIDDEN HOAXBUSTING TREASURE ................................. 128

## CHAPTER 4:
## THE BOOK TITLED
## *ALIAS BILLY THE KID*

MORRISON RISES FROM THE ASHES .................................. 129
FORMULATING THE HOAX ................................................ 132
TALL TALE TREASURE TROVE ............................................ 135
OTHER LIKELY SOURCES .................................................. 138
THE "BRUSHY" TEAM'S DILEMMAS .................................... 140

## CHAPTER 5:
## *ALIAS BILLY THE KID'S*
## HOAXING EXPOSED

MAKING A BETTER "BRUSHY" ............................................ 143
CREATING "BRUSHY'S" NARRATIVE .................................... 144
THE TITLE'S FAKE ALIAS .................................................. 146
THE PROLOGUE LAUNCHES THE HOAX ............................... 147
FAKING LIFE AS BILLY THE KID ......................................... 152
FAKING LIFE AFTER BILLY'S DEATH .................................... 191
FAKE PHOTO SECTION ...................................................... 193
FAKING EVIDENCE ............................................................ 195
"EPILOGUE": "BRUSHY'S" LAST SHOT ................................. 221
APPENDICES AND PARTING WORDS .................................... 222
SUMMARIZING *ALIAS BILLY THE KID'S*
   "BRUSHY BILL" IMPOSTER HOAX ................................... 223

## CHAPTER 6:
## TRUE-BELIEVERS CONTINUE
## THE "BRUSHY BILL" HOAX

WHEN DUPES REPLACE CHARLATANS .................................. 225
INTRODUCTORY MISINFORMATION ..................................... 226
MANGLED HISTORY OF BILLY THE KID ............................... 227
INTRODUCING THEIR MAN "BRUSHY" ................................. 231
EXPANDING A FAKE FAMILY TREE" .................................... 233
"BRUSHY" TALKS NONSENSE ............................................. 236
ALLEGED ANALYSES .......................................................... 248
FAKE "FORENSIC" PHOTO-COMPARISON ............................. 252
CONSPIRACY THEORIES .................................................... 254
THE JAMESON-BEAN OUTCOME ......................................... 264

## CHAPTER 6:
## "BRUSHY BILL" GETS TO HOLLYWOOD

A GREAT STORY ............................................................... 265

## CHAPTER 7:
## SUMMARIZING THE "BRUSHY BILL" HOAX

"BRUSHY BILL" AS A RIDICULOUS PARODY OF BILLY BONNEY .................................................. 267

# PART III:
# THE JOHN MILLER BILLY THE KID IMPOSTER HOAX

## CHAPTER 1:
## JOHN MILLER'S BILLY THE KID BID

RIDING ON "BRUSHY'S" COATTAILS ................................. 271
MANUFACTURING MILLER AS BILLY ............................... 272
BARE-BONES FAKE HISTORY OF BILLY THE KID ........... 275
MILLER'S LIFE AFTER BILLY'S DEATH .............................. 277
OLD-TIMERS SAY MILLER WAS BILLY .............................. 277
CONCLUDING FAKERY .......................................................... 281
SUMMARY ................................................................................. 282

# PART IV:
# THE "BILLY THE KID CASE" HOAX

## CHAPTER 1:
## CREATION OF THE "BILLY THE KID CASE" HOAX

LEGACY OF "BRUSHY BILL" .................................................. 285
DIABOLICAL DNA DECEPTION ........................................... 288
HOAX PROGRESSION ............................................................ 297

## CHAPTER 2:
## "BILLY THE KID CASE" HOAXERS AND HOAX DOCUMENTS

STARTING GATE BLOCKADES ............................................. 305
HOAXERS AND HOAX DOCUMENTS ................................. 313
HOAX INSTIGATOR: GOVERNOR BILL RICHARDSON ..... 314
LAWMEN "MURDER INVESTIGATORS":
  TOM SULLIVAN, STEVE SEDERWALL,
  GARY GRAVES, AND RICK VIRDEN ................................ 314
HOAX PUPPETEER: ATTORNEY BILL ROBINS III ............ 377
OFFICIAL HISTORIAN: PROFESSOR PAUL HUTTON ....... 388

FEDERAL HOAXER: U.S. MARSHALS SERVICE
    HISTORIAN DAVID TURK .................................................. 393
FAKE FORENSICS WITH DR. HENRY LEE ............................ 401
HOAX ENABLER: LINCOLN COUNTY ATTORNEY
    ALAN MOREL ................................................................... 421

## CHAPTER 3:
## ILLEGAL EXHUMATIONS OF JOHN MILLER AND WILLIAM HUDSPETH

DESCENT TO CRIMINALITY .................................................. 423
SHERIFF RICK VIRDEN LEADS THE EXHUMATIONS ........ 423
FAKING JOHN MILLER BELIEVERS: FELLOW HOAXERS
    DALE TUNNELL AND TOM SULLIVAN ............................. 425
TARGETING ARIZONA ........................................................... 427
THE SECRET FRENZIED DIG ................................................ 429
EXPOSED IN THE PRESS ....................................................... 430
THE HORROR SHOW OF RAVAGED GRAVES .................... 431
THE DNA TRAVESTY ............................................................. 432
THE PAPER TRAIL FOR ILLEGAL EXHUMATIONS ............. 433
BACK TO DIGGING UP CATHERINE ANTRIM ................... 440

## CHAPTER 4:
## "BRUSHY" GETS BACK IN THE MOVIES

THE HOAX MAKES THE CANNES FILM FESTIVAL ............ 441

## CHAPTER 5:
## TRYING TO DIG UP "BRUSHY BILL"

HEADING TO TEXAS WITH SHOVELS .................................. 443

## CHAPTER 6:
## STOPPING RICHARDSON'S "BRUSHY BILL" PARDON

THE PARDON PLOT ................................................................ 445
LAST MINUTE PARDON PETITION ...................................... 448
LEW WALLACE'S REAL DNA ................................................. 457
RIGHT UP TO THE END ........................................................ 462
BITTER "BIG BILL'S" LAST LIE ............................................ 464

## CHAPTER 7:
## EXPOSING THE
## "BILLY THE KID CASE" IN COURT

OPEN RECORDS SHOWDOWN.................................................... 465
SUMMARY OF OPEN RECORDS FIGHT ................................. 465
HOAXERS' LIES TO HIDE RECORDS ....................................... 467
THE LAWMEN'S MAJOR HOAX DOCUMENTS
   TO HIDE INCRIMINATING RECORDS ................................. 478
FORGING DR. HENRY LEE REPORTS ..................................... 498
THE JUDGE'S DECISIONS............................................................ 513
"BILLY THE KID CASE" HOAX UPSHOT ................................ 520

## PART V:
## THE RETURN OF "BRUSHY'S"
## TRUE-BELIEVER, W.C. JAMESON,
## AS A HOAXER

### CHAPTER 1:
### RETURN OF FAKERY IN
### BILLY THE KID: BEYOND THE GRAVE

AN ALLIANCE MADE IN HOAXER HEAVEN ........................ 523
HOAXBUSTING *BILLY THE KID: BEYOND THE GRAVE*..... 524
MAKING A BETTER "BRUSHY"................................................. 524
THE HOAXBUSTING MOON OF JULY 14, 1881 ..................... 526
CELSA GUTIERREZ AS OMNISCIENT NARRATOR ............. 528
THE "TRAVELING" ARMORY ................................................... 528
ATTACKING THE DEBUNKING................................................. 529
CONCLUSION: THE SAME OLD SCAM
   IN NEED OF NEW BLOOD ..................................................... 536

### CHAPTER 2:
### FURTHER FAKERY IN
### BILLY THE KID: THE LOST INTERVIEWS

FAKING "BRUSHY'S" WORDS..................................................... 537
UPGRADING THE "BRUSHY BILL" HOAX............................... 538
THE MYSTERY TRUNK AND TAPES......................................... 539
TRANSCRIBING THE "BRUSHY" TAPES ................................ 541
FAKING THE "BRUSHY" TRANSCRIPT .................................. 542
DISCUSSION .................................................................................. 562

## CHAPTER 3:
## DEFAMING IN *PAT GARRETT: THE MAN BEHIND THE BADGE*

THE "BRUSHY" HOAX'S HEART OF DARKNESS .................. 563
FAKING PAT GARRETT HISTORY ............................................. 565
STAGE SET FOR A MEGAHOAX .................................................. 579

# PART VI:
# COLD CASE BILLY THE KID MEGAHOAX

## CHAPTER 1:
## THE RETURN AS A MEGAHOAX

A KLEIDOSCOPE OF HOAXING .................................................. 583

## CHAPTER 2:
## FAKING BILLY THE KID HISTORY KNOWLEDGE

RETURN OF THE IGNORANCE OF
   *THE RETURN OF THE OUTLAW BILLY THE KID* ............ 585

## CHAPTER 3:
## FRAMING THE KID AS A COUNTERFEITER

RECYCLING AN OLD HOAX BY STEVE SEDERWALL .......... 609
REALITY OF BILLY AS A RUSTLER ......................................... 609
REALITY OF THE SECRET SERVICE AND THE KID .......... 610
REALITY OF WILLIAM BROCKWAY'S
   COUNTERFEITING GANG ...................................................... 614
STEVE SEDERWALL'S COUNTERFEITING ARTICLES ........ 618
THE RETURN OF SEDERWALL'S
   COUNTERFEITING FICTION ................................................. 623
A NON-EXISTENT CASE ............................................................. 652

## CHAPTER 4:
## FAKE LITTLE "INVESTIGATIONS

WEE NOT-AS-WRITTEN SCAMS ................................................ 653
ATTACKING PAT GARRETT'S AUTHORITY ........................... 653
FAKE DISCOVERY OF "BILLY THE KID" MONIKER ........... 656
FAKE DISCOVERY OF TOM O'FOLLIARD BEING
   TOM "FOLLIARD" ..................................................................... 657

## CHAPTER 5:
## FAKE "INVESTIGATION" OF STINKING SPRINGS

DISCOVERING A PORT-HOLE MAKING URINATION PLOT, A GUN, AND BAD MONEY, WHILE KEEPING A STRAIGHT FACE .............. 661

## CHAPTER 6:
## FAKE JAILBREAK "INVESTIGATION"

THE LEAD-UP .............. 667
THE "BILLY THE KID CASE" HOAX'S COURTHOUSE-JAIL FAKERY .............. 667
RETURN OF THE "BILLY THE KID CASE" AS SEDERWALL'S "INVESTIGATION" OF THE DEPUTY BELL SHOOTING .............. 669
RETURN OF THE "BILLY THE KID CASE" AS SEDERWALL'S "INVESTIGATION" OF GARRETT AS ESCAPE ACCOMPLICE .............. 675
ATTACKING PAT GARRETT BY "BRUSHY BILL" AND "BILLY THE KID CASE" HOAXES .............. 678

## CHAPTER 7:
## FAKING DEATH SCENE DOUBTS

THE MEGAHOAX'S HEART .............. 681
FAKING DISCREPANCIES .............. 682
FAKING A MAXWELL DOOR DISCREPANCY .............. 685
FAKING SHOOTING SCENE DOUBTS .............. 692
FAKING THE BODY'S REMOVAL .............. 694
FAKING A "PETER MAXWELL" .............. 695
NOTHING BUT FAKING .............. 698

## CHAPTER 8:
## FAKING NO INQUEST

HOAXERS VERSUS CORONER'S JURY REPORT .............. 699

## CHAPTER 9:
## THE RETURN OF FAKE FORENSICS

THE "BILLY THE KID CASE'S" HOAXED FORENSICS .............. 701
FAKING CARPENTER'S BENCH FORENSICS .............. 701
FAKING "MAXWELL FURNITURE" FORENSICS .............. 703

## CHAPTER 10:
## THE RETURN OF THE "BILLY THE KID CASE'S" EXHUMATION FAKERY

THE RETURN ATTACK ON JOHN MILLER'S BONES ........... 705
RETURN TO "BRUSHY" FOR "DNA FORENSICS" ................. 707

## CHAPTER 11:
## THE RETURN OF THE CONSPIRACY THEORIES

FANTASIZING PLOTS AGAINST "TRUTH" ............................. 709
SEDERWALL'S CONSPIRACY AGAINST HIMSELF ............. 710

## CHAPTER 12:
## FORGONE CONCLUSION

WHEN HOAXERS FOOL THEMSELVES ................................. 719

## PART VII:
## SUMMARY AND CONCLUSIONS

## CHAPTER 1:
## NOTHINGS PLUS NOTHING EQUALS NOTHING

MUCH ADO ABOUT NOTHING ............................................... 723

**ANNOTATED APPENDIX** ........................................................ 725

**ANNOTATED BIBLIOGRAPHY**

COMPREHENSIVE REFERENCES ............................................ 775
HISTORICAL ORGANIZATIONS .............................................. 775
   SANTA FE RING ................................................................. 775
   NORTH CAROLINA REGULATORS, 18TH CENTURY ..... 778
   LINCOLN COUNTY REGULATORS, 19TH CENTURY ..... 778
   SECRET SERVICE, 19TH CENTURY .................................. 778
NEW MEXICO TERRITORY REBELLIONS AGAINST
   THE SANTA FE RING ........................................................ 780
HISTORY OF WILLIAM HENRY BONNEY ............................ 783
OTHER HISTORICAL FIGURES (PERIOD) ............................ 792
OLIVER "BRUSHY BILL" ROBERTS
   BILLY THE KID IMPOSTER HOAX ................................... 818
JOHN MILLER BILLY THE KID IMPOSTER HOAX ............. 828
"BILLY THE KID CASE" HOAX" ............................................. 828
COLD CASE BILLY THE KID MEGAHOAX OF
   W.C. JAMESON'S 21ST CENTURY BOOKS ..................... 866

**INDEX** ........................................................................................ 875

# **PREFACE**

Howdy. I'm the old-timer pard of this here author, here to tell you that man's the only animal that can be skinned more then once. Cause I'm fictional, I sniff out fiction easy. Well, the gang pushing the fiction that Sheriff Pat Garrett never did shoot Billy the Kid is riding back into town with guns blazing. These fellas pushing loco old-timer "Brushy Bill" Roberts is now in cahoots with the fellas pushing their fake "Billy the Kid Case" calling Garrett a murderer. They's fixing to rustle Billy Bonney's history - with him being famous Billy the Kid; and them being nothing cept hankering after fame, and full of wind as a bull on corn.

On account of folks already knowing they's liars, they now call their tall tales *Cold Case: Billy the Kid*; figering changing pasture would make their scrawny calf look fatter. It's for folks who's easy to buffalo, or has a case of the slow, or is virgins - excuse the French - to reading books with real history.

As usual, this here author is locking horns with any campaign against truth when it comes to Billy. Seems she's got no cold feet to bust into such hot territory, since a ticket to the misty beyond seemed possible in her last fray with these same varmints. She took them on when she fought the "Billy the Kid Case," when it was started up by New Mexico's Governor Bill Richardson - so crooked a snake'd break his back trailing him; and so low that he was fixing to hand Texas New Mexico's famous Billy the Kid history for his publicity stunt for hisself. And she thought she stopped them. Hahaha.

Now, personally, I'd say this here author is barking at a knot. Old-timers with addled think boxes saying they's Billy the Kid has been around since the last century; and, even though they is as fake as a rustler's hair brand on a cow, they still find them suckers to bamboozle. And the "Billy the Kid Case" was just Santa Fe Ring shenanigans - meaning New Mexico officials being in cahoots to line their own pockets, which has not stopped since Billy's day. And nobody - I mean nobody - has ever broke that Ring. This here author has as much chance as a grasshopper in an anthill. So I'm hoping that she finally gets tired of Billy the Kid, since he just attracts trouble.

Vern Blanton Johnson, Jr.
Lincoln, Lincoln County, New Mexico

# AUTHOR'S FOREWORD

This book is to expose two Billy the Kid hoaxes which have now combined for a mutually reinforcing rerun in the 2018 book, *Cold Case Billy the Kid* by W.C. Jameson. They are the old "Brushy Bill" Roberts Billy the Kid imposter hoax, and the modern "Billy the Kid Case" forensic DNA hoax based on it. Both rest on fabricating that Pat Garrett did not kill Billy the Kid, and that Billy survived to old age. Both got press and profit by seeking the 1879 pardon promised to Billy by Governor Lew Wallace.

The first half of the 20th century was a heyday for old-timers promulgating Billy the Kid imposter hoaxes and fabricating personal contact with the Kid in his lifetime. It was also the time of minimal scholarly research, so their tall tales were built on outlaw mythology of the press, dime novel-style books, and their own imagination.

It has been my mission to expose this fakery because it masks the magnificence of the history of Billy Bonney, whose moniker Billy the Kid was devised by his enemies. His 1870's period in New Mexico Territory was marked by grass-roots uprisings against the corrupt land grabbing political and mercantile cabal of the Santa Fe Ring. The lost Lincoln County War of 1878, in part an Hispanic uprising, which made Billy famous, was the biggest and bloodiest, and crushed the freedom fighters' movement.

But with his brilliance, bi-culturalism, charisma, refusal to flee the Territory, and dare-devil escapes from imprisonment and assassination, Billy became the people's hero; and was a potential instigator of another Hispanic uprising. Pursued by the Ring - using Secret Service-assisted lawman, Pat Garrett - Billy's death by a hanging trial was inevitable. Only his escape, and defiant refusal to leave his young Fort Sumner lover, Paulita Maxwell, made a different death inevitable: his midnight ambush killing by Garrett in Paulita's brother's mansion's bedroom on July 14, 1881.

The first full-fledged Billy the Kid history hijacker was, surprisingly, a missionary nun to the frontier Southwest named Blandina Segale, who published her 1932 book, *At the End of the Santa Fe Trail*, with claims of a friendship with a demonic, scalping, highwayman outlaw Billy the Kid, "the greatest murder of the Southwest." I exposed her in my 2017 book: *Blandina Segale, The Nun Who Rode on Billy the Kid: Sleuthing a Foisted Frontier Fable*. Her scam lifted historic names and events from traceable sources. The give-away was her repeating those sources' errors.

That fakery of turning antiquated sources into first-person experience was used by the best known Billy the Kid imposter, Oliver "Brushy Bill" Roberts, and his hoaxing backer and eventual author, William V. Morrison; first for a failed 1950 pardon request to New Mexico Governor Thomas Jewett Mabry; then for a 1955 book: *Alias Billy the Kid*. I exposed imposter hoaxes in my 2010 book: *Billy the Kid's Pretenders, Brushy Bill and John Miller*.

In 2003, there arose arguably the most elaborate historic and forensic hoax ever attempted. Based on "Brushy Bill's" claim of surviving Pat Garrett's shooting, and backed by unlimited tax dollars from New Mexico's corrupt Governor, Bill Richardson, it claimed Garrett had willfully murdered an innocent victim to protect Billy, and filed a real murder investigation against him to prove his guilt by faked DNA matchings intended to show that Billy was actually "Brushy Bill," buried in Texas; and the innocent victim lay in Billy's Fort Sumner grave. I stopped it by years of litigation, and exposed it in 2010 and 2014 respectively in my books: *MegaHoax* and *Cracking the Billy the Kid Case: The Strange Plot to Exhume Billy the Kid, Convict Sheriff Pat Garrett of Murder, and Become President of the United States*.

In 2018, a "Brushy"-believer named W.C. Jameson allied with some "Billy the Kid Case" hoaxers for his book: *Cold Case Billy the Kid*; thus, uniting the "Brushy Bill" and "Billy the Kid Case" hoaxes under a concealing new name. It used the same fakery of Pat Garrett murdering an innocent victim; now called a "cold case," and glossed by additional pseudo-historical "investigations." Again, the goal was portraying "Brushy" as Billy, and history as being not as written.

So I wrote this book to demonstrate and debunk the diabolical intricacy of the culminating hoaxing. And the unpleasant labor of dealing with this outrageous junk was justified by the need to protect the real history of Billy Bonney and the Lincoln County War freedom fight from debasement to cartoonish fiction.

Gale Cooper, M.D.
Sandia Park, New Mexico

# METHODOLOGY

**PRIMARY DOCUMENTS:** For readers' reference, primary documents are presented; with italics for handwriting, two column newsprint for articles, and in distinctive font for books.

**COMMENTARY:** Author's notes and responses are provided in boldface; boldface is also used to highlight important claims by hoaxers; underlings and italics are added for emphasis; page numbers are given for cited text in books, or to refer back to pages in this book itself; and the "Appendix" and "Bibliography" are annotated.

# ACKNOWLEDGMENTS

Overriding is my debt to Billy Bonney, whose cause, courage, intelligence, and joie de vivre are my inspiration.

Special thanks goes to the honorable family of Oliver "Brushy Bill" Roberts. In 1987, his full brother's daughter, Geneva Roberts Pittmon, one of his family care-takers with whom he lived, exposed him in a letter to the Billy the Kid Outlaw Gang's founders as a 20 year too young imposter. And "Brushy" was the maternal half great-granduncle of Roy L. Haws, who exposed him in his 2015 book, *Brushy Bill: Proof that His Claim to be Billy the Kid Was a Hoax*, providing "Brushy's" true genealogy. And, using Roberts family interviews, historian Don Cline, debunked "Brushy" in his 1988 unpublished book, *Brushy Bill Roberts: I Wasn't Billy the Kid.*

Historical bedrock is from books by Frederick Nolan on Billy the Kid, the Lincoln County War, and John Henry Tunstall. As valuable is Leon Metz's Pat Garrett biography and Jerry (Richard) Weddle's book on Billy Bonney's early adolescence.

Hoaxbusting appreciation goes to brave journalist, Jay Miller, who acted as my open records proxy in my early dangerous days of exposing Governor Bill Richardson's "Billy the Kid Case" hoax.

Special assistance came from Michael Sampson, at the National Archives Secret Service Library Counterfeit Division, concerning a Billy the Kid counterfeiting hoax in *Cold Case Billy the Kid*. Other National Archives divisions used were the Civilian Records Branch, the Justice Department, and the Department of the Interior.

Collections used were at the Las Cruces, New Mexico State University Library's Rio Grande Historical Collections' Herman B. Weisner Papers, ca. 1957-1992 and Blazer Family Papers, 1864-1965; the Albuquerque, University of New Mexico Center for Southwest Studies, University Library, Catron Papers; the State of New Mexico Office of Cultural Affairs Historic Preservation Division; the Office of the New Mexico State Historian; the Silver City Museum and Library; the Midland, Texas Nita Stewart and J. Evetts Haley Memorial Library and Historical Center; the Canyon, Texas Panhandle-Plains Historical Museum; and the Morgantown, West Virginia & Regional History Center at West Virginia University Libraries' Stephen B. Elkins Papers.

Collections used for William Bonney's and Lew Wallace's documents were the Santa Fe, New Mexico, Fray Angélico Chávez Historical Library; and the Indianapolis, Indiana Historical Society's Lew and Wallace Collection.

Billy Bonney's unique Spencerian penmanship was discussed with Mott Media; David Sull; and the Iowa, Ames Historical Society's curators, Dennis Wendell and Sarah Vouthilak.

# PART I

## HOAXES
## HIJACKING
## HISTORY

# CHAPTER 1
# HOAXING HISTORY

## OVERVIEW

This book exposes Billy the Kid imposters: tricksters hijacking his identity and history as a shortcut to fame and fortune. Madmen, imposters, charlatans, hoaxers, hucksters, forgers, windbags, and wannabes, they make a pathetic and unsavory lot; whose eventual championing by a corrupt, self-promoting, 21st century, New Mexico governor gave them access to the world stage. All insulted legitimate historical investigation. That makes this book a study of lying, from delusional to malicious; matched with the gullibility of hoodwinked victims.

More profoundly, this book is a testament to the actual history unknown to those pretenders: a Territory-wide freedom fight against the deadly Santa Fe Ring political cabal, that culminated in the Lincoln County War Battle, which made a grass-roots hero of young, charismatic, bi-cultural zealot, Billy Bonney; and marked him for killing as the mythologized outlaw Billy the Kid.

It is also a demonstration that historical research is both a science and an art, requiring the skill to find correct data, and the ability to analyze it to decipher events' meaning. The historical hoaxers covered here, trying to mimic investigations, demonstrate just how hard it is to uncover fact as opposed to foisting fiction.

This book is also a manual for hoaxbusting, illustrating the extremity of labor needed to sleuth and expose chicanery this massive. Nothing can be taken for granted, since, at this level of profiteering and sociopathy, no claimed source can be accepted as accurate, no document is above being forged, fallacious straw man reasoning and fake conspiracy theories substitute for evidence, and truths are hidden. The conniving promulgators, assembled here, rely on a normal reader's trust in authoritative information beyond their knowledge. But here, readers are hoaxers' victim-dupes, cynically sold flimflam, disguised as historical discoveries with attention-grabbing claims.

## *THE GROWTH OF THE OUTLAW MYTH*

Billy Bonney's true story began with corrupted history. Even his moniker, "Billy the Kid," was created by his enemies to vilify him as their outlaw-murderer creation. The time was the 1870's, when New Mexico Territory was in the throes of multiple grass-roots uprisings against the land-grabbing political cabal of the deadly Santa Fe Ring: the real outlaws hiding their villainy.

In 1872, legislators in Santa Fe rose up against the increasing Ring stranglehold, and were suppressed by the Ringite Governor. In 1876, to the southwest, was the Grant County Rebellion, in which citizens wrote a "Declaration of Independence" and tried to secede and join Arizona Territory to escape the Ring. From 1875 to 1877, Ring atrocities escalated to the north, in the Colfax County War, with assassination of the anti-Ring leader and with terrorized citizens' futile exposés to Ring-biased President Rutherford B. Hayes. The people's culminating defeat was the 1878 Lincoln County War, where Ring-beholden troops illegally enabled citizens' murder; and in which Billy Bonney became a grass-roots hero, emerging as a future threat with his bi-cultural links and potential for eliciting an Hispanic uprising.

The result was Billy's outlawing by the Ring, magnified by his 1879 pardon bargain with Governor Lew Wallace, who disreputably reneged under Ring pressure, and concealed his moral failure by self-justifying additions to the Ring's outlaw myth of Billy the Kid. By 1882, Sheriff Pat Garrett capitalized on his fame for killing Billy the year before by publishing his own outlaw myth rendition. That mold was not broken by the scholarly historians of the latter half of the 20th century, who merely plastered new findings onto that antique armature.

It has taken my research, analyses, and books to restore Billy Bonney to his freedom fighter glory, along with his compatriots, in that period when democracy was destroyed by the Ring's infiltration of the executive, legislative, judicial, and law enforcement offices; and when opponents were destroyed by malicious prosecutions, massacres, assassinations, and military suppression. The Ring's victor's option of writing history hid those magnificent rebellions. Likewise, I have exposed modern Ring politics keeping New Mexicans silenced by learned helplessness.

From the ashes of fear and falsehood, Billy Bonney, after death, rose nevertheless, keeping alive, by his extreme fame, the lure of his times, until the truth could emerge.

## EMERGENCE OF HISTORICAL PARASITES

There was a peculiar side-effect of Billy's posthumous fame: the emergence of mentally disturbed, attention-seeking old men, in the second quarter of the 20th century, who claimed to be him. Since Billy was fatally shot in Fort Sumner on July 14, 1881 by Pat Garrett, that necessitated these imposters' second fabrication: accusing Pat Garrett of killing the wrong man and covering it up.

This was also the period in which fascination for Billy's story was so insatiable that his old-timer contemporaries achieved publishing books with their own mundane life stories, simply by adding him. And the most glib Billy the Kid impersonators followed suit by attracting hoaxing profiteering authors.

The problem these fabricating historical parasites faced was insurmountable: scholarly history books about Billy Bonney's life, and the specifics of the dramatic events in which he participated, had not yet been written. There was only the antiquated outlaw mythology of the 19th century, with its seepage into the early 20th century. So cribbing fake fables was the imposters' undoing. But their salvation was an equally benighted public, unable to distinguish hoaxes from truth, and eager for tales of Billy the Kid.

## PUBLICIZED PRETENDERS

One pretender outdistanced the others because he got an energetic huckster promoter, a publicity hook, and a book. Born in Arkansas, and named Oliver Pleasant Roberts, his delusions and attention-seeking endowed him with multiple famous Old West identities, among them Billy the Kid; though he named himself "Brushy Bill." His discoverer was a traveling salesman named William V. Morrison, who impersonated a lawyer, and had already unsuccessfully floated an Old West imposter tale about himself. Morrison was a hardworking showman. He researched his day's documentation of Billy the Kid. And he saw its publicity hook: Billy's lost pardon for Lincoln County War indictments. Morrison would seek that pardon for "Brushy" from New Mexico's current governor. Though this scheme ultimately failed, it kindled public imagination, yielded his book on "Brushy," and rippled out over time to get true-believer converts, who doggedly peddled the lies and held dear conspiracy theories as to "Brushy's" rejection.

A second imposter, an Arizonian named John Miller, has no known believers, was phlegmatic in self-promotion as Billy the

Kid, and got an equally lethargic author. He was long ignored, but burst into public awareness as one object in the biggest, most elaborate, internationally publicized, and best funded historic-forensic hoax ever perpetrated: the 2003 "Billy the Kid Case." And his illegal exhumation, along with the random man buried beside him, marked the hoaxes' descent from devious to criminal.

## THE "BILLY THE KID" CASE HOAX

The "Billy the Kid Case," beginning in 2003, was a self-serving publicity stunt of corrupt New Mexico Governor Bill Richardson and his major political donor, who was a "Brushy Bill" believer.

It was a murder investigation against Pat Garrett, with modern CSI glamour of DNA matchings from exhumations. The covert intent was anointing "Brushy" as Billy. That it was historically indisputable that Garrett killed Billy, and that no forensically valid, Billy the Kid DNA existed anywhere for DNA matching, were kept secret. The scam's genius was to legitimize exhumations by claiming they were part of a filed "cold case" murder investigation against Garrett for killing the innocent victim. And Lincoln and De Baca County Sheriffs Departments' lawmen became Richardson's agents for the fake investigation.

My fighting that hoax in district courts stopped the exhumations of Billy and his mother, then revealed its DNA fraud. And I wrote exposé books. Without all that, the history would have been destroyed, beyond retrieval, by these hoaxers.

## THE "COLD CASE BILLY THE KID" MEGAHOAX

In 2018, longstanding "Brushy"-believer and author, W.C. Jameson, partnering with past "Billy the Kid Case" hoaxers, combined the "Brushy Bill" and "Billy the Kid Case" hoaxes in his book: *Cold Case Billy the Kid*. His objective was to cast doubt on the recorded history - even including imposter John Miller as a survivor possibility - to propose once again that his man "Brushy" was actually Billy Bonney. Its pernicious result was resuscitating both scams in the public forum, and necessitating this book.

# CHAPTER 2
# THE HOAXES' IMPASSABLE HURDLES

## THE CORONER'S JURY REPORT

The survival hoaxes were over before they started because of the Coroner's Jury Report for the inquest of July 15, 1881 identified Pat Garrett's victim on July 14, 1881 as William H. Bonney. Originally in Spanish **[Figure: 1]**, its translated conclusion was published in the July 23, 1881 *Rio Grande Republican* in Garrett's announcement to Acting-Governor William Ritch.

The Report described San Miguel County Justice of the Peace Alejandro Segura, as *ex officio* coroner: *"[I]mmediately upon receiving said information [of a murder in Fort Sumner] I proceeded to the said place and named Milnor Rudolph, Jose Silva, Antonio Sevedra, Pedro Antonio Lucero, Lorenzo Jaramillo and Sabal Gutierres a jury to investigate the case."*

The body was identified: *"[The jury] found the body of William Bonney alias "Kid" with a shot in the left breast."*

The eye-witness was interviewed: *"[T]hey examined the evidence of Pedro Maxwell, which evidence is as follows: "I being in my bed in my room, at about midnight on the 14th day of July, Pat F. Garrett came into my room and sat down. William Bonney came in and got close to my bed with a gun in his hand and asked me "who is it" and then Pat F. Garrett fired two shots at the said William Bonney and the said William Bonney fell near my fire place and I went out of the room and when I came in again about three or four minutes after the shots the said William Bonney was dead."*

The jurymen's verdict stated: *"[T]he deed of said Garrett was justifiable homicide."*

That Report also confirmed its being filed with the District Attorney of the First Judicial District, William Breeden, to confirm no murder charges needed to be prepared against Garrett.

# THE TRANSLATED CORONER'S JURY REPORT

Territory of New Mexico ) Precinct No. 27
County of San Miguel )

To the District Attorney of the First Judicial District of the Territory of New Mexico,

Greetings:

On this 15th day of July, A.D. 1881, I, the undersigned, Justice of the Peace of the above named precinct, received information that a murder had taken place in Fort Sumner, in said precinct, and immediately upon receiving said information I proceeded to the said place and named Milnor Rudulph, Jose Silva, Antonio Sabedra, Pedro Antonio Lucero, Lorenzo Jaramillo and Sabal Gutierres a jury to investigate the case and the above jury convened in the home of Luz B. Maxwell and proceeded to a room in the said house where they found the body of William Bonney alias "Kid" with a shot in the left breast and having examined the body they examined the evidence of Pedro Maxwell, which evidence is as follows:

"I being in my bed in my room, at about midnight on the 14th day of July, Pat F. Garrett came into my room and sat at the end on my bed to talk with me. A little while after Garrett sat down, William Bonney came in and got close to my bed with a gun in his hand and asked me "Who is it Who is it?" and then Pat F. Garrett fired two shots at the said William Bonney and the said Bonney fell near my fire place and I went out of the room and when I came in again about three or four minutes after the shots the said Bonney was dead."

The jury has found the following verdict:

We the jury unanimously find that William Bonney has been killed by a bullet in the left breast in the region of the heart, the same having been fired from a pistol in the hand of Pat F. Garrett, and our verdict is that the act of said Garrett was justifiable homicide and we are unanimous in the opinion that the gratitude of all the community is due to the said Garrett for his deed and is worthy of being rewarded.

M. Rudulph, President
Anto Sabedra
Pedro Anto Lucero
Jose x Silba
Sabal x Gutierrez
Lorenso x Jaramillo

All which information I put at your disposal.

Alejandro Segura Justice of the Peace

Territorio de Nuevo Méjico ⎱ Precinto N° 27.
Condado de San Miguel ⎰ del 4°no y Distrito judicial
  Al Procurador ~~General~~ del Territorio de Nuevo
Méjico                                    Salud.

    Este dia 15 de Julio, A.D. 1881, recivi
yo, el abajo firmado, Juez de Paz del Precinto arriba
escrito, informacion que habia habido una muerte
en Fuerte Sumner en dicho precinto e immediata-
mente al recivir la informacion procedí al
dicho lugar y nombré á Milnor Rudulph,
José Silva, Antonio Saavedra, Pedro Antonio
Lucero, Lorenzo Jaramillo y Sabal Gutierres
un jurado para averiguar el asunto y ven-
nier el dicho jurado en la casa de
Luz Maxwell procedieron á un cuarto
en dicha casa donde hallaron el cuerpo
de William Bonney alias "Kid" con un balazo en el pecho en el lado yzquierdo del pecho
y habiendo ecsaminado el cuerpo ecsaminaron
la evidencia de Pedro Maxwell cuya evidencia es como sigue " Estando yo acostado en

FIGURE: 1. Original Spanish Coroner's Jury Report of July 15, 1881 for William H. Bonney aka Kid (Courtesy of the Indiana Historical Society, Lew Wallace Collection)

mi cama en mi cuarto a cosa de media noche El dia 14 de Julio entró á mi cuarto Pat. F. Garrett y se sentó en la orilla de mi cama á platicar conmigo. A poco rato que Garrett se sentó entró William Bonney y se arrimó á mi cama con una pistola en la mano y me preguntó "Who is it? Who is it?" y Entónces Pat. F. Garrett le tiró dos balazos á dicho William Bonney y se cayó el dicho Bonney en un lado de mi fogon y yo salí del cuarto cuando volví á entrar yá en tres ó cuatro minutos despues de los balazos estaba muerto dicho Bonney."

El jurado há hallado el siguiente dictámen "Nosotros los del jurado unanimemente hallamos que William Bonney há sido muerto por un balazo en el pecho yzquierdo en la region del Corazon tirado de una pistola en la mano de Pat. F. Garrett y nuestro dictámen es que el hecho de dicho Garrett fué homicidio justificable y estamos unánimes en opinion que la gratitud de toda la

comunidad es devida á dicho Garrett
por su hecho y que es digno de ser recompensado."  
      *[firma]*  
       Presidente

    Antº Saavedra  
     Pedro Antº Lucero  
    Jose + Silba  
    Tobal + Gutierrez  
    Lorenzo + Jaramillo

Todo cuya informacion pongo á
conocimiento de V.

      Alejandro Segura  
      Juez de Paz

# *PAT GARRETT'S LETTER TO THE GOVERNOR*

On July 15, 1881, Pat Garrett sent a letter, with enclosed copy of the Coroner's Jury Report, to Acting-Governor William Ritch confirming his killing of Billy Bonney. It was quoted in July 23, 1881's Las Cruces *Rio Grande Republican* as "Kid the Killer Killed, Wm. Bonney alias Antrim, alias Billy the Kid, Fatally Meets Pat Garrett, the Lincoln County Sheriff." It stated: "Below is given Sheriff Garrett's report as made to Acting Governor Ritch which contains also the verdict of the coroner's jury [with the reporter giving an English translation, but explaining: 'The verdict is given in Spanish in Garrett's report']."

Garrett's quoted letter stated:

Fort Sumner, N.M., July 15, '81 - To his Excellency the Governor of New Mexico:

"I have the honor to inform your Excellency that I had received several communications from persons in and about Fort Sumner, what William Bonney, alias the Kid, had been there, or in that vicinity for some time.

"In view of these reports I deemed it my duty to go there, and ascertain if there was any truth in them or not, all the time doubting their accuracy; but on Monday, July 11, I left home, taking with me John W. Poe and T.L. McKinney, men in whose courage and sagacity I relied implicitly, and arrived just below Fort Sumner, on Wednesday, 13th [sic]. I remained concealed near the houses, until night, and then entered the fort about midnight, and went to Mr. P. Maxwell's room. I found him in bed, and had just commenced talking to him about the object of my visit at such an unusual hour, when a man entered the room in stockinged feet, with a pistol in one hand and a knife in the other. He came and placed his hand on the bed just beside me, and in a low whisper, "who is it?" (and repeated the question) he asked Mr. Maxwell.

I at once recognized the man, and knew he was the Kid, and reached behind me for my pistol, feeling almost certain of receiving a ball from his at the moment of my doing so, as I felt sure he had now recognized me, but fortunately he drew back from the bed at noticing my movement, and, although he had his pistol pointed at my breast, he delayed to fire, and asked me in Spanish, "Quien es? Quien es?" This gave me time to bring mine to bear on him, and the moment I did so I pulled the trigger and he received his death wound, for the ball struck him in the left breast and pierced his heart. He never spoke, but died in a minute. **It was my desire to have been able to take him alive, but** his coming upon me so suddenly and unexpectedly leads me to believe that he had seen me enter the room, or had been informed by someone of the fact; and that he came there armed with pistol and knife expressly to kill me if he could. Under that impression I had no alternative but to kill him or to suffer death at his hands.

I herewith annex a copy of the verdict rendered by the jury called in by the justice of the peace (ex officio coroner), the original of which is in the hands of the prosecuting attorney of the first judicial district."

(The verdict is given in Spanish in Garrett's report, and upon being translated is as follows:

"We the jury unanimously say that William Bonney came to his death by a wound in the breast in the region of the heart, fired from a pistol in the hand of Pat F. Garrett, and our decision is that the action of said Garrett, was justifiable homicide; and we are united in opinion that the gratitude of all the community is due to said Garrett for his action, and he deserves to be compensated."
(Signed) M. Rudolph, Foreman,
Antonio Savedra,
Pedro Antonio Lucero,
Sabal Gutierres,
Lorenzo Jaramillo

I am Governor, very respectfully your Excellency's obedient servant,
Pat F. Garrett

## *THE ISSUE OF NO CULPABILITY*

Pat Garrett's quoted letter of July 15, 1881 to Acting-Governor William Ritch also functioned to confirm his innocence of murder. **It confirmed that he had followed proper legal procedure and sent the original Coroner's Jury Report to District Attorney for the First Judicial District William Breeden, responsible for San Miguel County, in which was homicide site Fort Sumner;** and who would have checked the verdict: "[O]ur verdict is that the action of said Garrett was justifiable homicide." That this killing was accepted as self-defense, is proved by prosecutor Breeden filing no murder charge against Garrett, and later assisting the processing of his reward payment.

Garrett's letter to Ritch had stated: "I herewith annex a copy of the verdict rendered by the jury called in by the justice of the peace (ex officio coroner), **the original of which is in the hands of the prosecuting attorney of the first judicial district."**

## THE ISSUE OF REWARD

Garrett's letter to Acting-Governor William Ritch also initiated the process of collecting his reward. The Coroner's Jury Report had presented no problem with its conclusion stating: "[W]e are unanimous in the opinion that the gratitude of all the community is due to the said Garrett for his action, and he deserves to be rewarded."

As will be further discussed below, since it was misstated in service of the "Brushy Bill" hoax, issuing the reward was complicated by two variables: its being a private reward made by past-Governor Lew Wallace, and its not being a dead-or-alive offer. The reward offer, published by Wallace in December 22, 1880's *Las Vegas Daily Gazette*, and May 3, 1881's *Santa Fe Daily New Mexican*, had stated: "I will pay $500 reward to any person or persons who will capture William Bonney, alias The Kid, **and deliver him to any sheriff of New Mexico.** Satisfactory proofs of identity will be required."

To cover that Bonney was now dead (i.e., not deliverable alive), Garrett's letter to Ritch explained that capture had been impossible, and killing the only option: **"It was my desire to have been able to take him alive, but his coming upon me so suddenly and unexpectedly leads me to believe that he had seen me enter the room, or had been informed by someone of the fact, and that he came there armed with pistol and knife expressly to kill me if he could. Under that impression I had no alternative but to kill him or to suffer death at his hands."**

And the "Kid the Killer Killed" article showed agreement; stating: "William Bonney, alias 'the Kid,' is dead. No report could have caused more general feeling of gratification than this, and when it was further announced that the faithful and brave Pat Garrett, he who had been the mainstay of law and order in Lincoln county, the chief reliance of the people in the dark days, when danger lurked at every hand, has accomplished the crowning feat of his life by bringing down the fierce and implacable foe single-handed, the sense of satisfaction was heightened to one of delight."

## LOCATING THE REPORT

After the Coroner's Jury Report fulfilled its uses, it was filed poorly. In 1935, in his book, *Wranglin' the Past: Reminiscences of Frank M. King*, in the chapter titled "The Kid's Exit," "Frank M. King published that Garrett's letter to Acting Governor William Ritch had recently been located in old files of the Secretary of

State of New Mexico. And the finding of that Report made the November 30, 1950 front page of the *Alamogordo News* as "Fort Sumner Jury Thought The Kid Had Been Killed." It stated that the report had been found in 1932 by a then-deceased New Mexico state employee, Harold Abbott, in the State capitol basement. Abbott had made copies for himself and others, including his brother George Abbott. The article stated:

Although the perennial controversy over whether the infamous Billy the Kid still lives, has again arisen, at least one Alamogordo man, Frank Phillips, 84, claims personal knowledge of his death in 1881 at the hands of the late Sheriff Pat Garrett, and George Abbott, also of Alamogordo has in his office at the Pioneer Abstract Co., a photostatic copy of the verdict of the coroner's jury which viewed the remains of the late Wm. Bonney

Some twenty years ago, when the late Harold Abbott, brother of George, was an employee of the state land office in Santa Fe, he, with other employees, were going over some old records in the basement of the state capitol. There they ran across, **in the San Miguel court records**, the original copy of the coroner's jury, dated July 15, 1881, and written in Spanish. The document covered three pages of which they made photostatic copies.

As the reader will see from the document, translated below, the six men serving on the jury and the Justice of the Peace who empanneled them, seemed convinced that Wm. Bonney, known as "Kid," was quite dead, and that he had been killed by Pat Garrett.

The most recent controversy arose when a firm of El Paso lawyers appealed to Governor Mabry for a full pardon for Wm. Bonney, who claims that the man killed at Fort Sumner by Pat Garrett was another outlaw, and not the Kid at all; that the Kid left the country, assumed the name of ["Brushy Bill"] Roberts, and has lived in Old and New Mexico all this time.

The documentary evidence of the Kid's death is translated as follows:

Territory of New Mexico
San Miguel County
Precinct No. 27
To the attorney of the 1st Judicial district of the Territory of New Mexico:
Greetings: [The English Translation followed]

# STATUTE OF LIMITATIONS FOR MURDER

The second hurdle for imposter hoaxes was needing a real homicide case against Garrett to claim his "cold case" covered-up murder of an innocent victim. But that was in 1881. So claimed was that New Mexico had no statute of limitation for murder.

But New Mexico had that statute. The 1876 *Acts of the Legislative Assembly of the Territory of New Mexico* established a **10 year limitation on prosecution for murder** after the alleged crime. This appeared in the 1882's *The General Laws of New Mexico* Edited by L. Bradford Prince, under "Limitation of Criminal Actions, Acts of the Legislative Assembly of the Territory of New Mexico, Twenty-Second Session, Chapter 13. Section 1."

With the killing on July 14, 1881, the possibility of prosecution ended in 1891. The statute stayed in effect as (NMSA) 1953, 40A-1-8(3). It stated:

### CHAPTER XIII.

AN ACT to provide the limitations of criminal actions.

### CONTENTS

Sec. 1. Limitation; - murder, within ten years; 2d, manslaughter, six years; 3d, perjury and other felonies, three years; 4th, misdemeanors, two years; 5th, violation of revenue laws, three years

Sec. 2. Provides if defendant absconds or secretes himself the limitation shall not hold for that time.

*Be it enacted by the Legislative Assembly of the Territory of New Mexico:*

SECTION 1. No person shall hereafter be prosecuted, tried, or punished, in any court of this Territory; unless the indictment shall be found, or information filed therefore as hereinafter limited and provided.

**First. For murder, within ten years from the time of the offence or act was committed.**

Second. For manslaughter, or any other killing of a human being, except murder in the first degree, within six years from the time the offence was committed.

# CHAPTER 3
# MORE HISTORICAL RECORDS HURDLES

## A MOUNTAIN OF RECORDS

Billy the Kid history fabricators picked an impossible period to hoax. It had a huge store of historical records generated by Billy and the uprisings against the Santa Fe Ring. But for mid-20th century imposters, most were still undiscovered, and the scholarly history books were not yet written. That forced fabricating their life as Billy. Duped true-believers later ignored accumulating facts, and merely made conspiracy theories. And 21st century forensic fraudsters relied on public ignorance for their lying.

For validating truth, there existed Billy's extensive recorded words and writings, plus his contemporaries' autobiographical publications describing him in detail. An undisputed tintype of him at age 20 is famous. In addition, 1870's New Mexico Territory grass-roots uprisings against the Santa Fe Ring generated massive output of letters, petitions, exposés, newspaper articles, court transcripts, a federal investigation with depositions and reports, a military court of inquiry, and Secret Service reports; all giving intimate details of Billy's world.

What did exist for imposters was history's junkyard: lurid dime novel-style publications cashing in on Billy the Kid mythology, and windbag oldsters spinning malarkey for self-aggrandizement, or trading hearsay and rumor for attention. Fortunately, for exposing the impersonators, their parroting of others' fakeries exposed their own. And even coaching of them by hoaxing authors from the few legitimate sources required their remembering a mind-boggling complexity and profusion of events. Their limited intelligence made that hard task unworkable.

Modern pretender promoters responded to this information hurdle by ignoring the historical record, or accusing historians of a conspiracy against them. In truth, these hoax promoters relied on public ignorance of the facts which laid bare their fabrications.

# ANTIQUATED SOURCES FOR HOAXING

It is important to take stock of sources available to the old-timer Billy the Kid malarkey spouters and imposters, to expose their scamming. Most flagrant was "Brushy Bill" Roberts, with authors coaching and editing to fraudulently claim he knew things not printed, or that he was illiterate so could not read-up on things printed. Ergo, he must have been there as Billy the Kid!

## *AVAILABLE TO IMPOSTERS*

Billy the Kid imposters in the second quarter of the 20th century knew about mythologized falsified fame of an outlaw boy named Billy the Kid, who murdered a man for each of his twenty-one years, and was killed by a Sheriff named Pat Garrett.

For more life details, there were just a few quasi-historical books. There was a 1927 reprint of Pat Garrett's 1882, ghost-written, dime novel-style *The Authentic Life of Billy the Kid The Noted Desperado of the Southwest, Whose Deeds of Daring and Blood Made His Name a Terror in New Mexico, Arizona, and Northern Mexico*. Adding minimally more was Walter Noble Burns's 1926 book, *The Saga of Billy the Kid*, based on Garrett's 1882 version. Robert N. Mullin and Maurice Garland Fulton were early researcher/writers, but no salvation for pretenders, who were left just with some historical names and a few big events.

To manufacture Billy himself, there were his pardon bargain letters with Governor Lew Wallace in the Lew Wallace Collection of the Indiana Historical Society at Indianapolis, with two more in personal possession of Wallace's grandson, Lew Wallace Jr. And known was his April 15, 1881 letter to Attorney Edgar Caypless, which existed only as a copy in New Mexico's Lincoln Museum.

And there were apparently available some pages of the 1879 Fort Stanton military Court of Inquiry for Commander N.A.M. Dudley, but lacking Billy Bonney's full testimony.

And because the historic town of Lincoln - site of the Lincoln County War Battle - has remained largely intact, it could be visited to fabricate past participation in events there. But lost for that trickery was the entire town of Fort Sumner, including the Maxwell family mansion in which Billy was killed, with only a few foundations of outlying buildings remaining. And the diagrams of the old fort seem to have been unavailable to the early hoaxers.

## *LATER SCHOLARLY HISTORY BOOKS*

The imposters were dead by the renaissance in Billy the Kid scholarship in the second half of the 20th century. In 1957, William Keleher's *Violence in Lincoln County 1869-1881* published both the original and translated Coroner's Jury Report. The unsurpassed scholarly researcher of the period, Frederick Nolan, published his *The Life and Death of John Henry Tunstall* in 1965; *The Lincoln County War: A Documentary History* in 1992; and *The West of Billy the Kid* in 1998. Billy's early adolescence in Silver City, New Mexico Territory, and Bonita, Arizona Territory, were unavailable until 1993 with Jerry Weddle's book, *Antrim is My Stepfather's Name: The Boyhood of Billy the Kid*. Other modern historians were Joel Jacobsen in 1994 with *Such Men as Billy the Kid: The Lincoln County War Reconsidered*; Philip Rasch with his 1995 compendium, *Trailing Billy the Kid*; and Robert Utley, with his 1989 *Billy the Kid: A Short and Violent Life*.

My own 21st century books, using major historical collections and new interpretations, added understanding of the role of the Santa Fe Ring from its 1866 origin, to its bloody Territorial take-overs of the 1870's, and its continuation to the present. There are 2012's *Billy the Kid's Writings, Words, and Wit;* 2017's *The Lost Pardon of Billy the Kid: An Analysis Factoring in The Santa Fe Ring, Governor Lew Wallace's Dilemma, and a Territory in Rebellion*; and 2018's *The Santa Fe Ring: The Making of an American Monster*. And, in multiple books, I have made it my mission to expose the profiteering hoaxes, from early 20th century origins to the present, that ride on Billy the Kid's coattails.

There also exists the marriage record of Billy's mother and step-father by Reverend David F. McFarland, in his Santa Fe, First Presbyterian Church's entry of March 1, 1873 listed in the *"Ledger: Session Records 1867-1874. Marriages in Santa Fe New Mexico. Mr. William H. Antrim and Mrs. Catherine McCarty."* Unpublished, it was unknown to the pretenders; so they had no clue about Billy's mother's name or brother, Josie, listed in it.

Pat Garrett himself got a major biographer, Leon Metz; whose *Pat Garrett: The Story of a Western Lawman* came out in 1974, and countered the defamation intrinsic in the pretender hoaxes based on Billy the Kid's not being killed by him on July 14, 1881.

And some of these later sources would reveal subsequent fakery, since the next generation of hoaxing authors surreptitiously used the new facts to fix-up the old scammers.

# KEY FIGURES AND OFFICIAL DOCUMENTS

Furthering imposter discrediting, were key figures in Billy's life, along with a multitude of depositions, court transcripts, and daily notes - all exposing their hoaxing by their ignorance of them.

## *INVESTIGATOR FRANK WARNER ANGEL*

The Frank Warner Angel depositions and reports on the murder of John Tunstall, the Lincoln County troubles, and corruption of public officials were discovered in 1956 by historian Frederick Nolan. Attorney Angel, an energetic and observant chronicler, was sent in May of 1878 by President Rutherford B. Hayes, and via the Departments of Justice and the Interior, to investigate the February 18, 1878 murder of John Henry Tunstall, as well as Territorial corruption. He produced a prodigious amount of first-hand documentation, including Billy Bonney's own June 8, 1878 deposition.

So, left for posterity, were Angel's 39 depositions and reports: October 4, 1878's *In the Matter of the Examination of the Causes and Circumstances of the Death of John H. Tunstall a British Subject*; October 4, 1878's *In the Matter of the Lincoln County Troubles*; October 3, 1878's *In the Matter of the Investigation of the Charges Against S.B. Axtell Governor of New Mexico*; and October 2, 1878's *Examination of Charges against F. C. Godfroy, Indian Agent, Mescalero, N. M.*

Aware of the Santa Fe Ring, but obstructed in its exposure by the corrupt administration of President Rutherford B. Hayes, frustrated Angel provided incoming Territorial Governor Lew Wallace with a secret notebook listing people's Ring affiliations; some of which Billy himself would have known.

As to real Billy Bonney, like all victims of the Santa Fe Ring, he would have been fully aware of Angel as a ray of hope. And he knowingly risked his life to give his deposition to Angel to get justice for his assassinated and admired employer John Tunstall. And real Billy would have seen the injustice that the Ring was left untouched except for scapegoating removal of one lower-tier member: Governor Samuel Beach Axtell.

The imposters, of course, lacked any notion of the specifics of Ring atrocities, or of Billy's articulate deposition about them.

## ATTORNEY IRA E. LEONARD

Billy's best friend in a high place was Attorney Ira E. Leonard, widow Susan McSween's attorney against past Commander N.A.M. Dudley for murdering her husband and arson of her home in the Lincoln County War Battle. Leonard, bravely took her case against Dudley right after the Ring murdered her first lawyer: Leonard's office-mate: Attorney Huston Chapman.

Leonard met Billy in March of 1879 when Billy was in his sham arrest in Lincoln for his Lew Wallace pardon bargain; and Leonard witnessed Billy's fulfilling that bargain by testifying in the April, 1879 Grand Jury against Attorney Huston Chapman's murderers. Reporting on Billy's behalf to Wallace in a letter of April 20, 1879, Leonard stated: *"I will tell you Gov. that the prosecuting officer of this Dist. [William Rynerson] is no friend to the enforcement of the law.* **He is bent on going for the Kid & ... is proposed to destroy his testimony & influence.** *He is bent on pushing him to the wall. He is a Dolan [Ring] man and is defending him by his conduct all he can."*

Leonard also aided the prosecution at Dudley's Fort Stanton Court of Inquiry, and would have heard Billy risking his life while testifying devastatingly against that past Commander; and consequently became his loyal attorney into 1881.

During Leonard's 1879 litigation against Commander N.A.M. Dudley, he sustained a near assassination by the Ring. Billy, nearby in his Patrón house sham arrest, would have known about that April 25, 1879 attempt.

Leonard also continued to assist Billy's pardon hope, even facilitating a possible one from the Secret Service. He then represented him in his 1881 Mesilla hanging trial, getting Billy's federal indictment for the "Buckshot" Roberts killing quashed; but quitting after a likely Ring death threat; leaving Billy with Ring-biased court-appointed attorneys.

But this central advocate in Billy's life was unknown to the pretenders, except for token name-dropping.

## COMMANDER NATHAN AUGUSTUS MONROE DUDLEY AND SUSAN McSWEEN

Comparable in magnitude to the Angel reports, is the Court of Inquiry for possible court martial for Fort Stanton's Commander N.A.M. Dudley. It has over a hundred testimonies of people involved in the Lincoln County War, including Billy's own, given on May 28th and 29th of 1879. Others speaking through time include the plaintiff herself, Alexander McSween's widow, Susan McSween, whose pivotal and courageous role in the post-war Lincoln County struggle was unknown to the pretenders. She would have seemed a heroine to Billy; and his testimony in the Dudley Court of Inquiry was on her behalf.

Billy's testimony, on his own anti-Ring initiative, in an honest court, would have achieved Dudley's court martial: Billy saw three of his white soldiers, likely officers, under order to shoot at least one volley at civilians, including Billy, escaping the burning McSween house. The imposters, of course, knew nothing of this.

Additionally, the foul-mouthed racism of "Brushy Bill" towards Dudley's black troops was belied not only by Billy's lack of it, but by the fact that he would have known that black 9th Cavalrymen, Private James Bush and Sergeant Huston Lusk, had, like him, risked their lives to testify against Dudley in the Court of Inquiry.

## SECRET SERVICE OPERATIVE AZARIAH WILD

Sent to New Mexico Territory from September to December of 1880 by the Secret Service, a Treasury Department branch, ostensibly to track counterfeiters, but, in fact, to eliminate anti-Ring Billy Bonney and remaining Regulators, New Orleans based Operative Azariah F. Wild, was one of 40 in the country. He wrote daily reports; thus, recording information about Billy Bonney in a format like the following; giving the date for the events documented, then the date on which he wrote the report:

### U.S. Treasury Department
**SECRET-SERVICE DIVISION**

_New Orleans_ District

**James J. Brooks,**
   **Chief U.S. Secret Service**

Sir: I have the honor to submit the following, my report as _Chief_ Operative of this District for _Monday_ the _29th_ day of _December,_ 18_79,_ written at _New Orleans, Louisiana,_ and completed at _9_ o'clock _A_ M on the _30th_ day of _December,_ 18_79_

Wild was duped by Ringmen into believing that Billy Bonney headed a counterfeiting and rustling gang. So Wild helped Pat Garrett become both Sheriff of Lincoln County and a Deputy U.S. Marshal to track down Billy. But Billy's attorney, Ira Leonard, proposed to Wild that Billy would testify against the actual counterfeiters in exchange for a pardon. Billy even wrote to Wild confirming the offer. On October 8, 1880, Wild described it:

> *I left Fort Stanton at 7 o'clock A.M. on the stage and reached Lincoln the County seat at 8:30 A.M. ... The object of my visit to Lincoln was to see Judge Ira Leonard ... In my report of October 5th ... I spoke of an outlaw whose name was Antrom alias Billy Bonney. During the Lincoln Co. War he killed men on the Indian Reservation for which he has been indicted in the territorial and the United States Court. Gov. Wallace has issued a proclamation granting immunity to those not indicted but as Antrom has been indicted the proclamation did not cover his (Antrom's) case and he (Antrom) has been in the mountains as an outlaw ever since a space of about two years time.*
>
> *Governor Wallace has since written Antrom's attorney on the subject saying he should be let go but has failed to put it on shape that satisfied Judge Leonard Antrom's attorney.*
>
> *It is believed and in fact is almost known that he (Antrom) is one of the leading members of this gang.*
>
> ***Antrom has recently written a letter to Judge Leonard which has been shown to me in confidence that leads me to believe that we can use Antrom in these cases provided Gov. Wallace will make good his written promises and the U.S. Attorney will allow the case pending in the U.S. Court to slumber and give him (Antrom) one more chance to reform.***
>
> *I have promised nothing and will not except to receive and propositions he Leonard and his client see fit to make and submit them to U.S. Attorney Barnes.*
>
> *Judge Leonard has written Antrom to meet him (Leonard) at once for consultation.*
>
> *The chances are that the conversation will take place within the next week I will report fully to you and submit whatever propositions they see fit to make to US. Attorney Barnes for such action as he deems proper to take.*

Ringites' interventions, however, made Wild decide to arrest Billy at the pardon meeting. Canny Billy, however, robbed the mail coach carrying Wild's reports, discovered Wild's fatal plan, and avoided the meeting. But he lost the second pardon chance.

The imposters were unaware of the Secret Service, of Azariah Wild, and of how close Billy actually came to getting his pardon at last. Obviously, Billy himself knew all that.

## *THE FRITZ INSURANCE POLICY CASE*

The imposters were unaware of the Santa Fe Ring's malicious prosecution of Attorney Alexander McSween for embezzling - with fraudulent entanglement of John Tunstall by wrongly claiming a business partnership - in the case of life insurance recovery for Emil Fritz, the deceased original partner in Lincoln's mercantile monopoly called "The House." Billy was certainly aware, having almost shot corrupt Sheriff William Brady's deputies doing the property attachments for the case at Tunstall's store, and then being eye-witness to Brady's posseman murdering Tunstall with excuse of those attachments. All that was the subject of Billy's June 8, 1878 deposition to Frank Warner Angel, and was the precipitant to the Lincoln County War uprising against the Ring - unknown to the impersonators, and fully known to Billy Bonney who became the people's hero in the ensuing lost freedom fight.

## *SHERIFF WILLIAM BRADY*

Lincoln County Sheriff William Brady was the Ring enforcer for the Fritz insurance policy case's fake embezzlement charge. Its documents still exist: the Action of Assumpsit to permit seizure of McSween's possessions, the Writ of Attachment (which falsely claimed a McSween-Tunstall partnership, making Tunstall's possessions seizeable also), and the inventory of items which Sheriff Brady attached. Billy, and the other Regulators, would have been aware of these machinations - and outraged.

As important, the case was part of a larger Ring scheme to kill Tunstall and McSween. Brady was such a danger to McSween, that Deputy Adolph Barrier - from McSween's arrest site in Las Vegas for the embezzling case - kept him in personal custody to protect him. After Barrier departed, and McSween was about to return to Lincoln for his Grand Jury trial, the Regulators - including Billy - knew Brady and his deputies would assassinate him that return day of April 1, 1878; since Brady had murdered Tunstall just 42 days earlier. So they ambushed Brady and his deputies. Brady and Deputy George Hindman died. (The killings of Brady and Hindman - as well as the Regulator killing of Tunstall murder posseman, Andrew "Buckshot" Roberts - constituted Billy's indictments for which he made the pardon bargain, then stood trial.) It was for the Brady killing that Billy got his hanging sentence in Mesilla on April 9, 1881.

The pretenders had no knowledge of Brady's role in the Lincoln County War, or the reason for Brady's ambush killing, or the Regulators existence, or Billy's reasonable mitigating defense that the ambush was done to save Alexander McSween's life.

## A.P. "PACO" ANAYA

A.P. "Paco" Anaya was a Fort Sumner friend of Billy's. His 1991, posthumously printed memoir held the truth in his title: *I Buried Billy*. Anaya was one of the 200 Fort Sumner residents who held a candle-light vigil for Billy's body on the night of July 14-15, 1881, all having identified him. Real dead Billy ends the imposters' and "Billy the Kid Case" promulgators' hoaxes.

## PAULITA MAXWELL

Unknown to the imposters was the romance of Billy and Paulita Maxwell, Billy's secret sweetheart in Fort Sumner. She was the daughter of deceased Lucien Bonaparte Maxwell, past owner of the 2 million acre Maxwell Land Grant and founder of Fort Sumner. Joining his young lover was the reason for Billy's post-jailbreak return to Fort Sumner - and almost certain death - rather than escaping to Old Mexico. And Billy was killed in the Maxwell mansion by Pat Garrett's ambush in her brother's bedroom.

Their love story was confirmed in an unpublished letter by historian, Walter Noble Burns. On June 3, 1926, he wrote to Jim East, one of Pat Garrett's Stinking Springs possemen:

> *I also know that the Kid and Paulita were sweethearts – at least I heard that story on most good authority many times. But I was unable to write it frankly because my publishers were afraid any such statement might lay them open to a libel suit.*

## *THE SANTA FE RING*

Pivotal to New Mexico Territory's 1870's history were the freedom fights against the rapaciously expanding Santa Fe Ring. Its Territorial "boss" was Thomas Benton Catron; his Washington, D.C. "co-boss" was Stephen Benton Elkins. Tunstall and McSween, aware of the Ring, would have informed Billy and Tunstall's other employees.

On April 27, 1877, writing to his family, Tunstall stated: *"Everything in New Mexico, that pays at all (you may say) is worked by a "ring."* (Nolan, *Life and Death*, of *John Henry Tunstall*, Page. 213)

Alexander McSween's February 23, 1878 letter to just-murdered Tunstall's father, John Partridge; stated: "[Tunstall] **understood well from the U.S. Attorney [Catron] to the lowest magistrate that there was a combination and determination to keep down independence. This combination is known as the "Santa Fe Ring." To the branch of the Ring down here he had become particularly obnoxious owing to the fact that he was acquiring so much land, and because I aided him."** (Nolan, *Documentary History of the Lincoln County War*, Pages 206-207)

The day before the start of the Lincoln County War Battle, and five days after outlaw John Kinney was used by Ringite Lincoln County Sheriff George Peppin for the massacre of McSween-side Hispanic residents of San Patricio, Billy wrote his July 13, 1878 "Regulator Manifesto" to Catron's brother-in-law, Edgar Walz, managing his Lincoln County Carrizozo cattle ranch, It stated: *"We are all aware that your brother-in-law,* **T.B. Catron sustains the Murphy-Kinney party** *... Steal from the poorest or richest American or Mexican, and the* **full measure of the injury you do, shall be visited upon the property of Mr. Catron."**

On November 14, 1878, soon after arriving in the Territory as Governor, Lew Wallace wrote to his friend Absalom Markland: *"I came here, and found a "Ring" with a hand on the throat of the Territory. I refused to join them, and now they are proposing to fight me in the Senate. Ex Delegate Elkins is head-center in Washington.*

Billy's attorney, Ira Leonard, knowledgeable about the Ring, wrote to Lew Wallace on May 20, 1879 about "The House's" partners, Lawrence Murphy and James Dolan: *"They were a part and parcel of the Santa Fe Ring that has been so long an incubus on the government of this Territory."*

Norman Cleaveland was a descendant of a Ring-fighting family in the Colfax County War. In his 1971 book, *The Morleys: Young Upstarts of the Southwest*, he wrote: "When my grandparents, William Raymond Morley and Ada McPherson Morley, pioneer New Mexicans, were in their twenties they were confronted with **an "establishment" known as the Santa Fe Ring**. By comparison, present-day establishments would rate rather as societies of butterfly collectors. (Cleaveland, p. viii)

The Santa Fe Ring is also in D.W. Meinig's 1998 *The Shaping of America: A Geographical Perspective on 500 Years of History, Volume 3: Transcontinental America 1850 - 1915*. Meinig wrote:

> In the 1870's anticipation of railroad connections to the East began to alter the prospects [in New Mexico] for profits and position. Slowly forming over the years, the "Santa Fe Ring" now emerged into full notoriety: "it was essentially a set of lawyers, politicians, and businessmen who united to run the territory and to make money of this particular region. Although located on the frontier, the ring reflected the corporative, monopolistic, and multiple enterprise tendencies of all American business after the Civil War. Its uniqueness lay in the fact that, rather than dealing with some manufactured item, they regarded land as their first medium of currency." "Land" meant litigation, and "down the trail from the states came ... an amazing number of lawyers" who, "still stumbling over their Spanish, would build their own political and economic empire out of the tangled heritage of land grants." And so, somewhat belatedly, a general repetition of the California situation got under way, and with the same general results: "eventually over 80 per cent of the Spanish grants went to American lawyers and settlers." Important differences were the presence in New Mexico of a much greater number of Hispanic peasants and communities well rooted on the land, the considerable resistance and violence generated by this American assault, and the sullen resentment created in an

increasingly constricted and impoverished people who felt they had been cheated out of much of their lands. In contrast to common representations it was not a case of vigorous, expanding society moving upon "a static culture," for "the Hispanos were still settling and conquering New Mexico, ever-extending their control" when the Anglos arrived. Here even more starkly than in California the conflict arose not just out of simple imperial position and crass chicanery but out of the clash of two fundamentally different sets of values, perceptions, and motivations. For ordinary Hispanos land was simply basic to a comfortable existence: "enough land to farm, enough pasture for stock, enough game to hunt, enough wood to burn, and enough material to build," all "to help one live as one ought to live" - including the continuity of such life generation after generation. Although operating to a great extent on tradition and custom, this was not the simple, "primitive" society most Anglos took it to be; it had its own laws relating to land and water, its own complexities of status, politics, and factions. To the Anglos land was a commodity to buy and sell, to exploit as quickly as possible, a means of profit and propellant of one's personal progress. Furthermore, "American land policy featured precise measurement and documentation, assumed individual ownership, and came out of a tradition that expected western land to be open for settlement." And it came out of eastern lands - out of the humid woodlands of Europe and America - and its assumptions about settlement and family farms, its rigid uniform rectangular survey system, its laws relating to water, cultivation, and seasonal use were incongruous with the needs and practices of Hispano farming and stock raising in the arid southwest. The most vulnerable parts of the Hispano system were the common lands, essential to the grazing economy, but often used without title, or held by a patron who ultimately sold or lost his title, or by a community grant that was readily challenged under American law and likely to be declared by the courts to be public land subject to routine survey and sale. This process of Anglo encroachment went through several phases over several decades but reached an important victory in an early court approval of the Maxwell Grant, an infamous case wherein the original 97,000 acres was inflated to nearly 2 million covering a huge county-sized area of prime piedmont lands. Well before the owner had certain title to this baronial tract he sold it to London speculators, and once the country that had "seemed worthless to Kearny's soldiers" became "an item in the stock exchange and a topic of interest in a dozen investment houses in Europe," the invasion of New Mexico had taken on a new momentum.

Unaware of the Ring's historical role and land-grabbing, except lifted, for name-dropping from an editor's note in Pat Garrett's *The Authentic Life of Billy the Kid*, the imposters missed real Billy's world - with his anti-Ring cause and the Ring's outlaw myth campaign to have him killed as "Billy the Kid."

## *THE BILLY BONNEY TINTYPE*

Billy appears in the flesh, at about age 20, in a full-length tintype photograph, thought to have been taken in Fort Sumner; forcing any imposter to match-up physically, and yielding failure by mismatch.

Ignorance that tintypes were right-to-left reversed, left mimicking impersonators claiming *left-handedness*, since Billy's *right hand* his cocked over his Colt 44's butt. Imposters also seized naively on details: like Billy's right ear happening to be pushed down by his jaunty rightward tilt of his hat brim, by claiming deformities in their *left* (tintype-reversed) ear! Small hands were claimed by impersonators to go along with the fable that Billy escaped the Lincoln courthouse-jail by slipping off his handcuffs, when his actual hand, cocked beside his gun butt, looks muscular and normal-sized.

Most repugnant, however, are photo-analysis "experts"-for-hire who matched aged imposters, "Brushy Bill" and John Miller, to that tintype to claim Billy the Kid identity matchings for each of these men, who bore no resemblance to Billy.

# PUBLIC IGNORANCE AS SALVATION

The old imposters, their scamming authors, and modern-day "Billy the Kid Case" hoaxers got a hearing only because of public ignorance of Billy the Kid's complex history. That enabled those fraudsters to spin Billy the Kid tales based on the Santa Fe Ring's original outlaw mythology of Billy the Kid, which had proliferated as mainstream books and movies.

Unknown, to this day, is that the Lincoln County War was a freedom fight of poor Anglo homestead farmers and disenfranchised Hispanic people against the land grabbing Santa Fe Ring seeking cattle ranching and mercantile monopolies. Unknown, to this day, is Billy Bonney's bi-cultural and bi-lingual role in bridging those two victimized sub-cultures, and bringing in Mexican fighters from nearby towns of San Patricio and Picacho into that War's final battle. Unknown, to this day, was Billy's future risk to the Ring as a potential leader of another uprising (along with equally zealous Hispanics, like his best friend, Yginio Salazar). Unknown too was Billy's more immediate risk to the Ring by testifying against its terrorist assassins - unless he was eliminated first. Certainly unknown, except by an occasional dropped name, were almost all the other historical participants in that unsung period when New Mexicans were willing to risk their lives to fight for their democratic rights.

So Billy the Kid's massive fame and popularity, plus massive ignorance about him, added up to an ideally non-critical but receptive audience for old imposters and modern hoaxers. But the antique oblivion and meaningless misinformation relied on by all these charlatans, is destined for failure and deserved ridicule, as the magnificent history of Billy Bonney and his compatriots becomes more commonly known. And juxtaposing the hoaxed claims of the imposters with known history ends their frauds.

And paralleling the exposure of Billy the Kid fakery, is righting the wrong done to famous lawman, Pat Garrett by the fraudsters, whose impersonations depended on claiming their own survival by fabricating that, by accident or by intent, he murdered an innocent victim to permit Billy the Kid to escape and live to old age. In fact, as will be seen, Garrett is the focus of the hoaxes most vicious lies, as attempt was made to paint him as the most evil of lawmen: murdering for ill-gotten lucre and fame.

# CHAPTER 4
# HISTORY OF BILLY BONNEY

## REAL HISTORY

Central to debunking the misinformation in the Billy the Kid imposter hoaxes, is Billy Bonney's history. It is a complex, colorful, traumatic life of a brilliant, charismatic, teenaged, literate, bi-cultural resistance fighter against the Santa Fe Ring; fit amazingly into just 21 years. Most of it was unknown to his old-timer impersonators. All of it was a problem to the modern "Billy the Kid Case" hoaxers.

\*\*\*\*\*\*\*\*\*\*\*\*\*\*

In a hot, full-mooned, New Mexico Territory night as bright as day, the 21 year old, homeless youth, Billy Bonney, with trusting stockinged feet, approached the porticoed, two story, Fort Sumner mansion of the Maxwell family, at about a quarter to mid-night.

That day, July 14, 1881, was the third anniversary of the Lincoln County War's start, which had left him branded as the outlaw, "Billy the Kid;" though, to himself, he was a freedom fighter: the last Regulator and that War's only participant to be convicted and sentenced to hanging.

That July night, he intended to cut a dinner steak from the side of beef hanging, at the patrón's generosity, on the mansion's north porch. But first he would check in, as requested, with that patrón and town owner, Peter Maxwell, at his south porch's corner bedroom.

Asleep in that mansion was Billy's secret lover, Maxwell's sister, Paulita, seventeen, and just pregnant with Billy's child. Also there, lived a never-emancipated Navajo slave, Deluvina; purchased, as a child, by Peter's and Paulita's fabulously wealthy, deceased father, Lucien Bonaparte Maxwell. Then, the family lived in Cimarron, a New Mexico Territory town in Colfax County, which Lucien had created on his and his wife's almost two million acre land grant; later named after himself.

That was before Lucien was cheated in the sale of that Maxwell Land Grant by unscrupulous lawyers, Thomas Benton Catron and Stephen Benton Elkins, who used their profits to propel their Santa Fe Ring. As Billy knew, that corrupt collusion of public officials still held New Mexico Territory in a stranglehold. As a hero in the failed Lincoln County War of 1878, Billy had fought that Ring. If Billy was thinking about his mortal danger, he knew its source was the Ring. If he thought about injustice, its focus would have been his promised pardon withheld by departed Territorial Governor Lew Wallace.

That July of 1881 day was 2½ months since Billy's jailbreak escape from his scheduled hanging on May 13th. He knew that Lincoln County Sheriff Pat Garrett would be in pursuit. Garrett had captured him on December 22, 1880 at Stinking Springs for his hanging trial. And in Billy's April 28, 1881 escape from Garrett's Lincoln jail, he had shot dead his deputy guards: James Bell and Robert Olinger. Garrett would kill him on sight.

When first tracking Billy in late 1880, Garrett had killed Billy's friends, Tom O'Folliard and Charlie Bowdre - missing Billy only by accident in two consecutive ambushes: at Fort Sumner and Stinking Springs. In fact, at the Stinking Springs capture of Billy and his companions, Garrett killed Bowdre by mistaking him for Billy: the prize for which the Ring had made Garrett a Sheriff.

To be near Paulita, Billy had recklessly chosen return to Fort Sumner, instead of fleeing to Old Mexico, the natural choice given his bi-culturalism. But he relied on the Maxwell family's protection, as well affection of the townspeople he had known since late 1877. It would take betrayal to bring his death.

Billy's life had been traumatic. Illegitimate, he was a second son, born on November 23, 1859, in New York City, as William Henry McCarty. Raised in Indiana with his brother, Josie, by his mother, Catherine, he became "Henry Antrim" after she married an Indiana man, William Henry Harrison Antrim, in 1873, after they relocated to New Mexico Territory. Antrim became a miner; and the family lived in Silver City. He was a rejecting father, evicting Billy at 14½ to homelessness when Catherine died of tuberculosis in 1874. But Billy's longing for a father remained, and he sometimes used the name "Antrim" for himself.

In Silver City's school, he learned Spencerian script. He also became fluent in Spanish; and, atypically, was equally comfortable in Anglo and Hispanic sub-cultures in those racist times. By 1975, 15½ year old Billy spent his last year in Silver City doing petty thievery, and butcher shop and hotel work; while altercations with local boys revealed his violent temperament.

By September, Silver City Sheriff, Harvey Whitehill arrested him for burglary, and laundry and revolver robbery; his adult accomplice having escaped. Facing ten years hard labor - the statutes making no provision for juveniles - he achieved his first dramatic escape: through the jail's chimney. He fled across the border to Arizona Territory's little town of Bonita.

In Arizona, as Henry Antrim, Billy again combined work - as a cook at a small hotel - with crime: stealing military blankets, saddles, and horses; while fatefully developing shootist skills. In 1876, incarcerated at local Fort Grant's guardhouse with his older, thieving accomplice, John Mackie, he escaped through a roof ventilation space. But he defiantly stayed in Bonita, relying on his rustling charges being dropped on a technicality, his first demonstration of risky behavior for his wish to have a "home."

On August 17, 1877, Billy's life again changed horrifically. His argument at Bonita's Atkins Cantina with a bullying blacksmith, Frank "Windy" Cahill, escalated to his fatally shooting that unknowably unarmed man. Billy escaped on a stolen horse. The Coroner's Jury declared him - as Henry Antrim - guilty of homicide, though in absentia; ignoring self-defense. So at 17½, Billy was almost hanged for murder. He escaped back to New Mexico Territory with an alias: William Henry Bonney - Billy Bonney. "Bonney" was likely his mother's maiden name.

In New Mexico Territory, by the next month of September, 1877, Billy attached himself to familiar sociopaths in Jessie Evans's murderous and rustling Santa Fe Ring-affiliated gang. And since all Ringites ended up immune to prosecution and profited financially, intelligent and energetic Billy, unknown to history, would have likely had a wealthy and long life.

But Billy had a conversion. He met kind, wealthy Englishman, John Henry Tunstall, a Ring competitor. By the next month, October of 1877, he left Jessie Evans's gang to become Tunstall's youngest ranch hand. Tunstall's men affectionately nick-named him "Kid." Tunstall became the lost father found; even gifting him, under the Homestead Act, with a ranch on the Peñasco River in partnership with another employee, half-Chickasaw Fred Waite. That was likely Billy's proudest and most optimistic moment.

Billy had stumbled into a noble cause: ending Ring oppression. His gunman skill now elevated him as a protector of the good. His hair-trigger temper became vehemence for justice. And the town of Lincoln, as well as Tunstall's ranch on the Feliz River, became home. But Billy's tragic destiny was unrelenting. After only 4½ months, this idyllic time ended with Tunstall's Ring murder.

Lincoln, site of the future Lincoln County War, had already sustained Ring abuses through mercantile monopoly of "The House": a huge, two-story adobe, general store run by its local Ring bosses, Emil Fritz, Lawrence Murphy, James Dolan, and John Riley for secret partner, Ring boss, Thomas Benton Catron. They bled cash-poor Mexicans and Anglo homesteaders with usurious credit. Redress was impossible, since law enforcement and courts were Ring-controlled. Terror reigned. In 1875, when rancher, Robert Casey, defeated Murphy in a Lincoln election, he was assassinated the same day. Three weeks later, Lincoln's anti-Ring, Mexican community leader, Juan Patrón, was shot by Riley; though accidentally surviving as a limping cripple.

Hope for change began in late 1876 with arrival in Lincoln of English merchant, John Henry Tunstall; persuaded to settle there by a resident attorney, Alexander McSween, a Ring opponent, but once legal counsel to "The House." Tunstall planned to defeat the Ring by fair mercantile and ranching competition.

But Tunstall's plans coincided with boss Catron's monopolistic thrust into Lincoln County: secretly owning a Pecos River cow camp fronted by "The House," and creating his Carrizozo Land and Cattle Company after taking dying Murphy's ranch in 1878.

By 1877, Tunstall built, just a quarter mile northeast of "The House," a general store and bank. And he began two cattle ranches to wrest from "The House" its beef and flour contracts to local Fort Stanton and Mescalero Indian Reservation. He even exposed Ringite Lincoln County Sheriff William Brady's embezzlement of tax money to buy rustled cattle for Catron's ranches. So Tunstall and McSween got on the Ring's hit list.

Ringmen preferred to kill with guise of legality. So they entangled Tunstall in fabricated criminality, starting with false prosecution of McSween, who was then attorney for the estate of "The House's" partner, Emil Fritz, who died intestate in 1874, but had two local siblings and a life insurance policy. The Ring seized on that policy. In 1877, McSween had successfully litigated to get its $10,000 proceeds from its withholding New York City insurance company, minus $3,000 to the collections firm - leaving

$7,000 minus his fees. Knowing that the House faced bankruptcy from Tunstall's competition, and would extort that sum from Fritz's local heirs, he retained it while seeking heirs in Germany.

In December of 1877, McSween left on business to St. Louis with his wife and with Tunstall's business associate, the cattle king, John Chisum, then also president of the bank in Tunstall's store. The Ring pounced, declaring McSween an absconding embezzler of the Fritz insurance money. Ring boss Catron, then U.S. Attorney, issued his arrest warrant for capture. Chisum was also jailed in retaliation for backing Tunstall. On February 4, 1878, McSween had his hearing in Mesilla under Ringite District Judge Warren Bristol (later Billy's hanging judge), who indicted him for embezzling; intending his incarceration and killing in Lincoln by its Ringite Sheriff, William Brady. McSween was saved by the honorable Deputy Sheriff, Adolph Barrier, from his Las Vegas, New Mexico, arrest site, who kept him in personal custody.

But Judge Bristol had set the Ring's traps for assassination of McSween and Tunstall. His indictment did two things. First, he set the bail at $8,000, with approval only by Ringite District Attorney William Rynerson; who refused all bondsmen to leave McSween open to Sheriff Brady's fatal custody at any time.

The second was Tunstall's trap. Bristol attached McSween's property to the sum of $10,000 - falsely deemed the embezzled total - to ensure the money if he was convicted at that April's Grand Jury. Then Bristol lied that Tunstall was in partnership with McSween, to attach Tunstall's property also. And Bristol empowered Sheriff Brady to do attachment inventories at their properties. The intent was harassment to provoke Tunstall and his men to violence to justify his killing in "self-defense."

But Tunstall merely said that any man's life was worth more than all he owned. Billy, with Tunstall three months, must have been overwhelmed by this novel idealism.

Tunstall's businesses had bankrupted "The House," making boss Catron emerge its mortgage owner. And the April Grand Jury would likely exonerate McSween. So the Ring acted urgently, using the embezzlement case's property attachment.

On February 18, 1878, when Tunstall sought to transfer his fine horses, which were immune to the attachment, from his Feliz River Ranch to Lincoln, Brady called it theft of attached property and sent his big posse of Deputies, Ring rustlers, and Jessie Evans's outlaw gang after him and his men, including Billy. Tunstall, becoming isolated, was murdered, his horse slain; with both corpses mutilated. This martyrdom, coupled with more Ring outrages, triggered the Lincoln County War.

Sheriff Brady refused to arrest the murderers. So anti-Ring Justice of the Peace John "Squire" Wilson issued warrants for James Dolan, Jessie Evans, and his other possemen. For service, he appointed Billy and Fred Waite as Deputy Constables under Town Constable Atanacio Martinez. Billy had already given Wilson an affidavit as to first-hand knowledge of the murderers. But Brady shielded them by putting Billy, Waite, and Martinez in Lincoln's pit jail. And he confiscated Billy's Winchester '73 carbine - likely a gift from Tunstall.

Next, "Squire" Wilson defied the Ring by deputizing Tunstall's foreman, Dick Brewer; who, in turn, made Tunstall's men, including now-released Billy, his possemen to serve those murder warrants. Billy, then 18, was still a lawman.

Meanwhile, Attorney Alexander McSween, in mortal danger from Brady and the Ring, went into hiding with Deputy Sheriff Barrier; mostly in the nearby Hispanic town of San Patricio.

By March of 1878, Dick Brewer's posse had captured Tunstall murder possemen, William "Buck" Morton and Frank Baker, who were shot attempting escape. Billy was in the firing group.

**At that point, including "Windy" Cahill, Billy Bonney was now involved in three killings.**

The Ring hit back. Ringite Governor Samuel Beach Axtell, by illegal proclamation, removed Wilson's Justice of the Peace powers to retroactively outlaw Dick Brewer's posse; then declared Sheriff William Brady to be Lincoln County's only law enforcer.

Enraged, Tunstall's men named themselves "Regulators" after pre-Revolutionary War freedom fighters. Included were Tunstall men - Billy; Fred Waite; John Middleton; Jim "Frenchie" French; farmer cousins, George and Frank Coe; and homesteader, Charlie Bowdre - and a John Chisum cattle detective, Frank MacNab. Dick Brewer was chosen as leader. Only one month after Tunstall died, Billy was being schooled in politics of revolution.

The Ring's next chance to assassinate McSween was April 1, 1878, when he returned to Lincoln for his Grand Jury embezzlement trial. That morning, to save him, Regulators with carbines, and Billy with only a revolver, ambushed Brady and his three deputies from behind an adobe corral wall at Tunstall's store. Brady and his Deputy George Hindman died. Recklessly, Billy, with Jim French, ran out to retrieve his confiscated

Winchester '73 carbine from Brady's body. Both got leg wounds from firing surviving deputy, Jacob Basil "Billy" Matthews. But Billy regained his symbol of father-figure Tunstall. (It is likely the carbine held in Billy's famous tintype two years hence.)

Three days later, on April 4, 1878, Deputy Dick Brewer, seeking stolen Tunstall horses, led Billy, John Middleton, Fred Waite, Frank Coe, George Coe, and Charlie Bowdre to Blazer's Mill - a privately owned, way station and grist mill within the Mescalero Indian Reservation. Accidently encountered was Tunstall murder posseman, Andrew "Buckshot" Roberts, for whom they had a warrant. Roberts fired his Winchester carbine at Bowdre, who shot him in the belly. Roberts's bullet had hit Bowdre's belt buckle, ricocheted, and wrenched George Coe's revolver, mutilating his trigger finger. Another Roberts shot hit Middleton's chest, though Middleton survived. Then Roberts killed Brewer, later dying himself from Bowdre's wound. Billy had not fired a shot. Roberts had demostrably resisted arrest murderously, necessitating self- defense response. But Ring boss Catron, as U.S. Attorney, seized on this killing to file his federal indictment against the Regulators, including Billy, claiming the murder site was the Mescalero Reservation, under federal control.

**Billy's murder involvement now totaled six men; though only "Windy" Cahill was demonstrably by his hand.**

At the April, 1878, Lincoln County Grand Jury, McSween was exonerated for embezzling. He continued his anti-Ring fight backed by the Regulators, though they had never been paid; John Chisum having dishonestly reneged. Revolutionary fervor sufficed. And Billy, their hot-headed fearless zealot, was becoming an inspiration - with McSween as his new father substitute.

McSween's lawful tactic was seeking high-level intervention, since murder of a foreign citizen could elicit a Washington, D.C. investigation. He filed a complaint with the British ambassador and to President Rutherford B. Hayes, accusing U.S. officials of murdering Tunstall. In response, investigating attorney, Frank Warner Angel, was sent by the Departments of the Interior and Justice. Arriving May 4, 1878, Angel took 39 depositions. Billy, volunteering for one, entered the national stage.

Public optimism of Ring defeat further grew when the Lincoln County Commissioners appointed neutral John Copeland, as Sheriff replacing Brady. He even deputized Regulator, Josiah "Doc" Scurlock, to recover Tunstall's horses, stolen by the Ring.

Still a lawman, Billy was on Scurlock's posse. And Wilson, ignoring Axtell's proclamation, continued as Justice of the Peace.

Optimism was short-lived. New Regulator leader, Frank MacNab, was killed in ambush on April 28, 1878 by Ringite Seven Rivers rustlers. By May 28th, because John Copeland forgot to post his tax collecting bond, Governor Axtell, by another proclamation, removed him and appointed as Sheriff, Ringite George Peppin, Brady's deputy, present at Brady's killing.

War fervor built, with furious Regulators and Mexicans calling themselves "McSweens." Billy's affiliation with local, firebrand youth, Yginio Salazar, and Billy's closeness to Hispanic residents of nearby San Patricio and Picacho, had arguably brought them all into the McSween alliance. By April 30, 1878, McSweens were skirmishing with Ring partisans, known as "Murphy-Dolans."

McSween again hid, often in San Patricio. In revenge, Sheriff George Peppin, with John Kinney's Ring-rustler gang from Mesilla, on July 3, 1878 massacred residents and destroyed farm animals and property there. On July 13th, the "Regulator Manifesto" was sent to Catron's brother-in-law, then managing his Carrizozo cattle ranch, threatening retaliation against Catron himself. Signed only "Regulator," it was likely created by Billy.

The Lincoln County War's culminating Battle began the next day: July 14, 1878. McSween, with 60 men - Regulators and Hispanic residents of San Patricio and Picacho - occupied Lincoln. Reflecting McSween's intended peaceful victory was that his wife, Susan, and her sister with five children, remained in his double-winged house; along with the sister's attorney husband's law intern, Harvey Morris.

McSween's men took strategic positions in houses throughout the mile-long town, most of whose inhabitants had fled. When Seven Rivers and John Kinney outlaws joined James Dolan and Sheriff George Peppin, Billy; his friends, Yginio Salazar and Tom O'Folliard; and San Patricio men - José Chávez y Chávez, Ignacio Gonzales, Florencio Chávez, Francisco Zamora, and Vincente Romero - rushed to McSween's house, joining guard, Jim French.

Though Ring men occupied foothills south of Lincoln, they were held at bay for five days by shooting McSweens. Regulators were about to win. But McSween did not realize that Fort Stanton's new Commander, Lieutenant Colonel N.A.M. Dudley, was beholden to the Ring. McSween was also reassured by the Posse Comitatus Act, passed the month before in Washington, barring military intervention in civilian disputes.

On July 16th, Commander Dudley began his invention by sending to Lincoln, for "fact-finding," 9th Cavalry Private Berry Robinson, who was almost hit in the mutual gunfire. Next, on July 18th, James Dolan used Ringite Lincolnite, Saturnino Baca, to claim his wife and children were at risk from the McSweens.

The next day, July 19th, violating the Posse Comitatus Act, Dudley marched on Lincoln with 39 troops - white infantry, black 9th Cavalry, and white officers - two ambulances; a mountain howitzer cannon; and a Gatling machine-gun, that period's most awesome weapon. Panicked McSweens - except for those in his besieged house - fled north across the nearby Bonito River. Dudley himself threatened McSween with razing his house if any soldier was shot. He then left three soldiers there to inhibit its defenders' shooting from it, and ordered three more to accompany Sheriff Peppin as a shield. Next, by death threats, he forced Justice of the Peace Wilson to write arrest warrants for McSween and his men as attempting murder of Private Robinson to feign reason for his intervention. Then he encamped at the east side of Lincoln.

Backed by the participating troops, Sheriff Peppin's outlaw posseman set fire to McSween's house's west wing. His family was evacuated after Dudley refused McSween's wife's plea to save him.

By nightfall, the McSween house conflagration - worsened by an exploding keg of gunpowder for bullet-making - left all trapped in the east wing. At about 9 p.m., escape was attempted into fire-lit shooting Ringites. With Billy was law intern, Harvey Morris, whom he saw fatally shot. And before Billy escaped across the Bonito River, at the property's rear - to rescue by fellow Regulators - he witnessed Dudley's treasonous crime: three of his white soldiers, imbedded with the assailants, under orders, fired a volley at those escaping. Arguably, they had even killed Morris.

Shot dead were Alexander McSween, Francisco Zamora, and Vincente Romero. Yginio Salazar survived with two bullets in his back. Symbolizing horror, McSween's starving, yard chickens ate the eyeballs of his corpse. Again was Ring murder and mutilation in Lincoln County to gain treacherous victory.

No one knew that Ring influence extended to Washington, D.C. Investigator Frank Warner Angel, after documenting crimes of Governor S.B. Axtell, U.S. Attorney Catron, and Sheriff Brady's posse, nevertheless concluded falsely in his report - likely under duress - that no U.S. officials were involved in Tunstall's murder. As part of the cover-up, Catron resigned as U.S. Attorney. And President Hayes scapegoated Governor Axtell, replacing him with

Civil War General Lew Wallace. But Angel secretly tried to get justice by writing for Wallace a notebook listing Ringites, and sending him an exposé on the Santa Fe Ring printed in 1877.

Though most Regulators fled the Territory, Billy stayed and carried out the Regulator Manifesto's guerrilla stock rustling with Tom O'Folliard and Charlie Bowdre - who had relocated to Fort Sumner with his wife Manuela. For his stolen stock, Billy used non-Ring outlets: Pat Coghlan in the western part of the Territory; and Dan Dedrick. Dedrick was a counterfeiter and rustler owner of Bosque Grande, a ranch 12 miles south of Fort Sumner. With his two brothers, he also owned a livery stable in White Oaks, a town about 45 miles northwest of Lincoln. Those brothers were another stock outlet for Billy. Billy also sold rustled horses in Tascosa, Texas; where he wrote a subsequently famous, bill of sale to friendly a doctor, Henry Hoyt, for an expensive sorrel horse - likely dead Sheriff Brady's. He also got money by gambling. He was again a homeless drifter. That would now be permanent.

Amidst public hope, on October 1, 1878, new Governor, Lew Wallace took office. A high-achieving elitist, he was the son of an Indiana governor; a Civil War Major General; an Abraham Lincoln murder trial prosecutor; author of best-selling novel, *The Fair God*; and was writing *Ben-Hur A Tale of the Christ*. He had sought an exotic ambassadorship, like to Turkey, not governorship of backwater New Mexico Territory. So, to dispatch quickly with Lincoln County "troubles" without confronting the Santa Fe Ring, he issued, a month after arriving, an Amnesty Proclamation; though excluding those already indicted. Billy had been indicted for the Brady, Hindman, and Roberts murders.

There were more sources of hope. The new Sheriff, George Kimbrell - having been appointed to replace Sheriff George Peppin, who resigned - was anti-Ring. And McSween's intrepid widow, Susan, had brought to Lincoln Attorney Huston Chapman to charge Commander N.A.M. Dudley with the Lincoln County War Battle's murder of her husband and arson of her home.

In that atmosphere of legal scrutiny, James Dolan made peace overtures, first to Susan McSween, then to Billy - a proof of that teenager's Ring threat. Billy and his Hispanic compatriots could yield another uprising - as T.B. Catron feared.

The Billy-Dolan peace meeting was fatefully scheduled on the February 18, 1879 anniversary of Tunstall's murder. It ended in calamity. As James Dolan; Billy; Jessie Evans and Jessie's new gang member, Billy Campbell; and Billy's Regulator friends, Tom O'Folliard and Josiah "Doc" Scurlock, walked Lincoln's dark street after the meeting, they encountered Chapman. Dolan and Campbell fired at point-blank range, killing him, then ignited his clothing. Billy was again an eye-witness. And again there was murder and mutilation in Lincoln County.

Chapman's murder forced Governor Wallace to go to Lincoln - after procrastinating for five months after arriving. Once there, he avoided Ring confrontation, using the Ring's own concoction of vague "outlaws and rustlers" causing trouble. The Ring had given him a list of Regulators as "outlaws;" with Billy on it as "the Kid."

Focus on Billy - likely through Dolan - made Wallace put the astronomical reward of $1,000 on his head. Billy responded with his pardon plea, writing on March 13, 1879, to offer Wallace his eye-witness testimony against Chapman's murderers in exchange for annulling his Lincoln County War indictments. It was Billy's bold and calculated risk to negate Ring power over himself.

His articulate pardon plea letter, in his personalized Spencerian script, led to his March 17, 1879, nighttime meeting with Wallace in Justice of the Peace Wilson's Lincoln house. Evidence indicates that Wilson was covertly backing Billy's plea. And Billy believed Wallace agreed to his pardon bargain.

To avoid assassination before testifying, Billy requested from Wallace a sham arrest (He had already seen Ring assassinations of John Tunstall, Alexander McSween, Harvey Morris, Francisco Zamora, Vincente Romero, and Huston Chapman.) He was kept in the home of his Lincoln friend, Juan Patrón, the town Jailer. Wallace, housed next door, interviewed him and got his additional letter about Lincoln County War issues.

Billy fulfilled his pardon bargain the next month by testifying in the Grand jury. He got indictment of Chapman's killers, with James Dolan and Billy Campbell for first degree murder, and Jessie Evans as accessory. But Ringite District Attorney William Rynerson, colluding with Judge Bristol, had his trial venue for his indictments switched from Lincoln to Doña Ana County to guarantee a hanging verdict. Still Wallace issued no pardon.

By that April of 1879, Alexander McSween's widow, Susan, retained Attorney Ira Leonard, Chapman's office-mate from Las Vegas, to prosecute Dudley. So Dudley, under likely advisement from Catron, who had represented him for past court martials, got defamatory affidavits to diminish her credibility. And he requested a military Court of Inquiry, where judges would be biased, and where he would be defended by Catron's law firm member, Henry Waldo. And on April 25th, the Ring tried unsuccessfully to assassinate Ira Leonard to stop the case.

Wallace, having removed Dudley as Commander, testified against him in the 1879 Court of Inquiry, though without confronting the Ring. Billy testified also, for his own anti-Ring agenda. He devastatingly reported the three white soldiers firing a volley at him and escaping others: meaning officers; meaning under Dudley's orders; meaning violating the Posse Comitatus Act and justifying court martial, and even hanging. His courage made Ira Leonard take him as client.

By July of 1879, the biased Court of Inquiry exonerated Dudley. And Billy, with no pardon and imminent transport to Mesilla for a hanging trial, exited his bogus jailing.

The Ring recouped. By October of 1879, Susan McSween lost her civil trial against Dudley in Mesilla, to which her venue had been changed by Judge Bristol. That month, Bristol also voided James Dolan's Chapman murder indictment based on no witnesses daring to appear for a trial. Dolan, certain of immunity, had even taken over Tunstall's store. Tunstall's ranch property was given by the Ring to Dolan, Riley, and Rynerson; and Billy's Peñasco River ranch went to Jacob Basil "Billy" Matthews, head posseman for Tunstall's murder. And there was a more subtle Ring victory: Lew Wallace's humiliation in the Court of Inquiry made him shun Lincoln County "troubles" and Billy's pardon.

Billy's future killer, Patrick "Pat" Floyd Garrett, had arrived in New Mexico Territory's Fort Sumner in 1878. Born to an Alabama plantation family, relocated to Claiborne Parrish, Louisiana, when 9½ - and Billy was just born - he had even been willed a slave. After the Civil War, he drifted to Texas, where he possibly murdered a black man, before becoming a buffalo hunter from 1876 to 1878 with two partners and a kid named Joe Briscoe. Garrett murdered Briscoe, but claimed self-defense. He never met fellow buffalo hunter, John William Poe; but later, his, Poe's, and Billy's histories would merge on the night of July 14, 1881.

In Fort Sumner, tall Garrett met transient kid, Billy Bonney, gambling at Hargrove's or Beaver Smith's Saloons. They were given townspeople's nicknames, "Big Casino" and "Little Casino," for their poker playing and height discrepancies.

The original Fort Sumner was built in 1865 by the U.S. government on desert flatlands east of the Pecos River for soldiers guarding Bosque Redondo: a concentration camp for 3,500

Navajos and 400 Apaches, until their scandalous starvation caused release of the Navajos to their homeland in 1868; the Apaches having already escaped. In 1870, Fort Sumner was purchased by Lucien Bonaparte Maxwell, one of the Territory's richest men. Converting it into a town around its parade ground, and using its thousands of acres for sheep raising, he settled there with his wife, Luz Beaubien; daughters, including Paulita; and son, Peter. Retained was the military cemetery for his family. Eventually it received Billy's body, to lie beside Pat Garrett's earlier shooting victims: Billy's Regulator pals, Tom O'Folliard and Charlie Bowdre. Maxwell died in 1875, leaving the town to his wife and son, Peter; who became the family's ruin through mismanagement. But when Pat Garrett and Billy Bonney gambled there, Fort Sumner was still thriving.

Before buying Fort Sumner, Maxwell's wealth came from his marriage to Luz Beaubien, an heiress of the almost two million acre Beaubien-Miranda Land Grant, buying its shares from her siblings. In 1870, he then sold it as the Maxwell Land Grant. But he was cheated by his robber baron attorneys, Thomas Benton Catron and Steven Benton Elkins, who resold it for double the money. That profit fortified their Santa Fe Ring, as they enriched themselves with railroads, banks, and mines. Catron eventually owned six million acres - more than anyone in U.S. history. In the Lincoln County War period, he was Billy's lethal enemy, with the Ring branding him as the murderous outlaw "Billy the Kid" to justify killing him. By 1912's New Mexico statehood, Catron became one of the two first senators.

By 1878, before the Lincoln County War, Pat Garrett and Billy Bonney led separate lives, though connected by Fort Sumner's Gutierrez sisters: Juanita, Apolinaria, and Celsa. Billy befriended Celsa, married to her cousin, Saval Gutierrez, a Maxwell sheep herder. Billy's July 14, 1881 death walk would start at their house. Garrett married Juanita, who died soon after of a possible miscarriage. Two years later, in 1880, he married Apolinaria, with whom he would father eight children. It was a double marriage with his Fort Sumner, best friend, Maxwell's foreman, Barney Mason, later a spy assisting Garrett's capture of Billy.

In 1878, Garrett had been desperate for employment. At Fort Sumner, he drove a wagon for Peter Maxwell; helped a local hog raiser, Thomas "Kip" McKinney; and bartended at Hargrove's Saloon. Then came 1880 and the opportunity of his life. For Lincoln County's November election, the Ring needed a compatible

Sheriff. To qualify, Garrett moved with his wife, Apolinaria, to that county's town of Roswell; adding, as a boarder, an unemployed journalist named Ashmun "Ash" Upson. In 1882, Upson would ghostwrite Garrett's book about killing Billy the Kid.

By 1880, the Ring's outlaw myth propaganda had advertised Billy's gunman reputation. That almost succeeded in his killing on January 3, 1880 at Fort Sumner's Hargrove's Saloon. A Texan bounty hunter named Joe Grant tried to shoot him in the back. Saved by Grant's gun's misfiring, Billy retaliated fatally. Obvious self-defense, that killing was not legally pursued.

**Billy was now linked to murders of seven men: Frank "Windy" Cahill, William Brady, George Hindman, Andrew "Buckshot" Roberts, William "Buck" Morton, Frank Baker, and Joe Grant.**

That 1880, when his now-famous tintype photograph was taken in Fort Sumner, Billy may have heard first mythological whispers of his outlawry. The Ring was setting its legal trap for eliminating him. In addition to murderer and rustler, he would be framed as a counterfeiter to use the Secret Service, a branch of the U.S. Treasury Department, with funding and power to track him down. Catron's Lincoln County agent, James Dolan, initiated the investigation by reporting receipt of a counterfeit $100 bill in his Lincoln store. And Catron or Elkins were the likely contact to Secret Service Chief, James Brooks.

By September 11, 1880, Secret Service Special Operative Azariah Wild was sent to Lincoln. Dolan's counterfeit bill, falsely linked to Billy, actually came from two youths, Billy Wilson and Tom Cooper, employed by the real counterfeiter, Dan Dedrick. But they occasionally rustled with Billy and his regulars: Tom O'Folliard, Charlie Bowdre, and a "Dirty Dave" Rudabaugh. Billy himself used Dedrick as an outlet for rustled stock, along with Dedrick's brothers at their White Oaks livery.

Gullible Operative Azariah Wild was led to believe by James Dolan and Catron's brother-in-law, Edgar Walz - then managing Catron's Carrizozo cattle ranch - that Billy was in the country's largest counterfeiting and rustling gang. In December of 1880, the *New York Sun*, with leaked Wild reports, featured Ring propaganda of Billy in: "Outlaws of New Mexico. The Exploits of a band headed by a New York Youth, War Against a Gang of Cattle Thieves, Murderers, and Counterfeiters." He was alias "the Kid." The Ring had launched his national outlaw myth.

The Ring's plot almost backfired when Wild was told by Attorney Ira Leonard that his client, Billy Bonney, would testify against the counterfeiters. On October 8, 1880, Wild wrote in his daily report to Chief James Brooks that he himself would arrange a pardon for Billy in exchange for that testimony. But Wild confided that pardon plan to his Ringite informers, who convinced him that Billy, staying in Fort Sumner, was the gang's leader! In his report for October 14, 1880, Wild wrote that he intended to arrest those desperados. By then, Billy was cautious. He held up the stagecoach with Wild's mail, read that report, and avoided apprehension by avoiding the meeting with Leonard and Wild. But another pardon was lost.

The Ring was determined to eliminate Billy. The next option was getting a Lincoln County Sheriff willing do it. The current Sheriff, George Kimbrell, who had assisted in Billy's sham arrest, was a McSween-side sympathizer. The Ring chose Pat Garrett. Secretly, Wild worked with him to form a dragnet to capture Billy and his "rustler-counterfeiter gang;" while, for the upcoming sheriff's election, Garrett was advertised as a law-and-order man to new gold-rush settlers in White Oaks, unaware of Lincoln County War issues, but a third of Lincoln County's voters.

In the November 2, 1880 election, Pat Garrett got 358 votes to Kimbrell's 141. Wild, convinced by his Ring contacts that Kimbrell protected the "Kid gang," also gave Garrett immediate Territorial power for the capture by appointing him Deputy U.S. Marshall. Unaware, Billy would have wrongly thought that Garret's lawman authority was limited to Lincoln County, not Fort Sumner's San Miguel County, where he stayed.

And unaware of his locally publicized "outlawry," Billy still brought stolen horses to the Dedrick's White Oaks livery. On November 22, 1880, a White Oaks posse ambushed him, Tom O'Folliard, Billy Wilson, Tom Pickett, and "Dirty" Dave Rudabaugh at nearby Coyote Spring, shooting dead two of their horses before Billy's group escaped. Five days later, that posse attacked them again at the way station ranch of "Whiskey" Jim Greathouse, 45 miles northeast of White Oaks; accidentally killing one of their own men, Jim Carlyle, but blaming Billy.

That accusation prompted Billy's only letter of 1880 to Governor Lew Wallace. On December 12[th], he wrote, denying his outlawry and murdering of Jim Carlyle. He even described his Robin Hood role of seeking justice for the downtrodden. Wallace never answered. Instead, on December 22, 1880, he placed a

Las Vegas *Daily Gazette* notice: "Billy the Kid: $500 Reward." He would repeat it in the *Daily New Mexican* on May 3, 1881, after Billy's jailbreak. His betrayal of the pardon bargain was complete.

By December of 1880, dreadful days began for Billy. U.S. Marshall Pat Garrett, backed by Azariah Wild, had assembled Texan posses to ride after Billy, since New Mexicans, to whom he was an anti-Ring hero, refused. Garrett's first ambush was on December 19, 1880, when Billy, Tom O'Folliard, Charlie Bowdre, Billy Wilson, Tom Pickett, and Dave Rudabaugh rode into Fort Sumner. O'Folliard was shot dead. The rest escaped.

Billy's group tried to flee the Territory in a snowstorm; but stopped, about 16 miles from Fort Sumner, on December 21, 1880, at a rock-walled, windowless, shepherds' line cabin at Stinking Springs. There Garrett ambushed them the next morning, killing Charlie Bowdre, whom he mistook for Billy, his intended victim. The rest surrendered. It would be seven months before Garrett succeeded in his mission to kill Billy.

Garrett transported his prisoners by train, via Las Vegas, New Mexico, to the Santa Fe jail. Billy remained there from December 27, 1880 to March 28, 1881, because the Ring awaited completion of the railroad to Mesilla to impede any rescue. But he almost escaped by tunneling out with fellow prisoners.

From his cell, Billy wrote four unanswered letters to Wallace, in 1881, pleading for his pardon: writing on March 4th: *"I have done everything that I promised you I would, and you have done nothing that you promised me."* On March 2nd, he had threatened: *"I have some letters which date back two years and there are Parties who are very anxious to get them but I will not dispose of them until I see you."* Wallace never got over that audacity or his own guilt, reworking the pardon obsessively till the end of his life in vindictive fictionalized articles on the outlaw "Billy the Kid."

Billy's first Mesilla murder trial, under Ringite Judge Warren Bristol, began on March 30, 1881, with jurors unaware of Lincoln County War's issues, and without any Lincolnites daring to be witnesses for his defense. Attorney Ira Leonard represented him for past U.S. Attorney Catron's June 21, 1878 federal indictment, Case Number 411, the United States versus Charles Bowdre, Josiah Scurlock, Henry Brown, William Bonney alias Henry Antrim alias the Kid, John Middleton, Steven Stevens, John Scroggins, Frederick Waite, and George Coe for the murder of Andrew "Buckshot" Roberts. It was first because the Ringites likely considered it air-tight.

But, surprising everyone, Leonard got it quashed as invalid, since the federal government had no jurisdiction over Blazer's Mill, the murder site; because private property, like it, was under Territorial jurisdiction. Its being surrounded by the federally-controlled Mescalero Reservation was irrelevant.

Remaining were only the Brady and Hindman Territorial indictments; and, though Billy been firing in the group of Regulators, he had only a revolver lacking accurate range.

But, suddenly, Ira Leonard withdrew, likely after a Ring threat. That was disastrous for Billy. He got Ring-biased, court appointed attorney, Albert Jennings Fountain, who considered him an outlaw, along with co-counsel John D. Bail, a Ringite Catron friend.

On April 8th and 9th of 1881, was Billy's Brady murder trial. His Spanish-speaking jury, given no translator, heard only prosecution witnesses - including James Dolan. After Judge Bristol's biased instructions (with translator) made Billy's mere presence equal to firing the fatal shot, the jury found him guilty of first degree murder; its sole punishment being hanging. On April 13th, Judge Bristol set Billy's hanging date for May 13th, to limit time for appeal. Billy was to be hanged in Lincoln by its Sheriff, Pat Garrett.

From the Mesilla jail, Billy wrote to Attorney Edgar Caypless - conducting his replevin case against Stinking Springs posseman, Frank Stewart for stealing his racing mare at Stinking Springs - hoping to get money from her sale to pay for an appeal.

Ironically, the new Lincoln jail, where Billy was incarcerated to await hanging, was in the past "House," which Catron had sold to Lincoln County for its courthouse, with second floor as jail.

On April 21, 1881, Billy arrived to Sheriff Garrett's custody. For his 24 hour guard, Garrett deputized a White Oaks man, James Bell, and a Seven Rivers man, Bob Olinger. Garrett's further precaution was shackling Billy at wrists and ankles, with securing to a floor ring - all to guarantee his hanging death.

But on April 28th, with Garrett away collecting White Oaks's taxes, Billy escaped. He used a revolver from an accomplice's putting it in the outhouse, or by seizing Bell's. A likely accessory was caretaker, Gottfried Gauss: Tunstall's past cook, and witness to Ring's Lincoln County War atrocities. Billy shot Bell dead as the man fled down the jail's stairway to sound alarm.

Deputy Bob Olinger, across the street at the Wortley Hotel with jail prisoners, either heard the shot or was directed to the ambush. Billy was at the second-floor window, and killed him with his own Whitney double-barrel shotgun.

Billy then spent hours using a miner's pick, supplied by Gauss, to break his leg chain to enable riding; while gathered loyalist Lincoln townspeople, in passive resistance, did nothing to stop him. He finally rode away on a pony supplied by Gauss.

As of that April 28, 1881 escape, Billy was involved in the murder of nine men; James Bell and Robert Olinger adding to Frank "Windy" Cahill and Joe Grant as Billy's only provable killings.

Of the dead, Billy would have said that that Cahill's and Grant's killings were in self-defense; that he was a legal posseman at the group shooting of escaping arrested Tunstall murderers, William "Buck" Morton and Frank Baker; that his gun lacked range to hit Sheriff William Brady or Deputy George Hindman, and their killings by the Regulators were to save Alexander McSween from murder by them; that he had not shot Andrew "Buckshot" Roberts, a Tunstall murderer and murderer of Dick Brewer firing at his group, and killed solely by Charlie Bowdre in self defense; and that Deputy James Bell, after refusing to be tied, had tried to run for help, so was killed to save himself from unjust hanging (and Bell had been on the White Oaks posse, and possibly killed Jim Carlyle, then falsely accused him).

Only Seven Rivers rustler, Bob Olinger, would have been admittedly hated as being in each Lincoln County War period crime - Tunstall's murder, Frank MacNab's ambush murder, and the War's skirmishes and battle. Billy's rage was so great, that he smashed apart Olinger's shotgun to throw it on his corpse, delaying his own escape.

That count of nine killed men - with only four certain - remained as Billy's final true tally.

Billy's escape route was across the Capitan Mountains to the Las Tablas home of his friend, Yginio Salazar. He next went south, possibly intending to go to Old Mexico, and visited friendly rancher, John Meadows. But he reversed, going northeast to Fort Sumner and Paulita, where he hid in the Maxwell's sheep camps, confident of protection by the Maxwells and townspeople. He was unaware that Pat Garrett was paying Maxwell foreman, Barney Mason, as a spy, through Secret Service Agent Azariah Wild.

Garrett's two deputies for the pursuit of Billy to Fort Sumner - John William Poe and Thomas "Kip" McKinney - did not know Billy. Poe, a buffalo hunter, past Deputy U.S. Marshall in Texas, cattle detective, and recent White Oaks settler, had met Garrett during the Wild-assisted tracking of the "Kid gang." McKinney knew Garrett from their 1878, hog farming days.

Once in Fort Sumner, Garrett, doubting Billy's presence as too foolhardy, was urged by Poe to stay. On July 14, 1881, Poe, a stranger to the townspeople, did recognizance of the town; and also checked with Sunnyside postmaster, Milnor Rudulph, seven miles to its north. Poe became convinced Billy was nearby. That night, he, Garrett, and McKinney planned an ambush in Peter Maxwell's bedroom, with Maxwell as traitor. Unknown accomplices likely directed Billy to Maxwell's bedroom, where Garrett waited, with Poe and McKinney outside to kill Billy if he managed to escape through the door to the porch.

Near midnight, Billy proceeded from the converted barracks house of Celsa and Saval Gutierrez, carrying their butcher knife across the parade ground to cut a dinner steak in light of the almost-full huge moon, hovering at the horizon. He first went toward Maxwell's bedroom; but seeing Poe, asked in Spanish who he was, then entered.

Inside, to Maxwell, in bed as decoy, Billy asked again in Spanish who was there, possibly sensing Garrett in the darkness. Garrett then fired. Next, he fired wild. But the first shot was fatal. In terror, Maxwell ran out, almost getting shot by Poe, primed for back-up killing. Then Garrett returned to the room, with Poe and McKinney, and made sure Billy was dead.

The townspeople held a night vigil for Billy in their carpenter's shop. The Coroner's Jury, the next day on July 15, 1881, had as **President, Postmaster Milnor Rudulph, a loyal Ringite who had helped take over the Legislature in 1872 to block anti-Ring bills.** Bi-lingual, Rudulph wrote the Coroner's Jury Report in Spanish. The frightened juryman had no alternative but to sign his conclusion: *"[O]ur verdict is that the deed of said Garrett was justifiable homicide and we are unanimous in the opinion that the gratitude of all the community is due to the said Garrett for his deed and he is worthy of being rewarded."*

Ring terrorism was now complete. Silence fell for a generation before any dared contradict the Santa Fe Ring's outlaw mythology of Billy the Kid.

# BILLY BONNEY'S CHAMPIONS

In the 20th century, Billy Bonney's aging Lincoln County War period contemporaries finally felt safe enough to contradict the Santa Fe Ring's outlaw myth propaganda in print. They confirmed his brilliance, charisma, ease in both Anglo and Hispanic subcultures in those racist times, and fluency in Spanish. He had a zealot's fervor in the Lincoln County War, in which he was a freedom fighting soldier. And neither he, nor his champions, would have seen him as an outlaw. He was a deputized pursuer of John Tunstall's murderers, then a hunted risk to the Ring.

## FRANK AND GEORGE COE

John Tunstall's employees, local Homestead Act farmers, cousins Frank and George Coe, 26 and 21 respectively, nicknamed new, 17 year old ranch hand, Billy Bonney, as "Kid." By 1878, after Tunstall's murder, they became his fellow Regulators. After the lost Lincoln County War Battle, they fled to the Territory's northwest, near Farmington.

## FRANK COE

As an old-timer, Frank Coe wrote about Billy in an unpublished letter to a William Steele Dean, dated August 3, 1926. He emphasized Billy's multiculturalism, and above-average height (5'6" was average), belying his mythologized "shortness": "[He was] 5ft 8in, weight 138 lb stood straight as an Indian, fine looking a lad as I ever met. He was a lady's man, the Mex girls were all crazy about him. He spoke their language well. He was a fine dancer, could go all their gaits and was one of them. He was a wonder, you would have been proud to know him."

On September 16, 1923, Frank Coe - like Billy, considering himself a Regulator soldier - gave a quote to the *El Paso Times*: "[Billy] was brave and reliable, one of the best soldiers we had. He never pushed his advice or opinions, but he had a wonderful presence of mind; the tighter the place the more he showed his cool nerve and quick brain."

Frank Coe also related Billy's shootist preoccupation: "He never seemed to care for money, except to buy cartridges with … and he always used about 10 times as many as any one else."

## GEORGE COE

In 1934, George Coe, Frank Coe's cousin and fellow farmer, published *Frontier Fighter: The Autobiography of George Coe Who Fought and Rode With Billy the Kid*. He described employer, John Tunstall's, paternal affection for Billy: "Tunstall seemed really devoted to the Kid. One day I was in Lincoln and I asked him about Billy. 'George, that's the finest lad I ever met," he said. "He's a revelation to me every day and would do anything to please me. I'm going to make a man out of that boy yet. He has it in him.' "

George Coe also emphasized Billy's charisma: "Billy came down to the Dick Brewer Ranch on the Ruidoso. He was the center of interest everywhere he went, and though heavily armed, he seemed as gentlemanly as a college-bred youth. He quickly became acquainted with everybody, and because of his humorous and pleasing personality grew to be a community favorite. In fact, Billy was so popular there wasn't enough of him to go around. He had a beautiful voice and sang like a bird. One of our special amusements was to get together every few nights and have singing. The thrill of those happy evenings still lingers – a pleasant memory – and tonight I would give a lot to live through one again. Frank Coe and I played the fiddles, and all of us danced, and here Billy, too, was in demand."

About Lincoln County War fighting, George Coe quoted Billy to show the boy's militant fervor in its freedom fighting: "As for ... giving up to that outfit, we'll die first." Billy himself exhibited that brave bellicosity in his March 20, 1879 pardon bargain letter to Governor Lew Wallace; writing: *"I am not afraid to die like a man fighting but I would not like to be killed like a dog unarmed."*

George Coe gave a telling anecdote about Billy's teasing bravado which occurred around April 3, 1878 in the lead-up to the Lincoln County War Battle. It shows how this teenager inspired grown men, and foreshadowed Billy's undaunted and ironic press interviews which he gave after his capture and after his unjust Mesilla hanging trial: "We made a big bonfire, and sat around swapping lies and bragging ... Then we talked about riding into Lincoln and setting in short order all the difficulties that were troubling the people there. We were a brave band as we told it.

Our guns, which formed the most important part of our possessions, had been placed carelessly around against nearby trees. Billy sized up the situation and, looking for a little fun and excitement with an inexperienced bunch of greenhorns, he slipped about five or six cartridges out of his belt and tossed them into the fire. In less than a minute they began to go off, and such a mad dash for tall timber you have never seen ... I looked back as I ran, and there stood the Kid with his arms folded, perfectly unconcerned ... "Well, you're a damn fine bunch of soldiers. Run like a bunch of coyotes and forget to take your guns. I just wanted to break you in a little before we met the enemy, and, boys, I'm sure proud of your nerve."

## *YGENIO SALAZAR*

Quoted in Maurice Garland Fulton's 1926 *The Saga of Billy the Kid*, Billy's good friend, Ygenio Salazar stated: " 'Billy the Kid' ... was the bravest fellow I ever knew. All through the three-days' battle [sic – six day Lincoln County War Battle] he was as cool and cheerful as if he were playing a game instead of fighting for his life." (Fulton, Page 144)

## *GOTTFRIED GAUSS*

German-born Gottfried Gauss, 56 at Billy's great escape from Lincoln's courthouse-jail, was part of Billy's Lincoln County history from that teenager's October of 1877 arrival as a John Tunstall ranch hand - when Gauss was Tunstall's cook - through the Lincoln County War period, and to Billy's 1881 jailbreak, when Gauss was the Lincoln courthouse-jail's caretaker and likely supplier of Billy's escape revolver.

Gauss's anti-Ring stance went back to 1876 when he was employed in the Ring's store called "The House," and was cheated out of his wages and profits from its brewery, which he ran.

Billy himself mentioned Gauss in his June 8, 1878 deposition to Washington Investigator Frank Warner Angel as being at Tunstall's Feliz River ranch before Tunstall's ambush-murder, as well as during an earlier intimidation of its ranch hands by Sheriff William Brady's possemen. Billy's transcriptionist wrote: "*The persons at the ranch were R. M. Brewer, John Middleton,*

*G. Gauss, M. Martz, R.A. Widenmann, Henry Brown, F.T. Waite, W<u>m</u> McClosky and this deponent.*" The night before Tunstall made his fatal return ride with his men and horses to Lincoln from that ranch, he assigned Gauss to stay. Thus, Gauss witnessed the arrival of Sheriff William Brady's posse, on its way to murder John Tunstall. By shared traumas, he was Billy's steadfast friend.

On March 1, 1890, in an interview with the *Lincoln County Leader* about Billy's 1881 jailbreak, Gauss implied enabling by non-intervening Lincolnites, as well as his own sympathy for Billy. Gauss may even have directed Deputy Bob Olinger to the courthouse's east side, where Billy shot him. Gauss stated:

I was crossing the yard behind the courthouse, when I heard a shot fired then a tussle upstairs in the courthouse, somebody hurrying downstairs, and deputy sheriff Bell emerging from the door running toward me. He ran right into my arms, expired the same moment, and I laid him down, dead. That I was in a hurry to secure assistance, or perhaps to save myself, everybody will believe.

When I arrived at the garden gate leading to the street, in front of the courthouse, I saw the other deputy sheriff Olinger, coming out of the hotel opposite, with the four or five other county prisoners, where they had taken their dinner. I called to him to come quick. He did so, leaving his prisoners in front of the hotel. When he had come up close to me, and while I was standing not a yard apart, I told him that I was just after laying Bell dead on the ground in the yard behind. Before he could reply, he was struck by a well-directed shot fired from a window above us, and fell dead at my feet. I ran for my life to reach my room and safety, when Billy the Kid called to me: "Don't run, I wouldn't hurt you – I am alone, and master not only of the courthouse, but also of the town, for I will allow nobody to come near us." "You go," he said, "and saddle one of Judge (Ira) Leonard's horses, and I will clear out as soon as I have the shackles loosened from my legs." With a little prospecting pick I had thrown to him through the window he was working for at least an hour, and could not accomplish more than to free one leg. He came to the conclusion to wait a better chance, tie one shackle to his waistbelt, and start out. Meanwhile I had saddled a small skittish pony belonging to Billy Burt (the county clerk), as there was no other horse available, and had also, by Billy's command, tied a pair of red blankets behind the saddle ...

When Billy went down the stairs at last, on passing the body of Bell he said, "I'm sorry I had to kill him but I couldn't help it."

On passing the body of Olinger he gave him a tip with his boot, saying, "You are not going to round me up again." And so Billy the Kid started out that evening, after he had shaken hands with everybody around and after having a little difficulty in mounting on account of the shackle on his leg, he went on his way rejoicing.

## **HENRY HOYT**

Henry Hoyt was a 24 year old medical doctor, working as a mail rider, when he met Billy Bonney in Tascosa, Texas, three months after the lost Lincoln County War Battle. Billy and fellow Regulators, Charlie Bowdre and Tom O'Folliard, were selling horses, rustled in retaliation from Ringmen, as forewarned in Billy's "Regulator Manifesto" letter of July 13, 1878 to Catron's Carrizozo cattle ranch manager and brother-in-law, Edgar Walz.

Billy gifted Hoyt a horse, likely dead Sheriff William Brady's, writing a legally protective bill of sale, dated October 24, 1878. Hoyt admired Billy's intelligence and bi-culturalism. In his autobiographical, 1929 book, *A Frontier Doctor*, he wrote: "After learning his history directly from himself and recognizing his many superior natural qualifications, I often urged him, while he was free and the going was good, to leave the country, settle in Mexico or South America, and begin all over again. He spoke Spanish like a native and although only a beardless boy was nevertheless a natural leader of men. With his poise, iron nerve, and all-around efficiency properly applied, he could have made a success anywhere."

And, as Hoyt recorded in *A Frontier Doctor*, he also witnessed Billy the following year in Las Vegas, New Mexico, in company with Jesse James; though Billy denied to him any outlaw alliance.

## JOHN P. MEADOWS

A cattle rancher living in New Mexico Territory from early 1880, John P. Meadows, when an old-timer, gave interviews to historians about having known Billy; and performed about it in an historical pageant called "Days of Billy the Kid in Story, Song and Dance" on February 26, 1931 in Roswell, New Mexico. Subsequently, he used his "Days of Billy the Kid" act for serialized newspaper accounts in the *Roswell Daily Record* on March 2nd, 3rd, and 4th of 1931. That year, he also typed a 78 page manuscript with information about Billy. And from August 8, 1935 to June 25, 1936, the *Alamogordo News* printed almost forty reminiscence articles by him. These recollections are collected in a 2004 book titled *Pat Garrett and Billy the Kid as I Knew Them: Reminiscences of John P. Meadows*. It gives insight into how Billy inspired the older men. Meadows stated: "When he was rough, he was as rough as men ever get to be, yet he had a good streak in him."

## E.C. "TEDDY BLUE" ABBOTT

E.C. "Teddy Blue" Abbott, a cowboy about Billy's age, roving through New Mexico Territory in 1878, and having merely heard of him, recorded Billy's atypical multi-culturalism.
It implied Billy could instigate a Hispanic revolt against the land-grabbing, Anglo, Santa Fe Ring minority. "Boss" Thomas Benton Catron himself confirmed that fear of uprisings in his February 10, 1913 *Washington Times* article stating, "Mexicans ... were perfectly equal to starting five new revolutions in five days." And Catron's anxiety connected to the Ring's mission to eliminate Billy by fabricating his outlaw myth.
In 1955, as an old-timer, "Teddy Blue" Abbott published *We Pointed Them North: Recollections of a Cowpuncher*. Open about his own racism, Abbott reported, as common knowledge, the existence of two sides, with Billy as the Mexican's hero, writing: "The Lincoln County troubles was still going on, and you had to be either for Billy the Kid or against him. It wasn't my fight ... it was the Mexicans that made a hero of him."

## *A.P. "PACO" ANAYA*

A Fort Sumner friend of Billy's, three years younger, was A.P. "Paco" Anaya, whose posthumous manuscript about Billy was published in 1991 as *I Buried Billy*. In it, about Billy's bi-culturalism, Anaya stated: "Billy liked better to be with Hispanics than with Americans." (Anaya, Page 82)

# CHAPTER 5
# REAL BILLY BONNEY IN HIS OWN WORDS

## SPEAKING THROUGH TIME

The real Billy Bonney was spectacularly brave, brilliant, and literate; and he left a big paper trail proving all that. His dull-witted imposters were left with an unattainable standard to mimic. And he certainly would not have referred to himself by the hated Santa Fe Ring moniker outlawing him for hanging as "Billy the Kid" - which his impersonators used for themselves.

The quantity of written and recorded records by Billy Bonney is incredible for a minor historical figure; explained, in part, by his anti-Ring political activism, which yielded his deposition and court testimonies. Additionally, his unusual charisma made people save his letters or documents.

So surviving were his 1878 affidavit and deposition on the murder of John Henry Tunstall, and his testimony in the 1879 military Court of Inquiry for possible court martial for Commander N.A.M. Dudley. His pardon bargain letters and interview with Governor Lew Wallace were retained by Wallace when he left the Territory, and were almost the only civilian documents Wallace kept. They ended up in his collected papers, donated to the Indiana Historical Society. Likewise, Dr. Henry Hoyt kept the Bill of Sale that Billy wrote out for him for a sorrel horse. And as big news in his day, Billy had press interviews.

Quotes of his doltish imposters exist, with devastating mismatch of their unschooled fractured grammar and ignorance of the contents of his known documents - unless coached by exposure to them. But the imposters' undoing was that they were impersonating a mythological, dime novel version of an outlaw: an uncouth, unschooled lout, as was expected by their second quarter of the 20th century audiences. The real Billy was beyond their conception.

# AFFIDAVIT AND DEPUTIZING

A key factor Billy Bonney's history was his lawman status in pursuing John Tunstall's killers. On February 19, 1878, the day after Tunstall's murder, Billy and Tunstall's foreman, Dick Brewer, gave eye-witness affidavits to Lincoln Justice of the Peace John "Squire" Wilson, to enable his writing arrest warrants. It is the first time Billy's voice is publicly heard. He named Tunstall's killers as Sheriff Brady's possemen: *"James J. Dolan, Frank Baker, Jessie Evans, George Davis, A.H. Mills, W.S. Morton, [William] Moore, George Hindman, [Frank] Rivers, Pantaleon Gallegos, divers other persons unknown."* It yielded Wilson's February 19th legal arrest warrants, stating:

*Territory of New Mexico )*
*County of Lincoln )*

*Be it remembered that before the undersigned Justice of the Peace in and for the County and Territory aforesaid, personally came R.M. Brewer &* **W. Bonney** *who being duly sworn according to law deposeth & saith that at the County and Territory aforesaid on the 18th day of February 1878 in and upon the [presence] of J.H. Tunstall, Robt A. Widenman[n], R.M. Brewer,* **William Boney** *[sic] & John Middleton, then and there in the Peace of the Territory an assault was made with divers deadly weapons to wit with Winchester Guns and Colts Revolvers, and divers other deadly weapons by James J. Dolan, Frank Baker, Jessie Evans, George Davis, A.H. Mills, W.S. Morton, [omitted first name] Moore, George Hindman, [Frank] Rivers, Pantaleon Gallegos, divers other persons unknown and did then and there as affiant believes wounded & killed J.H. Tunstall contrary to the statute in such case made and provided against the Peace & dignity of the Territory.*

*R.M. Brewer*
**William Bonney.**

After Sheriff Brady refused to serve them, Wilson concluded that *"there being then and there no officers to serve such warrant the undersigned as directed by law, in such cases specially empowered Richard H. Brewer to serve the same endorsing such deputation on said last mentioned warrant."* Wilson wrote:

The Territory of New Mexico )
County of Lincoln             )

I, John B. Wilson justice of the Peace in and for precinct N⁰ 1 Lincoln County, New Mexico, do hereby certify that on or about the 19th day of February 1878 **W. Boney** [sic] and R.M. Brewer filed in my office affidavits charging John [James] J. Dolan, J. Conovair, Frank Baker, Jessie Evans, Tom Hill, George Davis, A. [Andrew] L. ["Buckshot"] Roberts, P. [Panteleon] Gallegos, T. Green, J. Awly, A.H. Mills, "Dutch Charley" proper name unknown, R.W. Beckwith, William Morton, [Deputy] George Hindman, J.B. Matthews and others with having murdered and killed one John H. Tunstall at the said County of Lincoln on or about the 18th day of February 1878, that on or about the 20th day of Feby 1878, I secured warrants on said affidavits for the arrest of the parties above named and directed the same to the Constable of for precinct N⁰ one in said County to wit: Atanacio Martines [Martinez].

That on or about the 20th day of Feby 1878 said warrant was returned "not served" that on or about the said last mentioned day the undersigned issued an alias warrant for the apprehension of the above named persons, and there being then and there no officers to serve such warrant the undersigned as directed by law, in such cases specially empowered Richard H. Brewer to serve the same endorsing such deputation on said last mentioned warrant.

In testimony whereof I have hereinto set my hand at Lincoln Precinct N⁰ 1 Lincoln County, N. Mexico this 31st day of August 1878.

                    John Wilson, Justice of the Peace

This enabled Special Constable Dick Brewer to deputize Billy and Fred Waite as Deputy Constables under Lincoln Town Constable Atanacio Martinez to serve the warrants. To block the arresting, Sheriff William Brady then illegally locked them in Lincoln's pit jail, and confiscated Billy's Winchester '73 carbine.

## DEPOSITION TO FRANK WARNER ANGEL

On June 8, 1878, Billy gave his eloquent eye-witness deposition, with characteristic meticulous attention to detail, on John Tunstall's murder, to Investigator for the Departments of Justice and the Interior, Frank Warner Angel, with Lincoln

Justice of the Peace John "Squire" Wilson, as witness. In it, Billy stated information unknown to the imposters: that he had a ranch on the Peñasco River along with another Tunstall employee, Fred Waite; that he knew about the injustice of the case against Tunstall; and that the horses being herded back to Lincoln were exempted from the case's attachments.

Lacking that still-undiscovered deposition, imposters had to fabricate Tunstall's murder scene and its motive.

And proving his Regulator zeal to attain justice, Billy was risking his life by coming to Lincoln after Ringite Governor Samuel Beach Axtell's illegal proclamation outlawing the Regulators, and after receiving his own April Grand Jury indictments for Regulator killings in the Lincoln County War. He then signed the document, as witnessed by Angel and Wilson; which Angel's transcriptionist recorded as follows:

Territory of New Mexico )
County of Lincoln            )
                                      )

William H. Bonney was duly sworn, deposand says that he is a resident of said county, that on the 11th day of February A.D. 1878 he in company with Robt. A. Widenmann and Fred T. Waite went to the ranch of J. H. Tunstall on the Rio Feliz, that **he and said Fred T. Waite at the time intended to go to the Rio Peñasco to take up a ranch** for the purpose of farming. That the cattle on the ranch of said J. H. Tunstall were throughout the County of Lincoln, known to be the property of said Tunstall; that on the 13th of February A.D. 1878 one J.B. Matthews claiming to be a Deputy Sheriff came to the ranch of said J.H. Tunstall in company with Jesse Evans, Frank Baker, Tom Hill and [Frank] Rivers, known outlaws who had been confined to the Lincoln County jail and had succeeded in making their escape, John Hurley, George Hindman, [Andrew] Roberts and an Indian aka Poncearo the latter said to be the murderer of Benaito Cruz, for the arrest of murderers of whom (Benaito Cruz) the Governor of this Territory offers a reward of $500. Before the arrival of said J.B. Matthews, deputy Sheriff, and his posse, having been informed that said deputy sheriff and posse were going to round up all the cattle and drive them off and kill the persons at the ranch, the persons at the ranch cut portholes into the walls of the house and filled sacks with earth, so that they, the persons at the ranch, *should they be attacked or murder attempted, could defend themselves, this course being thought necessary* **as the sheriffs posse was composed of murderers, outlaws, and desperate characters none of whom has any interest at stake in the County, nor being residents of said County.** *That said Matthews when within about 50 yards of the house was called to stop and advance alone and state his business, that said Matthews after arriving at the ranch said that he had come to attach the cattle and property of A.A McSween, that* **said Matthews was informed that A.A. McSween had no cattle or property there,** *but that if he had he, said Matthews could take it. That said Matthews said that he thought some of the cattle belonging to R. M. Brewer whose cattle were also at the ranch of J.H. Tunstall, belonged to A.A. McSween, that said Matthews was told by said Brewer that he Matthews could round up the cattle and that he, Brewer, would help him. That said Matthews said that he would go back to Lincoln to get new instructions and if he came back to the ranch he would come back with one man. That said Matthews and his posse were then invited by R.M. Brewer to come to the house to get something to eat.*

*Deponent further states that Robert A. Widenmann told R.M. Brewer and the others at the ranch, that he was going to arrest Frank Baker, Jesse Evans and Tom Hill said Widenmann having warrants for them. That said Widenmann was told by Brewer and the others at the ranch that the arrest could not be made because if it was made they, all the persons at the ranch would be killed and murdered by J.J. Dolan and their party. That said Evans advanced upon said Widenmann, said Evans swinging his gun and catching it cocked and pointed directly at said Widenmann. That said Jesse Evans asked said Widenmann whether he Widenmann, was hunting for him, Evans, to which Widenmann answered that if he was looking for him, he, Evans, would find it out. Evans also asked Widenmann whether he had a warrant for him; Widenmann answered that it was his (Widenmann's) business. Evans told Widenmann, that if he ever came to arrest him (Evans) he, Evans would pick Widenmann as the first man to shoot at, to which Widenmann answered that that was all right, that two could play at that game. That during the talking Frank Baker stood near said Widenmann, swinging his pistol on his finger, catching it full cocked pointed at said Widenmann.*

*The persons at the ranch were R. M. Brewer, John Middleton, G. Gayss [Gauss], M. Martz, R.A. Widenmann, Henry Brown, F.T.*

Waite, Wm McClosky and this deponent. J.B. Matthews after eating started for Lincoln with John Hurley and Ponceano the rest of the party or posse saying they were going to the Rio Peñasco. Deponent started to Lincoln with Robert A. Widenmann and F.T. Waite and arrived at Lincoln the same evening and again left Lincoln on the next day, February the 14th in company with the above named persons, having heard that said Matthews was going back to the ranch of said J.H. Tunstall with a large party of men to take the cattle and deponent and Widenmann and Waite arrived at said ranch the same day.

Deponent states that on the road to Lincoln he heard said Matthews ask said Widenmann whether any resistance would be offered if he Matthews returned to take the cattle, to which said Widenmann answered that no resistance would be offered if the cattle were left at the ranch but if an attempt was made to drive the cattle to the Indian Agency and kill them for beef as he, said Matthews had been heard to say would be done, he, said Widenmann, would do all in his power to prevent this.

Deponent further says that on the night of the 17th of February A.D. 1878 J.H. Tunstall arrived at the ranch and informed all persons there that reliable information had reached him that J.B. Matthews was gathering a large party of outlaws and desperados as a posse and the said posse was coming to the ranch, the Mexicans in the party to gather up the cattle and the balance of the party to kill the persons at the ranch. It was thereupon decided that all persons at the ranch excepting G. Gauss, were to leave and Wm McClosky was that night sent to the Rio Peñasco to inform the posse who were camped there, that they could come over and round up the cattle, count them and leave a man there to take care of them and that Mr. Tunstall would also leave a man there to help round up and count the cattle and help take care of them, and said McClosky was also ordered to go to Martin Martz, who had left Tunstalls ranch when deponent, Widenmann and Waite returned to the town of Lincoln on the 13th of February and asked him said Martz to come to the ranch of said Tunstall and aid the sheriffs posse in rounding up and counting the cattle and to stay at the ranch and take care of the cattle.

Deponent left the ranch of said Tunstall in company with J.H. Tunstall, R.A. Widenmann, R.M. Brewer, John Middleton, F.T. Waite, said Tunstall, Widenmann, Brewer, Middleton and deponent driving the loose horses, Waite driving the wagon. Said Waite took the road for Lincoln with the wagon, the rest of the *party taking the trail with the horses.* **Deponent says that all the horses which he and the party were driving, excepting 3 had been released by sheriff Brady at Lincoln that one of these 3 horses belonged to R.M. Brewer, and the other was traded by Brewer to Tunstall for one of the released horses.**

Deponent further says, that when he and the party has traveled to within about 3 miles from the Rio Ruidoso he and John Middleton were in drag in the rear of the balance of the party as just upon reaching the brow of a hill they saw a large party of men coming towards them from the rear at full speed and that he and Middleton at once rode forward to inform the balance of the party of the fact. Deponent had not more than barely reached Brewer and Widenmann who were some 200 or 300 yards to the left of the trail when the attacking party cleared the brow of the hill and commenced firing at him, Widenmann and Brewer. Deponent, Widenmann and Brewer rode over a hill towards another which was covered with large rocks and trees in order to defend themselves and make a stand. But the attacking party, undoubtedly seeing Tunstall, left off pursuing deponent and the two with him and turned back at the caño in which the trail was. Shortly afterwards we heard two or three separate and distinct shots and the remark was then made by Middleton that they, the attacking party must have killed Tunstall. Middleton had in the meantime joined deponent and Widenmann and Brewer. Deponent then made the rest of his way to Lincoln in company with Robt. A. Widenmann, Brewer, Waite and Middleton stopping on the Rio Ruidoso in order to get men to look for the body of J.H. Tunstall.

Deponent further says that neither he nor any of the party fired off either rifle or pistol and that neither he nor the parties with him fired a shot.

*William H. Bonney*

*Sworn and subscribed before me this eighth day of June A.D. 1878.*

*John B. Wilson*
*Justice of the Peace*

# "REGULATOR MANIFESTO"

On July 3, 1878, during the multiple skirmishes in the Lincoln County War, and leading to the final Battle, there occurred a retaliatory Santa Fe Ring massacre at anti-Ring San Patricio: the Hispanic community which was like bi-cultural Billy's second home. On July 13, 1878, ten days after it, Billy took action: challenging the Ring, in what I named the "Regulator Manifesto." It is the anti-Ring declaration of the Lincoln County War Battle, starting the next day. It is signed only "*Regulator.*"

Existing as a copy, it was first attributed to Charles Bowdre by early historian, Maurice Garland Fulton, who claimed implausibly that its recipient, Ring head, T.B. Catron's, brother-in-law, Edgar Walz, recognized Bowdre's handwriting. But I believe it was Billy's production, either dictated to Bowdre, or wrongly attributed to him by Walz. And it heralds Billy's future retaliative guerrilla rustling from Ringites, like Catron and Walz. It stated:

*In Camp, July 13, 1878.*
*Mr. Walz. Sir: - We are all aware that your brother-in-law, T.B. Catron sustains the Murphy-Kinney party, and take this method of informing you that if any property belonging to the residents of this county is stolen or destroyed, Mr. Catron's property will be dealt with as nearly as can be in the way in which the party he sustains deals with the property stolen or destroyed by them.*
*We returned Mr. Thornton the horses we took for the purpose of keeping the Murphy crowd from pursuing us with the promise that these horses should not again be used for that purpose. Now we know that the Tunstall estate cattle are pledged to Kinney and party. If they are taken, a similar number will be taken from your brother [in-law, Catron]. It is our object and efforts to protect property, but the man who plans destruction shall have destruction measured on him. Steal from the poorest or richest American or Mexican, and the full measure of the injury you do, shall be visited upon the property of Mr. Catron. This murderous band is harbored by you as your guest, and with the consent of Catron occupies your property.*
                                            *Regulator*

# HOYT BILL OF SALE

After the lost Lincoln County War, refusing to leave the Territory, like most Regulators, Billy earned money by gambling and retaliatory rustling from Ringites, as threatened in his July 13, 1878 "Regulator Manifesto." He would not have considered himself a common rustler - as he later labeled Seven Rivers rustlers to Governor Lew Wallace in a March 23, 1879 interview.

Billy used non-Ring outlets for stock, and sold horses himself in Tascosa, Texas. There, on October 24, 1878, he "sold" to Dr. Henry Hoyt a sorrel horse - likely Sheriff William Brady's Dandy Dick, stolen from Catron's Carrizozo ranch. He priced it high for its bill of sale, which demonstrated legalese he had possibly learned from Alexander McSween; and with proper witnessing by saloon owners, James E. McMasters and George J. Howard. That skill would be used in 132 days to write his first pardon plea letter to Governor Lew Wallace.

Billy's abilities impressed Hoyt enough for him to keep the document. On April 27, 1929, Hoyt sent its copy to Lew Wallace Jr.; writing: "I am one of the very few men living who was well acquainted with that famous outlaw 'Billy the Kid' and for many years supposed I had the only specimen of his handwriting in existence [until learning about the Lew Wallace letters], **a Bill of Sale for a horse he presented me with, and wrote out himself,** to protect me should my ownership ever be questioned, a very important matter in that part of the world at that period. This paper I have preserved all these years."

The Hoyt Bill of Sale stated:

*Tascoso Texas*
*Thursday Oct 24th 1878*

*Know all persons by these presents that I do hereby Sell and deliver to Henry F. Hoyt one Sorrel Horse Branded BB on left hip and other indistinct Branded on Shoulders for the sum of Seventyfive $ dollars in hand received*
*W HBonney*

*Witness*
*Jas. E. McMasters*
*Geo. J. Howard*

# LETTER OF MARCH 13, 1879 TO LEW WALLACE

On approximately March 13, 1879, Billy began his pardon plea to Governor Lew Wallace, offering eye-witness testimony against Ringite murderers of Attorney Huston Chapman on February 18, 1879 for an exchange, since Wallace's November 13, 1878 Amnesty Proclamation had excluded those indicted, like him. Noteworthy is that Billy asked to *"annuly"* - meaning annul - his indictments for the murders of William Brady, George Hindman, and Andrew "Buckshot" Roberts. That was correct: a pardon is post-sentencing; annulment is before. And Billy's ability to spell even "indicted," contrasts the pretenders' low literacy. He wrote:

> *To his Excellency the Governor.*
> *General Lew. Wallace*
> *Dear Sir I have heard that You will give one thousand $ dollars for my body which as I can understand it means alive as a witness. I know it is as a witness against those that murdered Mr. Chapman. if it was so as that I could appear at Court, I could give the desired information. but I have indictments against me for things that happened in the late Lincoln County War and am afraid to give up because my Enimies would Kill me. the day Mr. Chapman was murderded I was in Lincoln, at the request of good citizens to meet Mr. J.J. Dolan to meet as Friends. So as to be able to lay aside our arms and go to Work. I was present when Mr. Chapman was murdered and know who did it and if it were not for these indictments I would have made it clear before now. if it is in your power to Annully those indictments I hope you will do so so as to give me a chance to explain. please send me an annser telling me what you can do. You can send annser by bearer.*
>
> *I have no wish to fight any more indeed I have not raised an arm since Your proclamation. as to my Character I refer to any of the Citizens, for the majority of them are my Friends and have been helping me all they could. I am called Kid Antrim but Antrim is my stepfathers name.*
> *Waiting for an annser I remain*
> *Your Obedient Servant*
> *W.H. Bonney*

## LETTER OF MARCH 20, 1879
## TO "SQUIRE" WILSON

Billy began a flurry of March 20, 1879 letters by writing to Justice of the Peace John "Squire" Wilson to check with Lew Wallace about his planned feigned arrest for his pardon bargain, since many of the men he was supposed to testify against for the Huston Chapman murder had escaped from their Fort Stanton imprisonment. He wrote from his safe-haven:

>   <u>San</u> <u>Pa</u>tricio
>                       Thursday 20<sup>th</sup> 1879
>   Friend Wilson.
>              Please tell You know
>   who that I do not know what to do, now
>   as those Prisoners have escaped. So send word
>   by bearer. a note through You it may be he has made
>   different arrangements if not and he still wants it the same
>   to Send :William Hudgins [Hudgens]: as Deputy, to the
>   Junction tomorrow at three Oclock with some men you know
>   to be all right. Send a note telling me what to do
>                                    WHBonney
>   P.S. do not send Soldiers

## LETTER OF MARCH 20, 1879
## TO LEW WALLACE

Wallace responded to Wilson with arrangements, and enclosed a vague *"note"* for Billy about their *"understanding."* Billy responded with a precautionary scenario for his sham arrest:

>   *San Patricio*
>   *Lincoln <u>County</u>*
>   *Thursday 20<sup>th</sup> <u>1879</u>*
>   *General. Lew. Wallace:*
>              *Sir. I will keep the appointment*
>   *I made. but be Sure and have men come that*
>   *You can depend on I am not afraid to die like a man fighting but*

*I would not like to be killed like a dog unarmed. tell Kimbal [Kimbrell] to let his men be placed around the house and for him to come in alone: and he can arrest us. all I am afraid of is that in the Fort we might be poisoned or killed through a window at night. but You can arrange that all right. tell the Commanding Officer to watch )Let Goodwin( he would not hesitate to do anything there Will be danger on the road of Somebody Waylaying us to kill us on the road to the Fort. You will never catch those fellows on the road Watch Fritzes. Captain Bacas ranch and the Brewery they Will either go to Seven Rivers or to Jicarillo Mountains they will stay around close untill the scouting parties come in. give a spy a pair of glasses and let him get on the mountain back of Fritzes and watch and if they are there there will be provisions carried to them. it is not my place to advise you, but I am anxious to have them caught, and perhaps know how men hide from Soldiers, better than you. please excuse me for having so much to say*

*and I still remain Yours Truly*
*W H. Bonney*

P.S.
*I have changed my mind Send Kimbal [Kimbrell] to Gutieres just below San Patricio one mile, because Sanger and Ballard are or were great friends of Camels [Billy Campbell's] Ballard told me ~~today~~ yesterday to leave for you were doing everything to catch me. it was a blind to get me to leave tell Kimbal [Kimbrell] not to come before 3 oclock for I may not be there before*

## **THE LEW WALLACE INTERVIEW**

For his sham arrest in Lincoln, Lew Wallace and Billy were housed next door to each other; with Billy in his friend, jailor Juan Patrón's, house, and Wallace at José Montaño's. On March 23, 1879, Wallace interviewed Billy, asking nothing about the Lincoln County War. At this period, Wallace was also collecting information about Territorial outlawry, and Billy seems to have responded to that quest by telling him about the Santa Fe Ring's network of cattle rustlers, who fulfilled the beef contracts for Fort Stanton and the Mescalero Indian Reservation; which were held by the local Ring front, "The House," then controlled by James J. Dolan and John Riley. Noteworthy is Billy's vast fund of local information and geography. The notes stated:

William Bonney ("Kid")
*relative to arrangement
with him.
Notes:*

3-23-1879

## Statements by Kid, made Sunday night March 23, 1879

1. There is a cattle trail beginning about 5 miles above Yellow Lake in a cañon, running a little west of north to Cisneza del Matcho (Mule Spring) and continuing around the point of the Capitan Mountains down toward Carrizozo in the direction of the Rio Grande. Frank Wheeler, Jake Owens and Dutch Chris are supposed to have used this trail taking a bunch of cattle over. Vansickle told K. so. They stopped and killed two beavers for Sam Corbett – hush money to Vansickle to whom they gave the beavers. Vansickle also said the Owens-Wheeler outfit mentioning "Chris" Ladbessor using this trail for about a year, but that lately their horses had given out, and of 140 head which they started to work they had only got through with 40. That now they were going to the Reservation to make a raid on the Indian horses to work on.

### The Rustlers.

The "Rustlers," Kid says: were organized in Fort Stanton. Before they organized as "Rustlers" they had been with Peppin's posse. They came from Texas. Owens was conspicuous amongst them. **They were organized before the burning of McSween's house**, and after that they went on their first trip down the county as far as the Coe's ranch and **thence to the Feliz where they took the Tunstall cattle.** From the Feliz they went to the Pecos, where some of them deserted, Owens amongst them. (Martin, known to Sam Corbett) was in charge of the Tunstall cattle, and was taken prisoner, and saw them kill one of their own party. On the same trip they burnt Lola Wise's house, and took some horses. Coe at the time was ranching at the house. On this trip they moved behind a body of soldiers, one company, and a company of Navajo Scouts. They moved in sight of the soldiers, taking horses, insulting women. Lorenzo Trujillo (Jus. Peder) Juan Trujillo, Jose M. Gutierres, Pancho Sanchez, Santos Tafoya, are witnesses against them. They stopped on Pecos at Seven Rivers. Collins, now at Silver City, was one of the outfit – nick-named the Prowler by the cowboys. At Seven Rivers. There joined them Gus Gildey (wanted at San Antonio for killing Mexicans) Gildey is carrying the mail now from Stockton to Seven Rivers – James Irvin and

Reese Gobles, (rumored that their bodies were found in a drift down the Pecos) – Rustling Bob (found dead in the Pecos, killed by his own party) – John Selman (whereabouts unknown) came to Roswell while [Captain] Carroll was there –

The R's [Rustlers] stayed at Seven Rivers; which they left on their second trip via the Berenda for Fort Stanton. On their return back they killed Chavez boys and the crazy boy, Lorenzo – and the Sanchez boy, 14 years old. They also committed many robberies. They broke up after reaching the Pecos, promising to return when some more horses got fat.

## Shedd's Ranch

The trail used going from Seven Rivers to Shedd's was round the S.W. part of the Guadalupe Mts. by a tank on the right hand of trail: from Shedd's the drives would be over to Las Cruces Jesse Evans, Frank Baker (killed) Jim [James] McDaniels (at Cruces, ranging between Cruces and El Paso) Reed at Shedd's bought cattle from them – also sold cattle to E.C. Priest, butcher in Cruces. "Big Mose" (at Cruces last heard from) and [blank], deserter from cavalry – (went to Arizona)

## Mimbres

Used to be called Mormon City – situated 30 miles on the road to Cruces from Silver City south. A great many of what are known as "West Harden gang" are there. Among them Joe Olney, known in Mimbres as Joe Hill; he has a ranch in old Mexico somewheres near Coralitos. He makes trips up in this country: was at Penasco not long ago.

## San Nicholas Spring

Is about 18 miles from Shedd's Ranch on the road to Tularosa, left hand road. There's a house at the spring and about 4 or 5 miles from it N.W. is another corral of brush and a spring, situated in a cañon. There Jim [James] McDaniels used to keep stolen Indian horses. McD. one of the Rio Grande posse. Kid says the latter is still used.

## The Jones Family

Came from Texas. Used to keep saloon at Fort Griffin. The family consists of the father, Jim Jones, John Jones, boy about 10 years old, a girl about 13, and the mother. Marion Turner lives with the family, and he killed a Mexican man at Blazers Mill "just to see him kick." He had no cattle **when the War started**. The Jones, John and Jim, killed a man named Riley, a partner of theirs, on the Penasco 3 or 4 years ago.

# THE "BILLIE" LETTER TO LEW WALLACE

On a likely March 24, 1879, Billy wrote a letter to Wallace about Lincoln County War events. It exists now as a one-page fragment, signed "Billie." I dated and authenticated it in my 2012 book, *Billy the Kid's Writings, Words, and Wit*. It stated:

*... on the Pecos. All that I can remember are the So Called Dolan Outfit but they are all up here now. and on the Rio <u>Grande</u> this man Cris Moten I believe his name is he drove a herd of 80 head one Year ago last December in Company with Frank Wheeler Frank <u>Baker</u> deceased Jesse Evans George Davis alias Tom Jones. Tom Hill, his name in Texas being Tom Chelson also deceased, they drove the cattle to the Indian Reservation and sold them to John Riley and JJ Dolan. and the cattle were turned in for Beef for the Indians the Beckwith family made their boasts that they came to Seven Rivers a little over four years ago with one Milch Cow borrowed from John Chisum they had when I was there Year ago one thousand six hundred head of cattle. the male members of the family are Henry Beckwith and John Beckwith Robert <u>Beckwith</u> was killed the time McSween's house was burned. Charles [blank] Robert Olinger and Wallace Olinger are of the same gang. their cattle ranch is Situated at Rock Corral twelve miles below Seven Rivers on the Pecos. Paxton and Pierce are Still below them forty miles from Seven Rivers there are four of them Paxton: Pierce: Jim Raymers, and Buck Powel. they had when I seen them last about one thousand head of cattle: at Rocky Arroyo there is another Ranch belonging to [blank] Smith who Operated on the Penasco last year with the Jesse Evans gang those and the places I mentioned are all I know of this man Chris Moten at the time they stole those Cattle was in the employ of <u>Dolan</u> and <u>Co</u>. I afterwards Seen Some of the cattle at the Rinconada Bonita on the reservation those were the men we were in search of when we went to the Agency. the Beckwith family were attending to their own Business when this War started but G.W. Peppin told them that this was John Chisums War. and so they took a hand thinking they would lose their Cattle in case that he Chisum won the fight. this is all the information I can give you on this point*

*Yours Respectfully Billie*

## LOST GRAND JURY TESTIMONY

Billy fulfilled his side of the Lew Wallace pardon bargain by testifying against the murderers of Attorney Huston Chapman - James Dolan, Billy Campbell, and Jessie Evans - in the April 1879 Lincoln County Grand Jury. By doing that, he was also implicating the Santa Fe Ring and risking his life. His testimony achieved those men's murder indictments (James Dolan and Billy Campbell for murder; Jessie Evans for accessory to murder).

That testimony was confirmed in *The Grant County Herald* of May 10, 1879, as reprinted from the Mesilla *Thirty Four*: "At the recent term of court in Lincoln, about 200 indictments were found. Among them, Col. Dudley and George W. Peppin for burning McSween's house, **Dolan and Campbell for the Chapman murder, in which the Kid is the principal witness.**"

## TESTIMONY AGAINST N.A.M. DUDLEY

Proof of Billy Bonney's anti-Ring commitment was his testifying against past Fort Stanton Commander N.A.M. Dudley on May 28th and 29th, 1879, since it was not part of his pardon bargain, and it risked his life. But he was seeking justice for Dudley's illegal military intervention in the Lincoln County War Battle, enabling the murders of Billy's compatriots: Alexander McSween, Harvey Morris, Francisco Zamora, and Vincente Romero. Billy twice made the unprotected, nine mile trip from his Lincoln sham custody to the courtroom in the Fort Stanton Adjutant's office for his court appearances.

His Regulator zeal, plus his courage and intellectual brilliance, made him unshakable under Dudley's lawyer's abusive cross-examination. Billy's precise and devastating testimony alone should have yielded a court martial after this interchange: "*How many soldiers fired at you? ... Three ... How many shots did those soldiers fire, that you say shot from the Tunstall building? ... I could not swear to that on account of firing on all sides, I could not hear. I seen them fire one volley ... Were the soldiers which you say fired at you as you escaped from the McSween house on the evening of July 19th last, colored or white? ... White troops.*"

A volley meant the three soldiers fired in unison. That required Dudley's order. "White" meant they were officers. That directly linked Dudley to ordering his soldiers to murder civilians. That was his treasonous Posse Comitatus Act violation. So dangerous was this evidence, that Dudley's lawyer's closing argument devoted a large part to a false attack on Billy.

Noteworthy, is that the Ring had already bestowed his outlaw moniker, "Billy the Kid;" and Billy was still uncertain about it under questioning. His transcript stated:

WILLIAM BONNEY, *a witness being duly sworn, testified as follows.*

    *Q. by Recorder. What is your name and place of residence?*
    *Answer. My name is William Bonney. I reside in Lincoln.*
    *Q. by Recorder. Are you known or called Billy Kidd, also Antrim?*
    *Answer. Yes Sir.*
    *Q. by Recorder. Where were you on the 19th day of July last and what, if anything, did you see of the movements and actions of the troops in that city, state fully?*
    *Answer. I was in the McSween house in Lincoln, and I saw soldiers come from the post with the sheriff's party, that is the sheriff's posse joined them a short distance below there, the McSween house. Soldiers passed on by and the men dropped off and surrounded the house, the sheriff's party. Shortly after, the soldiers came back with Peppin, passed the house twice afterwards. Three soldiers came and stood in front of the house, in front of the windows. Mr. McSween wrote a note to the officer in charge asking what the soldiers were placed there for. He replied saying that they had business there, that if a shot was fired over his camp, or at Peppin, or at any of his men, that he had no objection to blowing up, if he wanted, his own house. I read the note myself, he handed it to me to read. I saw nothing further of the soldiers until night. I was in the back part of the house.* **When I escaped from the house three soldiers fired at me from the Tunstall store, outside corner of the store.** *That's all I know in regards to it.*
    *Q. by Recorder. Did the soldiers that stood in front of the windows have guns with them while there?*
    *Answer. Yes Sir.*
    *Q. by Recorder. Who escaped from the house with you and who was killed at the time, if you know, while attempting to make their escape?*
    *Answer. Jose Chavez [Chávez y Chávez] escaped with me, Vincente Romero, Francisco Zamora and McSween.*
    *Q. by Recorder. How many persons were killed in that fight that day, if you know, and who killed them, if you know?*

*Answer. I seen five killed, I could not swear to who killed them, I seen some of them that fired.*

*Q. by Recorder. Who did you see that fired?*

*Answer. Robt. Beckwith, John Hurley, John Jones,* **those three soldiers, I don't know their names.**

*Q. by Recorder. Did you see any persons setting fire to the McSween house that day, if so, state who it was, if you know?*

*Answer. I did, Jack Long, and there was another man I did not recognize.*

*Recorder stated he had finished with the witness.*
*Cross examination.*

*Q. By Col. Dudley. What were you, and the others there with you, doing in McSween's house that day?*

*Answer. We came here with McSween.*

*Q. By Col. Dudley. Did you know, or had you not heard, that the sheriff was endeavoring to arrest yourself and others there with you at the time?*

*Answer. Yes Sir. I had heard so, I did not know.*

*Q. By Col. Dudley. Then were you not engaged in resisting the sheriff at the time you were in the house?*

*Objected to by Recorder. The Court has already ruled that nothing extraneous from the actual occurrence that took place, and Col. Dudley's actions in connection therewith, should be further inquired into ... it cannot be a matter of defense of Col. Dudley or justify his actions however much the parties may have been resisting the sheriff or civil authorities.*

*Lt. Col. Dudley, by his Counsel, states he does not deem it necessary to make reply to the objection.*

*Objection sustained.*

*Q. By Col. Dudley. In addition to the names you have given, are you also known as the "Kid?"*

*Answer. I have already answered that question, Yes Sir, I am, but not "Billy Kid" that I know of.*

*Q. By Col. Dudley. Were you not and were not the parties with you in the McSween house on the 19th day of July last and the days immediately preceding, engaged in firing at the sheriff's posse?*

*Court objects to the question.*

*Lt. Col. Dudley, by his Counsel, asks, does the Court intend to rule here, that after once gone into this matter of firing into the McSween house by the testimony of this witness, it is not permissible to show all the circumstances under which this firing took place ...*

Court cleared and closed.

Court opened and its decision announced ...

The Court directs the case to proceed calling attention to its previous rulings which were deemed sufficient by explicit.

Q. By Col. Dudley. Whose name was signed to the note received by McSween in reply to the one previously sent by him to Col. Dudley?

Answer. Signed N.A.M. Dudley, did not say what rank, he received two notes, one had no name signed to it.

Q. By Col. Dudley. Are you as certain of everything else you have sworn to as you are to what you have sworn to in answer to the last proceeding question?

Answer. Yes Sir.

Q. By Col. Dudley. From which direction did Peppin come the first time the soldiers passed with him?

Answer. Passed up from the direction of where the soldiers camped, the first time I saw him.

Q. By Col. Dudley. What direction did he come from the second time?

Answer. From the direction of the [Wortley] hotel from the McSween house.

Q. By Col. Dudley. In what direction did you go upon your escape from the McSween house?

Answer. Ran towards the Tunstall store, was fired at, and there turned towards the river.

Q. By Col. Dudley. From what part of the McSween house did you make your escape?

Answer. The northeast corner of the house.

**Q. By Col. Dudley. How many soldiers fired at you?**

**Answer. Three.**

Q. By Col. Dudley. How many soldiers were with Peppin when he passed the McSween house each time, as you say?

Answer. Three.

Q. By Col. Dudley. The soldiers appeared to go in company of threes that day, did they not?

Answer. All that I ever saw appeared to be three in a crowd at a time after they passed the first time.

Q. By Col. Dudley. Who was killed first that day, Bob Beckwith or McSween men?

Answer. Harvey Morris, McSween man, was killed first.

Q. By Col. Dudley. How far is the Tunstall building from the McSween house?

Answer. I could not say how far, I never measured the distance. I should judge it to be 40 yards, between 30 and 40 yards.

**Q. By Col. Dudley. How many shots did those soldiers fire, that you say shot from the Tunstall building?**

Answer. *I could not swear to that on account of firing on all sides, I could not hear. I seen them fire one volley.*

Q. By Col. Dudley. What did they fire at?

**Answer. Myself and Jose Chavez [Chávez y Chávez].**

Q. By Col. Dudley. Did you not just now state in answer to the question who killed Zamora, Romero, Morris, and McSween that you did not know who killed them, but you saw Beckwith, John Jones, **and three soldiers fire at them**?

Answer. Yes Sir. I did.

Q. By Col. Dudley. Were these men, the McSween men, there with you **when the volley was fired at you and Chavez by the soldiers**?

Answer. Just a short ways behind us.

Q. By Col. Dudley. Were you looking back at them?

Answer. No Sir.

Q. By Col. Dudley. How then do you know they were just behind you then, or that they were in range of the volley?

Answer. Because there was a high fence behind, and a good many guns to keep them there. I could hear them speak.

Q. By Col. Dudley. How far were you from the soldiers when you saw them?

Answer. I could not swear exactly, between 30 and 40 yards.

**Q. By Col. Dudley. Did you know either of the soldiers that were in front of the window of McSween's house that day? If so, give it.**

Answer. No Sir, I am not acquainted with them.

Redirect.

Q. by Recorder. Explain whether all the men that were in the McSween house came out at the same time when McSween and the others were killed and the firing came from the soldiers and others?

Answer. Yes Sir, all came out at the same time. **The firing was done by the soldiers until some had escaped.**

Recorder stated that he had finished with the witness.

*Q. by Col. Dudley. How do you know if you were making your escape at the time and the men Zamora, Morris and McSween were behind you that they were killed at that time, is it not true that you did not know of their death or the death of either of them until afterwards?*

*Answer. I knew of the death of some of them, I did know of the death of one of them. I saw him lying down there.*

*Q. by Col. Dudley. Did you see any of the men last mentioned killed?*

*Answer. Yes Sir, I did, I seen Harvey Morris killed first, he was out in front of me.*

*Q. by Col. Dudley. Did you not then a moment ago swear that he was among those who were behind you and Jose Chavez [Chávez y Chávez] when you saw the soldiers deliver the volley?*

*Answer. No Sir, I didn't think I did. I misunderstood the question if I did. I said he was among them that was killed not behind me.*

*Witness then withdrew ...*

In Billy's second day of testimony on May 29th, he confirmed that Dudley's white officers fired at escaping McSweens, including himself; and that visibility came from the burning McSween house that made the area *"almost light as day."* The transcript stated:

*Q. by Court. Were the soldiers which you say fired at you as you escaped from the McSween house on the evening of July 19th last, colored or white?*

*Answer. White troops.*

*Q. by Court. Was it light enough so you could distinctly see the soldiers when they fired?*

*Answer. The house was burning. Made it almost light as day for a short distance all around.*

## LETTER OF DECEMBER 12, 1880 TO LEW WALLACE

After Governor Lew Wallace betrayed the pardon bargain, Billy was publicly outlawed in lurid press. On December 12, 1880, he wrote to Wallace to deny a December 3, 1880 *Las Vegas Gazette* article by J.H. Koogler, titled "Desperadoe's Stronghold."

Billy's letter made clear that he did not consider himself an outlaw. He wrote: "*I noticed in the Las Vegas Gazette a piece which stated that, Billy "the" Kid, the name by which I am known in the Country was the captain of a Band of Outlaws who hold Forth at the Portales.* **There is no such Organization in Existence. So the Gentleman must have drawn very heavily on his Imagination.**" In addition, the letter shows his self-assured legal knowledge, describing to Wallace that he considered the posse illegal, for lack of proper arrest warrants: "*I asked for their Papers [warrants] and they had none. So I concluded that it amounted to nothing more than a mob.*"

By that December 12th, he had endured Secret Service pursuit, another lost pardon through a possible Secret Service bargain, two White Oaks posse ambushes, and a false murder accusation for Jim Carlyle. Seven days later, Garrett's posse would ambush Billy's group near Fort Sumner, killing Tom O'Folliard, intending to kill him. Ten days away was Billy's Stinking Springs capture, where Garrett would shoot dead Charlie Bowdre when mistaking him for Billy. Billy wrote:

*Fort Sumner*
*Dec. 12th 1880*
*Gov. Lew Wallace*
*Dear Sir*

**I noticed in the Las Vegas Gazette a piece which stated that, Billy "the" Kid, the name by which I am known in the Country was the captain of a Band of Outlaws who hold Forth at the Portales. There is no such Organization in Existence. So the Gentleman must have drawn very heavily on his Imagination.** *My business at the White Oaks at the time I was waylaid and my horse killed was to See Judge Leonard who has my case in hand. he had written me to come up, that he thought he could get Everything Straightened up I did not find him at the Oaks & Should have gone to Lincoln if I had met with no accident. After mine and Billie Wilsons horses were killed we both made our way to a Station, forty miles from the Oaks kept by Mr Greathouse. When I got up the next morning The house was Surrounded by an outfit led by one Carlyle, Who had come into the house and Demanded a Surrender. I asked for their Papers [warrants] and they had none. So I concluded that it amounted to nothing more than a mob and told Carlyle that he would have to Stay in the house and lead the way out that night. Soon after a* *note was brought in Stating that if Carlyle did not come out inside of five minutes they would Kill the Station Keeper )Greathouse) who had left the house and was with them. in a Short time a Shot was fired on the outside and Carlyle thinking Greathouse was Killed jumped through the window. breaking the Sash as he went and was killed by his own Party they thinking it was me trying to make my Escape. the Party then withdrew.*

*they returned the next day and burned an old man named Spencer's house and Greathouses also*

*I made my way to this Place afoot and During my absence Deputy Sheriff Garrett Acting under Chisum's orders went to the Portales and found Nothing. on his way back he went by Mr Yerby's ranch and took a pair of mules of mine which I had left with Mr Bowdre who is in Charge of mr Yerby's cattle. he (Garrett) claimed that they were stolen and even if they were not he had no right to Confiscate any Outlaws property.*

*I had been at Sumner Since I left Lincoln making my living Gambling the mules were bought by me the truth of which I can prove by the best citizens around Sumner. J.S. Chisum is the man who got me into Trouble and was benefited Thousands by it and is now doing all he can against me There is no Doubt but what there is a great deal of Stealing going on in the Territory. and a great deal of the Property is taken across the [Staked] Plains as it is a good outlet but so far as my being at the head of a Band there is nothing of it in Several Instances I have recovered Stolen Property when there was no chance to get an Officer to do it.*

*one instance for Hugo Zuber Post office Puerto de Luna. another for Pablo Analla Same Place.*

*if Some impartial Party were to investigate this matter they would find it far Different from the impression put out by Chisum and his Tools.*

*Yours Respect*
*William Bonney*

## SANTA FE JAIL LETTER: JANUARY 1, 1881

After capture, Billy was kept in the Santa Fe jail, awaiting transport to Mesilla for his hanging trial. On January 1, 1881, four days after arriving, he wrote to Lew Wallace:

*Santa Fe*
*Jan 1st 1881*

*Gov. Lew Wallace*
*Dear Sir*
*I would like to see you for a few moments if You can spare the time.*
*Yours Respect.*
*W.HBonney*

## SANTA FE JAIL LETTER: MARCH 2, 1881

On March 2, 1881, Billy sent his second jail letter, which Wallace considered "blackmail." Billy wrote:

*Santa Fe Jail New Mex*
*March 2nd 1881*
*Gov. Lew Wallace*
*Dear Sir*
*I wish you would come down to the jail to see me. it will be to your interest to come and see me.* **I have some letters which date back two years, and there are Parties who are very anxious to get them but I shall not dispose of them until I see you. that is if you will come immediately**
*Yours Respect*
*W<u>m</u> H Bonney*

## SANTA FE JAIL LETTER: MARCH 4, 1881

On March 4, 1881, Billy wrote his third jail letter in tragic confirmation of the pardon's betrayal: "*I have done everything that I promised you I would, and You have done nothing that You promised me.*" Billy wrote:

> Santa Fe. In jail.
> March 4th 1881
> Gov. Lew Wallace
>
> Dear Sir
>     I wrote You a little note the day before yesterday but have received no annser. I Expect you have forgotten what you promised me, this Month two Years ago. but I have not, and I think You had ought to have come and seen me as I requested you to. **I have done everything that I promised you I would, and You have done nothing that You promised me.**
>
>     I think when You think the matter over, You will come down and See me, and I can then Explain Everything to You.
>
>     Judge Leonard, Passed through here on his way East, in january and promised to come and See me on his way back. but he did not fulfill his Promise. it looks to me like I am getting left in the Cold. I am not treated right by [U.S. Marshal John] Sherman. he lets Every Stranger that comes to See me through Curiosity in to See me, but will not let a Single one of my friends in, not Even an Attorney.
>
>     I guess they mean to Send me up without giving me any Show. but they will have a nice time doing it. I am not entirely without friends.
>
>     I shall Expect to See you Sometime today
>     Patiently Waiting
>     I am Very truly Yours, Respect.
>     W<u>m</u> H. Bonney.

## SANTA FE JAIL LETTER: MARCH 27, 1881

On March 27, 1881, Billy wrote to Wallace for the last time, emphasizing the pardon bargain, possibly hoping that it would be issued after sentencing in the Mesilla trial. He wrote:

> Santa Fe New Mexico
> March 27th/81
> Gov Lew Wallace
> Dear Sir
>     for the last <u>time</u> I ask: Will you keep Your promise. I start below tomorrow. Send Annser by bearer.
>     Yours Respt
>     WBonney

# LETTER TO ATTORNEY EDGAR CAYPLESS

After Billy's unjust hanging sentence for the Regulators' killing of Sheriff William Brady, handed down by Ringite Judge Warren Bristol on April 13, 1881, Billy wanted to appeal. Two days later, on April 15th, he wrote to Las Vegas attorney, Edgar Caypless, whom he had earlier hired on contingency to file his audacious replevin (rustling) suit for recovery of his bay mare from Pat Garrett's posseman, Frank Stewart, who had stolen her at Billy's Stinking Springs capture. Billy hoped to sell her to pay an appeal lawyer, with grounds that his Spanish-speaking jurymen had been deprived of a translator.

Caypless prevailed in the replevin case, but only after Billy's death; and he kept the mare's sales price as fee.

For his last known letter, Billy wrote:

*Dear Sir. I would have written before this but could get no paper. My United States case was thrown out of court and I was rushed to trial on my Territorial charge. was convicted of murder in the first degree and am to be hanged on the 13th day of May. Mr. A.J. Fountain was appointed to defend me and has done the best he could for me. He is willing to carry the case further if I can raise the money to bear his expense. The mare is about all I can depend on at present so hope you will settle the case right away and give him the money you get for her. If you do not settle the matter with Scott Moore [to whom Frank Stewart sold the mare] and have to go to court about it either give him [Fountain] the mare or sell her at auction and give him the money. please do as he wishes in the matter. I know you will do the best you can for me in this. I shall be taken to Lincoln tomorrow. Please write and direct care of Garrett, sheriff. excuse bad writing. I have my handcuffs on. I remain as ever*

*Yours respectfully,*
*W.H. Bonney*

# NEWSPAPER INTERVIEWS

Billy Bonney's press interviews occurred after his Stinking Springs capture, and after his Mesilla hanging verdict. He was already nationally famous, and making ironic commentary like in his April 3, 1881's Santa Fe *Daily New Mexican's* "Something About the Kid": "At least two hundred men have been killed in Lincoln County during the past three years, but I did not kill all of them."

On December 27, 1880, the *Las Vegas Daily Gazette* published editor, Lucius "Lute" Wilcox's, article about the Stinking Springs capture and prisoner transport to Las Vegas, titled: 'The Kid. Interview with Billy Bonney The Best Known Man in New Mexico." Billy teased his outlaw myth; stating about onlookers: "Well, perhaps some of them will think me half man now; everyone seems to think I was some sort of animal." Wilcox wrote:

With its customary enterprise, the *Gazette* was the first paper to give the story of the capture of Billy Bonney, who has risen to notoriety under the sobriquet of "the Kid," Billy Wilson, Dave Rudabaugh and Tom Pickett. Just at this time everything of interest about the men is especially interesting, and after damning the men in general and "the Kid" in particular through the columns of this paper we considered it the correct thing to give them a show.

Through the kindness of [San Miguel County] Sheriff Romero, a representative of the *Gazette* was admitted to the jail yesterday morning.

Mike Cosgrove, the obliging mail contractor, who has met the boys frequently while on business down the Pecos, had just gone in with four large bundles. The doors at the entrance stood open, and the large crowd strained their necks to get a glimpse of the prisoners, who stood in the passageway like children waiting for a Christmas tree distribution. One by one the bundles were unpacked disclosing a good suit of clothes for each man. Mr. Cosgrove remarked that he wanted "to see the boys go away in style."

"Billy the Kid," and Billy Wilson who were shackled together stood patiently while a blacksmith took off their shackles and bracelets to allow them an opportunity to make a change of clothing. Both prisoners watched the operation which was to set them free for a short while, but Wilson scarcely raised his eyes, and spoke but once or twice to his compadres. **Bonney on the other hand, was light and chipper, and was very communicative, laughing, joking and chatting with the bystanders.**

"You appear to take it easy," the reporter said.

"Yes! What's the use of looking at the gloomy side of everything. The laugh's on me this time," he said. Then looking about the placita, he asked: "Is the jail at Santa Fe any better than this?"

This seemed to trouble him considerably, for as he explained, "this is a terrible place to put a fellow in." He put the same question to every one who came near him and when he learned that there was nothing better in store for him, he shrugged his shoulders and said something about putting up with what he had to.

**He was the attraction of the show, and as he stood there, lightly kicking the toes of his boots on the stone pavement to keep his feet warm, one would scarcely mistrust that he was the hero of "Forty Thieves," romance which this paper has been running in serial form for six weeks or more.**

"There was a big crowd gazing at me wasn't there?" he exclaimed, and then smiling continued: "Well perhaps some of them will think me half a man now; everyone seems to think I was some kind of an animal."

He did look human, indeed, but there was nothing very mannish about him in appearance, for he looked and acted like a mere boy. He is about five feet, eight or nine inches tall, slightly built and lithe, weighing about 140; a frank and open countenance, looking like a school boy, with the traditional silky fuzz on his upper lip, clear blue eyes, with a roguish snap about them, light hair and complexion. He is, in all, quite a handsome looking fellow, the only imperfection being two prominent front teeth, slightly protruding like a squirrels' teeth, and he has agreeable and winning ways.

On December 28, 1880, for the *Las Vegas Gazette*, from inside the train to Santa Fe, for "Interview with the Kid," Billy's steely self-control is evident when one realizes it was detained by a mob, either to lynch or to rescue him. The article stated:

We saw him again at the depot when the crowd presented a really war like appearance. Standing by the car, out of one of the windows from which he was leaning, he talked freely with us of the whole affair:

"I don't blame you for writing of me as you have. You have had to believe others' stories, but then **I don't know as anyone would believe anything good of me, anyway,**" he said. "**I really wasn't the leader of any gang.** I was for Billy all the time. About that Portales business, I owned the ranch with Charlie Bowdre. I took it up and was holding it because I knew that at some time a stage line would run there, and I wanted to keep it for a station. **But I found that there were certain men who wouldn't let me live in the country and so I was going to leave.**

We had all our grub in the house when they took us in, and we were going to a place six miles away in the morning to cook it and then light out. I haven't stolen any stock. I made my living by gambling, but that was the only way I could live. **They wouldn't let me settle down; if they had I wouldn't be here today,**" and he held up his right arm on which was the bracelet.

"Chisum got me into all this trouble and then wouldn't help me out. I went up to Lincoln to stand my trial on the warrant that was out for me, but the Territory took a change of venue to Dona Ana, and I knew I had no show, and so I skinned out ...

If it had not been for the dead horse in the doorway I wouldn't be here in Las Vegas. I would have ridden out on my bay mare and taken my chances of escaping. But I couldn't ride over that for she would have jumped back **and I would have got it in the head**. We could have stayed in the house but there wouldn't have been anything gained by that for they would have starved us out. I thought it was better to come out and get a square meal - don't you?"

The prospects of a fight exhilarated him, and he bitterly bemoaned being chained. "If I only had my Winchester, I'd lick the whole crowd" was his confident comment on the strength of the attacking party. He sighed and sighed again for the chance to take a hand in the fight and the burden of his desire was to be set free to fight on the side of his captors as soon as he should smell powder.

As the train rolled out, he lifted his hat and invited us to call and see him in Santa Fe, calling out "*adios.*"

Billy's loyal attorney, Ira Leonard, protectively accompanied him on the train ride to Mesilla, via the Rincón depot. From there, they took the stagecoach ride to Las Cruces. With them were guards and prisoner, Billy Wilson, also transported to Mesilla. At Las Cruces, a crowd had gathered to see the famous outlaw, Billy the Kid. The arrival was covered in the April 3, 1881 Santa Fe *Daily New Mexican* in: "Something About the Kid." It stated:

An extract of a letter written by W.S. Fletcher from Mesilla to a gentleman in the city reads about as follows: Tony Neis and Francisco Chaves, deputy U.S. Marshals, arrived Thursday night with **Billy, the Kid,** and Billy Wilson. They met an ugly crowd at Rincon, where some threats were made, but Tony's crowd were too much for them. **At Las Cruces an impulsive mob gathered around the coach and someone asked which is "Billy the Kid." The Kid himself answered by placing his hand on Judge Leonard's shoulder and saying "this is the man."** The Kid weakened somewhat at Las Cruces, where he found quite a number of Lincoln County men, who were to appear against him as witnesses.

[AUTHOR'S NOTE: Billy had no defense witnesses. The prosecution had Ringites James Dolan, Saturnino Baca, and Sheriff William Brady's deputy, Billy Matthews; and subpoenaed Lincolnite, Isaac Ellis.]

**He says at least two hundred men have been killed in Lincoln County during the past three years, but that he did not kill all of them.** I think twenty murders can be charged against him. He was arraigned yesterday (Wednesday) before the United States court for the murder of Roberts, on the Mescalero Apache reservation, in 1878. Judge Leonard was assigned to his defense. Judge Newcomb gave notice that he had three other indictments for murder against him, and it looks as if he had no show to get off. His counsel asked today for time to send to Lincoln, which was granted, so that his trial will not commence for at least ten days. Billy Wilson's case is before the grand jury. He is charged with passing counterfeit money. He has retained Judge Thornton as his counsel. He seems to have friends here while the Kid has none.

No mails between Rincon and Doña Ana for the past week. Mosquitoes and flies abound and weather hot as blazes.

Billy's articulate response to the hanging verdict was in an April 16, 1881 article in the *Mesilla News*. He summarized Santa Fe Ring injustice: "I think it hard that I should be the only one to suffer the extreme penalty of the law." He called his court "mob law;" ending with facetious "personal advice": "If mob law is going to rule, better dismiss judge and sheriff and let all take chances alike." And he said sarcastically: "Advise persons never to engage in killing." About Lew Wallace's pardon, he said curtly: "Don't know that he will do it." The article stated:

Well I had intended at one time not to say a word on my own behalf because persons would say, "Oh he lied." Newman, editor of the *Semi-Weekly*, gave me a rough deal; he created prejudice against me, and is trying to incite a mob to lynch me. He sent me a paper which showed it; I think it a dirty mean advantage to take of me, **considering my situation and knowing that I could not defend myself by word or act. But I suppose he thought he would give me a kick down hill.** Newman came to see me the other day. I refused to talk to him or tell him anything. But I believe the *News* is always willing to give its readers both sides of a question. **If mob law is going to rule, better dismiss judge and sheriff and let all take chances alike.** I expect to be lynched going to Lincoln. **Advise persons never to engage in killing.** Considering the active part Governor Wallace took on our side and the friendly relations that existed between him and me, and the promise he made me, I think he ought to pardon me. Don't know that he will do it. When I was arrested for that murder he let me out and gave me freedom of the town, and let me go about with my arms. When I got ready to leave Lincoln in June, 1879, I left. **I think it hard that I should be the only one to suffer the extreme penalty of the law.**

For his secret transport to Lincoln for hanging, to prevent his partisans' rescue, in darkness, on April 17, 1881, Billy was taken by wagon from the Mesilla jail. April 20, 1881's *Newman's Semi-Weekly* reported his departure, with Billy, as usual, joking:

On Saturday night about 10 o'clock Deputy U.S. marshal Robt. Ollinger [sic] with deputy sheriff David Wood and a posse of five men (Tom Williams, Billy Mathews [sic], John Kinney, D.M. Reade and W.A. Lockhart) started for Lincoln with Henry Antrim *alias* the Kid. The fact that they intended to leave at that time had been purposely concealed and the report circulated that they would not leave before the middle of the week in order to avoid any possibility of trouble, it having been rumored that the Kid's band would attempt a rescue. They stopped in front of our office while we talked to them, and we handed the Kid an addressed envelope with some paper and he said he would write some things he wanted to make public. **He appeared quite cheerful and remarked that he wanted to stay until their whiskey gave out, anyway.** Said he was sure that his guard would not hurt him unless a rescue should be attempted and he was certain that it would not be done, unless, perhaps, "those fellows at White Oaks come out to take me," meaning to kill him. **It was, he said, about a stand-off whether he was hanged or killed in the wagon ...** He was hand-cuffed to the back seat of the ambulance. Kinney sat beside him, Olinger on the seat facing him, Mathews on the seat facing Kinney, Lockhart driving, and Reade, Wood and Williams riding along on horseback on each side and behind. The whole party was armed to the teeth and anyone who knows the men of whom it was composed will admit that a rescues would be a hazardous undertaking. Kid was informed that if trouble should occur he would be shot first and the attacking party attended to afterwards.

# CONCLUSION

The real Billy Bonney's high intelligence, literacy, and fund of knowledge,- proved by his own writings and recorded words - contrasts the mental dullness and ignorance of information of his imposters; and is their undoing.

# PART II

## THE "BRUSHY BILL" ROBERTS BILLY THE KID IMPOSTER HOAX

# CHAPTER 1
## CREATORS OF THE "BRUSHY BILL" IMPOSER HOAX

### THE "BRUSHY BILL" HOAX

The most elaborate and enduring Billy the Kid imposter hoax, began with a deranged mid-twentieth century old-timer named Oliver Pleasant Roberts, self-named "Brushy Bill." His becoming "Billy the Kid" arose from his alliance with two men, each now dead: a con-artist traveling salesman named William Vincent Morrison; and a wannabe historian and English teacher, named Charles Leland Sonnichsen. Their 1955 book promoting that impersonator, *Alias Billy the Kid*, became "Brushy's" subsequent believers' bible.

Severely limited by lack of scholarly Billy the Kid history books, those three hoaxers had to rely on fabricating "Brushy's" Billy the Kid persona with known historical names and pseudo-history built around them; adding coaching and "sight seeing" trips to Lincoln for him. It did not work, either in their attempt to get him a modern-day governor's pardon as Billy the Kid; or for their book presenting him as Billy. But his total mismatch to Billy Bonney did not faze his later promoters, who declared real Billy's history was just a fake conspiracy of historians against him!

The "Brushy" scam relied on readers' ignorance of the true history, and their misguided image of Billy Bonney derived from the Santa Fe Ring's dime novel-like outlaw myth publications. The flimflam had two parts: "Brushy" must be Billy because he knew things-not-printed; and "Brushy" must be Billy because he was illiterate and could not read-up on things-printed. Both were lies. But the biggest lie was hiding that he was born 20 years *after* Billy Bonney. That was the hoaxes' biggest problem. Another problem was that people were not as dumb as they hoped.

# THE "BRUSHY BILL" HOAX TRIUMVIRATE

It took three men with complementary skills to create a Frankensteinian Billy the Kid. There was "Brushy Bill" Roberts, crazy enough to play the character; William V. Morrison, willing to research and coach; and C.L. Sonnichsen, posing as an historical expert vouching for the gambit. The upshot was their 1955 book, *Alias Billy the Kid*, promoting "Brushy" as Billy, and rationalizing the three men's failure to get him accepted as such.

## *OLIVER P. ("L.") "BRUSHY BILL" ROBERTS*

By the time Oliver Pleasant "Brushy Bill" Roberts entered the world stage in 1950, at 71, he had manifested handicaps of mental illness, vocational disability, and sociopathic deviancy. As reported by his family member Roy L. Haws, in his 2015 book, *Brushy Bill: Proof that His Claim to be Billy the Kid Was a Hoax*, in 1936, "Brushy" had altered his birth year from 1879 to 1868, and changed his name from Oliver P. to Oliver L. Roberts for identity fraud to collect Texas's newly offered Social Security benefits. (Haws, Page 24)

But "Brushy" compensated for his personal failures by tall tales of wild adventures as Old West fictional personas. According to historian, Don Cline, for his 1988 unpublished manuscript, *Brushy Bill Roberts: I Wasn't Billy the Kid*, "Brushy" "yearned for the wild, adventuresome life of the outlaws he heard and read about." (Cline, Page 91) And "Brushy's" family member, Roy L. Haws, even located a 1949 movie with early cowboy Lash LaRue, titled "Son of Billy the Kid," in which Pat Garrett does not kill Billy, who then becomes law-abiding - like "Brushy's own script. Haws speculated it fueled "Brushy's" fable. (Haws, Page 90)

The specifics of "Brushy's" pathology can only be surmised by his dependence on care by family members or his four wives, and his erratic employment in menial jobs. His long-winded tall tales match confabulation, a disorder in which absent knowledge is filled in by over-elaborated autobiographical or historical fables. It appears in diseases of memory, like dementias; and also in psychosis - like telling tales of being Napoleon. Would "Brushy" have known he was lying? His benefits fraud proves his capacity for his willful deceit. But being "Billy the Kid" was delusional.

So "Brushy" may have suffered from a schizophrenic disorder, with delusions of grandeur to counter his sad reality.

Self-named also as "Kid Roberts," "Texas Kid," "Rattlesnake Bill," "Hugo Kid," and "William Henry" Roberts (to match William Henry Bonney), he also claimed to have been a Jesse James gang member, a Roosevelt's Rough Rider, a Buffalo Bill Cody Wild West performer, a Pinkerton Detective, a bronco rider, a friend of Bell Starr, a Deputy U.S. Marshall, a rancher in Mexico, and an associate of Pancho Villa.

And he collected similarly disturbed, imposter friends. As will be seen, one was a Jesse James imposter; another presented himself as Lincoln County War badman, Jessie Evans. "Brushy's" family member, Roy L. Haws, for his 2015 *Brushy Bill: Proof that His Claim to be Billy the Kid Was a Hoax*, found a letter "Brushy" had written to a Kit Carson impersonator named Oran Ardious Woodman, who called himself "Uncle Kit Carson, Father of Billy the Kid." In a seeming *folie a deux* - two sharing delusion - on April 1, 1949, "Brushy" wrote to Woodman as "your son, O.L. Roberts," about Billy the Kid visiting him in Hico, Texas. (Haws, Pages 113-114) Haws felt that "Brushy" copied Woodman's own fakery: including an altered birth date, claiming employment by John Chisum, being a Rough Rider, and being in Buffalo Bill's and Pawnee Bill's Wild West Shows. (Haws, Pages 116-117)

"Brushy was discovered in 1949 through his imposter network by William V. Morrison; then was coached and promoted by Morrison as a cash cow for a publicity-grabbing gubernatorial pardon and future movie deals as Billy the Kid. One can surmise that Morrison, in his greedy urgency, over-taxed this fragile man with high-pressure prompting and exposure to public ridicule with the failed pardon, possibly contributing to his fatal December 27, 1950 heart attack, at 71 years, 4 months, and 1 day.

"Brushy's" actual life was researched through Roberts family interviews by historian, Don Cline, for his 1988 unpublished manuscript, *Brushy Bill Roberts: I Wasn't Billy the Kid*. Cline also used the Roberts family Bible, which listed "Brushy's" parents and siblings, all of whom Cline stated he confirmed by census reports and death certificates. (Cline, Page 110) Born as Oliver Pleasant Roberts on August 26, 1879 to a farming family in Arkansas, which moved to Texas between 1882 and 1884, "Brushy" was the fifth child of his twice married father, "H.O." Roberts; whose first wife, Caroline Dunn, died after two children. "Brushy" was the third child of his father's second wife, Sara Elizabeth Ferguson

Roberts, who then had five more. "Brushy" was the "black sheep," "a drifter ... uninhibited story teller obsessed with cowboys and outlaws, and the town character ... not able to take care of himself ... He always lived with members of his family or not far from them." (Cline, Page 92) "Throughout his life he worked as a farm laborer and [at] odd jobs. On occasion, his brother Tom Roberts would hire him."

"Brushy's" niece, Geneva Pittmon, his full brother, Tom's, daughter, wrote to Cline on April 27, 1988: "I don't know of any job he ever held except for farm work and that was not on welfare then." (Cline, Pahe 110) Clumsy, "Brushy" got injuries with scars, which he would claim were bullet or knife wounds to credulous listeners.

Cline dated "mental deterioration" in 1910, which he called "delusional Paranoia, Grandiose Type." (Cline, Page 93) He dated "Brushy's" first impersonation to 1918, when he claimed to be Jesse James's brother, Frank; which allegedly alienated his care-taker full brother, Tom Roberts. (Cline, Page 94) Between 1919 to about 1921, "Brushy" lived in Oklahoma and Arkansas with his sister, Cordelia, or his parents. In 1920 or 1921, he moved to Canton, Texas, to live again with his brother, Tom, and his family. In 1922, he disappeared, making-up that he had ridden in a Madison Square Garden rodeo and had been in the news. (Page 95) In 1925, he disappeared again, returning with the same claim. At his returns, Tom; Geneva Roberts Pittmon, Tom's daughter; or other family members housed him, while he did menial jobs. His last known work, in about 1929, was in a turkey processing plant. That year he made his third marriage, and moved to Comanche and Hamilton, Texas. There he was taunted for his tall tales, and fled to Gladewater, Texas. (Cline, Page 96)

In Gladewater, in about 1930, "Brushy" apparently developed his Billy the Kid persona. To Cline, the Roberts family confirmed that "Brushy" had no buck teeth like Billy the Kid. (Cline, Page 98) That his impersonating Billy crossed into delusion is implied by family reports of his fearing that signing his Social Security checks would get him arrested as the Kid; though Cline confirmed that he did sign them. (Cline, Page 96) In Gladewater, "Brushy" got his first converts, a duped wealthy oilman, named Dewitt Travis, and a man named Robert E. Lee. (Cline, Page 97)

After his third wife's death in 1944, on January 13, 1945, "Brushy" married Malinda E. Allison, from Hico, Texas. Cline stated that she was aware of his delusions. (Cline, Page 98)

Cline concluded: "When [the] Kid died Brushy was only twenty-three months old and wetting his diapers in Arkansas." (Cline, Page 123) Cline wrote that the "1880 federal census for Arkansas, Sebastion County, Bates Township, June 1, 1880, lines 27-33 shows Brushy at age 10 months that years [sic]. Included were his family Henry Roberts, Sarah Elizabeth Ferguson Roberts and their children Elizabeth, Samantha, Martha, Benny, Mary C. and young Oliver P. Their birth dates and birth places verified by the family Bible and on their death certificates. Brushy was twenty years too young to be Bonney." (Cline, Page 135)

"Brushy's niece, Geneva Pittmon, gave Cline a February 2, 1988 letter from one of her sisters about an author named William Tunstill pressuring the Roberts family to verify "Brushy's" claim. The sister wrote: "These people (meaning the Tunstills) seemed to think the story about him being Billy the Kid is true and it happened when he was younger and we didn't know anything about it. [That was based on "Brushy's" added 20 years.] I told them I didn't believe a word of it and I know it didn't happen that way." (Cline, Pages 103-104) Noteworthy, however, is that hoaxing William Tunstill would subsequently publish a fabricated genealogy pretending there was an Oliver L. Roberts, who was 20 years older than Oliver P. Roberts. And that was clung to by Brushy's" future believers.

## *WILLIAM VINCENT MORRISON*

The man who discovered "Brushy," and was second author of his book, *Alias Billy the Kid*, was William V. Morrison, his hard-working hoax accomplice. Much like "Brushy," he had fictionalized achievements for a lackluster life. An amateur historian and traveling salesman, he called himself an attorney; and capitalized on being a descendant of Ferdinand Maxwell, the oldest brother of New Mexico Territory's famous Lucian Bonaparte Maxwell, owner of the two million acre Maxwell Land Grant; then owner of Fort Sumner.

Morrison's background was investigated by Don Cline, for his 1988, unpublished, *Brushy Bill Roberts: I Wasn't Billy the Kid*. He stated that Morrison claimed to have attended law school in his home town of St. Louis, but: "we discovered he never graduated from a constituted law school nor [did he] apply to the bar association of any state to practice law." (Cline, Page 70) In *Alias*

*Billy the Kid*, Morrison claimed he worked on legal matters in Florida, but the Florida Bar Association had no mention of him. (Cline, Page 70) And he claimed he did legal work for the R.W. Waters Law Firm in Beaumont, Texas, but he was not listed in their firm or the Texas Bar. (Cline, Pages 70-71) Cline found that in 1940-1945 St. Louis directories, he listed himself as a sales clerk or salesman. (Cline, Page 70) But for his Missouri Historical Society membership, he called himself a lawyer. (Cline, Page 70)

Cline found that when Morrison moved to El Paso, Texas, in 1950, city directories, from then to his 1978 death, listed him as a salesman; bankruptcy liquidator; or, after retiring, as selling real estate. (Cline, Page 71) And Morrison was identified by the press as a "traveling salesman" in his 1950 pardon quest for "Brushy."

Cline also interviewed some of Morrison's employers. (Pages 71-73) The widow of J.J. Vance Microfilm Service's owner, where he worked from 1954 to 1955, said she remembered only that he talked about a man who said he was Billy the Kid.

Arthur Graves of Car Parts Depot, hired Morrison as an auto parts salesman, while thinking it odd that a man calling himself a lawyer would take such a low-paying job. Importantly, Morrison gave Graves different versions about "Brushy" than appeared in *Alias Billy the Kid*. He told Graves that "Brushy" had come to see him at his St. Louis office about getting a pardon; though his book stated that Morrison traveled to Hico in 1949 to meet "Brushy." Graves met "Brushy," and did not believe he could speak Spanish (like Billy the Kid). And "Brushy" told him that "many of the old outlaws (all of whom were his friends) were still alive and living in New Mexico in the same village. They had a get-together once a year for a big party." [This may have referred to his fellow imposter friends.] And it was Graves who introduced Morrison to Sonnichsen, because he had taken a course with him at the College of Mines at the University of Texas at El Paso. That meant, at the time of Morrison's pardon quest, he was an auto parts salesman.

Cline learned that, while still selling car parts, Morrison also worked for a Bill Cardon of Dautrich Reality Company from 1960 to 1970, whom he also told he was a lawyer. In this period, Morrison was also a bankruptcy liquidator.

Cline interviewed Pat Garrett's biographer, Leon Metz, who wrote to him on July 2, 1988 saying that he got to know Morrison when he lived near him in El Paso. To Metz, Morrison contradicted his attorney claim, stating that "he was not an attorney and had never claimed to be," and had only investigated bankruptcy proceedings. Interestingly, Metz added that Morrison had also been trying to prove "something different about Pancho Villa and (maybe) Jesse James" (Cline, Page 74), names that would later come up in "Brushy's biographical "memories."

Cline also interviewed, by letter, co-author C.L. Sonnichsen, who stated on June 30, 1988: "I believe, without evidence, that Bill Morrison had a law degree. I have a vague recollection that he told me he earned it at night school in St. Louis. He called himself a non-practicing lawyer. He specialized in bankruptcy cases." (Cline, Page 73)

Cline also noted Morrison's extensive promotional efforts. (Cline, Pages 75-76) After failing to get a gubernatorial pardon for "Brushy," Morrison tried with President Harry S. Truman; and, failing that, tried to get his tapes of "Brushy" and *Alias Billy the Kid* into Truman's presidential library. A March 17, 1954 letter to a Carl Breihan gave Morrison's attempts to sell "Brushy's" story to movie producers; television shows; and cowboy actor, Gene Autry.

Morrison's August 30, 1977 obituary, with information presumably provided by his family, stated: "[He was] "a resident of El Paso for 29 years. He had been associated in the George Hervey Real Estate Co. and in Cardon Real Estate Co. for many years. He was also a retired Bankruptcy Referee for the United States District Court. Mr. Morrison was also a member of the Historical Societies in Missouri, Illinois, and El Paso."

Morrison is idolized by "Brushy's" believers as a hero. But his endeavor to sell "Brushy" as Billy reveals he relied on duplicity as a short-cut to fame and fortune. Part of his escape from deserved exposure, came from his sheer labor and glib tricks, which were beyond the conception of most readers. That left "Brushy" saddled with hoaxing blame that Morrison should share.

## *CHARLES LELAND SONNICHSEN*

The most surprising hoaxer was C.L. Sonnichsen, an English teacher, who wrote about folklore and had published a few books on minor Old West figures. He became the first author of *Alias Billy the Kid*, and his credentials arguably got it published. His quirk seemed to be ambition: creating a contrarian niche in the famous Billy the Kid history, in those early days of scholarly research, which itself was beyond his capacity.

His admiring biographer, Dale L. Walker, wrote in his 1972 *C.L. Sonnichsen: Grassroots Historian*, that Sonnichsen was born on September 20, 1901. He got his B.A. at the University of Minnesota, and an M.A. and Ph.D. at Harvard University, specializing in 17th century English literature. He chaired the English department at Texas College of Mines and Metallurgy for 41 years. After retiring in 1972, he moved to Tucson, Arizona, and edited the *Journal of Arizona History*. He was also president of the Texas Folklore Society, and in the Texas State Historical Association, received writing awards. But just one book is remembered: his *Alias Billy the Kid*. He died on June 29, 1991.

In 1949, he was teaching English in the Texas College of Mines and Metallurgy when Morrison brought "Brushy" to meet him. He liked the act, glossed with huckster Morrison's claim that "Brushy," an illiterate, had inexplicable knowledge of Billy the Kid. And Sonnichsen, as one of the first to witness "Brushy" parroting Morrison's fakery, proved he possessed more hubris than history by thinking "Brushy" sounded like the real deal.

Sonnichsen's biographer, Dale L. Walker, wrote: "Roberts was decked out in a fringed buckskin jacket and a Stetson decorated with meshed horseshoes. After talking to him and Morrison - who had already completed most of the important research spadework - **Sonnichsen too became convinced that the old man was not an absolute fake. He seemed to know too much not at least to have been there during the times and in the places of the unfolding of Billy the Kid's desperate career.**"(Walker, Page 65) Walker quoted flowery Sonnichsen: "Here was a Western Lazarus, risen from the dead with a six-shooter in each hand, who was willing to tell of his experiences behind the veil ... Brushy Bill knew too much to have been an outsider. **He was not a literate man and could not have read up on the subject.** His recollections were too detailed and precise to have come from oral sources. He must have been there, in the flesh, when these things happened." (Walker, Pages 65-66) Recall that Sonnichsen had also taken imposter Morrison at his word that *he* was a lawyer. (Walker, Page 64) That uncritical gullibility added to Sonnichsen's complexity as a hoaxer, since he seemed to believe his own fakery.

Sonnichsen's first reaction to the scam is presented in *Alias Billy the Kid*, with "Brushy's" spouting about "negro soldiers from Fort Stanton [taking] positions on the hillside and joined in the firing that day when the Murphy men burned McSween's house." (*Alias Billy the Kid*, Page 12) But there were never black soldiers on the hillside firing on the McSween side in the Lincoln County War Battle. And Sonnichsen never checked. Demonstrated was Sonnichsen's hubris-gullibility-contrarian muddle.

In turn, Morrison, in his tireless promotion of himself and "Brushy" as Billy the Kid, also exaggerated his ally, Sonnichsen, as ranking among the contemporary Billy the Kid historians. This can be seen in Morrison's May 7, 1954 fawning letter to historian, Philip J. Rasch (a copy of which he sent to Paul Blazer, grandson of Joseph Blazer, whom Morrison was also courting), which stated: "People in the class of you, [Robert] Mullin, **[C.L.] Sonnichsen**, [Maurice Garland] Fulton, etc., represents [sic] the exception in the minority, who desire to see the true facts and records prevail."

Biographer, Dale L. Walker, convinced by Sonnichsen, in his 1997 *Legends and Lies: Great Mysteries of the American West*, backed the "Brushy" hoax under " 'I'm Billy the Kid,' The Case of 'Brushy Bill' Roberts" (Walker, Pages 111-136). Walker plugged Sonnichsen as a "a brilliant Harvard-educated English professor and historian [who] knew about the Lincoln County War and **counted among his friends some of the greatest authorities on it and on Billy the Kid** ... the result was a small but respectable collaborative effort, *Alias Billy the Kid* (1955), a fair and balanced work." (Walker, Page 134) He repeated Sonnichsen's "final word" on "Brushy" as Billy the Kid: "If it were not true, it ought to be." (Walker, Page 136) Walker betrayed the historical ignorance needed to be taken in (like calling Sheriff William Brady "James"). And he ignored that Sonnichsen's "greatest authorities" friends, had already condemned that hoax from 1950 onward.

But was Sonnichsen a true hoaxer? Important in assessing his complicitness, is the test of time. From the 1955 publication of *Alias Billy the Kid*, to his death in 1991, advances in Billy the Kid history confirmed "Brushy's" fakery. But when interviewed for a 1998 book by "Brushy Bill"-backing authors, W.C. Jameson and Frederick Bean, he was unrepentant. According to their book, *The Return of the Outlaw Billy the Kid*, he told them he had been vilified, but had gotten "never one shred of evidence to disprove Roberts' claim." (*The Return of the Outlaw Billy the Kid*, Page 200) And Jameson, who stayed in contact with Sonnichsen from 1962, when he was in his English class, till the man's 1991 death, recounted in his 2012 "Brushy"-backing book, *Billy the Kid: The Lost Interviews*, that Sonnichsen told him that he had warned Morrison to be prepared for historians trying to perpetuate the "status quo" of the "legend." And Sonnichsen had encouraged Jameson to do more work on the man Sonnichsen called "William Henry Roberts" ["Brushy's" made-up name]. (*Billy the Kid: The Lost Interviews*, Pages 29-30) Demonstrated was Sonnichsen's rationalization of "Brushy's" defeat: conspiracy theorizing impervious to facts. That settled whether he was a complicit or inadequate. He was both.

But there was more. According to Jameson, Sonnichsen authored *Alias Billy the Kid* using Morrison's notes and taped interviews of "Brushy." (*Billy the Kid: The Lost Interviews*, Pages 28-29) And, without disclosure, he had altered them! As Jameson wrote: "It became clear that Sonnichsen used a relatively small amount of the information ... [and he] heavily edited Roberts' grammar, even adding and deleting words ... In other places, Sonnichsen merely summarized." (*Billy the Kid: The Lost Interviews*, Pages 42) Jameson, thus, guilelessly revealed willful fixing-up of "Brushy" to match Billy Bonney. And, as will be seen, for *Alias Billy the Kid*, Sonnichsen provided his obscure sources as footnotes, apparently confident readers would not check his claims from them. When one does check, revealed is brazen fabrication of their contents. Sonnichsen was, indeed, a hoaxer; smugly posing as a thorn in legitimate historians' side.

## CREATING THE HOOK AND THE BOOK

The path to a book was long and twisting for the hoaxing trio. After meeting "Brushy," huckster Morrison had recognized in his kaleidoscope of identities, one with a publicity hook: he would seek for him, from the modern Governor of New Mexico, the pardon promised by Governor Lew Wallace to Billy the Kid.

To succeed, like Dr. Frankenstein, Morrison grafted onto "Brushy" all the Billy the Kid parts he could find. As he wrote to the Indiana Historical Society, on October 28, 1950, while copying its Billy the Kid archives: "Nearly two years have been consumed in my research, and I can scarcely realize that it has been completed." As revealing for the hoax, was Morrison's start, two years earlier.

# CHAPTER 2
# "BRUSHY BILL'S" BEGINNING AS BILLY

## A PASSEL OF PRETENDERS

The birth of the "Brushy" hoax united Old West pretenders. In *Alias Billy the Kid*, Morrison claimed that, in 1948, when doing probate research for a law firm in an inheritance case, he interviewed a Floridian named Jim Hines, who told him *he* was part of Lincoln County War history. Since Morrison had the same gambit, he told Hines that *he* was related to famous Lucien Maxwell, adding that Billy the Kid had worked for the Maxwells. (Page 3) This was a fitting beginning, since a Lucian Maxwell connection was indirect and Billy never worked for Maxwells. But Hines one-upped by sharing that *he* knew Pat Garrett had not killed Billy the Kid, because he now lived in Texas. (Page 3)

Next, Morrison, beating odds, claimed to meet, in undescribed circumstances, a Missourian named J. Frank Dalton, who told him *he* was Jesse James; knew Jim Hines; actually outlaw, Jessie Evans; and knew Billy the Kid was an O.L. Roberts ("Brushy Bill"), living in Hamilton, Texas. In one fell swoop, Morrison got a stable of old-timer imposters.

First he focused on Dalton. Don Cline, in his 1988 *Brushy Bill Roberts: I Wasn't Billy the Kid*, stated that Dalton was "Brushy's" friend, first himself claiming to be Billy the Kid (Cline, Page 35), before switching to Jesse James. (Cline, Page 41) Cline stated that in 1950, Morrison promoted Dalton as Jesse James, with "Brushy" as a confirming "witness." Morrison got them a New York appearance on human interest "We the People" radio show, called "everybody's soap box." In 2015, "Brushy's relative, Roy L. Haws, in his *Brushy Bill: Proof that His Claim to Be Billy the Kid Was A Hoax*, also cited "Brushy's" September 6, 1949 interview with radio personality Morrey Davidson, in which he claimed J. Frank Dalton was Jesse James. (Haws, Page 140)

His "We the People" "witness" stint got "Brushy" on the front page of his hometown *Hico News Review* of January 20, 1950, in reporter Carolyn Holford's " 'Brushy Bill' Is Back From Gotham." It makes no claim of "Brushy" as Billy the Kid, though it shows Morrison's earliest promotional efforts; "Brushy's" presentation of his Old West personas; and the lucrative potential, with the trip being "all expenses paid." That credulous coverage may have even emboldened Morrison to abandon his developing Dalton hoax, with its legal petition merely seeking to change his name back to Jesse James - with "Brushy" as his witness - and to switch to a bigger prize of creating "Brushy's" future pardon scam as Billy the Kid. The article stated:

O.L. (Brushy Bill) Roberts returned the first of this week to chat with hometowners about his trip to New York after spending a week as one of the "corroborating witnesses" who are supporting a man known as J. Frank Dalton in his claims to being the real Jesse James.

"Brushy Bill" is well known around Hico as a typical cowboy who dresses in Western regalia ...

Roberts gives his birthplace as Buffalo Gap in Taylor County in Taylor county. After living in this section as a boy, he returned to Hico in 1941 "to spend the rest of his life."

He was also a guest of Dalton's last September when he attended a party to celebrate the 102$^{nd}$ birthday of the man at his home in Meramac Caverns, Stanton, Missouri, where Jesse James had a hideout during the Civil War. **He was given both trips with all expenses paid**.

Dalton is one of the many claimants to the title of the notorious outlaw. **He says he has been known since 1882 as J. Frank Dalton, and had** **a petition in the Union, Mo. Circuit Court to change his name back to Jesse Woodson James**. To support the claim, these witnesses were called to New York, and two of them appeared on a broadcast "We the People" to tell of early recollections of Jesse James.

**In telling about his trip, "Brushy Bill" told several people that this man is the real Jesse, and said that he can recognize him from previous meetings**.

Among the experiences in his younger days Roberts recounts riding in Wild West shows with Buffalo Bill Cody, breaking wild cattle in South America, serving as a bronc rider in the Cheyenne Roundup of 1899, working on a Mexican Ranch during the Mexican revolution, and doing scout duty in the Black Hills of the Dakotas.

These are only a few of his tales of the "wild west," and he claims to have a collection of documents to authenticate them.

The next month, on February 3, 1950, "Brushy" was again on the *Hico News Review's* front page, in "Cornering Jesse James," still flogging J. Frank Dalton. "Brushy's" media magnetism would not be lost on Morrison, who had been coaching him since 1949 on Billy the Kid history and historic sites. With a big photo of "Brushy" and Dalton, came the short article: "Shown at top of picture is O.L. (Brushy Bill) Roberts of Hico, who, with another crony, lower left, and others, made a recent trip to New York to identify a man claiming to be the real Jesse James. The man known as Frank Dalton passed his 102$^{nd}$ birthday at Hotel Henry Hudson. He said that the man who was killed, thought to be James, was Charles Bigelow.

Morrison continued his J. Frank Dalton as Jesse James gimmick, long after his promoting of "Brushy" as Billy the Kid. On March 17, 1954, he wrote to a Carl W. Breihan in St. Louis, giving a copy to one of his "Brushy Bill" dupes, Paul Blazer, the grandson to the Lincoln County War figure, Dr. Joseph Blazer. Morrison informed Breihan, that a man named Al Jennings told him "that Dalton was really Jesse ... I would like to study the pictures again, the ones that Mr. [N.H.] Rose [owner of "The Famous N.H. Rose Collection Old Time Photographs"] showed to me, to satisfy my mind whether or not the body they buried could have been Jesse. At that time, we debated the difference of appearance and length and breadth of the face with the heavy dark beard on the purported corpse. In pictures of Jesse there was an apparent longer face with narrow chin and light shaggy growth of beard with different forehead line. I notice in your book where Homer Croy states that Mrs. James was sent to Missouri by Jesse, Jr., to file a suit against Dalton and that she obtained a judgment. This is the first I have heard of this suit." Possibly the push-back of the James family deflated Morrison's own push.

## BETTING ON "BRUSHY"

"Brushy," already a local Hico, Texas, character, had showman potential, parading in his fringed cowboy jackets, in possible emulation of "Uncle Kit Carson" and his own delusions. And he claimed to match Billy the Kid physically. Morrison recognized that he just lacked historical knowledge to perform that part.

## *FAKING SPECIAL KNOWLEDGE*

Transforming "Brushy" into Billy the Kid, may have seemed easy to huckster Morrison, who devised two sound bites: knowing things-not-printed, and illiteracy preventing reading-things-printed. That would create a wow factor, if "Brushy" could recite detailed historical renditions about Billy the Kid's life. Morrison must have anticipated three hitches: doing research, coaching "Brushy," and having him remember his lines.

Morrison spelled out his ploy of special knowledge as a clincher for identity in a June 29, 1955 letter to a William Waters (with a copy sent to Paul Blazer, Joseph Blazer's grandson). Morrison stated: "I will say that I conferred with specialists in the medical and legal professions, and those on other scientific fields, before arriving at my ultimate conclusion [that "Brushy" was Billy]. I do not believe that it would have been physically and humanly possible for anyone to have located the information and retained it in his mind over such a great period of time as would have been necessary in Roberts' case."

It was an argument for what Morrison thought was the perfect ruse. But he missed its fatal flaw: it depended on the limited and error-filled resources of his day. The give-away would be "Brushy's" repeating tell-tale errors from traceable sources. Conversely, "Brushy" parroting verbatim from Billy's writings of 70 years past, would reveal fakery. But Morrison was so confident of the scheme, that he would eventually listed the prompt sources as footnotes in *Alias Billy the* Kid, to pretend that they had corroborated what "Brushy" had said; thus, inadvertently giving away exactly what "Brushy" had been fed!

## **MORRISON'S RESEARCH**

William V. Morrison's "Brushy" hoax took great labor. Except for being delusional that he was Billy the Kid, "Brushy" was basically a *tabula rasa* for facts. As it would turn out, under pressure, he also had a bad memory for his coached history as Billy. But Morrison would not realize that until too late.

Morrison described his research to one of his research sites, the Indianapolis, Indiana Historical Society, on October 28, 1950, while "researching" its Billy the Kid archives. He wrote:

"Nearly two years have been consumed in my research, and I can scarcely realize that it has been completed." He was confident that this would be portrayed as corroboration for "Brushy," instead of cribbing.

## THE INDIANA HISTORICAL SOCIETY FOR BILLY THE KID'S LETTERS

Morrison's "research" included Billy's famous letters to Governor Lew Wallace. Morrison's correspondence with the Indiana Historical Society in Indianapolis, was to its William Henry Smith Memorial Library's librarian, Caroline Dunn; and to Lew Wallace, Jr., Lew Wallace's grandson. He wanted originals of Billy Bonney's letters; and he had urgent need, since he was in final preparations for the gubernatorial pardon plea.

As will be seen, he had already traveled to Lincoln, New Mexico, from his El Paso, Texas, home to do research there, and to take "Brushy" on site for coaching. As he wrote to the William Henry Smith Memorial Library on October 9, 1950: "Upon my return from Lincoln, N.M., today I have your telegram ... While in Lincoln I copied most of the letters in which I am interested. I am enclosing herewith copies for your information and assistance in locating the original to be photostated and certified by your office." And he would mention using the Lincoln Museum in Lincoln, and Maurice Garland Fulton papers.

Morrison's communications with the Indiana library began on October 6, 1950 in a Western Union telegram. It can be surmised that, by then, his plot was enfolding to request the Billy the Kid pardon for "Brushy" from New Mexico's then Governor, Thomas Jewett Mabry. Morrison's telegram stated:

> URGENT NEED OF PHOTOSTATIC COPIES CORRESPONDENCE BETWEEN GOVERNOR LEW WALLACE AND WM BONNEY BILLY THE KID ALSO GOVERNORS REPORT OF MEETING ON THURSDAY NIGHT MARCH 1879 ADVISE WILL FORWARD CHECK COVER COSTS =

He wanted copies of the original Billy the Kid letters. In October of 1950, he sent them his typed version of Billy's first pardon request letter of approximately March 13, 1879, from the Lincoln Museum. At that point, Morrison did not give his source, but Billy's spelling errors in the original had been corrected. It was annotated by the Indiana Historical Society archivist: "*Copy of transcript sent by Wm V. Morrison El Paso, Texas, Oct 1950 Mr. Lew Wallace [Jr.] thinks he has original.*"

On October 7, 1950, responding to his telegram of the day before, Librarian Caroline Dunn wrote:

Mr. William V. Morrison
1312 Arizona St.
El Paso, Texas

My dear Mr. Morrison:
  We have microfilm of Bonney-Wallace correspondence and can have prints made for you. Cheaper than Photostats. About $5.00 to $5.50. Check can be sent after work is done.
  Presume by "Governors report of Meeting on Thursday night March 1879" you mean newspaper article from The World, June 8, 1902, "General Lew Wallace writes a romance of 'Billy the Kid' most famous bandit of the plains?"
  Think it is not on film, but can add to group by film or Photostat.
                              Librarian
Would appreciate knowing purpose for which you desire material.

On October 9, 1950, Morrison responded by letter to the library; writing:

Dear Sir:

  **Upon my return from Lincoln, N.M., today** I have your telegram of the 7th in answer to my wire of the 6th, for which please accept my thanks.
  **While in Lincoln I copied most of the letters in which I am interested. I am enclosing herewith copies for your information and assistance in locating the original to be photostated and certified by your office.**
  Also, there is a letter written by Bonney to Squire Wilson, at whose home in Lincoln the Governor met Wm Bonney on the night of

March 23, 1879 [sic – March 17], by pre-arrangement. This letter is dated at San Patricio, Thursday 20, 1879, and signed, WHBonney.

I am not interested in the printed article appearing in the World, June 8, 1902. I desire a photostatic copy of the original notes made by Governor Wallace at the meeting under the date of Sunday night March 23, 1879. The enclosed statement was copied from a photostatic copy of the original notes in Lincoln Museum.

**[AUTHOR'S NOTE: Morrison gives his source for the letters' information.]**

The copies are to be offered in evidence in a proceeding.

**[AUTHOR'S NOTE: Demonstrated is Morrison's intent to use the letters for "Brushy's" pardon plea to the governor. To be noted is "Brushy's" illiteracy claim was to be backed by alleging the letters were written for him.]**

Therefore I desire photostats certified to by your office. Microfilm will not suffice. Colonel M.G. Fulton has a microfilm copy of the Wallace papers among his files in Lincoln, N.M.

**[AUTHOR'S NOTE: Demonstrated is Morrison's use of historian Maurice Garland Fulton's papers.]**

May I hear from you at your convenience?

Respectfully submitted,
Wm V. Morrison

Though Morrison had ignored the request about his purpose, Librarian Dunn put Lew Wallace's grandson, Lew Wallace Jr., in the loop; and responded to Morrison on October 13, 1950; writing:

My dear Mr. Morrison:
Your letter of the 9$^{th}$ received. Have checked [compared] transcripts [of his Lincoln copies] sent with original manuscripts. Locate all except two: March 13 [no year] Bonney to Wallace; April 15, 1881, Bonney to Caypless. Seems probable that the

last would not have been in Wallace collection. Can you give us further information about them; are there any records or notations on the copies in Lincoln which indicate location of originals? Of course if they are on film which Mr. Fulton acquired from us, we must have them, and I have overlooked them somehow.

Am checking with Mr. Lew Wallace great grandson [sic - grandson] of Gov. Wallace on possibility that he may have these two letters; his father had at least one Bonney letter which Mr. Fulton saw years ago. Will have the originals which we have photostated for you next week and we will certify each letter document. Presume you would wish statement of certification on back of first page of each group of photostats?

Very truly yours,<br>Librarian

On October 17, 1950, Morrison responded to Dunn; writing:

Dear Miss Dunn:

Your letter of the 13th received, for which please accept my thanks.

The "March 13th, Bonney to Wallace letter," should be among your collection. There is a photostatic copy of this letter in Lincoln Museum, Lincoln, N.M. I believe it bears the statement that the original is in the possession of the Indiana Historical Society. However, it may be in possession of Govenor Wallace's Grandson. It is presumed by Colonel Fulton that the letter was written March 13, 1879.

**[AUTHOR'S NOTE: Demonstrated is Morrison's meticulous research, even subtly correcting the librarian that Lew Wallace Jr. was a grandson, not great-grandson.]**

The Caypless letter eminated [sic] in Colorado. Colonel Fulton gave me a transcript.

**[AUTHOR'S NOTE: Again demonstrated is Morrison's research, though he is confused about specifics of Edgar Caypless's letter – so "Brushy would be too!]**

With reference to Certification, I suggest that a sheet, bearing certification, be attached to the documents.

Yours very truly,<br>
W<u>m</u> V. *Morrison*

By October 25, 1950, disregarding that his purpose was still concealed, the Indiana Historical Society sent him a bill for "17 sheets Photostats, Lew Wallace Collection" for $9.78 in the letter of Caroline Dunn sent him; stating:

My dear Mr. Morrison:
  Enclosed are the Photostats of the documents in the Wallace collection, with certification, as requested.
  Enclosed is a bill for them …
Governor Wallace's grandson, Mr. Lew Wallace, who is now living in Indianapolis, looked at the transcripts which you sent, and says that the family did have the letter of W.H. Bonney, March 13, to Wallace. He thinks that the letter, framed, is in his attic here, and hopes to get it out in the next few days. I talked to him again yesterday morning. But having waited a week for him, I thought we had better have ours done and send them to you. Mr. Wallace says, however, that when he does locate the other letter he will let me know and will be glad to furnish you photocopies of it, also.
  We are enclosing, also, the transcript.

Sincerely yours,<br>
Librarian

The enclosed carbon copy of the certification, listed the Billy Bonney documents sent to Morrison by Caroline Dunn. Missing were Billy's letters of March 13, 1879 and March 2, 1881 to Lew Wallace, in Lew Wallace Jr.'s possession. The certification stated:

Indianapolis, Indiana
October 25, 1950

I swear that the attached Photostats are true and correct copies of the documents listed below. In the Gen. Lew Wallace collection in the William Henry Smith Memorial Library of the Indiana Historical Society:

Lew Wallace to W.H. Bonney, March 15, 1879.
W.H. Bonney to Wilson, (March) 20, 1879.
W.H. Bonney to General Lew Wallace (March) 20, 1879.
"Statements by Kid, made Sunday night March 23, 1879".
Billie, portion of letter, probably 1880.

**[AUTHOR'S NOTE: This letter fragment was authenticated by me as dating to March 24, 1879.]**

William Bonney to Gov. Lew Wallace, Dec. 12, 1880.
W.H. Bonney to Gov. Lew Wallace, Jan. 1, 1881.
Wm. H. Bonney to Gov. Lew Wallace, March 4, 1881.
W. Bonney to Gov. Lew Wallace, March 27, 1881.

Librarian
Indiana Historical Society

Subscribed and sworn before me this 25th day of October, 1950.

Notary Public
My commission expires March 25, 1951.

On October 28, 1950, Morrison responded to Caroline Dunn:

Dear Miss Dunn:

This will serve to acknowledge receipt of your communication of the 25th, together with the Photostats of Documents from Lew Wallace Collection pertaining to "Billy the Kid."

I hope that Mr. Lew Wallace locates the letter that Wm Bonney wrote to his grandfather.

I am enclosing my check, signed in blank, to be filled in by you to cover costs of all Photostats, including the letter in possession of Mr. Lew Wallace.

**Your documents complete my file on this unusual case. Nearly two years have been consumed in my research, and I can scarcely realize that it has been completed.**

Being a member of the Missouri Historical Society, St. Louis, Missouri, I appreciate the valuable assistance rendered to research workers by various Historical Institutions.

Again I thank you for prompt attention to my requests.

                    Yours very truly,
                    *Wm* V. *Morrison*

On October 30, 1950, Lew Wallace Jr. finally responded somewhat suspiciously to Morrison; writing:

Mr. William V. Morrison
1312 Arizona,
El Paso, Texas.

Dear Sir:
      A photostatic copy is being prepared of the letter in my possession from William H. Bonney ("Billy the Kid") to Governor Lew Wallace and will be sent to you when completed.

Miss Dunn of the Indiana Historical Bureau has shown me your correspondence with her, and from it I am not able to understand the purpose for which you desire this Wallace MSS material. In one letter I believe you referred to a legal proceeding and in another to a "case". **I am pleased to cooperate with and assist all bona fide use of this historical data, but, as you can understand, I do not wish it to be used for any advertising, commercial or other purposes of that nature.**

May I therefore ask that you explain what will be done with this material. If we understand correctly that you are collecting evidence for a law suit, I believe it would be of historical value to have a transcript of the proceedings added to the Wallace collection in the Smith Memorial Library.

Very truly yours,
*Lew Wallace*

By November 10, 1950, still suspicious Lew Wallace Jr. answered Morrison's double-talk, with "**I do not care to assist any imposter to appear in the role of Billy the Kid.**" Wallace wrote:

Dear Sir:

Your letter of November 2 confuses me in some respects. **I cannot understand your reference to work "on the heirship of the father of certain persons" and your discovery that "the party in the interest was the same person as Billy the Kid."** Do you mean that you have proved that some person whom you know is a child or descendant of William H. Bonney?

I am also puzzled as to what you find lacking in proof of the death of Billy the Kid. If only documentary proof is missing, how many others have died in the American frontier without death certificates? In view of the Kid's sage he would be some ninety years old in 1950, and it is, of course, possible that a man of ninety years could be alive today, provided that he had not been killed seventy years ago.

**I do not care to assist any imposter to appear in the role of Billy the Kid or a child of Billy the Kid.** There is plenty of serious work in the world to be done by everybody.

Therefore, I would appreciate a clarification of this matter.

Your letter refers to a pardon of the Kid "as promised". **It is my impression (and at the moment of writing I do not have the time to check my memory) that Governor Wallace "promised" William H. Bonney that if he, Bonney, would give himself up and stand trial, Wallace would pardon him, if he were convicted.**

**[AUTHOR'S NOTE: This is a quote to remember. Lew Wallace Jr. is wrong: thinking that the pardon bargain was for Billy to stand trial, and get pardoned if convicted. This big error will later appear in "Brushy's" rendition of his pardon bargain as Billy.]**

I do not recall ever having seen an account of the Kid's story in which these conditions were shown to have been fulfilled, although the romanticizers of the Kid's life have intimated a broken pledge and bad faith.

**[AUTHOR'S NOTE: Neither Wallace nor Morrison know the pardon bargain details, so neither will "Brushy!"]**

The copies of these letters are therefore made available to you on the condition that you will permit me to examine you [sic] use of them in advance of such use in order to determine whether you allege that Governor Wallace broke his promise, and on the further condition that you will justly consider any fair criticism I may be able to make of your interpretation of the facts. Whatever you can prove I shall not object to.

Surely you realize that anyone dealing with history has a responsibility for the truth. I rely on your sense of that responsibility, as I hope you can rely on mine.

This letter does not constitute permission to publish these letters in any form.

                        Very truly yours,
                                *Lew Wallace*

On November 14, 1950, Caroline Dunn wrote to Morrison, who apparently never told his purpose to Lew Wallace Jr.; stating:

> My dear Mr. Morrison:
> In my letter to you of November 5 I said that I was returning the transcripts [he had made in Lincoln] and did not realize until some days after that they had not been enclosed, so here they are.
> I understand from Mr. Wallace that he has sent you a Photostat of the letter of March 13. We have paid for these Photostats also, so I am adding 87 cts. to the amount previously billed you, making a total of $9.78, which is the amount I am filling in on check No. 567, Oct. 27, which you sent me. I am cashing it myself, as the photostating was done by two companies, and I can thus pay them separately, and also pay our library $2.00 carriage charge.
> Very truly yours,
> Librarian

## *MORE RESEARCH AND PRACTICE*

As will be seen, other sources were Pat Garrett's *The Authentic Life of Billy the Kid* and Walter Noble Burns's *The Saga of Billy the Kid* (likely also read by "Brushy"); to writings by historians Robert N. Mullin and Maurice Garland Fulton, and Billy's contemporaries: Charlie Siringo, Jim East, and George Coe. Also used were magazine and newspaper articles. Added were archival documents - like a page of Billy's Court of Inquiry testimony, and Territorial Record Books.

Also, in 1949, Morrison interviewed Lincoln County residents for period "memories;" and, in 1949, he toured "Brushy," through Lincoln, with its courthouse-jail for the jailbreak scene.

Tellingly, when sources ran out, so did "Brushy's" "memory" - or his confabulations took over. And Morrison was equally helpless in that territory unchartered by documents or history books. So plain old lies were the order of the day, along with weird insolence that no one would ever notice the fakery.

# CHAPTER 3
# THE BILLY THE KID PARDON PRIZE

## PRIMED FOR THE PARDON PRIZE

Toward the end of 1950, William V. Morrison's sly stunt paid off: he actually got New Mexico Governor Thomas Jewett Mabry to agree to a pardon interview with "Brushy" - in company of Morrison, who brought with him the fruits of his labors, as described by Dale L. Walker in his 1997 *Legends and Lies*: "seventeen parcels of legal materials – transcriptions of his interviews, investigative findings, depositions, and several notarized statements from people who had known the Kid and testified that Roberts and the Kid were one and the same." (Walker, Page 132) Then all involved discovered the publicity magic of Billy the Kid: the entire charade became big news.

## *GOVERNOR THOMAS JEWETT MABRY*

The make-or-break for William V. Morrison's bid for his own glory depended on the 14th Governor of New Mexico: Thomas Jewett Mabry, an attorney at the tail-end of his tenure, which was from 1947 to 1951. Born in Carlisle County, Kentucky, three years after Billy Bonney was fatally shot by Sheriff Pat Garrett, Mabry was 66 when facing-off with odd old-timer, Oliver Roberts, lying to him about his age and identity; and his promoter, Morrison, doing the same. A Chief Justice of the New Mexico Supreme Court from 1939 to 1946, Mabry was familiar with testing evidence; and had a long career in public service, having also been in the New Mexico Senate, the Albuquerque City Commission, and a District Attorney for Albuquerque. And unlike the Billy the Kid Case's 30th Governor of New Mexico, Bill Richardson, then 3 years old, Mabry had integrity and respected the state's iconic Old West history. So he gathered Billy the Kid experts to assist his evaluation.

## PARDON REJECTED BASED ON NO BILLY THE KID TO PARDON

At the November 30, 1950 hearing, Governor Mabry stated: "I am taking no action, now or ever, on this application for a Pardon for Billy the Kid because I do not believe this man is Billy the Kid."

"Brushy's" tale of surviving the Garrett shooting was also clobbered that day by the *Alamogordo News's* publication of Billy Bonney's Corner's Jury Report, with sarcastic front page headline: "Fort Sumner Jury Thought The Kid Had Been Killed." It confirmed that the report was found in 1932 by a New Mexico state employee, in the State Land capitol basement.

Gathered as experts were Pat Garrett's sons, Oscar and Jarvis Garrett; Arcadio Brady, Sheriff Brady's grandson; Cliff McKinney, Kip McKinney's son; Wilbur Coe, Frank Coe's son; and historians Will Robinson and William Keleher of Albuquerque and J.W. Hendron of Santa Fe.

For them, "Brushy" performed deplorably. The December 1, 1950 *Albuquerque Journal's* " 'Billy the Kid' Bubble Bursts as Gov. Mabry Rejects Oldster's Claim," quoted Oscar Garrett: "Roberts was 'either a deliberate imposter or the victim of a delusion.' "

The November 30th *Santa Fe New Mexican's* "Billy the Kid Only a Phony It Turns Out," reported that "Brushy" "refused to admit to having killed anybody;" forgetting that Billy the Kid's killings were why he was there requesting a pardon! "[A]bout his escape from the Lincoln jail ... he denied he shot either of the two men killed ... His story was that he had been freed by friends." "His story of that night of July 14, 1881 at Fort Sumner was substantially this: A restaurant was out of meat. He was asked to go to Pete Maxwell's house and get some. He suspected a trap and declined. However Billy Barlow ...volunteered to go [and got shot]."

November 30th *El Paso Herald Post's* " 'Billy the Kid' Flunks in Talk With Governor," said: "He could not remember Sheriff Garrett's name or any particulars in the Lincoln county war." He claimed "he escaped from the Lincoln County jail at Lincoln earlier in 1881 with the help of some friends. He said he didn't "do any shooting" in the escape, but jumped on a horse and rode to a blacksmith shop three miles away to have the chain shackles removed."

The December 1, 1950 *Albuquerque Journal* reported in " 'Billy the Kid' Bubble Bursts as Gov. Mabry Rejects Oldster's Claim" that "Brushy" "did not remember, without prompting from Morrison, the name of Garrett ... Nor did he remember much about the famous Lincoln County cattle war in which Billy the Kid earned much of his infamous reputation ... He could not recollect the names of the important leaders in the Lincoln County fracas, nor the way the factions lined up ...At times he referred to Billy the Kid as "he," and at other times used the personal pronoun 'I.' Roberts said that when he previously escaped from the Lincoln County court house on April 28, 1881, he shot no one ... Roberts used his right hand in handling his cane, in drinking water from a glass, in buttoning his jacket and straightening his hat today. Tradition has it that the Kid was left-handed ... Roberts said both he and Barlow worked for John Chisum during the Lincoln County cattle war ...'Me and Billy Barlow,' Roberts declared, 'was as much alike as two blackeyed peas. You couldn't tell us apart' [which explained Barlow being shot instead of him]."

The November 30, 1950 *Santa Fe New Mexican's* "Billy the Kid Only A Phony It Turns Out" demonstrated that "Brushy" did not even know what the pardon was for: "I want to die a free man ... [T]hey'll put up a fine monument over my grave over in Texas. "Why?" Mabry inquired. Roberts said he had spent 10 years as a scout for an anti-horse thief association. That was why."

William V. Morrison was also exposed. The November 30, 1950 *Clovis News Journal's* "Mabry Terms "Billy" Outright Imposter," implied that Morrison was one too; stating: "William V. Morrison [is] an El Paso salesman. He had previously claimed to be a St. Louis lawyer." The November 30, 1950 *Santa Fe New Mexican's* "Billy the Kid Only a Phony It Turns Out," nailed him for prompting. When "Brushy" was asked if he knew another sheriff besides Brady, the reporter recorded: "What's his name?" ["Brushy"] asked, turning to Morrison. "Garrett," supplied Morrison." And December 1, 1950's *Albuquerque Journal's* " 'Billy the Kid' Bubble Bursts as Gov. Mabry Rejects Oldster's Claim" called him "a traveling salesman" from "St. Louis;" and clarified that the law firm supposedly petitioning for the pardon, merely represented Morrison: "El Paso law firm ... said it was acting solely as the legal representative for William V. Morrison, who was seeking the pardon on behalf of the man Morrison claimed was Billy the Kid." And the November 30, 1950 *Santa Fe New Mexican's* "Billy the Kid Only A Phony It Turns Out," brought up profiteering with "Brushy": "Not that I know of," he said when Mabry asked him if somebody were using him to 'promote something.' "

For proof, Morrison cited meaningless physical resemblance. He also had hearsay affidavits that "Brushy" was Billy from non-historical individuals.

It turned out that people were smarter than Morrison had reckoned, and "Brushy" was dumber than he had realized. It took a thick-skinned con-artist, like him, to be undaunted.

# "BRUSHY'S" PRESS

America had waited with bated breath for news about "Brushy." On November 25, 1950, a Sexton Humphreys wrote "'Pardon Me, I'm Alive,' Says Billy the Kid" for the *Indianapolis News*; stating:

### 'Pardon Me, I'm Alive,' Says Billy the Kid

The 1878 [sic – 1881] death of BILLY THE KID is "nothing but a legend," says an attorney who asks New Mexico Governor THOMAS J. MABRY for a pardon for him. The attorney, Ted Andress, says William Henry Roberts, alias William Henry Bonney, William H. Antrim, the Kid, Billy the Kid and A.L. [sic] Roberts still is alive at an undisclosed address and is now 90. The petition says he surrendered because the territorial Governor, Crawfordsville's LEW WALLACE, of "Ben Hur" fame, promised him a pardon. But the pardon was never given and Billy, under conviction for murdering a sheriff, broke for freedom. The "legend" is that he was killed in the escape attempt [sic], but the petition says that he was only wounded and got to Mexico, that it was a companion that was killed.

From Indianapolis, Indiana, on the November 30, 1850 day of decision, the United Press reported anticipation for *The Indianapolis News* under "Pardon My 6-Shooters. Billy the Kid? Governor to Decide." It stated:

### Pardon My 6-Shooters Billy the Kid? Governor to Decide

SANTA FE, N.M., Nov. 30 – A page out of the old West comes to life today when a grizzled old man who claims to be the fabulous outlaw, "Billy the Kid," matches wits with the Governor of New Mexico.

Governor Thomas Mabry will get out of a sickbed to confer with several distinguished historians and "Billy" over his application for a pardon in connection with the 1878 murder of Sheriff William Brady.

It has long been presumed that the legendary gunman was shot to death by Sheriff Pat Garrett July 14, 1881. But periodically since that date "Billys" have come forth to claim ownership of the silver six-guns that killed 21 frontiersmen.

The latest claimant, unseen so far by newspapermen and New Mexico officials, has been both verified and denied by elderly Southwesterners who claim to be former companions of "The Kid."

Mrs. Martile Able, of El Paso, Tex., says he "has the same keen blue eyes" as Billy. Fevero [sic] Gallegos, of Ruidoso, N.M., said he is "still as fast on the draw, despite age."

Both agreed in sworn affidavits that he possesses the same small hands and large wrists, supposedly physical characteristics of the pint-sized outlaw.

However, the aged cowpuncher Ben Cisneros said he "couldn't possibly be Billy the Kid." Cisneros said he "saw Billy in a casket in Ft. Sumner after Sheriff Garrett shot him."

Governor Mabry indicated that he wants to meet the new Billy and decide once and for all if the notorious gunman is still alive, or in a grave near Ft. Sumner, N.M. where hundreds of tourists have gazed on him for many years.

The latest Billy came suddenly to life when an El Paso law firm last week wrote Mabry seeking a pardon, "because the applicant, now past 90 years of age, wishes to spend his remaining years in peace."

The lawyers claimed Billy had not really been killed by Sheriff Garrett, but only wounded. He was then nursed back into health by a Mexican woman, and later escaped to old Mexico where he lived up to now, they said.

Then poured in news of "Brushy's" flop. From Clovis, New Mexico, Mabry's home town, the *Clovis News Journal* of Thursday, November 30, 1950, minced no words, declaring: "Mabry Terms "Billy" Outright Imposter." It also implied that Morrison was one too; stating: "William V. Morrison [is] an El Paso salesman. He had previously claimed to be a St. Louis lawyer." On the front page, it stated:

### MABRY TERMS "BILLY" OUTRIGHT IMPOSTER

SANTA FE. AP – Governor Thomas J. Mabry said Thursday he believes a 91-year-old man who claims to be Billy the Kid is an imposter.

"No action will be taken on his petition for a full pardon for Billy the Kid because I don't believe this man is Billy the Kid," the governor said at the end of a 45 minute interview with the man in the governor's office.

"Brushy" was a "phony" in the November 30, 1950 *Santa Fe New Mexican* article by an Art Morgan: "Billy the Kid Only A Phony It Turns Out." Under "Brushy's" photo in a fringed Western jacket it said he "couldn't remember enough of the youthful outlaw's career to convince the governor and newsmen of his right to the title." The article stated:

### Billy the Kid Only A Phony It Turns Out
#### By Art Morgan

A pardon for Billy the Kid, famous killer of New Mexico's - Lincoln county "war" in the late 70's and early 80's, today was refused by Gov. Tom J. Mabry. The Governor announced his decision after an hour's interview with Ollie or Henry Roberts (address withheld) at the executive mansion this afternoon. Roberts allowed as to how he was the Kid who, historians say, Sheriff Pat Garrett shot to death on the night of July 14, 1881, at Fort Sumner. "I don't think he is Billy the Kid," the governor said. "I am taking no action, now or ever, on this petition for a pardon."

In the presence of a group of newspaper reporters, Roberts told Mabry it was not he but a pal, Billy Barlow, whom Garrett killed on that night at Pete Maxwell's house at Fort Sumner. "You couldn't tell us apart," said Roberts. **Instead of a six-shooter, he handled a cane with his right hand. (Tradition, not verified, says the Kid was a southpaw.)**

Roberts recounted convincingly incidents in the Kid's life, when he was doing the talking. However, when Mabry asked pointed questions the answer frequently was: "Sixty-nine years is a long time to remember."

Dressed in a fringed buckskin jacket, levis and boots, Roberts turned once or twice to **William V. Morrison, St. Louis businessman who accompanied him for prompting**

The Kid is reputed to have slain 21 men in the 21 years of his life. Roberts **refused to admit to having killed anybody.**

Roberts said he didn't know who killed Sheriff William Brady at Lincoln April 1, 1878. Four men were shooting at one another at the time, he said.

"If a man is shooting at you don't you shoot back?" he asked Mabry.

Well I don't know," said the governor.

"It was a case of dog eat dog," Roberts said.

It was for the Brady killing that the Kid was sentenced to hang.

Questioned about his escape from the Lincoln jail, after the death sentence had been passed, **he denied he shot either of the two men killed in that incident. His story was that he had been freed by friends.**

His story of that night of July 14, 1881 at Fort Sumner was substantially this:

**A restaurant was out of meat. He was asked to go to Pete Maxwell's house and get some. He suspected a trap and declined.** However Billy Barlow, who was "half-shot," volunteered to go.

Roberts heard shooting and ran to Maxwell's yard. Men shot at him and he shot back. A bullet creased his skull, knocking him out. A Mexican woman who, who lived in the back of the yard, dragged him into her house and revived him. Soon afterward he lit out for the Mexican border.

"I see a mark there," said Mabry when Roberts told of the wound.

Oscar Garrett, Odessa, Tex., and Jarvis Garrett, here on a visit from South America – sons of Pat Garrett – sat in on the meeting.

Asked if he had any questions to ask, Oscar said he wouldn't "dignify the occasion" by asking any.

Roberts insisted on wearing his hat when cameramen took his picture ….

In his youth The Kid supposedly lived with his mother, Kathleen [sic] Antrim, at Silver City. Roberts said today she was not his mother, but his aunt.

He also "corrected" The Kid's biographers on another point. He was not born in New York, but in Buffalo Gap, Tex.

**Roberts also knew another sheriff, besides Brady. "What's his name?" he asked, turning to Morrison.**

"Garrett," supplied Morrison.

**[AUTHOR'S NOTE: This is an example of "Brushy's" expectation of Morrison's coaching.]**

Roberts, replying to Mabry, said he had "a good many girls," Garrett's wife's sister, Celsa Gutierrez, was one of his favorites, he said …

Did you ever steal any cattle?" Mabry asked.

Roberts answer was a loud "No."

Introduced to Cliff McKinney, Carlsbad, a mist dimmed Roberts' bright blue eyes. Roberts was informed McKinney was the son of T.C. (Kip) McKinney, who was with Garrett on that night of July 14, 1881, at Fort Sumner.

Saying McKinney, as well as Garrett, had earlier been a friend of his, Roberts choked up.

"God bless you," he said, clinging to McKinney's hand.

**[AUTHOR'S NOTE: This is "Brushy's" spontaneous confabulating, since neither Garrett nor McKinney were Billy's friends; but "Brushy" can even feign emotions.]**

Roberts said he would be 91 on his next birthday …

**"Not that I know of," he said when Mabry asked him if somebody were using him to "promote something."**

**[AUTHOR'S NOTE: The profiteering motive was obvious to Mabry.]**

"I want to die a free man," he added. "When I do they'll put up a fine monument over my grave over in Texas.

"Why?" Mabry inquired.

Roberts said he had spent 10 years as a scout for an anti-horse thief association. That was why.

[AUTHOR'S NOTE: Roberts demonstrated his chaotic thinking with inability to stick to his Billy the Kid tale, and switched to another of his personas.]

"Brushy" "flunked" for the November 30th *El Paso Herald Post* article by Vernon Smylie, with: " 'Billy the Kid' Flunks in Talk With Governor." It was on the front page with "U.S. Considers Use of A-Bomb." (Billy the Kid was big news!) Smylie wrote:

### "Billy the Kid" Flunks in Talk With Governor
### by VERNON SMYLIE
#### Herald-Post Santa Fe Correspondent

SANTA FE, Nov. 30. – Governor Thomas Mabry believes a 91-year-old man who claims to be Billy the Kid is an imposter.

Governor Mabry said he intends to take no action on a request by an El Paso law firm to grant a full pardon to the man.

"In my opinion, the man is not Billy the Kid," the governor said.

Governor Mabry, New Mexico historians and relatives of men who had been historically associated with the Kid, questioned the man in the governor's mansion today.

The man who claims he was the notorious outlaw was represented by **William V. Morrison, an El Paso salesman. He had previously claimed to be a St. Louis lawyer**.

The man gave his name as Ollie Roberts or Henry Roberts. He told the Governor that he used both names.

Roberts said that he did not want to tell his address or any of the details of where he lived for many years.

The petition presented the Governor by the El Paso law firm of Andress, Lipscomb and Peticolas, for a pardon for Billy the Kid maintained Roberts has been living with the Yaqui Indians in Mexico.

Roberts told Governor Mabry that he was born in Buffalo Gap, Texas. Historians say it is a "well determined fact" that Billy the Kid was born in New York.

Roberts said he left home at the age of 14 because "his father was mean to him." He then went to New Mexico, he said.

"The fellow that was killed was named Billy Barlow," Roberts said. "I was with him. We looked like two peas in a pod.

"Billy Barlow drank a heap. I never drank. Couldn't go for that rotgut beer.

"I figured it was a trap at the Maxwell house. I stayed away. It was Barlow that went."

**Has Scar on Head**

History does not mention Billy Barlow as an associate of the Kid's.

Governor Mabry asked Roberts where he was at the time of the shooting.

"I ran out in the yard," Robert's answered. "Two men started shooting at me. One bullet cut me across the head."

[AUTHOR'S NOTE: There was no "yard" in Fort Sumner; there was a large parade ground with perimeter buildings.]

Roberts paused to show the governor a scar on the top of his head. "I fell into a Mexican woman's yard," he continued. "It wasn't far from the shooting. She doctored my wounds."

Roberts wore a buckskin coat, blue denim pants, cowboy boots and a Western-style hat. He had a loud handkerchief around his neck.

**Who Was Pat Garrett?**

When he arrived at the governor's mansion, Roberts wanted to lie down. The governor took him to a couch and talked with him privately for about 20 minutes. Then they went to a dining room, where historians and relatives of men involved in the Fort Sumner shooting were waiting.

Governor Mabry and Roberts sat at the dining table. The governor questioned him again for another 20 minutes. Roberts was foggy. **He could not remember Sheriff Garrett's name or any particulars in the Lincoln county war.**

Roberts said that he was married, but that his wife is critically ill. When the governor asked him whether his wife called him Ollie or Henry, Roberts said, "She calls me Billy."

Cliff McKinney, son of Kip McKinney who was at the Maxwell house the night of the shooting, also questioned Roberts.

**Son Refuses Questions**

Will Robinson, an Albuquerque historian, asked Roberts several questions. Later Robinson said Roberts is not Billy the Kid.

The governor offered to let Oscar Garrett of Odessa, son of Sheriff Garrett, question Roberts, but Garrett said, "I don't intend to dignify this claim with any questions."

Among those present at the interview were Arcadio Brady, grandson of Sheriff Brady of Lincoln County, the man who Billy is charged with having killed, and Jarvis Garrett of Las Cruces, another son of Sheriff Garrett.

**Not Like History**

The old man said **he escaped from the Lincoln County jail at Lincoln earlier in 1881 with the help of some friends. He said he didn't "do any shooting" in the escape, but jumped on a horse and rode to a blacksmith shop three miles away to have the chain shackles removed from his body.**

History and records reveal, however, that in that escape Billy the Kid killed two guards and shot another.

[AUTHOR'S NOTE: Only guards, James Bell and Bob Olinger, were shot.]

**Shot With His Hat On**

At one time during the questioning, Roberts pounded on the table and demanded: Don't you dare take any pictures of me with my hat off.

The December 1, 1950 *Albuquerque Journal's* front page had "'Billy the Kid' Bubble Bursts as Gov. Mabry Rejects Oldster's Claim." It called Morrison a "traveling salesman," said the law firm only represented him, and "Brushy" flubbed basic questions about the Lincoln County War and Pat Garrett. It stated:

### 'Billy the Kid' Bubble Bursts as Gov. Mabry Rejects Oldster's Claim

SANTA FE, Nov. 30 (AP) – The bubble burst today for the buckskin-clad vain little man who claims he is 91 years old and is the one and only, the true Billy the Kid.

Governor Thomas Jewett Mabry rejected both the man's claim to being Billy the Kid and his request for a "full and complete pardon so I can die a free man."

For the time being at least, history books will continue to record that Billy the Kid, the West's most notorious juvenile delinquent punk, was shot to death by Sheriff Pat Garrett at Fort Sumner, N.M., July 14, 1881.

At that time the Kid was 21 years old and boasted that he had killed 21 men.

**"I am taking no action, now or ever, on this application for a pardon for Billy the Kid because I do not believe this man is Billy the Kid," Governor Mabry** said after a 45-minute interview with the aged man, who alternatively referred to himself as Billy the Kid, Billy Roberts, Henry Roberts, and Ollie Roberts.

Pardon Requested

**The request for the pardon was first presented to Governor Mabry last week by an El Paso law firm, which said it was acting solely as the legal representative for William V. Morrison, who was seeking the pardon on behalf of the man Morrison claimed was Billy the Kid.**

[AUTHOR'S NOTE: The law firm represented Morrison, not "Brushy," as Morrison would later claim.]

It was Morrison who brought Roberts to today's interview, in the executive mansion where the governor has been confined for the week with a severe cold. Their interview was arranged after Mabry said he would take no action at all on the pardon request until he had a personal interview with the man claiming to be Billy the Kid.

Roberts refused to say where he had been living or is living at the present time and **Morrison, who described himself as a traveling salesman and gave his permanent home as St. Louis**, said Roberts refusal to reveal his permanent address stemmed from a current serious illness of Roberts' wife.

The governor's disbelief was shared by more than a score of newsmen, state historians and descendants of men who figured in the Billy the Kid saga who attended the interview.

That disbelief was nourished on many things:

**Couldn't remember**

**Roberts did not remember, without prompting from Morrison, the name of Garrett.**

Nor did he remember much about the famous **Lincoln County cattle war in which Billy the Kid earned much of his infamous reputation.**

He could not recollect the names of the important **leaders in the Lincoln County fracas, nor the way the factions lined up.**

**At times he referred to Billy the Kid as "he," and at other times used the personal pronoun "I."**

**Roberts said he was born in Buffalo Gap, in Taylor County, Texas, and that the family later moved to Hamilton County, Texas.**

But J.W. Hendron, Santa Fe historian and author of a book about **Billy the Kid, says it is a "well-documented fact" that Billy the Kid was born in New York City, Nov. 23, 1859.**

Roberts said that when he previously escaped from the Lincoln County court house on April 28, 1881, he shot no one.

History and county records, however, detail that the Kid killed two guards and shot a third in that escape.

**[AUTHOR'S NOTE: Billy Bonney shot just his two guards: James Bell and Bob Olinger.]**

Roberts used his right hand in handling his cane, in drinking water from a glass, in buttoning his packet and straightening his hat today. Tradition has it that the Kid was left-handed.

**[AUTHOR'S NOTE: Billy Bonney was ambidextrous; with the left-handedness a misunderstanding of his right to left reversed tintype.]**

**Garrett Kin Scoffs**

Oscar Garrett, of Odessa, Tex., son of the sheriff who history says shot the Kid to death, declined to question Roberts, adding "I don't want to dignify this claim with any questions."

His brother, Jarvis, here on a visit from South America, also scoffed at Robert's [sic] claim that he was Billy the Kid.

After today's interview, Oscar Garrett declared

Roberts was "either a deliberate imposter or the victim of a delusion."

Garrett also said that Robert's [sic] claim is a "slur on the character of my father and on every pioneer in New Mexico at that time.

Pat Garrett reported to Territorial Governor Lew Wallace that he had killed the Kid and claimed the $500 reward offered for the Kid.

"I have never capitalized on being Pat Garrett's son," Oscar Garrett said. "I just want to see the record kept straight ..."

Balding and extremely sensitive about it, Roberts at one time pounded on the dining room table in the Governor's mansion, where the interview was held, and demanded:

**Poses With Hat**

"Don't you dare take any pictures of me with my hat off. I won't have pictures taken with my hat off."

He then carefully set his hat on his head, threw back his shoulders, and posed proudly for picture after picture.

Roberts, resplendent in a yellow buckskin jacket and a bright green-figured bandana, declared that the man killed by Pat Garrett was a man named Billy Barlow.

**Roberts said both he and Barlow worked for John Chisum during the Lincoln County cattle war.**

"Me and Billy Barlow," Roberts declared, "was as much alike as two blackeyed peas. You couldn't tell us apart."

The night he was supposed to have been killed, Roberts said, Barlow wanted him to go to the Pete Maxwell home, where history records Billy the Kid died with his boots on in front of Pat Garrett's blazing guns.

**"There was a trap"**

"But Barlow drank a heap and he was half shot at the time. He went right into the trap and was killed, not me."

Roberts refused to answer questions about being wounded in gun battles at Mocking Bird Gap and at Stinking Springs. These were put to him by Will Robinson, pioneer New Mexico newsman who is himself past 80 and known as a historian of the Lincoln County war.

Roberts said he was wounded many times and showed a scar on his bald head. He said he got that scar in a gun fight in the Maxwell house. He said he ran to the Maxwell house after he heard shots there. A shot creased his skull and knocked him out.

He said he was treated for that wound by "a Mexican woman and by Celsa Gutierrez." He described Celsa Gutierrez as Pat Garrett's sister-in-law and said she was his (Robert's [sic]) sweetheart at the time. While he was being treated, he said, Barlow's body was being passed off as his.

**"So Much Alike"**

"That's because we were so much alike."

Morrison, meanwhile, told newsmen that he first became interested in the Billy the Kid case when he was associated with the R.R. Roberts accounting and law firm in Beaumont, Texas. He said Roberts and the man who claims to be Billy the Kid are distant relatives.

"**We are satisfied,**" **Morrison said, "that this man is not an imposter, but is the real Billy the Kid."**

Morrison and Roberts headed back to Albuquerque after the interview with the governor. They spent last night at an Albuquerque hotel and came to Santa Fe this morning for the interview.

Morrison would not comment on what he intends to do now in the affair.

Historian William Keleher debunked "Brushy" in the December 1, 1950, *Albuquerque Journal*, as "Will A. Keleher, History Student, Sure Kid Was Shot." Keleher later put a photocopy of Billy's Coroner's Jury Report in his book 1957 titled *Violence in Lincoln County: 1869-1881*. The article stated:

### Will A. Keleher, History Student, Sure Kid Was Shot

Will A. Keleher, Albuquerque attorney and former newspaperman, was asked what he thought of the Governor's decision to disregard the latest pretender's attempt for recognition. Keleher, who made an extensive study of Billy the Kid's history, said:

"I'm not surprised to learn the death of Billy the Kid was considered once more. If the Kid wasn't killed at Fort Sumner on July 14, 1881, a lot of intelligent people living at the time were badly fooled." He continued:

"A list of the people who knew the facts of the case at that time contains many impressive names. For instance, Sheriff Pat Garrett, who killed him; John W. Poe, a later highly respected banker of Roswell and who, along with Kip McKinney, rode with Garrett's posse; George Coe and Frank Coe, Pete Maxwell, Paulita Maxwell Jaramillo, and Charles Siringo, who later became a famous Pinkerton detective.

"There was also Governor Miguel A. Otero who believed the Kid was the one they buried and Ash Upson, a reporter from the New York Tribune who also investigated the crime.

"Two nationally known writers investigated the death and wrote about it. Emmerson Hough, one time resident of White Oaks, in Lincoln county, had a book called "The Story of the Outlaw," published and Walter Noble Burns, who wrote the "Saga of Billy the Kid."

Other old-timers who knew quite a lot about the days when the 21-year-old outlaw was riding high in Lincoln County, were inclined to agree with Keleher.

The rejection continued as front page news. December 30, 1950's *Lubbock Morning Avalanche*, a month later, announced: "Billy the Kid is Called Imposter by New Mexico Chief." It stated:

### 'BILLY THE KID' IS CALLED IMPOSTER BY NEW MEXICO CHIEF

SANTA FE, N.M. Nov. 30 (AP) – Gov. Thomas J. Mabry today branded a 91-year-old man claiming to be Billy the Kid an imposter and denied his petition for a pardon.

"No action will be taken on his petition for a full pardon because I don't believe this man is Billy the Kid," the Governor said after a 45-minute interview at the executive mansion.

The decision means that history books will continue to record that the notorious outlaw died at the age of 21 under the flaming guns of Pat Garrett, famous New Mexico sheriff, at Fort Sumned [sic] in 1881.

Giving his name at [sic] Ollie Henry Roberts, the aged man appeared for the unusual interview wearing buckskins and a western hat. He told his story to more than a score of interested persons.

Without prompting from his representative, William V. Morrison of St. Louis, Roberts was unable to recall the name of Sheriff Garrett. He was similarly vague on details of the Lincoln county cattle war, in which his famous reputation was earned.

Roberts differed with the history books on Billy the Kid's birthplace, too. He said he was born at Buffalo Gap, in Taylor County, Texas. Historians say it is a "well documented fact" that the Kid was born in New York City.

Obviously sensitive about his baldness, the claimant at one time during the questioning demanded that no pictures be taken of him with his hat off. But he posed willingly enough with the hat on.

The Governor, ailing with a cold, got out of a sick bed to conduct the interview. It resulted from an appeal by an El Paso, Tex., law firm for a full pardon for the outlaw.

## HIDDEN HOAXBUSTING TREASURE

This failure did not end the "Brushy Bill" hoax. But it was last time anyone would be allowed to see the real "Brushy Bill" in action. William V. Morrison and C.L. Sonnichsen had learned their lesson. That made "Brushy's" hearing's flubs hoaxbusting treasure - before his backers' surreptitious fix-ups began.

# CHAPTER 4
# THE BOOK TITLED
# *ALIAS BILLY THE KID*

## MORRISON RISES FROM THE ASHES

To a legitimate petitioner, exposing of "Brushy" as an imposter by Governor T.J. Mabry and experts would have yielded bowing out. But to William V. Morrison, the message was: hitting pay-dirt. "Brushy's" press was front page. As P.T. Barnum said, "Without promotion something terrible happens: Nothing!" So after the pardon hook, Morrison pushed a "Brushy" book! He even had a writer: C.L. Sonnichsen, unfazed by real historians' ridicule.

Then fate provided Morrison with what no con-man can create: luck. Brushy died in on December 27, 1950. That embarrassing old fool who said Billy the Kid had *killed no one, forgot Pat Garrett's name,* guessed Fort Sumner's *restaurant was out of steak* on July 15, 1881, and called Billy *he* not *me*, was out of the way.

The *Hico News Review* of January 5, 1951, announced "Notorious Character is Buried." No Roberts family member came. But Morrison was there proclaiming: "There is considerable evidence on both sides of the [Billy the Kid] question;" though he admitted (for the last time) that there was "a noted discrepancy in the reported age of Brushy Bill." The article stated:

In striking contrast to colorful tales of his checkered career on the frontier, the earthly remains of O.L. Roberts lay in Barrow-Rutledge Funeral Chapel last Friday afternoon. Friends gathered to pay their last respects to a departed citizen ...

"Brushy Bill," as he called himself, had recounted his last tale about Indian battles and wild horse riding. His robust health had broken suddenly. His heart failed, and he dropped dead at noon Wednesday on the streets he had trod so often with a bearing erect and stalwart. Dressed in Western style ... he had explained a yen for such garb by telling his listeners innocent tales of derring-do while hobnobbing with famous desperados of pioneer days.

In a neat, plain business suit, his body rested before the assemblage ...

[Two of the pallbearers came] from East Texas with lifelong friend, **De Witt Travis of Longview, to attend the services. Another close acquaintance, W.A. Morrison of El Paso, was present to help console the widow, Mrs. Malinda F. Roberts** ...

Burial was in Littleville Cemetery, 20 miles south of Hico. He had made his home [there] in Hamilton at various times.

"**Brushy Bill" had recounted often that his placer of birth was Buffalo Gap in Taylor County, and the time was December 31, 1868, stating that he was born on the last day of that year. If correct, that would belie current tales being aired by daily newspapers linking his identity with that of a famous early-day character.** There is considerable evidence on both sides of the question.

On November 30, 1950, he had appeared before the governor of New Mexico, according to his friend, Morrison of El Paso, who said he accompanied him. The governor denied their appeal in spite of evidence consisting of a 17-page brief, a 2-page letter of testimonial from the law firm of Andres, Lipscomb and Petticolas of El Paso, and 22 instruments containing what was presented as documentary proof of the contention that he was, in fact, Billy the Kid.

"**We are not basing our claim on hearsay,"** Morrison emphatically stated in an interview with the News Review editor, "but on evidence which I have assembled over a period of years. It is taken from official records and affidavits, and will be on file for the proper parties to inspect." He stated that he expected to continue his efforts to piece the evidence together, with Mrs. Roberts' permission, and said he made three trips to Hico and one to Hamilton for interviews with the late Mr. Roberts during the past year and a half. He went through the background of the case meticulously, and said that his proof was more convincing than the fact that there was a discrepancy in the reported age of the old man.

[DeWitt] Travis, who has journeyed here frequently from Longview to visit his old friend, took a similar attitude as to his identity. "I am 62 years old," he stated, "and I have known who Billy was as long as I have known anything. Our fathers fought together in the Civil War, and we have made it a point not to discuss this man's past until just recently."

**[AUTHOR'S NOTE: Travis was exposed as "Brushy's" dupe by Don Cline in his book,** *Brushy Bill Roberts: I Wasn't Billy the Kid.* **(Cline, Page 97)]**

This claim was corroborated by his two companions accompanying him from East Texas for the funeral.

Contradictory claims have been made in statements and letters to the News Review, bearing testimony to the claim that the rustic character known so well in and around Hico was a law-abiding citizen. And there is no evidence here, where he has made his residence for most of the last decade, to support any contention otherwise.

Peace be to his ashes.

## *RATIONALIZING THE LOST PARDON*

First, sly Morrison turned the lost pardon into martyrdom; hiding "Brushy's" total mismatch with Billy in the Mabry hearing.

On April 3, 1954, to a Carl W. Breihan, then writing a Billy the Kid biography, Morrison floated his fakery (and sent a copy to loyalist Paul Blazer, who saved it). His double-talk was that: a Coroner's Jury Report did not exist, so there was no proof Billy the Kid had been killed; so "Brushy" had no legal judgment to contest in a real court; so requesting pardon was his only option. Then Morrison fabricated a catch-22: Governor Mabry could not pardon him without proof of death,! So a legal technicality explained refusal! Morrison wrote: "It was most unfortunate that ["Brushy" and I] did not have the opportunity to prove our case in a court of law for the reason that we could not dig up a cause of action. You know that they never made a legal coroner's verdict. Therefore it was not possible to file an action against the non-existent judgment. So, the Pardon was the only legal declaration that could be made. They had no cause of action against Billy Roberts for the reason that there was no proof that Garrett killed anyone in Fort Sumner on July 14, as contended."

Morrison added "Brushy's" being intimidated: "It is difficult for anyone to realize the intimidation meted out to Billy Roberts that day in Santa Fe, unless they were present during the working over. And no one present had ever seen the Kid about whom they thought they knew so much."

On April 12, 1954, to historian Philip J. Rasch, Morrison sent his fabricated version of the pardon failure, fishing for allies; but ultimately failing with him. This time, Morrison added a conspiracy theory blaming the Santa Fe Ring! He wrote: "I don't believe there was any secret why the Garrett faction opposed a legal hearing. They were put on notice that there was no legal record or evidence to support the contention that Garrett's Posse had killed anyone on that memorable July 14, 1881. And probably, that had acknowledged that I conferred with legal authority in New Mexico in an endeavor to prove up their purported coroner's verdict, or the first verdict - not mentioned by the Ring - in an attempt to file suit to then have it set aside. I was advised that it would be impossible to prove up the lost instrument at this late date. Therefore, the idea was abandoned and the Petition for Pardon was the only manner in which to make a declaration. The Santa Fe Ring had failed to make a legal record of the purported killing at the time. However, they did almost everything else in an attempt to collect the $500 reward [presumably for Pat Garrett]."

## FORMULATING THE HOAX

### *KEY FAKERY*

One can see the progressing book's fabricated claims in a December 3, 1953, El Paso Rotary Club lecture on "Billy the Kid," which Morrison gave, with introduction by Sonnichsen (a copy of which was sent to Paul Blazer). Morrison stated: "During my talk I hope to dispose of the two purported coroner's verdicts **[fabricated claim]**, and I hope to prove, among other things, That: The Kid was not killed by Garrett or anyone else; No official coroner's verdict was rendered; The Kid was a product of the times; Governor Wallace broke his agreement to pardon the Kid after the Kid had performed fully; The Kid's trial was unfair; The Kid lived for many years before appearing and applying for a pardon in 1950, which was refused by Governor Mabry without considering the indisputable records and evidence; At no time did anyone come forward with legal evidence to invalidate Billy Robert's [sic] claim; Billy Roberts was actually Billy the Kid as he claimed to be." Morrison concluded: "Garrett's posse purportedly killed an unidentified man in July or August, 1881 … In fact, there is no legal evidence in San Miguel County to prove that they killed anyone at that time."

Of course, the "Brushy" hoax rested on claiming that Garrett lied about killing Billy the Kid, and that no Coroner's Jury Report identified William Bonney. Since those claims were fake, Morrison fabricated an absurd and error-filled plot based on the Santa Fe Ring falsifying documents, and giving Garrett the reward money, to hide that he did not kill the Kid and that "Brushy" was Billy.

Later used by Sonnichsen in *Alias Billy the Kid*, this scam can be seen full-blown in Morrison's letter of May 7, 1954 to historian Philip J. Rasch, whom he was trying to convert to "Brushy" belief (and which he copied to Paul Blazer). Morrison wrote: "[Y]ou can understand that little credence can be placed on those papers controlled by the Ring at that time. I am sure you are probably aware **of** the fact that Catron was a dominant figure in the Lincoln County War, even though it might not have been written up. Also that Green, Garrett's attorney [sic] in the reward issue [for killing the Kid], was editor of Catron's New Mexican that printed the Government publications. And that Thornton, Catron's law partner, was the member of the legislature that pushed the act for relief of Garrett for killing the Kid in August [this was a transcriptionist error seized on by Morrison and Sonnichsen, though July was also correctly used] and not on that memorable July 14 as Garrett would have you believe. All of this was done in less than a year from the time they claimed the Kid was killed, which they could not prove at the time. And none of it was reported in their paper as it actually happened, Why not? Certainly the Editor, Mr. Greene, knew about it … In fact, all writers still contend that the killing took place on that memorable July 14, except Sonnichsen and Morrison, who have reproduced the record, the Official Act. Why has it gone untouched all of these years?

Certainly they had never intended for old man Roberts to come along seventy years later and dig it out, or did they? ... **Garrett did not kill anybody in the month of July or August 1881."**

**[AUTHOR'S NOTE: Carried away by his lying, Morrison forgot "Brushy's" key Billy Barlow tale!]**

Soon after the book was released, Morrison presented its made-up claims on June 29, 1955, to William Waters (sending a copy to Paul Blazer): "A man was killed by mistake in July – not in August – by a member of Garrett's posse on the outside --- not in Maxwell's house --- but excusing Garrett as the killer; he was buried the next day and not on the second day after the killing as reported; he had used an alias, Billy B. Barlow; he had worked on a ranch near Mule Shoe, Texas; was not an outlaw and he had not fought in the war; was a relative of the old Clements family from Texas; Garrett paid for this mistaken murder with his life in 1908, and that Wayne Brezel [sic - Brazel] did not kill Garrett ... I have two objectives in this case. Did Garrett kill anyone that night? Was Roberts Billy the Kid."

On April 17, 1954, sending Paul Blazer a copy, Morrison wrote to Fred Gipson, then editor of *True West* magazine: "Garrett's posse claimed to have killed a man on that memorable July 14, 1881 ... but they left no evidence to support the contention that they had killed anyone at that time. I have the proof." (This had an irony that Morrison, dying in 1977, would not live to see: by 2003, that magazine, under then editor, Bob Boze Bell, participating in the "Billy the Kid Case" hoax, would back "Brushy" and fake forensics, trying to make him Billy the Kid.)

## *STRATEGIZING PERSONAL PROFIT*

By March 17, 1954, the year before publication of *Alias Billy the Kid*, grandiose Morrison, already imagining big bucks, was lying in a letter to a Carl W. Breihan in St. Louis, giving its copy to Paul Blazer. Morrison made-up that "Mr. Wm. Keleher, the attorney-historian-author, in Albuquerque, has definitely decided that my theory is the correct one. He is accepting my records in the case of Billy the Kid." And Morrison could see a golden future for himself; adding: "At present, I am dickering on movie and television rights on my work." And he added something that did not make it to his hoax, but lived on with its descendants: he bemoaned not getting "the opportunity to remove the remains [in the Billy the Kid grave] for scientific investigation."

On March 31, 1954, Morrison got an answer from Gene Autry; after trying to sell his "information on Billy the Kid" to that movie cowboy; though it was a rejection. But he sent it to his fan, Paul Blazer, who saved it with the family papers.

By April 6, 1955, exuberant Morrison announced the publication of his *Alias Billy the Kid* to Paul Blazer: "The book will be reviewed this month and go on sale on May first, then autographing party is scheduled at White House on May 21. Also, television program in El Paso on KTSM as soon as I get there." "Brushy's" own P.T. Barnum was counting on his circus maxim: "There's a sucker born every minute."

## TALL TALE TREASURE TROVE

By November 30, 1950, Morrison had a treasure trove of sources used to prepare "Brushy" for his Billy the Kid act. And he had recordings of "Brushy;" and visits to Lincoln, and its courthouse-jail. They were all grist for *Alias Billy the Kid*.

It would take 67 years from "Brushy Bill's" death, for the specifics of that information hoard to be revealed. For his 2012 book titled *Billy the Kid: The Lost Interviews*, "Brushy"-believing author, William Carl "W.C." Jameson, related that between the summer of 1949 and December 1950, Morrison had taken notes, and made eight six-inch tape recorder reels, of his "Brushy" interviews. (Jameson, Page 28) Jameson also confirmed "Brushy's" own notes, kept in "Big Chief writing tablets;" which Jameson's co-author and "Brushy"-believer, Frederick Bean, had relocated in 1989. (Jameson, Pages 34, 36). What Jameson did not recognize, was that these were tools of the hoax: "Brushy's" recorded prompts and rehearsal tapes; though Jameson only noted that "Brushy" oddly kept repeating things over-and-over!

## *THE PROMPT FOOTNOTE SOURCES*

At the heart of the "Brushy Bill" hoax was claiming he knew things-not-printed; and was too illiterate to read things-printed. In fact, *Alias Billy the Kid* inadvertently revealed the sources that Morrison used from 1948 to 1950 to coach "Brushy" for his role as Billy Bonney.

Overconfident that theirs was the "perfect crime," Morrison and Sonnichsen had used them as *Alias Billy the Kid's* footnotes from books, magazines, articles, court filings, executive record books, and interviews (there being no bibliography). As footnotes, the sources were linked directly to supposedly esoteric information "Brushy" was mouthing. Hoped was that they proved corroboration, not cribbing. But that scam blew-up, because the sources, limited in their day to dime-novel fantasies, hearsay, rumors, and old-timer wind-bag malarkey, had glaring errors. So the give-away was "Brushy's" parroting those errors!

Additionally, lifted commonly known historical names and major events completed "Brushy's" "memories" as Billy the Kid. And, revealingly, although five years had passed from his death to the book's publication, the sources stopped at 1950, so were there to prompt him for the pardon attempt, and to make his practice interview tapes.

Books were global sources, and also referenced in footnotes. So available to "Brushy" (who could read and write) and his team were Pat Garrett's 1927 edition of *The Authentic Life of Billy the Kid*; Walter Noble Burns's 1926 *The Saga of Billy the Kid*, based on Garrett's original 1882 edition; John William Poe's 1933 *The Death of Billy the Kid*; George Coe's 1934 *Frontier Fighter. The Autobiography of George Coe Who Fought and Rode With Billy the Kid*; and other authors for specific scenes.

## *THE HEARSAY AND CONFABULATED SOURCES*

The art, science, and accuracy of historical writing rely on ability to distinguish hard evidence. Since there existed no valid evidence that "Brushy" was Billy, Morrison and Sonnichsen were left with hearsay sources. According to thefreedictionary.com legal definition, hearsay is: "law evidence that is not within the personal knowledge of a witness, such as testimony regarding statements made by someone other than the witness [whose] accuracy cannot be verified through cross-examination." Or as the

*Merriam-Webster Dictionary* states about hearsay: "evidence based not on a witnesss's personal knowledge." Again, the giveaway was the errors in the sources, which "Brushy" parroted.

The prompt source scam had another flaw: vast areas of Billy the Kid history with no source materials. That left "Brushy" on his own to confabulate. Likewise, confabulated sources of other addled or attention-seeking old-timers were fed to "Brushy," to parrot, and to inadvertently condemn him by their errors.

## *POST-"BRUSHY" SOURCES*

Important for hoaxbusting, is that Morrison continued his research for "Brushy's" "special knowledge" after "Brushy's" 1950 death. A key source was Paul Blazer, grandson of Joseph Blazer, whom Morrison convinced that "Brushy" was Billy, and who retained all Morrison's communications with his family papers.

Joseph Blazer, owner of the private property Blazer's Mill within the Mescalero Indian Reservation, was a Lincoln County War period figure, since the killing of Andrew "Buckshot" Roberts occurred at his building housing his office, a post office, and quarters of the Indian Agent Frederick Godfroy. His family papers were subsequently donated to New Mexico University's Las Cruces campus as the "Blazer Family Papers."

Morrison's letters document his visits with Paul Blazer in Mescalero, New Mexico, on his New Mexico research trips. From him, Morrison got photographs for scene reconstructions. For example, a photo caption on Blazer's Mill reads: "The old Blazer homestead, built in 1869, by Dr. Blazer, burned in 1883. Leased to Godfroy, Indian Agent, with Blazer retaining two rooms at N.W. corner, at rear near tree. The first floor window was cut into a door, and it was from this door that Buckshot Roberts made his brave stand against 13 men, until mortally wounded by the Kid [sic] in April, 1878. Roberts aimed Dr. Blazer's 45-70 Springfield rifle from the door and hit Brewer as his head came up from behind a log at the mill … killing Brewer instantly."

On April 18, 1952, Morrison, fine tuning his fakery, wrote to Paul Blazer, "I was very much interested in hearing you say Billy the Kid was ambidextrous."

# OTHER LIKELY SOURCES

For the cause of the Lincoln County War, and about the Santa Fe Ring, "Brushy's" day's sources were in the dark. So his parroted errors point to sources not listed, but likely used.

## *CAUSE OF THE LINCOLN COUNTY WAR*

"Brushy" consistently misstated the Lincoln County War as a cattle war or "great cattle feud." (Page 50) It was the going formula in his day, and erroneously reduced the citizens' uprising against the Santa Fe Ring to a local business conflict. As Morrison stated in his December 3, 1953 speech to the El Paso Rotary Club, with C.L. Sonnichsen giving the introduction: "This private [Lincoln County] war was created by friction between the Murphy-Dolan and Tunstall-McSween-Chisum factions, each of which was wresting trade from the other. The Murphy faction was controlled by the Santa Fe Ring, which was backed by politicians from the governor on down, and including the county officers."

That portrayal came from 1926's *The Saga of Billy the Kid* by Walter Noble Burns, who called it a "ugly local feud" between "A.G. [sic -L.G.] Murphy," who had "virtual lock on the cattle business in Lincoln County," and cattleman, John Chisum. Mentioned too is that the Murphy side had "the patronage of politicians and businessmen in Santa Fe." (Burns, Page xxiii). So, without understanding the uprising, "Brushy" and his authors inserted the Santa Fe Ring and corrupt politicians as simply on the Murphy side.

Other possible sources, not listed, are Ralph Emerson Twitchell, for his 1912 multi-volume *The Leading Facts of New Mexico History*. Twitchell, himself fabricating; wrote: "In [Lincoln County] a feud was begun which, in the annals of New Mexico, is known as the "Lincoln County War." The cause of this trouble and era of crime can be **traced to the rivalry existing between prominent cattlemen at the time living in Lincoln and the Pecos valley, respectively ... This was the basis for the war ...** The beginning of the so-called Lincoln county war occurred when John H. Tunstel [sic] was killed by a sheriff's posse seeking to levy an attachment upon property belonging to Tunstel [sic]. **The latter had a friend and employe [sic], William H. Bonney, later famous as "Billy the Kid"**

## *NAME-DROPPING THE SANTA FE RING*

The Santa Fe Ring was likely lifted by Morrison from the 1927 edition of Pat Garrett's *The Authentic Life of Billy the Kid.* He (and coached "Brushy") were limited by its minimal information; missing entirely that the Lincoln County War as a freedom fight against its corrupt monopolistic control.

For his 1882 first edition, cautious Garrett did not name the dangerous Ring; but he stated: "It is not the intention here to discuss the merits of the imbroglio or to censure or uphold either one faction or the other, but merely to detail such events of the [Lincoln County] war as ... [Billy the Kid] took part in. The principles in this difficulty were on one side John S. Chisum, called the Cattle King of New Mexico, with Alexander A. McSween and John H. Tunstall as important allies. On the other side were the firm of Murphy & Dolan, merchants in Lincoln, the county seat, backed by nearly every small cattle owner in the Pecos Valley. **This latter faction was supported by Thomas B. Catron, United States Attorney for the Territory, a resident of Santa Fe, one of the eminent lawyers of the Territory, and a considerable owner in the Pecos region.**" (Garrett, Page 52)

For the 1927 reprint of Garrett's book, annotating historian, Maurice Garland Fulton, added the Ring; writing: "Garrett is one of the few writers of the Lincoln County War who has had the frankness and courage to mention Catron's name in connection with it. [Catron] is the figure that looms up behind the Murphy and Dolan faction. As the president of the powerful First National Bank at Santa Fe, he furnished the money needed by Murphy and Dolan in their business, of course taking mortgages which at the close of the War gave him possession of their store and its stock of goods. Catron was also a cattle raiser, and in some sense a dominating figure in that industry in the western part of the county. **Besides all this he was a powerful member of the clique of politicians and business men called in those** days the "Santa Fe Ring," which largely controlled the Territory of New Mexico." (*The Authentic Life of Billy the Kid*, Fulton Note, Page 59)

"Brushy's cribbed version stated: "The Murphy bunch had the backing of the Santa Fe Ring, which included Tom Catron, U.S. District Attorney, and his brother-in-law. **[AUTHOR'S NOTE: This incorrect addition came from reading that Edgar Walz, Catron's brother-in-law, managed his Carrizozo cattle ranch. But Walz was not a Ring head.]** Of course, they were not out in the open with it, but during the cattle war Old Tom took over the Murphy-Dolan property. All the politicians belonged to the Santa Fe Ring, even judges and attorneys." (*Alias Billy the Kid*, Page 25)

## THE "BRUSHY" TEAM'S DILEMMAS

Besides his being 20 years too young, and knowing no intimate Billy the Kid history, "Brushy" and his team faced other built-in dilemmas for manufacturing him as Billy the Kid: the real Billy was highly literate and fluent in Spanish; and their day's publications painted him as a monstrous serial murderer.

### *THE LITERATE-ILLITERATE DILEMMA*

Existence of Billy the Kid history books, necessitated lying that "Brushy" was illiterate to avoid the reading-up in the things-already-printed problem. In a July 12, 1955 letter to historian, Robert Mullin, (with its copy to Paul Blazer), Morrison said "Brushy" "`could not read.`" Sonnichsen joined in, as quoted in Dale L. Walker's 1972 biography, *C.L. Sonnichsen: Grassroots Historian*: "['Brushy Bill'] was not a literate man and could not have read up on the subject." (Walker, Page 64)

But Sonnichsen and Morrison did not stick to that, since their book refers to "Brushy's" literacy as: "writing an autobiography" (Page 11), "correspondence" (Page 14), keeping "notebooks" that "covered practically the entire West," (Page 20) and having "copious notes" on his life after the Fort Sumner shooting. (Page 50) Authors Jameson and Bean, in their 1998 book, *The Return of the Outlaw Billy the Kid*, having seen "Brushy's" notebooks, say he wrote with a "scrawl," and had bad grammar and misspellings (*The Return of the Outlaw Billy the Kid*, (Page 204); which means he was literate!

In *Alias Billy the Kid*, Morrison and Sonnichsen also quoted "Brushy's" literate May 24, 1949 letter to Morrison to show that he was secretive about being Billy. "Brushy" wrote: "She said she had three affidavits that people knew me in 1887 ... These men said I was Billie [sic] the Kid ... I ain't putting out nothing ... I don't like for other people to meddle with my business." (Page 59) And "Brushy" is described as "writing up his history the way he wanted it told." (Page 59) His composition books and loose-leaf notebooks, going back to 1925, are cited as repositories, apparently with his imaginings before they met him. Noteworthy, is that Sonnichsen wrote: "Roberts' account of these early days is hard to follow." (Page 20) They were profuse: mad ramblings about roaming through Arizona, Montana, Oregon, Oklahoma Indian Territory, Wyoming, and Nebraska, and Old Mexico; being with outlaws, rustlers, Cheyenne and Arapaho Indians; and employment as a bronco buster and ranch worker. And that was before age 17!

And "Brushy's" relative, Roy L. Haws, for his 2015 book, *Brushy Bill: Proof That His Claim to Be Billy the Kid Was a Hoax,* provided a fully literate letter by "Brushy," dated April 1, 1949, from Dora, New Mexico, to a tall tale teller who was his possible inspiration: an Oran Ardious Woodman, who claimed to be Kit Carson. "Brushy" wrote: We are doing fine. Hope this finds you the same. The wind blows every day and its cold – Wheat looks good ... Cattle they are fat." (Haws, Page 113)

"Brushy" was a man who could, indeed, read, write, and study-up for the biggest role of his life!

## *THE BI-LINGUAL DILEMMA*

As *The Authentic Life of Billy the Kid* stated: "[Billy] talked Spanish as fluently as any Mexican." (Garrett, Page 8) Dr. Henry Hoyt, in his *Frontier Doctor;* stated: "He spoke Spanish like a native." Billy was also bi-cultural, and may be credited with bringing Hispanic fighters into the Lincoln County War Battle. "Brushy" did not speak Spanish; and there was no faking that; though one of his later authors tried. (See pages 526, 532 below)

## *THE SERIAL MURDERER DILEMMA*

"Brushy's" day's fictionalized sources portrayed Billy the Kid as a wanton killer. As Walter Noble Burns wrote for his 1926 *The Saga of Billy the Kid*: "[Billy] placed no value on human life ... He killed a man as nonchalantly as he smoked a cigarette. Murder did not appeal to Billy the Kid as tragedy; it was merely a physical process of pulling a trigger ... In his murders, he observed no rules of etiquette ... As long as he killed a man he wanted to kill, it made no difference to him how he killed him. It is impossible now to name twenty-one men that he killed, though, if Indians be included, it is not difficult to cast up the ghastly total." (Burns, Pages 57, 61) And Pat Garrett's *The Authentic Life of Billy the Kid* stated: "The Kid had **a devil lurking in him**. It was a good-humored jovial imp, or a cruel and **bloodthirsty fiend**, as circumstances prompted. **Circumstances favored the worser angel, and the Kid fell** ... Those who knew [Billy] best will tell you that in his most savage and dangerous moods his face always wore a smile ... [H]e killed and laughed." (Garrett, Page 21)

And *Alias Billy the Kid* had a secret impasse. It was too early for knowing that the Lincoln County War was just one freedom fight among the Territorial uprisings against the Santa Fe Ring.

So it was unclear to the hoaxing triumvirate why "Brushy," as Billy, killed at all - though revenge for Tunstall's killing was floated. Nevertheless, for his things-not-printed trick - from cribbed sources - "Brushy" has Billy killing John Chisum's cowboys at $5 per head to reduce Chisum's financial debt to him. This is monstrous. If such a person existed, as a youth or old man, he would, and should, be reviled. And a pardon for his deeds would be preposterous. So "Brushy's" hoaxers simply hoped readers would not notice this monster-Billy problem.

# CHAPTER 5
# *ALIAS BILLY THE KID'S* HOAXING EXPOSED

## MAKING A BETTER "BRUSHY"

A dastardly deception in the "Brushy Bill" hoax was his authors' manufacturing a better "Brushy" to match Billy. The pardon hearing proved he failed the things-not-printed trick: with his Lincoln County War ignorance, killing of no guards in his jailbreak, forgetting Pat Garrett, and the Fort Sumner steak restaurant for July 14, 1881. So a secret fix-up campaign began.

But it took 62 years after *Alias Billy the Kid's* publication, for it to be revealed. "Brushy"-believer, W.C. Jameson, in his 2012 book, *Billy the Kid: The Lost Tapes*, stated that Sonnichsen used Morrison's taped interviews to write *Alias Billy the Kid*. (Jameson, Page 29) That should mean "Brushy's" words. But no. Jameson's past co-author, Frederick Bean, had transcribed them in 1989. When Jameson compared that transcript to *Alias Billy the Kid*, he realized: "Sonnichsen used a relatively small amount of the information contained therein. It was also apparent that Sonnichsen, a long-time college professor of English literature, **heavily edited** Robert's grammar, even **adding and deleting** words for clarity. In other places, Sonnichsen merely summarized what Roberts said." (Jameson, Page 42) Jameson missed that this meant that Sonnichsen had created a fictional "Brushy" to hide real and incoherent imposter "Brushy."

Of course, Morrison had also tried to make "Brushy" a better "Billy": coaching, touring historic sites, and rehearsing answers on tape. As Jameson naively noted: "[On tape] Roberts related the same event as many as three times … some contained information others did not. Roberts repeated himself often, sometimes three or four times within only a few minutes." (Jameson, Page 43) This is called practicing one's lines!

## *ALIAS BILLY THE KID AS FORGERY EVIDENCE*

In truth, the last time real "Brushy" was viewed by the public was at his November 30, 1950 pardon hearing. And the hoax's deceitful fix-ups snowballed with later authors, "upgrading" his "knowledge" with new historical information, cleansing his racism, gentrifying his speech, and even making him bi-lingual! So *Alias Billy the Kid* is key a for hoaxbusting, since it still reflected his ignorance - shared by his authors - even though their fix-ups made sure there was no steak restaurant in Fort Sumner! So, the book provides a baseline for exposing the later, cynical, more out-of-control, forged fix-ups of "Brushy's" already glossed script.

## CREATING "BRUSHY'S" NARRATIVE

"Brushy's" narrative cobbled together his pre-Morrison multi-persona fabrications and genealogy, with Morrison's coaching from sources and touring historic sites; as well as making tapes of "Brushy's rehearsed parroting and confabulations in response to his prompting questions. And that was called "interviewing."

Morrison's cited "interviews" with "Brushy" in *Alias Billy the Kid*, are those of May 24, 1949 at uncertain location; June 16 and 17, 1949, in Hico, Texas; and on August 18, 1949, at Carrizozo and Lincoln. (Footnote 5, Page 21) (In a July 12, 1955 letter to historian, Robert Mullin, the date is given as the August 19, 1949, rather than August 18th). An April of 1950 trip throughout New Mexico is also cited, in which Morrison took "Brushy" to get supposedly verifying affidavits of his being Billy the Kid from non-historical people. (Pages 70-72) Carrizozo was clarified later in the book as having the courthouse for Morrison, with "Brushy," "to go through the records;" but the date of that endeavor was changed to "August, 1950." (Page 40) Morrison also referred to "later expeditions" of taking "Brushy" back to Lincoln. (Page 45)

As claimed by "Brushy"-believer W.C. Jameson in his 2012 book titled *Billy the Kid: The Lost Interviews* - who had also consulted with Sonnichsen - from the summer of 1949 to December of 1950, Morrison had taken notes on "Brushy's" renditions, and had eight six-inch reels of taped interviews with him; which were all given to Sonnichsen from which to write *Alias Billy the Kid*. (*Billy the Kid: The Lost Interviews*, Page 23)

## *DUPING THE PUBLISHER*

The "Brushy"-Morrison-Sonnichsen hoax, fusing Morrison's years of research, "Brushy's parroting and confabulations, and C.L. Sonnichsen's editing, deceptively purports that its densely massed names, places, and events came from "Brushy's memory, "proving" he must be Billy the Kid, because the information was "never printed." Assumed was ignorance of his pseudo-historical babble and his actually printed sources. And, as a precaution, he was called illiterate. That scam, plus touting Sonnichsen as a Harvard professor, got the book a publisher In fact, Sonnichsen's glib "Was he Billy the Kid? If not, who was he?" made the cover.

The publisher was the University of New Mexico Press, (the same state University from which the "Billy the Kid Case" hoaxers got their "Brushy"-backing "official historian" 48 years later). The "Publisher's Foreword" broadcasted the "never-printed" ploy, gushing: "the most skeptical readers ... have been amazed by what Brushy Bill knew ... It was generally believed, for example, that there was a federal charge outstanding against Billy the Kid. Brushy Bill said the case 'was thrown out of court.' Legal records, when found, proved Brushy Bill's statement."

**FAKE CLAIM:** The duped publisher did not realize that the "legal records" were merely "Brushy" parroting Billy Bonney's April 15, 1881 letter to Attorney Edgar Caypless - copied by Morrison from the Lincoln Museum; stating: *"My United States case was thrown out of court and I was rushed to trial on my Territorial charge."*

Furthermore, a footnote in *Alias Billy the Kid* reveals their additional source: Historian, Maurice Garland Fulton's, Note C, page 194, in the 1927 edition of Pat Garrett's *The Authentic Life of Billy the Kid*. It is paraphrased to explain that the murder site, Blazer's Mill was on private property, so Attorney Ira Leonard convinced the judge that it was not under federal jurisdiction. (*Alias Billy the Kid*, Page 77) This trickery is the gist of *Alias Billy the Kid*, whose conning come-back was that the listed sources were to check 'Brushy.' " But the truth was that when the script ran out, so did "Brushy's" "memories." And when the sources had errors, "Brushy" echoed them.

## THE HOAX FORMULA

*Alias Billy the Kid's* hoaxing unravels when facts are interpolated, errors are highlighted, and the sources are revealed. On its own, it is a surrealistic mélange of historical names and basic events jumbled in "Brushy's" fallacious confabulations, yielding no evidence that he was Billy Bonney.

At 90 text pages, including eight pages of photographs for "photo-comparisons" with Billy Bonney, it has an authors' sales pitch "Prologue;" a body of "Brushy's" "own words," as "narrated" by Morrison; and concludes with "Be He Alive, or Be He Dead," "In Black and White," and "Epilogue," offering fake conspiracy theories that are still fodder for "Brushy's" converts. A 40 page "Appendix" mixes real Billy Bonney's documents with meaningless hearsay affidavits vouching for "Brushy" as Billy.

The "Publisher's Foreword" states: "What if Garrett lied about killing Billy, and shot an innocent victim instead?" And the "Prologue" recycles Morrison's original punch line: "Brushy Bill" wanted "Billy the Kid's" gubernatorial pardon. That was the hoax's formula in a nutshell - and it would be recycled for the "Billy the Kid Case" hoax 48 years later.

But the book's errors were fatal and revealing - with one so audacious that it would lay bare the hoax's *modus operandi*. But it would be decades until "Brushy's" true-believer authors, the "Billy the Kid Case" hoaxers, and my research would reveal Morrison's terrible, telling, and terminating mistake - right at the death scene that was intended to prove "Brushy" was Billy Bonney.

## THE TITLE'S FAKE ALIAS

For their book, Morrison and Sonnichsen created a title that inadvertently distilled their chicanery into four words: *Alias Billy the Kid*. Real Billy Bonney did not use Billy the Kid as an alias, a truth unknown to "Brushy" and his team. The error may have been poached from one of their book's source footnotes of a 1943 *Frontier Times Magazine* article titled "A Story of 'Billy the Kid,'" which reproduced an August 10, 1881 article, from the *Laredo Times*, titled "Killing of 'Billy the Kid.'" The apocryphal article stated:" "Information from Lincoln County is that **William Bonney, alias, 'Billy the Kid,'**" who escaped from Lincoln jail on August 30 last, while under sentence of death, has added three more victims to his already large list." In truth, that moniker was only used in outlaw myth press, like this example.

And real Billy was aware of it, and objected in his December 12, 1880 letter to Lew Wallace; stating: "*I noticed in the Las Vegas Gazette a piece which stated that,* **Billy "the" Kid, the name by which I am known in the Country** *was the captain of a Band of Outlaws who hold Forth at the Portales. There is no such Organization in Existence. So the Gentleman must have drawn very heavily on his Imagination."*

## THE PROLOGUE LAUNCHES THE HOAX

The 12 page "Prologue" featuring the knowing-things-not-printed trick, alleges "Brushy's" pardon was lost because of his being rattled by press and hostile experts; and has him dying on December 27, 1950 as a victim of injustice. (Page 10)

Author Sonnichsen introduces Morrison as a "graduate lawyer;" Missouri Historical Society member; and "direct descendant of Ferdinand Maxwell, brother of the famous Lucien Bonaparte Maxwell." (Page 3) Given is Morrison's 1948 tale of finding Jim Hines as Lincoln County War participant, Jessie Evans, who alerted him to Billy the Kid living in Texas (Page 3); then Morrison's finding "Brushy" there, in Hamilton, after direction by J. Frank Dalton, as Jesse James. (Page 4) This trail of old men with delusions of Old West grandeur is a test for reader credulity. It is a fitting introduction to "Brushy," whom Morrison finally found in June of 1949. (Page 4)

Morrison is recorded as moving to El Paso for "Brushy's" research, and engaging the firm of Andress, Lipscomb, and Peticolas there to make "Brushy's" petition based on Billy the Kid having testified for the pardon bargain, and that he was not killed by Pat Garrett; so the governor should pardon him now. (Page 8)

FALSE: Historian Don Cline, in his unpublished manuscript titled *Brushy Bill Roberts: I Wasn't Billy the Kid*, stated that "Brushy" was not the firm's client; and Ted Andress became *Morrison's* attorney: Cline wrote: "The law firm had made a telephone call to Governor Thomas J. Mabry to arrange the meeting but it made clear that their sole client was William V. Morrison who was acting as agent/promoter for Brushy Bill Roberts. Their only interest in the affair was to arrange the meeting, not to represent their client in any legal matters." (Cline, Pages 7, 141) Cline also pointed out that New Mexico had a statute of limitations on murder. For Billy, it would have expired. He needed no pardon! (Cline, Pages 75, 142)

Sonnichsen presented meeting "Brushy," becoming convinced by his knowing-things-not-printed trick about shooting "negro" soldiers on the foothills "when the Murphy men burned McSween's house" [which was false]; and then getting deceased "Brushy's" materials to write the book. (Page 12) He calls himself "a hobbyist in Southwestern history and folklore" - which he should have realized made him unqualified to handle the complex history of Billy Bonney and the Lincoln County War period.

## *FAKING PHYSICAL MATCH*

"Brushy" obviously had to match Billy by age and appearance. Morrison was cited for the 20 year add-on, stating that upon first meeting "Brushy" in Texas in 1949 (when Roberts was 69), he "was amazed to see a man 90 years old in excellent physical condition." Physical likeness is concocted from the famous Billy the Kid tintype. So Morrison claims "Brushy Bill's" *"left ear"* protruded "noticeably farther from the head than the right ear." In the tintype, Billy's hat is rakishly tilted to the *right*, so its brim pushes out his *right* ear. But Morrison, unaware of a tintype's right-to-left reversal, puts a "funny" ear on his man's left. Saying "Brushy" was toothless, avoids Billy's protruding front teeth. (Page 6) "Brushy's" small hands and big wrists are claimed for shackle-slipping in escapes; and "Brushy" flexed his thumbs for Morrison to do a "slip through handcuffs" trick. (Pages 4, 6)

It should be noted that Morrison thought small hands was a clincher. In his April 19, 1954 letter to historian Philip J. Rasch, now in the Blazer family papers, complaining of the injustice of the Mabry pardon hearing; he wrote: "I was not permitted to interrogate anyone or produce any evidence - except Billy ["Brushy"], who stood there through the intimidation, waving those unusually small hands with large wrists - and no one seemed interested I his peculiar physical makeup."

POSSIBLE SOURCES: Real Billy had no evidence of "small hands," as shown by his regular-sized right hand seen in his tintype. But a Billy fable from Pat Garrett's *The Authentic Life of Billy the Kid* involved shackle-slipping: "His hand was small and his wrist large; so it was difficult to keep a pair of handcuffs on him." (Garrett, Page 116)

That myth was promoted by Lew Wallace, in his outlaw myth articles on Billy the Kid, in which he covered-up his betrayal of the pardon bargain by claiming that Billy escaped the sham jailing in Lincoln; when, in fact, Billy merely departed that arrest after Wallace refused the promised pardon. In *New York World Magazine* on June 8, 1902, Wallace published "General Lew Wallace Writes a Romance of 'Billy the Kid' Most Famous Bandit of the Plains," which stated: "**The manacles slipped like magic from his wrists. The guards stood stupefied, and "Billy the Kid," laughing mockingly, walked leisurely from the jail yard, through the gate and across the street.**"

That myth was also used for the great escape. Russ Kistler's *Las Vegas Daily Optic* of June 15, 1881 published "The Land of the Petulant Pistol, 'Scenes' where Life and Land are Cheap ... Billy the Kid as a Killer;" stating: "**[Billy] had worked his bracelet off and snatched the officer's pistol.**"

A 1935 book by a Frank M. King, titled *Wranglin' the Past: Reminiscences of Frank M. King*, stated the common fable about shackle-slipping, as used here in the jailbreak: "**After the Kid had killed [Bell], he slipped the handcuffs off over his extremely small hands.**" (King, Page 170)

Examining willingly striped-down "Brushy," Morrison found 26 scars claimed from bullets and knives. Billy had one scar. For that, "Brushy" says the one on his hip "was from the time I run into the street in Lincoln to take the **guns** off the body of Sheriff Bill Brady. Billy Matthews **ran behind an adobe wall** and fired. His shot went through the flesh of this hip and then hit **Wayte** [sic]." (Page 5) "Fred and I jumped the wall ... I pulled my pearl-handled .44 off his body." (Page 27)

FALSE: This was a failed things-not-printed trick. In fact, it was Billy and the Regulators who ambushed Brady *from behind an adobe wall*. Jacob Basil "Billy" Matthews, a Deputy Sheriff, next fired at them from *inside the Cisneros house* when Billy ran out with a companion to retrieve his single gun - a Winchester '73 carbine - from Brady's body. The carbine had been confiscated after John Tunstall's murder by Brady in a brief arrest of Billy; though "Brushy" fabricated two "pearl-gripped .44 revolvers." The shot companion was Jim "Frenchie" French, not Fred Waite (another known Regulator). "Brushy" throws in, apparently from movie Westerns of his day, "I wore my pistols in the scabbard with the butts toward the back. I fanned the hammer at times." (Page 6) Double-holstered guns and fanning were not used by real Billy.

Ambidextrousness, a known Billy trait, is claimed, but ruined by "Brushy's" claiming to favor the left (Page 6), repeating his tintype reversal error. In fact, in the tintype, Billy's *right* hand is cocked beside his Colt revolver's butt - showing he favored the right!

## *REVEALING HOAX UNDERPINNINGS*

To entice, the "Prologue" gives knowing-things-not-printed tricks. But they merely reveal "Brushy's" mismatch with Billy, his failed confabulations around known names and events, and the use of cribbed sources; as follows:

**INARTICULATE "BRUSHY":** When "Brushy" is quoted, he reveals the mismatch with Billy: **"I done wrong like everyone else in those days."** (Page 5) An unschooled rustic matched 1950's readers' Billy the Kid expectation; but was incompatible with the actual literate and articulate freedom fighter Billy Bonney, who objected to being called an outlaw.

**FAKING MURDER TRIAL SUBPOENA KNOWLEDGE:** "Brushy" states that his hanging trial witnesses lacked subpoenas. In fact, the subpoena of reluctant Lincoln resident and prosecution witness, Isaac Ellis, still exists. Furthermore, as a defendant, real Billy would not have that information, which apparently reflected Morrison's "research" having failed to find any.

**SOURCING A LEW WALLACE ARTICLE FOR A QUOTE:** As to facing his murder trial without the Governor Wallace pardon, "Brushy" is quoted: " 'But they didn't hang me, they didn't.' " he concluded. **"I wasn't born to hang.'** " (Page 7) That quote was lifted from a Lew Wallace article, available at the

Indiana Historical society, titled "Gen. Wallace's Feud with Billy the Kid, When the General Was Governor of New Mexico and Billy Bonne Was the Most Dangerous Western Outlaw;" stating: "He was convicted for murder and sentenced to be hanged. When the sentence was read, he arose in court and said: " 'Judge, that doesn't frighten me the least bit. **Billy the Kid was not born to be hung.**'... [He later escaped.] He called back as he spurred the animal into a gallop: "**Tell the judge that I said "Billy the Kid' was not born to be hung.**"

**SOURCING A BILLY LETTER FOR A QUOTE:** About the Garrett posse chase-down, "Brushy" is quoted: "I was never afraid to die like a man fighting, but I did not want to be shot down like a dog without a chance to fight back." That was his paraphrasing of Billy's actual and literate quote - *"I am not afraid to die like a man fighting but I would not like to be killed like a dog unarmed"* - from his March 20, 1879 letter to Governor Lew Wallace, which Morrison first got from the Lincoln Museum, then the Indiana Historical Society.

**BILLY THE KID AS AN ALIAS:** Claimed are "Brushy's" "aliases": "Ollie L. Roberts, Brushy Bill Roberts, Rattlesnake Bill, Texas Kid, Hugo Kid, William Antrim, William Bonney, Billy the Kid." (Page 9) But Billy Bonney never used Billy the Kid as an alias; being called just "Kid" by friends. And William Antrim was Billy's actual name after his mother's marriage.

**ADMITTING LITERACY:** Though the hoax rested on the illiteracy claim, "Brushy's" ability to read and write breaks through repeatedly in the book. In the "Preface," Morrison needed to establish that he had enough "Brushy" quotes to write for him after his death. So it is stated: "["Brushy"] made some attempts at writing his autobiography." (Page 11)

**THE FAKED SHOOTING NEGRO SOLDIERS:** "Negro" soldiers from Fort Stanton are described by "Brushy" as taking "positions on the hillside and joining in the firing that day when the Murphy men burned McSween's house." (Page 12) This is wrong. During the Lincoln County War Battle on July 19, 1878, the only day troops were present, only Sheriff George Peppin's white possemen attacked McSweens from the south foothills. And the only soldiers that fired on McSweens were three white ones, as Billy himself testified in the military court of inquiry against their commander. Furthermore, to hide "Brushy's" racism, Sonnichsen had substituted "negro" for "nigger;" accidently retained later.

**SOURCING A BILLY LETTER FOR THE JIM CARLYLE KILLING:** "Brushy's" claim that Billy did not kill Jim Carlyle in the Greathouse Ranch encounter, but he was killed by his fellow possemen (Page 12), was lifted from Billy's December 12, 1880 letter to Lew Wallace, which Morrison, with "Brushy" in tow, had gotten from the Lincoln Museum. Morrison then got a copy of the original from the Indiana Historical Society.

**FABRICATING THE DEATH/SURVIVAL SCENE:** Alluded to is the scene of "Brushy" surviving the Fort Sumner shooting of Billy the Kid, which he calls a "battle" with Pat Garrett's shooting possemen. (Page 6) It, and the book's later renditions of that scene, are key to cracking the "Brushy"-Morrison hoax - but it would take decades until some "Brushy"-believers and "Billy the Kid Case" hoaxers provided "Brushy's" actual fatal words.

## FAKING LIFE AS BILLY THE KID

*Alias Billy the Kid*, purporting to be a first-person account, lacked intimate information for autobiography. But for "Brushy Bill's Story," Oliver P. Roberts was on the firing line for a life tale of 44 pages - in his supposed own words. And, as discussed, there were unsolvable impasses. "Brushy" and his team were ignorant about Billy Bonney's early years, why the Lincoln County War was fought, or that Billy was a firebrand zealot in the grass-roots anti-Ring uprisings. So they were stuck with trying to minimize Billy the Kid's outlaw myth of serial killer-rustler. That made "Brushy's" confabulations a necessity. So that delusional, grammatically impaired, cowboy obsessed, lying, racist, old-timer, not only demonstrated no match for Billy, but was also a caricature that insulted the historical figure he was miming.

### *FAKING A GENEALOGY*

To be Billy Bonney, "Brushy" needed two decades of aging and a fictionally back-dated family to match. His genealogy, clearly by "Brushy" himself, proved his cunning sociopathy. Only after his death, and continued publicizing of his hoax, did his embarrassed Roberts family relatives reveal his actual August 26, 1879 birthdate - in contrast to Billy Bonney's on November 23, 1859.

But the fact that in the mid-20th century, real Billy's known history started in 1877 (at his age of 17-18), enabled "Brushy" to fill in a family for Morrison. And, as discussed, "Brushy" had already added 10 years to his life, and the middle initial "L" (instead of "P") for his Social Security benefits fraud. Ten more years were added to be Billy. So when "Brushy" met Morrison, he was 80 year old Oliver L. Roberts for his benefits checks, but was William Henry Roberts, and 90 years old, for Morrison.

Not the illiterate as claimed for his hoax, from Walter Noble Burns's quasi-fictional 1926 *The Saga of Billy the Kid*, "Brushy" apparently got false information that Billy Bonney's parents were named "**William H. and Kathleen Bonney.**" (Page 14; Burns, Page 70) He, thus, wrongly thought "Bonney" was a family name. In truth, Billy's father was a McCarty, and his mother was Catherine - with unknown maiden name. "Bonney" was an alias devised by Billy in 1877 from unknown inspiration.

"Brushy" contributed: "I was born at Buffalo Gap [Texas] on December 31, 1859." And mouthing a prompt - or simply a write-in by Sonnichsen- added "[T]hey have no proof on record that Billy the Kid was born in New York." (Page 15) That added age was obvious to those acquainted with "Brushy," including his last wife, and made Morrison admit at his funeral, as reported in the *Hico News Review* of January 5, 1951, that there was "noted discrepancy in the reported age of Brushy Bill." In fact, "Brushy's" wife put his benefits fraud date of December 31, 1868 on his tombstone!

**FAKING: Billy Bonney's real birth location and date came credibly from Ash Upson, ghostwriter of Pat Garrett's *The Authentic Life of Billy the Kid*. (Garrett, Page 1) Journalist Upson likely learned it when living as a boarder with Billy's family in Silver City. In addition, Lew Wallace, who got to know Billy for their pardon bargain in 1879, consistently wrote that Billy was born in New York in his subsequent articles about Billy the Kid.**

Slyly, "Brushy" did not claim Burns's "Kathleen Bonney" as his mother; minimizing risk of misstating history that could be checked. Instead, he made-up a half-sister of his mother, whom he called Katherine (or Kathleen) Ann Bonney; and claimed she raised him in Silver City. (Pages 14-16)

"Brushy's" real, too young parents obviously needed cover-up. So he created an older fictional family, woven with actual family names and fictional geography. There was a made-up Texas Army of the Revolution grandfather named Ben Roberts from Kentucky, a made-up abusive rancher father named James Henry, J.H. or

"Wild Henry" or "Two Gun" Roberts. This J.H. Roberts married a fictional Mary Adeline Dunn, derived from the name of "Brushy's" real father's real deceased first wife, Caroline Dunn. "Brushy" then made up that they settled in Buffalo Gap, Texas, where he was born on made-up December 31, 1859 as made-up William Henry Roberts. Then made-up J.H. Roberts departed as a confederate for the Civil War, and also joined William Quantrill.

Made-up was that when Mary Adeline Dunn died when "Brushy" was three, her half-sister, Katherine Ann Bonney, came from Indian Territory to take him to Trinidad, Colorado, then Santa Fe. As a "Brushy"-Morrison linking to Billy Bonney history, they had "Brushy" end up in Silver City in the mid-1860's, with his "Aunt Bonney" marrying a man named Antrim. (Pages 14-16)

**SOURCES AND FAKERY: For his unpublished *Brushy Bill Roberts: I Wasn't Billy the Kid*, historian Don Cline located one of "Brushy's" likely sources. The story and history of Ben Roberts was lifted from *Rangers and Sovereignty*, a popular book by Texas Ranger Capitan Dan W. Roberts, son of Ben. (Cline, Page 15) Cline also pointed out that being taken to Silver City in 1861 or 1862 by "Aunt Bonney" made no sense, since it was formed in 1871! (Cline 19)**

"Brushy" claimed he was called "Kid Roberts" in Silver City," until he left in 1872 to go back to Texas to see family. (Page 16)

**FAKERY: "Brushy" and team did not know the historical mother's name of "Catherine McCarty Antrim;" or that she died when Billy was 14½; or that Billy was not in Silver City until 1873, or that he departed in 1875 in a jailbreak.**

For his tale, "Brushy" has his returned father, J.H. Roberts, marry an Elizabeth Ferguson, as his step-mother. (He used his own history, since Sara Elizabeth Ferguson was his real mother's name.) Then he claimed Aunt Bonney, died also, apparently to match real Catherine Antrim's death.

As will be seen from a later book using his words, tape recorded by Morrison, "Brushy" also covered for the Oliver L. Roberts name (which he used for his Social Security benefits fraud). He said that an Ollie L. Roberts was his younger cousin, who had been killed. And when he took that Ollie's possessions back to Ollie's parents, they mistook *him* for their son. And he was taken in by them. Like the rest of his lies, "Brushy's" real relatives eventually exposed that whooper also.

## ROBERTS FAMILY EXPOSÉS

From 1987 to 2015, "Brushy's" long-suffering Roberts family exposed his hoax, and provided his actual genealogy.

### *GENEVA PITTMON*

Morrison did not live to see his fakery tumbled by 69 year old Geneva Pittmon, "Brushy's" niece. Her relative, Roy L. Haws, in his 2015 *Brushy Bill: Proof That His Claim to Be Billy the Kid Was a Hoax*, stated her grandparents, Henry Oliver Roberts and Sara Elizabeth Ferguson, were "Brushy's" parents; and she was the daughter of their son, Thomas Ulce Roberts, "Brushy's, full brother. (Haws, Page 52) She told Don Cline, for his 1988 book, *Brushy Bill Roberts: I Wasn't Billy the Kid*, that disabled "Brushy" lived with her, among other family members. (Cline, Page 95)

On December 16, 1987, Geneva Pittmon exposed "Brushy" to the founders of the Billy the Kid Outlaw Gang: Marlyn Estes Perez Bowlin and her husband, Joe Bowlin, who ran the Old Fort Sumner Museum at the cemetery where Billy Bonney is buried. She refuted his claim with the genealogy page of the family Bible; concluding *"My uncle was Not Billy the Kid ... He was born Aug 26, 1879."* She wrote:

Dec. 16, 1987

*Dear Sir: the reason you are not finding my family is you don't have the right name. My grandfather was H.O. Roberts - married to ~~Sara~~ Shara Elizabeth Ferguson on May 14, 1876. Oliver P. Roberts was Brushy Bill's name. I don't know what the P was for. He was born Aug. 26, 1879. I have the family Bible record.*

*My husband thinks I should not tell you anything unless I know just what are your interest in my family?*

*A William A. Tunstill P.O. Box 995 Roswell New Mex 88201 is also writing me asking questions which I have not written. He also has come up with a Ben Roberts and my great grandfather who was from [Kentucky?] and settled near Austin, 1835. I would also like for this to be settled as I know*

my uncle Oliver was
not <u>Billy</u> the <u>Kid</u>

*Mrs Geneva Pittmon*

## *MARY JUNE ROBERTS AND CORDELIA ROBERTS*

Don Cline, in his 1988 unpublished book, *Brushy Bill Roberts: I Wasn't Billy the Kid*, quoted Mary June Roberts, "Brushy's" niece and another daughter of Tom Roberts, "Brushy's" younger brother "with whom "Brushy" lived most of his adult life." (Cline, Page 11) Interviewed by Cline on January 28, 1888, Mary June Roberts stated: "Grandpa [O.H.] Roberts never fought in any war. Grandma was his second wife and Oliver's mother. Oliver never had a stepmother." (Cline, Page 11) And contrary to *Alias Billy the Kid's* claim that "Brushy" was secretive about being Billy, Cline wrote: "His family has stated they heard all his stories many times." (Cline, Page 14)

Interviewed by Don Cline in 1988, "Brushy's sister, Cordelia Roberts, also denied his various identity claims. (Cline, Page 49)

## *ROY L. HAWS*

In 2015, "Brushy's" relative, Roy L. Haws, published *Brushy Bill: Proof That His Claim to be Billy the Kid Was a Hoax*. He exposed "Brushy's" genealogy as an "incredible farce." (Haws, Page 13) And later "Brushy" hoaxers would build on misstating the family's having two branches resulting from "Brushy's" father, Henry Oliver Roberts's two marriages, with "Brushy" from the second. Haws descended from the first marriage. (Pages 19-20)

Haws stated: "Brushy was, in fact, my maternal half great-granduncle and was just under two years of age the night Pat Garrett is said to have killed Billy the Kid." (Haws, Page 14) Haws calls the family "Brushy" gave to Morrison "all false and completely fabricated. He did not have a father named John or James Henry Roberts, did not have a mother named Mary Adeline Dunn, did not have a birth name of William Henry Roberts, did not have a grandfather named Ben, and certainly was not born in Buffalo Gap, Texas on December 31, 1859. Brushy's actual birth name was indeed the identity he used throughout life in census, marriage, divorce, death certificates, and all public documents. **His true name was Oliver Pleasant Roberts, son of Henry Oliver and Sara Elizabeth Ferguson Roberts, born August 26, 1879 in Bates, Arkansas.**" (Haws, Page 28)

Haws gave a real genealogy. (Haws, Pages 136-138) "Brushy's" paternal grandfather was Joseph Roberts (1797-1857). His dirt-farmer father was Henry Oliver Roberts (1852-1924); a child in the Civil War - no soldier as "Brushy" claimed!

Henry Oliver Roberts first married **Caroline Dunn**, who died. They had Samantha Belle (1871) and **Martha Vada** (1872). Next he married **Sara Elizabeth Ferguson** (1856-1924) in 1876 in Arkansas. Their children were Andrew Berry (1877), Mary C. (1878) **Oliver Pleasant "Brushy" (1879)**, John W. (1881), Lonnie V. (1884), Thomas Ulce (1885, father of Geneva Pittman), Nora (1892), and Joseph Irvin (1895).

Roy L. Haws descended from **Martha Vada Roberts**, the daughter from Henry Oliver's his first marriage. She married Dudley Heath, and had **Vada Bell Heath**. Vada's marriage to a D.L. Goff, yielded **Eulaine Faye Goff**. Eulaine married Leonard Haws, with **Roy L. Haws** the youngest of three sons. Vada Bell Heath next married Joseph Emerson, producing **Paul Emerson** (who knew "Brushy"). **Key was Roy Haws's mother, Eulaine Faye Goff Haws, who was tricked into vouching that her Caroline Dunn branch from Henry Oliver was a different family, having a man named Oliver L. "Brushy Bill" Roberts, who was not Oliver Pleasant Roberts!**

As mentioned, Haws stated that "Brushy" had first changed his birth to December 31, 1868, and middle initial to L. in 1936 for benefits fraud. (Haws, Page 24) Don Cline, in his 1988 *Brushy Bill Roberts: I Wasn't Billy the Kid*, said "Brushy" faked additional ages. "In 1941 he told the Hico editor [of the *Hico News Review*] he was born in 1867 ... In 1949 he was wire recorded [in Meramac Caverns, Missouri] as stating he was 85 but a year later in the meeting with the Governor of New Mexico he had somehow reached 91 ... He told his last wife he was born in 1868 and this was placed on his death certificate and headstone." (Cline, Page 69)

Haws showed "Brushy's" linking his faked Roberts family to his real one with a lie "of finding his dead cousin, Ollie, [actually himself] killed in a horse theft incident in about 1892 ... [W]hile returning Ollie's belongings to Ollie Roberts' family (Brushy's actual true family) in Sulphur Springs, Texas, he was accepted as a long lost son by Ollie's mother (Brushy's actual mother)." Haws scoffs that this tall tale meant a man in his thirties (his faked age) was accepted as a 13 year old! (Haws, Pages 24, 27)

Haws also recorded that "Brushy's" four wives were Anna Lee (married 1909, divorced 1910); Mollie Brown (married 1912, died 1919); Luticia Ballard (married 1929, died 1944); and Malinda E. Allison (married 1945, died 1952).

## PAUL EMERSON AND CORA HEATH

Roy L. Haws added insider perspective in *Brushy Bill: Proof That His Claim to be Billy the Kid Was a Hoax* with his chapter titled "What the Family Thought of Brushy." Cited is Geneva Pittmon's December 16, 1987 letter of denial. (Haws, Page 52) Quoted also is an e-mail Haws got from his half uncle, Paul Emerson, of Houston, Texas, who met "Brushy," dressed as a cowboy, when he was a teenager, and "Brushy" was visiting Martha Vada Roberts Heath - Paul's grandmother and "Brushy's" half-sister - in Jacksonville, Texas. Paul informed Haws that Martha told him "Brushy" was not Billy the Kid. (Haws, Page 53)

Also, Haws presented a denial of "Brushy" from family member Cora Heath (Martha Vada Roberts Heath's second eldest daughter). Cora Heath's denial had been presented in a letter that Paul Emerson wrote on August 2, 1986 to "Brushy"-backing author, William Tunstill. Emerson informed Tunstill that he had found a note written by her on a clipping about "Brushy's" death; stating: "O.L. Roberts was my mother's brother. He was around 75 years of age when he died and he was not Billy the Kid." (Haws, Page 54)

## FAKING EARLY ADOLESCENCE

### THE 12 YEAR OLD MURDERER DILEMMA

Not till 1993, would Billy Bonney's early adolescence be known from Jerry Weddle's *Antrim Was My Stepfather's Name*, filling in Billy's dramatic and traumatic Silver City and Arizona years. So necessity mothered invention by "Brushy's" confabulations.

Knowing his day's claim that Billy Bonney left Silver City at 12, "after committing his first murder" (Page 16), "Brushy," who liked to minimize Billy as a killer, used it for the departure age.

**PROMPT SOURCES FOR ERROR:** The age of 12 came from sources cited in *Alias Billy the Kid's* footnotes. Pat Garrett's 1927 edition of his quasi-fiction *The Authentic Life of Billy the Kid*, and Walter Noble Burns's 1926 *The Saga of Billy the Kid*, which copied from Garrett's 1882 edition. Garrett's book stated: "When young Billy was about twelve years of age, he first imbrued his hand in human blood ... As Billy's mother was passing a knot of idlers on the street, one of the loafers made an insulting remark about her. Billy heard it, and quick as thought, with blazing eyes, he planted a stinging blow on the blackguard's mouth [and subsequently fatally stabbed him]." (Garrett, Page 5) Burns stated: "It was at Silver City, when twelve years old, that Billy killed his first man." (Burns, Page 72)

In fact, real Billy exited Silver City at age 15½ in a jailbreak, to escape trial for burglary and robbery at a Chinese laundry, in which, with an adult accomplice, he stole clothes and revolvers. He crossed the border to go to Bonita, Arizona Territory. There was no murder.

### FAKING EARLY ADOLESCENT YEARS

There were no sources for Billy Bonney's early adolescence. So "Brushy" confabulated wildly about being in Texas from 1872 with his father, "Wild Bill" Roberts; herding cattle to Oklahoma Indian Territory in 1874; and working for outlaw, Belle Starr, who introduced him as "Texas Kid" to the James and Younger gangs. (Pages 17-18)

FAKERY: Don Cline, in his *Brushy Bill Roberts: I Wasn't Billy the Kid*, stated that Myra Belle Shirley Reed took the name Bell Starr in 1880; and was not in Oklahoma in 1874. (Cline, Page 32)

"Brushy" then returns to Silver City, where his aunt Kathleen Bonney dies; returns to Indian Territory and becomes a cattle rustler; goes to Dodge City, Kansas; and then goes to Black Hills of South Dakota, to Arizona, to Montana, to Oregon, to Wyoming, and to Nebraska as a "bronco buster." (Page 20)

Then "Brushy" claims, in April of 1877 he returned to Arizona and worked at "the Gila ranch." (Page 21)

PROMPT SOURCE'S ERROR: Walter Noble Burns's *The Saga of Billy the Kid* had made-up that Billy became an "expert cowboy" in Arizona. And *The Authentic Life of Billy the Kid* also stated that Billy was there. (Garrett, Page 8)

"Arizona" also inspired old-timer malarkey as shown by a footnote giving "Brushy's" source as a 1929 *The Texas Monthly* magazine article by a Ramon F. Adams, titled "Billy the Kid's Lost Years: Cyclone Denton Tells of Bonney's Life as a Cowboy in Arizona." Adams interviewed "Cyclone" Denton, who made-up that he "knowed Billy," when they worked together at the "Gila Ranch" in Arizona.

"Brushy" then goes to Mesilla, New Mexico Territory, and encounters Lincoln County War badman, Jesse [sic- Jessie] Evans, whom he says he knew in 1870 or 1871 in Silver City, and went with him to Old Mexico when he left in 1872, where he broke a Mel Segura from jail. (Page 21)

PROMPT SOURCE'S ERROR: Neither real Jessie nor real Billy were in Silver City then, and Billy only rode with outlaw Jessie Evans and his boys in September of 1877.

The Jesse misspelling was from *The Authentic Life of Billy the Kid*, which yielded "Brushy's" fabrication: "During the latter portion of Billy's residence in Silver City, he was the constant companion of Jesse Evans, a mere boy but as dangerous as many an older ... desperado ... This youthful pair made themselves well known in western Texas, northern and eastern Mexico, and along the Rio Grande in New Mexico, by many deeds of daring crime." (Garrett, Pages 5, 20) That book also provided "Brushy" with the Old Mexico and the "Melquiadez Segura" fables. (Garrett, Pages 15, 34)

For his 1877 fakery, "Brushy," still in fictional company of Jessie Evans, goes to Mesilla, and meets up with "Jimmy McDaniel, Billy Morton, and Frank Baker." (Page 21)

PROMPT SOURCE'S ERROR: The name-dropping is from *The Authentic Life of Billy the Kid* as "James McDaniels, William Morton, and Frank Baker." (Garrett, Page 30)

"Brushy" also name-dropped Tom O'Keffe, to put himself into real Billy's return to New Mexico Territory. (Page 21)

THE MISSED REAL HISTORY: "Brushy" missed real Billy's crisis-filled early adolescence. Moving to Silver City in 1873 with his mother and stepfather, William Henry Harrison Antrim, he was made homeless by Antrim at her tuberculosis death in 1874. In 1875, at 15½ he escaped to Arizona Territory from Silver City's jail, where he was held for stealing revolvers and clothes from a Chinese laundry, and escaped to avoid 10 years in prison with hard labor. In Arizona from September of 1875 to August of 1877, as Henry Antrim, he was refused employment at Hooker Ranch, but got a job as a cook in the Hotel de Luna in Bonita. From there, he also stole Fort Grant's horses and tack, with an adult accomplice, John Mackie. In March of

1877 he was held, with Mackie, at Fort Grant for the thievery, but escaped, though remaining in Bonita. On August 17, 1877, fighting with blacksmith, "Windy" Cahill, Billy fatally shot him in likely self-defense. But Cahill was unarmed, and the Coroner's Jury declared it unjustified homicide, meaning likely hanging. Billy escaped back to New Mexico Territory, assuming a self-created alias: William Henry "Billy" Bonney.

## *FAKING RETURN TO NEW MEXICO TERRITORY*

A crossing of the Guadalupe Mountains with Tom O'Keffe is given, with a "fight" with Apaches, and reaching the Pecos River settlements of real Billy Bonney's 1877 history. (Pages 21-22)

PROMPT SOURCES' ERRORS: Unaware of the escape to avoid hanging, "Brushy" used sources. *The Authentic Life of Billy the Kid* gave the name Tom O'Keffe. (Garrett, Page 37-47) A footnote had Eve Ball's article, "Billy Strikes the Pecos," from the 1949-50 *New Mexico Folklore Record* (likely from folklorist Sonnichsen). But "Brushy" was misled for his "fight" claim by Ball's writing that Apaches "struck." In fact, O'Keffe, alone, was ambushed by Apaches, who stole Billy's horse, leaving Billy on foot. "Brushy" also misunderstood "Mountains;" confabulating that his feet got cut up from "mountain brush." In fact, the Guadalupes, in this region, are just a flat, sloping, sparsely vegetated, rocky plain down to the Pecos River.

## *FAKING LINCOLN COUNTY HISTORY*

### **FAKING EARLY EMPLOYMENT**

At the Pecos River, lacking sources, "Brushy" has only historical name-dropping. He states: "Jim and John Jones were working for Chisum, so I went to work for them - I think up at Bosque Grande. Frank McNab [sic - MacNab] was foreman ... I worked for Maxwell for a short time at Bosque Redondo." (Page 22)

FAKERY: The Jones boys did work for Chisum prior to 1877, but, in late 1877, were making a Roswell store with their father, Heiskell. MacNab, no foreman, was a cattle detective with consortium Hunter and Evans, which had bought John Chisum's herd. Bosque Grande, not Bosque Redondo (which was Fort Sumner's Apache and Navajo concentration camp before Lucien Maxwell bought it as a town), was Chisum's original ranch, south of Fort Sumner; and was not connected to Billy until 1879 or 1880, when Billy sold rustled stock to its new owner, Dan Dedrick (to whom he gave the famous tintype). By then, John Chisum was living near Roswell at his South Spring River Ranch. And Billy never worked for the Jones family, Chisum, or the Maxwells.

Then "Brushy" said he worked with Jessie Evans at "Murphy's Seven Rivers camp that winter [of 1877] (Page 22).

**PROMPT SOURCE'S ERROR:** The source footnote is Charles Siringo's 1920 largely fiction book, *History of Billy the Kid*, which lifted from Pat Garrett's *The Authentic Life of Billy the Kid*. It stated: "McDaniels, Morton and Baker ... persuaded [Billy] to join the Murphy and Dolan outfit, and become one of their fighting cowboys. This he agreed to do and was put on the pay-roll at good wages." (Siringo, Page 32)

And real Billy never worked for Murphy and Dolan's "House" or the Pecos Cow Camp.

As to Jessie Evans, "Brushy" fabricated that they were "like brothers," and that he "tried to spring him from jail in Stockton one time after they killed Chapman." (Page 23)

**PROMPT SOURCE'S ERROR:** The misunderstood footnote source was the Adjutant General's files from the State Library in Austin, Texas. It described real Jessie Evans's letter, written when he was incarcerated at Fort Stockton, Texas, <u>in August of 1880</u> for murder of a Deputy Texas Ranger, and tried to contact "Billy Antrum" [sic] to free him. The letter was intercepted, never reaching Billy. And there was no jailbreak. And it was unrelated to Attorney Huston Chapman's murder in February of 1879. And the "they" killing Chapman, included Jessie Evans himself!

Real Billy rode with Jessie Evans and his boys only in September of 1877. Billy did not work at the Dolan (not Murphy) cow camp, which was south of Seven Rivers. By October of 1877, Billy was hired by John Tunstall.

Sources let "Brushy" name some Tunstall employees; though he added unrelated names from Billy's 1880 history: Dave Rudabaugh, Tom Pickett and Wilson (missing first name of Billy). (Page 24) "Brushy" added that he had stopped at Tunstall's to get something to eat, and got hired (Page 23)

PROMPT SOURCE FOOTNOTE: George Coe's 1934 autobiography, *Frontier Fighter*, is parroted: "[W]ith kindly feeling [Tunstall] was drawn to the boy and invited him to lunch." (Coe, Page 49)

### FAKING LINCOLN COUNTY TROUBLES

Ignorant of specifics that led to the Lincoln County War, "Brushy" and team are left faking, using only vague references to mercantile competition of John Tunstall with the Murphy enterprise, and that the Ring backed the Murphy side.

So "Brushy" and his authors can only spray names and misinformation, relying on sources' misrepresentation of the conflict as a local cattle war. *The Authentic Life of Billy the Kid* stated: "It is not the intention here to discuss the merits of the imbroglio or to censure or uphold either one faction or the other, but merely to detail such events of the war as ... [Billy the Kid] took part in. The principles in this difficulty were on one side John S. Chisum, called the Cattle King of New Mexico, with Alexander A. McSween and John H. Tunstall as important allies. On the other side were the firm of Murphy & Dolan, merchants in Lincoln, the county seat, backed by nearly every small cattle owner in the Pecos Valley. **This latter faction was supported by Thomas B. Catron, United States Attorney for the Territory, a resident of Santa Fe, one of the eminent lawyers of the Territory, and a considerable cattle owner in the Pecos region.**" (Garrett, Page 52)

PROMPT SOURCE: The already cited Maurice Garland Fulton editor's note about Catron and the Santa Fe Ring was in Pat Garrett's 1927 edition of *The Authentic Life of Billy the Kid*. (See pages 139-140 above)

"Brushy" erroneously calls McSween Tunstall's partner in his businesses. (Page 24) Then, keeping to that erroneous cattle conflict theme, "Brushy" confabulated recklessly that McSween had worked previously for Murphy to prosecute "Chisum's cowboys for cattle rustling," but quit when he learned Chisum was taking back cattle Murphy rustled from him! (Page 24)

**PROMPT SOURCE'S ERROR:** This mistake is lifted from *The Authentic Life of Billy the Kid.* (Garrett, Page 52)

In fact, the Ring's weapon, unknown to "Brushy's" team, was malicious prosecution of Tunstall's Lincoln friend, Attorney Alexander McSween (a past attorney for "The House" who quit in 1876 because of disgust at their corruption) for a fake embezzling case of the life insurance proceeds of deceased past "House" partner, Emil Fritz. The Ring <u>falsely</u> named McSween as Tunstall's partner, in order to harass Tunstall also in the malicious prosecution - to either force him to flee the Territory, or to justify killing him in self-defense if he fought back.

"Brushy" makes up that Tunstall's men were employed by Chisum to steal back Chisum's cattle from Murphy (Page 24) in a conflict in which "each accused the other of cattle stealing." (Page 25)

**PROMPT SOURCE'S ERROR:** This comes from Walter Noble Burns's *The Saga of Billy the Kid* wrongly stating that Chisum employed McSween to prosecute Murphy's cattle thieves. (Burns, Page 38)

"Brushy" adds that the Santa Fe Ring's head, Tom Catron, took over the Murphy-Dolan property during that "cattle war." (Page 25)

**PROMPT SOURCE:** This is cribbed from Maurice Garland Fulton's editorial note in Pat Garrett's *The Authentic Life of Billy the Kid.* It stated: "[Catron] furnished the money needed by Murphy and Dolan in their business, of course taking mortgages which at the close of the War gave him possession of their store and its stock of goods." (Garrett, Page 59)

"Brushy" states the Fritz insurance policy conflict was about McSween's law fee. And he says Murphy attached Tunstall's property because of the partnership with McSween. (Page 25)

**FAKERY AND PROMPT SOURCE'S ERROR:** In fact, real; Billy, who knew the injustice of the malicious prosecution, was so enraged by the Ring's fake partnership claim concocted to harass Tunstall, that on February 10, 1878, he almost shot at Sheriff William Brady's deputies doing the attachment at Tunstall's store.

Also, the embezzlement case was by Fritz's brother and sister, not Murphy; that error being lifted from Walter Noble Burns's *The Saga of Billy the Kid*. (Burns, Page 46)

THE MISSED REAL HISTORY: Most important, "Brushy" and his team were unaware that Tunstall was ranching on the Peñasco, as well as the Feliz, River. Missed was real Billy's proudest moment: being gifted with a Peñasco River ranch by Tunstall - as Billy described in his June 8, 1878 Frank Warner Angel deposition, unavailable to these hoaxers. Found by historian Frederick Nolan, it was cited in 1956 in his article, "Sidelight on the Tunstall Murder," a year after *Alias Billy the Kid* was published.

## FAKING JOHN TUNSTALL'S MURDER AND IMMEDIATE AFTERMATH

John Tunstall's murder is threadbare, since it lacked real Billy's eye-witness deposition about it! "Brushy" has a posse, but it is headed by "Billy Morton" (Page 25), not the correct Chief Deputy Jacob Basil "Billy" Matthews. And he thinks Tunstall was herding horses to Lincoln to "surrender them until the case was cleared up;" though they killed him "in cold blood." (Page 25),

PROMPT SOURCE'S ERROR: Billy Morton was lifted from *The Authentic Life of Billy the Kid*. (Garrett, Page 61).

And "Brushy" and team had no idea of the big picture. Tunstall's horses were not part of the attachment, so he was taking them from his Feliz Ranch. His action was merely used as an excuse for Ringite Brady's posse to complete their mission of assassinating him – as real Billy knew. And missing also was the terrorist intent of the murder: with Tunstall's horse shot dead also, with desecration of Tunstall's hat being put on the horse's head.

For the aftermath, "Brushy" has only the attempted arrest of the murderers (Page 26), and attending Tunstall's funeral. (Page 26)

FAKERY: Missed are all the key events for real Billy: the day after Tunstall's assassination, he gave an affidavit to Justice of the Peace John "Squire" Wilson identifying the murderers; and Sheriff Brady shielded the murderers and illegally jailed deputized Billy and Fred Waite, from

February 20 to 23, 1878, to block their serving the murderers' warrants. That was why Billy did not attend Tunstall's funeral. That was also when Brady confiscated Billy's Winchester '73 carbine, later retrieved by Billy from ambushed Brady's corpse.

Furthermore, missed is the political outrage at Ring murder of Tunstall that galvanized citizens for the Lincoln County War. AND, IT SHOULD BE NOTED THAT THE REGULATORS, OF WHICH BILLY WAS THE YOUNGEST MEMBER, WERE UNKNOWN TO BRUSHY AND HIS TEAM.

Unaware of the Regulators, "Brushy" thinks Billy simply sought revenge for "this dirty deed." (Page 26) Pursuit is of "Billy Morton, the leader of the mob, and [Frank] Baker." (Page 26) "Brushy" adds wrongly that they had been "good pals of mine," when he worked with them at Murphy's cow camp. (Page 26)

**FAKERY:** "Brushy" and team are unaware of the anti-Ring Regulator movement, and of McSween becoming its leader.

On the ride back to Lincoln, captives Morton and Baker are killed trying to escape; and "Brushy" says that the way back to Lincoln is "the north road over the mountains." (Page 26)

**FAKERY:** "Brushy" guesses that going to Lincoln required crossing over the Capitan Mountains, being ignorant of the military road around their eastern terminus that was actually used by Billy and the other Regulators. "Brushy" likely got that mistake from his Morrison tour, where the east to west range looks like a barrier to Lincoln.

## FAKING THE MURDER OF SHERIFF BRADY

"Brushy," confused about Sheriff William Brady's motivation, confabulated: "Sheriff Brady was gunning for me with warrants for cattle stealing." (Page 27)

**PROMPT SOURCE'S ERROR:** This was "Brushy's" take on equally wrong *The Authentic Life of Billy the Kid's*: "Sheriff Brady held warrants for the Kid and his associates charging them with the murders of Morton, Baker, and Roberts." (Garrett, Page 78) "There was apparently no motive for it except that Brady harassed the Kid and his followers." (Garrett, Note B, Page 82) (Note that Garrett's/Upson's misinformation has Roberts killed before Brady.)

For the Brady ambush, "Brushy" has him accompanied by Hindman (no first name) and Billy Matthews, whom he calls the County Clerk (Page 27); and states he was aiming for him, so should not have been accused of Brady's murder. (Page 28).

**PROMPT SOURCES' ERROR:** Billy Matthews was a Brady deputy, not a clerk, as Billy stated in his own deposition to Investigator Frank Warner Angel about Tunstall's murder.

The source footnote was a Pat Garrett statement that Billy would have tried to get Matthews; and was from a 1936 book by Miguel Otero, titled *The Real Billy the Kid*; as well as the same fiction being in *The Saga of Billy the Kid*. (Burns, Page 105)

Knowing Billy had taken a gun from Brady's corpse, "Brushy" calls it a "pearl-handled .44." (Page 27)

**PROMPT SOURCES' ERROR:** This gun retrieval comes from *The Saga of Billy the Kid*, where Walter Noble Burns makes up that Billy just wanted to steal a new six-shooter. (Burns, Page 106) And Burns was copying *The Authentic Life of Billy the Kid*, which stated that Billy and his fellows went to the bodies to steal guns. (Garrett, Page 80) In reality, Billy retrieved his confiscated Winchester '73 carbine, likely a gift from Tunstall.

Knowing from sources that an adobe wall was involved in the ambush, "Brushy" guesses that Billy Matthews was shooting from behind one when hitting himself, as Billy, and Fred Wayte (sic - Waite) when they ran out to retrieve the gun. (Pages 27-28)

**FAKING AND SOURCE'S ERROR:** In fact, Matthews, having escaped the ambush gunfire, was shooting from inside the Cisneros house; and Billy had run out from behind the adobe wall of Tunstall's corral, accompanied by Jim "Frenchie" French. The Waite error, along with its misspelling, was lifted from *The Saga of Billy the Kid*. (Burns, Page 106)

Lack of sources, however, resulted in "Brushy's" missing the high drama that Frenchie was shot through the thigh, got the bullet removed by town doctor Taylor Ealy desperately using a poker, and real Billy's hiding Frenchie under floorboards in Tunstall's store until the Regulators could sneak him out of town.

THE MISSED REAL HISTORY: Missed by "Brushy" and his accomplice authors, was the big picture of the ongoing fight against the Santa Fe Ring, in which the Regulators, including Billy, ambushed Brady to save Alexander McSween from murder by him and his deputies when McSween returned that day to Lincoln for his upcoming Grand Jury trial for his fake embezzlement charge.

### FAKING THE "BUCKSHOT" ROBERTS KILLING

Unaware of the Regulator movement, "Brushy" sticks to a "cattle war" for the killing of "Buckshot" Roberts in Blazer's Mill. He fabricates a back-story of "Buckshot" getting into an argument with himself, as Billy, and Charlie Bowdre at a his house in San Patricio, followed by Matthews shooting at them. (Page 28)

FAKERY AND PROMPT SOURCE'S ERROR: In reality, Billy had no house in San Patricio, though he spent time there. "Brushy" likely got the idea from *The Authentic Life of Billy the Kid's* calling it "a favorite resort for the Kid." (Garrett, Page 85) It was also the address on Billy's March 20, 1879 pardon bargain letter to Lew Wallace.

More subtly, if "Brushy" had a house there, he would have known about its horrific event that inspired real Billy's "Regulator Manifesto" and the Lincoln County War Battle itself: the July 3, 1878 terrorist massacre of San Patricio's men, women, and children by Ringite Sheriff George Peppin, using outlaw John Kinney's murderous rustler gang as his "posse"

So "Brushy" claims revenge after the nasty argument at his San Patricio house as the reason for his shooting at "Buckshot" Roberts at Blazer's Mill.

PROMPT SOURCE'S ERROR: This was cribbed from equally unaware *The Authentic Life of Billy the Kid*; which stated: "[Billy's] hunger for vengeance was by no means satiated" [and he shot at Roberts]. (Garrett, Pages 74-75)

In fact, real Billy did not fire at all. "Buckshot" was killed by Charlie Bowdre's single shot to his belly. Missed is "Buckshot's" actual carnage, in which he first shot at Bowdre, maimed George Coe by that ricocheting bullet, shot John Middleton in the chest, and ended with killing Dick Brewer.

## FAKING THE LINCOLN COUNTY WAR BATTLE

The Lincoln County War Battle gets a big Sonnichsen-Morrison plug: "**The three-day battle in Lincoln, July 17, 18, and 19, 1878, was the end of the struggle for the McSween faction. It was a bloody business, and Brushy Bill Roberts described it as if every detail had been burned into his memory with a branding iron.**" (Page 29)

PROMPT SOURCE'S ERROR: The War went from the 14th – to 19th, so it was six days long. The error source was *The Saga of Billy the Kid*'s chapter heading for it: "The Three Day Battle." (Burns, Page 114) And, unknown to "Brushy" and his team, was that its immediate precipitant was Ringite Sheriff Peppin's San Patricio massacre of July 3rd, to punish Hispanic residents for backing the Regulators.

Unaware that the War was a freedom fight, "Brushy" sticks to his "cattle war" scenario. He recites that the Murphy store stole cattle from Chisum, and "we'd get them back from him." He states that Chisum had promised to pay the men "$500 apiece to fight for them." (Page 29)

PROMPT SOURCES' ERRORS: An aped source was *The Authentic Life of Billy the Kid*: "[Billy and his companions] said that Chisum owed them $600 each, for services rendered during the War." (Garrett, Page 118) A version of the fable appears in *The Saga of Billy the Kid*. (Burns, Page 177)

The footnote source for this fakery is a 1943 *Frontier Times* magazine's "A Story of Billy the Kid;" reprinted in an August 10, 1881 *Laredo Times* article titled "Killing of 'Billy the Kid.' " It stated: "[After killing some Chisum cowboys after the War, Billy said to one,] "I want you to live and take a message to old John Chisum for me. Tell him during the Lincoln County War he proposed to pay me $5 a day for fighting for him. I fought for him, and never got a cent. Now I intend to kill his men wherever I meet them, giving him credit for $5 every time I drop one."

And that tall tale article was, in turn, cribbed from Lew Wallace's June 18, 1881 Billy the Kid outlaw myth article in the Crawfordsville *Saturday Evening Journal* as "Billy the Kid, General Wallace Tells Why the Young Desperado of

New Mexico Wanted to Kill Him. A Dashing and Daring Career in the Land of the Petulant Pistol." It stated: "[Billy] worked for John Chisum, the cattle dealer, in the late Lincoln county trouble, and claiming he has never received the promised $5 per day for his services, he is hunting down and killing Chisum's herdsmen, and giving their employer credit for $5 for each man killed."

Then "Brushy" gives a threadbare version of the Lincoln County War Battle, with only basics and glaring errors. Repeated is his racist error of black shooting soldiers: "[S]ome of his <u>nigger soldiers</u> were up on the side of that hill firing on us with the Murphy men." (Page 30) Fabricated by "Brushy" was: "Some of the Murphy men were just across the river, which run past the north of the house." (Page 31) "Brushy" added his confabulation that when they escaped from the burning house's kitchen, "Bob Beckwith and some of them niggers started to come in;" and he claimed he, as Billy, shot Beckwith. (Page 31)

**PROMPT SOURCES' ERRORS:** In fact, there were never Murphy-side assailants at the Bonita River and behind McSween's house. That was lifted from *The Saga of Billy the Kid.* (Burns, Pages 124-125) From Burns, Brushy also lifted the house lay-out (Burns, Page 128), and "Brushy" copied that the escape was through the kitchen. (Page 31; Burns, Page 136) "Brushy's" lifted falsehood that Billy shot Beckwith came from *The Authentic Life of Billy the Kid.* (Garrett, Page 101) In fact, posseman Beckwith was killed by friendly fire after Alexander McSween's men escaped, when Beckwith was serving a warrant on trapped McSween, who was just then gunned down by Peppin's possemen. And black cavalrymen were not in the fighting.

**THE MISSED REAL HISTORY:** Missed from Commander Dudley's July 19, 1878 march into Lincoln is his intentionally terrifying Gatling gun and howitzer cannon - that caused flight of all the McSween men, except those trapped in his besieged house (including Billy)! Missing is that trapped in the house were Susan McSween, her sister, and her sister's five young children. Missed was the exploding keg of gunpowder that demolished the front of the house. Missing from the escape from the burning house are Dudley's three white soldiers firing at those escaping, including Billy, who saw them fire a volley at them.

Listed by "Brushy" were men escaping the burning building as: "[Chavez] and I ran toward Tunstall's store, was fired at, and then turned toward the river." (Page 31)

**PROMPT SOURCE:** Lifted from real Billy's May 28, 1879 Dudley Court of Inquiry testimony, was Billy's answer to the escape route: "*Ran towards the Tunstall store, was fired at, and there turned towards the river.*"

But missed was Billy's testimony's punch-line that should have gotten Dudley court martialed for Posse Comitatus Act violation, if the court was not corrupt: that he saw three white soldiers embedded with Sheriff Peppin's possemen treasonously firing a volley at himself and the other McSween civilians as they escaped!

Racist "Brushy" concluded: "If we could have kept them niggers out there at Stanton, we would have whipped Peppin's posse." (Page 30)

**THE MISSED REAL HISTORY:** Real non-racist Billy, a self-appointed prosecution witness in the Court of Inquiry against Dudley, would have correctly blamed Dudley. And Billy would likely have known that, like himself, Dudley's black 9th Cavalrymen, Private James Bush and Sergeant Huston Lusk, on May 30-31, 1879, (the day after his own testimony ended) had risked their lives to testify *against* Dudley as ordering them to protect Sheriff George Peppin, and, thus, enable the arson of McSween's house.

### *FAKING THE HUSTON CHAPMAN MURDER*

"Brushy's" problem with the murder of Susan McSween's attorney, Huston Chapman, was both lack of sources and erroneous coaching by Morrison.

One can see Morrison's ignorance about the murder in the El Paso Rotary Club talk he gave on December 3, 1953. Thinking Billy the Kid was a leader in the War, he stated: "The Kid and James J. Dolan, **surviving leaders of the two factions**, had gathered in Lincoln to arbitrate. At the close of a favorable agreement, attorney Chapman, representing the widow of McSween, was killed by Dolan's men."

"Brushy stated: "When we came out of the saloon that night in Lincoln we run into Chapman, the lawyer for Mrs. McSween. Campbell and Dolan killed him in cold blood. I was standing there with them and saw who killed him. (Page 33)

PROMPT SOURCE'S ERROR: "Brushy's" omission of Jessie Evans was from *The Authentic Life of Billy the Kid*'s error that Jessie Evans was merely a witness (Garrett, Page 113); when, in fact, real Billy testified against Jessie and got him indicted as accessory to Chapman's murder.

## *FAKING THE WALLACE PARDON BARGAIN*

"Brushy" garbles the Lew Wallace pardon bargain; stating: "I was standing there with them and saw who killed [Chapmen] ... I heard that Governor Wallace had offered a thousand dollars for me if I would come and testify. I wrote him back that I would come in if he would annul those indictments against me." (Page 33)

PROMPT SOURCE: Used is real Billy's letter of March 13, 1879 to Wallace from the Indiana Historical Society; stating: "<u>I have heard that You will give one thousand $ dollars for my body which as I can understand it means alive as a witness</u>. I know it is as a witness against those that murdered Mr. Chapman. if it was so as that I could appear at Court, I could give the desired information ... <u>I was present when Mr. Chapman was murderded and know who did it</u> ... if it is in your power to Annully those indictments I hope you will do so so as to give me a chance to explain." In fact, Wallace had merely offered the thousand dollar award for Billy's capture as a local outlaw. It was Billy who proposed the testifying against Chapman's murderers as a pardon bargain to get his Lincoln County War indictments annulled.

PROMPT SOURCES' ERROR: "Brushy" and team wrongly thought that Wallace initiated the pardon bargain. That error was in *The Saga of Billy the Kid*. (Burns, Page 152)

That error also came from a Billy the Kid outlaw myth article by Lew Wallace, used as a footnote elsewhere in the book, and available to Morrison at the Indiana Historical Society. It was Wallace's June 8, 1902 *New York World Magazine* article titled: "General Lew Wallace Writes a Romance of 'Billy the Kid' Most Famous Bandit of the Plains: Thrilling Story of the Midnight Meeting Between Gen Wallace, Then Governor of New Mexico, and the Notorious Outlaw, in a Lonesome Hut in Santa Fe." Wallace lied: "When I reached New Mexico [to become Governor] it was declared on every hand that "Billy the Kid" had been a witness to the murder. Could he be made to testify? "That was a question on the tip of every tongue. "I had been sent to the Southwest to pacify the territory; here was an opportunity I could not afford to pass by. Therefore I arranged the meeting by note deposited with one of the outlaw's friends, and at midnight was ready to receive the desperado should he appear."

For Billy's first pardon meeting with Wallace, "Brushy" and team float the "things-never-printed" trick, with "Brushy's" confabulation: "We didn't meet like they say we did in the daytime at Patron's." (Page 34)

FAKERY AND PROMPT SOURCE'S ERROR: The meeting was on March 17, 1879, at night, at the Lincoln house of Justice of the Peace John Wilson. "Brushy" garbled Walter Noble Burns's fiction of that meeting in *The Saga of Billy the Kid*, in which Juan Patrón is present with Wallace, General Hatch, and army officers. (Burns, Page 152)

Also, "Brushy" did not know the bargain; confabulating: "He promised to pardon me if I would stand trial on my indictments in district court in Lincoln, testify before the grand jury in the Chapman case, and testify against Dudley." (Page 34)

PROMPT SOURCES' ERROR: The bargain was solely Billy testifying against Chapman's murderers in the April of 1879 Grand Jury in exchange for annulment of his indictments for Brady, Hindman, and Roberts.

This error came from Morrison's wrong prompting, as seen later in his December 3, 1953 El Paso Rotary Club talk: "The governor met the Kid in Lincoln and agreed to pardon the Kid if convicted on his indictments, provided, that: The Kid submit to arrest; plead to his indictments in Lincoln County ... District Court; testify before the Grand Jury; furnish statements in general; and to cooperate fully with the governor."

The standing trial error was in *The Saga of Billy the Kid*. (Burns, Page 156) The Dudley testifying error was elaborated from *The Authentic Life of Billy the Kid*: "The Kid was a witness before the court of inquiry which convened at Fort Stanton in April, 1879 [sic – May, 1879], to investigate Col. Dudley's activities with his soldiers during the three days' fight in Lincoln." (Garrett, Note A, Page 126)

"Brushy" further confabulated: "Also [Wallace] wanted me to testify against Colonel Dudley in his court-martial trial at Stanton." (Pages 33-34)

**FAKERY:** Billy testified against Dudley at his own initiative. And the Court was not a court martial, just an inquiry as to possible future court martial.

"Brushy" continued by name-dropping in utter ignorance. He cited the grand jury, but, thinking Billy was on trial, said that Ira Leonard was not there to represent him. (Page 34)

**PROMPT SOURCE'S ERROR:** Billy needed no lawyer. He was a prosecution witness against Chapman's murderers. The error came from the Morrison-Sonnichsen misreading of the cited footnote of the 1879 grand jury minutes, which had Billy's name, and guessing he was a defendant.

Adding even worse error, "Brushy" name-drops that the Court appointed Colonel Fountain to represent him. (Page 34)

**FAKERY:** This was 1879. Albert Jennings Fountain was only Billy's court appointed lawyer in April of 1881 in Mesilla after Billy's attorney, Ira Leonard withdrew after a likely Ringite death threat.

## *FAKING THE PURSUIT PERIOD*

### UNAWARE OF NEAR-KILLING BY JOE GRANT

A big event missed by "Brushy" and team is Billy Bonney's January 3, 1880 near killing by possible Texan bounty hunter, Joe Grant, in Fort Sumner's Hargrove's Saloon. Grant's gun misfired, and Billy killed him in self-defense. It was not legally pursued.

## UNAWARE OF A SECOND PARDON BARGAIN

Missing for lack of its still undiscovered source, is Billy's second chance at a pardon from the Secret Service in October of 1880. It is in the daily records of Secret Service Agent Azariah Wild, in the National Archives Treasury Department records. Wild had almost arranged a new pardon contingent on Billy's testifying against Territorial counterfeiters. That pardon was sabotaged by Billy's Ring adversaries. And Billy himself learned Wild's plan to capture him instead after robbing a mail-coach to get Wild's reports. Real Billy would remember all that!

## FAKING THE JIM CARLYLE KILLING

Lack of sources left blank 1880, until real Billy's December 12, 1880 letter to Wallace about Jim Carlyle's killing at the Greathouse Ranch ambush; with his accusing Carlyle's fellow possemen. So "Brushy" parrots that claim. (Page 36) Cited also is the prompt footnote: Maurice Garland Fulton's article in *The New Mexico Folklore Record's* 1949-1950 volume, titled "Billy the Kid in Life and Books," in which Fulton called the killing unsolved.

Since the location of the Greathouse Ranch was unknown until the 1980's, "Brushy" *completely forgets* where it was, blaming old age! (Page 35) And, lacking a source, he omits Billy's Coyote Spring ambush by the White Oaks posse immediately before the one at Greathouse's ranch.

## FAKING KNOWLEDGE OF PAT GARRETT

Unaware that the Secret Service had backed Pat Garrett for Sheriff, "Brushy" and team make up that Garrett was backed by John Chisum. To feign special knowledge about Garrett, "Brushy" claims that, as a buffalo hunter, Garrett killed his partner in an argument about dividing buffalo hides. (Page 36)

PROMPT SOURCE'S ERROR: Cited was a prompt footnote *Alamogordo News* article, dated March 8, 1936, by old-timer John Meadows, titled "My Association with Pat Garrett, Pioneer Peace Officer of N.M., As Told By John P. Meadows To A Representative of the Alamogordo News," which erroneously stated that, as a buffalo hunter, Garrett killed his partner, "Glenn" [sic].

First of all, real Billy would not have known. And Meadows was blowing windbag malarkey. Garrett did not kill his partner. His 1876 murder was of Joe Briscoe, a teenager with their hunting group. And it was not known until 1890, when Garrett's partner, Willis Skelton Glen, wrote in his unpublished manuscript titled: 'Pat Garrett As I Knew Him on the Buffalo Ranges," that Garrett killed Joe Briscoe in an apparent fit of depressive irritability, and then successfully claimed self-defense.

Noteworthy, however, is that "Brushy" denies a friendship with Garrett. That would present a problem for the "Billy the Kid Case" hoaxers, decades later, when they would fabricate that "friendship" as key to "Brushy's" July 14, 1881 "survival."

## *FAKING THE CAPTURE AND TRANSPORT*

### **FAKING THE PAT GARRETT CAPTURE**

Ignorant of Lincoln County War issues, the Ring's role, or the Secret Service-backed election of Pat Garret, "Brushy" and team have no idea why Garrett pursued Billy. "Brushy" wrongly guessed the Jim Carlyle murder (Page 36); when it was with warrants for the Lincoln County War murder indictments for Brady, Hindman, and Roberts.

For Garrett's December 19, 1880 ambush of Billy and his friends entering Fort Sumner with killing of Tom O'Folliard, "Brushy" claims that he, as Billy, was not present (Page 36), and fakes special knowledge that Kip McKinney was there, and was O'Folliard's cousin. (Page 37)

UNLISTED POSSIBLE PROMPT SOURCES: Name-dropped Kip McKinney was not present, being only a Deputy for Garrett in Fort Sumner for Billy Bonney's killing.

The erroneous hearsay that O'Folliard and McKinney were cousins came from the fact that both were from Uvalde, Texas; and a female cousin of McKinney's married a possible family member of O'Folliard. (This genealogy is discussed in detail below at pages 657-660.)

Also, a 1935 old-timer windbag book by a Frank M. King, titled *Wranglin' the Past: Reminiscences of Frank M. King*, made that cousin claim, stating: "T.C. McKinney's full name was Thomas Christopher McKinney, but was known to his intimates as 'Kip.' He was a cousin of Joe T. McKinney, the noted peace officer who faced the dangers of the Tonto Basin 'war" in Central Arizona ... <u>Kip was also a cousin of Tom O'Folliard</u>, who was one of the main supports of Billy the Kid until Pat Garrett killed him at Fort Sumner some time before the Kid was put out of business." (King, Page 173)

And a further prompt was likely misreading of Pat Garrett's vague connecting of O'Folliard and McKinney in his *The Authentic Life of Billy the Kid* in O'Folliard's death scene; stating: "[O'Folliard] also asked [Barney] Mason to tell McKinney to write to his grandmother in Texas and inform her of his death." (Garrett, Page 173) That did not mean they were cousins, but that they knew each other, and McKinney could get a message back to his family.

For the Stinking Springs capture, sources were used.

PROMPT SOURCES: Shot Charlie Bowdre erroneously dies beside the rock house's horses (Page 37), as in Walter Noble Burns's *The Saga of Billy the Kid*. (Burns, Page 211) For the shot horse in the doorway, used was *The Authentic Life of Billy the Kid*, with Garrett stating: "[J]ust as the horse was fairly in the door opening, I shot him dead, partially barricading the outlet." (Garrett, Page 179) Another was a footnote citing Lew Wallace's June 8, 1902 *New York World Magazine* article, "General Lew Wallace Writes a Romance of 'Billy the Kid' Most Famous Bandit of the Plains." In it, Billy says: **If it had not been for the dead horse in the doorway I wouldn't be here in Las Vegas. I would have ridden out on my bay mare and taken my chances of escaping. But I couldn't ride over that for she would have jumped back and I would have got it in the head."**

### FAKING A SCENE AT THE MAXWELLS

"Brushy" creates an elaborately confabulated post-capture scene. He name-drops Garrett's posseman, Jim East, as taking him, as Billy, into the Maxwell house at the request of Mrs. Maxwell's "Indian servant;" and calls East "a friend of mine from Tascosa, Texas." He adds that, at this time, he traded the Billy the Kid tintype in his pocket to that servant in exchange for her scarf (which he showed to Morrison). (Page 38)

PROMPT SOURCE ERROR: The prompt footnote, described as from Sonnichsen, is a May 20, 1926 letter by Garrett's posseman, Jim East, to a W.H. Burgess, stating that the Maxwells tried to get Billy unshackled from fellow prisoner, Dave Rudabaugh, to get him alone for a supposed farewell, but to help him to escape. But Jim East was not real Billy's friend, being only Garrett's posseman.

And the non-historical scarf trade was a lifted fictional tale from *The Saga of Billy the Kid*. (Burns, Page 195) And the known tintype was given by Billy in 1880 to counterfeiter, Dan Dedrick, who took it to California, and willed it to family. Its provenance was so iron-clad that collector Bill Koch paid $2.3 million for it in 2010.

Footnoted also is Walter Noble Burns's June 5, 1926 letter to W.H. Burgess about the Maxwell house incident, stating that Paulita was Billy's sweetheart. Sonnichsen is listed as providing it; but apparently misread it as: "Burns omitted the incident because it made Paulita out to be Billy's sweetheart, and Paulita (then living) objected." (Page 38) In fact, Burns confirmed that Billy and Paulita were lovers, but stated concern about his publisher; writing: "I also know that the Kid and Paulita were sweethearts - at least I heard that story on most good authority many times. But I was unable to write it frankly because my publishers were afraid any such statement might lay them open to a libel suit." But Sonnichsen's discarding of Paulita led to "Brushy's" confabulating Celsa Gutierrez as his sweetheart - and missing the accidental chance of real history.

## *FAKING THE SANTA FE JAIL STAY*

For the Santa Fe jail stay, "Brushy" just paraphrases Billy's jail letters (which are in a footnote), which Morrison got in his "research;" like: "I wrote to Governor Wallace to come and talk to me, but he failed to do so." (Page 39)

THE MISSED REAL HISTORY: Lacking a source, "Brushy" missed the near-tunneling out escape by Billy and his cellmates, and Billy's being placed in solitary confinement in a windowless cell until transport to Mesilla for his trials.

## *FAKING THE MESILLA HANGING TRIALS*

Billy's Mesilla hanging trial gets color from Billy's April 15, 1881 letter to Attorney Edgar Caypless, in Morrison's possession, which so impressed *Alias Billy the Kid's* publisher, and was "remembered" by "Brushy" as: "In April I pleaded to the federal indictment and it was thrown out of court." But that was all "Brushy" and team knew.

PROMPT SOURCE: Real Billy had written: *"My United States case was thrown out of court and I was rushed to trial on my Territorial charge."*

The ignorance was Morrison's, as shown in his December 3, 1953 El Paso Rotary Club talk: "The Kid's Federal Indictment had been dismissed, on plea to the jurisdiction of the court, on April 6, 1881." This doubletalk hid that he had no idea what happened. The date was actually March 30, 1881, the Attorney was Ira Leonard, the case was "Buckshot" Roberts's killing, and the indictment was quashed because U.S. Attorney T.B. Catron had called the federally-controlled Mescalero Indian Reservation its site. But the site was the Territorially-controlled private property of Joseph Blazer. So it was quashed as not a federal case, but a Territorial one.

"Brushy" also used the Caypless letter to claim court appointment of A.J. Fountain as Billy's lawyer, adding: "**He done all he could for me.**"(Page 39)

PROMPT SOURCE: Billy's letter stated: *"Mr. A.J. Fountain was appointed to defend me and has done the best he could for me."* Also, *The Authentic Life of Billy the Kid* presented the same issue of the "Buckshot" Roberts killing being on private land, not federal Reservation land; thus, quashing the erroneous indictment. (Garrett, Note C, Page 194)

THE MISSED REAL HISTORY: For lack of a source, the key event was missed: Billy's trauma that his attorney, Ira Leonard, then abruptly quit, under likely Ring death threat, after getting that indictment quashed.

And one can trace the error to Morrison. His March 17, 1954 letter to *Arizona Highway's* editor, Raymond Carlson, while boasting about himself as a great researcher using "modern methods of digging out true facts for posterity," he stated: "[U]ntil my research uncovered the actual records, every writer, including a New Mexico attorney-author [William Keleher], insisted that Ira E. Leonard represented the Kid at his trial in Mesilla.

Mr. Burns went so far as to quote the eloquent plea to the jury by Leonard, when Leonard was not even there." And Morrison gave copies of this to a Carl W. Breihan in St. Louis and to Paul Blazer.) This is an excellent example of "Brushy's" tales fueled by Morrison, and paralleling his ignorance - here about a momentous event for real Billy and his loyalist, Ira Leonard.

A story about Billy's famous bay racing mare is then mutilated by the team's ignorance. "Brushy" confabulates: They didn't sell my mare up at Scott Moore's in Las Vegas. He was a friend of mine, but now he said I owed him money to board." (Page 39)

PROMPT SOURCE: A footnote references the Caypless letter as the source, with Billy's quote: *"The mare is about all I can depend on at present so hope you will settle the case right away and give him [Fountain] the money you get for her. If you do not settle the matter with Scott Moore and have to go to court about it either give him [Fountain] the mare or sell her at auction and give him the money."*

The *"settle the matter with Scott Moore"* was the source of "Brushy" making up "board." In reality, Garrett's posseman, Frank Stewart, had stolen the mare from Billy at the Stinking Springs capture, and had illegally sold her to Scott Moore, the owner of luxurious Moore's Hotspring's Hotel in Las Vegas, New Mexico Territory. Billy wanted to sell her to pay for a new attorney after Ira Leonard's withdrawal from his case - as Billy described in the Caypless letter; writing: *"[Fountain] is willing to carry the case further if I can raise the money to bear his expense."* Unknown to "Brushy" and team is why Billy contacted Caypless: he was Billy's attorney for his replevin (rustling) case against Frank Stewart for that mare.

For the Brady killing, "Brushy" merely calls the trial "crooked;" but he and his team had no idea of the issues. So "Brushy" confabulated that he wanted "Hank Brown" as a defense witness, but Pat Garrett would not get him. (Page 39)

PROMPT SOURCES: A source footnote for "crooked" trial is Maurice Garland Fulton's article in *The New Mexico Folklore Record's* 1949-1950 volume titled "Billy the Kid in Life and Books." In it Fulton argues that the trial was unjust, and that, by comparison, James Dolan, murderer of

Attorney Huston Chapman had gotten his case dismissed by intervention of T.B. Catron and his law firm.

Another possible source footnote for "crooked" trial was a 1935 book by a Frank M. King, titled *Wranglin' the Past: Reminiscences of Frank M. King*, stating: "It is history what happened to the Kid in Judge Warren H. Bristol's court. Billy's witnesses had all either been killed or were afraid to appear in court to testify. The prosecution had a bunch of the Murphy gunmen to swear against him ... The Kid didn't have a chance and he knew it. He had often said he would never be given a fair trial in a New Mexico court where the Murphy-Dolan influence was strong. I myself, have often wondered how a jury could have found the Kid guilty of murdering Brady, when a battle was going on and others were firing at the time. The Kid claimed he didn't shoot Brady."

THE MISSED REAL HISTORY: In reality, Henry Newton Brown (not "Hank") was no potential defense witness; he was Billy's fellow Regulator, also indicted for the Brady killing; and had fled the Territory.

If real Billy had a wish-list for witnesses in his defense, he would have wanted John "Squire" Wilson, the Lincoln County War period Justice of the Peace who knew that Brady was a Ringite who had refused to arrest Tunstall's murderers and had necessitated the Regulator movement to get justice; himself deputizing Billy to serve arrest warrants. Billy would have also wanted Juan Patrón, the Hispanic community leader and jailor, in whose house he stayed for the sham arrest, who had formed a Citizen's Committee to protest Brady's shielding Tunstall's killers. And he would have wanted subpoenaed prosecution witness, Isaac Ellis, cross-examined as to the Lincoln County War skirmishes against McSween's men, in which Ellis provided his Lincoln house as refuge.

"Brushy" confabulated that the Brady trial lasted a week, when it was just two days, April 8-9, 1881.

PROMPT SOURCE: But the prompt footnote of the Doña Ana County Court Minutes let "Brushy" give the sentence day as April 13th, with hanging set for May 13th.

## *FAKING TRANSPORT TO THE LINCOLN JAIL*

A good example of "Brushy's almost verbatim parroting of a source to fake special knowledge is his description of being transported, as Billy, from the Mesilla jail to the Lincoln jail. (Page 79) Possibly because the cribbing was so extreme, a "corroborating" footnote was hidden.

"Brushy" stated: "John Kinney ... sat on the back seat beside me. Billy Matthews ... sat across and facing Kinney. Deputy U.S. Marshal Bob Olinger ... sat beside Matthews facing me ... Dave Woods and a couple of other guards rode horseback, one on each side, and the other rode behind the ambulance. They told me if anyone attacked they would kill me first then catch the other fellows. We left Mesilla a little before midnight so no one would know where we were ... It took about five days to make the trip to Fort Stanton, where Garrett picked me up and took me to the jail in Lincoln." (Page 40)

PROMPT SOURCES: Used was an April 20, 1881 *Newman's Semi-Weekly* article; stating:

On Saturday night about 10 o'clock Deputy U.S. marshal Robt. Ollinger [sic] with deputy sheriff David Wood and a posse of five men (Tom Williams, Billy Mathews [sic], John Kinney, D.M. Reade and W.A. Lockhart) started for Lincoln with Henry Antrim *alias* the Kid. The fact that they intended to leave at that time had been purposely concealed and the report circulated that they would not leave before the middle of the week in order to avoid any possibility of trouble, it having been rumored that the **Kid's band would attempt a rescue.** They stopped in front of our office while we talked to them, and we handed the Kid an addressed envelope with some paper and he said he would write some things he wanted to make public. He appeared quite cheerful and remarked that he wanted to stay until their whiskey gave out, anyway ... It was, he said, about a stand-off whether he was hanged or killed in the wagon ... **He was hand-cuffed to the back seat of the** ambulance. Kinney sat beside him, Olinger on the seat facing him, Mathews on the seat facing Kinney, Lockhart driving, and Reade, Wood and Williams riding along on horseback on each side and behind. The whole party was armed to the teeth and anyone who knows the men of whom it was composed will admit that a rescues would be a hazardous undertaking. **Kid was informed that if trouble should occur he would be shot first and the attacking party attended to afterwards.**

That scenario was also in *The Authentic Life of Billy the Kid*, and was used by "Brushy" for the destination. Garrett stated: "[Billy] was brought from Mesilla to Lincoln by Deputy Robert W. Ollinger [sic] and Deputy Sheriff David Woods of Dona Ana County, and turned over to me by them at Fort Stanton, nine miles west of Lincoln." (Garrett, Page 189; Note D, Page 196)

## FAKING THE GREAT ESCAPE

The next big historical event was real Billy's escape from the Lincoln County courthouse-jail. "Brushy's" rendition reveals the mechanics of Morrison's hoaxing: using known information, touring "Brushy" in Lincoln; and getting input from a confabulating old-timer Lincoln County resident, Severo Gallegos, whom Morrison had interviewed. Gallegos was later used for a fake Affidavit that "Brushy" was Billy. (See pages 186-187; 197-199) Added are staged histrionics of "Brushy's" crying, and being able to identify old-style shackles. (Page 49)

Morrison had taken "Brushy" to Lincoln and that courthouse-jail. Oddly, *Alias Billy the Kid* first stated that Morrison took him there on August 18, 1849, during their Carrizozo courthouse for records research. (See page 144 above) But when describing the jailbreak, the visit date is changed to "August, 1950" for both Lincoln and Carrizozo courthouses. (Page 40) That should be noted, because the issue of Morrison-Sonnichsen fix-up editings, will later be apparent. Here the issue is that in either 1949 or 1950 Morrison toured "Brushy" to prepare for his pardon hearing. And Morrison also described "later expeditions" of taking "Brushy" back to Lincoln, so the coaching was intense. (Page 45)

## FAKING THE COURTHOUSE-JAIL

For the courthouse-jail, "Brushy" says its second floor was changed - though it matched Billy's day - adding that in 1881 there were no outside stairs to the upstairs balcony. (Page 42)

PROMPT SOURCE: The lack of external stairs came from *The Authentic Life of Billy the Kid*: "[A]t the south-west corner of the building was a door leading to a small hall and broad staircase, which was the only means of access to the second story." (Garrett, Page 190) And "Brushy" saw the new stairs in his Lincoln tour.

"Brushy" states the armory was directly across from Garrett's north-end office along the north to south hall. (Page 42) It was actually at that hall's opposite south end. Opposite Garrett's office was a room with the Tularosa Ditch War prisoners, which led to the long Masonic Hall room of the past "House."

## FAKING KILLING OF THE DEPUTY GUARDS

Basic known information about the guards, Bob Olinger and James Bell, is given. For the escape, "Brushy" uses both of the possible scenarios. For gun-placed-in-outhouse one, "Brushy" wrongly identified an accomplice as **Sam Corbett**. (Page 43)

PROMPT SOURCE ERROR: To be recalled first, is that in the Mabry hearing, "Brushy" denied killing the guards!

The prompt footnote cited for the incorrect Sam Corbett name was a July, 1936 *Frontier Times* interview of a Leslie Traylor of Galveston, Texas, titled "Facts Regarding the Escape of Billy the Kid." As a Billy the Kid history buff, he visited Lincoln and Fort Sumner in 1933 and 1935, getting old-timers' hearsay for escape scenarios. He got the "Sam Corbett" name from a Francisco Salazar, "who came to live in Lincoln after Billy escaped" and married one of Saturnino Baca's daughters. Salazar said he was told by his brother-in-law, Bonificio Baca, "that Sam Corbett left the gun in the jail latrine for the Kid, that when the Kid and Bell went to the jail latrine during the mid-day, when Ollinger [sic] had the other prisoners across the street for their mid-day meal, the noted desperado secured the gun and concealed it on his person, and on returning to the guard room the Kid was naturally in the lead, and as he ascended the stairway he quickly turned around and shot Bell through the heart, who was near the top of the stairway."

In fact, Sam Corbett was just John Tunstall's past shopkeeper. The accepted accomplice was Gottfried Gauss, the building's caretaker, and Billy's anti-Ring friend.

"Brushy" then abandoned the hidden gun version, and claimed his shackle-slipping trick for using a cuff to hit Bell; then shooting Bell as he ran down the stairs. (Page 44) Olinger is then shot from the window in an equally known scenario.

### FAKING CUTTING LEG SHACKLE CHAIN

For releasing the leg shackles, "Brushy" said: "I told Goss [sic] to cut this chain between my legs. He tried to cut it with a saw. I told him to get the ax and cut it ... I held a .44 on him. He cut the chain as I stood over a rock." (Pages 44-45)

**FAKERY AND PROMPT SOURCE:** Besides the mistaken confabulation that Gauss was an enemy needing a pointed gun, or the chain breaking occurring outside, the scenario was lifted from *The Saga of Billy the Kid*, and retained Walter Noble Burns's erroneous spelling as "Old Man Goss." (Burns, Page 251) That fable also came from Morrison's October 11, 1949 interview with Lincoln old-timer Severo Gallegos, who was referenced in a prompt footnote as stating: "Goss, the jail cook, cut the chain on the leg irons." (Page 45) Gallegos, as will be seen below was a windbag who also used *The Saga of Billy the Kid*.

Knowing Billy went out on the balcony, "Brushy" creates him threatening the people: "I called out that if anyone was looking for a six-foot grave, that they should follow me." (Page 45)

**THE MISSED REAL HISTORY:** "Brushy's" fakery misses the dramatic and key part of Billy's escape. In reality, Billy asked Gottfried Gauss for a miner's pick, and took desperate hours using it himself, inside the courthouse, to break the chain. During that, Lincolnites assembled across the street from the courthouse, and Billy periodically went out on the balcony to address them, stating that he was standing pat against the world. Tellingly, no one stopped him. Though the Lincoln County War had been lost, this was one way the people could still save their hero.

## FAKING THE ESCAPE HORSE

"Brushy" constructs his erroneous escape horse tale around Morrison's October 11, 1949 interview of Lincoln old-timer Severo Gallegos. "Brushy" stated: "Goss [sic] caught the horse behind the jail in the pasture. He and the **Gallegos boy** saddled the horse and took him to the front of the jail ... I went back downstairs and out the front of the jail, where the horse was tied. I jumped for the saddle, but slid off the other side hanging to the rope. The **Gallegos kid went down the road and took a rope off a yoke of steers in the field and tied it to my saddle.** I got on the horse and rode out of Lincoln." (Page 45)

PROMPT SOURCE'S ERROR: The source footnote for the horse fable and the meaningless "rope" is Morrison's October 11, 1949 interview of then 84 year old Lincoln County windbag, Severo Gallegos. Gallegos's malarkey stated: "Billy called to me [through the upstairs window] to help catch that horse back there. Goss [sic] ... then caught the horse in the yard. He led the horse up and I helped saddle him. Then Goss took the horse around to the front and into the street, where he was tied. Billy ... got on the horse. The horse started to buck, and Billy fell off and held to the rope. He told me to go down the road and get the rope from Prisciano, who had a rope tied over the horns of the cow near Dad Peppin's place ... I tied it around the neck of the horse and threw it on the saddle horn." (Page 45)

Gallegos was garbling a fictionalized mention of himself in *The Saga of Billy the Kid*, in which he and another child, "Miguel Luna," were described as playing marbles on the street and witnessing Billy's escape; and a Manuel Blandano as giving Billy a rope to picket the escape pony. (Burns, Pages 262-263)

Severo Gallegos was a known Lincoln County eccentric, aggrandizing himself with tall tales of Billy the Kid. In his August 6, 1948 *Ruidoso News* interview with reporter Mary Nell Taeger, he also gave the horse scene, which Morrison may also have lifted as his prompt source for "Brushy." Gallegos described himself as having "**a prominent part in the escape of Billy the Kid and remembers every incident as if it were yesterday instead of sixty years ago ... [After Billy shot "George, the jailor" [Bob Olinger] Billy yelled to me saying**

'Severo, don't run ... come help Gus (the cook in the jail) get a horse and saddle from the corral ... I ... caught the horse ... a fine big one ... black with a white nose ... took him back to Billy ... walking to the horse we had saddled he mounted ... that horse started bucking ... hadn't been ridden while he was in jail ... then Billy called to me 'Severo, see that man in the field plowing with the steers ... and the rope around their horns ... go get it!' I ran to the field ... asked for the rope ... brought it back to the Kid he threw it around the neck of the horse ... the saddle horn ... and was off into Ventura Canyon."

Contrary to the "rope" tale lifted by "Brushy"-Morrison from Severo Gallegos, the actual event had a different object: a red blanket. And the actual horse was a white pony belonging to Court Clerk Billy Burt. Billy realized that his rattling leg chains might spook the pony, so he had Gauss wrap the blanket over the saddle. However, that proved slippery, and when the horse bucked, Billy slid off; then remounted and rode away.

### FAKING THE ESCAPE ROUTE

Billy's escape route was unknown, so "Brushy" had no script, except that the Capitan Mountains were crossed. "Brushy said: "[I] walked over the mountain. My guns began to get heavy and I hung one of them in the fork of a tree." (Page 46)

PROMPT SOURCE: *The Saga of Billy the Kid's* fable stated Billy was "weighed down" by guns stolen from the armory, and "traveling over the mountain roads was wearying," so he "lightened his load by hiding one of his six-shooters in the forks of a juniper tree." (Burns, Page 256)

Also, Billy was riding Billy Burt's pony, which he had promised would be returned, he was not crossing on foot.

Used then is known information that Billy went to his friend Yginio Salazar (Page 46); except it is spelled "Higinio," a mistake Yginio's bi-lingual, literate friend, real Billy, would not make. And "Brushy's" confabulated scene with Ygenio makes-up why Billy did not go to Old Mexico. Unaware of Billy's sweetheart, Paulita Maxwell, that made him choose Fort Sumner to be with her, "Brushy" fabricated that he wanted to stay to kill John Chisum, Barney Mason and Pat Garrett. (Page 46) But name-dropping Barney Mason was out of place, since he was later a possible spy helping Garrett determine that Billy was in Fort Sumner for the resulting ambush killing.

## *FAKING THE FORT SUMNER STAY*

When "Brushy" gets to Fort Sumner, sources cease; so he confabulated around known names; claiming to stay at the home of Charlie Bowdre's widow. (Pages 47, 48)

**FAKING: In fact, Manuela Bowdre had left Fort Sumner after Garrett killed Charlie on December 22, 1880.**

Keeping to his revenge fable, "Brushy" confabulated a scene of going to Chisum's South Spring River Ranch to kill him, though encountering only a "Mexican cowboy - still getting mileage out of his Chisum fabrications around Billy's letter and the Lew Wallace article - though that trip would have been 78 miles each way (and real Billy was actually hiding in sheep camps near Fort Sumner to be with Paulita). "Brushy" also fakes meeting Barney Mason at a sheep camp.

**PROMPT SOURCE: A footnote gives the source of fable: Bell Hudson's 1949 book *Billy the Kid*, edited by his daughter, Mary Hudson Brothers, which also has sheep camp hide outs. (Page 47)**

Confabulating with name-dropping, "Brushy" gets into trouble. He states that Pat Garrett and Barney Mason "were related by marriage" (Page 47), garbling that, as friends, they had celebrated a double marriage. He adds that Mason rustled stock with him, as Billy, but that was untrue. "Brushy" also states: "I knew Celsa and Pat's wife [name not given], **who were sisters to Saval Gutierrez**, before Pat came to this country. Celsa was one of my sweethearts when I was in Fort Sumner. **Her brother Saval,** lived in Fort Sumner ... [Saval] went up to Cañaditas and got Celsa for me. She wanted to go to Mexico with me." (Page 47)

**FAKERY: This fatal error concerns a married couple so well known to real Billy that he began his death walk from their house: Saval and Celsa Gutierrez. "Brushy's" "sisters-to-Saval" error nicely reveals hoax underpinnings. Knowing from *The Saga of Billy the Kid* that Saval Gutierrez *was* Garrett's *brother-in-law* (Burns, Page 279), "Brushy's" lying got into trouble because of the coincidence that both Celsa and Saval had the last name of Gutierrez, so he called them siblings. In fact, they were *married cousins*. And Saval was Garrett's brother-in-law *by***

*marriage* to two of Celsa's sisters: first Juanita, who died, then Apolinaria. "Brushy" even spins the tale of Celsa wanting to run off with him - with Saval facilitating!

"Brushy" also says he hid out at the Yerby Ranch, where, he claims, Yerby kept horses and mules for him when Charlie Bowdre worked there. (Page 48)

PROMPT SOURCE: The source was Billy's December 12, 1880 letter to Lew Wallace; stating *"During my absence Deputy Sheriff Garrett Acting under Chisum's orders went to the Portales and found Nothing. on his way back <u>he went by Mr Yerby's ranch and took a pair of mules of mine which I had left with Mr Bowdre who is in Charge of Mr Yerby's cattle</u>."* But that was not a hide-out. Thomas Yerby held some of Billy's rustled stock when Charlie Bowdre worked there; but Yerby was not Billy's friend.

## *FAKING A DEATH SCENE*

Then comes the make-or-break Fort Sumner death scene, for which there were three well known elements: bright moonlight; Billy walking to the Maxwell house to cut himself a steak from the hanging side of beef there; and his going into Peter Maxwell's bedroom where hiding Pat Garrett fatally shot him in ambush. The chapter title is "Death by Moonlight."

For his survival, "Brushy" has an "innocent victim" mistaken for himself (as Billy the Kid) by Pat Garrett. That victim was his claimed partner, Billy Barlow.

POSSIBLE SOURCE: Barlow is non-historical. But "Brushy's" family member, Roy L. Haws, in his 2015's *Brushy Bill: Proof That His Claim To Be Billy the Kid Was a Hoax*, found the "Billy Barlow" name in a 1930's song called "Cutty Wren." (Haws, Page 91) It was also in a popular Southwestern ballad called "Billy Barlow," derived from an old English version. (Haws, Page 90)

"Brushy's" killing scene occurs after a Jesus Silva (the dropped name of Peter Maxwell's foreman) was cooking a meal for him and Billy Barlow; and Barlow wanted "fresh beef." (The Mabry hearing's local steak restaurant has been purged!) Sensing a "trap," "Brushy" lets Barlow go alone to the Maxwell house, where his is **shot on the back porch**, not inside the bedroom! (Page 49)

SHOCKING PROMPT SOURCE: First of all, real Billy was alone in the house of Saval and Celsa Gutierrez, when he went to get meat, carrying their butcher knife.

But shockingly revealed accidentally is why "Brushy" had Barlow oddly shot on the back porch: "BRUSHY" CREATED HIS BARLOW SHOOTING SCENE FROM C.L. SONNICHSEN'S PROMPT, proving Sonnichsen invented the hoax's key lie. It went like this: Sonnichsen had used a hearsay source stating Barlow was shot *outside the bedroom*. But Sonnichsen wrongly thought Maxwell's bedroom was at the *back porch*. So to be *shot outside the bedroom*, meant being *shot at the back porch*. That is why he coached "Brushy" to put Barlow there.

The footnote gives Sonnichsen's source as his April 15, 1944 interview of Jack Fountain, the son of Albert Jennings Fountain. Jack told him that Pat Garrett had told him that Billy was at the "house of a woman across the street" and went to get the beef. And the beef was in a "little outer room" beside Peter Maxwell's bedroom. From that spot, Billy asked Peter, in his bedroom, who was there, and was told, "Nobody." Jack said, "Garrett, in the room, had a perfect target of Billy outside the room. So he shot him dead." (Page 49) Sonnichsen - proving his misunderstanding of the layout - added that there are many versions, but this is best, since it "places the victim outside Maxwell's bedroom."

Proved is Sonnichsen's incompetence as an historian. And proved is that he was doing shoddy, conspiracy theory-oriented research about Billy the Kid five years before partnering with Morrison! Jack's fake descriptions are give-aways. The actual side of beef hung on the cool north porch, on the *opposite side of the house* from Maxwell's south-eastern corner bedroom. Neither beef nor bedroom were at a "back porch." And there was no house "across the street." The Maxwell mansion faced a large parade ground with buildings around its perimeter. But, as usual, "Brushy" stuck to his prompts for confabulating.

Also, neither the hoaxing team, nor Jack Fountain, knew the Fort Sumner town's layout. And when "Brushy" and Morrison visited in 1949, there were no buildings left. So "Brushy" confabulated that when he heard shots he ran through a gate into Maxwell's back yard (to stick to the Jack/Sonnichsen back porch fable) and shot at "shadows along the house." He was then shot by unnamed assailants through the mouth, his left shoulder, and across his forehead. He stumbles "into the gallery of an adobe behind Maxwell's yard fence," where a Mexican woman pulls him inside. (Page 49)

Then Celsa enters to tell him they were passing-off Barlow's body as his, and "they would not leave Maxwells for the night ... [because] [t]hey were afraid of being mobbed." (Page 50)

**PROMPT SOURCE: Celsa's statements about Garrett and his deputies would have been unknown to her. They are lifted from John W. Poe's 1933 *The Death of Billy the Kid*": "We spent the remainder of the night on the Maxwell premises, keeping constantly on our guard, as we were expecting to be attacked by friends of the dead man." (Poe, Page 44)**

But the error that would tumble the "Brushy Bill" hoax's house of cards was carefully hidden here. Following the "**Death by Moonlight**" chapter title, "Brushy" is quoted for the shooting scene: "I ran through the gate into Maxwell's back yard **in the bright moonlight.**" (Page 49) The moonlight was correct, and came from a source footnote: Garrett's Deputy, John W. Poe's, 1933 *The Death of Billy the Kid*, which stated: **"[T]he moon was shining very brightly.**" (Poe, Page 28) That was also in *The Saga of Billy the Kid*: **"The Kid's figure stood out clearly in the moonlight.**" (Burns, Page 281) It would take 43 years to recognize how fatal to "Brushy's" hoax that night's moonlight had been.

## FAKING LIFE AFTER BILLY'S DEATH

For life after the shooting, "Brushy" provided other delusional personas. And "illiteracy" is abandoned, with the claim that information came from his "copious notes" (Page 50); and his "jobs" - like a Pinkerton detective - required literacy.

"Brushy" was recorded as going first to El Paso, Texas, then Mexico, where he claimed to live two years with Yaqui Indians. Dressed like an Indian, he moved to Grand Saline, Texas, and drove a salt wagon, before returning to Mexico in 1883, then returning to Texas as the Texas Kid to work at a cattle company. He claimed he was arrested in Kansas City as Billy the Kid, but freed by friends. He then broke horses, and went to the Black

Hills of South Dakota to guard stage lines. There he said he was called "Brushy Bill" for riding in brushy hills. He rode for Buffalo Bill on his North Platte, Nebraska, ranch. In 1888 he became a Pinkerton detective to pursue horse thieves; and worked four years for Judge Parker in Fort Smith, Arkansas. But Don Cline, in his unpublished *Brushy Bill Roberts: I Wasn't Billy the Kid*, stated that Parker was dead by that time. (Cline, Page 41) "Brushy" claimed that, in 1892, he became a Deputy U.S. Marshal countering train robberies and encountered the Dalton gang. In 1889 he won $10,000 in the cowboy roundup in Cheyenne riding a horse named Cyclone and being known as "the Hugo Kid." In 1890, he became a boxer in Cincinnati, Ohio, then a bronco rider in Old Mexico, before going to Fort, Worth, Texas. In 1893, as a bronco rider, he went to Argentina to break horses. In 1894 he caught ponies in the Shetland Islands. That year he also became a marshal again, serving three years, during which he also rode in Wild Bill's and Pawnee Bill's Wild West shows. From 1895 to 1897, he ranched in Old Mexico as "the Hugo Kid." In 1898, he was a Roosevelt Rough Rider, and went to Cuba as the "Texas Kid," becoming a scout and being in charge of the horses, but was accused of shooting officers and was discharged. In 1899, back in Old Mexico, President Diaz seized his ranch in a 12 day shoot-out. From 1902 to 1904, he made his own Wild West show, before returning to Old Mexico in 1907 to make a new ranch. In 1910 he joined the revolution and rode with Pancho Villa, before escaping to Brownsville, Texas. In 1912 he married in Texas, making ranches in Oklahoma and Arkansas. He returned to Texas to work in oil fields and as a plainclothesman to fight bank robbers. Widowed, he remarried in 1925. Widowed again in 1944, he remarried that year. He then met Morrison. (Pages 51- 58) Provided is a "Brushy" quote used for the hoped-for Mabry pardon: "I've been a good useful citizen and I think I deserve a break." (Page 58) It would resurface in 54 years in the mouth of a hoaxing attorney in the "Billy the Kid Case," and then claiming to speak for Billy the Kid, as not killed by Pat Garrett, and as having "led a long and law-abiding life."

**FAKERY: "Brushy's" absurd and peripatetic tales were ripe for debunking. Don Cline, in his 1988 book, *Brushy Bill Roberts: I Wasn't Billy the Kid*, noted that he was told by "Brushy's" family that when Frank James (Jesse's brother), died in 1915, "Brushy" claimed *he* was Frank James, though that man had been 36 years older than himself**

[foreshadowing his Billy the Kid persona and age change]. (Cline, Pages 34-35, 59 ) Furthermore, the family told Cline, that "Brushy" had lived his life near or with family in Texas, Arkansas, and Oklahoma; and was never out of the country for his claims of Mexico, Argentina, Cuba, or the Shetland Islands. (Cline, Pages 35, 51) His mental disability apparently required ongoing family custodial care. His niece, his brother Tom's daughter, wrote to Cline that in 1918 "Brushy" was living with his parents in Oklahoma and Arkansas, until they died. Then he lived with his brother, Tom, and his wife. And a niece, named Mary, stated "Oliver was so much trouble to Mother and Dad that Mother asked me if I would take him and keep him. So we did." And other relatives also cared for him. (Cline Page 61) Cline checked records, finding no verification of his Pinkerton Detective and Rough Rider claims. (Cline, Pages 51-54)

"Brushy's" post-July 14, 1881 life was also debunked by his relative, Roy L. Haws, in his 2015 *Brushy Bill: Proof that his Claim to be Billy the Kid Was a Hoax*. He documented date mismatches for the claimed identities.

## FAKE PHOTO SECTION

Since "Brushy" was not Billy, Morrison's photo section lacks reality; but it summarized the book's lies by repetition as labels.

The photo used for "Katherine Ann Bonney" was accepted in "Brushy's" day as Billy's mother, Catherine McCarty Antrim. It is referenced in a *Alias Billy the Kid's* source footnotes as from Maurice Garland Fulton's article in *The New Mexico Folklore Record's* 1949-1950 volume titled "Billy the Kid in Life and Books;" as "Mrs. Antrim, [Billy the Kid's] mother." But, unknown to Sonnichsen and Morrison, it was fake - though embarrassingly vouched for by "Brushy" as his Silver City aunt who raised him! According to Frederick Nolan's *The West of Billy the Kid:* "The original was owned by the George Griggs family, who exhibited it at their Billy the Kid Museum. It was called the Kid's mother sometime in the late 1930's, when Eugene Cunningham, author of the book, *Triggernometry*, identified it as such to photographic collector Noah H. Rose in order to obtain from Rose another photograph ... he eventually confessed that he had no idea who the woman was."

Another woman is labeled as "Brushy's" mother named Mary Adeline Dunn. "Brushy's" relative, Roy L. Haws identified her, in his *Brushy Bill: Proof that His Claim to Be Billy the Kid Was a Hoax*, as actually a picture of "Brushy's" real mother: Sara Elizabeth Ferguson Roberts. (Haws, Page 29)

A Seven Rivers boys tintype is labeled as having been identified by "Brushy" as being taken in Dodge City in fall of 1877, with the claim that Bill and Sam Jones identified him in it as Billy the Kid. That is a lie. An earlier *Alias Billy the Kid* footnote admits that in "Brushy's" July of 1950 visit to the Jones brothers (a Morrison trip seeking Affidavits claiming he was Billy, and refused by the Jones boys), it was *"Brushy" who told them* that one figure was himself as Billy the Kid, and was given a copy. (Page 22) And the person "Brushy" called himself, as Billy, was actually Marion F. Turner, as identified by historian Eve Ball; and cited in Frederick Nolan's 1998 *The West of Billy the Kid*.

An historical photo of Fred Waite is misspelled as Fred Wayte, and called the man who was shot with Billy at the Brady killing - when the shot companion was actually Jim "Frenchie" French.

An illustration of the Billy the Kid tintype has an insert of the scarf for which "Brushy" claimed he traded it.

Other photographs are a randomly meaningless hodgepodge: a revolver of "Brushy's," a non-historical revolver claimed taken from Billy "when he surrendered to Garrett," the towns of Lincoln and Fort Sumner, the Lincoln courthouse, the Maxwell mansion, and Fort Sumner's barracks.

Then come photographs of "Brushy Bill" himself; the first, of him on a horse, claims to be age 30. Then there is a five photo collage, supposedly of "Brushy," labeled bizarrely "A Study in Ears;" though the one on the upper left is Marion Turner (not "Brushy"), cut from the Seven Rivers boys' photo, but labeled as "Brushy" at 17. In the center is a boy labeled as "Brushy" at 14, noteworthy for no sign of buck teeth. The bottom left crayon drawing labeled as "Brushy" at 27, looks like the dark-haired boy, though with a handle-bar mustache. The top right is of gray-haired "Brushy," called 55 years old. The bottom right is of "Brushy" labeled as 85 (with the 20 year added fix-up). Its point is a "protruding left ear," based on the hoaxers' tintype error of seeing the left-to-right reversed tintype ear pushed forward by Billy's rakishly tilted hat brim.

And a 1989 professional analysis at the Lincoln County Heritage Trust denied photo-match of "Brushy Bill" and real Billy.

# FAKING EVIDENCE

Having failed to convince experts and historical families in the pardon hearing, having provided no real evidence in their book that "Brushy" was Billy the Kid, and having belied their own claim of his illiteracy blocking studying-up, Morrison and Sonnichsen resorted to rationalizations, hearsay, and conspiracy theories to argue for his being Billy Bonney in chapters: "The Tangled Web," "Black and White" and "Epilogue."

## "THE TANGLED WEB": FAKING PROOF

Morrison and Sonnichsen offer fake rationalizations, some revealing their own lying, and none valid as evidence; as follows:

**"Brushy's" knowledge proved he was Billy the Kid.** (Page 60) (In fact, "Brushy" had no special knowledge beyond cribbed sources; whose errors and omissions he replicated.)

**Brushy's" was secretive because he was impersonating cousin Ollie Roberts while being Billy the Kid.** (Pages 60-61) (In fact, he *was* Ollie Roberts, as was shown by Roy L. Haws in his 2015 *Brushy Bill: Proof that his Claim to be Billy the Kid Was a Hoax.*) (See pages 154, 157)

**Pawnee Bill knew "Brushy" was Billy the Kid, as proved in a June 22, 1938 El Paso *Herald* article.** (Page 62) That is a lie. That tiny, 30 line, article, titled "Frontiersmen Track Reports 'Kid' is Alive," was one in a flood of early 20th century Billy the Kid fables. It said merely that Major Gorden W. (Pawnee Bill) Lillie of Pawnee, Oklahoma, and other members of the National Frontiersmen's Association were "seeking to verify reports the Kid escaped to Mexico instead of falling under Pat Garrett's guns." It had nothing to do with Pawnee Bill knowing "Brushy" or his claim. Pawnee Bill was a Wild West showman, in brief partnership with "Buffalo Bill" Cody - both names lifted by "Brushy" for his post shooting personas' confabulations.

**"Brushy" claimed that a Tom Waggoner, Judge Parker, a man named Longwell, a Tex Moore, John Selman, Jesse [sic] Evans, Tom Pickett, people in general from Montana to Missouri knew he was Billy the Kid.** (Pages 62-63) "Brushy's" confabulations are not evidence, nor is there evidence that these people claimed that he was Billy the Kid.

## *"BE HE ALIVE, OR BE HE DEAD": FAKING SURVIVAL EVIDENCE*

For this chapter, Sonnichsen and Morrison tried to contradict the Mabry hearing's imposter label by claiming old-timers vouched for "Brushy" as Billy the Kid. But offered are just random rumors that the Kid was not killed by Garrett, and five meaningless Affidavits obtained by Morrison. It was all hearsay junk, discarded by legitimate historians. The other possibility is worse: the willful intent to trick readers by faking evidence.

### MEANINGLESS SURVIVAL RUMORS

Meaninglessly presented are a woman from Seven Rivers claiming Billy had dinner at her house three days after the Garrett shooting; another living in "Peñasco country" from 1887 to 1889 claiming Billy was known to be hiding there; a man from the Whipple, Arizona, Veterans' Hospital having heard that Garrett had killed a Mexican boy instead in a plot with Billy; and a Manuel Taylor telling someone that Garrett had killed a young cattle detective instead of Billy. (Pages 65-67)

Hearsay articles were cited to fake corroboration. (Pages 67-69) A June 23, 1926 El Paso *Herald* one was quoted to say that someone in Alamogordo heard that George Coe did not believe Billy was killed, and people in Lincoln did not believe it either. Dishonestly omitted is the title: "**Billy the Kid, Alive Is Ridiculed by Oldtimers**;" the actual gist being that the killing was historically verified, and Garrett and the Fort Sumner residents knew Billy and identified him when "the body lay in state for several hours." The parts quoted by Sonnichsen are at its end to illustrate ridiculed claims. Reused was the Pawnee Bill 1938 "Frontiersmen Track Reports 'Kid' Is Alive" El Paso *Herald* article (carelessly dated as 1937) to claim that people were searching for Billy as alive; and having nothing to do with "Brushy." And an article by a Wilbur Smith, in an April of 1933 *New Mexico Magazine*, claimed that Billy's friend, Ygenio Salazar, believed he had not been killed. (Page 69) That is true. But Ygenio, as an old-timer, thought a school teacher from Mexico, who had visited him, was Billy the Kid. But Ygenio was unreliable, sadly being a morphine addict from the pain of the two bullets left in his back from the Lincoln County War Battle.

And Sonnichsen accepted any preposterous claim. For example a C.C. McNatt of Alamogordo, "who was in the vicinity of

Lincoln when the Kid was supposed to have been killed ... recalls that settlers there at the time doubted the story of the Kid's demise." (Page 67) In fact, Lincoln was 150 miles from the Fort Sumner killing, and the claim is not even McNatt's; it was hearsay from equally fantasizing others.

### MEANINGLESS SURVIVAL AFFIDAVITS

An equally dishonest thrust was inducing five people, with no connection to real Billy Bonney, to sign meaningless Affidavits that "Brushy" was Billy the Kid. Three came from Morrison's taking "Brushy" on an April of 1950 trip to New Mexico and Texas; and two were from friends of "Brushy's." They are printed in full in *Alias Billy the Kid's* "Appendix."

### *AFFIDAVIT OF SEVERO GALLEGOS*

Called by Sonnichsen "one of the best prospects" (Page 70), Severo Gallegos was the only affiant from Lincoln County. He was the old-timer Morrison had previously interviewed in Ruidoso, New Mexico, on October 11, 1949 for his apocryphal tale of getting a rope for Billy's escape horse, which was later parroted by "Brushy." (Page 45) Gallegos, living in Lincoln at the time of Billy's escape, was 11 or 12 years younger than Billy (giving birth dates of 1867 or 1868) and had no direct contact with him.

It should be noted that Billy was barely in Lincoln himself for child Gallegos to see. Billy's employment with John Tunstall was only 4½ months before Tunstall's murder by the Ring. Then, Billy was mostly at Tunstall's Feliz River Ranch. After the murder, Billy was imprisoned by Sheriff William Brady in Lincoln's pit jail from February 20-22, 1878. Outlawed soon after with the other Regulators, Billy only came secretly to Lincoln on June 8, 1878 to give his deposition to Frank Warner Angel on Tunstall's murder. And he was in his sham arrest, with Grand Jury testifying, for his Governor Lew Wallace pardon bargain from March to June of 1879 - none of which were known to Gallegos.

Gallegos proved himself to be a self-aggrandizing windbag in an interview he gave to a Mary Nell Taeger for a two-part article in the *Ruidoso News* titled "Severo Gallegos Tells His Story of His Family's Friend 'Billy the Kid,' " on July 30 and August 6, 1948. It appears that Morrison found the article, then sought Gallegos for a prompt source interview on October 11, 1949. (Page 45) But the article, which Morrison did not cite, destroyed Gallegos's credibility.

In the July 30th part, Gallegos garbled *The Saga of Billy the Kid* to claim Billy told him and his family that, at age 13, he killed his step-father for abusing his mother, which resulted in his being jailed. Then Gallegos wildly fabricated, unaware of the Lincoln County War, capture by Pat Garrett, or Billy's Mesilla hanging trial. He had child Billy escape that step-father killing jailing to come to Ruidoso (which did not yet exist), make friends with Frank and George Coe, hide in caves, and befriend his own family. His family then saved Billy from a posse in San Patricio, and he hid Billy's horse. Then Gallegos said his father killed a man, was put in Lincoln's jail, and Billy promised to rescue him.

The August 6th part completes the lies. Gallegos has Billy dressed as a woman get into the jail, tie the jailor, and release his father and all the other prisoners from behind "iron bars" [though the courthouse-jail had no cells]. His Billy, in hiding again for unclear reasons, is captured in the Gallinas Mountains [in the northwest, where Billy never was], escapes by killing a Deputy Sheriff Johnnie Hurley [made up], then is surrounded in a fortress-like stone house in the mountains [garbling of Stinking Springs] where he surrendered and was put in jail in Lincoln. Then Gallegos inserted himself into Billy's escape, first as playing marbles with friends [from the reference to himself in *The Saga of Billy the Kid*] seeing Billy kill "jailor George" [sic-Robert Olinger], and seeing Billy breaking "every one [of the armory guns] over a big rock in the yard." [This is a garbling of Billy smashing Olinger's Whitney double barrel shotgun after shooting the man, then throwing the pieces out the second floor window at the corpse.]

**Then Gallegos gave his horse-rope tall tale, which Morrison fed to "Brushy" to parrot:** "Billy yelled to me saying, "Severo ... come help Gus(the cook in the jail) [sic - Gauss] get a horse and saddle from the corral ... I went to the corral ... caught the horse ... a fine big one, black with a white nose [in truth, Gauss brought County Clerk Billy Burt's pony]... took him back to Billy. Right then Billy came out with every gun in the jail ... the one he killed George with too ... he broke every one over a big rock in the yard. [He is confabulating around the fact that, after killing Olinger from the second story, Billy smashed his Whitney double shotgun and threw it down at his body]. [Mounting the horse it] started bucking ... then Billy called to me 'Severo, see that man in the field plowing with the steers ... and the rope around their horns ... go get it.' I ran to the field ... asked for the rope ... brought it back to the Kid ... he threw it around the neck of the horse ... the saddle horn ... [this maneuver makes no sense] and was off across the field into Ventura Canyon." Following this horse lie, Gallegos claimed that "Gus" [sic - Gauss] took him upstairs in the courthouse and found a dead jailor on the steps. [In fact, Deputy Bell got to the back door; from there, Gauss dragged him outside.]"

As to getting Gallegos to sign the Affidavit, Morrison applied pressure. (Pages 70-71) First meeting "Brushy," Gallegos refused, saying correctly that he was too young. So Morrison told the attention-craving old-timer that he would take him back if he could identify him as Billy. That time, Gallegos - who in reality had never been up close to Billy or spoken with him - identified him by "small brown spots" in his eyes, by "Brushy's" standing straight, and talking like Billy. His affidavit repeated his lies from his *Ruidoso News* interview articles (Pages 117-118), with added ones. He claimed Billy was an expert shootist - though he had no proof that "Brushy" was. He also made up that he brought Billy food in the Lincoln jail. In fact, Gallegos, if legitimate, would have been the obvious person to address "Brushy" in Spanish. He did not. And "Brushy" would have failed that test.

For his 1988 unpublished book, *Brushy Bill Roberts: I Wasn't Billy the Kid*, historian Don Cline stated that Morrison first used this Gallegos's Affidavit in the Governor Mabry hearing, but that Gallegos was discredited by his preposterous *Ruidoso News* interview. (Cline, Pages 145-146)

**But concealed was that Gallegos was certain of the Billy the Kid killing, stating in his *Ruidoso News* interview: "We always knew he was dead ... he would have come to see my brother Chavez ... they were always such amigos."**

## *AFFIDAVIT OF MARTILE ABLE*

Morrison, posing as "Brushy's" lawyer, took him to El Paso, Texas, to meet an 89 year old, bedfast Martile Able, who claimed that she and her husband, John Able, had been the Kid's friends [non-historical]. She gave no historic specifics, stating only that "Billy would come to our house [of indeterminate location] when he was on the dodge." (Pages 71, 119-120) Her affidavit stated that she and her husband were Texans, who lived on a ranch near Carlsbad, New Mexico [no date given, and where Billy never was], then returned to Texas. She also claimed they knew Billy in Pecos, Texas [where he never was], and he visited them [location unstated] up to 1902. She said photos of young "Brushy" looked like her "Billy" in 1880 in Pecos, Texas. Unsurprisingly, "Brushy" then told her tales of Pecos life! This tomfoolery resulted in her meaningless Affidavit.

## AFFIDAVIT OF JOSÉ B. MONTOYA

In Carrizozo, New Mexico, Morrison and "Brushy" met with 80 year old José B. Montoya, a non-historical figure, who had been previously interviewed by Morrison; and for his Affidavit claimed he had **seen Billy at a bullfight in Juarez, Mexico, in 1902.** He added that an unnamed man in El Paso had told him Billy had been seen there. (Page 72)

Like Severo Gallegos, Montoya made up that he knew Billy in Lincoln, that Billy stayed with his family in the Capitan Mountains, and had his own fake tale of throwing quarters in the air while Billy shot them. He added some commonly known Lincoln County history unrelated to Billy. Like the other affiants, he declared "Brushy" to be Billy without any cited examples of proof except that "he looks the same." (Page 122)

Don Cline, in his 1988 book, *Brushy Bill Roberts: I Wasn't Billy the Kid*, from Roberts family interviews, stated that **in 1902 "Brushy" was "living with his family in west Texas, which is verified by census reports."** (Cline, Page 153)

## AFFIDAVIT OF DEWITT TRAVIS

The last two meaningless affidavits were by people who merely knew "Brushy," and believed his tall tales. An oddity was DeWitt Travis, born in 1889, ten years younger than "Brushy," and was his oilman friend from Longview, Texas. Inexplicably, Travis swore that he knew "Brushy" all his life.

But historian Don Cline in his 1988 book, *Brushy Bill Roberts: I Wasn't Billy the Kid*, stated that Travis had not met "Brushy until 1930 or 1931 when "Brushy" moved to Gladewater, Texas. Cline also pointed to Travis's claim that his and "Brushy's" fathers fought together in the Civil War, though "Brushy's" father was not in the War, being nine years old when it began. (Cline, Page 165) And Travis claimed his mother was friends with "Brushy's," though "Brushy's" mother's name is not given. And he repeated "Brushy's" tales of multiple personas, and demonstration of shackle-slipping. (Pages 124-125) To make sense of Travis's misinformation, Cline theorized that Travis had signed a document already prepared by Morrison. (Cline, Page 165)

In his affidavit, Dewitt Travis also cited "Brushy's" multiple scars, quoting "Brushy's" tale about being shot by Garrett's posse on July 14, 1881, and while retrieving a gun from Sheriff Brady's corpse. **Travis also claimed that "Brushy" had big "eye teeth" like "tusks," that were removed by a dentist. (Pages 74, 124)**

Eye teeth are the upper canines. Real Billy had protruding incisors, the front teeth. This bit of accidental truth was enough to sink "Brushy!"

## *AFFIDAVIT OF ROBERT E. LEE*

The last affiant was a 76 year old Robert E. Lee from Baton Rouge, Louisiana. (Pages 126-129) Claiming no knowledge of Billy Bonney, he was acquainted with "Brushy's" group of Old West impersonators, and merely took "Brushy's" word that he was the Kid. Lee stated the last time he had seen "Brushy" was in "New York City in January, 1950 ... at the Jesse James Press Conference [when Morrison was passing off J. Frank Dalton as Jesse James]." Along with "Brushy," he may have also been a "witness" cited by the press, whom Morrison brought along to vouch for Dalton as Jesse James.

Lee's Affidavit summarized "Brushy's" tales and aliases. Giving no Billy the Kid history, Lee claimed that he himself had worked at Buffalo Bill's ranch and at his Wild West Show as his bodyguard; and that "Brushy" had worked there in 1893 as a rider in the show. Lee stated Buffalo Bill had fought Indians with "Brushy's" father, and had known "Brushy's" mother and the Roberts family in Texas. Lee provided his own tall tale that he met "Brushy" in 1889 near Fort Selden, New Mexico, where, as Billy the Kid with his "band of thieves," "Brushy" rescued him from kidnappers.

## *REFUSED AFFIDAVITS*

The only people with credible contact with Billy Bonney refused to give Morrison Affidavits. On July 2, 1950, Morrison took "Brushy" to meet Sam and Bill Jones, brothers of John and Jim Jones - who are erroneously claimed to have worked with Billy at Chisum's ranch. When shown a photograph of four Seven Rivers boys, "Brushy" identified Marion Turner as himself. The Jones brothers refused to sign affidavits, stating correctly that "Brushy" gave "no conclusive proof." (Page 72)

## FAKING ADDITIONAL SPECIAL KNOWLEDGE

Still trying the knowing-things-not-written trick, Sonnichsen added one from "Brushy's" Affidavit-seeking trip with Morrison. When passing Santa Fe's Palace of the Governors, "Brushy" was reported (apparently from Morrison's notes) to say that he had been taken there from the jail "so people could make fun of me."

(Page 73) Brushy" added: "[The governor "wouldn't come down to the jail here and talk to me ... [H]e forgot how I helped him and wouldn't come down here to talk to me. He thought I was helpless and they were going to hang me." (Page 73)

PROMPT SOURCES: "Brushy" was parroting the display, but missed that it occurred in the Santa Fe jail cell. The prompt was real Billy's letter of March 4, 1881 to Lew Wallace which stated: "*I am not treated right by [U.S. Marshal John] Sherman. <u>he lets Every Stranger that comes to See me through Curiosity in to See me, but will not let a Single one of my friends in</u>, not Even an Attorney.*" It also stated: "<u>I Expect you have forgotten what you promised me, this Month two Years ago. but I have not, and I think You had ought to have come and seen me as I requested you to ... I guess they mean to Send me up without giving me any Show. but they will have a nice time doing it. I am not entirely without friends</u>."

Another prompt was a brief February 10, 1881 *Santa Fe New Mexican* article about U.S. Attorney John Sherman taking curiosity-seekers to the jail to view Billy.

## "IN BLACK AND WHITE" FAKING SUSPICION OF GARRETT AND CORONER'S JURY REPORT

The obvious make-or-break for the "Brushy" hoax was proving that Pat Garrett had not killed Billy the Kid. But he said he did; and the Coroner's Jury Report proved it. So faked was Garrett's being a liar, and the Report's not existing.

Morrison had heralded their fabrication two years before *Alias Billy the Kid's* publication, on December 3, 1953, by defaming Garrett in his El Paso Rotary Club talk, introduced by Sonnichsen. He stated: "Garrett had made a trip into [San Miguel County] Sheriff Romero's jurisdiction in an attempt to capture the Kid. Garrett's posse purportedly killed an unidentified man there in July or August, 1881. But, did they call in Sheriff Romero and turn the matter over to him? There's no legal evidence that they did. In fact, there is no legal evidence in San Miguel Court to prove they killed anyone at that time."

## BILLY IRRELEVANTLY AS A GOOD GUY

First, in a clumsy attempt to show history was not as written (to segue into the Garrett attack), Billy the Kid is described as being a good guy; though this was irrelevant to his being killed on July 14, 1881, or his being "Brushy Bill." It appears to be Sonnichsen's pseudo-historical creation.

Cited are a December 8, 1948 *New Mexico Magazine* article and a March 22, 1932 Silver City *Independent* article from Robert Mullin's papers about interviews with Louis Abraham of Silver City who said Billy had not committed murder there, but had "robbed a Chinaman and was put in jail;" which Sonnichsen calls "petty theft." (Page 77)

**FAKERY: Omitted is that "Brushy" never mentioned this, and it was not petty theft. It was robbery and burglary, the penalty for which, if Billy had not escaped, was thirty-nine stripes to his bare back and 10 years hard labor - with no exceptions for juveniles in the Territorial Kearny Code.**

Next Billy is claimed not to have shot "Buckshot" Roberts, or a Mescalero Indian Agency clerk named Morris Bernstein, or Jim Carlyle. (Pages 77-78)

Then listed are Billy's "grievances," all irrelevant to "Brushy's" being Billy. (Pages 80-81) Ignorant of the pardon bargain, Sonnichsen says Billy agreed to stand trial in Lincoln for Brady's murder; and he makes-up that Billy's change of trial venue to Mesilla made him leave jail, because the pardon deal was just for standing trial in Lincoln.

**PROMPT SOURCE: The source footnote is Lew Wallace's June 8, 1902 *New York World* outlaw myth article titled "General Lew Wallace Writes a Romance of 'Billy the Kid' Most Famous Bandit of the Plains," which says no such thing, but was from Morrison's Indiana Historical Society "research."**

The Santa Fe Ring is name-dropped as treating Billy badly with corrupt officials like District Attorney Rynerson and Judge Warren Bristol, and mean press, like Simon Newman's article in his *Semi-Weekly*; for which the source is listed as Garrett's book. The Mesilla trial for the Brady murder is called unfair, because enemies testified, it was not proved Billy shot Brady, and the judge made verdict of first degree murder necessary. Added is that Billy got the death sentence. (Page 82)

**FAKERY:** Sonnichsen is mimicking being an historian, while unaware of the correct defense that the Regulators had to kill Brady to stop his murdering Alexander McSween, returning to Lincoln within the next few hours.

Blather follows about Garrett's death warrant *after* Billy's jailbreak being useless, and Garrett having "no papers" to arrest Billy on July 14, 1881; though, admittedly, none were needed. (Page 82) Sonnichsen concludes his meaningless nonsense with: "THERE IS NO ACTUAL PROOF OF THE DEATH OF BILLY THE KID." (Page 82)

## REAL BLACK AND WHITE PRESS

Sonnichsen dishonestly concealed the reality of massive press - in black and white - around the country announcing the death of Billy the Kid - with no reason to make it up. Here are a few examples.

On July 18, 1881, *The Las Vegas Daily Optic's* headline was: "'The Kid' Killed! He Meets His Death at the Hands of Sheriff Pat Garrett, of Lincoln County." It gave identification of the body, as confirmed in the correctly cited Coroner's Jury Report: "An inquest was held on his body today [sic] and the verdict of the jury was 'justifiable homicide' and that Pat Garrett ought to receive the thanks of the whole community ... and that he is truly worthy of a handsome reward."

The July 21, 1881 *Santa Fe Daily New Mexican,* in "Garrett Exonerates Maxwell," confirmed Peter Maxwell as a witness to the shooting, and addressed rumors that he had hidden Billy the Kid in Fort Sumner before the killing. Garrett was quoted: "[H]e does not think that Maxwell was in with the Kid ... He says that Pete acknowledged that fear kept him from informing on the Kid."

The July 22, 1881 *Las Vegas Daily Gazette,* in "Words of Commendation and Encouragement," stated: "Immediately on the receipt of the news of the killing of Billy 'the Kid' by Sheriff Garrett, prominent citizens of Roswell and the lower Pecos wrote us giving particulars and expressing satisfaction. [One wrote] The words, 'God bless Pat Garrett for his good work' will escape many a lip, and people will never cease to love him for his great achievements."

The August 10, 1881 *The New York Sun,* reprinting from the *St. Louis Globe-Democrat,* published "The Life of Billy the Kid. His Name Was Billy McCarthy, And He Was Born in New York" – information which eliminated "Brushy" just by its headline!

It stated: "Before the words ["Quien es"] were off his lips Pat Garrett's bullet was through his heart, and 'Billy the Kid,' the terror of New Mexico, lay gasping, a quivering corpse."

Of course, Sonnichsen was also hiding the history of his own time: that on November 30, 1950, in response to that day's Governor Mabry hearing, the front page of the *Alamogordo News* announced: "Fort Sumner Jury Thought The Kid Had Been Killed." It confirmed that the original report had been found in 1932 by a state employee in the State capitol basement. He had made copies for himself and others. Sonnichsen could probably have gotten one for himself!

## ATTACKING PAT GARRETT'S AUTHORITY

Beginning his defamation of Pat Garrett, Sonnichsen denied his lawman authority; though that was irrelevant as to his killing Billy. Sonnichsen claimed that, as Sheriff of Lincoln County, he had illegally "stepped out of his own bailiwick when he entered [Fort Sumner's] San Miguel county." He claimed Garrett did not turn Billy over to the local sheriff, Hilario Romero, as required, because they had a feud. (Page 82)

**WRONG: Sonnichsen is ignorant that Garrett was also made a Deputy U.S. Marshal by the Secret Service in late 1880. So he was not confined to Lincoln County for his "bailiwick," was not beholden to San Miguel County Sheriff Romero, and had Territory-wide authority. (Later "Brushy" hoaxers would quibble erroneously about the *correctness* of his Deputy U.S. Marshal appointment, as is debunked on pages 327, 653-656 below.)**

## HIDING THE CORONER'S JURY REPORT

The fatal "black and white" proof against "Brushy," was the existing July 15, 1881 Coroner's Jury Report confirming that Garrett killed Billy Bonney; with its inquest identifying the body and determining the legal status of the homicide as self-defense.

So Sonnichsen lied. He said it never existed, or was "two" invalid versions, or Morrison could not find it, or its irregularity prevented Garrett from getting his reward - for a nonsensical leap that this meant Billy Bonney was not killed; and Billy Barlow was killed instead. Highlighting Sonnichsen's ridiculousness, is that the Coroner's Jury Report for Sheriff William Brady has not been located. So by his illogic, Brady was not dead either!

But in *Alias Billy the Kid's* "Appendix" is the translated Coroner's Jury Report (Pages 108-109) labeled: "Report of the Coroner's Jury (translation of a Photostat copy of a **purported original which was never filed in San Miguel County)."**

**FAKERY**: Typical of Sonnichsen's style is snideness - like "purported original" - instead of giving real evidence to the contrary. And his claim that it was not filed in San Miguel County is typical of his incompetence, since the quoted first line of that report, right below this claim, gives its filed location: "To the attorney of the first Judicial District of the Territory of New Mexico." As discussed above, that meant it was sent to District Attorney/ Attorney General William Breeden in Santa Fe. (See pages 7, 13 above)

Concealed also is the November 30, 1950 *Alamogordo News's* "Fort Sumner Jury Thought The Kid Had Been Killed," about the 1932 find of the Report, and its distributed copies. (See pages 15, 116, 206 above) Historian, Maurice Garland Fulton, donated one, certified on January 18, 1951, to the Indiana Historical Society's Lew Wallace Collection, from which Morrison could have gotten a copy himself! And a copy was also in the Lincoln Museum. Its Spanish photostatic copy was subsequently printed by William Keleher in his 1957 *Violence in Lincoln County: 1869-1881*, along with a translation. (See page 8 above) But Sonnichsen never recanted his misinformation.

### THE TWO-CORONER'S REPORTS SCAM

To discredit the validity of the Report, Sonnichsen alleged two coroner's juries, generating no "official record." His source was an A.P. Anaya telling a George Fitzpatrick, editor of the *New Mexico Magazine*, that a first report had been lost and that Garrett and another man wrote one with different jurymen's names. (Page 83)

Sonnichsen's motive was to call Garrett a liar, since Garrett had paraphrased the Report in his *The Authentic Life of Billy the Kid*; stating: "On the following morning, the alcade, Alejandro Segura, held an inquest over the body, M. [Milnor] Rudulph of Sunnyside being foreman of the coroner's jury. Their verdict [in the Report] was that William H. Bonney came to his death from a gunshot wound, the weapon being in the hands of Pat F. Garrett; and that the fatal wound was inflicted by the said

Garrett in the discharge of his official duty as sheriff and that the homicide was justifiable." (Garrett, Page 219)

**FALSE EVIDENCE:** Sonnichsen was unaware that Anaya confirmed Billy's death. A.P. "Paco" Anaya, Billy's friend, wrote a manuscript titled *I Buried Billy*. Published posthumously in 1991, it proved Billy's vigil and burial. Anaya wrote: "I, the writer, and my brother, Higinio Garcia, and several others of those that were there, dressed Billy with those clothes then we laid him on a high bed ... [A]nd on the next day we buried him." (Anaya, Page 132) But beyond that, Anaya knew no history, his book being mere windbag malarkey - like his two coroner's juries tale - information to which he would not have been privy.

### MORRISON'S NOT-FINDING-IT EXCUSE

Sonnichsen also absurdly alleges that Morrison's not finding the report in public repositories proved it had never been filed. And a footnote about its copy being in the Lincoln Museum is facetiously called a "purported copy of this purported death certificate" (Page 83), like for the Report in the "Appendix."

### SCAM OF HIDING THE CORONER'S JURY REPORT'S PROPER DISPOSITION BY PAT GARRETT

Sonnichsen hides Pat Garrett's proper legal disposition of the Coroner's Jury Report, to create his fake argument of its not existing, and to call Garrett a liar. But his own footnote of the *Executive Record Book* presented its correct disposition.

**THE REAL HISTORY:** Countering Sonnichsen's fakery of the Report's not existing, or not being "filed," was Pat Garrett's proper disposition of it to the correct authorities.

The immediate issue was that he had killed a man; so he had to establish justification. He was also justifying getting the offered reward.

Both issues were covered in his July 15, 1881 letter to Acting-Governor William Ritch (Governor Lionel Sheldon was then traveling). Garrett made clear his disposition of the Coroner's Jury Report: "I herewith annex a copy of the verdict rendered by the jury called in by the justice of the peace (*ex officio* coroner), <u>the original of which is in the hands of the prosecuting attorney of the first judicial district [William Breeden]</u>."

So, as stated in the Coroner's Jury Report itself, Garrett sent its original to his potential prosecutor, District Attorney Breeden, responsible for the First Judicial District, which included San Miguel County's Fort Sumner; and who was also Territorial Attorney General. Breeden needed the confirmation that the killing was immune to his prosecution, with the jurymen attesting: "*[O]ur verdict is that the action of said Garrett was justifiable homicide.*" So the original was in Breeden's files.

Garrett's letter to the governor had to address another technicality, which had to do with the reward. (And he properly enclosed a copy of the Coroner's Jury Report for him.) The reward, as originally promised by Lew Wallace, was not a dead-or-alive offer. The December 22, 1880's Las Vegas *Daily Gazette*, and May 3, 1881's *Daily New Mexican*, had both stated: "**I will pay $500 reward to any person or persons who will capture William Bonney, alias The Kid, and deliver him to any sheriff of New Mexico. Satisfactory proofs of identity will be required.**" So the fact that there was not a capture, but a killing, had to be addressed. So Garrett did, explaining his self-defense necessity. He wrote: "It was my desire to have been able to take him alive, but his coming upon me so suddenly and unexpectedly leads me to believe that he had seen me enter the room, or had been informed by someone of the fact, and that he came there armed with pistol and knife expressly to kill me if he could. Under that impression I had no alternative but to kill him or to suffer death at his hands."

This Garrett letter to the Governor was published in July 23, 1881's *Rio Grande Republican* as "Kid the Killer Killed." It stated:

William Bonney, alias 'the Kid,' is dead. No report could have caused more general feeling of gratification than this, and when it was further announced that the faithful and brave Pat Garrett, he who had been the mainstay of law and order in Lincoln county, the chief reliance of the people in the dark days, when danger lurked at every hand, has accomplished the crowning feat of his life by bringing down the fierce and implacable foe single-handed, the sense of satisfaction was heightened to one of delight. The following is Sheriff Garrett's official report to the chief executive of the territory.

It is as follows. – Fort Sumner, N.M., July 15. – "To his Excellency the Governor of New Mexico. – I have the honor to inform your Excellency that I had received several communications from persons in and about Fort Sumner what William Bonney, alias 'the Kid,' had been there, or in that vicinity for some time. In view of these reports I deemed it my duty to go there and ascertain if there was any truth in them or not, all the time doubting their accuracy; but on Monday, July 11, I left home, taking with me John W. Poe and T.L. McKinney, men in whose courage and sagacity I relied implicitly, and arrived just below Fort Sumner on Wednesday, the 13th. I remained concealed near the houses until night, and then entered the fort at about midnight, and went to Mr. P. Maxwell's room. I found him in bed and had just commenced to talk to him about the object of my visit at such an unusual hour, when a man entered the room in stockinged feet, with a pistol in one hand and a knife in the other. He came and placed his hand on the bed just beside me, and in a low whisper, "Who is it?" (and repeated the question) he asked Mr. Maxwell. I at once recognized the man, and knew he was 'the Kid,' and reached behind me for my pistol, feeling almost certain of receiving a ball from his at the moment of my doing so, as I felt sure he had now recognized me, but fortunately he drew back from the bed at noticing my movement, and although he had his pistil pointed at my breast, he delayed to fire, and asked me in Spanish, "Quien es? Quien es?" This gave me time to bring mine to bear on him, and the moment I did so I pulled the trigger and he received the death wound, for the ball struck him in the left breast and pierced his heart. He never spoke, but died in a minute. <u>It was my desire to have been able to take him alive, but his coming upon me so suddenly and unexpectedly leads me to believe that he had seen</u>

me enter the room, or had been informed by someone of the fact, and that he came there armed with pistol and knife expressly to kill me if he could. Under that impression I had no alternative but to kill him or to suffer death at his hands. I herewith annex a copy of the verdict rendered by the jury called in by the justice of the peace (*ex officio* coroner), the original of which is in the hands of the prosecuting attorney of the first judicial district.

## SCAM OF CLAIMING GARRETT'S REWARD WAS WITHHELD FOR AN IMPROPER REPORT AND NO IDENTIFIED BILLY THE KID

To attack the Coroner's Jury Report from another angle, Sonnichsen faked that Garrett's $500 Billy the Kid reward was withheld for lack of proof of the killing. (Pages 84-86) But this just proved Sonnichsen's incompetence in reading primary documents, or his lying. The simple truth was that the legislature merely had to convert Wallace's personal reward offer to a Territorial reward. That was done. Garrett was paid.

But Sonnichsen lied that Acting-Governor William Ritch refused payment **because of no record of the reward on file**, hissing snidely that this was "truly amazing ... strange and wonderful" as he revved-up for a conspiracy theory. (Page 84) For it, he misquoted Ritch's report of July 21, 1881 in the "Executive Record Book" of July 25, 1867-November 8, 1882 (even though it was his own footnote source!). (Page 84). Sonnichsen's dishonest intent was to manufacture a conspiracy theory that there was something irregular or concealed about the Coroner's Jury Report, then to leap to a conspiracy of the report not existing for premeditated concealment that the corpse was not Billy the Kid's – ergo, "Brushy" was surviving Billy!

THE REAL HISTORY: Garrett's meeting with Acting-Governor Ritch on July 20[th], was reported by the July 21, 1881 *Santa Fe Daily New Mexican*. Ritch was quoted as **"willing to pay the amount, and would be glad to do so,"** but the delaying issue was that proper procedure had to be followed first. The article stated:

> Yesterday afternoon Pat. Garrett; accompanied by Hon. T.B. Catron and Col. M. Brunswick, called upon acting-Governor Ritch in regard to the reward offered by ex-Governor Lew Wallace for the Kid. The reward was fixed at five hundred dollars, and the offer was published in the papers. <u>Governor Ritch announced that he was willing to pay the amount, and would be glad to do so, but that he would have to look at the records first</u>. He was not in the city when the offer was made, and had never received any notification of it, consequently did not know whether or not it was on record. In consequence of the state of affairs, the question of the reward was not settled.

But Sonnichsen, ignorantly or deceptively, identified Attorney Breeden's legal opinion to Ritch about its processing as Ritch's words; then claimed Ritch refused the reward! (Page 84)

THE REAL HISTORY: The only delay in payment, as Ritch made clear, was converting Wallace's offer. So he sought the legal opinion of Territorial Attorney General William Breeden (also District Attorney of the First Judicial District and recipient of the original Coroner's Jury Report for William Bonney). Then he quoted Breeden's opinion in his Executive Record Book entry. Breeden agreed that the reward was a private offer, claiming Wallace had not filed it with his office or that of the Territorial Secretary, converting it to a Territorial offer. Breeden stated (though Sonnichsen called his words Ritch's, and took them out of context): "<u>In addition, we will add as fact that there was no record whatever in this [Attorney General's] office or at the Secretary's office of there having been a reward offered as set forth by Attorney General, nor was there any reward or file in said offices of a corresponding reward in any form</u>." So the issue was just conversion of Wallace's private reward to a Territorial reward. But dishonest Sonnichsen faked that as <u>no reward offered at all</u>, or the reward was withheld on irregularity, which he implied meant no Report or no corpse!

Ritch's official response (misquoted by Sonnichsen) was entered on July 21, 1881 in *Executive Record Book 2,* as "In the matter of the application by Patrick F. Garrett for a reward claimed to have been offered May-1881 for the capture of Wm Bonney alias "the Kid." Ritch wrote:

*Executive Department*
*Territory of New Mexico*
*July 21st 1881*

July 20th 1881 Pat F. Garret *[sic- throughout]* Sheriff of Lincoln County appeared and presented a bill for $500. claiming it as a reward offered on or about the 7th of May 1881 by the late Governor Lew Wallace, for the capture of said Bonny *[sic, throughout]*.

As evidence of said offer having been made the affidavit of publication thereof made by Chas. H. Green *[sic – Greene]* the editor and manager of the Daily <u>New Mexican</u> was presented with said bill, as also was presented a statement of the proceedings and verdict of a coroner's jury at Fort Sumner in San Miguel County upon the body of the said Bonny, captured as aforesaid, and a statement of Garret directed to this office of his doings in the premises.

Upon examination of said papers it was deemed important that the opinion of the Attorney General be taken thereon and they were at once transmitted to that office. On the following day the papers with the opinion of Hon. Wm Breeden Attorney General were filed.

**[AUTHOR'S NOTE: Garrett's request was sent for legal opinion to Attorney General Breeden. Breeden's answer was then excerpted by Ritch in his response - printed smaller here to distinguish it from Ritch's words.]**

Said opinion is quite full. We quote the closing paragraphs as sufficient in this connection, to with

"The offer by the Governor, or the notice thereof, which is all there is to show such an offer, is as follows –
Billy the Kid
$500 Reward
"I will pay five hundred dollars reward to any person or persons, who will capture William Bonny, alias the Kid, and deliver him to any Sheriff of New Mexico. Satisfactory proof of identity will be required.
Lew Wallace
Governor of New Mexico"

"This certainly appears to be the personal offer of Governor Wallace, and it seems he did nothing to indicate that it was intended as an executive act on behalf of, and to bind the Territory.

"If the reward should be paid, it is very probable that the Legislature would approve the payment if so desired, and that no objection would be raised, or that it will provide for its payment if it remained unpaid, at the next session thereof;

[AUTHOR'S NOTE: Breeden saw no problem with the Legislature's eventual approving of reward payment.]

*but if the Governor [Ritch] should now direct the payment of the claim, he would doubtless expose himself to the charge of misappropriation of the Territorial funds, in case the Legislature should refuse to ratify or approve the payment."*

[AUTHOR'S NOTE: So Breeden said if Ritch paid the reward himself *before proper procedure of legislative approval*, it could be criticized as misappropriating funds. The text then returned to Ritch's own words.]

*In addition we will add as a fact that there was no record whatsoever; either in this office or at the [Territorial] Secretary's office of there having been a reward offered as set forth by Attorney General, nor was there any record or file in said offices of a corresponding reward in any form.*

[AUTHOR'S NOTE: Ritch confirmed that Wallace had not converted his reward offer into a Territorial offer.]

*The opinion of the Attorney General appearing to be consistent with the law and the facts. Decision is rendered accordingly and the Governor [Ritch] declines to allow the reward at this time. Believing however, that Mr Garret has an equitable claim against the Territory for said reward, the action at this office will simply be suspended until the case can properly be represented to the next Legislative Assembly.*

*Ritch*
*Act Governor NM*

[AUTHOR'S NOTE: Ritch confirmed that the reward was justified, but had to be converted to a Territorial reward.]

It may be noted that Ritch had forgotten that he had recorded Wallace's reward eight months earlier, when he was Territorial Secretary! Wallace had told him about it by letter on December 13, 1880. Then Ritch himself made its

December 13, 1880 entry in "Executive Record Book 2, July 25, 1867-November 8, 1882 on page 473. Wallace wrote:

**Executive Office**
SANTA FE., N.M.
*Dec. 13*     1880

Hon. W.G. Ritch
Loc. New Mexico.
Sir:
Be good enough to prepare a draft of proclamation of reward $500. for the capture and delivery of William Bonney, alias the Kid to the Sheriff of the County of Lincoln County.

Yours, truly,
Lew Wallace
Governor

Ritch had written in the "Executive Record Book":

Dec 13 [1880]
Reward

Territory of New Mexico ) Indictment in
vs                       ) Lincoln co. Dist. Court
William Bonney           ) for murder
   alias "The Kid"

Executive Office
Territory of New Mexico

Whereas William Bonney, alias "The Kid" charged under indictment issued from the District Court in and for the county of Lincoln of the crime of murder committed in said county: And whereas the said William Bonney, alias "The Kid" is a fugitive from justice

Now Therefore Lewis Wallace, Governor of the Territory, by virtue of the power and authority vested in me by law and believing the ends of justice will be served thereby do hereby offer a reward of five hundred dollars ($500.) for the apprehension and arrest of said William Bonney, alias "The Kid" and for his delivery to the Sheriff of Lincoln County at the county seat of said county.

*In witness Whereof I have set my hand and have caused the great seal of the Territory to be hereto affixed this 13th day of December 1880.*
*Lew. Wallace,*
*Governor N.M.*

*By the Governor*
*Wm Ritch, Secretary N.M.*

## SCAM OF NO PUBLISHED REWARD NOTICES

Sonnichsen next made up that no printed notices of the reward existed. (Page 85) But he had merely checked papers with the wrong dates of December 24, 1880 for the *Las Vegas Gazette*, and May 7, 1881 for the *Santa Fe New Mexican*! He had incompetently missed the correct December 22, 1880 Las Vegas *Gazette* front page notice, and its May 3, 1881 *Daily New Mexican* repeat!

**THE REAL HISTORY: On December 22, 1880, nine days after Wallace gave his reward notice in the Executive Record Book, he published his reward notice in the *Las Vegas Gazette*'s front page. After Billy's escape from the Lincoln courthouse-jail, Wallace reprinted it in the May 3, 1881 *Daily New Mexican*. It stated: "BILLY THE KID $500 REWARD, I will pay $500 reward to any person or persons who will capture William Bonney, alias The Kid, and deliver him to any sheriff of New Mexico. Satisfactory proofs of identity will be required. LEW. WALLACE, Governor of New Mexico."**

But Sonnichsen leapt from faking no reward notices to claiming that proved no Coroner's Jury Report - supposedly meaning no corpse's identity. Then using Ritch's same July 21, 1881 "Response of Acting Governor William Ritch to Pat Garrett's Reward Petition," Sonnichsen wrote that Ritch knew "the shaky character of the purported death certificate ... [which] cannot now be, and perhaps never could never have been produced." (Page 85)

**LYING: Sonnichsen, thus, maliciously and willfully hid from the readers that the Coroner's Jury Report was given in evidence to Ritch by Pat Garrett for his reward, as reported by Ritch, who wrote on July 21, 1881: "*As evidence of said offer having been made the affidavit of publication thereof made by Chas. H. Green [sic – Greene] the editor and manager of the Daily <u>New Mexican</u> was presented with said***

bill, *as also was presented a statement of the proceedings and verdict of a coroner's jury at Fort Sumner in San Miguel County upon the body of the said Bonny, captured as aforesaid,* and a statement of Garret directed to this office of his doings in the premises." That meant confirmation by the Territory's highest officials of the legal identification of the body as Billy Bonney's.

## FAKING A SANTA FE RING CONSPIRACY OF THE LEGISLATURE FOR GARRETT'S REWARD

Still laboring dishonestly in attempt to convert the simple delay in paying Garrett his reward to a conspiracy to conceal that he did not kill Billy the Kid, and the corpse of Billy Barlow was concealed by no Coroner's Jury Report, Sonnichsen next focused on the Legislature as being controlled by the Santa Fe Ring.

In fact, Sonnichsen had no idea of the Ring's role in Billy the Kid history. He was merely name-dropping from Maurice Garland Fulton's footnote about it being a corrupt cabal, in his 1927 annotation of Pat Garrett's *The Authentic Life of Billy the Kid.* (See pages 139-140 above). In fact, the specifics of the Ring, and the Territory-wide grass-roots uprisings against it in the 1870's were not elucidated until my 2017 *The Lost Pardon of Billy the Kid: An Analysis Factoring In the Santa Fe Ring, Governor Lew Wallace's Dilemma, and a Territory in Rebellion* and my 2018 *The Santa Fe Ring Versus Billy the Kid: The Making of an American Monster.*

But Sonnichsen stated that Ring bad guys were helping bad guy Garrett get the reward through the Legislature, because the Ring was against good guys Ritch and Wallace, who were Ring opponents trying to stop Garrett getting it. (Pages 85-86)

**FAKERY:** Sonnichsen is just writing fiction. As seen above, the issue of Garrett's reward was merely of converting Wallace's private offer to a Territorial one by legislative act. But Sonnichsen is lying to build his fake conspiracy.

In fact, Ritch was a Ringite, as Lew Wallace was warned in a 1878 secret notebook listing Ringites, given to him by Investigator Frank Warner Angel. The entry stated: "*Ritch W.G. Santa Fe Sec Territory, Axtel man, otherwise reliable.*" Governor S.B. Axtell was a central Ringite. And Wallace refused to oppose the vindictive Ring anyway to protect his own political future. And by the time of Garrett's reward request, he had left the Territory.

For his conspiracy theory, Sonnichsen again misrepresented Acting-Governor William Ritch's July 21, 1881 response to Garrett's reward request, which mentioned Charles W. Greene. Sonnichsen made-up that Greene was **"Garrett's lawyer,"** and **"an important Ring man."** (Page 85) This innuendo was apparently to prove Ring backing of Garrett. So Sonnichsen stated that the Ring's being "opposed to Billy the Kid ... may explain, at least partly, why Charles W. Greene asked the legislature to do what Ritch would not or could not do. A bill was introduced to afford Garrett 'relief.'" (Page 86)

**THE REAL HISTORY:** Sonnichsen is lying wildly. In fact, Charles W. Greene was not Garrett's lawyer. He ran a printing company. Ritch had referenced Greene as giving an Affidavit about *having printed Lew Wallace's reward notices.* Ritch was merely establishing proof that the reward notices existed as Garrett had claimed. Ritch stated: *"As evidence of said [reward] offer having been made the affidavit of publication thereof made by Chas. H. Green [sic – Greene] the editor and manager of the* <u>Daily New Mexican</u> *was presented with said bill."* Greene also published the *Santa Fe New Mexican*, which ran one of Wallace's two reward notices. It was a Ring-biased paper, but that is irrelevant to the reward issue. (Greene had also printed, for Wallace, reward posters for "the Kid," billing Wallace on May 20, 1881.) Greene had nothing to do with asking the legislature for a Garrett reward.

And there was nothing sinister about the progress of Garrett's request to the legislature. As Ritch made clear in his July 21, 1881 response to the request, the body was identified, since he had a copy of the Coroner's Jury Report with *"verdict of a coroner's Jury at Fort Sumner in San Miguel County upon the body of the said Bonney, captured as aforesaid."* And Ritch paraphrased Attorney General William Breeden's response to the request: *"[I]t is very probable that the Legislature would approve the payment if desired, and that no objection would be raised."* That meant Breeden too had no doubt about the body being Billy Bonney's.

Desperately seeking any supposed irregularity, Sonnichsen stated: "It is interesting to note that the act credits Garrett with killing William Bonney 'on or about the month of August, 1881.'"

(Page 86) So not saying July specifically, means to Sonnichsen that the killing never happened; rather than a minor vagueness in an act not passed until February 18, 1882.

THE REAL HISTORY: The actual "Act for the Relief of Pat. Garrett," of February 18, 1882, made clear the straightforward process, with the delay being a mere "technicality;" stating: "Garrett is justly entitled to the above reward, and payment thereof has been refused upon a technicality." There issue was not the body identity - there was no doubt it was William Bonney's - but the nature of the homicide, which was found justifiable and compatible with the reward. It stated:

AN ACT FOR THE RELIEF OF PAT. GARRETT
CONTENTS

SECTION 1. Authorizes payment of $500 reward for the arrest of "the Kid."

WHEREAS, The Governor of New Mexico did, on or about the 7th day of May, A.D., 1881, issue certain proclamation in words and figures as follows, to-wit:

"I will pay five hundred dollars reward to any person or persons who will capture William Bonney, alias 'The Kid,' and deliver him to any sheriff of New Mexico. Satisfactory proof of identity will be required."

(Signed)                 Lew. Wallace
                         Governor of New Mexico.

AND, WHEREAS, Pat. Garrett was at that time sheriff of Lincoln county, and did, on or about the month of August, 1881, in pursuance of the above reward, and by virtue of a warrant placed in his hands for the purpose, attempted to arrest said William Bonney, and in said attempt did kill said William Bonney at Fort Sumner, in the county of San Miguel, in the Territory of New Mexico, and wherefore, said <u>Garrett is justly entitled to the above reward, and payment thereof has been refused upon a technicality</u>. Therefore

*Be it enacted by the Legislative Assembly of the Territory of New Mexico:*

SECTION 1. The Territorial Auditor is hereby authorized to draw a warrant upon the Territorial Treasurer of the Territory of New Mexico, in favor of Pat. Garrett for the sum of five hundred dollars, payable out of any funds in the Territorial treasury not otherwise appropriated, in payment of the reward of five hundred dollars heretofore offered by his Excellency, Governor Lew. Wallace, for the arrest of William Bonney, alias "The Kid."

SEC. 2. This act shall take effect and be in force from and after its passage.

Approved February 18, 1882,

And, once returned, Governor Lionel Sheldon even said, in his February 14, 1882 letter to the Legislature, that *he* would have paid it outright: *"It is a claim which I think I should have paid if it had not been understood that the matter was to be referred to the legislature before it came into my hands."* (he had been out of the Territory from July 3, 1881 to August 27, 1881, leaving more timid Ritch in charge). Sheldon wrote:

𝔈𝔵𝔢𝔠𝔲𝔱𝔦𝔳𝔢 𝔒𝔣𝔣𝔦𝔠𝔢,
𝔗𝔢𝔯𝔯𝔦𝔱𝔬𝔯𝔶 𝔬𝔣 𝔑𝔢𝔴 𝔐𝔢𝔵𝔦𝔠𝔬,
Santa Fe, *February 14<sup>th</sup> 1882*

*Hon Lewis Baca*
*President of the Council*
*In the matter of the claim of Sheriff Garrett Lincoln county for the reward offered for the capture of "the Kid" so called, I am of the opinion that he is entitled to payment. He could not technically comply with the terms of the reward because when he met the "Kid" in Maxwell's room it is very certain that one or the other would be killed. It was not a reward the payment of which depended on conviction. The Kid had been convicted and was under sentence to be hanged. Garrett was in pursuit with an intention to capture if it could be done normally but under the circumstances of their meeting capture was pout of the question. It will not do to the technical in this case because men will not be willing to take risks and*

*proper services in the protection of society against bad men if captious objections are interposed to avoid the discharge of public observations. <u>The case under consideration is too notorious and remarkable to be made a precedent for the refusal to pay for services performed substantially in compliance with the provisions of high authority.</u>*

<u>*It is a claim which I think I should have paid if it had not been understood that the matter was to be referred to the legislature before it came into my hands.*</u>

*Very Respectfully*
*Lionel A. Sheldon*
*Governor of New Mexico*

So, contrary to Sonnichsen's lies, the Coroner's Jury Report for William Bonney ended up getting additional scrutiny by the Acting-Governor, the Territorial Attorney General, the Governor, and the Legislature; which all agreed that Garrett killed Billy the Kid, and therefore deserved the reward.

**THE MISSING HISTORY: Sonnichsen was unaware that the Ring wanted Billy dead as an anti-Ring zealot. From the Ring's angle, Garrett was paid *because* he killed Billy.**

### CONCLUDING WITH FAKE "DOUBTS"

Sonnichsen concludes ridiculously - based on his own lies about the Coroner's Jury Report and Garrett's reward - that foul play had occurred in 1881 because no one expected "Brushy Bill's" appearance to question it! (Page 86) That craziness segues to his irrelevant "doubts" as to Billy's guilt (for what is unstated) and the governor's right to deny the pardon. So he concludes that Billy's death and burial are also in doubt! And all his fakery and stupid misreadings, for Sonnichsen, added up to a cry that "Brushy" deserved "his day in court in order that his representatives could produce whatever was down in black and white for or against him." (Page 86)

Omitted is that "Brushy" had his Mabry hearing, and deservedly lost. Proved, however, was that Sonnichsen was trying to insert himself into the famous history of Billy the Kid, as well as to trump his naysayer historian colleagues. And though he failed, his fake conspiracy theories would become gospel to the next generation of "Brushy"-believers.

# "EPILOGUE": "BRUSHY'S" LAST SHOT

The "Epilogue" lumped together Sonnichsen's conspiracy theories in lieu of any evidence for the claim of "Brushy" as Billy.

Admitting that the survival claim required a cover-up conspiracy of Fort Sumner residents from July 14, 1881 to the present (Page 89), Sonnichsen backs that, claiming people there would have protected Billy. For irrelevant example of that loyalty, Sonnichsen quoted John W. Poe's 1933 *The Death of Billy the* Kid: "[I]f the object of my visit had been known, I should have stood no chance for my life whatever." (Page 89) But he omits Poe's stated belief in his book that only a few rough local Americans were in sympathy with the Kid, "while the remainder [of the town of 200-300 people] stood in terror of him" (Poe, Pages 18-19), which removed the 100% needed for Sonnichsen's conspiracy. More importantly, Sonnichsen omitted Poe's documentation of Billy's corpse being taken for the night vigil, and profuse identifications by townspeople. Poe wrote: "Within a short time after the shooting, quite a number of the native people had gathered around, some of them **bewailing the death of their friend**, while several women **pleaded for permission to take charge of the body, which we allowed them to do.** They carried it across the yard to a carpenter shop, where **it was laid out on a workbench**, the women placing lighted candles around it according to their ideas of properly conducting **a 'wake' for the dead.**" (Poe, Page 41-42)

After hiding Poe's eye-witness quote which was enough to sink *Alias Billy the Kid's* ship of fools, Sonnichsen claimed survival was supported by rumors. (Page 89)

And he repeated his Santa Fe Ring conspiracy theory. His illogic, with fake premises, went like this: If the Ring handled Garrett's reward money claim, then they wanted Billy to go away because he was "the hottest political potato." If so, Garrett fearing "imminent danger of mob violence, went along with a fiction which allowed Billy to get away and start a new life." (Page 90)

**FAKERY: As stated above, the Ring wanted Billy dead, and got him dead. And the "mob violence" was lifted, out of context, from Poe's fear of Fort Sumner residents' reprisal on the night Garrett killed Billy. As Poe stated in** *The*

*Death of Billy the Kid:* "We spent the rest of the night on the Maxwell premises, keeping constantly on guard, as we were expecting to be attacked by friends of the dead man." (Poe, Page 44)

The "Epilogue" ends with Sonnichsen's rehashing the "Brushy" hoax's claims - already debunked here: "Brushy" knew too much; and he was illiterate, so he could not have read-up. Sonnichsen finishes with his taunting quote: "[I]f Brushy Bill Roberts wasn't Billy the Kid, then who was he?" (Page 90) That left open the answer: not Billy Bonney.

## APPENDICES AND PARTING WORDS

*Alias Billy the Kid's* "Appendices" reveal more of its sources: Wallace's Amnesty Proclamation, Billy Bonney's change of venue, documents on Billy's Mesilla trial, Wallace's Death Warrant, the translation of Billy's Coroner's Jury Report, letters to Morrison from New Mexico District Courts denying possession of the Coroner's Jury Report, Lew Wallace's reward offer, Pat Garrett's reward claim saying it was Wallace's personal offer, and five Affidavits claiming "Brushy" as Billy.

The book ends with quoting "Brushy's" June 16, 1949 Morrison interview in Hamilton, Texas (Pages 130-131), which proved that Sonnichsen and Morrison had wisely limited his own words, because his gab is just hair-raising errors.

FICTION: "Brushy" said, 'Jesse [sic - Jessie] Evans knew that Garrett didn't kill the Kid.' **[AUTHOR'S NOTE: "Brushy" made the same third-person mistake in the Mabry hearing, by saying "he" for Billy, instead of "me."]**

FACT: The outlaw, Jessie Evans, would have known nothing of the sort. In 1881, he was in jail in Huntsville, Texas; and absent from New Mexico Territory since his March, 1879 escape from his Fort Stanton incarceration for the Huston Chapman murder.

FICTION: "Brushy" said: "Jim East, I knew him too. He was a friend of mine."

FACT: Jim East was a Pat Garrett posseman, hunting down Billy, and at his Stinking Springs capture - not Billy's friend. It came from confabulating around Walter Noble Burns's own fiction in *The Saga of Billy the Kid* in which he has Billy wanting to give East a gun because he was a nice man. (Burns, Page 216)

FICTION: About Lew Wallace, "Brushy" concludes clumsily: "I done everything I promised him to do."

FACT: Real Billy's prompt-letter of March 4, 1881 to Wallace said beautifully: *"I have done everything that I promised you I would, and you have done nothing that you promised me."*

In the end, *Alias Billy the Kid* only proves a pig's ear cannot make a silk purse, a real historian can act like a fool, and even the best con-man is only as good as his snare.

## SUMMARIZING *ALIAS BILLY THE KID'S* "BRUSHY BILL" IMPOSTER HOAX

Coaching from available sources, hoaxing authors William V. Morrison and C.L. Sonnichsen manipulated Oliver Pleasant Roberts, a mentally disabled septuagenarian, with pre-existing grandiose delusions of Old West personalities, including Billy the Kid, into parroting pseudo-memories to pass as Billy Bonney. The motive for all three was self-aggrandizement. The corollary of the hoax was defamation of Sheriff Pat Garrett as an unpunished murderer of an innocent victim, instead of Billy the Kid.

Hiding damning evidence of the Coroner's Jury Report and multiple identifications of dead Billy, the hoax fabricated "Brushy's" 20 year age enhancement with fictional genealogy, and feigned special knowledge and illiteracy to hide reading-up.

The failure was demonstrated by "Brushy's" lack of special knowledge separate from coaching, with its parroted source errors; and with erroneous confabulations when prompts were absent. There was no match with real Billy's birth, family history, literacy and letters, and Spanish fluency. Absent was decisive information in real Billy's life: his Peñasco River Ranch; deputizing, the Regulators; the San Patricio massacre; the Lincoln County War freedom fight against the Ring; his deposition, pardon bargain, and court testimonies; his near killing by Joe Grant, the Secret Service pursuit with possible second pardon; his anti-Ring guerrilla rustling; and his true-love, Paulita Maxwell.

As to "Brushy's" authors, William V. Morrison was a con-artist promoter, devising the hoax; prompting, touring, and rehearsing "Brushy" as Billy; and generating fake identity Affidavits. C.L. Sonnichsen was a slipshod amateur historian, intentionally hoaxing the text by altering "Brushy's" words, adding dishonest conspiracy theories, and hiding debunking evidence; to seek personal fame with the apparently cynical attitude that history was nothing but "myth" anyway.

The scam worked. Morrison sent *Alias Billy the Kid* to past president Harry S. Truman (1945-1953), and proved the hoax was destined for the big-time. On May 19, 1955, Truman responded (and Morrison sent a copy to Paul Blazer):

Dear Mr. Morrison:

I can't tell you how much I appreciate the Number 1 copy of ALIAS BILLY THE KID. I read it from cover to cover and it is one of the most interesting documents I have ever come across. I have read a great many of the things written about him and other Westerners, including the great and the desperadoes and this book is the most satisfactory arrangement with supporting documents that I have ever seen.

It is too bad that the old man who called himself "Billy the Kid" could not have lived long enough to see another Governor of New Mexico. He might have obtained a just decision.

That Number 1 copy pleases me immensely. You can be sure it will be placed in my Library when it is finished. I am hoping to have a whole section devoted to Western Lore.

Sincerely yours,
*Harry S. Truman*

It would take 48 more years before a corrupt aspirant to that Presidency would revive the hoax to publicize himself. And he would follow Truman's prophesy of being another Governor of New Mexico; and his hook would be a pardon for "Brushy Bill" as Billy the Kid. But first, "Brushy" accumulated a duped following.

# CHAPTER 5
# TRUE-BELIEVERS CONTINUE THE "BRUSHY BILL" HOAX

## WHEN DUPES REPLACE CHARLATANS

Hoaxes evolve from charlatan creators to dupes. In 1998, 43 years after C.L. Sonnichsen's and William V. Morrison's *Alias Billy the Kid*, "Brushy" got true-believer authors. William Carl "W.C." Jameson, a country music performer, and, now deceased, Frederic Bean, a novelist, who published *The Return of the Outlaw Billy the Kid*, dedicated to Sonnichsen and Morrison. As Jameson said in their book: "This amazing story captivated me such that for the next twenty-eight years I investigated it at every opportunity." (Page vii) Both stated: "We believe the case for William Henry Roberts ["Brushy's" made-up name] as Billy the Kid is stronger than the case against it." (Page 207)

Jameson and Bean, converted by Morrison's knowing-things-not-printed trick; wrote: "Roberts' recollections of people, places, and events were too 'detailed and precise' for a semiliterate man to have come from sources other than from personal experience." (Page 165) This revealed their quirk. Since the hoax's 1950's origin, scholarly books had been published; but their faith was immune to facts. "Brushy" was gospel.

To them, missing was just more "proof." So they would add "scientific" photo-comparisons of "Brushy" with Billy the Kid's tintype. They would expand Sonnichsen's conspiracy theories. But key to their starry-eyed strategy was letting "Brushy" speak for himself through Morrison's interview tapes. (Page vii) Not till Jameson's 2012 book, *Billy the Kid: The Lost Interviews*, was it explained that Bean got them in 1989 from "Brushy's" last wife's family, made a transcript, then returned them. As Jameson wrote:

"I was convinced I was looking at the words of the outlaw, Billy the Kid." (*The Lost Interviews*, Page 43)

Uncensored "Brushy" was bad for their mission, but great for hoaxbusting. As Jameson guilelessly reported in *Billy the Kid: The Lost Interviews*, Sonnichsen had *"heavily edited"* "Brushy" from those tapes. (*The Lost Interviews*, Page 42) (Sonnichsen knew that "Brushy" in the raw was what Governor Mabry saw in the pardon hearing - along with his Fort Sumner steak restaurant!) But even in *Alias Billy the Kid*, Sonnichsen had left untouched some of "Brushy's" atrocious grammar and racism (the "niggers" on the foothills), since they fit the crude 1950's image of Billy the Kid.

But Sonnichsen's admitted editing was corrupting, inspiring Jameson's and Bean's fix-ups. They added historical names - like "Regulators" - unknown to "Brushy." William Tunstill's 1988 book, *Billy the Kid and Me Were the Same* added to the fake genealogy.

Nevertheless, *The Return of the Outlaw Billy the Kid* froze "Brushy" in the amber of their adoration for all to see. And what was revealed, by comparing their text to *Alias Billy the Kid's*, were the sly changes in that book and theirs. Real "Brushy" was disappearing, and trickery was emerging, making their book hoaxbusting treasure. And, as Jameson descended to overt rewrites in later books, he would hide this more naive foray.

## **INTRODUCTORY MISINFORMATION**

For the "Prologue," the holy of holies were rolled out: the corpse was not Billy the Kid; Garrett lied; and the pardon hearing was unfair. So Pat Garrett is misrepresented as **"thinking" he shot the Kid**; Poe as saying he **"shot the wrong man;"** Garrett as ordering Poe and McKinney to guard the closed bedroom door to **prevent viewing of the body;** and Poe as wondering why Garrett said the body was Billy the Kid. (Pages x-xi) The pardon hearing is faked as presenting compelling evidence that "Ollie L. Roberts" was Billy the Kid. (Page xi)

The "Introduction" begins the hoax's lies: "Brushy" knew "more than most scholars." (Page 4) Salesman Morrison is called a "graduate lawyer" (Page 3) and an "attorney." (Page 4)

**FAKERY: They knew Morrison was no lawyer. In his 2012 book, titled *Billy the Kid: The Lost Interviews*, Jameson stated that on March 8, 1985 - 13 years *before The Return of the Outlaw Billy the Kid* - he interviewed now deceased**

Morrison's daughter who told him Morrison was a paralegal, with a degree from mail-order college LaSalle, in Chicago, Illinois; and did work related to wills, bankruptcy, and taxes; and Jameson called him a "glorified law clerk." (*Billy the Kid: The Lost Interviews*, Page 32) By his 2016 *Pat Garrett: The Man Behind the Badge*, on its page 85, Jameson called Morrison a "paralegal investigator." That confirmed that Morrison was a faker; and Jameson and Bean knew it all along, and still called him a "lawyer" and an "attorney" to trick readers.

The "Shadows of Doubt" chapter has their claims. To Jameson and Bean, since "Brushy" *was* Billy the Kid, but was called an imposter by historians, there must be conspiracies to hide truth; as evidenced by his knowing-things-not-printed trick, coupled with illiteracy yielding the couldn't-study-up trick. Then they lie that he "stunned researchers" by his knowledge of Billy the Kid's life, looked just like him, had scars like him, and his genealogy proved the source of the name "Bonney." (Pages 13-15) Actually proved is only that they had bought the "Brushy Bill" hoax hook, line, and sinker; and were abandoning scruples to get converts.

## MANGLED HISTORY OF BILLY THE KID

"The 'Accepted' History of Billy the Kid" chapter is proclaimed history "that gained acceptance among a fraternity of historians" (Page 18), in contrast to "Brushy's" tales; which, if they differed, were truths proving historians' misinformation. But provided is just a chaos of errors, even mixing in of some of "Brushy's" own mistakes from *Alias Billy the Kid*. The utter ignorance exhibited shows why Jameson and Bean fell prey to the "Brushy" hoax.

There is a fictional early adolescence, with Billy at 14 sent to a New York Children's Aid Society to live with a William E. Antrim, who marries a woman named Catherine (no last name), and moves with her and her son, Joseph, to Silver City, where she died of T.B. There is Billy's Chinese laundry theft and his Arizona "Windy" Cahill killing - though with him erroneously arrested - before getting to his Tunstall job, erroneously as a hired gun, in Lincoln County. There, actually dead Emil Fritz is at the Murphy-Dolan store; and Murphy, rather than the Ring, controlled Sheriff William Brady. This goulash of name-dropping and misinformation, can be seen in the example below:

At one point, Murphy retained lawyer McSween to collect on a $10,000 life insurance policy on partner Fritz, who died while on a trip to Germany. McSween collected the money but refused to hand it over to Murphy. Under orders from Murphy, Sheriff Brady attempted to seize some of Tunstall's cattle as partial payment.

Tunstall decided he needed to confer with Brady and arrange an appointment with him in Lincoln. On 18 February 1878 John Tunstall, riding a buckboard and accompanied by several of his hired gunmen, including Billy the Kid, headed for Lincoln. As they approached the town of Ruidoso, the gunmen spotted a flock of turkeys and set off in pursuit. Seconds later, a group of men led by Jesse [sic] Evans rode up to Tunstall in the wagon and shot him dead.

Tunstall's hired hands, led by Dick Brewer, vowed vengeance and organized themselves into a vigilante group they called the Regulators. (Pages 20-21)

Here are the mistakes:

**Murphy did not hire McSween as an attorney.** McSween was hired to collect the life insurance of deceased Emil Fritz by his siblings, the Administrators, Charles Fritz and Emilie Scholand.

**McSween only collected part of the money**, the rest was kept by the New York City law firm, Donnell and Lawson, as fee for their collection services from the life insurance company.

**McSween refused to hand over the money to James Dolan, not Murphy.** Murphy was dying of alcoholism. The money was for Fritz's heirs; not Dolan. Dolan separately litigated falsely to get it, but his claim was rejected by Probate Judge Florencio Gonzales. McSween kept the money while searching for other eligible heirs in Germany as probate law required.

**Sheriff Brady did not attempt to seize Tunstall's cattle as partial payment.** The mistake is "payment." The Ring made a malicious prosecution case again McSween, with Tunstall added falsely as his business partner. The embezzling complaint against McSween was filed February 4, 1878; with the Grand Jury not until that April. To guarantee the alleged $10,000 in question until the trial's outcome, a Writ of Attachment (meaning appraisal) of both men's property was made to ensure the sum existed in kind to pay the debt if McSween lost. Tunstall's cattle were for the Writ's appraisal, not payment.

**Tunstall did not head to Lincoln on February 18, 1878 to confer with Sheriff Brady.** Knowing that his cattle would be attached that day at his Feliz River ranch, and that his horses were exempted, he was merely taking them to Lincoln. But it was used as an excuse for Ringite Brady to murder him, ahead of the upcoming Grand Jury's likely exonerating of him and McSween.

**Tunstall did not ride on a buckboard.** Tunstall was on horseback with his men. His horse was killed with him.

**Tunstall's men were not gunmen per say.** They were his ranch hands at his Feliz and Peñasco River properties. Billy himself had been given a Peñasco River ranch, along with Fred Waite, as part of Tunstall's plan for mutual ranching along those rivers to the Pecos River. At this stage, there was no overt fighting. Tunstall was building his business.

**They were not approaching the town of Ruidoso.** It did not exist then.

**The murder did not occur at a wagon.** Tunstall was attacked on his horse (according to real Billy's own deposition!).

**The Regulators were not an outlaw vigilante group.** After Tunstall's murder, his men were deputized by Justice of the Peace John Wilson to arrest his murderers, because Lincoln County Ringite Sheriff William Brady was shielding them. After being illegally outlawed by Ringite Governor S.B. Axtell, in his March 9, 1878 Proclamation, they continued their legal mission to make arrests, calling themselves Regulators.

**Vowed vengeance** was not the Regulator cause. They were part of grass-roots uprisings in New Mexico Territory in the 1870's against the Santa Fe Ring's corrupt and terrorist take-overs.

Total misinformation continued. Sheriff Brady's murder is described as for "vengeance," rather than the Regulators' saving McSween from murder by him later that day. (Page 21) The Regulators' Blazer's Mill killing of "Buckshot" Roberts is attributed to seeking "sanctuary" there; when it was a Ring stronghold, no "sanctuary;" and they were there seeking stolen Tunstall stock. (Page 21) McSween is wrongly claimed as overseeing Tunstall's businesses. (Page 21) The Lincoln County War is merely a cowardly McSween barricading himself in his Lincoln house with Regulators to await an attack by Dolan. Sheriff Peppin requests McSween's surrender (for what is unclear), and a five day battle occurs, involving Fort Stanton soldiers. On July 19th, Peppin's deputies set fire to McSween's house and the occupants flee. McSween is killed and Billy the Kid becomes the Regulators' head. (Pages 22-23) The Dolan peace meeting becomes one with Jesse [sic] Evans instead; and ends with Evans's and Dolan's murder of Huston Chapman, wrongly called an attorney hired by Susan McSween *to prosecute the Dolan faction* - instead of Commander Dudley. (Page 23) Missed is Billy Campbell as another murderer - as testified to by real Billy!

Things only got worse. Everything was wrong. Lew Wallace is upset by the Murphy-Dolan beef contracts and Chapman murder, so meets with Billy to break up "the corrupt faction." Wallace promises pardon only for the Brady killing if Billy testifies about the Chapman murder. **[The actual pardon was to be for Brady, Hindman, and Roberts indictments.]** Billy testified and got Evans and Dolan indicted but District Attorney Rynerson jailed Billy. (Page 23) **[Billy was already in sham arrest in 1879 the pardon bargain. He was not jailed by Rynerson.]** The made-up Rynerson jailing is confused with Billy's Santa Fe jailing in 1881, so Billy is portrayed as writing his jail letters to Wallace then, next escaping jail. (Page 23) **[The jail letters were in 1881, and Billy did not escape in 1879: he walked out of a sham arrest.]** Unrelated incidents in 1879 and 1880 get mixed up. Billy's departure (called an escape) from the sham Patrón house arrest (on June 17, 1879), is called "a short time later" to his "January 10 [sic -3], 1880" killing of Joe Grant. And that killing is attributed to "an argument," (Page 23) **[It was just a gunslinger attempt by "Texas Joe" Grant, to shoot Billy in the back.]** Pat Garrett's 1880 election as sheriff leads to the White Oaks posse attacking Billy and his group in the Greathouse ranch with the killing of Jim Carlyle with Billy blamed. (Page 24) **[The Secret Service is missing.]** That ambush makes Billy hide in Fort Sumner and enables Garrett's ambush of him and his "gang," with Tom O'Folliard killed. (Page 24) For the Stinking Springs capture, shot Charlie Bowdre, mistaken for Billy, falls dead beside the rock house (Page 24) **[instead of staggering into the ravine]**. Billy's Mesilla hanging trial is portrayed as only for the Brady killing and on April 26th (Page 25) **[when it was on April 8-9, 1881; and this left out the "Buckshot" Roberts hearing]**. Judge Warren Bristol is called a Murphy-Dolan man (Page 25), **[when he was a Ringite]**. Billy's courthouse-jail escape has a gun hidden in the outhouse, with Bell shot on the stairs during

Billy's return. The Olinger killing and Billy's use of a pickax to break the leg chains is given. (Page 25) Billy's destination of Fort Sumner has town owner, Peter Maxwell, betraying him to Garrett because of "the outlaw's affections for his servant girls!" (Pages 25-26) **[This is made-up.]**

For a July 14, 1881, Maxwell bedroom shooting of Billy, (Page 26), Billy starts in Celsa Gutierrez's house; though she is called one of Maxwell's "servant girls." Billy goes to the side of beef on the porch where deputies Thomas McKinney and John Poe, are "**lurking in the dark.**" Then he enters the bedroom.

**REVEALING ERRORS:** This is not "accepted" history. It is "Brushy's" parroting of Sonnichsen's fake construct that the side of beef was beside Maxwell's door; which Sonnichsen then wrongly placed at the "back porch." That is why "Brushy" made-up that Billy Barlow was shot on the back porch. (See pages 189-190 above)

Noteworthy too is "Brushy's" error about "**the dark.**" Here, Jameson's and Bean's ignorance will be a boon for hoaxbusting: they are unaware of the bright moonlight! So when it comes to "Brushy's" own quotes, they will not do fix-ups if he sticks to "**the dark!!!**"

## INTRODUCING THEIR MAN "BRUSHY"

Jameson and Bean rely on the original "Brushy" hoax, calling him William Henry Roberts (the name he made up). They state that others had claimed to survive Garrett's shooting, but only he had "intimate and confounding Lincoln County War connections" (Page 27); and he had other old-timers who believed he was Billy the Kid. (Page 28)

Morrison enters as a probate attorney; a Missouri Historical Society member; a descendant of Ferdinand Maxwell (brother of Lucien Maxwell, and uncle of Peter Maxwell); and expert on Billy the Kid history. He meets a Joe Hines, who was Jessie Evans, who tells him Billy the Kid was living in Texas. He meets another unnamed old-timer in Missouri (his being J. Frank Dalton as Jesse James from the original hoax is omitted, likely because real Jesse was proved to be in his Kearny, Missouri, grave by DNA testing in 1995, ending Dalton's imposter scam). This Missourian knew Billy the Kid was O.L. Roberts of Hamilton, Texas. So in June of 1949, Morrison went there to meet him. (Pages 28-29)

That meeting presents the *Alias Billy the Kid* tricks that duped Jameson and Bean: fake physical similarities, shackle slipping, and supposed "incredible knowledge of New Mexico history" (Page 33); while too illiterate to study-up. So Morrison believes "Brushy" was Billy and deserved a pardon. And when Morrison took "Brushy" to sites, he had knowledge unknown to historians; so, if not Billy, he was his compatriot! (Page 34)

C.L. Sonnichsen appears as "a noted Southwestern historian," who joined Morrison to write 1955's *Alias Billy the Kid*.

Mentioned is that in 1950, the Governor refused "Brushy's" pardon request, because Billy the Kid "researchers" and Pat Garrett's descendants called him an imposter. Omitted was that, among his total failures, was inability to speak Spanish like Billy.

Updated "Brushy" is called "semi-literate" to encompass his jottings for Morrison. They quote his saying about Billy's letter of March 13, 1879 to Lew Wallace: "I had a friend who spelled it out in a letter for me, what I wanted from Governor Wallace." (Pages 56-57) And real Billy's Spanish fluency is hidden.

**FAKERY: As discussed, that lie broke-down with identical writing; witnesses seeing Billy write; and writing in multiple situations, including solitary confinement in jail.**

To this recitation of *Alias Billy the Kid* gospel, Jameson and Bean added their true-believer twist. They were sure that the solution to converting readers was to let them hear "Brushy" talk; unaware that this was the fiasco Morrison and Sonnichsen had labored to prevent by sly editing of his alleged words! But, through them, "Brushy" would speak from "actual tape recordings made by Morrison." Then, strangely, they say those words came to them from "transcriptions given by Roberts' step-grandson" "Bill Allison," rather than Jameson's later claim of being made by Bean from "Brushy's" tapes *provided by* Allison. (Pages 35, 37)

**LYING: For some reason, Bean's getting the original tapes from Allison, then *transcribing them himself* - as Jameson claimed in his 2012 *Billy the Kid: The Lost Interviews* - here had Allison doing the transcribing. As will be seen, fabricating and misstating are part of the Jameson-Bean style. In fact, by the *Lost Interviews* book, the existence of *The Return of the Outlaw Billy the Kid* - with its accidental revelations of hoax-revealing truth - would be hidden.**

# EXPANDING A FAKE FAMILY TREE

The Geneva Pittmon problem of 1987, had been a disaster for the "Brushy's" accumulating dupes; with her being a close relative and giving his parents as H.O. Roberts and Sara Elizabeth Ferguson and his birthday as August 26, 1879; thus, his being an infant at Billy's fatal shooting.

Jameson and Bean tackled that crisis of truth in chapter called "Birth and Genealogy," by relying on "Brushy"-backing hoaxer, William A. Tunstill's 1988 book, *Billy the Kid and Me Were the Same*. (Pages 37-39) Tunstill's underhanded solution had been to claim that Oliver P. was a different person than Oliver L. - so their "Brushy" - was from a different family; was born in Buffalo Gap, Texas, on December 31, 1859; and had the relatives "Brushy" had claimed. To counter Pittmon's Roberts family Bible, there was claimed to be *another family Bible* from a **Martha Vada Roberts Heath**, and "genealogical papers" from a **Eulaine Haws** of Tyler, Texas. (Pages 90-91)

**FAKERY**: It would take till 2015, 17 years after their book, for "Brushy's" Roberts family relative, Roy L. Haws, to publish his book, *Brushy Bill: Proof His claim to Be Billy the Kid Was a Hoax*, showing that there were not two Roberts families. "Brushy" was his maternal half great-grand-uncle. <u>Martha Vada Roberts Heath</u> was his great-grandmother, and <u>Eulaine Haws</u> was his mother!

As discussed, the Roberts family had two branches from Henry Oliver Roberts's two marriages. Martha Vada was his daughter from his first marriage to Caroline Dunn; so half-sister to "Brushy" who came from Henry Oliver's second marriage to Sara Elizabeth Ferguson. Martha Vada Roberts married Dudley Heath; their daughter, Vada Bell Heath, married D.L. Goff. Their daughter, <u>Eulaine</u>, married Leonard Haws becoming <u>Eulaine Haws</u>. (Haws, Page 137)

Haws revealed that Tunstill conned his mother, Eulaine. Haws wrote: "After reviewing numerous pieces of correspondence between Mr. Tunstill and my mother, I now realize that she mistakenly aided Mr. Tunstill by acknowledging the false genealogy provided her. In the early 1980's, Mr. Tunstill communicated often with her over a period of five years [and] successfully convinced my mother of the validity of his false Roberts family genealogical creations." (Haws, Page 41) Haws also accused *The Return of the Outlaw Billy the Kid* for perpetuating Tunstill's fake Roberts family genealogy. (Haws. Page 39)

Tunstill's fake genealogy was used by Jameson and Bean: "The origin of the name Bonney has long eluded and confused Billy the Kid researchers ... Roberts had an answer, and his claims have subsequently been supported by a genealogy taken from the family Bible of the late Texas resident **Martha Vada Roberts Heath.** Heath was the daughter of Henry Oliver Roberts (brother to James Henry Roberts) and Caroline Dunn (sister to Mary Adeline Dunn). According to genealogy records provided to the authors by Heath descendants and researcher William A. Tunstill, William Henry Roberts' aunt Catherine Bonney (b. 1829) was the daughter of a man named Bonney (first name unknown) and an unnamed wife." (Pages 89-91)

This fakery shows evolution of fix-ups to match Billy. So Jameson and Bean, possibly trusting Tunstill; wrote: "Following the death of Bonney, the wife married William Dunn and the two begat Mary Adeline, Catherine Bonney's half-sister. The Heath genealogy shows Catherine Bonney first married a man named Michael McCarty, who died in the War Between the States. They had a son, Joseph. Catherine subsequently married William Antrim in Santa Fe in 1873." (Page 91)

**FAKERY: The dishonest fix-ups are corrected spelling of "Catherine" for Aunt Bonney, a Michael McCarty (the last name of real Billy's father), a son Joseph (like real Billy's brother), and a marriage to a William Antrim, correctly in Santa Fe and in 1873 (to match Billy's mother's marriage). All this had been unknown to "Brushy;" and, in fact, disproved him by his ignorance.**

This brings up the mysterious and claimed "Heath Bible." (Page 91) Jameson and Bean state: "Brushy's" genealogy claims are supported "by **the family Bible of the late ... Martha Vada Roberts Heath.**" (Page 91) And they claim "**genealogy records provided to the authors by Heath descendants.**" (Page 91) Their diagram of the family tree is labeled: "Genealogy of William Henry Roberts (Billy the Kid) reconstructed from information taken from the family Bible of the late Martha Vada Roberts Heath as well as from Heath family papers." (Page 90) Its having the names Bonney, **McCarty**, and Antrim is claimed as the source of names used by Billy the Kid. (Page 91)

THE HOAX'S FAKE MYSTERY BIBLE: It took 19 years - until the 2012 publication of Jameson's *Billy the Kid: The Lost Interviews* - for the tale of this "Heath Bible" to unfold; albeit with a different story. There, it was claimed to have been found in 1989 by Frederick Bean in a trunk of "Brushy's," belonging to his step-grandson, Bill Allison. Supposedly it also had Morrison's interview tapes and "Brushy's" notebooks.

But "Brushy" never claimed a supporting family Bible. And he never used the name McCarty, unknown in his day. In fact, a Sonnichsen *Alias Billy the Kid* footnote mentions and abandons a name "McCartney" when citing "Brushy's" use of "Bonney": "Young Billy Roberts lived with Mrs. Bonney (later Mrs. Antrim) and her mother ... and passed as her son." (*Alias Billy the Kid*, Page 16) The footnote to that stated: "Another story, current in Silver City, says that Billy the Kid was really named McCartney." (*Alias Billy the Kid*, Page 16)

But think about it. How could this fake Bible, with William Tunstill's 1988 fake genealogy, be found in 1989 by Bean in the trunk belonging to "Brushy," who died in 1950?

Also, Roy L. Haws never mentioned that his Martha Vada Roberts Heath descendant mother, Eulaine Haws, gave Jameson and Bean "genealogy records," for their genealogical fakery as they claim in *The Return of the Outlaw Billy the Kid*.

So the unanswered question is: who planted or made-up this modern forgery (if it exists at all) in the claimed "Brushy"-Allison trunk? Frederick Bean was the trunk's alleged 1989 finder, and would have known about the 1987 Pittmon family Bible claim and the 1988 Tunstill family tree fakery. And, Bean and Jameson, claimed to possess additional Heath genealogical records. This leaves Bean and Jameson as the "Bible's" possible creators. If so, that would put *The Return of the Outlaw Billy the Kid* in a darker light of malicious hoaxing to advance "Brushy" as Billy the Kid by purposeful tricking of readers. And their belief in "Brushy" may have felt like justification

# "BRUSHY" TALKS NONSENSE

"Brushy" talks, but not entirely in his own words. Jameson and Bean admit "inserting important historical and geographical references [for] clarity." (Page 37) Fortunately, their historical ignorance spares "Brushy's" big errors, exposing the Morrison-Sonnichsen fix-ups of the same tapes for *Alias Billy the Kid*..

## *EARLY TRAVELS WITH "BRUSHY"*

"Brushy's" early history fixes-up his original confabulations. His aunt, now spelled Catherine, instead of Kathleen Ann Bonney, takes him on unnamed travels until marrying Antrim - with newly added first name of William - in Santa Fe, in corrected date of 1873, with moving to Silver City, where "Brushy" has his fake friendship with Jesse [sic] Evans. Sticking to age 12 for leaving Silver City for no particular reason, "Brushy" returns to his Roberts family for two years, being called "Kid" Roberts because he was small. He then leaves his abusive "Wild Henry" Roberts father, becoming the Texas Kid, traveling the mid-west, working with Belle Starr, encountering Jesse James and the Younger brothers, and returning to Silver City for his fake aunt's dying as Catherine Ann Bonney Antrim. (Pages 39-41)

## *FAKING THE LINCOLN COUNTY PERIOD*

"Brushy's erroneous confabulations, plus fix-ups to match real history, have him go, in 1877, to Arizona work *near* the Gila *River* (fixed-up from the Gila *Ranch*, but still not real Billy's history), where he meets Jesse [sic] Evans and Lincoln County War outlaws. (Page 41) He then crosses the Guadalupe Mountains on foot to Seven Rivers where he joins Jim and John Jones herding cattle for John Chisum, then works for Pete Maxwell at Bosque Redondo (added for name-dropping, but actually the Apache and Navajo concentration camp before Lucien Maxwell bought it to make the town of Fort Sumner). (Page 41) Then "Brushy" works for Frank Coe near the Ruidoso River, then for Jesse [sic] Evans, then for the Tunstall Ranch on the Feliz River; where among the listed workers is added Dave Rudabaugh from 1880. (Page 42)

For the Lincoln County War period, everything is wrong; but with the let-"Brushy"-speak policy, his ignorance is now shown.

But, the dishonest fix-up is adding the Regulators. (Page 45) The conflict is about supplying beef to the Mescalero Indian Reservation. Tunstall and McSween are partners owning a Lincoln store competing with Murphy and Dolan. They accused each other of cattle stealing, but the Murphy side was backed by Santa Fe Ring and by Sheriff Brady. (Pages 42-43)

"Brushy" stated: "I remember how it all started ... Lawyer McSween had been hired by the Murphy bunch to prosecute some of the Chisum cowboys for rustling cattle, but when he found out the Chisum boys were only taking back Chisum cows that were stolen by Murphy's men, [McSween] switched sides and joined up with John Tunstall. The Murphy-Dolan Ring operated a store where they sold supplies to the ranches, and then John Tunstall came along and opened his own store. That's where the trouble really started, between the two stores. McSween formed a partnership with Tunstall when he worked the case for Emil Fritz." (Page 43)

**FAKERY: Everything is wrong. McSween represented the Fritz estate. He had no partnership with Tunstall. He had been a Murphy-Dolan lawyer, but for their mercantile business. The "Murphy bunch" were themselves stealing Chisum's cattle for their beef contracts. McSween was not working for Murphy and Dolan when Tunstall came; having quit in opposition to their corruption. The Fritz life insurance money case had nothing to do with Tunstall. It was being done by McSween before his arrival; but was made the Ring's embezzlement case to attack McSween and enable Tunstall's murder. There was no "Murphy-Dolan Ring;" "The House" was a front for T.B. Catron.**

### MAULING THE FRITZ INSURANCE POLICY CASE

Next shown is that "Brushy" had mauled the Emil Fritz life insurance money case far worse than Sonnichsen had revealed. "Brushy" stated: "There was a settlement when Fritz died and the Murphy-Dolan Store claimed that Fritz owed a bill of goods. McSween got the settlement money and the Murphy bunch claimed it, so they rode over to Mesilla and got a court order in the form of a **writ that would give them some of the goods in McSween's and Tunstall's store and a herd of blooded horses out at Tunstall's ranch.**" (Page 44)

**FAKERY AND DISHONEST FIX-UP:** Everything is wrong. It was an embezzlement case against McSween by Fritz's New Mexico heirs claiming he kept Emil Fritz's life insurance policy money. Dolan made a *separate* case to get the money by claiming Fritz owed it to "The House;" but lost in probate court. The "writ" was for property attachment on McSween; with Tunstall falsely added as his partner, to attach his property too, against future payment if McSween lost the embezzlement case in the Grand Jury.

And "Brushy's" quote is a fixed-up from *Alias Billy the Kid*, in which he stated: "Tunstall had a herd of fine horses of his own. <u>He decided that he would drive the horses over to Lincoln and surrender them until the case was cleared up.</u>" (*Alias Billy the Kid*, Page 25) And that was wrong too!

## MAULING TUNSTALL'S MURDER

"Brushy" confabulates Tunstall's murder: "We sat on our horses off in some brush watching when Dolan and his boys rode up on Tunstall [and killed him] ... I swore that day at the funeral that I would make them pay for the dirty deed." (Pages 44-45)

**FAKERY:** Everything is wrong. And real Billy gave the facts in his Frank Warner Angel deposition. He and the others fled at the posse's arrival, and did not see the killing. And he was not at Tunstall's funeral, having been illegally jailed by Sheriff Brady.

## MAULING THE MORTON AND BAKER KILLING

For pursuit of Tunstall's killers, the Jameson-Bean dishonest fix-up is adding Regulators, unknown to "Brushy." For the Morton and Baker killing, "Brushy" stated that, after their capture, they were taken to Lincoln, by "**the north road, over the mountains.**" And he alone shoots them. (Page 47)

**FAKERY:** This is wrong. "Brushy" had made-up the route from his Morrison touring of Lincoln, thinking the east to west Capitan Mountains were a barrier to cross to the town. He was unaware that the Regulators took the military road, skirting their eastern terminus. And the Regulators shot escaping Morton and Baker as a group.

## MAULING THE BRADY KILLING

The Sheriff Brady murder scene adds to "Brushy's" confabulation that Brady was pursuing him, as Billy, for "cattle theft," with a fix-up that "Brushy," as Billy, was arrested for that crime, had his "pearl-handled .44" confiscated, then was released on bond. (Page 47)

FAKERY: The fix-ups are a dishonest attempt to match Billy's historical arrest by Brady, but are wrong. Brady was not after Billy; Billy did not steal cattle in that period; the arrest was illegal detention of deputized Billy, Fred Waite, and Town Constable Atanacio Martinez to block their serving arrest warrants on Tunstall's murderers; and Brady confiscated Billy's Winchester '73 carbine.

The Brady ambush, retains "Brushy's" confabulations about aiming for Billy Matthews, and going with Fred Waite (fixed-up from "Wayte") to retrieve his pearl-handled .44, "taken from me when he arrested me on cattle-rustling warrants." And shooting Mathews [sic] hits them from "behind an adobe wall down the street." (Page 49)

FAKERY: This is all wrong. As already discussed, "Brushy" had no idea why Brady was ambushed. There were no warrants on Billy. The gun taken was a Winchester '73 carbine. The Regulators were behind an adobe wall. Billy Matthews fired from the Cisneros house. And the motive was saving McSween from murder by Brady when he returned to Lincoln later that day in anticipation of his Grand Jury Trial.

## MAULING THE "BUCKSHOT" ROBERTS KILLING

New "Brushy" confabulations are added: that "Buckshot" Roberts "was worse than any of them;" that he raided San Patricio with "Murphy's gang;" that "Brushy" "shot it out" with "Buckshot;" and that the incident ended with Bowdre shooting "Buckshot." (Page 50)

FAKERY: This is all wrong. The missed point is that "Buckshot" resisted arrest for his murder warrant as a Tunstall murder posseman, first shot at Bowdre, then was shot by Bowdre. No one else shot at "Buckshot." And Bowdre's shooting was arguable self-defense.

### MAULING THE LINCOLN COUNTY WAR BATTLE

The Lincoln County War keeps "Brushy's" original confabulations; but with fix-ups of adding "Regulators" to escort McSween into Lincoln; adding two more days to "Brushy's" three day War; and using "black," or no mentioned skin color, instead of racist "Brushy's" "nigger" soldiers. But added is "Brushy's" error that Mrs. McSween asked for aid from Dudley "[w]hile the house was burning." (Pages 52) And, for Billy's escape route, "Brushy" says the men crossed the *Peñasco* River - 100 miles to the south of the *Bonito* River, which they did cross! (Page 52)

FAKERY: Confirmed are "Brushy's" erroneous *Alias Billy the Kid* confabulations. But exposed are sly Jameson-Bean fix-ups to fake that he knew about the Regulators, knew length of the battle (though they are wrong too, since it lasted six days), and was not a crude racist. And "Brushy's" ignorant name-dropping is revealed by the crossing of the *Peñasco* River - a 100 miles south of the *Bonito* River, which they did cross! And, like "Brushy," Jameson and Bean have no idea why the battle was fought.

## *FAKING THE LEW WALLACE PERIOD*

### MAULING THE CHAPMAN MURDER

Huston Chapman's murder has "Brushy's" "Me and Tom were standing right there and saw the whole thing." (Page 56) But what he "saw," was: "**Mrs, McSween and her lawyer, Chapman,** walk up to Evans and Dolan and Chapman [and kill him]." (Page 56)

FAKERY AND FIX-UP: This is wrong. Chapman was alone, accidentally met the group, and was killed. And missing is that, horrifically, Dolan poured liquor from his flask to set fire to his clothing. And real Billy testified to the correct scene, getting Dolan, Campbell, and Evans indicted!

And proved is the Morrison-Sonnichsen fix-up of this extreme gaffe. Their book's "Brushy" said: "When we came out of the saloon that night ... we run into Chapman, the lawyer for Mrs. McSween." (*Alias Billy the Kid*, Page 33) They had done a complete rewrite to remove "Brushy's" fatal error of adding Susan McSween, which was now revealed!

## MAULING THE PARDON BARGAIN

For the Wallace pardon bargain, "Brushy's" original confabulation got a funny twist: "Governor Wallace had **offered a thousand dollars to the outlaw** if he would turn himself in and testify about the illegal activities of the Dolan faction." (Page 56) "Brushy" was quoted: "One day a fellow brought word that Governor Wallace had offered a thousand dollars if I would come in and **give myself up for the murder of Chapman**." (Page 56) Then added was: "testify about the murder of Chapman." (Page 56) And "Brushy" was utterly confused, even unaware of what indictments needed to be annulled, making up that "[t]hey had fresh warrants out on us for rounding up [Chisum's] cattle [as owed payment]. (Page 57)

FAKERY AND FIX-UP: This is all wrong. Proved is that "Brushy" had no idea whatsoever of the pardon bargain.

This proves that Sonnichsen-Morrison had done a complete fix-up. Their book's quote was: "I was standing there with them and saw who killed [Chapmen] ... I heard that Governor Wallace had offered a thousand dollars for me if I would come and testify. I wrote him back that I would come in if he would annul those indictments against me." (*Alias Billy the Kid*, Page 33) So Sonnichsen-Morrison had lifted the words from Billy's first pardon plea letter, of March 13, 1879, and "Brushy" never mouthed them himself! That letter stated: "*I was present when Mr. Chapman was murderded and know who did it and if it were not for these indictments I would have made it clear before now. if it is in your power to Annully those indictments I hope you will do so so as to give me a chance to explain.*"

The next problem was Billy's letter to Wallace in light of "Brushy's" claimed "illiteracy." "Brushy" says: "I had a friend who spelled it out in a letter for me, what I wanted from Governor Wallace." (Pages 56-57)

FAKERY: This proves "Brushy" participated in the illiteracy scam, putting it on the Morrison rehearsal tapes, while both knew from his notebooks and letters that he was not illiterate. But they knew he could not have written with Billy's beautiful script or articulateness.

Jameson and Bean hide "Brushy's" confabulation that the Wallace pardon meeting was at Juan Patrón's house in the daytime (*Alias Billy the Kid*, Page 34), instead of "Squire" Wilson's. The provided quote proves dishonest fix-up: "We shook hands on it before Tom and I **left Squire Wilson's that night.**" (Page 58) (And real "Brushy" would have said: "Tom and me!")

But they retain "Brushy's" ignorance of the deal: "The governor promised to pardon me if I would stand trial on my indictments in Lincoln. I also agreed to testify against Dudley at his court-martial hearing at Fort Stanton, and testify before the grand jury in the Chapman case." (Page 58)

**FAKERY: Standing trial on indictments and testifying against Dudley were not in the bargain.**

Kept are "Brushy's" errors that Wallace promised to appoint his personal attorney, Ira Leonard, to defend him for indictment trials; that Leonard did not come; that Albert J. Fountain was appointed by the court; that the bargain was to stand trial in Lincoln; and that the change of venue meant Wallace reneged on the deal, causing "Brushy" to leave before testifying. (*Alias Billy the Kid*, Page 34) But a dishonest Jameson-Bean fix-up has "Brushy" correctly testify against Chapman's murderers. (Page 58)

**FAKERY: "Brushy," Jameson, and Bean were all lying. And "Brushy" had disastrously garbled the pardon's 1879 Grand Jury with the 1881 Mesilla trial with Fountain.**

Given is "Brushy's" quote allegedly describing Wallace's broken promise at the time of the Grand Jury: "They pinned the whole affair [Brady shooting] on me because they wanted to get rid of Billy the Kid. The governor broke his word to me. I did what I promised I would do, but he didn't keep his promise to me." (Page 59)

**FAKERY: Confused "Brushy," for the 1879 pardon deal, with its <u>Lincoln County</u> Grand Jury testimony as Billy's part of the bargain, was incorrectly using the Billy prompt letter of March 4, 1881 from the Santa Fe jail, about anticipating his <u>Mesilla</u> hanging trials, and needing the pardon; saying: "*I have done everything that I promised you I would, and you have done nothing that you promised me.*"**

## MANGLING THE JIM CARLYLE KILLING

Ignorant of why Billy was being pursued, and unaware of Secret Service participation as contributing to the Greathouse Ranch ambush, "Brushy" made-up the adversary as the "Murphy bunch" who had deputized a "James Carlyle ... to head up the posse and hunt us down" as cattle rustlers. That lead to his fabrication of Carlyle telling Billy: "I wear a badge and that's all I need to bring you in." Then Carlyle is killed in friendly fire. And "Brushy" flees to Las Vegas. (Pages 60-61)

**FAKERY: In truth, Jim Carlyle, a blacksmith and White Oaks posseman under Deputy Will Hudgens, went into the ranch house to negotiate with Billy. The rest of the scene is from Billy's prompt letter of December 12, 1880 to Lew Wallace about Carlyle's killing by fellow possemen.**

**But revealed is how "Brushy" built on his prompts. In the letter, Billy writes: "*I noticed <u>in the Las Vegas Gazette</u> a piece which stated that, Billy "the" Kid, the name by which I am known in the Country was the captain of a Band of Outlaws*. That gave "Brushy" his <u>Las Vegas destination</u>!**

## *FAKING PAT GARRETT KNOWLEDGE*

For chapter titled "Enter Garrett," the authors give "Brushy's" faking of special knowledge from *Alias Billy the Kid*: "Garrett] had come over from Texas after he had shot his partner in an argument over some buffalo hides" (Page 61); all being unaware of the actual Joe Briscoe killing. And "Brushy" had no idea of why Garrett was pursuing Billy, so he guessed: "As soon as Garrett got elected, with this killing of Carlyle tacked on me, [he] had an excuse to come after me;" when it was for the Brady, Hindman, and Roberts indictments. (page 61)

## *FAKING BILLY'S CAPTURE AND JAILING*

For Garrett's killing of Tom O'Folliard, "Brushy" falsely includes, in the tracking posse, a Deputy Tip [sic] McKinney, as O'Folliard's cousin; with newly revealed confabulation that "when the dying [O'Folliard] begged for water, the deputy refused to give him any." (Page 62) And after the capture, "Brushy" claimed he spoke with "Tip" McKinney about Tom O'Folliard's death. (Page 63)

**FAKERY:** Nothing is true. As discussed, Kip McKinney was not present at the ambush or Stinking Springs, and was not O'Folliard's cousin.

The Stinking Springs capture has a dishonest Jameson-Bean fix-up that Billy and his group were Regulators. (Pages 62-63)

**FIX-UP REVEALED:** Original "Brushy" and team did not know about Regulators. But Jameson's and Bean's fix-up adding them was wrong. The Regulators disbanded two years earlier. Except for past Regulators Billy and Charlie Bowdre, the other captives were just petty criminals.

"Brushy" describes shot Bowdre's being mistaken for him: "Charlie wore a **big hat like mine.** (Page 62)

**FUTURE FAKERY:** As Jameson's hoaxing increased in later books, "big hat" would fix to "sombrero" to match Billy.

"Brushy's" post-capture scene at the Maxwell house had been worse than *Alias Billy the Kid* let on. "Brushy" flubbed his Jim East letter prompt for a meeting with Luz Maxwell and Paulita. He really said: "Mrs. Maxwell asked them to unchain me from Rudabaugh so I **could go in the other room to be with the Indian girl [from his tintype exchange fable].**" (Page 63)

**FIX-UP:** Sonnichsen had faked "Brushy's" quote to mimic accuracy: **"After we went in the house, Mrs. Maxwell asked them to cut me loose from Rudabaugh so I could go into another room with her daughter."** (*Alias Billy the Kid*, Page 38)

For the Santa Fe jailing, three letters to Governor Wallace are mentioned as unanswered – there were four.

## *MANGLING THE MESILLA TRIALS*

For Mesilla, the "Buckshot" Roberts case is entirely omitted.

**FIX-UP:** Oddly, this was the case Morrison and Sonnichsen had used to "prove" "Brushy's" special knowledge as: **"In April I pleaded to the federal indictment and it was thrown out of court. Judge Leonard represented me on this indictment. He got it thrown out by the judge."** (Page 39) This leaves open that this quote was shockingly created by them for their book, since it was not in the transcript used by Jameson and Bean as being "Brushy's" actual quotes.

The Brady trial reproduces "Brushy's" errors in *Alias Billy the Kid*, but now includes "Brushy's" near verbatim repeat of a prompt source: "**Even Pat Garrett admitted to Miguel Otero that he doubted I ever fired a shot at Brady because it was more likely that I would have tried to get Matthews, since I hated him.**" (Page 67)

HOAXING REVEALED: Demonstrated is "Brushy's" studying-up by prompt sources from Morrison and Sonnichsen for rehearsal tapings. He was parroting a source footnote in *Alias Billy the Kid*, which quoted from Miguel Otero's 1936 book, *The Real Billy the Kid*; and stated: "Pat Garrett told Miguel Otero that he 'doubted if the Kid had even fired at Brady because it was more likely that he would have tried to get Matthews, whom he hated." (*Alias Billy the Kid*, Page 28) Obviously, real Billy would not have known what Miguel Otero wrote. Sonnichsen had caught that, and edited it out for *Alias Billy the Kid*.

## *SILENCING "BRUSHY" FOR THE GREAT ESCAPE*

For the Lincoln jailing and escape, Jameson and Bean end "Brushy's" quotes, and just summarize, using the Severo Gallegos escape horse and rope fable. Fixed-up is Goss, to "Godfrey Gauss" (though it was Gottfried); and Higinio Salazar is Ygenio. (Page 69)

Retained are *Alias Billy the Kid's* errors of "Brushy" staying with Charlie Bowdre's widow (who had left Fort Sumner the year before), and at "Yerby's," where Billy did not stay. (Page 72) And Barney Mason is still wrongly called Garrett's brother-in-law, when he merely had a double marriage with Garrett. Celsa Gutierrez is still called Garrett's sister-in-law, wanting to marry "Brushy;" and her actual husband, Saval, is still thought to be her brother because of the shared Gutierrez name. (Pages 71-72)

## *"BRUSHY'S" DEATH SCENE*

To Jameson and Bean, the death scene was the holy grail. So their faith in "Brushy's" words, combined with their historical ignorance, give a view of him in the raw, comparable to his Mabry pardon hearing fiasco. This version would not be seen again as Jameson wised-up more and fixed-up more for his later "Brushy"-backing books. But now they opened a can of worms for "Brushy!"

## ACCIDENTALLY LETTING "BRUSHY" REVEAL HIS HOAXBUSTING MOON PROBLEM

The chapter "William Henry Roberts' Story Part I: 1859-1881," just uses *Alias Billy the Kid's* death scene summary, with no quotes; and mindlessly repeats: "Billy, **easily seen in the moonlit yard**, immediately drew return fire from the lawmen." (Page 73)

Hoaxbusting treasure is in the chapter "Quien es? A Reexamination of the Shooting in Fort Sumner" (Pages 101-133) where "Brushy" finally speaks. **And he says July 14, 1881's night was dark!** And, as discussed above, in reality, the near-full moon, hovering at the horizon, made it light as day!

Revealingly, "Brushy's" dark night was **not in *Alias Billy the Kid*.** Sonnichsen, as supposedly quoting "Brushy" for the death scene," in the chapter he titled "Death **By Moonlight**," wrote: "I ran through the gate into Maxwell's back yard **in the bright moonlight**." (*Alias Billy the Kid,* Page 49)

So Jameson and Bean had naively copied *Alias Billy the Kid's* "Brushy" being "**easily seen in the moonlit yard.**" (Page 73) But unaware of the moon's significance, they left it untampered when quoting "Brushy's" own transcript: "[After hearing the shot from Pete Maxwell's place] I pulled one of my .44's and ran through the door, **trying to see in the dark.** Two more shots came from the shadow beside the Maxwell house. **I couldn't find a target. It was too dark to see.**" (Page 112) "Brushy stuck to darkness with: "emptying my six-shooter at the shadow where I saw the muzzleflash." (Page 113) And "Brushy" used the darkness to explain the accidental killing of Barlow: "Garrett knew by now that he'd **killed the wrong man in the dark.**" (Page 117) Also, "Brushy" had Celsa say: "They took the body of your friend inside the house and they say it is yours ...**Your partner looks very much like you in the dark.**" (Page-117)

CRACKING THE "BRUSHY BILL" IMPOSTER HOAX: Thus, "Brushy's" dark night moon error, in one fell swoop, proved not only that he was not present in Fort Sumner on the night of July 14, 1881, but that Sonnichsen and Morrison had willfully, dishonestly, and despicably fixed-up and concealed his fatal error to perpetrate their hoax of his as being Billy the Kid. And by Jameson's next books, his newly fixed-up bright moonlight would prove his fall into active hoaxing himself.

## ACCIDENTALLY LETTING "BRUSHY" REVEAL THE REST OF HIS DEATH SCENE ERRORS

Jameson and Bean also provided the rest of "Brushy's" hoax-revealing claims; as follows:

"Brushy" said he had been hiding at "the Yerby Ranch." (Page 105) **[Billy was in Maxwell's sheep camps.]**

"Brushy" said: "Pat's wife was a sister to my friend, Saval Gutierrez, and Saval told me that Pat was after me – he heard it from his sister." (Page 106) "She was another of Saval's sisters, named Celsa, and she had been a sweetheart of mine." (Page 116) **[Celsa and Saval were husband and wife.]**

"Brushy" said he and Billy Barlow went to Jesus Silva's house in Fort Sumner. **[Billy was at Celsa and Saval's house; Barlow was fictional; and Silva was name-dropping Maxwell's foreman.]**

"Brushy" said, after hearing three shots, he ran to "Maxwell's back porch." (Page 113) **[The back porch was unrelated; but "Brushy" got it from Sonnichsen's prompt source claiming the bedroom was there with the side of beef beside it.]**

"Brushy" said "too many guns were shooting at me;" and that he emptied his .44. (Page 113) **[There were over 200 residents, and no such gunfire was heard.]**

As wounded, "Brushy" said: "I ran past a little adobe shack down the alley from Pete Maxwell's" from which a Mexican woman took him in. (Page 114) **[He was unaware that Fort Sumner's buildings were arranged around the perimeter of the Fort's original parade ground.]**

"Brushy" quoted Celsa: "They took the body of your friend inside the house." (Page 116) **[He tried to match the historical scene.]**

"Brushy" has Celsa present the Barlow hoax with the murdered and concealed innocent victim: "Pat is telling everyone you are dead. They took the body of your friend inside the house and they say it is yours. Some men from the town have already been sent to dig a grave by lantern light ... Your partner looks very much like you in the dark except for his beard ... Pat says they will bury the body in the morning. If the coffin is closed, who will guess that you are not inside it?" (Pages 116-117)

FUTURE HOAXING: Remember this. When omniscient quoting appeared in a future Jameson book, it would be a forgery in the mouth of a new character, and would be an expanded vehicle for using the characters to present the hoax's conspiracy theories and to add information to match hoax claims! (See pages 561-562 below)

## *LIFE AFTER BILLY'S DEATH*

For "Brushy's" life after Billy's death, Jameson and Bean abandon "Brushy's" quotes (Page 75) and give *Alias Billy the Kid's* version of peripatetic travels and Wild West name-dropping; with Judge Parker now fleshed-out as: " 'Hanging Judge' Isaac C. Parker at Fort Smith, Arkansas. (Pages 76-77)

The Governor Mabry pardon fiasco is rationalized as "Brushy" being rattled by reporters, being scared by historical family members and alleged armed guards; being old; and being rejected because his answers "conflicted with accepted notions." (Page 83) Recycling Morrison's original double-talk, they claim the pardon was refused "without a legal hearing." (Page 84)

In the chapter "Tracking William Henry Roberts" they try to validate "Brushy's" post-Billy's shooting life, but they conclude that lack of records and his claimed 12 aliases made the quest impossible. (Page 93) They do, however, think a badge he owned showed he worked for the Anti-Horse Thief Association. And a medal was claimed by hoaxing author, William Tunstill, to be from the Spanish War. They conclude slyly: "[W]e were unable to disprove any of Roberts' contentions." (Page 100)

## **ALLEGED ANALYSES**

In their chapter titled "Evidence For and Against William Henry Roberts as Billy the Kid" (Pages 135-163), Jameson and Bean try to mimic a real investigation as to "Brushy's" being Billy the Kid by claiming physical similarities, "Brushy's" "revelations," anecdotal evidence, and identification Affidavits. But they first conclude: "There exists a great deal of evidence that leads to conclusion for some that William Henry Roberts was, in fact, Billy the Kid." (Page 135) (But even the "William Henry" was fake!)

## *FAKING PHYSICAL SIMILARITIES*

Parroted are *Alias Billy the Kid's* error-filled and fake "physical similarities," including shackle-slipping and scars. Misstated is Dewitt Travis's big eye teeth (canines) claim (*Alias Billy the Kid*, Page 74) to lie that "Brushy" had "protruding front teeth" like Billy. Claimed is "Brushy" prominent ears matched Billy's (though that error came from the tintype's right ear being pushed out by the tilted hat brim). (Page 136) They do a dishonest fix-up by removing Morrison's gaffe about a funny "left" ear (from misunderstanding the tintype's right one). (Page 136)

## *FAKING "BRUSHY'S" "REVELATIONS"*

For claiming special knowledge, Jameson and Bean do the not-reading-things-printed trick, by calling him "semiliterate," "could barely read" (Page 137); and repeat his confabulation: "I had a friend who spelled it out in a letter for me, what I wanted from Governor Wallace." (Pages 56-57) But aware of his notebooks and letter to Morrison in *Alias Billy the Kid*, they say he had "barely legible scrawl." (Page 137) (That, of course, made him literate with bad handwriting; and canceled out his match with real Billy's beautifully modified Spencerian handwriting).

And they provide no "Brushy" revelations, just his name-dropping, parroting from sources, and observations from Morrison's tours. Worse, they dishonestly fix-up his quotes from *Alias Billy the Kid*, to conceal errors they catch, and his racism.

Repeated would be Lincoln town itself, from "Brushy's" 1949 and 1950 field-trips there with Morrison; as well as miscellaneous claims: like "shooting black soldiers," and citing the federal versus territorial indictment for the Mesilla trial from real Billy's Caypless letter. And the hearsay affidavits from *Alias Billy the Kid* are repeated.

### LINCOLN TRIP REVELATIONS

Lincoln "revelations" are about just two sites: the old Lincoln County courthouse-jail and the McSween house. Unrecognized by Jameson and Bean, "Brushy" was confabulating from his Morrison sight-seeing tours, and made the fatal error of a "north road, over the [Capitan] mountains." (*Alias Billy the Kid*, Page 47)

### FAKING THE COURTHOUSE-JAIL

For the courthouse-jail revelations, given is "Brushy's" report of the well-known later addition of stairs to the second-story balcony. (Page 138) Repeated is his wrong location of the armory as opposite Garrett's office (now with a diagram!). (Pages 138, 141) For the escape, "Brushy" erroneously names Sam Corbett as an accomplice, and does his shackle-slipping and striking of Deputy Bell. (Pages 146-147) Given is *Alias Billy the Kid's* fake Severo-Gallegos-Kid-helping-escape fable (Page 150); and "Brushy's" parroting of Morrison's interview with Yginio Salazar's adopted daughter who gave the known information that Yginio cut off Billy's shackles. (Page 151) So there are no revelations.

### FAKING THE McSWEEN HOUSE

For the McSween house revelations, claimed is "Roberts' intimacy with the layout of the McSween house and yard could only have come from personal experience." (Page 144) After the Lincoln County War Battle arson, the house is gone. "Brushy" claimed a kitchen window, a corral fence, and a woodpile; which is called "amazing." (Page 143) That was it!

For filler, added are "Brushy's" fake "Murphy men ... just across the river" - where no attackers were. (Page 142) And for the escape, Jameson and Bean dishonestly rewrite his *Alias Billy the Kid* racist fabrication: "We opened the back door and looked out just as **Bob Beckwith and some of them niggers started to come in**" (*Alias Billy the Kid*, Page 31); to: "We opened the back door and looked out just as **Bob Beckwith with some of those soldiers tried to rush us.**" (Page 142) Then there is "Brushy's" parroting of Billy's Dudley Court of Inquiry testimony about escaping people (Page 145), but with missing the key fact of shooting white soldiers. There are no revelations.

### FAKING THE SHOOTING BLACK SOLDIERS

Covering-up racist "Brushy's "nigger soldiers" as "black troopers," Jameson and Bean, while dishonestly adding the name "Regulators," claim the common knowledge that Fort Stanton's 9th Cavalry was black was unknown until "Brushy!" (Page 144) And they are unaware that "Brushy" missed that they rode horses, or that there were white infantrymen, a Gatling gun, and a howitzer cannon; and that, for Lincoln, he had lied that "nigger" troopers fired from the hillside. There are no revelations.

## FAKE REVELATION OF FEDERAL VERSUS TERRITORIAL INDICTMENTS

Taken in by the knowing-things-not-printed trick, Jameson and Bean repeat "Brushy's" parroting of real Billy's April 15, 1881 letter to Attorney Edgar Caypless about his federal indictment thrown out of court, then being tried for his Territorial charge. (Page 145) This is no revelation.

## FAKE REVELATION OF THE JIM CARLYLE KILLING

Taken in by the knowing-things-not-printed trick, Jameson and Bean repeat "Brushy's" parroting of real Billy's December 12, 1880 letter to Lew Wallace about the Jim Carlyle killing. (Page 148) This is no revelation.

## FAKE REVELATION OF THE INDIAN GIRL AND SCARF

Taken in by the knowing-things-not-printed trick, Jameson and Bean repeat "Brushy's" confabulating about trading the Billy the Kid tintype for a scarf from an Indian girl at the Maxwell house (Page 148) - as lifted from Walter Noble Burns's fable in his 1926 *The Saga of Billy the Kid*. This is no revelation.

## *FAKE EVIDENCE FROM ANECDOTES*

Anecdotes, or hearsay, are not evidence in law or historical investigation. But Jameson and Bean present an absurd list of them, thinking they link "Brushy" and Billy; as follows:

1) Once, on a Hico, Texas, street, a mother called to her child, "Billy!" And Roberts turned. (Page 152) (The authors forgot that *they and he* claimed his name was both "Brushy *Bill*" and "*William* Henry"!)

2) In 1990, the grandson of a Pinkerton detective, said, in 1945, his grandfather called out to "Brushy": "Bonnie [sic] ... you're under arrest." (Pages 153-154) (This proves that in 1945 there were at least two Texas eccentrics.)

3) In 1983, a Texan wrote a letter saying that Garrett's blind daughter told him Pat did not shoot Billy. (Page 154) (This is why hearsay is meaningless.)

4) Yginio Salazar is cited as believing Billy was not killed. (Page 154) That is true. But Yginio had no first-hand knowledge. His belief came from a visit he got years later from a teacher from Mexico - not "Brushy." That pretender, with forgotten name,

disappeared. By then, Yginio was an unreliable morphine addict, from pain of the two, Lincoln County War bullets, still in his back.

5) In 1948, someone told someone in Las Cruces, New Mexico, that Billy was not shot by Garrett, because he saw him in Mexico in 1914. He knew Billy, he said, when they lived in Silver City from 1868 to 1871. (Page 155) (Real Billy lived in Silver City from 1873 to 1875.)

## *FAKE AFFIDAVITS THAT "BRUSHY" WAS BILLY*

*Alias Billy the Kid*'s five Affidavits by non-historical people are repeated, and are still meaningless. (Pages 155-161)

## *IGNORING CONTRARY EVIDENCE*

Having ignored real history books or primary documents, Jameson and Bean end with "Evidence Against William Henry Roberts as Billy the Kid," and claim: "The only available evidence for Billy the Kid being shot and killed in Fort Sumner on 14 April 1881 is the word of Pat Garrett." (Page 161) Their foregone conclusion is: "[T]he case "for Roberts being Billy the Kid is considerably stronger than the case against." (Page 162)

## FAKE "FORENSIC" PHOTO-COMPARISON

Jameson's and Bean's jewel in their crown for "Brushy" was supposed to be updating his evidence with modern science. To them, that meant their 1990 "Photo-Comparison Study" using "computer technology" - which, they said, replicated the CIA, FBI, Interpol, and Scotland yard - to compare a photos of "Brushy" from *Alias Billy the Kid* to the correctly named Dedrick-Upham Billy the Kid tintype. (Page 165) The resulting silly study would ultimately yield Jameson's empty boast, in a 2003 *True West* magazine article about "Brushy" being Billy, that "history needed to be rewritten." (See pages 299-300 below)

For the study, they picked a Dr. Scott T. Acton, at the Department of Electrical and Computer Engineering and the Laboratory for Vision Systems and Advanced Graphic Laboratory at the University of Texas; and claimed no expertise for him.

And there was a starting-gate problem. A year before their study, one had been done by the Lincoln County Heritage Trust: the Lincoln, New Mexico, museum which, at that time, housed the Billy the Kid tintype. That study was headed by world-famous forensic anthropologist, Clyde Snow, along with a Thomas G. Kyle of the Los Alamos National Laboratory, and historical experts, comparing the tintype to the over 150 alleged photographs of Billy the Kid, along with a control of 100 photographs of random men. Historian, Don Cline, in his unpublished 1988 *Brushy Bill Roberts: I Wasn't Billy the Kid*, referenced that study. It concluded that "Brushy" was not Billy based on eye position, nose, chin, and ears - namely everything on his head! And another pretender, John Miller, did as badly. (Cline, Page 169)

Jameson and Bean, of course, opposed this study. Concealing that Clyde Snow was in charge, they attacked Thomas Kyle as in an "economic" conspiracy to maintain the historical "status quo." They meaninglessly questioned his equipment and statistical methods. And they got mean: saying that, for him, the whole thing had been "more like a hobby." Finally, they declared that ears should not have been used! (Page 166-172)

## *THE ACTON STUDY*

Jameson and Bean enthuse about Dr. Scott Acton's "state of the art facilities," and inventory his equipment. Thus, revealed is his shockingly old computer system from 1972 and 1976, and apparently unimpressive 92% success rate ("success" not being defined). Furthermore, Acton is cited bizarrely as consulting with his school's "Psychology Department" to determine a "method for scientific comparison of facial structure!" (Page 174)

Accidentally further demeaning Acton, guileless Jameson and Bean give his data and his quote that "the similarity between the facial structure of Roberts and the man in the ... tintype is indeed amazing." (Page 178) What was amazing, was how Acton reached his conclusion.

His clowning began with "mouths." He used old "Brushy's" death-year picture (*Alias Billy the Kid*, Page 173); though tintype Billy was about 20, and *Alias Billy the Kid* had comparably young photos (which looked nothing like Billy, and might explain their avoidance). Acton's chosen "Brushy" has a fish-tail mustache which *covered his mouth*! Nevertheless, Acton's "mouth breadth" measurements, give tintype Billy an "80" and "Brushy" an "82." (Page 175) And Billy's "mouth" was as fake as "Brushy's," since Acton did a "restoration of the Dedrick-Upham photograph of Billy the Kid." (Page 177) The tintype has black spot blemishes on the mouth. Acton used them to stretch real Billy's small mouth. And "Brushy's" Acton "restoration" used his mustache shadow to fake a long straight mouth (since none was visible). (Page 176) These pseudo-mouths yielded his "amazing" "80 to 82" match!

Wisely, Scott Acton abided by the "Jameson-Bean law," and omitted "Brushy's" ears, unlike Billy's. Though in Acton's doctored picture, Billy's missing left ear is added, along with added rolled rims on both ears - to emulate "Brushy's!"

This leaves one with an opinion of Dr. Scott Acton, identical to Jameson's and Bean's opinion of Thomas Kyle.

But they conclude that Acton proved "a very close match" between "Brushy" and Billy. (Page 179) (Omitted, however, is the obvious: even if there had been a real likeness, everything else about "Brushy" was a mismatch! In fact, such people can get employment as stunt doubles!)

## CONSPIRACY THEORIES

Having presented their testament with "Brushy's" sacrosanct words, Jameson and Bean attack the philistines who denied their truth, that he was Billy the Kid, by expanding the Morrison-Sonnichsen gospel of conspiracy theories.

### *CONSPIRACY OF HISTORIANS*

Jameson and Bean acknowledge that historians called "Brushy" an imposter. But the mountain of contradictions, elicits only accusations that historians want to maintain the *status quo*, refuse to admit to being wrong so long, and perpetuate myth and misinformation. (Pages 15, 185-186) They state: "There exists a confederacy of Billy the Kid researchers and writers, an informal alliance composed of a number of adherents to the prevailing and accepted theories regarding the death of the outlaw ... The alliance dismissed Roberts ... The truth is, however, their efforts were never supported by valid scientific and historical research." (Pages 15-16) So they will give the readers examples to prove that plot against "Brushy."

## CONSPIRACY OF GARRETT
### FAKING DEATH SCENE SUSPICION

Obviously the key person to denounce is Pat Garrett, who knew Billy and killed him. So Jameson and Bean lie that the only evidence that he killed Billy "was the word of Pat Garrett." (Page 14) "None of the so-called facts relating to the death of Billy the Kid at the hands of Pat Garrett have ever been supported by concrete, or even competent evidence." (Page 125) For proof, they make-up discrepancies to claim a conspiracy.

So Garrett's seeing two figures in the peach orchard, and later realizing one was Billy on the killing night (Page 105), is called suspicious because Poe did not have that in his book.

**MEANINGLESS: Poe's 1933 *The Death of Billy the Kid* was published 52 years after the event. This minor and insignificant observation was recorded by Garrett right after it for his *Authentic Life of Billy the Kid*, coming out the next year. There is nothing suspicious.**

They question Billy's asking Maxwell: "Quien es?" They wrote: "If Billy the Kid, an Anglo, had entered Maxwell's bedroom and encountered the resident, who spoke excellent English, why would he question him in Spanish? It is likely that a person of Mexican heritage would be more inclined to speak Spanish instead of English." (Page 123)

**PREPOSTEROUS: This is not only absurd, but contrives to make Barlow match their claim of his Mexican identity. And it hides that bi-lingual Billy, disguising himself, would use Spanish with bi-lingual Maxwell about a stranger in the room. There is no discrepancy.**

They question why Billy did not shoot the deputies on the porch since "there was a full moon - light enough for anyone to see" (forgetting that their man "Brushy" said it was a dark night)!

**MEANINGLESS: They forget Poe's own statement that strangers could be in town, with him thinking that approaching Billy could be Maxwell's guest. (Page 110) Billy would have been equally uncertain of who they were, which is why he asked Poe: "Quien es?" He would have had no idea that they were deputies, or its being a trap. His walking into it, proved that! There was no discrepancy.**

The attempt is made to turn Poe's book's initial disbelief after the shooting ("Pat, the Kid would not come to this place; you have shot the wrong man") (Page 112) into actual doubt that he killed the Kid, by claiming that Poe accepting it was Billy Bonney was based "entirely on what he was told by Garrett." (Page 198)

**FAKERY: Omitted is Garrett's response: "I am sure that that was him, for I know his voice too well to be mistaken." (Page 112) And omitted is that Peter Maxwell, Deluvina Maxwell, 200 townspeople in the vigil, and the Coroner's Jurymen, all of whom, Poe was aware, identified the body as Billy Bonney's. There was no discrepancy.**

They state that the only witnesses to the shooting were Pat Garrett and Peter Maxwell, with John Poe and "Kip" McKinney, falsely discounted because they were outside the room. They then claim that "Maxwell contributed very little relative to describing what actually took place in the room." (Page 119)

**FAKERY: This hides that Maxwell knew, and could identify Billy, and made a definitive Coroner's Jury Report statement on July 15, 1881: "[The jurors] examined the evidence of Pedro Maxwell, which evidence is as follows: "I being in my bed in my room, at about midnight on the 14$^{th}$ day of July, Pat F. Garrett came into my room and sat down. William Bonney came in and got close to my bed with a gun in his hand and asked me "who is it" and then Pat F. Garrett fired two shots at the said William Bonney and the said William Bonney fell near my fire place and I went out of the room and when I came in again about three or four minutes after the shots the said William Bonney was dead."**

They state that there was confusion "about whether the body had fallen inside the room or out on the porch." (Page 188)

**FAKERY: There is no historical confusion. This is made-up using "Brushy's" "back porch" fabrication, which parroted Sonnichsen's fabrication which confused the location of the bedroom and side of beef. (See pages 189-190) There is no discrepancy.**

They claim a discrepancy about immediate disposition of the body by alleging the carpenter's shop vigil contradicted the Coroner's Jury's viewing the body in the Maxwell house. (Page 188)

FAKERY: There was no contradiction. The vigil was at night; the body would have been carried into the house in the morning for the inquest.

They allege that Poe's account of the body being taken to the carpenter's shop was countered by a book by Charles Frederick Rudulph titled *"Los Billitos: The Story of Billy the Kid and his Gang,"* published by a Louis Leon Branch in 1980 from Rudulph's 1880 manuscript. They claim that Rudulph stated that the body was on the floor for the coroner's jury.

FAKERY: Charles Rudulph did not say that. In his book, he wrote: "Alejandro Segura, justice of the peace, had been happy to see his friend [Milnor] Rudulph, whom he knew was of unquestionable integrity and clear thinking. He appointed him to head the coroner's jury, and together they picked other prominent level-headed leaders of the community to fill the remaining five seats. They met over the Kid's body and with no argument or dissent unanimously agreed on the following report given below." (Rudulph, Page 252) [The Coroner's Jury Report is provided in English. (Rudulph, Page 253)] And Rudulph claimed his father, Milnor, brought him along: "Hearing the news, Milnor Rudulph called Charley from his bed, and together they sped through the night to Fort Sumner." (Rudulph, Page 252) In fact, Charles Rudulph fully confirmed, from his being present the morning after the shooting, that the body was identified as Billy's by Garrett, Peter Maxwell, Deluvina Maxwell, Luz Maxwell, townspeople, and the coroner's jury headed by his father - whom he calls "six honorable men [who] affixed their signatures and marks to the post mortem of William Bonney, 'Billy the Kid.'" (Rudulph, Pages 253-254) There was no discrepancy.

Jameson and Bean ruminate about the caliber of the gun carried by Billy, or there being no gun. A hearsay account of Lucien Maxwell's great-granddaughter is used to claim that fear that Billy was alive made the men have Deluvina go in first to check before entering themselves. (Pages 119-123)

MEANINGLESS: That only adds another eye-witness, since Deluvina and Billy were friends! There is no discrepancy.

Then they use "Brushy" for evidence! They state: "William Henry Roberts maintained that the man who went to Maxwell's room was a friend named Billy Barlow."

**MIXED-UP:** "Brushy's" version was that Barlow <u>was shot on the back porch, not the bedroom</u>. As "Brushy" stated: "From the corner of my eye I saw the body lying on the back porch ... I knew it had to be Barlow." (Page 113) "Brushy" then had the Celsa character describe taking the body to the Maxwell house: "They took the body of your friend inside the house and they say it is yours." (Pages 116-117)

But, still trying to make the body Barlow's, Jameson and Bean add fakery unused by Morrison and Sonnichsen, and absent in *Alias Billy the Kid*; writing: "It has been stated by Sonnichsen that Barlow may have been half Mexican." (Page 123)

**FAKERY:** This is Sonnichsen's hoaxing, building on the article, also cited by Jameson's and Bean, by journalist, Singleton M. Ashenfelter, on July 23, 1881 titled "Exit 'The Kid'" in his newspaper, *The New Southwest*, in which he made-up that corpse Billy had a beard and "**stained his skin to look like a Mexican.**" Jameson's and Bean's Bibliography cites their interview with Sonnichsen dated June 25, 1991 in Oklahoma City, Oklahoma, when he seems to have told them this. It is irrelevant to reality.

Then they claim there was another version of the shooting, and quote Sonnichsen's hearsay interview of April 15, 1944 with Jack Fountain, A.J. Fountain's son. (Page 124)

**FAKERY:** They are repeating Sonnichsen's use of Jack's fake interview placing the side of beef beside Maxwell's door, which led Sonnichsen to think all this happened at the back porch, resulting in "Brushy's" back-porch-Barlow confabulation. But Jameson and Bean miss that Jack confirmed that Pat shot Billy. There was no discrepancy.

They use a hearsay claim from Morrison that an unnamed man called the law firm doing "Brushy's" pardon case to say that McKinney told Garrett in a saloon "that he should know that he had not killed anyone that night." (Page 126)

**MEANINGLESS: Hearsay is not valid evidence.**

This meaningless conglomeration elicits the Jameson-Bean conclusion: "[N]o credible evidence exists to indicate what actually occurred in Pete Maxwell's bedroom around mid-night on 14 July 1881. Or who was killed." (Page 126)

### FAKING GARRETT AS DISHONEST

They claim the history of Billy the Kid is "flawed" and "suspect" because it is based on Pat Garrett's 1882 book, *The Authentic Life of Billy the Kid*, which contained errors and proved he was a "liar." (Pages 182, 187-188, 197)

FALSE: The history is not based on Garrett's 1882 dime novel-style book. More importantly, Jameson and Bean have avoided real history books and original documents - like Billy's own writings and words, and depositions of participants - that prove "Brushy's" ignorant mismatch.

They try character assassination, claiming: Garrett was "overrated," "never succeeded in anything," and "was a man of questionable veracity and integrity." (Page 197-198) And, since he was "an aspiring political figure," he wanted to keep secret killing the wrong man. (Pages 125, 189)

MEANINGLESS: Garrett's personality had nothing to do with whether he killed Billy. And they made-up that he lacked integrity and killed the wrong man.

### *CONSPIRACY OF GARRETT'S REWARD*

Jameson and Bean lift Sonnichsen's *Alias Billy the Kid* fabrication that Garrett was denied the Billy the Kid reward money because of lack of a Coroner's Jury Report and lack of proven corpse identity (Page 14); **instead of the innocuous truth that payment was delayed simply by need to convert Lew Wallace's private reward into a Territorial one by legislative act, since he had already left the Territory.** (See pages 14, 211-215 above)

"Brushy" is quoted as a source: "Garrett realized his mistake and was making a try at collecting the reward that was out on me anyway." (Page 117) And Sonnichsen's fakery is repeated about Acting-Governor Ritch denying the reward, with their faking that Garrett never got it. (Page 129) They also add the reward was denied because he had not killed Billy, or "the death certificate was never found," or Billy was unarmed, or the Legislature gave him the money because they were "his henchmen." They add, like Sonnichsen, suspicion that the Legislature wrote August, not July, for the killing date. (Page 129)

**FAKERY: This is Sonnichsen's fakery, with their added fakery. Noteworthy, is that Jameson, in his later books, would continue to repeat the absurd "August" clerical imprecision in the legislative act for Garrett's reward, as if it was suspicious evidence and meaningful. And the fact is that the reward was granted because all was in order.**

## *CONSPIRACY OF THE CORONER'S JURY*

The hoaxers' bugaboo, after Pat Garrett, was the Coroner's Jury Report of July 15, 1881; with its profuse evidence of existing - with its English translation even in *Alias Billy the Kid* - and its identification of the body as Billy Bonney's. So Jameson and Bean make-up conspiracies to hide all that.

### CONSPIRACY OF MILNOR RUDULPH

Jameson and Bean sought suspicion about Coroner's Jury President, Milnor Rudulph. So, for John Poe's July 14, 1881 recognizance to Sunnyside's Postmaster, Milnor Rudulph, about Billy, they portray him as "a friend of the Kid." (Page 102) Poe's observing that Rudulph was "nervous out of fear of the Kid," to them meant Rudulph was "protective of the Kid" against lawmen, and gave misleading information. (Page 189) Or maybe he and Garrett had plotted to make the Kid seem "officially dead." (Page 191) So Jameson and Bean conclude that he was part of a conspiracy to hide Billy's survival to let him go free. (Page 190)

**FALSE: As discussed, Rudulph was an Ringite, who in 1872, as Speaker of the House, assisted the Ring's take-over of the Legislature to block anti-Ring bills; thus, precipitating what I named the 1872 Legislature Revolt: the first anti-Ring uprising in the Territory. Rudulph was Billy's enemy, and likely feared reprisal from him for betrayal. (See page 49 above) And Rudulph would have had no way of knowing that Poe was a lawman. And Rudulph's son, Charles, had ridden on a Garrett posse to capture Billy.**

## CONSPIRACY OF CORONER'S JURYMEN

For their conspiracy theory, Jameson and Bean fabricate that the inquest was "shrouded in confusion and mystery" (Page 126), make-up "suspicions," and conclude: "There is, in fact, no legal proof of the death of Billy the Kid." (Page 129)

But their "proof" of no proof was preposterous and fabricated! They claimed the inquest was fast. (Page 126) [Why not?] They claimed Garrett did not put the body on public display. (Page 126) [For whom? It was an isolated town, and its more than 200 residents had already conducted a vigil for it that night.] They wanted the body photographed. (Page 126). [By whom? Rural people in 1881 did not have cameras.] They recycled Sonnichsen's A.P. Anaya malarkey of two coroner's jury reports. (Pages 126-127) [But Anaya had no access to knowing about any report; and they were apparently unaware that he was real Billy's friend and, in his manuscript, claimed to be an eye-witness preparing dead Billy for burial, in his book published posthumously in 1991 as *I Buried Billy*.] They claimed: "To date, no one has ever seen the document." (Page 127) [The photostatic copy of the original report is in William Keleher's 1957 *Violence in Lincoln County*, cited in their own Bibliography.] They questioned spelling of the signers' names, and make-up that the report was a forgery by Garrett. (Page 128) [But Garrett, as the homicide suspect, would have had no access to writing the report.] They claimed that the Report "never made it to the official records of San Miguel County," and "Justice of the Peace Segura never made an entry regarding the report in his own books." (Page 118) [As discussed above, the original Report was sent to District Attorney of the First Judicial District William Breeden. It would have been stored with his records in Santa Fe, where it was found in storage in the basement of Santa Fe's State capitol in 1932. (See pages 14-15, 116, 205, 700) Segura was irrelevant.] Added is that Morrison was told there was no filed report by an August 14, 1951 letter from a Fourth Judicial District Attorney Jose E. Armijo. [That was because it was not filed there! And Morrison must have known, then hid, that on "Brushy's" pardon hearing day of November 30, 1950, the *Alamogordo News* reminded readers that the Report had been found 20 years earlier, identifying dead Billy Bonney!]

## *CONSPIRACY OF BURIAL*

The burial receives the same faked "suspicion and misinformation in vain attempt to contradict reality. Jameson's and Bean's foregone conclusion is: "There has long been uncertainty relative to whose remains, if anyone's, is buried at the Fort Sumner site." (Page 132) [**But the uncertain gravesite within Fort Sumner's cemetery has nothing to do with Billy Bonney having been killed.**]

Claimed is that the body was seen only by Garrett, Poe, McKinney, "and two or three other people." (Page 130) [**This omits Peter Maxwell, Deluvina Maxwell, over 200 townspeople in the night vigil, and the coroner's jury president and five jurymen.**] Leon Metz, Garrett's biographer, is misrepresented as saying in his *Pat Garrett: The story of a Western Lawman*, that Garrett could have passed off the body. (Page 130) [**Metz's book confirmed that Garrett killed Billy.**]

They give the fake corpse identity created by Grant County journalist S.M. Ashenfelter on July 23, 1881, in his *The New Southwest's* "Exit 'The Kid', that the corpse was dark-skinned, like a Mexican, and bearded. (Page 119) So they solemnly, preposterously, and with what they call "scientific style," cite a book on sexual maturity (with "SMR's – Sexual Maturity Ratings") to compare Ashenfelter's corpse to fair beardless Billy, to show the impossibility of his transformation from fair and blue-eyed to dark-skinned and bearded. So they conclude that the body could not have been Billy's. (Page 131) [**They forgot that Billy Barlow was *their* victim, and "Brushy" said *they* looked the same! And Grant County put Ashenfelter about 250 miles from the fast Fort Sumner burial, so he obviously faked his "outlaw" description for his readership.**]

Hearsay tales follow about non-historical people claiming a Mexican that looked like Billy had been shot, or a Maxwell hired hand was shot, or that the wagon carrying the casket had an "armed guard" so no one could see the body. (Pages 132-133)

The uncertain location of the Fort Sumner Billy the Kid grave is called suspicious (Page 132), rather than mere neglect. And Yginio Salazar of Lincoln is fabricated as being one of Billy's pallbearers and not knowing the gravesite. (Page 133) [**For the future, this uncertain site admission is important, because the "Billy the Kid Case" hoax would fake its certainty.**]

## *MOTHERS OF ALL CONSPIRACY THEORIES*

By the book's end, Jameson and Bean were out-of-control with conspiracy theories to explain their lost cause. They claim:

**All Fort Sumner people were in a conspiracy.** They tricked Garrett into thinking he had killed Billy, since they were "friendly and sympathetic to the Kid ... [and they perpetuated] the masquerade well into the twentieth century because they knew the Kid was still alive." (Page 189) This scenario is "Brushy's" own, since Jameson and Bean state: "According to Roberts, the two (Jesus Silva and Deluvina) decided to perpetuate a deception, perhaps allowing Garrett to believe the victim was, in fact, the wanted outlaw." (Page 189)

**FAKERY: More than absurdity ruins this; it needs Garrett unable to recognize Billy. But Garrett knew him; captured him at Stinking Springs; and transported him by train to Las Vegas, then Santa Fe, for jail. And, as Sheriff, Garrett imprisoned him in his Lincoln jail, awaiting his hanging.**

**All of New Mexico is in a conspiracy.** The reason given is "tourism." If Billy was a Texan, the loss would be "millions of dollars each year." (Page 191) So, Governor T.J. Mabry had been in cahoots with the assembled historians and descendants to call "Brushy" an imposter for economic reasons. (Pages 192-193)

**IRONY: That governors protect Billy the Kid tourism would be proved false in five years, when corrupt Governor Bill Richardson made the "Billy the Kid Case" hoax, to, indeed, give Texas the history and make "Brushy" Billy. And Jameson was in that hoax as a "Brushy"-backer.**

The Lincoln County Heritage Trust, a Lincoln museum which then held the Billy the Kid tintype, was in a conspiracy. The reason given is that its 1989 photo-analysis denied a match of "Brushy" as Billy the Kid. (Page 195) Again, according to Jameson and Bean, it was tourism dollars that made the director, Bob Hart, lie to protect his job; and the Trust was, according to them, a big business. (Page 195)

**FAKERY: Jameson and Bean are hiding the sophisticated nature of Dr. Clyde Snow's investigation, that legitimately found no photo-match for "Brushy."**

A television program "Who Was Billy the Kid" on "Prime Time Live" (date not given) **was a conspiracy**, because presenter, Sam Donaldson, who acknowledged tourism value of Billy the Kid, was "a resident of Lincoln County," and there was no one on the program to back "Brushy." (Pages 196-197)

**FAKERY: There should be no one representing "Brushy" in legitimate Billy the Kid history, since he was an imposter.**

## THE JAMESON-BEAN OUTCOME

At the end of Jameson's and Bean's meaningless game, the score was still "Brushy" zero. But "Brushy" was undergoing a dishonest transformation unreported to readers. From pardon-"Brushy" killing no one, forgetting Pat Garrett, and claiming an out-of-steak restaurant in Fort Sumner; to *Alias*-"Brushy" with his racist "niggers" and Lincoln County cattle war; he had become *Return*-"Brushy," posthumously having a new genealogy with a McCarty and a Catherine Antrim, knowing about the Regulators, and being cleansed of racism and bad grammar. But *Return*-"Brushy" was permitted to speak real "Brushy's" own words, so he spouted his tale of the dark and moonless night of July 14, 1881 that would destroy them all.

# CHAPTER 6
# "BRUSHY BILL" GETS TO HOLLYWOOD

## A GREAT STORY

In the Hollywood world of make-believe, fact and fiction can be blurred without guilt, with sole claimed objective of entertainment, and real objective of getting rich. "Brushy Bill" was a perfect fit, once recognized by a screenwriter with adequate indifference to truth - and that was not hard to find. So "Brushy's" fabrications became mainstream, misleading the mass public beyond the wildest dreams of his hoaxers and true-believers.

When gauging a good story, one has to admit that "Brushy Bill's" fantasy tale hits an archetypal nerve. There is defying of death after a life of daring-do; then continuing a life of daring-do. There is the wish-fulfilling discovery that an ordinary old coot was the most famous outlaw of them all in his secret past. But it took Hollywood 40 years to notice; so dead "Brushy Bill" and dead William Morrison saw not a penny. Though C.L. Sonnichsen had one year of life left to see the foul fruits of his labor.

The 1990 movie, "Young Guns II" was by screenwriter, John Fusco. His "Brushy," as Billy the Kid, is spared death by Pat Garrett because they are friends. This man-to-man friendship, so strong that Garrett would murder an innocent victim so Billy could live free, was as moving as it was fake. Not only did real Garrett kill real Billy, but they merely knew each other in passing from Fort Sumner. And they had near lethal contact after Garrett had twice tried to kill him, but accidentally murdered Tom O'Folliard and Charlie Bowdre instead. Then they were together in the grim aftermath of Billy's Stinking Spring's capture and later imprisonment in Lincoln awaiting hanging, which there is no doubt that Garrett would have carried out.

But John Fusco's fakery got him more than box office success. "Brushy Bill" true-believers and future "Billy the Kid Case" hoaxers were poised to make him their hero: like the second coming of William V. Morrison and C.L. Sonnichsen. So he was sought out at the 2003 start of the "Brushy Bill"-based "Billy the Kid Case" hoax, and interviewed for that hoax's promoting, glossy *True West* magazine's August/September edition. Staff writer, Janna Bommersbach, used Fusco for her article titled "Digging up Billy. If Pat Garrett didn't kill the Kid, who's buried in his grave?"

The answer was supposed to be "a stranger" - or even Billy Barlow - and John Fusco was positioned for that punch line. Instead, apparently satiated by his $44 million profit, he was frustratingly honest, saying that he did not believe "Brushy" was Billy; but his movie had made a lot of money!

So traveling salesman, pseudo-lawyer, con-man William Morrison, had been right all along: "Brushy" was a great product. And John Fusco became the hoax's actual beneficiary. A huckster like Morrison, though believing actual Billy the Kid history, he ran with the show-business option of making-up whatever he wanted - even out-Brushying "Brushy." And he arguably did more damage to Billy the Kid history than all the hoaxers combined. But he gave them dreams of never before conceived heights of greed. And he gave them a hook that "Brushy," Morrison, W.C. Jameson, and Frederick Bean had missed: a bromance.

So his "Young Guns II" has an old "Brushy Bill" narrating his story to a young historian. Emilio Estevez is Billy, a leader of an outlaw gang, known as the Regulators. Cattle king John Chisum, pays Pat Garrett to kill Billy. As Billy's super-friend, Garrett only pretends to do the deed. So Billy rides off to life as "Brushy." And the public thought Fusco's fiction was fact.

The lesson was not lost on W.C. Jameson and the "Billy the Kid Case" hoaxers that the formula of "Pat did not kill Billy" was now a proven bonanza. And there was another hook as good as the knowing-things-not-printed trick. It was the man-to-man-love trick to explain the killing of the innocent victim. They were poised for its encore - Fusco or no Fusco. All they needed was a governor as indifferent to the truth as Fusco had been. Then the best hook of all could be offered again: the pardon of Billy the Kid.

# CHAPTER 7
# SUMMARIZING THE "BRUSHY BILL" HOAX

## "BRUSHY BILL" AS A RIDICULOUS PARODY OF BILLY BONNEY

The answer to C.L. Sonnichsen's provocative dare - "If he wasn't Billy the Kid who was he?" - is: He was Oliver Pleasant Roberts, a septuagenarian, mentally disabled, attention-seeking, racist, coarse-spoken, confabulating, delusional, Social Security benefits fraudster born on August 26, 1879 in Arkansas; among whose multiple self-created personas was "Brushy Bill;" who was promoted by opportunist and profiteering authors to create a Billy the Kid imposter hoax, which concomitantly defamed Sheriff and Deputy U.S. Marshal Pat Garrett and obscured the true history of the Lincoln County War freedom fight and its hero, Billy Bonney. And his December 27, 1950 fatal heart attack likely culminated the stress of his forced impersonation.

Building on this fragile man's original scribbled notebooks of identity cues - from Frank James to a Pinkerton detective - his clever huckster backer, William V. Morrison, himself a glory-seeking imposter, thought he had hit pay-dirt. His hoax strategy was to support "Brushy's" fabricated old age and genealogy, and to enhance exponentially his historical sources, with added on-site tours, to flesh out his Billy the Kid persona; as "Brushy" dutifully scribbled prompt notes and made rehearsal tape recordings. Added was English teacher and aspiring historian, C.L. Sonnichsen, for more sources, flakey conspiracy theories, and ultimately for book-writing. "Brushy" was to be sold as an illiterate, incapable of reading-up, yet knowing things not printed. And, promisingly, he could contribute as a creative confabulator. Counted on, was his being able to retain his backer's coaching to perform under scrutiny for a gubernatorial pardon to seal him as Billy the Kid.

Morrison and Sonnichsen missed the scheme's fatal flaws. It did not occur to them that the history of Billy the Kid was still largely unwritten, leaving huge gaps for contradictory discoveries. Worse, the prompt sources for special knowledge had tell-tale errors revealed if parroted. Worse, "Brushy" had limited memory, especially under pressure. Worse, he failed abysmally his pardon hearing. And, though his death in the next month removed him and his limitations, creating a better "Brushy" for their *Alias Billy the Kid* book did not remove their hoax's built-in vulnerabilities for exposure. And the conversion, decades later, of true-believer authors, W.C. Jameson and William Bean, with their *The Return of the Outlaw Billy the Kid*, only made things worse, because their innocent faith led them to present "Brushy's" own words, which revealed his chaotic ignorance and mistakes.

Hoaxbusting the "Brushy" material shows no match whatsoever with Billy Bonney. And his ridiculous caricature, woven together from dime novel-style books, cowboy movies, and other windbag old-timers, is an insult to brilliant, charismatic, freedom fighting zealot Billy Bonney and his cohorts.

The worst insult, however, was to Billy Bonney's killer, Sheriff Pat Garrett, defamed in every way the hoaxers could conceive, to manufacture doubt about his having killed Billy on July 14, 1881. And the insult to history was denying the irrefutable existence of Billy Bonney's Coroner's Jury Report, extinguishing the hoax by facts.

There was more. The progression of the hoax from 1950 to 1998 demonstrated its dark side of deterioration to conspiracy theories and secret fix-ups to hide "Brushy's" mismatch and glaring errors. There was also sly and dishonest updating by addition of pseudo-science, with fake photo-analyses. And all this chicanery foreshadowed far worse to come.

Fueled by media attention and fiction posing as fact, like "Young Guns II," the hoax burgeoned with greedier developments and implementation by racketeering profiteering political corruption, becoming the 2003 "Billy the Kid Case" hoax; and ultimately W.C. Jameson's 2018 megahoax book: *Cold Case Billy the Kid*. This unsavory future trajectory would lead to illegal concealment of public records, lying about law enforcement status, forensic DNA fraud, illegal exhumations desecrating remains and robbing graves, and forging official records to conceal wrongdoings. The "Brushy" hoax was bad from the beginning, and its evolution magnified its rotten core.

# PART III

## THE JOHN MILLER BILLY THE KID IMPOSTER HOAX

# CHAPTER 1
## JOHN MILLER'S BILLY THE KID BID

### RIDING ON "BRUSHY'S" COATTAILS

Obscure Billy the Kid imposter, John Miller, dead since 1937, with no known believers, only made it to wider public awareness by riding on the pretender trend successfully carried out by the "Brushy Bill" hoax. In 1993, Miller got an author named Helen Airy for her *Whatever Happened to Billy the Kid?* A short and lethargic hoaxlet, with the "Brushy" premise of Pat Garrett shooting an innocent victim and Billy surviving, it would have remained as uninspiring as John Miller himself, except for a surprising development. The "Billy the Kid Case" hoax, started in 2003, became desperate for bones for its fake forensic DNA matchings, after I legally blocked those hoaxers from the sought graves of Billy Bonney and his mother, Catherine Antrim.

So, in 2005, for fodder for their TV production company, they illegally exhumed concession prize John Miller as "Billy the Kid." Possibly they thought it would prime the media pump to facilitate the goal: digging up "Brushy." It failed; and only corrupt political intervention saved the hoaxers from deserved felony convictions.

I exposed these hoaxers in my 2014 book, *Cracking the Billy the Kid Case Hoax: The Strange Plot to Exhume Billy the Kid, Convict Sheriff Pat Garrett of Murder, and Become President of the United States*. But it gave John Miller a place in the burgeoning "Brushy" hoax. Miller would even make it into W.C. Jameson's "Brushy"-backing 2018 *Cold Case Billy the Kid*, as a measure of his desperation to fabricate any example indicating that history was not as written, and that Garrett may have shot someone other than Billy on July 14, 1881. And, by then, he was in league with the "Billy the Kid Case" hoaxers; so John Miller and his wee hoax made it into their megahoax. And, as will be seen, another random man, named William Hudspeth, made it also, as illegally dug up by being buried beside the equally unmarked Miller grave.

# MANUFACTURING MILLER AS BILLY

With her rudimentary history knowledge, Helen Airy relied on a few history books and old-timer interviews of Miller's friends, who recalled that he and his wife had said he was Billy the Kid. And the Millers convinced their adopted Navajo son, Max Miller; so he believed that too. (Page 14) That was Airy's "proof."

## *THE BIRTH BARRIER*

As with Oliver "Brushy Bill" Roberts, age was John Miller's impassable obstacle. He was born in December of 1850; making him nine years older than real Billy. Miller, as Billy, would have been older than "his" boss John Tunstall, who himself died at 24 in 1878. Miller would have been the same age as Pat Garrett. And no one would have called him "Kid;" which was transmogrified to the famous "Billy the Kid" moniker in outlaw myth press. In consequence, his author, Helen Airy, did not directly mention that inconvenient truth. So she lied, saying Miller was 21 on August 8, 1881, when he married (Pages 9, 11) - and was actually 30!

And his birthdate was easily available to her, being at the Arizona Pioneers' Home in Prescott where he was placed on March 12, 1937 after he broke his right hip - as she herself stated in her book. Miller died at 87, on November 7, 1937 of complicating pneumonia after that injury. He was buried in their Pioneers' Home Cemetery on November 9, 1937. (**Remember that fatal broken hip. It will figure dramatically in his fabricated inclusion in "Billy the Kid Case" hoaxing** .)

In addition, John Miller's birthplace was Fort Sill, Texas, to a Comanche mother - all unconnected to Billy Bonney. But, totally unaware of the history, Miller was untroubled by factual discrepancies during his life, merely giving hints that made those close to him think he was the Kid. And he sought no profit from it.

## *FAKING GARRETT SHOOTING SURVIVAL*

Helen Airy starts her book with a tiny sly death scene: "It was near midnight on July 14, 1881, when Sheriff Pat Garrett shot someone in Pete Maxwell's darkened bedroom in the old officers' quarters in Fort Sumner, where Maxwell lived." (Page 9) Why that "someone" was not Billy is missing; though later, to John Miller, is attributed a tale of an accidental killing of an Indian-dressed-similarly death scene.

Airy adds that there was a cover-up of the victim's identity. What makes her think that? She says Garrett and a coroner's jury identified Billy, but there were "doubts." (Page 9) She mentions an unreferenced, unknown document, and says: "When he was asked to sign an affidavit that it was the Kid he had shot, Garrett refused to sign." (Page 9) She also malingers: "McKinney and Poe accused Garrett of shooting the wrong man" (Pages 9, 13) adding McKinney to her own distortion of John Poe's statement of initial identity concern in his 1933 book, *The Death of Billy the Kid*, explained by his not knowing Billy.

Airy concludes: "But all through the years since that night, there have been doubts that it really was Billy the Kid's body they buried the next day." (Page 9) Why doubts? Airy says unnamed people "saw Billy" after the death date **[meaningless hearsay]**; some Coroner's Jurymen signed with an X **[so what, they were illiterate]**; there was "irregularity" in filing the Coroner's Jury Report **[untrue]**; and the corpse was seen by only a few people **[untrue]**. For witnesses, she lists Garrett and his deputies, "immediate family members" **[there were none]**, and adds snidely: "supposedly, members of the coroner's jury" **[snideness is not an argument]**. With no conspiracy theory, she declares: "Surely there was reason to wonder."

The rest of Helen Airy's 175 page book is about John Miller's irrelevant life after July 14, 1881; though little flash-backs of blighted Billy history are given - and prove nothing.

## *ROMANCE AND MURDER AS "BILLY THE KID"*

It appears that John Miller's hoax was a team effort with his wife, Isadora, "a dark-eyed Mexican girl." To friends and neighbors, she claimed that he, as "the Kid," had been shot "**some days before the shoot-out at Pete Maxwell's house**," - without elaboration - and she tended his wounds and hid him from "officers" in her Fort Sumner house's mattress. (Page 9) But, for unstated reason, the Santa Fe Ring of "unscrupulous and treacherous men" and Thomas Benton Catron were after him, as well as Governor Lew Wallace [actually gone from the Territory]." (Pages 11, 13)

Airy calls Isadora the widow of Charlie Bowdre, admitting that the widow's actual name was Manuela (Page 12); and unaware that she had left Fort Sumner after her husband's murder by Garrett in 1880. She states that Miller married Isadora on August 8, 18881; but debunking author, Jim Johnson, in his 2006 book, *Billy the Kid: His Real Name Was ...* states that census reports show the marriage was in 1885 or 1886. (Johnson, Page 2)

But why should anyone think John Miller was Billy?

Airy says there were similarities: blue eyes, prominent front teeth, heavy eyebrows (which she says were like his mother's, though he claimed she was a Comanche Indian, not Catherine Antrim). He had the pretenders' requisite small hands and thick wrists for shackle-slipping, a trick he did for friends, saying: "Billy the Kid could do that." (Pages 10, 144) Airy descended to the ridiculous, adding that Miller wore a hat like Billy's (from the tintype), carried a gun, had a bad temper, and tended to point his rifle at people! (Page 11) Wisely unmentioned was Miller's long scrawny neck, since Billy had a short thick one.

John Miller himself, apparently, barely mouthed Billy history. But he would strip to show friends twelve supposed bullet scars on his chest; though real Billy had just a thigh wound from Deputy Jacob Basil Matthews at the Regulators' Sheriff Brady ambush shooting.

To back physical identity, Helen Airy gives photos of wax busts made by a sympathetic artist named Deborah Robinson, who stated: "I aged the sculpture [of Billy the Kid] to a man of about sixty years ... In my opinion, John Miller and Billy the Kid were the same person." (Pages 161-162) The sculptures demonstrate that, by reconstructing Billy and John Miller a resemblance can be faked (as well known to Dr. Scott Acton, who faked the same way for his "Brushy" photo-comparison study!). But that does not prove identity as Airy claims.

Another Airy "proof" would have outraged real Billy. Miller's last shooting victim was a Mexican worker. (Pages 15, 19) Billy's bi-culturalism was famous. As cited above, "Teddy Blue" Abbott, a cowboy contemporary of Billy's, wrote in his 1955 book, *We Pointed Them North*: "The Lincoln County troubles was still going on, and you had to be either for Billy the Kid or against him. It wasn't my fight ... it was the Mexicans that made a hero of him." (See page 55 above) And as Henry Hoyt wrote in his 1929 book, *A Frontier Doctor*: "He spoke Spanish like a native."

## BARE-BONES FAKE HISTORY OF BILLY THE KID

Having presented nothing to indicate that John Miller was Billy Bonney, Helen Airy gave a brief summary of her day's Billy the Kid history. But she made no attempt to say that Miller claimed any of it. And, though she gave some Silver City and Arizona history, she made no attempt to reconcile it with Miller's known history from his November 8, 1937 *Prescott Courier* obituary, which stated: "[H]e was adopted as an infant or very young boy by an Indian tribe after one of his parents had been killed outright and the other burned to death as a sacrifice by the Indians." (Cited in Jim Johnson's 2006 *Billy the Kid: His Real Name Was ...* Page 9)

To her, Billy the Kid was a "gunslinger" (Page 19), and the Lincoln County War was the "bloodiest range war of them all." (Page 22) Tunstall and McSween are incorrectly called partners, and the strife was mercantile competition with the Murphy firm, backed by T.B. Catron (Page 22) - in a description apparently relying on Maurice Garland Fulton's note in Pat Garrett's 1927 edition of *The Authentic Life of Billy the Kid*. After Tunstall's murder, Billy's killing motive is listed as revenge, as is that of the Regulators. (Page 23) For her, the Lincoln County War is a fabricated three day battle, with McSween's men surrounding a building with Sheriff Peppin's men; until Fort Stanton's Colonel Dudley, by show of might, forced McSween's men to flee in the night (Page 24) **[It was actually the morning of his arrival.]** For the burning building escape, Billy takes command.

Unaware of Huston Chapman's murder, Billy's pardon bargain, or real Billy's letters, Airy has him writing to Governor Wallace that he had wanted justice done, and volunteering to tell a court about Lincoln County troubles. (Page 24) Unsure of what went wrong, she makes-up that people got tired of thinking about the Lincoln County War, so nothing came of testifying or pardon. (Page 24) She also makes-up: "Billy the Kid was the only member of the Regulator gang who was not pardoned by Governor Wallace at the end of the Lincoln County War." (Page 147) **[No Regulators were pardoned.]**

In her version, Billy became a cattle rustler tracked by Pat Garrett, and had a ranch for stolen cattle in Las Portales. (Page 24) That proved that Airy used the December 22, 1880

*New York Sun* outlaw myth article titled: "Outlaws of New Mexico. The Exploits of a Band Headed by a New York Youth. The Mountain Fastness of the Kid and His Followers - War Against a Gang of Cattle Thieves and Murderers."

Ignorant of all intervening events, Airy covered the Stinking Springs capture and the Santa Fe jailing. There she had Billy writing to Wallace that he had letters going back two years that certain parties wanted to see. (Page 25) She apparently got that from a June 23, 1900 *The Indianapolis Press* article titled: "Gen. Wallace's Feud with Billy the Kid, When the General Was Governor of New Mexico and Billy Bonne Was the Most Dangerous Western Outlaw;" which stated: "He had been in jail a week when he addressed me: 'Governor, why haven't you come to see me?' I paid no attention to it. A few days later there was a second note: 'Governor, I have some papers you would not want to see displayed. Come to the jail.' " And it was in the June 8, 1902 *New York World Magazine* in "General Lew Wallace Writes a Romance of 'Billy the Kid' Most Famous Bandit of the Plains;" which stated: "Then the outlaw sent him a note. The note said: 'Come to the jail. I have some papers you would not want to see displayed.' "

For the Mesilla trial, she leaves out the "Buckshot" Roberts case; and, for Brady's trial, makes-up that Judge Warren Bristol was controlled by the "Brady crowd" and "cowed the local Mexican jury." (Page 25) For the great escape, she uses the gun in the privy scenario, with a slipped shackle weapon to kill Bell; and shooting Olinger with his own shotgun. (Page 26)

For the Fort Sumner shooting, she gave "Brushy Bill's" version of being at a dance! And the victim is an Indian mistaken for Miller. She called conventional history "Garrett's version."

Then she tried to manufacture doubts. She says the Kid would not go into a darkened room; makes-up that Poe said Garrett was not a good enough shot to hit the Kid; makes-up that Poe and McKinney accused Garrett of shooting the wrong man; says people saw Billy after the death date; and makes-up that years after the death date rewards were offered for arrest of Billy. (Page 27) The coroner's jury is attacked as "hastily recruited," with illiterate signatures with an X, no one viewing the body, and no official report filed. (Page 27)

Oddly, Airy makes no attempt to reconcile the death scene with John Miller's claim of being shot days before that event; so his attackers and their motives remain a mystery.

## MILLER'S LIFE AFTER BILLY'S DEATH

Miller's irrelevant life with his wife is covered, as a rancher for over 30 years in McKinley County's Ramah, in northwestern New Mexico, originally a Mormon settlement, between the Zuni and the Ramah Navajo Indian Reservations, with Airy editorializing that he lived in fear that Catron and the Santa Fe Ring were after him. (Pages 38, 147) For a 1900 census for Valencia County, New Mexico Territory, he lied about his birth date, making it 1857. (Page 39) And in the 1910 census, he changed his age to 58. Airy states all this was to throw off people seeking him as Billy the Kid! (Page 39) In the 1900's he moved to Arizona with his wife, living in Buckeye, where his wife died. (Page 154) After marriages to two Navajo women, and living in Borrego Pass, he was admitted to the Prescott, Arizona Pioneers' Home on March 12, 1937 after falling off a roof and breaking his right hip. (Page 146) Dying eight months later, he was buried in the Pioneers' Home Cemetery.

## OLD-TIMERS SAY MILLER WAS BILLY

Having offered nothing to indicate that Miller was Billy the Kid, Helen Airy uses old-timer recollections, padding her book with details of their irrelevant lives. Most of them merely say he *told them or others they knew* that he was Billy the Kid.

### *HERMAN TECKLENBURG*

The oddest story teller is a Herman Tecklenburg, who confabulated that he knew John Miller in Fort Sumner as Billy the Kid; and was later his "most trusted friend." (Page 42)

On August 9, 1944, Tecklenburg, then a janitor, but claiming to have been a cowpuncher and Indian hunter, gave an interview for the *Gallup Independent*, to a Wesley Huff, titled: "Did Garrett Kill Billy the Kid? Herman Tecklenburg Says No; Billy Lived on Ranch at Ramah 35 Years Ago and Visited Him." Tecklenburg stated: "They shot somebody over in Fort Sumner, and they buried him there and put an end to the hunt for Billy the Kid. But it wasn't Billy they shot. He and his Mexican wife escaped over into Old Mexico ... [Later] he was ranching it down near Ramath. They all knew of him down there as Billy the Kid, but never spoke of it for fear of getting him in trouble. He was a prince. Big shots made him out to be an outlaw because they couldn't handle him. Down at Ramath he was known as John Miller." (Page 43) He told Huff that " '[i]t was in his cowpunching days that he became acquainted with Billy the Kid in Fort Sumner ... Billy the Kid would kill and butcher a maverick and ride all night leaving cuts of it with the poor people so they could eat ... All they have to do is say something bad about Billy and I see red. I knew him as a friend and he was no cow thief or bad man ... Them was the kind of men who made the West' ... Mr. Tecklenburg said that Billy the Kid lived as John Miller at his Ramah ranch until about 25 years ago ... when he sold out and moved near to Phoenix. "

Jim Johnson, in his 2006 book, *Billy the Kid, His real Name Was* ... exposed Tecklenburg's lying through family records, showing that he was born in Germany on June 9, 1869, and immigrated to the United States as a teenager, **arriving on June 5, 1884.** (Johnson, Page 4) Thus, in 1880 and 1881, he was in Germany, not in Fort Sumner as "Billy the Kid's friend."

## *FRANK BURRARD "BURT" CREASY*

Frank Creasy, was a hired ranch hand of John Miller's. He alleged that Miller told him his history as Billy the Kid. It is Helen Airy's only sample of Miller's fabrications.

The first part of Creasy's narrative had Miller's garbling from Pat Garrett's *The Authentic Life of Billy the Kid* or Walter Noble Burns's 1926 *The Saga of Billy the Kid*; parroting: "[I]n 1871, when he was twelve years old ... [a] deputy sheriff apparently insulted Billy's mother for which Billy promptly shot him and fled to the hills." (Page 91) Garrett's and Burns's books stated: "When young Billy was about twelve years of age, he first imbrued his hand in human blood" [after an insult to his mother.]"

Creasy continued his malarkey: "[B]illy made his next appearance in Arizona four years later in 1875, when he killed another man in a gunfight and later had a shoot-out with three Indians and a white man over a dispute in a horse trading deal. He killed all four ... [Then he appeared] in New Mexico during the famous Cattle War of the West, where he was arrested and thrown into Lincoln jail, from which he escaped, killing his guard and a deputy sheriff in the process." (Page 92)

Creasy claimed that a $10,000 reward was made for Billy, dead or alive. And he next appeared in 1880, when, in the company of an Indian boy who looked like him, he **went to Lincoln** to visit his Mexican sweetheart. Hearing that a side of beef hung next door, the Indian went there to steal some meat. Creasy continued his total misinformation: "Pat Garrett, who was the marshal of Lincoln at the time, and a well known bounty hunter, heard that Billy was in town and along with two of his deputies laid in waiting near the side of beef. **When the Indian boy stepped up onto the veranda of the house, he was shot down by Pat Garrett, who had apparently mistaken him for Billy.** Billy [Miller] told me once that he and the Indian were dressed alike to confuse people. Pat Garrett was afraid of the reaction of townspeople and immediately buried the body. [And he collected the $10,000 reward.] (Page 92)

Creasy concluded: "Billy [Miller] hearing the shooting, and after finding out what happened he immediately left with the Mexican girl, whom he later married." (Page 92)

Important is not only the total misinformation - including the shooting in **Lincoln instead of Fort Sumner**, 150 miles away in San Miguel County - but that totally ignorant Helen Airy thought it was correct! Creasy's fabrications inspired her to a vehement crescendo of conspiracy theory hoaxing. She wrote: "To date, American historians maintain Sheriff Pat Garrett **killed Billy the Kid in Lincoln County, New Mexico.** But according to Creasy's account Garrett killed the wrong man, concealed the error and collected the reward ... For reasons unknown, historians in the United States failed to follow up on the leads Frank Creasy furnished about John Miller's claim that he was Billy the Kid." (Page 92)

## *BILL CROCKETT*

Bill Crockett, speaking for Miller's adopted son, Max Miller, his friend; stated: "I do believe John Miller was truly William Bonney, alias Billy the Kid ... Max told me many times that Miller had told him about the Lincoln County War and Pat Garrett, who Miller said was his good friend. Miller said there was a Mexican shot and buried in the coffin that was supposed to be the Kid." (Page 155) **[But Miller had told Frank Creasy that the victim was his Indian friend dressed like him.]**

## OTHER OLD-TIMERS

Helen Airy's other meaningless interviews with old-timers demonstrated that it was common in their day to fake personal knowledge of Billy the Kid to shine by reflected glory.

An Apollas Boaz Lambson's son, Eugene Lambson, said, when he was a boy, his father knew John Miller in Ramah, and Miller "talked a lot about Billy the Kid, but never admitted he was Billy the Kid." And he once pointed a rifle at them before he recognized who they were. But he had no memory of Miller's tales. (Page 48) He did recall his father telling him he knew Pat Garrett too, who told him that Billy the Kid was hiding in Pete Maxwell's house, so Garrett knocked on the door and a Mexican youth opened it, and Garrett shot him dead. Then he told Billy the Kid and his girlfriend "to pack up and leave Lincoln County forever." (Page 50) From this fakery, Helen Airy concluded absurdly that when John Miller and his wife went to El Paso for supplies, they were actually socializing with Pat Garrett as friends! (Page 50)

An Atheling Bond claimed Miller was Billy the Kid because Miller's wife, adopted Navajo son, the son's children, and Herman Tecklenburg told him so. (Page 56) He recalled that Miller told stories of Billy the Kid's gun fights, and would show them his 12 "bullet hole" scars. (Page 51)

A Blanche Lewis, as a child, was taken to the Millers and was frightened because John Miller talked a lot about guns, had many on the wall, and said he was Billy the Kid. (Page 60)

In about 1883, an Emma Tietjen, one of Mormon Earnest Tietjen's wives, was frightened by some rough men who came to the house when she was alone, so she hit one over the head with a bowl of butter. And one of the men told her she had hit Billy the Kid; though no one said he was John Miller. And nothing was done to her. To Helen Airy, that proved Billy was alive after the 1881 Fort Sumner shooting, was chivalrous to women, and was John Miller! (Page 62)

A woman named Feliz Bustamante was a neighbor of the Millers and spent time in their home as a girl. And the Millers talked about Billy the Kid. (Page 72) Airy interjected that the Kid was basically good, and so was John Miller. (Pages 72-73)

An Andrew Vander Wagen was a missionary, and stated that John Miller was thinking of stealing his horse, but decided not to, and then attended his sermons. He thought both that Miller was Billy the Kid, and that he was "not right in the head"

(Pages 77, 79)– the latter opinion being the only true statement Airy gleaned from her old folks' interviews.

Georgie Jackson was given a different version that eliminated any thought of Miller as Billy; stating; "[Miller] told us he was on the run with his wife ... [H]is mother was a Comanche Indian, and his father was a white man ... He lived in Texas with his mother and the Comanche Indians until he was grown ... Miller knew Billy the Kid and ran with him on some of his escapades." (Pages 143-144) Airy ignores the implication of this total negation of Miller as Billy.

A Joe Conley stated that Miller was always critical of Billy the Kid stories in various publications, saying: "[T]hey were wrong] and I ought to know because I was there." And when Conley stated that Miller said he had been a horse thief and raided a town, Helen Airy interjected that this must refer to when he was in Lincoln County as the outlaw Billy the Kid. (Page 145)

Miller's neighbor, a Carl Baxter, stated: "I believe that John Miller knew Billy the Kid." (Page 147)

And an unnamed source added that Miller also knew John Chisum, and worked for "the Chisum brothers." (Page 146) To ignorant Airy, it was amazing that Miller knew that Chisum had brothers, missing the point that Billy never worked for them.

## CONCLUDING FAKERY

Pretending that her nonsense proved something, Helen Airy launched a conspiracy theory that "the testimonies that Billy the Kid had escaped death in Fort Sumner [she forgot that Bernard Creasy said Miller said it was in Lincoln] were silenced [because] the myths surrounding Billy the Kid and Pat Garrett were too overwhelming." (Page 147) She wildly fantasized that maybe Susan McSween, "Cattle Queen of the Pecos," had helped Miller escape New Mexico; or even got money for him from John Tunstall's family. (Pages 159-160) She claimed Miller had a trunk with Billy the Kid's letters, but it was lost. She claimed Isadora was Manuela Bowdre, because she was short and Mexican.

Without an iota of evidence, or even claiming John Miller said anything like her claim, Airy rhapsodized: "John Miller in his youth was known throughout the world as the brave young man who was called Billy the Kid, who in a bloody war known as the Lincoln County War, heroically took on the Santa Fe Ring conspiracy." (Page 148) And she bemoaned that people had made money from the story, but not John Miller, because he was forced to hide out from the Ring.

Airy has a small "Afterward" with hearsay claims by non-historical people, much like the fake Affidavits in "Brushy Bill's hoax. So a woman whose father lived near Fort Sumner in the early 1900's said a Mexican he worked for told him he saw Billy the Kid in bullfights in Mexico after the death date. Someone from Albuquerque was told by a man who died in 1935 and said he worked for Pete Maxwell, that an Indian who died the night before the supposed shooting of Billy was buried as him. A man told his family that he was Billy the Kid's friend, and helped bury the body, and it was not Billy's. A granddaughter of Sheriff William Brady told someone that someone told her that Garrett had not killed Billy, but had killed a "wanderer" to let Billy escape. And George Coe is claimed as not believing Billy was shot, though he had no way of knowing. (Pages 162-163)

For fake press reports of Billy sightings after his death, Airy presented tabloid-like *El Paso Times* articles from the 1920's to 1960's. For example, the Fort Sumner Billy the Kid grave is said to have been "marked by a rude cross, that was to prove to Billy's sister that he was still alive." (Page 165) **[But Billy had no sister. And he was dead!]**

Airy concluded whimsically: "And so William Bonney, alias Billy the Kid, alias John Miller, alias The Old Man, alias Old Dad, died alone and was buried in the Arizona Pioneer [sic] Home Cemetery in Prescott. But John Miller won the last round. He was not hanged by the lackeys of the Santa Fe Ring." (Page 148)

## SUMMARY

Presenting no evidence whatsoever that John Miller was Billy Bonney, Helen Airy's book nevertheless bears striking resemblance to the more labor-intensive "Brushy Bill" hoax; with a faked birthdate, fabricated historical events, falsified physical match, reliance on hearsay, and explanations by conspiracy theorizing rather than real evidence.

# PART IV

## THE "BILLY THE KID CASE" HOAX

# CHAPTER 1
# CREATION OF THE "BILLY THE KID CASE" HOAX

## LEGACY OF "BRUSHY BILL"

The "Billy the Kid Case" hoax was enormous, spawned in 2003 from William V. Morrison's original scam; and its covert goal was to fulfill his huckster's dream of a gubernatorial pardon for imposter "Brushy Bill" Roberts. Proved in the years since the failed Governor T.J. Mabry pardon hearing, were two things: the fable was a money-maker and media magnet (think "Young Guns II"), but it was historically ridiculous. So it took special people to take on a re-run: self-serving sociopaths. True-believers, like W.C. Jameson, were rolled out for saccharine sincerity; while the perpetrators conducted thug history by might makes right.

But Morrison's ghost hovered. His May 19, 1955 letter from duped past president Harry S. Truman, was prescient; stating: "It is too bad that the old man who called himself "Billy the Kid" could not have lived long enough to see another Governor of New Mexico. He might have obtained a **just** decision." Truman was right about a future Governor; he just erred that the decision needed was **"just."** The scheme was a perfect match for corrupt Governor Bill Richardson; seeking national publicity for a craved presidential run, and seeking pay-to-play for a major political donor who was a Texan "Brushy"-believer.

And master promoter Morrison had already invented the hook after the failed pardon: digging up Billy the Kid. Right after his *Alias Billy the Kid* came out, Morrison wrote to a William Waters on June 29, 1955 (sending a copy to his fan, Paul Blazer): "You believe that the Kid was killed, but you say, " 'shouldn't we pay a little more attention to the body buried in the grave,' and I agree with you. **We should pay a lot of attention to the body buried.** If we could have found a cause of action to get into court, one of the first orders would have been to exhume the remains. In the absence of a coroner's verdict [his fake claim], **we did not have the necessary cause of action.** I am giving serious thought to a plan that may enable a legal exhumation. **If so, I firmly believe that a scientific investigation would determine that it was not the body of the Kid and that the lead slugs did not pass through the pistol Garrett had claimed he used that night.** This will not prove Roberts' claim, but it will prove that the Kid was not killed by Garrett."

But Morrison, just a traveling salesman, could not think his way around the legal obstacle of "[no] necessary cause of action." Digging up human remains needs a reason overriding sanctity of a grave, and needs someone with legal standing: the right to make a case in a court - usually kin of the deceased.

The brilliant and devious solution likely came from Richardson's potential recipient of "Brushy's" Billy the Kid crown: a law partner in a multi-million dollar personal injury firm: Bill Robins III. The second category able to breech the moral barrier of exhumation is law enforcement - if exhumation is needed to solve a crime. That fit the "Brushy"-Morrison-Sonnichsen claim that Pat Garrett murdered an innocent victim, Billy Barlow, and was never punished because of his cover-up. SO ALL THAT WAS NEEDED WAS OPENING A REAL MURDER CASE AGAINST GARRETT TO GET IN THE GRAVE!

The next hurdle involved conscience: violating a grave for no reason, and lying that there was no statute of limitations for murder in New Mexico. But with Santa Fe Ring politics unbroken from the days of Billy the Kid, it was easy to find morally vulnerable profiteering lawmen to file that murder case.

Then came the next hook, possibly a group effort by the growing cabal: to claim modern DNA forensics would prove Billy the Kid was not in his Fort Sumner grave, by matching those remains with his mother's in Silver City. That both graves were just tourist markers, did not faze these reprobates who intended to fake the DNA results to get whatever match they desired anyway. That, of course, necessitated a "forensic" expert in the mold of W.C. Jameson's and Frederick Bean's, who did their photo-match of "Brushy" and Billy; or Helen Airy's sculptor, who twinned John Miller and Billy. So they got notorious Dr. Henry Lee. And complicit judges for exhumation permits were recruited by Richardson's appointments.

The fraudulent forensics was to tie in the loose end of the pardon - fake matching of DNA from Billy's mother to "Brushy" (though he said she was not *his* mother) to make him Billy; then pardoning him for having led a long and law-abiding life. And his history would supersede the real history, while Governor Bill Richardson would become the first American governor to hand his state's iconic history to another state for personal gain.

It looked like the perfect crime - and crime it was, because intended was getting away scot-free from unjustified wanton desecration of graves. And after generations of helplessly facing impenetrable Ring corruption, New Mexican's could be counted on to do nothing, believing resistance was futile and dangerous.

But there was an unanticipated problem: me. I had moved to New Mexico in 1999 to write a novel on Billy the Kid, Paulita Maxwell, the Lincoln County War, and the Santa Fe Ring. Its first draft was then completed, and had used over 40,000 pages of archival documents and books. I knew the history. As an M.D, psychiatrist doing forensic consulting in murder cases, I had access to the most sophisticated DNA experts in the country. I knew the science. And I had recognized the magnificence of the unsung freedom fight, of which Billy Bonney was an inspirational hero. To protect the true history, I was willing to take the risk against these dangerous bullies.

It was a "Brushy Bill" hoax on an astronomical scale, appearing in national and international press and a TV documentary. It was Lincoln County Sheriff's Department Case 2003-274; called by its promulgators the "Billy the Kid Case."

I blocked it by litigation against its illegal exhumations. And I blocked it by open records litigation revealing its DNA frauds. And I exposed it in my 2014 book: *Cracking the Billy the Kid Case Hoax: The Strange Plot to Exhume Billy the Kid, Convict Sheriff Pat Garrett of Murder, and Become President of the United States.* It would take 15 years for it to attempt a come-back disguised by another name as "Cold Case Billy the Kid," in W.C. Jameson's 2018 book, as he still struggled, now in league with low-level "Billy the Kid Case" hoaxers, to make "Brushy" Billy the Kid.

# DIABOLICAL DNA DECEPTION

The "Billy the Kid Case" hoax entered at a stratospheric level; though decades of "Brushy's" ridicule necessitated covert action. On June 5, 2003, Governor Bill Richardson announced his scam to the world in a front page *New York Times* article titled "122 Years Later, The Lawmen Are Still Chasing Billy the Kid." Its irresponsible reporter, Michael Janofsky, mouthed that Richardson was simply doing an investigation about pardoning Billy the Kid. But Richardson's "experts," unbeknownst to the public, were just "Brushy"-believers and complicit lawmen.

So Janofsky wrote that Richardson was seeking **"evidence to a long-held alternative theory that Garrett shot someone other than the Kid and led a conspiracy to cover up his crime;"** and that a Jannay Valdez, owner of a "Billy the Kid ["Brushy Bill"] Museum" in Canton, Texas, said: **"I'm absolutely convinced that Garrett killed someone else and that Brushy Bill was the Kid." Listed lawmen were Lincoln County Sheriff Tom Sullivan, and his Deputy, Steve Sederwall, filing the murder case against Pat Garrett**; as well as a Texas law firm for the case [**Attorney Bill Robins III**]. Richardson's spokesman [Billy Sparks] stated **"the state would assist by clearing any legal hurdles to gain access to the mother's body."** With feigned CSI glamour, Janofsky concluded that if "Brushy" was not a match, they could check John Miller. As to the pardon, Janofsky wrote that Governor Lew Wallace had promised it. Hidden was that "Brushy" was discredited since 1950, and that Billy the Kid's and his mother's graves were just tourist markers without valid remains for DNA. The article stated:

LINCOLN, NEW MEXICO – For more than 120 years, Pat Garrett has enjoyed legendary status in the American West, a lawman on a par with Wyatt Earp, Bat Masterson, even Matt Dillon. As sheriff here in Lincoln County in 1881, Garrett is credited with shooting to death the notorious outlaw known as Billy the Kid, a killing that made Garrett a hero. For years, a patch bearing his likeness has adorned uniforms worn by sheriff''s deputies here.

**But now, modern science is about to interrupt Garrett's fame in a way that some say could expose him as a liar who covered up a murder to save his own skin and reputation.**

Officials in New Mexico and Texas are working out plans to exhume and conduct genetic tests on the bodies of a woman buried in New Mexico who was believed to be the Kid's mother and a Texas man known as Brushy Bill Roberts, who claimed to be the Kid and died in 1950 at the age of 90. If test results suggest that the two were related, it would add new evidence to a long-held alternative theory that Garrett shot someone other than the Kid and led a conspiracy to cover up his crime.

Such skepticism is hardly uncommon. Disputes over major events in the Old West have engaged historians almost since they happened. The debate over Billy the Kid is one of the longest-running.

Beyond renewing interest in the Kid saga, the possibility that testing could enlarge Garrett's reputation or destroy it has even caught the fancy of Gov. Bill Richardson of New Mexico, who has offered state aid for the investigation and a possible pardon that an earlier New Mexico governor had once promised the Kid for a murder he committed.

"The problem is, there's so much fairy tale with this story that it's hard to nail down the facts," said Steve Sederwall, the mayor of Capitan, N.M., who is working with Lincoln County's current sheriff, Tom Sullivan, to resolve the matter. "All we want is the truth, whatever it is. If the guy Garrett killed was Billy the Kid, that makes him a hero. If it wasn't, Garrett was a murderer, and we have egg on our face, big time."

No matter what the genetic testing may show - and it might not show much of anything – it is hard to overstate the prominence of Garrett and the Kid in Western lore, especially here in southeastern New Mexico where their lives converged during and after the gun battles for financial control of the region that were known as the Lincoln County War. The Kid's notoriety grew after he and friends on one side of the conflict killed several men in an ambush, including Garrett's predecessor, Sheriff William Brady. For that, the Kid was hunted down, captured by Garrett, found guilty of murder and taken to the Lincoln jail, where he was placed in shackles to await hanging. He was only 21.

Today the tiny town of Lincoln, population 38, is a memorial to what happened next. More than a dozen buildings, including one that housed the jail, have been preserved as a state monument that attracts as many as 35,000 visitors a year.

**Historians generally agree that the Kid, born Henry McCarty and known at times as William H. Bonney, escaped after it became apparent that Gov. Lew Wallace had reneged on a promise to pardon him in exchange for information**

about another killing in the county war. On April 28, 1881, the Kid managed to get his hands on a gun, kill the two deputies assigned to watch him and leave the area on horseback.

But then the stories diverge, providing fuel for two major theories of where, when, and how the Kid's life ended.

The version embraced here and supported by numerous books and Garrett relatives is that the Kid made his way to a friend's ranch in Fort Sumner, about 100 miles northeast of Lincoln. The ranch owner, Pete Maxwell, was also a friend of Garrett and somehow got word to Garrett that the Kid was in the area. After arriving, Garrett posted two deputies at the door.

As the Kid approached on the night of July 13 [sic], he spoke a few words in Spanish to the deputies, who did not recognize him. But Garrett, waiting inside, knew the voice. When the Kid walked in, Garrett turned and shot him in the heart.

William F. Garrett of Alamogordo, N.M., who is Garrett's grand-nephew, said years of research, including conversations with his cousin Jarvis, the last of Garrett's eight children, convinced him there is "no question about it" that his great-uncle killed Billy the Kid at Maxwell's. Jarvis died in 1991 at the age of 86.

"He was hired to get the Kid, and he got the Kid," Mr. Garrett said in an interview. "uncle Pat was a person of integrity who did his job. He was a law abider, not a law breaker."

But just as the story of Garrett as hero has flourished over the years, so have others, including the tale of Brushy Bill of Hico, Tex. His trip to New Mexico in 1950 to seek the pardon he said he was denied nearly 70 years before gave new life to an alternative possibility, that Garrett had not killed the Kid at all, but a drifter friend of the Kid's named Billy Barlow.

This story holds that Garrett and the Kid may have been in cahoots for some reason and that Garrett had stashed a gun at the outhouse at the jail that the Kid used to kill the deputies and escape. Even if only part of that is true, it would strongly suggest that Garrett killed the wrong man.

**Speaking with the same person as Garrett's great-nephew, Jannay P. Valdez, curator of the Billy the Kid Museum in Canton, Tex., said he had no doubt that Garrett killed someone else and that Brushy Bill was the Kid.** "I'm absolutely convinced," he said here on Monday after meeting with Mr. Sederwall to discuss theories and how to begin the kind of genetic testing that has been used to ascertain lineage of other historical figures like Thomas Jefferson and Jessie James. "I'd bank everything I have on it."

As longtime friends, Mr. Sederwall and Sheriff Sullivan decided they wanted to settle the matter once and for all but could do so only through scientific analysis. To justify the effort that would require much of their time and, perhaps at some point, taxpayer money, they needed an official reason. So in April, they opened the first-ever investigation into the murders of the two deputies shot in the Kid's escape, James W. Bell and Robert Olinger, to examine what happened at the jail and Maxwell's ranch.

**[AUTHOR'S NOTE: Janofsky is parroting the hoax. The deputy murders and Garrett's killing of the Kid are unconnected, but the hoaxers made-up that Garrett helped the escape.]**

As Mr. Sederwall said, "There's no statute of limitations on murder."

**[AUTHOR'S NOTE: This announces the real murder case; but hidden is New Mexico's having had a statute of limitation.]**

The goal now, he said, is to compare genetic evidence of Catherine Antrim, believed to be the Kid's mother, who died of tuberculosis in 1874 and is buried in Silver City, N.M., and of Brushy Bill, who lived out his life in Texas. A Dallas firm [sic Houston] has agreed to help, and a spokesman for governor Richardson said the state would assist by clearing legal hurdles to gain access to the mother's body.

The Kid was buried at Fort Sumner, N.M., although the whereabouts of the grave are uncertain; he has no known living relatives. Mr. Valdez said he had already secured permission to exhume the body of Brushy Bill, who is buried 20 miles from Hico in Hamilton, Texas.

But solving the mystery might not be so simple. For one thing, Mr. Valdez said he was certain that the woman buried in Silver City was but "a half aunt." And even if tests disqualify Brushy Bill as Billy the Kid, other "Kids" have emerged over the years, including a man named John Miller, who died in 1937 and is buried in Prescott, Ariz. Mr. Sederwall said that efforts would be made to exhume his body as well.

The investigators conceded that much is riding on their quest. Sheriff Sullivan, a tall, strapping man who carries a turquoise-handled .357 magnum on his right hip, said he, like so many others in the West, revered Garrett for gunning down the Kid. The uniform patch with Garrett's likeness was his design. Now, the legend is threatened.

**"I just want to get to the bottom of it," said Sheriff Sullivan**, who is retiring next year. "My integrity's at stake. So's my department's. So's what we believe in and even New Mexico history. If Garrett shot someone other than the Kid, that makes him a murderer and he covered it up. He wouldn't be such a role model, then, and we'd have to take the patches off the uniforms."

On June 10, 2003, Richardson held a press conference, with a press release repeating his Janofsky fakery. Present were key hoaxers: Lincoln County's Sheriff Tom Sullivan and Deputy Steve Sederwall; De Baca County's Sheriff Gary Graves; Attorney for exhuming the mother, Sherry Tippett; and University of New Mexico professor Paul Hutton, appointed by Richardson as the hoax's "historical advisor." Richardson revealed that Lincoln County Sheriff's Department murder case against Pat Garrett had been flied as No. 2003-274. The press release promised use of forensic DNA to prove that the Kid deserved a pardon. It stated:

**State of New Mexico**
*Office of the Governor*

**Bill Richardson**
Governor
For immediate release
6/10/03

Contact: Billy Sparks
telephone number

### GOVERNOR BILL RICHARDSON ANNOUNCES STATE SUPPORT OF BILLY THE KID INVESTIGATION

SANTA FE – Governor Bill Richardson today outlined how the state of New Mexico will support the investigation efforts to investigate the life and death of Billy the Kid.

Governor Richardson delivered the following remarks during a news conference today in the State Capitol:

This is an important day in the history of New Mexico and the American West. I am announcing my support and the support of the state of New Mexico for the investigation into the life and death of Henry McCarty, also known as William Bonney. To millions around the world, he was called Billy the Kid. How he captured the world's imagination is well worth exploring. His life, though ended at the age of 21, is part of what makes New Mexico and an American West, unique.

**My goal is to shed new light on old history.**

**I am pleased to be joined here by Lincoln County Sheriff Tom Sullivan, Capitan Mayor Steve Sederwall, DeBaca County Sheriff Gary Grays [sic - Graves]. Grant County Attorney Sherry Tippett, University of New Mexico History Professor, Doctor Paul Hutton and State Police Major Tom Branch.**

**Let me tell you how this all came about.**

**Last month I was contacted by Lincoln County Sheriff, Tom Sullivan and Capitan Mayor, Steve Sederwall, to support reopening the case. Case number 2003-274 seeks to answer key**

questions that have lingered for over 120 years surrounding the life and the death of Billy the Kid.

This episode in the history of New Mexico and the history of the old west is both fact and legend and continues to stir the imagination and interest of people all over the world.

**By utilizing modern forensic, DNA and crime scene techniques, the goal of the investigation is to get to the truth.** In the process, the reputation of Pat Garrett, still a hero in Lincoln County law enforcement, hangs in the balance. **The question is did Sheriff Garrett kill Billy the Kid at Fort Sumner, New Mexico on July 14. 1881?**

This investigation will also seek to shed new light on the events surrounding the escape of Billy the Kid from the Lincoln County Jail on April 28, 1881. The shooting of Deputies J.W. Bell and Bob Olinger by Billy the Kid has never been officially investigated. Where did Billy get his gun and what really happened?

I have contacted the national Labs, Los Alamos and Sandia and have been assured that they will volunteer their support in this effort. Los Alamos Lab can assist us by providing ground penetrating radar, DNA expertise and technical forensic assistance. Sandia Labs will allow their experts to volunteer their time to help us uncover the facts.

The State Police will help supervise the investigation and crime scene analysis of the evidence uncovered in the investigation.

**I have also asked University of New Mexico Professor of History and Executive Director of the Western History Association, Doctor Paul Hutton, to serve as our historical advisor.** Dr. Hutton has served as President of the Western Writers of America and has won several national honors for his works on western history.

I intend to hold hearings at Fort Sumner, Lincoln, Silver City and Mesilla. I will appoint a defense counsel and a prosecutor to present the evidence. **[Never done.]**

**As Governor, I will examine the events surrounding the alleged offer of a pardon to Billy the Kid by former New Mexico Governor Lew Wallace. I will evaluate the evidence uncovered and make a decision.**

There is no question that this story deserves our attention and that the history of New Mexico and the American West is important to all of us. If we can get to the truth we will. I have total confidence in the team you see here today to conduct a professional, honest and exhaustive investigation of the facts and report back to me and to the rest of the world what really happened here in New Mexico.

The benefits to our state and to the history of the West far outweigh any cost we may incur. I expect the actual cost to be nominal. Just since this investigation was announced, it has sparked news articles about New Mexico and Lincoln County from New York to London to India. Getting to the truth is our goal. But, if this increases interest and tourism in our state, I couldn't be happier.

I understand that Movie Producer Ron Howard has donated the cabin used in shooting his movie "The Missing", being shot in Santa Fe, to Silver City. The cabin is a replica of a Billy the Kid era home. The cabin will be delivered to Silver City this week.

The potential benefit from this investigation to all of New Mexico is already being felt and is well worth the effort.    #30#

Proved was Richardson's scorn of the public. No relevant DNA existed! Even in 1997, "Brushy"-promoting author, Dale L. Walker, in his *Legends and Lies*, had written: "[Frederick] Bean knew that the exhumation of the Kid's grave in Fort Sumner was **unlikely to provide any evidence and would probably not even produce any bones** due to the repeated floodings of the nearby Pecos River. In any event, no known blood relatives of the outlaw survived and so DNA testing was not an option." (Walker, Page 134) In their 1998 book, *The Return of the Outlaw Billy the Kid*, W.C. Jameson and Frederick Bean had written: "Billy the Kid's current gravesite is not even authentic ... The original wooden marker, often used by drunks for target practice, disappeared ... **The current marker is a tourist attraction, nothing more**, and it is estimated it lies several yards from the original burial site." (Jameson and Bean, Pages 132-133) So all this was ignored.

Also insurmountable, was that the exhumation of Billy the Kid had already been legally blocked. In 1962, the family of Charles Bowdre, buried beside Billy, successfully sued, blocking any exhumation, then and forever, of Billy the Kid, as potentially disrupting Charlie's remains. And the grave of Billy's mother, Catherine Antrim, had no valid remains at all. So all this was ignored.

As to exhumation petitions for the murder investigation against Pat Garrett, there was no murder to investigate. Billy's Coroner's Jury had declared Garrett's killing of him not a crime; swearing on July 15, 1881: *"our verdict is that the deed of said Garrett was justifiable homicide."* Proof that this was legally valid is that no charges were filed against him for murder, and he was granted Lew Wallace's reward. Additionally, the statute of limitations to prosecute him expired in 1891. So this was ignored.

Instead, Richardson and cohorts declared that Garrett had murdered an innocent victim as grave-filler, instead of Billy the Kid. To "convict" him, a "cold case" investigation was instigated to see if the victim - instead of Billy - lay in the Fort Sumner grave. (Note that W.C. Jameson's 2018 rerun of this hoax used that claim to rename the defeated "Billy the Kid Case" as *Cold Case Billy the Kid*.) Ignored was zero historical basis for the claim.

Then, by lying that there was no statute of limitations for murder, they filed real murder case No. 274-2003 against Garrett in the Lincoln County Sheriff's Department (where Garrett had been Sheriff) and Case No. 03-06-136-01. in the De Baca County Sheriff's Department (for Fort Sumner's Billy the Kid grave). The objective was the exhumation of Billy the Kid. His DNA was to be compared with his exhumed mother's DNA in Silver City, to see if he matched her. Hidden from the public was that New Mexico's Office of the Medical Investigator (OMI) refused exhumation permits based on no valid DNA available from either grave.

But what about the pardon? **The "DNA" (though there was none) of the mother would also be matched to "Brushy," in his Hamilton, Texas, grave. If "Brushy" matched mom, then *he* was Billy the Kid; and, by extrapolation, the remains in the Fort Sumner grave could not be Billy, so they were the innocent victim, and Garrett was a murderer.** So slyly slipped in "Brushy" just looked like part of their murder case, instead of its purpose. And since there would be no real DNA anyway, they planned to claim any matchings they wanted with their complicit forensic expert.

But what about the pardon? Hoax Attorney, Bill Robins III, gave the link in the Grant County District Court in his January 5, 2004 "Pre-Hearing Brief" petitioning to dig up Catherine Antrim. His fakery began with stating that his client was dead Billy the Kid! (Note that a corpse cannot be a client.) And, speaking for Billy, he claimed "Billy" had and interest in "his legacy." Then Robins slipped in "Brushy." **The diabolically clever hoax, possibly Robins's own brain-child, was to claim the fake "DNA match," and then claim "Brushy" deserved the gubernatorial pardon as Billy the Kid for having led a long and law-abiding life.** So Robins wrote: **"Should the DNA extracted from Ms. Antrim confirm that one of the potential Kids was in fact Billy the Kid, undersigned counsel will be able to make an even stronger argument for pardon by citing to the long years of law abiding life."**

## *THE BOTTOMLESS BUDGET*

Here is where the bottomless budget came into play. Recall that William V. Morrison struggled with his Indiana Historical Society $9.78 bill for Billy the Kid records for coaching "Brushy." Now, behind "Brushy" were limitless taxpayer dollars for fueling this hoax. Ultimately, it would use the Governor and his office staff; District Courts in Grant, De Baca, and Sandoval Counties; the Lincoln County and De Baca County Sheriffs Departments; and would pay attorneys defending its Sheriffs and Deputies a half-million dollars to stonewall my records requests for seven years to hide their fake DNA records from me to cover up their hoax and its illegal exhumations.

## *THE CAST OF HOAXERS*

Limitless also were on-paper credentials of the hoaxers, all secretly backing "Brushy" as a favor to Richardson. Besides Richardson and Attorney Robins, there was state-salaried University of New Mexico history professor, Paul Hutton, appointed by Richardson as the official historian, and writer-producer of its hoax-promoting History Channel program. The lawmen were Lincoln County Sheriff Tom Sullivan, who deputized for the case the Mayor of Capitan, Steve Sederwall. After Sullivan's tenure, his Undersheriff, Rick Virden, was elected Sheriff; and he deputized both Sullivan and Sederwall to continue it under him. Taxpayer-funded Lincoln County Attorney Alan Morel hid the hoax from the County Commissioners. In De Baca County, Sheriff Gary Graves participated. And Ted Hartley, the District Court Judge there, like Henry Quintero in Grant County for the mother's grave, had just been appointed by Richardson to back the exhumation of Billy the Kid there. And the U.S. Marshals Service Historian in Washington, D.C., David Turk, actively participated. Editor-in-Chief of the *Albuquerque Journal*, Kent Walz, publicized the hoax profusely, with no rebuttals. And Editor-in-Chief of the glossy Old West magazine, *True West*, Bob Boze Bell, not only backed the hoax, but also promoted "Brushy" with W.C. Jameson. And Jameson appeared in Professor Hutton's documentary to push "Brushy" as Billy. By 2005, Arizona Governor Janet Napolitano paved the way for illegally exhuming John Miller in the historic, state controlled Arizona Pioneers' Home Cemetery in Prescott. For that foray, a Dave Tunnell, a self-styled "psycholinguistic expert" friend of Deputy Sederwall, was enlisted as a "forensic expert" front. And for a real forensic expert to carry out all the DNA fakery, they enlisted Dr. Henry Lee, of O.J. Simpson trial infamy, and detested by colleagues as a publicity hound doing sleazy "show-biz" forensics. But the "star quality" of this shady gang intimidated opponents and dazzled the press. It seemed impossible that they were all colluding liars.

## HOAX PROGRESSION

The "Billy the Kid Case" hoax became arguably the most elaborate historical fraud ever perpetrated. But what made it nearly unbeatable was Bill Richardson's megalomaniacal determination to win. So every time I legally blocked the schemes, his empowered minions merely rewrote the hoax and persisted; cynically assuming the public would not notice fakery or failures. The progression, thus, became increasingly absurd, desperate, and ultimately criminal; with nasty push-back of conspiracy theories. But the Richardson umbrella of immunity from legal consequences never sprang a leak - and gave me first-hand opportunity to experience the same Santa Fe Ring corruption that had yielded the Lincoln County War freedom fight history of Billy the Kid.

### *FROM FAKERY TO FELONIES*

Few New Mexicans dared to oppose Richardson and his hoax. It fell to me to stop the steamrolling behemoth. I hired attorneys to block the exhumations of Billy and his mother through honorable mayors standing for their towns of Silver City and Fort Sumner. We won by 2004 based on no valid graves, opposition of the OMI, historic certainty that Pat Garrett killed Billy the Kid, and the precedent case blocking the Fort Sumner exhumation. That had no effect on the "Billy the Kid Case" hoaxers. They merely fabricated a new source of "DNA."

In 2004, they announced they had found the carpenter's bench on which shot Billy the Kid had been laid out. This ignored their first hoax version in which Billy, as "Brushy," was not laid out; and the laid out corpse was the "innocent victim" or Billy Barlow. Ignored too, was that there was no certain proof that the bench was the real one. Their bench surfaced in 1926, 45 years after Billy's killing, for a little Billy the Kid tourist display by a teenaged Maxwell family member. Since the Maxwell's lost Fort Sumner by 1884 in calamitous ruin of their fortunes, there was no evidence they saved the actual bench. And worst of all for the hoaxers, if Billy was laid out, he was dead: end of story.

So the hoaxers descended into the ridiculous. They claimed Billy *was* laid out, but *played dead*, while bleeding on the bench. Then Garrett substituted the murdered innocent victim as Billy climbed off to bench to escape as "Brushy." The hoaxers were pushing their luck with public credulity and stupidity. And even "Brushy," in his wildest confabulations, did not venture into this crazy scenario. But the punch-line was "bled on the bench."

Their "forensic expert," Dr. Henry Lee, was willing to say that its rust stains (expected on a carpenter's bench) looked like blood to him. So he tested for the "blood DNA of Billy the Kid." It should be noted that the chemical test he used was for iron, so it would be positive for rust, as well as blood. And even if it was the actual carpenter's bench, and even if it had recoverable DNA after 124 years, there existed no proven DNA of Billy the Kid (called reference DNA) to test it against for validity as being *Billy's DNA*. In other words, they had nothing.

But Lee was willing to find blood anywhere he was directed. So the lawmen had him "investigate" the courthouse, from which Billy escaped before hanging. This was to give a gloss of CSI to the increasingly obvious silliness. As may be recalled, Billy Bonney fatally shot Deputy James Bell when Bell fled down the back stairs. So Lee noted that under the second-floor boards, and down the wall under the steps, were brown stains - as could be seen on the wall by any tourist, including me, and looked like a second floor flood of rusty water that had streamed down. So Lee tested it for "blood," got a positive with his iron test, and the hoaxers made-up that it was Deputy Bell's blood! Then they claimed that this "investigation" proved Bell was shot on top of the stairs instead of the bottom, because the drips came from upstairs. Of course, no DNA was extracted; no verified Bell DNA existed to match it with if there had been any; and if it was blood instead of a flood of water, there had been a massacre of dozens on that second floor! Anyway, as a "finding," it was meaningless. But it was in the Sonnichsen-Jameson-Bean tradition of fabricating tiny fake discrepancies to claim "suspicion." So the hoaxers claimed that since Garrett said Bell was killed *on* the stairs, instead *on the top* of the stairs, he was a liar; which meant he never killed Billy the Kid! And the press dutifully reported this junk.

But Lee was not finished. Told the hoax scenario that Garrett did not kill the Kid, he made-up a "crime scene" from unsubstantiated furniture provided to him by the hoaxers. It was from the same teenaged Maxwell family member's 1926 "museum." She labeled it as from Peter Maxwell's bedroom, and it was in a newspaper photo in 1937. So Lee went to work. Examining a bed headboard, he claimed Garrett had lied that his second shot went through it, since there was no bullet hole. Lee omitted that there was also no headboard! It was just a frame around air! There was no place for any bullet hole!

Then Lee outdid himself. He "examined" what he called a washstand, finding two holes in it. Though it was not in actual history of the shooting, Lee fabricated that the holes were from a bullet shot by Garrett crouching on the floor and shooting over his back! And that proved, to Lee, that Garrett was a crawling coward! Hidden by Lee was that the washstand is unsubstantiated, the "crime scene" Maxwell house no longer exists to know where furniture was placed; the "washstand" is just a toy-sized little cube requiring the Garrett crouching; it had no bullet it; the holes could come from anytime in its history; and he made-up the entire scene. It was not forensics. It was fraud.

By then, the hoax's official historian, Professor Paul Hutton, had written and co-produced, with Bill Kurtis Productions, 2004's History Channel "Investigating History: Billy the Kid," about the "mystery" of the killing of Billy Bonney. A milestone in hoaxing, it included - beside's narrator Hutton's fakery and ignorant mangling of actual history - almost all the "Billy the Kid Case" hoaxers, including Richardson and Robins. W.C. Jameson even appeared to back "Brushy."

Jameson had already participated, in November of 2003, in hoaxing Editor-in-Chief Bob Boze Bell's *True West* magazine for "Was Brushy Bill Really Billy the Kid? Experts face off over new evidence." in a "debate" with Pat Garrett's biographer, Leon Metz. For it, Jameson parroted Morrisonisms, and waved Dr. Acton's fake photo-comparison, along with "Brushy's" made-up name: "On one side, passionate supporters of the historical status quo assert Roberts was a fraud, yet to date they have provided no logical, definitive proof ... Roberts was an illiterate man, yet he was astonishingly intimate with the people, geography, architecture and events of Lincoln County, New Mexico, in the late 1870s-early 1880s – an intimacy that could have come only from being present and involved ... After Roberts' image was compared to the only known photograph of Billy the Kid, **one researcher concluded that William**

**Henry Roberts was, in all likelihood, Billy the Kid, and as such, history needed to be rewritten."**

The obvious direction was to "Brushy's" grave. But I had warned Hamilton officials about the hoax and its having no valid DNA for matchings, so no exhumation of "Brushy" was permitted.

But, by then, the hoaxers were desperate for any results; and Bill Kurtis's TV cameras were poised for another production. The only available victim was John Miller, underground in the Arizona Pioneers' Home Cemetery, with his fatal broken hip, and with corrupt state Governor, Janet Napolitano indifferent to violating graves for a publicity stunt. And Dr. Rick Staub, the director of Dr. Henry Lee's regular DNA processing lab, Orchid Cellmark, in Texas, was eager to collect bones with himself on camera. So wanton desecration of graves and grave robbing joined the "Billy the Kid Case" hoax's repertoire. Under Lincoln County Sheriff Rick Virden, the on-site perpetrators were his Deputies Tom Sullivan and Steve Sederwall. Concealed from authorities was that they had no DNA of Billy Bonney to compare with any remains to justify any exhumation - besides the fact that John Miller was not Billy the Kid, and never claimed their playing-dead-carpenter's-bench-bleeding for DNA scenario. For that gambit, hoaxer, Dave Tunnell, posed for the press as a John-Miller-as-Billy-believer. And Sheriff Sullivan "became" one too!

Then it got worse. Knowing they were crossing the line to potential indictments, they behaved with extreme secrecy, rushing a backhoe into the cemetery, and working into the night with flashlights. Then it got worse. There were no grave markers. It was just an open field. So they descended to barbaric depths, plowing into one grave, collapsing its coffin and grabbing bones. In doubt that they were in the right grave, they demolished the adjoining one. Skulls, femurs, a pelvis, and other bones from both graves, were horrifically dismembered for Rick Staub's bone bags. Deputy Steve Sederwall even posed for a ghastly trophy photo holding a skull. That picture made the papers.

Miller's dead neighbor, the random desecrated man, was named William Hudspeth. (Imagine that he was your beloved relative, now with demolished remains and destroyed grave.)

Following these atrocities, the hoaxers claimed to have gotten John Miller's DNA for matching with carpenter's bench "DNA;" and that he had buck teeth, like Billy the Kid. But, at that point, they had a problem besides felonious desecrations and grave-robbing. To feign a real forensic investigation, they had hired a

Maricopa County Office of the Medical Investigator forensic anthropologist named Dr. Laura Fulginiti. Somehow thinking that the fiasco was legitimate, and honest herself, she dutifully wrote a complete report of both exhumations. [APPENDIX: 9] It denied the hoaxers' claims of John Miller's skull having buck teeth. It had no teeth! So Bill Kurtis had ended up filming a crime scene.

By 2006, a duped French film maker, with visions of Young Guns II, had filmed the Lincoln County lawmen in New Mexico, and had gotten Chris Kristopherson (Sam Pekinpaugh's Billy the Kid from his movie "Pat Garrett and Billy the Kid") as narrator. It made the Cannes Film Festival, and while facing possible indictment for Miller/Hudspeth felonies, Rick Virden's Deputies, Sullivan and Sederwall, were wined and dined in France, where the film got an award; and they were taken seriously.

The hoax was so out-of-control that I had to do something. First I made a RICO case with the FBI against Richardson and the rest of his colluding public officials. In 1970, Congress had passed that Racketeer Influenced and Corrupt Organizations Act to enable prosecution of all members in a criminal cabal. It prosecuted conspiracy for the same criminal objective; stating: "If conspirators have a plan which calls for some conspirators to commit the crime and others to provide support, the supporters are as guilty as the perpetrators." But the corrupt U.S. Attorney, David Iglesias, (removed soon after for shielding Richardson in his other pay-to-play schemes) blocked the FBI from pursuit. Meanwhile, the Maricopa County District Attorney's office investigated the Miller-Hudspeth exhumations, while I informed on the hoax. I also reported Dr. Henry Lee to the American Academy of Forensic Sciences (AAFS) Ethics Committee as perpetrating a hoax. They shielded him.

## *CALLING THE DNA BLUFF IN COURT*

It was left to me to stop the destruction of the history of Billy the Kid. In 2006, under the open records act, I demanded the Lincoln County lawmen's DNA records from the carpenter's bench, the courthouse floorboards, and the bones of John Miller and William Hudspeth. Rick Virden was then Sheriff, with Tom Sullivan, and Steve Sederwall as his Deputies for the "Billy the Kid Case." For intimidation, complicit Lincoln County Attorney Allan Morel, with the lawmen, then reported me to the U.S. Marshals Service as a terrorist - presumably to their fellow hoaxer there, its historian, David Turk. And they also claimed they had no DNA records at all! So I reported that to the Maricopa County District Attorney's office, in hopes of precipitating prosecution for illegal exhumations without DNA for justification; but the only result was cover-up through Governor Napolitano.

In 2007, I hired a law firm to litigate, under open records law, against Virden, Sullivan, and Sederwall for the DNA records. So these hoaxers rewrote the hoax again. Since only public officials are required to turn over public records, **they claimed that they had been private hobbyists all along, dabbling in the history!** Of course, "private hobbyists" do not operate out of sheriff's departments and cannot dig up graves.

But five sets of my apparently pressured attorneys tried to throw my case, as the hoaxers stonewalled, and the judge permitted it. I finally went *pro se*, and won; though the lawmen hid their DNA records throughout. But I had discovered that they had forged Dr. Lee's reports to trick the court that the case was a private hobby. So the judge made them give me Lee's actual report. It made no conclusion about obtaining the DNA of Billy the Kid. And I got the hidden results of the bench/Miller/Hudspeth DNA extractions and matchings from my co-plaintiff, who, in 2012, subpoenaed them from Orchid Cellmark Lab. They showed that no valid DNA - except from random man Hudspeth!

And the hoaxers' attorneys would ultimately pocket a half-million taxpayer dollars in fees for hiding the DNA records available for cost of postage at the time of my request.

## *THE FAKE PARDON THRUST*

By 2010, Governor Richardson's two terms were coming to a close. He was still determined to win the "Billy the Kid Case." So he played his last card: the pardon of Billy the Kid. And he linked it to his seven year "investigation." That translated into lying that "Billy the Kid Case" findings had established that "Brushy" was Billy the Kid, and deserved a pardon for his long and law-abiding life. In July of 2010, anticipating this, I contacted Pat Garrett's family. Though the case defamed him, they had been silent. Fortunately, his grandson, Jarvis Patrick "J.P." Garrett (from his son Jarvis, who had been in Governor Mabry's hearing) took action, arranging a family meeting with Richardson (who told them he would not meet if they brought me). J.P. Garrett got

Richardson to sign an agreement that he would not claim his grandfather killed an innocent victim.

But it was not over. Richardson simply attacked from another angle. He used his attorney from one of his past pay-to-play cases, a Randy McGinn, to claim *she* was an amateur historian, petitioning *herself* for a pardon for Billy the Kid based on past Governor Lew Wallace's "promise." It was now December 14, 2010, with Richardson having just 17 days left in office. My belief was that in a pardon, Richardson would again turn to "Brushy," fulfilling his original intent to hand over the history to Texas.

So I contacted Lew Wallace's great-grandson, William N. Wallace, a past *New York Times* reporter. He threatened Richardson with a law suit for defaming his family name.

On the 31st, Richardson told the waiting press that he had come to his decision. He lied that his "investigation" had revealed that Billy the Kid was an outlaw, so he could not pardon him!

## *THE CONCLUDING LITIGATION*

At that point, the "Billy the Kid Case" was not over. I still had five more years of my own litigation against the lawmen to get their fake DNA records. As it would turn out, though I prevailed, the state's corrupt high courts were concomitantly making decisions to shield corrupt officials from whistleblowers, like me, by removing penalties to wrongful records concealers, like my lawmen defendants! That meant the judiciary illegally rewrote the open records statute to claim that a records requester had to prove *personal injury* to get a penalty against violators; though getting public records is a citizen's right, and the penalties were written into the statute to force corrupt officials to comply. It had nothing to do with personal injury. And, of course, whistleblowers, are not litigating for personal injury, but to expose corruption. And the judiciary is not allowed to write statutes; that is done by the legislature.

But my compliant District Court judge removed all penalties to Virden and Sederwall (by then Sullivan had died) to block the $966,000 damages owed to me as a prevailing plaintiff. I appealed, and was denied up to the Supreme Court. Who was its chief Justice? Charles "Charlie" Daniels, appointed by Richardson, a major donor of Richardson's; and his wife is Attorney Randy McGinn, last to join the "Billy the Kid Case" hoax to save it in its zero hour with her "amateur historian pardon petition."

The "Billy the Kid Case" hoax was on a magnitude beyond any conception, tapping into the state's pervasive Santa Fe Ring corruption dating back to 1866, and conducted with soulless and conscienceless venality and smug certainty of Santa Fe Ring invulnerability of unchecked power.

All along, there had been a sincere fan of the "Billy the Kid Case": W.C. Jameson. It was the closest he, or any of "Brushy's" true-believers had ever come to realizing their dream of seeing him declared Billy the Kid. The termination of the case and its pardon dashed hopes and dreams. And with his usual gullibility and idolization of authority figures, Jameson must have believed the forensic claims of the hoaxers, and their bogus conspiracy theory explanations for their being blocked.

So, in 2006 and in 2012, Jameson wrote more "Brushy"-backing books, on "Brushy's" Morrison tape recordings and against Pat Garrett; but now with the hoaxers' unscrupulous influence. And in 2018, once again as "Brushy's indefatigable soldier, he renewed his quixotic foray, now joined by many of the past "Billy the Kid Case" hoaxers, to try again for the brass Ring of "Brushy" being Billy, by fusing their "Billy the Kid Case" hoax with the "Brushy" hoax for his *Cold Case Billy the Kid* book, built on the quicksand of their forensic hoax. And since *Cold Case Billy the Kid* relied on the original hoaxers and their lies about the content of their case's records, those individuals and documents require exposure. But Jameson, in usual blissful ignorance, and the participating hoaxers, in usual conniving exploitation, would never again mention the now blighted name of the "Billy the Kid Case" or its once famous file number Case 2002-274. They would proceed as if their infamy had never happened.

# CHAPTER 2
# "BILLY THE KID CASE" HOAXERS AND HOAX DOCUMENTS

The "Billy the Kid Case" hoaxers produced profuse press and legal documents for fake DNA claims and illegal exhumation attempts, which reveal the case as a rerun attempt to make "Brushy Bill" Billy the Kid. They also reveal the irony that there was no match to "Brushy's" own hoax, which lacked Catherine Antrim as Billy's mother, and shot-playing-dead-Billy-bleeding-on-bench with Garrett as his best buddy willing to murder for him. Nevertheless, desperate W.C. Jameson would eventually see it as advantageous to join forces with them - and ignore all that.

## STARTING GATE BLOCKADES

The "Billy the Kid Case" was a forensic fraud with covert goal of crowning "Brushy," by faked DNA matchings. Pat Garrett's fabricated murder of the innocent victim was to be proved by matching DNA from Fort Sumner's Billy the Kid grave to the Silver city mother's DNA; with no match meaning a stranger was in Billy's grave; ergo, Garrett killed Billy Barlow. Then "Brushy's" DNA would be matched to Catherine Antrim's DNA; with a match proving she was his mother; ergo, he was surviving Billy

But reality was the blockade. Catherine Antrim's gravesite was just a tourist marker, over overlapping plots, without verifiable remains. And matching her "DNA" with "Brushy's" was meaningless, since he claimed she was not his mother. And Billy the Kid's grave was not only of uncertain location (the marker being for tourists), so could yield no valid DNA for matchings; but was also legally blocked from exhumation by a prior test case, and by current refusal of the New Mexico Office of the Medical Investigator (OMI) to issue exhumation permits for a publicity stunt scamming DNA claims.

## THE LOIS TELFER TEST CASE FOR EXHUMING BILLY THE KID

Kept secret from the public was that the exhumation of Billy the Kid's gravesite had been blocked since 1962 based on its uncertain location and possible disruption of other remains. So when the "Billy the Kid Case" hoaxers hit Fort Sumner in 2004, the exhumation of Billy the Kid had been blocked by legal precedent for over 42 years. A prior exhumation attempt had been stopped by a judge; and the reasons were unchanged.

That case, Petition No. 3255, begun in 1961, had been filed by a Lois Telfer, alleging unproved Billy kinship, but seen as a publicity-seeker. Her petition was "For the Removal of the Body of William H. Bonney, Deceased, From the Ft. Sumner Cemetery in Which He is Interred for Reinterment in the Lincoln, New Mexico, Cemetery." **[APPENDIX: 1]**

But Billy's gravesite was known to be contiguous to Charlie Bowdre's. And Bowdre's father's brother's descendant, Louis Bowdre, was still alive. He went to Fort Sumner to testify his opposition on grounds of disrupting his deceased relative's remains. On April 6, 1962, District Judge E.T. Kinsley, Jr. agreed and blocked any exhumation. Ignoring that Kinsley decision, Attorney Bill Robins III and his fellow "Billy the Kid Case" hoaxers were returning for a re-run.

Unbeknownst to them, however, I took the precaution of contacting Louis Bowdre; by then in his 80's and blind, but still willing to fight. And after his death in 2005, his role as family historian passed to the younger generation. And that person told me, with fervor that echoed passionate Charlie Bowdre himself: "I will protect my grandfather's wish to my dying day."

## OMI'S REFUSED EXHUMATION PERMITS

Further blockage to digging up the mother's and Billy the Kid's graves was refusal of the OMI to issue exhumation permits for useless DNA and likely disruption of adjacent bodies.

Governor Richardson anticipated a problem with the OMI, on the University of New Mexico Health Sciences Center campus. Its head, Dr. Ross Zumwalt, and its forensic anthropologist, Debra Komar, were ethical. So he had his recent appointee, University of New Mexico President David Harris, remove their attorney to obstruct their opposition of the exhumation petitions.

And the hoax's Silver City attorney, now deceased Sherry Tippett, working for Richardson, met with the OMI staff, then lied to him through Richard Gay, his Assistant to the Chief of Staff, in her July 11, 2003 "Memorandum RE: Exhumation of Catherine Antrim." Tippett stated: "This is a summary of the work I have performed to date on the exhumation of Catherine Antrim from Memory Lane Cemetery in Silver City … **Research conducted by Dr. Debra Komar, of the Office of Medical Investigations [sic] (OMI) now indicates that the body of Mrs. Antrim can be moved without disturbing any other bodies in the cemetery.**"

Then Sherry Tippett lied again about having the OMI's exhumation permission in her October 3, 2003 Grant County Case No. MS 2003-11 "In the Matter of Catherine Antrim, Petition to Remove Remains" for Judge Henry Quintero. Importantly, in this first exhumation petition, Tippett made clear the lawmen's titles and that the case was against Pat Garrett for murder. (The hoaxers would later deny both.) Tippett wrote:

<u>PETITION TO EXHUME REMAINS</u>

Comes now **Petitioners Tom Sullivan, Sheriff of Lincoln County, Steve Sederwall, Deputy Sheriff of Lincoln County, and Gary Graves, Sheriff of De Baca County**, by and through their attorney, Sherry J. Tippett, hereby Petitions this Court to enter an Order directing the New Mexico Office of Medical Examiners [sic- Investigator] (hereinaftee "OMI") to disinter the remains of Catherine Antrim for the purpose of obtaining DNA samples. This petition is made in conjunction with investigation No. 2004-274 [sic] filed in Lincoln County and case number 03-06-136-01 filed in De Baca County, **for purpose of determining the guilt or innocence of Sheriff Pat Garrett in the death of William Bonney aka "Billy the Kid."**

Catherine is the undisputed mother of William Bonney. Catherine Antrim is buried in Silver City, NM at the Menorial [sic] Lane Cemetery …

In the case at hand, there is no known direct descendant of Catherine Antrim or William Bonney alive today.

Section 24-14-23 C NMSA (1978) states that a permit for disinterment and reinterment shall be required to disinterment [sic] of a dead body or fetus except as authorized be regulation or otherwise provided by law. This statute further states that the permit shall be issued by the state registrar or state medical investigator to a licensed funeral service practitioner or direct disposer. Dr. Debra Komar, Forensic Anthropologist with the OMI has performed a significant amount of research on the burial history and exact location of the remains of Catherine Antrim including visiting Memorial [sic] Lane Cemetery and performing records research in both New Mexico and Arizona. **Dr. Komar is confidant that Mrs. Antrim's remains can be exhumed without disturbing the remains of other bodies laid to rest in Memorial [sic] Lane Cemetery.** Disturbance of any other remains is unacceptable to the OMI staff. Dr. Komar is a world renowned Forensic Anthropologist who has previously worked for the united nations in the exhumation of mass buries [sic] in eastern Europe. Several meetings have taken place between the Petitioners, counsel of Record and OMI Director and Forensic staff as well as UNM Counsel Angela Martinez. **All parties are in agreement that an Order should be entered by this court prior to exhumation**.

The Petitioner respectfully requests this Order be entered as soon as possible to begin the exhumation by early to mid November. The coordination of several public and private agencies will be necessary to complete the exhumation.

         Respectfully submitted,
         Sherry J. Tippett
         Attorney for Petitioners

In fact, multiple remains were in potential risk, since the Antrim gravesite was the overlap of 12 other burials. And one grave was contiguous, and was Donna Jenice Amos's, from 1989. And its tire-track rutted desecration by the hoaxers' first film crew had outraged the decedant's sister, Joani Amos-Staats, who joined her own Petition to Silver City's Petition in Opposition - the case I had made with the Kennedy Han Law Firm.

### RESPONSE OF THE OMI

Sherry Tippett's failing, besides perjury, was underestimating the OMI. In response to Richardson's gagging attempt, Dr. Ross Zumwalt hired a private attorney, William Snead. Snead filed the OMI's January 12, 2004 response implying Tippett's lying, and refusing to permit exhumation. [APPENDIX: 2]

Snead stated: "**Contrary to the statements contained in the petition [of Sherry Tippett], Debra Komar, Ph.D., the forensic Anthropologist referred by petitioner, does not believe that Ms. Antrim's remains can be exhumed without disturbing the remains of** other bodies also interred in Memory Lane Cemetery ... **Contrary to the petition, the Office of Medical Investigators does not agree that an order should be entered allowing exhumation.** After a detailed and scientific investigation described in the affidavits [of Drs. Zumwalt and Komar] attached hereto, it is the scientific opinion of the OMI that any such attempted exhumation has very little possibility of contributing any information to the petitioner's alleged investigation, threatens the disturbance of unrelated burials, is a very great waste of public resources and a distraction of the OMI from its mandated work."

### OPPOSITION AFFIDAVITS BY ZUMWALT AND KOMAR

Snead's exhibits of the January 9, 2004 Affidavits of Dr. Ross Zumwalt **[APPENDIX: 3]**, as head of the OMI, and of Dr. Debra Komar **[APPENDIX: 4]**, its forensic anthropologist, stated that there was no valid DNA to be obtained from the mother's gravesite, it being only the location of multiple overlapping plots.

Dr. Zumwalt concluded that the mother's remains were not necessarily in her gravesite, which held 12 other bodies; that that comparison with Billy the Kid remains was useless because the site was not confirmed; that comparison with "Brushy Bill" made no sense because mitochondrial DNA only shows descent from the mother, and he claimed a different mother; that other remains would be disturbed; and that permission would not be granted.

He stated: "[I]f the purpose of exhuming Catherine Antrim is to provide a "known" standard for DNA testing, **the fact that she cannot be positively identified [because her unverified remains were moved from another location in 1881] renders all DNA tests suspect** ... If attempt is made to exhume the supposed body of Catherine Antrim from the burial site with her name, it is probable with a reasonable degree of scientific probability that the remains of other individuals will be disturbed. The burial site with Catherine Antrim's name is Plot D-27 at Memory Lane Cemetery. **This plot is the resting place of twelve (12) other known individuals** [who might be disturbed or confused with her remains] ... **If the purpose of the exhumation of the remains of Catherine Antrim is to compare her DNA to the remains of the believed Billy the Kid, those remains are not likely to be obtained in my opinion**. Based upon research performed by the OMI, the exact location of the Billy the Kid grave is not known, in my opinion, to a reasonable degree of scientific probability ... **If the purpose of extracting mtDNA [mitochondrial DNA] from the supposed remains of Catherine Antrim is to obtain a sample to compare against**

Brushy Bill Roberts in Texas, such a comparison, in my opinion, is also scientifically flawed. Based on research to date, I am unaware that Mr. Roberts ever claimed to be the biological child of Catherine Antrim. Thus, a test between his mtDNA and the putative remains of Catherine Antrim would have no scientific basis to a reasonable degree of scientific probability ... Based on the fact that DNA testing of the putative remains of Catherine Antrim would have no probative value and the fact that an exhumation would likely disrupt other burial sites, **an exhumation of Catherine Antrim is scientifically unsound in my opinion.**"

Dr. Debra Komar, in her Affidavit, confirmed the uncertain location of the mother's and Billy Bonney's gravesites, the unacceptable risk of disturbing other remains, and the meaningless plan to match mitochondrial DNA (meaning maternal DNA) with "Brushy Bill," since he never claimed Catherine Antrim as his mother.

## THE KOMAR DEPOSITION

In addition, on January 20, 2004, Dr. Debra Komar gave a 224 page deposition for the Sixth Judicial District Court Case No. MS 2003-11, "In the Matter of Catherine Antrim" to my Kennedy Han attorney, Adam Baker, in opposition to the lawmen hoaxers' exhumation petitions. Present were the hoax's attorneys, Sherry Tippett and Bill Robins III. In the deposition, Komar was described as "a world-renowned forensic anthropologist who has previously worked for the United Nations in the exhumation of mass burials in Eastern Europe." (Page 11)

She highlighted that "Billy the Kid is not buried in an isolated situation, but that he shares his burial with two other individuals" (Pages 17-18); and "there seems to be disagreement as to the placement of the bodies [of Tom O'Folliard, Charles Bowdre, and Billy Bonney] relative to each other; and some disagreement as to the placement of those bodies within the cemetery." (Page 22)

As to Silver City's Catherine Antrim remains, Komar described their relocation from within the city limits to outside them, to an uncertain location in Memory Lane Cemetery; with added problem that disruptive flooding had also occurred. (Pages 24-25) She explained that a John Miller [not the John Miller Billy the Kid imposter], who purchased the in-town cemetery, had his handymen move some of the bodies, likely without caskets, from it to an undocumented location in Memory Lane. (Pages 25, 27-28) And the untrained workers, handling decomposing remains, would not necessarily know which was Catherine Antrim. Komar stated: "We know she's been moved. We know there's been flooding. We know when she was moved, it was in a completely uncontrolled set of circumstances. And therefore, to hold her up as some sort of standard [for DNA identification] becomes scientifically unacceptable." (Page 38) Added was that her current plot listed presence of 12 other individuals. (Page 52)

As to the Fort Sumner Billy the Kid grave, where flooding "literally washed bodies out of the ground" (Page 45), there was "not a specific place where we would put a shovel in the ground ... [because the grave location is uncertain and] remains themselves may no longer still be there." (Page 69)

As to "Brushy," since he never claimed to be Catherine Antrim's son, Komar said: "[Y]ou might as well compare his [mitochondrial] DNA to mine. It would mean as much." (Page 77)

She concluded about the "Billy the Kid Case's" sought DNA of Billy and his mother: "**So if you ask the opinion of myself and the Office of the Medical Investigator why is this being done or what scientifically valid conclusions can be drawn from it, I can't find any**." (Page 81)

Attorney Bill Robins III cross-examined as to Catherine Antrim. He absurdly claimed that he was "defending Billy the Kid" (Page 97), and oddly stated, "I'm an historian." (Page 135) He ignored the OMI's contention of invalid DNA and disturbing other remains; instead, to fake validity, quibbled about soil samples, the original grave marker, how to avoid other graves, or how long DNA lasted. Dr. Komar responded: "[W]e're arguing that we can't do that .. given that we can't then prove it's Catherine Antrim." (Page 139) She repeated the OMI's refusal: "If the purpose of using Catherine is to provide [DNA] identification for someone else that must be, for a forensic standard, based on positive identification to begin with." (Page 142) "We don't exhume historical people for the sake of doing it." (Page 143) Robins even revealed his agenda by questioning matching Catherine to "Brushy." (Page 149) Komar responded that "Brushy" did not claim she was his mother, and mitochondrial DNA is so imprecise that it can get false positives merely from being white Europeans and having the same small gene combination by chance (Page 150), which is not enough for the claim that "Brushy" was Billy. She stated: "DNA won't conclusively prove what you are trying to say" (Page 152); which was that "Brushy" was Billy the Kid.

As to Billy the Kid, the same problems applied. And there was the addition of the removal of the supposed body of a soldier from the cemetery's military past, with the chance that Billy's body, not his, had been accidentally removed at that time! (Pages 70-72) So the following interchange occurred:

**ROBINS QUESTION: You don't think Billy the Kid is buried at Fort Sumner, do you?**
**KOMAR ANSWER: I don't know. I have reason to suspect perhaps not. (Page 144)**

Komar was just repeating her Affidavit contention that "[b]ased upon research performed by the OMI, the exact location of the Billy the Kid grave is not known." **But this interchange would subsequently be seized upon out of context and dishonestly misstated by the "Billy the Kid Case" hoaxers and in W.C. Jameson's** *Cold Case Billy the Kid* **to claim that she had said Billy the Kid was buried elsewhere; ergo, he was "Brushy Bill" buried in Hamilton, Texas!**

In fact, Komar was also referring to her earlier statements in the deposition, in which she said about Billy: **"[T]he remains may no longer still be there. Even if they were buried there at one point."** (Page 69) She was referring to her finding references to Billy's remains being stolen to sell soon after burial, or other digging in the area finding no remains. (Page 70) Or, in 1904, a Willie E. Griffin was hired to remove soldiers from that old military cemetery to move to Santa Fe's National Cemetery, and knew that one was supposed to be buried in association with the contiguous graves of Billy, Charles Bowdre, and Tom O'Folliard. He found only two bodies, and took one. So he may have accidentally taken Billy! (Page 71-72)

Under equally meaningless questioning by Attorney Sherry Tippett, Dr. Komar pointed out that doing exhumations as a criminal investigation of necessity involved the OMI, and the OMI demanded scientific validity. Komar stated: **"There is a big difference in the level of standard and what's expected if something is done as an academic versus a criminal investigation. If you want to continue to call it a criminal investigation, it mandates the involvement of our office."** (Pages 201-202) Komar had hit the hoaxers' bind: having no provable kin to request exhumations, the only way to conduct their exhumation scam was as the bogus murder investigation they had invented.

As Attorney William Snead concluded in Komar's deposition, as to the OMI's position: "We're opposed to the principle of digging someone up where it's not going to lead to scientifically probative evidence." (Page 203) And as to the taxpayer cost, just for her time of hundreds of hours used-up by then by the meaningless "Billy the Kid Case," it was at $2,800 per day. (Page, 223)

## *THE HOAXERS' RESPONSE TO OPPOSITION*

Since the "Billy the Kid Case" was not a legally or scientifically legitimate endeavor, its promulgators merely ignored the exposed legal and forensic meaninglessness. Instead, Richardson relied on his recently appointed, corrupt judges in Silver City and Fort Sumner, Henry Quintero and Ted Hartley respectively, to push through the exhumations. And that is what they tried to do. And the hoaxers took the precaution of replacing bumbling Attorney Sherry Tippett with central hoaxer, Attorney Bill Robins III, to argue for exhumation of Billy and his mother.

Only the brilliant legal opposition of the Kennedy Han Law firm, which I had engaged to back the respective Mayors of Silver City and Fort Sumner trying to protect their cemeteries, stopped digging which would have fraudulently claimed whatever Richardson wanted, and would have made "Brushy" Billy.

But the hubris of the hoaxers yielded a gigantic paper trail for their spectacular historic-forensic hoax.

## **HOAXERS AND HOAX DOCUMENTS**

The "Billy the Kid Case" hoaxers were massively productive, with press statements, legal documents, forensic reports, and a TV program, which all proved their fakery, collusion, and links to the "Brushy Bill" and John Miller imposter hoaxes.

To counter the cover-up expurgations common in New Mexico's corrupt officialdom, I reproduced most of the hoax documents in my 2014 book, *Cracking The Billy the Kid Case Hoax: The Strange Plot to Exhume Billy the Kid, Convict Sheriff Pat Garrett of Murder, and Become President of the United States.* Court filings are also under that title in my website GaleCooperBillytheKidBooks.com. This book presents the documents recycled, along with false and misleading claims, in W.C. Jameson's 2018 book, *Cold Case Billy the Kid*, where they were used to imply that "Brushy Bill" was Billy the Kid.

# HOAX INSTIGATOR: GOVERNOR BILL RICHARDSON

Blame for the "Billy the Kid Case" hoax rests squarely with its initiator: New Mexico's corrupt Governor, Bill Richardson; then contemplating a 2008 run for the Presidency, and seeking national self-promotion by using Billy the Kid. More reprehensible was his covert backing of "Brushy Bill," to give his state's iconic Old West history and tourism to Texas, as an apparent pay-to-play for his major donor-backer, Attorney Bill Robins III, a "Brushy"-believer.

## LAWMEN "MURDER INVESTIGATORS": TOM SULLIVAN, STEVE SEDERWALL, GARY GRAVES, AND RICK VIRDEN

Governor Bill Richardson enlisted and shielded two Sheriff's Departments to conduct his hoax. To attack past Lincoln County Sheriff Pat Garrett, he got now deceased Lincoln County Sheriff Tom Sullivan, who deputized the Mayor of Capitan, Steve Sederwall, as an accomplice. The next sheriff, Rick Virden, continued the hoax, deputizing Sullivan and Sederwall for it.

For assault on Fort Sumner's Billy the Kid grave, Richardson got De Baca County Sheriff Gary Graves. But Grant County Sheriff, Raul Holguin, proved incorruptible, and protected Billy's mother's Silver City grave. On August 29, 2006, Holguin told me that, in 2003, Sheriff Graves had pressured him to join. Holguin said, "I was appalled. It was clearly a publicity stunt. The woman deserved to lie in peace."

Lincoln County Sheriff Tom Sullivan opened murder Case No. 2003-274, and De Baca County Sheriff Gary Graves filed its counterpart as Case No. 03-06-136-01. Sullivan's deputized Mayor of Lincoln County's Capitan, Steve Sederwall, later claimed authorship of their major documents; among them Case 2003-274's "Probable Cause Statement," accusing past Lincoln County Sheriff Pat Garrett of the murder of the "innocent victim" instead of Billy the Kid. And Sullivan's Undersheriff, Rick Virden, participating from the start, would eventually become Sheriff, deputizing Sullivan and Sederwall, attempting to dig up "Brushy," and achieving the illegal exhumation of John Miller and the random man lying beside him: William Hudspeth.

## *THUG HISTORY: MIGHT MAKES RIGHT*

"The Billy the Kid Case" hoax made thugs "historians." Taking to their role like fish to land, and dressed like Old West cowboy caricatures, the lawmen substituted brawn for brains, and tried to power through the exhumations by intimidation and lying - all they had to work with, since they had no real evidence.

They were terrifying, so I stayed anonymous as long as I could, for fear of being killed if they realized that I was behind all the efforts to stop them. Of course, the biggest thug was Richardson himself. But it was the lawmen who stood at the firing line.

### TOM SULLIVAN AND STEVE SEDERWALL

There were many examples of Sullivan's and Sederwall's roughness. They had not anticipated the resistance I had organized in Silver City. So, in 2004, after their June 2004 disinvite by its officials for the big local event: the Millie and Billy Ball (the invitation apparently came from their zany attorney, Sherry Tippett), reporter, Levi Hall, in the June 12, 2004 *Las Cruces Sun* wrote: "Sederwall said he no longer had any plans to help Silver City and was going to let the whole town 'drain dry.' " The duo also snarled to Mary Alice Murphy and Melissa St. Aude in the *Silver City Daily Press* of June 10, 2004. Sederwall was quoted: "Tom and I will go on as if Silver City doesn't exist ... We're going to call the governor and tell him we're not going to Silver City."

When they learned the Fort Sumner's Mayor, Raymond Lopez, would oppose them, Lopez told me he got this Sederwall call: "Get your head out of your ass. We're getting this [the Billy the Kid exhumation] done whether you want it or not." Feisty Lopez answered: "I've been beaten up by smaller men than you (Sederwall is 6'5"), and I'm still not afraid."

On September 21, 2004, when Lincoln County Commission Chairman Leo Martinez confronted them about using the Sheriff's Department to conduct a hoax, Dianne Stallings of the *Ruidoso News* reported Sullivan's racist attack on restaurant owner Martinez in "Showdown in the County Seat: shouting match erupts at County Commissioners meeting over investigation of Billy the Kid." Stallings wrote: "Sullivan [said], "I don't tell you how to make burritos. Don't tell me how to run the sheriff's department." And on September 23, 2004, *Lincoln County News* reporter, Doris Cherry in "Lincoln County War heats up over 'Billy: Capitan Mayor [Sederwall] Tracks His Kind of ' ------ ' To County

Commission Meeting. Tells Jay Miller where to go; wonders why Commissioner has his panties in a wad." She quoted Sederwall as saying that Leo Martinez's questioning "smells of Jay Miller ... a sleaze-bag reporter from Santa Fe." [Jay Miller was proxying my open records investigations on them to protect my anonymity.] Cherry added from Sederwall: " 'The sheriff has no documentation,' the mayor [Sederwall] said. 'I have them.' He then went on to say that he will not release the documents, not as mayor or as a commissioned reserve deputy. 'He (Miller) can go to hell because I will not turn the (documents) over because once they are turned over they become public documents.' "

Sullivan's and Sederwall's letterhead for my own 2006 open records request said: "You Believin' Us Or Them Lyin' Whores."

Locally, Tom Sullivan a three time sheriff, then sheriff's deputy, was seen as an alcoholic lout with a bad back. By rumor, in the 1980's, he allegedly got that bad back when driving off with a woman who was not his wife (with her being voluntary or involuntary seems uncertain). Her male relatives caught up, and allegedly beat him. He was rescued by his deputies, who later got promotions. Possibly being Sheriff was not enough fun. For the Billy the Kid Case, Sullivan became an actor for nine months in 2004 for movie about it - collecting his sheriffs' 24 hour per day on-duty pay. He played Sheriff William Brady. Subsequently, he showed his lack of gravitas in the December 27, 2007 affidavit of my process server, DeWayne Zimitski, for my open records case to get the DNA records he was hiding. Zimitski wrote: "Mr. Sullivan came to the door ... and told me ... to get off his fucken property."

Of the lawmen, 6'5" Capitan Mayor and Lincoln County Deputy Sheriff Steve Sederwall was the most scary. Lincoln County locals nick-named him "Snake," and avoided encounters with him. An erstwhile hat maker, lawman in Texas and California, and Bureau of Land Management employee in New Mexico, he was arrested in 1983 in Oklahoma for alleged "assault and battery" in "Case CRM-83-55 State of Oklahoma versus A.B. McReynolds, Jr., John (Nick) Moore and Steve Sederwall." Its February 9th Affidavit by a Ray Kirkland stated: "I investigated an Assault and Battery upon one Darryl Gene Williams and ascertained that A.B. McReynolds, Jr., John (Nick) Moore and Steve Sederwall assaulted and hit, acting in concert with each other, the said Darryl Gene Williams. That this incident took place at Christ's Forty Acres in Honobia, in LeFlore County, Oklahoma, and was without just or excusable cause." Not convicted, when facing this case in a 2008 lost Lincoln County Sheriff's election, Sederwall allegedly stated that it was a *different* "Steve Sederwall." But February 17, 1983's *The Daily Oklahoma* article, "5 Charged in Beatings," had "Steve Sederwall" as age 30, as an aide to A.B. McReynolds Jr., President of the Board of Christ's 40 Acres Christian mission, then in conflict with its director, Riley Donica; who litigated against him. Subsequently, Donica's aide, Darrel Williams, was beaten on February 8, 1983, at mission headquarters by the accused, including Sederwall.

This case was used on October 16, 2008, by a group calling itself "Concerned Citizens of Lincoln County," who took out a full page ad in the *Lincoln County News* as "Should Lincoln County Have Grave Concerns Over A Person Like Steve Sederwall Running for Sheriff?" He was cited as charged in "assaulting Preacher Darryl Gene Williams;" with a reprint of Oklahoma's February 8, 1983 Case CRM-83-55. The "Concerned Citizens" then gave the resume he had submitted in 2002 when running for the Village of Capitan Mayor, and asked: "Does the resume he submitted then have key differences than his current resume posted on his website now that he'd rather Lincoln County residents view in the race for Lincoln County Sheriff?"

Firstly, that resume's birth date of September 2, 1952 matched the age 30 of "Steve Sederwall" in the Oklahoma beating case. And, in descending chronology, he called himself a retired freelance Western writer; past president of the Beaver Bank Hat Company and past owner of the Thievin' Vaqueros Hat Company; a past "Special Agent in the U.S. Department of the Interior responsible for "the western United States;" a past Los Alamos County police supervisor; a past police sergeant in Lake of Ozarks, Missouri; a past Los Angeles police officer; a past owner of a log home dealership (in the 1983 beating period, but with no location given); and a Garland, Texas, policeman. The "Concerned Citizens" noted that his claimed 30 years of law enforcement experience was not supported by his employment dates. Also, his tenure as Mayor of Capitan had yielded suits against him as: "20 tort claims were filed against the Village of Capitan with 10 being either litigated or arbitrated; resulting in over $350,000 in payments."

One was his 2004 verbal attack on his political opponent for a District 1 County Commission seat - a widowed mother named Debra L. Ingle, who was operation supervisor of the Lincoln County Solid Waste Authority - by naming her a "whore and cocaine dealer" - shortened to "cocaine whore." On June 15, 2004 Ingle sued him for defamation in the Twelfth Judicial District Court in "Ingle vs Sederwall (and Village of Capitan) No. D-1226-

CV-200400147." She won. The county paid damages. And for my later open records litigation against him and his fellow lawmen hiding public records of their fake Billy the Kid investigation, taxpayers footed a half-million dollars just for their attorneys representing them as public official sheriffs and deputy sheriffs - while Sederwall lied to the Court that he was just a "hobbyist."

As to his claim of being a "federal investigator," the October 16, 2008 "Concerned Citizens" article cited that it was for the Bureau of Land Management, starting in 1991, with his getting "disability retirement" based on stress by 1995. He returned in 2000, but sued "the BLM for 'mental, emotional and psychological distress' ... and he's still collecting the checks." He was listed as also suing the Village of Capitan, the Beaver Hat Company, the Lincoln County Clerk, and "numerous others."

As to attacking me, Sederwall worked behind-the-scenes. In September of 2009, he called the publisher of the first edition of my "Billy the Kid Case" hoax book, titled *MegaHoax*; trying, but failing, to stop its publication. He repeated that maneuver in November of 2012, after my advertisement for all my Billy the Kid books came out in *Wild West* magazine. He contacted Editor-in-Chief Greg Lalire, and had him to promise that my books on the hoax would not be reviewed there. But Lalire still accepted my ads; and informed me about the call. Sederwall had also tried double-barrels: having his fellow hoaxer, U.S. Marshals Service Historian David Turk (under Homeland Security) contact Greg Lalire with the same implied threat. Later, he and Tom Sullivan, with colluding Lincoln County Attorney Alan Morel, reported me to the U.S. Marshal's Service as a terrorist for filing my open records request - presumably with co-hoaxer Turk as recipient.

Also, Sederwall seems to have tried his Debra Ingle approach for an article defaming me in fellow "Billy the Kid Case" hoaxer and editor Bob Boze Bell's *True West* magazine of August/September 2010. I was portrayed as a conspiracy theorist blocking "Billy the Kid Case" truth, and was painted by artist, Boze Bell, as a wild-haired madwoman shrieking at Billy's grave. The article claimed I was insanely coming to Lincoln County to mutilate their horses! (That horse fabrication may have come to Sederwall from his past job with the Bureau of Land Management dealing with horse abuse cases.)

Though low on the totem pole of "Billy the Kid Case" hoaxers, Sederwall was active in "investigations" and writing, culminating by being featured in 2018's *Cold Case Billy the Kid* megahoax.

## GARY GRAVES

De Baca County Sheriff Gary Graves's worst thuggery was not connected to the Billy the Kid Case. On his own, he made New Mexico history by being the first (and only) sheriff ever recalled.

Grave's come-uppance began with the September 13, 2004 De Baca County Tenth Judicial Court "Case No. CV-04-00019, In the Matter of De Baca County Sheriff Gary Graves. Petition for Order Allowing Recall Vote." It was filed by five men (Dennis Cleaver, Jay Paul, Allen Sparks, Ellis Jones, and Rex Pope) and local attorney, Steve Doerr. Graves was accused of malfeasance and misfeasance; using public property as his own; threatening, harassing, and intimidating residents; violating prisoners' rights at the De Baca County Detention Center; not keeping financial records; and misappropriating money and property entrusted to his Sheriff's Office. On September 14, 2004, Fort Sumner's *De Baca County News* printed: "De Baca County Citizens' Committee Files Petition for Recall of Sheriff Gary Graves." It said: "Spokesman Dennis Cleaver said the recall is an effort to restore law enforcement and end more than 21 months of intimidation and harassment of De Baca County citizens."

Graves's Sheriff's Association refused to represent him. So his fellow "Billy the Kid Case" participant, Attorney Bill Robins III, came all the way from Texas to protect him!

His recall hearing, under a Judge Joe Parker, was documented by Scot Stinnett, owner of the *De Baca County News*. The headline on September 1, 2005 was: "Testimony paints Graves as 'above the law.' " Graves's head dispatcher/administrative assistant, Linda Boyd, gave incidents called "sickening" (alleged sexual comments), and scary (in which Graves sped his county vehicle with her and her son inside). De Baca County Jail Supervisor Lynita Lovorn testified that Graves bound prisoners with duct tape. He allegedly also seized $2,000 from a Mexican woman following a traffic stop, gave the woman $50 travel money, and kept the rest.

Robins used Graves's alleged deputy, A.J. Haley, to call Lovorn a liar. But Haley had come from Utah to be "deputized" by Graves for that testimony! Judge Parker kicked him out.

The Billy the Kid Case came up only in prosecution questioning as to whether Graves was continuing it. He said yes.

Judge Parker ruled that the recall could proceed. Fort Sumner's tiny population voted 576 to 150 to oust him. Attorney Robins appealed the recall in both the Appellate and Supreme Courts of New Mexico. He lost.

## RICK VIRDEN

After Sheriff Sullivan's term ended in 2004, his Undersheriff, Rick Virden, was elected Sheriff. Like the other two, he had skeletons in his closet. He was believed to have stolen expensive railroad ties in the worst kept crime secret in Lincoln County. He was rumored to have been shielded by the local District Attorney, with possible collusion of then Attorney General, Patricia Madrid.

Virden learned my name in 2006 by my open records request to him; and, with Lincoln County Attorney Alan Morel and Sullivan and Sederwall, reported me (as a terrorist?) to the U.S. Marshals Service (presumably hoaxer Turk) for doing it.

### THE LAWMEN'S' ROUGH PHOTOGRAPHER

An October 6, 2005 *RuidosoNews.com* article by Julie Carter, titled "Follow the Blood: In the Billy the Kid Case, Miller Exhumed," had a photo of Steve Sederwall holding John Miller's alleged skull. Its photo-credit was Lionel Lippman. Lippman, now deceased, was Sederwall's friend. "Lonnie" had served time. The Texas Department of Public Safety Conviction Records Database for Lionel Whitby Lippman had a trio of arrests in Bexar County's San Antonio. The first was on February 17, 1970 for "vehicular theft;" the second, on July 7, 1970, for "assault with attempt to commit rape;" and the last, on June 11, 1973, for "forgery and passing." So "Lonnie" was a thug too.

## *MAJOR HOAX DOCUMENTS BY LAWMEN*

### "MAYOR'S REPORT" OF STEVE SEDERWALL

Steve Sederwall had already announced the "Billy the Kid Case" murder case in his May, 2003, *Capitan Village Hall News* "Mayor's Report," beating the Governor by a month, and revealing hoax preparations. His focus was "Brushy Bill;" even claiming that Billy Barlow was in the Fort Sumner grave. He also announced that a sub-investigation would be the murder of Deputy James Bell by Billy the Kid. This report came to his constituents in their monthly water bill. Its showmanship and sound-bites left traveling salesman, William V. Morrison, in the dust. Low in hoax hierarchy, Sederwall would prove valuable and hardworking. And his association with W.C. Jameson in 2006, would inspire Jameson's continuation of the hoax in his 2018 book, *Cold Case Billy the Kid*. Sederwall's "Mayor's Report" stated:

... On April 28, 2003, at five minutes after noon, one of our citizens, Sheriff Tom Sullivan fired two shots in Lincoln, New Mexico. The floor under my feet shook at each report of his pistol. The gun smoke hung in the air just as in a western novel would describe it. As I heard the shots a cold chill ran down my back knowing that J.W. Bell heard the shots that killed him.

A 122 years before, just minutes after twelve, noon, on April 28, 1881, two lawmen lay dead, in the yard of the courthouse in Lincoln, New Mexico, from gunshot wounds. Quicker than it took New Mexico breeze to clear the gunsmoke, history was clouded with the myth of the shooting and escape of William H. Bonney a.k.a. Billy the Kid from the make-shift jail where he awaited the date with the hangman.

Sheriff Sullivan and I have opened a case into that shooting in 1881. As part of the investigation Sheriff Sullivan fired off two rounds from a .45 Long Colt to see if the shots could be heard from the Wortley Hotel. To our surprise the black powder rounds loaded for us by Virgil Hall could be heard in nearly every part of town.

**This investigation came about after Sheriff Sullivan and I talked about a man by the name of Brushy Bill Roberts. In 1950 Roberts ["Brushy Bill"] came to the Governor of New Mexico with his attorney [sic - William Morrison, not an attorney]; saying he was Billy the Kid. He said that Pat Garrett shot a man by the name of Billy Barlow and buried his body claiming to be that of Billy the Kid. Roberts said he lived out a life within the bounds of the law under an assumed name and wanted a pardon that was promised to him by Governor Wallace.**

**[AUTHOR'S NOTE: This is the hoax's first known reference connecting the "Billy the Kid" hoax's claim that Garrett did not kill the Kid, to the "Brushy Bill" Roberts hoax.]**

**On the surface of this story [Brushy Bill Roberts's] you would say "so what?" But if you look at this man's claim he is saying our Sheriff Pat Garrett is a murderer. Garrett knew the Kid and killed someone else. What this says also is that Pete Maxwell who said the body is of The Kid is a co-conspirator in a murder. There is no statute of limitations on Murder [sic], so the Lincoln County Sheriff's Office has opened a case to pursue the investigation. If Brushy Bill Roberts is Billy the Kid then history changes. But if he is lying, we need to clear Garrett's name.**

[AUTHOR'S NOTE: Confirmed is the case as a filed murder investigation, with a "Brushy" emphasis. Demonstrated is the sly double-talk that would characterize the hoax. Here, the absurd claim is made that the murder case against Pat Garrett was being done to clear his name of murder – though they were the accusers, and murder cases are not done to prove someone innocent! Also, New Mexico *did* have a statute of limitations that had expired for prosecuting Garrett in 1891!]

I feel this investigation will put a positive light on the county, our town and the state in whole. Tom Sullivan and I have been in touch with the Governor's office and he is behind us. People who are conducting DNA on victims of the World Trade Center have agreed to complete DNA tests for us on remains of persons believed to be Billy the Kid. We have a filmmaker creating a made-for-TV story about this investigation. We have recruited some of the best investigators in the country from other states to assist in this investigation. The Sheriff and I feel this should not only clear up a 122-year-old mystery but also bring money into our village ...

Tom Sullivan and I know it is a crazy idea but won't it be fun.

## PROBABLE CAUSE FOR GARRETT AS A MURDERER

The key to the "Billy the Kid Case" hoax- and to faking "Brushy Bill's" survival tale - was getting legal access to historic graves to fabricate self-serving DNA matches. That meant filing real murder investigations. The legal intent of a Probable Cause Statement is establishing, with probability, the guilt of a suspect.

The December 31, 2003 "Probable Cause Statement for Case No. 2003-274" is eleven pages of single-spaced footnoted text, combining double-talk, lies, and mock erudition. Steve Sederwall subsequently claimed to have written it. But Attorney Bill Robins III may contributed, since he used the same wording a month before its December signing in reporter Louie Fecteau's November 19, 2003 *Albuquerque Journal's* "No Kidding: Governor Taps Lawyer for Billy." Robins stated: "[I]t was hard to tell who the good guys were." The Probable Cause Statement has: "[I]t was hard to tell who the good guys were." Also hoaxer, U.S. Marshals Service Historian David Turk, provided fake research.

It had two thrusts to establish Pat Garrett as a murderer of an "innocent victim" on July 14, 1881. The first used fabricated "suspicions," misinformation, and false forensic DNA claims, to claim Garrett's guilt.

The second thrust was fabrication of a murder motive for Garrett by a sub-investigation of Billy Bonney's jailbreak murders of his deputy guards, James Bell and Robert Olinger. Used were meaningless "what-ifs": *If* Garrett gave Billy the revolver used for the jailbreak, he and Billy *might* have been friends. And *if* they were friends, Garrett *might* again have helped Billy escape in Fort Sumner by killing an innocent victim. But the ifs" had no evidence. And there was no historical friendship between Garrett and Billy. So substituted were only old-timers' malarkey of post-death sightings of Billy. In fact, Garrett had no motive to assist Billy's jailbreak, and was not in Lincoln that day.

Subsequently, however, when I was litigating against the hoaxers, this sub-investigation was called the *total* Case 2003-274 by them to hide their attack on Garrett, and to hide its connected DNA records. Also, this sub-investigation had its own fake CSI forensics and DNA claims about "Bell's blood."

But for the "Probable Cause Statement," Sederwall and Sullivan claimed that Garrett was guilty, as would be proven by DNA comparisons of remains of Billy the Kid and his mother (to show Garrett's unknown victim lay in Billy the Kid's grave).

An addendum of two pages was an affidavit by a Homer Overton, addressed to Sheriff Sullivan, swearing that Garrett had not shot the Kid; but crumbling under Overton's confabulated dates. (It was comparable to the fake affidavits of *Alias Billy the Kid*, attesting that "Brushy" was Billy.)

The upshot is that the "Probable Cause Statement" presented no reason to assume that Garrett did not kill the Kid. But its labor in production take one's breath away. One can guess that expecting no opposition, the hoaxers had written it for their complicit judges who were expected to rubber-stamp their exhumations, but might have wanted backing to bear scrutiny.

Importantly, it would much later emerge, as I pursued the hoaxers with my open records investigations, that there had been a first and rejected "Probable Cause Statement," titled "Lincoln County Sheriff's Office, Lincoln County New Mexico, Case: William H. Bonney, a.k.a. William Antrim, a.k.a. The Kid, a.k.a. Billy the Kid: An Investigation into the events of April 28, 1881 through July 14, 1881 - seventy-seven days of doubt." Its authorship was uncertain. But it overtly promoted "Brushy Bill;" and it was apparently rejected in lieu of Sederwall's and Sullivan's more circumspect treatment of that hoax intent. The official "Probable Cause Statement" follows.

# LINCOLN COUNTY SHERIFF'S DEPARTMENT
## CASE # 2003-274
## Probable Cause Statement

In the struggle dubbed the "Lincoln County War" investigators [Sullivan and Sederwall] soon learned that nothing was as seemed.

**[AUTHOR'S NOTE: For lack of any evidence, this is the familiar "suspicion" used by Billy the Kid imposters' authors.]**

As they poured through the volumes of information, documents, paperwork, reports, county records, books and examined newly discovered evidence, it became apparent no clear lines could be drawn as to who was working with or for whom. What first appeared to be clear quickly became clouded as new information was uncovered,

**[AUTHOR'S NOTE: No new evidence is ever presented.]**

it's difficult to judge who the "good guys" and the "bad guys" were. One would think that the Lincoln County Sheriff's Department would be on the side of the law. However, it was a duly sworn posse of Lincoln County Deputies that shot and killed John Tunstall, in what investigators in clean conscience can only cauterize [sic] as an unprovoked murder.

**[AUTHOR'S NOTE: Tunstall's murder is irrelevant. It occurred when William Brady was Sheriff of Lincoln County; and was 3½ years before Garrett killed the Kid. Of course, Brady's dishonesty is irrelevant to Garrett as a murderer.]**

Evidence shows that posse-men, Hill and Morton

**[AUTHOR'S NOTE: Error: Tom Hill was not Brady's official posseman; he was in Jessie Evans's outlaw gang. Brady, in writing, swore he used no known outlaws on that posse.]**

committed murder when "*Hill called to him* (Tunstall) *to come up and that he would not be hurt; at the same time both Hill and Morton threw up their guns, resting their stocks on their knees; that after Tunstall came nearer, Morton fired and shot Tunstall through the breast, and then Hill fired and shot Tunstall through the head ...*" [1]([1]Deposition of Albert Howe, Angel Report) Although these deputies were acting under the color off the law they were not acting within the law. This behavior permeates the Lincoln County War and investigators will not make judgments on that behavior but rather uncover the facts and present the facts without varnish.

**[AUTHOR'S NOTE: Repeating that lawman can be dishonest, is irrelevant to proving Garrett a murderer.]**

No one from the Governor to the District Attorney to the Sheriff of Lincoln County is beyond suspicion of deception and covering up the true facts in this case.

**[AUTHOR'S NOTE: Vague "suspicion" is irrelevant to Garrett.]**

This can be seen in a number of examples. In a letter to Riley and Dolan of the Murphy-Dolan faction from District Attorney W. L. Rynerson of the 3$^{rd}$ Judicial District, the attorney clearly demonstrates he himself plays a part in the hostile actions when he writes, *"Shake that McSween outfit up until it shells out and squares up and then shake it out of Lincoln. I will aid to punish the scoundrels all I can."*[2] ([2]Rynerson letter to Riley and Dolan, Feb. 7 [sic], 1878, University of Arizona Special Collection)

**[AUTHOR'S NOTE: Error: The letter is dated February 14, 1878; is about murdering Tunstall; and is irrelevant to Garrett.]**

When investigators began to look at the murder of Deputy Sheriff J.W. Bell and Deputy Robert Olinger on April 28, 1881, it was found that much of the information we now know as "history" came from Pat F. Garrett's book, "The Authentic Life of Billy the Kid" published in 1882.

**[AUTHOR'S NOTE: Error: Bell/Olinger eye-witness murder information was not claimed by Garrett, who was away at White Oaks; but was from, Gottfried Gauss, the caretaker.]**

Investigators learned that much of this history is flawed for the reason historian Robert Utley writes: *"Although not many copies of the Authentic Life were sold, it nevertheless had a decisive impact on the Kid's image. More than any other single influence, the Garrett-Upson book fed the legend of Billy the Kid. As the legend blossomed, writers turned to the Authentic Life for details. Ash Upson's fictions became implanted in hundreds of " histories" that followed. For more than a century, only a few students thought to question the wild fantasies that flowed from Ash's imagination. In the evolution of the Kid's image, the Authentic Life is a book of enormous consequence."*[3] ([3]Robert M. Utley. Billy the Kid a short and violent life. University of Nebraska Press, 1989.)

**[AUTHOR'S NOTE: Utley is merely describing evolution of the legend, not history. And Garrett's book confirms his shooting of Billy. All subsequent scholarly historians, including Utley, confirmed that Garrett fatally shot Billy the Kid.]**

On March 23 [sic – 17], 1879, Governor Lew Wallace met with William Bonney (Kid) in Lincoln. In this meeting it is demonstrated that Wallace convinced the Kid that it would be to his advantage to work for the government.

**[AUTHOR'S NOTE: Wrong. Billy proposed to Wallace, by a letter of about March 13, 1879, to give eye-witness Grand Jury testimony against the murderers of Huston Chapman in exchange for Wallace's annulling his Lincoln County War indictments. But a straw man argument is being set up.]**

The Kid becomes, what would be referred to in today's terminology as a "Confidential Informant." In Governor Wallace's hand we read "Statements made by Kid, Made Sunday night March 23, 1879."[4] ([4]Statements by Kid, Lew Wallace Collection, Indiana Historical Society Library) It was through this meeting Wallace devised a plan and attempted to deceive when he and the Kid entered into an agreement where by the Kid would appear to have been arrested.

**[AUTHOR'S NOTE: Claiming attempt "to deceive" is a misleading switcheroo. The hoaxers admitted Billy's confidential informant status. The arrest plan was devised by both Wallace and Billy to prevent his being killed before his testimony against Chapman's murderers. But the hoaxers are still pumping the irrelevant claim that everyone was deceptive. Of course, that was irrelevant to Garrett as murderer.]**

The Kid later talks of this and says he was allowed to wear his guns and he left when he wanted to leave.

David S. Turk, Historian for the United States Marshals Service has discovered other such deceptions in his study of official records.

**[AUTHOR'S NOTE: Referring to "other such deceptions" is fake. Turk's "other deceptions" are never given. And Turk, an active "Billy the Kid Case" hoaxer, contributed his own fake Probable Cause addendum to the hoax. (See pages 397-401)]**

It is commonly believed

**[AUTHOR'S NOTE: Misstatement: It is a *known*.]**

that Lincoln County Sheriff Pat F. Garrett arrested the Kid in December of 1880 in Stinking Springs near Fort Sumner. But the records show that Garrett was elected in November of 1880 and did not take office until January of 1881.[5] ([5]Lincoln County Commissioners Records, November 8, 1880).

**[AUTHOR'S NOTE: This leads to a fake claim that he did not have proper authority to capture Billy.]**

He went to Fort Sumner as a Deputy United States Marshall, but even that Commission and authority are now questioned. Secret Service Special Operative Azariah F. Wild of New Orleans writes in his daily logs *"I this day went to Lincoln to meet Capt. Lea & Garrett who are to organize the Posse Comatatus (sic) to make a raid on Fort Sumner to arrest counterfeiters."*[6] ([6]Report of Azariah F. Wild, November 11, 1880, Record Group 87, National Archives) Garrett shot and killed Charles Bowdre and Tom O'Folliard during the chase and arrested the Kid. Later, Secret Service Special Operative Azariah F. Wild writes to his superior and admits he was deceptive in his commission of Garrett. *"I will respectfully state that I applied to Marshall Sherman to appoint P.F. Garrett as a Deputy Marshall to which he paid no attention. I was in great need of Mr. Garrett [sic – Mr. Garrett's aid] at that time and took one of the Commissions Sherman sent to John Hurley (he having sent two) and substituted P.F. Garrett the very man who has rendered the Government such a valuable service in killing and arresting these men who I was in pursuit."*[7] ([7]Report of Azariah F. Wild, January 4 [sic -3], 1881, Record Group 87, National Archives)

**[AUTHOR'S NOTE: This fakes doubt about Garrett's commission. In fact, Wild, needing Garrett's aid, got paperwork from U.S. Marshal John Sherman; but two commissions were for John Hurley. So he crossed out Hurley's name on one, and added Garrett's. It was not done secretly, since Wild put it in his daily report to Secret Service Chief James Brooks. And it was accepted. Also, Sederwall recycled this fakery in W.C. Jameson's 2018 book titled *Cold Case Billy the Kid*.]**

No one in 122 years has been able to speak with clear certainty where the gun came from that William Bonney used to kill Deputy J.W. Bell.

**[AUTHOR'S NOTE: A switch to a sub-investigation begins to fake Garrett as Billy's escape accomplice.]**

With the information investigators have seen they question Garrett's involvement in the Kid obtaining a weapon.

**[AUTHOR'S NOTE: There is no "information," just fake "what-ifs": *If* Garrett was Billy's friend, he helped him escape. *If* he did that, he would later kill the innocent victim to help Billy escape again.]**

It would go to reason that if the body in Fort Sumner is anyone other than William Bonney then Garrett no doubt had a hand in allowing the Kid to escape on July 14, 1881.

[AUTHOR'S NOTE: This is fakery. No one says anyone but Billy was buried. It is just hoaxing.]

If the body at Fort Sumner is anyone other than William Bonney, then Garrett, whether by accident or design, is responsible for homicide of the person resting in that grave.

[AUTHOR'S NOTE: Here are more meaningless "what ifs."]

If it is not Bonney in the grave at Fort Sumner it would also go to reason that Garrett would be looked at as a suspect in furthering the escape of the Kid on April 28, 1881 when the two Lincoln County Sheriffs were murdered.

[AUTHOR'S NOTE: Here is the switcheroo. Now the fake "what-ifs" are used as fact: that Garrett helped Billy escape. **THIS FAKERY IS THE HOAXERS' SOLE PROBABLE CAUSE FOR GARRETT AS A MURDERER.** In fact, no evidence has been given; and none exists. And Pat and Billy were not friends.

[AUTHOR'S NOTE: What follows next is built on the hoaxers' lying that (1) they established Garrett's murder motive, and that (2) they established need to check Billy's grave for Garrett's "innocent victim."]

Although the investigation will deal with what happened in the Lincoln County court house on April 28, 1881, this writing will deal with the alleged shooting of William Bonney at Fort Sumner on the night of July 14, 1881.

[AUTHOR'S NOTE: Do not let this fast-one slip by. The deputy murders "sub-investigation" at the courthouse consisted merely of: (1) firing a gun inside to test if it could be heard across the street; and (2) bringing in a forensic consultant, Dr. Henry Lee, whose finding of "blood" on the upstairs hallway floorboards was a hoaxer lie. Lying more, the hoaxers said the "blood" was Bell's. Olinger was left out. Also left out is that this "investigation" has nothing to do with the gun used to shoot Bell. And, even if it did, that would have nothing to do with whether Garrett gave it to Billy, or whether Garrett murdered an innocent victim 2 ½ months later. The "upstairs blood," though irrelevant, will be debunked later with the rest of the fake forensic claims.]

[AUTHOR'S NOTE: At this point, the hoaxers abandon the deputy murders and the Garrett murder motive. But they pretend that they: (1) established Garrett's Billy friendship; (2) Garrett's escape weapon involvement; (3) Garrett's murder motive; and (4) Garrett's murder of the innocent victim.]

This writing will set forth probable cause as to why investigators question who is in the grave in Fort Sumner and seek DNA from Catherine Antrim.

**[AUTHOR'S NOTE: Probable cause of Garrett as a murderer has not been established. But this double exhumation is the hoaxers' goal.]**

**[AUTHOR'S NOTE: What follows is the hoaxers' attempt to fake that someone other than William Bonney was shot by Garrett. It is back to "what-ifs": *If* there was any inconsistency in reporting of events around the murder, something is "suspicious;" ergo, Garrett killed someone else. But the hoaxers only fabricate some "inconsistencies."]**

The detractors of this investigation hold up the statements of Lincoln County Sheriff Pat F. Garrett, Deputy Sheriff John W. Poe, and the Coroner's Jury report as proof it is William H. Bonney that Sheriff Garrett shot and killed on July 14, 1881 and that the Kid is buried in Ft. Sumner.

**[AUTHOR'S NOTE: Hidden are the multiple corpse identifications. Later, in this document, in slip-ups, the hoaxers accidentally present more of them!]**

Historian Philip J. Rash [sic - Rasch] tells the story history puts forth about the shooting of the Kid in the following manner:

*Garrett led them to the mouth of Taiban Arroyo, arriving after dark on 13 July. When Brazil failed to appear, Poe, who was unknown in the area, agreed to ride into fort Sumner the next morning to see what he could learn. Finding the inhabitants suspicious and uncommunicative, he proceeded to Sunnyside, about seven miles north, to visit Milnor Rudolph, the postmaster and an old friend of Garrett's. Rudolph was nervous and evasive. He denied all knowledge of the Kid's whereabouts, but Poe was sure he was concealing something.*[8] (*[8] Poe, John W. The Death of Billy the Kid.* New York: Houghton Mifflin Company, 1933) *There is a curious story that while the officer was on the way to Sunnyside, John Collins (Abraham Gordon Graham), a former member of Billy's gang, headed to Lobato's camp to warn the outlaw that officers were in the vicinity. On the way he met the Kid, bound for Fort Sumner. "Billy," he warned, "don't go down there. I just saw Poe, and no doubt Pat Garrett and a posse are around town looking for you."*

**[AUTHOR'S NOTE: Recall that Poe was unknown to the locals; so this irrelevant hearsay further lacks credibility.]**

The Kid merely laughed and answered, "Oh, that's O.K. I'll be alright," and rode on, leaving Collins badly puzzled."[9] ([9]Ben Kemp. *Dead Men, Who Rode Across the Border.* Unpublished. No date.)

That night Poe rendezvoused with Garrett and McKinney at La Punta de la Glorietta [sic], four miles north of Fort Sumner. Poe's report of both his failure to learn anything definite and his suspicions that there was so much smoke there must be some fire only increased the sheriff's skepticism. After some discussion he commented that the Kid was a frequent visitor to the house of Celsa Gutierrez (sister of Pat's wife Polineria [sic] Gutierrez) and suggested that they watch her home. Their vigil proved fruitless. As midnight approached Garrett and Poe decided that there was only one other possible source of information - Peter Maxwell, the town's most prominent citizen.

The officers arrived at his home about 12:30 AM on Friday, the 15[th] [sic]. Pat instructed Poe and McKinney to wait outside while he went in to talk to Maxwell. Sitting down on the edge of the bed, he asked in a low voice whether the Kid was on the premises. Maxwell became very agitated, but answered that he was not. At that point a bare headed, bare footed man in his shirt sleeves, carrying a butcher's knife in his left hand and a revolver in his right sprang through the door and asked Maxwell who the two men outside were.

Maxwell whispered, "That's him."

**[AUTHOR'S NOTE: Note the hoaxer slip-ups in presenting this source: (1)** *This* **Garrett cannot recognize Billy, though they claimed he and Billy were such good friends that Garrett killed for him; and (2) Maxwell identifies the victim as Billy!]**

Sensing a third person in the room, the intruder backed toward the door, at the same time demanding, "Quien es? Quien es?"

Pat jerked his gun and fired twice.[10] [11] ([10]*Las Vegas Daily Optic*, July 18, 1881. [11]*Santa Fe Daily New Mexican*, July 21, 1881) As the man fell Maxwell plunged over the foot of the bed and out the door, closely followed by the sheriff. Maxwell would surely have been shot by Poe if Garrett had not struck the latter's gun down saying, "Don't shoot Maxwell." He added, "That was the Kid that came in there onto me, and I think I have got him."

**[AUTHOR'S NOTE: This is Peter Maxwell's second dead Billy identification; and is not contradicting Garrett's statement.]**

Poe was not so sanguine. "Pat," he answered, "the Kid would not come to this place, you shot the wrong man." All was quiet inside. After some persuasion Maxwell brought a tallow candle and placed it on the outside of the window sill. By its light the body of a man could be seen.

*Deluvina Maxwell, a Navajo servant, entered the room, examined the body, and found that it was indeed the Kid's.*

[AUTHOR'S NOTE: This is a third identification of Billy! And Deluvina knew him, as he hoaxers later confirm themselves. She also reported his killing in a June 24, 1927 interview by J. Evetts Haley. And Poe's quote, in his 1933 book, *The Death of Billy the Kid*, expressed initial disbelief of Billy's coming there – and he did not know him. It does not disprove the victim.]

*Garrett's first shot had struck him in the left breast just above the heart; the second had gone wild. Later it was learned that Billy had been staying at the house of Juan Chavez.*

[AUTHOR'S NOTE: A fourth Billy identification!]

*Becoming hungry, he had gone to Maxwell's to slice a steak from a yearling Pete had killed that morning.*

*The corpse was taken to a carpenter's shop and laid on the work bench.*

[AUTHOR'S NOTE: The carpenter's bench would later became the hoaxers' focus for faking DNA claims.]

*Fearing an assault from Billy's friends, the officers remained awake and on guard the rest of the night. However, it passed without incident.*

[AUTHOR'S NOTE: The townspeople join the list confirming the body as Billy's, and are called "Billy's friends." Note also that Garrett does not try to conceal the body of the supposed innocent victim of his "murder."]

*When morning came, Justice of the Peace Alejandro Segura convened a jury, with Rudolph as president.*

[AUTHOR'S NOTE: The Justice of the Peace convened the Coroners Jury. Later the hoaxers will switch this fact.]

*They rendered a verdict that William Bonney, Alias "Kid," had been killed by Garrett and were "unanimous in the opinion that the gratitude of the whole community is due the said Garrett for his act and that he deserves to be rewarded".*

[AUTHOR'S NOTE: Note that the job of a Coroners' Jury was to identify the body. They did. Billy was known to them. The hoaxers already quoted historian Philip Rasch saying Rudolph was nervous when interviewed by Poe - indicating he knew Billy, and knew he was in the area. Crucial also is that the Coroner's Jury declared the killing justifiable homicide. That closed the case legally. Re-opening it is double jeopardy.]

*That afternoon Jesus Silva and Vincente Otero dug a grave for the outlaw in the old military cemetery.*[12] ([12]Philip Rasch. *Trailing Billy the Kid* by Philip J. [sic - Rasch] Outlaw-lawman research series Volume 1, University of Wyoming, Laramie, Wyoming, 1993.)

On face value this looks to be the truth. However, if you study the statements of the eye witness [sic] and the documents they do not match up and both can not be true.

**[AUTHOR'S NOTE: This is to fake "inconsistencies."]**

Deputy John Poe says the following:

*It was understood when I left my companions in the morning that in case of my being unable to learn any definite information in Fort Sumner, I was to go to the ranch of Mr. Rudolph (an acquaintance and supposed friend of Garrett's) whose ranch was located some seven miles north of Fort Sumner at a place called "Sunnyside," with the purpose of securing from him, if possible, some information as to the whereabouts of the man we were after. Accordingly I started from Fort Sumner about the middle of the afternoon for Rudolph's ranch,*

**[AUTHOR'S NOTE: Remember "in the middle of the afternoon." It will later be switched to Poe leaving for Rudulph's at night.]**

*arriving there sometime before night. I found Mr. Rudolph at home, presented the letter of Introduction which Garrett had given me, and told him that I wished to stop overnight with him.*[13] ([13]Poe, John W. Billy the Kid. Privately published by E.A. Brininstool. Los Angeles, CA.)

**[AUTHOR'S NOTE: With this unpublished, Brininstool source - and reasonable assumption of its unavailability to readers – the hoaxers are about to construct a fake argument.]**

In this part of Deputy Poe's statement he tells us he was sent to Rudolph's ranch by Garrett because Rudolph was *"an acquaintance and supposed friend of Garrett's,"* that the ranch was located seven miles north of Ft. Sumner, at Sunnyside. Poe also tells Rudolph he is going to spend the night at the ranch.

**[AUTHOR'S NOTE: The fakery here is leaving out part of the quote. Brininstool information is as follows: There was no "Brininstool book." Poe wrote his account, including the Rudulph episode, for Charles Goodnight in 1917. In 1919; and an Edward Seymour in New York contacted Goodnight for information on the Kid. Goodnight referred him to Poe. Poe sent his account of Billy's death to Seymour, who sent it to Brininstool, who published it in British *Wild World Magazine*, in December of 1919, later making it a brochure. It was also used in in Poe's book, *The Death of Billy the Kid*, which the hoaxers**

earlier cited. On its page 22, Poe states he <u>declined</u> the invitation to spend the night. But the hoaxers omitted its pages 25-26. There, Poe states: "Darkness was now approaching, and I said to Mr. Rudulph that inasmuch as myself and my horse were by this time pretty well rested, having had a good meal, I had changed my mind, and instead of stopping with him, would saddle up and ride during the cool of the evening to meet my companions. This I accordingly did, much, I thought, to the relief of Rudulph." So there was no inconsistency ]

In Sheriff Garrett's statement he gives about the same facts of where he was headed and how far it was from Ft. Sumner. Garrett differs with Poe in one area when he says he "arranged with Poe to meet us that night at moonrise" rather then spend the night with Rudolph, as can be seen below:

[AUTHOR'S NOTE: This is to fake Garrett as making contradictions. But Poe *did not* spend the night. The hoaxers merely hid Poe's quote saying that he did not spend the night.]

*I advised him* (Poe) *also, to go to Sunnyside, seven miles above Sumner, and interview M. Rudolph Esq. In whose judgment and discretion I had great confidence. I arranged with Poe to meet us that night at moonrise, at La Puenta de la Glorietta, four miles north of Fort Sumner.*[14] ([14]Garrett, Pat F. The Authentic Life of Billy the Kid. University of Oklahoma Press, Norman. Oklahoma. 2000)

[AUTHOR'S NOTE: That was it: the hoaxers' alleged inconsistency: whether Poe did or did not spend the night at Milnor Rudulph's! But both Poe and Garrett agree that Poe did not. There was no inconsistency. Nevertheless, this hoaxer flimflam is later repeated on the same subject.]

Deputy Poe then gives his account of when he says he first saw the Kid when he writes:

*I observed that he was only partly dressed, and was both bareheaded and bare-footed - or rather, had only socks on his feet, and it seemed to me that he was fastening his trousers as he came toward me art a very brisk walk.*

*As Maxwell's was the one place in Fort Sumner that I considered above suspicion of harboring "The Kid," I was entirely off my guard, that thought coming into my mind that the man approaching was either Maxwell*

**[AUTHOR'S NOTE: This quote dovetails with Poe's question about the correct man, since he could not identify Billy. Also note Poe's lack of alarm. It will be misstated by the hoaxers.]**

*or some guest of his who might have been staying there. He came on until he was almost within arm's length of where I sat before he saw me, as I was partly concealed from his view by the post of the gate. Upon his seeing me he covered me with his six-shooter as quick as lightening, sprang onto the porch, calling out in Spanish, "Quien es?" (Who is it?), at the same time backing away from me toward the door through which Garrett only a few seconds before had passed, repeating his query, "Quien es?" in Spanish several times. At this I stood up and advanced toward him, telling him not to be alarmed: that he should not be hurt, and still without the least suspicion that this was the very man we were looking for.*

This statement raises many questions with investigators. Poe says he sees a man *"partially dressed, and was bare-headed and bare-footed - or rather, had only socks on his feet, and it seemed to me that he was fastening his trousers as he came toward me art a very brisk walk."* Then the man covers him with his six shooter. Where did the man put the *"six-shooter"* when he was *"fastening his trousers"*?

**[AUTHOR'S NOTE: This is an accidentally hilarious hoaxer contrivance of the impossibility of doing two things at once! Actually, one can hold a revolver and button one's pants. And Billy was a gunman and ambidextrous, so even more able! Amazingly, this silliness would be repeated by Sederwall for W.C. Jameson's 2018 book, *Cold Case Billy the Kid*.]**

He did not stop and lay it down because Poe says he *"he came toward me art a very brisk walk."*

**[AUTHOR'S NOTE: Triple tasking!]**

Another question that investigators struggle with is would it not go without saying Poe would have had a description of the Kid as he ventured into Ft. Sumner to scout around and gather information. It is beyond reason that he would go searching for a man without at least having a description of the man for whom he was searching?

**[AUTHOR'S NOTE: It is not beyond reason. Garrett was not an experienced lawman. And Poe's task was not to search for Billy, but to find out from locals about Billy's whereabouts.]**

In a town of about 200 people, many of which were Hispanic would Poe be unable to recognize the Kid from this description as he claims?

**[AUTHOR'S NOTE: What description? It seems Poe had none. Also, this is racist. Many people of Hispanic background could be as fair as Billy.]**

Deputy Poe continues his statement with these words:

*As I moved toward him trying to reassure him, he backed up into the doorway of Maxwell's room, where he halted for a moment, his body concealed by the thick adobe wall at the side of the doorway, from whence he put his head out and asking in Spanish for the fourth or fifth time who I was. I was within a few feet of him when he disappeared into the room.*

When the Kid asks Poe who he is in Spanish and has his pistol pointed at the deputy, what is Deputy McKinney doing at this time? Why is he not shouldering his rifle, and at least deploying to the side to cover his partner Deputy Poe from this very real threat? Today the shooting policy for police officers is tight and narrow: in 1881 a shooting policy was non-existent. Investigators believe the deputies had to have a description for whom they were searching. With a threat such as Poe describes, a man with a gun, added to the description of the most wanted man in New Mexico, there would have been cause for both deputies to have fired on the suspect.

**[AUTHOR'S NOTE: Here comes fakery. Who says Poe had the description, or thought the gun was a threat? Back then, most men were armed. Poe even shows lack of alarm by reassuring the stranger. This fakery was repeated by Sederwall for W.C. Jameson's 2018 book, *Cold Case Billy the Kid*.]**

Even if the deputies chose not to fire, would they have allowed the man who was threatening their lives with a gun

**[AUTHOR'S NOTE: Note this switcheroo from a fake claim of alarm at "threatening their lives," to making it a fact.]**

to walk in on the unaware Sheriff in the dark? If they chose to allow the man with a gun to walk in on the Sheriff would these seasoned lawmen

**[AUTHOR'S NOTE: Kip McKinney was just a hog farmer.]**

not at least have warned the Sheriff of the danger?

**[AUTHOR'S NOTE: No danger is established.]**

In Garrett's statement he relates the following:

*From his step I could perceive he was either barefooted or in his stocking feet and held a revolver in his right hand and butcher knife in his left.*

*He came directly towards me. Before he reached the bed, I whispered, "Who is it Pete?"*

**[AUTHOR'S NOTE: If Garrett cannot recognize Billy, there goes the hoaxers' best-buddies-murder-plot case centerpiece! Note also that Maxwell provides another Billy identification!]**

*But I received no response for a moment. It struck me that it might be Pete's brother-in-law. Manuel Abrea, who had seen Poe and McKinney and wanted to know their business. The intruder came close to me, leaned both hands on the bed, his right and almost touching my knee, and asked in a low tone: "Who are they, Pete?" At the same moment Maxwell whispered to me, "That's him!" Simultaneously the Kid must have seen, or felt, the presence of a third person at the head of the bed. He raised quickly his pistol, a self cocker, within a foot of my breast. Retreating rapidly across the room he cried: "Quien es? Quien es? (Who's that? Who's that?) All this occurred in a moment. Quickly as possible I drew my revolver and fired, threw my body aside, and fired again. The second shot was useless: The Kid fell dead ..."*

Investigators find it hard to believe that Garrett could see a 6 inch knife in the Kid's hand.

**[AUTHOR'S NOTE: That night had a bright moon. When Billy opened the door, a held weapon would have been visible.]**

Yet the Kid could not see a six foot, five inch man.

**[AUTHOR'S NOTE: It was dark in the room. Note that at this half-way point in the Probable Cause Statement, with killing done, nothing indicates the victim was not Billy.]**

Deputy Poe talks about what happened after the shooting of the Kid. He writes:

*Within a very short time after the shooting, quite a number of the native people had gathered around, some of them bewailing the death of their friend,*

**[AUTHOR'S NOTE: From Poe's *The Death of Billy the Kid*, comes this hoaxer slip-up: These people, who can recognize Billy, will later be given his body to lay out.]**

*while several women pleaded for permission to take charge of the body, which we allowed them to do. They carried it to the yard to a carpenter's shop, where it was laid on a workbench, the women placing candles lightened around it, according to their ideas of properly conducting a "wake" for the dead.*

**[AUTHOR'S NOTE: By this point, there are profuse eye-witness identifications of Billy!]**

Investigators keep Deputy Poe's statement in mind as they studied the Coroner's Jury Report:

*Greetings:*

*On this 15th day of July, A.D. 1881, I, the undersigned, Justice of the Peace of the above named precinct, received information that a murder had taken place in Fort Sumner, in said precinct, and immediately upon receiving said information I proceeded to the said place and named Milnor Rudolph, Jose Silva, Antonio Sevedra, Pedro Antonio Lucero, Lorenzo Jaramillo and Sabal Gutierres a jury to investigate the case and the above jury convened in the home of Luz B. Maxwell and proceeded to a room in the said house where they found the body of William Bonney... alias "Kid"...with a shot in the left breast and having examined the body they examined the evidence of Pedro Maxwell, which evidence is as follows: "I being in my bed in my room, at about midnight on the 14th day of July, Pat F. Garrett came into my room and sat down. William Bonney came in and got close to my bed with a gun in his hand and asked me "who is it" and then Pat F. Garrett fired two shots at the said William Bonney and the said William Bonney fell near my fire place and I went out of the room and when I came in again about three or four minutes after the shots the said William Bonney was dead."*

**[AUTHOR'S NOTE: This is a definitive Jury, plus Maxwell , making identifications of the victim as William Bonney.]**

*The jury has found the following verdict: We the jury unanimously find that William Bonney has been killed by a shot on the left breast near the region of the heart, the same having been fired with a gun in the hand of pat F. Garrett and our verdict is that the deed of said Garrett was justifiable homicide and we are unanimous in the opinion that the gratitude of all the community is due to the said Garrett for his deed and is worthy of being rewarded.*

M. Rudolph, President          Anto, Sevedra(signature)
Pedro Anto. m. Lucero (signature)
Jose Silba (x)        Sabal Gutierrez (x)        Lorenzo Jaramillo (x)

*All said information I place to your knowledge.*

*Alejandro Segura Justice of the Peace (signature)*

[AUTHOR'S NOTE: This is a legally binding document confirming victim identification. To reopen the case is double jeopardy. Further confirmation of jurymen's certainty, is that no murder indictment was later made with the District Attorney of the First Judicial District Attorney against Garrett.]

Investigators remembered Deputy Poe's statement and Sheriff Garrett's statement as to where Poe had been that night.

[AUTHOR'S NOTE: The hoaxers hope the reader believed their faked contention that Poe spent the night at Rudulph's. What follows is more fakery to manufacture "inconsistencies."]

Earlier that evening

[AUTHOR'S NOTE: The time was afternoon, as quoted by the hoaxers earlier, and tagged by me to prepare for this switcheroo where they need night for their fake argument.]

Garrett had dispatched Deputy Poe to interview M. Rudolph in Sunnyside, seven miles north of Fort Sumner. Poe says he left Rudolph and rode to meet Garrett and McKinney. All records show that the shooting took place about midnight and Historian Philip I. Rash [sic] sets the time at 12:30 AM on July 15$^{th}$. If this were true then the time does not allow for the statement of Poe and the coroner's jury report to both be true.

[AUTHOR'S NOTE: Their hoaxers' time switcheroo is done to discredit the Coroner's Jury Report: their bugbear. But, even if granted them, it does not work because of the length of the ride. Poe could cover the 7 miles to Sunnyside in 1½ hours. Puenta de la Glorietta was 4 miles north of Fort Sumner on the way. So Poe's return journey to meet his companions was only 3 miles, or about 45 minutes: easy to meet them by evening: a fact he and Garrett confirmed. No time inconsistency exists.]

If, after the shooting, Garrett had to get some order to the scene, locate a rider to ride to Sunnyside to get Rudolph,

[AUTHOR'S NOTE: The above Coroner's Jury Report clearly states that the appointment - and contacting - of Rudulph was a legal duty performed by the appropriate official: Justice of the Peace, Alejandro Segura; certainly <u>not</u> Garrett, then a suspect as to his legality in Billy Bonney's killing.]

and the rider then had to get his horses [sic] caught, saddled and ready to go all of which would take the better part of an hour,

[AUTHOR'S NOTE: Timing here is faked. Maxwell had a stable and workers. A horse could be readied quickly.]

the time would be 1:30 am.

[AUTHOR'S NOTE: The hoaxers are faking time "inconsistency. Yet they know that the Coroner's Jury met sometime during daytime of the 15th. There was no need for extreme urgency; and no evidence that it occurred.]

It would take a rider who was in shape, on a good horse, and riding fast, an hour and a half to cover the seven miles to Rudolph's ranch, putting the time at 2:30 am. Adding an hour for the rider to wake Rudolph up and for Rudolph to catch his horse and saddle the horse the time would be 3:30 am. If Rudolph was in good shape, on a good horse it would be another hour and a half on the return trip to Fort Sumner putting the time at 4:30 am. Add another hour to put together a jury, and the time is now 5:30 am. This is if everyone worked smoothly.

In the jury's report we find the words:

*... a jury to investigate the case and the above jury convened in the home of Luz B. Maxwell and proceeded to a room in the said in said house where they found the body of William Bonney alias "Kid"...*

Either the jury found the Kid in the Maxwell's home, or he was not given to the women to put on the carpenters workbench as Poe says, or the jury report is deceptive.

[AUTHOR'S NOTE: The hoaxers hope they convinced readers of that conclusion to fake an inconsistency. But there was enough time to carry the corpse from the Maxwell house, across about 300 yards of parade ground, to the carpenter's shop. In the morning, it could be returned to the Maxwell's house for the jurymen. This fakery was recycled by Sederwall for W.C. Jameson's 2018 book, *Cold Case Billy the Kid*.]

Deputy Poe also says:

*The next morning we sent for the justice of the peace,*

[AUTHOR'S NOTE: Here is undone the fakery of the night riding by giving this quote about the next morning.]

*who held an inquest over the body, the verdict of the jury being such as to justify the killing, and later, on the same day, the body was buried in the old military burying ground at Fort Sumner.*

If the Kid's body was taken to the carpenter shop then the jury did not find the body at Maxwell's house as stated and makes investigators wonder why they would lie in the report.

[AUTHOR'S NOTE: This fabrication leads to a "lie" accusation. But nothing indicates that the body was not brought to the house from the carpenter's shop. But the hoaxers are still trying to discredit the Coroner's Jury Report by fake "contradictions;" though, of course, that is irrelevant to establishing the victim's identity.]

Deputy Poe says something else that raised investigators suspicions when he writes about the shooting itself:

[AUTHOR'S NOTE: This switcheroo distracts from the sly misstatements slipped past. And though the hoaxers never say what is "suspicious" in Poe's quote – which is merely repeating Garrett's description - they are setting the stage for their fake "investigation" to be described next.]

*An instant later a shot was fired in the room, followed immediately by what everyone within hearing distance thought was two shots fired, the third report, as we learned afterward, being caused by the rebound of the second bullet which had struck the adobe wall and rebounded against the headboard of the wooden bedstead.*

[AUTHOR'S NOTE: Let us take stock now. Nothing so far indicates a victim other than profusely identified Billy Bonney. Nor are there any "contradictions." Later, when exhumations were blocked, the hoaxers contradicted this document: stating Billy *was* shot, laid out on the bench, but played dead to bleed as a source of DNA, before evil Garrett switched him with the murdered innocent victim!]

[AUTHOR'S NOTE: Note that the second bullet hit the headboard. But the hoaxers will do fake forensics on a washstand instead! So next is a faked CSI-style investigation.]

On August 29, 2003, Deputy Sederwall of the Lincoln County Sheriff''s Department

[AUTHOR'S NOTE: Sederwall calls himself a deputy; years later, when hiding the case's DNA documents from my open records case, he would lie that he did the case as his "hobby!"]

located the carpenter bench where the Kid's body was placed on July 14, 1881.

[AUTHOR'S NOTE: Error: earliest morning of July 15th]

On September 13, 2003, investigators located all the furniture that was in Pete Maxwell's bedroom the night of the shooting, July 1881.

[AUTHOR'S NOTE: Though this information is irrelevant to the claim of whether Billy was Garrett's victim, this Maxwell furniture - including the carpenter's bench - became pivotal to the survival of the hoax after exhumations were blocked. But the furniture's connection to the historical scenes is not iron-clad. Maxwell family sold Fort Sumner at public auction on January 15, 1884 to Lonny Horn, Sam Doss, Daniel Taylor and

The Maxwell house was torn down in 1887; and its lumber was used to build the Pigpen Ranch south of Melrose, New Mexico.
After the 1884 sale, Peter Maxwell moved outside town (see page 697), dying there in 1898. His furniture would have been from that house. One of Peter's sisters, Odile, married a Manuel Abreu, settling near the town. She had family furniture, but Peter's would have come after his death. In about 1926, her 15 year old daughter, Stella, made a little "Billy the Kid Museum" in a shack for tourists. Stella labeled Odile's furniture as from Maxwell's bedroom and the vigil's carpenter's bench. But, as she told historian Richard Weddle in old age, she merely got the bench from a local. (See page 402) The Museum closed in 1936. In 1940 she put the furniture in her Santa Rosa gas station run with her husband, Kenneth Miller. It was again stored before being moved, in 1959, to their converted chicken coop in Albuquerque. Her son, Mannie Miller, showed it to the hoaxers. He died on March 20, 2011; and it was sold to a collector. In fact, all one can say is that 45 years after Billy's killing, Stella made unprovable claims about furniture for profit, with the cheap-looking items more likely from Perer's new bedroom. And the random bench was never in the family.]

Among these items is the headboard of the bed that was in Maxwell's room that night. There is no bullet hole in the headboard.

[AUTHOR'S NOTE: That finding, though irrelevant to the victim, is part of the hoaxer's fake forensics and was created to contradict Poe's eye-witness statement that the headboard was hit. The fakery omitted mention that Stella Abreu's museum's headboard was just a thin frame around a huge opening of the missing headboard. There is no place for a bullet hole! This fakery would be recycled by Sederwall in W.C. Jameson's 2018 book, *Cold Case Billy the Kid*.]

In a statement made by Deluvina Maxwell she says the following:

*... There was a washstand with a marble top in Pete Maxwell's bedroom, which Garrett had seen in the moonlight and shot at, thinking it was Bonney trying to get up.*

[AUTHOR'S NOTE: This is a faked Deluvina quote. Its footnote states: "[15]Deluvina Maxwell's story as related to Lucien B. Maxwell grandchildren, unpublished." This is just hearsay, without even a source. It is being used to fake legitimacy of the hoaxers' claim that the washstand was shot by Garrett.]

*It was an old Spanish custom that the night before the burial of a person, people would take turns staying with the body and reciting prayers. William Bonney had a proper funeral. The people took turns and stayed through the night.*

[AUTHOR'S NOTE: Another body identification as Billy!]

*He was buried in the old government cemetery in Fort Sumner. For many years Deluvina left flowers on his grave in the summer time.*[15]

[AUTHOR'S NOTE: This third person statement again shows the quote was not Deluvina. But she did lay flowers for decades, proving the body was Billy's!]

Deluvina lends credibility to the story of the Kid's body being laid on the carpenter bench.

[AUTHOR'S NOTE: Here is a hoaxer slip that ends their case: Billy's corpse on bench! And it ends "Brushy's" hoax too! To get out of that problem, the hoaxers later fabricated that Billy was just "playing dead!"]

In the items investigators located on September 13, 2003 was that wash stand.

[AUTHOR'S NOTE: This washstand is unsubstantiated as from Pete Maxwell's bedroom - as is the rest of the furniture from Stella Abreu's Billy the Kid Museum. And this washstand is implausibly toy-sized. Furthermore, eye-witness Poe said the headboard was hit. But what follows is a fake "crime scene investigation" using the unsubstantiated washstand.]

The was stand was dark in color and 29 1/2 inches wide, with a splash board on the back that measured 5 inch at the middle and tapered down to the ends in a decorative curve. From front to back the wash stand measured 16 inches. It stood 29 inches with three drawers with rusted locks on each drawer. There was what appeared to be a bullet hole through the stand.

Deputy Sederwall removed a .45 caliber pistol round from his deputy weapon and noticed the round was just a little bit bigger than the hole. The night of the shooting Sheriff Garrett was shooting a Colt Single Action Army Revolver, Serial Number 55093, caliber .44/40.[16] ([16]Typed letter from P.F. Garrett dated April 16, 1906. James H. Earl Collection, from County Clerk's office, El Paso, Texas.)

[AUTHOR'S NOTE: Note that there is no bullet, just holes. Claiming .44/40 ammunition is fakery to match Garrett's known weapon's caliber. Actually, there is no link to Garrett or to Maxwell's bedroom. There is even no link to anyone being shot, since accidental discharges happened in New Mexico where owning guns was common from the 19th century to the present – the time frame for "shooting" the tiny washstand!]

The bullet pierced the left side of the washstand, both sides of the drawer and exited out the right side of the stand.

The bullet struck the left side of the stand 22 1/4 inches on the center up from the bottom and 6 1/2 inches on the center of the back of the stand. The bullet exited to the right side 20 1/2 inches on the center up from the bottom and 6 1/2 inches on center from the back of the washstand. On the inside of the left side panel the wood was somewhat splintered indicating that was where the bullet entered the stand. On the right side panel the outside of the panel was splintered indicating the exit of the bullet.

The owner of the washstand, whose name investigators do not wish to release at this time

**[AUTHOR'S NOTE: The hoaxers later named Mannie Miller.]**

says it was inherited along with the bed from Maxwell's bedroom. The discovery of this evidence makes Deluvina's statement believable.

**[AUTHOR'S NOTE: Historically real or not, the furniture examination is irrelevant to Garrett's victim's identity.]**

Many questions remain. Why would the coroner's jury report and the eye witness reports be so at odds?

**[AUTHOR'S NOTE: They are not at odds. The hoaxers simply made up some "discrepancies." But the hoaxers were heading to additional fakery, once again to attack the hated Coroner's Jury Report that undid their hoaxing.]**

A hint can be found in a document discovered in July of 1989 by Joe O. Bowlin.

**[AUTHOR'S NOTE: This is a low blow to a dead man. Joe Bowlin, with his wife Marlyn, founded the Billy the Kid Outlaw Gang to "preserve, protect, and promote the history of Billy Bonney and Pat Garrett." This hoax would have been anathema to Joe Bowlin. What follows misstates a book Bolin published posthumously for its old-timer author, A.P. "Paco" Anaya.]**

The document is a story, according to Louis Anaya of Clovis, New Mexico as told to his father, Paco Anaya, a friend of Billy the Kid.

**[AUTHOR'S NOTE: Note the admitted friendship of Paco Anaya and Billy. It will catch the hoaxers in another slip-up about the victim being Billy.]**

This story was translated from Spanish and then printed in book form. In this transcript you will find the following:

*Also, I will have to tell you a lot in reference to the reports that Pat Garrett made about the sworn declaration that appears in the records of the Secretary of State and more, concerning what he said about the*

Coroners Jury that investigated the death of Billy the Kid when Pat killed Billy.

In this report, I find that the Coroners Jury that investigated the death of Billy the Kid when he was dead is not part of the same report that acted as a Coroners Jury, neither the form or the verdict of the Coroners Jury. The verdict is recorded in the office of the Secretary of State in Spanish, and they (the jury) are not the same men. There are two that did not even live in Fort Sumner.[17] ([17]Anaya, A. P. *I Buried Billy.* Creative Publishing Company. 1991.)

Paco Anaya goes on to list the members of the Jury that he remembered holding the inquest over the body. They are not the same as the jury report as is held up as proof that Garrett killed the Kid.

**[AUTHOR'S NOTE: This is the two coroner's jury report claim made up by windbag "Paco" Anaya, spewing malarkey for his manuscript devoid of historical knowledge. He was used first as an "expert" in the "Brushy Bill" hoax; and subsequently recycled as a staple in all Billy the Kid imposter hoax books to follow – including W.C. Jameson's *Cold Case Billy the Kid*]**

One of the differences is Illeginio Garcia [sic - poor legibility - unclear spelling] as the Jury President and not M. Rudolph.

Paco Anaya says that Garrett wrote the first version in English himself. Anaya says that Garrett later came back and wrote another report in Spanish with the help of "Don Pedro Maxwell and Don Manuel Abrea," [sic - Abreu] Maxwell's brother-in-law.

This makes the investigators ask, if Garrett wrote the verdict is that why the words are found, *"...we are unanimous in the opinion that the gratitude of all the community is due to the said Garrett for his deed and is worthy of being rewarded"*?

It should be noted that in the Coroners Jury Report that Garrett puts forth

**[AUTHOR'S NOTE: Note the switcheroo. Garrett did not "put forth" the Coroner's Jury Report. It was a legal document done by authority of Justice of the Peace, Alejandro Segura. Garrett was the *subject* of their investigation. The document was available to him after he was cleared of wrongdoing, to send to District Attorney William Breeden. And it surely was not available to humble citizen Anaya. But the hidden punch line is that Anaya's posthumously published book was titled *I Buried Billy*, confirming the body as Billy Bonney's. ]**

it is interesting to note that two of those listed were in Garrett's wedding, Sabal Gutierrez is his brother-in-law, and Garrett admits in his statement that Rudolph is a close friend.

**[AUTHOR'S NOTE: Note the lie. Garrett did not pick the jurymen; the Justice of the Peace did. All the fakery has done nothing to show that Garrett murdered anyone but Billy.]**

**[AUTHOR'S NOTE: Next is the hoaxer' last try: using fellow hoaxer, David Turk, for useless hearsay and his fancy title.]**

David Turk, Historian for the United States Marshal's Service has pointed out other documents

**[AUTHOR'S NOTE: Only one document is presented; though Turk came to New Mexico in December of 2003, possibly to assist in writing this Probable Cause Statement.]**

bringing into question Garrett's involvement in the Kid's escape.

**[AUTHOR'S NOTE: Note the switcheroo. Who said Billy escaped? He was dead.]**

Mr. Turk has produced a Works Progress Administration, Federal Writer's Project interview where the following statement was taken:

*The people around Lincoln*

**[AUTHOR'S NOTE: The killing was 150 miles from Lincoln; and Turk's old-timer reports are useless hearsay. He also supplied the hoax with his own slip-shod and pretender-oriented booklet titled "U.S. Marshals Service and Billy the Kid."]**

*say Garrett didn't kill Billie (sic) the Kid. John Poe was with Garrett the night he was supposed to ... said that he didn't see the man that Garrett killed.*

**[AUTHOR'S NOTE: Besides the fact that Poe's statements all refer to seeing the victim, Poe did not know Billy.]**

*I can take you to the grave in Hell's High Acre, an old government cemetery, where Billie (sic) was supposed to be buried and show you the grave.*

*The cook at Pete Maxwell's was always putting flowers on the grave and praying at it. This woman thought a lot of Billie (sic), but after Garrett killed the man at Maxwell's home her grandson was never seen again*

**[AUTHOR'S NOTE: No "grandson" was part of this history.]**

*and Billie (sic) was seen by Bill Nicholi an Indian scout. Bill saw him in Mexico.*[18] ([18]Frances E. Tolly [Totty], comp. "Early Days in Lincoln County," Charles Remark Interview. February 14, 1938, Works Progress Administration, Federal Writer's Project, Folklore-Life Histories, Manuscript Division. Library of Congress.)

[AUTHOR'S NOTE: So this sole "evidence" that Garrett did not kill Billy is old-timer malarkey 57 years later, by someone unconnected to the event, and titled as "folklore."]

[AUTHOR'S NOTE: Next comes the conclusion pretending they proved their contentions.]

Discovering the headboard of Maxwell's bed that does not have a bullet hole in it, as Deputy Poe says it did, leads investigators to question if Poe was in fact in the room after the shooting of William Bonney as he said.

[AUTHOR'S NOTE: Omitted is that the headboard is just an empty frame. And claiming if it was not shot, Poe was not in the room" is absurd; and also irrelevant to victim identity.]

However, the discovery of the Maxwell wash stand with the bullet hole through it indicates someone was shot in Maxwell's room on the night of July 14, 18821.

[AUTHOR'S NOTE: Why? A shot washstand does not mean a shot person - or anything at all about who Garrett shot.]

The question remains as to who is in William H. Bonney's grave at Fort Sumner.

[AUTHOR'S NOTE: No question remains. This is all fakery.]

Investigators believe with the conflicts of Sheriff Pat F. Garrett and Deputy John Poe and the fact that these statements are at odds with the Jury Report as shown above,

[AUTHOR'S NOTE: This is fakery. The "conflicts" do not exist; and had nothing to do with whom Garrett shot.]

coupled with the evidence discovered by deputies,

[AUTHOR'S NOTE: There has been no legitimate evidence.]

probable cause exist [sic] to warrant the court to grant investigators the right to search for the truth in criminal investigation 2003-274 through DNA samples obtained from Catherine Antrim.

[AUTHOR'S NOTE: Without any probable cause of a murder, the hoaxers, contrived their objective: exhumation of Billy and his mother.]

[AUTHOR'S NOTE: Signatures follow; typed and written.]

Steven M. Sederwall: Deputy Sheriff, Lincoln County (12/31/03)

Tom Sullivan: Sheriff Lincoln County (12/31/03)

## THE OVERTON AFFIDAVIT

Attached to the "Probable Cause Statement" was a two page, typed, old-timer affidavit prepared for Sheriff Tom Sullivan by a Homer Overton in the mold of the fake identity Affidavits used by William V. Morrison for *Alias Billy the Kid*.. To be noted is that Overton is lying, for whatever reason. It should be noted that Pat Garrett's widow, Apolinaria Gutierrez Garrett, died in 1936, four years *before* Overton's alleged conversation with her in 1940 (b.1861 - d.1936)! She is buried in the Masonic Cemetery in Las Cruces, New Mexico, where Pat Garrett also lies.

Overton's windbag malarkey includes fabrications of a Pat Garrett report to Texas Rangers, a corpse with blasted face, and, of course, Garrett's murder of someone other than Billy the Kid.

Overton's claims also insult Pat Garrett's widow's reverential protection of Garrett's legacy. After Garrett's death in 1908, she even legally fought and reclaimed from a saloonkeeper his revolver used to kill Billy the Kid. She was the last person in the world to tell random, 9 year old child, Homer Overton, that Pat had not shot the Kid - even if she had not been four years dead! Homer Overton wrote:

December 22, 2003

Tom Sullivan
Lincoln County Sheriff
P.O. Box 278
Carrizozo, NM 88301

Tom,

It was good talking to you on the phone and, as promised, I am sending this letter as promised to present this Statement of Facts.

Fact: I was born in Pecos, Texas in the year 1931 and lived there until the later [sic] part of 1941. In the summer of 1940, I was invited to spend the summer with Bobby Talbert and his mother, who had moved from Pecos to Las Cruces, New Mexico earlier that year.

**[AUTHOR'S NOTE: Time specificity of Overton's age plus the date fixes Overton in Las Cruces in 1940 – not earlier.]**

The time I spent there was wonderful, but one thing happened that summer that made the summer unforgettable.

Bobby's next door neighbor was a lady who introduced herself as Mrs. Garrett, the widow of Pat Garrett. Mrs. Garrett would invite us over to have iced tea with mint leaves in it, and told us stories about her life with Pat. I recall her having a parrot that had belonged to Pat which she said was very old. She told us some parrots live to be over 100 years.

That afternoon, she brought out a gun to show us and said it had belonged to Pat. As I recall, the gun appeared to be a Colt single action revolver. At that point I asked her if that was the gun used to kill Billy the Kid. At this point she got an unusual look on her face and stated that she was going to tell us something we would have to promise to keep it secret, and never to tell anyone. We both promised, and until this day I have never told anyone but my immediate family.

Mrs. Garrett proceeded to tell us the following facts concerning her husband and Billy:

Mrs. Garrett said, "Pat did not shoot Billy". She said there was a very close relationship between Pat and Billy, almost like a father and son relationship. She further stated that the night Pat was supposed to kill Billy, that they were in Ft. Sumner and had made a plan to make it look like Pat killed Billy so Billy could go to Mexico and live with no one looking for him any more. She said that Pat had seen a drunk Mexican lying in the street on his way to talk to Billy. So they planned to use the Mexican and claim that he was in fact Billy the Kid. She didn't state if the Mexican was dead or not, but said that they shot him in the face so he couldn't be recognized. They dressed him in Billy's clothes and Pat signed a paper for the Texas Rangers stating that he had killed Billy the Kid and that this was his body. The Mexican was then buried in Fort Sumner and identified as Billy.

Mrs. Garrett struck me as being very sincere when she told us this and she stated that she had never told anyone before. I have kept this secret for sixty-three years and feel it is time to disclose this story. I hope it will be helpful to you in your quest to find the truth about Billy, as I believe what Mrs. Garrett told us that day was the absolute truth.

All that I have told you is as I recall it related to me sixty-three years ago when I was nine years old. It made such an impression on me that I have remembered it in detail these sixty-three years.

Sincerely,
Homer D. Overton
AKA: Homer D. Kinsworthy
CONTACT INFORMATION

Witnessed by: Jerry Raffee, NOTARY
on December 27th 2003

SEAL AFFIXED

# THE ABANDONED "SEVENTY-SEVEN DAYS OF DOUBT" PROBABLE CAUSE STATEMENT

A document which the lawmen hoaxers hid, and I got by my open records litigation against them, revealed the "Brushy Bill" core of the "Billy the Kid Case" hoax. Likely created around April of 2003, it is a draft of a never-used "Probable Cause Statement" for Pat Garrett as the murder suspect. "LATEST" is handwritten on its front page, as if drafts were attempted. It was titled: "Lincoln County Sheriff's Office, Lincoln County New Mexico, Case: William H. Bonney, a.k.a. William Antrim, a.k.a. The Kid, a.k.a. Billy the Kid: An Investigation into the events of April 28, 1881 through July 14, 1881 - seventy-seven days of doubt." I nick-named it the "Seventy-Seven Days of Doubt Document." Typed-in for future signatures are: "Tom Sullivan: Sheriff, Lincoln County Sheriff's Office; and Steven M. Sederwall: Deputy Sheriff, Lincoln County Sheriff's Office."

Its intent was promoting "Brushy Bill" as Billy the Kid. "Brushy's" "survival" is the "evidence," or probable cause, for Garrett's not having killed Billy. So, according to the fledgling "Billy the Kid Case" hoax, Billy Barlow was their corpse in Billy's Fort Sumner grave - and intended recipient of their hoax's "high-tech, modern, CSI, DNA forensics."

The "Seventy-Seven Days of Doubt" version is pure conspiracy theory where "Brushy" is king; with John Miller fleetingly referenced for "survival suspicion." And with guilelessness and ignorance matching true-believers W.C. Jameson and Frederick Bean, it uses "Brushy's" unscreened quotes as proof. **So "Brushy's" fatal mistake of the *dark night* of the July 14, 1881 killing scene appears again, as in *The Return of Billy the Kid*;** after having been altered to "bright moonlight" by the original Sonnichsen-Morrison team for *Alias Billy the Kid*.

But its actual author is unclear. **The person was unaware of the history, for example, calling Paulita (Peter Maxwell's sister), his "teenage daughter."** Mere guesses for authoring are amateur historian Attorney Bill Robins III, since needed was a "Brushy"-believer. Or it could have been W.C. Jameson (since he had the "Brushy" transcript); or David Turk, who contributed another big "Brushy"-oriented pamphlet.

Importantly, the "Seventy-Seven Days of Doubt Document" lets uncensored "Brushy" talk, giving another window into his mad and florid confabulated death scene. The document stated:

# LINCOLN COUNTY SHERIFF'S OFFICE
# LINCOLN COUNTY, NEW MEXICO

Case: *William H. Bonney*, a.k.a. **William Antrim**, a.k.a. **The Kid**, *a.k.a.* **Billy the Kid**

**An Investigation into the events of April 28, 1881 through July 14, 1881 - seventy-seven days of doubt.**

Just minutes after twelve, noon, on April 28, 1881, two lawmen lay dead, in the yard of the courthouse in Lincoln, New Mexico, from gunshot wounds. In less time then [sic] it took the New Mexico breeze to clear the gunsmoke, history was clouded with the myth of the shooting and escape of William H. Bonney, a.k.a. Billy the Kid from the makeshift jail, where he awaited a date with the hangman.

The following is a thumbnail sketch of the most widely excepted [sic] account of the events of the escape, capture and shooting death of William H. Bonney a.k.a. Billy the Kid.

## The Last Days of William H. Bonney

On August 17, 1877, in George Atkin's cantina near Camp Grant, Arizona, William H. Bonney, who answered to "The Kid" found himself in an altercation with Francis P. "Windy" Cahill over cards or Cahill's woman, no one is quite sure as newspapers report both. It's reported that Windy Cahill called The Kid a "pimp", and in response The Kid dubbed Cahill a "sonofabitch". Infuriated, Cahill reportedly grabbed the Kid and The Kid shoved his pistol into Cahill's stomach, sending a hot round into his belly. With Cahill on the floor, The Kid fled on a stolen horse. Cahill died the next day. A coroner's jury headed by Miles Wood found the shooting by The Kid to be *"criminal and unjustifiable"*. The Kid now being a bona fide outlaw drifted across the line into New Mexico's Lincoln County where he signed on as a cowboy working for London born rancher John Tunstall.

Tunstall and his lawyer friend Alexander McSween had decided to challenge the chock-hold [sic] monopoly L.G. Murphy & Company had on Lincoln County. Murphy and his associates, with the backing of the "Santa Fe Ring" ran Lincoln County as they pleased and verticality [sic] unchecked until Tunstall's challenge. The Santa Fe Ring, with their powerful political and financial backing and through Murphy controlled the sheriff, maintained a buddy-buddy relationship with the military and appropriated by means both legal and illegal most of the government money out of the Mescalero Apache Indian Agency near Fort Stanton. When Tunstall wouldn't back down and his challenge became to [sic] powerful for the Murphy faction to turn their heads to, Tunstall was killed. His death on February 18, 1878 fanned the spark that raged into the white-hot flame that became the famed and bloody Lincoln County War.

As history goes Bonney was insignificant as a man, but there exist [sic] no better example of how legends of the west are born and continue to grow. By participating in a number of bloody shootouts, included [sic] the assassination of Lincoln County Sheriff William Brady and one of his deputies, on April 1, 1878, Bonney was catapulted from his status of an unknown drifter to the undisputed leader of the Tunstall-McSween faction and into history becoming bigger the [sic] life.

**[AUTHOR'S NOTE: Though starting when Bonney was 17 ½ (not his last days!), the intent is to feign historical knowledge, but fails. Billy was never the leader of the Tunstall-McSween faction. The fakery intentionally blurs history and "legend," to pretend that actual history *was* legend, to segue to the fakery that history was not as written. But all this is irrelevant to any probable cause of Pat Garrett murdering an innocent victim.]**

After newly elected Lincoln County Sheriff Pat Garrett captured Bonney at Stinking Springs, east of Fort Sumner, just before Christmas 1880, Bonney was held in the jail in Santa Fe for several months and then taken to La Mesilla, New Mexico for trial.

The Dona Ana County, District Court records reveal on April 13, 1881, William H. Bonney was convicted of the April 1, 1878 murder of Lincoln County Sheriff William Brady. United States District Judge, Warren Henry Bristol, of the Third Judicial District, sentenced Bonney to be confined in Lincoln County until Friday, May 13, 1881. Looking down from the bench, the judge proclaimed, *"between 9 a.m. and 3 p.m., William Bonney, alias Kid, alias William Antrim, be taken from such prison to some suitable and convenient place of execution within said county of Lincoln, by Sheriff of such county and that then and there, on that day and between the aforesaid hours thereof, by the sheriff of said county of Lincoln, he, the said William Bonney, alias Kid, alias William Antrim, be hanged by the neck until his body be dead."*

On April 21, 1881, Bonney was transported back to Lincoln under heavy guard. Because Lincoln had no adequate jail Bonney was incarcerated in the upstairs of the old Murphy-Dolan store, recently bought by the county to be used as the courthouse. A staircase led up to a hallway that ran north to south across the middle section of the building. The room ahead and to the left of the hallway was being used as the sheriff's office. Off the sheriff's office, with access only through the sheriff's office was the room where Bonney was confined.

With no bars on the windows of this room, Sheriff Garrett had special leg shackles made, and Bonney was chained to the hardwood floor at all times. In addition, Garrett assigned Lincoln County Sheriffs Deputy J.W. Bell and Deputy United States Marshall [sic] Bob Olinger, to guard the prisoner twenty-four hours a day. On the floor Bonney's guards drew a chalk line across the center of the room, a line which Bonney was forbidden to cross or he would be shot by the guards.

On Wednesday, April 27, 1881 Sheriff Pat Garrett left Lincoln on a tax-collecting mission to White Oaks, New Mexico. Just after twelve, noon, the next day, Thursday, April 28, Deputy United States Marshall [sic] Olinger escorted all the prisoners with the exception of Bonney to the Wortley Hotel, across the street from the courthouse, for their midday meal, leaving Deputy Sheriff Bell in charge of Bonney.

No eye witness record can be found of the escape of Bonney with the exception of the following statement made by the courthouse caretaker Gottfried Gauss, published in the *Lincoln County Leader* on January 15, 1890, nearly a decade later.

*I was crossing the yard behind the courthouse, when I heard a shot fired then a tussle upstairs in the courthouse, somebody hurrying downstairs, and deputy sheriff Bell emerging from the door running toward me. He ran right into my arms, expired the same moment, and I laid him down, dead. That I was in a hurry to secure assistance, or perhaps to save myself, everybody will believe.*

*When I arrived at the garden gate leading to the street, in front of the courthouse, I saw the other deputy sheriff Olinger, coming out of the hotel opposite, with the four or five other county prisoners, where they had taken their dinner. I called to him to come quick. He did so, leaving his prisoners in front of the hotel. When he had come up close to me, and while I was standing not a yard apart, I told him that I was just after laying Bell dead on the ground in the yard behind. Before he could reply, he was struck by a well-directed shot fired from a window above us, and fell dead at my feet. I ran for my life to reach my room and safety, when Billy the Kid called to me: "Don't run, I wouldn't hurt you – I am alone, and master not only of the courthouse, but also of the town, for I will allow nobody to come near us." "You go," he said, "and saddle one of Judge (Ira) Leonard's horses, and I will clear out as soon as I have the shackles loosened from my legs." With a little prospecting pick I had thrown to him through the window he was working for at least an hour, and could not accomplish more than to free one leg. He came to the conclusion to wait a better chance, tie one shackle to his waistbelt, and start out. Meanwhile I had saddled a small skittish pony belonging to*

*Billy Burt (the county clerk), as there was no other horse available, and had also, by Billy's command, tied a pair of red blankets behind the saddle ...*

*When Billy went down the stairs at last, on passing the body of Bell he said, "I'm sorry I had to kill him but I couldn't help it." On passing the body of Olinger he gave him a tip with his boot, saying, "You are not going to round me up again." And so Billy the Kid started out that evening, after he had shaken hands with everybody around and after having a little difficulty in mounting on account of the shackle on his leg, he went on his way rejoicing.*

There are numerous theories about the killing of Deputy J.W. Bell. One is that he was coming up the stairs when shot. Another theory is Bell was running down the stairs and was at the bottom of the stairs and heading to the doorway when Bonney shot him. Garrett's testimony seems to be the most solid. Garrett says, *"Bell was hit under the right arm, the bullet passing through his body and coming out under the left arm. The ball had hit the wall on Bell's right, caromed passed through his body, and buried itself in an adobe (wall) on the left. There was no other proof besides the marks on the walls."*

Garrett later said of Olinger, that he was *"hit in the right shoulder, breast and side. He was literally riddled by thirty-six buckshot."* Each pellet weighed four grams - nearly a quarter pound of lead in all hit Olinger.

It's hard to determine how many shots were fired at Bell from Bonney's pistol. In the 1920's Maurice G. Fulton saw the building and states there were *"any number of bullet holes"*. Fulton had a photograph taken in the 1930's prior to the restoration, which shows three.

With only two people on the stairway that day numerous versions of what happened have been brought forth, and debated. One theory in the Kid's escape is that he slipped his irons, which were double the usual weight, over his small wrists and hands. He turned on Bell striking the deputy over the head with the irons and grabbing the deputy's pistol. This theory could have come from the following article.

In the *Grand County Herald's*, May 14, 1881 edition an article appeared quoting an "anonymous bystander" as testifying about the Kid's escape. *He had at his command eight revolvers and six guns. He stood on the upper porch in front of the building and talked with the people who were in Wortley's, but he would not let anyone come towards him. He told the people that he did not want to kill Bell but, as he had to. He said he grabbed Bell's revolver and told him to hold up his hands and* surrender; that Bell decided to run and he had to kill him. He declared he was "standing pat" against the world; and while he did not wish to kill anybody, if anybody interfered with his attempt to escape, he would kill him.

In this statement the "anonymous bystander" claims Bonney says he took Bell's pistol from him and used it to kill the deputy. In Garrett's book *The Authentic Life of Billy the Kid*, Garrett writes this about the escape:

*From circumstances, indications, information from Geiss (also spelled Gauss – the courthouse caretaker) and the Kid's admissions, the popular conclusion is that:*
*At the Kid's request, Bell accompanied him down stairs and to the back corral. As they returned, Bell allowed the Kid to get considerably in advance. As the Kid turned on the landing of the stairs, he was hidden from Bell. He was light and active, and with a few noiseless bounds, reached the head of the stairs, turned to his right, put his shoulder to the door of the room used as an armory (thought locked, this door was well known to open by a firm push), entered, seized a six-shooter, returned to the head of the stairs just as Bell faced him on the landing of the staircase, some twelve steps beneath, and fired. Bell turned, ran out into the corral and towards the little gate. He fell dead before reaching it. The Kid ran to the window at the south end of the hall, saw Bell fall, then slipped his handcuffs over his hands, threw them at the body, and said: "Here, damn you, take these, too."*

Garrett's account seems to have to [sic] many holes to be taken as truth in this matter. At the beginning of Chapter XXII, where this account is found Garrett begins, *On the evening of April 28, 1881, Olinger took all the other prisoners across the street to supper, leaving Bell in charge of the Kid in the guard room.* It is a known fact that the escape did not happen in the evening as Garrett writes but just after noon.

Frederick Nolan, in his commentary notes at the side of the page in this book, points out the following: *The "popular" conclusion set forth here - that Bell would have allowed the Kid latitude and time he needed to perform these maneuvers - has already been examined. That he could have moved "noiselessly" when wearing manacles and leg irons defies belief. And would Billy have waited until after killing Bell before he "slipped his handcuffs over his hands?" Either the Kid struck Bell over the head with his handcuffs, grabbed Bell's gun and killed him with it, or, far more plausibly, someone hid a pistol in the outhouse privy, which*

*Billy retrieved and, when they got inside, killed Bell with it.*

When Garrett describes The Kid shooting Olinger he says that ... *Olinger appeared at the gate leading into the yard, as Geiss appeared at the little corral gate and said, "Bob, The Kid has killed Bell." At the same instant the Kid's voice was heard above: "Hello, old boy," said he. "Yes, and he's killed me too," exclaimed Olinger, and fell dead with eighteen buckshot in his right shoulder and breast and side.*

It is doubtful that Olinger would have time to say the words that Garrett contributes [sic] to him before the Kid cut him down, making Garrett's account difficult to be taken as true accounting of the events.

**[AUTHOR'S NOTE: Though lacking crafty finesse of the final Probable Cause Statement, this author likewise uses Garrett's ghostwritten, dime-novel-style book to try to discredit him. But it remains irrelevant to Garrett as a murderer.]**

Garrett also says about The Kid in his account – *He took deliberate aim and fired the other barrel, the charge taking effect in nearly the same place as the first; then breaking the gun across the railway of the balcony, he threw the pieces at Olinger, saying: "Take it, damn you, you won't follow me any more with that gun."*

This doubtful this happened. [sic] The account of The Kid breaking Olinger's shotgun on the balcony is not found elsewhere. Added to the fact that Olinger's shotgun was a Whitney, serial number SN903, and is now on loan to the *Texas Ranger Hall of Fame* in Waco, Texas from the James H. Earl Collection; the shotgun is in tact [sic].

**[AUTHOR'S NOTE: Error. Deputy Bob Olinger's Whitney double-barreled shotgun there is broken at its waist, and repaired, at some unknown time, by a wrapping of copper wire. Its curator at the Texas Ranger Museum, attesting to the description, is Don Agler. This is another irrelevant attempt to discredit Garrett.]**

The version which seems the more popular, is that Bonney, retrieved a pistol that had been hidden in the outhouse by a "friend." History has theories but no firm answers to the identity of the "friend" who put the pistol in the outhouse.

**[AUTHOR'S NOTE: Error. This seems to be a confusion of the Bell killing with Olinger's, for which the Whitney was used.]**

After the Kid shot and killed both of his guards he gather [sic] weapons, and left Lincoln about 3 p.m. on a stolen horse. The Kid's whereabouts from the date of his escape until just before his death, as nearly every aspect of the case, is still debated. The Kid later showed up in Ft. Sumner, New Mexico. **Pete Maxwell's teenage daughter, Paulita,**

[AUTHOR'S NOTE: Error. Paulita was Peter Maxwell's sister. Also, using Paulita contradicts the "love tales" of "Brushy Bill" (Celsa) and John Miller (Isadora), and eliminates them as Billy contenders!. But revealed is the writer's historical ignorance.]

was supposedly in love with the Kid and he with her, which seems to be the most likely motive for him to return to Ft. Sumner.

On the night of July 14, 1881, after searching the area around Ft. Sumner Lincoln County Sheriff Pat Garrett and his deputies John Poe and Thomas C. "Kip" McKinney were about to ride back to Lincoln. Before leaving they thought it a good idea to check with Pete Maxwell. In Garrett's account of this he takes credit for wanting to check with Maxwell before giving up the chase, Deputy Poe differs with Garrett. In Deputy Poe's account written in 1919 we see the events through his eyes.

*Garrett seemed to have but little confidence in our being able to accomplish the object of our trip, but said that he knew the location of a certain house occupied by a woman in Fort Sumner which the Kid had formerly frequented, and that if he was in or about Fort Sumner, he would most likely be found entering or leaving this house some time during the night. Garrett proposed that we go to a grove of trees near the town, conceal our horses, then station ourselves in the peach orchard at the rear of the house, and keep watch on who might come or go. This course was agreed upon, and we entered the peach orchard about nine o'clock that night, stationing ourselves in the gloom or shadow of the peach trees, as the moon was shining very brightly. We kept up a fruitless watch here until some time after eleven o'clock, when Garrett stated that he believed we were on a cold trail; that he had very little faith in our being able to accomplish anything when we started on the trip. He proposed that we leave the town without letting anyone know that we had been there in search of the Kid.*

*I then proposed that, before leaving we should go to the residence of Peter Maxwell, a man who up to that time I had never seen, but who, by reason of his being a leading citizen and having a large property interest should, according to my reasoning, be glad to furnish such information as he might have aid us [sic] in ridding the country of a man who was looked on as a scourge and curse by all law-abiding people.*

*Garrett agreed to this, and there-upon led us from the orchard by circuitous by-paths to Maxwell's residence, which was a building formerly used as officers' quarters during the days when a garrison of troops had been maintained at the fort. Upon our arriving at the residence (a very long, one-story adobe, standing end to the flush with* the street, having a porch on the south side, which was the direction from which we approached, the premises all being enclosed by a paling fence, one side of which ran parallel to and along the edge of the street up to and across the end of the porch to the corner of the building).\, Garrett said to me, "This is Maxwell's room through the open door (left open on account of the extremely warm weather), while McKinney and myself stopped on the outside. McKinney squatted on the outside of the fence, and I sat on the porch.

It should be here that up to this moment I had never seen Billy the Kid, nor Maxwell, which fact in view of the events transpiring immediately afterward, placed me at an extreme disadvantage.

It was probably not more than thirty seconds after Garrett had entered Maxwell's room, when my attention was attracted, from where I sat at the little gateway, to a man approaching me on the inside of and along the fence, some forty or fifty steps away. I observed that he was only partially dressed and was both bareheaded and barefooted, or rather had only socks on his feet, and it seemed to me that he was fastening his trousers as he came toward me at a very brisk walk.

As Maxwell's was the one place in Fort Sumner that had considered above suspicion of harboring the Kid, I was entirely off my guard, the thought coming to my mind that the man approaching was either Maxwell or some guest of his who might be staying there. He came on until he was almost within arm's length of where I sat, before he saw me, as I was partially concealed from his view by the post of the gate.

Upon seeing me, he covered me with his six-shooter as quick as lightening, sprang onto the porch, calling out in Spanish "Quien es" (Who is it?) - at the same time backing away from me toward the door through which Garrett only a few seconds before had passed, repeating his query, "Who is it?" in Spanish several times.

At this I stood up and advanced toward him, telling him not to be alarmed, that he should not be hurt; and still without the least suspicion that this was the very man we were looking for. As I moved toward him to reassure him, he backed up into the doorway of Maxwell's room, where he halted for a moment, his body concealed by the thick adobe wall at the side of the doorway, form [sic] whence he put his head and asked in Spanish for the fourth time who I was. I was within a few feet of him when he disappeared into the room.

After this, and until after the shooting, I was unable to see what took place on account of the darkness of the room, but plainly heard what was said on the inside. An instant after the man left the door, I heard a voice inquire in a sharp tone, "Pete, who are those fellows on the outside?" An instant later a shot was fired in the room, followed *immediately by what anyone within hearing distance thought were two shots. However, there were only two shots fired, the third report, as we learned afterward, being caused by the rebound of the second bullet, which had struck the adobe wall and rebounded against the headboard of a wooden bedstead.*

*I heard a groan and one or two gasps from where I stood in the doorway, as of someone dying in the room. An instant later, Garrett came out, brushing against me as he passed. He stood by me close to the wall at the side of the door and said to me, "That was the Kid that came in there onto me, and I think I got him". I said, "Pat, the Kid would not come to this place; you have shot the wrong man".*

*Upon saying this, Garrett seemed to be in doubt himself as to whom he had shot, but quickly spoke up and said, "I am sure it was him, for I know his voice to [sic] well to be mistaken". This remark of Garrett's relieved me of considerable apprehension, as I had felt almost certain that someone whom we did not want had been killed.*

The next day Billy the Kid was buried in Fort Sumner. Or was it the Kid in the grave?

**[AUTHOR'S NOTE: Poe's initial uncertainty about Billy's identity, is this writer's only "evidence" of victim identity doubt. Omitted are all witnesses, the Coroner's Jury, and Poe's acceptance. ]**

## What Happen [sic] to William H. Bonney a.k.a. Billy the Kid?

Soon after the shooting in Maxwell's home on July 14, 1881, the rumor took life that Garrett shot the wrong man and that he knew he shot the wrong man but covered it up.

**[AUTHOR'S NOTE: This "Seventy-Seven Days Document" is transparently tailored to fit the pretenders.]**

Some even say that Garrett had an empty coffin buried the next day in Fort Sumner. Some say Garrett wrote the book *The Authentic Life of Billy the Kid*, in which he demonizing [sic] Billy the Kid, to prop up his waning popularity that was being eroded by the rumor that he killed The Kid in less than a fair fight or that he did not kill The Kid at all.

**[AUTHOR'S NOTE: These contentions, without sources, appear made-up, and are not evidence.]**

To this day the rumor still has life that Billy the Kid never died that night.

**[AUTHOR'S NOTE: Nothing has been presented to support that "rumor."]**

Most everything we know about William H. Bonney a.k.a. Billy the Kid is what is know [sic] about him in during the last three years of his life. The date and place of his birth, who his father was, where he lived, as a child is still a mystery. Most of what we do know and what we call history is flawed by myth. Even where he is buried is the subject of controversy these 122 years later.

**[AUTHOR'S NOTE: This "what-if" illogic tries to make Bonney's death uncertain, by manufacturing "uncertainties" in his earlier history.]**

In England is a grave with the name William H. Bonney on the headstone, where is it said [sic] Billy the Kid is buried. The story is that the Tunstall family, in apparition [sic] of his help and loyalty to John Tunstall, brought the Kid back to England where he lived a long life dying of old age.

**[AUTHOR'S NOTE: This is so bizarre, it seems a delirium, rather than an argument. It does indicate the author lacks ability to sort fact from fiction.]**

**[AUTHOR'S NOTE: The case for Garrett's murder of an innocent victim ends here without proof; and segues to the pretenders.]**

## John Miller

**[AUTHOR'S NOTE: At this preliminary stage - years before the hoaxers needed John Miller's exhumation to keep their hoax afloat - he was of minimal interest; their focus being "Brushy Bill." This disinterest is reflected in the following cursory text - and its negative presentation was kept secret when the hoaxers headed with backhoe to John Miller's grave, suddenly claiming *he* was Billy the Kid.]**

In 1993 Helen Airy published a book by Sunstone Press entitled *What* [sic- Whatever] *Happened to Billy the Kid*. In this book the claim is made that a John Miller who died on November 7, 1937, at six-thirty in the evening, in the Pioneer [sic] Home in Prescott, Arizona and was buried in the Prescott Pioneer home cemetery [sic], was Billy the Kid. In Airy's book Miller is quoted as saying, *"there was a Mexican shot and buried in the coffin that is supposed to be the Kid."*

In her book *What* [sic- Whatever] *Happened to Billy the Kid* these accounts are found:

Page 162 paragraph 2 - *Ann Storrer of Belen writes: "My father, Charlie Walker, grew up around Fort Sumner during the early 1900's. A Mexican he used to work for told him that he saw Billy the Kid at the bullfights in Mexico long after he was supposed to be dead. The rumor around Fort Sumner was that Pat Garrett and Bill [sic] the Kid were good friends and Garrett tried to stop everyone from killing Billy. My father believed there was never a body in the grave.*

*Page 162 paragraph 3 and 4 - Arleigh Nation of Albuquerque supplied the Following story; "A man by the name of Trujillo, who died in 1935 at the age of ninety-five told Nation he worked for Pete Maxwell at the time Billy the kid was supposed to have been killed. He said the day before the shoot-out they dressed up an Indian, who had died the night before, to look like the Kid. The Indian was buried in the grave that was said to have been the Kid's.*

*Nation, who is a Billy the kid Buff, also said a neighbor of his who lived in Lincoln, Mrs. Syd Boykin, told him that the kid stayed as [sic] her home in Lincoln many times after he was supposed to have been dead.*

Airy states that a John Collins claimed to have been a friend of Billy the Kid. Collins says that he helped bury the corpse of the man Garrett killed on July 14, 1881, and it was not Billy the kid.

Arley Sanches interviewed Nadine Brady, of Adelino, New Mexico, and whose grandfather was Sheriff William Brady, who was shot by the Kid, for a story, which appeared in the *Albuquerque Journal* on September 8, 1990. Nadine says one old timer told her Garrett didn't shoot Bonney. He told her Garrett and Bonney were friends and Garrett invented a story to help his friend escape. A wanderer was killed and buried, and Garrett told everyone he had shot Billy the Kid.

Airy says Frank Coe, a friend of Billy the Kid during the Lincoln County War, believed to the day of his death that Billy was still alive, and spent a great deal of time tracing reports that he had been seen.

*The El Paso Herald Post,* June 29, 1926 reported a story that a "government official" re[ported that "Billy the Kid and Garrett framed an escape" from Lincoln, New Mexico. The government official claimed the Kid was still alive in this article.

*The El Paso Times*, July 26, 1964, reported that retired Immigration and Naturalization Service Inspector, Leslie Traylor of San Antonio, Texas claimed Billy the Kid was a man named Henry Street Smith. Traylor said he traced Smith and believes him to be buried under the name of John Miller who died in 1935 in Prescott, Arizona.

**[AUTHOR'S NOTE: Airy's John Miller hoax was debunked above. The writer here, however, does not appear to argue for Miller as Billy. And no death scene is presented, that being the purpose of a probable cause statement for a murder case!]**

## William Henry Roberts a.k.a. Brushy Bill Roberts

**[AUTHOR'S NOTE: Next is the attempt to establish Oliver "Brushy Bill" Roberts as Billy the Kid. Noteworthy is use if his fake "William Henry" from *Alias Billy the Kid*. Though he surfaced throughout the hoax, it was given as "survival suspicion," not the case's goal. The very fact that this "Seventy-Seven Days of Doubt Document" was kept secret, indicated hiding of that motive. Apparently, it was intended to have that conclusion arise from the fake forensic DNA matchings. But the effusions that follow here show the "Brushy" bias as well as access to the transcript of "Brushy's" Morrison interviews. And the contradiction of his non-bench death scene, presented in detail below, was not yet anticipated; since the hoaxers expected the Billy and mother exhumations to go through, followed by a faked match to "Brushy." So switching to the bench scenario for "blood DNA" was unanticipated.]**

Before Sheriff Pat Garrett could clean his pistol the bogus Billy the Kid's began to crop up everywhere. Some were too ridiculous to take notice of and some convinced a few people but were forgotten with the passage of time. Out of all the men to come forward to claim they are Billy the Kid the one that caused the most stir and gained national and even worldwide attention was Brushy Bill Roberts.

To this day Roberts' claim is being taken seriously by many. In Hamilton, Texas, where William Roberts is buried there stands a sign that proclaims that his grave is "The Authentic Grave Site of Billy the Kid." A plaque states that he spent the last part of his life attempting to get a "promised pardon" from the New Mexico Governor. Just weeks before Roberts death he and his attorney [sic - William Morrison, not an attorney] approached the Governor of New Mexico and asked for a pardon for the Kid, who Roberts claimed to be. Dubious of Roberts claims the Governor granted no pardon.

**[AUTHOR'S NOTE: This "Brushy" pardon focus exposes the otherwise inexplicable linking of DNA to pardon in the hoax. Making "Brushy" Billy by the fake match, would then lead to a pardon for an alleged long law-abiding life as Billy the Kid.]**

The story goes that in 1948, William V. Morrison was working as an investigator for a law firm. Morrison was a graduate attorney [sic - Morrison was not an attorney] and it was said that he had a "good nose for evidence". He was a member of the Missouri Historical Society and a descendant of Ferdinand Maxwell, the brother of Lucien Bonaparte Maxwell and uncle of Pete Maxwell. **[AUTHOR'S NOTE: Morrison's fabrication.]** Because of this, Morrison possessed a keen interest in New Mexico history.

During this time Morrison was sent to Florida to investigate an inheritance claimant by the name of Joe Hines. Hines' brother, in North Dakota, had passed away and Hines claimed to be the sole inheritor of some property. As Morrison interviewed the old man the story did not match with the facts Morrison possessed. After more questions Joe Hines told Morrison his name, Hines, was an alias. Hines claimed his real name was Jesse [sic] Evans and he was a survivor of the Lincoln County War.

**[AUTHOR'S NOTE: This is the pure "Brushy" hoax, straight from *Alias Billy the Kid*. Indicated is that the writer was a true-believer, like Bill Robins III or W.C. Jameson, or an opportunistic copier, merely seeking publicity and profit from winning.]**

Morrison being proud of his ancestral connection to New Mexico history mentioned to Hines (Evans) that Billy the Kid worked for the Maxwells at one time

**[AUTHOR'S NOTE: Morrison's fake claim about Billy.]**

and added that the Kid was shot and killed in Maxwell's house on July 14, 1881. To that Hines replied, "Garrett did not kill the Kid on July 14, 1881, or any other time." Hines went on to say, "In fact Billy was still living in Texas last year. The reason that I know is that a friend of mine, now living in California stops over to visit with me here every summer. He and Billy and me are the only warriors left of the old Lincoln County bunch.

**[AUTHOR'S NOTE: Besides the total fakery, real outlaw-murderer-rustler Jessie Evans would not have called himself a Lincoln County War "warrior."]**

Later that year Morrison became acquainted with another man in Missouri who said he knew who all the parties were and gave Morrison an address of a man named O.L. Roberts who lived in Hamilton, Texas. In June of 1948 Morrison drove to Hamilton, Texas and met Roberts. On their first meeting Roberts told Morrison that the Kid was his half brother and was still alive in Old Mexico. The next day Morrison came back to Roberts home and Roberts sent his wife to a neighbor's house saying he and Morrison had business to discuss.

After Mrs. Roberts left the house Morrison claims Roberts pointed his finger at him and said, "Well, you've got your man. You don't need to look any farther. I'm Billy the Kid. But don't tell anyone. My wife doesn't know who I am. She thinks my half brother is Billy the Kid, but he died in Kentucky many years ago. I want a pardon before saying anything about this matter. I don't want to kill anyone anymore, but I'm not going to hang." Morrison goes on to write that Roberts told his story and tears coursed down his cheeks, as he said, "I done wrong like everyone else did in those days. I want to die a free man. I do not want to die like Garrett and the rest of them, by the gun. I have been hiding so long and they have been telling so many lies about me that I want to get everything straightened out before I die. I can do it with some help. The good Lord left me here for a purpose and I know why He did. Now will you help me out of this mess."

Morrison wanted proof that Roberts claims were true and knew the scars the Kid would have on his body. Morrison had Roberts strip and from the scars on Roberts' body Morrison was convinced that he was talking to the true William H. Bonney.

Roberts tells Morrison in detail how he escaped death at the hands of Sheriff Pat Garrett the night of July 14, 1881. In a statement Roberts records the following:

**[AUTHOR'S NOTE: To follow are "Brushy's" words from pages 105-117 of W.C. Jameson's and Frederick Bean's 1998** *The Return of the Outlaw Billy the Kid.* **They claimed to have gotten the transcript from "Brushy's" step-grandson, Bill Allison. Thus, indicated is possible participation of W.C. Jameson.]**

**[AUTHOR'S NOTE: Do not miss the attempted validation of "Brushy" that this document represents. His words are being used as "evidence" in** *a real law enforcement case* **to show probable cause that Garrett was a murderer, since** *he* **survived; ergo, Garrett** *must have murdered innocent Billy Barlow.***]**

*I rode into Fort Sumner from Yerby's a few days before Garrett and his posse rode in. When they rode in that day, I had spent the day with Garrett's brother-in-law, Saval Gutierrez. Nearly all the people in this country were my friends and they helped me. None of them liked Garrett. It was dark that night, but there was enough moonlight to make shadows. Me and my partner Billy Barlow, rode up to Jesus Silva's house when we reached Fort Sumner. We had been staying at the Yerby Ranch laying low for a while. Word was all around that Pat Garrett and a posse were after me. Pat's wife was a sister to my friend Saval Gutierrez, and Saval told me that Pat was after me, that he heard it from his sister.*

*Things were mighty hot in Lincoln County for me right about then, but I wasn't running from it. I meant to have a talk with Pat Garrett and set things straight between us if I could. We used to be friends ... We hid our horses in the barn and walked up to Jesus' back door. Barlow was nervous about being in Fort Sumner with me and I couldn't blame him much. Jesus came to the back door when I tapped on it with the barrel of my six-shooter. When he saw that it was me, he grinned and let us in. I told Jesus we were hungry. We'd been out in the hills all day, scouting* around Fort Sumner for any sign of Garrett and his posse. "I have nothing but cold frijoles, compadre," Jesus whispered as he closed the door. Barlow made a sour face. "I want some meat," he said, "we have been living on beans and tortillas all week. Ain't you got any beef?"

According to Roberts statement Jesus Silva told Barlow that Pete Maxwell had some meat hanging on his porch. Barlow wanted to get the beef to cook but Roberts told him it was too dangerous and they should not move from the house. Barlow would not listen. According to Roberts statement Barlow took a butcher knife and left the house to head to Maxwell's to get the beefsteak. While Roberts and Jesus were lighting the wood stove they hear [sic] gunfire in the direction of Pete Maxwell's place. Roberts' statement goes on to describe the following events:

*I pulled one of my .44's and ran through the door, trying to see in the dark. Two more shots came from a shadow beside the Maxwell house. I couldn't find a target to shoot at. It was too dark to see. I ran toward Maxwell's back porch. I heard another gunshot and felt something hit me in the jaw. I stumbled and kept on running with a broken tooth rolling around my tongue. I tasted blood and spit the mess out of my mouth as I started emptying my six-shooter at the shadow where I saw the muzzleflash. From the corner of my eye I saw a body lying on the back porch ... I knew it had to be Barlow.*

*My partner had walked right into a trap, and the trap had likely been set for me. I pulled my other .44 and ran toward the porch to check on Barlow, but I ran into a wall of gunfire. I knew I wasn't going to make it to my partner. Too many guns were shooting at me. I didn't have a chance. I turned for a fence across the back of Maxwell's yard and dove for it when a bullet caught me in the left shoulder. I jumped over the fence and landed hard on the far side, with the echo of gunshots all around me, ringing in my ears. I staggered into an alley that ran behind the house, firing my .44 over my shoulder until it clicked empty. My mouth and shoulder were bleeding and I lost track of where I was, but I knew I had to get away from Maxwell's before they killed me. I heard a shout and another gunshot. Something passed across my forehead like a hot branding iron. I was stunned. I lost footing and fell on my face in the darkness. I knew I was hurt bad and wondered if I would make it out of this scrape alive.*

*I forced myself up again, wiping the blood from my eyes with my shirtsleeve as I stumbled headlong down the ally. I didn't know how bad the head wound was, only that it was bleeding and I couldn't see. It wouldn't matter if the found me in the alley just then, they were bent on killing me, to be sure. If I fell again I knew they'd find me and finish the job, so I kept running down the ally as hard as I could, barely able to see where I was going. I heard them shouting to each other behind me, arguing over something, but I was too woozy to think about what they were saying and too frightened to care. The gunshot to my head had knocked me senseless. I kept on staggering and running down the alley, trying to get away. Blood was pouring into my eyes; I couldn't see a thing. I ran past a little adobe shack down the alley from Pete Maxwell's. I supposed all the shooting woke everybody up, because a door opened just a crack when I ran behind the adobe and I could see a lantern light spilling from the doorway across the alley.*

*I stumbled toward the light not knowing what else to do. I needed help and the open door was the only place I could find, hurt like I was. A Mexican woman pulled me inside. She saw the blood on my face and threw her hands over her mouth. She closed the door quickly and helped me to a chair. I sleeved the blood from my eyes, watching her, loading my Colts.*

In Roberts' statement he identifies the woman as Celsa Cutierriz [sic - Gutierrez] who he had known previously. Ms. Cutierriz [sic] helped Roberts and kept him at her home that night. Roberts says that later Ms. Cutierriz [sic] had Frank Lobato saddle his horse and bring it around in the alley so he can [sic] escape. Before Roberts was able to leave Ms. Cutierriz [sic] told him it was rumored about Fort Sumner that Sheriff Garrett was telling everyone he had killed the Kid.

Roberts says, *I started puzzling over what Celsa told me. Garrett was trying to pass off Barlow's body as that of Billy the Kid. I wondered how he figured to get away with it. Garrett knew by now that he'd killed the wrong man in the dark. Billy Barlow looked a lot like me, the same general description, with blue eyes like mine. But in the daylight, a lot of folks who knew me would know they had the wrong body. I couldn't figure it, unless Garrett realized his mistake and was making a try at collection [sic] the reward money that was out on me anyway ...*

Roberts says it was 3 a.m. when Celsa brought his horse up to the house. He says he left with Frank Lobato. Roberts stayed in a camp south of Fort Sumner until his wounds healed and the first of August he rode to El Paso, Texas.

**[AUTHOR'S NOTE: "Brushy's" error-filled hoaxing has been debunked earlier, but his expansive dialogue demonstrates excellently the relentless floridness of his confabulations and imagination. Noteworthy for the "Billy the Kid Case" hoaxers, however, is that his death scene with back-porch-Barlow points to an early phase of their own faking, where they were not yet**

concealing the major discrepancies between his "death scene" tale and their own.]

## Questions About the Case

There seems [sic] to be problems with every account of the escape of Billy the Kid from the make shift [sic] jail in Lincoln and the shooting at Fort Sumner by Pat Garrett. In every account there remain questions as to what really happened.

**[AUTHOR'S NOTE: The above used the hoaxers' fakery of "vague, though unfounded, suspicions" instead of actual evidence - which they lacked. What follows are fake "what-ifs" to make unwarranted leaps to hoaxed conclusions – called by the writer "Questions." It represents the writer's last chance to fake a link of Garrett to a "probable cause" of murder.]**

**[AUTHOR'S NOTE: For clarity, the illogical transitions are put in boldface. The breath-taking leap of the scam is seen when the "what-ifs" of the outhouse version, lead to a fake, implied accusation that Garrett reported the gun from armory version to hide that *he* was the pistol-giving "friend."]**

1. In the historical account of the escape of Billy the Kid, from the courthouse in Lincoln, **it's believed** that a "friend" placed a pistol in the outhouse for Billy to use in his escape. The identity of the "friend" who placed the pistol in the outhouse has gone nearly unasked. **If** this version is true, and a "friend" left a pistol in the outhouse to aid in Bonney's escape that "friend" is a coconspirator to the murder of Bell and Olinger. This "friend" also should have been charged with two counts of homicide but remained at large. **Why** didn't Sheriff Garrett pursue the question of the idenety [sic] of the "friend" who hid the pistol? Garrett says the Kid took the pistol from the armory. **If** the story of the pistol in the outhouse is true did Garrett have a reason to say it was from the armory?

2. **If** Roberts account and claim about the night of July 14, 1881, is to be believed then Lincoln County Sheriff Pat Garrett was not the hero that history portrays him as. Instead, he becomes a murderer who killed Billy Barlow and covered up that killing and passed off Barlow's body as that of Billy the Kid. With the sign in at [sic] Brushy Bill's grave site claiming to the [sic] grave site of Billy the Kid they are in short saying Pat Garrett lied. Did Garrett lie?

**[AUTHOR'S NOTE: This earliest version of the "Billy the Kid Case" hoax relies heavily on "Brushy;" later discrepancies between the evolving hoax and "Brushy's" tales would be concealed by the hoaxers. Here, certainty of winning without**

bearing scrutiny, apparently yielded a devil-may-care attitude.]

[AUTHOR'S NOTE: This earliest version of the hoax also is unabashedly vicious in accusing Garrett of heinous crimes. Later, under scrutiny, the hoaxers would lie that the case was to protect Garrett's honor against "others" who had accused him!]

3. **If** Roberts claims are believed, it beings up other questions? [sic] He claims in his statement when talking about Pat Garrett, *"we use* [sic] *to be friend"* [sic]. **If** Garrett and Roberts were friends did Garrett and Garrett [sic] allowed The Kid out of friendship to escape from Fort Sumner, *did he also* arrange his escape from Lincoln? Did Garrett question why **his friend, the Kid**, with all the others involved in all the killing was the only one to be convicted and sentenced to hang? The Kid **mentions this** in an interview that was published in the *Mesilla News* on April 15, 1881 when he said, *Think it hard that I should be the only one to suffer the extreme penalties of the law."*

[AUTHOR'S NOTE: Here, "Brushy" is the authority, with "what-ifs" that fabricate Garrett as Billy's "friend" and "accomplice." In addition, lied is that Billy's mention had anything to do with Garrett, rather than to his own sense of injustice.]

4. **Did** Garrett arrange having the pistol put in the outhouse by the "friend" **and is this** why he did not search for the coconspirator to the murder of the two lawmen? **If this is the case then** Garrett is also a coconspirator in the murder of those two lawmen.

[AUTHOR'S NOTE: More meaningless "what-ifs."]

5. In the Lincoln County Courthouse Caretaker Gauss' statement he quotes Bonney as saying about Bell, *"I'm sorry I had to kill him but couldn't help it."* This statement must raise the question did Bonney, when he produced the pistol he retrieved from the outhouse

[AUTHOR'S NOTE: Sly switcheroo from "what-ifs" to using the outhouse as a fact.]

order Bell to surrender? Did Bell panic and instead of throwing up his hands, turn and run causing Bonney to shoot him?

[AUTHOR'S NOTE: This parrots the historically accepted version. Later in the hoax, for fake forensics, it would be switched to Billy striking Bell with a shackle to cause "blood" on the hallway.]

6. Other questions come to mind in this investigation, some about Gauss. It should be noted that Gauss had worked with Tunstall, so had Bonney. Gauss and Bonney shared the same table as they took meals, slept on the same floor and spent a great deal of time together when Bonney was in the courthouse under guard. It goes to reason that Gauss was sympathetic

towards Bonney. With that in mind it could be pointed out that there were a number of things missing from Gauss's account. Gauss made no reference to how Bell was killed, and leaves out the fact that Bonney used Olinger's own shotgun to kill him. If Bonney retrieved a pistol from the outhouse it had to be prearranged with Bonney and the "friend" as to what date and where to place the pistol in order for Bonney to find it. Since Gauss spent so much time with Bonney would he not have heard something about the plot?

**[AUTHOR'S NOTE: This is failed hoaxing! With Gauss as the accomplice, Garrett is innocent – undoing the scam!"]**

7. Since the caretaker Gauss worked outside it is not outside the realm of possibility that he saw who put the pistol in the outhouse?

**[AUTHOR'S NOTE: The historical reality of Gauss being the accomplice never made it to the final hoax.]**

8. It is known that Bonney ate his meals at the courthouse and the only time he was allowed to leave was to use the outhouse. Bell and Olinger took turns escorting the prisoners to the hotel for lunch, leaving the other in charge of Bonney. Bonney as well as the others would have known that Olinger would be escorting the prisoners to lunch that day. Bonney was aware that out of the two guards Bell was the one to make his escape move on since Bell was easy going and seemed to get along with him. Bonney also knew that Olinger had killed men in the past and had threatened to kill him. **Had Garrett and the Kid discussed this and chose Bell** as the deputy for Bonney to make his move thinking Bell would just give up giving the Kid an hour to escape while Olinger was eating?

**[AUTHOR'S NOTE: "What-if" blather with a fake conclusion.]**

9. If Garrett was part of the plot for the Kid's escape **is that why** he rode to White Oaks on a "tax collecting" trip, to give himself an alibi?

**[AUTHOR'S NOTE: More 'what-if" fakery.]**

10. **If Garrett were part of the plot to allow the Kid to escape he would have reason to chase the Kid. He could not afford for the Kid to tell of his involvement in the two killings of the lawmen. Garrett also has a weak link in the plot, that being the "friend" who put the pistol in the outhouse. If Roberts' story is true, is Billy Barlow the one who put the pistol in the outhouse under orders of Garrett? In Roberts' accounting he shows up at Fort Sumner with no one but Barlow. Did he meet Barlow after he rode out of Lincoln and move on [sic] to Fort Sumner?**

[AUTHOR'S NOTE: The culmination of "what-if" fakery.]

11. **If** Garrett shot Billy Barlow in the dark, by mistake, on July 14, 1881, and Barlow was the only one who could tell the story of Garrett's involvement other than the Kid, would Garrett not know the Kid would run to keep from hanging?

[AUTHOR'S NOTE: This incoherent reverie, appears to contradict the Pat-Billy friendship on which this hoax relies. ]

12. In Deputy John W. Poe's statement as he lays out the shooting in Maxwell's house on July 14, 1881, he says "... Garrett came out, brushing against me as he passed. He stood by me close to the wall at the side of the door and said to me, That was the Kid that came in there onto me, and I think I got him.' I said, "Pat, the Kid would not come to this place; you have shot the wrong man.' Upon my saying this, Garrett seemed to be in doubt himself as to whom had shot ..." Did Garrett kill the wrong man by mistake and cover it up?

[AUTHOR'S NOTE: The writer forgot that backing "Brushy" means no bedroom murder scene – but a Barlow-on-back-porch one. Also forgotten is that "Brushy's" scene had enough gunfire to rival the Alamo.]

[AUTHOR'S NOTE: Similar to the final "Probable Cause Statement," this "question" hides the multiple identifications of Billy, following this moment of doubt in a darkened room.]

13. Most researchers and historians have accepted without much question, the statement that Billy the Kid was born Henry McCarty, in New York on November 23, 1859. It should be noted that the first time this information comes to light is in Pat Garrett's book *The Authentic Life of Billy the Kid.*

[AUTHOR'S NOTE: Error. This was outlaw myth press in Billy's lifetime, while he was pursued by Garrett and Secret Service Agent Azariah Wild. It was in "Outlaws of New Mexico. The Exploits of a Band Headed by a New York Youth. The Mountain Fastness of the Kid and His Followers - War Against a Gang of Cattle Thieves and Murderers." December 27, 1880. *The Sun.* New York. Vol. XLVIII, No. 118, Page 3, Columns 1-2.]

In the book the evidence for this claim is sited [sic] to have come from a birth announcement that appeared in the New York Times on November 25, 1859. In 1950 William Morrison the attorney [AUTHOR'S NOTE: **Morrison was not an attorney**] for William (Brushy Bill) Roberts claims he asked the *New York Times* about the announcement and the Times replied that no information about birth announcements appeared in that issue. A ghostwriter by the name of Marshall Asmon [sic - Ashmun

Upson is credited with writing Garrett's book. It might also be worth mentioning the date November 23, is the birth date of Marshall Asmon [sic - Ashmun] Upson. Is it by chance that Upson and the Kid have the same birthday or by design?

**[AUTHOR'S NOTE: Irrelevant, but a clumsy manufacturing of fake "suspiciousness," instead of evidence.]**

14. As stated above most believe Billy the Kid was born in New York. This information also appeared for the first time in Garrett's book. [AUTHOR'S NOTE: See *New York Sun* 1880 article reference above.] It is also believed that Billy the Kid was shot and killed in 1881 at the age of 21. However, according to the United States Bureau of Census, 1880 census, Fort Sumner, San Miguel County, William Bonney says differently. Between June 17 and 19, 1880, while taking census records at the Fort, Lorenzo Labadie, a former Indian Agent, noted the vital statistics of one William Bonney, who was living next to Charlie Bowdre and his wife Manuela, leaving us to believe this to be the William Bonney of Lincoln County fame. What is interesting about the entry is that he gave his age as twenty-five, and his place of birth not New York but Missouri.

**[AUTHOR'S NOTE: Irrelevant, but clumsy fake "suspiciousness." Also, it is thought that Manuela Bowdre gave the interview and the incorrect information.]**

The attorney Morrison asked Roberts why Garrett would say he was born in New York. Roberts told him that is what he told the "Coe boys" when he first came to New Mexico. Roberts went on to say he never saw New York until he was a grown man.

**[AUTHOR'S NOTE: Morrison was not an attorney.]**

**[AUTHOR'S NOTE: Irrelevant, since "Brushy" was not Billy.]**

### Conclusion

If history is correct and William H. Bonney a.k.a. Billy the Kid was shot and killed by Lincoln County Sheriff Pat Garrett on July 14, 1881, at the house of Pete Maxwell in Fort Sumner, and was buried the next day in Fort Sumner, then Brushy Bill Roberts is a fake and nothing more than a story teller of the first order.

**[AUTHOR'S NOTE: Again, this early document points to "Brushy" as Billy; which would later be more hidden.]**

However, if it is not the body of William H. Bonney buried in Fort Sumner then Lincoln County Sheriff Pat Garrett killed the wrong man on July 14, 1881. He covered up that killing with help from others such as

Pete Maxwell. If it is not Bonney buried at Fort Sumner then Garrett is a murderer and Maxwell is a knowing coconspirator to that homicide.

**[AUTHOR'S NOTE: This is an early hoax attempt at a conspiracy theory. Instead of the "Garrett friendship," is presented "Brushy's" accidental killing of the innocent victim version. And Maxwell is added as a cover-up conspirator, without motive or evidence – or truth.]**

If Brushy Bill Roberts were William H. Bonney then one would have to assume that the body in the grave is that of Billy Barlow as Robert's claims. If that is true Sheriff Garrett could quite possibly be a coconspirator of the double murder of two lawmen that occurred during the Kid's escape from Lincoln.

**[AUTHOR'S NOTE: This illogical jump even leaves "Brushy" behind, since he never claimed Garrett as a jailbreak accomplice, or a "friendship" with Garrett to explain not being killed on July 14, 1881 to enable escape.]**

The Lincoln County Sheriff's Department believes, with the unanswered question as to who is buried in Fort Sumner

**[AUTHOR'S NOTE: This is fakery. The victim is not doubted.]**

there remains serious doubt as to what involvement Sheriff Pat Garrett played in the escape of Billy the Kid from Lincoln that resulted I the deaths of two lawmen.

**[AUTHOR'S NOTE: This is fakery. There is no evidence that Garrett assisted the jail escape of Bonney, though it is an early version of the final "Probable Cause Statement's" fake Deputy Bell killing investigation.]**

If the body of William H. Bonney is buried in Fort Sumner the claims of William Roberts'' and others alleging to have been Billy the Kid are unfounded and the name of Pat Garrett is cleared of any wrong doing in this incident. It is the duty of the Lincoln County Sheriff''s Office to clear this mystery and possible crime off the books of history in a professional manner and to allow the guilt to fall where it belongs.

**[AUTHOR'S NOTE: The imposters are easily debunked without exhumations. And no one is accusing Garrett, except imposters and hoaxers – and without basis. ]**

Billy the Kid's mother is buried in Silver City, New Mexico. To exhume her body could provide the DNA to solve this 122-year-old mystery. Her DNA would hold the key to the true answer as to where William Bonney is buried and if Pat Garrett was a murderer or a Sheriff doing his duty.

If those in Hamilton, Texas believe Roberts is in fact Roberts [sic] this DNA should prove their claim. If he is not the town of Hamilton, Texas needs to take down the signs that the grave of Roberts is "The Authentic Grave Site of Billy the Kid." However, if Roberts is William Bonney then history should be rewritten showing what really happened in Lincoln County and Fort Sumner.

If Bonney is buried in Fort Sumner the History stands and the name of Sheriff Pat Garrett would be cleared and he did not kill some incendet [sic] person in Fort Sumner and would appear he had no hand in the escape of William Bonney from Lincoln and the death of Olinger and Bell.

Lincoln County Sheriff, Tom Sullivan and the Lincoln County Sheriff's Office believe it our duty to put this mystery to rest after 122 years of doubt. Since these questions continue to nag at our conscience, and since there is no statute of limitations on Murder we feel this investigation should answer the question of "is Pat Garrett a murderer?" or a Sheriff doing his duty and wrongly accused of a crime?

**[AUTHOR'S NOTE: No probable cause has been established to implicate Pat Garrett of murder of the innocent victim - the purpose of this document. But much evidence was revealed that the "Billy the Kid Case" hoax was a modernized version of the "Brushy Bill" hoax.]**

In Pat Garrett's book *The Authentic Life of Billy the Kid* he pens these words - "*Again I say that the Kid's body lies undisturbed in the grave - and I speak of what I know.*"

It is the intention of the Lincoln County Sheriff's Office to prove one way or the other if these words are true.

_____

Tom Sullivan: Sheriff
Lincoln County Sheriff's Office

_____

Steven M. Sederwall: Deputy Sheriff
Lincoln County Sheriff's Office

_____

Date

## *HAPLESS HOAXER SHERIFF GARY GRAVES*

De Baca County Sheriff Gary Graves was enlisted for the hoax as on-site lawman for the Fort Sumner Billy the Kid exhumation. But once signed on, it seems he got heebie-jeebies. For example, his entire parallel murder case against Pat Garrett, Sheriff's Department Case No. 03-06-136-01, disappeared forever - and was rumored to have been kept in his police car trunk!

As discussed, he was ultimately recalled for unrelated crimes. But for the Billy the Kid Case" he defied his County Commissioners' letter of September of 2003 from Chairman Powhatan Carter III, Joe Steele, Tommy Roybal; and County Clerk Nancy Sparks. It said: "The De Baca County Commissioners are in full support of the Village of Fort Sumner's stand against exhuming the Body of Billy the Kid. We feel this is a waste of time and especially money." So Graves ignored them.

Graves's problem was being in way over his head. For his fake role as a "history buff," he was interviewed by hoax-backing *True West* magazine's reporter, Jana Bommersbach, for "Breaking Out More Shovels: Fort Sumner's Sheriff Commits to Exhuming the Kid," for their January/February 2004 issue. Boomersbach declared: "If anyone knows Billy the Kid, it's the sheriff in the town that claims to hold the outlaw's grave."

Then it was Graves's turn: "You've got your die hards that are scared of their shadow and say leave it alone," says Sheriff Graves in his soft twang during a phone interview from his home. "The mayor says he wants nothin' to do with it" ... "I'm not anybody's 'yes-man,' " Sheriff Graves says. "I think it's great." Then Graves hit a wall of ignorance. Wildly, he guessed that the case was to decide if Garrett killed Billy "legal" or "illegal" - whatever that meant. If "illegal," then Garrett was "a murderer!"

Then he simply fantasized: "I don't think he killed him in the Maxwell house," the sheriff says. "And I think they held him until dark and then killed him." He suspects Garrett came gunning for Billy, [Both Graves and Bommersbach seem to think Billy was tracked only for killing the deputies] not so much to catch a cop killer as to protect himself and his complicity with the outlaw. "I think Pat Garrett was afraid people would hear the real story," he says. "I kind of feel ol' Pat

Garrett might have been behind the escape," says Graves, as he notes the lingering suspicions that the sheriff had planted a gun to help Billy."

As if recalling lines, Graves then became a "researcher," as Boomersbach recorded his desperate fabrications: "Why does the sheriff feel the story is a legacy of lies? He says he's uncovered two major points that fuel his suspicions: While Billy the Kid was in Fort Sumner, he was involved with Pat Garrett's sister-in-law [and] Garrett's long-rumored friendship with the Kid is allegedly underscored by paperwork that has the men buying property together." Obviously, this "paperwork" - unknown before that moment - never appeared.

And "researcher" Graves finished his unintended demolition of the Billy the Kid murder case by adding that he did not believe the tales of "Jim" [sic - John] Miller or "Brushy Bill!" Boomersbach dutifully recorded as Graves blew his punch line for exhumation: "[T]he real Billy the Kid was killed in his town some 120 years ago."

Possibly being recalled from the craziness ended up being a relief to Graves. But his fellow hoaxers eventually faked his recall as being punishment for his "Billy the Kid Case" involvement, and made him a martyr for their "truth."

## *EXHUMATION PETITIONS AS LAWMEN*

The only way to legally exhume human remains is by kin permission or for a law enforcement case. Thus, having structured the "Billy the Kid Case" as a real murder investigation against Pat Garrett, the lawmen were featured on every exhumation petition for Catherine Antrim and Billy the Kid with their official Sheriff or Deputy titles. This is noteworthy, because, when I finally cornered them in open records litigation in 2007, they shamelessly lied, claiming they had been just private amateur historian hobbyists (though hobbyists cannot dig up graves)!

Demonstrating their later lying, is their exhumation petition of July 26, 2004 for Billy the Kid. It was by one of their lawyers, and was titled "County of De Baca, State of New Mexico, Tenth Judicial District. In the Matter of William H. Bonney A/K/A 'Billy the Kid.' Cause No. CV-04-00005." In it, Acuña called them "law enforcement officers" 13 times in his mere five page filing! Acuña wrote:

## PETITIONER'S [sic] RESPONSE TO
## THE VILLAGE OF FT. SUMNER'S MOTION TO DISMISS

COME NOW Petitioners Sullivan, Sederwall and Graves by and through their attorneys of record The Jaffe Law Firm (Mark Anthony Acuña, Esq.) and for their response to the Village of Fort Sumner's Motion to Dismiss sate as follows:

### INTRODUCTION

**Tom Sullivan, Steve Sederwall and Gary Graves are law enforcement officers**. Prior to the filing of the Petition for Exhumation of the Remains of Billy the Kid, a.k.a. William H. Bonney, **Sullivan, Sederwall, and Graves acting in their capacity as law enforcement officers initiated Investigation No. 2004 [sic] –274 filed in Lincoln County and Case No. 03-06-136-01 filed in De Baca County.** The principle purpose of opening the investigation and the case was to determine the guilt or innocence of sheriff Pat Garrett in the death of Billy the Kid.

**[AUTHOR'S NOTE: The fact that Case No. 2003-274 was a murder investigation against Pat Garrett would later be hidden by the hoaxers – both by calling the case only an investigation of Billy the Kid's jailbreak shootings of the deputy guards, or calling the whole case their "hobby."]**

Initially, as part of their on-going investigation, **Sederwall, Sullivan, and Graves, in their capacity as law enforcement officers petitioned the Sixth Judicial District Court for exhumation of the remains of Billy the Kid's mother, Katherine [sic] Antrim**. As a part of the on-going investigation, the Petition to Exhume Katherine [sic] Antrim was intended to obtain DNA samples for purposes of comparing those DNA samples with DNA samples that were hoped to be obtained upon the exhumation of the remains of what are thought to be that of Billy the Kid. After filing of the Petition to Exhume the remains of Katherine [sic] Antrim, a second petition was filed in the Tenth Judicial Court for purposes of the exhumation of Billy the Kid's remains and for purposes of obtaining DNA samples to compare with those samples obtained from the remains of Katherine [sic] Antrim. Sederwall, Sullivan, and Graves, all joined in on the Petition to Exhume the remains of Billy the Kid as Co-Petitioners and in their capacity as **law enforcement officers** engaged in an on-going investigation.

Petitioners assert that they maintain standing in the instant action as **law enforcement officers** engaged in the investigation of criminal violations, namely, the alleged killing of Billy the Kid by the legendary Sheriff, Pat Garrett. Moreover, Petitioners assert that as **law**

**enforcement officers** they are duly authorized to investigate the death of Billy the Kid to determine 1) the guilt or innocence of sheriff Pat Garrett, and 2) to determine whether or not foul play was involved if there were violations of criminal statutes or laws. Acting in their capacity as **law enforcement officers** on behalf of the public and the public's best interest, Petitioners further assert that they are the real parties in interest to this suit and, therefore, maintain proper standing to prosecute these claims.

## ARGUMENT

### Petitioners are Law Enforcement Officers Currently Conducting Active Investigations Regarding the Death of Billy the Kid and, therefore, they have Standing.

New Mexico Rule of Civil Procedure 1-017 states in pertinent part that "every action shall be prosecuted in the name of the real party in interest ... for a party authorized by statute may sue in that person's own name without joining the party for whose benefit the action is brought; and when a statute of the state so provides, an action for the use or benefit for another shall be brought in the name of the state.

Moreover, Section 29-1-1 states impertinent [sic] part that ...

"It is hereby declared to be the duty of every Sheriff, Deputy Sheriff, Constable and every other peace officer to investigate all violations of the criminal laws of the state which are called to the attention of any such officer or which he is aware, and it is also declared the duty of every such officer to diligently file a complaint or information, if the circumstances are such to indicate to a reasonably prudent person that such action should be taken, and it is also declared his duty to cooperate with and assist the Attorney General, District Attorney or other prosecutor, if any, if any in all reasonable ways ... Failure to perform his duty in any material way shall subject such officer to removal from the office and payment of all costs of prosecution."

In the instant case, Petitioners Sullivan, Sederwall, and Graves acting in their capacity as **law enforcement officers** pursuant to Section 29-1-1, were not only authorized to commence the investigation into the death of William H. Bonney, a.k.a. Billy the Kid, but were duty-bound to fulfill their responsibilities as **law enforcement officers** to investigate the circumstances surrounding the death of Billy the Kid. Indeed, Petitioners initiated the investigations into the death of Billy the Kid based upon inconsistent and incongruous facts and information surrounding the death of Billy the Kid and raising suspicion as to the truth of the circumstances surrounding the killing of Billy the Kid. Under the circumstances, Petitioners had a duty to investigate or be subject to removal of office subject to Section 29-1-1.

Furthermore, pursuant to Rule 1-017, Petitioners acting in their capacity as **law enforcement officers**, are real parties in interest to the instant causes of action. Plaintiffs are authorized by statute, that is, Section 29-1-1, to being this action in their own names on behalf of and for the benefit of the public in their capacities of investigating **law enforcement officers**.

### CONCLUSION

Therefore, based upon all the foregoing, it is clear that the Petitioners acting in their capacity as **law enforcement officers** and engaged in an active investigation regarding the death and alleged killing of Billy the Kid by Sheriff Pat Garrett, and of standing in this case and are real parties in interest.

Wherefore, Petitioners respectfully request that the court issue its order denying the Village of Ft. Sumner's Motion to Dismiss as against Petitioners; that the court allow Petitioners to remain in the instant action and for such other further and proper relief as the Court deems just and proper."

       Respectfully submitted by:
       The Jaffe Law Firm
       Mark Anthony Acuña
       Attorneys for Petitioners Sullivan,
        Sederwall & Graves

## HOAX PUPPETEER: ATTORNEY BILL ROBINS III

The *New York Times* article of June 5, 2003 foreshadowed key hoax participant, Attorney Bill Robins III, under a "Dallas" law firm connected to Governor Richardson. In fact, Robins was second partner in a Houston one; with reported, yearly, multi-million dollar personal injury, product liability, and medical malpractice settlements. He and his firm, Heard, Robins, Cloud, Lubel & Greenwood LLC, also were Richardson's major political donors for his gubernatorial runs and his intended presidential bid in 2008. And, in 2004, they had been presidential candidate John Kerry's top donors in his September quarter. They were kingmakers. Richardson knew it. And Robins knew it. They felt above the law, and made a mockery of the courts for their "Billy the Kid Case."

Calling himself a Billy the Kid historian on his website when the "Billy the Kid Case" began, Robins appeared to be a "Brushy"-believer, rather than a hoaxer. I concluded that the "Billy the Kid Case" was Richardson's payback to him. And if "Brushy" being Billy was to be Robins's pay-to-play prize, contemplate this: Mad "Brushy" may have risen to a king-maker - or president-maker!

It also seemed likely that Robins was responsible for the legal creativity of achieving exhumations by a real murder case, using "Brushy" as evidence for the survival claim, and using the pardon hook as the goal - thus, finally overriding past Governor Mabry.

Robins's first public entry in the Billy the Kid Case may have been forced: to take-over from faltering Silver City attorney, Sherry Tippet. And he was not circumspect about "Brushy." On November 19, 2003, an AP internet article for Silver City, titled "Lawyer Appointed to Represent Dead Outlaw," quoted him: "Robins says he's excited to represent the Kid. His first duty as Billy's lawyer will be to intervene in the Silver City case to exhume the body of Billy's mother, Catherine Antrim. DNA testing is supposed to show whether Antrim was related to Ollie "Brushy Bill" Roberts. If Antrim is related to Roberts, that would mean Billy the Kid is buried in Hico [sic - Hamilton], Texas - not Fort Sumner."

Robins was also a financial backer of the "Billy the Kid Case," as I learned in 2004 because I was paying Kennedy Han law firm's costs for fighting the hoaxers' exhumation petitions. So I had paid the airfare and hotel costs for historian, Frederick Nolan, as a witness in a Silver City hearing in November of 2003. But Attorney Sherry Tippett requested an extension. Unsure if it would be granted, Frederick Nolan had to come anyway. Judge Henry Quintero did give the extension; but for her short notice, he sanctioned *her* to pay Nolan's bills. That led to the Kennedy Han firm informing me on April 28, 2004, who really paid Tippett's bill: **"This is to confirm our receipt of payment in the amount of $830.59, issued by Heard, Robins, Cloud, Lubel and Greenwood LLP, deposited on March 1, 2004, as payment in full for reimbursement of travel and lodging expenses incurred by Mr. Frederick Nolan."** Later, then-Sheriff Tom Sullivan would hide Tippett's cost coverage as well as Robins's contribution, in answer to one of my open records requests, as being from a "secret private donor!"

After replacing Tippett, Robins led the exhumation attacks on both the mother's and Billy's graves. To counter the absolute legal obstacles of the 1962 Lois Telfer case's blockade on exhuming Billy the Kid, and the OMI's opposition to both exhumations, on January 5, 2004, he filed his "Billy the Kid's Pre-Hearing Brief" in

Grant County. And on March 5, 2004, to clear the way for Richardson's recently appointed, pocket judge in De Baca County, Ted Hartley, he used the plaintiffs' option of removing a judge without cause to get honest Judge Ricky Purcell replaced by corrupt Hartley.

But an attorney needs a client to appear in a court. The client Robins chose proved his scorn of the law, the public, and the sanctity of graves. **His client was the dead Billy the Kid, "co-petitioner" with the lawmen for his own exhumation!** This, of course, ignored that a corpse has no legal standing in court. But for complicit judges, Henry Quintero in Silver City and Ted Hartley in Fort Sumner, Robins channeled "Billy," and spoke for him without their objection! And "Billy," of course, wanted his mother and himself dug up to protect his "legacy." And, as will be seen, the "legacy" Billy was "protecting" was that an innocent victim, not himself, had been killed on July 14, 1881 on a "dark and moonless night" (the fatal "Brushy" error that gave away Robins's "Brushy" thrust). And "Billy" claimed he had led a long and law-abiding life, so deserved a pardon (Robins's second give-away for his "Brushy" thrust). There was one other problem. Robins was not licensed to practice in New Mexico. So he added New Mexico lawyer, David Sandoval, to legitimize his outrages.

So for the March 4, 2004 "Notice of Excusal" dead Billy spoke": **"COMES NOW Co-Petitioner, William H. Bonney aka "Billy the Kid," by and through counsel Bill Robins III** and David Sandoval, and pursuant to 1978 NMSA Section 38-3-9 exercises his peremptory challenge and excuses the Honorable District Judge Ricky D. Purcell from this proceeding." Winning looked like a slam-dunk!

## *SPEAKING FOR BILLY THE KID IN SILVER CITY*

Robins had already channeled dead Billy on January 5, 2004, before Judge Henry Quintero for "In the Matter of Catherine Antrim, Billy the Kid's Pre-Hearing Brief." **[APPENDIX: 5]** It revealed, for the first time, the hoax's link of DNA matching and pardon. Hoaxed matching would claim an innocent victim in Billy's grave, and the mother would match "Brushy." With those fake forensics, Richardson would then pardon "Brushy" as Billy. As Robins wrote: "**Should the DNA extracted from Ms. Antrim confirm that one of the potential Kids ["Brushy"] was in fact Billy the Kid, undersigned counsel will be able to make an even stronger argument for pardon by citing to the long years of law abiding life."**

So Bill Robins III's outrageous Brief had his client, dead Billy the Kid, as a co-petitioner for exhumation of his own mother, joining Sheriffs Sullivan and Graves, and Deputy Sederwall, and backing the pretenders as legitimate; writing:

[T]he very question of [Billy the Kid's] life and death will be impacted by the results of the Petitioners' [lawmen's] investigation [into the Garrett murder and DNA].

### B. *The Planned Request For Pardon Confers Standing Here*

Undersigned counsel intends to ask Governor Richardson that he pardon Billy the kid for the murder conviction of Sheriff Brady on several known bases including the fact that then Territorial Governor Lew Wallace reneged on his promise to pardon the Kid. There were at least two individuals that laid claim to Billy the Kid's identity years after his alleged shooting by Garrett. **Both of them apparently led long and peaceful and crime-free lives** ...

The reasons that the exhumation is sought is to disinter the remains of Billy the Kid's mother for the extraction of Mitochondrial DNA.

As such, Ms. Antrim presents the only source of such DNA. Should the exhumation be denied, Billy the Kid will be forever denied the opportunity to make use of modern technology to shed light on his life and death. **Should the DNA extracted from Ms. Antrim confirm that one of the potential Kids was in fact Billy the Kid, undersigned counsel will be able to make an even stronger argument for pardon by citing to the long years of law abiding life.**

Convinced he was above law or decency this smug rogue presented the following examples of fakery in his "Billy the Kid's Pre-Hearing Brief;" writing:

(1) COMES NOW, Bill Robins, III and David Sandoval, of the law firm of Heard, Robins, Cloud, Lubel & Greenwood, LLC, and on the behalf of the estate of William H. Bonney, aka "Billy the Kid."

**[AUTHOR'S NOTE: The first claim is representation of Billy's "estate." First of all, Billy had no estate - meaning posthumous property for probate court. Secondly, property has nothing to do with exhuming his mother. Thirdly, this cover of something that sounds legal - like an estate - will next be switched to Billy talking for himself through Robins. Note that Attorney Sandoval was present to provide the New Mexico law license which Robins lacked, making him complicit in the hoax.]**

(2) This is an interesting proceeding in that the relief sought here is not exclusively judicial. "[N]ormally a district court would not become involved in such matters unless a protesting relative or interested party files an injunction or takes some other legal action to halt the autopsy or disinterment,"

**[AUTHOR'S NOTE: Robins's Brief is not "judicial" at all. It is pseudo-historical rambling with an irrelevant idea of a pardon. And its legal citations are all irrelevant filler.]**

(3) Petitioners [Lincoln County Sheriff Tom Sullivan and his Deputy, Steve Sederwall] should thus be commended for bringing this Court into the picture.

**[AUTHOR'S NOTE: Robins is trying to legitimize fellow hoaxers. Note also their law enforcement titles.]**

(4) As will be shown clearly, Billy the Kid's interests are real, legitimate, proper for consideration, and we respectfully ask the Court to recognize them as such.

**[AUTHOR'S NOTE: Segueing into speaking for Billy, Robins does a switcheroo from "estate" to "interests." But a dead person has no interests, being dead - meaning legally non-existent.]**

(5) To the extent that the Court remains concerned **with the presence of Billy the Kid in this litigation**, it is a matter that can be more properly addressed pursuant to legal requirements of standing and intervention, which the discussion below shows the Kid satisfies.

**[AUTHOR'S NOTE: This is now the switcheroo point for Billy himself entering the courtroom. Robins even claims that Billy has "standing," meaning the legal right to be present in court.]**

(6) The governor has the "power to grant reprieves and pardons." Undersigned counsel intends on seeking a pardon for Billy the Kid. Certainly Governor Richardson is within his inherent appointment power to hire counsel to advise him on the merits of such a pardon.

**[AUTHOR'S NOTE: Tricky Robins omits that pardon advising gives him no legal justification to be in this court seeking exhumation of Catherine Antrim. He has no real client.]**

(7) Counsel's appointment here is in the nature of an appointment as a public defender

**[AUTHOR'S NOTE: Now cagy Robins makes up that he was appointed by Richardson as a "public defender" for Billy. But only the judge can legally appoint an attorney for an indigent client in court - and, obviously, the client has to be alive.]**

(8) Billy the Kid's interest here is his legacy. As noted in previous briefing the very question of his life and death will be impacted by the results of the Petitioners' investigation.

**[AUTHOR'S NOTE: Here, dead Billy has "told" channeling Robins that *he* cares about "his legacy." Besides being absurd, that is not what "interest" means: which is legal justification for a case, not sentimentality of an historical nature.]**

(9) Undersigned counsel intends to ask Governor Richardson that he pardon Billy the kid for the murder conviction of Sheriff Brady on several known bases including the fact that then Territorial Governor Lew Wallace reneged on his promise to pardon the Kid.

**[AUTHOR'S NOTE: The pardon issue, though irrelevant to exhuming Catherine Antrim, is here segueing into "Brushy Bill" territory with "several known bases" that will apply to "Brushy" and not to Billy Bonney.]**

(10) There were at least two individuals that laid claim to Billy the Kid's identity years after his alleged shooting by Garrett. Both of them apparently **led long and peaceful and crime-free lives.**

**[AUTHOR'S NOTE: Here is the jump to "Brushy." And the "several known bases" for pardon are his long, peaceful, and crime-free life. The second pretender, John Miller, was added by the hoaxers to obscure their "Brushy" focus.]**

(11) The reasons that the exhumation is sought is to disinter the remains of Billy the Kid's mother for the extraction of Mitochondrial DNA. As such, Ms. Antrim presents the only source of such DNA. Should the exhumation be denied, Billy the Kid will be forever denied the opportunity to make use of modern technology to shed light on his life and death.

**[AUTHOR'S NOTE: Now Billy is himself in court, pleading, through Robins's mouth, for modern technology to help him. But do not miss the greater absurdity: this is a pretender argument by channeled "Brushy," wanting *his* life and death vouched for as Billy the Kid. And "Brushy's" real problem is hidden by Robins: mitochondrial DNA proves a mother relationship; "Brushy" *denied* she was his mother!]**

(12) Should the DNA extracted from Ms. Antrim confirm that one of the potential Kids was in fact Billy the Kid, **undersigned counsel will be able to make an even stronger argument for pardon by citing to the long years of law abiding life.**

[AUTHOR'S NOTE: **This was the sentence that proved to me that the "Billy the Kid Case was a "Brushy Bill" hoax, along with its plot: claim a match by faking DNA, then pardon "Brushy" as Billy the Kid. Note again the fakery that neither "Brushy" nor John Miller claimed Ms. Antrim was their mother – so mitochondrial DNA matching was meaningless unless the results' claims were faked**.]

(13) This Court has allowed the intervention of the Town of Silver City in this matter. The municipal politicians there have apparently authorized the Town's Mayor to oppose the exhumation. Billy the Kid acknowledges the existence of case law that accords standing to the owners of the cemetery concerned in such proceedings.

[AUTHOR'S NOTE: **Do not miss that speaking, channeled, dead Billy Bonney even has legal expertise on "case law" about court standing!**]

(14) What is of interest here, is that such standing is often given to the cemetery owner because it may be the only entity that can represent the wishes of the deceased, an element typically considered in whether to order an exhumation ...

As expected, the Mayor here opposes the exhumation and is positioned to present evidence in support of its objection. Whether or not that truly represents the interests of Ms. Antrim can never be known. Given the identity of the decedent and the time that has passes since her death, the Mayor cannot possibly have any direct evidence of Ms. Antrim's wishes. As such, the evidence that is presented by the Mayor can be viewed as best, supposition, or at worst, utterly unreliable.

[AUTHOR'S NOTE: **Do not miss the bizarreness of this argument. The Mayor, whose legal duty is to protect remains in a cemetery under his authority, according to Robins, needs to mind-read corpse Catherine to find out if *she* wants to be dug up. But Attorney Robins, the channeler, is about to come to the rescue and speak for the dead woman also!**]

(15) One is left to question why such a party with such a remote interest and lack of express knowledge about the decedent's wishes is conferred standing while the interests of Billy the Kid go unheard if this Court denier him standing. Allowing such a party to appear and present evidence while denying the same opportunity to a party that has been appointed to represent the interests of the decedent's son does not seem prudent nor fair

[AUTHOR'S NOTE: **This argument is so crazy that a reader might be tempted to rationalize that it cannot be as crazy as it sounds. Attorney Robins is saying that dead Billy has more** credibility to let his wishes be known than the live Mayor, whose obligation it is to protect the cemetery. And Robins can speak for the exact wishes of the dead, unlike the more supernaturally limited Mayor.]

(16) 1st Factor Public Interest, Billy the Kid's name is forever tied to New Mexico and to that of another legendary figure of the Old West, Sheriff Pat Garrett. **A commonly held version** of history paints a picture of an ambush in which Garrett killed the Kid in Ft. Sumner where most believe the Kid still lies at rest. **This version has been questioned. It is the investigation into whether Garrett killed the Kid that has prompted these investigators to seek exhumation.**

**[AUTHOR'S NOTE: This is pure "Brushy Bill" hoaxing. Only "Brushy's" believers question Pat Garrett's killing of Billy. Since "Brushy" was not Billy, there is no "public interest," meaning public value in the case. There are only the self-serving motives of the hoaxers, and the "Brushy" goal of puppeteer Robins.]**

(17) 2nd Factor, the Decedents wishes. In spite of Silver City's position to the contrary, we simply do not know what the decedent's wishes would be. Given the present circumstances, however, where her remains could possibly provide critical evidence to be used by modern day advocates to clear her son's name, one might easily surmise that Silver City's dogged attempt to resist exhumation would not be appreciated by Ms. Antrim.

**[AUTHOR'S NOTE: Now Robins is channeling Billy's mother enough to know that Silver City's blocking her exhumation would "not be appreciated" by her! For Robins, she is a "Brushy"-believer too! And she is angry! And corrupt Judge Henry Quintero never objected at all to Robins's making a mockery of his court. He was just basking in his undeserved Richardson appointment for a desired judgeship.]**

(18) 3rd Factor, Surviving Relatives Wishes. There are no relatives of Ms. Antrim currently before the Court ... The closest party currently before the Court is in fact Billy the Kid as represented by the undersigned counsel. As is apparent from the arguments set forth in this brief, the kid's [sic] interests would be furthered by the exhumation.

**[AUTHOR'S NOTE: Here is Robins channeling dead Billy again to say that he wants his mother dug up as part of his agenda!]**

(19) **Billy the Kid believes that the evidence adduced at the exhumation hearing will certainly support an order of exhumation here.**

[AUTHOR'S NOTE: Robins has crossed into the "Exorcist" movie's territory. He has disappeared. Only dead Billy is talking now through Robins's mouth. And *he* is "Brushy." The creepy thought is that Robins might not be faking. He may really think he *is* "Brushy Bill" incarnate.]

20) The foregoing has established that the undersigned counsel may legally and properly appear in these proceedings on behalf of, and to represent the interests of Billy the Kid.

[AUTHOR'S NOTE: Robins has established nothing whatsoever to justify his being in court as a channeler of dead Billy; nor has he established any reason for exhumations. But he has proved New Mexico's intractable corruption of collusive cronyism.]

(21) Respectfully submitted this 5th day of January, 2004.
Heard, Robins, Cloud, Lubel & Greenwood, L.L.P.

Bill Robins III
David Sandoval
Address and Telephone Numbers
**ATTORNEYS FOR BILLY THE KID**

## *SPEAKING FOR BILLY IN FORT SUMNER*

On February 26, 2004, Attorney Robins, with Attorneys David Sandoval and Mark Acuña, filed the "Tenth Judicial Court of De Baca County Case No. CV-2004-00005, Petition for the Exhumation of Billy the Kid's Remains." **[APPENDIX: 6]** Dead Billy is listed as a co-petitioner with the hoax's lawmen: "Gary Graves, Sheriff of De Baca County, Tom Sullivan, (Sheriff) and Steve Sederwall (Deputy Sheriff) of Lincoln County, New Mexico. (hereinafter the 'Sheriff-Petitioners')."

For digging up Billy, Robins used hoaxer style of vague suspicion, like: "This was also a time whose history was not accurately nor completely written." Or, as he made-up: "For generations now, the life of Billy the Kid has been the subject of historical debate. Perhaps the most significant lingering question involves whether Billy the Kid was indeed shot by Sheriff Pat Garrett in an ambush."

"Brushy Bill" makes his expected grand entrance under Section "IV. Historical Background." with introduction of the pretenders. Robins stated: "The debate has been sparked at various times in the past by at least two individuals who laid claim to his identity. **Ollie "Brushy Bill" Roberts** resided in Hico, Texas and claimed to be Billy the Kid. John Miller, in Arizona also died still claiming he was Billy the Kid. Co-Petitioners are in the initial phases of pursuing exhumations of these individuals as well."

"Brushy" is emphasized with Robins's ignorant true-believer plug of repeating his "dark night" confabulation for the Fort Sumner murder scene's actual bright moonlight; and by adding the pardon as deserved by "Brushy" for a reformed long life. So Robins stated about the shooting that the "ambush [was on] **one dark night** in Ft. Sumner;" and he claimed that the question that needed to be answered was **"whether the Kid went on to live a long and peace-abiding life elsewhere**."

To justify exhumation, Robins called the July 14, 1881 killing of Billy the Kid an "historical quandary" – but it was only a "quandary" for "Brushy" believers! He stated: "The investigation ["Billy the Kid Case"] has renewed questions as to whether Billy the Kid lies buried at the fabled grave-site in Ft. Sumner. Allowing the exhumation of the remains at Ft. Sumner grave site for extraction of DNA to be compared with that of Ms. Antrim's will likely finally provide definitive answers to this **historical quandary**."

Robins's lying becomes clear when one recalls that the month before, on January 9, 2004, the OMI issued the Affidavits of Drs. Zumwalt and Komar stating the graves' DNA was invalid. And Robins himself participated in the Komar deposition of January 20, 2004, in which she said the same thing. Obvious is the intent of the hoax to fake results, since real ones were impossible.

Also, contemplate this weirdness when contemplating Robins's filings: When he was channeling dead Billy the Kid, he was actually channeling dead, talking "Brushy Bill" Roberts! So dead 'Brushy" was seeking *his own* pardon, while *still pretending* to be real Billy Bonney, by using demon-possessed Attorney Bill Robins's tongue in Silver City and Fort Sumner courts!

So Robins now had Billy the Kid (secretly as "Brushy") request his own exhumation from Richardson's pocket-judge, Ted Hartley.

## *FOILING THE EXHUMATION SCHEME*

The hoaxers were no match for the Kennedy Han Law firm which I had brought in to represent the Mayors of Silver City and Fort Sumner. They made clear that there was neither forensic nor historical justification for the exhumation.

But truth had to contend with trickery. Silver City Judge Henry Quintero apparently colluded with Bill Robins III to get the hoaxers where they wanted to be: Billy the Kid's Fort Sumner grave. So on February 24, 2004, Robins filed "In the Matter of Catherine Antrim: Billy the Kid's Brief on the **Question of Ripeness;**" arguing that Billy should be dug up first; because having *his* DNA would then justify digging up his mother.

So Quintero - as aware as Robins that the OMI refused exhumation permits based on no valid DNA being available from the mother's or Billy's graves - promptly, on April 2, 2004, declared the mother's exhumation **not ripe** - meaning not ready - in his "Sixth Judicial District Court, State of New Mexico, County of Grant. No. MS 2003-11, In the Matter of Catherine Antrim. Decision and Order." He wrote: **"[The Court] finds that the Decision should be entered on ripeness for judicial review of exhumation of Catherine Antrim's remains ... Due to substantial uncertainty surrounding the recovery of the Kid's remains, only if the Petitioners are successful in locating the Kid's burial site and collecting his DNA may they again petition this Court for a review of Catherine Antrim's matter." [Note that later, after that trick failed in Fort Sumner, the hoaxers would lie that by digging up Billy first, Quintero had meant digging up "Brushy" or John Miller!]**

For the Fort Sumner hearing, I flew in historian, Frederick Nolan, as a witness; and had Charles Bowdre's relative, Louis Bowdre - the original opponent to the Telfer exhumation attempt - ready to testify again against it; though old and blind.

But my work on another front had paid off. Brave Lincoln County Commission Chairman Leo Martinez had confronted the lawmen about conducting a hoax through the Lincoln County Sheriff's Department. With Fort Sumner about to recall Sheriff Gary Graves, Tom Sullivan feared recall for himself - meaning no retirement benefits. So the lawmen accepted defeat by withdrawing their petition. On September 24, 2004, their attorney, Mark Acuña, filed "Tenth Judicial District Court, State of New Mexico, County of De Baca. No. CV-04-00005. In the Matter of William H. Bonney aka 'Billy the Kid.' Stipulation of Dismissal With Prejudice." "With prejudice" meant that they could not come back to exhume Billy Bonney.

That was not as good as it sounded. The hoaxers had already come up with a new scheme, and had found a forensic expert disreputable enough to back them if TV cameras were rolling and he was featured. All that was needed was rewriting the hoax for another fake source of DNA.

# OFFICIAL HISTORIAN: PROFESSOR PAUL HUTTON

Appointed by Governor Bill Richardson as the hoax's official historian, University of New Mexico history professor, Paul Hutton, was listed in the Lincoln County Sheriff's Department file in the lawmen's "Contact List for "William H. Bonney Case # 2003-274" as one of the main "investigators." **[APPENDIX: 7]**

Hutton fulfilled his role by making the hoax's key media contacts: Bill Kurtis of Bill Kurtis Productions, and forensic expert, Dr. Henry Lee. As Steve Sederwall stated in his June 26, 2012 deposition in my open records litigation: "[T]he way I met Bill Kurtis was through Paul Hutton. Paul Hutton wanted me to be on some investigative history ... I said, "You know, I'm looking at bringing Henry Lee out here ... Tell Kurtis I'll let him film it if he wants to, or whatever, if he can get Henry out here." So [Hutton] jumped on it." Sederwall had also alluded to Hutton's setting up the "deal" with Bill Kurtis; stating in my litigation's January 21, 2011 Evidentiary hearing that: "I got a call from Paul Hutton, a historian up in Albuquerque, teaches at the University. He was writing a deal for Bill Curtis [sic]. He wanted us [Sederwall and Sullivan] to interview with Bill Curtis [sic] ... Paul and I were friends ... So Curtis [sic] contacted us and wanted to know if he could follow the investigation ... That's when Bill Curtis [sic] got involved, and **Curtis [sic] paid to bring Dr. Lee to New Mexico.**" [Transcript 1/21/11, pp. 164, 168].

## "INVESTIGATING HISTORY: BILLY THE KID"

The first, in the hoaxers' anticipated tv series of "Billy the Kid Case" fake forensics with exhumations, was the collaboration of Paul Hutton, as writer and co-producer, with Bill Kurtis for a 2004 History Channel documentary titled: "Investigating History: Billy the Kid. It preserved, like in a chunk of amber, all the major hoaxers as participants. They declared the hoax's tenets: Garrett's victim was not Billy; the body was kept secret; there was no Coroner's Jury Report; friend Garrett helped Billy escape; and tourist interests blocked truth-seeking exhumations for DNA. Added was that the "investigation" was to assist Governor Bill Richardson's decision as to pardoning Billy. It was pure "Brushy Bill" hoaxing.

## A PROFITEERING PLOT

From the start, Hutton saw the program as his cash cow: the first in his series. He boastfully confirmed it to a *University of New Mexico Campus News* reporter, Carolyn Gonzales, for her February 16, 2004 article titled "Hutton Writes Wild Frontier Stories for History Channel." Gonzalez wrote: "His role has evolved into fulltime scriptwriting for "Investigating History" ... Hutton pitched **the idea of the series** to the History Channel after working with Governor Bill Richardson to try to verify the Kid's identity through a DNA comparison with his mother ... Richardson, who dubbed Hutton "Doc," appointed him historian on the Billy the Kid issue."

For it, Hutton also created a hoax mantra: "the mystery of Billy's murder." When interviewed on April 24, 2004 by a Rick Nathanson for the *Albuquerque Journal* weekly television guide, "Entertainer," Hutton was quoted: "[P]eople are always intrigued by mystery, and this has always been one of the great mysteries of the Old West. **The great mystery in this case is, of course, who is buried in Billy the Kid's grave in Fort Sumner.**" Setting up Garrett as murder of an innocent victim, Hutton called him "Billy's good friend." He also straddled the fence, stating: "I'm pretty sure that Pat Garrett shot Billy the Kid that night at Pete Maxwell's house." Left out was that his program claimed the opposite.

## THE PROGRAM'S OVERVIEW

For his travesty, Hutton had Richardson as an "historical investigator" assembling "experts" as a "pardon team" for Billy the Kid. They were fellow hoaxers: Sheriff Tom Sullivan, Deputy Steve Sederwall, *True West* magazine Editor-in-Chief Bob Boze Bell; and "Brushy's" believers, Bill Robins III and W.C. Jameson. For the final credits, Hutton listed "Frederick Nolan;" though, Nolan told me it was without his participation or knowledge.

Hutton narrates, as *Alias Billy the Kid's* cover looms: "Over the years that story has gained some credence." W.C. Jameson states that the "Coroner's Jury Report was never found," and there was "no evidence jurymen saw the body." Steve Sederwall adds, "If "Brushy Bill" is Billy the Kid, it comes down to this ... Garrett had to have let him escape in Fort Sumner."

As to the pardon, Hutton states: "New Mexico Governor Bill Richardson is ready to make things right." Then, Richardson himself says: "I might pardon him." But *that* will be based on [Attorney Bill] Robins's "investigation."

Since I had been relentlessly, though anonymously, exposing their exhumation-seeking hoax in district courts, Hutton switched the "Billy the Kid Case" from proving Pat Garrett a murderer of the innocent victim, to a "homicide investigation" to see if Billy the Kid "deserved" a pardon for his killings. And the Garrett murder case was turned into "Brushy" hoax-style defamation of bad guy Garrett tracking Billy "for the reward."

Faking hoaxers' expertise, Hutton has Sheriff Sullivan "discover" that Billy was promised a pardon; has himself and Bob Boze Bell as "historians" on the "Governor's pardon team;" and has Bill Robins III doing pardon legalities. Deputy Sederwall is a Capitan Mayor wondering if "Brushy" was Billy. And Richardson declares his commitment to "science," "tourism," and New Mexico.

## A TRAVESTY OF HISTORICAL IGNORANCE PLUS "BILLY THE KID CASE" AND "BRUSHY" HOAXING

Hutton's presentation, relying on "Brushy Bill" and "Billy the Kid Case" hoaxes, seeks to cast doubt on the Fort Sumner death scene; to make Pat Garrett a liar; and to denigrate legitimate historians. The film starts with Billy approaching a dark Maxwell house (no bright moonlight), while Hutton intones: "This is one of the most controversial moments in the history of the Old West: history's version of the last seconds of Billy the Kid ... Pat Garrett fires into the darkness ... Billy the Kid is dead when he hits the floor - or is he?" He then doubts a successful shot in the dark; and sneers: "The story is almost too good ... that the Kid ... would come strolling into this room unarmed and right into the hands of the law enforcement official ... is just too bizarre." **[But Billy was armed; and was likely sent to the ambush, since he was just going to the opposite side of the house to cut a steak.]**

Concealing all corpse identifications, Hutton calls the killing "a mystery;" quotes Poe's initial doubt, as if denying corpse identity; calls the killing "Garrett's version;" and lies that eye-witness, Pete Maxwell, never gave his version." He concludes that it was "unlikely" that Billy the Kid was shot.

*Alias Billy the Kid* is then backed by Hutton; Jameson denies the Coroner's Jury Report; and Sederwall declares that Garrett let Billy "escape in Fort Sumner."

Hutton proclaims: "Some suggested that it was more likely that Pat Garrett, Billy's friend, let him go ... burying someone else in his place" **[hoaxing friendship and "innocent victim"]**. Bob Boze Bell (subtitled as "Editor, True West Magazine") sneers that: "Friends of Pat Garrett conducted what they called an autopsy. But there were no photographs." He adds that they said

Garrett deserved the reward. [**Jurymen were not his friends, they identified the body as Billy's, and nobody had a camera.**] Boze Bell says Garrett did the killing in "secrecy," and buried the body the next day. [**There was no secrecy. The body had a vigil and legal inquest.**]

Hutton calls history "Garrett's version;" says that the only eye-witness was Pete Maxwell, "who was never interviewed" [**hiding Maxwell's Coroner's Jury testimony, and the townspeople's corpse vigil**], and lies that Poe "contradicted" Garrett's statement. [**Poe was merely initially unsure that Garrett had shot Billy, whom he could not recognize.**]

Hutton's "history" is pure "Brushy" hoax. He says Billy's mother died when he was 12 [**actually 14½**]; and outlaw, Jessie Evans, was Billy's "old side-kick" [**Billy rode with Jessie one month, September of 1877, before being hired by John Tunstall.**] He says John Tunstall and Alexander McSween were in partnership in Tunstall's Lincoln store [**there was no partnership**]; and says the James Dolan House filed a civil case against Tunstall. [**The case was against McSween, was filed by the Fritz heirs, was both a civil breech of contract and a criminal embezzlement; and Tunstall's property was attached by false claim of partnership with McSween**] He says after Tunstall's murder, Sheriff William Brady was shot in revenge [**when he was actually ambushed by the Regulators to prevent his murdering McSween**]; and says "only" Billy was charged with Brady's shooting [**when the murder defendants included all the shooting Regulators**].

For the Lincoln County War, he says the McSweens lost by being "divided up" in the town [**when they were strategically well placed, held the town for five days, and lost only because of military intervention – which Hutton omits**].

As to the pardon, Hutton is clueless. He calls Governor Lew Wallace's Amnesty Proclamation "for everyone;" [**when Billy was excluded with those indicted**]. He thinks Billy's testimony in the 1879 Grand Jury *failed* to indict Dolan for the Chapman murder because the district attorney was Dolan's friend. [**Thus, missed was the reason real Billy had deserved pardon: for achieving the indictments of Dolan, Campbell, and Evans!**]

Hutton says Lew Wallace made Garrett Sheriff [**when he was backed by the Santa Fe Ring and Secret Service**]; and says he wanted to be sheriff to get the $500 reward [**when it was offered over a month *after* he was elected**].

About the Stinking Springs capture, he wrongly says it was the day after Garrett's ambush of Billy's group at Fort Sumner **[which was December 19, 1880; with capture on the 22nd].**

As to Billy's jail letters to Wallace, he says they were written in Lincoln's courthouse-jail **[not the correct Santa Fe jail].**

<u>But the most egregious and most damaging part of Hutton's TV fraud is his "Billy the Kid Case" hoax re-enactment with Garrett, as deputy murder accomplice, placing the revolver in the outhouse to enable Billy's killing of the deputy guards. No one accused Garrett of this horrific crime before the hoax. Hutton contaminated public awareness irrevocably by this faked scene.</u>

Ongoing errors continue in re-enactment scenes. For example, after Brady is shot, Billy runs out to steal *Brady's* Winchester carbine; when he was retrieving his own confiscated gun.

Hutton announces that the "investigation" will solve if Billy was really killed by Garrett and if Governor Richardson should pardon him. Sullivan appears as a "researcher" who discovered that Wallace reneged on his promise to pardon Billy "which could have ended the Lincoln County War." **[So *he* "discovered" the famous Wallace pardon promise! But *he* called it connected to the Lincoln County War - the year before!]** Hutton intones: "New Mexico Governor Bill Richardson is ready to make things right." Richardson declares: "I might pardon him." But he wants truth "through science." Bill Robins, as the attorney seeking pardon evidence, says Billy "should never have been charged."

Sullivan, with his sheriff's badge, says he tried to settle the matter, but was "opposed by tourism interests" in Silver City and Fort Sumner, which he calls "obstruction of justice." Billy Sparks, Richardson's spokesman, says: "People want to prevent any truth that is not their truth." A Dennis Erickson, Ph.D. Science Policy Advisor *in Richardson's Office*, says there are ways of locating graves through "ground-penetrating radar." **[Hidden is OMI blockage, irrelevance of radar, and uncertain gravesites.]**

Richardson says: "I might pardon him." But *that* will be based on Robins's "investigation." He adds: "When I traveled around the world, there was curiosity about the wild West and I know that's tourism, that's economic development for us." **[Hidden is his pay-to-play intent to give that history to Texas!]**

In conclusion, "Investigating History: Billy the Kid" was "Billy the Kid Case" hoaxing, with its covert "Brushy" pardon thrust.

## *HOAXING PERSONAL INNOCENCE*

Ignoring evidence, by June 20, 2006, Paul Hutton denied any connection to the "Billy the Kid Case" or to being its "historian." Answering my inquiry proxied through journalist, Jay Miller, he wrote: "I was never the 'state historian' (as *True West* put it) on this project and had absolutely nothing to do with the production of any written materials on it outside of some initial talking points I emailed the governor's office before the first press conference ... As to my work on the History Channel and how I came to any conclusions in the Billy the Kid program, that is really none of your business." And he called the "Billy the Kid Case" a "positive effort to promote our state nationally."

There was actually no doubt about Hutton's being the hoax's historian. Jay Miller had also contacted Hutton's mentor: historian, Robert Utley. No confidentiality was requested, so Miller e-mailed me Utley's September 16, 2004 answer: "I am truly disappointed in your governor ... he should be held accountable for the dumb things he is doing in the Billy dustup. When his aid tried to enlist me as 'historical advisor,' I told him to tell Richardson to stay out of this or he would get in deep doodoo. So they got Paul Hutton, my protégé, who loves the outrageous." When I spoke with Utley himself in November of 2005, he bemoaned that betrayal of historical ethics by the man he called his "protégé": Paul Hutton.

In fact, Hutton continued to milk his hoax participation. Still faking, he validated the carpenter's bench. He then made a Billy the Kid show in Albuquerque featuring it by claiming its "blood."

## **FEDERAL HOAXER: U.S. MARSHALS SERVICE HISTORIAN DAVID TURK**

A shocking and secret "Billy the Kid Case" participant was Washington, D.C., based U.S. Marshals Service Historian David Turk, involved in the hoax from its 2003 start, and coming to New Mexico to help the hoaxers destroy Pat Garrett's reputation. To put his participation in perspective, as the Marshals Service Historian, he was attacking its most famous Old West Deputy U.S. Marshal. But Turk declared him a murderer of an innocent victim, with "Brushy Bill" as a possible surviving Billy the Kid.

Turk was the only historian backing Case 2003-274 in its "Probable Cause Statement;" with his fake "proof" being an old-timer's hearsay claim about a post-death Billy the Kid sighting. Also, since the Statement's footnotes were obscure National Archive documents on microfilm (like Azariah Wild's Secret Service reports), Turk may have provided them.

Later, in the forensic scam being conducted by Dr. Henry Lee with an old carpenter's bench, Turk used his title as expertise to fake its "validation" as the one on which Billy was laid out. He was also present, in 2004, at Lee's fake forensic investigation of the Deputy Bell killing at the Lincoln courthouse (where Turk was misrepresented as an actual U.S. Marshal, either by Lee's mistake or intentional misinformation). He was also acknowledged for his assistance in the 2018 "Brushy"-backing book, *Cold Case Billy the Kid* by W.C. Jameson.

Turk must have known he was a subversive, hiding his participation in the "Billy the Kid Case;" while his irresponsible department covered up for him for years of my Freedom of Information Act requests through my journalist proxy, Jay Miller (to maintain my anonymity). But on June 22, 2005, a William E. Bordley, Associate General Counsel/FOIPA Officer, sent Turk's job description: "Conducts historical research in order to prepare and edit historical articles for publications and exhibits on USMS history ... Develops fact sheets, brochures, pamphlets, and books on the history of the USMS. Research is conducted both on and off site." Participating in a filed, New Mexico, murder case stretched that job description; and its being a hoax topped off the impropriety!

The eye-opener was Turk's taxpayer funding for hoaxing. In New Mexico from December 5, 2003 to December 9, 2003, when the "Probable Cause Statement" was allegedly being written by Steve Sederwall, he traveled to Silver City, Lincoln, Las Cruces, Santa Fe, Ruidoso, Albuquerque, and Tijeras; spending $848.42 of taxpayer money for travel, lodging, car rentals, and cell phone, while collecting $1,967.00 of his yearly salary of $84,127.00.

As to his U.S. Marshal's Service response to Turk's hoax participation, its attorney, William Bordley, double-talked: "Regarding Item 6 of your request, Mr. Turk's role in this matter is to research and gather information relative to the Billy the Kid case to ascertain the historical accuracy of the U.S. Marshals Service involvement in the events relating to the Billy the Kid case." So I had Jay Miller ask outright: Did Turk author the "Probable Cause Statement?" The shock answer came in a month. Turk had written a secret report as part of the "Probable Cause Statement.

## *DAVID TURK'S SECRET REPORT*

In answer to my open records request through proxy journalist, Jay Miller, on August 24, 2005 a Mavis DeZulovich FOI/PA Liaison, Office of Public Affairs for the U.S. Marshals Service, responded with a tantalizing tidbit: "Mr. Turk is not the author of the Lincoln County Sheriff's Department Probable Cause Statement 2003-274. **However, mention is made in that document to information contained in a research report authored by Mr. Turk entitled: "The U.S. Marshals Service and Billy the Kid."** So Turk's quote in the Statement was from *his own* research report! But he was hiding that incriminating report.

So, on August 18, 2004, I wrote, for Jay Miller to proxy, an open records request to Sheriff Tom Sullivan for all records in *his* files pertaining to David Turk. Sullivan refused to give any records, but claimed he did not have to since *they* were exempt as being part of his *ongoing criminal investigation* in Case 2003-274, the "Billy the Kid Case!" So Sullivan indirectly proved Turk's records and participation!

In April of 2006, I called Turk myself, terrified, knowing his division was part of Homeland Security, and certain he was some kind of crack-pot. I made up the name "Wilma Jordan" and a Polish accent, requesting a copy of his "The U.S. Marshals Service and Billy the Kid." He said it was in "departmental revision."

On June 2, 2006, I called back. He now claimed to be doing "revisions" himself, with indefinite delay. So I asked, "Zo, do you tink Pad Garred *did nod shood* Billy de Kid?" Bull's eye. "The facts do not fit together," said Turk. "Vy is dis your interest?" Wilma asked. Turk said because it involved murders of U.S. Marshals when Billy escaped in October of 1880. "Wilma," like Pandora, could not resist temptation. She said they were *Deputy* Sheriffs, and it was *April* 28th of *18-81*.

On June 15th, "Wilma" wrote Turk, wanting more information on why Garrett did not kill the Kid. And she wanted that report.

Turk's answer, on July 3, 2006, was intended to scare the stuffing out of nosy "Wilma Jordan": he had tracked her down, and supplied her address! Amazingly, there *really was a Wilma Jordan in New Mexico*! It was *her* address! (I hope she does not have a Polish accent.) This proves that some Homeland Security tax dollars go to employee research to protect their own backside's security. And Turk directed "Wilma" to a Steve Sederwall (!), with his telephone number provided! And, of course, there never came a copy of "The U.S. Marshals Service and Billy the Kid." I learned that afterwards, Sederwall himself was asking around if anyone knew about a Polish woman who had called David Turk. At least I got confirmation that I had done the accent right!

And Nikki Cedric stated that the pamphlet would be sent "when it is ready for distribution." It never came.

On September 11, 2006, through Jay Miller, I tried Nikki Cedric again as: "Re. Follow-up to your August 31, 2006 response to my Freedom of Information Act request No. 2004USMS7634 in reference to David Turk, Historian for the U.S. Marshals Service; and request for clarification." I asked if he provided the sources for the "Probable Cause Statement." Responses ceased forever.

## THE EXPURGATED TURK REPORT

February of 2007 brought hope. Turk had published "Billy the Kid and the U.S. Marshals Service" in hoax-promoting *True West* magazine! I got it. It proved his "revisions" were expurgations, being just about U.S. Marshals in the Lincoln County War period.

But it had a telling peculiarity. After the conventional Billy the Kid death scene, Turk emerged spouting the "Billy the Kid Case's" "Brushy" hoax's familiar script. He faked Pat Garrett as the sole witness, claimed an innocent victim, and babbled about Billy's post July 14, 1881 survival. He wrote: "That traditional account [of the killing] - as told by Garrett himself (with the help of a ghostwriter) in the *Authentic Life of Billy, the Kid* - **has been questioned many times over the years with some accounts suggesting that the Kid got away to live another day or decades, and others indicating that somebody else besides the Kid died in Maxwell's bedroom.**" So he concluded "decades" of Billy's survival following Garrett's killing of an innocent victim!

## GETTING TURK'S ACTUAL SECRET REPORT

Finally, on September 3, 2008, the Turk mystery was solved - as a part of my long, open records litigation against the hoaxer lawmen. For Sheriff Rick Virden's September 8, 2008 deposition, we subpoenaed his file for Case 2003-274. Though he had expurgated the forensic DNA records I was after, its last 26 pages were the *actual, David Turk, The U.S. Marshals Service and Billy the Kid!*

The cover had a galloping Old West rider with a big marshal's badge. Its date was December 2003: the signing date of the "Probable Cause Statement!" It was titled: "United States Marshals Service Executive Services Division: Research Report, Submitted by David S. Turk." Page one gave me what I wanted: "Research Report: The U.S. Marshals Service and Billy the Kid. **To Be Added in its Present Entirety, with Exhibits, to Lincoln County, New Mexico Case # 2003-274.**"

So David Turk had created an addendum for the "Billy the Kid Case's Probable Cause Statement," using his title and government money to defame a famous Deputy U.S. Marshal for a hoax! And he had contributed his own, major hoax document! And its style implied him as possibly assisting the actual "Probable Cause Statement," besides his hearsay old-timer quote. And it shows that he was supplying National Archive documents for the hoax.

## THE TURK ADDENDUM

Providing no historical evidence, David Turk backed the "Billy the Kid Case" hoax premise of Pat Garrett as murderer of an innocent victim. For filler, he discussed U.S. Marshals in the Lincoln County War period (including Garrett). But abruptly, based on a few WPA hearsay interviews from the 1930's (of people unconnected to the event), he concluded that Billy the Kid's killing "fueled speculation over the precise outcome."

Turk's *The U.S. Marshals Service and Billy the Kid* is called a "Research Report." It had a cover page, 9 pages of text; bibliographic "Endnotes;" and "Exhibits" consisting of a Turk article titled "How much did it cost to find Billy the Kid?;" a "National Police Gazette" May 21, 1881 article on Billy's escape; and a May 30, 1881 letter from Attorney Sidney Barnes (one of Billy's Mesilla prosecutors) about Billy's Mesilla trial and his later escape. (Turk's general and irrelevant information on U.S. Marshals is omitted here.)

The only parts of Turk's "Research Report" that also appear in the "Probable Cause Statement" are his Frances E. Totty, WPA quote about "Billie" being seen after the death date; and his "Endnote" sources, like Secret Service Operative Azariah Wild's reports. But Turk's report - that he tried so hard to hide - was part of the 2003-274 case file, as "probable cause" that Pat Garrett was a murderer of an innocent victim instead of Billy the Kid.

Below is the report that Turk knew should be hidden because it revealed him as disreputable and subversive incompetent.

# Research Report: The U.S. Marshals Service and Billy the Kid

Submitted by David S. Turk, Historian
December 2003

"**Research Report: The U.S. Marshals Service and Billy the Kid**. To Be Added in its Present Entirety, with Exhibits, to Lincoln County, New Mexico Case # 2003-274."

## Purpose of Research [Page 1]

There is renewed interest in examining the crimes and final resting place of William H. Bonney, also known as Henry Antrim, Henry McCarty, or Billy the Kid.

**[AUTHOR'S NOTE: The only "renewed interest" was from the "Billy the Kid Case" hoax and loony conspiracy theorists.]**

Two Sheriffs' Offices in New Mexico reopened an investigation, with the approval of the Governor of New Mexico. In September 2003 Steve Sederwall, Mayor of Capitan, and Deputy Sheriff, Lincoln County, New Mexico, contacted me on research matters relating to the Lincoln County War.

**[AUTHOR'S NOTE: Turk claims Sederwall as contact.]**

Given the integral role of the U.S. Marshals Service, and the dual roles between our two institutions during the time of Billy the Kid, and further that Pat Garrett was a Deputy U.S. Marshal during the pursuit of the Kid, and that another Deputy U.S. Marshal (and Lincoln County officer), Robert Olinger, was shot and killed by the Kid during his escape, it is relevant to the agency's historical interest to research those portions of the case pertinent to it to ensure accuracy.

**[AUTHOR'S NOTE: The report gives no information to doubt conventional history. It does not "ensure accuracy!"]**

The primary investigation of Lincoln County, New Mexico State No. 2004-274 [sic] is being conducted by Lincoln County Sheriff Tom Sullivan, De Baca County Sheriff Gary Graves, and Steve Sederwall, but the following findings add significantly to the data being collected in revisiting Billy the Kid.

[AUTHOR'S NOTE: No reason is given for "revisiting Billy the Kid," except hearsay death rumors 56 years after the event.]

## Overview of Research Focus [Page 1]

The following research relates to the prominent roles of the U.S. Marshals Service in the Lincoln County War ... Finally, there is a study on the deaths of Deputy Marshal Olinger and Lincoln County Officer J.W. Bell, followed by Billy the Kid's subsequent escape. The Works Progress Administration interviewed several Lincoln residents during the late 1930's in this regard ...

[AUTHOR'S NOTE: The oddness of this statement is easy to miss; but each part is irrelevant to the others. Out of nowhere, will come Turk's "suspicions" that the Kid was not Garrett's murder victim.]

## Deputy U.S. Marshal Garrett and His Agency Status [Page 4]

[AUTHOR'S NOTE: This page, about Garrett's U.S. Marshal status has Secret Service Agent Azariah Wild's praise of Garrett to his Chief. All is irrelevant to Garrett's murder victim.]

## Key Event: Billy the Kid's Escape and the Deaths of Bell and Olinger [Page 8]

On April 28, 1881, [sic - missing word] made his famous escape from Lincoln. Accounts of the events were recalled later by witnesses. A contemporary news account from *The National Police Gazette* dated May 21, 1881, followed a generally accepted recollection pattern with some minor inconsistencies. Deputy U.S. Marshal Olinger and guard J.W. Bell ... were holding the Kid in the jail. Olinger dined at a local establishment, and during his absence the shackled prisoner hit Bell with handcuffs. He then grabbed Bell's revolver and shot him in the chest ... Just as he [Olinger] entered a small gate leading through the jail fence, the Kid shot him with a double-barreled gun, filling his breast of shot and killing him.

[AUTHOR'S NOTE: Note that the *National Police Gazette*, published in New York, was merely a dime novel tabloid, and not a legitimate historical source. Also, Turk presents Billy the Kid's escape without Garrett's participation.]

## Differing Accounts on Death of Billy the Kid [Pages 8 - 9.]

Deputy U.S. Marshal and Lincoln County Sheriff Pat Garrett pursued Billy the Kid for several months after the deaths

[AUTHOR'S NOTE: About 2 ½ months.]

of Deputy Olinger and J.W. Bell. The end of the chase appeared to be at Pete Maxwell's ranch on July 15 [sic], 1881.

[AUTHOR'S NOTE: This is "Brushy" hoax-style sly innuendo of "suspicion" without evidence. And the date was July 14, 1881.]

What occurred at the Maxwell Ranch fueled speculation over the precise outcome. There appears [sic] to be many questions to answer.

[AUTHOR'S NOTE: This is full-blown, hoax conspiracy theory, with vague "suspicion." No evidence is given.]

According to the WPA interview of Francisco Trujillo in May 1937, Garrett was negotiating capture of the Kid with Pete Maxwell himself. Josh Brent's father was one of the Sheriff's deputies, stating that Garrett said "that he sure hated to kill the boy, but he knew it was either his life or the boy's life."

[AUTHOR'S NOTE: The "Billy the Kid Case" hoaxers omitted this hearsay from the Statement. But, as a hoax connoisseur, I say they missed a great hoax quote – even though it is groundless! It was a chance to fake the Pat-Billy friendship.]

Yet another resident stated,

> The people around Lincoln say Garrett didn't kill Billie [sic] the Kid. John Poe was with Garrett the night he was supposed to ... [sic] said that he didn't see the man that Garrett killed. Ican [sic] take you to the grave in Hell's Half Acre, a old government cemetery [sic], where Billie [sic] was supposed to be buried to show you the grave.
>
> The cook at Pete Maxwell's was always putting flowers on the grave and praying at it. This woman thought a lot of Billie [sic], but after Garrett killed the man at Maxwell's home her grandson was never seen again and Billie [sic] was seen by Bill Nicoli? And indian scout. Bill saw him in old Mexico.

[AUTHOR'S NOTE: This hearsay was put in the "Probable Cause Statement" with attribution to Turk.]

The recollections took a legendary bent, even extending to events that occurred after those at the Maxwell ranch. Josh Brent stated that Garrett told his father that after he killed the Kid, "that a fellow from the east wrote him and said that he would pay $5000.00 for the trigger finger of the boy."

[AUTHOR'S NOTE: Irrelevant pseudo-historical filler like in the "Probable Cause Statement."]

Other Related Fact [Page 9.]

A sidelight from this period was the debunking of one widely-held story that Billy the Kid killed twenty-one men by the age of twenty-one. U.S. Attorney Barnes stated in a letter to the Attorney General, dated May 30, 1881, that while the Kid "has killed fifteen different men & is only twenty one years of age."

[AUTHOR'S NOTE: This irrelevant hearsay by one of Billy's Mesilla prosecutors, who had no way of knowing; was used to fake historical savvy, as in the "Probable Cause Statement."]

So U.S. Marshals Service Historian David Turk was a "Billy the Kid Case" hoaxer, abusing the prestige of his federal title.

# FAKE FORENSICS WITH DR. HENRY LEE

My blocking the exhumations of Billy Bonney and his mother with the Kennedy Han Law Firm, and Fort Sumner and Silver City Mayors, Raymond Lopez and Terry Fortenberry, caused the Billy the Kid Case" hoaxers not to stop, but to rewrite the hoax! Version one had Billy *not shot* by his friend, Pat Garrett, who killed an innocent victim instead. But now, with no "DNA" from Billy and his mother, the hoaxers were desperate for any "DNA" claim to continue the hoax by digging up "Brushy" and John Miller.

So hoax version two arose (without admission), to use the only object they had possibly connected to Billy history: the carpenter's bench. The scam was to say it still had shot Billy's blood, from which they could get his DNA! Since Billy was *not shot* in version one, so was not laid out on the bench (with the body being the innocent victim), with sociopathic scorn of their audience as idiots, the hoaxers did a switcheroo. Now Billy *was shot* by friend Garrett, just to *play dead* and bleed on the bench (for future DNA recovery), then to sneak away and be replaced, by Garrett, with the murdered innocent victim. When this happened during Billy's body's being in a 200 person town vigil was omitted. Omitted too was that their man "Brushy" had no playing-dead-on-bench tale.

Version two's leg-work was left to Sheriff Tom Sullivan and his Deputy, Steve Sederwall. Their December 31, 2003 "Probable Cause Statement," had claimed finding the bench; stating:

"On August 29, 2003, Deputy Sederwall of the Lincoln County Sheriff's Department located the carpenter bench where the Kid's body was placed on July 14, 1881." Then, it was used to fake "discrepancies" to call Garrett a murderer, and to feign "investigating." Now the entire hoax rested on its three long planks with legs.

So the hoaxers had two needs: verifying the bench; and finding a sleazy enough, name recognition "forensic expert" to play along with faking DNA to desecrate graves for a publicity stunt. They got both. For the unaware public, fellow hoaxers, Paul Hutton and David Turk, made-up that the bench was real. And limelight-seeking Dr. Henry Lee got on board to claim, blood, DNA, and anything else they wanted.

## *THE INVALID CARPENTER'S BENCH*

The carpenter's bench was not forensically valid, since its being the real one is unprovable. As discussed, it was found in the Albuquerque converted chicken coop of Mannie Miller, son of Stella Abreu Miller, who had it in her 1926-1936 Fort Sumner Billy the Kid Museum, with supposed Peter Maxwell bedroom furniture. (See page 341 above) It had no provenance from 1881 to 1926; during which were Fort Sumner's sale in 1884, and Peter and Luz Maxwell's deaths in 1898 and 1900 respectively.

In this tragic fall of Lucien Bonaparte Maxwell's dynasty, it is inconceivable that anyone kept a bench from the town's carpenter's shop (Stella's had three crude planks and measured 86" x 28" x 31¼" high); or even kept Peter's bedroom furniture. In fact, after the town's sale, caused by his mismanagement, he lived in a little house outside of Fort Sumner for 16 years before death. The "furniture" could have been from his bedroom there!

And the bench's uncertainty is further confirmed. According my personal communication with historian, Jerry (Richard) Weddle, who interviewed Stella in her old age at the Albuquerque chicken coop storage, the bench had not been kept by the family. She had gotten it in 1926 from a Fort Sumner local for her Museum. She showed it to early historian, Robert Mullin; and another historian, Maurice Garland Fulton, photographed it. That is how it became *the* carpenter's bench of the death scene.

By 1936, Stella's museum closed; but, for May 31, 1937, a reporter, Dee Blythe, for the *Clovis, New Mexico Evening News-Journal*, wrote "Billy the Kid Landmarks Fast Vanishing: Historic Spots Hard to Find; Markers Needed." With photos, it stated:

"Nearby [a post office] is the house of Manuel Abreu and Mrs. Stella Miller, children of Mrs. Odelia Abreu, youngest of the daughters of Pete Maxwell. They have treasured quite a few relics of the old days, particularly with reference to Billy the Kid, but these relics are all jumbled together into one small room of the house. The collection includes the <u>carpenter's bench on which Billy the Kid's body was laid to cool</u>, the bed beside which Pat Garrett sat talking to Pete Maxwell that fateful night; a rifle once owned by the Kid; <u>a washstand that was struck by Garrett's second shot</u>; <u>the lamp Deluvina Maxwell held to see if the Kid was dead</u> ... Last year, for awhile these relics were on display in a building on highway 60 in Fort Sumner; but the arrangement was unsatisfactory and they were brought back to their out-of-the-way resting place." Assumedly, this history came from Stella; so noteworthy is her incorrect inclusion of the washstand as shot; adding likelihood to the carpenter's bench being bogus.

It would not be until 1959, 22 years after Stella's museum closed, when her son, Manuel "Mannie" Miller - who had moved from Fort Sumner to Albuquerque in 1944 - took what was left of the past museum's contents to store in his back-yard converted chicken coop, where the "Billy the Kid Case" hoaxers found them. And their storage in the interval from 1944 to 1959 involved exposure to high temperatures, the elements, and flooding: disastrous for claiming preservation of Billy's blood as the hoaxers were about the do.

In 2011, after Mannie Miller's death, I met his nephew, Kenny Miller, Stella Abreu Miller's grandson, and Lucien Maxwell's great-great grandson, the new caretaker. He showed me the objects in the coop. Included was Stella's home-made sign about "outlaw" Billy the Kid - not what Billy's day's Maxwells would have called him, casting more doubt on authenticity of her objects. Pandering to tourists, it said: "FOR YOUR INFORMATION THIS MUSEUM IS OWNED BY THE NIECE AND NEPHEW OF PETE MAXWELL. IT WAS IN HIS HOME WHERE BILLY THE KID WAS KILLED BY SHERIFF PAT GARRETT WE WILL ASSURE AND NOT MISREPRESENT ANY ONE WHO IS INTERESTED IN THE SOUTH-WEST AND ITS NOTORIOUS OUTLAW BILLY THE KID. THERES NOT JUST ONE OR TWO ANTIQUES BUT SEVERAL THINGS OF INTEREST DATED BACK 18-81 AND TERRITORIAL DAYS."

But Kenny Miller told me the key truth: the family has no doubt that Pat Garrett killed Billy the Kid.

But claiming "blood" - not necessarily *real* blood - was the hoaxers' only bench concern. So they faked it. On August 14, 2004, for the *Lincoln County News*, reporter Doris Cherry's "Forensics 101 for 'Billy,'" quoted Sederwall: "The bench has been in the Maxwell family descendents since 1881 and has been stored out of weather, protecting the blood evidence ... **Only once was the blood**

**exposed to the elements, when a family member who took the bench without family approval returned it to the Maxwell family home in Fort Sumner and left it outside to get rained on once.** So the odds of finding blood evidence were very good."

The "rained on" part was not good for blood! It got worse. For an October 6, 2005 *RuidosoNews.com* article, hoax loyalist, Julie Carter, wrote "Follow the Blood: In the Billy the Kid Case, Miller Exhumed." She stated: "The Maxwell compound and everything in it was reportedly washed away in a flood of 1906. The photo of the bench was taken in 1926 by historian Maurice Fulton ... Since 1959, they [Maxwell family] had stored the historical furniture and household items in an old chicken coop." The "washed away" in a 1906 flood, and unknown location from 1881 to 1926 were also bad! And added was the gap from Fulton's 1926 photo, to transport in 1959 to Mannie Miller's back yard chicken coop.

For "validation," hoaxer Paul Hutton "authenticated" it. Then, in 2007, for his Albuquerque Museum of Art and History Billy the Kid show, with curator, Deb Slaney, he labeled it as having "human blood." U.S. Marshals Service Historian David Turk gave another fake authentication. On August 8, 2006, via Jay Miller, my Freedom of Information Act request to Turk's agency asked how he could authenticate it. On August 31, 2006, Nikki Cedric at Public Affairs answered: "Mr. Turk ... has seen the said workbench; *however, he did not state that any particular person was on the bench. This is for the lab to determine.* The bench does match descriptions given in other sources and he believes it to be the one described."

So on April 19, 2006, hoax-backing reporter, Julie Carter, in *RuidosoNews.com*, reported in "Digging up Bones": "**UNM History professor Paul Hutton and U.S. Treasury [sic - Marshals Service] historian Dave Turk have both authenticated the bench.**"

But no amount of hoaxer lying could change that the bench was forensically useless for Billy the Kid DNA. Nevertheless, the lawmen hoaxed wildly. Providing himself a master con-artist, Steve Sederwall, falsely declared: "Dead men don't bleed." So Sederwall's shot Billy survived, but bled on the bench!

Hoax loyalist reporter, Julie Carter, for her October 6, 2005, *RuidosoNews.com* article "Follow the Blood: In the Billy the Kid Case, Miller Exhumed," quoted Sederwall's whoppers: "**Whoever was laid on that, whether it was Billy the Kid or not,**" said Sederwall, "**he left his DNA." The investigators said the amount of blood found on the bench indicated that whoever was on that bench must have been still alive. "Dead men don't bleed," explained Sederwall. "and we witnessed a large amount of blood.**" The hoaxers were back in business with a new hoax and exhumation hopes.

## *DR. LEE WAS THE PERFECT DNA MATCH*

Deputy Steve Sederwall had contacted Dr. Henry Lee through fellow hoaxer, "Billy the Kid Case" official historian, Paul Hutton; as Sederwall testified in his June 26, 2012 deposition for my open records litigation against the lawmen: "Paul Hutton wanted me to be on some investigative history … I said, "You know, I'm looking at bringing Henry Lee out here … Tell Kurtis I'll let him film it if he wants to, or whatever, if he can get Henry out here." So [Hutton] jumped on it."

Henry Lee jumped on it too, getting the flood of publicity that accompanies media magnet, Billy the Kid; and that Lee craves for what his scornful colleagues call his "show-biz" forensics: choosing cases for their limelight. And he had national name recognition by helping O.J. Simpson walk free in his 1996 murder trial. As to reputation for veracity, that was another story.

Prosecutor, Vincent Bugliosi, in his book, *Outrage: The Five Reasons Why O.J. Simpson Got Away With Murder*, called Henry Lee "nothing short of incompetent." Bugliosi was avoiding "liar." An example from *Outrage* was Lee's testifying that "crime-scene" shoe "imprints" on murder victim Nicole Simpson's walkway did not match O.J. Simpson's incriminatory, "size-12 Bruno Magli bloody shoe prints" - also at the scene. But the smaller "prints" Lee used, according to Bugliosi, had been hardened into the concrete during its laying "ten years earlier!"

Helpful Dr. Lee resurfaced for the 2007 murder trial defense for music impresario, Phil Spector; accused, and ultimately convicted, of fatally shooting actress, Lana Clarkson. But Attorney Sara Caplan - in Spector's first defense team - testified to the judge, Larry Paul Fidler, that, at the crime scene, Lee bottled dead Clarkson's torn-off fingernail, which indicated possible struggle - not Spector's defense's claim of her committing suicide. Then that fingernail disappeared. Judge Fidler declared destruction of evidence. The CNN.com AP headline of May 25, 2007 was: "Famed expert's credibility takes a hit at Spector trial."

Lee's involvement in a 2016 documentary, "The Case of JonBenet Ramsey," accusing her nine year old brother, Burke Ramsey of murdering her, resulted in Burke's $750 million defamation suit, which included Lee. On January 5, 2019, Dailymail.com reporter Maxine Shen wrote: "CBS and the brother of JonBenet Ramsey settle their $750m defamation lawsuit to the 'satisfaction of both parties.' " It stated: "Beyond CBS and the documentary production company Critical Content, LLS, Burke's lawsuit named **forensic scientist Henry Lee** and forensic pathologist Werner Spitz among several others who appeared in the broadcast."

So Henry Lee was the perfect "expert" to keep secret that no verifiable DNA of Billy the Kid existed on the planet – and find some. He sham-tested for "blood" wherever he was pointed; and made up crime scene scenarios however he was directed - as long as Bill Kurtis Productions kept filming.

Lee was part of the "Billy the Kid Case" hoaxers' team from 2004 onward; even acknowledged in 2018's *Cold Case Billy the Kid*. Wearing a cowboy hat in a 2010 photo, he was even a "posse" member in Steve Sederwall's then website, called BillytheKidCase.com selling Case 2003-274 public documents.

Lee was funded by Bill Kurtis, who wrote to Sederwall a letter (eventually an exhibit in my open records litigation) stating: "This letter is provided as official verification that Kurtis Productions, LTD located in Chicago, Illinois paid all expenses for Dr. Henry Lee and his participation in the making of the documentary *Investigating History: Billy the Kid*. Dr. Lee was flown to New Mexico on July 30, 2004 and departed on August 1, 2004 at the expense of Kurtis Productions, LTD."

Lee's joining the "Billy the Kid Case" was announced by hoax-backing *Albuquerque Journal* reporter, Rene Romo. On August 2, 2004, Romo splashed, "Forensic Expert on Billy's Case: Questions Remain on Outlaw's Fate" Romo declared: "Dr. Henry Lee, one of the nation's leading forensic scientists ... has added the Billy the Kid slaying to his case files ... "This is an extremely interesting case of some historical importance,' Lee said in an interview ... 'That's why I agreed to spend some of my own time to work with them ... **It's basically a worthwhile project and legitimate.**"

So famous Dr. Lee called the "Billy the Kid Case" "a worthwhile project and legitimate." What else was the public to think? And Romo confirmed: "Lee's expenses were paid by Illinois-based Kurtis Productions, headed by Bill Kurtis, host of the History Channel series 'Investigating History.'"

Lee's profit motive was further elucidated in the August 12, 2004 *Lincoln County News* article by Doris Cherry: "Forensics 101 for 'Billy." She quoted Sheriff Tom Sullivan: "Along with Sullivan and Lee were a crew from Curtis [sic] Production Company filming for the History Channel and Court T.V. **Dr. Lee also has a show produced by Curtis [sic] Production.**"

So Billy the Kid DNA exhumations and "matchings" were to be churned out by Lee and Kurtis for their enterprise. No wonder Lee called the project "worthwhile." He was intending an exhumation franchise for himself.

But the public was fed a different bill of goods via the hoaxers. By April 13, 2006, deceived reporter, Leo W. Banks of the *Tucson Weekly*, in "The New Billy the Kid?" had Lee pleading; as in: "Everybody wants a piece of the Kid, even a celebrity like Henry Lee ... when he heard about the Kid dig-up efforts, **he called Sederwall to volunteer his services.**"

The "Billy the Kid Case" hoaxers plugged Lee extravagantly. Rene Romo's August 2, 2004 *Albuquerque Journal* article even used their "Probable Cause Statement's" complicit historian: "You're getting the top guy ... I think that will go a long way to finding out what happened in Lincoln," said **David S. Turk**, historian with the U.S. Marshals Service ... who is cooperating on the case."

Added was that a Calvin Ostler, a Utah Medical Examiner - would participate. Unmentioned, was that Ostler was Lee's business partner. So Lee-Turk-Ostler did ricochet validation, without public awareness that they were all in cahoots for a trash "documentary" by Bill Kurtis and Professor Paul Hutton - all doing their job for Governor Bill Richardson.

## *THE DNA DEAD END*

By the time Dr. Henry Lee arrived on the scene, it was indisputable that no valid DNA existed for the "Billy the Kid Case." In forensics, that means "reference DNA." It has 100% certainty of belonging to the person in question; and is *the only DNA valid for identity matching.*

The carpenter's bench "blood DNA' was worthless, because it could not be "reference DNA." It would be like a random fingerprint, with no actual fingerprints existing of the individual in question to compare with it. And the OMI had declared Billy's and his mother's graves useless for "reference DNA."

However, legitimate DNA forensics were not Dr. Henry Lee's worry. His worry was *DNA film footage.* Anything that could be claimed as linked to Billy the Kid sufficed. The bench was just fine for Dr. Lee. And when Lee looked at the bench, unsurprisingly, he found "blood."

Rene Romo's August 2, 2004, *Albuquerque Journal's* "Forensic Expert on Billy's Case" gave this new hoaxed finding: "Lee, assisted by Calvin Ostler ... performed tests on the bench that Sederwall believes to be the one on which the Kid's body was laid out after Garrett gunned him down. Preliminary results indicated **trace evidence of blood**, but, without further testing, it is not certain whether the blood was human, Lee said."

In fact, it was not even certain that it was blood! Since I too had seen the bench; it just looked like a few rust-colored discolorations - like expected on a carpenter's bench.

By August 12th, reporter Doris Cherry, for her *Lincoln County News*, "Forensics 101 for 'Billy,' " wrote: "Dr. Lee proved the good odds by utilizing a laser to bore into the wood of the bench to take samples and he took scrapings from the top and underneath of the bench. **'Then he swabbed it with the chemical that changes color to indicate the presence of blood,' Sullivan said.**"

The hoaxers were just hoaxing. Lee, as stated in his report, which I got after years of open records litigation against the record-hiding lawmen, was merely using Luminol, a non-specific chemical that fluoresces with iron-containing substances. Besides blood, it lights up for rust, paints, and cleaning agents - all more likely on a carpenter's bench than blood. **And no other testing would *ever* be done** by that hoaxing group to verify blood - or to connect it to Billy Bonney (which was impossible).

Next the hoaxers got carried away. Romo's original **"trace,"** in his August 2, 2004, "Forensic Expert on Billy's Case," started bleeding like stigmata. In Doris Cherry's "Forensics 101 for Billy," **Sullivan stated that Lee "found a lot of blood."** For Julie Carter's "Follow the Blood," **Sederwall said: "We witnessed a large amount of blood;" and he creatively lied that it proved "an upper chest wound."** By April 13, 2006, "blood" was almost dripping off the bench. Leo Banks of the *Tucson Weekly*, in "The New Billy the Kid," reported that **Sederwall said the bench was "saturated!"**

Obviously the hoaxers hid Lee's actual report. But after five years of open records litigation against the lawmen, on January 31, 2012, I got it. At 25 pages, it was dated February 25, 2005, and titled "Forensic Research & Training Center Forensic Examination Report." **[APPENDIX: 8]** Its header listed "Requested by: Lincoln County Sheriff's Office, New Mexico; Investigation History Program, Kurtis Production." "Local Case No." was "2003-274." The "Report To:" was Steve Sederwall, Lincoln County Sheriff's Office, New Mexico." Recorded for the "forensic investigation team" were: "Calvin Ostler, Forensic Consultant, Riverton, Utah;" "Tom Sullivan, Sheriff, Lincoln County, New Mexico;" "Steve Sederwall, Deputy Sheriff, Lincoln County;" and "David Turk, US Marshall [sic], United States Marshall [sic] Service." The carpenter's bench was reported under "Item # 1 Workbench." Lee concluded:

After a detail examination of the evidence and review of all the results of field testing, the following conclusion was reached.

1. Brownish dark stains were observed on different areas of the workbench. These areas were subjected to chemical presumptive blood tests. Some of those samples give a positive reaction. These results indicate the presence of Heme or Peroxidase like activity with those stains testing positive, **which suggest that those stains could be bloodstains**. Further DNA testing could reveal the nature and identity of these blood-like stains.

Lee had proved himself a true "Billy the Kid Case" hoaxer by omitting more likely rust. And his lab, Orchid Cellmark, does not test for blood. And finding DNA would not even connect it to those stains, since no controls were done for DNA from non-stained areas. Nor were controls taken from all people present at his testing to check for *their* contaminating DNA (think sneeze!). Lastly, Lee was lying that "[f]urther DNA testing could reveal the nature and identity of these blood-like stains." There was no reference DNA of Billy the Kid, or of any kin, to compare with any DNA found - the only way of claiming "bench DNA' as Billy's.

## *"BLOOD OF BILLY THE KID" GETS A DNA LAB*

Next, Dr. Henry Lee had to turn his fake "blood of Billy the Kid" into the fake "DNA of Billy the Kid." So he sent his bench swabbing and scraping specimens to Orchid Cellmark Lab.

Reporter, Doris Cherry, in her August 12, 2004, "Forensics 101 for 'Billy' " stated: "Each swab and all scrapings from the bench were sealed in preparation to shipping to the Orchard Selmark [sic - Orchid Cellmark] Lab in Dallas. Sullivan said Dr. Lee uses the lab for most of his work, and the lab is also famous for its forensic work to determine DNA of the 9-11 victims."

Kept secret was that Orchid Cellmark does not test for blood; that objects in a human environment pick up human DNA; that no controls were done; and, of course, no reference DNA existed. Soon, the rightfully nervous, out-of-control hoaxers called the lab's name "secret."

In fact, Orchid Cellmark had "secrets." On August 9, 2004, I had contacted its then director, Mark Stolorow, explaining the "Billy the Kid Case" hoax. He was amused. On August 18th, we spoke again. Stolorow was defensive. Orchid Cellmark, he told me, was under a "gag order" on the case. Dr. Lee was now in charge!

Three months later, Orchid Cellmark was caught faking DNA computer data on another case. That scandal appeared on November 18, 2004, in "TalkLeft.com," as "Fraud alleged at Cellmark, DNA Testing Firm." It stated: "This is shocking to the forensic community which has always believed that raw data cannot be electronically manipulated." It concluded: "Bottom line: A lot of defendants will be seeking retesting by an independent lab when the prosecution is relying on results by Cellmark." That scandal reduced Orchid Cellmark to one lab in Farmers Branch, Texas.

Mark Stolorow was replaced as Orchid Cellmark's director by Dr. Rick Staub. Unlike Stolorow, he seemed indifferent to scandal. And, as will be seen, his lab found no DNA at all in Henry Lee's bench specimens! **But that did not stop the hoaxers from claiming they had the DNA of Billy the Kid for identity matching, and doing exhumations based on it!** And Dr. Lee, in charge of the forensics, never objected. And Dr. Rick Staub was right there in Arizona with his bone bags, along the backhoe, to take dismembered body-parts back across state lines to Texas. After all, Bill Kurtis Productions was filming another TV program; and he would be featured along with famous Dr. Lee!

## LEE ATTACKS GARRETT, A WASHSTAND, AND A HEADBOARD

Dr. Henry Lee knew he was in an alleged investigation against bad guy murderer, Pat Garrett. So he did his best to make Garrett look bad by fake "forensics." Lack of a crime scene to investigate - with the Maxwell house torn down in about 1887 - left the hoaxers with only young Stella Abreu's "museum" furniture.

The lawmen's "Probable Cause Statement" had introduced a "washstand" from her collection to fabricate that Garrett lied that his second shot hit Maxwell's headboard. In his 1933 *The Death of Billy the Kid*, Poe had reported that: "[A] shot was fired in the room, followed immediately by what everyone within hearing distance thought were two other shots. However, there were only two shots fired, the third report, as we learned afterward, being caused by the rebound of the second bullet, which had struck the adobe wall and **rebounded against the headboard of a wooden bedstead**."

So, by fake "what-if" reasoning, the lawmen claimed that *if* Garrett lied about hitting the washstand, he lied about the corpse's identity!

About the washstand, they gave their fake "Probable Cause Statement" Deluvina Maxwell quote: *"There was a washstand with a marble top in Pete Maxwell's bedroom, which Garrett had seen in the moonlight and shot at, thinking it was Bonney trying to get up."* **[This hid that it was made-up quote by Lucien Maxwell's "grandchildren," in uncited source. (See page 341 above) And hidden is her confirming victim Billy on June 24, 1927 to historian J. Evetts Haley: "I came here about [1869] and was here when Billy the Kid was killed ... I did not see Billy the night after he was killed, but I saw him the following morning."]**

But all that was important was having it. As the "Probable Cause Statement" said: "On September 13, 2003, investigators located all the furniture that was in Pete Maxwell's bedroom the night of the shooting, July 1881. **In the items investigators located on September 13, 2003 was that wash stand.**"

This supposed "washstand" was a little wooden box, the size of a toy! **[FIGURE: 2]** Its measurements by Lee were: 28¾" x 16", x 30" high. It had no marble top. But it had the claimed bullet holes. So, with Dr. Lee on board, and willing to claim anything he was told, they recycled their washstand-headboard scam as a "forensic investigation" to incriminate Garrett as a liar.

Lee fabricated a crime scene for them - based on no existing room, no authenticated furniture, disregard of the historical record, and the toy's tiny height. Hoax-helping reporter, Rene Romo, presented Lee's "washstand" fakery in his August 2, 2004 *Albuquerque Journal*'s "Forensic Expert on Billy's Case." stating:

> Lee and the investigators [Sullivan, Sederwall, and Calvin Ostler] also examined a washstand that was purportedly struck by a bullet when Garrett shot the Kid in a bedroom of the outlaw's friend, Pete Maxwell, in Fort Sumner ... Lee and the investigators used laser technology Saturday to determine the trajectory of the bullet as it entered the left side of the washstand and exited the right at a downward angle. Given the washstand's likely location in the room, the investigation has already cast some doubt on Garrett's account of the fatal shooting, Sederwall and [Calvin] Ostler said.
>
> 'The evidence we are seeing does not corroborate the popular legend,' Ostler said. 'Something's askew' ...
>
> **One simple explanation that Lee offered is that Garrett may have shot defensively at the Kid as he fled and struck the washstand from the side instead of head on. Garrett's official story may have omitted that embarrassing detail. "You don't want to paint yourself as a chicken," Lee suggested.**

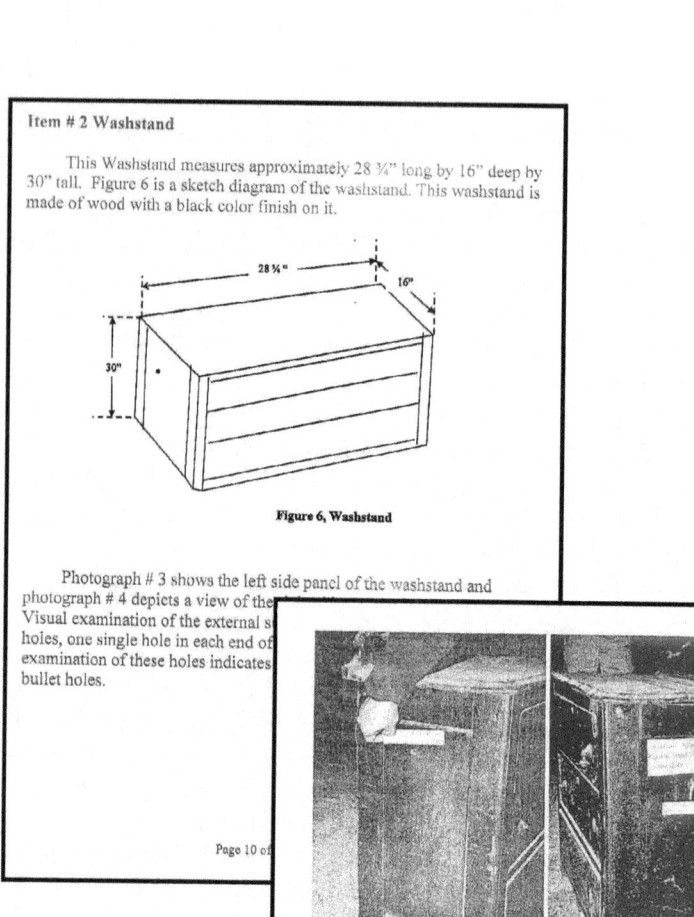

FIGURE: 2. "Washstand" from Stella Abreu's Fort Sumner Billy the Kid Museum, 1926-1936

There was also no bullet for dating, no provable relationship of the washstand to Garrett or to Billy or to Peter Maxwell or to the shooting. And Lee fabricated his groveling Garrett from the little box being toy-sixed. In his February 25, 2005 report titled "Forensic Research & Training Center Forensic Examination Report" under "Item # 2 Washstand," he fabricated: "The angles produced in the examination tell us two things: First, the bullet was fired from no more than 41" from the floor given the reported limitations of the room. The room was reported to be 20' by 20'; the maximum distance is assumed to be 20'. If the firearm was a maximum of 41" off the floor it is unlikely that the shooter was standing. It is more likely the shooter was kneeling, squatting, or close to the floor. Second, the horizontal angle is such that if the Washstand was positioned so that the back was against the wall, the shot could not have been fired from more than approximately 40 inches from the Washstand, because the wall would have been in the way. The angle of trajectory intersects the back plane of the Washstand at approximately 45 3/16", and no more than 46". Lee's conclusion reflected his well-known caution about putting his lies in writing: "Two bullet holes were located on the side panels of the Washstand. The hole on the left side panel is consistent with a bullet entrance hole while the hole on the right side panel is consistent with a bullet exit hole. However, it is not possible to determine when those bullet holes were produced at this time."

The lawmen also gave Dr. Lee Stella's museum's headboard to "investigate." Important for their fake argument of Garrett as a liar, was claiming it had no bullet hole as claimed by him and Poe. So that is what Lee gave them.

Lee's February 25, 2004 report titled "Forensic Research & Training Center Forensic Examination Report" - which I got during the open records litigation against the hoaxing lawmen - under its topic, **"Item # 2 Headboard:"** stated: **"No bullet hole and no observable damage, no sign of bullet ricocheted type of defects were found on the Headboard. No blood or biological materials were observed on the Headboard."**

What Lee left out, is that Stella's "headboard" is just a rim around a huge hole. **[Figure: 3]** There was no headboard to have the hole! So Lee and Calvin Ostler had lied to Rene Romo for his August 2, 2004 *Albuquerque Journal*'s "Forensic Expert on Billy's Case" by stating: "The evidence we are seeing does not corroborate the popular legend."

FIGURE: 3. Headboard without its center from Stella Abreu's Fort Sumner Billy the Kid Museum, 1926-1936 (Courtesy of Kenny Miller)

Deputy Steve Sederwall was soon spouting Dr. Lee's Garrett-is-a-liar fable in Julie Carter's October 2005, "Follow the Blood": "Using high-tech lasers and other modern crime scene methods, investigators learned that the shooting of the Kid in Pete Maxwell's bedroom was not in the way history has portrayed it. Tests indicate that Garrett fired his second shot from the doorway while on his knees and with his left hand on the floor, firing back over his shoulder ... Being blinded by his first shot, it appears he was in a great hurry to get out of the room and fell to the floor.' He [Sederwall] added: 'To find the furniture from Maxwell's bedroom was great. But to have Dr. Lee recover usable evidence was truly a historical find.' "

This Lee washstand and headboard "investigation" alone demonstrates why, in 2006, I filed a complaint against him with the American Academy of Forensic Sciences Ethics Committee for perpetrating a forensic hoax; and why they dishonestly covered-up for him as their media star.

## FAKE FORENSICS FALLOUT OF WASHSTAND

A footnote to this washstand fakery came 12 years later. In an article in the September, 2016 *Wild West History Association* magazine, a James and Margaret Bailey wrote "Billy the Kid Death Scene: Reviewing Ballistic Evidence," innocently thanking, among others, "Billy the Kid Case" hoaxer, Paul Hutton, who, in 2007 (along with the carpenter's bench he falsely labeled with "human blood"), had put Lee's washstand in his Albuquerque Museum of Art and History Billy the Kid show.

The Bailys sole knowledge was that, in 2004, Bill Kurtis Productions, interested in Stella Abreu's collection, used "internationally respected forensic scientist, Dr. Henry C. Lee, and two of his associates, Calvin D. Ostler ... and Kim Ostler ... to conduct forensic tests on the washstand" to investigate the shooting scene. (Bailys, Page 33) So the Bailys thought the washstand was an actual part of the shooting scene.

Consequently, they did a "forensic investigation" around the washstand, unaware that its holes were make at an unknown time on a unproven box. And it made them add a third shot, by denying Poe's claim of a rebound at the headboard. (Bailys, Page 41) Worse, they backed three shots by lying: "Pete Maxwell reported during the inquest Billy also fired." (Page 40) In fact, Maxwell stated: "*William Bonney came in and got close to my bed with a gun in his hand and asked me "who is it" and then Pat F. Garrett **fired two shots at the said William Bonney and the*** *said William Bonney fell near my fire place."* So they concealed that the witness in the room reported only two shots!

Using their faked three shots, the Bailys made-up their own washstand tale. They denied Pat Garrett's conclusion that a spent shell in Billy's pistol was not recently shot (Bailys, Page 49) by claiming he did not mention if the gun was hot; omitting that he was an experienced buffalo hunter and knew what to look for. Furthermore, he had no motive to hide a shot by Billy. As he stated in *The Authentic Life of Billy the Kid*, Billy's not having fired made him feel guilty, as if Billy nobly chose not to kill him.

So with no authenticated room, and the toy-height washstand, they make-up trajectories and decide that Garrett mistook the washstand for Billy and shot at it! (Page 42) **And they made-up that it was Billy who fired first and hit the headboard first to kill "the stranger."** (Page 43) This omitted that Billy did not know it was an ambush, trusted safety of the Maxwell house, merely asked Peter Maxwell, "Quien es?" and was immediately shot by Garrett.

So trusting Henry Lee's faked inclusion of a shot washstand, the misled Bailys had Billy insanely shoot at a possible visitor right after asking "Quien es?" and almost kill Maxwell by hitting his headboard before being shot dead by Garrett. Then Garrett fired the third shot thinking a tiny box was Billy. This is a good example of the rotten fruits of the rotten hoax.

## *LEE'S DEPUTY KILLING "INVESTIGATION"*

Next on Dr. Henry Lee's agenda for the hoaxers (and presumably for future TV viewing) was Billy Bonney's April 28, 1881 jailbreak killing of Deputy James Bell: the "Billy the Kid Case" hoax's sub-investigation in its "Probable Cause Statement" to defame Garrett; here presented as his being a liar.

As may be recalled, that sub-investigation was preposterous fabrication of Garrett's motive for killing the innocent victim. Its fake "what-if" reasoning went: *if* Garrett gave Billy the escape gun, then he was Billy's friend, and would later kill to save him in Fort Sumner. Since there existed no Garrett friendship, no giving of the gun, and no known weapon, Lee's job was to manufacture "suspicion" about the jailbreak, in the hope that it cast "suspicion" on Garrett himself. So Lee used Garrett's report from Gottfried Gauss that Billy shot Bell as the man escaped down the stairway; and that he found Bell dying, and dragged him out the back door.

For their fakery, the lawmen took Lee to the old Lincoln courthouse on August 1, 2004. Lee tested for "blood" on upstairs floorboards and a wall. Of course, he found "blood."

Lee's original report of February 25, 2005, titled "Forensic Research & Training Center Forensic Examination Report" **[APPENDIX: 8]**, had this "investigation" under "Examination of Lincoln County Court House." Listed as present were "Calvin Ostler, Forensic Consultant, Riverton, Utah;" "Tom Sullivan, Sheriff, Lincoln County, New Mexico;" "Steve Sederwall, Deputy Sheriff, Lincoln County;" and "David Turk, US Marshall [sic], United States Marshall [sic] Service;" and Bill Kurtis of Bill Kurtis Productions - presumably getting his TV footage.

The staircase is called "repainted," when it was actually *replaced* in the 1980's. Lee gave a photo of the "target area" showing brown drips on the wall under the stairway. Not only do they look like rusted water from a broken pipe or leaking roof, but the upstairs hall has nothing to do with the historical shooting.

To test those stains, Lee used O-tolidine: like Luminol, a non-specific chemical test for iron-containing compounds - like rust or blood. So cagy Lee calls the drips *"blood-like* stains;" and states they merit "presumptive blood tests." So, in his report's "Conclusions," he stated: "[T]hose stains could be bloodstains." Omitted is that for the amount of dripping, a massacre was needed on the second floor, not one man bleeding; and that from 1881 to 2004, the mess would have been cleaned up.

And, as an expert, Lee should obviously have asked if there were Bell remains or Bell kin for "reference DNA" to establish if "blood" was Bell's. The answer is: no remains and no kin. Nevertheless, hoaxing Lee, indifferent to real forensics, concluded: "Various stains were observed on the surface and underside of the floorboards. **Chemical tests for the presence of blood were positive with some of these stains. These results indicate presence of Heme or Peroxidase like activity with those stains tested positive, which suggests that those stains could be bloodstains. Further DNA testing could reveal the nature and identity of those blood-like stains**."

The day after Lee's fake "investigation," on August 2, 2004, in the *Albuquerque Journal's* "Forensic Expert on Billy's Case," the hoaxers' mouthpiece, Rene Romo, reported the find of Deputy Bell's "blood!" And Lee had reconstructed a "crime scene" of Bell's killing - though neither blood nor a link to Bell existed! Romo wrote: "Lee and the investigators Sunday afternoon also found several positive indications of blood residue below floor-boards at the top of a stairwell in the old Lincoln County courthouse. Such evidence could support Sederwall's theory that **the Kid fatally shot deputy J.W. Bell there, at the top of the stairs,** in his infamous escape from the Lincoln County jail. **That version would also contradict Garrett's account that the Kid, at the top of the stairs, shot Bell who was at the bottom of the stairwell."**

*Lincoln County News* reporter Doris Cherry followed suit with her August 12, 2004 "Forensics 101 for 'Billy' ": **"Sullivan said that after studying the courthouse and the shooting he contended Bell was really killed at the top of the stairs, not near the bottom of the stairs as legend has it."** Cherry did note Sheriff Sullivan's admitting that, lacking any Bell kin, DNA testing could not confirm "blood" as his.

But the hoaxers claimed that Bell was shot on *the top, versus middle, of the stairway,* based on no blood, no stairway from the period, and no connection to Bell!

On March 13, 2010, erstwhile Deputy, Steve Sederwall, appeared in a National Geographic International TV program, produced by British Parthenon Entertainment for the Discovery ID channel, to give this top-of-stairs scam to call Garrett a liar, therefore a likely murderer of an innocent victim!

## *HIDING LEE'S RECORDS AND LAB RESULTS*

The lack of any DNA for continuing their hoax, did not faze the hoaxers. What they wanted was lack of Dr. Lee's DNA records availability to expose their hoaxing! So they hid his Orchid Cellmark DNA extraction results, while fabricating DNA claims.

And no one worked harder to hide the records than hoaxing Henry Lee himself. On March 27, 2006, I had written, for my journalist proxy, Jay Miller, a request about Lee's DNA testing for Case No. 2003-274. On May 1, 2006, Lee answered on official stationery of State of Connecticut Department of Public Safety, Division of Scientific Services, under his title "Chief Emeritus." He used cagey semantics, for which he was famous, to shift responsibility to the Lincoln County Sheriff's Department for a hide-the-ball game. So he confirmed that he had written a single report of his investigations, but it was in the possession of Case 2003-274's lawmen. So it should be obtained from them! Of course, they refused to turn over any report. Lee wrote: **"I completed my examination of the evidence and submitted my report to the Lincoln County Sheriff's Department."**

Lee's letter stated:

Dear Mr. Miller:

In response to your letter dated March 27, 2006 regarding Forensic Consultation in the New Mexico Billy the Kid Case. To set the record straight, **the Lincoln County Sheriff's Department contacted me**. They requested a forensic expert to perform preliminary identification and scene reconstruction. This was a pro bono forensic consultation case. **[AUTHOR'S NOTE: Bill Kurtis Productions was paying him, and anticipated a documentary with him in it.]** We examined a wooden bench, and floorboards at the courthouse.

I completed my examination of the evidence and submitted my report to the Lincoln County Sheriff's Department. If you want a copy of the report, you should contact the Lincoln County Sheriff's Department directly.

Since **I did not conduct any DNA testing on the evidence** and the Lincoln County Sheriff's Department sent samples directly to a private laboratory for analysis **[AUTHOR'S NOTE: Lee is concealing Orchid Cellmark Lab]**, I am sorry but I do not have answers to your questions regarding DNA.

Sincerely,
Dr. Henry Lee

Lee was unaware that past Orchid Cellmark Lab Director Mark Stolorow had told me their case was under Lee, and that Lee had put the results under gag order! There was no wonder that the hoaxers hid the records. They exposed their faked claims, but would ultimately reveal the criminality of their exhumations.

## *LEE'S SECRET DNA RESULTS AND HOAXER LIES*

Ultimately, by open records litigation and subpoena of Orchid Cellmark Lab, on April 20, 2012, I got the 133 pages of Lee's DNA records. They laid bare the audacity and criminality of the "Billy the Kid Case's" hoaxers. October 15, 2004's "Laboratory Report, Forensic Identity, Mitochondrial Analysis, Results and Conclusions" for its Case 4444-001B-004B (for Case 2003-274) for the carpenter's bench **SHOWED LEE'S SPECIMENS HAVING NO DNA! THE HOAXER'S CLAIM TO HAVE BENCH-BLOOD-DNA OF BILLY THE KID FOR DNA MATCHINGS WAS A LIE!** And they knew it by October 15, 2004. There was no justification to dig up anyone at all in their "investigation!"

And Lee's Deputy Bell shooting courthouse investigation - already fake since there was no Bell reference DNA to compare with any other DNA - likewise yielded **no valid DNA from Lee's floorboard specimens**, as reported in that October 15, 2004 "Laboratory Report, Forensic Identity, Mitochondrial Analysis, Results and Conclusions." One specimen yielded no DNA, and his second specimen showed a useless **"mixture of two or more mitochondrial profiles. Consequently no sequence data are reported."** The conclusion was: "[P]rofiles are therefore inconclusive." **And even if there had been valid floorboard DNA, there was no Bell DNA with which to compare it.**

Before these results were known to me, for years the lawmen hoaxers would lie that it was the *carpenter's bench* that had "DNA," which came from two individuals (taken to mean Billy and the unidentified victim, like Billy Barlow). Erstwhile Deputy, Steve Sederwall, eventually testified in my open records litigation on January 21, 2011 and February 4, 2013, that they had needed "$50,0000" to separate mixed DNA, so had not proceeded! Even that was a lie.

In fact, DNA expert and President of San Francisco's Lexigen, Dr. Simon Ford stated: "Mixed DNA results are very common in forensic casework," and the meaning of "two or more ... profiles," **merely means "at least two;" not that there are two**. And the only way to sort out a mixed specimen to use reference DNA of all possible individuals in the sample. (But Bell's DNA was not available.) And if the DNA had degraded, no separate individuals could be identified in the mix anyway. Dr, Ford added: "[B]ased on DNA technology alone, there is no way of knowing from which kind of cell a particular DNA profile originated **[meaning DNA results cannot prove a blood source]**.

As to the $50,000 claimed by Sederwall, Dr. Ford stated: "Most labs charge about $1,000 for testing an evidence sample or reference sample. Some labs have a surcharge of between $300 and $500 for "difficult" samples, such as bone or tissue. The interpretation (matching and statistical calculation) is usually included in the cost of the testing."

## *BIG PICTURE FOR LEE'S FAKED FORENSICS*

Even if the hoaxers had gotten DNA from Lee's specimens, they had no reference DNA of Billy or Bell to claim it as theirs. But the lie that they had Billy the Kid's carpenter's bench "DNA" would become the basis for digging up John Miller (with added William Hudspeth), and for trying to dig up "Brushy Bill."

# HOAX ENABLER: LINCOLN COUNTY ATTORNEY ALAN MOREL

As the Billy the Kid Case hoax progressed, Lincoln County Attorney Alan Morel - nicknamed by locals "the little weasel" - covered up the hoaxing lawmen. From 2004, he wrote fake open records responses claiming they had no DNA records, mislead his County Commissioners about the liability, and finally participated in years of stonewalling to hide records in my litigation.

Morel was a thug like Sullivan, Sederwall, and Virden; threatening journalist Jay Miller with an harassment case for requesting records from Sheriff Tom Sullivan. And by October of 2006, he tried to intimidate me in his response for Sheriff Rick Virden, by allowing Virden to report me as a terrorist via the U.S. Marshals Service; being unaware that I knew it was likely a bluff using fellow hoaxer, David Turk. By 2013, about the huge, open records litigation bill, Morel allegedly told his County Commissioners, "It's not our worry. It comes from taxpayers."

## *STOPPED BY COMMISSIONER LEO MARTINEZ*

In 2004, Alan Morel's shielding was confronted by Lincoln County Commissioners Chairman Leo Martinez, who had learned the hoax's implications from me. On September 21, 2004, in his County Commissioners' meeting, with thuggish Sheriff Sullivan and Deputy Sederwall shouting obscenities, Martinez asked his County Commissioners to stop Sheriff Sullivan's pursuit of the Billy the Kid Case, which he said was not a "real law enforcement matter." He implied that Morel had burdened the County with incurred liability from the case.

Commissioner Martinez cited Sullivan's lack of authorization by the County Commissioners to do the case; his improper use of departmental resources and sheriff's time; and his denying records requests based on "secret private donors" constituted buying a murder case, meaning vigilante law! He demanded that Sullivan stop the case or resign.

The next day, September 22, 2004, a huge, *Ruidoso News* front page headline was: "Showdown in the County Seat: shouting match erupts at County Commissioners meeting over investigation of Billy the Kid." Reporter, Dianne Stallings, described boorish and racist Sullivan: Shouting and pounding the podium, Lincoln County Sheriff Tom Sullivan attempted unsuccessfully Tuesday to drown out questions from County Commissioner Leo Martinez over his publicity-generating investigation of two 123-year old murders ... **Sullivan [said], "I don't tell you how to make burritos. Don't tell me how to run the sheriff's department.** This is nothing but a personal attack."

The next day, September 23rd, the *Lincoln County News* weighed in with Doris Cherry's "Lincoln County War heats up over 'Billy: Capitan Mayor Tracks His Kind of ' ------- ' To County Commission Meeting. Tells Jay Miller where to go; wonders why Commissioner has his panties in a wad." Sullivan attacked journalist Jay Miller, who was doing the open records investigation on them to protect my anonymity. So Sullivan was quoted as saying that Leo Martinez's questioning "smells of Jay Miller ... a sleaze-bag reporter from Santa Fe." And heated-up Sederwall revealed their plot to hide their incriminating records. Doris Cherry quoted him: " **'The sheriff has no documentation," the mayor [Sederwall] said. "I have them."** He then went on to say that he will not release the documents, not as mayor or as a commissioned reserve deputy. 'He (Miller) can go to hell because I will not turn the (documents) over because once they are turned over they become public documents.' " And Sullivan and Sederwall lied franticly: denying use of public money or even their law enforcement roles.

But reporter Diane Stallings, in her September 22, 2004 *Ruidoso News* "Showdown in the County Seat" revealed the County Commissioners' own notorious corruption, which kept a crook like Alan Morel as their County Attorney. Stallings wrote: "When he [Martinez] called for a motion to sever any association, no other Commissioners responded." With Morel present, they had shielded the obscene hoaxers and continued the hoax.

Nevertheless, Martinez got results. Tom Sullivan had just one option. Sheriff Gary Graves faced recall. If that happened to him, he would get no retirement benefits. So just three days before Judge Ted Hartley's Hearing in Fort Sumner, on September 24, 2004, the "law enforcement petitioners" - Graves, Sullivan, and Sederwall - filed in his De Baca County Court, through their attorney, Mark Acuña, to withdraw *with* prejudice their Billy the Kid exhumation case! "With prejudice" meant they could *never* meet Judge Henry Quintero's stipulation of getting DNA from the Billy the Kid grave in order to exhume Catherine Antrim.

So Alan Morel's crookedness accidentally ended the exhumations of Billy the Kid and his mother.

# CHAPTER 3
# ILLEGAL EXHUMATIONS OF JOHN MILLER AND WILLIAM HUDSPETH

## DESCENT INTO CRIMINALITY

Bill Richardson did not back down on his plot to pardon "Brushy" Bill;" even though my push-back had been unexpected. Nor were his Case 2003-274 lawmen deterred by having no DNA of Billy the Kid for identity comparisons. He backed them, as did Bill Kurtis, with his production company; and Dr. Henry Lee, with his Orchid Cellmark Lab. By this point, they just wanted to film any exhumation to keep the case going. A vulnerable grave was in the state-controlled Prescott, Arizona, Pioneers' Home Cemetery, under corrupt Governor Janet Naploitano, willing to back Richardson's publicity stunt. So, in 2005, the hoaxers descended to desecration of graves and graverobbing, confident of protection from on high, and of the next TV "documentary" in their series. So Billy the Kid imposter, John Miller's, repose was about to end, with a horrific twist of an added corpse.

## SHERIFF RICK VIRDEN LEADS THE EXHUMATIONS

After Lincoln County Sheriff Tom Sullivan's term ended in 2004, his Undersheriff, Rick Virden, a "Billy the Kid Case" peripheral participant, was elected Sheriff. He immediately deputized Sullivan and Sederwall to continue Case No. 2003-274.

With over 30 years in State Police, as Sheriff in Otero County, and Undersheriff in Lincoln County, Rick Virden took corruption in stride. He was also a rumored unpunished thief - of railroad ties: the worst kept crime secret in Lincoln County. And as

Sheriff, he had solved no real cold case murders - like the "Cotton" and Judy McKnight killings (some locals even implicated him). But it is no rumor that he was the lawman directly responsible for the illegal exhumations in the "Billy the Kid Case."

During my open records investigation of him, Virden wrote on his official departmental letterhead, on November 28, 2005, to my journalist proxy, Jay Miller: "We are interested in the truth surrounding Billy the Kid." Virden stated:

Dear Mr. Miller,

We are interested in the truth surrounding Billy the Kid and are continuing the investigation, utilizing volunteers that have investigative experience **and at no cost to Lincoln County.**

**[AUTHOR'S NOTE: With my investigation, the hoaxers started claiming no taxpayer cost. In fact, they used the governor's office, sheriff's departments, district courts, and almost a million dollars to pay my lawyers and theirs for my open records litigation in which I won.]**

**Tom Sullivan and Steve Sederwall are Deputies with the Lincoln County Sheriff's Department.**

Tom Sullivan and Steve Sederwall belong to the Reserve Deputy Unit.

Tom Sullivan and Steve Sederwall **are assigned to investigate the shootings of William H. Bonney and Deputies Bell and Olinger.**

As you acknowledge in your letter, there is an ongoing investigation being conducted. When the investigating officers conclude their investigation, I will gladly avail to you all of the information you request in case # 2003-274.

**[AUTHOR'S NOTE: The hoaxers hid Dr. Henry Lee's DNA report by claiming immunity of an ongoing real murder investigation.]**

R.E. Virden
Lincoln County Sheriff

From the 2003 start of their "Billy the Kid Case," the hoaxers had John Miller half-heartedly in their sights, as was seen in their already-cited "Seventy-Seven Days of Doubt" initial draft of a "Probable Cause Statement" for their Lincoln County Sheriff's Department Case No. 2003-274. There, Miller's brief presence was for "survival suspicion," and as a foil for "Brushy Bill."

By 2005, with their faltering hoax, "Johnny" Miller looked much better to the hoaxers. They hid his 10 years too old death certificate proof from the Arizona Pioneers' Home Cemetery, which author, Jim Johnson, also published in his 2006 book, *Billy the Kid: His real Name Was* ... It gave Miller's birth as in Fort Sill, Texas in December, 1850 and death at 87 on November 7, 1937 at 6:30 PM. The cause of death was a "fracture of the neck of the right femur and bronchopneumonia." (Johnson, Page 7) **[Remember that broken hip. It would become key in the hoax.]**

The hoaxers also hid that Miller had no playing-dead-on-the-carpenter's-bench scene - and even denied being present on July 14, 1881, for his fabricated Garrett-killing-an-Indian tale. Nonetheless, scorning their audience as idiots, the hoaxers waved their flag of bleeding-playing-dead-Billy-on-the-bench-DNA from famous forensic expert Dr. Henry Lee - though it was non-existent for matching with anyone. So there was no basis, by history or by DNA, to justify his exhumation. So the hoaxers hid that too, but proceeded with great secrecy.

## FAKING JOHN MILLER BELIEVERS: FELLOW HOAXERS, DALE TUNNELL AND TOM SULLIVAN

A hoaxer problem with John Miller was that he had no believers. So fellow hoaxer, Dale Tunnell, became his fan, via Helen Airy's 1993 *Whatever Happened to Billy the Kid?*

A March 13, 2006 Internet article about Tunnell, on helenair.com, by a Robert Struckman, was "Bitterroot man hopes to uncover the truth about Billy the Kid." A major hoax document, it was another hoax rewrite apparently in response to my open records requests to the lawmen hoaxers as public officials. Now they claimed they were "amateur historians" with private records, immune to the open records act. For John Miller, their exhumation "permission" had been shaky; and their "forensic data" fake. So, for Struckman, Tunnell became an "amateur historian" too. Struckman wrote: "[Tunnell] would like to confirm the story put forth by Airy. **Like him, she was an amateur historian who bucked the official story.** Academics scoffed at her account. 'I'd like to prove her correct,' he said."

Also calling himself a "forensic criminologist," Tunnell tried to upgrade imposter, John Miller. Struckman recorded:

> Tunnell's interest in the famous outlaw was piqued when he read a 1993 book by Helen Airy entitled, "Whatever Happened to Billy the Kid" ...
>
> "Even if it [DNA matching] comes back positive, there will be more work to do," Tunnell said. He hopes to find conclusive documentation placing Miller at or near Fort Sumner in July of 1881 or connecting his wife, Isadora, to a relationship there ...
>
> Tunnell has found enough material to poke holes in the official histories, he said ...
>
> "I want to set the record straight. If Billy the Kid , from 1881 to 1937, lived the life of an honest man, a hardworking fool, then I say he paid his debt to society," Tunnell said.

A credibility gap remained. Hiding their Garrett murder case, made exhumation seem like just a favor to Miller: setting *his* record straight! Reminiscent of hapless hoaxer, fired De Baca County Sheriff Gary Graves, Dale Tunnell became confused by the tangled fakery. So he made an unintentionally funny comment to Struckman: ""It's possible," Tunnell said, "that Garrett conspired with Billy to fake the death. Maybe **Billy never laid, wounded, on the carpenter's bench**. Maybe another body was buried in Billy's place." Oops, "Doctor" Tunnell! Without Billy on the bench, there goes Lee's blood-DNA-of-Billy-the-Kid." There goes digging up John Miller solely for a DNA match to it!!!

Struckman ended with back-up from hoaxing Deputy Tom Sullivan, who had also just become a John Miller believer:

> After getting permission [no legitimate permit for exhumation for DNA matching was obtained] to exhume Miller's body, DNA samples were taken. The DNA analysis will be done by Dr. Henry Lee, founder of the Forensic Science Program at the University of New Haven and chief emeritus of the Connecticut State Police, Sullivan said.
>
> What if the DNA matches the wooden bench?
>
> "We'll change history. I don't know. Arizona would have the real Billy the Kid," Sullivan said.

And unbeknownst to Dale Tunnell, he was also to be the hoaxers' patsy. When they were first investigated by the Prescott Police Department for digging up John Miller and his adjoining neighbor, then were passed to the Maricopa County District Attorney to pursue charges, Tom Sullivan and Steve Sederwall blamed the exhumation on him!

# TARGETING ARIZONA

Confident of Richardson's shielding if things went wrong, the hoaxers faked legality (and hiding having no DNA for identity matching) by using a perceived loophole in Arizona exhumation law: the **supervisor of a state cemetery** could approve an exhumation *to identify remains*. The simple statutory intent was to ensure correct grave markers - not to investigate a deceased person's delusional claims of being someone else.

As a forensic front, Dale Tunnell, had been on the original "Contact List for Case # 2003-274 as "Criminal Investigator, State of Arizona, Phoenix, Arizona." In a Prescott Police Department report that I got from its Detective Anna Cahall at the start of a criminal investigation into the exhumation, Tunnell was described as Steve Sederwall's 15 year friend. During that post-exhumation period, reporter Robert Struckman's March 13, 2006 "Bitterroot man hopes to uncover the truth about Billy the Kid," quoted him as owning an Arizona company called Forensitec; and being "a Ph.D. in forensic criminology ... pursuing a second doctorate in general psychology ... [a] retired federal investigator ... a deputy sheriff in 1974 in Lincoln County ... [an] investigator with the Arizona Department of Corrections, [and] a federal agent with the U.S. Department of Interior."

Checking Forensitec on the internet, yielded "Forensitec - Forensic Psycholinguistic Patterning," with Tunnell as "President and founder." Instead of a PhD, he is a "a doctoral learner in General Psychology," and the "World's Foremost Authority in Forensic Language Analysis." This apparently meant he read psychology books and identified liars (ironic given his hoax participation, and indication he was no "doctor").

For their "supervisor of a state cemetery," their dupe was Arizona Pioneers' Home Cemetery Director Jeanine Dike, an apparent referral from Governor Napolitano's Office. Sederwall and Tunnell took her on: Tunnell as the forensic expert from Forensitec; Sederwall as the cop. Avoiding the name, "John Miller," they told her they had to dig up "William Bonney!"

That they landed Jeanine Dike hook, line, and sinker is seen by her chummy e-mail of May 3, 2005 to Tunnell - as "Dale" - with "Subject: Disinterment of Wm Bonney." "I am so glad for you that things are coming together for the forensic study on Wm Bonney. I am asking Dale Sams to contact Mountain View Cemetery and make arrangements for the disinterment and reinterment to take place on

May 19, 2005 at 10 AM ... I wish you the best and I hope your anticipated results are correct. It has been a pleasure working with you."

The next day, May 4, 2005, dazzled Dike cleared the way with her employee, Dale Sams, e-mailing him to make arrangements for "disinterment and reinterment." For billing, she provided Tunnell's Forensitec address. (Another later e-mail from the Pioneer Home's next Supervisor, Gary Olsen, to Napolitano's Office, stated that Tom Sullivan had paid the exhumation bills. Two years later, under oath in his deposition in my open records litigation, Sullivan revealed who did pay: Bill Richardson.)

The same May 4, 2005, Dale Sams contacted a George Thompson, at an adjoining cemetery, on their Arizona Pioneers' Home's official letterhead, with "Governor Janet Napolitano" under the Arizona state seal. The subject was "Disinterment." Sams wrote: "George: An excavator wants to disinter William Bonney on May 19 at 10 am at the Pioneers' Home Cemetery ... Please have someone there to dig up Mr. Bonney. **I'm not sure where he's located but this company believes he's there.**"

That was the slipshod start to ravishing the grave of John Miller for no reason in a supposedly state-protected historic cemetery. And none of them questioned why the hoaxers swore them to secrecy, as Gary Olsen, the Director after Dike, reported to Janet Napolitano's office: "Representatives from APH [Arizona Pioneers' Home] were in attendance during the process - some were asked to sign a confidentiality agreement and asked to remain silent by Sullivan and Sederwall."

Everyone complied, as seen in an e-mail sent by Sederwall on July 6, 2005, to Misty Rodarte, the Arizona Pioneers' Home Administrator present at the dig. The subject was "Billy the Kid." With pure hoaxing, Sederwall stated:

> Thanks for calling the other day. It is too funny how these people react to someone looking for the truth. Thanks for not talking to anyone about it that is just what we are doing [sic]. Here is the update: Rick [Staub] from the [Orchid Cellmark] lab called me the other day. They have recovered DNA from the grave to the right as you stand at the foot of the graves. They are working on the grave on the left now. **When they recover DNA from that grave they will compare them both with the work bench we recovered last year.** I will keep you up to speed on it and we will not wait. Tell all the wonderful folks out there we said hello.

# THE SECRET FRENZIED DIG

John Miller's eternal rest had ended on May 19, 2005, when the hoaxers secretly and violently backhoed his grave and coffin, frenetically grabbing bones into the night, and handing them to on-site Orchid Cellmark Lab Director, Dr. Rick Staub, who, with them, was being filmed by Bill Kurtis Productions.

Present with the hoaxers was moonlighting, Maricopa County, forensic anthropologist, Dr. Laura Fulginiti, who had been nervously added to bolster their fellow hoaxer and fake forensic expert, Dale Tunnell. An apparent dreamboat, Fulginiti took their word about "permission," and noticed nothing amiss by their frenzied digging (to maintain secrecy). She even shrugged off plowing into an additional grave, in what would become the hoax's greatest secret. So exhumed, torn apart, and stolen for Rick Staub's bone bags was also random man William Hudspeth. But there was an unforeseen problem with Laura Fulginiti: she was honest, and dutifully recorded everything they did.

Going through the motions of a legitimate investigation (and before they got in trouble for its illegalities and lied that they were not involved in the digging), the lawmen prepared the "Lincoln County Sheriff's Department Supplemental Report for Case No. 2003-274 for the Exhumation of John Miller." I got it from Prescott Police Department Detective Anna Cahall after the exhumation became a matter of criminal investigation. It was a great source list for perpetrators and witnesses.

Signed by Steve Sederwall on Sheriff Rick Virden's official form, it began like this:

## LINCOLN COUNTY SHERIFF'S DEPARTMENT SUPPLEMENTAL REPORT

Case # : 2003-274
Date: Thursday, May 19, 2005
Subject: Exhumation of John Miller
Location: Arizona Pioneers' Cemetery, Prescott, Arizona
Report By: Steven M. Sederwall

On Thursday, May 19, 2005, at approximately 1:00 pm the following met at the Arizona Pioneers' Cemetery at Prescott, Arizona.

**Investigators:**

Steven M. Sederwall, Lincoln County Deputy Sheriff

Following Sederwall, was Tom Sullivan as "Sheriff of Lincoln County, Retired," then Dale Tunnell as an "Arizona State Investigator." In line was "**Dr. Rick Staub, Orchid Cell Mark** [sic]**, DNA**," proving the lab head himself was there for the bones.

The remaining "Investigators" were listed as "Mike Poling, Yavapai County Sheriff's Deputy [a random lawman who happened on the scene to give forensic expert, Laura Fulginiti, specimens from another case, but was slyly added to the list to fake presence of Arizona authority; and was later claimed by the lying hoaxers to be responsible for the exhumation!]; Laura Fulginiti, Forensic Scientist - Anthropologist; Kristen Hartnett, Forensic Scientist - Archeologist; Misty Rodarte, Arizona Pioneers' Administration."

Then came "Others Present." They were Pearl Tenney Romney, Anthony Rodarte, Diana Shenefield, Jesse Shenefield, Russ Hadley, Toby Deherra Jr., Pat Sullivan, Linda Fisher, Billie Martin, Dale Sams, and Clara Enest. All but Pat Sullivan, Tom Sullivan's wife, had Arizona addresses listed.

Lastly, under "Bill Kurtis Productions," were cameramen, Joel Sapatori; and the soundman, Greg Gricus.

And Steve Sederwall posed for the trophy photo taken by his buddy, forger-rapist Lionel Lippman, for hoax-backing reporter, Julie Carter's, October 6, 2005 *RuidosoNews.com* article, "Follow the Blood: In the Billy the Kid Case, Miller Exhumed."

Subsequently, the Case 2003-274 lawmen perpetrators would deny any participation in the exhumation.

## EXPOSED IN THE PRESS

Besides the risk of Dr. Fulginati's honesty, the hoaxers got their first skeptical reporter: the *Tucson Weekly's* Leo W. Banks. In his April 13, 2006 article "The New Billy the Kid?" he noted that the graves were unmarked; so, unsure of Miller's location, they simply guessed. But after digging up one grave, they felt uncertain, and dug up the adjoining one and took its remains too - just to be safe! The secret of William Hudspeth was out. Banks wrote:

> The Miller exhumation began about 1 p.m. on May 19 last year, and didn't end until about 7:30 that night, with investigators examining the last of the remains by flashlight. A backhoe did most of the heavy labor, after which the diggers worked by hand to avoid damaging the coffins or the remains.

But they soon learned that the coffins had already collapsed with age, which had also made the bones extremely fragile. Each piece was carefully photographed, measured and cleaned, then placed on a white sheet on the ground.

Dr. Laura Fulginiti, a well-known forensic anthropologist from Phoenix, supervised the dig. She describes the atmosphere as collegial and charged with excitement as they removed the tobacco-colored bones from the ground.

"At one point, they were holding up the skull and comparing it with pictures of Billy," Fulginiti says. "They recited the story to each other, and when we found something that matched, like the scapula (shoulder) fracture, they were like little kids. They were really invested in this, and that added to the enthusiasm."

But the effort was anything but clear-cut.

In the first place, Miller's grave held no marker or headstone, and neither did the grave closest to his. To determine where Miller's plot should be, the investigators used a map provided by the Pioneers' Home, which pinpointed the location to within 20 square feet.

As Tunnell acknowledges, ground shift and weather patterns can sometimes move bodies underground, and Miller had been 6 feet under almost 70 years. How certain were they of digging in the right place? "Probably upwards of 90 percent," says Tunnell.

## THE HORROR SHOW OF RAVAGED GRAVES

Not until my open records litigation, with subpoena of Orchid Cellmark Lab's records, was the extent of the graves' ravishment made apparent. Its Case No. 4444 (for Case 2003-274) January 26, 2009's "Laboratory Report, Forensic Identity, Mitochondrial Analysis: Evidence Received," confirmed the dismemberment of John Miller in the "South Grave," and William Hudspeth in the "North Grave." Torn from their bodies and arguably destroyed for no reason for Dr. Rick Staub's bone-bags for transport back to Texas were: Miller's "skull and mummified brains," Miller's "pelvis," Miller's "left femur," Hudspeth's "mandible and teeth," and Hudspeth's "right femur." Even part of Miller's shattered casket had been taken. There was not much left in the graves.

And DNA extraction destroys much of the bones to get results. And the hoaxers would have known all along that they had no DNA of Billy the Kid to compare with anything. And they all had to know that one of the two bodies represented straightforward wanton desecration and graverobbing of a random man (since there could not be two John Miller's).

And Bill Kurtis Productions was filming all along. But this time he documented a crime scene. I was told the rumor that he subsequently destroyed or hid his footage.

## THE DNA TRAVESTY

Of course, the Orchid Cellmark records were fiercely hidden by the hoaxers and Dr. Rick Staub. But my open records litigation, with subpoena of Orchid Cellmark Lab's records, gave the results they obtained from their horror show exhumations.

Dr. Rick Staub, hiding that there was no Billy the Kid DNA for matching to justify exhumations, had told Leo Banks, for his April 13, 2006 *Tucson Weekly* article "The New Billy the Kid?" that no DNA had been obtained from the John Miller specimens, and the only DNA came from random man, William Hudspeth. Nevertheless, by 2009, Orchid Cellmark claimed DNA extracted from John Miller's *and* William Hudspeth's femurs; meaning by then there had been a possible fix-up - like Orchid Cellmark's other DNA faking case: its scandal as reported in November 18, 2004's "TalkLeft.com," as "Fraud alleged at Cellmark, DNA Testing Firm," with fraudulent manipulation of data.

The Orchid Cellmark results of DNA testing from the Miller/Hudspeth exhumations were in January 26, 2009's "Laboratory Report - Forensic Identity – Mitochondrial Analysis," using the subsets of its in-house Case 4444 (for its Case No. 2003-274 specimens). Under its Case 4444-011, John Miller's left femur from the South Grave was reported as having "a mitochondrial DNA profile obtained." For pulverized William Hudspeth, Case 4444-012 from his North Grave's mandible and teeth indicated a useless mixed sample: "Consequently no sequence data are reported ... [P]rofiles are therefore inconclusive." However, **Hudspeth's Case 4444-013 North Grave's right femur yielded the "mitochondrial DNA profile obtained,"** originally admitted by Dr. Staub to reporter Leo Banks. Of course, there was no Billy the Kid DNA anyway for determining identity matching (since the carpenter's bench yielded none). So they had nothing.

Nevertheless, to Governor Napolitano, the hoaxers made-up a DNA match for John Miller. It was a double-talk lie, claiming a match of 80%; which has no forensic meaning - a match is 100%, meaning identical. And it was merely submitted to her office; and I got it by open records request. It was not publicized. The hoaxers were hedging their bets, and hoping against convictions.

# THE PAPER TRAIL FOR ILLEGAL EXHUMATIONS

The Arizona gambit created a perfect paper trail for convicting the hoaxers. Wanton desecration of human remains and graverobbing were felonies. And with usual hubris and sense of invulnerability, they had everything in writing.

An Arizona citizen, amateur historian, David Snell, started the ball rolling. Hearing the rumor of intended exhumation at the Arizona Pioneers' Home Cemetry, he kept checking until he observed its unmarked, open field rutted with tracks.

## *A CRIMINAL CASE FOR GRAVEROBBING*

On March 11, 2006 - just two days before Dale Tunnell's glib Miller as Billy article - Snell had filed his complaint about the May 19, 2005 exhumation with the Yavapai County Attorney, Shiela Polk. He had stated:

> I feel it is my duty to report to you that grave robbers are plying their trade in Yavapai County. There individuals' crimes are being committed openly, knowingly, and with contempt for state and county law regarding exhumations. In the course of their nefarious activities, these parties have compromised and ultimately corrupted various officials and public employees. To date, all the parties involved in these crimes have been exempted from any sort of criminal investigation, let alone prosecution ...
>
> Now that these circumstances have been brought to your personal attention, I have every confidence that the good citizens of Yavapai County, and Arizona, can be assured of timely and effective action against these ghoulish scofflaws who loot our people's final resting places for personal gain.

On April 12, 2006, reporter Joanna Dodder in *The Daily Courier* of Prescott, printed "Officials Could Face Charges for Digging Up Alleged Billy the Kid." She quoted David Snell: "This is some kind of good ol' boy back-slappin' beer-drinkin' crusade ... He's [Billy's] buried in Ft. Sumner, where he's always been."

Imperiled, Tom Sullivan and Steve Sederwall ditched their fake, Tunnell-generated, amateur historian identities and the Kid's deputy killing case, and shape-shifted back to Lincoln

County Deputy Sheriffs doing a cold case murder investigation against Pat Garrett. Dodder wrote: "Former Lincoln County Sheriff Tom Sullivan said he and the others plan to compare DNA from Miller's bones with DNA from blood that came from a bench on which Billy the Kid lay after Lincoln County Sheriff Pat Garrett shot him on July 14, 1881, in Ft. Sumner, N.M. ... Sullivan and former Capitan, N.M., mayor Steve Sederwall now are commissioned as Lincoln County deputies, Sullivan said. They are in the midst of a 3-year-old investigation into whether Billy the Kid actually is buried in Ft. Sumner ... Sullivan and his fellow former lawmen are on a mission to find the real Billy using modern-day technology."

Grasping at straws, they even lied that the "Billy the Kid Case" was done *to protect Pat Garrett*! For hoax-backing reporter, Rene Romo's, November 6, 2005, *Albuquerque Journal* article titled "Billy the Kid Probe May Yield New Twist," Romo wrote: "Sederwall acknowledges that what started out as an effort to defend the honor of Garrett against claims that the famous Lincoln County sheriff did not kill the Kid may have taken a new direction."

Joanna Dodder's April 12, 2006's *The Daily Courier's* "Officials Could Face Charges for Digging Up Alleged Billy the Kid" reported the progression to the Prescott City Prosecutor; with the hoaxers' excuse that "permission" came from confused Pioneers' Home Director, Jeanine Dike (omitting that behind her for cover-up were Governors Napolitano and Richardson. Dodder wrote:

> Now Prescott City Prosecutor Glenn Savona is trying to figure out whether someone violated the law and whether the city or state has jurisdiction since the State of Arizona owns the Pioneers' Home Cemetery.
>
> Complicating matters is the fact that the person who apparently gave Sullivan permission to dig up the grave, former Pioneers' Home Superintendent Jeanine Dike, is away on a Mormon mission until June 2007 ...
>
> **Dike apparently agreed to let Sullivan and others dig up Miller's unmarked remains under a relatively new state law that allows the action without a court order and permit if it's for "internal management," according to a Prescott Police Department report.**
>
> "It doesn't look like the request came for an internal issue," Savona said. That law doesn't allow people to take the remains, either, he added ...
>
> The only other way to legally disinter the body is to get a permit from the Yavapai County Community Health Services Department after getting a court order or family permission
>
> Fulginiti and others told police that Tunnell assured them he had permission to conduct the dig.

Cornered, the hoaxers portrayed themselves as martyrs for the truth. Hoax-backing reporter, Julie Carter's, October 6, 2005 "Follow the Blood" *Ruidoso News* article quoted Sederwall: "In the light of the evidence, we see that the history of Billy the Kid will change. **Those with monied interest in history remaining the same will not be happy ... As a cop I know when people fight to keep you from looking at something, they are always trying to hide something. The Lincoln County War is still going on.**"

And, apparently hoping discovery trumped criminality, they desperately pretended that their "investigation" was real. For Rene Romo's November 6, 2006's *Albuquerque Journal's* "Billy the Kid Probe May Yield New Twist," Sederwall was quoted: ""If that Miller] DNA matches the work bench, I think the game is over ... If not," he said, "investigators will try to obtain permission to exhume the remains of Roberts, who is buried in Hamilton, Texas."

**But something impressive was necessary immediately. So the lawmen hoaxers announced that the skeleton of John Miller looked just like Billy the Kid!.** So hoax-backing Romo wrote: "**Sederwall ... said Miller's skeletal remains were intriguing. He said Miller had buck teeth, like the Kid, and an old bullet wound that entered his upper left chest and exited through the scapula.**" And Joanna Dodder, for her April 12, 2006 *The Daily Courier,* quoted Sullivan: "**A shoulder bone from Miller's grave already indicates damage consistent with that of a gunshot wound that The Kid suffered ... The skeleton's protruding teeth and small stature also are consistent with Billy ... Since Garrett was friends with The Kid, he might have shot him and then let him escape.**"

## *PILTDOWN MAN HOAX REDUX*

The hoaxers were inadvertently rerunning the most famous skeleton hoax of all: Piltdown Man. Between 1908 and 1912, an amateur anthropologist named Charles Dawson, claimed to have found Charles Darwin's coveted "missing link" between apes and men in and near Piltdown gravel quarry in East Sussex, England. Possible, though unproved, hoaxer, Dawson, hoped his discovery would yield him a fellowship in the British Royal Society. He had "discovered" parts of a human-like skull, an ape-like jawbone, a hominid-seeming canine tooth; plus an ivory tool and Stone Age animal teeth - for a Stone Age touch. "Museum experts" assembled the skull and jawbone into a creature they named *Eanthropus dawsoni,* to honor Dawson. Popularly called "Piltdown Man," it held its spot in humans' family tree for over 40 years.

In 1953, Sir Kenneth Oakley, using a new fluorine absorption test, proved Piltdown Man was a fake composite of a medieval human skull and an antique orangutan's jawbone - all stained to match. And the ape's jawbone's teeth were filed to fit the skull.

For their own Piltdown Man hoax, the hoaxing lawmen had turned to reporter, Leo Banks, and tried to seduce by: "We're giving Arizona Billy the Kid!" For his April 14, 2006 *Tucson Weekly* article, "The New Billy the Kid?" Deputy Tom Sullivan took over for fake Miller fan, Dale Tunnell, to be the Helen Airy convert, and was quoted: "Helen Airy's book triggered it for me … It made a lot of sense. I read it and thought, 'We have another Billy the Kid.' " And Sederwall and Sullivan performed their "high-tech forensic" routine, flaunting famous Dr. Lee and the carpenter's bench - now "saturated with blood." Banks quoted: "When we found the bench and the other evidence, we thought, 'Let's forget about these other bodies,' " says Sullivan, referring to Catherine Antrim and the Kid. "Let's do Miller. And if that doesn't work, we'll go down to Texas and do Brushy Bill."

As discussed, Banks had researched the "Billy the Kid Case," and had discovered their digging up of the random man (later identified as William Hudspeth). So he called their roving extravaganza "airship Billy." And he exposed that Sullivan's and Sederwall's "Billy the Kid" skeleton claims were made by mixing-up up Miller's and the random man's bones! He had interviewed Dr. Laura Fulginiti. She denied the skeletal claims! Banks wrote:

> Fulginiti says the first body she studied had buck teeth and the scapula fracture that caused such a commotion with investigators.
> As Sederwall told the *Weekly*, "We were shocked when we got him up. He had buck teeth just like the Kid and a bullet hole in the upper left chest that exited the shoulder blade."
> Sullivan made a similar statement, suggesting this might be the man Garrett shot the morning of July 14, 1881.
> **But when contacted by the *Weekly*, Fulginiti didn't support their enthusiasm. "There was evidence of trauma on the scapula, but I couldn't tell whether it was from a gunshot wound or not," she said.**

She also said the buck teeth were from what Banks named "Scapula Man" [Hudspeth] from his non-shot right scapula! And Miller's skull had no teeth. Fulginiti had researched Miller as dying of a broken hip. So Banks called him "Hip Man."

Banks also contacted Orchid Cellmark Lab, discovering: **"The DNA expert present at the exhumation, Dr. Rick Staub, of**

**Orchid Cellmark Labs in Dallas, was unable to extract useable DNA from Hip Man [Miller]. But he did get a usable sample from Scapula Man [Hudspeth].**" This was the admission that John Miller's bones had yielded no DNA.

When confronted by Banks, Sullivan and Sederwall were left clumsily lying that hired forensic expert Fulginiti was wrong.

**Nevertheless, it was obvious that, for their own Piltdown Man, the hoaxers had assembled a "John Miller as a Billy the Kid" from William Hudspeth's bones.** That was how random man, William Hudspeth - his coffin smashed and corpse dismembered, with Dr. Rick Staub of Orchid Cellmark stealing his bones to grind to oblivion for meaningless DNA extraction - entered Billy the Kid history.

## THE INCRIMINATING FULGINITI REPORT

And dutiful Dr. Laura Fulginiti reported it all. Duped into thinking Dale Tunnell was a forensic expert conducting the exhumation, as "Dr. Tunnell," she titled her June 2, 2005 report: "Re: Exhumation, Pioneer Home Cemetery, Prescott, Arizona for "Dale L. Tunnell, Ph.D. [sic], Forensitec." **[APPENDIX: 9]** I got its copy from the Prescott Police Department.

In her official report, Fulginiti described the scene, while the hoaxers feverishly dug before they were caught. She had written:

On May 19, 2005 at approximately 1230 hours I am asked to assist in the exhumation of the remains of an individual known as Mr. John Miller by Dr. Dale Tunnell, President, Forensitec. The purpose of my involvement is to aid in the exhumation process as well as to assess any skeletal remains recovered. The exhumation takes place at the Arizona Pioneer [sic] Home Cemetery, Iron Springs Road in Prescott Arizona in the presence of Dr. Tunnell, several of his associates, members of the Arizona Pioneer Home staff and Kristen Harnett M.A., AMSU graduate student.

**[AUTHOR'S NOTE: The unmarked grave first exhumed was later called the South Grave, and was John Miller's.**

Dr. Tunnell located the alleged gravesite of Mr. Miller prior to our arrival on the scene ... At approximately 1400 hours, a backhoe began to remove the sod overlying the alleged grave, which was oriented in an East-West direction, with the head to the West. When fragments of wood began to be removed, the grave was excavated using a shovel ... The left femoral shaft, minus the head, was removed, examined, and packaged for DNA analysis [the role of Rick Staub, Director of Orchid Cellmark].

**[AUTHOR'S NOTE: Tunnell then changed his mind, and they dug up the adjacent, North Grave of William Hudspeth]**

Dr. Tunnell, in consultation with the cemetery staff and his other associates determined that the adjacent grave to the North was likely that of Mr. Miller and excavation shifted to that gravesite ... The backhoe removed the overlying sod until fragments of wood began to be unearthed. The excavation shifted to shovels and the top of the casket was identified. Excavation proceeded using trowels and hand tools until various aspects of the skeleton were identified and cleared ... Skeletal elements were measured for depth and location, removed from the grave and examined ... **There were extensive healed traumata on the right scapula** ... The remains were photographed, samples were harvested for DNA (tooth and femur) [Note and the skull had teeth] remains were returned to the grave and reburied.

**[AUTHOR'S NOTE: Fulginiti then had doubts about the North Grave's remains being John Miller's.]**

Anecdotal historical information suggested that Mr. John Miller had died from complications of a fractured hip while recuperating in the Arizona pioneer Home. The individual in the north grave, while having extensive pathological conditions, particularly in the upper body, did not have discernible pathology of the *os coxae* [pelvis].

**[AUTHOR'S NOTE: The North Grave's body had no pelvic damage to go with John Miller's broken hip. So they ravished the South Grave again.]**

The south grave was excavated by shovel to the point where the remnants of the casket lid were identified. Excavation resumed using trowels and hand tools until the left femoral head was identified.

The head of the femur was misshapen with bony remodeling, suggesting an **antemortem injury** ... The ischium [part of the pelvis] tapered to a point with lack of union to the pubis [another part of the pelvis], suggesting a healing fracture of the ischiopubic ramus. **This evidence led the team to believe that the individual in the south grave was, in fact, more consistent with the known facts regarding the Medical history of Mr. John Miller and additional DNA samples were recovered (femur, scalp [?], matter from inside the braincase).**

**[AUTHOR'S NOTE: The South Grave was confirmed as Miller's because of its broken hip.]**

The maxillae and mandible were recovered but were edentulous [had no teeth at all].

**[AUTHOR'S NOTE: So Miller had NO TEETH. Random man Hudspeth had the "buck teeth" claimed as Billy the Kid's!"]**

This was how Fulginiti revealed that the body in the North Grave its the bad scapula and alleged buck teeth was not Miller's! That was how she revealed that William Hudspeth had been dug up also. And the bad scapula and buck teeth were his! And his damaged scapula was the right one, not the left! And its damage was not from a bullet! So the hoaxers were switching "Scapula Man" (William Hudspeth) for John Miller ("Hip Man") for their fables to the press; a well as switching his right scapula as a left one!

## *THE CRIMINAL INVESTIGATION*

Great effort went into blocking the criminal investigation for desecration of graves and graverobbing begun by David Snell. Yavapai County's Prescott City Prosecutor Glenn Savona had proved inconveniently honest by pointing out that the "internal management" statute did not apply; nor did any law allow taking the remains to Texas. Also, he had found no needed court order from Yavapai County Community Health Services Department or family permission. He pointed to felonies.

So the hoaxers got out of Yavapai County. They lied that Deputy Mike Poling, who had come on site to give Dr. Laura Fulginiti specimens from another case, then lent his metal detector at their request, was responsible for the exhumation! That meant that Yavapai County might have to prosecute *him*: making a conflict of interest. So the case was transferred to Maricopa County.

Since I was providing information at each stage, I was informed of the other ploy used by the hoaxers. They also claimed that Arizona Pioneers' Home Supervisor Jeanine Dike and Dale Tunnell were responsible. So Maricopa County opened Case No. 2006020516 against Dike and Tunnell! But I was told the names were just a filing formality.

In actuality, it would emerge that Governor Bill Richardson and Governor Janet Napolitano were pressuring Maricopa County's Chief Prosecutor Andrew Thomas to stop the case.

Unaware, from June 9, 2006 to October 17, 2006, I supplied the assigned Maricopa County Prosecutor, Deputy Attorney Jonnell Lucca, with hoax information, hoaxer names, the lack of DNA to justify any exhumation. Nevertheless, this corrupt official wrote to me on October 17, 2006: "Dear Dr. Cooper: This letter is to inform you that the Maricopa County Attorney's Office has **declined to file charges against Jeanine Dike and Dale Tunnell** as there is no reasonable likelihood of conviction in this case. There is no further information regarding the decision. Thank you for your interest in the case." So she pretended they were the only suspects. And she hid the felonious desecration and graverobbing of William Hudspeth.

She had folded under Richardson's thuggish, Santa Fe Ring-style racketeering. I owned a telling e-mail (obtained from its Lincoln County public official recipient) dated May 16, 2006 by gloating Steve Sederwall, feeling immune. It was signed with a smiley face symbol and "Steve." He stated:

> Well **we have the governor reaching out to the Arizona [sic- missing word, Prosecutor?]** to stop this investigation. They thought we had the DNA [sic - illegible word follows] and they tried to get the FBI to get John Millers bones back with a warrant and get the DNA. They think we are going to announce that John Miller is the kid in France [an upcoming secret trip promoting the hoax]. We will not give them a break. They are now trying to get is [sic - us?] worked up about grave robbery charges. But being good cops we have all the docs that show the state of Arizona did the dig not us. How funny. if [sic] they do something stupid and file on us we sue and Arizona well [sic] be the state of Tom and Steve.

## BACK TO DIGGING UP CATHERINE ANTRIM

So confident of immunity were the hoaxers, that even before Deputy Attorney Jonnell Lucca closed their case, they were using the John Miller exhumation to claim that they had gotten DNA justifying the exhumation of Catherine Antrim. For hoax-backing Julie Carter's October 6, 2005 *Ruidoso News* article, "Follow the Blood," Sullivan lied that Silver City Judge Henry Quintero wanted *any* Billy the Kid DNA - not just from Fort Sumner. He stated: "A judge in Silver City told the investigators to come back if they had enough evidence to warrant the need for Catherine Antrim's (the Kid's mother) DNA. With the DNA results from the blood on the table and soon the results of Miller's DNA, investigators will likely take the judge up on that offer ... The officials in Ft. Sumner and Silver City thought we would just roll over and play dead. We didn't and this case is far from over." That bravado translated into going after "Brushy" himself. But first, they would make an astounding announcement.

# CHAPTER 4
# "BRUSHY" GETS BACK IN THE MOVIES

## THE HOAX MAKES THE CANNES FILM FESTIVAL

In 2006, the hoaxers had been keeping a huge secret. The John Miller exhumation was merely a warm-up of their fake forensics. They were well on their way to crowing "Brushy" as Billy the Kid. They had completed a movie with a French film crew - with Tom Sullivan as Sheriff William Brady - and with narration by Kris Kristofferson, who had played Billy the Kid in the Sam Peckinpah movie, "Pat Garrett and Billy the Kid." It was to be a rerun of 1990's "Young Guns II" by John Fusco.

Of all the "Billy the Kid Case" hoax's dupes, the biggest had been French film-maker Anne Feinsilber. Inspired by the hoaxers', June 5, 2003, *New York Times* article, "122 Years Later, The Lawmen Are Still Chasing Billy the Kid." with its quote of "Brushy" believer, Jannay Valdez, ("I'm absolutely convinced that Garrett killed someone else and that Brushy Bill was the Kid"), Feinsilber created a nearly million dollar film, "Requiem for Billy the Kid," about "the mystery of the murder of Billy." And "Brushy Bill" Roberts hovered as "Billy as a murder scene escapee."

Feinsilber's film went on to be screened at the 2006 Cannes Film Festival and won an award.

I learned about this disaster to legitimate history just before Tom Sullivan and Steve Sederwall departed to be honored guests at the Festival. Sederwall had referred to it in his May 16, 2006 e-mail: "They think we are going to announce that John Miller is the kid in France." In fact, Governor Richardson planned to name them Ambassadors from New Mexico to announce DNA matchings implying "Brushy" as Billy. Through a contact, I managed to block Richardson's move. So they kept their mouths shut about DNA. But they still went to France.

## *REQUIEM FOR REAL HISTORY*

Anne Feinsilber's "Requiem for Billy the Kid" got wide publicity; and it gave the "Billy the Kid Case" hoaxers the chance to disseminate misinformation about their own endeavor.

On May 21st, from *Variety* magazine, came the review of "Requiem for Billy the Kid" by a Todd McCarthy. He said:

> With Sam Peckinpah's Billy, Kris Kristofferson re-enlisted to portray the Kid delivering his account of what happened between him and Pat Garrett in 1881, pic goes on a photogenic search for the "truth" about the young killer. Seems there has always been a rumor that Billy escaped and lived to a ripe old age, and Tom Sullivan, who was sheriff of Lincoln County when pic was shot in the fall of 2004, describes his efforts to exhume the body of Billy's mother for DNA, efforts shot down by a judge whose motives Sullivan describes as baldly financial.

A May 25th review by Dave McCoy of MSN Movies, as "L 'Ouest Américain," wrote: "Feinsilber follows up on a rumor that Pat Garrett shot the wrong man and Billy the Kid actually isn't buried where it's said he is."

Feinsilber's damage was further evidenced on a May 6, 2006 Internet version of *The Hollywood Reporter* in reviewer, Ray Bennett's, "Bottom line: A story well told." He wrote:

> History has it that **Sheriff Pat Garrett, a reformed villain,** gunned down William Bonney, also known as Billy the Kid, at Fort Sumner, where his grave has a much-visited marker. Some say, however, that **the friendship between Garrett and Bonney** led the lawman to let the outlaw go and another man's body lies beneath his headstone. **Could Billy the Kid have lived to see two world wars and driven a car?** Feinsilber sets out to discover the truth and she finds several people in New Mexico whose grandparents were said to have known Bonney. Competing factions would like to exhume the bodies of Billy and his mother Catherine, who died of tuberculosis when Billy was 14, in order to prove once and for all when he died. Such myths fuel tourism, however, and the mystery has remained unsolved.

With this hoax victory, Pat Garrett became a "reformed villain," the friendship between Garrett and Billy was real, a stranger's body likely lay in Billy's grave, the exhumation would have solved the questions, but the "mystery" was being left unsolved to "fuel tourism." And "Brushy" was in the running.

# CHAPTER 5
## TRYING TO DIG UP "BRUSHY BILL"

### HEADING TO TEXAS WITH SHOVELS

In 2007, Governor Bill Richardson, seemed to have no adequately corrupt Texas contact; because Hamilton's mayor and town council refused exhumation of "Brushy Bill."

That Texas onslaught, like the Arizona one, was under Sheriff Rick Virden, with his Deputies, Tom Sullivan and Steve Sederwall. And they had another hurdle, compliments of me. In 2006, was my American Academy of Forensic Sciences Ethics Complaint against Dr. Henry Lee for hoaxing. Though the unethical Ethics Committee covered-up, Lee apparently stopped the hoaxers using his name for the carpenter's bench DNA scam. So they could claim no DNA for matching with "Brushy's."

Nevertheless, Virden tried, writing that year on his official stationery to Mayor Roy Rumsey, misspelling his name, but using lawman clout to try and get the job done. Virden wrote:

> Hamilton Texas
> Mayor Roy Ramsey
>
> Mayor Ramsey,
>
> This letter will inform you that Tom Sullivan and Steve Sederwall are both commissioned deputies with the Lincoln County New Mexico Sheriff's Department.
>
> They have been investigating case # 2003-274. Their investigation has been funded by them personally and has been conducted on their own time.
>
> Mr. Mayor, should you have any questions please do not hesitate to contact me.
>
> R.E. Virden
> Lincoln County Sheriff

Virden's double-talk was trying to cover all hoax bases. The "funded by them personally," came from my years of open records exposure of their tax-dollar squandering. And, "their own time" was part of their new switcheroo that it was not a law enforcement case at all, but their private hobby! That scam was to hide the DNA records from me, since turn-over was only legally demanded of public officials, not private citizens. That left Virden absurdly telling Rumsey that he was sending his deputies for his New Mexico murder case - which was really a hobby - but those deputies could dig up "Brushy," though his jurisdiction was Lincoln County, New Mexico; and certainly not Texas!

Mayor Rumsey did not have to decipher this craziness, since I had already told him that the circus was coming to town. Deputy Steve Sederwall met with him. Rumsey told me that he told Sederwall: "If 'Brushy Bill' is Billy the Kid, I'm Pancho Villa."

Rumsey added for the press in a May 5, 2007 *Houston Chronicle* article titled "DNA could solve the mystery of Billy the Kid": "Roberts was 'just a big windbag who went around telling stories. Few people, if anybody, believed him."

Sederwall had floated the hoax's new spin. The *Roswell Daily Record*, using a Stephenville, Texas, article, wrote on May 2, 2007, "Billy the Kid Exhumation a Possibility." "Sederwall said if DNA is allowed to be obtained from Roberts, investigators will pursue exhuming the body of Catherine McCarty Antrim, who researchers have confirmed was Billy the Kid's mother." (Omitted is that this was blocked by Judge Quintero.)

On May 4th, for the hoax-backing *Albuquerque Journal's* "Manhunt for Real Billy the Kid Goes On: Deputy hopes DNA will finally reveal outlaw's true identity." Sederwall again blew smoke. "Those (Hamilton City) people want to know, they are not afraid ... You talk to Fort Sumner and they want to pull pistols on us. You talk to Hamilton City and they're like, 'Sure, we'd like to know.' "

On May 10, 2007, Hamilton's Town Council unanimously opposed exhumation; even though Texas's own "Brushy Bill" believer, Jannay Valdez, still pitching after his stint for Richardson for the June 5, 2003 *New York Times*, spoke for it.

But what if the hoaxers had gotten "Brushy's bones? Even Henry Lee might have returned with that lure. (Some old-timer could claim: "Didn't Gramps say that Billy the Kid had vomited on his saddle?") And Orchid Cellmark's Dr. Rick Staub, could have "matched" Billy-vomit-DNA to "Brushy"-bones-DNA. Then there could be another TV show, and Bill Robins III could get the faked "Brushy" pardon. But, so far, I had kept the hoaxers at bay.

# CHAPTER 6
# STOPPING RICHARDSON'S "BRUSHY BILL" PARDON

## THE PARDON PLOT

By 2010, it was rumored that Governor Bill Richardson, now at the end of his two terms, was going to pardon "Billy the Kid." This megalomaniac wanted to win at last.

So I had a painful dilemma. Billy Bonney had deserved the Lew Wallace pardon. But Richardson was likely to pardon "Brushy," with a hoaxed claim of having proved it by "DNA." With its international press, he would destroy Billy's real history. So I had to stop what I most wanted: the pardon of Billy the Kid.

In July of 2010, I contacted the Garrett family, which, to date, had not responded to the "Billy the Kid Case." Most proactive was Jarvis Patrick "J.P." Garrett, Pat's grandson from the second marriage of Pat's youngest son, Jarvis (who had testified against "Brushy" in the Mabry hearing).

Our window of opportunity to save the history was just weeks. The world was waiting. On July 11, 2010 India's *Press Trust of India Hindustan Times* and Pakistan's *Daily Express*, fed hoax claims, printed "Billy the Kid 'to be pardoned.'" It stated:

> Billy the Kid was 19th century America's most infamous frontier outlaw who killed 21 men in Lincoln County War. Now, the Wild West's "Robin Hood" may get a posthumous pardon, 129 years after he was supposedly gunned down by Sheriff Pat Garrett, a media report said. Experts and historians believe the outlaw may not have been the man who died in Fort Sumner, New Mexico, on July 14, 1881, in a shoot-out that has become part of frontier folklore and material for Hollywood producers.

Instead, many now believe Garrett, a lawman who is ranked alongside Wyatt Earp, accidentally killed the wrong man and lied to cover up his mistake.

**On hearing reports of his death, it is thought the Kid, born Henry McCarty, but also known to have used the names Henry Antrim and William H Bonney, retired as a gunslinger and fled to Texas where he outlasted both world wars and died, at the ripe old age of 90, in 1950.**

Now, the myth surrounding the gambler, cattle rustler and outlaw, who has no known family survivors, could be laid to rest at last as forensic experts want to exhume the body of the man buried in Hamilton under the assumed name of Ollie "Brushy Bill" Roberts, the *Daily Express* reported.

Above the grave is a monument that unequivocally identifies Roberts as Billy the Kid. And, if it proves to be accurate, New Mexico Governor Bill Richardson has pledged that he will grant a formal pardon to the fugitive of many names, the report said.

He said: "The evidence that will clinch this will be if genetic tests match samples from another grave in Silver City, New Mexico, we believe contains the body of Billy the Kid's mother Catherine Antrim."

On Saturday, July 24, 2010, came Richardson's front page *Albuquerque Journal* salvo by hoax-backing Rene Romo as: "Gov. Weighs Pardon for Billy the Kid." Romo gave only Richardson's lies, without warning of state history destruction:

RUIDOSO- The history of Billy the Kid is fueled with enduring debates: Was he a hero fighting for justice in a corrupt landscape? Or was he a scoundrel, unworthy of respect, who sank to the level of his enemies?

It might seem politically questionable for Gov. Bill Richardson, on his way out of office, to wade into the debate, but the governor appears to be doing just that. And think of the field day his critics will have if the governor pardons a serial cop killer.

The Governor's Office confirmed that, during the spring meeting in Santa Fe, Richardson asked syndicated columnist Jay Miller to put out feelers to historians and others enthralled with the history of the Lincoln County War and to assess the reaction to a pardon for the Kid.

After the Lincoln County War, Gov. Lew Wallace offered to pardon the Kid if he testified about heinous crimes. The Kid did, but Wallace never held up his end of the bargain, and the outlaw subsequently killed two Lincoln County deputies in his infamous escape from the Lincoln County jail.

A spokeswoman for the governor said last week that there's nothing new about Richardson's consideration of the pardon and the idea just "came up" during the meeting with [Jay] Miller.

But someone close to the highly publicized Lincoln County investigation of the Kid's 1881 slaying told me he was contacted in recent months by someone from the Governor's office asking for his reaction to the idea of a pardon.

Richardson first talked about a pardon back in 2003 during a press conference in Santa Fe to announce the Lincoln County Sheriff's Department had opened an investigation into the Kid's slaying on July 14, 1881, by Sheriff Pat Garrett.

The idea, investigators said, was to try to refute, by DNA evidence, claims by several men, such as John Miller and Brushy Bill Roberts, widely regarded as imposters who professed to be the Kid after the historical record said the outlaw had been killed. Those claims, the thinking went, cast doubt on Garrett's character, and modern forensic tools could lay the stories to rest.

**[AUTHOR'S NOTE: Romo absurdly spun the hoax as a murder case against Garrett *to prove him innocent*. Also added is fake anti-pretender spin.]**

In any event, publicity about a new investigation was said to be good for New Mexico tourism.

**[AUTHOR'S NOTE: The lie is omits that casting doubt on the history and its sites destroys tourism.]**

But critics lambasted the case. Officials in Silver City and Fort Sumner fought off legal efforts to dig up the remains of the outlaw's mother and the Kid himself in the hunt for DNA. They said the investigation just fed doubts about established history and undermined the value of Billy's Fort Sumner grave as a tourist site.

**[AUTHOR'S NOTE: Romo conceals the true obstacle – no real DNA - while using the hoaxers' usual conspiracy theory of obstructing and venal local officials.]**

There are even disagreements about whether a pardon would boost state tourism today.

"Leave him (Billy the Kid) alone," said former Mayor Juan Chavez. "As far as pardoning, what good will it do now? He's dead."

The investigation has since ground to a halt, beset by lawsuits and the rebuffed attempt to dig up the remains of Brushy Bill.

**[AUTHOR'S NOTE: "Lawsuits" meant my litigation for their fake DNA records. Romo also hides that "Brushy's" exhumation was blocked by no DNA to justify it.]**

But I had prepared a letter for the Garrett family to give to Richardson, and leaked it to Santa Fe AP reporter Barry Massey, who interviewed them, writing his July 30, 2010, article which started the salvation of the true history. Titled: "Billy the Kid to be Pardoned, 130 Years Later? Lawman's Grandchildren Outraged; "Would You Issue a Pardon For Someone Who Made His Living As A Thief?" (Obviously, the Garretts were not fans of Billy the Kid!) It had the first mention of me: "Gale Cooper, an amateur historian who lives near Albuquerque, said a pardon by Richardson would be the 'culmination of the hoax that contended Pat Garrett was a nefarious killer and Billy was not buried in his grave.' Cooper has written a book, 'MegaHoax,' to debunk claims that Garrett killed someone other than the Kid."

By August 4, 2010, in his Executive Office, Richardson met with the Garretts, and signed their petition (prepared by me) to promise not to pardon "Brushy" as Billy the Kid. (He had told the family that he would not meet with them if they brought me.)

But devious Richardson apparently thought he could evade that guarantee by using the Lew Wallace pardon promise to segue back to pardoning "Brushy" for his long law-abiding life.

## **LAST MINUTE PARDON PETITION**

In his zero hour, Richardson concocted a new twist for his hoax by enlisting his own attorney, who had defended him in his huge pay-to-play Grand Jury trial in which he had been indicted, then saved in a cover-up in 2009 by President Barack Obama (who, in part, owed "super delegate" Richardson his presidential election), and using Attorney General Eric Holder.

The attorney was Randi McGinn. Attorney Bill Robins III, in his deposition of January 6, 2011 for my open records case, called her *his* friend too. She was married to Attorney Charlie Daniels, appointed by Richardson in November of 2007 as a state Supreme Court Chief Justice. (Noteworthy is that from 2003 to 2007, I had asked Daniels to represent me in hoax opposition, and kept him up-to-date. So he knew about the hoax when his wife joined it.) Of course, Richardson and McGinn kept their hand-in-glove relationship secret. So, out of the blue, came "amateur historian" McGinn, petitioning Richardson to pardon Billy the Kid!

On December 14, 2010 - only seventeen days to December 31, 2010's end of Richardson's term, Randi McGinn, on her Albuquerque law firm's official letterhead of McGinn, Carpenter,

Montoya & Love, P.A., via hand-delivery to Shammara Henderson, Legal Counsel Office of the Governor, presented, by letter and attachments totaling six pages, her error-filled "Application for Pardon for Henry McCarty, aka William Bonney or Billy the Kid." It is a major hoax document, on the order of the "Probable Cause Statement." McGinn's cover letter stated:

Dear Ms. Henderson:
   Enclosed please find an application for Henry McCarty, who was known in New Mexico by the name of William Bonney and later became known as Billy the Kid.
   Please let me know if I need anything further to advance this pardon application.
                                        Best regards,
                                        Randi McGinn

************ *

## PARDON APPLICATION FOR HENRY McCARTY, AKA WILLIAM BONNEY and BILLY THE KID

**General information:**
Applicant Name: <u>Henry McCarty, aka Billy the Kid, William H. Bonney, Henry Antrim, Kid Antrim, Billito, El Chivato</u>
Date of Birth: <u>Precise dob unknown, circa 1859</u> Soc. Security No. <u>N/A</u>
Address/City/State/Zip Code: Deceased. Buried in Fort Sumner, New Mexico
Home Phone #: <u>   N/A   </u> Work Phone #: <u>   N/A   </u>
Dept. of Corrections Inmate #: <u>   N/A   </u>
Education: <u>Through the age of 16 [sic-15½] in Silver City, New Mexico</u>
Employment:

| | |
|---|---|
| 1874 | Age 15-16 [14½- 15½] – After his mother's death, worked as a hotel employee, Silver City, N.M. for room and board and for landlord who said he was the only employee who never stole anything.**[Also worked at butcher shops]** |
| 1875-1877 | Seasonal ranch hand in Arizona Territory at various ranches **[No. A cook and petty rustler]**. |
| 1877-2/18/78 | Ranch hand for John Tunstall at the Rio Feliz Ranch in Lincoln County, N.M., until Mr. Tunstall was killed **[also a Tunstall employee after the murder]** by a "posse" **[was a real posse under Brady]** of armed men sent by Sheriff William Brady on February 18, 1878 |

March, 1878    Member of a posse called "the Regulators" to capture and arrest the men who murdered John Tunstall. Arrest warrants for the killers issued by Justice of the Peace John Bautista Wilson were withdrawn by Governor Samuel B. Axtell.

**Crime location:**
List conviction: <u>Only one of the 6-7 suspected shooters to be tried and convicted of murder in the shooting death of Sheriff William Brady on April 1, 1878, as Brady walked down the streets **[one street]** of Lincoln, New Mexico with 3 other men to inform the assembled grand jurors **[no Grand Jurymen were assembled; a notice was allegedly to be posted at the court]** that the grand jury investigation into the death of John Tunstall was canceled **[was delayed]** and would not occur that day. One other man, George Hindman, was also shot and died. Present to testify as witnesses before the grand jury about the killing of John Tunstall were some of the Regulators, John Middleton, Fred Waite, Frank McNab **[MacNab]**, Henry Brown, Jim French, William Bonney and Rob Widenmann **[they were in town for the ambush; they were outlawed, not testifiers]**.</u>

<u>Although 5 men were ultimately indicted for the killing of John Tunstall by the Grand Jury which re-convened **[convened]** on April 13, 1878 – Jesse **[Jessie]** Evans, Miguel Segovia, Frank Rivers, James J. Dolan, and Billy Matthews – none of these men were ever tried or convicted. Nor was any other person ever tried and convicted of any of the dozens of killings which occurred during the Lincoln County War between February, 1878 and March, 1879 **[Lincoln County War was February 18, 1878 to July 19, 1878]**.</u>

Sentence: <u>Death by hanging</u>. Date sentenced: <u>April 13, 1881</u>
Date(s) probation/parole ended: <u>N/A Shot by Sheriff Pat Garrett on July 13, 1881 **[July 14, 1881 ... she missed the famous date in the history!!!]**</u>
List additional conviction(s) on the lines below:
<u>None. However, killed 2 men, deputies Jim **[James]** Bell and Bob Olinger, during his escape from custody on April 28, 1881, while awaiting imposition of the death sentence at the jail on the second floor of the Lincoln County courthouse. Shot dead by Sheriff Pat Garrett before he could be tried on those crimes. **[omits the other murders]**</u>

**Questions:**
Have you met all sentencing requirements? <u>N/A</u>
Are you requesting restoration of firearm privileges? <u>No</u> State reasons __

**Additional attachments:**
 1. Factual Statement of historical basis for gubernatorial pardon and clemency.

*Randi McGinn*, Pardon Applicant               *December 14, 2010*

## Factual Basis to Pardon Billy the Kid

A promise is a promise and should be enforced. It is particularly important to enforce promises and deals made by government officials, law enforcement officers or the governor of a state made in exchange for a citizen risking his life to testify against a criminal who committed murder.

Such a promise was made by New Mexico Governor Lew Wallace **[Billy thought there was a "promise;" he was likely tricked]** to the man known in New Mexico as William Bonney, aka Billy the Kid, at the end of the Lincoln County War **[a year later]**. Mr. Bonney kept his end of the bargain by testifying before a grand jury against the men who murdered attorney Huston Chapman on February 18, 1879. Governor Wallace did not keep his end of the deal **["deal" may have been a "trick"]**, which was to pardon Mr. Bonney for all outstanding charges, including the impending indictment related to the death of William Brady **[indictments were for "Buckshot" Roberts, William Brady, George Hindman]**. This injustice should be corrected.

On February 18, 1879, the anniversary of the murder of John Tunstall, Mr. Bonney's former employer and mentor, both sides in the year-long Lincoln County War **[the War was 6 months]** met to negotiate a truce **[the Dolan-Billy meeting was merely a peace meeting between *them*]**. The new governor, Lew Wallace, who replaced the old, corrupt governor, Sam Axtell, on October 2 **[sic- October 1st]**, 1878, had issued an amnesty proclamation on November 13, 1878, which pardoned all offences committed during the Lincoln County War, except for those with pending prosecutions. With an indictment pending against him for the April 1, 1878 deaths of Sheriff Brady and Mr. Hindman **[and the April 4, 1878 murder of "Buckshot" Roberts]**, William Bonney was one of the few Lincoln County residents who was not given retroactive amnesty for the dozens of killings which had been committed during the conflict **[none of the McSween-side fighters were given amnesty]**.

Both sides of the Lincoln County War – those on the Dolan/Murphy "House" side and those from the Tunstall/McSween/Chisum side – met after the Governor's amnesty proclamation to negotiate a treaty. **[This is made-up. The February 18, 1879 meeting was of Dolan and some of his thugs and Billy and some of his friends.]** The prime mover behind the meeting, the person who wanted peace in Lincoln County, was William Bonney, who sent a letter to the other side proposing a truce. **[This is made-up. The February 18, 1879 meeting was proposed by Dolan, following pressure from Susan McSween's lawyer, Huston Chapman, who was threatening litigation against Commander Dudley. Dolan, thus, first made a peace offer to her; then to Billy, as arguably representing the Hispanic faction in the War.]** At the meeting, the parties agreed that the fighting would end and none of the parties would testify against any of the others, on pain of death. Unfortunately, after the written treaty was signed [**This is made-up**], Jesse [**Jessie**] Evans and Jimmy Dolan broke out whiskey to celebrate and, in short order, there were 20 [**This is made-up**] armed, drunken cowboys [**Dolan was no cowboy, Evans and Campbell were outlaws**] stumbling down Lincoln's one street. The only sober one was William Bonney, who did not drink alcohol.

Into this drunken celebration walked a one-armed lawyer named Huston Chapman, who was coming back from a neighbor's house [**he was in town representing Susan McSween. He was going from her house to Juan Patrón's, where he was staying**]. He was confronted on the street by drunken Billy Campbell, from the Murphy/Dolan House [**Campbell was one of Jessie Evans's outlaw gang**], who pulled out his pistol, pressed it to Chapman's chest [**Dolan did that**], and demanded that he "dance." When Chapman refused, he was shot from the front by Mr. Campbell and from behind by Jimmy Dolan. [**This is wrong. Dolan shot Chapman point-blank in the chest; and Campbell fired at Chapman as he fell. The shots were from Chapman's front.**] He was set on fire and burned in the street where he lay.

The death of the lawyer, Chapman, finally convinced Wallace to travel to Lincoln, which he did two weeks after the shooting. Although the federal troops at the Governor's disposal were quickly able to capture Campbell, Dolan and accomplice Jesse [**Jessie**] Evans, and hold them in the fort, he could not find anyone to testify against them. It was then that the Governor received a letter from W.H. Bonney stating that Mr. Bonney had been present and was an eyewitness to the shooting of the lawyer, Chapman, and, despite the risk of death, was willing to testify against the killers if the Governor would annul the pending charges against him, including the indictment for the murder of Sheriff Brady [**Billy asked only for annulling his indictments from the Lincoln County War.**].

Governor Wallace wrote back to Mr. Bonney and asked to meet him at a private residence, indicating that: "I have the authority to exempt you from prosecution if you will testify to what you say you know." [**This promises nothing. It is just cagy Wallace's confirmation of his authority.**]

Mr. Bonney came to the private, nighttime meeting. [**Justice of the Peace John Wilson was present.**] At that meeting, after representing that he had the power to give him absolute protection, Governor Wallace promised Mr. Bonney that, if he testified fully against Billy Campbell and the other shooters before the grand jury meeting in 2-3 weeks, "In return for your doing this, I will let you go scot free with a pardon in your pocket for all your misdeeds." [**This is made-up. The actual conversation is unknown. The quote is taken from a fictional article Lew Wallace wrote in 1902 – 23 years later – for** *New York World Magazine*, **titled "General Lew Wallace Writes a Romance of 'Billy the Kid' Most Famous Bandit of** the Plains." It has no correct facts - even stating that the meeting occurred in Santa Fe.]

Several hours after this meeting and agreement [typical hoaxer style of first making up information, later presenting it as true. McGinn – or whoever wrote this – has not proved any pardon agreement], Jimmy Dolan, Jesse [Jessie] Evans and Billy Campbell "escaped" from the Fort Stanton guardhouse. [Only Evans and Campbell escaped. The date was the next day: March 18th. Dolan was released legally, by habeas corpus, on April 13th.] After the escape, Mr. Bonney wrote another letter to Justice of the Peace John Wilson, where the governor was staying [Wallace was staying in the Montaño family home to the east of Wilson's; the meeting was in Wilson's], asking him to find out whether, now that the prisoners had escaped, the governor was still interested in their deal. [Billy did not cite a "deal." Billy's total letter stated: "*San Patricio Thursday 20th 1879 Friend Wilson. Please tell You know who that I do not know what to do, now as those Prisoners have escaped. So send word by bearer. a note through You it may be he has made different arrangements if not and he still wants it the same to Send :William Hudgins: as Deputy, to the Junction tomorrow at three Oclock with some men you know to be all right. Send a note telling me what to do WHBonney P.S. do not send Soldiers*"] Governor Wallace responded:

> The escape makes no difference in arrangements. To remove all suspicions of understanding, I think it better to put the arresting party in charge of Sheriff Kimball, who shall [sic - will] be instructed to see that no violence is used. This will go to you tonight.

[Actually, with lawyer's slyness, Wallace had decisively crossed out, in his own unused draft, "*I will comply with my part if you will with yours*;" as if taking no chances by putting a "promise" in writing. So Wallace actually wrote in his first and unsent draft: "*The escape makes no difference in arrangements. I will comply with my part if you will with yours. To remove all suspicions of arrangement understanding, I think it better to put the arresting party in charge of Sheriff Kimball, who will be instructed to see that no violence is used. This will go to you tonight.*]

Mr. Bonney wrote back [this is edited for grammar and punctuation]:

> Sir. I will keep the appointment I made but be sure and have men come that you can depend on. I am not afraid to die like a man fighting but I would not like to be killed like a dog unarmed. Tell Kimbal to let his men be placed around the house and for him to come in alone: and he can arrest us All I am afraid of is that in the Fort we might be ... killed through a window at night. But you can arrange that all right ... It is not my place to advise you, but

*I am anxious to have them caught, and perhaps know how men hide from soldiers better than you."*

Based on the plan devised with Governor Wallace to protect the safety of their eyewitness, Sheriff George Kimball **[Kimbrell]** made a mock arrest of Mr. Bonney on March 23, 1879 **[March 22, 1879]**. Shortly thereafter, Mr. Bonney kept his word and testified before the grand jury which, with an eyewitness, indicted Billy Campbell, Jimmy Dolan and Jesse **[Jessie]** Evans for the murder of lawyer Huston Chapman.

Despite his promise **[no promise has been proven here]**, Governor Wallace returned to Santa Fe without granting William Bonney a pardon. After getting the testimony he needed for the indictment, the local District Attorney William L. Rynerson did not enforce the governor's promise **[the pardon had to be in writing; Wallace never did that; as he did for Billy Matthews, for example]** and immediately pressed the prosecution of his eyewitness, William Bonney, even changing venue out of his hometown, Lincoln, where he was well liked by much of the citizenry. Mr. Bonney was out of jail at the time the indictments were returned in another county and was never pursued by Sheriff Kimball **[Kimbrell]**, who knew firsthand of the Governor's broken promise. **[This is made-up. Kimbrell favored the McSween side, including Billy. There is no evidence he was privy to a pardon promise - only the fake arrest.]** Over the next 21 months, while the local and national press gave him the catchy nickname, Billy the kid, and built him into a Western legend, Mr. Bonney started a small ranch near Portales, New Mexico. **[This is made-up. In Billy's December 12, 1879 letter to Wallace, Billy states:** *"I had been at Sumner Since I left Lincoln making my living Gambling…".***]**

**[Omitted by McGinn – or whoever wrote this – is Wallace's scornful March 31, 1879 letter to Secretary of the Interior Carl Schurz, during the actual period of the alleged pardon "deal," and when Billy was in the fake arrest in jailer, Juan Patrón's house. Wallace stated:** *"A precious specimen nick-named "The Kid," whom the Sheriff is holding here in the Plaza, as it is called, is an object of tender regard. I heard singing and music the other night; going to the door, I found the minstrels of the village actually serenading the fellow in his prison."***]**

On December 13, 1880 **[December 22, 1880 in the** *Las Vegas Gazette***]**, Wallace announced a reward of $500 for the capture of the man now known as Billy the Kid. By December 24, 1880 **[December 22, 1880]**, Sheriff Pat Garrett and his posse had tracked William Bonney to Stinking Springs, near Ft. Sumner, where he was captured and taken into custody.

On January 1, 1881, William Bonney wrote the governor from jail asking him to come and see him. When there was no response to the request or a second note on March 2, he wrote a third letter on March 4, 1881 **[with Billy's grammar again corrected by the writer]**:

Dear Sir:

... I expect you have forgotten what you promised me, this month two years ago, but I have not, and I think you had ought to have come and seen me as I requested you to. I have done everything that I promised you I would, and you have done nothing that you promised me.

... I am not treated right by (his jailor) **[U.S. Marshal John Sherman's name is given by Billy, not his jailor's]**. He lets every stranger that comes to see me through curiosity in to see me, but will not let a single one of my friends in, not even an attorney. I guess they mean to send me up without giving me any show ...

There was no response to that or a fourth letter. By that time, because the story of "Billy the Kid" had captured public attention and there was pressure not to pardon an "outlaw," the governor did not keep his promise.

One month later, on April 8, 1881, Mr. Bonney was put on trial for the murder of Sheriff Brady with a recently appointed public defender, Colonel A.J. Fountain, who had just quit his job as a newspaper editor. He was convicted on April 13, 1881 **[April 9, 1881]** and sentenced to death **[April 13, 1881]**.

The Old West wasted no time in carrying out death sentences and there was no appeal. **[Billy tried to get money for an appeal with Attorney Edgar Caypless, but could not sell his horse, stolen at Stinking Springs by a Garrett posseman. The issue was needing to hire Fountain for the appeal.]** Three days after his sentence, Mr. Bonney was moved to Lincoln to be hanged. There, he was held in custody in the building owned by "the House" **["The House" had already been sold by 1880 to Lincoln County for a new courthouse-jail]**, the powerful business faction behind the killing of his former boss, rancher John Tunstall. Shortly before he was to be executed, On April 28, 1881, while Sheriff Pat Garrett was out of town, William Bonney escaped, in the process killing 2 deputies, Jim **[James]** Bell and Bob Olinger, who were left to guard him.

On July 13, Sheriff Pat Garrett carried out the death sentence **[This is the most bizarre error in this document, ending suspicion of a typo when July 13th, rather than 14th, was used earlier – missing the most famous date in Billy the Kid's history! And the death sentence was hanging, not random killing instead of recapturing]** when he tracked Mr. Bonney to where he was hiding at the Maxwell house **[There is no evidence that Billy was hiding in that house; and he approached it from another location]** near Ft. Sumner **[in Fort Sumner]** and shot him. William Bonney was dead at 22 **[21; another error of a famous fact]**.

Submitted by: Randi McGinn                December 14, 2010

*Sources of Historical Information:*
Joel Jacobsen, "Such Men as Billy the Kid"
Frederick Nolan: "The Billy the Kid Reader," *The West of Billy the Kid*"
Mark Lee Garner, "To Hell on a Fast Horse"
Pat F. Garrett's, "The Authentic Life of Billy the Kid" (additional author – Frederick Nolan
Interview with Drew and Elise Gomber
Review of Historical records, visits to scene and museums.

## THE McGINN PARDON TRICK

Given to the public via Richardson's gubernatorial website to justify his planned pardon, the McGinn Petition used familiar "Billy the Kid Case" hoaxer guise of expertise (here legal), and historical errors for its "a promise is a promise" presentation. That the pardon issue was complex is presented in my 2017 *The Lost Pardon of Billy the Kid: An Analysis Factoring in the Santa Fe Ring, Governor Lew Wallace's Dilemma, and a Territory in Rebellion*. There is no doubt that Billy fulfilled the bargain, and Wallace reneged. But, Richardson, since 2003, had avoided the exploration of real history or real historians to come to a legitimate decision about pardoning Billy the Kid.

Instead, this McGinn petition was a bait and switch trick. The only "investigation" Richardson had backed since 2003 was the "Billy the Kid Case" hoax. No contribution had been made to explain a pardon on the basis of Wallace's "promise." The only argument had been for pretenders: Garrett shot the innocent victim; Billy the Kid earned a pardon by a long law-abiding life. All indication was that this was just Richardson's evasion of his signed agreement with the Garrett family.

## PRESS RELEASE FOR PARDON PETITION

On December 16, 2010, Richardson sent out a press release to resuscitate his hoax with Attorney Randi McGinn's Petition. It was titled: "Governor Bill Richardson to Consider Billy the Kid Pardon Petition." He added another ploy: calling it a "limited pardon" - only for the Sheriff Brady killing. To slip all that through, Richardson and Randy McGinn shape-shifted to Old West history aficionados. It stated:

SANTA FE – Governor Bill Richardson today announced his office has received a formal petition for the pardon of Billy the Kid which he will consider and make a decision before the end of the year. Governor Richardson is seeking input on the petition and has set up a website and email address where history buffs, experts, and other interested parties and the general public can weigh in on its merits.

The petition centers around the widespread belief that Territorial Governor Lew Wallace promised Billy the Kid a pardon in return for damning testimony The Kid gave during a murder trial. The petition is narrow in scope and does not argue for a blanket pardon of all of Billy the Kid's activities ...

"As someone who is fascinated with New Mexico's rich history, I've always been intrigued by the history of Billy the Kid and, in particular, the alleged promise of a pardon he was given by Territorial Governor Lew Wallace," Governor Richardson said. "I will diligently review this new petition and all the facts available regarding an agreement between Billy the Kid and Governor Wallace before rendering any decision" ...

Independently, nationally prominent trial attorney Randi McGinn was designated to review both the history and prior petitions to ascertain whether there was sufficient basis for the matter to be seriously considered. Ms. McGinn, a New Mexico resident and western history enthusiast, agreed to undertake this voluntarily and at no cost to taxpayers. After concluding her review, Ms. McGinn submitted a formal petition on December 14, 2010 ...

"I look forward to hearing what others have to say about the petition. I also hope that it will spark renewed interest in New Mexico's history and how the days of Billy the Kid and the Lincoln County War helped shape our state," Richardson added.

## LEW WALLACE'S REAL DNA

Governor Bill Richardson's mistake, when trying to trick the Garrett family, was forgetting that there might be more, real, living, Old West DNA in the form of Wallaces. Lew Wallace and his wife Susan had one son: Henry. Henry had two sons, one having died in World War II. The other, Lew Wallace Jr., had a son, William N. Wallace, and two daughters.

After the McGinn petition, I rushed to find these great-grandchildren. At the Indiana Historical Society, one repository of

Lew Wallace's papers, no Wallace family contact had occurred for 15 years. But someone remembered their state was Connecticut. So I called every Wallace there. And I found Lew Wallace's great-grandson, William N. Wallace, the last male descendant.

With trepidation, I phoned. Everything depended on him.

William N. Wallace, an author and retired *New York Times* journalist in his 80's, was imperious (as was probably Lew himself); but was indignant about the insult to "the General," as he called his ancestor. Amusingly, he also thought Richardson's office was in the "Palace of the Governors" (as had been Lew Wallace's). And William N. Wallace's e-mail address was a *Ben-Hur* character's name; all leaving me feeling like I was in a time-warp and had contacted Lew Wallace himself.

By December 16, 2010, William N. Wallace, using historical talking points from me; a copy of Richardson's August 9, 2010 letter to the Garrett family; the McGinn Pardon Petition; and contacts with AP reporter Barry Massey, a "German Worldwide TV outfit," and the *L.A. Times*, wrote his letter to Richardson.

Governor Richardson –

Your imminent action – issuing a pardon to William H. Bonney, aka Billy the Kid – does not sit well with me, the great grandson of General Lew Wallace and his only remaining male heir. Such action would declare Lew Wallace to have been a dishonorable liar.

Your proposed deed, based on an alleged "broken" promise of then Governor Wallace, is without any rational reasoning. There is no concrete evidence that Governor Wallace ever made any such pardoning promise to Billy the Kid.

The petition filed on this matter lacks any credible supporting evidence. Also, its source, Attorney Randi McGinn, has meager qualifications and possible conflicts of interest in my opinion. Is one to believe that Ms. McGinn thought up this petition all by herself out of her compassion for someone who may have taken as many as 22 lives in federal territories two centuries back? It is not a petition. It is a deceit.

Lew Wallace was an American hero of his time. His honors are many. His statue is one of the just 100, two for each state, in the National Statuary Hall of the United States Capitol, his representing the state of Indiana.

You may have walked across that impressive rotunda. New Mexico's representatives there are Chavez and Pope, each of who would make far more effective objects of tourism enhancement than the questionable pardon of Billy-the-Kid, a convict. Your other motives in issuing the pardon are unclear to me.

Why would a retiring governor choose to defame a distinguished predecessor 130 years later?

By your intended action, you desecrate, defile, debase and dishonor an American hero in favor of a convicted murderer.

Furthermore such an action may have no legal standing because New Mexico, at the time of Governor Wallace, was a territory, not a state, and thus under federal jurisdiction.

I intend to make public my views. (My distribution list is competitive.)

My background: Yale University Bachelor of Arts degree (major in American history); New York City Journalist, 1949-1999 (*New York Times*, 1964-1999); published author of 11 books.

William N. Wallace

## *REPORTER MASSEY WRITES AGAIN*

Santa Fe AP reporter, Barry Massey, followed his Garrett family article with an August 21, 2010 William N. Wallace one headlined: " 'Billy the Kid' pardon effort draws Wild West showdown." It popped up in remote corners like Wilkes-Barre, Pennsylvania's *The Times Leader*. Massey wrote:

SANTA FE, N.M. (AP) — New Mexico Gov. Bill Richardson has stirred up a historical hornet's nest with his talk of pardoning the Old West outlaw Billy the Kid.

The latest to come out against it is a descendant of the territorial governor who once met with the Kid but never granted him clemency 130 years ago.

William N. Wallace, great-grandson of Civil War Gen. Lew Wallace, said he sees no solid historical foundation for Richardson to offer a posthumous pardon for the Kid, also known as William H. Bonney and Kid Antrim.

"There was nothing in my lifetime knowledge of Gen. Lew Wallace, my great grandfather, that ever suggested that he intended to give William H. Bonney ... a pardon," the 86-year-old Wallace said in a telephone interview from his home in Westport, Conn.

Richardson is considering a pardon to make good on an alleged promise by Gov. Wallace to provide some form of clemency for the Kid in exchange for his testimony about killings during the Lincoln County War ...

The historical record surrounding the supposedly promised pardon - like many events during New Mexico's turbulent frontier days - is ambiguous and open to conflicting views.

There's no written documents "pertaining in any way" to a pardon in the archive of Wallace's papers maintained by the Indiana Historical Society, according to staff members who sent an e-mail and letter to Richardson last week.

"If Gen. Wallace did not intend to give William H. Bonney a pardon, there is no reason why Gov. Richardson should consider giving William H. Bonney, a murderer, a pardon," said Wallace's great-grandson, a retired New York Times sports writer.

Descendants of Sheriff Pat Garrett - the lawman who shot and killed the Kid on July 14, 1881 - met with Richardson earlier this month to oppose a pardon. The governor told them he accepts historical accounts of the Kid's death.

Richardson has made no decision, said chief of staff Eric Witt. Before the governor would issue any pardon, Witt said, he'd start a formal inquiry and solicit comments from historians and others. The governor's term runs through Dec. 31.

Wallace went to New Mexico in 1878 to help bring an end to the violence of the Lincoln County War. After arriving, he offered general amnesty to those involved in the bloodbath unless they already were under indictment.

That excluded the Kid, who faced murder charges, including for killing a Lincoln County sheriff.

A tantalizing part of the pardon question is a clandestine meeting that Wallace had with the Kid in Lincoln in March 1879.

Letters written by the Kid leave no doubt the Kid wanted Wallace to at least grant him immunity from prosecution if he agreed to testify about killings he had witnessed.

The letters suggest the Kid was looking for a way out of a life of crime. Wallace, in arranging the meeting, responded to the Kid: "I have authority to exempt you from prosecution if you will testify to what you say you know."

The Kid delivered on his testimony. But Wallace never granted any form of clemency, even after the Kid was later convicted of murder and sentenced to hang.

As the Kid awaited his execution in 1881 - and as Wallace prepared to leave New Mexico to become ambassador to Turkey - the Las Vegas, N.M., Gazette asked the outgoing governor about prospects that he would spare the Kid's life.

Wallace replied, "I can't see how a fellow like him should expect any clemency from me."

The Kid escaped from the Lincoln County jail but Garrett tracked him to a ranch near Fort Sumner, N.M.

In the early 1900s, a few years before Wallace died, a pardon for the Kid resurfaced in newspaper articles in which Wallace described his secret meeting with the Kid. Wallace, by then, had achieved literary fame as the author of the historical novel, "Ben Hur."

Wallace's great-grandson questions the accuracy of the newspaper accounts, saying a number of facts are wrong. They describe the meeting between Gov. Wallace and the Kid, for instance, as taking place in Santa Fe rather than Lincoln.

"I am smelling a rat right off the bat," William Wallace said.

Doug Clanin of Anderson, Ind., who retired after serving as editor of the Wallace papers for the Indiana Historical Society, said Gov. Wallace became quite famous and in his later years was adept at "improving on old stories" as he entertained audiences on a lecture circuit.

Historian Frederick Nolan, who lives in London and has written extensively about the Lincoln County War, said in an e-mail that "there does not seem to me to be the slightest doubt that Wallace indeed made some kind of promise to the Kid" and that was at least immunity from prosecution, which could have set aside two indictments for murder.

As for a posthumous pardon, Nolan said, "Speaking for myself, I'd sort of like to see the Kid pardoned because - at the time the 'arrangement' was made - he surely merited at least as much consideration as all the others who took advantage of Wallace's amnesty. But the moment passed and so, I think, did the Kid's entitlement to a whitewash."

## *RICHARDSON'S ATTEMPTED SAVE*

Fighting back, Richardson reverted to his earliest, but abandoned, hoax approach: "pardon hearings." A September 6, 2010 *NY Times Opinion Section Contribution* by an ignorant hostile historian named Hampton Sides, titled "Not-So-Charming Billy," announced a "pardon hearing" for November in Lincoln, with period costumes and Richardson as judge. It never happened.

## *WILLIAM N. WALLACE'S FINAL SALVO*

On September 16, 2010, William N. Wallace e-mailed me: "Ms. Cooper - Barry Massey of the AP has ready from me a reaction quote should Gov. Richardson go ahead with the pardon, a condemning quote. Massey has informed the governor's staff that he has the quote and will use it." Richardson, unaccustomed to intimidation, had to weigh consequences of his scam. He wanted a political life after December 31, 2010. Was the hoax worth his future?

# RIGHT UP TO THE END

December 27, 2010 was the rumored date for Richardson's pardon announcement. But it had only uncertain press. For "CBS News," Edecio Martinez wrote: "Billy the Kid to be Pardoned 130 Years Later?" It pressured Richardson; stating: "Descendants of Old West lawman Pat Garrett and New Mexico Territorial Gov. Lew Wallace are outraged that Gov. Bill Richardson is considering a pardon for Billy the Kid, saying Wallace never offered a pardon, and a petition seeking one is tainted because it comes from a lawyer with ties to Richardson." So Randi McGinn shape-shifted for the reporter from amateur historian to a lawyer seeking weird work - no longer *pro bono*, but for pay: "McGinn said her only tie to the administration is that she volunteered to look into the pardon issue for a fee."

So my exposing her had worked. But could a man with no conscience be stopped?

On December 29, 2010, AP writer, Mark Guarino, wrote: "Outgoing New Mexico Gov. Bill Richardson is considering a pardon for celebrated outlaw Billy the Kid. An informal e-mail poll shows support. But time is running out." For this article, official hoax historian, Paul Hutton resurfaced to back pardoning (omitting his 2004 "Investigating History: Billy the Kid" in which "Brushy" was the "Billy" to be pardoned).

On December 29, 2010, Richardson floated a last-ditch oddball solution via a Glen Levy at TIME NewsFeed.com as "Will Billy the Kid Be Pardoned? Governor Has Until Friday." For it, Richardson's Deputy Chief of Staff Eric Witt - a talking head in Hutton's hoax 2004 History Channel program - stated: "We're not offering a blanket pardon for everything he did."

December 30, 2010 brought FoxNews.com's Kelly David Burke's "Billy the Kid Pardon?" Missing the irony, he wrote that Richardson - with only one day to go - says: "I want to see "some concrete evidence ... on whether ... the pardon promise, potentially a promise by Governor Lew Wallace, was valid and documented."

Left with only drama of time running out, on December 30, 2010, Richardson, through his spokesperson, Alarie Ray Garcia, gave his press release titled "Governor Richardson to Announce his decision on Billy the Kid Pardon Request Tomorrow." Deflecting fall-out to Randi McGinn's "request," it stated: "Governor Bill Richardson will announce his decision regarding a pardon of Billy the Kid tomorrow, Friday, December 31$^{st}$ live on ABC's Good Morning America. The announcement is expected at approximately 7:10 am ET/5:10am MT."

On December 31, 2010, Jessica Hopper reported for "ABC Good Morning America": "Gov. Bill Richardson: 'I've Decided Not to Pardon Billy the Kid.'" Her article proved that my fear of Richardson's using the pardon to validate his eight year "Billy the Kid Case" hoax had been correct. But he kept his mouth shut about "Brushy." Hopper wrote:

> In 2003, Richardson, a history buff, first said that he would consider pardoning the famous outlaw. He finally made up his mind today. **"It was a very close call. I've been working on this for eight years. The romanticism appealed to me to issue a pardon,** but the facts and the evidence do not support it and I've got to be responsible especially when a governor is issuing pardons," Richardson said. **Richardson said that Billy the Kid's decision to continue to kill after the pardon wasn't granted to him impacted his decision.**

After my Garretts-Wallace onslaught, I pictured that historically imbecilic Richardson asking around: "What's my excuse for no pardon? Oh! The Kid killed deputy guards? I'll use that."

On December 31st, FoxNews.com printed: "Richardson Declines to Pardon Outlaw Billy the Kid." It built on my input to J.P. Garrett and William N. Wallace; stating from J.P. that "Richardson appointed McGinn's husband to the state Supreme Court;" and from William N. Wallace that: "McGinn has 'meager qualifications' and possible conflict of interest."

Again, on December 31st, Kathryn Watson of *The Washington Times* headlined: "Alas, no pardon for Billy the Kid: New Mexico's Richardson says close call." For her, Richardson was a "history buff" reacting to the deputy killings. With hypocrisy lost to all but me, Richardson intoned: "We should not neglect the historical record and the history of the American West."

The *Los Angeles Times*, with a Rick Rojas, gave Richardson's final spin: "No Pardon for Billy the Kid. New Mexico Gov. Bill Richardson Says." 'The romanticism appealed to me ... but the facts and evidence did not support it.'" Richardson had "Albuquerque lawyer Randi McGinn" fall on her sword with an ungranted "pardon petition." She claimed no regrets, and spookily channeled Bill Robins III: "It's great being Billy the Kid's lawyer."

## BITTER "BIG BILL'S" LAST LIE

By January 1, 2011, loser Richardson took out his rage on Billy the Kid for *New York Times* reporter, Marc Lacey's "For 2nd Time in 131 Years, Billy the Kid is Denied Pardon." Richardson stated: "If one is to rewrite a chapter as prominent as this, there had better be certainty as to the facts, the circumstances and the motives of those involved," Mr. Richardson said in announcing that he would not tamper with the history **of a man whose life was spent 'pillaging, ravaging and killing the deserving and the innocent alike.'** "

Billy himself might answer Richardson - his worst enemy since Santa Fe Ring bosses of his day - as he did a *Mesilla News* reporter on April 16, 1881, three days after his hanging sentence: "I think it a dirty mean advantage to take of me, considering my situation and knowing that I could not defend myself by word or act. But I suppose he thought he would give me a kick down hill."

I would add: "Billy had dodged his most dangerous bullet yet."

# CHAPTER 7
# EXPOSING THE "BILLY THE KID CASE" HOAX IN COURT

## OPEN RECORDS SHOWDOWN

Cleverly making the "Billy the Kid Case" a real murder investigation to dig up graves, the hoaxers forgot it meant that its public official lawmen were subject to open records law.

By 2006, I took over records requests from my journalist proxy, Jay Miller. It took me seven years to get records available the day I started. During litigation, five sets of my *own* attorneys tried to throw my case. Then I went *pro se* and won. But the judge and the state's high courts blocked the statute's penalty to the lawmen. The system was rigged for crooks to protect crooks.

But I got what I wanted: proof of no valid DNA, meaning illegality of their exhumations. And I got more than I wanted: facing head-on the terrifying thuggery of the empowered lawmen.

## SUMMARY OF OPEN RECORDS FIGHT

Since the "Billy the Kid Case" hoaxers merely rewrote the hoax every time I blocked them, I realized the only way to end their scam was by exposing their fake DNA claims by getting their actual DNA documents. When journalist, Jay Miller, was my proxy from 2004 to 2006, they refused all records turn-overs by the open records exemption of Case 2003-274 being an ongoing criminal investigation. This was fakery, since that exception's intent was to prevent a suspect from escaping; and Pat Garrett, dead since 1908, was going nowhere. **(But remember the criminal investigation claim.)**

In 2006, under my name, I began my open records requests to the responsible records custodian, Sheriff Rick Virden. He used fellow hoaxer, Lincoln County Attorney Alan Morel, to respond. They tried to scare me off by claiming to report me as a terrorist! So I got a lawyer in 2007 to do the requests.

Through Morel, Virden lied to my lawyer that he had no records whatsoever for Case 2003-274, and claimed Tom Sullivan and Steve Sederwall had them. Through Morel, Sullivan and Sederwall then **lied, claiming it was not a law enforcement case, but was their private hobby** (immune to the public records act), and its records were their private "trade secrets;" thereby brazenly reversing the law enforcement exception they had used for years to deny me records through proxy, Jay Miller.

Improper withholding of public records triggers litigation, so, in October of 2007, my lawyer filed "Sandoval District Court Case No. D-1329-CV-2007-1364, Gale Cooper et al v. Rick Virden, Lincoln County Sheriff and Custodian of the Records of the Lincoln County Sheriff's Office; and Steven M. Sederwall, Former Lincoln County Deputy Sheriff; Department; and Thomas T. Sullivan, Former Lincoln County Sheriff and Former Lincoln County Deputy Sheriff.

Demanded were the DNA records of Case 2003-274. That meant Dr. Henry Lee's specimens from the carpenter's bench and courthouse floorboards; Rick Staub's bones from exhumed John Miller and William Hudspeth; Orchid Cellmark Labs' DNA extractions from the carpenter's bench, the floorboards, John Miller, and William Hudspeth; and Orchid Cellmark's matchings of Miller and Hudspeth DNA to bench DNA. My lawmen defendants - with unlimited tax dollars to pay for attorneys as public officials (while claiming to be hobbyists) - got two law firms, who split the case for apparent double billing (Virden with one, Sullivan and Sederwall with another).

Though the judge eventually declared them public officials and ordered records turn-overs, the lawmen ignored him, with Virden saying he did not know how to get them, and Sullivan and Sederwall saying they were private. And, contrary to a legitimate court, the judge did not hold them in contempt; instead, permitting years of stonewalling, as I had to get rid of five sets of my own lawyers for not properly representing me.

Then things got worse. The hoaxers did turn over Lee reports; except they forged them to look like their private investigation to trick the judge! I caught them; so the judge again demanded turn-over. So, after five years, I got Lee's single report. But that was just his specimen recoveries. The lawmen hid Orchid Cellmark Lab's records which proved their fraudulent claims and illegality of exhumations. So my co-plaintiff used an attorney outside the public records act to subpoena the records. Orchid Cellmark turned over 133 pages proving no usable DNA.

Then things got worse. The last of my attorneys betrayed my case, and I had to go *pro se* and fight alone. I prevailed. But the judge shielded the lawmen, removing all penalties for wrongful records withholding, to punish me by blocking my deserved near million dollars. But he did sanction them for the forgeries.

I took the case to the state Court of Appeals and Supreme Court, who not only upheld no penalties, but removed the one for forgeries. To understand this Santa Fe Ring-style corruption, note that the Chief Justice of the Supreme Court was Charlie Daniels: appointed by Richardson; a major Richardson political donor; and husband of Richardson's Attorney Randi McGinn: who did the hoax's final "Pardon Petition."

To stymie the usual Santa Fe Ring-style cover-up expurgation, I put the major filings on my GaleCooperBillytheKidBooks.com website. And I published two exposé books reproducing the documents: 2012's *Billy the Kid's Pretenders, Brushy Bill and John Miller*; and 2014's *Cracking the Billy the Kid Case Hoax: The Strange Plot to Exhume Billy the Kid, Convict Sheriff Pat Garrett of Murder, and Become President of the United States*.

## HOAXERS' LIES TO HIDE RECORDS

### *SHELL GAMES TO HIDE RECORDS*

To hide their incriminating records from me, Virden, Sullivan, and Sederwall lied wildly. After years of calling themselves "cops" doing the "Billy the Kid Case," creating all documents under Lincoln County Sheriff's Department Case No. 2003-274 as Sheriff or Deputy Sheriff, and refusing records to my proxy, Jay Miller, by the exclusion for an "ongoing criminal investigation," they now called the case a private hobby. And, after years of boasting about their DNA evidence, and digging up bodies based on it, Virden now said he had no DNA records at all. This ignored that, as records custodian, he was required to get them from Dr. Henry Lee or Orchid Cellmark. But he was playing hide-the-ball.

## CALLING THE CASE ONLY THE BELL MURDER

Since Case No. 2003-274's murder investigation against Pat Garrett had generated the DNA records, the hoaxers claimed the case was just the Deputy Bell's shooting - which had no DNA!

They did not realize I was behind all past anti-hoax litigation, so I had all their records. I had their "Probable Cause Statement" for Pat Garrett as a murder suspect, with the Bell shooting as a sub-investigation as to his friendship with the Kid.

I had Bill Richardson's June 10, 2003 press release: "Last month I was contacted by Lincoln County Sheriff, Tom Sullivan and Capitan Mayor, Steve Sederwall, to support reopening the case. Case number 2003-274 ... is [to determine] did Sheriff Garrett kill Billy the Kid at Fort Sumner, New Mexico ... on July 14. 1881?"

I had all their exhumation petitions about Garrett being a murderer. As their Attorney, Sherry Tippett, stated in her October 3, 2003 Case No. MS 2003-11 "In the Matter of Catherine Antrim, Petition to Remove Remains;" stating: "This petition is made in conjunction with investigation No. 2004-274 [sic] filed in Lincoln County and case number 03-06-136-01 filed in De Baca County, for purpose of determining the guilt or innocence of Sheriff Pat Garrett in the death of William Bonney aka "Billy the Kid."

So hoaxing Lincoln County Attorney Alan Morel, responded to my records request on April 27, 2007 for Sheriff Rick Virden by lying: "The Lincoln County Sheriff's Office has extremely limited information pertaining to the case you are inquiring about, Case Number 2003-274. **Case 2003-274 involves an investigation into the escape of William H. Bonney and the murder of two Lincoln County Deputies, namely James W. Bell and Robert Olinger of April 28, 1881.**"

And four years into litigation, Sullivan and Sederwall's attorney Kevin Brown, was still lying to the court about the Deputy killing sub-investigation for a January 21, 2011 Evidentiary Hearing, in which he claimed: "**[T]he investigation that was opened was a follow-up investigation of the escape of William Bonney and the double homicide of James and Robert Olinger. I forgot the other guy's name.**" [Transcript 1/21/11, p. 27] That segued into Brown's lying that the carpenter's bench was not in that courthouse killing; ergo, it was not part of the Case 2003-274's records I was requesting! So Brown claimed everything else - including that carpenter's bench - was a private hobby. He stated: "Steve Sederwall – **this didn't have anything to do with the courthouse investigation** ... on his own, paying his own expenses, located this workbench in Albuquerque ... On July 31st, Dr. Lee examined the workbench. **It wasn't part of the courthouse investigation.** And DNA samples he took were given to Calvin Ostler. Cal Ostler sent the DNA to Orchid Cellmark Lab ... Steve Sederwall's position is that the workbench was personal.." [Transcript 1/21/11, pp. 28-29, 31] In fact, that finding of the bench was in the "Probable Cause Statement," with Sederwall as deputy and as its author; stating: "**On August 29, 2003, Deputy Sederwall of the Lincoln County Sheriff's Department located the carpenter bench where the Kid's body was placed on July 14, 1881.**"

Sheriff Rick Virden used the Deputy Bell lie, testifying in the January 21, 2011 Evidentiary hearing that "[t]he documents that I have were documents that says [the case was] ... the escape of William Bonney." [Transcript 1/21/11, p. 137]

But Steve Sederwall, who claimed he wrote the "Probable Cause" statement for Garrett as a murderer, testified in January 21, 2011's Evidentiary Hearing: "The way I saw 2003-274, was Sheriff Sullivan opened up a case ... and it was a follow-up on the escape and homicide of James Bell and Robert Ollinger [sic]." [Transcript 1/21/11, pp. 148-149]

The judge did not buy that trick. For the January 21, 2011 Evidentiary Hearing he stated: "I'm going to find that the investigation in this case of Billy the Kid and the double homicide of James Bell and Robert Olinger and the investigation of the death of Billy the Kid are related. I'm going to find that these investigations were under the auspices of the Lincoln County Sheriff's Office. I'm going to find that any report, lab results, and anything coming out of this investigation are public documents." [Transcript 1/21/11, p. 192]

## *VIRDEN CLAIMING TO HAVE NO RECORDS*

As the Sheriff then conducting Case No. 2003-274, Rick Virden was the custodian of its records under open records law.

So, through crooked Attorney Alan Morel, he claimed no records. First Morel responded to me on April 27, 2007: "Neither Sheriff Virden nor the County of Lincoln maintains any public records that are responsive to [your requests]." On May 11, 2007, Morel added: "**Neither Lincoln County nor the Lincoln County Sheriff's Office maintains any records of any kind whatsoever pertaining to Case No. 2003-274.**" In fact, after years of litigation, Virden finally turned over his hidden file of hundreds of pages - though expurgated of DNA records.

Virden also claimed that his Deputies, Tom Sullivan and Steve Sederwall had his records, and would not give them back! So Attorney Morel, on April 27, 2007 wrote: "The Lincoln County Sheriff's Department is unaware of what information Mr. Sullivan and Mr. Sederwall may or may not have within their possession."

In the litigation, Virden's lawyer, Henry Narvaez, lied that Virden was not responsible for records not in his possession. In the hearing of November 20, 2009, his firm's lawyer stated: " [W]e simply cannot produce something we don't have and never did." [Transcript 11/20/09, p. 19]. In fact, New Mexico's Inspection of Public Records Act NMSA 1978, Chapter 14, Article 2 under its section 14-2-6 "Definitions" (A) stated: "custodian" means any person responsible for the maintenance, care or keeping of a public body's public records, **regardless of whether the records are in that person's actual physical custody and control**" [and] (F) "public records" means all documents ... that are used, created received, maintained or held by **or on behalf of** any public body and relate to public business" (with intent to prevent the shell game Virden was playing).

In his "Summary Judgment" of March 12, 2010, the judge did not accept their lies, and declared for me that: "Defendant Lincoln County Sheriff opened the investigation and continued the investigation [and] [a]ll evidence, documentary or otherwise, resulting from this investigation is public record [and] Defendants are ordered to turn over to Plaintiffs all information which has been collected as a result of the investigation which is the subject matter of this cause of action."

## *VIRDEN'S FAKED RECORDS RECOVERY TRIES*

For my initial records requests, Sheriff Rick Virden faked records recovery attempts. He claimed to have asked Sullivan and Sederwall for the records of *his own murder case*, No. 2003-274, and said they refused to give them back! So he did nothing.

Pressured in litigation, on October 26, 2010, he wrote on official letterhead to Dr. Henry Lee, using my open records case's number (not his Case 2003-274), asking for a floorboard report. He stated: "It is my understanding that on May 22, 2004, Steve Sederwall requested you to review evidence that came from a forensic investigation of the old Lincoln County Courthouse in New Mexico in connection with the death of Billy the Kid. You reviewed the evidence and generated a 9 page report dated February 25, 2005, signed by you and Calvin Ostler, Forensic Consultant. If you generated any other reports as a result of your review, I would appreciate you providing copies to me."

On November 12, 2010, Lee answered: "This letter is in response to your letter dated October 26, 2010. My only report issued in regards to the death of Billy the Kid was issued on February 25, 2005. No other report has been issued by me in regards to this case." Then Virden never requested that report from Lee!

To fake impossibility of getting Orchid Cellmark records, Virden coordinated with his fellow hoaxers, as discussed below (See pages 477-478), by claiming he did not know how to access the case in their system.

Do not miss the brazen fakery of this 40 year lawman claiming he had all records of his filed murder case stolen by his deputies, took no action except asking for their return, was unable to get his case's report from its forensic expert, and had no idea how to get them from their forensic lab.

## *PRETENDING TO BE HISTORY HOBBYISTS*

To escape public officials' requirement to turn over public records, the lawmen pretended to have been just hobbyists!

So, on June 21, 2007, with Attorney Morel, Deputies Tom Sullivan and Steve Sederwall gave me a major hoax document: their 18 page "Memorandum" to Sheriff Rick Virden with 11 Attachments, both resigning their deputyships, and claiming to be private hobbyists! They stated: "We have been told that the letter from Gail [sic] Cooper's attorney is her attempt to gain the information we spent years gathering to add to a book she is attempting to sell. We will continue our investigation. **Now we choose to put an end to the harassment and political pressure by tendering our resignations as Deputies of the Lincoln County Sheriff's Department, effective this date.**" (See "Memorandum" below, pages 485-498) Then Virden claimed he had no way to get records from them.

For his deposition of August 18, 2008, Sullivan lied through his attorney, Kevin Brown, that records from Dr. Lee's and Orchid Cellmark's DNA work were "irrelevant" to my request because: "It's not a public record ... And it could be covered by the trade secret privilege." (Deposition 8/18/08, p. 117) To put this in context, Sullivan had been refusing my records requests for years based on its *being a law enforcement case*. For example, on October 8, 2003, he responded to my then attorney, Randall Harris, on official Lincoln County Sheriff's Office letterhead, with "denial Letter, Billy the Kid Case": "**This is an ongoing investigation and until the investigation is completed and closed [the records] will not be** available for release, as per Section 14-2-1(A)(4) of the inspection of Public Records Act which protects law enforcement records."

In the September 9, 2010 Hearing for Mandatory Disclosure and Production of Records, Sederwall's attorney, Kevin Brown, stated: "[O]ur position is going to be that Steve Sederwall is an amateur historian ... whatever he's doing on his own cannot be considered a public document." [Transcript 9/9/10, p. 16]

Rick Virden joined the hobbyist lie, testifying in a January 21, 2011 Evidentiary Hearing: "This [murder] investigation was done by those two reserve deputies from the start, on their own, with their own funds, by themselves." [Transcript 1/21/11, p. 105] He was hiding the full-powered **commissioned deputy cards** he had issued Sullivan on January 1, 2005, and Sederwall on February 25, 2005 to enable their doing exhumations. He hid his November 28, 2005 letter to my proxy, journalist Jay Miller; stating: "**Tom Sullivan and Steve Sederwall are Deputies with the Lincoln County Sheriff's Department ... Tom Sullivan and Steve Sederwall are assigned to investigate the shootings of William H. Bonney and Deputies Bell and Olinger.**" He hid his May 19, 2005 "Supplemental Report for Case # 2003-274, Subject: Exhumation of John Miller," with its "**Investigator**" as "**Steven M. Sederwall, Lincoln County Deputy Sheriff.**" And he hid his 2007 letter to Hamilton, Texas, Mayor Roy Rumsey, trying to dig up "Brushy" exhumed: "Mayor Ramsey [sic], This letter will inform you that **Tom Sullivan and Steve Sederwall are both commissioned deputies with the Lincoln County New Mexico Sheriff's Department. They have been investigating case # 2003-274.**"

## SEDERWALL'S "HOBBYIST" TESTIMONIES

The most brazen "hobbyist" claims were by Deputy Steve Sederwall, who claimed *he* was doing the investigation himself.

### *LYING ABOUT DR. LEE AS HIS PRIVATE CONTACT*

When Sederwall finally turned over alleged reports of Dr. Henry Lee about the carpenter's bench and courthouse floorboards, (which he had forged to make them look like his hobby case!), he testified on January 21, 211, for an Evidentiary Hearing, that he had gotten the reports at home as a private citizen hobbyist, working with a group he called the "posse." The transcript recorded Sederwall:

A. Dr. Lee called me is how it went down. He called me, and I told him ... we would try to get him involved, that would be great, because **this whole affair thing was done by – we call it a posse.** It is done on their own time and their own dime. And Dr. Lee, when we found the workbench and other items, and then we wanted to do the CSI down at the courthouse, so we called him --- I think Bill Curtis [sic] called and arranged him to come out.
Q. So did you personally ever receive a copy of Exhibit E [furniture investigation, including carpenter's bench]?
A. Yes, sir.
Q. How did you receive it?
A. Dr. Lee mailed it to me ... At my house.
Q. When you received a report at your house ... you weren't acting as a Lincoln County investigator, were you?
A. No, Sir.
Q. When you received the report, who did you think it belonged to?
A. It belonged to me. It was sent to me ...
[And the same questioning and answering was repeated for Exhibit F, the courthouse floorboard investigation.] ...
Q. Have you ever called Orchid Cellmark to talk about things?
A. Yes, sir.
Q. Tell me about those calls.
A. The first one, we asked Dr. Lee who would be some one to deal with, and he told us Orchid Cellmark. So I discussed it with them, and told them we couldn't pay them. **We were looking at a historical event, just a bunch of guys with backgrounds as criminal investigators** ... They said that would be fine. (Transcript 1/21/11, pp. 169-171)

In fact, as Lee had responded in his May 1, 2006 letter to Jay Miller: "To set the record straight, **the Lincoln County Sheriff's Department contacted me**. They requested a forensic expert to perform preliminary identification and scene reconstruction ... **We examined a wooden bench, and floorboards at the courthouse. I completed my examination of the evidence and submitted my report to the Lincoln County Sheriff's Department**." And when Lee gave his affidavit for my case, on August 31, 2012, he swore that he had worked for the Lincoln County Sheriff's Department: He stated: "In approximately late July and early August of 2004, I assisted with the collection of samples from various locations thought to be locations where there may have been residue of biological material, which could be **relevant to an** investigation into the death of William Bonney, a/k/a Billy the Kid, then being performed by the Lincoln County, New Mexico, Sheriff's Department."

## *LYING ABOUT ORCHID CELLMARK LAB*

Sederwall also claimed that, as a hobbyist, he was in direct contact with Orchid Cellmark's Director, Dr. Rick Staub, about Lee's carpenter's bench specimens. Sederwall lied: "[Staub] told me it was blended, that there was two DNA ... Before they could do anything with it, they would separate it .(See pages 419-420 above for **no bench DNA** and mixed DNA actually being from floorboards)... [Staub] said, 'We are talking about probably $50,000." (See page 420 above) (Transcript 1/21/11, p. 172) In his June 26, 2012 Deposition (TR, p. 561), cornered on his hobbyist ploy, incorrigible Sederwall gave a smart-alack reply: **not feeling like a deputy in his mind!** My attorney's questioning was as follows:

Q. This is a letter to [Jay] Miller from Virden. It says that you - Tom Sullivan and Steve Sederwall are assigned to investigate the shootings of William H. Bonney and Deputies Bell and Olinger? ...

A. Yes, sir ... I've never - this is the first time I've seen this letter ... Rick Virden **never gave me an assignment other than, can you go watch a horse barn, and help transport prisoners**, and work the Lincoln Days ...

Q. With the probable cause statement that I just read you and the questions and answers, we know that you were acting as a Deputy Sheriff at the time you went with Henry Lee to get the scrapings, weren't you? ...

A. **In my mind, I was, not that night, acting as a Deputy Sheriff. ... Because I'm a Deputy Sheriff, doesn't mean that I am acting on their behalf. I was not. I wasn't sent up there to do this. I was just looking. I'm a Deputy Sheriff, yes. I'm also a grandpa ...**

In truth, when I got the Orchid Cellmark records on April 22, 2012, they proved that Lee's specimen bags for the carpenter's bench and floorboards were labeled for "Chain of Custody" with Case No. 2003-274, the Arizona exhumations were listed as part of Case 2003-274, and the contact person was Calvin Ostler, Lee's partner and co-signer of Lee's report for Case No. 2003-274.

## REALITY OF 100% LAW ENFORCEMENT CASE

Until my records request litigation, it had never occurred to the hoaxers to claim that they were not lawmen; that being the authority required for the sought exhumations.

So when their first attorney, Sherry Tippett, wrote her October 3, 2003 Grant County Case No. MS 2003-11 "In the Matter of Catherine Antrim, Petition to Remove Remains," she made clear their lawmen's titles and that the case was against Sheriff Pat Garrett for murder. Tippett wrote:

### PETITION TO EXHUME REMAINS

Comes now **Petitioners Tom Sullivan, Sheriff of Lincoln County, Steve Sederwall, Deputy Sheriff of Lincoln County, and Gary Graves, Sheriff of De Baca County**, by and through their attorney, Sherry J. Tippett, hereby Petitions this Court to enter an Order directing the New Mexico Office of Medical Examiners [sic- Investigator] (hereinaftee "OMI") to disinter the remains of Catherine Antrim for the purpose of obtaining DNA samples.

And, on July 26, 2004, was Attorney Mark Acuña's "County of De Baca, State of New Mexico, Tenth Judicial District, In the Matter of William H. Bonney A/K/A 'Billy the Kid' Cause No. CV-04-00005" **[APPENDIX: 14]**, in which his five page filing called Sullivan, Graves, and Sederwall "law enforcement officers 13 times *to deny that they were 'hobbyists!'* As Acuña stated: Sederwall, Sullivan, and Graves, all joined in on the Petition to Exhume the remains of Billy the Kid as Co-Petitioners and **in their capacity as law enforcement officers** engaged in an on-going investigation ... Petitioners assert that they maintain standing in the instant action **as law enforcement officers** engaged in the investigation of criminal violations, namely, the alleged killing of Billy the Kid by the legendary Sheriff, Pat Garrett.

When Sheriff, Tom Sullivan boasted to reporter, Rene Romo, for the December 9, 2003, *Albuquerque Journal's* "Kid's Mom May Stay Buried." Romo wrote: **"This summer, the sheriffs of Lincoln and De Baca counties opened a criminal investigation into the death of William Bonney aka Billy the Kid to resolve claims that Lincoln County Sheriff Pat Garrett killed someone other than the famous outlaw at Fort Sumner on July 14, 1881."**

When journalist Jay Miller proxied my records requests, he was refused by Lincoln County Attorney Alan Morel with the law enforcement case exception, like on May 19, 2004: **"Sheriff Sullivan** maintains that the case involving Billy the Kid is an ongoing criminal investigation and, as such, the records you requested pertaining to the investigation are not subject to disclosure at this time pursuant to the Public Records Act, Sec. 14-2-1, Subparagraph A 4."

And the lawmen flaunted their status. On October 21, 2005, Tom Sullivan's letter to the *RuidosoNews.com* editor stated: "Frederick Nolan dismisses the modern day law enforcement technologies we have used to recreate the crime scene in Pete Maxwell's bedroom on the night that Pat Garrett allegedly shot "the Kid" as nothing but "stunts." And now Robert Utley refers to us as "loony guys" and "two nut cases" ... Our investigation contradicts their theories written in their books. It appears that our critics all suffer from the same "kindergartenmentality." [sic] Why are they so afraid of the truth? ... **Steve and I were both sworn in as sheriff's deputies by Sheriff Rick Virden shortly after he took office.**"

## *LYING THAT ORCHID CELLMARK GOT BLOOD*

Key to the hoax, after I blocked its exhumations of Billy and his mother, was claiming they got Billy's blood from the carpenter's bench for DNA. In his Deposition of August 18, 2008, Steve Sederwall testified to my attorney that Director Rick Staub told him that Orchid Cellmark confirmed blood from the carpenter's bench. (Deposition 8/18/08, p. 43) Sederwall stated:

> Q. Do you know if [Orchid Cellmark] tested for blood?
> A. They did.
> **Q. Did they find blood?**
> **A. They did.**

In fact, when the Orchid Cellmark records were subpoenaed in April of 2012, they had no testing for blood; and their actual testing found *no DNA at all* from Dr. Lee's bench samples.

## *FAKING NO ACCESS TO ORCHID CELLMARK DNA RECORDS*

The lawmen defendants hid the Orchid Cellmark DNA records, knowing they showed no bench DNA to justify exhumations. (Complicit were Dr. Henry Lee and Orchid Cellmark Director Rick Staub, who wanted the records hidden as much as the lawmen.) They used their two scams of Sullivan and Sederwall being private hobbyists, and Virden not knowing how to get them.

## SULLIVAN AND SEDERWALL

For his August 18, 2008 deposition, Tom Sullivan, pretending to be a private hobbyist, refused to give any records as his "trade secret privilege;" stating: "There's DNA evidence from the bench and there's DNA evidence from John Miller ... It's probably at Orchid Cellmark." (Deposition 8/18/08, p. 107) In his Deposition that day, Steve Sederwall, also posing as a private hobbyist, acknowledged that Orchid Cellmark's contact person was Calvin Ostler: "Henry Lee's assistant ... He took possession of [the specimens]. He sent it to Orchid Cellmark." (Deposition 8/18/08, p. 43)

## VIRDEN

To get the Orchid Cellmark records, Sheriff Rick Virden, their custodian under open records law, merely had to request them for his Case No. 2003-274. But he fabricated that he could not get them because he was not the Lab's "designated client." In fact, a "client" name is a lab formality to access cases with multiple investigators. But Virden and Orchid Cellmark hid that the client was Lee's partner, Calvin Ostler. And Virden hid that in his own case file's "Contact List" for the Lab had its Director, Rick Staub.

So Virden, faked a records request by using "client." On October 26, 2010, on official letterhead, he requested to records using *my litigation's* irrelevant case number, D-1329-CV-2007-1364, instead of *his own identifying Case 2003-274*! Then he double-talked: "It is my understanding that in the spring or summer of 2004, Steve Sederwall sent a blood sample(s) to Orchid Cellmark Lab gathered from a forensic investigation of the old Lincoln County Courthouse in New Mexico and possibly related to the death of Billy the Kid. If you reviewed the blood sample(s) and generated any reports, or have in your possession any documents related to the blood sample(s) sent to you by Steve Sederwall, I would appreciate you providing copies to me." Since this was nonsense, no response came from the Lab.

On November 2, 2010, Virden called Orchid Cellmark's Customer Liaison for Forensics, Joan Gulliksen, lying that *Sederwall* had sent specimens to their Lab (as if their client), and not asking for his contact, Director Staub. She told Virden that he therefore needed Sederwall's written permission for records release! She followed-up by letter: "Orchid Cellmark is in receipt of your letter requesting DNA documents relating to Billy the Kid. The case file is confidential and available only to our client. For those documents to be handed over, I would need written permission on Letterhead from our client authorizing us to release those documents." Then Virden did nothing; avoiding contact with Dr. Staub or Dr. Lee to either get the records, or to get the name of the client on file, which Lee or Staub could provide. But Virden's complicit Narvaez Law Firm attorney responded on November 4, 2010 to my attorney: "Orchid Cellmark Labs is refusing to turn over any documents to the Sheriff's Department because the Sheriff's Department is not its client."

The hoaxing misled my judge think Sederwall was the "client." In his order for the January 21, 2011 Evidentiary Hearing, declaring the records public, he ordered Sederwall to get them; stating: "Defendant Steven Sederwall shall through counsel, within 15 days of January 21, 2011, in writing request and authorize Orchid Cellmark Laboratory to provide to Sheriff Virden a complete copy of its entire file ... related to the investigations of the homicide of Billy the Kid and/or the double homicide of James Bell and Robert Olinger ... Sheriff Virden is to then provide to Plaintiffs' counsel everything he receives in response to the request to Orchid Cellmark."

So, for Sederwall, his attorney, Kevin Brown, simply faked a request letter on February 3, 2011; writing "I have been ordered by the court to write you and have you produce and DNA results you have resulting from an event which occurred on July 21, 2004." This scam had no case, no listed records, and a made-up date! Then Attorney Brown claimed he got no response; and ceased further requesting. And the judge did not file for contempt.

That is why my co-plaintiff, separate from open records law, subpoenaed the Orchid Cellmark records on April 6, 2012.

## THE LAWMEN'S MAJOR HOAX DOCUMENTS TO HIDE INCRIMINATING RECORDS

The documents created by the "Billy the Kid Case" hoaxer lawmen to hide their forensic DNA records of Case 2003-274 demonstrate their conscienceless deceit and smug certainty of immunity. From the thousands of pages of responses, depositions, transcripts, and judge's decisions, I selected a few to illustrate their chicanery.

The examples are of further interest because the hoaxers, with Steve Sederwall in the lead, recycled them to bamboozle gullible "Brushy"-believing author, W.C. Jameson, for his 2018 book *Cold Case Billy the Kid*, in which they all attempted to resuscitate their "Billy the Kid Case" under that new "cold case" name.

## *RESPONSE TO MY FIRST RECORDS REQUEST*

In 2006, when I ended my anonymity and began my open records investigations on my own, after two years of journalist Jay Miller's proxying my requests. I started with Sheriff Rick Virden.

On September 29, 2006, complicit Lincoln County Attorney Alan Morel delayed response, calling my request "excessively burdensome." He had already threatened Jay Miller with an harassment case for records requests on Sheriff Tom Sullivan.

Virden's response, on October 11, 2006, tried to intimidate me by fury, threats, and retaliation from Virden, Morel, Sederwall, and Sullivan. I did not retreat, but was terrified.

Alan Morel's mailing was thick, though he denied existence of any requested records. But to legitimize Case No. 2003-274, he provided the deputy cards for Sullivan (issued January 1, 2005) and Sederwall (issued February 25, 2005), proving they were commissioned deputies with full powers. And Virden denied involvement with the Arizona exhumations.

Then Morel got rough. (Remember that they had not yet heard of me. So they thought I was a mere intimidatable citizen.) So Morel labeled attachments as "Exhibits," as if in litigation; and wrote: "I have also attached to this response two e-mails from Steven M. Sederwall to Jay Miller, dated September 19, 2006, and September 20, 2006 as Exhibit 3. **I do not believe they are responsive to any of your requests for records**, but I decided to include them, as they were provided to me by Mr. Sederwall." Thug Sederwall's September 19, 2006 e-mail stated: " Jay, Is there a reason you're obsessed with our investigation? ... I am sure your [sic] aware this story is not what history claims, are you worried it will destroy New Mexico's cash cow?"

Morel's letter continued: "In addition, I have attached a copy of a letter dated September 30, 2006, with the heading 'The Dried Bean,' which was written to me on September 30, 2006. This correspondence is attached as Exhibit 4. Although I do not believe that the enclosed correspondence is responsive to any request for public records that you forwarded to me [Virden], I have, nevertheless, attached the correspondence, **as it has already been forwarded to outside parties - namely the U.S. Marshal** [sic] **Service** and Jay Miller.

That "Exhibit 4" was purposefully terrifying. The Marshals Service is under Homeland Security. So I was reported for doing an open records request - as if I was a terrorist! I guessed their contact was fellow hoaxer, U.S. Marshals Service Historian David Turk; frightening anyway for his bizarre irrationality.

The "Exhibit 4" letter was to Morel, dated September 30, 2006, and co-signed by Sullivan and Sederwall. Its obscene letterhead was: "The Dried Bean: 'You Believin' Us or Them Lyin' Whores'." So I was the "lyin' whore," in recycling of Sederwall's defamatory "cocaine whore" bestowed on Debra Ingle. Addressing the exhumation, they lied: "None of the 'promulgators' [them] so much as entered the grave of Mr. Miller. We did however examine some of the remains with our eye. **[Author's note: Sederwall's hands were "eyeball-holding" John Miller's skull in his newspaper photo!]**

However, this unsavory crew thought *I was Jay Miller*. So "The Dried Bean" calls me "Miller/Cooper," or "Miller." Assuming my ignorance, they even lied that Frederick Nolan backed them.

At this time, I was working with Maricopa County Prosecutor, Jonell Lucca, about the illegal John Miller/William Hudspeth exhumations. So, from Morel, I got what I wanted for her: a written denial by Virden, Sullivan, and Sederwall that they possessed no DNA records to justify their Arizona exhumation for "DNA matching." Unfortunately, she was as corrupt as they were.

### THE MOREL COVER LETTER

Attorney Alan Morel's October 11, 2006 open records response to me on behalf of Sheriff Virden stated:

Dear Dr. Cooper:

Please be advised that your Freedom of Information Act request dated September 22, 2006, to the Lincoln County Records Custodian and Lincoln County Sheriff Rick Virden has been forwarded to me for review and response. By way of information, I am the attorney for the County of Lincoln and, as such, represent the various elected officials of Lincoln County, including the Lincoln County Sheriff. The following represents Lincoln County Sheriff Rick Virden's response to your request for information ...

Prior to responding to your request for information, I met with Lincoln County Sheriff Rick Virden and obtained his verbal and written responses to your requests, which are incorporated herein.

I must point out that I do not agree or disagree with the opinions you expressed in the first three pages of your request for public records ... Your opinions simply aren't relevant to the records you have requested.

**[AUTHOR'S NOTE: I had stated that Virden had misused the criminal investigation exception to withhold records.]**

Response Item 1. A copy of a deputy sheriff commission issued to Tom Sullivan on January 1, 2005, is attached ... [Author's Note: Signed by R.E. Virden, Sheriff and by Donna Harkey; expiration date 5/20/08.]

Response Item 2. A copy of a deputy sheriff commission issued to Steven Sederwall on February 25, 2005, is attached ... [Author's Note: Signed by R.E. Virden, Sheriff and by Donna Harkey; expiration date 5/20/08.]

Responses Items 3 and 4. [Author's Note: Denial as "no public records" of law enforcement certification for Sullivan, then Sederwall.]

Responses to Items 5 and 6. Sheriff Virden did not assign or authorize Tom Sullivan to perform any exhumations, whether in Prescott, Arizona, or elsewhere. In speaking with Tom Sullivan (Steven Sederwall), Mr. Sullivan (Steven Sederwall) advised me that he did not personally perform any exhumations in Prescott, Arizona, or elsewhere. By further response, neither Sheriff Virden nor Lincoln County maintains any public records that are responsive to Item 5 (6).

Responses to Items 7 to 23. Neither Sheriff Virden nor Lincoln County maintains any public records that are responsive to Item (7-23).

**[AUTHOR'S NOTE: Items requested were about the Arizona exhumations: forensic DNA reports, funding, and permissions.]**

... I have also attached to this response two e-mails from Steven M. Sederwall to Jay Miller, dated September 19, 2006, and September 20, 2006, as Exhibit 3. **I do not believe they are responsive to any of your requests for records, but I decided to include them,** [author's boldface] as they were provided to me by Mr. Sederwall. In addition, I have attached a copy of a letter with the heading "The Dried Bean," which was written to me on September 30, 2006. This correspondence is attached as Exhibit 4. **Although I do not believe that the enclosed correspondence is responsive to any request for public records that you forwarded to me, I have, nonetheless, attached the correspondence, as it has already been forwarded to outside parties - namely the U.S. Marshals Service and Jay Miller.**

### "THE DRIED BEAN" ATTACHMENT

Morel's "Exhibit 4," written on September 30, 2006 by Sullivan and Sederwall, was their major hoax document, "The Dried Bean." Their uneasiness can be seen as they rolled out all their fabrications: Case 2003-274 was only for the Deputy Bell killing, it cost no taxpayer money, and they were at the Arizona exhumation as mere observers. They stated:

# THE DRIED BEAN
## "YOU BELIEVIN' US OR THEM LYIN' WHORES"

Mr. Alan Morel: Attorney at Law
Lincoln County Attorney
ADDRESS

September 30, 2006

Dear Mr. Morel:

Lincoln County Sheriff Virden forwarded a FOIA request on the Billy the Kid [sic] signed by Gale Cooper. We will do our best to answer these questions for you and give you some background on this case.

When we (Sheriff Tom Sullivan and I) opened this case to examine the death of two Lincoln County Deputies there had been no official investigation. Those upset with our investigation hold up Sheriff Pat Garrett's 1882 book *"The Authentic Life of Billy the Kid"* to say Garrett's writing, since he was the Sheriff, should stand as the official report. However, Garrett's account is fraudulent in fact.

Frederick Nolan, one who has come out publicly against our investigation, writes in *"The Authenticated Life of Billy the Kid an annotated edition"* by Oklahoma Press [sic] in 2000, *"It will surprise hardly anyone to hear that much of this text is farrago of nonsense."* Nolan goes on to say, *"But careless inaccuracy, slanted historical accounting, deliberate untruth, and downright cover-up are less forgivable, especially when purveyed under the implicit imprimatur of Garrett's name."* A statement with which we investigators agree. This presents a question. Why do the self-proclaimed arm-chair historians including Gale Cooper M.D. and Jay Miller, fear a bright light being shown [sic] on a subject that most agree is a lie?

When we began this case we agreed we would not expend any money from the public coffers or burden the County with this investigation. We do not drive government vehicles, or make copies at the government's expense. We do not sit at a government desk, use government pen or paper or computers, and not ever [sic] a government paper clip has been used. We do not work out of a government office; it is our telephones we use, our paper we write on (this is my letterhead); we use our computers, and our filing cabinets. It is our vehicles with which we use to travel. With our credit cards we pay for meals and lodging. This case has taken thousands of man hours none of which has been billed to anyone including the local, county, state, or federal government, and we have spent thousands of dollars on copying of records, all paid for with our money.

**We have Fulton Collection, Cline Collection, copied files of the National Archives, W.G. Ritch Collection, Lew Wallace Collection, Hailey** [sic - Haley] **Collection as well as many others,** at great expense, all of which we absorbed. Many historians have answered questions we posed in our search for the truth and many more have blocked our efforts. Using investigative methods we have uncover [sic] a great number of artifacts relating to this case, artifacts passed over and missed by historians and others such as Gale Cooper who *"followed all aspects of the Billy the Kid case."*

We have not entered into contracts as we are men of the west and a handshake has served us well in these matters. In the matter of John Miller Lincoln County provided nothing, not travel monies, not film or camera to take a picture. There is no contract between Lincoln County or anyone. There is no contract between the "promulgators" as Cooper and Miller insist in calling us and anyone. We merely observed the dig and introduced the State of Arizona to the lab we used and advised the lab we would allow our findings to be compared with Mr. Miller. In return the State of Arizona said we could use the comparison of Miller's DNA and our findings in our quest for the truth.

**[AUTHOR'S NOTE: This is their claim of Arizona doing the dig.]**

There was no agreement between Lincoln County and the State of Arizona. None of the "promulgators" so much as entered the grave of Mr. Miller. We did however examine some of the remains with our eye.

What is feared is that the "myth" and "legend" of Billy the Kid as written will change. This is a valid concern, with the information we now hold the "myth" and "legend" will surely be destroyed. This is what drives Jay Miller in his e-mail I have attached.

In any correspondences or written document in a crime investigators search for patters [sic], cadence of the writing, use of words or phrases, similarities and charters [?] in the writings. This is how investigators can know if the writer of a ransom note and a threat letter are from the same writer. In Jay Miller's September 3, 2003 [sic] letter to Stewart Bluestone the New Mexico Deputy Attorney General Miller uses the word "promulgators" in describing us no less than seven (7) times. In his letter to the New Mexico Attorney General Patricia Madrid Miller uses the word "promulgators" as in letters he has written to the [sic] Steve Sederwall in his capacity as Mayor and the United States Marshals Service. In Gale Cooper's letter of September 22, 2006 the word "promulgators" is used ten (10) times. Investigators have combed through the volumes of letters that Miller has sent us in the form of FOIA and have documented a great deal of other structure and phrases that would demonstrate that the Cooper letter and Miller's writings are from the same writer.

Our agreement was to bring our findings to the Sheriff when complete and not burden his office with the matter. In the September 22, 2006 Cooper/Miller letter they write "There cannot be a real murder investigation against a dead man. Pat Garrett died in 1908." Which brings us to wonder why the preachy, wordy letter questioning an investigation that "cannot be a real murder investigation"?

[AUTHOR'S NOTE: Responding to my allegation of inappropriate use of the criminal investigation exception.]

Here are the answers to the questions that Cooper/Miller pose.

[AUTHOR'S NOTE: What follows is a list of my 23 items requested, all denied; with added claim that: "Lincoln County did not perform one or more exhumations in Prescott, Arizona Pioneers' Home Cemetery at any time in 2005."]

We feel that Miller has crossed the line into harassment and we have grown weary of his actions. We will be in contact with the United States Marshals Service on this issue also he has papered them with the same long word [sic] letters and they too are weary of these "promulgators".

Sincerely,
Tom Sullivan & Steve Sederwall

Cc: Lincoln County Sheriff Rick Virden
   **United States Marshals Service**

[AUTHOR'S NOTE: This appears to be a use of fellow "Billy the Kid Case" hoaxer, U.S. Marshal's Service Historian David Turk, for intimidation of me, since the U.S. Marshals Service is part of Homeland Security. This also demonstrates that Attorney Morel was complicit in that intimidation attempt.]

   Jay Miller

[AUTHOR'S NOTE: They Cc'd Jay Miller, because, at this stage, they were still unsure if the records request had came from him, since this was the first time they became aware of me. So they were adding him for intimidation also, to cover all bases!]

## *"INVESTIGATION MEMORANDUM"*

In April of 2007, I hired a law firm to do the records requests. But the hoaxers, emboldened after escaping the illegal Arizona exhumations unscathed, refused turn-over by various lies.

On June 22, 2007, Attorney Alan Morel denied Virden's having any records, claiming Sullivan and Sederwall had them.

He also enclosed a June 21, 2007 document, titled "Memorandum, Subject: Billy the Kid Investigation," addressed to "Rick Virden, Lincoln County Sheriff," from "Steven M. Sederwall & Thomas T. Sullivan." It was signed by Virden, Sullivan, and Sederwall. It is a major hoax document. Written by Sullivan and Sederwall, it was seven footnoted pages, plus 11 Attachments, portraying themselves as martyrs for the truth. Against them was fabricated a conspiracy of Governor Richardson Bill Robins III, historians, the OMI's Debra Komar, Silver City and Fort Sumner mayors, Jay Miller, and me. And it promoted "Brushy," as if spitefully letting the cat out of the bag. It concluded with resignation as Deputies, and keeping the records as private property. But none of this fake hysteria was legal justification to withholding Case 2003-274's records from me.

## **"MEMORANDUM: BILLY THE KID INVESTIGATION"**

This June 21, 2007 "Memorandum" is on the level of the "Probable Cause Statement" for labor-intensive fabrications.

To: Rick Virden, Lincoln County Sheriff
From: Steven M. Sederwall & Thomas T. Sullivan
Subject: Billy the Kid Investigation
Date: Thursday, June 21, 2007

On April 28, 2003 we began a quest for the truth, looking into the *"escape of William Bonney and the double homicide of James Bell & Robert Olinger.* [Footnote 1: Lincoln County Call sheet pulled by Sheriff Sullivan April 28, 2003.] We chose this as a private venture and did not want to burden the county financially. The idea was to being modern science and police investigation methods to uncover the truth of the escape of the Kid and murder of our deputies. We had planned to file a report with the Sheriff at the end of the investigation, a report which the public could then access if they so desire.

[AUTHOR'S NOTE: Hoaxed is Case 2003-274 as the Deputy killing, the concealing of the Garrett murder case, and faking themselves as private hobbyists.]

At the beginning of the investigation, it became known that career law enforcement officers were investigating a century old cold case involving Billy the Kid and the case began to generate a great deal of press.

[AUTHOR'S NOTE: This is untrue. Publicity was from claiming Pat Garrett did not kill the Kid, and from Governor Richardson's press release to the *New York Times* calling it a real murder investigation with Case Number 2003-274.]

With the enormous amount of publicity generated by the investigation Governor Bill Richardson was prompted to call a press conference. On Tuesday, June 10, 2003 he told the world of his intentions; *"I am announcing my support and the support of the state of New Mexico for the investigation into the life and death of Henry McCarty, also known as William Bonney".*

[AUTHOR'S NOTE: This is fake time inversion; Richardson's article and press conference created the publicity.]

He told the roomful of reporters, *"By utilizing modern forensics, DNA and crime scene techniques, the goal of the investigation is to get to the truth. In the process, the reputation of Pat Garrett, still a hero to Lincoln County law enforcement hangs in the balance. The question is did Sheriff Garrett kill Billy the Kid at Fort Sumner, New Mexico on July 14, 1881"* The Governor went on to say, *"If we can get to the truth we will."*

[AUTHOR'S NOTE: They are contradicting their starting claim of the deputy investigation. They are also beginning a devil-made-me-do-it accusation of Richardson as the prime mover of the Billy the Kid Case.]

On September 1, 2003, the Governor, behind the scenes, supported the investigation, by instructing Billy Sparks to hand Sheriff Sullivan three checks, from private backers, totaling $6,500.00. [Footnote 2: Three checks handed to Sheriff Sullivan in Governor's office by Billy Sparks] Standing at the threshold of the Governor's office, Sparks said, *"The governor wants to insure this investigation goes forward."*

[AUTHOR'S NOTE: This is their vindictive exposure of Richardson's "buy a sheriff scheme!" The checks, presented in Attachment 2, show the payees as the Lincoln County Sheriff's Department Case number, or state "Billy the Kid Investigation." The hoaxers are, thus, revealing what they had called "secret private donors" and those donor's improper write-offs as "charity."]

The Governor also asked investigators to contact Ft. Sumner and get them *"on board."* On Friday, June 13th, Sederwall drove to Ft. Sumner and spoke with Mayor Raymond Lopez. Lopez liked the idea of worldwide attention on his village and felt it would help boost tourist dollars. He handwrote a note to the Governor, on Ft. Sumner letterhead saying, *"Mr. Steve Sederwall and I have talked and feel that we are on the same page on this Billy the Kid deal. He'll bring the information to you on the talk we had."* [Footnote 3: Handwritten note by Mayor Raymond Lopez on Ft. Sumner letterhead]

At the time investigators did not know if DNA could be obtained from a grave after 100 years, so after the Governor's news conference Sederwall met with Dr. Debra Komar an investigator with the New Mexico Office of the Medical Investigator's office. During this meeting Dr. Komar said considering the terrain, topography and climate of Silver City she judged chances of obtaining DNA from Catherine Antrim would be somewhere in the ninety percent range. Dr. Komar said she would begin investigating the graves. She and her boss were excited about working on this historical investigation.

**[AUTHOR'S NOTE: The hoaxers have now switched to the Garrett murder, and from the Fort Sumner grave to the mother's. Importantly, they are hiding Dr. Komar's OMI position, in her affidavit and deposition: that the graves of Billy and his mother had no forensically valid DNA.]**

On June 17th, 2003, something happened that shocked the investigators. In a Ft. Sumner grocery store, Ft. Sumner's ex-mayor, David Bailey approached DeBaca County Sheriff Gary Graves and told him the Billy the Kid investigation *"had to stop."* Bailey said that if the Sheriff's [sic] were to exhume the grave of the Kid there would be a problem. Bailey said, *"You do not know what you are going to find but I do."*

On Friday, October 10, 2003, investigators were in Grant County District Court requesting a court order to exhume the body of Catherine Antrim, who is known as William H. Bonney's mother. Investigators wanted to obtain her DNA. Attorneys for Silver City and Ft. Sumner opposed the exhumation, so the judge scheduled a hearing on the matter, set for August of 2004.

**[AUTHOR'S NOTE: This hides that the exhumations were all part of Case 2003-274, with themselves as its lawmen petitioners, with Sheriff Gary Graves.]**

The same day in a special meeting of the town of Silver City, Councilman Steve May objected to the exhumation by saying, *"Who cares? Who cares if it's Billy the Kid buried in Fort Sumner or if it's Brushy Bill in Texas? We might regret this if the DNA shows it's not Billy the Kid. We could shoot ourselves in the foot."*

Fear quickly spread through the "Billy the Kid" community. Anyone with an interest to protect, museum owners, authors, and entire towns became afraid of what the investigation would uncover and how it would affect their livelihood. The newspapers were full of their fears, libelous accusations and paranoia.

**[AUTHOR'S NOTE: Blocked exhumations are faked as a "afraid-of-the-truth-conspiracy;" while hiding the OMI's permit refusals, and my attorneys' arguing no historical basis to claim Garrett did not kill the Kid.]**

*"What will happen if no DNA from that grave matches DNA from the Silver City site? How do we explain that? Might it be better to leave well enough alone?"* – **Jay Miler, syndicated columnist, *Inside the Capital* [sic], July 25, 2003.**

*"I think it would have a truly negative impact if that's not Billy the Kid over there* (Fort Sumner) – **Silver City Councilman Steve May, Silver City Sun News, October 11, 2003.**

*"This is an industry for us,"* Lopez said. *"It's no different from Intel, or Sandia Labs, or Kirkland Airforce Base. It's that big for us. We don't have much to live off other than the legend, so we have to protect it."* – **Fort Sumner Mayor, Raymond Lopez, November 18, 2003, MSNBC News.**

The investigation has the *"potential to destroy the existing legend and mystery and folklore surrounding Billy the Kid, badly damage the state's tourism industry, and severely impact the economy of the state, and damage the reputation of the Governor's Office."* – **Letter to New Mexico Governor Bill Richardson signed by the Silver City Town Counsel [sic], June 21, 2004.**

**[AUTHOR'S NOTE: This was Silver City's citizens' petition, ignored by Governor Richardson, indifferent to destruction of legitimate history - here called "legend" by the hoaxers – while he pursued his "Brushy Bill" as Billy the Kid scheme.]**

*Silver City and Fort Sumner face a loss of part of their Billy the Kid legend if DNA analysis is unable to show a match between bones dug up in the two communities." ?"* – **Jay Miler,** *Inside the Capital* [sic]**, July 2, 2004.**

*"And if bodies are exhumed and no matching DNA is found, as the Office of the Medical Investigator predicts, the effect on these communities will be considerable, especially on Fort Sumner."* – **Jay Miler,** *Inside the Capital* [sic]**, September 19, 2004.**

The comments were published nearly daily. Their words told us they feared the Kid was not buried in Ft. Sumner. Most of the history of the escape of the Kid as well as his alleged killing by Garrett was built on a foundation set forth in Garrett's book. Historian Robert Utley pointed out in his book, *Billy the Kid a short and violent life:* "Although not many copies of the *Authentic life* were sold, it nevertheless had a decisive impact of the Kid's image. More than any other single influence, the Garrett-Upson book fed the legend of Billy the Kid. As the legend blossomed, writers turned to the *Authentic life* [sic] *for the authentic details. Ash Upson's fictions became implanted in the hundreds of 'histories' that followed.*

**[AUTHOR'S NOTE: This recycles their Utley misquote from the "Probable Cause Statement," where he is not talking about scholarly history, but growth of the legend.]**

Investigators were searching for the truth in this story and the fact that Garrett was not truthful in his accounts was not brought to the table by investigators but historians themselves. Just as Utley voiced Garrett was not truthful, in an August 8, 2000 interview with the Associated Press, Historian Frederick Nolan made the statement that Garrett's version of the Kid's death *"may have been the biggest lie of all."*

**[AUTHOR'S NOTE: This is a misstatement of Nolan, who was, like Utley, commenting on Garrett's book's dime novel style, but not denying that Garrett fatally shot Billy. They knew Nolan condemned their hoax, but were faking that Nolan called Garrett's report of the killing a lie.]**

Yet when it became know [sic] investigators planned to use science, fear prompted the only thing that could be done to protect the books, museums, throw insults, such as, *"The three sheriffs trying to dig up Billy and his mother are a slippery bunch of varmits."* [sic] – **Jay Miler,** *Inside the Capital* [sic], **August 9, 2004.**

It was from there that the campaign to discredit the investigation and investigators was launched. Even Nolan saying that Garrett lied, feared his repeated version of the history was being questioned wrote an editor of the *Ruidoso News*. He said, *"This project is a complete and utter nonsense, and I Wouldn't be at all surprised if Sheriff Sullivan and Mayor Sederwall are already wishing they'd never got started on this benighted project."* The next day Nolan garnered more press by appearing on CCN *Live Saturday* with Frederika Whitfield, talking ill of the investigators.

As the unchecked fear spread, investigators were trying to make contact with Dr. Komar at the OMI's office but she refused to return the calls. We were advised by the girl answering the phone that she had instructions not to send our calls to Dr. Komar. The girl stated that Dr. Komar had "lawyered up" and we would have to talk to her attorney. We had never heard of a medical investigator retaining an attorney to deal with investigators.

**[AUTHOR'S NOTE: This omits the OMI's blockade based on forensically useless DNA. The hoaxers are fabricating a "conspiracy against truth" by the OMI in what follows.]**

We didn't understand until January 20, 2004, when Bill Robins an attorney appointed by the Governor for the Kid, deposed Dr. Komar. She was asked by Robins, on page 144 lines 7 – 10 of the record, *"You don't think Billy the Kid is buried at Fort Sumner, do you?"* Dr. Komar replied, *"I don't know. I have reason to suspect perhaps not."*

**[AUTHOR'S NOTE: As discussed above (see page 312), they have taken out of context Komar's response about the Billy's body possibly not being present because of flooding, or accidental removal with soldiers' bodies**

It was at this point we believed Dr. Komar had discovered information, maybe some of the same information we had, about the Kid's grave. We wondered if the fear of harming New Mexico's tourist industry had caused the state to apply pressure to Dr. Komar and told her not to talk to us, in hopes this case would die and the myth would live.

**[AUTHOR'S NOTE: Their "conspiracy" involves Dr. Komar and "the state;" though she merely explained that there was no valid Billy the Kid DNA available in Fort Sumer. But the hoaxers want to claim she knew Billy was buried elsewhere as "Brushy!" Sederwall repeated this scam in 2018 in W.C., Jameson's book, *Cold Case Billy the Kid*. (See pages 710, 714-716 below)]**

Since doctor Komar had obtained a lawyer and refused to talk, we wrote a letter to the OMI's office under the *New Mexico Open Records Act* asking for Dr. Komar's records. Unlike our part of the investigation, it was government money that financed her studies and paid her trips to gain information, which we reasoned would make the records public.

**[AUTHOR'S NOTE: They were harassing Komar to force her to say Billy was never buried in Fort Sumner. Amusingly, they make-up that, unlike her, they were private and immune to public records requests!]**

After nearly 5 months of letters back and forth to the OMI's office we were provided with only a list of who was buried in Silver City. We knew that Dr. Komar had more records than the state admitted because she had stated this fact when deposed by Robins. We pointed out the state had paid for her trips and we knew there was more information, we received a response saying, *"The remainder of the material requested in your public records act request is in the possession of Dr. Komar, a faculty member of the University of New Mexico, and constitutes her intellectual property under federal copyright law and the University of New Mexico's Intellectual Property Policy."* [Footnote 5: Letter from Salvatore J. Giammo, Director of Public Affairs HSC Custodian of Public Records, address to Sullivan and Sederwall, dated April 12, 2007]

It became clear the state was hiding information and was not going to share it with investigators. The nagging question remained, what was the information and why did the state feel a need to hide it?

**[AUTHOR'S NOTE: Fabricated is something "hidden." The hoaxers knew the OMI's Affidavits and Komar Deposition confirmed invalid DNA in the Billy and mother graves.]**

Friday April 2, 2004, the judge in Silver City came out with a surprise ruling, not waiting for the August hearing; his ruling startled investigators would have to provide the court with DNA from Fort Sumner before he would allow the investigators to obtain DNA from Catherine Antrim.

**[AUTHOR'S NOTE: This is jump back to 2004 to fake "Komar-concealed-information" as the cause of the case's transfer to Fort Sumner; not the truth that the Judge Quintero colluded with Attorney Bill Robins III to call the case "not ripe" – meaning he wanted Billy's DNA first to justify digging up the mother for matching, as a ploy to get the case there, since they were losing in Silver City to my Kennedy Han Law Firm's attorneys. (See Page 387)]**

What no one realized was that by September 20, 2003, we had located the workbench on which Garrett claimed to have laid the Kid's body. Through our discussions with the CSI experts we felt the Kid's DNA could be obtained from that bench. We also knew historians, from as far back as the 1920's, knew the grave was not located behind the "museum and gift shop" as Ft. Sumner had led tourist [sic] to believe. [Footnote 6: Notes entitled "Bonney Grave, Ft. Sumner", by Fulton found in the Robert N. Mullin Collection, Haley Memorial Library] We also knew that digging into that empty grave would be fruitless.

**[AUTHOR'S NOTE: The hoaxers are lying about Billy's grave not being in Fort Sumner's cemetery, instead of its merely having no certain location to justify exhumation (as well as the Lois Telfer 1962 blockade). Instead they make their hoax switch to the invalid bench as a DNA source. And they still conceal that the bench was part of Case 2003-274, not their private hobby; and that it yielded no DNA.]**

Without contacting us and immediately after the judge ruled, Attorney Bill Robins filed to exhume the Kid in Ft. Sumner. The fight was on again with the village of Ft. Sumner filing motions to block Robins' attempt to look in their grave. On Wednesday July 22, 2004, Billy Sparks of the Governor's office called Sederwall at home. Sparks asked if the investigators would *'pull out of Fort Sumner"* and if so the Governor would consider it a *"personal favor."* Sparks said Silver City and Ft. Sumner were putting a great deal of pressure on the Governor to stop the dig because they feared it would destroy their tourism.

**[AUTHOR'S NOTE: Besides the continued surprising biting of the hands that had fed them, this fabricates the Fort Sumner withdrawal reason. It occurred after County Commissioner Leo Martinez threatened Sullivan with recall for continuing the hoax with public money and without County Commissioners' approval. And they well knew of Robins's filing, since they were its lawmen petitioners!]**

Sederwall called Mayor Lopez and attempted to talk to him about the issue and tell him it was not our desire to harm tourism in New Mexico. When Sederwall identified himself Lopez shouted, *"fuck you!"* and hung up. This was the last time any of the investigators talk [sic] to Mayor Lopez.

**[AUTHOR'S NOTE: This may be Sederwall's reworking his original threat to Lopez as: "Get your head out of your ass. We're getting this done whether you want it or not."]**

That Friday we called our attorney and told him attorney Robins had filed the case on our behalf and we wanted to withdraw it. Which he did and we sat back quietly as Ft. Sumner was shorn in the press throwing a party where Frederick Nolan declared it a victory for "truth."

**[AUTHOR'S NOTE: Omitted is that the Fort Sumner case had proceeded for months under their attorney, Mark Acuña, that Robins was Billy's, not their, attorney, and they withdrew days before the September 27, 2004 Hearing because of Leo Martinez's and press exposure.]**

During the investigation the village of Fort Sumner, the town of Silver City and the city of Hamilton, Texas, in an effort to protect tourism, fought the investigation so DNA could not be recovered.

In the case of Hamilton, Texas, Brushy Bill Roberts died under the name of Oliver L. Roberts and his date of birth, on his official death certificate sets out he was born on December 31, 1868 [Footnote 7: Death certificate of Ollie L. Roberts], which would make the man 12 years old in 1881 when the Kid shot and killed James Bell and Robert Olinger.]

**[AUTHOR'S NOTE: This lie about Hamilton being a tourism conspiracy, conceals that digging up "Brushy" was refused by its County Commissioners based on the hoaxers' refusing to provide DNA records to prove they had anything for its justification (which they did not have).]**

Roberts died a pauper and was buried at county expense and above his grave was placed a homemade marker of cement. [Footnote 8: Old Tombstone of Ollie L. Roberts] However, the investigators found a new tombstone on a grave located in the middle cemetery [sic] on the first row, in a very prominent place. We wondered if that grave is empty and there only for tourists. We wondered if the man was in fact buried in the back of the cemetery.

The new marker was donated and placed by the owner of the Billy the Kid Memorial Museum in Hamilton. [Footnote 9: New Tombstone for "Henry William Roberts"] Roberts name has changed from Ollie L. Roberts as listed on his death certificate and old tombstone to *Henry W. Roberts* on the new tombstone. As well, his date of birth has changed from December 31, 1868, to December 31, 1859. This would make him 21 in 1881 rather than 12 and would coincide with the history of Billy the Kid.

On May 20, 2005 [sic- May 19, 2003], the only body to be exhumed who claimed to be Billy the Kid was that of John Miller. The state of Arizona exhumed Mr. Miller and the samples were received by Dr. Rick Staub of Orchid Cellmark labs in Dallas for recovery of DNA.

**[AUTHOR'S NOTE: This is the reworking of their Arizona exhumation fiasco as "the state did it." And slyly concealed is the horrific desecration and grave-robbing of William Hudspeth. And omitted, of course, is that they did the exhumations for Case 2003-274 under their official titles, while claiming Dr. Lee's fake bench DNA for matching.]**

Investigators agree the investigation of Billy the Kid has garnered more press and has been more troublesome than any thing we have encountered in the past. Countless letters have been written to the Village of Capitan, Orchid Cellmark, Dr. Henry Lee's office, Lincoln County, the Lincoln County Sheriff, Lincoln Counties [sic] Attorney, the New Mexico Attorney General, the United States Marshal's [sic], newspapers, magazines and to investigators in an attempt to disrupt or stop the investigation. The majority of these letters were written by Dr. Gail [sic] Cooper or Jay Miller.

**[AUTHOR'S NOTE: Now the conspiracy against the truth turns to me and Jay Miller, leaving out that the "letters" were open records requests for their fake DNA records. It is also a lead-in, at this early stage of open records requesting as prelude to litigation, to claim that the requesting is legal harassment – as fellow hoaxer Attorney Alan Morel had already threatened to try to stop earlier the Jay Miller requests.]**

Miller weighed into the fight the first time on June 6, 2003 with an article accusing Governor Richardson of attempting to get publicity for the state for the investigation. Had Jay Miller read the press release, he would know that Governor Richardson admitted that fact up front.

Miller wrote letter after letter requesting files and documents concerning the financing of the investigation **but there were no records as it was privately funded by law.** Yet, Miller continued to write letter after letter. In a two month period, Jay Miller wrote the United States Marshals office, the Lincoln County Sheriff, the Lincoln County Attorney, James Jimenez, New Mexico Secretary Department Finance and Administration, the New Mexico Governor, and countless others complaining about Sederwall and Sullivan and each rambling letter, required a response. At one point he complained to the Attorney General Sederwall was *'impersonating a police officer.*

[AUTHOR'S NOTE: They are misstating the open records requests, as I know, since I wrote them! The issue was that they had no grounds for withholding the records; and murder investigations are not privately funded!]

The attacks did not center only on Sederwall and Sullivan but on anyone who dared look at the Billy the Kid Case. When Ft. Sumner heard Sheriff Gary Graves was part of the investigative team a campaign began attacking his career. On November 30, 2003 Mayor Ramon [sic] Lopez Mayor of Ft. Sumner was quoted in the paper saying Sheriff Graves was trying to start a "war" with the city over the grave of Billy the Kid. In the end, the Mayor and Ft. Sumner successfully removed Sheriff Gary Graves from office. Sheriff Graves became the first sheriff in New Mexico to be removed by a recall vote and the last sheriff taken out by Billy the Kid.

[AUTHOR'S NOTE: This lies that Gary Graves's recall for malfeasance and misfeasance, unrelated to the Billy the Kid Case, was because of it. And Mayor Lopez did not participate. It was a citizens' group that got the necessary signatures, after Graves had stolen a prisoner's money and had repeatedly terrorized residents.]

Both the village of Ft. Sumner and the City of Hamilton, Texas own a grave marked "Billy the Kid" to draw in tourist dollars. The fact remains that a man can have but one grave. Since it is a governmental entity that owns both graves and both governments have fought to keep investigators obtaining DNA from their grave that would prove where Bonney rests, it would go to reason one or both, of these governmental agencies are guilty of perpetrating fraud against the public.

[AUTHOR'S NOTE: Omitted for this fake tourism conspiracy theory, was that they had no DNA of Billy the Kid to match with any remains. And their whole case was a hoax.]

On February 9, 2007, Sederwall and Jay Miller had lunch together in Santa Fe. Without hesitation Sederwall answered any and all questions Miller posed. Miller explained what encouraged him to fight the investigators in the Billy the Kid Case. Miller said he was born in Silver City and knew *"a lot of people up there."* He said he had received a telephone call from someone in Silver City, he chose not to identify, and the caller wanted his help to stop the investigation and the exhumation of the Kid and his mother. Miller said he began to produce the newspaper articles and the massive amount of letters knowing that we would have to answer each of them. He said that a Dr. Gail [sic] Cooper was involved and wrote most of the letters.

Miller admitted if the investigation continued it would jeopardize tourism in both Silver City and Ft. Sumner. The meeting was pleasant and as the men parted company they shook hands. Miller walked away but stopped, turned and said of Catherine Antrim, *"you know she's not in that grave don't you?"*

Even though Ft. Sumner and Hamilton know, in their hearts, Billy the Kid can have only one grave, they continue to fight the discovery of the truth and continue the fraud in the name of commerce. The Governor bending to the pressure from Ft. Sumner and Silver City turned his back on his promise to find the truth. This past week another letter, requiring an answer, came to the Sheriff requesting the information we have gathered in this investigation. **We have been told the letter from Dr. Gail [sic] Cooper's attorney is her attempt to gain the information we have spent years gathering to add to a book she is attempting to sell.**

**[AUTHOR'S NOTE: Now revealed is their new tactic for withholding the DNA documents: by calling them proprietary "research," or private property immune to open records law, which is for public officials' public documents - like those of a filed Sheriff's Department murder case like 2003-274! Also, the accusing of me as wanting to get their information for a book I am writing, is intended to mean that they had made spectacular new findings that I wanted to use myself! That was part of the open records "trade secret" exclusionary clause they would later misuse in litigation. That clause applies to private businesses doing work for the state; and needing to protect their unrelated proprietary information in cases of open records litigation. The hoaxers were straight-forward public officials, generating public records.]**

We will continue our investigation. Later, we shall make the decision if and when we will release the information. Now, we choose to put an end to the harassment and political pressure by tendering our resignations as Deputies of Lincoln County Sheriff''s Department, effective this date.

**[AUTHOR'S NOTE: Quitting as its Deputies, does not convert Case 2003-274's records from public to private.]**

Respectively Submitted,
Steven M. Sederwall, Thomas T. Sullivan [written and typed]

## "MEMORANDUM ATTACHMENTS"

Though a hodge-podge irrelevant to justifying records withholding, revealed by the cornered hoaxers are apparent bribery checks from Bill Richardson and Bill Robins III for Case No. 2003-274, as well as the Case's "Brushy Bill" direction.

**ATTACHMENT 1:** "Lincoln County Call sheet requested by Sheriff Tom Sullivan on April 28, 2003 as 'Follow up investigation Escape of William Bonney and double homicide of James Bell & Robert Olinger"

**[AUTHOR'S NOTE: Faking that Bell's killing was Case 2003-274]**

**ATTACHMENT 2:** "Checks handed to Sheriff Sullivan in the State Capital [sic] by Billy Sparks"

**ATTACHMENT 3:** "Handwritten letter by Mayor Raymond Lopez to Governor Bill Richardson on Village of Fort Sumner letterhead"

**ATTACHMENT 4:** "'Statement by DeBaca County Sheriff Gary Graves dated July 20, 2003"

**ATTACHMENT 5:** "Letter from the Office of Public Affairs of the OMI's office"

**ATTACHMENT 6:** "Notes by Historian Marcie [sic - Maurice] Fulton found in the Robert N. Mullin collection, indicating that "what Ft. Sumner claims is the Kid's grave is not possible"

**[AUTHOR'S NOTE: Amusing, since getting into that "not possible" grave for "Billy the Kid DNA" was their Case's intent for DNA. This confusion is accounted for by trying to back Billy being buried elsewhere as "Brushy."]**

**ATTACHMENT 7:** "Brushy Bill Roberts Certificate of Death showing his name and date of birth has been changed to fit the history of the Kid"

**[AUTHOR'S NOTE: Amusing, since they were trying to dig him up as being Billy the Kid. Shown is that the hoaxers were mere profiteers, riding any bandwagon for self-gain.]**

**ATTACHMENT 8:** (photo) "Original headstone of Ollie L. Roberts in Hamilton, Texas Cemetery"

**ATTACHMENT 9:** (Photo) "New Headstone put up by the owner of the Billy the Kid Memorial Museum, dates and name has changed. Sederwall on the right and Lucas Speer on the left, note the plastic tube under Sederwall's arm directing tourist [sic] to the museum"

**ATTACHMENT 10:** (Copy) "Flyer found in plastic tube affixed to Brushy Bill's grave in Hamilton, Texas"

**ATTACHMENT 11:** (Photocopies) "Commission cards of Deputy Steven M. Sederwall and Deputy Thomas T. Sullivan from the Lincoln County Deputy Sheriff office"

**[AUTHOR'S NOTE: Contradicting their "private hobbyist" ploy, and even their ploy of being "reserve" deputies, are their presented regular deputy commission cards.]**

## FORGING DR. HENRY LEE REPORTS

The hoaxers knew well that the Dr. Henry Lee report that I sought about his carpenter's bench investigation was fatal to their case. I knew they had it from Lee's May 1, 2006 letter to Jay Miller which confirmed that he had "**examined a wooden bench, and floorboards at the courthouse**," that he had "**submitted my report [single]**," and that he had sent it "**to the Lincoln County Sheriff's Department**." So the lawmen first claimed that they never got it. To be noted, is that open records law requires also turning over records *not in direct possession*; so even if they "lost" it, all they had to do was get me a copy from Lee.

The judge agreed, and ordered them to turn over the Lee report. But unbeknownst to me and the judge, that started their frenzy of forging Lee reports to cover up their two big lies: (1) They had based refusal to turn over records by lying that they had done Case 2003-274 not as public officials, but as private hobbyists. (2) Their illegal Arizona exhumations were done by claiming they had Lee's "blood-DNA" of Billy the Kid from the carpenter's bench for DNA identity matching with remains to see if they were Billy.

As it would turn out, Lee's report exposed their lying. But at the start, that was not known, and forgeries were inconceivable.

### *FLOORBOARD REPORT NUMBER ONE*

On February 18, 2010, my then attorney called me to say that he had received *the* Lee report from Steve Sederwall's lawyer, Kevin Brown. I drove with pounding heart to his office, and was handed nine pages, with photos. **[FIGURE: 4]** Dated February 25,

2005, it was an official-looking report about *seeking "blood" at the old Lincoln courthouse upstairs landing for the Deputy Bell killing*. Attorney Brown's cover letter stated: "Our position is that the document Mr. Sederwall obtained from Dr. Lee is not a public record ... However to resolve this matter, I am enclosing the document Mr. Sederwall obtained from Dr. Lee. This should resolve all claims against both Mr. Sederwall and Mr. Sullivan ... If you do not believe all claims against both Mr. Sederwall and Mr. Sullivan are now resolved ... please return the document to me without making any copies."

The report's title was "Forensic Research and Training Center Forensic Examination Report: Examination of Lincoln County Courthouse. Forensic Examination Report" Its header stated its "Date of Request: May 22, 2004;" and that it was "**Requested By: Steve Sederwall, and Bill Kurtis Productions;**" with "**Report To: Steven M. Sederwall.**" It stated: "On Sunday, August 1, 2004, the forensic investigation team examined the old Lincoln County Court House in Lincoln, New Mexico. **Present at the scene were Steve Sederwall, Tom Sullivan, David Turk, Bill Kurtis, and Gary Wayne Graves**. The target area of examination is located on the top landing of the stairs of the old courtroom." No mention was made of Case 2003-274! No one had an official title! And the case was done for "Steve Sederwall!"

Its **"Results and Conclusions"** section stated: "Various stains were observed on the surface and the underside of the floorboards. Chemical tests [with O-Tolidine] for the presence of blood were positive with some of those stains. These results indicate the presence of oxidas [sic - oxidase] activity with those stains tested positive, which suggests those stains could be bloodstains. Further DNA testing could reveal the nature and identity of that blood like stains [sic - on grammar]."

Signers were "**Dr. Henry C. Lee**, Chief Emeritus, Connecticut State Forensic Laboratory, Distinguished Professor, University New Haven" and "**Calvin D. Ostler**, Forensic Consultant, Crime Scene Investigator" (Lee's business partner, and in the Utah Medical Examiner's Office).

I told my attorney to return the report to Kevin Brown as unrequested. *I had asked for the carpenter's bench report*. Oddly, Sederwall had claimed in his deposition of August 18, 2008 that he had *a 12 page Lee bench report*, and had not mentioned this 9 page floorboard one. But he had then refused turn-over, claiming it was part of his private hobby. And all the lawmen in this report had no titles, as if it was the private hobby as claimed by the hoaxers. But the outrageous idea of forgery never occurred to me.

## *A FLOORBOARD REPORT AS EXHIBIT F*

On March 9, 2010, my attorney held a Presentment Hearing before the judge to demand the DNA records and to report that no requested records had been turned over. Sheriff Rick Virden lied through his Narvaez Law Firm attorney that he was not "required to produce documents that we are not in possession of."

Sederwall lied through his Attorney, Kevin Brown, that Lee's report met my request, and **was his only Lee report**. Brown stated: "I didn't want to disregard the Court's ruling, and so I obtained the particular document that Sederwall had that we were talking about. I presented it to [Dr. Cooper's attorney], and I said, I think this is going to resolve all the matter. If you disagree, return it back to me and we'll just go further. It was returned back to me, and I was told that this isn't what you requested ... **I will state to the Court, the document which I have here, which I would mark as an exhibit or do whatever, is the only document that Sederwall received**." It was marked **Exhibit F**. [FIGURE: 5] As an exhibit, it was part of the court record, but not shown to me in court. *But it seemed obvious that it was the same floorboard report I had already been given and rejected.*

## *FLOORBOARD REPORT NUMBER ONE AGAIN*

On April 6, 2010, my attorney faxed me Virden's turn-over of the same floorboard report that was already given to me by Attorney Brown on February 18, 2010. Virden's Narvaez Law Firm attorney's cover letter stated: "Attached is the Forensic Examination Report from Dr. Lee ... Please be advised that this report was never in Lincoln County's possession, and the only reason we have a copy of it is because Mr. [Kevin] Brown provided it to us."

On April 12, 2010, Virden's attorney sent a second letter: "This letter is to follow up my phone conversation with [Dr. Cooper's attorney] this morning regarding a document pertaining to the Billy the Kid investigation that he believes has not been produced. [In] Mr. Sederwall's deposition he testified that he received a copy of Dr. Lee's report 'about the workbench' ... Mr. Sederwall testified that it was perhaps 10 [sic - 12] pages in big font ... The report Mr. [Kevin] Brown produced seems to fit the above description, with one exception. It is a report authored by Dr. Lee that is 9 pages long in big font. However it appears to be an examination of floorboards rather than a workbench. Could Mr. Sederwall simply have been mistaken ... about the nature of the report? ... [I]f the only remaining dispute in this case is about whether there exists a second report ... we could either have an evidentiary hearing and allow Judge Eichwald to decide, or ... [Dr. Cooper's attorney] could subpoena Dr. Lee and have him produce any reports he authored dealing with Billy the Kid."

The Narvaez Firm was lying that Virden was required only to turn over records in possession, and ignoring his statutory requirement to get Lee's report from Lee, if he did not have it. Furthermore, they were playing games that Sederwall meant "floorboard" not "bench" report as the only record he had. The Narvaez Firm also said *I* should subpoena Lee's records - when open records law required Virden to recover them.

Nevertheless, it seemed that the crooked lawmen were all talking about the same Lee floorboard report.

## *THE CARPENTER'S BENCH REPORT*

On November 10, 2010, with my all-day Evidentiary Hearing looming, Steve Sederwall shockingly pulled another Dr. Lee report out of a hat - this time, the carpenter's bench report!

Its cover letter was to my attorney from his lawyer, Kevin Brown (keeping a straight face after telling the judge in the March 9, 2010 Presentment Hearing that Sederwall had *only one* report). Brown's letter stated: "Enclosed please find a copy of another report dated February 25, 2005 which deals with the examination of furniture by Dr. Lee ... It is our position that the documents produced are not public records. It is our position that if the documents are public records, they are protected by the trade secret privilege ... Nevertheless, these documents are being produced in attempt to resolve this matter."

Oddly, this report looked different from the Lee floorboard report, having ornate font in its title. **[FIGURE: 6]** One would assume a standard presentation by an expert. **And it lacked any "Results and Conclusions" section whatsoever - a forensic report's purpose!** It was titled "Forensic Research & Training Center Forensic Examination Report, Examination of furniture from Pete Maxwell's of July 15, 1881." It was 16 pages, and was signed by Lee and Calvin Ostler. Its header had no law enforcement information; and the "Requested by" section was expanded from the floorboard report's "Steve Sederwall, and Bill Kurtis Productions" to "Steve Sederwall, Capitan, New Mexico, paid for by Investigating History Program, Kurtis Production."

Its "Introduction" stated: **At the request of Steve Sederwall of Lincoln County, New Mexico, Bill Kurtis and Jamie Schenk of**

Kurtis Production, Dr. Henry Lee went to New Mexico on July 31, 2004 to assist in the re-investigation of the case of Billy the Kid. The forensic investigating team participating in re-investigation consist the [sic] following individuals: [listed as] **Steve Sederwall, Investigator; Tom Sullivan, Investigator; Dr. Henry Lee, Chief Emeritus of the Connecticut State Police Forensic Laboratory; Calvin Ostler, Forensic Consultant, Riverton, Utah; Kim Ostler, Crime Scene Assistant, Riverton, Utah; David Turk, U.S. Marshall [sic], United States Marshall Service [sic]. In addition, Mike Haag, Firearm examiner from Albuquerque Police Department Crime Lab, also provided valuable technical assistance in the investigation.** The forensic investigation team arrived at the Manny [sic - Mannie] Miller residence, located at (address removed), Albuquerque, New Mexico, at 18:20 hours on Saturday, July 31, 2004. Upon arrival we were presented with three pieces of evidence: a worktable, a washstand, and a headboard. Investigator Sullivan, Investigator Sederwall, and members of Bill Kurtis Productions had removed the three pieces of evidence from a storage building at the rear of the residence. Each item was inspected visually and macroscopically."

Listed were three separate investigations titled: "Item #1 Workbench," "Item # 2 Washstand," "Item # 3 Bed Headboard."

**WORKBENCH:** For the carpenter's bench, Lee's testing for "blood" on the top was listed on page 6 as by Phenopathlien and Ortho-tolidine. And page 9 listed testing the underside of the bench with Luminol. (All are for iron compounds - like blood or rust - with rust being more likely on a carpenter's bench.) And it had something fatal for the hoaxers on page 9; stating: "Swab samples of area number '3' and area number '4' were collected for DNA testing. Two swabs were taken from each area and placed in two separate swab boxes, one box was labeled for area number '3' and one box was labeled for area number '4'. **These two samples were transferred to Lincoln Sheriff Department.** In addition, scraping samples were also taken from these two areas. These samples were placed in two evidence envelopes [**AUTHOR'S NOTE: When I did get Orchid Cellmark's evidence envelopes by 2012 subpoena, they were, indeed, labeled as for Case 2003-274**] and were transferred to Lincoln Sheriff Department."

**WASHSTAND:** This had its photograph and had diagrams of the supposed bullet holes for the trajectory discussed by Lee in his press interviews at the time.

**HEADBOARD:** With no photograph or diagram, it merely stated: "A piece of headboard was examined. No bloodlike stains was observed. No bullet hole was found. No evidence of damage was noted." [This omitted that the entire headboard was missing, having only a rim; thus, without a place for that bullet "damage!"]

Although one would have expected Dr. Lee to prepare standardized reports, although Sederwall had originally said the report was 12, not 16, pages, and although law enforcement titles were missing for requester Sederwall and the investigators, the report did prove that the evidence samples went to the Lincoln County Sheriff's Department - contradicting the hoaxers' private hobby claim. There was no way of imagining that this revealing information was just careless rewriting for a forged document intended to prove the private hobbyists claim.

## *FLOORBOARD REPORT AS EXHIBIT F AND CARPENTER'S BENCH REPORT AS EXHIBIT E*

For my January 21, 2011 Evidentiary Hearing, which had yielded the nervous flurry of turning over Lee reports to avoid contempt, Attorney Kevin Brown, for Sullivan and Sederwall, still ignored the Court's decision as to their being public officials, calling them "hobbyists." And he lied that Case # 2003-274 was just the deputy murder investigation, which had produced no DNA records - meaning there were no records to give me.

Then Brown segued into his intended clinchers to the judge to show open records compliance and prove the amateur historian hobby. He said Sederwall's investigation with the carpenter's workbench was private, and its specimens were sent to Orchid Cellmark by report signer Calvin Ostler.

**As proof, Brown then dramatically handed over to the Court the workbench report as Exhibit E and repeated hand-over of the floorboard report as Exhibit F.**

Brown added, to address records hiding, in case the judge stuck to its being a public official case: "[O]nce we start talking about DNA, its existence or creation of documents, we are going to be getting into a recognized exception in the Public Records Act, which is trade secret privilege." The intent of this dishonest maneuver was to hide the fatally incriminating, also requested, Orchid Cellmark Lab records of DNA extraction and matching results from me as being Sullivan's and Sederwall's private "trade secrets."

## *THE LEE TURN-OVER REPORTS' SHOCKER*

As I have mentioned, my own attorneys kept trying to throw my case; which necessitated my replacing them. Having gotten rid of the attorney who got the floorboard and carpenter's bench reports, I went to a meeting with my new attorneys to review the old attorney's boxes of my case's files.

As a layman, I was permitted only the court sessions' transcripts (for which I paid); but only an attorney could get the transcripts' Exhibits. So I wanted to review them to know what had been entered for the record. But in going over the defense Exhibits from my January 21, 2011 Evidentiary Hearing, I was struck by defense Exhibit E (for carpenter's bench) and Exhibit F (for floorboards). I had only seen the supposedly same ones given to my attorney before that hearing.

I have near-photographic memory. **I exclaimed, "This floorboard report is completely different from the floorboard report Sederwall turned over to my attorney on February 18, 2010, and gave to the Narvaez Law Firm on April 6, 2010!"** [Figure: 4 and Figure: 5] This Exhibit F floorboard report had a completely different title font. The font on this Exhibit F floorboard report matched the ornate font on the carpenter's bench report's title, which Sederwall had turned over on November 10, 2010 (and then gave to the Court as Exhibit E). I thumbed through Exhibits E and F. Now *neither* had a "Results and Conclusions" section - though that first turned-over Lee floorboard report had one!

From my papers I took out that first Lee report to show these new attorneys the numerous alterations and changes between the first floorboard report, and the Exhibit F floorboard report given to the court. Noted were:

1) The "Requested by" phrase on the face of each report was different, showing on Exhibit 1 that Steve Sederwall and Bill Kurtis Productions requested the Report, while Exhibit F stated that it was requested by "Steve Sederall, Capitan, New Mexico, paid for by Investigation History Program, Kurtis Production."

2) The first paragraph had been changed in Exhibit F with additional descriptions of persons added as being present during the examination.

3) The photograph reference numbers had been changed, the text changed and some deleted.

4) The reference numbers on the diagrams had been changed throughout the report.

5) All of the "Results and Conclusions" on page 9 of the first floorboard report had been deleted from the Exhibit "F" floorboard report given to Court at the January 21, 2011 hearing.

Then, with all laid out together, I realized that the Lee and Ostler signatures were superimposable - cut and pasted onto the reports. **SO THE DEFENDANTS WERE FORGING DR. LEE REPORTS!** No wonder that since 2010 Sederwall had been pulling them like rabbits from a magician's hat. He was nervously re-working them in repeated fix-ups for court, while faking turn-over compliance, and thinking his scam would not be noticed.

**This was a bombshell. It proved Sederwall was giving me and judge fake records as genuine, proved evidence tampering, and proved contempt of the judge's orders for turn-over. In fact, no real records had been turned-over!**

## THE AUTHENTIC LEE REPORT

In his February 23, 2012 "Order" for my "First Motion to Supplement the Record and For Sanctions," requesting the authentic Lee Report and sanctions for the forgeries, the judge ordered: "Defendant Sederwall is to produce all original Reports received from Dr. Henry Lee with his original signature on them."

So Sederwall gave another Lee report! On January 31, 2012, my attorney and I met in Attorney Kevin Brown's office. Brown kept a straight face. This was the seventh "only one report" he was giving. This one had a different font **[FIGURE: 7]**, was 25 pages, with black-and white photos; and came with the same manila envelope Sederwall had been presenting since 2008 as holding his "one" Lee report - using its home mailing address to claim it came to him as a hobbyist!

Titled "Forensic Research & Training Center Forensic Examination Report" **[APPENDIX: 8]**, this report combined all investigations into one report - just as Lee had claimed in his letter to Jay Miller.

Its sections were: "Item #1 Workbench," "Item # 2 Washstand," "Item 3 (now labeled) **A piece of** Headboard," Item # 4 "Examination of Lincoln County Court House," and "Results and Conclusion." And it proved all the other reports were forgeries, rewritten by lifting, omitting parts, and changing parts.

The eye-opener was its heading and "Introduction." After repeating the "Date of Report as February 25, 2005, as in the other "Lee reports," **it gave the law enforcement information expurgated from the others, including case number and lawman titles.** It stated:

Requested By: **Lincoln County Sheriff's Office, New Mexico**
Investigating History Program, Kurtis Production
**Local Case No. 2003-274**
Date of Report: February 25, 2005
Report to: **Steve Sederwall**
**Lincoln County Sheriff's Office, New Mexico**

**Introduction**

At the request of **Steve Sederwall of Lincoln County Sheriff's Office, Lincoln County**, Bill Kurtis and Jamie Schenk of Kurtis Production, [sic – and] Dr. Henry Lee went to New Mexico on July 31, 2004 to assist in the re-investigation of the case of Billy the Kid. The forensic investigation team participating in re-investigation consist [sic –of] the following individuals:

Dr. Henry Lee, Chief Emeritus of the Connecticut State Police Forensic Laboratory
Calvin Ostler, Forensic Consultant, Riverton, Utah
Kim Ostler, Crime Scene Assistant, Riverton, Utah
**Tom Sullivan, Sheriff, Lincoln County New Mexico**
**Steve Sederwall Deputy Sheriff, Lincoln County New Mexico**
David Turk, US Marshal, United States Marshall [sic] Service

In addition, Mike Haag, Firearm examiner from Albuquerque Police Department Crime Lab, also provided valuable technical assistance in the investigation.

The forensic investigation team arrived at the Manny [sic] Miller residence, located at (address given here, not removed like in Exhibit E version), Albuquerque, New Mexico, at 18:20 hours on Saturday, July 31, 2004. Upon arrival we were presented with three pieces of evidence: a worktable, a washstand, and a headboard. The three pieces of evidence had been removed from a storage building at the rear of the residence by **Sheriff Sullivan, Deputy Sederwall**, and members of Bill Kurtis Productions. Each item was inspected visually and macroscopically. The following were found [with findings given].

This report repeated Lee's giving his samples to the Lincoln County Sheriff's Department. **And it had the "Results and Conclusion" section which was removed from "Lee reports" Exhibits E and F.** It had only Lee's claim of "blood-like" stains (as far as Lee himself dared hoaxing in writing, though he had dishonestly left out rust as the likely source); **and did not claim actual blood - as the hoaxers had announced.** The "Results and Conclusion" section stated:

> After a detail [sic] examination of the evidence and review of all the results of field testing, the following conclusion [sic] was reached.
>
> 1. Brownish dark stains were observed on different areas of the workbench. These areas were subjected to chemical presumptive blood tests. Some of those samples give a positive reaction. These results indicate the presence of Heme or Peroxidase like activity with those stains testing positive, which suggest that those stains could be bloodstains. Further DNA testing could reveal the nature and identity of these blood-like stains.
>
> 2. Two bullet holes were located on the side panels of the Washstand. The hole on the left panel is consistent with a bullet entry hole while the hole on the right side panel is consistent with a bullet exit hole. However, it is not possible to determine when those bullets were produced at this time. The angles produced in examination tell us two things:
>
> First, the bullet was fired from no more than 41" from the floor given the reported limitations of the room. The room is reported to be 20' by 20'; the maximum distance is assumed to be 20'. If the firearm was a maximum of 41" off the floor it is unlikely that the shooter was standing. It is more likely that the shooter was kneeling, squatting, or close to the floor.
>
> Second, the horizontal angle is such that if the Washstand was positioned so the back was against the wall, the shot could not have been fired from more than approximately 40 inches from the Washstand, because the wall would have been in the way. The angle of trajectory intersects the back plane of the Washstand at approximately 45 3/16", and no more than 46".
>
> 3. No bullet hole and no observable damage, no sign of bullet ricocheted type of defects were found on the Headboard.

4. The floor boards on the 2$^{nd}$ floor stair landing area of the court house have been repaired. Different types of wood and nails were used on this area.

5. Various stains were observed on the surface and underside of the floor boards. Chemical tests for the presence of blood were positive for some of those stains. These results indicate the presence of Heme or Peroxidase like activity with those stains tested positive, which suggests that those stains could be bloodstains. Further DNA testing could reveal the nature and identity of those blood-like stains.

The motive for forgeries was obvious: hiding the law enforcement case confirmation to fake a private hobby; and hiding Lee's non-committal conclusions about blood or DNA to fake legitimacy of the Arizona exhumations.

This report also proved Lee's hoaxing. Recall that Bill Kurtis was filming a series about Garrett not having killed Billy the Kid. So Lee used unsubstantiated "crime scene" objects, like the washstand, and faking of no bullet hole in the headboard fragment. And Lee suggested blood, when rust was the obvious source of his reagents' iron-triggered reactions.

Nevertheless, Dr. Henry Lee did not back the hoaxers' open records evasion of Case 2003-274 was their private hobby. When Lee gave his Affidavit for my case, on August 31, 2012, he swore that the work he did was for the Lincoln County Sheriff's Department for a case on the killing of William Bonney. He stated: "In approximately late July and early August of 2004, I assisted with the collection of samples from various locations thought to be locations where there may have been residue of biological material, which could be **relevant to an investigation into the death of William Bonney, a/k/a Billy the Kid, then being performed by the Lincoln County, New Mexico, Sheriff's Department.**" That meant Lee himself understood that the courthouse floorboard investigation was related to the "death of William Bonney" as the sub-investigation of the Garrett murder case to claim that the location of Bell's bleeding would contradict Garrett's version, making him a liar; ergo, also future murderer of the innocent victim.

For his June 26, 2012 deposition, incorrigible rogue Sederwall, when asked by my attorney, "Did you make up that report?" answered: "No, I did not make up the report. **The report has been massaged, it's been changed, it's been worked on. That's what's been done.**" (Deposition Sederwall, 6/26/12; p. 561)

# Forensic Research & Training Center

## Forensic Examination Report

Date of Request:   May 22, 2004

Requested By:   Steve Sederwall, and Bill Kurtis Productions

Date of Report:   February 25, 2005

Report to:   Steven M. Sederwall

**Examination of Lincoln County Court House:**

On Sunday, 8/1/04, the forensic investigation team examined the old Lincoln County Court House in Lincoln, New Mexico. Present at the scene were Steve Sederwall, Tom Sullivan, David Turk, Bill Kurtis, and Gary Wayne Graves. The target area of examination is located on the top landing of the stairs of the old courtroom.

1. The staircase has been repainted several times over the years.

2. The 2$^{nd}$ floor hallway floor was recovered with wooden floor board. These floor boards were removed. The original floor was exposed. Photograph #1 shows an overall view of hall floor after the removal of new floor board.

3. Photograph #2 shows the target area, which is at the top landing of the stairs where presumptive blood tests were done. The area measured approximately 28 7/8" deep by 43 ½ "wide.

4. Figure 1 is a sketch diagram shows the general dimensions of this staircase.

5. Photograph # 3 depicts the location and condition of the floor boards in the target area.

FIGURE: 4. Title page of first forged Dr. Henry Lee floorboard report; titled "Examination of Lincoln County Court House;" dated February 25, 2005; 9 pages long

# Forensic Research & Training Center

## Forensic Examination Report ©

Date of Request:     May 22, 2004

Requested By:        Steve Sederwall, Capitan, New Mexico, paid for by
                     Investigation History Program, Kurtis Production

Date of Report:      February 25, 2005

Report to:           Steven M. Sederwall

### Examination of Lincoln County Court House:

On Sunday, 8/1/04, the forensic investigation team examined the old Lincoln County Court House in Lincoln, New Mexico. Present at the scene were Steve Sederwall, Tom Sullivan, United States Marshal's Historian David Turk, Producer Bill Kurtis, and Gary Wayne Graves of De Baca County, New Mexico. The target area of examination is located on the top landing of the stairs of the old courtroom.

1. The staircase has been repainted several times over the years.
2. The $2^{nd}$ floor hallway floor was recovered with wooden floorboard. These floor boards were removed. The original floor was exposed. Photograph #6 shows an overall view of hall floor after the removal of new floor board.

EXHIBIT F

FIGURE: 5. Title page of second forged Dr. Henry Lee floorboard report; titled "Examination of Lincoln County Court House;" dated February 25, 2005; 9 pages long; submitted to Court on January 21, 2011 as Exhibit F

# Forensic Research & Training Center

## Forensic Examination Report ©

Date of Request:    May 22, 2004

Requested By:       Steve Sederwall, Capitan, New Mexico paid for by
                    Investigation History Program, Kurtis Production

Date of Report:     February 25, 2005

Report to:          Steven M. Sederwall

## Examination of furniture from Pete Maxwell's of July 15, 1881:

### Introduction

At the request of Steve Sederwall of Lincoln County, New Mexico, Bill Kurtis and Jamie Schenk of Kurtis Production, Dr. Henry Lee went to New Mexico on July 31, 2004 to assist in the re-investigation of the case of Billy the Kid. The forensic investigation team participating in re-investigation consist the following individuals:

> Steve Sederwall, Investigator
> Tom Sullivan, Investigator
> Dr. Henry Lee, Chief Emeritus of the Connecticut State Police Forensic Laboratory
> Calvin Ostler, Forensic Consultant, Riverton, Utah
> Kim Ostler, Crime Scene Assistant, Riverton, Utah
> David Turk, US Marshall, United States Marshall Service

FIGURE: 6. Title page of forged Dr. Henry Lee carpenter's bench report; titled "Examination of furniture from Pete Maxwell's of July 15, 1881," dated February 25, 2005; 16 pages long

# Forensic Research & Training Center

## Forensic Examination Report

Date of Request: May 22, 2004
Requested By: Lincoln County Sheriff's Office, New Mexico
Investigation History Program, Kurtis Production
Local Case No. 2003-274
Date of Report: February 25, 2005
Report to: Steve Sederwell
Lincoln County Sheriff's Office, New Mexico

### Introduction

At the request of Steve Sederwell of Lincoln County Sheriff's Office, Lincoln County, Bill Kurtis and Jamie Schenk of Kurtis Production, Dr. Henry Lee went to New Mexico on July 31, 2004 to assist in the re-investigation of the case of Billy the Kid. The forensic investigation team participating in re-investigation consist the following individuals:

Dr. Henry Lee, Chief Emeritus of the Connecticut State Police Forensic Laboratory
Calvin Ostler, Forensic Consultant, Riverton, Utah
Kim Ostler, Crime Scene Assistant, Riverton, Utah
Tom Sullivan, Sheriff, Lincoln County, New Mexico
Steve Sederwall Deputy Sheriff, Lincoln County, New Mexico
David Turk, US Marshall, United States Marshall Service

In addition, Mike Haag, Firearm examiner from Albuquerque Police Department Crime Lab, also provided valuable technical assistance in the investigation.

FIGURE: 7. Title page of authentic and sole forensic report of Dr. Henry Lee for Lincoln County Sheriff's Department Case 2003-274; titled "Forensic Examination Report;" dated February 25, 2005; 25 pages long

## *JUDGE'S RULING ABOUT THE FORGERIES*

For his May 15, 2014 "Findings of Fact and Conclusions of Law and Order of the Court," the judge ruled on Sederwall's forgeries; though the penalty for them that he awarded to me was later removed by the corrupt appellate courts to shield the lawmen of all penalties; though forgeries were not denied. For his "Findings of Fact," the judge wrote:

> 26. In his June 26, 2012 deposition Sederwall admitted to: removing law enforcement information from later Lee reports; called the twenty-five (25) page Lee report he first received from Lee as original; and admitted to knowing that the Orchid Cellmark client was Calvin Ostler [to request the records].
>
> 29. At an Evidentiary Hearing conducted on December 21 [sic – 18], 2012 and February 4, 2013 ... [w]itness Seterwall [sic], still calling Case 2003-274 his private hobby, admitted to altering the first Lee report's header to remove Case 2003-274 information; and admitted to creating the other report versions given to the Court and lacking law enforcement information.
>
> Conclusions of Law:
>
> 27. Defendants' conduct in providing altered records as discussed in Findings of Facts 25, 26, and 29 and Conclusions of Law 18 is wanton, willful, and in bad faith.
>
> 28. Based on Defendants' conduct, Plaintiff Cooper is entitled to punitive damages in the amount of one hundred thousand dollars ($100,000.00) against Defendants.

## THE JUDGE'S DECISIONS

Throughout the case, the judge's decisions were against the lawmen. On November 20, 2009, in the hearing for "Summary Judgment," the judge said: "I'm going to find that Sheriff Sullivan and Deputy Sederwall were, in fact ... employees of the County – of Lincoln County Sheriff's Department ... I'm also going to find that this investigation, when it was opened, as continued by the Lincoln County Sheriff's Department, anything that comes out of it is, in fact, public record. I'm going to order that all of the information that was received, including Dr. Lee's report and any lab report, if it exists, be turned over to the plaintiffs." [Transcript 11/20/09, p. 28]

At the end of the District Court litigation, when I was *pro se*, the judge declared that I had won, and presented his May 15, 2014 "Findings of Fact and Conclusions of Law and Order of the Court." Key points exposing the "Billy the Kid Case" hoaxers under "Findings of Fact" were:

4. The matter in controversy is for enforcement of the New Mexico Inspection of Public [Records] Act, Section 14-2-1 et seq. NMSA 1978 (IPRA) and concerning the Defendants' refusal to turn over requested DNA records of Lincoln County Sheriff's Department Case No. 2003-274, "Billy the Kid Case," ("Case 2003-274").

5. Case 2003-274 is a murder case, filed in 2003 in the Lincoln County Sheriff's Department by Sheriff Tom Sullivan (hereinafter Sullivan) and his commissioned Deputy Steve Sederwall (hereinafter Sederwall) to be solved by forensic DNA acquisitions and matching, and accusing the suspect Pat Garrett of murdering an innocent victim instead of Billy the Kid; with a sub-investigation of Billy the Kid's double homicide of Deputies James Bell and Robert Olinger.

6. From 2003 to 2004, Case 2003-274's New Mexico exhumation attempts on Billy the Kid and his mother for matching DNA were legally blocked so no DNA was obtained.

7. In 2004 Billy the Kid's DNA was allegedly obtained for Case 2003-274 by Dr. Henry Lee (hereinafter Lee) from an old carpenter's bench on which Billy the Kid [was] laid after being shot. Lee's specimens were sent for DNA processing to Orchid Cellmark Lab (hereinafter Orchid Cellmark) in Texas.

8. In 2005 newly elected Lincoln County Sheriff Rick Virden (hereinafter Virden) deputized Sullivan and Sederwall to continue Case 2003-274 by exhuming Billy the Kid's identity claimants John Miller and "Brushy Bill" Roberts for DNA match with Lee's bench DNA to solve the Garrett murder.

9. On May 19, 2005, for Case 2003-274, John Miller and William Hudspeth were exhumed in Arizona and their bones were taken to Orchid Cellmark for DNA extractions and for DNA matching to the carpenter's bench DNA.

10. From April 24, 2007 to June 26, 2007 Plaintiff Cooper made IPRA [open records] records requests from Sheriff Virden for Case 2003-274 through her then attorney ... ("request phase"). Requested records were for:

A. Lee's DNA recoveries from the carpenter's bench;
B. Orchid Cellmark's DNA extractions from Lee's specimens;
C. Orchid Cellmark's DNA extractions for the two Arizona bodies; and
D. Orchid Cellmark's DNA matchings for the carpenter's bench [DNA] to the bodies [DNA].

11. In the request phase, no records were given and their denials were improper: without valid IPRA exceptions; with Sullivan and Sederwall after having resigned their deputyship on June 21, 2007 admitting to records possession, but calling them private hobby "trade secrets;" with Virden denying having any Case 2003-274 records; and with Virden not attempting to recover records from Sullivan, Sederwall, Lee, or Orchid Cellmark.

12. The case at hand [litigation] for enforcement of IPRA [open records] was filed on October 15, 2007.

13. In their August 18, 2008 depositions Sullivan and Sederwall admitted knowing that the requested records existed, and admitted that Sederwall possessed Lee's carpenter's bench report.

14. On September 3, 2007 [sic – 2008], by subpoena duces tecum, Virden turned over his Case 2003-274 file of one hundred ninety-three (193) pages; lacking requested records, but with documents confirming the DNA investigation and having contact information for records recovery.

15. In his September 8, 2008 deposition Virden denied knowledge of requested records.

16. On November 20, 2009 Partial Summary Judgment was issued in favor of Plaintiffs and against Defendants [lawmen] declaring the records requested were public, were created in official capacities, and should be turned over.

17. On February 18, 2010 Sederwall turned over to the Plaintiffs an unrequested nine (9) page Lee report on courthouse floorboards. Its header had no link to Case 2003-274. It was signed by Lee and Calvin Ostler. In the March 9, 2010 Presentment Hearing, the Court was told that this floorboard report was the only Lee report in Sederwall's possession.

18. On October 26 2010 Virden first made records requests to Lee and Orchid Cellmark but never followed up to recover the records after Lee responded that he had one report, and Orchid Cellmark responded that it would send the records if released by their client.

19. On November 10, 2010 Sederwall turned over to the Plaintiffs a sixteen (16) page Lee report on the carpenter's bench but [it] was lacking a link to Case 2003-274.

20. An Evidentiary Hearing was held on January 21, 2011 and Virden argued that he could not turn over records that were not in his direct possession and which he did not know existed. Sederwall's Lee courthouse floorboard report was entered as Exhibit "F," and the carpenter's bench report was entered as Exhibit "E." At this hearing the Court reminded the parties that the Partial Summary Judgment previously entered on November 20, 2009 found that the Defendants and the investigation were official and connected to the Lincoln County Sheriff and that all evidence was public record and that all information should be turned over to Plaintiffs.

20. [sic – numbering incorrect] In July, 2011 Cooper recognized that the Lee courthouse floorboard report (entered as Exhibit "F") was a rewrite of the alleged same floorboard report given on November 10, 2010, and that this rewriting also put in doubt the authenticity of the carpenter's bench report (Exhibit "E").

21. At a September 23, 2011 Presentment Hearing Cooper alerted the Court of the discrepancies in the Lee reports.

22. On January 17, 2012 a Hearing on Sanctions was conducted and Plaintiffs stated that there were no records productions and allegations of altered Lee reports. Production of the original Lee report was ordered ...

23. On January 31, 2012 Sederwall turned over a twenty-five (25) page "original" Lee report combining the courthouse floorboard and the carpenter's bench. Its header identified Lee's work as for Case 2003-274.

24. On March 20, 2012 [Cooper's co-plaintiff] subpoenaed the Orchid Cellmark records for Case 2003-274, receiving one hundred thirty-three (133) pages on April 20, 2012. The records included DNA results from Lee's specimens and from the two exhumed Arizona bodies ...

**26. In his June 26, 2012 deposition Sederwall admitted to: removing law enforcement information from later Lee reports; called the twenty-five (25) page Lee report he first received from Lee as original; and admitted to knowing that the Orchid Cellmark client was Calvin Ostler [for records recovery].**

27. In his June 27, 2012 deposition Virden admitted to: waiting three (3) years into litigation to write record requests to Lee and Orchid Cellmark; not requesting from Lee the report when Lee wrote back that he had one; and not trying to find out the client's name after Orchid Cellmark wrote back that it was required to send Virden the requested records ...

29. At an Evidentiary Hearing conducted on December 21 [sic – 18], 2012 and February 4, 2013 Virden admitted: that the subpoenaed Orchid Cellmark DNA records were from Case 2003-274 but gave no valid explanation for waiting three (3) years to begin records recovery or for not following up on the resulting responses to get the records. **Witness Seterwall [sic], still calling Case 2003-274 his private hobby, admitted to altering the first Lee report's header to remove Case 2003-274 information; and admitted to creating the other report versions given to the Court and lacking law enforcement information ...**

Key points exposing the "Billy the Kid Case" hoaxers under "Conclusions of Law" were:

1. Section 14-2-5 NMSA 1978 states, "The intent of the legislature in enacting the Inspection of Public Records Act is to ensure as the policy of the State of New Mexico, that all persons are entitled to the greatest possible information regarding the affairs of government and the official acts of public officers and employees" ...

3. Cooper's status as an author is irrelevant in requesting records under IPRA and [she] is entitled to receive document[s] which were requested.

4. Without statutory justification, no requested records were produced by the Defendants.

5. The requested records exist, and have been recoverable from the time of the request phase ...

9. In both the request and enforcement phases, Virden's records recovery refusal[s] have been misplaced and ignored IPRA by arguing that recovery pertains only to records in direct physical possession. Section 14-2-6(A) NMSA 1978 states enforcement custodial responsibility "regardless of whether the records are in that person's actual physical custody and control" ...

10. Virden was obligated to recover records from it [sic- his] deputy agents. *Ronald A. Coco, Inc. v. St Paul's Methodist Church of Las Cruces, N.M., Inc.*, 78, N.M. 97, 99, 428 P.2d 636, 638

(1967), states, in part, "Unquestionably, insofar as an agent's acts are with the agent's authority they are in legal contemplation of the acts of the principal."

11. Ignorance of records existence was argued by Virden to refuse recovery. Ignorance is not an IPRA exception under Section 14-2-1(A) (1-8) NMSA 1978. Virden's lack or [sic - of] knowledge of records is disingenuous, since his deputies admitted to records possession, his Case 2003-274 file showed DNA investigations and recovery options, Lee responded to Virden and Lee had the record, and Orchid Cellmark responded to Virden that it had the records ...

12. Virden ignored Section 14-2-7(E)(5) NMSA 1978, "the responsibility of a public body to make available public records for inspection." Virden waited three (3) years into litigation to seek records, then did not actually try to recover them from Lee and Orchid Cellmark. To prevent stonewalling, IPRA has time based damages in NMSA Section 14-2-11. IPRA damage provisions are intended to encourage public entities' prompt compliance with records requests. *Derringer v. State*, 133 N.M. 721, 68 P.3$^{rd}$ 691 9(Ct. App. 2003).

13. As public officials, under Section 14-2-5 NMSA 1978, Sullivan and Sederwall had to provide records as, "an integral part of the routine duties of public officers and employees."

14. As commissioned deputies, under Section 13[sic - 14]-2-11(B)(2) NMSA 1978, along with Virden, they were "responsible for the denial of records." As Virden's deputies, they were his agents. "A person may appoint an agent to do the same acts and achieve the same legal consequences by performing of an act as if he or she had acted personally." 3 Am. Jur. 2d Agency Section 18, at 422 (2002). Section 4-41-9 NMSA 1978 states, "The said deputies are hereby authorized to discharge all the duties which belong to the office of sheriff, that may be placed under their charge by their principals, with the same effect as though they were executed by the respective sheriffs."

15. Sullivan and Sederwall said they were hobbyists and the records were private property. Sullivan's and Sederwall's argument of being "unsalaried "reserve deputies" is irrelevant to the records responsibility, since "an agent is a person who, by agreement with another called the principal, represents the principal in dealings with third persons or transacts some other business ... for the principal, with or without compensation. UJI 13-401, NMRA.

16. In their June 21, 2007 "Memorandum" to Virden, Sullivan and Sederwall admitted to having Case 2003-274 records, but called them private property, while at the same time resigning their public official positions as deputies. Furthermore, from 2010 to 2012, Sederwall offered Case 2003-274 records for sale on his own billythekidcase.com website.

17. After being court-ordered, Sederwall made a non-specific records request for Orchid Cellmark on February 3 [sic – 5], 2011; later admitting in his June 26, 2012 deposition, that he knew Calvin Ostler was the Orchid Cellmark client contact for getting records released.

18. In his June 26, 2012 deposition, Sederwall admitted to willful involvement in altering Lee reports by rewritings to remove the original law enforcement information in Lee's "first" report sent to him as Lincoln County Deputy Sheriff. Section 14-2-6(F) NMSA 1978 defines "public records" as "all documents, papers, letters, books, maps, tapes, photographs, recordings and other materials, regardless of physical form or characteristics, used, created, received, maintained or held by or on behalf of any pubic body and related to public business, whether or not the records are required by law to be created or maintained." The plain language implication is that the records are to be "originals" of [sic – or] true "duplicates" of the original. Under Rule 11-1001(D) NMRA 1978, "an original of a writing is the writing itself. Rile [sic –Rule] 11-101(E) NMRA 1978 states "a duplicate is a counterpart produced by the same impression as the original … which accurately reproduces the original." Neither an "original" nor a "duplicate" report was presented, only altered records which do not comply with IPRA law.

19. The Defendants' actions and/or inactions in responding to Plaintiff's IPRA requests are in violation of IPRA law and subject to sanctions …

26. Defendants' conduct in not providing the requested records enumerated in Findings of Fact 10, is willful, wanton, and in bad faith.

27. Defendants' conduct in providing altered records as discussed in Findings of Facts 25, 26, and 29 and Conclusions of Law 18 is wanton, willful, and in bad faith …

**The judge ordered: "Judgment be entered in favor of Plaintiff Cooper against Defendants."**

# "BILLY THE KID CASE" HOAX UPSHOT

I stopped the hoaxers making "Brushy Bill" Billy the Kid and having him "pardoned" despite ruthless head hoaxer, Governor Bill Richardson; the enabling reporters, judges and attorneys; covered-up illegal exhumations; and the hoaxers' bottomless tax-dollar funded budget for the case and for fighting me in courts.

These cynical profiteering charlatans defamed famous Sheriff Pat Garrett by conducting a baseless murder case against him; and they damaged Billy the Kid history by disseminating fraudulent claims. They demeaned the Lincoln and De Baca County Sheriff's Departments by a corrupt endeavor. They abused forensic science by fake investigations. They scorned the dignity of courts by having the corpse of Billy the Kid as a petitioner, and hoodwinked the open records judge by forged forensic reports. They willfully, immorally and feloniously desecrated two graves; graverobbing and destroying remains for a publicity stunt.

The "Billy the Kid Case's" unchecked cronyism and corrupt shielding of fellow conspirators, became one more chapter in New Mexico's Santa Fe Ring racketeering going back to 1866.

In its wake were left two documentaries disseminating its lies: 2004's "Investigating History: Billy the Kid," and 2006's "Requiem for Billy the Kid."

And its unrepentant, unpunished, and unexposed perpetrators staged a come-back, 15 years after they started the "Billy the Kid Case," through "Brushy"-believer, W.C. Jameson, in his 2018 book: *Cold Case Billy the Kid*. And, before that, they had inspired Jameson's hoaxing for his "Brushy"-backing books, which followed his 1998 *The Return of the Outlaw Billy the Kid*.

As to Oliver "Brushy Bill" Roberts, he got another incarnation. There had been Pardon-"Brushy" with his Fort Sumner steak restaurant, forgotten Pat Garrett, and no killings. There had been *Alias*-"Brushy" with his crude grammar, racism, and dime novel "memories." There had been *Return*-"Brushy," cleansed and with a new family tree and posthumously updated Billy the Kid history. And now there was "Billy the Kid Case"-"Brushy," in a Pat Garrett bromance stimulating murder, while playing-dead-on-the-carpenter's-bench-to-bleed-for-DNA. And it was not over. "Brushy" was coming back with a new make-over, towing a bunch of "Billy the Kid Case" hoaxers, renamed as "Cold Case investigators."

# PART V

# THE RETURN OF "BRUSHY'S" TRUE-BELIEVER, W.C. JAMESON, AS A HOAXER

# CHAPTER 1
# RETURN OF FAKERY IN *BILLY THE KID: BEYOND THE GRAVE*

## AN ALLIANCE MADE IN HOAXER HEAVEN

In his 2018 book, *Cold Case Billy the Kid*, W.C. Jameson stated that he first met Steve Sederwall in 2006 at a book signing for his 2005 *Billy the Kid: Beyond the Grave*. Jameson had been a "Billy the Kid Case" hoax participant by his 2004 TV appearance in official hoax historian, Paul Hutton's, Discovery Channel "Investigating History: Billy the Kid." And Jameson's transcript of "Brushy's" Morrison tapes was quoted for the hoax's earliest "Probable Cause Statement" for Case 2003-274: the "Seventy-Seven Days of Doubt Document." Omitting that entire case, Jameson stated that he knew Sederwall "by reputation," from newspapers and TV, where "his aggressive investigations into a variety of Billy the Kid-related events ... were based on solid police work, and they differed, sometimes dramatically, from established history." Jameson added that Sederwall "irritated" "self-anointed experts," but ignored them. (*Cold Case*, Page v) So adulating Jameson now added Sederwall to his pantheon of "Brushy," Morrison, and Sonnichsen.

And the hoaxers' chicanery influenced him. By his 2005 *Billy the Kid: Beyond the Grave*, he was less the innocent who had co-authored 1998's *The Return of the Outlaw Billy the Kid*. Hoaxing, plus the "Billy the Kid Case's" "Brushy" push, had emboldened him to do clandestine fix-ups of "Brushy" for a new millennium of dupes. The means became justified by that end. So he hid his *The Return of the Outlaw Billy the Kid*, with its starry-eyed accidental exposures, and proceeded to contradict his old self.

## HOAXBUSTING "BILLY THE KID: BEYOND THE GRAVE"

In 2005, when W.C. Jameson published his *Billy the Kid: Beyond the Grave* to fix-up his 1998 *The Return of the Outlaw Billy the Kid*, though exposed to the "Billy the Kid Case" hoaxers, he was its lone author, acknowledging none of them.

He was, thus, relatively naïve, just before plunging into willful hoaxing in his future *Billy the Kid: The Lost Interviews*, *Pat Garrett: The Man Behind the Badge*, and *Cold Case Billy the Kid*. That makes his *Billy the Kid: Beyond the Grave* worth its weight in gold for hoaxbusting, because it has his last accidental exposure of the fatal error that sank "Brushy's" scam. After that, he would never make that revealing mistake again.

## MAKING A BETTER "BRUSHY"

Though rehashing *The Return of the Outlaw Billy the Kid*, Jameson made dishonest fix-ups to hide "Brushy's" most glaring blunders, attacked the piling-up proofs that "Brushy" was not Billy the Kid, blamed opposition on New Mexico tourism interests, and concluded that "Brushy" was Billy the Kid. Contradicting his earlier book, he hid its existence in *Billy the Kid: Beyond the Grave*, and his subsequent "Brushy" books. A better "Brushy" would now replace his old (and closer to the truth) version.

## FIXING-UP MORRISON AND THE FAILED MABRY PARDON

William V. Morrison is now no lawyer, but a "paralegal;" while still called a descendant of Ferdinand Maxwell (brother of Maxwell Land Grant owner, Lucien Maxwell).

Given is his finding of "Brushy" through Jim Hines (as Jesse [sic] Evans); but J. Frank Dalton is just "a Texan," his Jesse James claim hidden after James's 1995 validating DNA matching exhumation (though Dalton had been hidden as "a Missourian" in *The Return of the Outlaw Billy the Kid*!). Morrison's Mabry pardon petition is called unjustly rejected, but rocking "the world of Western American outlaw and lawman history [with its] stunning claim that another young man was mistaken for the Kid and was shot by Pat Garrett in Pete Maxwell's bedroom."

And C.L. Sonnichsen, listed as a noted Billy the Kid historian, is presented as backing "Brushy." (Page 51)

## *FIX-UPS AND NEW ERRORS FOR "BRUSHY"*

*Billy the Kid: Beyond the Grave* repeats original "Brushy" fakery, with "physical similarities;" the Billy Barlow shooting; a post-shooting multi-persona life; his things-not-printed trick, including black (no longer "nigger") soldiers; fake Lincoln revelations; fake Acton photo-match; and the fake Affidavits, with fake claim that "Lincoln County War veterans" identified him as Billy the Kid. Conspiracy theories and discrepancies for the shooting scene are recycled, as is fakery about no Coroner's Jury Report, and Garrett's reward being denied based on uncertain corpse identity and no Report.

But there is now an updated genealogy from a "Roberts family Bible" from "Brushy's" wife Malinda; with additional genealogical records from "Brushy's" step-grandson, Bill Allison. (Pages 6, 54) They add the names Bonney, Antrim, and McCarty.

**FIX-UPS: "Brushy's" genealogy is updated by a bogus different Roberts family Bible (as opposed to the Geneva Pittmon one) allegedly provided to Jameson's past co-author, Frederick Bean in the 1980's; though genealogy faker, William Tunstill is also cited as a bibliographic source for his 1988** *Billy the Kid and Me Were the Same.* **Fakery is indicated since the name "McCarty" was unknown to "Brushy" and team (with C.L. Sonnichsen citing, but not using, in** *Alias Billy the Kid* **that "Another story, current in Silver City, says that Billy the Kid was really named McCartney." (***Alias Billy the Kid***, Page 16))**

**Furthermore, there existed no separate Roberts family, as exposed by Roy L. Haws in his 2015 book,** *Brushy Bill: Proof that His Claim to be Billy the Kid Was a Hoax***, showing that his mother, Eulaine Haws, "Brushy's" relative, had been duped by author William Tunstill into vouching for the fabricated genealogy.**

And Jameson added a new lie, never repeated, that "Brushy's" being from Texas explained his "facility with Spanish" (Page 54); though "Brushy" had none.

"Brushy," called his made-up "William Henry Roberts," gets his most embarrassing Billy the Kid blunders get fixed up, though Billy's Silver City and Arizona years remain missing. For the

Tunstall period, a fix-up has "Brushy" calling himself "William Antrim" (Page 26); though, in fact, it was the start of real Billy's using Bonney. For the Lincoln County War Battle, "Brushy's" racism is cleansed by removing "nigger" for Dudley's soldiers. **An accidental reveal is "Brushy's" wrong confabulation that Pat Garrett was Sheriff Kimbrell's [misspelled Kimball] deputy *before* being elected sheriff** (Page 35); when, in fact, Garrett was deputized by Kimbrell after the election. The entire Santa Fe jail period is missing. The Lincoln courthouse-jail stay begins on April 6, when it was April 21, 1881, and ends with the "Brushy's" unchanged jailbreak tales.

For Fort Sumner, Jameson fixes-up "Brushy's" fatal Celsa-Saval siblings error, making **Celsa Gutierrez Saval Gutierrez's *wife*, not sister, and brother-in-law to Garrett *by Garrett's marriage to Celsa's sister***, though he holds to "Brushy's" tale of planning to leave with her! (Page 41) For "Brushy's" post-Billy-shooting, Jameson fixes-up the confabulations with meaningless updating. And the fake "revelations" about Lincoln town are repeated from his *The Return of the Outlaw Billy the Kid*.

## THE HOAXBUSTING MOON OF JULY 14, 1881

The hoaxbusting importance of *Billy the Kid: Beyond the Grave*, is revealed in Jameson's naive treatment of "Brushy's" moon problem, still unaware that it was "Brushy's" fatal error proving he was not in Fort Sumner on the night of July 14, 1881. For Jameson, as for "Brushy," the logic was an accidental killing by Pat Garrett, who mistook Billy Barlow for "Brushy" **because it was so dark.**

Thus, for this book, still relying on "Brushy's" original transcript, Jameson wrote: "**William Henry Roberts recalled that the night was dark but there was enough moonlight to make shadows.**" (Page 57) And after "Brushy was shot, Jameson quoted from "Brushy's" transcript: "**I lost my footing and fell on my face in the darkness.**" (Page 61) And from the transcript came "Brushy's" stating: "**Garrett knew by now that he killed the wrong man in the dark.**" (Page 64)

This dark night matched Jameson's *The Return of the Outlaw Billy the Kid*, which had "Brushy" say: "[After hearing the shot from Pete Maxwell's place] I pulled one of my .44's and ran through the door, trying to see in the dark. Two more shots came from the shadow beside the Maxwell house. I couldn't find a target. It was too dark to see." (*The Return of the Outlaw Billy the Kid*, Page 112) That dark night was repeated in that book in "Brushy's" quote explaining Billy Barlow's killing: **"Garrett knew by now that he'd killed the wrong man in the dark."** (*The Return of the Outlaw Billy the Kid*, Page 117)

"Brushy's transcript of the death scene was also used in the "Seventy-Seven Days of Doubt" Probable Cause Statement by "Billy the Kid Case" hoaxers, Lincoln County Sheriff Tom Sullivan and his Deputy, Steve Sederwall. Like Jameson, they were still unaware of "Brushy's" fatal error. So they quoted him: *"I had spent the day with Garrett's brother-in-law, Saval Gutierrez. Nearly all the people in this country were my friends and they helped me. None of them liked Garrett.* ***It was dark that night, but there was enough moonlight to make shadows.*** *Me and my partner Billy Barlow, rode up to Jesus Silva's house when we reached Fort Sumner."* Sullivan and Sederwall continued: "While Roberts and Jesus [Silva] were lighting the wood stove they hear [sic] gunfire in the direction of Pete Maxwell's place. Roberts' statement goes on to describe the following events: ***"I pulled one of my .44's and ran through the door, trying to see in the dark. Two more shots came from a shadow beside the Maxwell house. I couldn't find a target to shoot at. It was too dark to see.*** *I ran toward Maxwell's back porch. I heard another gunshot and felt something hit me in the jaw. I stumbled and kept on running ... I tasted blood and spit the mess out of my mouth as* ***I started emptying my six-shooter at the shadow where I saw the muzzleflash.*** *From the corner of my eye I saw a body lying on the back porch ... I knew it had to be Barlow ... My mouth and shoulder were bleeding and I lost track of where I was, but I knew I had to get away from Maxwell's before they killed me. I heard a shout and another gunshot. Something passed across my forehead like a hot branding iron. I was stunned.* ***I lost footing and fell on my face in the darkness.*** *I knew I was hurt bad and wondered if I would make it out of this scrape alive."*

But, as stated above, Morrison and Sonnichsen had recognized "Brushy's" error, likely from reading John William Poe's 1933 *The Death of Billy the Kid*, in which he stated about the July 14, 1881 night: **"[T]he moon was shining very brightly."** (Poe, Page 28) For *Alias Billy the Kid*, they even titled the chapter **"Death by Moonlight,"** and fixed-up "Brushy's" own words to: "I ran through the gate into Maxwell's back yard **in the bright**

**moonlight.**" (*Alias Billy the Kid*, Page 49) So, carelessly confused Jameson, forgetting "Brushy's" own transcribed words, which he had himself quoted, also used the Sonnichsen-Morrison text for his *Billy the Kid: Beyond the Grave* shooting scene; writing: "Roberts, **easily seen in the moonlit yard,** drew return fire from the lawmen." (Page 41)

But Jameson, in his upcoming alliance with "Billy the Kid Case" hoaxers, would never again reveal the moon error. But it was too late. **Every time they lied about "Brushy" claiming that night's bright moonlight," it branded their hoaxing.**

## CELSA GUTIERREZ AS OMNISCIENT NARRATOR

Claiming "Brushy's" quote, Jameson faked Celsa Gutierrez's omniscient description of the shooting aftermath; one real Celsa could not know. Pseudo-Celsa stated: Garrett and his deputies feared to leave Maxwell's house because Billy's friends would shoot them; Garrett set a trap expecting Billy's visit; Garrett killed Barlow but passed him off as Billy, except he had a beard; Garrett had the grave dug by lantern light; and Deluvina was crying to pretend Billy was shot. So "Brushy" realized that Garrett was hiding the corpse identity to collect the reward. (Pages 63-64)

"Celsa's" eerie clairvoyance would get even weirder in seven years in his 2012's *Billy the Kid: The Lost Tapes*; when Jameson would again have "Brushy's" mouthing the quotes, **but by a new character - Frank Lobato** – who added even more information lifted from Garrett's and Poe's books! (See pages 561-562 below)

## THE "TRAVELING" ARMORY

"Brushy's" faked armory location in Lincoln's courthouse helped to prove Jameson's transformation to a hoaxer. In *Billy the Kid: Beyond the Grave* it was still across the hall from Garrett's office as "Brushy" had confabulated, though in sequence with a fix-up of an added unlabeled room. So, mimicking a history book's illustrations, Jameson gave fake diagrams of the building as the Murphy-Dolan "House" (24$^{th}$ figure)," then as the courthouse (25$^{th}$ figure; no page numbers) (See page 570 for Jameson's leap from attempted fix-up to active hoaxing of corrected location.)

FIX-UP: The "diagram" of the second floor fixes-up "Brushy's" misconception that one room - which he called the armory - was opposite Garrett's office. But Jameson learned there were *two* adjoining rooms. So his made-up diagram has an empty room across the hall from Garrett's office, *leading to another called "armory."* This is important, because once Jameson became a full hoaxer, he would move the armory down the hall to its correct location to the left of the stairs, far from Garrett's office!

## ATTACKING THE DEBUNKING

Jameson addressed some of "Brushy's" debunking that followed the Mabry pardon rejection and *Alias Billy the Kid*, concluding that all were wrong; as follows:

1) **NO HANDWRITING MATCH:** Claimed is that "Brushy's" handwriting could not be compared with Billy's, because **Billy's was unknown**. Made-up is that since Billy had little education, he did not write his known letters. An alleged handwriting expert, Howard Chandler, is cited to claim Billy's letters were "written by at least two men" who were "law clerks." (Page 108)

FAKERY: First of all, Billy Bonney wrote all his letters, as I proved in my 2012 book: *Billy the Kid's Writings, Words, and Wit*, in which I compared each alphabet letter and demonstrated his uniquely modified Spencerian cursive script, a script he would have learned in his Silver City schooling. And he repeated the same errors in his letters: misspelling "answer" as "annser," and not capitalizing the first word after a sentence's period.

Jameson's so-called expert was likely responding to the fact that Billy's 1879 pardon bargain letters look somewhat different from his 1881 Santa Fe jail letters. That was caused by Spencerian handwriting's need for hand and forearm desk support to slide the pen. In jail, Billy lacked this option, so the writing is cramped. But the alphabet, and his typical errors remain unchanged. Also, Billy's brilliance and literacy were unknown to "Brushy's" hoaxers, so correctly spelling "indictment," for example, in his March 13, 1879 letter to Lew Wallace, was inconceivable; making the "expert" call him a law clerk!

Also, the "Brushy" hoax's rationalization of someone writing the letters for "Brushy," falls apart with the reality that Billy's doing his own writing was witnessed by others. Dr. Henry Hoyt, George Howard, and James McMasters witnessed his October 24, 1878 Bill of Sale. On April 27, 1929, Hoyt wrote to Lew Wallace Jr. about that it: "[F]or many years supposed I had the only specimen of his handwriting in existence, a Bill of Sale for a horse he presented me with, and wrote out himself." Billy's signature (matching the Bill of Sale's) was witnessed by Investigator Frank Warner Angel and Justice of the Peace John Wilson for signing his deposition on June 8, 1878. And Lincoln jailor, Juan Patrón, during Billy's sham pardon arrest in his house, gave him embossed stationery to write his March 24, 1879 while there.

The "Brushy" hoax's fabricated writer-assistant, always with the same handwriting, would need to be on call in far flung places from 1879 to 1881, including solitary confinement in the Santa Fe jail with Billy!

And "Brushy's" handwriting was known, to check for matching. Though calling him illiterate, Morrison had his "notebooks" and "correspondence" (*Alias Billy the Kid*, Page 14), and "copious notes" about his later personas. (*Alias Billy the Kid*, Page 50). Jameson (with Frederick Bean) called his writing as a "scrawl." (*The Return of the Outlaw Billy the Kid*, Page 204) And, in 2012, Jameson described "Brushy's" trunk, passed to his step-grandson, Bill Allison, which had his three Big Chief writing tablets, which Bean said had "Brushy's" bad handwriting in pencil. (*Billy the Kid: The Lost Interviews*, Pages 35-36) "Brushy's" scrawl did not match Billy's elegant script.

2) "BRUSHY" WAS OLIVER P. ROBERTS: Jameson denies Geneva Pittmon's December 16, 1987 letter (omitting her name); by arguing that "Brushy" could not have been Oliver P. because that man was born on August 26, 1879 in Arkansas, and "Brushy" was born on December 31, 1859! Jameson's authority is William A. Tunstill (with his 1988 book *Billy the Kid and Me Were the Same* in his bibliography). And claimed is that there was *another* Roberts family Bible found by Frederick Bean in the 1980's in "Brushy's" trunk giving the genealogy with McCarty, Antrim, and Bonney. (Page 108)

WRONG: True-believer Jameson cannot accept the logical response to the Pittmon letter: "Brushy" was 20 years too young to be Billy the Kid! And, unbeknownst to Jameson, waiting in the wings was another "Brushy" relative, whose mother, Eulaine Haws, had been duped by Tunstill into rewriting the family genealogy, which was now being called *the different Roberts family*. But in seven more years, her son, Roy L. Haws, would expose Tunstill's fraud in his *Brushy Bill: Proof That His Claim to Be Billy the Kid Was a Hoax*. As to the "Brushy" trunk's so-called Roberts family Bible, Jameson gives more of its description in his 2012 book, *Billy the Kid: The Lost Interviews*, and it is debunked there. (See pages 539-541, 543-544 below)

3) NO RECORD OF WILLIAM HENRY ROBERTS IN LINCOLN COUNTY: Jameson claims "Brushy" used the aliases William Bonney, Henry McCarty, and Henry Antrim. (Page 109)

FAKE FIX-UP: In *Alias Billy the Kid*, the least tampered "Brushy" hoax version, "Brushy" does not claim the aliases Henry McCarty and Henry Antrim, as yet unknown to him and his team. As will be seen, Jameson, in his 2012 *Billy the Kid: The Lost Interviews*, claimed the latter two were in "Brushy's" trunk's Roberts family Bible, which is debunked for that book. (See pages 539-541 below)

4) "BRUSHY" WAS LEFT-HANDED; BILLY WAS NOT: Jameson, learning Billy was not left handed, says "Brushy" was actually ambidextrous, like Billy the Kid. (Page 109)

FAKE FIX-UP: For *Alias Billy the Kid*, "Brushy" and Morrison used the Billy the Kid tintype's right-to-left reversal to fake "Brushy" as left-handed. In the Mabry hearing, "Brushy" was seen to favor the right. And Morrison may have done that fix-up for his book, because, on April 18, 1952, he wrote to Paul Blazer, "**I was very much interested in hearing you say Billy the Kid was ambidextrous.**" (*Alias Billy the Kid*, Page 6)

5) POE AND McKINNEY CONCURRED THAT GARRETT KILLED BILLY THE KID ON JULY 14, 1881: Jameson claims that Poe, who did not know Billy, eventually concurred; but McKinney did not. (Page 109)

**FAKERY:** Jameson is slipping in a conspiracy theory that the corpse was not identified as Billy the Kid. Poe and McKinney were irrelevant, since he was identified by Pat Garrett, Peter Maxwell, Deluvina Maxwell, about 200 townspeople, and the official Coroner's Jury inquest for their Report of July 15, 1881. As to McKinney, Jameson merely used Morrison's double hearsay account in a June 29, 1855 letter to a William Waters, claiming that McKinney's cousin had said that McKinney had told relatives that *he* McKinney had "killed the man in Maxwell's bedroom 'by mistake and that the Kid got away.'" **(Pages 70-71)** That this McKinney fakery does not match "Brushy's" fake back-porch-Barlow account is ignored by Jameson.

**6) BILLY BARLOW IS NON-HISTORICAL:** You guessed it: Jameson says Billy Barlow was an alias. (Pages 109-110)

**FAKERY:** "Brushy's" entire killing scene is fake. Barlow is irrelevant, as well as non-existent.

**7) ROBERTS COULD NOT SPEAK SPANISH:** Jameson says "Brushy" lived in Mexico, so he spoke Spanish. And Morrison and Sonnichsen claimed "passable" Spanish. (Page 110)

**FAKERY:** "Brushy" made-up being in Mexico. And one of the many reasons "Brushy" failed his Mabry pardon hearing was *that he could not speak Spanish*. And, the least tampered source, *Alias Billy the Kid*, does not claim his Spanish speaking. And real Billy spoke more than "passable" Spanish. In his 1929 book, *A Frontier Doctor*, Henry Hoyt wrote: "[Billy] spoke Spanish like a native."

For his 2006 "Brushy"-debunking *Billy the Kid: His Real Name Was...*", author Jim Johnson noted that in "Brushy's" tale of being on his ranch in Old Mexico in 1899, he claimed "old Diaz seized everything," and fifty Mexican soldiers came to take his stock. So "Brushy" and his friends send an interpreter to talk to them. Johnson says bi-lingual Billy would not have needed an interpreter. (Johnson, Page 71)

**8) NO RECORD OF "BRUSHY" WITH ROUGH RIDERS:** Of course, Jameson claims he used an alias. (Page 110)

**FAKERY:** The Rough Rider fakery was addressed in 2006 by Jim Johnson in his *Billy the Kid: His Real Name Was...* The problem was more than what name "Brushy" used.

"Brushy" had no first person knowledge. (Johnson, Pages 69-71) According to Johnson, "Brushy" did not know the transport specifics to Cuba; the Lieutenant Cook "Brushy" mentioned did not exist; and the "two months" of war "Brushy" confabulated were just June 22, 1898 to July 1, 1898. "Brushy" claimed being in charge of the horses, but there were *none*. It was a "dismounted cavalry unit." "Brushy" claimed a battle with "four officers shot in the back." There was no such battle. And "Brushy" left out the famous "charge up San Juan Hill!"

9) DON CLINE DISPUTED ANTI-HORSE THIEF ASSOCIATION EXISTENCE: Jameson said it did exist. (Page 110)

FAKERY: Existence would not prove "Brushy" was a member. And "Brushy" had bigger Don Cline problems. And Cline stated the badge "Brushy" claimed as from it, was fake. And Jameson seemed unaware of Cline's 1988 manuscript titled *Brushy Bill Roberts: I Wasn't Billy the Kid*. Cline, as discussed above, saw the entire "Brushy" endeavor as a scam using a mentally ill man.

10) BILLY THE KID HAD BUCK TEETH: Jameson says "Brushy's" "incisors" (meaning front teeth) were extracted in 1931. (Page 110)

FAKERY: To fake abnormal front teeth, Jameson is misquoting the source of the extracted teeth: Dewitt Travis, one of the five "Brushy" affiants from *Alias Billy the Kid*. Travis said "Brushy" had big "eye teeth" that were removed by a dentist. (*Alias Billy the Kid*, Pages 74) Eye teeth are the upper canines (fangs). In fact, eye-witness Travis correctly described "Brushy's" abnormality in his Affidavit as looking like "tusks," and "extracted in 1931 by Dr. Cruz, Gladewater, Texas." (*Alias Billy the Kid*, Page 124)

This lie reappeared in Jameson's 2012 book, *Billy the Kid: The Lost Interviews*, as yet another "Brushy" artifact in the "Brushy" trunk. Its two teeth, claimed as pulled in Gladewater, were falsely called "incisors" by Bean.

Billy's buck teeth came from the December 27, 1880 *Las Vegas Daily Gazette* article by Lucius "Lute" Wilcox, titled: 'The Kid. Interview with Billy Bonney The Best Known Man in New Mexico." Wilcox wrote: **"He is, in all, quite a** handsome looking fellow, the only imperfection being two prominent front teeth, slightly protruding like a squirrels' teeth." There is no mention of canine tusks!

**11) THE DEATH SCENE ACCOUNTS OF PAT GARRETT AND JOHN W. POE AGREE:** Jameson says they *did not* agree because of "discrepancies;" and since Poe did not know Billy, Garrett could have tricked him about corpse identity. (Page 110)

FAKERY: Jameson is using the "Brushy" hoax's faked "discrepancies" "proving" Billy's killing did not occur; as well as concealing the profuse identification of the body.

Matching Garrett's and Poe's accounts also made Jameson accuse them of conspiring to hide truth. That became most absurd in his 2012 *Billy the Kid: The Lost Interviews* and 2018 *Cold Case Billy the Kid*, which faked that Peter Maxwell's bedroom had no outside door! Since Garrett and Poe mention it, Jameson claimed they colluded to make it up, from which he declared that they made up killing of Billy the Kid! (See pages 573-574, 686-691 below)

**12) MORRISON WAS A FRAUD BY CLAIMING TO BE A LAWYER:** Jameson says that Morrison **never claimed to be a lawyer, but claimed to be an attorney**. And they are not the same, so he was telling the truth. Jameson defines "attorney" as a "person legally appointed to conduct business for another." He then states Morrison took paralegal correspondence courses from LaSalle College in Chicago. (Page 111)

FAKERY: Jameson is hiding that in his 1998 *The Return of the Outlaw Billy the Kid*, he had already advertised Morrison as both. Morrison is a "**graduate lawyer**" on its page 3, and an "**attorney**" on its page 4.

Jameson's "attorney" definition is made-up to hide Morrison's compulsive self-aggrandizing lying; which, of course, created his "Brushy" hoax. *The Free Dictionary* of legal terms states: "[Lawyer] is synonymous with attorney." The definition of "attorney," which Jameson claims Morrison was, in *The Free Dictionary* is: "a person admitted to practice law in at least one jurisdiction and authorized to perform criminal and civil functions on behalf of clients." Morrison, neither an attorney nor a lawyer, was a fraud.

His impersonating was continuous. It the November 30, 1950's *Clovis News Journal* for "Mabry Terms "Billy" Outright Imposter." was: "**William V. Morrison an El Paso salesman ... previously claimed to be a St. Louis lawyer.**"

For their 1955 book, C.L. Sonnichsen called him a "graduate lawyer." (*Alias Billy the* Kid, Page 3) He also reported that Morrison identified himself as "Brushy's" lawyer to impressionable, bedridden, 89 year old widow, Mrs. Martile Able, who had claimed her husband knew Billy the Kid. From her, Morrison sought an Affidavit that "Brushy" was Billy. Sonnichsen quoted an *El Paso* reporter (from an uncited article) as having her say: "**When Billy's ["Brushy's"] lawyer, William V. Morrison, of St. Louis**, brought Billy to the home of my grandson in the Lower Valley, he asked Billy, 'Do you know this lady?' " (*Alias Billy the* Kid, Page 71) Unsurprisingly, prompted "Brushy" said she was John Able's wife, clinching the scam.

Don Cline, for his 1988 unpublished book, *Bill Roberts: I Wasn't Billy the Kid*, confirmed that Sonnichsen stuck to that fable in a letter to him of June 30, 1988: "I believe, without evidence, that Bill Morrison had a law degree. I have a vague recollection that he told me he earned it at night school in St. Louis. He called himself a non-practicing lawyer." (Cline, Page 73) Cline also found that the Missouri Historical Society, to which Morrison belonged, listed him as a lawyer, apparently told by him. (Cline, Page 70) Cline also learned that, when selling car parts, Morrison worked for a Bill Cardon of Dautrich Reality Company from 1960 to 1970, whom he also told he was a lawyer. (Cline, Pages 72-73)

13) **THE LINCOLN COUNTY HERITAGE TRUST PHOTOANALYSIS FOUND NO MATCH OF "BRUSHY" TO BILLY THE KID:** Like in his 1998 *The Return of the Outlaw Billy the Kid*, Dr. Thomas Kyle is accused of an inaccurate study. Jameson blames "the Trust" having a "vested interest" in "Brushy" not being Billy to protect "tourist interests." (Page 113)

**FAKERY:** Omitted is that the study was done under the auspices of world-famous forensic anthropologist Clyde Snow; and "Brushy" showed no match to Billy Bonney.

# CONCLUSION: THE SAME OLD SCAM IN NEED OF NEW BLOOD

By his 2005 *Billy the Kid: Beyond the Grave* W.C. Jameson seemed to have hit a wall. There was a limit to how many times he could repeat the same "Brushy" tales, rationalizations, and conspiracy theories in different books; with a few sly fix-ups to modernize the fakery. And contrary evidence was piling up, striking at the heart of "Brushy's" claims. Jameson needed help.

By 2006, he got it, by his accidental meeting with "Billy the Kid Case" hoaxer, Steve Sederwall. And waiting in the wings were other promulgators of that case, still craving for the glory and gains that had seemed so close. With the "Brushy" hoax's desperate state, Jameson may have realized that compromise was necessary, since there was no match of his hoax to theirs – beyond a death scene's sparing of Billy the Kid. And their anti-establishment mantra of "history is not as written" appealed to his conspiracy theory bent.

So he allied with Steve Sederwall, apparently unaware that he had been accused of an Oklahoma assault on a defenseless man; had defamed a political opponent as a "cocaine whore;" was a Deputy Sheriff for the "Billy the Kid Case" hoax, authored that hoax's major documents, bullied the mayor of Fort Sumner in attempt to force exhuming Billy the Kid; lied that he was a hobbyist instead of a lawman; hid Case 2003-274's public records by calling them private "trade secrets," participated in illegal exhumations of John Miller and William Hudspeth through the Lincoln County Sheriff's Department; faked the results of those illegal exhumations for his own Piltdown man-style hoax; and forged forensic records to trick a court of law. And, apparently, for gullible Jameson, he shape-shifted to a random "federal investigator" interested in Billy the Kid crime scene forensics. And he offered buddies (unmentioned as fellow "Billy the Kid Case" hoaxers) who could also assist Jameson.

Jameson had hit the big leagues of hoaxing; and, replicating his response to the "Brushy"-Morrison-Sonnichsen scam, he was awed, enamored, duped, and corrupted.

# CHAPTER 2
# FURTHER FAKERY IN *BILLY THE KID: THE LOST INTERVIEWS*

## FAKING "BRUSHY'S" WORDS

In 2012, came W.C. Jameson's *Billy the Kid: The Lost Interviews*. It was intentionally misleading, as if based on newly found, convincing, "lost interviews" for Brushy Bill." In fact, they were the same taped 1949-1950 William V. Morrison interviews that C.L. Sonnichsen had used to write *Alias Billy the Kid*; and that Frederick Bean had located in 1989, and were quoted from his transcript in *The Return of the Outlaw Billy the Kid*. The change was in Jameson. He was now in league with hoaxers.

Tellingly, he enthused in his "Preface" about Steve Sederwall as a "retired federal investigator ... separating truth from legend ... who treated ... Billy the Kid-related events as historic cold cases ... [and got] information and facts heretofore unknown." Of course, the "Billy the Kid Case" is unmentioned. Oddly, however, the copyright page states: "The following is a work of fiction. Any resemblance to actual names, persons, businesses, and incidents is strictly coincidental." These are the book's only honest words, but by an unidentified person.

On the surface, the book seems to follow *The Return of the Outlaw Billy the Kid's* let "Brushy" speak for himself. Except, that book is now hidden, and the quotes are by a pseudo-"Brushy," himself mouthing new facts and the hoax's conspiracy theories!

And the little bibliography gives modern sources for its "prompting" upgrades. But absent were the works that disproved "Brushy;" like: Frederick Nolan's 1992 *The Lincoln County War: A Documentary* History for actual events; like Jerry Weddle's 1993 *Antrim is My Stepfather's Name's* on the Silver City and Arizona years; and like niece, Geneva Pittmon's fatal family Bible letter.

# UPGRADING THE "BRUSHY BILL" HOAX

For the "Foreword," a Daniel A. Edwards, as author of *Billy the Kid: An Autobiography*, claims "Brushy" was Billy the Kid. He adds that the Governor Mabry hearing was "treacherous," To him, Jameson is a savior with his 2004 *Billy the Kid: Beyond the Grave* [hidden is contradictory 1998 *The Return of the Outlaw Billy the Kid*]; and "federal investigator" Steve Sederwall did "extensive forensic studies" on Billy the Kid "crime scenes." So Edwards wants to end the "lie" about the death of Billy the Kid.

Jameson's "Preface" now unabashedly reveals the hoax's dark heart: defamation of Pat Garrett. He is called "dishonest, a debtor, an adulterer, a drunk, an inveterate gambler, and a [pathological] liar": all for the "Brushy" hoax's July 14, 1881 accusation of his murdering an innocent victim and covering it up.

And Jameson's "Brushy" hoax claims, are updated with deceptions to appeal to readers more knowledgeable than for the original 1950's hoax. "Brushy's" previous illiteracy claim for the things-not-printed trick, appears only as his "quote": "I don't rightly know what the history books say ... Malinda [his wife] reads me stuff ... She helps me write letters to my friends too." (Page 85) And the bi-lingual Billy obstacle is hidden.

Faked is that impressive evidence had accumulated proving "Brushy" was Billy; that only Garrett identified the Fort Sumner corpse; that there was no "inquest;" that the dark-skinned bearded body proved it was not Billy Bonney [using uncited Grant County newspaperman Singleton Ashenfelter's fake description]; that the burial was hurried to hide the body's identity; and that people saw live Billy after the burial.

Jameson repeats now "paralegal" Morrison's finding of "Brushy," has "Brushy" doing his tiny-hands-shackle-slipping trick; but now his 12 scars are reduced to just a hip one attributed to the Brady shooting scene.

The new Jameson also lies more freely. He claims that Morrison introduced "Brushy" to "veterans of the Lincoln County War" who "immediately recognized" him as Billy the Kid. (Page 11) There were none. He is faking the fake Affidavits of non-War participants in *Alias Billy the Kid*. And, this time around, they are hidden to block checking.

"Brushy's" confabulated Billy Barlow killing scene is given, but with a silly attempt to make sense of the Ashenfelter corpse, by calling Barlow looking so much like fair unbearded Roberts to be mistaken for him, except for dark skin and beard! Barlow is now killed in a vague location "near Pete Maxwell's bedroom," with "Brushy" rushing to the scene and getting some wounds, then being helped by two women and a Frank Lovato.

"Brushy's" multi-identity life after the killing scene is now fabricated as: "All of the claims have been investigated and verified." (Page 13) The pardon attempt with Governor Mabry is claimed as unjustly calling "Brushy" an imposter.

Importantly, Jameson now confirmed that Sonnichsen authored *Alias Billy the Kid* from Morrison's notes and interview tapes. He stated that Sonnichsen had been impressed by the things-not-written trick, and that "Brushy" looked like Billy. Repeated are the hoax's well-worn conspiracy theories to explain historians' rejection of "Brushy." New Mexico is again blamed for a conspiracy to protect tourism by the Lincoln County Heritage Trust's study proving no match of "Brushy" to the Billy the Kid tintype. The fake Acton study is again touted.

The new fakery from his *Billy the Kid: Beyond the Grave* is added with its "new" family Bible, with relatives having names McCarty, Bonney, and Antrim - with Jameson now lying that "Brushy" used the names for himself, when "Brushy" did not know the name "McCarty," and the names "Antrim" and "Bonney" were merely added for his fake Silver City aunt, "Kathleen."

## THE MYSTERY TRUNK AND TAPES

For *Billy the Kid: The Lost* Interviews, the mystery truck, first mentioned in Jameson's 2005 *Billy the Kid: Beyond the Grave*, got an expanded role, now claimed as containing the interview tapes for this *Lost Interviews* book, and the alternate Roberts family Bible, with the historical names (unknown to "Brushy").

The sequence of this trunk's emerging is suspicious. In the *Beyond the Grave* book, Jameson said Frederick Bean learned of it in the 1980's (now made specifically 1989) from "Brushy's step-grandson Bill Allison. But for their 1998 *The Return of the Outlaw Billy the Kid*, nine years after Bean allegedly got the trunk with "Brushy's Bible," there was no mention of "Brushy" having one. In that book, that alternate Bible is a possession of "the late Texas resident Martha Vada Roberts Heath," called "the daughter of Henry Oliver Roberts (brother to James Henry

Roberts) and Caroline Dunn (sister to Mary Adeline Dunn)." (*The Return*, Pages 89-91) And the new genealogy (including the name "McCarty," unknown to "Brushy") was attributed to "[Martha Vada Roberts] Heath descendants" and "researcher " William Tunstill. (*The Return*, Page 91)

**FAKERY: But Tunstill was a genealogy faker, and Martha Vada Heath Roberts's descendant, Roy L. Haws, in his 2015 book, *Brushy Bill: Proof His Claim to Be Billy the Kid Was a Hoax*, revealed her as part of Oliver Pleasant Roberts's family, being descended from his father's first wife, Caroline Dunn; with the rest of Tunstill's faked genealogy vouched for by his own duped mother, Eualine Haws, for Tunstill's 1988 book, *Billy the Kid and Me Were the Same*. And Sonnichsen made clear that the McCarty name was unknown to "Brushy" and team; writing: "Another story, current in Silver City, says that Billy the Kid was really named McCartney." (*Alias Billy the Kid*, Page 16)]**

Jameson's *Billy the Kid: Beyond the Grave* first mentioned the trunk as shown to Frederick Bean by Bill Allison in 1988 [sic - also said 1989] (*Beyond the Grave*, Page 84), and as having Morrison's interviews tapes. (*Beyond the Grave*, Page 6) Also, an alternate family Bible is claimed "in the possession of ["Brushy's"] wife Melinda [sic – Malinda];" and is claimed as validating "Brushy" about Aunt Bonney, by having a "Catherine" [fixed-up from Kathleen] Bonney. And it had a McCarty. (*Beyond the Grave*, Page 54)

For his *Billy the Kid: The Lost* Interviews, Jameson expanded the trunk's tale, it being the source of his "lost" "Brushy" interview tapes from 1949; though they were not "lost." Bean, he stated, got them from Bill Allison in 1989; so they had them for their 1998 *The Return of the Outlaw Billy the Kid*. But Jameson now calls it his own quest, first trying fruitlessly with Morrison's daughter in 1985 and 1994. Then he learned in 1994 that his future co-author, Frederick Bean, had gotten Morrison's materials in 1989 from Bill Allison, of Temple, Texas; who had contacted Bean to say his grandfather was Billy the Kid, and he had a trunk of "Brushy's." Allison stated he was "Brushy's" step-grandson, with his grandmother being Malinda Allison Roberts, whom Jameson called "Brushy's" third wife [though Roy L. Haws stated she was his fourth]. "Brushy's" trunk had been passed to Malinda's son ("Brushy's step-son"); then to *his* son, Bill Allison. (Pages 35-36)

As portrayed by Jameson, Bean opened the trunk like archeologist Howard Carter opening the sealed lost tomb of Tutankhamen. "Bean unlatched the trunk lid ... within were a jumble of objects ... Bean lifted them out one by one." (Page 36) According to Jameson, Bean found three Big Chief writing tablets with bad handwriting in pencil; the five Affidavits from the Morrison book; various photos of Roberts, with one claimed to be aunt Catherine Bonney [apparently the fake Catherine Antrim picture in Morrison's book]; an alleged Spanish War Service medal; an alleged Anti-Horsethief Association badge; two alleged "incisors" described as extracted by a dentist in Gladewater, Texas [misstating the canine teeth which Dewitt Travis, in his Affidavit of December 12, 1951, had described as "Brushy's" "peculiarly shaped teeth with two large teeth protruding outward from under the upper lip and a large tusk on each side of his upper jaw, the teeth having been extracted in 1931 by Dr. Cruz, Gladewater, Texas." (*Alias Billy the Kid*, Page 124) In *Alias Billy the Kid*, page 74, they are called "eye teeth," which are canines]; a .44 caliber revolver [with no serial number given for dating]; and eight six-inch reels of tape, labeled as Morrison interviews; and the alternate Bible with Bonney, McCarty, and Antrim. (Pages 37-38)

THE TRUNK-BIBLE MYSTERY: "Brushy's" trunk appeared to have his Morrison-period possessions, making the Bible appear dated to that time. The rest of the items were his props and prompts for his 1949-1950 Billy the Kid impersonation. But the Bible was never claimed by him; and is an obvious forgery from the William Tunstill 1988 period - when the trunk was allegedly located in 1989. The claim of its having been *in the trunk* appears fake. Though its 1980's creator remains uncertain. This is now a new level of hoaxing: forgery and planting evidence.

## TRANSCRIBING THE "BRUSHY" TAPES

Tracing the finding of the "Brushy" tapes in the mystery trunk, and getting them transcribed, reveal stages in the hoaxing of original "Brushy" into fixed-up pseudo-"Brushy" in *Billy the Kid: The Lost Interviews*. Jameson stated that Bean was lent Morrison's taped "Brushy" interviews by Bill Allison; and transcribed those not too deteriorated, making no copies. And

Bean apparently strove for accuracy; as Jameson wrote: "even spelling words as Roberts mispronounced them." (Page 40) Jameson reported Bean's true-believer and historically ignorant awe: reporting that "Brushy" spoke as if personally involved in events - as portrayed in *Alias Billy the Kid*. (Page 42) Then, noted by Jameson, was the above-mentioned revelation that Sonnichsen, working from those tapes for *Alias Billy the Kid*, unlike Bean, had "heavily edited" "Brushy's" grammar, and added words. (Page 42) That would mean Bean's transcript was more accurate.

Now deceased Bean ultimately gave Jameson his transcript. As Jameson wrote: "I was convinced that I was looking at the words of the outlaw, Billy the Kid." (Page 43) And that was the transcript that Jameson and Bean used to let "Brushy" speak in their 1998 *The Return of the Outlaw Billy the Kid* with its fatal dark night error. And it would have been the source for the "Billy the Kid Case's" "Seventy-Seven Days of Doubt Probable Cause Statement's" long quote repeating "Brushy's dark night death scene, possibly provided by Jameson.

But, by 2012, there was a new Jameson. He revealed something darker: he, like Sonnichsen, altered the transcript for his *Billy the Kid: The Lost Interviews*. He admitted "corrections" if there was a "wrong" word; elimination of "Brushy's" repeating himself multiple times in "only a few minutes;" substitution of politically correct words for "Brushy's" racist ones; and that he "blended elements" of narrations. (Pages 43-44)

**FAKING A TRANSCRIPT: Whether Jameson realized it or not, he was forging a transcript and destroying evidence in order to fake "Brushy" as Billy; as had C.L. Sonnichsen.**

In fact, a transcript is an identical copy, and a potential legal document. The *Merriam-Webster Dictionary* defines it as a "usually typed copy of dictated or recorded material," or "a reproduction of an original work." *Black's Law Dictionary* calls it an "official record ... copy." The whole point is its being *exactly the same as its original source*.

In fact, "Brushy's" bad grammar and racism are more proofs that he was not Billy. And the "**repeating himself**" was obvious rehearsal with Morrison for his Billy the Kid things-not-printed trick, as Morrison asked leading questions for prompting. Jameson has merely given his readers what his copyright page correctly called "**a work of fiction.**" This was a cross-over from true-believer to hoaxer.

# FAKING THE "BRUSHY" TRANSCRIPT

The format of the transcripts is Morrison asking questions, with answers by "Brushy." Not mentioned, obviously, is that the questions are a set-up for confabulating (also implying their rehearsal intent). As examples, Morrison asks: "Tell me what you remember about the incident at the Greathouse Ranch where Deputy Jimmy Carlyle was shot and killed, a killing that was attributed to you" (Page 91); or "You rode away and hid out at Stinking Springs then, didn't you? Tell me about the confrontation with Garrett and his posse." (Page 97)

As to "Brushy's" responses, Jameson's dishonest insertions of updated Billy Bonney history into his words, overlooked that "Brushy's" ignorance was already documented in *Alias Billy the Kid's* quotes. But Jameson was trying to elevate crass, racist, and ignorant "Brushy" into a better match for Billy. It is a mind-bending fictionalizing of "Brushy's" fictions! (Note that "Brushy's" own fakery that was really in the transcripts has already been debunked by me for *Alias Billy the Kid* and *The Return of the Outlaw Billy the Kid*, and is not repeated here.)

Fortunately, however, Jameson's true-believer bedazzlement and historical ignorance leave most of "Brushy's" error-filled confabulations untouched; while Jameson's added fix-ups are equally wrong or glaringly discovered after "Brushy's" day, and unknown to him in the earlier *Alias Billy the Kid* and *The Return of the Outlaw Billy the Kid*. So fix-ups stand out.

## FIX-UPS OF "BRUSHY" AS BILLY THE KID

Though fixing-up "Brushy" and his quotes, Jameson, as a believer, leaves his basic fabrications untouched.

1) Though not in *Alias Billy the Kid*, when "Brushy" and team would certainly have used it, the Bible from the mystery trunk now is used for his date of birth as December 31, 1859, and his fake genealogy. Bizarrely, Jameson portrays "Brushy" as, in the transcript, "pointing to the Bible" (Page 45), as if it was a video!

2) "Brushy" calls himself "William Henry Roberts," but says: "I mostly used names from some of my relatives like Antrim and McCarty and Bonney." (Page 45)

FAKING THE TRANSCRIPT: The "Brushy" quote about the historical names is added by Jameson from the fake Bible.

The name "McCarty" was unknown to "Brushy," who created the tape! *Alias Billy the Kid*, written from it by Sonnichsen, stated: "Young Billy Roberts lived with Mrs. Bonney (later Mrs. Antrim) and her mother until he was twelve years old, and passed as her son." Sonnichsen's footnote, proving "McCarty" was unknown to them, stated: "Another story, current in Silver City, says Billy the Kid was really named McCartney. See the *New Mexico Magazine* for December, 1948, reprint of an interview with H.H. Whitehill." (*Alias Billy the Kid*, Page 16)

And "Brushy" did not use the names McCarty, Antrim, and Bonney as his aliases. Antrim and Bonney were merely tacked on to his fake aunt Kathleen for name-dropping.

3) "Brushy" says: "**I told the Coe boys** (George and Frank) that Mrs. Antrim was my mother and I wanted to go back home and see her." (Pages 46-47)

FAKING THE TRANSCRIPT: The actual transcript, given in *Alias Billy the Kid*, merely had Morrison prompting "Brushy" with the Coe names. Morrison asks: "You told the Coe boys you that were born in New York?" "Brushy" answers: "Yes, and I told them Mrs. Antrim was my mother." (*Alias Billy the Kid*, Page 15) By faking the quote as "Brushy's" bringing up the "Coe boys" *himself*, Jameson faked knowledge that "Brushy" did not have.

4) "Brushy" says about the Fritz life insurance policy case: "They [Murphy] had a lot of trouble about McSween's law fee too. <u>McSween got the settlement money and the Murphy bunch claimed it. They rode over to Mesilla and got a court **order in the form of a writ** that would give them some of the goods in McSween's and Tunstall's store and a herd of blooded horses out at Tunstall's ranch. Sheriff William Brady was given the papers and he served them on McSween, padlocking the store until it was settled.</u>" (Pages 64-65)

FAKING THE TRANSCRIPT: This rewrite added everything underlined. Besides making unsophisticated "Brushy" sound like an attorney (!), it added technical information unknown to him and his team, who were utterly confused about the Fritz insurance case and its legal maneuvers (though Jameson was also ignorant).

The actual unsophisticated transcript in *Alias Billy the Kid* stated: "They had a lot of trouble about McSween's law fee. Finally Murphy got a judgment or attachment against McSween and started to pick up partnership property of Tunstall's. We turned the cattle over to the law. Tunstall had a herd of fine horses of his own. He decided that we would drive the horses over to Lincoln and surrender them until the case was cleared up." (*Alias Billy the Kid*, Page 25)

5) "Brushy" says: "Tunstall was a good man. He had been good to me and treated me like a gentleman." (Page 66)

**DISHONESTLY RECYCLED QUOTE:** For his 2018 book, *Cold Case Billy the Kid*, even more dishonest Jameson would recycle this quote (which was also in *Alias Billy the Kid*) by attributing it to real Billy Bonney, without letting his reader-victims know it was actually by "Brushy Bill!"

6) "Brushy" says: "Dick Brewer was a foreman at the Tunstall Ranch, so it was up to him what we would do about the way they shot John. That day at the funeral we asked Brewer how we ought to go about settling the score." (Page 68)

**FAKING THE TRANSCRIPT:** This quote was not in *Alias Billy the Kid*, and appears made-up by Jameson. And it is wrong. It was up to Sheriff Brady to make arrests. When he did not, Tunstall's men organized as the Regulators, and Justice of the Peace John Wilson wrote out arrest warrants for them to serve. And Billy *was not at Tunstall's funeral*. Brady had arrested and imprisoned him and Fred Waite as deputies of Town Constable Atanacio Martinez, and confiscated Billy's Winchester '73 carbine.

7) "Brushy" says: "We'd have won that war, too, if those (black) soldiers of Dudley's had been kept out." (Page 78)

**FAKING THE TRANSCRIPT:** Racist "Brushy" actually said about the Lincoln County War Battle: "We'd have won the war too, if those nigger soldiers of Dudley's had been kept out." (*Alias Billy the Kid*, Page 29)

8) "Brushy" says: "The real battle broke out when we took over Montoya's house across the street from the tower." (Page 78)

**TRANSCRIPT FIX-UP:** In *Alias Billy the Kid*, "Brushy" cites "Montaña's house." (*Alias Billy the Kid*, Page 30) Both names are wrong. It was José Montaño's house.

9) "Brushy" says: "They started firing on us as we rode in that day, so we fought back at them. The battle lasted three days. It was July, and on the 19th, on the last day, Colonel Dudley rode into town with those (black) soldiers." (Pages 78-79)

**FAKING THE TRANSCRIPT:** In *Alias Billy the Kid*, "Brushy" did not have the date, and was racist, stating: "They started firing on us as we rode in that day, so we fought back at them. On the last day, Colonel Dudley rode into town with those nigger soldiers." (*Alias Billy the Kid*, Page 30)

10) "Brushy" says: "If we could have kept them (black) soldiers out at Stanton, we could have whipped Peppin's posse all right." (Page 79)

**FAKING THE TRANSCRIPT:** Racist "Brushy" actually said in *Alias Billy the Kid:* "If we could have kept them nigger soldiers out at Stanton, we could have whipped Peppin's posse." (*Alias Billy the Kid*, Page 30)

11) "Brushy" says: "[Dudley] said that he did not have the authority to interfere, but some of his (black) soldiers was up on the side of the hill firing at us with the Murphy men." (Page 79)

**FAKING THE TRANSCRIPT:** Racist "Brushy" actually said in *Alias Billy the Kid:* "[Dudley] said that he did not have the authority to interfere. But some of his nigger soldiers was up on the side of that hill firing at us with the Murphy men." (*Alias Billy the Kid*, Page 30)

12) "Brushy" says: "We opened the back door and looked out just as Bob Beckwith and some of them (black soldiers) tried to rush us, started to come in." (Page 80)

FAKING THE TRANSCRIPT: Racist "Brushy" actually said in *Alias Billy the Kid:* "We opened the back door and looked out just as Bob Beckwith and some of them niggers started to come in." (*Alias Billy the Kid*, Page 31)

13) "Brushy" says: "McSween, Zamora, and Romero were driven back ... all three were killed by John Jones, John Kinney, and those (black) soldiers of Dudley's." (Page 81)

FAKING THE TRANSCRIPT: Racist "Brushy," mispronouncing Hispanic names, said in *Alias Billy the Kid:* "McSween, <u>Samora</u>, and Romero were driven back ... all three were killed by John Jones, John Kinney, and those nigger soldiers of Dudley's." (*Alias Billy the Kid*, Page 31)

14) "Brushy" says: "**Folliard [sic]**, Salazar, and the rest of our boys started through." (Page 81)

FAKING THE TRANSCRIPT: This is a fake rewrite of Tom O'Folliard's name, which would not be explicable until Jameson's 2018 *Cold Case Billy the Kid*. There it was revealed as Steve Sederwall's absurd "investigation" claiming he discovered the name was really "Folliard;" when he was just seeing a misspelling by a census taker. But this revealed that Sederwall was active behind-the-scenes for Jameson's *Billy the Kid: The Lost Interviews*.

In fact, this name discredited "Brushy," who, as Billy, should know his good friend's name: and "Brushy" always used "O'Folliard;" stating: "O'Folliard, Salazar, and the rest of our boys started through." (*Alias Billy the Kid*, Page 31)

But throughout this faked transcript, "Folliard" is substituted for "Brushy's" stated "O'Folliard," proving Jameson's forging and succumbing to bad influence.

15) "Brushy" says: "We didn't know it then, but the fight we lost at McSween's was the turning point for us in the war. With McSween and Tunstall dead, we didn't have a way to make a living. We drifted down to San Patricio for a while, but there were warrants out for us and we had to stay on the dodge. I was bitter about what they'd done to McSween and Tunstall." (Page 81)

**FAKING THE TRANSCRIPT: This complex explanation of the War was not in *Alias Billy the Kid*; appearing made-up.**

16) "Brushy" is quoted about "the winter of '79," being with Tom "Folliard" and meeting with J.J. Dolan and Jesse Evans "to talk about things," with a "fellow named Campbell along;" and that with "Tunstall and McSween dead, Tom and I didn't have much of a stake in things." And they shake hands. (Page 86)

**FAKING THE TRANSCRIPT: None of this is in *Alias Billy the Kid*, where "Brushy" never used Dolan's initials or "Folliard." It appears made-up for this book. In *Alias Billy the Kid*, "Brushy" merely stated: "In the winter of '79 we got together with Dolan and Evans and agreed to quit fighting each other." (*Alias Billy the Kid*, Page 33)**

17) "Brushy" says: "When we walked out of the saloon, we parted company. Just down the street, I saw Mrs. McSween and her lawyer, Chapman, walk up to Evans, Dolan, and Chapman." (Page 86)

**INADVERTENT REVEAL OF C.L. SONNICHSEN'S OWN FAKING OF THE TRANSCRIPT: This is likely the real transcription. Since Jameson is historically ignorant, this serious error of Susan McSween being present at the Chapman shooting went unnoticed; as well as having "Brushy" at a distance. Dishonest Sonnichsen had done his own fix-up for *Alias Billy the Kid*; writing: "When we came out of the salon that night in Lincoln we run into Chapman, the lawyer for Mrs. McSween. Campbell and Dolan killed him in cold blood. I was standing there." (*Alias Billy the Kid*, Page 33)**

18) "Brushy" has a long quote of Governor Wallace wanting to "clean" up the Lincoln mess, "looking into cattle contracts controlled by the Catron Ring up in Santa Fe," and wanting to stop "crooked dealings." So he tells Tom he wants a meeting with Wallace to see "if he is on the level," and to testify "about the murder of Chapman." Wallace agrees, and "Brushy" states: "I sent word back that I would come in if he would annul those indictments against me. I had a friend who spelled it out in a letter for me, what I wanted from Governor Wallace." (Page 87)

**FAKING THE TRANSCRIPT:** None of this is in *Alias Billy the Kid*, where "Brushy" is quoted as saying only: "I heard that Governor Wallace had offered a thousand dollars for me if I would come and testify. I wrote and told him I would come in if he would annul those indictments." (*Alias Billy the Kid*, Page 33) Furthermore, Jameson is now trying to fix-up the problem of real Billy's articulate first letter to Wallace, by here inserting the original "Brushy" hoax's fakery of someone writing for him.

It is noteworthy that "Brushy," his team, and Jameson were utterly confused about the pardon bargain, so Jameson left in the text "Brushy's" confabulation that the pardon bargain was for "standing trial on my indictments," "testifying against Dudley" at a "court martial," and testifying against Chapman. (Pages 88-89) The actual bargain was only for testifying against Chapman's assassins. Billy's Dudley testimony was on his own initiative, and the Dudley Court of Inquiry was not a court martial, but was to determine if one was justified.

19) "Brushy" is quoted about the arranged arrest with Sheriff Kimbrell, adding extensive text about testifying in a "board of Inquiry in Colonel Dudley's case," then being told he would be taken to Mesilla for trial, and leaving the jailing because of the unfair switch in the bargain. There is no testifying before the Grand Jury against Chapman's murderers. (Pages 89-90)

**FAKING THE TRANSCRIPT:** None of this is in *Alias Billy the Kid*, where "Brushy," for his made-up pardon bargain, mixed up Ira Leonard and Albert Jennings Fountain as his attorney for pleading not guilty to his indictments (which never occurred anyway, since it was not part of the pardon bargain), gets Dolan "and his men" indicted, and testifies in the "Dudley trial." (*Alias Billy the Kid*, Page 34)

Jameson appeared to make-up the quote, removing "Brushy's" Leonard-Fountain errors, and correcting his Dudley "court martial" to "board of Inquiry." But ignorant Jameson also deleted "Brushy's" claim of getting Chapman case indictments: the punch line of fulfilling the pardon bargain (and the key to showing the injustice in real Billy's history)! Instead, Jameson has "Brushy" exiting jailing before testifying; thus, breaking the bargain himself!

20) "Brushy," answering about the Greathouse Ranch ambush, gives a quote from Jim Carlyle after "Brushy" asks about a warrant: " 'Don't need one, Billy,' he said. "Everybody in the territory knows you're a wanted man for killing Sheriff Brady. I wear a badge, and that's good enough to bring you in.' "

FAKING THE TRANSCRIPT: None of this is in *Alias Billy the Kid*, in which "Brushy" merely said, "They sent in Carlyle to get us to surrender. He had no warrant." (*Alias Billy the Kid*, Page 34) This text appears to be made-up by Jameson to fix-up *Alias Billy the Kid's* confusion about why Billy was pursued. But it is wrong. Jim Carlyle was just a White Oaks resident in the posse of Deputy Sheriff Will Hudgens.

21) "Brushy" says: "Deputy Sheriff Kip McKinney, Tom's own cousin and one of Garrett's posse, wouldn't give Tom a drink of water." (Page 96)

FAKING THE TRANSCRIPT: *Alias Billy the Kid* stated: "His cousin, Kip McKinney, one of Garrett's posse, wouldn't give Tom a drink." (*Alias Billy the Kid*, Page 37) Adding "Deputy Sheriff" seems to be Jameson's fix-up. But McKinney was only deputized by Garrett for the Fort Sumner killing of Billy. "Brushy" himself made-up that he was just a posseman at the Tom O'Folliard killing.

22) "Brushy" says: "I had known McKinney some time before all the difficulties ... It turned out he was just another coward like the rest of them Murphy men and Garrett men. I learned years later that McKinney never lived down riding with Garrett, that it left a bad taste in his mouth for the rest of his life." (Page 96)

FAKING THE TRANSCRIPT: This is not in *Alias Billy the Kid*. It appears made-up by Jameson to defame Garrett.

23) "Brushy" says about the Bowdre shooting: "Charlie wore a large sombrero like mine when he stepped out the door that morning and I figured they must have thought Charlie was me." (Page 97)

FAKING THE TRANSCRIPT: *Alias Billy the Kid* stated: "He wore a large hat like mine. They thought it was me." (*Alias Billy the Kid*, Page 37) This is a Jameson fix-up by adding "sombrero," as well as the usual polishing of "Brushy's" wording. More subtly, "Brushy" was unaware of Billy's bi-culturalism, of which the sombrero was part.

24) "Brushy" says: "While I was [in the Santa Fe jail] I had a letter sent to Governor Wallace asking him to come and talk to me." (Page 101)

FAKING THE TRANSCRIPT: *Alias Billy the Kid* stated: "I wrote to Governor Wallace to come and talk to me." (*Alias Billy the Kid*, Page 39) This appears to be a Jameson fix-up of a "Brushy" gaffe: he could write. But it showed Jameson's ignorance that all Billy Bonney's letters are in the same handwriting, even in solitary confinement!

25) "Brushy" says: "I pleaded to the federal indictment. It was for killing Buckshot Roberts and I never did. It was thrown out of court." (Page 102)

FAKING THE TRANSCRIPT: *Alias Billy the Kid* stated: "I pleaded to the federal indictment and it was thrown out of court." (*Alias Billy the Kid*, Page 39) A fix-up is adding "Buckshot" Roberts, unknown to "Brushy" and team.

26) In answer to a Morrison question about anyone else arrested for the Sheriff Brady killing, a long text follows garbling previous pardon bargain text about "Judge Leonard" not being "there like the governor promised," "Colonel Fountain" being appointed as attorney, being before "the grand jury that brought in indictments" against Dolan and Chapman, testifying at Fort Stanton, being threatened with a trial at Mesilla, Judge Bristol being a "Murphy sympathizer and friend of Tom Catron at the head of the Santa Fe Ring," having to be a Mason to stand a chance, and leaving jail in Lincoln. (Pages 104-105)

FAKING THE TRANSCRIPT: This was not in the Mesilla trial in *Alias Billy the Kid*. It appears to be Jameson's rewrite of "Brushy's" (or Sonnichsen's) garbling of the 1979 pardon bargain trials and the 1881 Mesilla trial. The problem of all these fakers - from "Brushy" on down - is that they did not know the history they were attempting to mimic.

27) "Brushy" goes on about Peppin's Mesilla trial testimony being unfair; his trying to shoot Matthews, not Brady; Pat Garrett saying Governor Otero said Billy the Kid never shot at Brady; and nobody knowing who killed Brady; but he, as Billy, was blamed for his "reputation." (Pages 104-105)

**FAKING THE TRANSCRIPT: This is not in *Alias Billy the Kid* for the Mesilla trial, though it is made-up from that book's Sonnichsen footnote about Otero's claim. It appears to be Jameson's fix-up to show the Brady trial as unjust. But, like for "Brushy" and his team, he is too ignorant about the Regulator killing to make a correct argument.**

28) "Brushy" says about transport to Lincoln: "John McKinney, who fought against me in the war, sat on the back seat." (Page 106)

**FAKING THE TRANSCRIPT: *Alias Billy the Kid* stated: "John Kinney, who fought against me in the war, sat on the back seat." (*Alias Billy the Kid*, Page 40) It is not clear if Jameson wrongly fixed-up the correct "Kinney" name, or if "Brushy" got mixed-up in his name-dropping, and had been corrected with an earlier Sonnichsen fix-up.**

29) "Brushy" says for the jailbreak: "I could lay my thumbs flat against my palms and the irons would slide right off ... (Page 109) The date for my execution was only a few days away. I knew I had to make a break." (Page 111)

**FAKING THE TRANSCRIPT: This is not in *Alias Billy the Kid*. And it has a new error: from the jailbreak on April 28, 1881 to hanging date of May 13, 1881 was over two weeks, not a few days. Billy escaped seven days after arriving.**

30) "Brushy" says when escaping: "[O]ld man Gauss and someone else was standing near Bell's body." (Page 113)

**FAKING THE TRANSCRIPT: This is fixed-up from the *Alias Billy the Kid's* "Goss." (*Alias Billy the Kid*, Page 44)**

31) "Brushy" says: "I rode out of Lincoln to the west and up the canyon to the home of a friend who cut the bolts in my leg irons. It was 'ol Cipio Salazar. He was cousin to Ygenio ... Ol' Cipio had a time of it, he did." (Page 116)

FAKING THE TRANSCRIPT: This fix-up adds information and corrects spellings. *Alias Billy the Kid* stated only: "I got on the horse and rode out of Lincoln to the west and up the canyon to the home of a friend, who cut the bolts in my leg irons." (*Alias Billy the Kid*, Page 45) The new text lifts Sonnichsen's footnote, which stated: "Mrs. Bernardo Salazar, adopted daughter of Higinio [sic - Ygenio], told Morrison on October 11, 1949, that Higinio's [sic] cousin, Sepio Salazar, was the one who cut the bolts." (*Alias Billy the Kid*, Page 45)

## *FIX-UPS OF THE FAKE DEATH SCENE*

A weakness in the original "Brushy Bill" hoax, had been its threadbare death scene, lacking explanation for why his Billy Barlow was killed on the back porch, and omitting the Maxwell bedroom scene. Jameson's solution was his pseudo-"Brushy" mouthing Sonnichsen's conspiracy theories against Pat Garrett. And, apparently feeling above detection, he also had his pseudo-"Brushy" insert "Billy the Kid Case" hoax claims, either from his own involvement with the hoax, or from Steve Sederwall's input.

All this exposes active hoaxing and a forged transcript; with forgery defined by *Duhaime Legal Dictionary* as "[t]he making of a false document knowing it to be false with intent that it should be used or acted on as genuine to the prejudice of another." These are examples:

1) "Brushy" has a long passage before the Fort Sumner shooting saying he wanted to "have a talk with Mr. Pat Garrett" to set things "straight between us" because "[w]e used to be friends before the Lincoln County War." (Page 121)

FAKING THE TRANSCRIPT: This was not in *Alias Billy the Kid*. But it fabricates a friendship between "Brushy" and Pat Garrett like in the "Billy the Kid Case" hoax. "Brushy's" version merely had an accidental killing of Billy Barlow, when Garrett was trying to kill *him*.

2) "Brushy" says about the shooting: "I pulled one of my .44's and ran through the door, trying to see in the dark. I ran through the gate into Maxwell's back yard **into the bright moonlight**. Two more shots came from a shadow beside the Maxwell house. I started shooting at the shadows along the house." (Page 124)

## EXPOSING JAMESON AS A HOAXER BY HIS FAKED TRANSCRIPT: "Brushy's" fatal error was confabulating that July 14, 1881 had a dark night.

In fact it had unusually intense moonlight. That moonlight was the hoaxers' undoing, as they fraudulently rewrote his words to hide his fatal mistake. One should, however, note that "Brushy's confabulation was well thought out. His tall tale was that Billy Barlow was mistaken for him *because* the night was so dark, making the killing accidental. Bright moonlight was incompatible with his fabrication!

In *Alias Billy the Kid*, Morrison and Sonnichsen, taking no chances with reality, titled the death scene chapter "Death by Moonlight." (*Alias Billy the Kid*, Page 48) So "Brushy is quoted: "I ran through the gate into Maxwell's back yard in the bright moonlight." (*Alias Billy the Kid*, Page 49)

But for their 1998, *Return of the Outlaw Billy the Kid*, Jameson and Frederick Bean were just naïve true-believers, quoting from Bean's transcript of "Brushy's" tapes, as the gospel words of Billy the Kid. So they were accidentally honest.

But first they copied equally idolized Sonnichsen's fixed-up text for: "Billy, easily seen in the moonlit yard, immediately drew return fire from the lawmen." (*Return of the Outlaw*, Page 73) Then, unaware that the moonlight was fatal, they honestly quoted "Brushy" from the transcript: "[After hearing the shot from Pete Maxwell's place] I pulled one of my .44's and ran through the door, trying to see in the dark. Two more shots came from the shadow beside the Maxwell house. I couldn't find a target. It was too dark to see." (*Return of the Outlaw*, Page 112) And they repeated his dark night quote as his explanation for the killing of Barlow: "Garrett knew by now that he'd killed the wrong man in the dark." (*Return of the Outlaw*, Page 117) Thus, they accidentally proved the dishonest Morrison-Sonnichsen fix-up.

But a more debased Jameson now hid "Brushy's" error. To trick readers, as Morrison-Sonnichsen had intended, he deleted "Brushy's" disastrous quote from his *The Return of the Outlaw Billy the Kid*: "I pulled one of my .44's and ran through the door, trying to see in the dark. Two more shots came from the shadow beside the Maxwell house. I couldn't find a target. It was too dark to see." (*Return of the Outlaw*, Page 112) All that Jameson used for *Billy the Kid: The Lost Interviews* was: "I pulled one of my .44's and ran through the door, trying to see in the dark. I ran through the gate into Maxwell's back yard into the bright moonlight" – adding "bright moonlight," which "Brushy" never said. This is despicable and willful forgery to hide that "Brushy" could not have been in Fort Sumner on the night of July 14, 1881.

Nevertheless, hoaxing Jameson still seemed unaware of just how dangerous to the hoax the error was, since he was careless in "cleaning up" all "Brushy's quotes. Later in the text, he fabricated "Brushy" ruminating to Morrison about the Billy Barlow killing (adding "half-Mex" to Barlow's background to go with S.M. Ashenfelter's newspaper article's swarthy corpse). But Jameson has "Brushy" repeat the darkness: "Barlow looked a little like me but he was half-Mex. I could imagine Garrett couldn't tell us apart in the real dark, except Barlow had a beard." (Page 133)

3) "Brushy" is quoted about the location of the side of beef at Maxwell's house: "Silva said if one of us would go over to Maxwell's and get beef, he would cook it for us. He said Maxwell had one on his back porch hanging from a rafter hook, killed on the day before ..." (Page 123) "[After hearing shots] [f]rom the corner of my eye I saw a body lying on the back porch. A candle was lit in the alcove where the beef was hung and I knew it had to be Barlow." (Page 124)

## EXPOSING JAMESON AS A HOAXER BY HIS FORGED TRANSCRIPT:

In *Alias Billy the Kid* and *The Return of the Outlaw Billy the Kid*, "Brushy" says only: "One of their shots had killed my partner on the back porch." (*Alias Billy the Kid*, Page 49; *The Return of the Outlaw*, Page 113)

Revealed in Jameson's made-up quote is even more extreme hoaxing: fabricating these scenes as "Brushy's" words. He was trying to fix-up "Brushy's" and his team's fatal ignorance about the lay-out of Fort Sumner and the Maxwell house. So the "back porch" is a clue to hoaxing going back to Sonnichsen's and Morrison's prompting by sources that revealed themselves by fatal errors when "Brushy" confabulated by using them.

The problem these first liars had, was not knowing the location of Maxwell's bedroom or the side of beef. So Sonnichsen got that from a provided footnote. It was an apocryphal tale told to him by Jack Fountain (Albert Jennings Fountain's son) in an April 15, 1944 interview. Jack said that Garrett said <u>the beef hung beside Maxwell's bedroom from which Garrett saw Billy and killed him outside the room.</u> This is Jack's made-up Garrett quote: "The beef was <u>hanging in a little outer room from the vigas. There was a candle and materials for making a light in the niche in the wall.</u> [Billy] made a light and held it up while he cut. I was in Pete's room, talking. Billy heard something and asked Pete who was there. Pete said, 'Nobody.' <u>I looked out at a perfect target - Billy lighting himself up</u> with a candle... I thought if he ever got his gun it was him or me. My conscience bothers me about it now." (*Alias Billy the Kid,* **Page 49**)

When given to "Brushy" as a prompt, he simply confabulated that the connected bedroom and beef were at the "back porch." And, using the rest of Jack Fountain's fable, he put the shot victim (Billy Barlow) outside the room. So this explained "Brushy's" weird death scene's ignoring the shooting inside the Maxwell bedroom.

But equally ignorant Jameson, accepting "Brushy's" fable and Sonnichsen's fake footnote, fixed-up by putting the footnote into "Brushy's" mouth to make sense of the absurd scene. Instead, he proved he faked the transcript.

4) "Brushy" is "quoted" for a two page description of being shot and running down a long "alley" behind the Maxwell house to an "adobe shack." (Pages 125-126)

**FAKING THE TRANSCRIPT:** This is not in *Alias Billy the Kid*; which only stated: "I stumbled into the gallery of an adobe behind Maxwell's yard fence." (*Alias Billy the Kid*, Page 49) Morrison-Sonnichsen may have omitted it as too revealing of "Brushy's" utter ignorance of the Maxwell property and Fort Sumner buildings; or Jameson may have added it to justify "Brushy's" claims of being shot there, since he quotes him saying about one of his faked head wounds: "That's this scar here." (Page 125)

5) "Brushy" says about his rescue that when he came to he saw "another woman in the room ... She was another of Saval's sisters, named Celsa, and she had been a sweetheart of mine at one time." (Page 127)

FAKING THE TRANSCRIPT: This is not in *Alias Billy the Kid* at this location, but was "Brushy's" Celsa-Saval-sibling mistake, which he had given earlier in that book.

Fortunately, Jameson's utter historical ignorance limited his fix-ups of "Brushy's" fatal errors. In fact, Celsa was Saval Gutierrez's <u>wife</u>, with "Brushy" and his original team misled by his being called Garrett's brother-in-law by being married to one of Celsa's sisters, Apolinaria. But that did not make Apolinaria his sister. It made Garrett his brother-in-law by marriage.

6) "Brushy" quotes Celsa telling him that Garrett and his men stayed at Maxwell's house after the shooting: "She said, 'They are afraid to come out in the dark, afraid of being mobbed. They think some of your friends may try to shoot them. You have many friends here, Billy. Pat and his men say they won't leave the house until early daylight." (Page 128)

FAKING THE TRANSCRIPT: This fixed-up *Alias Billy the Kid's*: "She said they would not leave Maxwell's house for the night. They were afraid of being mobbed." (*Alias Billy the Kid*, Page 50) It was lifted from John W. Poe's 1933 *The Death of Billy the Kid*; which stated: "We spent the remainder of the night on the Maxwell premises, keeping constantly on our guard, as we were expecting to be attacked by friends of the dead man." (Poe, Page 44) Noteworthy is that real Celsa would not have known this information.

7) "Brushy" says: "Celsa confirmed what I had guessed. Garrett and a posse had been laying for me over at Maxwell's. They knew Pete and I were friends and that I'd stop by to see him if I was in this country. Me and Barlow rode into town late and I figured Mrs. Maxwell was already in bed by the time we got there. I aimed to talk to Pete in the morning." (Page 128)

FAKING THE TRANSCRIPT: This is not in *Alias Billy the Kid*. It appears made-up by Jameson to explain why "Brushy" went to Peter Maxwell's room. But his historical ignorance made him unaware that real Billy had been hiding-out, since his jailbreak, on Maxwell's property's sheep camps; so he had "Brushy" visiting "the country."

8) "Brushy" says: "Celsa said, 'Don't worry, Billy. Pat is telling everyone that you are dead. They took the body of your friend inside the house and they say it is yours. Some of the men in town have already been sent to dig a grave by lantern light. Jesus is building a coffin in the carpenter's shop. Deluvina Maxwell is crying and carrying on, but she knows Pat killed the wrong man ... Your partner looks very much like you in the dark except for his beard. His eyes are blue like yours, Billy. Pat says they will bury the body in the morning. If the coffin is closed, who will guess that you are not inside it?' I couldn't figure it right then, hearing what Celsa was saying about Garrett. Was he trying to pass off Barlow's body as mine? We were friends. He knew the body was not mine, so why was he telling everybody that he had killed me?" (Page 129)

FAKING THE TRANSCRIPT: This is not in *Alias Billy the Kid*, which merely stated: "Celsa came running in and said they had killed Barlow and they were passing off his body as mine." (*Alias Billy the Kid*, Page 50) Jameson appears absurdly to be making-up "Brushy's" dialogue to encompass the entire hoax: the body taken into the house (to correspond with history); Deluvina Maxwell being in on the conspiracy to hide the body's identity; the burial rushed by dishonest Garrett to hide corpse identity; and a resemblance of Barlow to "Brushy," with even the "beard" from S.M. Schenfelter's fake article on the body. But amusingly, Jameson forgets the "bright moonlight," and has Celsa to say: "Your partner looks very much like you in the dark."

Important to note is that even in Jameson's expanded death scene, there is no match to the "Billy the Kid Case" hoax, with which he was allying. The latter had Billy's best friend, Garrett, purposefully shoot *him* for playing dead on the carpenter's bench (to leave blood for DNA); then had Billy sneak off while evil Garrett *replaced him on the bench* with the murdered innocent victim - not necessarily Billy Barlow. Desperate Jameson had climbed in with incompatible bed-fellows, but now matched them in his scornful intent to trick his reader-dupes.

9) "Brushy" says in answer to a Morrison question about Garrett's claim of killing Billy the Kid: "I wondered how he figured to get away with it. I had lots of friends in town. Would they go along with Garrett's ploy. Garrett knew by now he had killed the wrong man in the dark ... [Barlow looked like me] [b]ut in daylight, a lot of folks who knew me would know they had the wrong body. I couldn't figure it, unless Garrett was making a try at collecting the reward ... [He] was out of his bailiwick in San Miguel County. Hilario Romero was sheriff there ... Sheriff Romero would have to appoint a coroner's jury to sign the death certificate, not Garrett ... [T]hey would have trouble rounding up a coroner's jury that didn't know what I looked like." (Pages 130-131)

**FAKING THE TRANSCRIPT: This is not in *Alias Billy the Kid*. It appears made-up by Jameson to put his and Sonnichsen's fake conspiracy theories in pseudo-"Brushy's" mouth: Garrett hid the corpse identity to collect the Billy the Kid reward; Garrett was out of his jurisdiction; and no Coroner's Jury had been called, since it was Sheriff Romero's responsibility.**

10) "Brushy" states that there was another reason for Garrett being in trouble: that Barlow had a .41 double action revolver, which he would not use because they jam. (Page 131)

**FAKING THE TRANSCRIPT: This is not in *Alias Billy the Kid*. It appears to be Jameson's fiction to set-up his future claim that Garrett lied about the gun with Billy's body. It is also wrong, since the .41 caliber, double action Colt Thunderer was used by Billy and others as a back-up hide-away, preferable to a single shot derringer, and would not cast doubt on Garrett's claim of its being with Billy.**

11) "Brushy" ruminates about Garrett digging a grave the night of the killing to hide that the body was Barlow's, since killing Billy the Kid would have made him famous and he would have showed off the body. And he claims gravedigger Jesus Silva, who knew him, kept secret the body's identity. (Pages 131-132)

**FAKING THE TRANSCRIPT: This is not in *Alias Billy the Kid*. It appears to be Jameson's fiction to set up his and Sonnichsen's conspiracy theorizing about Garrett hiding the corpse's identity for personal gain.**

12) "Brushy" says: "**It crossed my mind that Garrett might be trying to help me. We'd been friends once**, back when he first came to this country." (Page 132) "Brushy's" earlier confabulation for showing special knowledge that Garrett had been a buffalo hunter who killed a partner over hides is then inserted here as proof of "friendship." "Brushy" continues that, as Lincoln County Sheriff, Garrett had to pursue him, but wonders if "he saw his chance to let me get away clean and make a fresh start for myself" by pretending Barlow was Billy the Kid. (Pages 132-133)

## EXPOSING JAMESON AS A COMPLICIT "BILLY THE KID CASE" HOAXER BY HIS FAKED TRANSCRIPT:

This is not in *Alias Billy the Kid*, except for the erroneous description of buffalo hunter Garrett's killing, which was copied from "Brushy's" earlier confabulation based on a prompt source and in a different context. (*Alias Billy the Kid*, Page 36; See pages 175-176 above)

This shockingly appears to be Jameson's making-up quotes to make "Brushy" fit the "Billy the Kid Case" hoax - which relied on a fake Garrett friendship motive for the innocent victim killing to let Billy go free. It should be noted that this book first came out in 2012, and Jameson was a participant in the latter hoax since 2004; and hoaxer, Steve Sederwall, was also participating with him for this book. As will be seen, Jameson's unwieldy fusing of that hoax, and its hoaxers, to his "Brushy" hoaxing culminated six years later in his *Cold Case Billy the Kid*.

Used here, however, it contradicts original "Brushy's" own description of Garrett's effort to kill him as Billy the Kid. As Jameson's own "Brushy" text quoted: "My partner walked right into the trap, and the trap had likely been set for me ... I knew I had to get away from Maxwell's before they killed me." (Pages 124-125) And Jameson himself had first stuck to the theme of Garrett's intent to kill "Brushy" as Billy, by the quote: "Barlow looked a little like me but he was half-Mex. I could imagine Garrett <u>couldn't tell us apart in the real dark</u>, except Barlow had a beard." (Page 133) That meant Garrett intended to kill the Kid in the world according to "Brushy." Jameson could not keep his hoaxing straight.

13) "Brushy" is quoted that Garrett could keep the corpse identity secret because the only people who knew it was not him were Celsa, Jesus Silba, the Mexican woman who took him in, and a Frank Lobato; and they would keep a secret.

**FAKING THE TRANSCRIPT: This is not in *Alias Billy the Kid*. It appears to be Jameson's fiction to have pseudo-"Brushy" mouth conspiracy theories of Sonnichsen and himself. (Note that his fake list forgets his earlier fabrication of Deluvina in on the secret too!) Of course, this maintains the "Brushy" hoax's key lies of hiding the night vigil over Billy's body and his Coroner's Jury Report.**

14) "Brushy" states a flashback of a **Frank Lovoto** having checked Fort Sumner and reporting to him that Barlow's body had been taken to the carpenter's shop wrapped in a sheet to hide its identity; Poe could not recognize him, so could not identify the body; Garrett sealed the house to prevent viewing of the body; and a "coroner's jury was appointed to sign the death certificate so Garrett could file for the reward." "Brushy" adds that there were two coroner's jury reports, with the first lost and Garrett making people sign a second with different signers; that Milnor Rudulph was not the real president, and never viewed the body. And he says Garrett succeeded by burying Barlow in the Billy the Kid grave, and by taking the fake coroner's jury report to Santa Fe to get his reward. (Pages 134-135)

# EXPOSING JAMESON AS AN ACTIVE HOAXER AND COMPLICIT WITH THE "BILLY THE KID CASE" HOAX BY HIS FAKED TRANSCRIPT: This obviously fabricated flashback quote, is not in *Alias Billy the Kid;* and substitutes omniscient Lobato for omniscient pseudo-Celsa in *Billy the Kid: Beyond the Grave*. (See page 528 above) It is an awkward fix-up to match the "Brushy" hoax to the "Billy the Kid Case" hoax's faking DNA from the carpenter's bench by putting Barlow's body on it, hiding the body with a sheet to counter the townspeople's viewing, and announcing a fake coroner's jury merely to shield Garrett. For the "Brushy" hoax, it puts into pseudo-"Brushy's" mouth Sonnichsen's fake conspiracy theory of two coroner's jury reports.

This is now brazenly out-of-control hoaxing and forging. But it ridiculously requires sheepherder, Frank Lobato, to know insiders' information about a cover-up of the innocent victim. And, if real Lobato had found it out, it would prove general gossip among townspeople, and no postulated conspiracy of them to keep the secret!

At this point, Jameson's "transcript" goes on to "Brushy's" faked life after the death scene, and is irrelevant to Billy Bonney.

## DISCUSSION

In *Billy the Kid: The Lost Interviews*, W.C. Jameson created a fictionalized, grammatically-sophisticated, politically correct, pseudo-"Brushy," glossed with newly accurate historical spellings; all intended to fake a better match with real Billy, as well to enhance the original things-not-printed trick. An added contrivance was having pseudo-"Brushy" mouth the hoax's conspiracy theories. This is active hoaxing. And this is a forgery of "Brushy's" actual transcript. And, since hoaxer, Steve Sederwall's, input was implied by Jameson, it is not clear if any of this hoaxing is attributable to him.

Jameson's give-away for intentional and premeditated trickery was his altering his own rendition of "Brushy's" quoting the death scene in his 1998 *The Return of the Outlaw Billy the Kid*. There "Brushy" confabulated the night of July 14, 1881 as dark and moonless - eliminating any chance of his having been there. (And even Morrison-Sonnichsen had fixed that up for *Alias Billy the Kid* as "bright moonlight.") But Jameson undoes his earlier honesty to add "bright moonlight" for this *Billy the Kid: The Lost Interviews*. And, as if that chicanery broke the dam for honesty, out poured his fictionalized "Brushy" quotes supporting his and C.L. Sonnichsen's conspiracy theories, as well as the "Billy the Kid Case" hoax! Jameson had apparently crossed-over to no-holds-barred flimflam to attain his goal of "Brushy" as Billy. He was well on his way to creating his megahoax: his 2018 book, *Cold Case Billy the Kid*. But first, allied with "Billy the Kid Case" hoaxers, he attacked Pat Garrett. And this book ends: "Steve Sederwall's ongoing research and investigative work applied to Billy the Kid and the Lincoln County war continues to yield new and exciting results." ("Acknowledgments") Sederwall would now be in the driver's seat for this dupe.

# CHAPTER 3
# DEFAMING IN *PAT GARRETT: THE MAN BEHIND THE BADGE*

## THE "BRUSHY" HOAX'S HEART OF DARKNESS

W.C. Jameson's 2016 *Pat Garrett: The Man Behind the Badge*, represented a new direction in his pursuit of "Brushy" as Billy. It is a foray into faking that "history is not as written": the mantra of the "Brushy" and "Billy the Kid Case" hoaxes. And, though not a co-author, Steve Sederwall was his acknowledged source; as he wrote: "Intrepid investigator Steve Sederwall turned over more stones and found more pertinent information and evidence regarding Pat Garrett, Colonel Albert Jennings Fountain, Oliver Lee, Billy the Kid, and others than all the so-called experts put together." (Page 223) So the "Billy the Kid Case" hoax's forensic fakery is now incorporated into this book - with sly alterations to "Brushy's" original creation to match-up the mismatched hoaxes. And the florid misinformation by Jameson as author, may have been parroted from Sederwall instead.

The motive is defamation of Pat Garrett, with crazy illogic that, *if* he had character flaws, then he covered up killing an innocent victim; and that proved "Brushy" was surviving Billy the Kid! It obviously made no sense. But neither did the entire "Brushy Bill" hoax, stuck in early-20th century historical ignorance parroted by a mentally ill septuagenarian, and promoted by ambitious hucksters. And neither did the "Billy the Kid Case," seeking DNA from non-existent graves of Billy and his mother, and faking forensics with sham "crime scenes." And adding to ridiculousness, is that a quoted authority, contradicting Garrett's version of events, will now be "Brushy" himself - as "William Henry Roberts (aka Billy the Kid)!"

Amusingly, right from the start, wised-up Jameson was taking no more chances with "Brushy's" fatal error of the "dark night," which the more honest version of himself had reproduced in his 1998 *The Return of the Outlaw Billy the Kid*. He now officiously announced July 14, 1881's moon was full three nights earlier, in waning phase, with 87 percent brightness! (Page x)

As sneaky, Jameson now also relied on his own forged transcripts of William V. Morrison's 1949 taped "Brushy" interviews, as debunked above in his 2012 *Billy the Kid: The Lost Interviews*, in which his pseudo-"Brushy" mouthed the fake conspiracy theories used by the Morrison-Sonnichsen team, himself, and the "Billy the Kid Case" hoaxers. The original "Brushy" hoax was bloating into the monstrosity that would emerge in two more years, in his 2018 megahoax collusion with "Billy the Kid Case" hoaxers for his book: *Cold Case Billy the Kid*.

## *INTRODUCTORY MISINFORMATION*

Defaming of Pat Garrett begins with the basic "Brushy" hoax that his killing of Billy the Kid on July 14, 1881 was "the biggest lie of his life" (Page ix); the victim was a dark-skinned Mexican substituted for the Kid (Page ix); and historians perpetuate Garrett's lie. (Page ix) To this would now be added personality flaws, including being so careless he got himself murdered! (Page xi) Garrett's scholarly biographer, Leon Metz, is accused of doing no real investigation (Page 2); and Jameson recycles his conspiracy of historians to keep "status quo." (Page 5)

For naïve readers, fractured Lincoln County War history is presented by a "William Henry Roberts (aka Billy the Kid)!" (Page 25) "Brushy" provided: a Lincoln County War caused by the Fritz insurance policy; Murphy using Alexander McSween for policy collection (Page 19); a fake Tunstall's murder scene (Page 20); the Brady shooting having the retrieved pearl-handled .44 revolver along with "Waite" [corrected spelling of erroneous name] (Page 21); the Battle abruptly on July 14, 1878, with Sheriff Peppin searching for Regulators, and McSween riding in shooting (Page 22); the entry of Colonel Dudley with *black* cavalrymen [and Gatling gun now added], who route McSweens *and* set fire to the McSween house, forcing inmates' escape; and the "Brushy" as Billy, murder of Bob Beckwith. (Page 23) Jameson added weirdly that last out of the burning house came Susan McSween! (Page 23) "Brushy" continued with the Chapman killing with Susan McSween there too (Page 24); with having a pardon "letter drafted" for Wallace for testifying on the Chapman case; testifying against Dudley; and standing trial on his indictments, with District Attorney Rynerson's change of trial venue proving Wallace's betrayal. (Page 25) Jameson added the error that, in the pardon deal, Billy was kept in the "Lincoln County jail" (Page 25) instead of Juan Patrón's house (unknown to the "Brushy" team).

## FAKING PAT GARRETT HISTORY

For the "Brushy" and "Billy the Kid Case" hoaxes, Pat Garrett is the heinous lawman who got away with murder. Since this is a lie, considerable effort was expended fake his history to set-up the claim. Also fictionalized is Billy Bonney and John Poe history.

Garrett's known negatives are presented as if newly discovered: possibly killing a black man in Texas (Page 9); killing fellow hunter, Joe Briscoe, in claimed self-defense on the buffalo range (Page 13); testifying against his past buffalo hunter partner for inflated losses from a Native American raid (Page 15); being unfaithful to his second wife, Apolinaria [misspelled as Apolina] (Page 17); earning a low income (Page 50); drinking (Page 110); being an unsuccessful rancher (Page 111); being an unsuccessful irrigation company investor (Page 112-115); lacking "social graces" (Page 160); "difficult ... to do business with;" "impolite" (Page 164); and "proud and stubborn." (Page 163) To create a "Billy the Kid Case"-style friendship, Jameson claims that Billy and his gang paid for Garrett's wedding reception to Juanita Gutierrez. (Page 17)

**WRONG: This brief marriage, ended by Juanita's death within months, occurred in early 1878, when there existed no "Billy the Kid" and no gang. It was just two months after John Tunstall was murdered, and Billy was an 18 year old ranch hand, just made the youngest of the Regulators.**

Added maligning was that Garrett lied about Billy's great escape and was his possible accomplice (Page 61); murdered and covered-up an innocent victim instead of Billy the Kid (Page 71); gouged out his daughter Elizabeth's eyes in a drunken rage (Page 117); or infected her in utero with syphilis from his cavorting with prostitutes, leaving her blind. (Page 118)

Garrett's famous history, after his winning the 1880 Lincoln County sheriff's election, is either conventionally known, erroneous, fabricated, or given by "Brushy." Mixed in is erroneous Billy Bonney history. And Jameson hid that real "Brushy" was ignorant of the Secret Service intervention, which enlisted Garrett. To this bizarre potpourri, Jameson added faked forensic investigations by the "Billy the Kid Case" hoaxers, and new incorrect historical claims, possibly by Steve Sederwall.

Here are the mistakes:

1) Garrett's plan with Wild to track down an alleged gang of counterfeiters, is called a multi-pronged attack on White Oaks. (Page 30)

**WRONG: Attack was for Fort Sumner (where Billy was).**

2) A White Oaks capture is claimed to have been foiled by "outlaws" holding up a stage an finding Wild's reports about it, and making Wild fear for his life (Page 30);

**WRONG: Billy had held up one mail-coach, got Wild's report about arresting him, and ended their pardon negotiation. It had no other effect on Wild. And the incident canceled out "Brushy" by his ignorance of it!.**

3) The stage robbery is faked as the reason for Wild's enlisting Garrett's friend, Barney Mason, as a spy. This is called "strange," because Mason is alleged to be a "small-time outlaw." (Page 30)

**WRONG: Mason was Peter Maxwell's Fort Sumner foreman, and Wild and Garrett were seeking information about Billy's being in Fort Sumner with his supposed gang.**

4) Presented is Mason's offer by counterfeiter Dan Dedrick to do a cattle deal with counterfeit money. But the deal presented is a untrue: that Mason had a meeting with Dan Dedrick and "a man "named Duncan, who, according to Mason, had just arrived from New York and was carrying a suitcase filled with counterfeit money. According to Mason, the two men asked him to take the counterfeit currency to El Paso, purchase a herd of cattle, and deliver the livestock to Dedrick at Bosque Grande." (Pages 30-31)

**WRONG: In fact, for November 18th and 20th, 1880, Wild reported hiring Mason as a spy, then the Dedrick cattle**

deal. There was no "Duncan" from New York. Wild wrote: "*It appears from the statements of Garrett and Mason that he (Mason) is an experienced stockman and is now and has been for some time past in the employ of a man named Maxwell who resides at Fort Sumner. He (Mason) states that a few days ago one Daniel Dedrick who resides at Bosque Grande, and who has an interest with his brother Samuel Dedrick & West in a livery stable at White Oaks came to him and proposed [to hire him to take $30,000 counterfeit money to Texas, buy cattle there, take them to a place near Mexico to Dedrick and West, then leave the country].*

As will be seen, by Jameson's 2018 book, *Cold Case Billy the Kid*, this Mason deal was twisted into an elaborate fabrication by Steve Sederwall to prove Billy the Kid was a counterfeiter along with Jesse James! This appears to be a passing reference to this fakery. (See pages 621, 623, 639-642 below)

5) After Dedrick backed out of the cattle deal with Mason, Wild is described as going with a Garrett posse to Bosque Grande, Dedrick's ranch, "intent on capturing the counterfeiters," and hoping to capture Billy the Kid there. (Page 31)

**FAKERY: This is made-up.**

6) Garrett is described as having the assignment of capturing or killing Billy the Kid and Billy Wilson to stop rustling, apprehending horse thief, George Davis, and finding stolen mules at Thomas Yerby's ranch. (Page 31)

**WRONG: The George Davis from this period was a Jessie Evans gang member, and he was killed by in Texas by Texas Rangers in Fort Davis in August of 1880, before the Wild investigation.**

7) Wild is reported as dissatisfied with Garrett and sending Sheriff Kimball [sic - Kimbrell] and Deputy Marshal John Hurley. (Page 32)

**FAKERY: Wild did not use Kimbrell; writing in his daily report of October 16, 1880 that Kimbrell was seen playing cards with Billy, thus, being on his side.**

8) For the Greathouse Ranch posse encounter "William Henry Roberts (aka Billy the Kid)" appears for a quote about the killing of Jim Carlyle (Page 37)

**FAKERY: This is lifted from real Billy's December 12, 1880 letter to Lew Wallace, which is then paraphrased!**

9) Garrett's Texas posses, which had included Charlie Siringo and Frank Stewart, were then described as separate groups seeking Lew Wallace's Billy the Kid reward. (Page 38) And Garrett is described as sending Barney Mason to "head off Stewart, as if interfering." (Page 38)

**WRONG: The posses were under Garrett. And Barney Mason did not interfere with Stewart.**

10) The killing of Tom O'Folliard is quoted from "William Henry Roberts," as contradicting Garrett's version! (Page 40)

**FAKERY: Down the rabbit hole with "Brushy" as leader!**

11) For Stinking Springs, Jameson is no more aware than "Brushy" of the huge arroyo in the front of the rock house. And Jameson was facing the problem that the scene contradicted the "Billy the Kid Case" hoax's Garrett-Billy friendship; while "Brushy's" hoax lacked it. But both wanted to defame Garrett. And there was the reality that at Stinking Springs Garrett obviously tried to kill Billy when he accidentally shot Charlie Bowdre. So Jameson tried to include everything: "Though once friends, Garrett in his quest for success in the office of sheriff and with his eye on greater status, regarded the Kid as expendable." (Page 42)

**FAKERY: Two hoaxes in one is still a hoax.**

12) Garrett is called a liar for claiming he shot the tethering ropes of two outside horses at Stinking Springs, because it was hard to do. And proof that he did not is that William Henry Roberts did not mention it! (Pages 43-44)

**FAKERY: This is silly. Also, Garrett was a buffalo hunter, where Big Sharps rifles could hit at a half-mile; and might have actually accomplished this. And, if he exaggerated, it does not prove he murdered the innocent victim!**

13) After the capture, the famous December 28, 1880 *Las Vegas Gazette* article describing Billy as fair, with blue eyes, and protruding front teeth was quoted as proof that the Fort Sumner corpse looked different; so Garrett was a liar! (Page 46)

**FAKERY:** This is yet another re-run of S.M. Ashenfelter's article's fake, swarthy, bearded corpse.

14) A major gaffe is made for Billy's Santa Fe jailing in solitary confinement. Since his jail letters from it are known, and "Brushy's" fake illiteracy had to be maintained, Jameson wrote "the Kid had a letter drafted to ... Lew Wallace." (Page 48)

**WRONG:** In fact, there were four letters, and their handwriting was identical to that in the Hoyt Bill of Sale, his signature in his Frank Warner Angel deposition, and all his past letters to Lew Wallace and "Squire Wilson: another knock-out of "Brushy" and his lying team.

15) For the Mesilla trial, the courthouse is called someone's home. (Page 49)

**WRONG: It was a courthouse.**

16) A fatal error exposing Jameson's massive ignorance is his statement that the "Buckshot" Roberts case was dropped because the case "was weak and the prosecution feared the risk of acquittal." (Page 49)

**WRONG:** Even "Brushy" did better by using Billy's letter to Edgar Caypless of April 15, 1881, about the federal case being dropped. That was the end of his prompt; but, in reality, Attorney Ira Leonard had argued for Billy that the Blazer's Mill site was private property, thus Territorial jurisdiction, not federal. The case was quashed on the legal error of improper jurisdiction.

17) For the Brady trial, Jameson relied on "Brushy's" confabulations as his source. So he thought that Wallace reneged on providing Ira Leonard as an attorney, causing the Court to appoint Albert Jennings Fountain. (Page 49)

**WRONG:** Billy's loyal lawyer, Ira Leonard, representing him at his own honorable initiative, withdrew after getting the Roberts case quashed, likely after Ring death threat.

18) For the jailing in the Lincoln County courthouse, Garrett's fame is said to be based only on Billy. (Page 50)

**WRONG:** The tale of these two larger-than-life men, with intertwined fates, made them both famous.

19) Garrett is claimed to be so poor that he depended on collecting the Billy the Kid award; but it was denied; indicating he was a liar. (Page 50)

**FAKERY: This fabrication jumps the gun to the post-killing, with C.L. Sonnichsen's fake conspiracy theory and lies that Garrett was denied the reward because the body was not identified as Billy's since there was no legitimate Coroner's Jury Report. In fact, the Coroner's Jury Report was used as proof of justifiable homicide, the delay was in converting Wallace's personal reward offer to a Territorial one, and Garrett was paid. (See pages 147, 210-215 above)**

20) Then Garrett was declared enriched for killing Billy, and becoming a big spender lush; indicating he was no good! (Page 51)

**WRONG: Too silly for words. No words.**

21) For the Lincoln jailing, hoaxing Jameson fixes-up "Brushy's" faked armory across from Garrett's office, now putting it correctly on the opposite side of the stairway. (Page 52)

**FAKERY: Dishonest fix-up to hide that "Brushy" had no special knowledge, and faked the great escape.**

22) For the great escape, Garrett's version, as told to him by Gottfried Gauss, has the gun in the outhouse, and shot Bell dying after running down the stairway. This is claimed as a Garrett lie, because it is inconceivable that Deputy Bell would let Billy to get ahead of him on the stairs. (Page 54)

**FAKERY: At last, Jameson was in "Billy the Kid Case" hoax's territory; and possibly parroting Steve Sederwall.**

23) For the Deputy Olinger killing, Jameson puts Billy on the balcony, not at the east window; and has him break the shotgun on the "balcony railing." For the escape, he has Gauss give Billy a "file" to cut through his leg chains. (Page 55)

**FAKERY: This was faked as conventional history, so "Brushy" could later appear and give the "correct" version!**

24) For the escape horse, Jameson secretly relied on Steve Sederwall, as revealed by a misspelling that was not repeated until Jameson reused the tale for his 2018 *Cold Case Billy the Kid*. Claimed is that the escape horse got away and another prisoner, misspelled as "**Andrew Nimley**," retrieved it.

**WRONG:** The Tularosa Ditch War prisoner - spelled Andrew Nunnelly - did not participate as Sederwall claimed. (*Cold Case Billy the Kid*, Page 116) Since Jameson had not revealed Sederwall's input – exposed here only by his misspelling – making one wonder how much of the text was Sederwall's, rather than his.]

25) Jameson next provided "William Henry Roberts aka Billy the Kid's" version, for the first time revealing to the reader "Brushy's" strange tale, by claiming it came from his 1948 William V. Morrison interview when he was "eighty-eight years old" and had special familiarity with the building - though he repeated "Brushy's" lie that the building was extensively remodeled, while claiming "Brushy's" special knowledge left no doubt he was there. Repeated is "Brushy's" Sam Corbett-gun-in-outhouse-slipping-handcuffs fable. And given is a Bell-shot-on-the-stairs-dying-at-the-back-door scene; the Olinger shot through the window scene, the Gauss cutting the leg chain with an ax scene, the Severo Gallegos scene (but he now "ties" the horse - instead of "Brushy's" nonsensical actual tale); and Sonnichsen's Cipio Salazar fake shackle removing addition. (Pages 55-57)

**FAKERY:** Jameson's "Brushy" version mismatched Sederwall's "Nimley" version; and it got worse as he introduced the "Billy the Kid Case" forensic hoax itself.

26) The "Billy the Kid Case" hoax now enters full-blown in a chapter called "Crime Scene Investigation, Lincoln County Courthouse," with duped Jameson narrating for Steve Sederwall. Lincoln County Sheriff Department Case 2003-274 is concealed as a "police investigation." And Sederwall is shape-shifted to a nebulous "private detective" and "former policeman and criminal investigator for the United States Government" and a truth seeker suspicious about the historical version of the Deputy Bell killing; while making up that Sophie Poe said there was blood on top of the stairway, instead of the bottom. (Page 59) So, as an intrepid investigator, Sederwall takes Dr. Henry Lee, TV producer Bill Kurtis, U.S. Marshal David Turk, investigator Cal Ostler, and Gary Graves, oddly called Lincoln County Sheriff, (really De Baca County Sheriff; with co-hoaxer and real Sheriff, Tom Sullivan, omitted) to evaluate the courthouse. Lee does his presumptive tests for blood (omitting that they were also for rust). Of course, blood is claimed at the top of the stairs. (Page 59)

Cagy Sederwall rewards Jameson by adding "Brushy's" "Sam Corbett" as the hider of the outhouse gun. (Page 59) And "Brushy's" slipping handcuffs trick is used for the blow to get Bell bleeding in the right spot. (Page 60)

**FAKERY: This floorboard hoax has already been debunked on pages 328, 416-418, 420 above. Do not miss that the list of those present, and hiding of the report's being for Case 2003-274, come from Sederwall's forged Lee reports, whose made-up title matches this chapter's title. (See pages 509, 510 above) That forged report is not listed in this book's bibliography, but is brazenly present for the repeat of this fakery in Jameson's 2018** *Cold Case Billy the Kid.*

27) Garrett is now defamed using these fake claims, by Sederwall concluding that he was a liar or an incompetent lawman to hide the blood at the top of the stairs. (Page 61)

**FAKERY: Concealed is the "Billy the Kid Case" hoax's use of this Bell fakery as the preposterous Case 2003-274 sub-investigation as to Garrett's probable cause murder motive, to "prove" he was Billy's friend, because he lied about the Bell scene to conceal that he was Billy's escape accomplice; and, being such a good friend, he subsequently murdered the innocent Fort Sumner victim to save Billy.**

28) Garrett is further defamed by Sederwall's new "investigation," claiming that, as administer of Bob Olinger's estate, Garrett stole Olinger's possessions - in particular the Whitney double barrel shotgun the Kid had broken and thrown on Olinger's body. Though Sederwall admits that Garrett had considered the gun worthless when he apparently confiscated the parts. (Pages 61-62)

**FAKERY: This fakery is repeated in Jameson's 2018 in** *Cold Case Billy the Kid* **for the culminating megahoax. It is debunked there. (See pages 678 below)**

29) The key Fort Sumner shooting event gets much attention, it being both hoaxes' make-or-break. A fix-up is adding Paulita Maxwell as Billy's girlfriend to explain why Billy was there (though that was unknown to "Brushy," with his confabulated Celsa girlfriend). (Page 66) Information from Pat Garrett's *The Authentic Life of Billy the Kid* and John W. Poe's *The Death of Billy the Kid* is manipulated to fabricate discrepancies, from the

stake-out of the Maxwell house, to the shooting scene in Peter Maxwell's bedroom. Faked by Sederwall, is that **the bedroom had no door to the outside**, to claim that, since that door was in the accounts of Garrett, Poe, and Maxwell, they were all liars.

**FAKERY: The no outside door fakery came with an undated, unreferenced, untitled sketch in the glossy print section, claiming to be the Maxwell house. It was reused when this fake claim was repeated in** *Cold Case Billy the Kid***. It is debunked there. (See pages 689-691 below) But the diagram was of the 1860's Fort Sumner Commanding Officer's quarters. And ignored was that Lucien Maxwell rebuilt the building as his home in 1870, adding the door.**

30) Of course, the identification of the body is claimed as in doubt. (Pages 69-70) Fabricated are "discrepancies," "contradictions," no "inquest," Poe doubting the identity of the body, and a questionable "burial" to cast doubt on the historical version. (Pages 71-97) "William Henry Roberts aka Billy the Kid" as the expert, provides his alternative version with shot-back-porch-Billy-Barlow, though expanded from his original fable with Jameson's forged transcripts of his words from *Billy the Kid: The Lost Interviews*! (Page 72)

Garrett is defamed by fabricating "subsequent inquests" as serving to "generate doubt as to whom [he] actually shot and killed that night." (Page 71) And for doubting the bedroom scene, used are fake hearsay accounts of Charles Frederick Rudulph, from his reprinted manuscript in 1980's *Los Billitos: The Story of Billy the Kid and His Gang*; and of a Bundy Avant (misspelled as "Bud Avants," from his unreferenced old-timer malarkey in a 1978 *True West* article: "The Bundy Avant Story"); and C.L. Sonnichsen's hearsay interview with Jack Fountain. (Pages 80, 83) The conclusion is "[T]here is little corroborative, logical evidence on which to base the claim that Billy the Kid was shot and killed by Sheriff Pat Garrett on the night of July 14, 1881." (Page 84) And this means to Jameson that "Brushy" survived as Billy, with proof being William V. Morrison's original fake Affidavits. (Page 85) Concluded is that "no shred of evidence" proves Billy the Kid was killed on July 14, 1881, and "Pat Garrett lied about the entire incident." (Page 86) Jameson adds: "[C]ompelling evidence suggests the body was that of Billy Barlow." (Page 96)

**FAKERY:** This new fakery, apparently by Sederwall, to defame Garrett as a murderer, and to elevate "Brushy" as a surviving Billy, was repeated in two years in Jameson's culminating "Brushy" plus "Billy the Kid Case" megahoax: *Cold Case Billy the Kid*. It is for that book that I debunked these claims in detail.

31) The "Billy the Kid Case's" hoaxed forensics with Dr. Henry Lee's fake washstand investigation is first slipped in for the Maxwell bedroom death scene to ruminate about where Garrett's second shot ended up, while hiding that it hit the wall and bed's headboard. So Lee's fabricated washstand scenario is presented as if fact; saying that Garrett must be lying about his position in the shooting, since his bullet perforated a washstand "fifteen feet" away "at an angle that indicted he was on his knees in the far corner of the room when he fired." As to the search by Garrett, Poe and McKinney for the second bullet strike, it was claimed Garrett would have hidden the washstand holes, because they proved a different positioning than his lie. (Page 76)

**FAKERY:** This brazen hoaxing is intended to dupe readers into thinking it is accepted history. They are not informed that the "washstand" was an unsubstantiated little box with two holes from a teenaged girl's 1920's amateur tourist museum in a Fort Sumner shed, and alleging to have Peter Maxwell's bedroom furniture. Nor are readers told that the Maxwell house no longer exists, and the placement of that made-up "washstand" was also made-up by complicit hoaxer, Dr. Henry Lee. The intent here is defaming Garrett as a liar by fabricating a different shooting scenario. But it is still irrelevant to the body being Billy Bonney's, or to "Brushy" being Billy.

This washstand hoaxing is continued in the book's glossy print section, with an unattributed diagram of the alleged Maxwell bedroom, with a washstand positioned to go along with the hoax (as well as no outside door, to go with that other hoaxed claim).

32) The washstand hoax is continued in "Appendix II" as "Crime Scene Investigation: The Washstand." (Pages 206-207) Hidden is that it was part of Lincoln County Sheriff's Department Case No. 2003-274, "Billy the Kid Case." Instead, as mere "investigators," are listed, Steve Sederwall (first, with "Deputy"

hidden), Tom Sullivan (with "Sheriff" hidden), Kim [sic – Calvin] Ostler, Dr. Henry Lee, David Turk (as from the U.S. Marshals Service, but with "Historian" hidden to fake him as a Marshal), and Mike Haag (as a firearms examiner). They are to examine the washstand, claimed as from Peter Maxwell's bedroom on July 14, 1881. Its measurements and two holes are presented, with Lee's laser as showing a "bullet path." The conclusion is that Garrett "shot the holes in the washstand ... from a position that likely involved being on both knees with one hand on the floor for support while the opposite hand fired the revolver."

FAKERY: The exposé of this Lee's washstand hoax for Case 2003-274 is on pages 410-413 and 415 above. And Sederwall's forgery of Lee's report about it is on page 511 above. Jameson subsequently and unknowingly cited one of the forged reports for his *Cold Case Billy the Kid* book as by Henry Lee and titled "Forensic Examination Report (Examination of Furniture From Pete Maxwell's of July 15, 1881) 22 May 2004." (*Cold Case Billy the Kid.* Page 187)]

And, in 2016, this fakery had been proliferated in the September, 2016 *Wild West History Association* magazine by James and Margaret Bailey for "Billy the Kid Death Scene: Reviewing Ballistic Evidence," misled that the washstand was a legitimate historical object by "Billy the Kid Case" hoaxer, Paul Hutton. So they had it shot by Garrett; though they had him kill Billy as victim. (See pages 415-416 above)

33) The Coroner's Jury Report identifying William Bonney is concealed; and the claim of no certain report is made. (Pages 87-92) "Paco" Anaya's malarkey of two reports is used, plus Sonnichsen's fake conspiracy theories about Garrett's problem collecting his reward being based on no corpse identification. And the burial is claimed to have hidden the body, with "only a handful" of witnesses; along with the fake swarthy bearded body from fabricating newspaperman S.M. Ashenfelter. (Page 93)

FAKERY: This fakery attacking the reality of the existing Coroner's Jury Report for William Bonney is debunked under *Alias Billy the Kid*, where C.L. Sonnichsen invented the fraudulent conspiracy theories (See pages 205-215 above); and under *Cold Case Billy the Kid*, where it was repeated from this *Pat Garrett: The Man Behind the Badge* book. (See pages 699-700 below).

34) Case 2003-274 Billy the Kid exhumation attempt is shape-shifted by duped Jameson as: "An attempt by investigator and researcher Steve Sederwall to examine the space beneath the stone [Fort Sumner cemetery marker] in order to learn the truth was rejected by the Fort Sumner city council. Clearly they did not want to take the chance of the result indicating there was nothing there. In this case, tourism dollars were more important than truth." (Page 97)

**FAKERY: Jameson's confusion about the "Billy the Kid Case" is evident. Before his conspiracy theory of tourism interests blocking truth, he confirmed that the gravesite was unknown, and flooding destroyed any remains. (*The Return of the Outlaw*, Pages 132-133) That was before the "Billy the Kid Case" hoax depended on faking that valid DNA *was* available from that tourist-marked grave.**

35) To continue defaming Pat Garrett, his ghostwritten book, *The Authentic Life of Billy the Kid*, is unsurprisingly claimed as not an authoritative. (Pages 98-100) This leads to the usual fake reasoning: *if* Garrett had fiction in it, he also made-up the killing; so "Brushy" was Billy the Kid, and the body was Billy Barlow's!

**FAKERY: The book, written in 1882, was in dime novel style. The history of Billy Bonney was not yet explored by scholars. But the thing Garrett did know, and did relate, was his fatal shooting of Billy Bonney. And, as to being finicky about dime novel-style, Jameson was in no position to criticize. His corpse identification by Silver City newsman, Singleton M. Ashenfelter, was nothing more than fake dime novel fodder. And his "evidence," using old-timer malarkey and confabulations - "Brushy's being a good example – were as meaningless!**

36) Garrett's life after killing Billy Bonney continues with irrelevant micro-detail filler, apparently contributed by Steve Sederwall, to fake historical chops (like biographies of Albert Jennings. Fountain and Oliver Lee; and even the claimed history of the invention of the teddy bear!)

**FAKERY: The information overdose is an irrelevant attempt to bamboozle readers as to historical expertise. And that faked expertise is to make them accept the fake claims being made about Garrett.**

But even the Teddy bear's history is fake! Claimed is that, sometime after 1905, a one-eyed El Paso saloon owner and gambler named Tom Powers shipped President Teddy Roosevelt, "a wildlife lover," a bear cub from Mexico, which newspaper's called "Teddy's bear." So a "doll maker" made them as toys. (Page 167) In fact, Teddy Roosevelt was a big game hunter, and on a 1902 bear hunting trip in Mississippi, on invitation of its Governor, Andrew H. Longino, to ensure he bagged a bear, a small one was tied to a tree. Roosevelt spared it as an unsportsmanly killing. His act was made famous in a 1902 *Washington Post* cartoon by a Clifford Berryman. In 1903, a Brooklyn candy shop owner, Morris Michtom, whose wife Rose made stuffed animals, created a bear dedicated to Roosevelt as "Teddy's Bear." Its wild popularity enabled their founding of the Ideal Toy Company. And German toymaker Steiff soon had copies made. So one can say the Garrett history to follow, is nothing more than W.C. Jameson's and Steve Sederwall's teddy bear tales!

37) Garrett's post-killing Billy history is skewed to defamation. Meaningless catty swipes call him: "illiterate" (Page 102); "egoistic" (Page 102); "whoring" (Page 129); a bad rancher (Page 110); unable to solve the A.J. Fountain murder case privately or as Doña Ana County Sheriff (Pages 119 - 159); failing his ambush of Oliver Lee and Jim Gilliland and getting his deputy killed instead (Page 144); "inept" in sheriff's department paperwork (Page 160); being appointed an El Paso customs collector by President Theodore Roosevelt after promising not to drink (Page 162); getting into a fist-fight with a cattle inspector, with both charged with disturbing the peace (Page 164); losing his customs inspector job for hobnobbing with a gambler (Page 167); being a debtor (Pages 168-174); returning to his ranch in the San Andres Mountains because of "no where else to go" (Page 168); failing in mining speculation (Page 169); being in debt to T.B. Catron, and others (Pages 171-172); having trouble paying taxes on his ranch (Page 173-174); being unsuccessful as a real estate agent in El Paso, while being with a prostitute (Page 176); and conflicting with a Wayne Brazel who was renting his New Mexico ranch for his goat-raising because he "hated goats," and wanted to rent the land to a James Miller and a Carl Anderson, but could not settle a pay-out for Brazel to vacate (Pages 177-179).

**FAKERY: This blather about Garrett is irrelevant to his killing Billy Bonney on July 14, 1881.**

38) For Garrett's murder, a conspiracy theory is presented with Carl Anderson driving a buggy with Garrett, and Wayne Brazel meeting them along the way to Las Cruces, and arguing about the number of goats to be purchased. Anderson was reported as stopping the buggy to urinate; then Garrett doing the same and being fatally shot in the head and abdomen. Jameson added insult to fatal injury by labeling his death that of a "deadbeat drunk." (Page 182) Because Brazel was exonerated in his trial, meaningless rumination followed about other possible murderers and a cover-up involving smuggling Chinese laborers out of Mexico, and killing Garrett so he could not tell authorities. Jameson accused Oliver Lee and his nephew, Todd Bailey (who, astoundingly, was really born in Buffalo Gap, Texas - unlike "Brushy," though that irony is lost an grimly plodding Jameson with his back-up of Sederwall, blowing smoke). (Pages 183-199)

**FAKERY: None of this blather about who killed Garrett has anything to do with his killing Billy on July 14, 1881; and certainly has nothing to do with "Brushy" being Billy. Proved is only that Jameson was so wowed by Sederwall's smoke and mirrors, that he let him take over his book.**

39) For the "Conclusion" chapter, it is claimed that Garrett was famous for an act he "did not perform": killing Billy the Kid. Evidence was that he lied; had "character flaws;" was "unacceptable to polite society;" was a debtor; was "more of a criminal than was Billy the Kid," and less smart; did the Fountain murder case just for the money; and oddly, because he was "murdered by his enemies." Resistance to these "truths," was attributed to a "reigning clique" of historians. (Pages 200-201)

**FAKERY: Too silly for words. No words.**

40) In "Appendix I," a brief and manipulative history of "Brushy" is given (Pages 203-205, 215-216), with "paralegal" Morrison finding him as an 88 year old Billy the Kid, with alias Oliver L. Roberts. C.L. Sonnichsen is given as assisting the investigation as "a noted author, historian, and folklorist" (with Harvard added, and just an English teacher left out). The Mabry pardon hearing is omitted! Morrison and Sonnichsen write *Alias Billy the Kid*, with "remarkable evidence," but get hostile

response from historians, including death threats, to keep the "status quo." Subsequent research is said to prove that "Brushy's" genealogy had the names Antrim, McCarty, and Bonney; that his photo matched the Billy the Kid tintype; that his transcribed tapes (ala *Billy the Kid: The Lost Interviews*) proved the things-not-printed trick, since he was illiterate. Ergo, "Brushy" was Billy the Kid. And his fantastical life after the Fort Sumner shooting scene was exactly as he told it.

**FAKERY: True-believer Jameson's "Brushy" as Billy the Kid gospel is well-worn, but this fake and defamatory book against Pat Garrett did nothing to back or advance its claims. And when left to his own devices to advertise "Brushy," Jameson proved he had nothing more to add to that hoax that had long outlived its 1950's throwback expiration date.**

## STAGE SET FOR A MEGAHOAX

*Pat Garrett: The Man Behind the Badge,* represents another step downward for W.C. Jameson into active hoaxing. Having at least some awareness of the "Billy the Kid Case," and having been a participant, he willfully kept it secret from his readers; instead portraying one of its perpetrators, Steve Sederwall, as a random investigator of Billy the Kid history. So hidden was the agenda of hijacking Billy the Kid history for an imposter, as linked to defamation of Pat Garrett as a willful and never-punished murderer of an innocent victim.

It may be that gullible Jameson was yet again duped, but an author purporting to portray history owes to readers a degree of diligence in researching information and its sources. Ignorance and incompetence are not an adequate defense. Jameson is blameworthy for capitulating to more hoaxed information; without even caring to reconcile the divergent claims to his own contradictory "Brushy" beliefs. That leaves him in the league of the cynically opportunist "Billy the Kid Case" hoaxers themselves: merely strategizing trickery for personal aggrandizement or profit, with winning meaning duping.

The result in *Pat Garrett: The Man Behind the Badge* is a hodge-podge of disconnected and meaningless nastiness about that famous lawman, with Jameson permitting the takeover of his text to showcase Sederwall's bombastic and sham pronouncements as being valid investigations. But Jameson merely proved that, even with added hoaxing, "Brushy's" Billy the Kid impersonation could not be sustained.

Possibly it was Jameson's desperation that led to the next endeavor: giving Steve Sederwall, and some of his fellow "Billy the Kid Case" hoaxers, a new book in which to peddle their fakery under the new name of a "cold case" investigation. But the only cold case for "Billy the Kid Case" hoaxers was their never being prosecuted for the appalling, illegal, and meaningless John Miller and William Hudspeth exhumations and graverobbings.

But W.C. Jameson was about to speak for them all his 2018 *Cold Case Billy the Kid*, letting them flaunt their hoaxing in a hair-brained notion that their fake claims that "history was not as written" would translate into "Brushy" being Billy the Kid - since "history" definitely did not write that!

But all that Jameson was about to achieve was becoming the sole author of a megahoax; once again a dupe for the same kind of charlatans as lying huckster, William V. Morrison, and fake conspiracy-theorist-historian-wannabe, C.L. Sonnichsen.

# PART VI

## THE *COLD CASE* BILLY THE KID MEGAHOAX

# CHAPTER 1
## THE RETURN AS A MEHGAHOAX

### A KALEIDOSCOPE OF HOAXING

Sixty-eight years after "Brushy" and William V. Morrison failed to trick honorable Governor Thomas Jewett Mabry with their Billy the Kid imposter hoax, and 15 years after corrupt Governor Bill Richardson tried to trick the public with his "Billy the Kid Case" rerun of that imposter hoax, W.C. Jameson fused them, while adding more hoaxing, to create a megahoax.

Long past was Jameson's innocent rationalizing with Frederick Bean for 1998's *The Return of the Outlaw Billy the Kid;* replaced by his own fake fix-ups in his 2005 *Billy the Kid: Beyond the Grave*, his 2012 *Billy the Kid: The Lost Interviews*, and his 2016 *Pat Garrett: The Man Behind the Badge*; all of which hid that first book proving his hoaxing by their alterations. And he built on acquaintances with "Billy the Kid Case" hoaxers.

His "Acknowledgements" lists many of them: Gary Graves, Dr. Henry Lee, Lonnie Lippman, Rick Staub, Tom Sullivan, Dale Tunnell, and Dave Turk. (Page 181) Lippman's 2007 death, and Sullivan's in 2013, prove the long association. Featured is Steve Sederwall, as a major contributor to his book. (Page 181)

Jameson, as their narrator, show-cased Sederwall; writing: "His tenacity and thoroughness when taking on the study of historical topics is exceeded by no one I have ever encountered." Impressed by his cowboy costuming and 6'5" height, Jameson advertised him vaguely as a "cop," a U.S. government investigator, and a worker of crime scenes, with his own "investigative agency" for "western cold cases." (Page vi) Here, at last, was a partner for the Morrison-Sonnichsen history-is-not-as-written trick.

But even the title was a hoax. Like with *Alias Billy the Kid*, which was not Billy's alias; *Cold Case: Billy the Kid* had no cold case! There was just "Brushy's" fable that Pat Garrett killed Billy

Barlow; and the "Billy the Kid Case's" lie that Garrett killed an innocent victim to save Billy. The book is as unreal, with known events rewritten by fabricated evidence as "crime scene investigations;" accepted information given as discoveries; and "Brushy" being a quoted authority for events he never conceived!

## *"FOREWORD" AND "INTRODUCTION"*

Jameson dated his first meeting with badge-wearing Steve Sederwall to 2006, at one of Jameson's book-signing-readings about Billy the Kid not being killed by Pat Garrett. (Page v) Jameson stated he knew of Sederwall as an aggressive investigator of Billy the Kid events. (Pages v-vi)

For Sederwall, Jameson must have seemed like a dupe made in heaven. At the 2006 time of their meeting, Sederwall was in the midst of exposure for the 2005 illegal Arizona exhumations of John Miller and William Hudspeth as a Lincoln County Deputy Sheriff under Sheriff Rick Virden. So he shape-shifted for Jameson to a "private detective" "investigating western cold cases," with emphasis on Billy the Kid, since 1998. (Pages vi-vii) And the only whiff of me and my years of litigations exposing him and the hoax, was Jameson's acceptance of his martyr for the truth scam. As Jameson wrote: **"[H]e was once hauled into court by one of the rabid embracers of the status quo."** (Page x)

And, though the "Brushy" hoax did not match the "Billy the Kid Case" hoax, with its Garrett bromance and Billy-playing-dead-and-bleeding-on-bench, Jameson was in no position to quarrel with his new larger-than-life hero; who used fancy words like "crime scene" and "Deoxyribonucleic acid – DNA;" which he called Sederwall's "investigation kit." (Pages vii-viii)

So Jameson's lead-in quotes C.L. Sonnichsen's biographer Dale L. Walker's *Legends and Lies:* "All history is a mystery" (Page viii) Jameson adds that the "published" history of Billy the Kid is "fraudulent." The truth would now come from his mouthing of Sederwall; who, according to himself, had done the whole (unnamed) "Billy the Kid Case" himself, while thwarted by politicians - "up to and including the Governor of New Mexico" - panicked by *his* findings as risking tourism! (Page xviii)

# CHAPTER 2
# FAKING BILLY THE KID HISTORY KNOWLEDGE

## RETURN OF THE IGNORANCE OF *THE RETURN OF THE OUTLAW BILLY THE KID*

Presented Billy the Kid history is stuck in mid-20 century ignorance of "Brushy"-Morrison-Sonnichsen, with surreptitious fix-ups; and with Jameson's 1998 *The Return of the Outlaw Billy the Kid's* conspiracy theorist avoidance of history books and primary documents. Scholarly books are called "legend." (Page xiv) Hidden is that "Brushy's" imposter hoax was demolished by his family by 2015, three years earlier. Added are "crime scene investigations" by Steve Sederwall, to claim no past historian "possessed much insight"(Page 11); while narrator Jameson informs readers that Sederwall uses "tells" - a "cop term" to find "suspicious discrepancies" - in Pat Garrett's 1882 *The Authentic Life of Billy the Kid* and John W. Poe's *The Death of Billy the Kid*. (Page xvi) So Sederwall's history-is-not-as-written trickery becomes the backbone of *Cold Case Billy the Kid*.

### *FAKING EARLY YEARS*

Jameson claims that Billy the Kid's origins were unknown (Page 1), pretending that meant "Brushy's" years were Billy's.

**HOAXING:** By his 2018 publication date, Jameson knew "Brushy's" "early years" were debunked his Roberts family members: Geneva Pittmon, Roy L. Haws, Paul Emerson, and Cora Heath, removing him simply as 20 years too young. Also, Jameson hid Jerry Weddle's 1993 book, *Antrim is My Stepfather's Name*, with Billy's early adolescence and Arizona period, which exposed "Brushy's" fabrications.

## *FAKING TUNSTALL PERIOD*

For the Tunstall period (Pages 4-10) Lawrence Murphy's beef and mercantile monopoly and Santa Fe Ring involvement are attributed to competition with John Chisum. Arriving Tunstall is claimed to have partnered with another *Englishman,* Alexander McSween. [WRONG: McSween as British is a new error. He was born in Canada in 1843. And there was no "partnership." Tunstall was *falsely* named as his partner by Ringite Judge Warren Bristol, to enable malicious prosecution of him, along with McSween, with intent of forcing their flight or killing them.]

Tunstall's alliance with Chisum is cited. Using "Brushy's" fake history, Murphy is claimed as making a legal case against Tunstall [WRONG: the Emil Fritz heirs, not Murphy, made a legal case], allowing him to seize Tunstall's store goods and horses [WRONG: the property was attached as part of the Fritz case, unrelated to Murphy, and the horses were immune]. To avoid problems, Tunstall decided to deliver the horses himself to Lincoln. [WRONG: Tunstall was innocently taking the immune horses back to Lincoln.] On the way, Fred Waite, driving a wagon, separated from the group. [FIX UP: "Brushy" had Tunstall driving the wagon.] Tunstall is killed by a posse. [CONCEALED: The Frank Warner Angel report is cited in a fix-up; but hidden is that Billy Bonney gave the deposition on Tunstall's murder for it, likely because Billy's high literacy eliminated coarse-spoken "Brushy."] The murder is blamed on the "Murphy-Dolan faction." [WRONG: It was a Santa Fe Ring assassination, which is why it precipitated the Lincoln County War freedom fight.]

Jameson introduced Sederwall by claiming the murder *was not investigated*, so Sederwall can fabricate his "suspicions."

FAKED ASSERTION: The crime scene *was* investigated. Trackers, under John Newcomb, recovered Tunstall's corpse, described the two part crime scene, his body, and its wounds. One was a law enforcement official: Probate Judge Florencio Gonzales, who likely provided the findings to the Coroner's Jury, and subsequently gave them in his June 8, 1878 deposition to Frank Warner Angel.

The trackers identified the murder site by blood, and located Tunstall's hidden body 100 yards off the trail, with his killed horse beside him, and his hat on its head. They called it a *"burlesque"* desecration. They located his revolver beside his corpse, with two empty chambers. but lack of cartridge shells in them showed he had not fired. His skull was *"broken,"* there was a bullet entry at his breast, and a bullet entry at the back of his head, exiting the forehead. They also identified many fresh horse tracks, and concluded that the possemen passed the horse herd just to kill Tunstall; thus, pointing to intentional murder.

Sederwall's so-called "crime scene investigation" involved finding an old rifle casing with a metal detector. Of course, it was claimed as from the bullet that killed Tunstall! He also cited the Frank Warner Angel files, likely obtained from fellow hoaxer with easy access to the National Archives, U.S. Marshal's Service Historian David Turk (who had also helped him with the "Case 2003-274 Probable Cause Statement"); though Sederwall wrongly cited the deposition quotes as an Angel "report."

For his "investigation," Sederwall used an alleged Tunstall autopsy report, without given source, and allegedly by Fort Stanton Assistant Post Surgeon Daniel Appel. He excerpted quotes: "Wounded in the head, entered 3 in. behind and in the line with the superior border of the right ear, made its exit 1 ½ in. above the left orbit and ¼ in. left of the middle line of the forehead." (Page 14)

FLAWED EVIDENCE: Sederwall seemed unaware that Appel was an unreliable witness because of his Ring bias, shared by many at Fort Stanton. Even worse, Appel was motivated to destroy Tunstall and McSween, who had exposed the frauds at the Mescalero Indian Reservation being perpetrated by Appel's wife's father: Indian Agent Frederick Godfroy, in collusion with Lawrence Murphy, and his "House" partners, for their reservation contracts. Also reservation supplies were being stolen by Godfroy to be sold through "The House;" and rustled beef and mealy flour were accepted by Godfroy from "The House" for the Reservation. So Appel was biased to making the killing seem self-defense by Brady's posse, making his descriptions useless for crime scene reconstruction.

MISSED EVIDENCE: Sederwall missed Appel's biased and official version in his July 1, 1878 deposition to

Investigator Frank Warner Angel. [APPENDIX: 10] In it, Appel fabricated a scene of Tunstall on the ground and attacking the possemen, while irrationally maddened by venereal disease; forcing them to shoot him in self-defense through the shoulder and head. Appel stated that the shoulder wound did not kill him immediately, but threw him off his horse. He described the second bullet as "*entering the head about one inch to the right of the median line almost on a line with the occipital protuberance of [and] the left orbit.*" Omitted is the entry point - as to that front-to-back line. Given only is the trajectory of "*about one inch to the right of the median line*" [which is opposite to the quote used by Sederwall]; but implied is Tunstall's being shot from the front, with the trajectory on level with the left eye straight across to the centered bump (occipital protuberance) at the skull's base. Appel, noting the skull's circumferential fracture, remarked snidely: "*In my opinion the skull both on account of its being very thin and from evidence of venereal disease was likely to be extensively fractured from such a wound and this fracture in this case resulted entirely from said wound.*" But Appel hid that the head had been mutilated, a likely fracture contributor; lying "*There were no marks of violence or bruises on the body except the above two wounds.*"

MISSED EVIDENCE: Sederwall was also apparently unaware that Alexander McSween, expecting cover-up for the Ring-backed Brady posse, got Lincoln's unbiased town doctor, Taylor Ealy, to participate in the autopsy. Ealy confirmed mutilation of Tunstall's head, noted by the first tracker investigators, which indicated malicious intent. That is why the verdict was murder, as found by Tunstall's Coroner's Jury Report of February 19, 1878; signed by George B. Barber, John Newcomb, Robert M. Gilbert, Samuel Smith, Frank Coe, Benjamin J. Ellis, John B. Wilson, Justice of the Peace. It stated:

> *We, the undersigned Justice of the Peace and Coroner's Jury who sat upon the inquest held this 19th day of February 1878 on the body of John H. Tunstall, here found in precinct No. 1. of the County of Lincoln, Territory of New Mexico, find that the deceased came to his death on or about the 18th day of February 1878*

*by means of divers bullets shot and sent forth out of and from deadly weapons, and upon the head and body of said John H. Tunstall, which said deadly weapons were there and then held by one or more of the persons whose names are herewith written to wit, Jessie Evans, William Morton, Frank Baker, Thomas Hill, George Hindman, J.J. Dolan, and others not identified by the witnesses who testified before the Coroner's Jury.*

*We, the undersigned, to the best of our knowledge and belied from the evidence of the Coroner's Inquest, believe the above statement to be a true and impartial verdict.*

Sederwall also cited a few words of what he called "testimony provided by Billy the Kid," omitting that they were from Billy's deposition on June 8, 1878 to Frank Warner Angel.

**HIDING EVIDENCE THAT "BRUSHY" WAS NOT BILLY: Billy Bonney's long articulate deposition is another proof that coarse-spoken "Brushy" was not him; as well as the fact that "Brushy" and his hoaxing team were ignorant of that deposition, it being discovered in 1956 by Frederick Nolan. So "Brushy" never claimed to have given it as Billy.**

Nevertheless, Sederwall, using his unspecified "autopsy report," and unaware of Appel's bias or lying, made-up trajectory paths of bullets, much like Dr. Henry Lee's fake forensics for the washstand claimed from the Maxwell bedroom. Then, Sederwall, of course, claimed a cover-up; accusing the Sheriff's posse of one - as was obvious to the contemporaries and subsequent Billy the Kid historians! But Sederwall added: "**Judge Gonzales may also have been involved in the cover-up.**" (Pages 21-22) He cited Gonzales's eye-witness statement in his Angel deposition that the chest wound was from a rifle or carbine, and the head wound was from a pistol and traveled from back to front. So Sederwall accused him of making-up the firearms used.

**MISSED EVIDENCE: Sederwall's** accusing Florencio Gonzales of being in a "cover-up" (of what is uncertain) makes no sense. In fact, the real cover-up was blocking pursuit of Tunstall's Ringite murderers, because Sheriff William Brady and Governor S.B. Axtell shielded them.

Sederwall had missed the point of Florencio Gonzales's June 8, 1878 Angel deposition, while merely trying to show-off firearms knowledge. Gonzales was, anti-Ring, and was himself blocking *cover-up of Tunstall's Ringite assassination*. Gonzales had been the elected Lincoln County Probate Judge since 1875, and was a Tunstall-McSween ally from San Patricio, who had mitigated their Ringite malicious prosecution by denying the fake claim of James Dolan's "House" on the Emil Fritz estate for $76,000.

As Gonzales said in his Angel deposition: *"[If anyone] undertook to oppose L.G. Murphy & Co., they were either killed or run out of the County ... I have no doubt that the murder of John H. Tunstall was premeditated and designed by L.G. Murphy, J.J. Dolan, and J.H, Riley, commonly known as "The House" and carried out by their tools."* As to the murder, he testified: "<u>It has been claimed that Mr. Tunstall fired upon the posse</u> [by Appel and the Ring]... and that he fired two shots at them out of a Colt's Improved Revolver. We found his revolver quite close to the scabbard on the corpse. It must have been placed there by someone after Tunstall's death. We found two chambers empty, but there were no hulls or cartridge shells in the empty chambers [meaning no bullets shot from them] – the other four chambers had cartridges in them." As to the corpse, he testified: "On examination we found the skull broken. We found that a rifle or carbine bullet had entered his breast and a pistol bullet entered the back of his head coming out the forehead." [Gonzales then described the hidden body, with the killed horse] "*over 100 yards off the trail.*"

So Gonzales's deposition tried to make clear to the Washington, D.C., investigator that the killing was like a coupe de grâce, with a shot at the back of the head (contradicting Tunstall as an aggressor, removing doubt about Dr. Appel's ambiguous Angel testimony, and proving murder). Appel accidentally reinforced that scenario by claiming the chest strike would have thrown Tunstall off his horse, leaving him on foot for that final coupe de grâce shot. In addition, hiding the body, the killing of Tunstall's horse beside him, and the mocking *"burlesque"* of putting his hat on the horse's head, pointed to the viciousness of the murder. Sederwall missed it all by relying ignorantly on biased witness Appel with a malicious agenda.

Sederwall then claimed *he* had discovered that Tunstall was murdered; that William Morton was the murderer; that the sheriff's pose was acting unlawfully; and did a cover-up!

**FAKED DISCOVERY:** All that may have been news to W.C. Jameson - or even to Sederwall - but, with addition of more killers, Sederwall's is the conventional version of Tunstall's assassination! In fact, knowing that Sheriff Brady was complicit and was shielding the murderers, made the Regulators get murder warrants from Justice of the Peace John "Squire" Wilson to arrest the murderers, including William "Buck" Morton.

**IRRELEVANCE:** Of course, all this was irrelevant to Garrett not killing Billy, or "Brushy" being Billy. And it added nothing to the Tunstall killing. But it was in the "Brushy" hoax mode of claiming conspiracies to hide "truth," while faking special new knowledge - much like the original "Brushy"-Morrison things-not-printed-trick, or Sonnichsen's misstated primary records.

## *FAKED AFTERMATH OF TUNSTALL MURDER*

Naming his chapter "The Law Gets in the Way of Truth," Jameson continued to build hoped-for suspicions about written history. (Pages 24-27) So cited were cover-ups of Brady's posse's killing of Tunstall. Dishonest fix-ups were adding Billy's being deputized, and his illegal arrest by Sheriff Brady. And Sederwall was inserted as if discovering these basic historic facts!

**PROVING "BRUSHY" WAS NOT BILLY:** Billy's deputizing and arrest are damning to "Brushy," since they were unknown to him.

**IRRELEVANCE:** All this was irrelevant to Garrett not killing Billy, or "Brushy" being Billy. It was just "Brushy" hoax-style claiming of conspiracies to hide the truth.

### **FAKED REVENGE MOTIVE**

In this chapter, Jameson makes a bizarre and duplicitous switcheroo - without telling the reader. "Brushy's" confabulations are used as Billy Bonney's quotes! So Jameson wrote: "Billy the Kid stated, 'He had been good to me and treated me like a gentleman. I lost the best friend I ever had when they killed him.'" (Page 28) In *Alias Billy the Kid*, "Brushy stated: "Tunstall was a good man. **He had been good to me and treated me like a gentleman. I lost the best friend I ever had when they killed him.** I swore that day that I would make them pay with their lives for this dirty deed." (*Alias Billy the Kid*, Page 26)

Also copied by Jameson is "Brushy's" guess that the aftermath to the Tunstall killing was revenge. Added is that Justice of the Peace Wilson - called a "judge" – helped the revenge. But Wilson was not a judge, and his agenda, like the Regulators', was anti-Ring, which included arresting responsible Ringites.

Known history of the Morton Baker, and McCloskey killings, yields a Sederwall "investigation." (Pages 32-34) As expected, without certainty of the killing site in the vast open plain to the east of the Capitan Mountains, Sederwall found spent cartridges. He gives versions of the killings, from Regulator Frank "McNab" [sic - MacNab], James Dolan, a Lucius Dills, and Pat Garrett.

**FLAWED "CRIME SCENE INVESTIGATION":** Revealed is Sederwall's "what-if" fake reasoning, instead of evidence. He ruminates about *what if* Morton and Baker had their hands tied. *If* they had their hands tied, they could not snatch McCloskey's gun and kill him. And it is hard to ride a horse with tied hands. This silliness makes him conclude they were executed in revenge by Billy the Kid. But this is no investigation. It is just fantasizing to back "Brushy's" guess about revenge.

**IRRELEVANCE:** All this is irrelevant to Garrett not killing Billy, or "Brushy" being Billy. But it was in the "Brushy" hoax mode of claiming conspiracies to hide the truth.

### BILLY THE KID AS A GOOD GUY

An underlying theme of William V. Morrison's formulation of the "Brushy Bill" hoax, was that Billy the Kid was branded as an outlaw by the Santa Fe Ring. Ignorance left the theme undeveloped, but its motive was to paint "Brushy," as Billy, as a victim of injustice, deserving a pardon. That theme is in Jameson's chapter "The Evolution of an Outlaw." (Pages 35-40)

That formulation is correct, but neither "Brushy," nor Morrison, nor Sonnichsen, nor Jameson understood why. Missing was information that real Billy would have known: that there was grass-roots resistance to the Santa Fe Ring's corrupt political and economic domination and terrorist tactics - like the malicious prosecution of Alexander McSween and John Tunstall, and Tunstall's brutal assassination. And bi-cultural and bi-lingual Billy would also have seen it as an Hispanic cause, that being the population most victimized by the Ring's land grab of millions of acres of their grant lands (with Paulita Maxwell, his lover, having her family's two million acre Ring-stolen Maxwell Land Grant as the most famous example). That ignorance of Billy Bonney's actual world was key to understanding why the "Brushy" team were at a loss as to the cause of the Lincoln County War, and made up simplistic "revenge" for Tunstall's killing.

So Jameson blamed Garrett for Billy's outlaw reputation, calling him a "politician and constant self-promoter" with his *Authentic Life of Billy the Kid*. He also blamed Governor S.B. Axtell for his Proclamation outlawing the Regulators, stating that he was friends with Murphy and Dolan. He then stated erroneously, to show Axtell as bad, that "[he] had once been governor of Utah and was removed from that position for corruption." (Pages 37-38)

**WRONG AND "BRUSHY" BASHING: First of all, this debunks "Brushy," who knew nothing of the Regulators or their freedom fighting.**

**And Jameson confused Utah Governor Axtell's transfer to New Mexico, in 1875, to replace deceased Marsh Giddings as Governor, with Axtell's removal in late 1878, after the Lincoln County War, for corruption, as documented in Frank Warner Angel's report. The missed big picture is that Ringite Axtell was scapegoated by the Angel investigation under President Hayes to hide the larger responsibility of T.B. Catron and his Ring.**

Further guessing about why Axtell wrongly outlawed the Regulators, Jameson made up it was because Angel uncovered that he was in debt to Murphy, Dolan, and Riley of "The House."

**WRONG: In fact, the $1800 loan through John Riley, when Axtell assumed office, was a Ring bribe.**

This foray led Jameson to conclude that it was Axtell who made Billy the Kid an outlaw by his Proclamation.

**WRONG: Missed is the big picture that all Ring opponents were "outlawed." Axtell had similarly suppressed and**

supported terror in Colfax County from 1875 to 1877, causing the Colfax County War. And in Axtell's March 9, 1878 Proclamation, Billy was not singled out. The outlaw myth of Billy the Kid was still in the future - with Ring-controlled press and the next Governor, Lew Wallace himself. The big picture is that real Billy became politicized, and with his bi-culturalism threatened to instigate further uprisings after the Lincoln County War. But "Brushy," his team, and Jameson are unaware of the issues that made Billy a dangerous gadfly.

Jameson parlays his feeble foray into historical analysis to attack all historians by stating that they do not "probe for facts, and attempt to uncover the truth." (Page 40)

IRRELEVANCE: All this was irrelevant to proving Garrett's not killing Billy, or "Brushy's" being Billy. But Jameson was trying to repeat the "Brushy" hoax's historians being in a conspiracy against the truth.

PROVING "BRUSHY" WAS NOT BILLY: These feeble fix-ups proved "Brushy" was ignorant about the freedom fight, which eventually made the Ring machine kill Billy.

## *FAKING THE SHERIFF BRADY KILLING*

The Sheriff William Brady killing, called "the pivotal event of the Lincoln County War," is in "Blood and Mud." (Pages 41-51) Actually, the pivotal event was the killing of Tunstall, which yielded the Regulator movement, a hark-back to the pre-Revolutionary War first freedom fighters. [That Regulator's ambush now has fix-ups of Billy running out to retrieve "something," along with Jim French, instead of "Brushy's" Fred Wayte [sic]]. Questioning if the "something" was Billy's "rifle" [sic - carbine] or arrest warrants for Alexander McSween, Jameson slips in "a revolver" as a "something," to add unnamed "Brushy's fakery. And fixed-up is that Billy Matthews shot Billy and French [instead of "Brushy's" shot Wayte [sic]].

Claimed is that no investigation of the killings of Brady and Hindman occurred until "cop" Sederwall's (Pages 43-51); though cited is merely the commonly known cold wet day, Brady coming on horseback from his ranch, and his claim of putting up a courthouse notice while accompanied by four deputies.

But, like for "Brushy's" team, the motive for Brady's murder is unknown. Sederwall uses Francisco Trujillo's 1937 WPA fake hearsay from the "Probable Cause Statement" (see page 400 above) that McSween told Billy to stop Brady from arresting him. "Brushy" had guessed: "Sheriff Brady was gunning for me with warrants for cattle stealing." (*Alias Billy the Kid*, Page 27) And Sederwall uses historian Robert Utley to claim the Regulators wanted to get rid of Brady.

So Sederwall did a "crime scene" investigation, deciding killing in town was a bad way to keep a secret; weather was too bad for socializing; it was better to kill Brady coming from his ranch (which he boasts "cops" call a "kill zone"). **So Sederwall claimed the Regulators were there to testify in the Grand Jury**. And when it was delayed, they got angry at Brady for "obstructing justice;" so abruptly killed him. This was apparently an attempted defense, as to non-premeditation, but a "crime of passion."

**FLAWED ANALYSIS: Oddly, Sederwall used Attorney Randi McGinn's strange error from her Pardon Petition: that the Regulators were "[p]resent to testify as witnesses before the grand jury about the killing of John Tunstall."** (See page 450 above)

In fact, the Regulators were outlawed by Governor S.B. Axtell's March 9, 1881 Proclamation, giving Brady absolute power. That same March 9th, they had killed "Buck" Morton and Frank Baker. To come to Lincoln that April 1, 1878, risked their lives, indicating their desperate motive. And they were not, as Sederwall used, witnesses in the Grand Jury - which had not begun. As outlaws, they dared not testify. And Tunstall's murder had adequate evidence for the murder indictments that finally resulted.

Their act was premeditated killing of Brady before he murdered McSween that day, when he returned to Lincoln for his upcoming Grand Jury trial for his Ring-concocted embezzlement case. Brady hoped to kill him with guise of legal pursuit before his exoneration. The Regulators hid behind Tunstall's corral's adobe wall, and acted in unison when Brady and the deputies came into view in the brief time presented by the awkward position of the adobe wall and the blocking, long, eastward side of Tunstall's building. And walking abreast, and armed was key: they were heading to McSween's point of arrival to the east, confirming to the Regulators need to act.

**MISSED CORRECT DEFENSE ARGUMENT:** Sederwall seemed to argue non-premeditation by instantaneous "crime of passion" to mitigate the eventual first degree murder verdict Billy got in his Mesilla trial. But it was both incorrect and useless.

It would have been useless in Ringite Judge Bristol's Mesilla court, where his April 9, 1881 jury instructions for Billy trial for the Brady murder stated: "*If the design to kill is completely formed in the <u>mind but for a moment before inflicting the fatal wounds</u> it would be premeditated and in law the effect would be the same as though the design to kill had existed for a long time.*" Bristol deemed it still first degree murder, meaning hanging as the sole penalty.

The correct argument for a lesser degree, was the Regulators' conviction that deadly force was the only way to stop Brady's murder of McSween. In fact, if their response had been to <u>immediate</u> threat - like seeing Brady attacking McSween - it would be a defense for exoneration - like self-defense. But the gap of about three hours before McSween's arrival, required a mitigating defense based on their *certainty* that Brady would then kill McSween.

So trial evidence had to show that Brady was a proven murderer of McSween's friend, John Tunstall, just 42 days earlier. And Brady had made a death threat to Tunstall in McSween's presence, stating: "I won't shoot you now, you haven't long to run." Brady was also a rogue lawman, blocking arrest of Tunstall's killers, who were his own deputies and possemen. And he illegally imprisoned the Defendant, Billy Bonney, on February 20, 1878, to obstruct his arrest of Tunstall's killers in his capacity as a Deputy Constable appointed by Justice of the Peace John Wilson. And Brady was a known threat to McSween, having harassed him by property attachment for his embezzlement case far in excess of the $10,000 set for the trial. And McSween hid because of certainty of Brady's murderous intent, staying in protective custody of Deputy Sheriff Adolph Barrier, also certain of McSween's murder risk from Brady. On March 28, 1878, Brady, brought Fort Stanton soldiers to the ranch of John Chisum, in failed attempt to apprehend, and likely kill, McSween. And just four days later - the murder day - McSween would return to Lincoln for his eventual Grand Jury trial.

Also, on the murder day, Defendant Bonney had only a revolver, since Brady had confiscated his carbine; and all others had carbines. He could not attain the 60 yard range to Brady's position, so could not have been his killer. Furthermore, Defendant Bonney had no motive to kill Brady except in defense of McSween. To protect another from certain death is noble, and mitigates against a verdict of 1st degree murder, which is wanton and with malice aforethought. And it is the burden of the Territory, not the Defendant, to prove beyond reasonable doubt that the Defendant *did not* act in defense of another. The prosecution, using Brady's indicted fellow murderers as witnesses, failed to do that. So the jurors, with reasonable doubt as to whether the defendant acted justifiably in defense of another, cannot find him guilty of 1st degree murder, and are free to find the him not guilty - or, at most, guilty of 2nd degree murder, which spares his life.

Sederwall also faked discovery of "discrepancies," stating reports that Brady and Deputies were on foot were false because it is unpleasant to walk in the mud; and Brady was old. Also, they were described as walking abreast, but *only horses walk abreast*! So he fabricated a scene with Brady falling off his horse when being shot. And he cited a witness stating that "he saw "Brady 'fall into a sitting position.' " (Pages 49-50)

**FAKERY:** This is too silly for words. Nevertheless, here goes. The street was unpaved; walking on mud was a part of Old West life. The word "abreast," means side by side, or shoulder to shoulder - like Brady and the Deputies walked.

And Sederwall built his fakery on confusing shot George Hindman's "fall into a sitting position," with shot Brady. In fact, Hindman being upright, made Ike Stockton run from José Montaño's building for attempted rescue.

Added to his horseback scenario was Sederwall's fantasy that, in the escape, Billy stole Brady's horse. He then claimed that Billy sold Brady's horse to Henry Hoyt in the Bill of Sale.

**FAKE INVESTIGATION ACCIDENTALLY BASHING "BRUSHY":** Sederwall built on his own fakery that horses were involved, then used meaningless "what-ifs": *If* Billy stole the horse, he could have sold it to Hoyt in Tascosa, Texas. But this sale of an expensive sorrel for $75, on

October 24, 1878, merely lifts conventional history of the likely sale of Brady's sorrel horse Dandy Dick.

Missed by Sederwall is that, in the pre-Lincoln County War Battle period, Billy rode a gray horse; that the Hoyt sale was 206 days after the Brady killing; and in the post-Lincoln County War period of that sale Billy was doing guerilla rustling against Ringites, and was selling horses in Tascosa. Dandy Dick was likely stolen then, with other horses, from Catron's Carrizozo Ranch or the Ring-backing Charles Fritz ranch. As Billy had threatened in his July 13, 1881 "Regulator Manifesto" to Catron's ranch manager and brother-in-law, Edgar Walz: *"We are all aware that your brother-in-law, T.B. Catron sustains the Murphy-Kinney party ... Steal from the poorest or richest American or Mexican, and the full measure of the injury you do, shall be visited upon the property of Mr. Catron."*

And, of course, "Brushy" was unaware of this horseback Brady ambush (*Alias Billy the* Kid, Page 27), or of real Billy's guerrilla rustling. Further debunking "Brushy," Sederwall gave a photocopy of that Bill of Sale, in Billy's fine Spencerian handwriting, and with proper legalese. And he admitted its two witnesses, who were George Howard and James McMasters, owners of the local saloon. That alone was enough to end the "Brushy" hoax, since "Brushy" was not literate enough to create it, and the two witnesses - and obviously Hoyt - identified Billy as the writer. In fact, as discussed above, the Bill of Sale was the likely source for "Brushy's" Tascosa fabrication that Jim East was "a friend of mine from *Tascosa, Texas*." (*Alias Billy the* Kid, Page 38). Morrison likely knew of it from the Indiana Historical Society's Lew Wallace Collection, in which was Hoyt's copy of the October 24, 1878 Bill of Sale as sent to Lew Wallace Jr. on April 27, 1929.

But the big picture here is that Sederwall's "crime scene investigation" is just fantasizing. No witness ever reported ridden horses in the scene.

IRRELEVANCE: All this "crime scene" fakery was irrelevant to Garrett's not killing Billy, or "Brushy" being Billy. But it was in the "Brushy" hoax mode of faking special knowledge.

## *FAKING "BUCKSHOT ROBERTS' KILLING*

Jameson claimed the Regulators' Blazer's Mill killing of "Buckshot" Roberts furthered Billy the Kid's reputation, so it would be revisited "to demonstrate the difference between the manner in which this event has long been treated and what is more likely the truth as discerned by investigative analysis conducted by Steve Sederwall." The chapter is "The Shooting at Blazer's Mill." (Pages 52-55)

First presented is conventional history, unknown to "Brushy" and Morrison, though with the shooting scene a bit garbled. The location is the building used by owner, Joseph Blazer, and the Mescalero Indian Reservation Agent, who is correctly listed as corrupt. But missed was the key to the event: that "Buckshot" *shot first* while resisting arrest, hit Charlie Bowdre's cartridge belt buckle, with the bullet ricocheting and hitting George Coe's gun, and mutilating his thumb and trigger finger. "Buckshot," was shot in the abdomen by Bowdre, then shot John Middleton non-fatally in the chest, and killed Dick Brewer; dying himself the next day. The reason that the part which Jameson missed is important, is that the sequence made the killing of Roberts self-defense; and, furthermore, Billy Bonney was not involved.

But "Brushy's" confabulation had left a problem. Unaware of the Regulator movement, "Brushy" accounted for the shooting by confabulating an earlier argument with himself, Charlie Bowdre, and "Buckshot; followed by his own revenge shooting of "Buckshot" as Billy. (*Alias Billy the* Kid, Pages 27-28; using Pat Garrett's *The Authentic Life of Billy the Kid* fiction, Pages 74-75) So a scenario was needed to make Billy the killer. That was left to "cop" Sederwall. (Pages 54-55)

Admitted by Sederwall is that the Blazer's Mill building for the scene no longer exists. And for casting doubt on the historical version, the only "evidence" he had was three letters by Joseph Blazer's son, A.N. Blazer, to historian, Maurice Garland Fulton, claiming he had been an eye-witness to the April 4, 1878 shootings at age 13. His claim, unlike the history, was that "Buckshot" arrived **at night, and in minutes there was shooting.** Blazer's three letters' dates make them 52 years and 5 days after the scene, 53 years and 20 days after the scene, and 59 years, 4 months, and 23 days after the scene. Sederwall also referenced A.N. Blazer's non-historical tale, told to A.N. by his sister, that, Billy, returning to Lincoln after the hanging trial, had breakfast at Blazer's Mill, and had told her (not A.N.) a version, **with Billy shooting Roberts through the door in the room into which he had retreated.** Windbag A.N. Blazer even described the bullet wound as just above the left hip and a little up.

But relying on old-timer A.N. Blazer's malarkey, Sederwall made-up a "crime scene," with Billy sliding and falling on the boards on the way to the room and firing through the door from a prone position! Sederwall claimed corroboration from the no longer existing door with its unprovable bullet hole.

**FLAWED ANALYSIS: Sederwall used A.N. Blazer's childhood memory hearsay over a half-century later, and double hearsay with his sister; when the actual account was from the Regulators' eye-witness experience.**

Telling, is A.N. Blazer's malarkey about "Buckshot's" wound. In fact, he had a single abdominal one from Charlie Bowdre, as documented in U.S. Attorney Thomas Benton Catron's June 21, 1878 federal indictment of the Regulators - including Billy - for the killing and titled "The United States vs. Charles Bowdry [Bowdre], Doc Scurlock, Henry Brown, Henry Antrim alias "Kid," John Middleton, Stephen Stevens, John Scroggins, George Coe and Frederick Waite." [APPENDIX: 11] It stated: "*[He was shot] in and upon the right side of the belly of him the said Andrew Roberts one mortal wound of the depth of ten inches and of breadth of one half of an inch of which said mortal wound the Said Andrew Roberts then and there at the said Reservation instantly died [sic – the next day]: and so the Jury aforesaid upon their oaths as aforesaid do say that the Said Charles Bowdry, Doc Scurlock, Henry Brown, Henry Antrim – alias Kid – John Middleton, Stephen Stevens, John Scroggins, George Coe and Frederick Waite the Said Andrew Roberts in manner and form aforesaid feloniously, willfully, unlawfully of this malice aforethought and from a premeditated design to effect the death of the Said Andrew Roberts, did kill and murder.*"

Sederwall concluded his fake discrepancies by stating that "Buckshot" and Brewer were buried **in the same grave nearby**. So he did what he called "on-site examination;" and found two markers.

**FAKING DISCREPANCIES: Sederwall mixed-up the burial issue. There are two graves, but uncertainly marked.** When formal gravestones were finally added to this well-known tourist site, it was arbitrarily decided to make one grave Brewer's, and the other "Buckshot's." There is no discrepancy, just Sederwall's ignorance, and the irrelevant chance that that the corpses are reversed.

Sederwall may have lifted his error from a past Morrison letter. On April 27, 1953, Morrison shared the same confusion with Paul A. Blazer, writing: "I had heard that both of them were buried in the same grave. But your explanation that Brewer was buried the same day that he was killed and Roberts lived until the next day, being buried that afternoon ... convinced me that the legend is in error."

IRRELEVANCE: All this was irrelevant to Garrett not killing Billy, or "Brushy" being Billy. It is not even a real "crime scene investigation."

## *FAKING THE LINCOLN COUNTY WAR BATTLE*

The Lincoln County War chapter is titled "The Burning of the McSween House." (Pages 56-67) For it, Jameson presented names and events unknown to "Brushy;" thus, inadvertently discrediting his man, who confabulated a "three day" "cattle war."

Error-filled, it plucks wee fix-ups from modern history books, the Frank Warner Angel files, and Dudley Court of Inquiry testimonies. At its end, Jameson revealed it was actually Steve Sederwall's "analysis of the 'war;' " (Page 67) inadvertently placing the blame.

The Jameson-Sederwall duo did not realize the War was a six month fight against the Santa Fe Ring, that it began at Tunstall's assassination, had multiple skirmishes, and culminated in a six day battle in Lincoln. As unaware as imposter "Brushy," they missed both the horror and the magnificence of that final battle which imbued real Billy's remaining life with freedom fighting zeal. They did, however, did add more days to "Brushy's" three.

In the Jameson-Sederwall fantasy, the Regulators ride into Lincoln on July 14, 1878 for motives wrongly guessed as: they had warrants to arrest Tunstall's killers and to protect McSween.

WRONG: In fact, that day represented Alexander McSween's culminating show-down with the Ring, its local bosses at "The House," Ringite Sheriff George Peppin, and the Ring's allies of Seven Rivers boys and John Kinney's outlaw gang. Ring terrorism had been escalating.

On April 29, 1878, Seven Rivers boys, hiding in Charles Fritz's ranch ambushed Frank Coe and Regulator leader, Frank MacNab, murdering MacNab. On May 28, 1878, Governor Axtell made a Proclamation to remove unbiased Sheriff John Copeland, and replace him with Ringite George Peppin as Sheriff. And on July 3, 1878, just eleven days earlier, had been the retaliative terrorist massacre and property destruction at San Patricio by Sheriff George Peppin and John Kinney's outlaw gang to punish McSween's Hispanic sympathizers. Thus, most of the approximately 60 men who rode in for McSween were enraged, traumatized, Hispanic, and from San Patricio and Picacho, with a lesser number of Anglo Regulators. And the day before, Billy and the Regulators had sent the "Regulator Manifesto" to T.B. Catron's brother-in-law, Edgar Walz, making clear the anti-Ring intent.

Also, it was McSween's intention to take the town peacefully, and force James Dolan to move away. He was so confident of safety, that he had his wife, her sister with five young children, and his law intern at the house. His men occupied positions throughout the town; which Jameson adds to a list unknown to "Brushy" - though still missing the Tunstall store. Jameson also wrongly thought - using "Brushy" - that most of the men stayed with McSween, but it was initially only Jim "Frenchie" French.

Adrift, the Jameson-Sederwall duo create a bizarre fiction that the battle resulted from squabbling about trespassing on some McSween land in town, saying McSween got angry that Peppin's posseman were on his land in an old stone tower called the Torreon; and McSween also blamed Saturnino Baca, his tenant in a house on that land, and sent him an eviction notice. Claimed is that Baca, an "ex-sheriff," knew the law, so he sent for his friend, Fort Stanton Commander N.A.M. Dudley. And Dudley sent Post Surgeon Daniel Appel, who tried to negotiate as "a peacemaker," but the possemen would not leave the Torreon because it gave them "an advantage." So, according to the clueless duo, "the Regulators dug in for war."

**WRONG:** In the Battle's first day of July 14th, the Torreon was of no advantage, since McSween's men were positioned along Lincoln's single street, and could prevent attackers ascending the south foothills to shoot down at them. Saturnino Baca, McSween's tenant, but a Lincoln settler since 1867, was one of the few Hispanic Ringites, a traitor to his people; and McSween knew it. In a political alliance with T.B. Catron since 1868, Baca was also a hay supplier to "The House" in its earliest days in Lincoln in 1873, and a Murphy ally. And he had been a Probate Judge, not Sheriff. Lincoln's first Sheriff was Brady; then came John Copeland; then George Peppin. But on the Battle's first day, Baca was not yet actively involved. And Ringite Appel did not come to town until later; and as a Ring-biased fact-finder, not as a peacemaker.

The duo thought shooting began when Deputy Jack Long tried to serve warrants on McSween for attempted murder. (Page 58)

WRONG: Gunfire began with entry of shooting Ring-side Seven Rivers boys, joining the Peppin posse. That caused McSween's men, including Billy, to rush to his house as protectors. Also, the faking duo were unaware that Long's warrants for murder and attempted murder against McSween and Billy were invalid. They were written at Blazer's Mill on May 1, 1878 by then Justice of the Peace David Easton at James Dolan's and Billy Matthews's request after an April 30, 1878 Lincoln County War skirmish of Seven Rivers boys, coming to Lincoln to kill McSween, with McSween's men there to protect him.

Easton was T.B. Catron's Ring agent in Lincoln County. So Easton called the self-defense killings by the Regulators murder; though the Seven Rivers attackers were arrested by then Sheriff John Copeland. Easton's warrants named McSween, Billy, and others unknown, with murder and assault; with victims being four dead and one injured Seven Rivers men. But, fearing retribution, Easton then quit, invalidating his warrants! The key point, missed by the duo, is that there was no legal reason for the Peppin posse to attack McSween. And he had been exonerated for embezzling by the Grand Jury. That is why, on July 19th, when Commander Dudley marched on Lincoln, and realized this, he forced Justice of the Peace Wilson to write a warrant fabricating McSween's attempted murder of fact-finder, Private Berry Robinson on July 16th.

As to the duo's reference to evicting McSween's tenant Saturnino Baca, it occurred on July 15th, for his assisting Sheriff Peppin's possemen at the Torreon. Baca used that eviction notice for his pre-planned Ringite plot to evade the Posse Comitatus Act that barred military intervention in civilian matters, as passed the month before. The plot was to use its exception allowing intervention if women and children were in danger. So traitor to his people, Baca, wrote to Dudley that his pregnant wife and many children were in danger of McSween, and requested troops.

As to Post Surgeon Daniel Appel's coming to Lincoln, it was on July 15th, and he was no "peacemaker." A Ring tool, he had come at Dudley's orders for "fact finding," in further Ringite exploration of excuses to use troops against the McSween side.

It was at that point on July 15th, that the Ring side was adequately emboldened to send Deputy Jack Long to the McSween house with David Easton's invalid May 1st arrest warrants for McSween and Billy for the April 30th skirmish with the invading Seven Rivers boys. But Long was repelled by shots from inside. This was the point that the ignorant duo wrongly thought the war started.

But writing fiction, the duo next had departing failed "peacemaker" Daniel Appel encounter the John Kinney gang, whom they call "Seven Rivers Warriors" (confusing Kinney from Mesilla with the Seven Rivers boys). They add Jessie Evans, and say that Appel convinced Kinney to go to Lincoln - when Kinney and his gang from Mesilla were there for a pre-planned attack - along with Seven Rivers boys from the Pecos valley.

For the next day (of uncertain date, but with information compatible with July 16th), the duo have Sheriff Peppin station men on the south foothills to shoot unsuccessfully at "McSween's snipers." Claimed is that was when Peppin requested a howitzer cannon from Dudley.

**FLAWED:** Here the duo missed a crucial point. McSween's plan for a peaceful take-over was working. The south foothills were unattainable, with his men able to fire at any attempted ascent. That was why Peppin tried to get military intervention by a claim that violated the Posse Comitatus Act: arming civilians against civilians.

The duo then garble the next incident of July 16th. They state that Dolan and Kinney wrote Dudley making up that McSweens had fired on his soldier in town. And that made Dudley come.

**WRONG:** In fact, that July 16th, responding to Peppin's cannon request, Dudley sent 9th Cavalryman Private Berry Robinson as another fact-finder. The McSweens, stopping shooting for fear of hitting a soldier, gave a few Peppin men a chance to ascend the south foothills. Robinson was then likely fired upon by the Dolan side, was uninjured but thrown from his horse, and returned to Fort Stanton. The Dolan side claimed Robinson was attacked by McSweens. But that did not cause Dudley's immediate intervention.

For that same July 16th, the duo have McSween-side Fernando Herrera shoot Charles Crawford, a Peppin posseman on the south foothills; with good Surgeon Appel suddenly appearing in town to "risk his life" to give him aid - though Crawford died.

**WRONG:** The actual date was July 17th. And Appel was back in Lincoln in another "fact-finding mission," now with past Fort Stanton Commander George Purington, and five soldiers, with the excuse of Berry Robinson's shooting. Dudley was in a dilemma: afraid to act, but as an alcoholic incompetent, he was Ring-beholden, with T.B. Catron having already represented him for two prior court martials. He knew he was supposed to crush the uprising. So again the fact-finders recorded accusations against McSween, which McSween denied. It was in that context, that Appel - not risking his life because McSweens would not shoot at soldiers - picked up dying Charles Crawford. But the crucial big picture missed by the duo was that it was now the fourth day of McSween's occupation, and he was holding the town, with Peppin's posse neutralized.

For July 18th, the duo have McSween side's Ben Ellis shot in the neck, though it occurred the day before. They then describe town doctor [Taylor] Ealy, going to assist Ben, making clear that Mrs. Ealy was there too. And an unidentified "Sue Gates" accompanies her to get water.

**WRONG:** The duo were unaware that there were also two young Ealy children, or that Susan Gates was a teacher living with the Shield family in McSween's house, but had taken shelter with the Ealy's. In fact, they missed the whole Shield family. Living in a wing of McSween's two part house, was Susan McSween's sister Elizabeth, her five children, and her husband David, who was McSween's law partner. There also was McSween's law student, Harvey Morris. The missed *big picture is women and children*. It was the obligation, under the Posse Comitatus Act, for Dudley to protect women and children. But he would instead enable their life-threatening attack.

For the 19th, the duo had Dudley arrive at Lincoln with troops, including officers. Avoiding "Brushy's" racism, they avoid races! They do a fix-up by adding Dudley's Gatling gun, howitzer, ammunition load, and provisions, proving the "Brushy" and team's ignorance!

Showing-off, the duo digress - like "Brushy's" revelations about the obvious - and declare that Dudley later lied in a court of inquiry that he had come to protect women and children! Noted also is the well known fact that, the day before, Dolan and John Kinney had visited Dudley at Fort Stanton, and influenced him. As if shocked, the duo decide Dudley and Dolan were in a conspiracy(!) - which they define (!) - and decide they all lied!

**FAKERY:** The obvious is not discovery. In fact, Dolan's partner, John Riley, had been in Santa Fe; and one can presume he was strategizing the attack with T.B. Catron. The duo have missed the significance of the Lincoln County War and Battle was an uprising against the Ring, which was intentionally and ferociously crushed.

But thinking they discovered Dudley's "lying," the duo give known examples of his outrages in Lincoln, like refusing aid to Susan McSween - an conclude the obvious: Dudley had refused aid to women and children! And they had Dudley pointing a cannon at McSween's front door. (Page 65)

**WRONG:** With so many fix-ups, the duo got confused. The cannon was pointed at José Montaño's house. Thus, the duo missed the key point: Dudley's intentional act of terror, which caused flight of McSween's men throughout the town. The strategy was to besiege McSween's house to kill him, and everyone else there.

Now possessing the Dudley Court of Inquiry transcript, likely from fellow "Billy the Kid Case" hoaxer U.S. Marshals Service David Turk, the duo had real Billy's own testimony, which they cite - though hiding how differently real Billy talked compared to grammatically impaired "Brushy." But they tried to use what Billy said to fake an investigation. But Billy's testifying to three soldiers stationed at McSween's house by Dudley, is misunderstood as: "an attempt to draw fire."

**WRONG:** In fact, the key point that Billy was making was that the soldiers were stationed there to inhibit those inside from shooting, so as to give Peppin's men the advantage. Billy had also stated that Dudley left three soldiers to accompany Peppin as a shield.

For the burning of the McSween house, the duo have Peppin order his posse to commit arson. They then identify an Andy Boyle as the fire-setter, but are unaware he was a Seven Rivers boy - calling him a "cattle rustler from Texas."

**WRONG:** Andy Boyle was not the only fire-setter, as proved by the May 23, 1879 eye-witness testimony of Susan McSween at the Dudley Court of Inquiry. She stated: *"I then said to Mr. McSween that I believe that I would go down to his camp and talk with [Dudley] myself ... [O]n my way to his camp I saw [Sebrian] Bates, he being a colored servant of mine ... just in the act of picking up some lumber. At the time I saw three of Murphy's men ... I then asked what they were doing, they said ... [t]hat Peppin and Col. Dudley had sent them to carry lumber to our house to set it on fire ... I then begged them not to do so."*

Also missed is a key point that Dudley enabled the fire to be set around the McSween family's women and children. And the duo was unaware of the catastrophic event that added to the fire: the house's keg of gunpowder for reloading cartridges exploded, finally leaving the men in the last remaining room, the kitchen.

The duo describe the nighttime escape from the room. They state that the "**Kid said they had to jump over the body of Harvey Morris,** then ran towards the Tunstall Store and then turned towards the river." (Page 66)

**WRONG:** Jumping over Morris's body is invented here; and is not in "Brushy's" own quote copying Billy's testimony on running towards the Tunstall store and river (*Alias Billy the Kid*, Page 31), or Jameson's 1998 book (*Return of the*

*Outlaw Billy the Kid*, Page 54), or in real Billy's testimony. It opens the possibility that Jameson simply published verbatim whatever Sederwall made-up.

**FLAWED:** Most importantly, even with Billy's transcript in hand, the confused duo missed Billy's key testimony about the escape. And it was fatal to "Brushy," who had no idea of it. Real Billy reported seeing three white soldiers (likely meaning officers) fire a volley at those escaping; thus, making Dudley complicit with murder, as ordering his men to shoot at the escaping civilians.

The duo then give the killing of McSween and shooting of Yginio [now corrected from "Brushy's Higinio] Salazar.

**FLAWED:** Missed are the murders of McSween-side Vincente Romero and Francisco Zamora. Even the friendly fire shooting of Ring-side Bob Beckwith is omitted.

Unaware of the Battle's cause, the duo conclude feebly that Billy the Kid and his companions were disappointed because they did not get a chance to serve the warrants for Brady's murder, and had failed to protect McSween! And they floated the hoax's point that authorities cannot be trusted. Jameson provided Sederwall's conclusion that "more violations of the law were committed by the men responsible for law enforcement than by those who were identified as outlaws." That was to imply that also meant Garrett did not kill Billy!

**"BRUSHY" TAKES A BEATING:** All this was irrelevant to Garrett not killing Billy, or "Brushy" being Billy. Even worse, the duo had discredited "Brushy" by demonstrating that his confabulations had missed almost all of the Battle's events. Poor Jameson had even permitted omission of the jewel in "Brushy's" knowing-things-not-printed trick: black ("nigger") soldiers on the foothills shooting at the burning McSween house!

# CHAPTER 3
## FRAMING THE KID AS A COUNTERFEITER

### RECYCLING AN OLD HOAX BY STEVE SEDERWALL

W.C. Jameson's "Counterfeit Money" chapter (Pages 68-84), inserts an old hoax by Steve Sederwall, fabricating Billy the Kid as a Secret Service-pursued crook, in cahoots with Jesse James and William Brockway, in a national rustling-money laundering racket; and as a vicious murderer of an informer.

Oddly, Jameson missed that this scam demolished his man "Brushy," who, as Billy, not only had no idea of these activities; but also made him, as Billy, so despicable that a pardon was unthinkable. Possibly, mesmerized narrator Jameson thought Sederwall's theme was just history-is-not-as-written.

In fact, Sederwall's trick was simple: tracking the New York Brockway gang's counterfeit bill distributions nationally, then faking links to Billy Bonney. Like C.L. Sonnichsen's fraud about Pat Garrett's reward money, it relied on readers having no access to obscure cited documents, which are then misstated.

### REALITY OF BILLY AS A RUSTLER

Billy Bonney was a not a counterfeiter. After the lost Lincoln County War Battle on July 19, 1878, he made money by rustling, staying true to his July 13, 1878 "Regulator Manifesto": "*We are all aware that your brother-in-law, T.B. Catron sustains the Murphy-Kinney party ... Steal from the poorest or richest American or Mexican, and the full measure of the injury you do, shall be visited upon the property of Mr. Catron.*" One prize of his guerrilla rustling was dead Sheriff William Brady's sorrel horse, likely stolen from Lincoln County's Charles Fritz Ranch or T.B. Catron's Carrizozo Ranch, and "sold" in Texas to Henry Hoyt on

October 24, 1878. And John Chisum got retaliative rustling for his betrayal of John Tunstall and Alexander McSween by refusing aid of his 80 cowboys, and not paying the Regulators as promised.

Billy's gave his Robin Hood self-image in a December 12, 1880 letter to Governor Lew Wallace: *"There is no Doubt but what there is a great deal of Stealing going on in the Territory ...* **but so far as my being at the head of a Band there is nothing of it** *in Several Instances I have recovered Stolen Property when there was no chance to get an Officer to do it. one instance for Hugo Zuber Post office Puerto de Luna. another for Pablo Analla Same Place."* And he never sold to Ringites, like rustler John Kinney.

For his rustling roundups, he used fellow Regulators - Tom O'Folliard, Charlie Bowdre, and Josiah "Doc" Scurlock (until he left for Texas in late 1879) - as well as toughs also working for Dan Dedrick, owner of Bosque Grande ranch, near Fort Sumner, and one recipient of his stolen stock. Dedrick's brothers, Sam and Mose, also had a livery in White Oaks, and accepted Billy's stock.

Since Dedrick was a counterfeiter too, his men, that Billy used for rustling - Billy Wilson and Tom Pickett - also passed fake bills; though Billy did not. And Billy's association with the White Oaks livery also placed him where the Dedricks did their counterfeiting business in partnership with a W.H. West aka William Budd.

Billy also sold stock to Pat Coghlan at Seven Rivers. And in *The Authentic Life of Billy the Kid*, Pat Garrett related his sale of stolen Chisum cattle to Colorado buyers at the Alamogordo, New Mexico, ranch of Alexander Grzelachowski. (Garrett, Page 86)

Billy also got money with a gambling circuit from Fort Sumner, to Anton Chico, to Las Vegas; being charged in August of 1879 in a Las Vegas court for keeping a gaming table.

Home base was Fort Sumner, with "Doc" Scurlock and his wife living there, as well as Charlie Bowdre's wife Manuela; with Charlie himself working at the nearby ranch of Thomas Yerby. But Billy's location choice was weighed by friendliness of the Maxwell family and his secret liaison teenaged Paulita Maxwell.

## REALITY OF THE SECRET SERVICE AND THE KID

There was no indication that counterfeiting in New Mexico Territory was large scale. As I discussed in my 2018 book, *The Santa Fe Ring Versus Billy the Kid*, the complaint appeared to be a Santa Fe Ring ruse to bring in the Secret Service to eliminate the last of the Regulators - and Billy Bonney in particular - seen by it as a potential instigator of another Hispanic uprising - like the Lincoln County War. The Ring preferred to kill with a guise of legality (like the embezzlement case to assassinate Tunstall, and Fort Stanton troops to enable murdering Alexander McSween); and Secret Service Operatives could pursue crimes other than counterfeiting. By 1880, either T.B. Catron, or his Washington, D.C.-based co-boss, Stephen Benton Elkins, could have accessed Secret Service Chief, James Brooks, for their purpose.

Sent to the Territory in mid-September of 1880 was Operative Azariah Wild, who stayed till the end of December. Gullible and lazy - opposite to Investigator for the Departments of Justice and the Interior, Frank Warner Angel, the year before - and likely unaware of the mission, he relied on Ringite informers, like James Dolan and T.B. Catron's brother-in-law and Carrizozo ranch manager, Edgar Walz, who eventually duped him into linking Billy's rustling to counterfeiting as one big gang, so he would focus pursuit on Billy and the remaining Regulators.

Adding credence to Wild's mission being against Regulators, not counterfeiters, was that, Operatives Arthur L. Drummond and Wallace W. Hall were concomitantly capturing major counterfeiter William Brockway and his gang; but Chief Brooks never told Wild. Instead, given a few bills by Ringite James Dolan, Wild only identified local counterfeiters: Dan Dedrick, his brothers, W.H. West, William Wilson, and Thomas Cooper.

And he refused to accuse Billy. Reporting for October 5, 1880, he wrote: *"There is an outlaw in the mountains here who came here from Arizona after committing a murder there named William Antrom alias W$^{\underline{m}}$ Bonney alias Billy Kid with whom these cattle thieves meet, and by many it is believed that they (the cattle thieves and shovers of the queer) receive the counterfeit money.* **I have found no evidence so far to support their suspicions.**"

By his October 10, 1880 report, Wild localized counterfeiting to White Oaks and Bosque Grande: *"William Wilson is reported to be at Bosque Grande at Dedricks ranch.* **Dedrick is reported as being one of the leaders of the clan [gang], and partners with [W.H.] West in the coral [sic] at White Oaks.**"

For his October 18, 1880 report, Wild quoted an informer, James Devours, employed by Ringite Edgar Walz, as stating: "**[T]heir presses and plates are in this county** *... [and] they have near $200,000 struck.*" For October 28$^{th}$, Wild reported: " *I am perfectly confident that* **there is a counterfeit gang** *here who are making counterfeit $100- and $50- notes as I am of anything that I do not know absolutely certain, and that I have not seen with my own eyes."* And Wild believed the printing was local: *'The leading man of this gang is W.H. West ... He left here before I came ... and is now in Topeka Kansas. He is one of the proprietors of a coral [sic] or stable at White Oaks. He has as partners several brothers named Dedrick who own a ranch near Fort Sumner. <u>It is at this ranch that it is believed the plates and tools are at the present time</u>."*

About that local gang, Wild reported for November 20, 1880, that his hired spy, Barney Mason, told him that Dan Dedrick was hiring him to buy Texas cattle with bad money, and bring them back to sell for good money. But slipshod Wild, bad at keeping his mission secret, frightened off the counterfeiters. In his report for November 27, 1880, he wrote that W.H. West and Dan Dedrick told Mason that they were holding off the deal until the *"excitement and trouble"* ended. James DeVours *"left the country for safety;"* and Dan Dedrick moved permanently to California.

Then Wild's Ring minders diverted him. For his report completed on October 18th in Lincoln, under the influence of Dolan and Walz, he listed *"outlaws"* [past Regulators], indicted federally by Catron for the "Buckshot" Roberts killing [which Wild garbled as *"the Indian Agent"*], and now based in Fort Sumner. And Wild turned from real counterfeiters in White Oaks, and Dedrick's ranch with possible plates, to focus on *"Charles Bowdre ... Billie Kid ... Dr. Joseph G. Scurlock ...Henry Brown ... Thomas O'Folliard [and] James French."* Adding minor bill pusher Billy Wilson, he called them a rustling-counterfeiting gang; and applied unlimited lethality. So for his November 1, 1880 report for October 31st, still in Lincoln, he hysterically declared another Lincoln County War, with his intent to *"arrest or kill the whole business."*

Wild's being a Ring dupe is shown by his report for November 10, 1880 about making criminal, John Kinney - the Ringite rustler of Chisum's cattle, perpetrator of the San Patricio massacre with Sheriff George Peppin, and murderous posseman in the Lincoln County War Battle - a Deputy U.S. Marshal to aid his pursuit of the men he now called the *"Wilson & Kid gang."*

And Wild, backing Pat Garrett in the Sheriff's election, made him a Deputy U.S. Marshal, and paid for his informers and posses to attack the Regulators. Reporting for November 10, 1880 about planning a raid on Fort Sumner using Garrett and Texans *"to arrest counterfeiters,"* he claimed it would *"break up the worst (organization) gang of men that this country has."*

But Billy would have been unaware of his risk. Reminiscent of his March 23, 1879 interview with Lew Wallace which yielded "Statements by Kid," in which he reported the Territorial underworld to Wallace as Santa Fe Ring-associated rustlers and murderers, he contacted Wild through his lawyer, Ira Leonard. For October 6, 1880, Wild reported that Billy had offered to testify against the counterfeiters in exchange for a pardon. But loose-lipped Wild informed his Ringite minders, and was persuaded, instead, to arrest Billy. Wary Billy (by then having lived through the treacherous murders of John Tunstall, Dick Brewer, Frank MacNab, Alexander McSween, Harvey Morris, Francisco Zamora, Vincente Romero, and Huston Chapman; and near assassination of Ira Leonard) robbed the mail-coach to check Wild's reports. Learning of the arrest plan, he backed out of the offer.

By his report for November 4, 1880, duped and dull Wild called William Wilson and William Antrom [sic] alias "Billy Bony" [sic] alias "Billy Kid" the gang's leaders. For his report for November 10, 1880, he stated that Garrett's posses would **"*break up the worst (organization) gang of men that this country has.*"** In his report for December 24, 1880, Wild wrote murderously: *"I have this day received information of an almost positive nature that Deputy U.S. Marshal P.F. Garrett had the Kid and Wilson at his mercy and that **he will either kill or arrest them**."* By empowering Garrett with Texan posses, Wild achieved killings of Tom O'Folliard, Charlie Bowdre, and, indirectly, Billy Bonney. Without his backing, Billy would not have been captured. Wild succeeded in his Ring assignment, without ever realizing it.

A year after leaving New Mexico Territory, and with input from Chief James Brooks, Wild finally saw a link to counterfeiter, William Brockway's main bill distributor, James B. Doyle; not only in New Mexico Territory, but as also to bills found in his summer of 1880 investigation in Sherman, Texas.

From New Orleans, for October 16, 1881, Wild reported to Brooks: *"I have the honor to acknowledge the receipt of your letter of the 13th instant in which you state that James B. Doyle the notorious counterfeiter has a brother who has just returned home to Bradford Ill from Santa Fe, Las Vegas and White Oaks New Mexico. I shall without delay make the necessary inquiries as directed."* Defensively, Wild cited his Sherman investigation of counterfeiter, Walter B. Greenham, who had committed suicide, but had met with a "stranger" named "Kibby," who then went to Kansas City (as Wild had reported on June 11, 1880); and whom he now saw as James Doyle's brother, Frank Doyle. Wild wrote: *"[Being in Texas] was at a time when I had not the least idea of going to New Mexico. On or soon after my arrival in New Mexico* **I learned [W.H.] West of White Oaks ... whose place was the headquarters of William Wilson, Tom Cooper and William Antrom, alias "Billy the Kid"** *had gone to Kansas and Colorado on business and that on his return he brought back with him to White Oaks a man who claimed to hail from New York and that his name was* Duncan. *From the best description I could get at the time, this man answered the description well enough to have been the same man who called himself Kibby at Sherman Texas. It was after West returned to White Oaks in company with this man that an effort was made to employ Barney Mason to go into Texas with $30,000 counterfeit money to purchase cattle &c. ... Soon as I get a description or photograph of [Frank] Doyle I will have no trouble in tracing him in New Mexico provided he is known there and is the man who accompanied West back from Kansas to White Oaks."*

Defensive about his erroneously focused investigation, Wild had kept Billy in his list. In reality, from Texas to New Mexico, he had merely seen Brockway's bill distribution sites to pushers like Greenham, West, and Dedrick. None of this connected to Billy or the other Regulators. So one can say that it was gullible, careless, and duped Azariah Wild who became a Ring tool to enable one of the first uses of the Secret Service for political murder; inadvertently adding himself to the long list of the Santa Fe Ring's hired killers of opponents.

## REALITY OF WILLIAM BROCKWAY'S COUNTERFEITING GANG

William E. "Long Bill" Brockway alias Edward W. Spencer, who died in 1920 at 97, was the most famous bill counterfeiter ("coneyman") of the second half of the 1800's, starting before the Civil War; and already featured as the master in George P. Burnham's *American Counterfeiters* in 1875. Working from Brooklyn, New York, with his engraver accomplice Charles H. Smith, he used as his main distributor ("shover of the queer") Illinois-based James Brace Doyle. With Doyle's brother, Frank Doyle, brother-in-law, Nathan B. "Nate" Foster, and a John W.

Hays, they passed near-perfect counterfeit bills around the country. The March, 1882 *Government Counterfeiter Detector*, featuring James Doyle in "The Boss of the Boodle and King of 'Outside Men,'" hypothesized that Brockway might have put into "circulation all the counterfeits of the National Bank Hundreds, which for several years have bothered the experts," with some even "sent to Europe." By October 21, 1880, Secret Service Operatives Andrew L. Drummond, focusing on Brockway and Smith, and Wallace W. Hall, tracking James B. Doyle, had achieved their arrest.

On November 25, 1880, Brockway turned over his plates in exchange for no jail time. The *Government Counterfeiter Detector's* June 30, 1881 "Annual Report of the Secret Service Division of the United States Treasury Department" by Chief James J. Brooks, reported that there were "twenty-two finely executed counterfeit plates for printing United States bonds and state National bank notes, two expensive ruling machines, one press; $40,000 in counterfeits notes, much fiber paper and other property." Smith likewise got immunity. With postponements, James Doyle started a 12 year sentence in 1882.

The gang's counterfeit $100 notes were listed in the *Secret Service Currency Reference Information: 1860's-1880's,* and John S. Dye's *Government Counterfeiter Detector* of February, 1882 as being made from skeleton plates, to which Smith added title plates for six banks: Merchants National Bank of New Bedford, Massachusetts; Second National Bank of Wilkes Barre, Pennsylvania; National Exchange Bank of Baltimore, Maryland; National Revere Bank of Boston, Massachusetts; Pittsfield National Bank of Pittsfield, Massachusetts; and Pittsburgh National Bank of Commerce, Pittsburgh, Pennsylvania.

On August 4, 1895, Brockway was rearrested for counterfeiting. Sentenced to 10 years, he was released early; though apparently still dabbled in his criminal craft.

## TRACING BROCKWAY'S PUSHERS

Brockway's bill distributors, going from New York, to the mid-West and West, were James and Frank Doyle, Nate Foster, John Hays and William H. West. They sold to locals, who passed bills or money-laundered; as intended by the Dedricks by stock-buying. For themselves, the Doyles, Foster, and Hays purchased stores, a farm, saloons, and mines. **Despite their name-dropping in Sederwall's counterfeiting hoax, these distributors did not** do Dedrick-style money-laundering with cattle; nor were they "cattle buyers" in Colorado or involved in rustling.

Operative Wallace Hall followed these main distributors. About the Doyle brothers, he reported for October 10, 1881 that they had been associated with Brockway since he and Smith had visited them in Bradford, Illinois in 1875. Hall traced their bill-distributing travels. For October 10, 1881, he reported Frank Doyle, then in Bradford, had returned that July *"from a year absence in the south-west,"* with cited places as *"Las Vegas, Santa Fe and White Oaks New Mexico."* And Nate Foster, then in Blakely's Mills, Colorado, had also been in *"Las Vegas and Santa Fe, New Mexico, also Colorado Springs, Colorado."*

About John Hays, Hall reported on February 24, 1881 that a "boodle" (bunch of counterfeit bills) was found in his Moundville, Missouri, farms's haystack. Hays also passed bills in Missouri; and, in 1880, fellow-distributor, W.H. West, stayed at his farm and store. And James Doyle's wife, once he was apprehended, had moved to Deer Trail, Colorado, where her father had a cattle ranch. **[Note that both Colorado and this ranch would be misstated for Sederwall's hoax, to fake a cattle-buying-rustling- money-laundering site.]**

Hall's report for May 19, 1882 recorded their purchases. In about May of 1881, Nate Foster *"had a saloon in White Oaks New Mexico. That Hays Frank Doyle, and others ... were with him. Hays was engaged in mining ... in the vicinity of White Oaks, N.M. That Hays about a year ago [May, 1881] passed a cft hundred on a clothing merchant in Denver ... in payment of a clothing account of Nate Foster's."* And West passed the counterfeit hundreds in New Mexico (with real name William Budd). All were in Nevada, Missouri in 1880, before going to White Oaks. And Hall concluded that they had stored the bills in Hays's Moundville haystack.

For July 1, 1882, Hall traced James Doyle's wife's brother, Nate Foster, to Deer Trail, Colorado; thence to New York to get $20,000 in counterfeit $100 bills; James Doyle, taking them to Colorado and Frank Doyle. They passed some in Colorado. Then Frank Doyle, Nate Foster, and John Hays *"went to New Mexico and Texas where more of the notes were passed. Hays and some of the party later located in Nevada, Missouri. Eventually, however, again all went to New Mexico, and Texas, where they engaged in the saloon business, mining speculations, &c,&c."*

For October 7, 1882, Hall reported that *"young Doyle – James B's son – and Nathan Foster were in Colorado."* Thus, Brockway's "passers of the queer" were untouched, and now were in a new generation with "young Doyle."

As to the Brockway gang's bill distribution in New Mexico, from W.H. West in White Oaks, they went to the Dedricks; with Dan possibly also having plates and press at his Bosque Grande ranch. Their cattle-buying-money-laundering scheme was uncovered by Azariah Wild's spy, Barney Mason, and described in Wild's report completed on November 21, 1880. (See pages 627-628 below) They also used local pushers for smaller quantities of bills: men identified by Wild in his report completed on November 28, 1880: *"[My spy, Mason,] saw* **William Wilson** *on last Sunday night have a long talk with [W.H.] West, [Dan] Dedrick &* ***[Tom] Cooper****. That it was agreed that Cooper was to go to El Paso and return by the 16th of December. That Cooper had just purchased a fine horse at San Marical for which he (Cooper) paid $150 ... That he (Mason) was given to understand the horse was paid for in counterfeit money."*

Azariah Wild unwittingly linked the local counterfeiters to Brockway's gang by identifying the banks on notes when describing a defect of pin-holes in the paper. In his report for October 4, 1880, he listed them as the National Revere Bank of Boston, Massachusetts passed to William Dowlin, and the Merchants National Bank of New Bedford, paid to José Montaño. He also stated that a $100 bill passed by Wilson on August 5, 1880 to James Dolan was from the Merchants National Bank of New Bedford, Massachusetts. And that Cooper passed to the clerk of Dowlin & Delaney a counterfeit National Revere Bank of Boston Massachusetts. For October 10, 1880, he reported that past Indian Agent, Frederick Godfroy, got a $100 counterfeit bill from Wilkes Barre Second National Bank of Wilkes Barre, Pennsylvania, which traced to the banker husband of John Chisum's niece.

The big picture was that William Brockway's gang, James B. Doyle, Frank Doyle, Nate Foster, and John W. Hays, distributed bills in Illinois, Missouri, Colorado, Texas, and New Mexico Territory. For New Mexico, the courier was William Budd, alias William H. West, whose partners, the Dedrick brothers, planned to launder bills by stock sales; and, in turn, used minor pushers, like William Wilson, Tom Cooper, and Tom Pickett. None of this involved Billy Bonney. But the outcome was that none of the real counterfeiters got significant punishment. And non-counterfeiter Billy got death.

# STEVE SEDERWALL'S COUNTERFEITING ARTICLES

Steve Sederwall first presented his hoax in 2010 and 2015 articles fabricating a link between Brockway's counterfeiting and Billy Bonney's rustling as a national money-laundering scheme.

At the time, he was also forging Dr. Henry Lee reports for my open records litigation in the "Billy the Kid Case." On March 9, 2010, he provided his first forged Lee floorboard report. On November 10, 2010, he gave me his forged Lee carpenter's bench report. At January 21, 2011's Evidentiary Hearing, he gave the Court a second forged Lee floorboard report as Exhibit F, and the forged Lee carpenter's bench report as Exhibit E.

And it was on July 16, 2010 that he presented to the *Ruidoso News* his "discovery" that Billy the Kid was actually a national-level counterfeiter. Since the hoax was expanded for 2018's *Cold Case Billy the Kid*, it is more extensively debunked for it.

## "COUNTERFEIT BANK NOTE REWRITES CHAPTER OF BILLY THE KID"|

On July 16, 2010, "Billy the Kid Case" hoax-backing, reporter, Julie Carter, published "Counterfeit Bank Note Rewrites Chapter of Billy the Kid" in the *Ruidoso News*. A $100 bank note was captioned: **"The front view of a counterfeit bank note passed in Lincoln County by Billy the Kid and his gang. William Brockway ... printed it from the plate the Secret Service recovered the day before Thanksgiving in 1880. The plate had been engraved by Charles Smith, a government employee whose job was engraving Federal currency plates. The note was located by the United States Secret Service in their vault in Washington, D.C., January 2010."** Added was Sederwall's helper: U.S. Marshals Service Historian David Turk. This was Sederwall's tale:

> In January of 2010, Sederwall called the Secret Service and spoke with Michael Sampson, of the public affairs office [sic – archivist].
>
> "I told him I was looking for evidence that they might have in their vault from a case in the 1880's," Sederwall said. "He politely laughed, but after telling him why I was looking, I gave him the dates [sic- of] the counterfeit that Wilson had passed had been recovered, the name of the bank, along with the serial numbers of both notes that we found documented in [Billy] Wilson's [counterfeiting] indictments.

Sampson returned the call a day later with good news. "The notes were in a file with no paperwork," he said. Until now, no one had any idea what the notes were or why they were there." [So David Turk, being local, picked them up. And Sampson then helped them sort it all out "working the case backwards."]

**DECEPTION:** For this book, I called archivist Michael Sampson. He told me what actually happened. In 2010, Sederwall contacted him requesting counterfeit bills obtained by Azariah Wild in New Mexico Territory. Sampson told him there were none in the files. So Sederwall requested <u>any counterfeit bill from the period</u>. He was given a random bill. It had no documented connection to Wild or Billy; and was not filed as a Brockway bill, though it is from a bank used in Brockway's plates. But, on this lie, Sederwall built his hoax; along with his fellow "Billy the Kid Case" hoaxer, David Turk.

To be noted is that Billy was never accused of passing counterfeit bills. Wild saw him as a rustler and murderer, linked to counterfeiters in the "Wilson & Kid gang."

Sederwall next made-up that Wild found no plates in New Mexico, because there were 22 plates found for "three different Eastern banks;" which meant "organized crime ... much bigger than recorded by historians." So David Turk, like in his fake carpenter's bench authentication (see page 404 above), stated that the bills were made in New York, went to Chicago, "then branched out into Texas, Missouri, Colorado, New Mexico, and Mexico."

**FAKERY:** This introduces the turned-over Brockway plates. They had nothing to do with Billy Bonney.

Turk then made-up that the counterfeiters intended to "buy stolen cattle and use fake bills of sale to launder the money."

**FAKERY: This garbles Wild's report from spy, Barney Mason, of Dan Dedrick's cattle-buying money-laundering plot. Rustling was not involved. But Sederwall's hoax adds rustling, as for money-laundering, for a fake link to Billy.**

Next came disjointed claims. James Dolan, who reported getting counterfeit bills to the Secret Service, is called a counterfeiter himself, from an alleged August, 1880 letter to the Secret Service by a woman in Chicago. A non sequitor to 1878, claims the Secret Service was investigating counterfeiter William Brockway, and plate maker, Charles Smith. That leapt to:

"[The Secret Service] knew about the cattle theft operation run by the Kid and his gang used to launder some of the money."

FAKERY: Dolan as a counterfeiter came from a misreading Operative Wallace W. Hall's report for August 24, 1880 about a Miss N.M. Ferguson of Chicago and a counterfeit bill involving merchant Will <u>Dowlin</u>, not James <u>Dolan</u>.

Made-up is that the Secret Service claimed Billy had a rustling-money-laundering gang. Wild's late 1880 investigation only accused Billy of having a gang. That made Billy write on December 12, 1880 to Governor Lew Wallace: "*I noticed in the Las Vegas Gazette a piece which stated that, Billy "the" Kid, the name by which I am known in the Country was the captain of a Band of Outlaws who hold Forth at the Portales. There is no such Organization in Existence. So the Gentleman must have drawn very heavily on his Imagination.*"

Next thrown in was that in November of 1880, the Secret Service caught Brockway, Charles Smith, and James Doyle, the distributor; and found the 22 plates. **Sederwall stated: "Brockway provided answers to the Secret Service's questions, including how the bank notes were getting in to New Mexico and Colorado. Simply put, they were buying cattle from a group of cattle thieves in White Oaks, N.M.: Billy the Kid and his gang.**" So Sederwall claimed his "investigation" proved the Brockway counterfeiting gang was arrested by the Secret Service before Garrett even pursued them. So Garrett deserved no credit.

FAKERY: Made-up is that Brockway did rustling-counterfeit money-laundering. He printed and sold bills. It was the Dedricks' group that passed bills, and intended to buy cattle for money-laundering. Billy played no part.

Added is usual hoaxers' maligning of Garrett, by faking that capturing Brockway meant capturing his "gang" in New Mexico; when just minor passers, Billy Wilson and Tom Pickett, were captured with Billy Bonney.

Cited is a January 6, 1881 article of the Long Port, Indiana, *Long Port Journal* about Brockway's bills there. But Sederwall adds: "The information that enabled the Government officers to fix the handling of counterfeit money upon the Kid's gang came from a freighter named Smith. Soon afterward, while Smith was on his way from Las Vegas to Fort Sumner, with a load of freight, he was waylaid and murdered by some of the gang."

**FAKERY: Murdered Smith is a fable Sederwall lifted from fake press. This fakery is exposed in his recycling of it in *Cold Case Billy the Kid*. (See pages 648-649 below)**

The article ended with Sederwall's blather about the carpenter's bench, the shot washstand, and Billy's not taking a "rifle" from dead Brady's body; adding that he was "shedding new light on the story of Billy the Kid," and was making a website titled www.billythekidcase.com.

**BLOWING SMOKE: Sederwall was advertising Sederwall.** And his website was selling Case 2003-274's public documents, while he was hiding them in my open records litigation. That outrage helped me win. The Judge stated in his May 15, 2014 "Findings of Fact": "In their June 21, 2007 "Memorandum" to Virden, Sullivan and Sederwall admitted to having Case 2003-274 records, but called them private property ... Furthermore, from 2010 to 2012, Sederwall offered Case 2003-274 records for sale on his own billythekidcase.com website."

## *"BILLY THE KID'S BAD BUCKS"*

Five years later, Sederwall expanded his counterfeiting fiction in fellow "Billy the Kid Case" hoaxer and editor, Bob Boze Bell's *True West* magazine of June, 2015, as "Billy Bonney's Bad Bucks: Did the Kid Travel the Counterfeit Trail?" For it, Sederwall proclaimed: "With all we know about Billy the Kid, most do not know that he was part of a counterfeiting ring."

This time, he faked that Billy was in counterfeiting cahoots with Jesse James. **[Concealed was that the source was a possible 1879 sighting of Billy <u>eating a meal</u> with James in a Las Vegas hotel. And James was not a counterfeiter.]**

He also made-up that Billy was in a cattle rustling-counterfeit-money-laundering scheme with Brockway's pusher, John Hays. **[The fake reasoning had Hays in the Civil War, as was Jesse James; so that connected Hays to Billy via James. But Hays was not connected to James or Billy.]**

Then was claimed that Billy "had stolen cattle in the Panhandle for John Chisum's ranch, and the rancher had not paid him as promised. The Kid stole the cattle back." **[This fakery garbled Billy's claim that Chisum had not paid him and the Regulators promised wages in the Lincoln County War period, and may have rustled from him as a**

**consequence.**] As proof, a Lane Cook, called Tom Folliard's [sic] cousin, was cited as stealing Chisum's cattle to sell to Hays for counterfeit money, which Lane laundered in Kansas City, Missouri. **[This fake scenario was built on two separate lies: misstating old-timer Jim (Lane) Cook's 1936 book,** *Lane of the Llano's* **different tall tale (see pages 632-636 below); and making-up Tom O'Folliard's name and genealogy, then connecting it to Jim Cook. (See pages 657-660 below).]**

To get to New Mexico Territory, Sederwall made-up an elaborate fable with merchant, James Dolan, as a "cattleman" passing counterfeit bills in Tularosa in 1880, which brought in Secret Service Operative Azariah Wild, who caught him; making Dolan lie that he got the bills from Billy Wilson. **[This re-ran Sederwall's original garbling of a Miss N.M. Ferguson reporting a counterfeit bill connected to New Mexico's <u>Dowlin</u> [not <u>Dolan</u>] & Company, with one letter from M.J. <u>Dowlin</u> from <u>Tularosa</u>. (See pages 644-647 below)]**

This hogwash was Sederwall's lead-up to his faked find of a Wild investigation bill. This version had U.S. Marshals Service Historian David Turk "locate the sample of counterfeit that matched the bill described in [Billy] Wilson's 1881 indictment." **["Match" hides its being a random bill to trick the reader into thinking it was connected to Wild and Billy Bonney.]**

Then made-up is that "**four days** after Dolan pointed the finger at Wilson, the Kid offered to be a government snitch." **[There was no connection. Wild reported to Chief Brooks for September 20, 1880 that he had met in Santa Fe with U.S. Attorney Sidney Barnes and James Dolan, who reported the bill. Billy's pardon bargain of testifying against the counterfeiters was initiated by his attorney, Ira Leonard, weeks later, as Wild reported on October 8, 1880.]**

Sederwall alleged that Billy's "snitching" was because a "man named Smith [told Wild that] the Kid was reading his reports while they were in possession of mail carrier Mike Cosgrove." **[This fable lifted the fake report of Smith's murder in a December 22, 1880** *New York Sun* **article. The Kid's reading reports came from Wild's reporting, on October 21, 1880, Billy's single October 16, 1880 mail coach theft during the pardon negotiation, in which cautious Billy checked Wild's reports, learned his arrest plan, and stopped the negotiation. And Mike Cosgrove, a mail contractor, not a** mail carrier, was not connected, except for giving captured Billy a new suit, as described in a December 27, 1880 *Las Vegas Daily Gazette* article by Lucius "Lute" Wilcox about the Stinking Springs capture titled 'The Kid. Interview with Billy Bonney The Best Known Man in New Mexico."

Sederwall, however, using Cosgrove's giving suits and wrongly thinking he was a mail carrier, made-up that it was a ploy to get Billy alone to plead with him not to reveal that he had let Billy read Wild's reports! [**This is Sederwall's wild fictionalizing.**]

Sederwall ended with his 2010 fakery that Garrett had not broken "the counterfeit ring in Lincoln County," because it was broken by Brockway's arrest. He added that Billy's bad bills had bought Lincoln County businesses, livestock, and mining claims.

## THE RETURN OF SEDERWALL'S COUNTERFEITING FICTION

For *Cold Case Billy the Kid*, Sederwall, as mouthed by W.C. Jameson, inflated his hoax; declaring: "For reasons not understood ... every writer who treated the Lincoln County War and Billy the Kid either completely ignored or provided all too brief attention to the issue of counterfeit money." He added that involved in the counterfeiting were "Billy Wilson ... W.W. West, James J. Dolan ... Billy the Kid ... and Jesse James." (Pages 68-69)

**FAKERY: Counterfeiting was not a Lincoln County War event; the War being in 1878. Operative Azariah Wild came at the end of 1880. And Sederwall has falsely linked Billy, Dolan, and Jesse James to counterfeiters West and Wilson.**

Sederwall's hoax now had Billy the Kid partnering Jesse James in national-level counterfeiting with the Brockway gang in a money-laundering racket involving cattle rustled from John Chisum, sold in Colorado to Brockway's gang, and with Billy's murdering informer Sam Smith, who told Azariah Wild the plot.

### *PULP FICTION INSPIRATION*

Though not cited in the Bibliography, Sederwall's obvious source was the Ring's key Billy the Kid outlaw myth article in Billy's lifetime: the December 22, 1880 *New York Sun's* "Outlaws of New Mexico, The Exploits of a Band Headed by a New York

Youth, The Mountain Fastness of the Kid and His Followers - War Against a Gang of Cattle Thieves and Murderers - The Frontier Confederates of Brockway, the Counterfeiter." [APPENDIX: 12] Sederwall's use is proved by his lifting its error of Billy the Kid gang's murdering a freighter named Smith - much like nabbing "Brushy's" team's cribbing from their erroneous sources.

The article was mere pulp-fiction, as illustrated by its fictional Billy the Kid and Lincoln County War: "About three years ago a difficulty arose in Lincoln County, New Mexico, between the stockmen and the Indian agent on the reservation. The trouble arose in regard to some cattle that had been purchased for the Indians. Nearly every man in the county was under arms, and the troops were called out by Gov. Wallace to quell the disturbance. The Kid was mixed up in the affair, and had some narrow escapes. On one occasion he was hotly pursued and was obliged to take refuge in a house in Lincoln, which was surrounded by sixty solders. To the demand to surrender, he only laughed and shot down a soldier just to show that he was game. The house was set on fire, when the Kid, after loading up his Winchester Rifle, leaped from the burning building and made a dash for liberty. All the while he was running he kept firing from his Winchester, bringing down a number of his pursuers. Bullets whistled over his head, but he made his escape, and leaping on a horse was soon laughing at his pursuers. There is no telling how many men he has killed. He sets no value on human life, and has never hesitated at murder when it would serve his purpose."

Tacked on were William Brockway and his accomplice, James Doyle: "Government officials are now interested in the campaign [to catch the Wilson-Kid gang], for, in addition to their other crimes, the outlaws have put in circulation a large quantity of the counterfeit money manufactured by William Brockway, the forger. The bills were obtained by one of the gang named Doyle who formerly operated in Chicago, and counterfeit $100 bills in large numbers have been put in circulation among the stockmen and merchants in all that region."

**FAKERY: This article likely inspired Sederwall's hoax. But it likely just added New Yorker Brockway just as a local hook, with his being just arrested there in late October.**

## *FAKING A LINK TO A COUNTERFEIT BILL*

Sederwall repeated his July 16, 2010 *Ruidoso News* article's photo of a $100 bill which he had labeled as "a counterfeit bank note passed in Lincoln County by Billy the Kid and his gang." Now it was labeled as "[a] counterfeit hundred-dollar bill passed in Lincoln County, New Mexico, during the 1880's." (Page 77)

DECEPTION: This is the random bill from Secret Service archivist, Michael Sampson, with faked connection to Lincoln County, Azariah Wild, and Billy Bonney.

## *FAKING SOURCES AS A BROCKWAY LINK*

*Cold Case Billy the Kid's* Bibliography cites three Brockway articles and some Secret Service reports, misleadingly implying that they were sources for linking Billy to Brockway.

An October 24, 1880 *New York Times* article, "Old Counterfeiters Caught, Brockway and Two Others Arrested as J.B. Doyle's Accomplices," was about the Brooklyn, New York, arrests of Brockway as king-pin; Jasper Owens as printer; and William H. Smythe [sic - Charles Smith] as engraver. J.B. Doyle was the passer, apprehended at his transport of a valise of Brockway bills from New York to Chicago. That was it.

A May 6, 1882 *New York Times's* "Brockway's Forged Bonds: The Counterfeiter Telling How Doyle Got the Bonds - Curious Statements in Court," had Doyle's Chicago trial, with Brockway testifying that Doyle did not know the bills were bad. That was it.

Lastly was a syndicated "True Detective Stories," by Operative Andrew L. Drummond, titled "A Genius Who Went Wrong," from the December 20, 1908 *New York Herald* about his capture of Brockway; with Operative Wallace W. Hall's tracking of James Doyle; and Brockway and Smith with no jail time for surrendering the plates, and Doyle getting 12 years in prison. That was it.

Cited also were some Secret Service reports. Those of Andrew L. Drummond and Wallace W. Hall were about the Brockway case, with tracing his bills westward to Illinois, Missouri, Colorado, Texas and New Mexico Territory. Focus was on James Doyle as the major pusher, who, as Drummond stated in his report for June 3, 1881, *"traveled East and West quite often."* Hall, most involved in tracing bill distribution, was cited for his report of August 24, 1880 about a Miss N.M. Ferguson reporting a counterfeit bill gotten in New Mexico Territory; for his report for January 24, 1881 about counterfeit bills being found in a Moundville, Missouri, haystack on John W. Hay's farm, along with Hays's association with W.H. West and White Oaks; his report for October 10, 1881 which traced the Brockway-associated Doyle brothers to Las Vegas, Santa Fe and White Oaks New Mexico; his report for May 19, 1882 referencing Frank Doyle, Nate Foster, and John W. Hays as in Deer Trail, Colorado, and White Oaks, New

Mexico, with linking their bills from the Moundville, Missouri, haystack to the one gotten by Miss Ferguson in Santa Fe; his report for June 17, 1882 announced that James Doyle had finally started his prison term; his report for July 8, 1885 revealed that William Doyle, son of James Doyle, had counterfeit plates in the Bradford, Illinois, area; and his June 30, 1885 report stated that $100 counterfeit notes being passed in Denver, Colorado, were likely left over "*Foster-Doyle notes.*" And Azariah Wild's reports cited his Sherman, Texas, and New Mexico findings of local pushers, only later linked by him to Frank Doyle,

**FAKERY: The sources showed no link to Billy or rustling. They were used for name-dropping Brockway's history, and his gang members to make fake links to Billy the Kid.**

## *FAKING A LINK TO BILLY'S RUSTLING*

Sederwall's centerpiece in framing Billy Bonney as a counterfeiter, was his convoluted fabrication that Billy's rustling was actually a multi-state counterfeit money-laundering scheme, making Billy central to the Brockway gang's bill distribution.

### FAKING PAT GARRETT AS A SOURCE

Sederwall's hoax was built on faking one Pat Garrett quote. He claimed that Garrett stated that John Chisum owed Billy money for services in the Lincoln County War, so Billy and his "gang" accepted cattle in trade; then rebranded them and sold them "to a group of 'Colorado beef buyers" with Billy telling them "he was working for John Chisum;" but Chisum took them back. (Page 68) Sederwall asked why Billy changed brands if he worked for Chisum; and claimed that the Colorado beef buyers bought the cattle with counterfeit money, which was why they could not go to the law when Chisum took them back. (Page 69)

**FAKERY: This misstated Garrett to add the hoax's key lie: that "<u>Colorado beef buyers</u>" meant Brockway's pushers!**

**Also, Billy was not employed by Chisum. In 1878, when Chisum was in business with John Tunstall and was his Lincoln Bank president, Chisum offered to pay Tunstall's employees - like Billy. But he never did - even when they fought the Lincoln County War. And Chisum never traded cattle to Billy as payment. That is why Billy did retaliative rustling against him.**

Pat Garrett's actual quotation in *The Authentic Life of Billy the Kid* about Billy's settling up the Chisum debt was: "In April [of 1879], they returned to Fort Sumner and resumed depredations on loose stock ... In October of 1879, the Kid with O'Folliard, Bowdre, Scurlock, and two Mexicans rounded up and drove away from Bosque Grande ... one hundred and eighteen head of cattle, which were the property of Chisum. They drove them to Yerby's ranch in his absence, branded them, and turned them lose on the range ... They said Chisum owed them $600 each, for services rendered during the War. They afterwards drove those cattle to Grzelachowski's ranch at Alamo Gordo, and sold them to <u>Colorado beef buyers</u>, telling them they were employed in <u>settling up</u> Chisum's business. Chisum followed the cattle up, recovered them, and drove them back to his range." (Garrett, Page 118)

First of all, Garrett was not an historian. In April of 1879, Billy was still jailed in Juan Patrón's Lincoln house in the Lew Wallace pardon bargain, and did not leave until June. But Garrett made clear that Billy's retaliative rustling was for Chisum's debt, and not getting cattle in trade. So Billy rebranded them. Sederwall's claiming that Billy told the Colorado buyers that he "was working for" Chisum, misread Garrett's "settling up Chisum's business," which meant taking care of the debt his own way.

As to the unnamed "Colorado beef buyers," Sederwall based his hoax in pretending they were Brockway's Colorado pushers. But <u>*they* were not beef buyers</u>! And Billy's deal was made through Alexander Grzelachowski. And Chisum's recovery shows only that he proved ownership. Also, for Sederwall's fable, if Colorado buyers paid in counterfeits, Billy was a victim, not a counterfeiter!

Sederwall had lifted and modified rustling-counterfeit-money-laundering from the unrelated plot of real counterfeiter Dan Dedrick, as told to Azariah Wild by his Fort Sumner spy, Barney Mason. Reporting from Lincoln for November 20, 1880 on November 21st, Wild revealed the scheme <u>to buy cattle with bad money, with resale for good money</u>. To note, is that the bill courier was W.H. West, accompanied by a New Yorker, likely Brockway's Frank Doyle, as Wild decided a year later. All this had no <u>connection to Billy or to rustling</u>. Wild reported:

*He (Mason) states that a few days ago one Daniel Dedrick who resides at Bosque Grande, and who has an interest with his brother Samuel Dedrick & West in a livery stable at White Oaks came to him and proposed as follows:*

"*I (Daniel Dedrick) want to employ you (Barney Mason). That after a short conversation with Dedrick he (Dedrick) stated that he wanted me (Mason) to take a lot of counterfeit money down to the Rio Grande on Texas and buy up all the cattle. I (Mason) could bring them to a point near New Mexico turn them over to him (Dedrick) and West give them a square bill of sale of the same and I (Mason) to then leave the country and go to Mexico and from there wheresoever I pleased.*"

*That when West returned a few days since he brought with him $30,000 in counterfeit money which had been made from a new plate, and from which had not yet been "spotted."*

*Mason goes on to state that Daniel Dedrick informed him that when West recently returned to White Oaks that one man who hailed from New York came with him and was there at the time.* "*To the best of his memory he (Dedrick) called the man Duncan and that he was pretending to represent J.H. Hardin of New York.*"

*Mason stated that Dedrick informed him that they could get all the counterfeit money they desired from West, and that he was given to understand that the money came from the New York stranger who came with West on his return to White Oaks.*

*Mason states that William Wilson boards at his house when at Fort Sumner. That he has seen him [with] counterfeit money at various times. That he (Mason) knows he Wilson passed a $100- on a saloon keeper named [Beaver] Smith at Fort Sumner. That he (Smith) sent it to the bank and had it returned as counterfeit. That Wilson laughed at Smith and agreed to redeem it with good money although Wilson told him (Mason) that he was only letting the old man (Smith) down easy.*

In that same report for November 20, 1880, Wild made clear Billy's separate rustling, using Billy Wilson; writing: "*That William Wilson & Billy Kid left about the 15th inst with sixty head of stolen horses and went down the Canadian River to be gone two or three weeks. That on their return they would probably return to his [Mason's] house when he would turn them over to Patrick F. Garrett Deputy U.S. Marshal and Sheriff elect.*"

On November 28, 1880, for November 27th, Wild reported that the Mason deal was put on hold, with the gang apparently spooked by his investigation. Wild wrote: "[Mason] *saw West and Dedrick about the sending of him to purchase cattle on the Rio Grande with counterfeit money. That they say they will not do anything in the matter until the present excitement and trouble is over.*"

Garrett, knowledgeable, with Barney Mason as his friend, confirmed the money-laundering scheme, making clear it had no connection to Billy or rustling, in his 1882 *The Authentic Life of Billy the Kid*: "[Mason] told me that he had stopped at Bosque Grande ... at the ranch of Dan Dedrick and that Dan had read him a letter from W.H. West, partner of his brother, Sam Dedrick, in the stable business in White Oaks. The gist of the letter was that West has $30,000 in counterfeit greenbacks and that he intended to take this money to Mexico, there buy cattle with it, and then drive them back across the state line. He wanted to secure the services of a reliable assistant whose business would be to accompany him to Mexico, make sham purchases of the cattle as fast as they were bought, receive bills of transfer so that in case of detection the stock would be found in the legal possession of the apparently innocent party. West's letter went on to suggest Barney Mason as just the man to assume the role of scapegoat in these nefarious traffickings." (Garrett, Page 140)

But Sederwall slipped in Brockway's gang members: "The Secret Service learned that four men living in Colorado - James and Frank Doyle, John Hays, and Nate Foster - were **buying cattle with counterfeit money**." Then he made-up: "**They were the Colorado beef buyers mentioned by Pat Garrett** who paid for cattle delivered to them by Billy the Kid." (Pages 76-77)

FAKERY: Sederwall's hoax was built on his making-up that Brockway's gang bought "cattle with counterfeit money" and were the "Colorado beef buyers" Garrett mentioned.

In fact, Operative Wallace W. Hall traced the Doyles, Hays, and Foster to Colorado, among many places. But they were pushers. To frame Billy, Sederwall made-up a connection of cattle buying to rustling (unlike Dedrick's buying-with-bad-selling-for-good plot); used the pushers' "Colorado" location; and faked it made them "Colorado beef buyers" cited by Garrett. Made-up is that Billy delivered the cattle. And how rustled cattle could launder money is unexplained. In fact, Sederwall showed no link to Billy.

## *FAKING A NATIONAL COUNTERFEITER BILLY*

To fake Billy the Kid as operating on a national level, Sederwall cited Azariah Wild's summer of 1880 Sherman, Texas, investigation; and claimed Wild knew the counterfeiting extended beyond Texas. So Sederwall added New Mexico, and said the counterfeiting ranged from New York to the Southwest. (Page 71)

FAKERY: Sederwall was merely describing Brockway's national bill distributions to local pushers, unrelated to Billy. And rustling-money-laundering was not present.

Wild's Sherman, Texas, investigation was initially of local counterfeiting by a Walter Greenham, his family, and business associates. And there was no cattle plot. Wild's going to New Mexico at the end of that year for the West-Dedrick counterfeiting case was unrelated in his mind to his Sherman investigation.

A year later, however, with input on the Brockway gang by Chief James Brooks, Wild linked Greenham's Texas bills to Brockway's pushers, James Doyle and his brother Frank. (See pages 613-614 above). He then decided that Frank Doyle was also providing counterfeit bills to White Oaks's W.H. West, and thus to the Dedricks.

Sederwall cited Operative Wallace W. Hall's reports about John Hays's "boodle" in his Missouri farm's haystack, with his connections to Frank Doyle, Nate Foster, and New Mexico.

FAKERY: This is just more Brockway history, without any link to Billy the Kid. (See page 616 above)

## FAKING EVIDENCE FOR BILLY AS DOING MONEY-LAUNDERING RUSTLING IN CONNECTION WITH BROCKWAY'S GANG

Since no evidence existed that Billy's rustling connected to counterfeiting, money-laundering, or Brockway's gang, Sederwall faked it. First used in his June 2015 *True West's* "Billy Bonney's Bad Bucks," it had an alleged "eye witness" named **Lane** Cook. (Pages 71-72) [For that article, he made Lane Cook Tom O'Folliard's cousin, selling rustled Chisum cattle to a man named Hays to money-launder in Kansas City, Missouri.]

For this rerun, Sederwall rewrote his fable. He had Billy and Tom O'Folliard, in 1879, riding to the South Llano River ranch of a **Jim** Cook in "Texas Hill Country," and telling "old friend" Cook that John Chisum owed him and O'Folliard money, "and how they planned to collect." Cook is quoted as saying that Billy and Tom would go to the Pecos and round up 3,200 "of Uncle Johnny's steers," and give him a bill of sale for them. Cook was to drive them to Kansas to sell, pay himself, and return with the remaining money for Billy. Sederwall adds: "**The Kid specifically told Cook to sell the cattle in Honeywell, Kansas; take the money to Kansas city and deposit it; wait for three days; and then return to the bank and withdraw it.**" Cook did this and paid Billy $9,000.

Sederwall claimed that, to him, this is a "tell," because Kansas City was far away, and waiting three days was strange. So that meant "to have the money laundered;" meaning Cook had deposited bad money from the sale and gotten back good money.

That segued to Sederwall claiming: "Later the Secret Service pieced together the details of the criminal enterprise;" adding that it found "John Hays, [no first name] Doyle, and [no first name] Foster "at Deer Trail, Colorado, when the gang were operating in the counterfeit hundreds." He added it was Colorado because "**Hays's father-in-law owned a cattle ranch in Deer Trail ... Foster lived in Colorado ... [and] [t]hey were the 'Colorado beef buyers.** Buying and selling cattle was yet another way of laundering counterfeit money."

That segued to his claim that on June 8, 1880, the plot unraveled when the Vernon County bank in Nevada, Missouri, caught John Hays passing a counterfeit bill, which Hays admitted came from the "**Mastin Bank** in Kansas City." Tying this to his

Cook tale, Sederwall adds: "It was the **same bank** where Jim Cook deposited the money he received from the sale of John Chisum's cattle that had been stolen by Billy the Kid." (Page 72)

That segued to claiming the Mastin brothers founded the bank "with money from the Confederacy and that it catered to the beef industry." And the **Mastins**, as "Confederate sympathizers," were still trying "to collapse the Union's financial system" by saturating with bogus money. "Cook and Hays were laundering money at the **Mastin Bank** in Kansas City." (Page 73)

That segued to claiming the Secret Service exposed this when they found counterfeit money in John Hays's haystack. Added is that "Agent Wallace Hall learned from Nevada County residents that Hays had been shipping cattle from the west to Missouri. He also learned that Hays traveled to Kansas City on a number of occasions to deposit large sums of money at the **Mastin Bank**. It was determined that this was counterfeit money and the intention was to have it laundered at the bank." And the people doing it were in Deer Trail, Colorado. (Page 73)

That segued to claiming [no first name] Doyle and Foster fled to White Oaks. (Page 73)

**FAKERY:** This flimflam - like C.L. Sonnichsen's lies about the Coroner's Jury report and Garrett's reward - is a pinnacle of con-artistry. Like Sonnichsen's fakery, it needs dissection to show no connection to Billy, rustling, or money-laundering. But it was Sederwall's intent fake a rustling link counterfeit bill laundering.

1) **EYE-WITNESS COOK:** On "eye-witness," Jim (Lane) Cook, the fiction is built. The Bibliography cites James L. Cook's 1936 *Lane of the Llano: Being the Story of Jim (Lane) Cook as Told to T.M. Pearce*. Cook was an old-timer windbag. A 1936 review of his book by a J. Frank Dobie in *Southwest Review* called it "puerile invention." The Texas State Historical Society called it: "a bunch of the worst lies that would make Bill Burns, Zane Grey, and John Cook green with envy;" adding that historian, J. Evetts Haley, said he "failed to distinguish truth from fiction." Haley also wrote "Jim Cook: On the Frontiers of Fantasy" for Spring, 1964's *The Shamrock*, stating *he* wrote in the "frontiers of fantasy."

As examples, Cook claimed he worked for John Chisum, who stole cattle and horses *from him*. (Cook, Page 87) His

Lincoln County War fiction, adding himself, stated: "It was while I was working for Uncle John that trouble between rival cattle gangs started over at Lincoln. A band was stealing from Uncle John, and Chisum hired Billy the Kid to fight for him ... He promised Billy fifteen dollars a day as a fighter. The Kid rode in to Uncle John one day and said, 'Come on and go up to Lincoln with us. We're going to shoot up the town.' He had O'Folliard and five or six others with him ... Uncle John didn't go, but Billy and the rest of us did. When we got into Lincoln, the soldiers came in there with orders to get Billy dead or alive. We had to barricade ourselves in the McSween house. Mrs. McSween wasn't there. The boys played her piano and sang during the day while the bullets were coming into her house. McSween was killed when he stepped out the door to talk to the commander of the soldiers. Eventually the soldiers set fire to the roof, and at about twilight the Kid decided to make a break. There was a long adobe wall which ran to the house and down to the creek. We broke out along this wall – Billy, Tom O'Folliard, myself, and some others. The Negro soldiers had placed themselves around two sides of the wall, and they couldn't fire at us without shooting each other ... After this fight ... [Chisum] sold out everything he had to some St. Louis merchants." (Pages 88-89)

Cook's fiction used by Sederwall stated:

> [My wife and I] had not been long at home [at his ranch on the South Llano] when Billy the Kid and Tom O'Folliard came to see us. They said they believed they had a plan how we could get our money out of Chisum ... Billy said he and Tom would go back on the Pecos and round up thirty-two hundred of Uncle Johnny's big steers, bringing them across to Paint Rock Crossing on South Llano River; close to our ranch. He would give me a bill of sale for them; I was to drive them to Kansas and sell them, pay myself, and bring him and Tom what was left ...
>
> In about thirty days Billy came back and said the thirty-two hundred big steers were at Paint Rock Crossing ready for me. He handed me a bill of sale. It had a signature on it and the name was Uncle John's.

I drove the steers to Honeywell, Kansas, and sold them without a hitch. I put the money in the <u>Master Bank of Kansas City</u>. [My wife] and I sewed nine thousand dollars in big bills up in our clothing ... We met the boys at Portales Springs ... I said to Billy and the others: "Now when you get this money, you go out of the country ... and settle down. You know I'm your friend. I'm the best friend you boys have got." They didn't take my advice. I never saw Billy again. He was killed at Fort Sumner two years later." (Pages 91-92)

So Cook's tale - besides being made-up - was about <u>selling rustled Chisum cattle to give Billy $9,000</u>. It was not about counterfeiting. And the bank was the "<u>Master</u> Bank of Kansas City; not Sederwall's "<u>Mastin Bank</u>."

To segue to his money-laundering fable, Sederwall made-up that: "The Kid specifically told Cook to sell the cattle in Honeywell, Kansas; take the money to Kansas city and deposit it; wait for three days; and then return to the bank and withdraw it;" which was not in Cook's tale.

2) THE MONEY-LAUNDERING LEAP: Having himself made-up the elaborate Cook-Kansas-City-Mastin-deposit, Sederwall claimed it proved money-laundering!

3) IMAGINARY SECRET SERVICE CONNECTION: Building on his fable, Sederwall added a non sequitor: "Later the Secret Service pieced together the details of the criminal enterprise," to feign the Secret Service as revealing the Cook-Billy-rustling-laundering; instead of just its actual, and unrelated, exposure of the Brockway gang.

4) IMAGINARY CONNECTION TO BROCKWAY'S AGENTS: Having falsely thrown in the Secret Service, Sederwall switched to the Brockway investigation, changed the scene to Colorado, added Brockway's agents, a Doyle [Frank or James unspecified] and Nate Foster, and quoted without citation: "at Deer Trail, Colorado, when the gang were operating in the counterfeit hundreds;" as if this tracked Billy to Colorado. But the quote was Operative Wallace Hall's for May 13, 1882 that J.B. Doyle was with Frank Doyle, Nate Foster, John W. Hays and others at

Deer Trail, Colorado *"when the gang were operating in the cft hundreds."* It had nothing to do with Billy.

5) IMAGINARY CONNECTION TO A COLORADO CATTLE RANCH: Building on "Colorado," Sederwall made-up that "Hays's father-in-law owned a cattle ranch in Deer Trail ... Foster lived in Colorado ... [and] [t]hey were the 'Colorado beef buyers.' Buying and selling cattle was yet another way of laundering counterfeit money." But the father-in-law is faked. The real father-in-law with the ranch was James Doyle's wife's father. After Doyle's arrest, she had gone home to wait out the proceedings. And the statement that cattle transactions were to launder money, was lifted from the unrelated Dan Dedrick-Barney Mason plot reported by Azariah Wild for November 18th and 20th, 1880.

Most deceitful, is Sederwall's claim that Hays and Doyle "were the "Colorado beef buyers," going back to the starting point of his hoax with faking Pat Garrett's *The Authentic Life of Billy the Kid*, about Billy selling rustled Chisum cattle to "Colorado beef buyers" at Grzelachowski's ranch (Garrett, Page 118), to mean that Billy sold to Brockway's agent John Hays. Except Brockway's agents were not beef buyers. And "Colorado" did not mean it had to be them!

So faked was Billy as a counterfeiter, Jim Cook's Kansas sale, and link to Brockway's men in Colorado.

6) IMAGINARY MASTIN BANK LINK: Continuing his money-laundering fiction, Sederwall added the "Mastin Bank in Kansas City," with a long-winded anti-Union conspiracy adding Cook and Hays, as "the same bank where Jim Cook deposited the money" from Billy's cattle." The problem here was reading: Cook's tale used Master Bank not Mastin Bank – toppling Sederwall's house of cards.

7) IMAGINARY LINK TO HAYS'S HAYSTACK: Pretending he had linked Billy through Cook, Sederwall gave the Secret Service's find of counterfeit bills in John Hays's haystack. Faking cattle-selling as central to the Brockway gang, to link to Billy's rustling, he claimed that "Agent Wallace Hall learned from Nevada County residents that Hays had been shipping cattle from the west to Missouri [and that he deposited] sums of money at the Mastin Bank;" then fled with Nate Foster to White Oaks.

First of all, the "**Mastin Bank**" was faked, with its elaborate money-laundering by Confederates fable elaborating Sederwall's misreading of Jim Cook's, "**Master Bank**." And Operative Hall, expert on the gang, did not claim their west to east sale of cattle; instead reporting for May 13, 1882 on Nate Foster's having a **saloon in White Oaks, and John Hays** "*engaged in mining or some mining speculations at or in the vicinity of White Oaks.*" For July 1, 1882, he traced Frank Doyle, Foster, and Hays "*to New Mexico and Texas where more of the notes were passed ... Eventually, however, again all went to New Mexico, and Texas, where they engaged in the saloon business, mining speculations*" – not cattle-buying.

## FAKING A LINK OF WILD'S SHERMAN, TEXAS, INVESTIGATION TO A NATIONAL RUSTLING-COUNTERFEITING RING

Sederwall cited Azariah Wild's summer of 1880 Sherman, Texas, investigation, claiming a man named "Kirby [sic - Kibby] from New York" met with a man named "Walter Graham [sic – Greenham]" for a deal to supply money to buy cattle for resale with a percentage of the profits. But Wild learned that Kirby [sic] was James Doyle "linked to New York counterfeiters." Sederwall stated that Wild learned that "Grahm" [sic] was being sent packages of counterfeit notes from Chicago, to buy cattle "to be herded into Missouri and placed on a ranch in Vernon County owned by John Hays." So, Sederwall claimed, Wild realized the "counterfeiting enterprise he was investigating was not limited to Texas and New Mexico, but rather turned out to be a widespread activity ranging from New York across the country into the American Southwest." (Page 71)

**FAKERY: This was another faked linking of Billy, rustling, and Brockway's gang; this time by misstating Azariah Wild's Sherman, Texas, investigation from June 6, 1880 to July 10, 1880. It was unconnected to Wild's New Mexico Territory investigation from September to the end of December 1880, except that he was unwittingly witnessing different distribution sites of Brockway's bills through local passers. Wild himself reported for October 16, 1881 about Sherman: "*It] was at a time when I had not the least idea of going to New Mexico.*"**

When in Sherman, Wild depicted the gang as local wagon factory owners, Walter B. Greenham, who had just committed suicide, his partner, Calvin Jackson, their wives, the firm of M. Schneider Bros., the Planters and Merchants Bank, and Greenham's counterfeiting family in Maine and New Hampshire. They passed bills gotten by Greenham when in New York in the winter of 1879 (report for June 7, 1880) or from a New Yorker courier calling himself Kibby or Kibbey alias Murphy [Frank Doyle].

Contrary to Sederwall's claim, Wild did not claim that Kibby made a deal with Greenham to supply money to buy cattle for resale with profit sharing. What Wild stated for his report for June 4, 1880 was about another Texas case, separate from Greenham's; writing: *"Information has reached me of there being a man in Foces Co. buying up cattle and paying in part or all in counterfeit money ... That after taking them they dispose of them for what they can get."* And for June 22, 1880, Wild wrote about *"two brothers named John and Clive Merchant down in the neighborhood of Brown County engaged in the cattle business who are reported as men who handle counterfeit money when there is any in circulation."*

But Greenham used that technique for cotton. For his report of June 11, 1880, Wild wrote that Kibby accompanied Greenham in his buggy out to look at a cotton patch; the implication being its purchase with bogus money for resale.

As to the Greenham counterfeiters' connection to cattle, for June 12, 1880, Wild reported *"that Greenham just a short time before his death was at his place [in Pilot Grove, Texas] and purchased some cattle ... That Greenham said he was going to start a stock ranch in the Indian Territory."* And for June 14, 1880, Wild quoted the informer who reported the small deal Greenham had made: "He either sent over 108 or 110 head [to Indian Territory] before he killed himself." And the informer had seen his pickle jar in which he kept his 71 $100 presumably counterfeit bills.

Likewise, in that report, Wild wrote that the Schneider brothers' business was both mercantile and in cattle. Important to note, however, is that, like in the Dedrick-Mason plot, rustling was not involved.

And contrary to Sederwall's fiction that Greenham was being mailed packages of counterfeit bills from Chicago, to buy cattle "to be herded into Missouri and placed on a ranch in Vernon County owned by John Hays;" for his report for June 12, 1880, Wild had merely checked with the local; postmaster about *any* registered mail, and learned: *"The postmaster remembered a registered mail package a Quimby & Co. from Chicago, Ill."* Sederwall had made-up the rest to link Greenham with Brockway's agent, John Hays - something never stated by Wild.

It was not until Wild's October 16, 1881 report (a year after his time in New Mexico), that Chief James Brooks finally filled him in on the Brockway gang, and that Frank Doyle had been in Santa Fe, Las Vegas, and White Oaks. Then Wild decided Kibby was Frank Doyle, and surmised that when W.H. West from White Oaks had traveled *"to Kansas and Colorado on business and that on his return he brought back with him to White Oaks a man who claimed to hail from New York and that his name was Duncan."* Wild now decided that he was Frank Doyle also; and was the likely bill courier, because soon afterward *"an effort was made to employ Barney Mason to go into Texas with $30,000 counterfeit money to purchase cattle."*

Though Wild still persisted in that October 16, 1881 report to join incorrectly Billy's name to the West-Dedrick counterfeiters, he was merely describing the New Mexico outlet of some Brockway bills.

And Sederwall's statement that Wild realized the "counterfeiting enterprise" was not just in "Texas and New Mexico, but from New York across the country," was just about the Brockway gang, not Billy or rustling; though his intent was to trick the reader into believing a connection.

### FAKE LINKING OF BROCKWAY'S MEN TO BILLY

Sederwall then linked John Hays to White Oaks, New Mexico, where, on February 23, 1881 Hays quitclaimed his Missouri farm to an A. Kahn, with a deed notarized by a Frank Lea at the Lincoln County courthouse. Sederwall added that Lea's brother Joseph, from Roswell, New Mexico, had ridden - along with Frank and Jesse James - with William Quantrill. (Page 73)

FAKERY: Name-dropping Brockway's pusher John Hays, is an attempt to link him with Joseph Lea, and Jesse James.

But Joseph Lea did not ride with the James brothers. William Pennington's 1998 "Roster of Quantrill's, Anderson's and Todd's Guerrillas and Other 'Missouri Jewels,' " lists Lea as fighting only on August 21, 1863 for William Quantrill's pro-Confederate "bushwacker" massacre in Lawrence, Kansas. Frank James joined Quantrill in 1862, at 19, but did not fight in that battle. And Jesse James joined a year after the battle, in 1864, at 17.

Faked too is linking Joseph's brother, Frank Lea, to John Hays. But Frank Lea's notarizing of Hays's quitclaim, only means Frank did a professional service.

Building on his fake linking of Frank or Joseph Lea to Jesse James, Sederwall then contended that Frank Lea was Pat Garrett's friend; implying Garrett was in on the counterfeiting too.

FAKERY: Garrett's friend was Frank's brother, Joseph Lea, as documented by Garrett's biographer, Leon Metz, in his 1973 *Pat Garrett: The Story of a Western Lawman*. And Joseph Lea was an upstanding citizen. As Metz wrote: "News of [Garrett's] bravery and perseverance so impressed the Roswellians that John Chisum and <u>Captain Joseph C. Lea, the latter a prominent local resident who commanded universal local respect in Lincoln County</u>, approached Pat Garrett and induced him to move to Roswell in time to qualify for the election [as Lincoln County Sheriff]." (Metz, Pages 54-55) And none of this has anything to do with Billy Bonney.

## *FAKING A LINK TO JESSE JAMES*

To his "counterfeiting gang," Sederwall added Jesse James to prove "historians were wrong." His "proof" was Henry Hoyt's, *A Frontier Doctor*, in which Hoyt saw Billy with James at Moore's Hotsprings Hotel in Las Vegas, New Mexico Territory. (Page 70)

FAKERY: In fact, Hoyt merely claimed that, in late 1879, he saw Billy and James *eating together* at the Hotsprings Hotel. His publisher denied his claim in a footnote, though Hoyt stuck to it. (Hoyt, Page 111) But eating together does not mean counterfeiting together!

In fact, Hoyt described the whole encounter. Teenaged Billy was in Las Vegas for an boyish adventure of seeing passenger trains. Hoyt wrote: "I ... found at a corner table the only vacant seat in the room. Glancing at the three guests already there, I was perfectly amazed to recognize that the one to my left was Billy the Kid, urbane and smiling as ever. We shook hands, but neither mentioned a name. We were chatting away of old times in Texas [Tascosa in October of 1878] ... when the man on Bonney's left made a comment ... Whereupon Billy said, 'Hoyt, meet my friend Mr. Howard from Tennessee' ... Mr. Howard had noticeable characteristics. He had piercing steely blue eyes with a peculiar blink, and the tip of a finger on his left hand was missing. I mentally classed him as a railroad man ... After dinner we separated and Billy, taking me to his room, gave me, after pledging me to secrecy, one of the surprises of my life. Mr. Howard was no other than the bandit and train robber, Jesse James." (Hoyt, Pages 110-111)

And Hoyt confirmed no business relationship; writing: "Jesse James had been in seclusion for some time; [hotel owners] Mr. and Mrs. Moore were former friends whom he could trust, so he came out to size up the situation in a new territory. Billy also knew the Moores, and as he had not seen a passenger train since he was a youngster, he had slipped into Las Vegas, discarded his cowboy togs for an entire new city outfit of clothing, and was having the time of his life for a few days at the Hot Springs ... Jesse James was prospecting and preparing to make a move, and after meeting Billy and sizing him up made a tentative offer to join forces and hit the trail together. <u>Although both were outlaws ... their lives and activities were entirely different. Billy was never a train or bank robber ... His only peculations had been rounding up cattle and horses carrying someone else's brand ... His offences, for which he was now an outcast, were entirely traceable to the now historic Lincoln County War ... On account of the differences in their status and of the fact that a union with Jesse James would carry him away from the magnet at Fort Sumner [Paulita Maxwell], Billy turned down his proposal.</u>" (Hoyt, Pages 112-113)

Sederwall added that future New Mexico Territory Governor, Miguel Otero, claimed that the owner of Moore's Hotsprings Hotel had told him that Jesse James came there. (Page 70)

FAKERY: Henry Hoyt made that claim too, but it does not prove any criminal collusion of Jesse and with Billy. And Otero made no Billy the Kid claim; and Hoyt denied a link.

Sederwall cited a June 24, 1880 *Sacramento Daily Record-Union* article about a William Ralston being a counterfeiter, as well as being Frank James's brother-in-law Sederwall adds that Secret Service agent P.S. Tyrell [sic - P.D. Tyrrell], in July 8, 1881, stated that Frank James sold counterfeit coins. (Pages 70-71)

FAKERY: This has nothing to do with Billy or Jesse James. And Wild's case was for was counterfeit bills, not coins. Operative Patrick D. Tyrell stated for his report for July 8, 1881, completed July 10th, that an informer told him *"that Frank James had a large amount of counterfeit coin, and that he [the informer] could get all he wanted from James."* No link was made to Jesse James.

And Operative Wallace W. Hall, expert on Brockway's pushers in the West, referenced Jesse James in a September 1, 1882 report as just a *"robber and bandit."*

Sederwall then claimed that Frank James lived in Nevada, Missouri; that the population had ex-Confederates; that it was good for holding stolen cattle bought with counterfeit money; and that is why John W. Hays, a known counterfeiter, like Frank James, lived there. And in the Civil War, Hays and Frank James rode with William Quantrill. (Pages 71).

FAKERY: Lumping unconnected people with his made-up stolen cattle bought with counterfeit money is to trick the reader into believing a relationship existed with Brockway's pusher, John Hays, in Moundville, Missouri, and Frank James (with hoped-for implication of Jesse James). But William Pennington's 1998 "Roster of Quantrill's, Anderson's and Todd's Guerrillas and Other 'Missouri Jewels,' " lists only a John Hays (with no W.) and no dates of service or battles. Frank James joined Quantrill in 1862, at 19, but had minimal service. There is no evidence that the two would have met, if Brockway's Hays was actually among Quantrill's hundreds of men.

Sederwall quoted Azariah Wild's report of January 2, 1881: "Information on [ sic - of] the arrest of William Wilson, William Antrim [sic- Antrom] alias Billy the Kid, with several members of their gang by Deputy U.S. Marshal Patrick F.

Garrett has reached me." Sederwall said the report also stated: "There is no trouble in arresting Jesse James if he is not already arrested. I have put several men on his track who have been assisting me and would have arrested or caused his arrest when in New Mexico had I known he was wanted for any crime against the U.S. Government." (Pages 73-74) Sederwall claimed that Billy's and Jesse James's names being in the same report meant they were in cahoots in counterfeiting.

**WRONG**: Wild is not linking Billy and Jesse James. He reported after leaving New Mexico about a James rumor. And the Secret Service never had a case against him. In fact, Wild confirmed that he was not *"wanted for any crime against the U.S. Government"* - meaning counterfeiting.

**REALITY**: Jesse James had no criminal connection to Billy the Kid; and no source accuses James of counterfeiting.

Azariah Wild mentioned James twice. For his December 23, 1880, report about Stinking Springs capture of what the called the *"Kid & Wilson gang;"* he garbled him with Jessie <u>Evans</u> and Billy Campbell of Huston Chapman's murder notoriety; stating that Pat Garrett *"is still in pursuit of the balance of the outlaws: Jessie James is surely here under the name of Campbell."* Wild's second mention was in that report of January 2, 1881, when he was back in New Orleans; but it was a rumor not pursued.

Lew Wallace also mixed-up Jesse James with Jessie Evans in his Billy the Kid outlaw myth articles. On June 18, 1881 and June 23, 1900, for respective interviews in the Crawfordsville *Saturday Evening Journal* and *The Indianapolis Press* - with respective titles, "Billy the Kid, General Wallace Tells Why the Young Desperado of New Mexico Wanted to Kill Him" and "Gen. Wallace's Feud with Billy the Kid," he stated: **"A young lawyer named Chapman was murdered in Lincoln county, and for this were arrested four men, among whom was the notorious Jesse James, under one of his many names."** His June 8, 1902 *New York World Magazine's* "General Lew Wallace Writes a Romance of 'Billy the Kid'" had: **"[A] young attorney in Lincoln, had been murdered. Half a dozen men were arrested, accused of the crime. Among them was Jesse James."** And since Wallace had conferred with Wild in New Mexico, he may have been the one to confuse Wild.

## FAKING LINK OF BILLYS WILSON AND BONNEY

Sederwall cited the March 30, 1881 counterfeiting trial of Billy Wilson in yet another attempt to link Billy Bonney to counterfeiting. So he called Wilson a "close associate" of Billy's and "a member of the Regulators."(Page 74)

**WRONG: Wilson was neither a close associate of Billy's nor a Regulator. He was used as a minor pusher in Dan Dedrick's counterfeiting business; and he was one of the shady characters used by Billy for rustling, having likely met him, Tom Pickett, and possibly Dave Rudabaugh, through Dan Dedrick, one outlet for his rustled stock.**

Sederwall then rolled out his Merchants National Bank of New Bedford, Massachusetts, bill, and claimed his call to "Secret Service public affairs officer Michael Sampson ... led to the discovery in the secret Service Archives of **one of the bank notes passed by Billy Wilson.** A close examination of the bill by the Secret Service yielded the information that it had been the work of ace counterfeiter William E. Brockway." And it was his bills that ended up in Lincoln County. (Pages 74-75)

**FAKERY: This repeats the lie about the random bill from Mike Sampson, which was not connected to Wild's investigation, to Lincoln County, to Billy Bonney, to Billy Wilson, or to Brockway; though it had a bank he used.**

Building on his faked friendship of Billy Bonney to Billy Wilson, Sederwall again tried to link Billy to the counterfeiters by name-dropping a bunch of them. He said that Nate Foster and W.H. West used counterfeit money to buy White Oaks property. And "West bought the stable from **the Kid's friend Billy Wilson**," and Wilson was also living with Samuel Dedrick who "was also paying for cattle using counterfeit bills that he obtained from West." (Page 77)

**FAKERY: Starting from his made-up friendship of Billy Wilson and Billy Bonney, Sederwall fabricated a link of Billy Bonney to the other Brockway pushers connected to White Oaks. Additionally, he added the Dedrick cattle buying plot, though it was by Dan, not Samuel; and was unconnected to Billy Bonney or to rustling.**

Operative Wallace Hall's report for May 19, 1882 recorded that in about May of 1881, Nate Foster *"had a saloon in White Oaks New Mexico. That Hays Frank Doyle, and others ... were with him. Hays was engaged in mining or some mining speculations at or in the vicinity of White Oaks, N.M.* For July 1, 1882, Hall described Nate Foster and Frank Doyle passing bills in Colorado, then going to *"New Mexico and Texas where more of the notes were passed. Hays and some of the party later located in Nevada, Missouri. Eventually, however, again all went to New Mexico, and Texas, where they engaged in the saloon business, mining speculations, &c,&c."*

Even Pat Garrett was aware of the counterfeiters' investing. In *The Authentic Life of Billy the Kid*, he wrote: "Billy Wilson had sold some property to W.H. West and received in payment $400 in counterfeit money." (Garrett, Page 141)

None of this had anything to do with Billy the Kid.

## *FAKING JAMES DOLAN AS A COUNTERFEITER*

Sederwall, stated that on October 2, 1880, Wild got a counterfeit bill from James Dolan, allegedly from Billy Wilson; and Dolan was also holding four more bills for him. But Sederwall claimed that Wilson and Dolan were enemies; thus, Dolan framed Wilson, and was the counterfeiter himself. (Pages 77- 78) This recycled Sederwall's 2010 *Ruidoso News* counterfeiting article about a **Miss N.M. Ferguson from Chicago** writing an August of 1880 letter to the Secret Service accusing Dolan.

Claimed now was that on August 8, 1880, she wrote to Operative Wallace Hall reporting that counterfeit bills were being passed in New Mexico, and enclosed a note from "Fort Stanton, New Mexico, resident J.C. Delaney" which had a counterfeit bill enclosed. Hall's report of August 24, 1880 was quoted: *"[T]he Delaney letter, if true in its statements, gives some light as to who are operating in the counterfeit hundreds in that region."* Sederwall added: "Hall learned from Ferguson the name of the suspect who had passed the counterfeit bill to Delaney: James J. Dolan of Lincoln." (Page 76)

FAKERY: This fable was built on misreading Operative Halls report's of August 3, 1880, August 24, 1880, October 10, 1880, and July 1, 1882 about a Miss N.M. Ferguson of

Chicago getting a counterfeit $100 bill when in New Mexico. But the letters were <u>from</u> merchant <u>Dowlin</u>, not about merchant <u>Dolan</u>! And <u>she did not write the letters</u>. She <u>enclosed letters</u> she had received about the bill. One was from Delaney to her, and one was from M.J. Dowlin to Will Dowlin and Co. <u>Importantly, none of these letters now exist in the Secret Service files; so there is no known content about "who [were] operating in the counterfeit hundreds in that region."</u> Sederwall brazenly made-up that "Hall learned from Ferguson the name of the suspect who had passed the counterfeit bill to Delaney: James J. Dolan of Lincoln."

Hall's actual conclusion was merely that Miss Ferguson had gotten a Brockway bill, then being passed in New Mexico by his gang members. There was no connection to Billy the Kid or to James Dolan in his reports; as follows:

1) For August 3, 1880, from Chicago, Hall tried to find out if a Miss M.M. [later wrote N.M.] Ferguson had gotten an answer to her letter to a John C. Delaney in Fort Stanton, New Mexico, in which she had enclosed the counterfeit bill. For August 4th, Hall reported that he met with her, and she got no reply *"to her letter returning the cft $100 note to J.C. Delaney."* So <u>the only Ferguson letter merely informed Delaney about getting the bad bill</u>.

2) Hall's report for August 24, 1880, stated that he received from Ferguson a cover note with two enclosed response letters. <u>So there was a Ferguson note accompanying enclosed letters</u>. Hall stated that one letter was dated Fort Stanton, New Mexico, August 8, 1880, and was *"addressed to Miss Ferguson and signed J.C. Delaney. It referenced a $100 Revere Bank of Boston note and speaks of some persons in that section supposed to be 'shoving' them"* <u>So one letter was from J.C. Delaney to Ferguson.</u> Hall stated: *"Enclosed with this Delaney letter, I received a letter dated Tularosa Aug 5th, 1880, addressed to Messrs. Will Dowlin & Co and signed M.J. Dowlin. It also refers to the Ferguson cft hundred ... The Delaney letter, if true in its statements, gives some light as to who are operating in the counterfeit hundreds in that region."* <u>So the second enclosed letter was from M.J. Dowlin to Will Dowlin & Co.</u>

3) Hall's report for October 10, 1881, followed-up for Chief Brooks about Ferguson's matter: *"You will remember that almost one year ago cft $100 were put in circulation*

*about Santa Fe, New Mexico, and one of these cft hundreds was received from there by Miss N.M. Ferguson of this city [Chicago]. I forwarded you, on Aug 24, 1880 letters of J.C. Delaney and Will Dowlin & Co and M.J. Dowlin of New Mexico concerning cft $100 shovers, etc. etc."* Hall connected Ferguson's bill to the Brockway gang, hypothesizing they came from the "boodle" in John Hays's haystack; writing: *"Frank Doyle, brother of James [Doyle] is now in Bradford, Ill. Had returned in July, this year, from a year absence in the south-west. Mentioned Las Vegas, Santa Fe and White Oaks New Mexico as some of the places where [Frank] Doyle had spent a portion of his time. You will remember that almost one year ago cft $100 were put in circulation about Santa Fe, New Mexico, and one of these cft hundreds was received from there by Miss N.M. Ferguson of this city. I forwarded you, on Aug 24, 1880 letters of J.C. Delaney and Will Dowlin & Co and M.J. Dowlin of New Mexico concerning cft $100 shovers, etc. etc. ... [and] Frank Doyle was ... in that section at that time. again it might have been his 'boodle' found in the haystack near Nevada, Mo."*

4) Hall's report for July 1, 1882 referenced the Ferguson matter: *"With my report of August 24, 1880 I sent you two letters. One dated Fort Stanton Texas [sic] Aug 24, 1880, addressed to Miss N.M. Ferguson, signed J.C. Delaney; the other dated Tularosa Aug 5, 1880, addressed to Will Dowlin & Co, and signed by M.J. Dowlin. The cft [counterfeit] $100 referred to in these letters was no doubt passed by some of the Hays Foster party. I think you never returned these letters to me. I cannot find them in my files."*

The men involved in the Ferguson matter were merchants who likely got passed the bad bill. William "Will" Dowlin, with his brother Paul, had a mill on the Ruidoso River since about 1869, operating as Paul Dowlin & Co. In 1873, when L.G. Murphy & Co. were kicked out from their sutler store in Fort Stanton, Paul took it over as post-trader, and Will operated the mill; becoming, by 1876, Paul Dowlin & Brother. When Paul died in 1877, Will sold the mill, and kept the store. In about 1878, Will partnered with John C. Delaney. In 1879, they bought "The House" in Lincoln from T.B. Catron with a mortgage, but defaulted in December of 1880; and Catron sold it in January of 1881 to the county for its new courthouse and jail.

Azariah Wild, for October 4, 1880, had reported that William Dowlin had received a National Revere Bank of Boston, Massachusetts passed by William Wilson; also demonstrating Dowlin & Delaney's getting bad bills; like Wallace Hall reported for Miss N.M. Ferguson. But Wild never linked the bill to Brockway's gang when he was in New Mexico Territory. And there was no link to Billy.

## *FAKING BILLY AS AN EVIL SECRET SERVICE SNITCH, MURDERER OF AN INFORMER, AND CONSPIRATOR TO ROB MAIL*

Though one wonders why it is in this W.C. Jameson book - which was supposed to advertise "Brushy" - Sederwall's fiction of unredeemably evil Billy the Kid repeated his June, 2015 *True West* article: "Billy Bonney's Bad Bucks," in which **Billy offered to "snitch" against fellow counterfeiters to Azariah Wild because a "man named Smith" told Wild that "the Kid was reading his reports while they were in possession of mail carrier Mike Cosgrove."** This caused Billy's revenge murder of Smith. (Pages 78-79) Sederwall constructed this hogwash from unrelated parts: Billy's October of 1880 Secret Service pardon bargain attempt, an April of 1880 murder of a freight hauler named Sam Smith, and a December of 1880 Las Vegas jail visit to Billy of mail contractor, Mike Cosgrove.

### FAKING THE SECRET SERVICE PARDON BARGAIN

Billy's pardon bargain for testifying against counterfeiters was made-up as connecting him to Brockway's gang. Sederwall claimed: "In truth, all the Kid knew about the counterfeit ring involved Doyle and Hays, the Colorado beef buyers." (Page 78)

FAKERY: Billy was not a counterfeiter. And Sederwall had made-up that Billy's one time selling of cattle to Colorado buyers, meant that he sold to Brockway's men: Frank and James Doyle and John Hays – though they were just sometimes in Colorado and were not cattle buyers.

Wild's reports indicate Billy's pardon bargain testimony was to be against the Dedricks and their employees. At that time, Wild, saw the counterfeiting as local.

In his report for October 6, 1880, he presented a pardon for Billy in exchange for testimony. For October 9, 1880, he included a copy of his letter to U.S. Attorney Barnes about it. He also stated that Attorney Ira Leonard had revealed the counterfeiters in White Oaks and at Dan Dedrick's ranch - likely obtained by Leonard from Billy to advertise his testimony's value. And Billy wrote too, as he had to Lew Wallace, about *"being tired of dodging the officers."*

But Barnes was a Ringite, likely alerting Wild's minders, James Dolan and Catron's brother-in-law, Edgar Walz; because Wild abruptly concluded Billy was in the counterfeiting gang, and it centered in Fort Sumner. So his report of October 11, 1880 documented his requesting from Barnes arrest warrants for Regulators: Billy, Bowdre, Scurlock, and O'Folliard.

By October 16, 1880, savvy Billy checked on Wild himself. He robbed the mail-coach, would have read Wild's report about arresting, and refused the meeting; but lost his second chance at a pardon.

### FAKING SAM SMITH'S MURDER

Confusing dates, Sederwall continued his fiction of monster Billy the counterfeiter. For Billy as the murderer of Sam Smith, he cited a supposed *Santa Fe New Mexican* article of May 21, 1880 about Billy and his gang **murdering "a freighter named Smith" because Smith snitched to Wild about his counterfeiting gang.** Sederwall gave its alleged quote: "The information that enabled the Government officers to fix the handling of counterfeit money upon the Kid's gang came from a freighter named Smith. Soon afterward, while Smith was on his way from Las Vegas to Fort Sumner with a load of freight, he was waylaid and murdered by some of the gang." (Pages 78-79)

FAKERY: First of all, Wild was not in New Mexico Territory until late September of 1880; meeting with U.S. Attorney Sidney Barnes and counterfeiting victim, James Dolan, on September 20, 1880. So he was not there in May of 1880 to be snitched to by Sam Smith.

And Smith's April of 1880 murder had nothing to do with Billy the Kid. Sederwall's quote was actually from the December 22, 1880 *New York Sun's* "Outlaws of New Mexico, The Exploits of a Band Headed by a New York Youth" [APPENDIX: 18], which had likely inspired his hoax. But it was fake news. Smith was killed by Apaches.

Sam Smith's killing was well publicized in this period of Indian Wars in which Native American retaliations were feared. Though there was no *Santa Fe New Mexican* article of May 21, 1880 about the incident, as Sederwall claimed; there was May 21, 1881's *The Santa Fe Daily New Mexican's* "Mescalero Marauders," that reported Smith's murder by Mescalero Apaches. It stated: "**Last Thursday the stock ranch of Hon. T.B. Catron, of this city, known as the Carizoso [sic] ranch, was taken in by <u>a party of the [Mescalero Apache] Indians</u> ... The Indians were seen by the herders while killing the cattle, but the latter dared not attack them being outnumbered. As this ranch is only ten miles from the camp of White Oaks and thirty-five miles west of Fort Stanton, <u>it is more than probable that this party was the same which murdered Sam Smith, the freighter, near Pato Springs</u>.**"

The Pato Springs Apache murder of Sam Smith was also recorded in the 1880 *Annual Report of the Secretary of War* as on April 15, 1880; though that date varied in the press. *The Las Vegas Daily Gazette* of April 27, 1880 reported from Lincoln: "**I am sorry to state to you that the Indians from the agency and also Victorio's band are a bad racket. They killed Sam Smith, our freighter, who left Las Vegas loaded for us on the 8th and arrived at Patos on the 20th in the evening; and on the 21st he was killed at Dry Lake. The goods were taken, harness and all, also sheets of wagon.**" The May 4, 1880 *Sacramento Daily Record-Tribune's* front page had "Indian Depredations in Colorado and Dakota;" stating: "A freighter, Samuel Smith by name, was killed at Patos Springs on the 19th ultimo, by nine Indians, supposed to be Mescalero Apaches or Comanches.

### FAKING A CONSPIRACY WITH "MAIL CARRIER" MIKE COSGROVE

Recycling his June, 2015 *True West* article, "Billy Bonney's Bad Bucks," and building on his meaningless May 21, 1880 date for faking Billy's "murder of freighter Smith;" Sederwall made-up that "around this time" (i.e. May of 1880), Wild became aware that Billy "was stopping the mail coach and reading his reports." Sederwall then claimed this proved Billy's conspiracy with the "mail carrier" "in the tampering;" though he omitted his prior use of Mike Cosgrove's name. (Page 79)

FAKERY: Firstly, the May of 1880 date is fake, since Wild was not there until September of 1880. Also, Billy just robbed the mail coach once: to check on Wild's intentions during his pardon negotiation in October of 1880.

And there was no mail-theft conspiracy. The Mike Cosgrove he had accused was not a "mail deliverer," but a large-scale "mail contractor." Sederwall originally misread the famous December 27, 1880 *Las Vegas Daily Gazette* article by Lucius "Lute" Wilcox about the Stinking Springs capture titled 'The Kid. Interview with Billy Bonney The Best Known Man in New Mexico;" in which Cosgrave gave new suits to Garrett's prisoners, including Billy. It stated: **"Mike Cosgrove, the <u>obliging mail contractor</u>, who has met the boys frequently while on business down the Pecos, had just gone in with four large bundles [of suits]."** Mail contractor was a political appointment, and Cosgrove was likely publicizing himself. But in his *True West* article, Sederwall fabricated that Cosgrave's suit gift "proved" his conspiracy to let Billy read Wild's mailed reports, because he was getting Billy alone to ask him to keep it secret from Wild!

That Cosgrave was a mail contractor was presented in October 19, 1881's *Las Vegas Daily Optic*, for "Cosgrove's Contract," describing that his brother, Cornelius Cosgrove, on July 1, 1878, with a bid of $14,900, got the 442½ mile mail route contract from Las Vegas to Las Cruces; then added a route along the Pecos River to Roswell for an additional $2,517. In about July of 1879, Cornelius turned over the route to Mike. Since this was the period of Star Route scandals, the pay increase that the Cosgroves got of $73,997 was scrutinized. But Mike Cosgrove retained the route. The *Official Register of the United States Containing a List of the Officers and Employees in the Civil, Military, and Naval Service on the First of July, 1881, Volume II*, on page 209 lists his Star Service contract. And the 1888 *Miscellaneous Documents of the Senate of the United States for the First Session of the Fiftieth Congress. Volume II* confirms, on page 190, that a mail contractor was a political position, with appointment by the Second Assistant Postmaster-General.

As to <u>Mike Cosgrave's mail carrier</u>, an April 26, 1882 *Las Vegas Daily Optic* article, in the section "Optic Oracle," named his "buckboard driver" as hairy "Dutchy," who made news when he was shaved by a barber.

## FAKING LINK OF BILLY'S TESTIFYING OFFER AS PROOF OF HIS BEING A COUNTERFEITER

Sederwall claimed that Billy's willingness to be a prosecution witness against the counterfeiters, meant he *was* a counterfeiter.

FAKERY: This illogical conclusion hid that Wild had identified the New Mexico Territory counterfeiters in his October 10, 1880 report, writing: *"William Wilson is reported to be at Bosque Grande at Dedrick's ranch. Dedrick is reported as being one of the leaders of the clan, and partners with West in the Corral at White Oaks."* And, even when duped Wild included Billy, he saw him as an indicted murderer and rustler, joining forces with the counterfeiters – not passing counterfeit bills himself.

And Billy had gotten his information not from being a counterfeiter, but from associating with them: selling stock to Dan Dedrick and his brothers at the White Oaks livery, and using Billy Wilson and Tom Pickett for rustling.

Also, Pat Garrett, working with Wild, did not accuse Billy of counterfeiting; instead naming the same New Mexico Territory suspects in his *The Authentic Life of Billy the Kid* as Dan Dedrick, W.H. West, and Billy Wilson. (Garrett, Pages 140-142)

## *FAKING BILLY AS A COUNTERFEITER DOING WITNESS INTIMIDATION ON JAMES DeVOURS*

Building on his fiction of Billy murdering Sam Smith for informing on him, Sederwall added that Billy scared-off another witness named James DeVours, who was referenced in Azariah Wild's report of October 9, 1880; and who Sederwall called the "manager of the Carriso [sic] Ranch." (Page 78-79)

FAKERY: The manager of T.B. Catron's Carrizozo Land and Cattle Company ranch was his Ringite brother-in-law, Edgar Walz, not James DeVours.

Sederwall misstated Devours. As Wild reported, he was a low level counterfeiter and ranch employee. Wild's report for October 18, 1880, documented Walz's relating that DeVours would give information about the *"gang of counterfeiters"* if paid. But by his report for November 28, 1880, Wild admitted that the counterfeiters had gotten wind of his activities, and halted their Mason-cattle buying plot *"until the present excitement and trouble is over."* Dan Dedrick fled to California. And Walz's counterfeiting workers also fled. One, unnamed, left, with Tom Cooper, to El Paso. DeVours, Wild noted, *"left the country for safety."* All this was unrelated to Billy the Kid.

## *FAKING A LINK TO A.P. ANAYA'S "EVIDENCE"*

Sederwall concluded his case for Billy as a counterfeiter with A.P. "Paco" Anaya, a mainstay in "Brushy Bill" and "Billy the Kid Case" hoaxes for his windbag malarkey. Here used was his claim that Billy had a lot of cash because it was "spurious." (Page 79)

FLAWED EVIDENCE: Anaya's book, *I Buried Billy*, stated: "Billy and his pals always had a lot of money ... but this money was spurious money [which was printed from a plate he buried] that Billy Wilson had stolen in Washington when he was employed by the government [and they] printed about $5000." (Anaya, Pages 70-71)

Hidden are Anaya's other tall tales. For example, about John Chisum's debt to Billy, he made-up a bizarre scene in which he witnessed Billy meeting Chisum in a bar, and making him bite a pistol. ("You could hear the sound the teeth made on the barrel.") Then Billy beat up Chisum to make him pay. (Anaya, Pages 84-86)

## A NON-EXISTENT CASE

No evidence is presented by Steve Sederwall, as narrated by W.C. Jameson, to indicate that Billy Bonney was a counterfeiter, or was rustling to launder counterfeit money, or was linked to the Brockway gang, or murdered Sam Smith, or plotted with a mailman to read Azariah Wild's reports.

Of course, all this was irrelevant to Garrett not killing Billy. And Sederwall's showing-off fakery was damaging to promoting the "Brushy" and "Billy the Kid" hoaxes - the purpose of the book - by creating a creepy bad Billy in contradiction to his imposters' claims for themselves. And, obviously, all Sederwall's claims knocked "Brushy" out of the running by his ignorance of them.

# CHAPTER 4
## FAKE LITTLE "INVESTIGATIONS"

### WEE NOT-AS-WRITTEN SCAMS

Still mindlessly showcasing Steve Sederwall, W.C. Jameson ignored his portrayal of Billy as a major counterfeiter-witness-murderer; and called Billy's outlaw notoriety just bad press for "blue-collar variety" crimes, listed as: rustling, mail tampering, and revenge-related murders (Page 80); leaving out counterfeiting! To Jameson, that meant "Brushy," as Billy, was not so bad.

Jameson continued Sederwall's "cop finds," beginning with public officials being worse crooks than Billy, and adding fake claims for history-is-not-as-written; which, to fuzzy-headed Jameson proved that "Brushy" was Billy.

### ATTACKING PAT GARRETT'S AUTHORITY

A little Sederwall "investigation" claimed that Pat Garrett had *illegally* tracked Billy the Kid in 1880, because he was only a "sheriff-elect" under Lincoln County Sheriff George Kimbrell, and not a Deputy U.S. Marshal as history claimed.

Used was one of Secret Service Operative Azariah Wild's reports stating that Wild had received paperwork for two Deputy U.S. Marshal commissions for a John Hurley from Santa Fe's U.S. Marshal John Sherman. So he had crossed out one, and added Pat Garrett's name. Sederwall concluded that meant Garrett was not legally appointed, so had only authority in Lincoln County as a Deputy Sheriff. (Page 81) Thus, he could not make arrests in San Miguel County site of Fort Sumner.

**FAKE INVESTIGATION: Sederwall misstated Garrett's legitimacy in his Deputy U.S. Marshal appointment by Wild to head posses tracking the "Wilson and Kid gang."**

Garrett's biographer, Leon Metz, in his 1974 *Pat Garrett: The Story of a Western Lawman*, gave the circumstance: "Since United States marshals and deputy marshals were too frightened to help him, Wild ... compiled a list of brave citizens ... Among them ... [was] Pat Garrett ... [He] wrote [U.S. Marshal] Sherman saying that these men would do the work if Sherman would simply sign United States deputy marshal commissions for all of them. Sherman happily complied, sending everything the Treasury man asked for, except that he mistakenly dispatched two commissions for Hurley and none for Garrett. Wild rectified this error by scratching Hurley's name from one of the papers and substituting Garrett's."

Sederwall omitted that Wild informed Secret Service Chief James Brooks of this on January 3, 1881; and, as one of only 40 Special Operatives in the country, he had power to make appointments and pursue investigations as he chose - including capturing and killing suspects. He had already reported his difficulty getting warrants and commissions. On October 13, 1880, he wrote: "*Complaints are made here against Marshal Sherman that he is a drunkard and inefficient. But as I am not investigating the Marshal [note that Wild had that power over him] I will not complain if he will arrest or commission men who will make the arrests I want.*" Also, Lincoln County citizens refused, as he wrote on October 29, 1880: "*There is no one who I can get to assist me here that I can trust as every one ... who resides here, and who would otherwise assist me is scared that he will be killed.*" Pat Garrett was one of the few willing to help, as Wild reported to Chief Brooks on November 11, 1880. And by November 21, 1880, Wild reported that Garrett had enlisted his friend, Barney Mason, to infiltrate the counterfeiting gang as a spy.

What Sederwall took out of context, was that Wild, back in his New Orleans home base, was going over his New Mexico Territory case to complain about problems with U.S. Marshal Sherman, and having to correct his sloppy paperwork. Wild's January 3, 1881 report stated:

> *I am disposed to believe U.S. Attorney Barnes will and has done all he could, but he had a man as Marshal who is but little or no assistance to him, and*

*in fact I will state that had I gone there and found no U.S. Marshal I would have accomplished my work sooner and I believe more satisfactory to the government and to myself.*

*I will respectfully state that I appealed to Marshal Sherman to appoint P.F. Garrett as Deputy Marshal to which he paid no attention. <u>I was in great need of Mr. Garrett's aid at that time and took one of the Commissions Sherman sent to John Hurley (he having sent two) and substituted the name of P.F. Garrett the very man who has rendered the Government such valuable service in killing and arresting these men who I was in pursuit.</u>*

So Garrett's Deputy U.S. Marshal appointment was proper. Chief Brooks acceptance confirmed its legitimacy.

In addition, further debunking of Sederwall's defamation of Garrett, Wild had written a commendation letter, included in his report to Chief Brooks of January 25, 1881:

*Patrick F. Garrett Esq.*
  *Sheriff of Lincoln County*
    *New Mexico*

*Dear Sir:-*
  *Your letter dated Lincoln NM January 10<sup>th</sup> 1881 just received and noted.*

*1<sup>st</sup> Allow me to congratulate you, and your men for the success in bringing up, arresting and killing the worst band of outlaws in the United States ...*

*Your services to the Government have been of too great value to go unpaid or be treated in a miserly manner.*

*I have properly represented you and the services performed by you and your men to the Departments to which I belong, at Washington, and will continue to aid you all that is in my power until you are fully paid ...*
    *Very Respectfully*
     *Azariah F. Wild*
      *Operative*

Garrett himself referenced his Deputy U.S. Marshal appointment in his 1882 *Authentic Life of Billy the Kid*: "[Bob] Olinger and myself were both commissioned as deputy United States marshals and held United States warrants for the Kid and Bowdre for the killing of ["Buckshot"] Roberts on an Indian Reservation." (Garrett, Page 145)

## FAKE DISCOVERY OF "BILLY THE KID" MONIKER

Sederwall pretended to have discovered that the name "Billy the Kid" was first used in the *Las Vegas Gazette* (Page 81), (which Jameson should have noticed debunks "Brushy," who made-up it was his childhood alias because he was small!).

WRONG: This "find" came from Billy's December 12, 1880 letter to Lew Wallace, stating: "*I noticed in the Las Vegas Gazette a piece which stated that, Billy "the" Kid, the name by which I am known in the Country was the captain of a Band of Outlaws.*" But the showing-off was wrong.

The moniker "Billy the Kid" was first publicly used in the May 23, 1879 testimony of Susan McSween in the Dudley Court of Inquiry. She was being questioned by the prosecutor about requesting aid from Dudley by going to his camp. She stated: "*He said he ... did not intend to have anything to do with either party ... I then said it looked strange to me to see his men, or his soldiers I should say, guarding Peppin back and forth through town and sending soldiers around our house ... if he had nothing to do with it. He then got very angry and said it was none of my business, that he would send his soldiers where he pleased, that I have no such business to have such men as Billy the Kid, Jim French, and others of like character in my house. He then ... said that he had come to protect women and children. I then asked why he did not protect myself, my sister, and her children. He said I have no business, or we had no business, to be in that house, that he would not give us protection.*"

In fact, this testimony is so famous, that historian, Joel Jacobsen, used it to title his 1994 book *Such Men as Billy the Kid: The Lincoln County War Reconsidered*.

# FAKE DISCOVERY OF TOM O'FOLLIARD BEING TOM "FOLLIARD"

For a history-is-not-as-written "investigation," Jameson announced: "As a result of genealogical records and census records, detective Steve Sederwall learned [Tom O'Folliard's] **real name was Thomas O. Folliard**." (Page 82)

Claimed is Sederwall's discovery that Tom's father, was "Tom Folliard," emigrated from Ireland, married "Sarah Cook;" and had Tom after "**two and a half years**." (Page 82) They then moved to Monclova, Coahuila, Mexico, where the parents died of smallpox. John Cook (called Sarah's uncle) then took Tom to Uvalde, Texas.

Cited is: "The Uvalde census for 1870 lists 'Thomas <u>Folliard</u>, 9 years old," and other family members. Claimed as Sarah's parents were David Cook and Eliza Jane Cook; and that "**[t]his would make Eliza Jane Cook, the woman who raised him, Tom's grandmother. Eliza Jane's married name was McKinney; she was Kip McKinney's cousin. Kip McKinney and Tom Folliard [sic] were related**." (Pages 82-83) Sederwall concluded that with Tom raised in Uvalde, Kip McKinney being from there, and Garrett living there *from 1891 to 1900*, they were "all acquainted" (Page 83) [ignoring Tom being dead in 1880!]. Nevertheless, Sederwall gave dying O'Folliard's asking Garrett to put him out of his misery **as a friend**; and Garrett **denying he was his friend**. So Sederwall concluded Garrett was "stressing the business of friends a bit to hard, as if he were trying to **cover up the fact that he and Folliard [sic] had been friends**." (Page 84)

An anecdote has Thalis Cook, as "Folliard's" uncle, write about visiting him in New Mexico. But a Robert N. Mullin Collection letter by a Mrs. O.L. Shipman claimed Billy the Kid intercepted that letter, and told Thalis "he could not have Tom." (Page 83)

**FAKE AND FLAWED INVESTIGATION: This is not a true genealogical investigation with census reports, obituaries, and other kinship records. Sederwall just lifted from unsubstantiated sources; since O'Folliard's real genealogy is uncertain. Worse, Sederwall added errors.**

**Only one record exists, tentatively linked to O'Folliard: the 1870 census on September 26, 1870 in Zavalla County, Uvalde, Texas, used by Sederwall. [FIGURE: 8]**

Frederick Nolan cited it in his 2011 publishing of a 1940 manuscript by a Frank Clifford, titled *Deep Trails in the Old West: A Frontier Memoir*. But Nolan critiqued it as problematically listing Tom's age as 9 in 1870, which contradicted other claimed birthdays of 1854 and 1958. Also, the name used is "Folliard," making it not him or misspelled. Nolan concluded: "[A] lot more work needs to be done before we have anything remotely like an acceptable biography." (*Deep Trails*, Nolan, Page 276)

But Sederwall used unsubstantiated genealogies. A January, 1934 article by Jack Shipman in *Voice of the Mexican Border* magazine, "Brief Career of Tom O'Folliard Billy the Kid's Partner," lacking sources, gave an Irish immigrant father named Tom O'Folliard. As Sederwall lifted, it made-up Tom's birth "two and a half years" after his parents' marriage. Shipman claimed, without proof, that Tom was raised by John Cook and his sister, Margaret Jane Cook, till she married; then his living with John, till his marriage in 1875. Then Tom was with grandmother, "Mrs. David Cook." (Shipman, Page 216)

Philip J. Rasch's 1995 *Trailing Billy the Kid* (in *Cold Case Billy the Kid's* Bibliography) had "The Short Life of Tom O'Folliard," using Shipman's article. His Tom is born in Uvalde, Texas, to "Irish immigrant" Tom O'Folliard, and Sarah Cook; moves to Mexico, with the parents dying. Sarah's brother, John Cook, takes him to Uvalde to his sister Margaret Jane Cook, until her 1873 marriage. Then Tom lived with John Cook, until his marriage to "a Miss McKinney" in 1875; when he went to grandmother, "Mrs. James Cook." (Rasch, Page 77) The Thalis Cook tale is told, as Sederwall used. (Rasch, Page 81)

But these sources' Irish father was Tom O'Folliard. So Sederwall made-up his name as "Folliard" to match the census's misspelled "Folliard" to fabricate his "Folliard" discovery. And he faked that the son's middle initial was "O," as: Thomas O. Folliard! (Page 82)

That "Folliard" is wrong, is proved by contemporaries use of O'Folliard. Operative Azariah Wild, who tracked him in the "Wilson & Kid gang," wrote in his report completed on October 18, 1880: "*Thomas O'Falliard: [Came] [f]rom Texas here.*" Pat Garrett, who knew and killed him, wrote

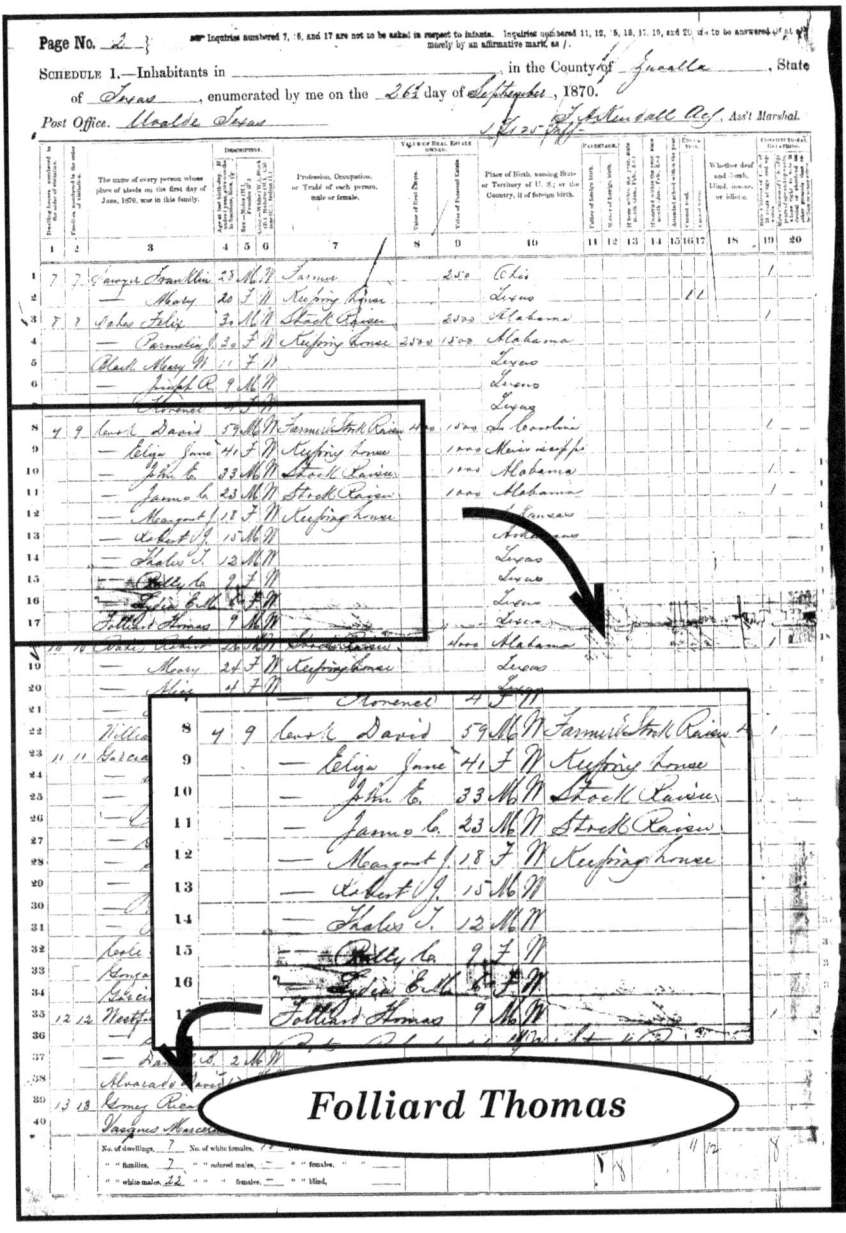

FIGURE: 8. U.S. Census Record 1870; recorded September 26, 1870; Zavalla County, Uvalde, Texas showing the possible Tom O'Folliard as "Folliard," but with questionable age of 9 years old. This spelling was used by the hoaxers to claim

in *The Authentic Life of Billy the Kid*: "[After the shooting] Mason came around the building just as O'Folliard was returning, reeling in his saddle. After we had laid him down inside, he begged me to kill him, saying that if I was a friend of his I would put him out of his misery. I told him I was no friend of his kind." (Garrett, Page 172) This quote also shows Sederwall's misstatement of the "friend" claim.

Sederwall added errors by calling Eliza Jane's married name McKinney, when it was her *maiden name*, with *married name* Cook. And he made-up that she and David Cook were O'Folliard's grandparents.

As to "Brushy's" cousin claim, Sederwall reduced it to "relative." The original "Brushy" team's prompt source was the 1935 book by Frank M. King, titled *Wranglin' the Past: Reminiscences of Frank M. King*; stating: "Kip was also a cousin of Tom O'Folliard." (King, Page 173) Another prompt, was Garrett's O'Folliard death scene; stating: "He also asked [Barney] Mason to tell McKinney to write to his grandmother in Texas and inform her of his death." (Garrett, Page 173) But that did not mean cousins, or even relatives.

Linking of Cook and McKinney families was explained in Frederick Nolan's note in Frank Clifford's *Deep Trials in the Old West*. He stated that, on April 4, 1875, Tom's uncle, John Enoch Cook married Elizabeth Francis McKinney, a cousin of Kip McKinney. Also, Tom's uncle, David Cook, had married, as second wife, Eliza Jane McKinney Cook. Nolan noted that possibly Eliza's father was a Collin McKinney, possibly Kip McKinney's grandfather, through Collin's son, Thalis McKinney. That would make her Kip's aunt. But none of this makes Tom and Kip blood cousins, but might explain dying Tom's knowing Kip could contact his Cook family.

RELATED SCAM: Sederwall used this faked genealogy for his "Lane Cook" as O'Folliard's cousin doing rustling-counterfeit-laundering with Billy. (See page 622 above.)

DESTROYING "BRUSHY": "Brushy," as Billy, always used "O'Folliard." (*Alias Billy the Kid*, Page 31; *The Return of the Outlaw Billy the Kid*, Pages 54, 55, 62) So this supposed "Folliard" name would represent more proof that "Brushy" was not Billy!

# CHAPTER 5
# FAKE "INVESTIGATION" OF STINKING SPRINGS

## DISCOVERING A PORT-HOLE MAKING URINATION PLOT, A GUN, AND BAD MONEY, WHILE KEEPING A STRAIGHT FACE

Just when you thought the hoaxing could not get more silly, it does. Contradicting the "Billy the Kid Case's" Garrett-Billy friendship, is Jameson's chapter "The Stinking Springs Incident" (Pages 85-91) in which Pat Garrett tries to kill him. Also given is conventional history of Billy and his group's hiding out at the Wilcox-Brazil ranch (Page 85), which was unknown to "Brushy."

For the actual Stinking Springs scene, it seems that the Jameson-Sederwall duo had never visited the site, since omitted is its most dramatic feature: the huge arroyo near the front of the rock house shelter in which Garrett and his posse hid. Instead, the scene was lifted from old-timer "Paco" Anaya's windbag malarkey in his posthumous 1991 book, *I Buried Billy*.

FAKING EVIDENCE: No legitimate historian or lawman would use A.P. "Paco" Anaya as a reliable witness. He is in the mold of the "Brushy Bill" team's Severo Gallegos, the garrulous old-timer windbag used by them for his apocryphal jailbreak scene and fake affidavit of "Brushy" as Billy." (See pages 186-187, 197-199 above)

Anaya's book, *I Buried Billy*, was printed posthumously in 1991 by founders of the Billy the Kid Outlaw Gang, Joe and Marlyn Bowlin, as an old-timer document given to them by his nephew, Sam Anaya in 1989. It had input from Paco's son, Louis Anaya, from a 1937 article in *Personal Adventure Stories* magazine titled "I Hid Out Billy the Kid." (*I Buried Billy*, Page 17) Sam stated it was completed in

Spanish in 1930 when Paco was "seventy less nine days." The Bolins had it translated. (*I Buried Billy*, Page 10)

The book's punch line is that Anaya witnessed Billy Bonney's burial, as well as knowing him in Fort Sumner after his great escape; though Paco was two years younger (born January 25, 1862). (*I Buried Billy*, Page 68) Besides that, the book is merely Anaya's, often ludicrous, fiction; though he claimed to know Billy since August of 1878 as a teenaged sheep herder in the Fort Sumner area. (*I Buried Billy*, Page 23)

An example of his tall tales is the Lincoln County War Battle. He stated that one day in August of 1878, Bob Beckwith came with 48 armed men to Alexander McSween, telling him he had come to fix things with him and the Murphys. "Bob followed McSween and Billy the Kid followed both into McSween's office. When McSween sat down he turned his back to Bob and then Bob drew his gun and shot him in the back. At the same moment Billy shot Bob in the head and he fell dead. At the same time, the other Texans outside started a fire in several parts of the house." (*I Buried Billy*, Page 30)

Another example of tall tales is that for Billy's Lincoln jailing, Billy's food is "very well cooked by the black cook, Gus, which was the cook's name." (*I Buried Billy*, 51) [Gottfried Gauss was white, German, the building's caretaker, and John Tunstall's past cook.] And about Stinking Springs, for which he would be used as Sederwall's source, Anaya thought it was December of 1879, and Billy was being pursued by Sheriff Pepen [Peppin] and 40 men. (*I Buried Billy*, Page 88)

But "cop" Sederwall based his "investigation" on Anaya's malarkey to fake a Stinking Springs "discovery."

For the capture, Jameson and Sederwall have the lawmen wait outside for daylight. A Garrett quote is given, based on his knowing that Billy wore a distinctive hat: "I told the posse that should the Kid make his appearance, it **was my intention to kill him**, and the rest would surrender." And Garrett's fatal shooting of Bowdre, mistaken for Billy, is given. (Pages 86-87)

ANAYA'S FAKERY: Again proving himself a useless historical source, Anaya lifted the historical hat incident to make-up his own hat story. He put Billy at a mail stop between Pinos and White Oaks, where Billy traded his hat with a Mexican. So the Pepen [sic] Posse [confused from the 1878 Lincoln County War Battle] saw it and killed the Mexican as Billy. (*I Buried* Billy, Page 90) Billy and his group fled to the Wilcox ranch, but Garrett and 40 Texans [in the 1880 posse] had a run-in with Tom O'Folliard and Tom Pickett; and Billy sent them smoke signals so they could meet-up again. (Anaya, Pages 94-97) And Anaya has no killing of O'Folliard!

For the Stinking Springs surrender, Sederwall claimed that he "discovered" that Billy had **urinated on the piled-up weapons** in the rock house before surrendering as the last person out (Page 88); with Tom Pickett as first out with a white cloth. (Page 87)

**FAKERY USING ANAYA'S FAKERY OF BODILY WASTE:** Sederwall relied on "Paco" Anaya's malarkey for his "urinating" discovery, but misread Anaya's text. Anaya wrote: "[W]hen Billy gave up, and as soon as Billy was secure, Pat went into the house to bring what they had there, and found that Billy had piled up all the rifles and pistols, as well as the gunbelts, and <u>did his business on them</u> and got them all covered. When Pat saw them he said to Billy, 'What did you do that to the weapons for?' And Billy answered, 'That's all they're good for when you can't use them.' " (*I Buried Billy*, Page 107)

But Anaya's dirty joke is about *defecation* to ruin the weapons. Urination, actually, was used by buffalo hunters, like Garrett, to cool hot barrels of their Sharps Big Fifties during multiple shootings into a herd, and would not have been seen as disgusting.

More important is that the real witness, Pat Garrett, gave no such scene with a urinating Billy last out, and first-out as white-flag-bearing Tom Pickett. Garrett stated in *The Authentic Life of Billy the Kid*: "Rudabaugh stuck out from the window a handkerchief that had once been white ... In a few minutes all of them - the Kid, Wilson, Pickett, and Rudabaugh – came out." (Garrett Pages 181-182)

But Sederwall was setting-up his fake "cop discoveries" that history is not as written.

Sederwall added to the scene, from an uncited source, the historically never reported information that the possemen heard the sound of porthole-making. (Page 88) His sly intent was to use his counterfeiter Billy hoax as evidence for a hoaxed "discovery" about Stinking Springs.

So Sederwall called the sound of "porthole-making" a "tell" because "writers and historians missed [that] in addition to pursuing the man who was convicted of killing Sheriff Brady and <u>gunning down two of his deputies</u>, Garrett was sent by the United States Secret Service in pursuit of counterfeiters." (Page 88)

FAKING A "DISCOVERY": First of all, Billy was accused of killing *one* Brady deputy: George Hindman. The other indictment, besides Brady, was for posseman, Andrew "Buckshot Roberts." Sederwall seems to be confusing Billy's April 28, 1881 Lincoln jailbreak with killings of Deputies Bell and Olinger, with the December 22, 1880 Stinking Springs capture. Also, it was a windowless, <u>solid, stacked rock house at Stinking Springs. Portholes could not be cut out,</u> like they were in the adobe McSween house in the Lincoln County War Battle; casting doubt on reality of the porthole claim. Also, being deep in the ravine at a distance in front of the house, the posse would not have been able to hear activity inside the house.

Also, Garrett's working with the Secret Service on a counterfeiting case is known history. His participation was given by himself, 137 years before Sederwall thought he discovered it. In *The Authentic Life of Billy the Kid*, Garrett stated: "In October [of 1880], Azariah F. Wild, a detective in the employ of the Treasury Department. hailing from New Orleans, La., visited New Mexico to glean information in regard to the circulation of counterfeit money, some of which had certainly been passed in Lincoln County." (Garrett, Page 139) But Garrett made clear in his book that his warrants, and consequent pursuit, were for Billy's murder indictments: "[Bob] Olinger [commissioned also through Azariah Wild] and myself were both commissioned as deputy United States marshals and held United States warrants for the Kid and Bowdre for the killing of ["Buckshot"] Roberts on an Indian Reservation." (Garrett, Page 145) And Garrett never claimed Billy as a counterfeiter.

But Sederwall was using his Billy-as-counterfeiter hoax, already debunked above. (See pages 623-639)

So Sederwall, pretending he discovered a connection to Garrett's pursuit and counterfeiting, and pretending that Billy was a counterfeiter, pretended that Billy worried that Garrett would find counterfeit bills on him; which, Sederwall stated, would make Garrett file "federal counterfeiting charges" against him. (Page 88) Sederwall added that the porthole-making sound was really burying counterfeit money along with a Colt .45! (Page 90)

FAKERY: This is Sederwall's usual fake reasoning by "what-ifs." He had not proved Billy was a counterfeiter - or a urinator, or a hole digger! Also, Billy already had a bigger federal indictment to worry about: past U.S. Attorney T.B. Catron's 1878 federal indictment No. 411 for the murder of "Buckshot" Roberts - with hanging as outcome.

Furthermore, the switcheroo from porthole-making to digging, is even more absurd as being heard from a windowless solid rock house by men at a distance in a deep ravine.

But, building on thin air, Sederwall quoted John Meadows from Billy's post-jailbreak, as saying Billy told him he could not yet leave the Territory for lack of money. So Sederwall made-up that Billy was referring to lack of counterfeit money stored in the Stinking Springs rock house! (Page 89)

FAKERY: This is still Sederwall's "what-ifs" to preposterous lengths: *if* Billy was a counterfeiter, *if* he hid counterfeit money in the Stinking Springs rock house, *if* he dug a hole to hide it, *if* he urinated on it, *if* he needed cash, *then* he might want to go back and get it!

Of course, missing is the reality that Billy was giving John Meadows misleading excuses for staying in the Territory. Unknown to "Brushy," and the rest of the hoaxers, and kept secret from Meadows, was Billy's romance with Paulita Maxwell. Meadows's ranch was south of Lincoln, with Billy possibly first intending to go to Old Mexico. He then turned northeast to Fort Sumner, Paulita, and certain death.

Sederwall then made-up that Billy piled the guns on the hole with counterfeit money to "camouflage" it; with the "urine" supposedly repelling squeamish Garrett. (Page 90) He added that historian Philip Rasch claimed that in 1932, Tom Pickett, sent an Ed Coles to dig up the money. But none was found. (Page 90) So Sederwall spewed "what-ifs": What if after the jailbreak Billy had retrieved the counterfeit money and gun? What if the gun got rusty after being in the ground? What if it was then useless?

Now guess if Sederwall found a gun? He states that in 1910, a child named Ralph Camp dug inside the rock house and found a rusted Colt .45 (with photo provided).

**FAKE "INVESTIGATION":** Sederwall built his "discovery" backwards by meaningless "what ifs" using the 1910 gun finding and "Paco" Anaya's Billy defecating fable, which he had confused as urinating.

Used also was Philip Rasch's 1995 *Trailing Billy the Kid*, which gave the Pickett-Cole tale of seeking money in the Stinking Springs cabin, but in the tale it is real money, and Rasch made clear Pickett's reputation for telling tall tales. (Rasch, Page 108)

Also, no serial number is given to check the gun's dating. And the rock house was a Maxwell sheep herders' line cabin, likely built after Maxwell bought Fort Sumner. So from 1870 to 1910, anyone could leave the gun there. No link is established to Billy, to counterfeiting, to urinating, to defecating, or to real history.

**IRRELEVANT:** All this was irrelevant to Garrett not killing Billy, or "Brushy" being Billy. And it disproved "Brushy" by his not claiming to be a counterfeiter, or a urinating-or-defecating-gun-and-bad-money-hider. But Sederwall was warming up for a rerun of the "Billy the Kid Case" hoax.

# CHAPTER 6
# FAKE JAILBREAK "INVESTIGATION"

## THE LEAD-UP

Both the "Brushy" and "Billy the Kid Case" hoaxes make their entry for Billy's post-capture events; with "Brushy" coyly featured without naming. For the Mesilla hanging trial in the chapter "Sentenced to Hang" (Pages 92-93), Jameson replicates the "Brushy" team's guess that the verdict was unjust because of lack of evidence; and introduces "Brushy" by hinting that the names in the trial - William Bonney, William Antrim, Kid Antrim, Kid, and Billy the Kid - were not his *real* name. (Page 92) Still hinting, he asserts that the man in Billy's coffin was not Billy; and recycles the absurd Sexual Maturity Ratings from his 1998 *The Return of Billy the Kid*, in response to Grant County newspaperman S.M. Ashenfelter's fabricated dark hairy corpse. Jameson then gets Billy to the Lincoln courthouse-jail with conventional history.

## THE "BILLY THE KID CASE" HOAX'S COURTHOUSE-JAIL FAKERY

The "Billy the Kid Case" hoax enters in Jameson's chapter "Escape." (Pages 95-101) Unbeknownst to Jameson, he was now its vehicle for resuscitation, after having built-up Steve Sederwall as doing "cop" investigations, and having acknowledged most of the other second tier "Billy the Kid Case" hoaxers for his book. And, hilariously, Sederwall now claimed the *entire* "Billy the Kid Case" as *his own personal investigation*, calling his fellow hoaxers his bystanders and assistants! And Jameson's own hoaxing continued as surreptitious fix-ups of the "Brushy" team's errors: so, for example, "Goss" is now correctly Gottfried Gauss, and the escape horse now belongs to court clerk, Billy Burt.

In fact, the jailbreak "investigation" was the "Billy the Kid Case" hoax's most ridiculous scam, as Sheriff Tom Sullivan's, and his Deputy, Steve Sederwall's, sub-investigation for Lincoln County Case 2003-274 against Pat Garrett, to fabricate his murder motive as friendship with Billy. Its fake forensics were done by Dr. Henry Lee; with Sederwall later forging Lee's so-called "Floorboard Reports" to fake them as his own private hobby.

But instead of the unsavory reality, readers got Jameson's clueless adulating: "Steve Sederwall revealed elements of this gripping event that had long escaped the notice of earlier researchers and writers" because Garrett's version had been used (Page 95); though, in fact, there are many versions of the escape, with none certain. Given is the "Garrett version" from *The Authentic Life of Billy the Kid* has the gun in the outhouse, Billy getting ahead of Bell on the steps, and shooting down the stairway at Bell. (Page 97).

**CONCEALING EVIDENCE: Since Garrett was away collecting taxes, he was not a witness; so he only quoted witnesses. The favored version, is of Gottfried Gauss leaving the gun in the outhouse; on returning, Billy getting first to the second floor hall ahead of his guard James Bell; then menacing Bell, and wanting to tie him. But Bell bolted down the stairs, was fatally shot by Billy, stumbled to the landing, and was escorted out the rear door by likely accomplice, Gauss, to be concealed.**

Jameson gives the shotgun shooting of returning Bob Olinger, and Billy's telling Gauss to saddle to escape horse; though there is an error that Billy "filed the shackles from one leg." (Page 98) In fact, Billy got a miner's pick from Gauss, and himself broke a link in the chain joining his leg shackles so he could ride.

Then, suddenly, as if finally released from holding his tongue, Jameson launched into the "Brushy Bill" hoax. As an alternative escape version, he cited one from a "William Henry Roberts aka Billy the Kid," as being from his own books: listed as 2005's *Billy the Kid: Beyond the Grave* and 2012's *Billy the Kid: The Lost Interviews* (with his pre-fix-up *The Return of the Outlaw Billy the Kid* concealed). He gives "Brushy's" version as slipping handcuffs in the jail room while Bell fetched the leg iron key, then striking Bell on the head with the cuff, grabbing his gun, then wanting to be taken to the armory, but with Bell running down the steps and being shot by him. Then he quibbles about one or two shots fired, and how it was hard to hit Bell on the stairway. The hole on the right side of the wall in descent is made-up as not from Billy's shot, but by a "hand drill" by historian Maurice Garland Fulton. (Pages 100-101)

Next arrives the "Billy the Kid Case" hoax, with Jameson's fabrication that Garrett was responsible for two deputies killed, and never did an "investigation" (Page 101) - whatever that was supposed to mean; since he had interviewed witnesses and described the victim's fatal wounds. And there was no doubt that Billy did the killings.

Of course, that led to announcing Steve Sederwall's now "applying modern crime-solving and investigative techniques" to the Bell "crime scene." And Jameson voiced his hidden hope for history-not-as-written: "Virtually every cold case contains new information if new eyes search and a fresh and open mind considers the evidence." (Page 101) The reader was being herded to the rabbit hole for the drop into the hallucinatory wonderland of "Brushy" himself; updated with imaginary DNA and corpses dug up for no reason except to appear in a TV program.

## RETURN OF THE "BILLY THE KID CASE" AS "SEDERWALL'S INVESTIGATION" OF THE DEPUTY BELL SHOOTING

Duped Jameson devoted two chapters to the "Billy the Kid Case's" fake forensic investigation: "Lincoln County Courthouse Crime Scene Investigation" (Pages 102-111), and "An Escape Plot." (Pages 112-119). Showcasing Steve Sederwall, the intent was to denigrate Pat Garrett as set-up for calling him an murderer of an innocent victim instead of Billy the Kid, after "Sederwall's cop instinct kicked into gear after studying Garrett's account of the [jailbreak] escape." (Page 102).

So Sederwall secretly recycled Case 2003-274's "Probable Cause Statement," which he wrote, then signed on December 31, 2003 as a Lincoln County Deputy (See pages 324-346 above); and he recycled his forged Dr. Henry Lee "Floorboard Reports," as cited by unaware Jameson in his "Bibliography."

Repeated was Sederwall's usual fake reasoning by "what-ifs": What if Pat Garrett killed the innocent victim? What if he helped Billy escape jail by giving him the gun? That means they were friends. That means Pat would kill for Billy. That means Pat *did kill* for Billy and is a murderer. (It should be noted that "Brushy" never claimed this plot.)

Here is the original Sederwall-authored, "Probable Cause Statement's" presentation of its Deputy James Bell killing sub-investigation:

> No one in 122 years has been able to speak with clear certainty where the gun came from that William Bonney used to kill Deputy J.W. Bell. With the information investigators have seen they question Garrett's involvement in the Kid obtaining a weapon.
>
> It would go to reason that if the body in Fort Sumner is anyone other than William Bonney then Garrett no doubt had a hand in allowing the Kid to escape on July 14, 1881.
>
> If the body at Fort Sumner is anyone other than William Bonney, then Garrett, whether by accident or design, is responsible for homicide of the person resting in that grave.
>
> If it is not Bonney in the grave at Fort Sumner it would also go to reason that Garrett would be looked at as a suspect in furthering the escape of the Kid on April 28, 1881 when the two Lincoln County Sheriffs were murdered.
>
> Although the [sub] investigation will deal with what happened in the Lincoln County court house on April 28, 1881, this writing [Probable Cause Statement] will deal with the alleged shooting of William Bonney at Fort Sumner on the night of July 14, 1881 [as the murder case].

Jameson was apparently unaware that this "investigation" addressed only the silly question of whether Bell died at the top or bottom of the stairway; or that Dr. Henry Lee's "floorboard investigation" was not only fake forensics, with no provable connection to Deputy Bell for lack of Bell's reference DNA for comparison; or that Sederwall forged Lee's report about it to hide its law enforcement nature and Lee's non-committal conclusions. But Jameson may have known that, on March 13, 2010, Sederwall, appeared in a National Geographic International TV program, produced by British Parthenon Entertainment for the Discovery ID channel, to present this top-of-the-stairs scam to call Sheriff Pat Garrett a liar.

But Sederwall, faking the "investigation" as solely his, rolled out its full forensic hoaxing for fake "suspicions," while keeping secret its silly top-of-the-stairs direction; as follows:

1) It was "suspicious" that Garrett described the scene, since he was away at White Oaks collecting taxes. **[But Garrett made clear he was recounting the escape from eye-witnesses.]**

2) It was "suspicious" that Garrett said the armory door could be opened by a "firm push." **[Concealed is that in** *The Authentic Life of Billy the Kid* **Garrett was just saying that "Lincoln did not then have a jail that would hold a cripple." Prisoners were merely housed on the second floor of the courthouse, and chained to steel rings in the floor. That is why Garrett took extra precaution with Billy by keeping him alone, with wrist and ankle shackles, and two 24 hour deputy guards (Bell and Olinger).]**

3) It was "suspicious that Garrett blamed Bell and Olinger. **[Why not? They were the responsible guards.]**

With himself as sole investigator, Sederwall then presented himself as the hero to "remedy the situation" of Garrett's "lying." On August 4, 2002, he leads New Mexico lawmen and forensic expert Dr. Henry Lee (presented in a photo wearing a cowboy hat along with Sederwall wearing a badge) to examine the area claimed for the Bell killing. (Page 104) Admitted is that the stairway was replaced. [Omitted is that the shooting of Bell had occurred on it - so there was no longer an evidence source!] Stating that the original floorboards on the second floor were then exposed for Lee, Sederwall has him perform his "presumptive blood tests" with o-Tolidine (Ortho-tolidine), called a test for blood (omitting it was for any iron-containing compound, like rust). Sederwall portrays Lee as swabbing the flooorboards, and **quotes him as saying: "Positive for blood."** (Page 105) Sederwall added: "The tests showed positive reactions for blood in several areas on the landing ... Lee's conclusion was that 'chemical tests for the presence of blood were positive with some of [the floorboard] stains." (Page 105)

LYING: Dr. Lee's quote and conclusion are fabricated by Sederwall, proving why, in the Lee reports he forged, he removed Lee's "Results and Conclusions" section to cover-up his own claiming whatever he wanted.

Lee, though a hoaxer himself, had approximated truth. So in his real report of February 25, 2005, he called the stains "blood-like" and "could be bloodstains." Lee concluded: "Various stains were observed on the surface and underside of the floor boards. Chemical tests for the presence of blood were positive for some of those stains. These results indicate the presence of Heme or Peroxidase like activity with those stains tested positive, <u>which suggests that those stains could be bloodstains</u>. Further DNA testing could reveal the nature and identity of those blood-like stains."

Most important, is that Sederwall, and likely Lee, knew that there existed no DNA of Bell to compare the "blood" to, since his gravesite is unknown and there are no kin. There was no way to prove blood, if found, was Bell's. And omitted is that the Lab, Orchid Cellmark, did not test for blood anyway.

**JAMESON AS INADVERTENTLY COMPLICIT:** Dupe Jameson cited Sederwall's forged Dr. Lee report in his Bibliography under "Reports" with yet another faked title and a new made-up date as "Forensic Examination Report (Lincoln County Courthouse), May 22, 2004." Lee's actual and sole report [APPENDIX: 8] was dated February 25, 2005 and titled "Forensic Research & Training Center Forensic Examination Report;" and combined all his investigations as: "Item #1 Workbench;" "Item #2 Washstand;" "Item #3 A piece of Headboard;" Item #4 "Examination of Lincoln County Court House;" and "Results and Conclusion."

Out-of-control Sederwall next lied that blood had been confirmed, claimed Bell's was the only bloodshed in the courthouse's history, made-up a "significant amount," and concluded the "blood" must be Bell's. (Pages 105-106; 110) He then made-up that Garrett must have lied because he did not mention so much blood on the second floor. (Page 106)

Sederwall then quoted witness Gauss about hearing a "tussle upstairs, somebody hurrying down the stairs," and Bell coming out the door to him. This is the conventional scene in which Bell struggled with Billy, ran down the back stairs, was shot on the way down, got to the back door at the base of the landing, and was taken outside by Gauss as he died. Sederwall stated that this meant Bell was "upstairs," because he ran downstairs. (Page 106)

**FAKERY: Running down the stairway, has nothing to do with proving bleeding on its top.**

Sederwall then misrepresented a quote of Sophie Poe, from her 1936 book titled *Buckboard Days*, about when she lived in the courthouse. As the wife of John William Poe, who replaced Pat Garrett as Lincoln County Sheriff, she commented on blood on its stairway - while forgetting that Bell was heading down, not up, when shot. She stated: "The back stairway ... which I had to travel many times during the day, was still stained with blood, a grim reminder of the day ... when Billy the Kid had shot and killed his guard, James W. Bell. Bell had been climbing those stairs and his body had fallen to the bottom of them." (Sophie Poe, Page 205) The place she referenced is preserved for tourists, as where the bullet passed sideways through Bell, striking the wall half-way down the stairway, to the right of a descent.

But Sederwall falsely claimed she referenced blood <u>on the second floor</u>. (Page 106) Then he quibbled about her saying that Bell had fallen "to the bottom of the stairs." She obviously meant that was were he collapsed. But Sederwall claimed she saw blood all the way from the top to the bottom of the stairs. Then he claimed Garrett lied by not describing that too.

**LYING: Sederwall is fabricating scenarios from made-up evidence. Bell was shot in the middle of the stairway while heading down, dying soon after he made it to the bottom.**

Sederwall faked "discrepancies" in Garrett's account; questioning slipped handcuffs, and ruminating about how to wipe yourself in the latrine if your hands were cuffed behind your back (which was never claimed for Billy). (Pages 107-108)

**FALLACIOUS ANALYSIS: Sederwall omits that Garrett might not have been given the true manner of escape, especially if Billy had an accomplice, like Gauss, supplying the information, and obviously concealing a plot. So any discrepancies that Garrett got second-hand would not implicate him of willful misinformation anyway.**

Sederwall then gives the gun-left-in-the-outhouse version, and ruminates about why Billy did not shoot Bell then. And he gives the known scenario that Billy wanted to take Bell prisoner, not kill him. But he adds Bob Olinger to that plan. And he makes-up scenes of Billy's confronting Bell with the gun, and wounding Bell's head, usually seen as Billy's attempt to subdue him to enable tying-up. But Sederwall fakes Bell's head's blood as being on the floorboards for Dr. Lee's fake forensics. (Pages 108-110)

By then, Sederwall had blood pouring out - much like he had lied for the carpenter's bench in the original hoax in escalating newspaper interviews. (See page 408) So he made-up that Lee had said "Bell lost a great deal of blood." (Page 110)

THEN CAME THE WHOLE POINT OF JAMESON'S BOOK: THE FUSING OF THE "BRUSHY" AND "BILLY THE KID CASE" HOAXES INTO A MEGAHOAX: SEDERWALL QUOTED "BRUSHY" HIMSELF FOR AN ESCAPE SCENARIO TO GO WITH FOR HIS FAKE FORENSICS! In the quote, Sederwall has "Brushy" ask to go to the latrine. While Bell goes to get the key, he slips out of his handcuff, hits and stuns returned Bell on the head, grabs his gun and key, and wants to be taken to the armory. On the way there, Bell runs for the stairway, pauses at the hall on top of the stairs so "copious amounts of blood" can fall. Then Billy's fatal bullet ricochets on the wall. So Sederwall says this explains the "blood" he and "his investigative team" found "a century and a quarter later."(Page 111)

FABRICATING "BRUSHY'S FABRICATION: This, at last, is the uniting of two liars: "Brushy" confabulating himself as Billy; and Sederwall fabricating himself as a valid investigator using "Brushy" for "evidence" that Bell-head-wound-blood was on the upstairs hallway.

But Sederwall is faking "Brushy's" tale. In fact, "Brushy" confabulated by combining two well known escape versions. He said "Sam Corbett [actually Tunstall's past shopkeeper] and his wife came in to see me. Sam had hid a six-shooter in the latrine. But I didn't need Sam's six-shooter. [He had Olinger leave, and himself alone with Bell in the east room where Billy was kept. Bell goes to Garrett's office to the west of it to get the key. He slips his shackle, and when Bell returns, he states] I hit him in the back of the head. He tumbled over on the floor ... [NOTE: "Brushy" said he hit Bell in the east room used for the incarceration, not the hallway scenario Sederwall made-up.] I told him to walk through [Garrett's] office and unlock the armory door." (*Alias Billy the Kid*, Pages 43-44) Then "Brushy" has Bell's flight down the stairs, and the shot hitting the wall, as "Brushy" would have seen himself on his Morrison tour.

And, a key discrepancy to note is that "Brushy" never claimed that Pat Garrett played a part in this escape. This was unique to the "Billy the Kid Case" hoax.

# RETURN OF THE "BILLY THE KID CASE" AS "SEDERWALL'S INVESTIGATION" OF GARRETT AS ESCAPE ACCOMPLICE

By the next chapter, "An Escape Plot," building on his fake courthouse forensics, and based on no real evidence at all, frothing and lying Jameson-Sederwall accuse Garrett of "perfidy;" to segue into sneering: "[H]e may have been more involved in the Kid's escape than we have been led to believe." (Page 112)

**A BAD FIT OF HOAXES: Since the "Brushy" hoax is a bad fit for the "Billy the Kid Case" hoax, contradictions like this arise: "Brushy" did not claim Garrett helped his escape, or that Garrett killed Billy Barlow to save him. But the "Billy the Kid Case" hoax, and now Sederwall, used the Bell killing to fake Garrett's friendship for Billy, for a future murder motive for Garrett.**

Adding to the basic "Billy the Kid Case" hoax, Sederwall, continued to attempt Garrett's character assassination by faking history-not-as-written. He faked "discrepancies" about Garrett's report of Billy's escape, with his usual "what ifs": What if Garrett had been away collecting taxes on purpose? (Pages 113-114)

**WRONG: Tax collecting was required. When new Sheriff John Copeland neglected filing his tax collecting bond in his first month, on May 28, 1878, Governor S.B. Axtell issued a Proclamation removing him as Sheriff, replacing him with Ringite George Peppin.**

Sederwall provided Garrett's report about the escape horse being Billy Burt's, Billy's promise to return it, and an "Andrew Nimley" [sic] retrieving it; and concluded Garrett lied because it was too much information. (Page 116)

He then tried a history-not-as-written trick to claim the escape horse was Garrett's. He cited old-timer windbag malarkey of a Gorgonio Wilson, a self-proclaimed eye-witness, who stated in an August 7, 1955 (!) *El Paso Times* article, when 89, that Billy called him from a window to saddle *Garrett's horse* for him. And the daughter of a non-historical Robert Corn said her father said Billy used *Pat's horse*. And in 1977, a Ygenio Salazar relative claimed *Garrett's horse*. (Page 116-117) So Sederwall concluded that sharing his horse meant Garrett and Billy were friends.

**FLAWED EVIDENCE:** First of all, the Tularosa Ditch War prisoner was Alexander Nunnelly, not "Andrew Nimley;" and he did not retrieve Billy's escape pony.

As to the escape horse, Sederwall used meaningless hearsay. And it involved hiding that Lincoln's townspeople eye-witnessed Billy's escape. And no legitimate witness reported Garrett's horse used for it. But, if his horse had been stolen for it, Garrett would have reported it himself. Also, he would have ridden his horse to White Oaks for his tax collecting, so it would not have been there.

Furthermore, Garrett wanting to give a detailed account about the embarrassing fact of the escape of his most important prisoner means just that. Sederwall is merely blowing smoke by calling it too much information.

And a crucial real discrepancy is to be noted: Sederwall just destroyed "Brushy" as Billy! "Brushy" had no Garrett horse tale. His tale was child Severo Gallegos getting Billy a rope for the horse, <u>which he called Ira Leonard's</u>. Worse, Gallegos, who Sederwall had just made a liar before dupe Jameson's eyes, was also "Brushy" and team's *only eye-witness Lincolnite* to give a "Brushy" as Billy Affidavit! And, marble-playing on the street, *he* was someone who could actually have recognized Garrett's horse!

Next, Sederwall presented known scenarios of Gauss's involvement in the escape, and of the Kid's going to the outhouse to get the gun; but rejected them as "lies." (Pages 117-118)

**FAKE ANALYSIS:** Since Sederwall is faking evidence to fabricate Garrett an accomplice in the escape (and ultimately a murderer of the innocent victim), he has to discount the likely and accepted truth that *Gauss* was actually Billy's accomplice. He gives no evidence that the Gauss-gun-in-outhouse scenario is "lies."

And he omits the likely motives for Gauss's willingness to risk his life by hanging as a murder accomplice of Billy's deputy killings. In fact, Gauss, was bitterly anti-Ring. He had first been employed in running the brewery for "The House" in its sutler store beginnings, and had been cheated out of his wages. As anti-Ring, John Tunstall's, cook, he would have met Billy by October of 1877, and had been present at every subsequent Ring atrocity. He was the only one left at Tunstall's Feliz River ranch when

Brady's murderous posse came looking for Tunstall, then murdered him. He knew about the illegal Proclamation of Governor S.B. Axtell to outlaw the Regulators, and might even have been at Tunstall's store at the Regulator's Brady ambush. And he would have known the horror of the murder of Alexander McSween, whom he knew, in the Lincoln County War Battle. He would have believed Billy's hanging sentence was unjust, especially since all the Ring murderers had been shielded from penalties. And he was now caretaker of the courthouse, in an ideal position to intervene. Furthermore, he was above suspicion, because Pat Garrett was a late entry to Lincoln County, and would have been unaware of his partisanship. Furthermore, it is obvious that Gauss and Billy would have used the outhouse plan when Garrett was out of town - as Garrett would have represented their greatest risk to success.

Adding to his fakery of Garrett as Billy's accomplice, Sederwall relied on his usual meaningless "what ifs;" now so bizarre they knock your sox off: What if Garrett made up that Billy was a bad outlaw to build himself up as a hero by contrast? What if Garrett blamed his deputies for incompetence to remove responsibility from himself? What if, on purpose, he did not seal off the town to further investigate the deputy killings? (Pages 118-119)

Jameson may then have pitched in from the "Brushy" hoax, that because Garrett sought "higher political office" he had to convince citizens he was competent. (Page 119) The Jameson-Sederwall duo conclude: "The evidence clearly shows that Garrett lied. The evidence is highly suggestive of [his] possible role in the escape plot."

IMPLICATIONS: All this fakery was irrelevant to Garrett not killing Billy, or "Brushy" being Billy. But one can guess that for gullible W.C. Jameson, this courthouse forensics blather and lying looked like real science and real "cop" investigations adding useful evidence. And saying bad things about Garrett was C.L. Sonnichsen's legacy from the "Brushy" hoax. And to fuzzy-headed Jameson, this may all have seemed helpful to his cause. Instead, possibly unbeknownst to himself, as sole author, Jameson was now perpetrating a massive hoax by inability to vet his own hoaxing sources.

# ATTACKING PAT GARRETT BY "BRUSHY BILL" AND "BILLY THE KID CASE" HOAXES

The fake jailbreak investigations set the stage for the core premise of the "Brushy Bill" survival hoax and the "Billy the Kid Case" murder hoax: that Pat Garrett murdered an innocent victim, then covered it up. The Jameson-Sederwall duo continued their attacks in the chapters "A Liar and a Thief." (Pages 120-124) and "Reluctant Pursuit." (Pages 125-130) Added were more fake Sederwall "cop investigations."

Important to recognize is that the two hoaxes formulated their bad guy Garrett differently. In the "Brushy" hoax, he was a tool of the Santa Fe Ring trying to kill Billy, and dishonestly collected a reward while hiding that he had accidentally murdered Billy Barlow instead. In the "Billy the Kid Case" hoax, Garrett was in a bromance with Billy, was an accomplice to Billy's jailbreak murder of his own deputy guards, and intentionally killed an innocent victim (risking his own life to future hanging) so Billy could live free (after he shot him for playing-dead-on-the-carpenter's-bench-to-bleed-for-Dr. Lee's-future-"blood-DNA").

To further defame Garrett, the duo called him a deadbeat, a debtor, a drunk, an adulterer, a con man, and a thief; much like they did in Jameson's 2016 *Pat Garrett: The Man Behind the Badge*. (Page 120)

So they accuse him of theft in handling dead Bob Olinger's estate, by keeping Olinger's guns, and giving his Whitney double-barrel shotgun to his friend, Joseph Lea! "Cop" Sederwall "discovers" in the list of clothes listed as valueless, Garrett's omission of hat, boots, and saddle. So he quoted Lilly Klasner from her book *My Girlhood Among Outlaws* (a posthumous memoir), saying after Olinger's death she got his six-shooter, field glasses and gauntlet. (Page 124) So Sederwall adds them to list omissions; even though he claimed earlier that the possessions should go to his family (and was possibly unaware that Klasner was Olinger's fiancé). This foolish drivel leads Sederwall to conclude that Garrett was a liar and a thief. (Page 124)

Garrett was next accused of not trying to capture Billy, since a May 12, 1881 *Las Vegas Gazette* article said he was near Fort Sumner; even though Garrett was also cited as saying he was working out a plan of action. (Pages 125-126)

OMITTING EVIDENCE: Omitted is the known fake reporting about Billy's location, since his whereabouts were unknown and he was big news. He was even accused, in the May 4, 1881 *Santa Fe Daily New Mexican*, of murdering Billy Matthews in "More Killing by Kid, When But a Short Distance From Lincoln, He Meets one of His Old Enemies, and Kills Him and His Companion. Two More Victims." Here are other examples. On May 5, 1881 in the *Santa Fe Daily New Mexican's* "Anything that the imagination can concoct," had Billy seen in Albuquerque. On May 13, 1881, the *Santa Fe Daily New Mexican* reported Billy in Chloride City. On May 19, 1881, the *Santa Fe Daily New Mexican* printed, "The Kid is believed to be in the Black Range." On May 19, 1881, the *Santa Fe Daily New Mexican* printed "Billy the Kid was last seen in Lincoln County." And on June 13, 1881, the *Las Vegas Daily Optic* had " 'Billy the Kid,' He is Reported to Have Been Seen on Our Streets Saturday Night."

As to Fort Sumner, the duo claim Billy was there because of Paulita Maxwell, Peter Maxwell's teenaged sister. (Page 127) This is important to note because it is a fix-up unknown to "Brushy," who fabricated Celsa Gutierrez there as his sweetheart.

Also cited is known history that Garrett did not believe Billy was in Fort Sumner, and that his Deputy, John W. Poe, convinced him to go there. But, to fake Garrett as unmotivated to capture Billy, Poe is portrayed as having to take the initiative.

HIDING EVIDENCE: Omitted is Garrett's explanation, in *The Authentic Life of Billy the Kid*, about using Poe for recognizance: "Poe was a stranger in the country, and there was little danger he would meet anyone at Sumner who might know him. So, after an hour or two spent in the hills, <u>I sent him to Fort Sumner to take observations. I advised him to go to Sunnyside,</u> seven miles above Sumner, and interview M. Rudulph, in whose judgment and discretion I had great confidence. It was understood that Poe would meet with us that night at moonlight." (Garrett, Pages 212-213)

Then, to portray Garrett as a liar, the approach to the Maxwell house is garbled from *The Authentic Life of Billy the Kid*, as to his seeing two figures in the peach orchard. Stated is: "As Garrett, Poe, and McKinney approached the houses, Garrett said, they 'heard the sound of voices conversing in Spanish,' though they were too far away to hear words distinctly. As they watched from hiding, 'a man rose from the ground in full view, but too fat away to recognize. He wore a broad-brimmed hat, dark vest and pants, and was in his shirt sleeves.' This man, claimed Garrett, was Billy the Kid, even though he previously stated he was too far away to recognize.' A few lines later, however, Garrett again wrote, 'The Kid by me unrecognized.' Did Garrett recognize the Kid or not?" This fake "discrepancy leads the duo to claim the incident never happened because Poe did not mention the scene in his own book. So Garrett lied. (Page 129)

FAKING EVIDENCE: What Garrett actually stated in *The Authentic Life of Billy the Kid* is that he, Poe, and McKinney, on foot, secretly entered the Maxwell's peach orchard which extended to some houses "occupied by Mexicans, not more than sixty yards from Maxwell's house. We approached these houses cautiously, and when within earshot heard the voices of people conversing in Spanish [i.e., they heard the Spanish voices of the people in the houses]. We concealed ourselves quickly and listened, but the distance was too great to hear words or even distinguish voices [i.e., referring to a couple at a distance in the orchard, too far to make out their words]. Soon a man arose from the ground, close enough to be seen but too far away to be recognized [i.e., the distant man, whose words could not be made out, rose]. He wore a broad-brimmed hat, dark vest and pants, and was in his shirt sleeves ... [H]e went to the fence, jumped it, and walked toward the Maxwell house. Little as we suspected it, this man was the Kid." [i.e., it would only be later, that Garrett would realize, likely by the outfit of the corpse he had shot, that it had been Billy). (Garrett, Page 214) Garrett makes clear he did not recognize Billy in the orchard: "When the Kid, who had been thus unrecognized by me, left the orchard, I motioned to my companions." (Page 215) And Poe merely left out this insignificant scene in his book decades later. Jameson and Sederwall were faking a "discrepancy."

# CHAPTER 7
# FAKING DEATH SCENE DOUBTS

## THE MEGAHOAX'S HEART

The Jameson-Sederwall duo (presumably assisted by the acknowledged additional hoaxers) present their hoax's make-or-break July 14, 1881 death scene in chapters "Shooting at Fort Sumner" (Pages 131-134) and "Discrepancies." (Pages 135-163)

Concealed is that "Brushy's" tale is totally different from the "Billy the Kid Case's." He had Billy Barlow accidentally killed in the dark night on the back porch. The "Billy the Kid Case" hoax had super-friend Pat Garrett shooting willing Billy to play dead on the carpenter's bench (to bleed for future fake DNA); then murdering the innocent victim to switch with Billy for burial.

Concealed also, is zero evidence supporting either hoax; and profuse evidence debunking them. So the duo rely on fake "discrepancies," fake "investigations," and Dr. Henry Lee's fake carpenter's bench and washstand forensics. The result is a megahoax, that disproves "Brushy" by its mismatch, and exposes its creators by its ridiculous lies.

Their hoaxed claim is that "researchers never noted the obvious and glaring discrepancies" in Pat Garrett's and John W. Poe's accounts of the shooting. There were none, but the Jameson-Sederwall duo propose to show them by breaking the death scene shooting to five parts: arrival of participants to Maxwell's room, shooting, post-shooting removal of body, the "inquests" [sic - there was just one] and burial. (Page 135)

Since the only relevant fact is the profuse identification of the body as Billy Bonney's - as was obviously omitted by these charlatans - the meaninglessness of their scam is obvious from the start. Important, however, are additions to the original hoaxes of this magahoax's new fake "cop investigations."

# FAKING DISCREPANCIES

Discrepancies are faked using Pat Garrett's 1882 *Authentic Life of Billy the Kid* and John W. Poe's *The Death of Billy the Kid*, to pretend they proved events did not occur. So the duo conclude that this "incident [shooting in the bedroom] as the two lawmen described it never took place." (Page 141) Examples follow:

**1) DEPUTIES OUTSIDE:** The duo claim it was suspicious for Garrett to enter the Maxwell's bedroom, while leaving his deputies outside, because it was too careless for searching for "the most dangerous outlaw in New Mexico." (Page 138)

**FAKING EVIDENCE: Omitted is that Garrett did not believe that Billy was in Fort Sumner, and was merely checking with Maxwell. Omitted is another possibility, that a trap was being set, with Billy being sent to Maxwell's bedroom for ambush. In that case, it was strategic to have the deputies outside in case Billy escaped out of the room.**

**2) IN SOX AND BUTTONING PANTS:** The approach of the stranger, in sox and buttoning his pants, is tackled by "cop" Sederwall, recycling this absurdity from his (concealed) Case No. 2003-274's "Probable Cause Statement" about it being too hard to hold a gun and a knife and button your pants; plus gravel would hurt your sensitive stockinged feet! (Page 139)

**FAKING EVIDENCE: Billy apparently could multi-task! And apparently he could tackle gravel too! Sederwall's silliness in the "Probable Cause Statement" stated:**

> [Poe stated] *At this I stood up and advanced toward him, telling him not to be alarmed ... and still without the least suspicion that this was the very man we were looking for.*
>
> This statement raises many questions with investigators. Poe says he sees a man *"partially dressed, and was bare-headed and bare-footed - or rather, had only socks on his feet, and it seemed to me that he was fastening his trousers as he came toward me art a very brisk walk."* Then the man covers him with his six shooter. Where did the man put the *"six-shooter"* when he was *"fastening his trousers"*?
>
> He did not stop and lay it down because Poe says he *"he came toward me art a very brisk walk."*

3) **SPEAKING SPANISH:** Sederwall cogitated that if approaching Billy said, "Quien es?" and non-Spanish-speaking Poe responded in English to reassure him, then bi-lingual Billy would have reverted to English. So Sederwall concludes that left just two possibilities: it was not Billy, or Poe lied! (Page 140)

**FAKING EVIDENCE:** Omitted is that Billy was the most hunted man in the Territory. Speaking Spanish to a stranger was his disguise. Furthermore, he probably used the language commonly, as he would with bi-lingual Peter Maxwell in the next a moment. And the disguise worked! Poe assumed he was a Maxwell worker. Sederwall's two "possibilities" are absurd.

Noteworthy is ongoing demolition of "Brushy" as Billy; here arguing based on being bi-lingual. "Brushy" was not.

4) **LETTING BILLY ENTER THE BEDROOM:** Sederwall claimed it was unimaginable that two deputies let a man with a knife and a gun walk into the bedroom with Garrett, without shouting a warning. And he imagines that Billy would have been more cautious, or even shot the deputies. (Pages 140-141)

**FAKING EVIDENCE: Fantasizing is not evidence.**

In fact, neither Poe nor McKinney knew Billy, and thought he was a Maxwell worker. Billy's gun was attributed to strangers alarming him, and could as easily be construed as a worker being protective of Maxwell, and rightly asking them in Spanish, "Who are you?" And none of the lawmen were expecting Billy to turn up at Maxwell's house, so were not alarmed. As Poe stated in his book: "As Maxwell's was the one place in Fort Sumner I considered above suspicion of harboring the Kid, I was entirely off my guard." (Poe, Page 34)

As to Billy being incautious, he was known for fearlessness. That is how he ended up in Fort Sumner, instead of hightailing it to Old Mexico after his jailbreak. And Fort Sumner had strangers passing through. It is absurd to think that he would automatically shoot them!

5) **ENTERING THE BEDROOM:** Garrett's statement that the person "sprang quickly into the door" is contrasted with Poe describing Billy backing towards the door, to claim Billy never entered the room! (Page 132)

FAKING EVIDENCE: Actually, the manner of entering is merely vantage. In his 1933 book, Poe described Billy as "<u>backed up</u> into the doorway of Maxwell's room, where he halted for a moment, his body concealed by the thick adobe wall at the side of the doorway." (Poe, Page 35) So Poe could not have seen Billy's final turn to enter the room face-forward as Garrett saw. There is no discrepancy.

6) THE VICTIM'S IDENTITY: After the shooting, Maxwell is presented as running out; Garrett as doubtful, saying, "I <u>think</u> I have got him;" and Poe being doubtful. (Page 133)

FAKING: Garrett did not say, "I think I have got him." In his book, he was certain: "I told my companions that <u>I had got the Kid</u>. They asked if I had not shot the wrong man. I told them I made no mistake, for I knew the Kid's voice too well." He explained the Deputies' doubt: "Seeing a bareheaded, bare-footed man, in his shirt sleeves, with a butcher knife in his hand, and hearing his hail in excellent Spanish, they naturally supposed him to be a Mexican and an attaché of the establishment, hence their suspicion that I had shot the wrong man." (Garrett, Page 217)

As to Poe, *he* is the one who gave quote the duo called Garrett's: " 'I think I have got him' ... I said, 'Pat, the Kid would not come to this place; you have shot the wrong man ...' Upon my saying this, Garrett seemed to be in doubt himself as to whom he shot, but quickly spoke up and said, 'I am sure that was him, for I know his voice too well to be mistaken.' " (Poe, Pages 37-38) And Poe confirmed: "**Upon examining the body, we found it to be that of Billy the Kid.**" (Poe, page 41) There was no discrepancy.

7) POST-SHOOTING SCENES: The scene is given of "native people" taking the body "to a carpenter shop where it was laid out on a workbench." Poe is quoted about staying in Maxwell's house for fear of attack by "friends of the dead man." (Page 134) Then appears "cop" Sederwall to say it all seemed suspicious to him that Garrett would let women take the body of such a famous outlaw, or that he would "cower" in Maxwell's house. To him that means Garrett was a bad leader - or worse. (Page 134)

FAKING DOUBT: Sederwall's fantasies are not evidence.

# FAKING A MAXWELL BEDROOM DOOR DISCREPANCY

This new hoax of Maxwell's bedroom having no outside door - used in *Pat Garrett: The Man Behind the Badge* (see pages 573-574 above) - is to destroy the historical death scene in one fell swoop, since all participants recounted it. A diagram is given and labeled "Floor plan of the Maxwell house," and has no door. And the building is called a one-story adobe. (Page 137) **[FIGURE: 9]**

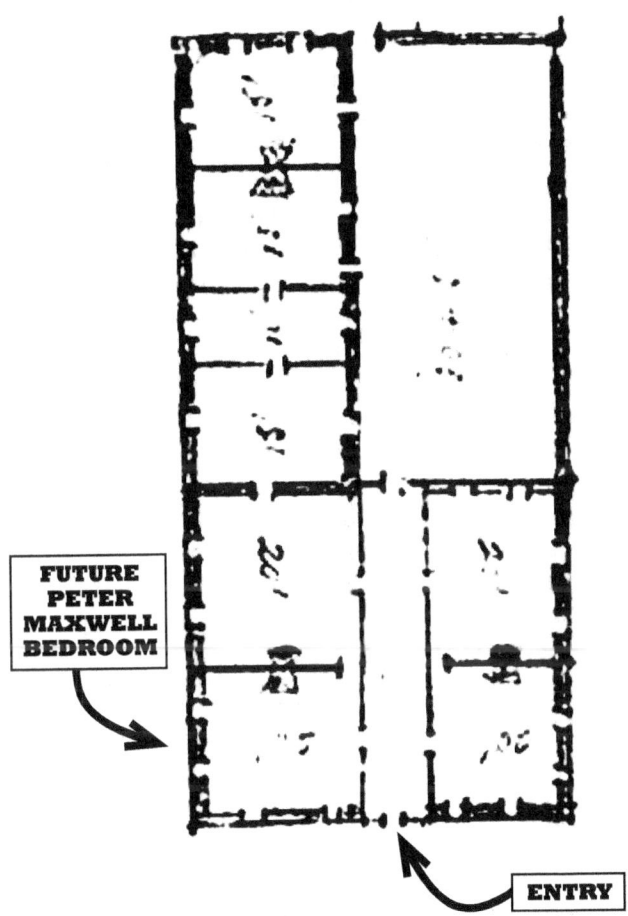

FIGURE: 9. Falsely used by the hoaxers as "Floor plan of Maxwell house" from the "National Archives" (Page 137); this diagram is from the National Archives as "Commanding Officer's Quarters, Fort Sumner, New Mexico Territory;" and its copy, so labeled, is at the Fort Sumner State Monument

To indicate that Garrett lied about the door, the hoaxers state: "**Garrett wrote, '[Billy] 'stepped onto the porch and entered Maxwell's room through the open door left open on account of the extremely warm weather.'**" (Page 131) And Poe's witnessing Billy enter through that door is cited as to his lying also. (Page 140) Added is that if there was a door, it was not open, as Garrett said, because scary animals could get in. (Page 138) So the duo conclude that Garrett and Poe were lying about the entire scene to conceal that Billy the Kid was never shot.

**FAKED INVESTIGATION:** The claimed "floor plan" is not Maxwell's bedroom, but is the original Fort Sumner Commanding Officer's quarters for the Bosque Redondo Indian Reservation from 1863 to 1868. Since its sources in the National Archives and at Fort Sumner State Monument label it as such, the hoaxers are faking its identification.

Omitted is that in 1870, when Lucien Maxwell bought Fort Sumner, he rebuilt it as his family home. As Robert Mullin wrote on the back of the Maxwell house photo: "*Pete Maxwell's House Fort Sumner ... Originally 1 Story Flat Roof, Officers Quarters. 2nd Floor Added By Maxwell.*"

The actual Maxwell house floor plan shows the outside door. [Figure 10] And the Maxwell house photograph, also shows that door in Maxwell's bedroom. [Figure 11]

And to claim, as did the hoaxing duo, that the door was not left open, is meaningless fantasizing.

And the Garrett quote is faked. He actually wrote: "When we reached the porch in front of the building, I left Poe and McKinney at the end of the porch, and about twenty feet from the door of Pete's bedroom, while I myself entered it." (Garrett, Page 215) The quote is actually distorted from Poe's book; stating: "'You fellows wait here while I go in to talk to [Maxwell].' Thereupon he stepped onto the porch and entered Maxwell's room through the open door (left open on account of the extremely warm weather), while McKinney and myself stopped on the outside." (Poe, Page 31)

Also, Poe described the further role of that door when he almost shot Maxwell: "A moment after Garrett came out of the door, Pete Maxwell rushed squarely onto me in a frantic effort to get out of the room." (Poe, Page 38) This contradicts the hoaxers' walking through the house fakery.

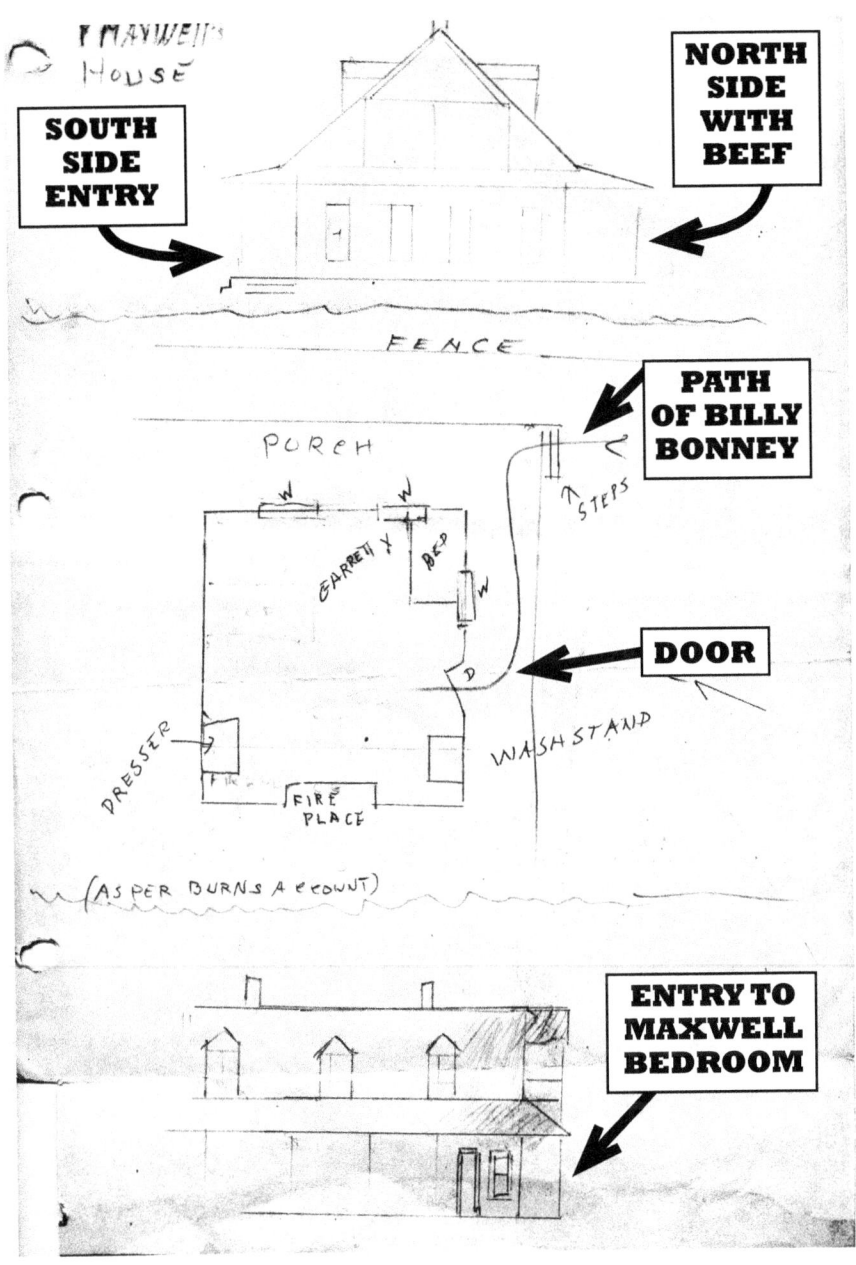

FIGURE: 10. Diagrams by Maurice Garland Fulton of the Maxwell's house, with Peter Maxwell's bedroom, and Billy Bonney's entry through its outside door. From the Midland, Texas, Haley Library, Robert N. Mullin Collection.

FIGURE: 11. Photograph of the Maxwell house showing Peter Maxwell's bedroom with a door to the outside. From the Midland, Texas, Haley Library, Robert N. Mullin Collection.

SOURCE FOR FAKE DOOR INVESTIGATION: This "investigation's" no door claim was lifted from an undated article by an unknown author (erroneously named as Gregory Scott Smith) titled "The Death of Billy the Kid: A New Scenario?" now in the Fort Sumner State Monument files. It used John L. McCarty papers of an October 22, 1942 interview titled "Kid Dobbs Interviews: An Interview with Garrett H. 'Kid' Dobbs at Farmington, New Mexico, on September 12, 1942, with Mel Armstrong and John McCarty, Thursday Morning, October 22, 1942, In the Presence of Mrs. Dobbs and Pat Flynn. J.D. White, Amarillo, Heard Part of the Final Statements of this Interview Re. Billy the Kid's Death."

Garrett H. "Kid" Dobbs merely spouted old-timer windbag malarkey. His fabrication, with the usual claim of knowing Billy the Kid, began with: "Billy told me ... he came from San Francisco, California, and had killed a chinaman out there for insulting his mother." Here is Dobbs's Lincoln County War Battle: "Once when a friend of Billy the Kid was killed, Billy went to Chisholm [sic] and volunteered to lead the Chisholm party at war ... They made a fight and Murphy's men set fire to McSwain's [sic] house ... Billy had killed four of Murphy's men during the fight ... [During the escape] McSwain [sic] was killed by Murphy. Mrs. McSwain [sic] yelled for her trunk in the house and Tom O'Folliard went back in and got it but burnt his whiskers."

For the death scene, Dobbs's fakery continued:

> Billy was hiding out in Pete Maxwell's house ...
>
> Maxwell wrote Garrett a letter saying he would turn over Billy to him. Garrett thought it might be a trick to trap him for Billy. <u>Pat had Frank Poe and Jim McIntosh, two deputies with him</u>. [Note ignorance of even of the famous deputies.] He told them he was afraid this was a trap and wasn't going up there until he spoke with Maxwell ... Garrett wrote a note to Maxwell and sent it to him by a Mexican boy telling him to meet them at the Mexican plaza 6 miles below Fort Sumner ...
>
> Garrett told Pete if it was a trap he would kill him too. He told Pete he was coming up that night.
>
> They arrived ay Maxwell's early before Billy came in from his daylight hiding and [Pat] told his deputies to bed down in one corner of Maxwell's yard. Pat went in to the house and waited in Maxwell's bedroom.

When Billy came in that night he saw the men in the yard and asked the cook who they were. The cook said they were some of Pete's sheepherders ...

In the meantime Maxwell had told the cook not to save any cold meat ... so the Kid would have to fix his own supper.

Billy asked the cook where the knife was ... Garrett could hear every word in the bedroom.

Then the Kid asked where the meat was and the cook said he guessed it was in the meat box. The Kid told him it wasn't. The cook told Billy it must be in Pete's bedroom then as Pete had brought some new meat out from town. [Note that Dobbs did not even know that Fort Sumner *was* the town.]

<u>The Kid had the knife in his left hand and started to the bedroom to get some meat. [Note that Billy walks through the house to get to the bedroom.] There was a broken-rock walk way just large enough for two to pass in the hall way from the kitchen to the bedroom. There was a dining room between the kitchen and bedroom. Garrett could hear the Kid coming on those rocks. He was sitting on the foot of the bed</u> [The interviewer here explains that the hall "ran east and west; and Pete's room was on the west] ...

It was warm weather and the bedroom window was open ... The door opened and Billy saw Pat move off the bed. Billy said: Como estes? (What's that) ...

Garrett ... fired and as Billy fell he fired over Pat's head and the bullet went in the ceiling ... Pat's shot went under Billy's heart ...

Pat and Pete ... told me how it happened many times as did the deputies.

For "The Death of Billy the Kid: A New Scenario?" the unknown author used this junk and added his/her ignorant research by attaching the National Archives floor plan. It was called "the original layout of the officers' quarters buildings, one of which became the Maxwell house [provided to show no outside door]. Taken in conjunction with the Dobbs interview [Billy walking through the house], it raises a whole new series of questions as to exactly how Billy the Kid was killed on that July night in 1881." This author was unaware that Lucien Maxwell rebuilt the house as two stories and added the outside door to what would be Peter's bedroom. And the equally ignorant hoaxers used that diagram for *Cold Case Billy the Kid*. (Figure – above). So the ignorant author concluded:

"We can posit an alternative scenario, based partly on what Dobbs said and partly on common sense. If the Kid was really after a hunk of steak he would have gone to the kitchen or the 'cool box' either in the storage or dining area or even outside in the courtyard, because it beggars belief that Maxwell would have a side of beef hanging in his bedroom. However, if the Kid was either going to or just leaving [his lover] Paulita either from the room next to Dona Luz - which would then require him to use the hallway just as Dobbs describes it – or alternatively from one of the two rooms on the northern side of the house, he would as he reached the front (eastern) doorway [believed by Smith, and used by the hoaxers, as the only entrance] – either from the inside or out – have seen the two strangers and acted just as Poe and Garrett described – skipping through the door [here an inside door] into Pete's bedroom to find out who they were – and Garrett was there waiting for him."

HOAXERS' PAST FAKE DOOR GAMBIT'": Sederwall had given this fake "evidence" for the no door scam for fellow "Billy the Kid Case" hoaxer and editor, Bob Boze Bell, for Bell's August, 2010's *True West's* "Caught with his Pants Down? Billy the Kid vs Pat Garrett, One Door Closes."

For it, Sederwall was a "retired lawman" giving "CSI" evidence that Billy was in Paulita's bedroom, "across from Pete's, when he heard two men (Poe and McKinney) talking outside." Using Dobbs's no outside door, Sederwall has Billy enter the bedroom from the hall. And his "CSI" proof is none other than hoaxing Dr. Henry Lee's Case 2003-274 fake washstand forensics, with Sederwall making-up his own version that "laser lines up perfectly with the hole [sic] in the washstand" if Garrett shot Billy, then ran out the inside door, and on his knees fired back in, hitting the washstand!

So Bob Boze Bell concluded: "[C]onventional wisdom is often misinformed, which I found out when Gregory Smith [the erroneously listed author of the article] discovered the original 1863 floor plans ... Apparently, windows, not doors, were located alongside these rooms. Lucien ... might have created doorways when he and his family moved in. Yet if Pete's room did not have an outside door, historians will certainly be forced to look at the event with new eyes."

To be noted is that opportunistic Sederwall here backs the victim being Billy Bonney!

# FAKING SHOOTING SCENE DOUBTS

The historical shooting scene is given, with Garrett's sitting on Peter Maxwell's bed when Billy entered; with Maxwell identifying him; and with Garrett shooting twice. Doubts are presented about Garrett's claim that Billy had a gun and knife, and the possibility he was unarmed. (Pages 142-143)

OMITTED EXPLANATIONS: Omitted are historically postulated explanations for Garrett's description of the shooting. His telling of a surprise encounter with Billy was likely to shield Maxwell from accusation of complicitness. It was possible that Peter Maxwell played traitor, setting up the ambush with Garrett, who was hiding in the dark room, with his deputies outside to shoot in case Billy escaped. With Billy's popularity in the town, it would have been a great risk to Maxwell if this had been revealed. This is supported by Poe's book, in which he described almost shooting Maxwell when he ran out the door; which would have only occurred if Poe was anticipating an escaping Billy, and was prepared to shoot him. (Poe, Page 39) And Poe reported the danger from Billy's partisans: "We spent the remainder of the night on the Maxwell premises, keeping constantly on our guard, was we were expecting to be attacked by friends of the dead man." (Poe, Page 44)

A further possibility is presented in Frederick Nolan's 1992 *The Lincoln County War: A Documentary History*. "Garrett found the Kid in bed with Paulita Maxwell and shot him *in flagrante delictu*; the authored version [given by Garrett] ... was then cooked up to protect the girl's reputation." (Nolan, Page 425)

Obviously, Garrett's possible need to protect other killing participants, has nothing to do with an unwarranted leap that the corpse was not Billy's.

Questioned are whether two or three shots were fired.

OMITTED EVIDENCE: Poe provided the explanation for the sound of three shots in his book: "An instant later a shot was fired in the room, followed immediately by what everyone within hearing distance thought were two other shots. However, <u>there were only two shots fired</u>, the third report, as we learned afterward, being caused by the rebound of the second bullet, which had struck the adobe wall and rebounded against the headboard of a wooden bedstead." (Poe, Pages 36-37) Garrett also addressed it in his book as first thinking Billy had fired one shot to his two. But Billy's revolver showed no shot fired. Garrett stated: "We searched long and faithfully – found <u>both my bullet marks</u> but no other." (Garrett, Page 218) And eye-witness Peter Maxwell testified on July 15, 1881 for the Coroner's jurymen: *"Pat F. Garrett <u>fired two shots</u> at the said William Bonney and the said William Bonney fell near my fire place."*

Then, added as "evidence" is the "Brushy" hoax's claiming Garrett had "high political ambitions": Sonnichsen's faked motive for hiding shooting an unarmed man. Added, while concealing addition of Billy Barlow fakery, is: "there is disagreement on whether the body of the slain man was inside or outside the room." (Page 143; and *Alias Billy the Kid*, Page 49)

**FAKING EVIDENCE: Garrett was not politically ambitious, and the corpse was in Maxwell's bedroom. Using the "Brushy" hoax's back-porch-dead-Billy-Barlow for this hoax is obviously not evidence.**

Omitting that the actual second strike involved Maxwell's headboard, given is Dr. Henry Lee's fake washstand forensics, with his positioning of Garrett on the floor and shooting.

Then, like Jameson's silly "Sexual Maturity Ratings," a Homeland Security "expert" is used to claim physiologic alterations in a shooter causing "fight or flight mode" and flinching, supposedly as confirmation of Lee's positioning to claim Garrett lied by reporting it differently. Also claimed is that he lied additionally by leaving out the washstand. (Pages 144-146)

**MAJOR HOAXING: This fakery uses the "Billy the Kid Case" hoax as evidence to call Garrett a liar, by its substitution of the unsubstantiated washstand for the shot headboard; and use of Dr. Henry Lee's fraudulent crime scene reconstruction based on it. (See pages 410-413 above) And Poe had confirmed that: "[T]he second bullet, which had struck the adobe wall ... [had] rebounded against the headboard of a wooden bedstead." (Poe, Pages 36-37)**

## FAKING THE BODY'S REMOVAL

Little is said about taking Billy's body from the bedroom to the carpenter's shop to avoid the townspeople's identifications of Billy.

Instead, a quote is taken from Garrett's July 15, 1881 "letter to the territorial governor": "It was my desire to have been able to take him alive, but his coming upon me so suddenly and unexpectedly led me to believe that he had seen me enter the room, or had been informed by someone of the fact, and that he had come there armed with pistol and knife expressly to kill me if he could." (Page 147) Trying to fake a discrepancy, there followed a convoluted rendition of Poe's stating that the room was too dark to make things out. And Poe is claimed to have had to go through the house to get to the bedroom. (Page 147)

FAKING EVIDENCE: Hiding numerous identifications of the corpse as Billy Bonney's, there is mere blather about Garrett's description, and Poe's blocking entry based on the already faked lack of an outside door.

But Garrett's quoted letter of July 15, 1881 to Acting-Governor William Ritch (as reprinted in the Las Cruces *Rio Grande Republican* as "Kid the Killer Killed, Wm. Bonney alias Antrim, alias Billy the Kid, Fatally Meets Pat Garrett, the Lincoln County Sheriff" (see pages 208-210 above)) debunked the Jameson-Sederwall duo's fakery by giving the shooting scene, and reprinting the Coroner's Jury Report's identifying the body and confirming justifiable homicide. Written to initiate his receiving the promised reward, Garrett may have added his necessity of killing to address Lew Wallace's offers on December 22, 1880's Las Vegas *Daily Gazette*, and May 3, 1881's *Daily New Mexican*, which had both stated: "I will pay $500 reward to any person or persons who will capture William Bonney, alias The Kid, and deliver him to any sheriff of New Mexico. Satisfactory proofs of identity will be required." It was not a dead-or-alive notice. So killing, instead of capture, had to be addressed. So Garrett did. Noteworthy is that this was also the letter confirming he had sent the original Coroner's Jury Report to First Judicial District Attorney William Breeden. And Breeden agreed to the justifiable homicide, and assisted in processing the reward through the Legislature. This alone destroyed the hoaxing duo's lies.

Next was quibbling about the body lying on its back or front, with Jesus Silva, Maxwell's foreman, quoted from Miguel Otero's **1936** book, *The Real Billy the Kid*, as the body being face down. So the duo questioned whether Silva entered first (Page 148) (with Jameson forgetting "Brushy" had no bedroom scene!).

FAKING EVIDENCE: With Garrett's shooting Billy from the front, he was likely thrust backwards, landing supine. And the hoaxers admit the room was next lit, and the body examined. And it could have been turned over then.

The Jesus Silva story came from an *Alias Billy the Kid* prompt footnote: a July, 1936 *Frontier Times* interview of a Leslie Traylor of Galveston, Texas, titled "Facts Regarding the Escape of Billy the Kid." Traylor, a history buff, interviewed old-timers in Lincoln and Fort Sumner in 1933 and 1935; including Jesus Silva about Garrett's shooting of Billy. He wrote: "Silva said he was at home when he heard the shot, and they sent for him, that when he arrived they were afraid to go into the room, and as he knew the Kid well and was not afraid, he went in with a light and found him dead, lying face downward with a pistol in one hand and a butcher knife in the other." So the real issue for the hoaxers to wrangle with is not face-up or down, but that Jesus Silva was yet another witness identifying the corpse as Billy Bonney's!

And Miguel Otero was a meaningless hearsay source, who wrote his book 55 years after the shooting!

There was no discrepancy.

And, by now, the hoaxers had presented the multiple body identifications as Billy: Garrett, Peter Maxwell, Jesus Silva, Deluvina, the townspeople's vigil, and the Coroner's Jury Report in the Garrett article's letter. Thus Garrett killed Billy. Thus, "Brushy" was not Billy. End of story.

## FAKING A "PETER MAXWELL"

A key witness was Peter Maxwell, with his Coroner's Jury testimony stating: *"Pat F. Garrett fired two shots at the said William Bonney and the said William Bonney fell near my fire place and I went out of the room and when I came in again about three or four minutes after the shots the said William Bonney was dead."*

So Sederwall tried to discredit Maxwell's fatal testimony by citing a 1978 article by a Bundy Avants [sic] (in an unreferenced publication) titled "The Bundy Avants [sic] Story," claiming to have spoken to Maxwell years after the shooting, with Maxwell telling him: Billy was not shot; Poe was not there; the body was of a Mexican; and Garrett kept it all secret. (Page 136)

FAKE EVIDENCE: The article is from a May-June, 1978 *True West* interview with old-timer Bundy Avant, spouting malarkey. In 1894, as a child, he came with his ranching family from Texas to Roswell, New Mexico; and moved to Capitan, when he was eight; then White Oaks in 1905 for farming. His Billy the Kid fakery begins with a fictional George Coe telling him he had retrieved murdered John Tunstall's body. Name-dropping Avant also faked John Chisum's brand as the "Long S," when it was the "Long Rail." He also said "Colonel Henry Fountain" was a family friend; when Fountain's name was Albert, and his little son, murdered with him, was Henry.

For his Peter Maxwell fabrication, <u>Avant had himself meeting an old man named "Pete," a cook at a ranch near the San Andres Mountains</u>. This pseudo-Pete says: "I've takin a likin' to you" ... I sensed he had something on his mind which had bothered him for a long time and he felt he had found someone to confide in." Avant says the man told him he was Pete Maxwell, and would tell Avant a secret, if he promised not to tell it "to a living sole as long as I'm alive." Pete then tells him, "Billy is not dead; I can take you to where he lives and has a nice family ... I'll tell you how it was ... There was no light in the house and Pat and I were in the dark when we heard someone come in. We both thought it was Billy. So when the man came in and sensed someone else was there beside me, he said, 'Quien es?' and Pat just fired. We heard the man fall. But when we struck a match and looked at him, we saw it was not the Kid ... Pat was pretty well shook up, as he didn't want it said he had killed the wrong man. It was a Mexican and we decided he was a drifter who would never be missed ... I agreed to keep quiet, too, as I could see it would give Billy a chance to slip away and start a new life, which he had been talking of doing." Avant says it must be true, because Maxwell would know.

In fact, Peter Maxwell lived near Fort Sumner until his death on June 21, 1898. [FIGURE: 12] His death, as a "Las Vegas" item, in June 28, 1898's *The Albuquerque Citizen*; stated: "**By parties arriving from Fort Sumner it was learned Saturday that Peter Maxwell died at his home near that place , an the morning of the 21 st, and was buried on the following day. He leaves a wife and one child. Peter Maxwell was the son of Lucien B. Maxwell, the original owner of the celebrated Maxwell land grant lying in Colorado and New Mexico. Peter Maxwell is well remembered in Las Vegas, where he was a frequent visitor in years past.**" Also, the coarse vernacular Bundy Avant faked for his pseudo-Pete is unlike that sophisticated and bi-lingual man born to Luz Trotier de Beaubien of Hispanic aristocracy, and Lucien Bonaparte Maxwell, of the prosperous and political Menard family.

FIGURE: 12. Peter Maxwell's house near Fort Sumner, where he lived after the town was sold; discrediting Bundy Avant's claim that he lived as a cook in a San Andres Mountains cow camp; from Midland, Texas, Haley Library, Robert N. Mullin Collection

Avant continued his Billy the Kid period lies with meeting John W. Poe at Roswell at a later date. Poe asks him what he thought of Garrett, and Avant "didn't think too highly of him." This pseudo-Poe, who was not present at the killing scene, tells Avant that he had been Garrett's deputy when Garrett killed Billy in Fort Sumner, but since "Pat, Billy, and I were good friends at one time," he wanted to pay his last respects [with Avant unaware that Poe had never met Billy until moments before the killing]. So Poe used two horses to ride to Fort Sumner that night. Avant says Garrett then refused to let Poe see the body; so Poe suspected foul play and turned in his badge. Avant concluded: "This made the second time in a period of three years that I had been told by two men, who of all people should know the facts, that Billy was not killed by Pat Garrett." (Avant, Pages 47-48)

This Bundy Avant fakery replicated garrulous Billy the Kid fakery of old-timer Severo Gallegos, featured in the original "Brushy" hoax; and old-timer Homer Overton's fake Affidavit used as evidence in 2003 by then "Billy the Kid Case" hoaxer, Sheriff Tom Sullivan, for an addendum to Case No. 2003-274's "Probable Cause Statement." (See pages 347-348 above) And it revealed the current fakery of the Jameson-Sederwall duo by using the same kind of junk as "evidence."

An interesting aside is that Avant described having "a little white pony called Billy Barlow" (Avant, Page 12), showing the prevalence of the name "Brushy Bill" picked for his own death scene confabulation.

## NOTHING BUT FAKING

The Jameson-Sederwall fakery, though adding more hoaxing to the original chicanery, added not a stitch of evidence to prove Pat Garrett did not kill Billy the Kid. And abandoning "Brushy's" back-porch-Billy-Barlow-shot-fetching-meat contrivance actually ended "Brushy's" run. One is left wondering what the hoaxers were trying to accomplish, besides the well-worn, hollow, meaningless, and failed history-is-not-as-written mantra of their respective hoaxes; along with Sederwall showing off his fake "investigations" and hijacking the "Billy the Kid Case" as his own.

# CHAPTER 8
# FAKING NO INQUEST

## HOAXERS VERSUS CORONER'S JURY REPORT

To face the July 15, 1881 Coroner's Jury Report, the Jameson-Sederwall duo had only faked discrepancies, fake "investigations," and fake conspiracy theories.

Recycled was Steve Sederwall's "Billy the Kid Case" hoax's "Probable Cause Statement," with his made-up time discrepancies for Justice of the Peace Alejandro Segura's contacting Sunnyside's Milnor Rudulph to fabricate that the Jury never even convened. (See debunking in pages 332-333, 338-339 above)

As in that "Probable Cause Statement," the body's location was questioned because the Report said: *"[T]he above jury convened in the home of Luz B. Maxwell and **proceeded to a room in the said house where they found the body of William Bonney alias "Kid."*** But the body was taken to the carpenter's shop vigil. So the location is called a lie. (Page 149)

**FAKERY: It is obvious that, after that wake, the body was returned to the Maxwell house for the inquest.**

It is claimed that Justice of the Peace Segura "instructed Rudolph to assemble a coroner's jury and serve as foreman." (Page 149)

**WRONG: Segura appointed Rudulph and the five jurymen, as he stated in the Coroner's Jury Report:** *"I, the undersigned, Justice of the Peace ... immediately upon receiving said information I proceeded to the said place and named Milnor Rudulph, Jose Silva, Antonio Sevedra, Pedro Antonio Lucero, Lorenzo Jaramillo and Sabal Gutierres a jury to investigate the case."*

The Report, as written by Milnor Rudulph, about "gratitude of the community" being owed to Garrett, is called "suspicious" to "cop" Sederwall, because it praises, while Fort Sumner people were angry at the killing, not grateful. (Pages 150-151)

**FALSE INTERPRETATION: Sederwall seems unaware that Rudulph, as discussed above, was a Ringite. (See pages 49, 630 above) He would have praised Garrett for stamping out the last anti-Ring rebel. And the jurymen, presumably terrified by this killing, would not have dared to object.**

The Report's existence is next "doubted" by claiming its not being filed in San Miguel County; "Paco" Anaya claiming two reports; the inquest being speedy; William Keleher's photocopy in Spanish [in his 1957 *Violence in Lincoln County*] as the "second coroner's report;" his English translation meant the victim spoke English; and that some signers misspelled names. So the duo doubt that the jurymen even saw the body. (Pages 150-151)

**HOAXING EVIDENCE: This just rewrites the "Brushy" hoax's C.L. Sonnichsen fakery (see pages 205-215 above), with a bit more added. As discussed, the original Report was sent by Pat Garrett to First Judicial District Attorney William Breeden, with its copy to Acting-Governor William Ritch. As Breeden's, it was filed in Santa Fe, where it was located in 1932 by state employee, Harold Abbott, in the State capitol basement. He made copies, eventually reproduced by historians, like William Keleher.**

Windbag "Paco" Anaya's "two reports" was fabrication, as was the rest of his posthumous book's Billy the Kid history. But, as stated, he did know one thing: Billy was killed by Pat Garrett; hence the title, *I Buried Billy*.

As to viewing the body, the Coroner's Jury Report confirmed it performed the inquest's legal duties: interviewing witness Peter Maxwell, identifying the body as Billy Bonney's, examining the wound, and concluding that the homicide did not require prosecution as being justifiable self-defense.

For their conclusion, the Jameson-Sederwall duo rely on their own fakery; and, of course, state that Garrett killed an innocent man, rushed through the inquest process to hide the body of the non-Billy victim by burial, and wrote the "second" [i.e., real] Coroner's Jury Report himself. And 'cop' Sederwall intones that "somebody (or somebodies) are lying" to hide the truth. (Pages 151-152)

# CHAPTER 9
## THE RETURN OF FAKE FORENSICS

### THE "BILLY THE KID CASE'S" HOAXED FORENSICS

Jameson and Sederwall, pretending they proved the corpse was unidentified (Pages 153-154), recycle Dr. Henry Lee's fake "Billy the Kid Case" forensics, while shape-shifting it as Sederwall's personal investigation; and hiding that he had forged Lee's reports for my open records case. So Sederwall calls Fort Sumner an active crime scene (Page 154), echoing the fake title of the book as a "cold case" involving Billy the Kid.

HOAXING: Fort Sumner was not a Pat Garret crime scene after the Coroner's Jury decision of July 15, 1881; stating: *"[O]ur verdict is that the deed of said Garrett was justifiable homicide."*

### FAKING CARPENTER'S BENCH FORENSICS

Steve Sederwall, as sole "investigator," of the pretend crime scene, presents the "Billy the Kid Case's" carpenter's bench hoax, with some additions. The bench is called an **important source of "bloodstains from the slain intruder"** (Page 155) - a new name for the innocent victim - **as a source of DNA**.

Research is claimed on the Maxwell house history (Pages 155-159), though it was never bench's location. Admitted is that the town was sold in 1884, and its buildings no longer stand. A new claim is that the Maxwell house's floorboards are in a house built by a Charlie Floor, and they could have blood DNA too (which accidently refuted the "Brushy's" back-porch-Barlow!). The furniture (bed, washstand, with added carpenter's bench) is traced to Peter Maxwell's sister Odelia, married to Manuel Abreu. Hilariously inserted is Bundy Avant's old-timer malarkey of meeting "Pete" in the San Andres mountains. (See page 696 above) So Peter Maxwell is portrayed as giving away his furniture after being reduced to "cooking for 'wagon outfits.' " It is then is traced to Odelia's and Manuel's daughter, Stella Abreu, for her "museum" (with a photograph of that shed-like building). The carpenter's bench photo by an unknown photographer from the Robert Mullin Collection is cited, but its date of about 1926 - 46 years after the shooting - is omitted. Given is Sederwall's tracing the bench to the Albuquerque home of Stella Maxwell's son, Mannie Miller, in his converted chicken coop. (Pages 158-160) [Oddly, a photo of the bench, labeled as in the "Steve Sederwall Collection" (Page 160) does not match the Mullins Collection photo, or the bench I saw in 2010 with Kenny Miller at deceased Mannie's chicken coop. The Sederwall one, is falling apart, with one of the top boards cracked. It may have been repaired, with possible board replacement, to match the one later photographed by Dr. Lee – adding to its invalidity for forensics.]

    Dr. Henry Lee was introduced as contacted by Sederwall; who lies that **"a number of locations" on the bench's top and bottom tested positive for blood** by "presumptive blood test reagents phenolphthalein and o-tolidine." **He attributes the "blood" to "two different human beings;" claiming future separation to presumably identify the "slain intruder."** (Page 163) A Lee report is not cited, but one is in the Bibliography as: "Lee, Dr. Henry. Forensic Examination Report (Examination of Furniture From Pete Maxwell's of July 15, 1881) 22 May 2004." (Page 187)

**HOAXING: Sederwall is lying. No blood was identified. Dr. Lee's sole report of February 25, 2005 merely hoaxed "blood-like" stains; and Orchid Cellmark Lab <u>got no DNA from the bench. The mixed sample was from floorboards</u>.**

    **The cited Lee report appears to be one of Sederwall's forged ones, with the date changed to May 22, 2004. The one given to me and the Court was titled "Forensic Research and Training Center Forensic Examination Report: "Examination of furniture from Pete Maxwell's of July 15, 1881," and dated February 25, 2005.**

    Sederwall's "**bloodstains from the slain intruder**" were his fabrication, repeating the "Billy the Kid Case" hoax's lie about the bench having "mixed DNA" of two people bleeding on the bench: first playing-dead-Billy; next, switched shot innocent victim (possibly Billy Barlow).

IRRELEVANT: Not only did this fakery give no proof that Garrett did not kill Billy, it contradicted "Brushy's" death scene with shot-Billy-bleeding-on-the-bench-for-DNA.

# FAKING "MAXWELL FURNITURE" FORENSICS

Sederwall, as sole "investigator," next had Dr. Henry Lee examine the headboard and the washstand.

## *HOAXING THE HEADBOARD*

Sederwall reminds the reader that Deputy Poe had said Garrett's second shot rebounded from the wall and hit the headboard of Maxwell's bed. But he states that Lee found "nothing resembling the impact of a bullet, even a scratch." So Poe is called a liar. (Pages 160-161) No mention is made of Lee's report, but the Bibliography cites "Lee, Dr. Henry. Forensic Examination Report (Examination of Furniture From Pete Maxwell's of July 15, 1881) 22 May 2004." (Page 187)

HOAXING: Sederwall is tricking readers, since the "headboard" is just a big empty hole with a thin frame, having no place for the bullet hit. But scorning readers' intelligence, he gives its photo. Wily Dr. Lee had omitted one in his February 25, 2005 report with its "investigation."

The Lee report in the Bibliography appears to be one of Sederwall's forged ones, with the date changed to May 22, 2004. The one Sederwall first presented to me was his fake "Forensic Research and Training Center Forensic Examination Report: "Examination of furniture from Pete Maxwell's of July 15, 1881," dated February 25, 2005. Its second forged version, with different font and deleted "Results and Conclusions," went to the Court as Exhibit E.

Lee's, actual report of February 26, 2005 had stated dishonestly: "No bullet hole and no observable damage, no sign of bullet ricocheted type of defects were found on the Headboard. No blood or biological materials were observed on the Headboard."

This is pure hoaxing by both Sederwall and Lee; as well as records forgery, as found by the Court, for Sederwall.

IRRELEVANT: All this fakery had nothing to do with Garrett not killing Billy, or "Brushy" being Billy.

## *HOAXING THE WASHSTAND*

Sederwall also repeated Dr. Henry Lee's fake washstand forensics. (Pages 161-163) A photo of it (Page 162) differs from the one photographed and diagramed by Lee in his February 25, 2005 report, by having a raised back rim - with Lee's picture being only a box. Described are the washstand's two holes. Lee's bullet trajectory is presented, with his fake claim of Garrett shooting from the floor. No report is mentioned, but the Bibliography cites: "Lee, Dr. Henry. Forensic Examination Report (Examination of Furniture From Pete Maxwell's of July 15, 1881) 22 May 2004." (Page 187)

HOAXING: The toy-sized washstand used, is implausible as being one from Maxwell's bedroom; or he would have had to wash himself preposterously crouched on the floor - like Lee's faked shooting Garrett! And neither Garrett nor Poe reported a washstand as struck by a bullet of Garrett's. So the trajectory is merely hoaxing of Garrett as shooting it, and of his position in the room.

The Lee report cited in the Bibliography appears to be one of Sederwall's forged ones, with date changed to May 22, 2004. It was given to me with a "Results and Conclusions" section absent.

Lee's report of February 25, 2005 was actually non-committal; stating: "Two bullet holes were located on the side panels of the Washstand. The hole on the left side panel is consistent with a bullet entrance hole while the hole on the right side panel is consistent with a bullet exit hole. However, it is not possible to determine when those bullet holes were produced at this time [meaning anytime from the 1870's to the 1900's]."

IRRELEVANT: All this was irrelevant to Garrett not killing Billy, or "Brushy" being Billy.

# CHAPTER 10
# RETURN OF THE "BILLY THE KID CASE'S" EXHUMATION FAKERY

## THE RETURN ATTACK ON JOHN MILLER'S BONES

By this point in *Cold Case Billy the Kid*, a reader might realize that it had no point, except for duped W.C. Jameson's show-casing of Steve Sederwall's fake "investigations," with a vague theme of history-is-not-as-written. It was about to get worse, as unleashed Sederwall would proclaim that John Miller matched Billy the Kid! (To hell with "Brushy!") And Case 2003-274's exhumation would be just Sederwall's personal "ongoing investigation" (Page 165); with dug up random man, William Hudspeth, obviously concealed.

### *FAKING THE JOHN MILLER EXHUMATION*

Reflecting Sederwall's breathtaking audacity, no background is given for John Miller: like being born in 1950; almost ten years before Billy, like knowing no Billy the Kid history at all, like dying soon after breaking a hip, and like being toothless. His exhumation is claimed to have been done on May 9, 2005 [sic – May 19] by an unnamed "forensic anthropologist" and "authorized by the state of Arizona." (Page 165)

**HOAXING: Hidden** is the report for that exhumation: "Lincoln County Sheriff's Department Supplemental Report," listing "Case # 2003-274, Date: Thursday, May 19, 2005, Subject: Exhumation of John Miller, Location: Arizona Pioneers' Cemetery, Prescott, Arizona, Report By: Steven M. Sederwall, On Thursday, May 19, 2005, at approximately 1:00 pm the following met at the Arizona

Pioneers' Cemetery at Prescott, Arizona. Investigators: Steven M. Sederwall, Lincoln County Deputy Sheriff."

Hidden is that the hired Maricopa County forensic anthropologist was Dr. Laura Fulginiti, who denied all the hoaxers claims. [APPENDIX: 9] Hidden is that the hoaxers had no Billy the Kid DNA to justify any exhumation for identity matching. Hidden is the wanton desecration of random man, William Hudspeth, buried beside Miller.

Sederwall shamelessly gives his Piltdown man-style hoax, harking back to that illegal exhumation when his felon buddy Lonnie Lippman (in Jameson's Acknowledgments) photographed him for Julie Carter's October 6, 2005 "Follow the Blood," holding the skull of John Miller (or William Hudspeth) like a trophy.

Sederwall lied: "**The right scapula of John Miller manifested a round hole. The anthropologist observed that it appeared to be a bullet hole that had healed**" and the bullet entered the upper chest and exited his back. He added that **Miller's right front incisor was placed somewhat in front of his left front incisor.**" So he concluded that this was Pat Garrett's bullet killing buck-toothed Billy the Kid. (Page 165)

HOAXING: Sederwall is recycling his fakery to reporter, Rene Romo, in his November 6, 2006's *Albuquerque Journal's* "Billy the Kid Probe May Yield New Twist." Romo wrote: "**Sederwall ... said Miller's skeletal remains were intriguing. He said Miller had buck teeth, like the Kid, and an old bullet wound that entered his upper left chest and exited through the scapula.**" Hidden, is that forensic expert, Dr. Laura Fulginiti, reported Miller having no teeth, and no damaged scapula. Hidden is that Sederwall was faking the results from random man, William Hudspeth, who had a damaged *right*, not *left* scapula, with Dr. Fulginiti denying the injury was from a bullet. (See page 436)

Sederwall then claimed he got DNA from Miller's remains "sufficient to conduct a test." (Page 165)

HOAXING: **Hidden was having no Billy the Kid DNA to compare with Miller's. Hidden was no need for DNA matching, since Miller had no historical match to Billy.**

Jameson was apparently unaware of the "Billy the Kid Case's" publicity, in which the conscienceless, profiteering hoaxers were willing to claim any remains as Billy the Kid's to keep the Bill

Kurtis cameras rolling. For Julie Carter's October 6, 2005 "Follow the Blood," Sederwall plugged Miller as Billy; crowing: ""In the light of the evidence, we see that the history of Billy the Kid will change. Those with monied interest in history remaining the same will not be happy ... As a cop I know when people fight to keep you from looking at something, they are always trying to hide something. The Lincoln County War is still going on."

For reporter Rene Romo's November 6, 2006's *Albuquerque Journal's* "Billy the Kid Probe May Yield New Twist," hoaxing Sederwall plugged Miller, as well as faking having DNA from the carpenter's bench; stating: "If that [John Miller] DNA matches the work bench, I think the game is over."

## RETURN TO "BRUSHY" FOR "DNA FORENSICS"

Finally, after 165 pages, Jameson got to extol his man. "Brushy" is described as dying in Hico, Texas, on December 27, 1950, "two days shy of his ninetieth birthday." He is praised for the knowing-things-not-printed trick, with "revelations" beyond knowledge of historians. He is claimed to have more credibility than Pat Garrett. The photoanalysis by Dr. Scott Acton is waved as claiming his "amazing" match to Billy the Kid. (Pages 165-167)

TRUE-BELIEVER BEFUDDLEMENT: This "Brushy Bill" imposter hoax has already been debunked above for C.L. Sonnichsen's and William V. Morrison's *Alias Billy the Kid*; and for Jameson's own *The Return of the Outlaw Billy the Kid*, and his other books. And Jameson's cross-over to active hoaxer, doing dishonest fix-ups of some of "Brushy's" glaring mismatches to Billy Bonney in his later books, is already exposed above also.

It will remain a mystery as to what Jameson thought he was accomplishing with this *Cold Case Billy the Kid* book, as he mouthed Steve Sederwall's out-of-control fakery, which had practically nothing to do with "Brushy;" which invented alternative events not dreamed of by "Brushy," which demolished "Brushy's" knowing-things-not-printed trick; which showcased the "Billy the Kid Case" hoax which mismatched "Brushy;" and which even pushed imposter John Miller, not "Brushy," as Billy the Kid.

## WISHING FOR "BRUSHY'S" DNA

Sederwall's fake forensics, inspired Jameson's focus on "Brushy's" DNA. Angered by Hamilton, Texas's, Mayor and City Council blocking "Brushy's" exhumation, he proclaimed the grave was just a tourist-marker anyway; with "Brushy's" being elsewhere in the cemetery; apparently meaning an uncertain site.

Jameson then had a pathetic wish: if only Sederwall had been allowed to get DNA from the Fort Sumner grave, and compared it to the carpenter's bench, the "controversy" would have been settled. (Page 167)

TRUE-BELIEVER BEFUDDLEMENT: Jameson appeared unaware that the "Billy the Kid Case" hoax claimed that Billy Bonney's playing-dead-blood-DNA was alleged to be on the carpenter's bench. That claim alone canceled out "Brushy," who had no such tale. And Jameson seems to have forgotten his own claim in *The Return of the Outlaw Billy the Kid* that the Fort Sumner Billy the Kid grave was just a fake tourist marker. As he and Frederick Bean wrote: "Billy the Kid's gravesite is not even authentic ... the original wooden marker ... disappeared ... Furthermore, because the majority of bodies in the cemetery were soldiers [and] were disinterred when the army removed them to the Santa Fe National Cemetery. There is more. On a number of occasions the Pecos River flooded ... carrying ... coffins ... <u>The current marker is a tourist attraction, nothing more, and it is estimated it lies several yards from the original burial site. The truth is, no one is actually buried under the stone.</u>" (*The Return of the Outlaw Billy the Kid*, Pages 132-133)

Jameson may also have been hoodwinked by Sederwall's tall tale of DNA of two people on the bench (when no DNA at all had been recovered), and concluded that one of those people must have been Billy Barlow. So Jameson wished *that DNA* could have been compared to the bones in the Fort Sumner grave to show Barlow was buried there as the innocent victim. He did not understand that even if a DNA match had been found, the mitochondrial DNA used by Orchid Cellmark has coincidental matches; and worse, without the proven reference DNA of Billy Barlow, no DNA from the bench or the grave can be called his. And Barlow did not exist!

# CHAPTER 11
## THE RETURN OF THE CONSPIRACY THEORIES

### FANTASIZING PLOTS AGAINST "TRUTH"

For duped W.C. Jameson, the only explanation for the blockade of Billy's and his mother's graves for exhumations was a conspiracy to hide the truth. That drew on his total belief in the other conspiracy theories invented by William V. Morrison and C.L. Sonnichsen to explain "Brushy Bill" Roberts's rejection in the Governor T.J. Mabry pardon hearing as an imposter. That drew on the conspiracy theories he and Frederick Bean had used in *The Return of the Outlaw Billy the Kid* to discount subsequent historical debunking of "Brushy." Furthermore, he also likely trusted that Steve Sederwall was his ally for proving "Brushy" as Billy the Kid, rather than merely an opportunistic profiteer.

So he next presented Sederwall's own self-promoting conspiracy theory, that hid Lincoln County Sheriff's Department Case No. 2003-274, and my open records litigation exposing its DNA frauds. In Sederwall's fable, he was a lone crusader, seeking truth from Billy's and his mother's graves and a carpenter's bench to settle the question of Garrett's killing and hiding an innocent victim, and was blocked.

Jameson harked back to his 1998 *Return of the Outlaw Billy the Kid's* conspiracy of historians, blaming Frederick Nolan and unnamed others for protecting the "status quo" and their "reputations as 'experts' [for refusal] to embrace a number of Sederwall's findings that contradict the legend." (Page 168)

**DUPED BEFUDDLEMENT: Jameson was unaware of parroting the "Billy the Kid Case" hoaxers' 2005, conspiracy theory sound-bite: "Why are they so afraid of the truth?" On October 21, 2005, Tom Sullivan's letter to the *RuidosoNews.com* editor stated: "Frederick Nolan dismisses the modern day law enforcement technologies we**

have used to recreate the crime scene in Pete Maxwell's bedroom on the night that Pat Garrett allegedly shot "the Kid" as nothing but "stunts." And now Robert Utley refers to us as "loony guys" and "two nut cases" ... Our investigation contradicts their theories written in their books. It appears that our critics all suffer from the same "kindergartenmentality." Why are they so afraid of the truth? ... Steve [Sederwall] and I were both sworn in as sheriff's deputies by Sheriff Rick Virden shortly after he took office."

But it was now 2018 for *Cold Case Billy the Kid*. Being hidden from Jameson also was the name Gale Cooper, my litigation exposing their DNA frauds and forged Dr. Lee records, and my exposé book, *Cracking the Billy the Kid Case Hoax: The Strange Plot to Exhume Billy the Kid, Convict Sheriff Pat Garrett of Murder, and Become President of the United States*. The issue had nothing to do with keeping the "status quo." The issue was that the hoaxers had no evidence whatsoever to change anything. The issue was that they had now tricked their latest dupe, W.C. Jameson.

## SEDERWALL'S CONSPIRACY AGAINST HIMSELF

For his chapter "Politics v. Truth," Jameson gave Sederwall a platform to attack his fellow hoaxers, and fabricate himself as a beleaguered, lone, "cop"-hero seeking truth. (Pages 168-171) For this fiction, Sederwall secretly recycled documents he, as a Deputy, with Sheriff Tom Sullivan, wrote for my open records case to hide "Billy the Kid Case" records: September 30, 2006's "The Dried Bean, You Believin' Us or Them Lyin' Whores;" and June 21, 2007's "Memorandum," which faked the OMI's Dr. Debra Komar's deposition. (See pages 490-491 above). So Jameson wrote: "The government of New Mexico, from the governor on down to public officials, has fought to keep the myths and legends of Billy the Kid and Pat Garrett alive;" and initiated a number of attempts to thwart any quest for the truth." (Page 168)

So gullible dupe Jameson presented incorrigible Sederwall's audacious, megalomaniacal, and astounding fable; as follows:

As Mayor of Capitan, who happened to be a "reserve" deputy in the Lincoln County Sheriff's Department, Sederwall went to Santa Fe with Sheriff Tom Sullivan for unstated reason. There, also for unstated reason, they met with Governor Bill Richardson and his communications director, Billy Sparks.

Sparks immediately whisked Sederwall away to the "parking garage" to tell him that "Fred Nolan had called the governor" and said the carpenter's bench was not real, and Richardson wanted Sparks to "talk with Sederwall about the situation." So all turned to Sederwall for help.

Since the bench was just located, Sederwall suspected that a spy had gotten to Nolan in England. Since history professor, Paul Hutton, had been present, that spy must have been him! And, by chance, Hutton was Richardson's Billy the Kid legend history advisor! So there were a lot of politicians, employees, and sycophants in bed together! (Pages 169-170)

So Sparks, still in the garage, needed Sederwall's help; since Fort Sumner officials, like Mayor Raymond Lopez, were upset that their "cash cow" would be ruined. (Page 170) And people feared carpenter's bench DNA would upset the legend. Sederwall, then still an idealist, thought Richardson would back the truth. But Sparks made clear that the governor had thought that Sederwall would merely "drive around, ask some questions, talk to the newspapers, and proudly declare that everything associated with the Billy the Kid legend was correct." But now it looked like intrepid Sederwall would do a DNA analysis that could "ruin the Billy the Kid legend." So idealist Sederwall abruptly realized, right in that garage, that this was all about politics and money, not truth! (Pages 170-171)

Billy Sparks then asked him to change *his* focus to a pardon for Billy the Kid. Sederwall, smelling a rat, got Sparks to admit the truth. The truth was that **Sederwall's "photograph and details about the ongoing investigation were showing up in 'every paper on the planet. [H]e was getting more publicity than Governor Richardson."** And they were afraid that Sederwall would find out that Pat Garrett had not killed Billy the Kid. And they wanted to hide this outcome. (Page 171)

Still in that fateful garage, Sederwall asked Sparks if the governor wanted to back out. Sparks said that Richardson wanted to be President of the United States, and wanted the publicity; and his attorney, Bill Robins III would file for the pardon for Billy the Kid "using Sederwall's investigations." So Sederwall could get "cop fun," and tourist dollars would flow in. Except they were now afraid of Sederwall's carpenter's bench. (Page 172)

Worse, Sparks knew about Sederwall's investigations into John Miller and "William Henry Roberts" as potential Billy the Kid's, as also risking the history. And Sparks admitted that they actually did not know where Billy the Kid was buried. (Page 172) **So Sederwall realized that he was doing such a good job as an investigator that they wanted him to stop, because it could interfere with Richardson being President of the United States.** (Page 172) Then Sederwall made clear his extreme danger, since everything depended on him. Sparks shared a "heads-up": "they [unnamed] have you in their crosshairs and before this is over ... [y]ou guys are going to feel the heat." (Page 172)

Sederwall later learned that his opponent was Fort Sumner Mayor Raymond Lopez, who had tried to get Richardson to stop his investigation. Evidence was that when Richardson's attorney, Bill Robins III, filed in Grant County to exhume Catherine Antrim to get her DNA **for Sederwall**, Lopez rushed there to stop officials from getting access. Lopez feared her DNA "would not match the DNA from the workbench." (Pages 172-173)

**GLITCH IN THE FABLE: In truth, Mayor Lopez had merely gone to Silver City to sit in on a Catherine Antrim exhumation hearing. His only action had been to stand for the village of Fort Sumner for the Case 2003-274's exhumation attempt there on the Billy the Kid grave. The "Billy the Kid Case hoaxers' opponent was me!**

Sederwall then made up a Silver City Town Council meeting about the threat of *his* getting the mother's DNA; with fear he would show that Billy the Kid was not buried in New Mexico; and that "Brushy Bill" Roberts was Billy the Kid. So Sederwall realized they too feared truth, and it was all for money. (Page 173)

Then the ruling of Grant County District Judge Henry Quintero, postponing exhumation of the mother, was quoted: "Only if the petitioners are successful in locating the Kid's burial site and collecting his DNA, may they petition this court for a review of Catherine Antrim's matter."

Sederwall claimed that meant Judge Quintero knew the plan was to compare the mother's remains with Miller and "Brushy Bill," and also knew Fort Sumner's grave would be blocked; **so he wanted Sederwall to dig up Billy wherever he was buried!** (Pages 173-174)

FAKERY: Besides bizarre rewrite of the entire case as his own, Sederwall misstated Judge Quintero's ruling of <u>April 2, 2004</u>, for "Sixth Judicial District Court, State of New Mexico, County of Grant. No. MS 2003-11, In the Matter of Catherine Antrim. Decision and Order."

Quintero called the case "not ripe," meaning not ready for decision, until Billy the Kid's remains in Fort Sumner had been dug up and DNA extracted for matching; because there was no other reason to dig up the mother. Complicit Quintero was responding to Attorney Bill Robins's filing six days earlier on <u>February 24, 2004</u>: "In the Matter of Catherine Antrim: <u>Billy the Kid's Brief on the Question of Ripeness</u>. Case No. MS 2003-11. Sixth Judicial Court, Grant County;" and to Robins's, David Sandoval's, and Mark Acuña's <u>February 26, 2004's</u> "Tenth Judicial Court of De Baca County, Case No. CV-2004-00005, In the Matter of William H. Bonney, aka 'Billy the Kid.' <u>Petition for the Exhumation of Billy the Kid's Remains</u>." But Sederwall also faked that Quintero's order meant digging up any "Billy the Kid" - like "Brushy" or John Miller - for DNA to match with the mother.]

Sederwall next made-up that Attorney Bill Robins III *then* filed for Fort Sumner's Billy the Kid exhumation, as if to purposefully interfere with Judge Quintero wanting Sederwall to dig up Miller and Roberts first. And Sederwall claimed surprise that his name had been included as a lawman exhumation petitioner by Robins. (Page 174)

FAKERY: Faking a conspiracy, Sederwall reversed the filings. In fact, first came the Robins filings on <u>February 24 and 26, 2004</u> for Fort Sumner's exhumation. Then, on <u>April 2, 2004</u>, Judge Quintero ordered that exhumation before the mother could be dug up.

Also, Sederwall's "surprise" at his name on the petition is silly; as lawmen petitioners for the exhumations, he, as Deputy Sheriff, and Tom Sullivan and Gary Graves, as Sheriffs, were on *all* the petitions in Grant and De Baca Counties, because their standing as lawmen doing a murder case was sole justification for doing exhumations.

Sederwall claimed that three days before the Fort Sumner hearing, Billy Sparks called him and told him to drop the exhumation petition in Fort Sumner; and that it needed his permission because he was a listed petitioner. He gave permission, and then claimed the Fort Sumner politicos had a party to celebrate the news. (Page 174)

**FAKERY: Sederwall was hiding that the withdrawal of the Fort Sumner exhumation petition was actually by Sheriff Tom Sullivan, who had just been threatened with potential recall by Lincoln County Commissioner Leo Martinez, for conducting a hoax through his Sheriff's Department, and without permission of the County Commissioners. And Sullivan knew that fellow hoaxer, De Baca County Sheriff Gary Graves, was facing recall for other malfeasances, but with added anger of his County Commissioners at his doing the "Billy the Kid Case" against their directive to him to stop.**

**The party was held by my victorious Kennedy Han law firm, and included Frederick Nolan, whom I had flown in to testify as to the history; Mayor Raymond Lopez, who stood for Fort Sumner; as well as local citizens like Billy the Kid Outlaw Gang founder, Marlyn Bowlin. As maintaining my anonymity and central role, I did not attend for my own safety against the thug perpetrators.**

Sederwall next fabricated the response of the OMI for this figment of his imagination. He claimed that he then told Billy Sparks that he had reason to believe that Billy the Kid was not buried in Fort Sumner, and there was no body in its grave. (Pages 174-175) For proof, he stated that Governor Richardson had assigned the state medical investigators office to the case. And he, Sederwall, gave them his theories and plans. Then, state medical investigator, Debra Komar, investigated the Fort Sumner grave and the Arizona grave of John Miller. After that, she refused his calls. (Page 175)

**So Sederwall concluded that this proved Komar found something in Fort Sumner or Arizona, and "the state of New Mexico wanted it covered up" from "the public."** He said he was determined to find the truth. So on January 20, 2004, Komar appeared in court under a subpoena, to give a deposition. He stated that her going to Fort Sumner's cemetery upset local officials. And he stated that she had testified that she had been prevented from contacting him, and her attorney in the deposition prevented her from telling him what she found. (Pages 175-176) **He concluded that her refusing to speak to him meant she**

"found something that would negate the legend of Billy the Kid if the information were released." (Page 176) He then lifted quotes from her deposition out of context: To the question, "You don't think Billy the Kid is buried at Fort Sumner, do you?" she said: "I don't know. I have reason to suspect perhaps not." (Page 176)

FAKERY: Sederwall is making-up the OMI investigation, and Debra Komar's testimony; and implying falsely that he obtained her deposition by subpoena.

In fact, the OMI investigation was not requested by Richardson, who had tried to block it, since the OMI opposed exhuming Billy and his mother as forensically useless for DNA. (See pages 308-313)

The OMI did not evaluate the grave of John Miller, it being in another state, and not part of the New Mexico exhumation petitions it was opposing.

Debra Komar, an OMI forensic anthropologist, before her deposition, gave a January 9, 2004 Affidavit [APPENDIX: 4] opposing the exhumations of Billy and his mother as forensically useless because of uncertainty of location of the remains in the Silver City and Fort Sumner cemeteries, and the risk of disturbing other remains.

Komar's deposition was subpoenaed by the Kennedy Han legal team I had brought in to oppose the exhumations, and taken by its attorney, Adam Baker. (See pages 310-313 above) Komar was cross-examined by Attorney Bill Robins III. She had concluded: "So if you ask the opinion of myself and the Office of the Medical Investigator why is this being done or what scientifically valid conclusions can be drawn from it, <u>I can't find any</u>." (Deposition, Page 81)

But Sederwall was recycling his fakery from his June 21, 2007 "Memorandum," in which he lifted her response to Attorney Robins about Billy's uncertain burial site out of context. (Deposition, Page 144) Komar's meaning was that Billy's buried body might no longer be present, with Fort Sumner's history of flooding, and possible accidental removal with soldiers' remains. Komar was merely repeating her Affidavit's contention that "[b]ased upon research performed by the OMI, the exact location of the Billy the Kid grave is not known." That meant location within the Fort Sumner cemetery. She was also referring to her earlier statements in her deposition, in which she said about Billy: "[T]he remains may no longer still be there. Even if they were buried there at one point." (Deposition, Page 69) She was citing references to Billy's remains being stolen to sell soon after burial, or past digging in the area finding no remains. (Deposition, Page 70) Or, in 1904, a Willie E. Griffin was hired to take soldiers' remains from that cemetery to move to Santa Fe's National Cemetery; and he knew that one was said to be buried in association with the contiguous graves of Billy, Charles Bowdre, and Tom O'Folliard. He found only two bodies, and took one. So he may have accidentally taken Billy! (Deposition, Page 71-72)

But Sederwall faked Komar as saying that Billy was never buried in Fort Sumner, and was buried somewhere else - like Texas as "Brushy" or Arizona as John Miller! (See page 490 above)

Sederwall concluded his fable with a claim that a David Bailey, a past Fort Sumner Mayor, had told De Baca County Sheriff Gary Graves that "Sederwall's investigation" had to be stopped, because he knew what was in the Billy the Kid grave, because he and a companion, on June 17, 2003, had dug it up and found nothing. And they had hidden their excavation by shoveling into adjoining graves. So Sederwall's concluding punch line was that there were no remains at the marked gravesite. (Page 177)

**FAKERY: Besides documenting a felonious crime by David Baily and an accomplice, Sederwall's claim merely substantiated the OMI's exhumation opposition based on no certain site for remains, if any still remained. And the 1962 Lois Telfer blocked exhumation case's Decision repeated the same site uncertainty.**

But Sederwall's digger Bailey story does not hang together. The Billy the Kid grave is surrounded by a thick-barred locked, iron cage, including its top. Its large interior surface is covered with concrete, and has three mounds to represent Billy, Charlie Bowdre, and Tom O'Folliard. And there are no adjoining graves to shovel into for cover-up. And the ground is hard-packed, since it is an inactive historical cemetery, with only a distant grave of Chino Silva, Jesus Silva's grandson, added in the 2000's. Also, Marlyn Bowlin, then running the Old Fort Sumner Museum at the cemetery, checked the graves daily, and would have seen the evidence of David Baily's crime.

MEANINGLESS EVIDENCE: Stating that no remains were available proves nothing.

In fact, the poorly marked graves in the cemetery are described by a Leslie Traylor of Galveston, Texas, in his July, 1936 *Frontier Times* interview of a, titled "Facts Regarding the Escape of Billy the Kid." Traylor, a history buff, interviewed old-timers in Lincoln and Fort Sumner in 1933 and 1935. Traylor wrote: "[T]he old cemetery near old Fort Sumner ... is now usually referred to as Hell's Half Acre. During the summer of 1935 I visited the old cemetery accompanied by Francisco Lovato, his son Pete, and a friend of theirs ... The old cemetery was originally surrounded by an adobe wall, but now is surrounded by a wire fence, the entrance being in the north side as before. Lucien B. Maxwell, the cattle king [sic] and father of Pete Maxwell, is buried in the old cemetery, but the exact site of his grave is unknown. His son Pete died in 1898 and there is a monument erected to his memory, supposedly near where is father is buried. The monument to Billy the Kid and his pals is badly defaced where Billy's name appears; the vandals still chipping off pieces of stone. I was told by Pete Lovato that his father helped Vincente Otero bury the remains of Thomas O'Folliard and Chas. Bowdre, who were killed in Dec., 1880, by Pat Garrett and his men, and that his father said that O'Folliard and Bowdre were not buried by the monument erected to the three pals, but were buried to the left of the entrance to the cemetery by the side of the old adobe wall, and now where the fence is ... Regardless of where the three pals were buried the monument serves its purpose just the same."

JAMESON'S DUPED BEFUDDLEMENT: One can picture dupe Jameson absorbing Steve Sederwall's hero myth of himself with open-mouthed amazement and starry-eyed adulation. Finally, his years of paranoia about a plot against the truth were vindicated.

But it seems inconceivable that Jameson bought the fable of Sederwall against the Richardson contingent wanting to maintain the "status quo." Jameson must have known about Richardson's own "Brushy Bill" thrust, featured in his "Billy the Kid Case" announcement on the

*New York Times* June 5, 2003 front page that started the scam. It featured Jannay Valdez, a major "Brushy"-believer vouching for "Brushy" as Billy the Kid. And Richardson's thrust was proving "Brushy" as Billy by modern forensic DNA. Also, Jameson himself participated as a talking-head in hoaxing professor, Paul Hutton's, "Brushy"-backing TV documentary, "Investigating History: Billy the Kid," to vouch for his man. And Sonnichsen's and Morrison's *Alias Billy the Kid* had been promoted by Hutton in that program for survival proof for the Garrett killing. And it featured all the main hoaxers, centered on Bill Richardson as the man contemplating the "pardon of Billy the Kid." It seems inconceivable, that Jameson would not have watched it as "Brushy's" next big chance to rectify the lost Governor Mabry pardon. It also seems inconceivable that Jameson could be convinced that the massively publicized "Billy the Kid Case" had been done solely by Steve Sederwall. But all that might be the level of oblivion needed to be a "Brushy"-believer. And Sederwall's martyr for the truth trick must have struck a cord with "Brushy's" untiring, often failing, and increasingly desperate warrior, W.C. Jameson himself.

# CHAPTER 12
## FOREGONE FAKE CONCLUSION

### WHEN HOAXERS FOOL THEMSELVES

Having been convinced himself by the fake forensics of the "Billy the Kid Case" hoaxers, and impressed by the flimflam "investigations" of "cop" Steve Sederwall, Jameson apparently believed that, in this rerun with his *Cold Case Billy the Kid*, "Brushy" was finally home free, as he depicted in his "Conclusion." (Pages 178-180) Smugly, he declared, "The historians got it wrong" because they believed legends instead of truth. But he despaired of convincing historians, because they refused to admit being wrong. He was certain that the state of New Mexico suppressed the truth. But he was as certain of his hysterical conclusion that although Steve Sederwall "will turn to dust ... the truth he uncovered ... will remain, will endure." (Page 180)

In fact, neither Jameson, Sederwall, nor the back-up team of other hoaxers in the wings, had offered any evidence whatsoever in *Cold Case Billy the Kid* to indicate that "Brushy" had been Billy Bonney, or that history was not as written. The "Billy the Kid Case" hoax had fared no better; though Steve Sederwall had repeated its lies as truths - while audaciously absconding with that case as his own!

**OUTCOME: By firing every bit of ammunition he had, and showing it was all blanks, W.C. Jameson inadvertently discredited the Billy the Kid pretender hoaxes, as well as the reprehensible hucksters who had sought to profit from riding the coattails of famous Billy the Kid.**

# PART VII

# SUMMARY AND CONCLUSIONS

# CHAPTER 1
# NOTHINGS PLUS NOTHING EQUALS NOTHING

## MUCH ADO ABOUT NOTHING

This had to be a long book to debunk the massive output of the Billy the Kid imposter hoaxes, all of it fake, but intricate and esoteric to trick readers unable to dissect out each lie.

But hoaxbusting actually needed just two birthdays, one almost-full moon, and one Coroner's Jury Report. Oliver Pleasant "Brushy Bill" Roberts was born on August 26, 1879, twenty years after Billy Bonney; making him a baby on July 14, 1881. John "Jonnie" Miller was born in December of 1850, nine years before Billy Bonney; making him no Kid on July 14, 1881. The near-full moon, hovering in giant illusion at the horizon on the light-as-day night of July 14, 1881, undid the "Brushy" and "Billy the Kid Case" hoaxes by their reliance on "Brushy's" faked dark and moonless night. And the Coroner's Jury report of July 15, 1881 identified Pat Garrett's shooting victim as William Bonney.

The opportunistic pretenders, masquerading as Billy the Kid himself or investigative historians, spanned the years from John Miller's 1930's to W.C. Jameson's 2018 *Cold Case Billy the Kid*. All were nothings, with nothing to offer, until they eventually sank into grave-robbing criminality just to keep TV cameras rolling.

But the inadvertent contribution of W.C. Jameson's *Cold Case Billy the Kid* megahoax was his embracing the "Billy the Kid Case" hoaxers, thereby putting them where they belonged: in the sleazy netherworld of his "Brushy Bill" pseudo-history, groundless conspiracy theories, ghoulish exhumation quests, and credulous dupes; removing their last vestige of legitimacy, falsely bequeathed by the most powerful charlatan of them all: their past promoter, New Mexico Governor Bill Richardson.

# ANNOTATED APPENDIX

APPENDIX: 1. Tenth Judicial District Judge E.T. Kinsley, Jr. "Decree for Lois Telfer's Case No. 3255, For the Removal of the Body of William H. Bonney, Deceased, From the Ft. Sumner Cemetery in Which He is Interred for Reinterment in the Lincoln, New Mexico, Cemetery" (Filed in 1961). (Incorporating Louis Bowdre's "Motion to Intervene" of 1961.) Filed April 9, 1962.

```
IN RE APPLICATION OF LOIS TELFER,
PETITIONER, FOR THE REMOVAL OF THE
BODY OF WILLIAM H. BONNEY, DECEASED,
FROM THE FT. SUMNER CEMETERY IN WHICH
HE IS INTERRED FOR REINTERMENT IN THE
LINCOLN, NEW MEXICO, CEMETERY.
No. 3255
```

## D E C R E E

This matter coming on for hearing in open Court at Fort Sumner, New Mexico, this 13th day of March, 1962, petitioner appearing by her attorney, C.C. Chase, Jr., respondents, Board of County Commissioners appearing in person and by Victor C. Breen, District Attorney of the Tenth Judicial District and John Humphrey, Jr., Assistant District Attorney, and respondent, Mrs. J.W. Allen appearing in person and by her attorneys Victor C. Breen and John Humphrey, Jr., and the intervener, Louis A. Bowdre, appearing in person and by his attorneys, Victor C. Breen and John Humphrey, Jr., and the County having heard the evidence presented and being fully advised in the premises,

FINDS:

1. That Charles Bowdre was killed at Fort Sumner, New Mexico in the year 1880.

2. That the said Charles Bowdre was thereafter buried in the Fort Sumner Cemetery, where his remains now war.

3. That William H. Bonney, alias Billy the Kid, was killed at Fort Sumner, New Mexico, on July 14, 1881.

4. That said William H. Bonney was thereafter buried in the Fort Sumner Cemetery, beside or very near the grave of the said Charles Bowdre, and that the remains of the said William H. Bonney are still buried in the said Fort Sumner Cemetery.

5. **That due to the lapse of time and natural causes, it is no longer possible to locate the site of the graves of the said William H. Bonney, deceased** , and the said Charles Bowdre, deceased.

6. That over the years, large numbers of persons have been buried in the said Fort Sumner Cemetery and that the said Cemetery as it now exists is very thickly planted with graves.

7. That a search for the grave of the said William H. Bonney, deceased, in order to disinter said body, will invariably lead to disturbing the remains of other persons, buried in said cemetery, including the said Charles Bowdre, deceased.

8. That petitioner Lois Telfer is the next of kin of said William H. Bonney, deceased.

9. That intervener, Lois A. Bowdre, is next of kin of said Charles Bowdre, deceased.

WHEREFORE, the Court makes the following

### CONCLUSIONS OF LAW

1. That the court has jurisdiction of the subject matter and of the parties hereto.

2. That the relief prayed for in the petition herein cannot be granted since the site of the grave for William H. Bonney, deceased, cannot be located.

3. That the relief prayed for in the petition herein cannot be granted since a search for the grave of the said William H. Bonney, deceased, in order to disinter said body, will inevitably lead to disturbing the remains of other persons, buried in said cemetery, including the said Charles Bowdre, deceased.

WHEREFORE IT IS ORDERED, ADJUDGED AND DECREED that said Petition of Lois Telfer be, and the same hereby is, dismissed and that the petitioner take nothing and that the action be, and hereby is, dismissed on the merits.

DATED this 6th day of April, 1962.

<u>E. L. Kingsley, Jr.</u>
DISTRICT JUDGE

## APPENDIX: 2. Attorney William Snead. "Response of Office of Medical Investigator to Petition to Exhume Remains of Catherine Antrim." January 12, 2004.

COMES NOW the Office of the Medical Investigator, (OMI) through its counsel, William E. Snead, and hereby responds to the Petition to Exhume Remains of Catherine Antrim. OMI provides this response as an organization affected by the relief sought in the Petition. The Petition seeks a court order compelling OMI to disinter the remains of Catherine Antrim.

In the summer of 2003, the Office of the Medical Investigator, (OMI) was asked to respond to three questions in connection with **a criminal investigation** (author's boldface) of the circumstances behind the death of Billy the Kid and any involvement of Pat Garrett. The three questions posed related to the bodies of Catherine Antrim and Billy the Kid: (a) could these bodies be located; (b) could the bodies be recovered; and (c) would the bodies be in a state such that a positive identification could be made.

The OMI, primarily through the work of its forensic anthropologist, Debra Komar, Ph.D. conducted research and investigation in an attempt to respond to the questions posed. The details of the investigative findings are summarized in the attached affidavit by the Director of the OMI, Ross E. Zumwalt, M.D. (attached hereto as <u>Exhibit 1</u>) and the Affidavit of the forensic anthropologist for the OMI, Debra Komar, Ph.D. (attached hereto as <u>Exhibit 2</u>).

**Contrary to the statements contained in the petition, Debra Komar, Ph.D., the forensic Anthropologist referred by petitioner, does not believe that Ms. Antrim's remains can be exhumed without disturbing the remains of other bodies also interred in Memory Lane Cemetery.** (author's boldface) In fact, there is very significant probability that, even assuming Ms. Antrim's remains can be identified (although it is scientifically improbable that Ms. Antrim's remains can even be identified), **other remains would necessarily be disturbed in any exhumation** because of the way other burials have occurred in the cemetery and due to the passage of time, flooding and other natural causes.

**Contrary to the petition, the Office of Medical Investigators does not agree that an order should be entered allowing exhumation. After a detailed and scientific investigation described in the affidavits attached hereto, it is the scientific opinion of the OMI that any such attempted exhumation has very little possibility of contributing any information to the petitioner's alleged investigation, threatens the disturbance of unrelated burials, is a very great waste of public resources and a distraction of the OMI from its mandated work.**

APPENDIX: 3. Ross Zumwalt, M.D. "Sixth Judicial Court, State of New Mexico, County of Grant. No. MS 2003-11 "In the Matter of Catherine Antrim. Affidavit of Ross E. Zumwalt, M.D." January 9, 2004.

## AFFIDAVIT OF ROSS E. ZUMWALT, M.D.

The undersigned Ross E. Zumwalt, M.D. upon oath states:

1. My name is Ross E. Zumwalt, M.D. I am the Director of the Office of the Medical Investigator (OMI), located on the campus of the University of New Mexico Health Sciences Center (HSC) in Albuquerque, New Mexico. A copy of my resume is attached as Exhibit A. My training, education and background qualifies me to make the statements contained in this affidavit.

2. In my capacity as Director of OMI, I was asked to investigate the following questions related to the bodies of William Bonney aka "Billy the Kid" and Catherine Antrim, the mother of William Bonney: (a) whether the bodies could be located; (b) whether the bodies could be recovered; and (c) whether the bodies would be in a state such that a positive identification could be made. The stated purpose of the request was to aid in a criminal investigation of the circumstances behind the death of Billy the Kid and any involvement by Pat Garrett.

3. **Based on research of Silver City cemetery records, the location of the body of Catherine Antrim may not be known to a reasonable degree of scientific probability.** According to cemetery records, Catherine Antrim was buried in 1874 in Silver City in a cemetery within the City limits. In 1877, the cemetery in which she was buried flooded. Records indicate that the floodwaters could have disturbed the burial sites within the cemetery. In 1882, as a result of a change in the city ordinance requiring burials outside the city limits, Catherine Antrim's body was removed to a new burial site. It is not certain to a reasonable degree of scientific probability that the body, which was exhumed and moved in 1882, was that of Catherine Antrim. **Accordingly, if the purpose of exhuming Catherine Antrim is to provide a "known" standard for DNA testing, the fact that she cannot be positively identified renders all DNA tests suspect to a reasonable degree of scientific probability.**

4. If attempt is made to exhume the supposed body of Catherine Antrim from the burial site with her name, it is probable with a reasonable degree of scientific probability that **the remains of other individuals will be disturbed**. The burial site with Catherine Antrim's name is Plot D-27 at Memory Lane Cemetery. **This plot is the resting place of twelve (12) other known individuals.** See Exhibit B. In addition to the known individuals within Plot D-27, present cemetery records list two hundred seventy six (276) other individuals known to be buried in Memory Lane Cemetery but whose exact location within the cemetery is listed in the records as "unknown." See Exhibit C. Similarly, cemetery records also indicate that there are **at least four hundred fifty five (455) additional individuals who are buried within the Memory Lane Cemetery in "unmarked graves."** See Exhibit D. Given the uncertainty of the original location of the aforementioned burials and the fact that the cemetery flooded in 1877; July 1899; July-August 1895, 1892 (twice); August 1904; October 1909, 1913, and 1915; it is impossible to say to a reasonable degree of scientific probability that the remains of some other individual(s) will not be encountered in the process of exhuming the supposed remains of Catherine Antrim.

5. Should the exhumation uncover remains, the process of DNA collection will destroy portions of the remains. The process of DNA collection involves cutting and destroying large portions of bone. The amount of bone and the extent of the destruction is dependent upon the number of extractions per test and the extent of preservation of the

remains. If independent tests of DNA are performed, which is generally considered to be scientifically sound, or if preservation of the remains is poor, which given the history is expected to be the case, significant destruction of the recovered remains is scientifically probable.

6. Should the exhumation uncover the supposed remains of Catherine Antrim and DNA samples can be obtained, prior studies show that the probability of successfully extracting mitochondrial DNA (mtDNA) from remains interred in excess of 120 years is extremely low. Support for this principle is found at Stone et al, 2001; Ivanov et al, 1966; Jeffreys et al, 1992; and Gill et al, 1994 (see references). Accordingly, given the age of the remains at this date, it is not certain to a reasonable degree of scientific probability that any DNA will be usable as a standard for comparison to any individual.

7. Because of these technical problems, it has been the long-standing practice of the OMI to decline to disturb any remains that have been buried in an excess of 50 years. Ms. Antrim's remains, as well as those of Billy the Kid, both greatly exceed this threshold period.

8. **If the purpose of the exhumation of the remains of Catherine Antrim is to compare her DNA to the remains of the believed Billy the Kid, those remains are not likely to be obtained in my opinion. Based upon research performed by the OMI, the exact location of the Billy the Kid grave is not known, in my opinion, to a reasonable degree of scientific probability.**

9. If the purpose of exhuming Catherine Antrim is to compare her DNA to individuals claiming to be potential living descendents of Billy the Kid, it is not possible, to a reasonable degree of scientific probability to do so. The only DNA sample that may be successfully extracted from Catherine Antrim would be mitochondrial DNA (mtDNA). This mtDNA sample provides proof of matrilineal lineage only - in other words, it only passes from mother to child and not from father to child. Billy the Kid would carry his mother's mtDNA; however, _his_ biological children would have received their mtDNA from their own mother and not Billy.

10. **If the purpose of extracting mtDNA from the supposed remains of Catherine Antrim is to obtain a sample to compare against Brushy Bill Roberts in Texas, such a comparison, in my opinion, is also scientifically flawed. Based on research to date, I am unaware that Mr. Roberts ever claimed to be the biological child of Catherine Antrim. Thus, a test between his mtDNA and the putative remains of Catherine Antrim would have no scientific basis to a reasonable degree of scientific probability.**

11. Based on the fact that DNA testing of the putative remains of Catherine Antrim would have no probative value and the fact that an exhumation would likely disrupt other burial sites, an exhumation of Catherine Antrim is scientifically unsound in my opinion.

FURTHER AFFIANT SAYETH NOT.

Ross E. Zumwalt, M.D.

APPENDIX: 4. Debra Komar, PhD. "Sixth Judicial Court, State of New Mexico, County of Grant. No. MS 2003-11 "In the Matter of Catherine Antrim. Affidavit of Debra Komar, PhD." January 9, 2004.

## AFFIDAVIT OF DEBRA KOMAR, PhD.

The undersigned Debra Komar, PhD. upon oath, states:

1. My name is Debra Komar, PhD. I am a forensic anthropologist employed by the Office of the Medical Investigator (OMI) at the Health Sciences Center (HSC) at the University of New Mexico in Albuquerque, New Mexico. A copy of my resume is attached as Exhibit A. My training, education and background qualifies me to make the statements contained in this Affidavit.

2. In my capacity as a forensic anthropologist for the OMI, I was asked to investigate the following questions related to the bodies of William Bonney aka "Billy the Kid" and Catherine Antrim, the mother of William Bonney: (a) whether the bodies could be located; (b) whether the bodies could be recovered; and (c) whether the bodies would be in a state such that a positive identification could be made. The stated purpose of the request was to aid in a criminal investigation of the circumstances behind the death of Billy the Kid and any involvement by Pat Garrett.

3. Based on research of Silver City cemetery records, the location of the body of Catherine Antrim may not be known to a reasonable degree of scientific probability. According to cemetery records, Catherine Antrim was buried in 1874 in Silver City in a cemetery within the City limits. In 1877, the cemetery in which she was buried flooded. Records indicate that the floodwaters could have disturbed the burial sites within the cemetery. In 1882, as a result of a change in the city ordinance requiring burials outside the city limits, Catherine Antrim's body was removed to a new burial site. It is not certain to a reasonable degree of scientific probability that the body, which was exhumed and moved in 1882, was that of Catherine Antrim. **Accordingly, if the purpose of exhuming Catherine Antrim is to provide a "known" standard for DNA testing, the fact that she cannot be positively identified renders all DNA tests suspect to a reasonable degree of scientific probability.**

4. If attempt is made to exhume the supposed body of Catherine Antrim from the burial site with her name, it is probable with a reasonable degree of scientific probability that **the remains of other individuals will be disturbed.** The burial site with Catherine Antrim's name is Plot D-27 at Memory Lane Cemetery. **This plot is the resting place of twelve (12) other known individuals.** See Exhibit B to Zumwalt Affidavit. In addition to the known individuals within Plot D-27, present cemetery records list two hundred seventy six (276) other individuals known to be buried in Memory Lane Cemetery but whose exact location within the cemetery is listed in the records as "unknown." See Exhibit C to Zumwalt Affidavit. Similarly, cemetery

records also indicate that there are **at least four hundred fifty five (455) additional individuals who are buried within the Memory Lane Cemetery in "unmarked graves."** See Exhibit D to Zumwalt Affidavit. Given the uncertainty of the original location of the aforementioned burials and the fact that the cemetery flooded in 1877; July 1899; July-August 1895, 1892 (twice); August 1904; October 1909, 1913, and 1915; it is impossible to say to a reasonable degree of scientific probability that the remains of some other individual(s) will not be encountered in the process of exhuming the supposed remains of Catherine Antrim.

5. Should the exhumation uncover remains, the process of DNA collection will destroy portions of the remains. The process of DNA collection involves cutting and destroying large portions of bone. The amount of bone and the extent of the destruction is dependent upon the number of extractions per test and the extent of preservation of the remains. If independent tests of DNA are performed, which is generally considered to be scientifically sound, or if preservation of the remains is poor, which given the history is expected to be the case, significant destruction of the recovered remains is scientifically probable.

6. Should the exhumation uncover the supposed remains of Catherine Antrim and DNA samples can be obtained, prior studies show that the probability of successfully extracting mitochondrial DNA (mtDNA) from remains interred in excess of 120 years is extremely low. Support for this principle is found at Stone et al, 2001; Ivanov et al, 1966; Jeffreys et al, 1992; and Gill et al, 1994 (see references). Accordingly, given the age of the remains at this date, it is not certain to a reasonable degree of scientific probability that any DNA will be usable as a standard for comparison to any individual.

7. Because of these technical problems, it has been the long-standing practice of the OMI to decline to disturb any remains that have been buried in an excess of 50 years. Ms. Antrim's remains, as well as those of Billy the Kid, both greatly exceed this threshold period.

8. **If the purpose of the exhumation of the remains of Catherine Antrim is to compare her DNA to the remains of the believed Billy the Kid, those remains are not likely to be obtained in my opinion. Based upon research performed by the OMI, the exact location of the Billy the Kid grave is not known, in my opinion, to a reasonable degree of scientific probability.**

9. If the purpose of exhuming Catherine Antrim is to compare her DNA to individuals claiming to be potential living descendents of Billy the Kid, it is not possible, to a reasonable degree of scientific probability to do so. The only DNA sample that may be successfully extracted from Catherine Antrim would be mitochondrial DNA (mtDNA). This mtDNA sample provides proof of matrilineal lineage only - in other words, it only passes from mother to child and not from father to child. Billy the Kid would carry his mother's mtDNA; however, <u>his</u> biological children would have received their mtDNA from their own mother and not Billy.

10. If the purpose of extracting mtDNA from the supposed remains of Catherine Antrim is to obtain a sample to compare against Brushy Bill Roberts in Texas, such a comparison, in my opinion, is also scientifically flawed. Based on research to date, I am unaware that Mr. Roberts ever claimed to be the biological child of Catherine Antrim. Thus, a test between his mtDNA and the putative remains of Catherine Antrim would have no scientific basis to a reasonable degree of scientific probability.

11. Based on the fact that DNA testing of the supposed remains of Catherine Antrim would have no probative value and the fact that an exhumation would likely disrupt other burial sites, an exhumation of Catherine Antrim is scientifically unsound in my opinion.

FURTHER AFFIANT SAYETH NOT.

Debra Komar, PhD.

APPENDIX: 5: Attorney Bill Robins III and Attorney David Sandoval. "Sixth Judicial District Court, State on New Mexico, County of Grant. Case No. MS-2003-11." "In the Matter of Catherine Antrim, Billy the Kid's Pre-Hearing Brief." January 5, 2004.

## IN THE MATTER OF CATHERINE ANTRIM, BILLY THE KID'S PRE-HEARING BRIEF

COME NOW, Bill Robins, III and David Sandoval, of the law firm of Heard, Robins, Cloud, Lubel & Greenwood, LLC, and on the behalf of the estate of William H. Bonney, aka "Billy the Kid",

**[AUTHOR'S NOTE: The Kid had no estate: posthumous property settled in a probate court. This fakery segues to Robins's calling dead Billy as his client as exhumation petitioner!]**

file this Pre-Hearing Brief and state as follows:

### I. INTRODUCTION

The Court asks the undersigned counsel to brief several questions as follows:

1. The Governor's right to assign an Attorney to Represent the Interests of Billy the Kid and the Associated Zone of Public Interest;

2. Who is the Real Party in Interest Represented by Counsel;

3. What Stake Does that Party Have in Intervening in This Cause;

4. Billy the Kid's Interest as Defined in the Law Relating to Standing; and

5. The Effect of *In Re: Application of Lois Telfer, for the Removal of the Body of William H. Bonney*

[AUTHOR'S NOTE: These questions by corrupt Judge Quintero are a parody. He well knows that Governor Richardson had no right to appoint an attorney to his court, knows that Robins has no "real party" as a client; knows that the dead do not appear in court and have no standing; and knows that the Fort Sumner Telfer exhumation case blocked all future exhumation attempts there by stating that the grave location was uncertain and contiguous remains would be disturbed.]

The Points and Authorities section below does so as follows: **Point One** provides introductory legal analysis, **Point Two** addresses Question 1, **Point Three** addresses Questions 2, 3, and 4, and **Point Four** addresses Question 5. **Point 5** supports the merits of the Petition for Exhumation.

## II. POINTS AND AUTHORITIES

### Point One
### Initial Discussion as to the Nature of This Proceeding

This is an interesting proceeding in that the relief sought here is not exclusively judicial.

**[AUTHOR'S NOTE: That is true. The following is just hoaxing.]**

New Mexico allows the state registrar or state medical examiner to issue permits for disinterment. 1978 NMSA §24-14-23D. The statute does not identify who may make such a request nor specify the showing that needs to be made in order to obtain the permit. Rather than proceeding with this simple and non-adversarial process, Petitioners here have invoked this Court's equity jurisdiction for an order allowing the exhumation of Billy the Kid's mother, Catherine Antrim. See, *Hood v. Spratt*, 357 So.2d 135 (Miss. 1978) (request for disinterment "is particularly one for a court of equity") citing *Theodore v. Theodore*, 57 N.M. 434, 259 P.2d 795 (1953).

"[N]ormally a district court would not become involved in such matters unless a protesting relative or interested party files an injunction or takes some other legal action to halt the autopsy or disinterment," *In Re Johnson*, 94 N.M. 491, 494, 612 P.2d 1302 (1980). Petitioners should thus be commended for bringing this Court into the picture and in doing so, offering the town of Silver City, a relative of another descendent buried in the cemetery, and the legal interests of Billy the Kid, an opportunity to participate in the process.

**[AUTHOR'S NOTE: This implies the hoax is a favor to Silver City - in court opposing exhumation - and a favor to dead Catherine Antrim. Also, Billy has no "legal interests," being dead!]**

The questions the Court asked briefed, however, suggest the possibility that the court may not allow Billy the Kid to be heard.

**[AUTHOR'S NOTE: At this point, the hoaxers were going through the motions, believing the judge was in their pocket.]**

As will be shown clearly, Billy the Kid's interests are real, legitimate, proper for consideration, and we respectfully ask the Court to recognize them as such.

**[AUTHOR'S NOTE: This is audacious lying.]**

A challenge to a governor's appointment power is made in a *quo warranto* proceeding.

**[AUTHOR'S NOTE: Robins is faking legitimacy of his appointment as dead Billy's attorney. In fact, only the judge can appoint an attorney for a client. This appointment was an example of Richardson's illegal abuse of power.]**

*New Mexico Judicial Standards Commission v. Governor Bill Richardson and Espinoza,* 134 N.M. 59, 73 P.2d 197 (2003); see also, 1978 NMSA. §§44-3-1 *et. seq.* (quo warranto action proper when "any person shall usurp, intrude into or unlawfully holds or exercise any public office, civil or military, or any franchise within this state.")

The *quo warranto* statute contains specific procedures that the Town has not properly followed, nor could follow because the Town is not a "private person."

**[AUTHOR'S NOTE: This fact demonstrates that Robins is misapplying the law to the town with his false argument.]**

Standing to bring such a proceeding lies first with the attorney general or district attorney. 1978 NMSA, §44-3-4; *Beese v. District Court,* 31 N.M. 82, 239 P. 452 (1925). Those public officials do not present any challenge here.

A private person can bring a *quo warranto* action only when he has requested the aforementioned public officials to bring action and they have refused. 1978 NMSA, §44-3-4. The only private person in this matter is Ms. Amos-Staadt [sic] and she has not challenged the Governor's appointment, much less shown compliance with the procedural requisites of the *quo warranto* statute.

As noted, the challenge to the Governor comes from the Town of Silver City. It simply has no standing to bring a *quo warranto* proceeding. 1978 NMSA, §44-3-4. The validity of Governor Richardson's appointment of the undersigned counsel is thus not before this Court.

**[AUTHOR'S NOTE: In fact, a legitimate judge would have made it his/her matter and kicked an inappropriately appointed lawyer representing a dead client out of court.]**

To the extent that the Court remains concerned with the presence of Billy the Kid in this litigation,

**[AUTHOR'S NOTE: Robins here switches from the "estate" of Billy the Kid to the dead Kid as client.]**

it is a matter that can be more properly addressed pursuant to legal requirements of standing and intervention, which the discussion below shows the Kid satisfies.

**[AUTHOR'S NOTE: Robins now fakes that dead Billy had court standing to justify his intervening.]**

*(Given the express direction to brief the question, however, the discussion below sets forth the proper gubernatorial powers at play here.)*

### C. The Governor's Powers

As noted above, the governor is the supreme executive officer of the state. There can be no question that in that capacity Governor Richardson has authority to engage the services of professionals to assist him in accomplishment of those duties. Lawyers are certainly within that group, as is witnessed by Geno Zamora, the Governor's chief legal counsel.

**[AUTHOR'S NOTE: Robins is here making a false argument by omission. The governor can engage an attorneys services. But the matter here is not services, it is the illegal nature of Robins's appointment to this court.]**

The source of power behind such appointments is likely found in the "inherent general power of appointment in the executive." *Matheson v. Ferry*, 641 P.2d 674, 682 (Ut 1982); *Hadley v. Washburn*, 67 S.W. 592 (Mo. 1902) (appointment of election commissioners is an inherent executive power); *Application of O'Sullivan*, 158 P.2d 306, 309 (Mont. 1945) ("the power of appointment is an executive function which cannot be delegated to the judiciary); *State v. Brill*, 111 N.W. 294, (1907) (legislature prohibited from requiring judges at appoint members to a board of control unrelated to the judiciary on a separation of powers theory grounded in the presumption that the power of appointment is inherently executive).

**[AUTHOR'S NOTE: Robins, spewing irrelevant cases, is omitting that the Constitution guarantees separation of powers: executive branch Richardson could not appoint him to a court!]**

This inherent power must also allow the Governor to appoint attorneys to address his concerns and/or further his interests outside his immediate circle.

**[AUTHOR'S NOTE: Robins gives dramatic proof that the "Billy the Kid Case" was Richardson's baby. Then he leaps to the motive of the publicity-seeking hoax: the Billy the Kid pardon.]**

The governor has the "power to grant reprieves and pardons." N.M. Const. Art. V Sec. 6. Undersigned counsel intends on seeking a pardon for Billy the Kid. Certainly Governor Richardson is within his inherent appointment power to hire counsel to advise him on the merits of such a pardon.

**[AUTHOR'S NOTE: Robins omits that pardon advising does not justify his appointment to this court seeking exhumation. It just makes him an amateur historian.]**

That the power extends to pardons of long-dead individuals is clear because our Constitution extends that power to pardon offences under the Territorial Laws of New Mexico. N.M. Const. Art. XXII Sec 5. (Footnote: Posthumous pardons are not unusual. In fact, Lenny Bruce was pardoned by Governor Patake in New York just last month.)

**[AUTHOR'S NOTE: Robins omits that pardon was at the discretion Governor's discretion. Richardson could pardon Billy if he wanted to. The rest was just a publicity stunt.]**

That the appointment is consistent with the statutorily granted powers is shown by consideration of two different status. Counsel's appointment here is in the nature of an appointment as a public defender; a portion of their work effort will go towards exposing the merits of a pardon. 1978 NMSA §§31-15-1, et. seq. The public defender department is within the executive branch and is headed [sic-by] an appointee of the governor. 1978 NMSA §§31-15-4A. The duty and function of the department is to have attorneys serve as defense counsel "as necessary and appropriate." 1978 NMSA §§31-15-7B(10).

**[AUTHOR'S NOTE: Robins is preposterously saying he is in an exhumation court to decide on a pardon.]**

The Governor has apparently deemed it necessary and appropriate to seek guidance from undersigned counsel on matters related to the Kid and potential pardon.

Similarly, the Governor has authority to request the appointment of prosecutorial attorneys. 1978 NMSA, Section 8-5-2B provides that a governor may request the attorney general to appoint counsel in "all actions civil or criminal" in which the governor believes the state is "interested." The governor's pardon power gives the state an interest [sic-in] legal matters involving a potential candidate for pardon and Governor Richardson could rely on Section 8-5-2B's power at the appropriate time. This should not be read to mean that Governor Richardson is assuming power to appoint attorneys to act on behalf of the State, a power that lies exclusively with the Attorney General. It is referenced here as another example of how the governor is authorized in several instances to procure the assistance of attorneys.

**[AUTHOR'S NOTE: Faking Robins has given no justification for his being in this court, a travesty which only a corrupt judge, like Henry Quintero, would have permitted.]**

## Point Three
## What Interests Are of Importance Here

A. *The Law of Standing*

As has been established, this is an action in equity. New Mexico's Supreme Court wrote: "The equity right of intervention in proper cases has always been recognized. The equitable test is, 'Does the intervener stand to gain or lose by the judgment.'" *Stovall v. Vesely*, 38 N.M. 415, 34 P.2d 862, 864 (1934).

**[AUTHOR'S NOTE: The actual test here is that Robins has no existing client to have an interest, since Billy is dead.]**

Billy the Kid's interest here is his legacy.

**[AUTHOR'S NOTE: Robins is out-of-control faking that dead Billy, for whom he can speak, is after a "legacy."]**

As noted in previous briefing the very question of his life and death will be impacted by the results of the Petitioners' investigation.

**[AUTHOR'S NOTE: Robins's fake argument reveals the thrust to make "Brushy Bill" Billy the Kid - and pardon him.]**

B. *The Planned Request For Pardon Confers Standing Here*

Undersigned counsel intends to ask Governor Richardson that he pardon Billy the kid for the murder conviction of Sheriff Brady on several known bases including the fact that then Territorial Governor Lew Wallace reneged on his promise to pardon the Kid.

**[AUTHOR'S NOTE: Now comes Robins's leap that cracked the hoax for me. He seemed to be talking about pardoning Billy Bonney, but segues to the pretenders - as if one *is* Billy, who deserves pardon. This is to be a rerun of the Governor T.J. Mabry hearing, with "Brushy" winning!]**

There were at least two individuals that laid claim to Billy the Kid's identity years after his alleged shooting by Garrett. **Both of them apparently led long and peaceful and crime-free lives.** [author's boldface]

As was recently recognized by the court in *Mestiza v. DeLeon*, 8 S.W. 3d 770 (Tx. Ct. App. - Corpus Christi - (1999) this interest is sufficient to properly confer standing. There an inmate imprisoned on murder conviction sought the exhumation of the victim's body on the basis that the exhumation could lead to new evidence to support a habeas corpus claim. While not deciding the merits, the Texas court determined that the inmate's interest in showing the improper conviction was sufficient to confer standing. That certainty is an analogous situation here.

The reasons that the exhumation is sought is to disinter the remains of Billy the Kid's mother for the extraction of Mitochondrial DNA.

As such, Ms. Antrim presents the only source of such DNA. Should the exhumation be denied, Billy the Kid will be forever denied the opportunity to make use of modern technology to shed light on his life and death.

**[AUTHOR'S NOTE: Do not miss that this is just a Billy the Kid pretender argument: namely that Billy's death is in question. Hidden is the historical certainty of Billy's killing by Garrett.]**

<u>Should the DNA extracted from Ms. Antrim confirm that one of the potential Kids was in fact Billy the Kid, undersigned counsel will be able to make an even stronger argument for pardon by citing to the long years of law abiding life</u>.

**[AUTHOR'S NOTE: THIS IS THE SENTENCE THAT CRACKED THE "BILLY THE KID CASE" HOAX. And here is the full-blown plot: prove a pretender by faking DNA, then pardon him; ergo, Oliver "Brushy Bill" Roberts – as Billy the Kid!]**

### C. A Comparison of Interests

This Court has allowed the intervention of the Town of Silver City in this matter. The municipal politicians there have apparently authorized the Town's Mayor to oppose the exhumation. Billy the Kid acknowledges the existence of case law that accords standing to the owners of the cemetery concerned in such proceedings.

**[AUTHOR'S NOTE: Do not miss Robins's sly and crazy switch from "Billy the Kid's estate" to channeling dead Billy, who is now speaking along with him - in apparent legal agreement!]**

What is of interest here, is that such standing is often given to the cemetery owner because it may be the only entity that can represent the wishes of the deceased, an element typically considered in whether to order an exhumation. *Theodore*, 57 N.M. at 438, *Estate of Conroy*, 530 A2d 212, 530 N.Y. S.2d 668 (N.Y.Super. 1988)

As expected, the Mayor here opposes the exhumation and is positioned to present evidence in support of its objection. Whether or not that truly represents the interests of Ms. Antrim can never be known. Given the identity of the decedent and the time that has passes since her death, the Mayor cannot possibly have any direct evidence of Ms. Antrim's wishes. As such, the evidence that is presented by the Mayor can be viewed as best, supposition, or at worst, utterly unreliable.

**[AUTHOR'S NOTE: Do not miss the bizarreness of this argument. In the real world, the Mayor is has to protect remains in a cemetery under his authority. But Robin is saying the Mayor actually needs to mind-read corpse Catherine to find**

out if she wants to be dug up. Or better, Robins implies, the Mayor should channel her, so she could speak in Court!]

One is left to question why such a party with such a remote interest and lack of express knowledge about the decedent's wishes is conferred standing while the interests of Billy the Kid go unheard if this Court denier him standing. Allowing such a party to appear and present evidence while denying the same opportunity to a party that has been appointed to represent the interests of the decedent's son does not seem prudent nor fair.

[AUTHOR'S NOTE: This argument is so crazy that a reader might be tempted to rationalize that it cannot be as crazy as it sounds. Robins is saying that dead Billy the Kid has more credibility to let his wishes be known, than the live Mayor whose obligation it is to protect his city's cemetery. And, by the way, Robins makes clear that he himself can tell the wishes of the dead, unlike the limited Mayor. And also, Robins claims, this speaking for the dead adds up to corpse Billy the Kid having standing in court – in fact, better justification to speak in Court than the Silver City Mayor himself!]

Point Four
The *Telfer* Case and Impact on This Case

The *Telfer* case is of no major consequence here.

[AUTHOR'S NOTE: This statement is evidence that Robins has nerve as well as nuttiness. The *Telfer* case was fatal to the Catherine Antrim exhumation. The 1962 blocked exhumation on the Billy the Kid grave by Lois Telfer established precedent that remains were in uncertain location, and exhumation could disturb contiguous bodies. Catherine Antrim was to be exhumed to match with Billy the Kid's DNA. But it was unattainable. So there was no reason to exhume her. In what follows, Robins hides all that.]

First, since neither of the parties here were parties there, the doctrines of res judica and collateral estoppel cannot possibly apply against the current litigants. *Brantley Farms v. Carlsbad Irrigation District*, 124 N.M. 698, 702, 954 p.2d 763 (1998).

Second, the body sought to be exhumed there was the purported body of Billy the Kid and not the subject of this request, his mother. Third, the basis for the request was that the Ft. Sumner burial site had been abandoned and not maintained for years. The petitioner's desire was to re-inter the body in a "decent and respectable burial place" in Lincoln, New Mexico. The factual and legal matters there are thus distinct to those here. That one was denied cannot serve to prohibit the exhumation of the other.

The opponents of exhumation may rely on the *Telfer* court's finding that "it is no longer possible to locate the site of the grave of the said

William H. Bonney" as a means to argue that the exhumation of Ms. Antrim for DNA would be futile. Even if such a factual finding was true and correct the technology available now as opposed to 1962 is such that a new factual inquiry would be likely to yield different results.

**[AUTHOR'S NOTE: This argument about "new technology" is fakery. Technology cannot show where Billy Bonney himself rests in Fort Sumner's cemetery, or prevent disturbing contiguous remains.]**

Even if the body buried in Ft., Sumner cannot possibly be exhumed for comparable DNA, a denial here is not called for. As has been mentioned there are at least two other individuals who claim to have been the Kid. Surely *Telfer* would not be a binding precedent to deny exhumations of grave sites in Texas or Arizona.

**[AUTHOR'S NOTE: Robins is arguing for exhuming pretenders, when they fail just based on invalid history.]**

Point Five<br>Exhumation is Proper

The Sheriffs invoke the jurisdiction of this Court in an attempt to exhume the remains of Catherine Antrim. The Court has express statutory authority to so order. It is a crime in New Mexico to knowingly and willfully disturb or remove remains of any person interred in a cemetery. 1978 NMSA, § 30-12-12. The criminal statute, however, recognizes three exceptions. Disinterment is allowed "pursuant to an order of the district court, the provisions of Section 24-14-23 NMSA 1978 or as otherwise permitted by law." This request falls into the first and last exceptions.

**[AUTHOR'S NOTE: Robins must know that the OMI was blocking exhumation and that Attorney Sherry Tippett lied about its permission. He is, thus. trying to get the court to act independently of the OMI.]**

The leading exhumation case in New Mexico is *Theodore*, 57, N.M. 434 and sets forth as follows:

**[AUTHOR'S NOTE: The irrelevant *Theodore* case, which follows, is about <u>digging up and relocating</u> a body - absolutely noting to do with the Antrim exhumation at hand.].**

> In determining whether authority to disinter a body **and bury it elsewhere** should be granted, controlling consideration seems generally to be given by the courts to the following factors, (1) the interest of the public; (2) wishes of the decedent; (3) rights and feelings of those entitled to be heard by reason of relationship; (4) the rights and principles of religious bodies or other organizations which granted the right to inter the body in

the first place of burial, and (5) the question of whether or not consent was given to the burial in the first place of interment by the one claiming the right of removal.(emphasis added).

The bolded language is important because it shows that *Theodore* is not directly on point.

**[AUTHOR'S NOTE: Robins even admits the Theodore case is irrelevant. In fact, his whole document is just fake filler.]**

The exhumation there was for the purpose of moving remains from one grave site (preferred by the decedent's brother) to another site (preferred by the plaintiff's widow). That is not the case here. Petitioners asking for an exhumation that is of importance in their investigation surrounding the Lincoln County Wars [sic] and the shooting of Billy the Kid.

The distinction renders some of the *Theodore* factors of no consequence and the others of limited precedential value. Since the Ms. Antrim remains will be replaced in the same burial site, the 4th and 5th factor, which involves the decedent's ties to the "first place of burial" sought to be abandoned are of no consequence here. The first three factors remain.

1st Factor Public Interest, Billy the Kid's name is forever tied to New Mexico and to that of another legendary figure of the Old West, Sheriff Pat Garrett. A commonly held version of history paints a picture of an ambush in which Garrett killed the Kid in Ft. Sumner where most believe the Kid still lies at rest. This version has been questioned. It is the investigation into whether Garrett killed the Kid that has prompted these investigators to seek exhumation.

**[AUTHOR'S NOTE: This is pure hoaxing The only ones to "question" history are the hoaxers themselves for their stunt. There is no "public interest" - meaning value - there is only the self-serving motives of the hoaxers - and definite "lack of public interest" by destroying New Mexican's iconic Old West history and its tourist sites.]**

2nd Factor, the Decedents wishes. In spite of Silver City's position to the contrary, we simply do not know what the decedent's wishes would be. Given the present circumstances, however, where her remains could possibly provide critical evidence to be used by modern day advocates to clear her son's name, one might easily surmise that Silver City's dogged attempt to resist exhumation would not be appreciated by Ms. Antrim.

**[AUTHOR'S NOTE: This is Robins at his most slippery. First of all, he is now near-channeling Catherine Antrim to express "her wishes." Secondly he is misstating Silver City's position. The Mayor has standing not to guess "wishes," but to protect the sanctity of her grave from exactly the groundless publicity stunt that this hoax represents. Thirdly, Robins is still faking**

"public interest." Fourthly, is his most outrageous thrust: that Catherine Antrim would want to be dug up to "prove" that her son was "Brushy Bill."]

3rd Factor, Surviving Relatives Wishes. There are no relatives of Ms. Antrim currently before the Court. This Court can take judicial notice from the *Telfer* case, that at least one of her claimed relatives was not adverse to the concept of exhumation since the disinterment of Billy the Kid was sought in 1962 [sic - 1961, denied in 1962]

[AUTHOR'S NOTE: Robins hid that Lois Telfer had no proven kinship to Billy the Kid, so had no true standing. And no opinion was expressed by her as the exhuming Catherine Antrim anyway.]

The closest party currently before the Court is in fact Billy the Kid as represented by the undersigned counsel. As is apparent from the arguments set forth in this brief, the kid's [sic] interests would be furthered by the exhumation.

[AUTHOR'S NOTE: Here again is Robins is channeling dead Billy to say that HE, BILLY THE KID (meaning more bizarrely: he "Brushy Bill" Roberts) wants his mom dug up!]

The "limitation of "currently before the Court" was used above because of undersigned counsel is aware of certain individuals who claim to be related to Ms. Antrim who at worst will likely testify in support of exhumation and may even attempt to intervene in this matter.

[AUTHOR'S NOTE: Robins is apparently referring to Elbert Garcia, a Santa Rosa, New Mexico, resident who wrote a book claiming to be Billy the Kid's grandson. Since his kinship was unproven, he was soon abandoned by the hoaxers.]

Billy the Kid believes that the evidence adduced at the exhumation hearing will certainly support an order of exhumation here.

[AUTHOR'S NOTE: Oops, Robins has crossed into the "Exorcist" movie's territory. He has "disappeared" as an entity; only dead Billy is talking now. The creepy thought is that Robins not be faking. He may really think he IS "Brushy Bill" incarnate.]

As such, Billy the Kid's mother's name, will forever be tied with other famous names and legendary figures: Czar Nicholas II of Russia and his family, John Paul Jones, President Zachary Taylor, Jesse James, Butch Cassidy and the Sundance Kid. All these individuals were themselves exhumed for various reasons. Other lesser known, or perhaps less colorful figures, have also been exhumed. They include Samuel Mudd (conspirator in the assassination of Abraham Lincoln), Haile Selassie (former emperor of Ethiopia), Czar Lazar (14th century Serbian monarch), Medgar Evers (civil rights leader, Carl A. Weiss (alleged assassin of Huey Long). Those whose exhumation has been proposed at various times in the past include, Meriwether Lewis. John Wilkes Booth, John F. Kennedy, Lee Harvey Oswald and J. Edgar Hoover.

**[AUTHOR'S NOTE: Exhumation of other famous people does not lend any justification to this exhumation attempt.]**

Clearly, exhumation as a truth seeking device has been used throughout history. Exhumation has also been the subject of case law and legal discourse. See, 61 U. Colo.L.Rev. 567, Evidentiary Autopsies, 1990; 21 A.L.R.2d. 538, *Annotation*, Power of a Court to Order Disinterment and Autopsy or Exhumation for Evidential Purpose in a Civil Case."

**[AUTHOR'S NOTE: Robins is using irrelevant cases. First of all, this is allegedly a criminal murder case, not a civil one. More important, the murder case is a hoax, since Pat Garrett killed Billy Bonney not an innocent victim.]**

The current state of knowledge and technology, and its expected refinement and expansion, will likely make it even more of a common occurrence in the future. It is proper to allow such an inquiry here.

### III. CONCLUSION

The foregoing has established that the undersigned counsel may legally and properly appear in these proceedings on behalf of, and to represent the interests of Billy the Kid. They are ready to present testimony and evidence to further support their interests that the exhumation of the Kid's mother, Ms. Catherine Antrim be allowed to proceed.

**[AUTHOR'S NOTE: Robins established nothing to justify his being in this Court, or to channel dead Billy. One is left with the creepy "They are ready ..." and wondering if "they" are Robins and his dead buddy Ollie Roberts, or just Robins and his co-counsel, David Sandoval - present with his New Mexico law license because Robins had just a Texas one.]**

Respectfully submitted this _5th_ day of January, 2004.

Heard, Robins, Cloud, Lubel & Greenwood, L.L.P.

By: _David Sandoval_
Bill Robins III
David Sandoval
Address and Telephone Numbers
**ATTORNEYS FOR BILLY THE KID**

**[AUTHOR'S NOTE: Really, in boldface, Robins and Sandoval are listed as Billy's lawyers! And New Mexico taxpayers footed the district court bills in Grant and De Baca Counties for these hoaxing charlatans.]**

APPENDIX: 6: Attorneys Bill Robins III, David Sandoval, and Mark Acuña. "Tenth Judicial Court of De Baca County. Case No. CV-2004-00005, In the Matter of William H. Bonney, aka 'Billy the Kid.'" February 26, 2004.

## PETITION FOR THE EXHUMATION OF BILLY THE KID'S REMAINS

COME NOW, Co-Petitioners, and respectfully request that this Court order that the body of William H. Bonney, aka "Billy the Kid" be exhumed, and in support of the Petition state:

### I. The Petitioners

1. The Co-Petitioners are Gary Graves, Sheriff of De Baca County, Tom Sullivan, (Sheriff) and Steve Sederwall (Deputy Sheriff) of Lincoln County, New Mexico. (hereinafter the "Sheriff-Petitioners").

2. Co-Petitioner Billy the Kid is one of the subjects of an investigation being conducted by the Sheriff-Petitioners. Bill Robins III and David Sandoval have been appointed by the Honorable Bill Richardson, Governor of the State of New Mexico, to represent the interests of Billy the Kid in the investigation.

### II. Jurisdiction and Venue

3. Jurisdiction is proper with this Court on the basis of 1978 NMSA Statute 30-12-12.

4. Venue is proper in this County on the basis that the remains that are the subject of this exhumation are located in deBaca [sic] County.

### III. Procedural Background

5. The Sheriff-Petitioners initiated investigation in their respective counties to set the historical record straight as to the guilt or innocence of the legendary Sheriff Pat Garrett in the death of Billy the Kid. The investigative files bear the numbers 03-06-136-01 (*deBaca* [sic] *County*) and 2003-274 (*Lincoln County*).

**[AUTHOR'S NOTE: During my open records case from 2007 to 2015, its law enforcement officers would lie, claiming the "Billy the Kid Case" was their "private hobby," and/or it was just the investigation of the deputy murders by Billy the Kid – to hide their Garrett murder case as Sheriffs and Deputies.]**

6. The remains of Billy the Kid's mother, Catherine Antrim, currently lie in a marked grave located in Silver City, New Mexico. The Sheriff-Petitioners previously filed a Petition to Exhume the remains of Catherine Antrim (hereinafter the "Antrim Petition") which is currently pending before the Honorable District Court Judge Quintero in the Sixth

Judicial District. Counsel for Billy the Kid filed a Petition to Intervene in support of that exhumation.

**[AUTHOR'S NOTE: Robins's client is dead Billy!]**

7. The purpose of the Antrim Petition is to disinter her remains to extract vital mitochondrial DNA to then be used to compare with the DNA sought to be extracted from the purported remains of Billy the Kid. Those purported remains of Billy the Kid lie in a cemetery in Ft. Sumner, New Mexico. A hearing on the merits of the Antrim exhumation is scheduled for August 16-18, 2004.

8. Exhumations, DNA extractions and comparisons have become an increasingly common and accepted investigatory method and tool in forensic criminology and historical investigation ...

## IV. Historical Background

**[AUTHOR'S NOTE: This section confirms the "Billy the Kid Case" as a "Brushy Bill" hoax, and another attempt at the lost Governor Mabry pardon.]**

9. Billy the Kid is New Mexico's best known Old West figure. He has even been called the best known New Mexican ever. The Kid is no doubt the stuff of legend, myth, and continuing popular attention.

10. The Kid lived during a complex and violent time in New Mexico history which included the "Lincoln County War." It was a time when the distinction between "outlaw" and "lawman" was blurred due to rival political factions having deputized their respective supporters. Billy the Kid himself was deputized during these times.

11. This was also a time whose history was not accurately nor completely written.

**[AUTHOR'S NOTE: This is hoaxer-style fake "suspicion," which is ultimately the fake "proof" used for "survival suspicion" and accusing Garrett of murdering the innocent victim, not Billy.]**

For generations now, the life of Billy the Kid has been the subject of historical debate. Perhaps the most significant lingering question involves whether Billy the Kid was indeed <u>shot by Sheriff Pat Garrett in an ambush **one dark night**</u> in Ft. Sumner **or whether the Kid went on to live a long and peace-abiding life elsewhere.**

**[AUTHOR'S NOTE: THIS IS THE DARK NIGHT GIVE-AWAY OF A "BRUSHY"-BELIEVER, LIKE ROBINS. Faking that "historical debate" exists, he is quoting "Brushy's" confabulation about the "dark night" as fact, ignorant of July 14, 1881's full moon. His motive, however, is to validate intended pretender exhumations.]**

12. The debate has been sparked at various times in the past by at least two individuals who laid claim to his identity. **Ollie** "**Brushy Bill**" **Roberts** [author's boldface] resided in Hico, Texas and claimed to be Billy the Kid. John Miller, in Arizona also died still claiming he was Billy the Kid. Co-Petitioners are in the initial phases of pursuing exhumations of these individuals as well.

**[AUTHOR'S NOTE: Amusingly and revealingly, Robins affectionately and familiarly calls Roberts "Ollie."]**

13. The Sheriff-Petitioners' investigation has certainly fueled debate as to whether or not Pat Garrett's version of events surrounding his claimed killing of Billy the Kid is in fact historically accurate. The investigation has renewed questions as to whether Billy the Kid lies buried at the fabled grave-site in Ft. Sumner. Allowing the exhumation of the remains at Ft. Sumner grave site for extraction of DNA to be compared with that of Ms. Antrim's will likely finally provide definitive answers to this historical quandary.

**[AUTHOR'S NOTE: As discussed, these DNA claims are fake, and were the basis of the Office of the Medical Investigator's refusal of exhumation permits.]**

## IV. Claim for Relief, *Exhumation of Remains*

14. Co-Petitioners repeat and re-allege the foregoing paragraphs 1-13 as if fully set herein.

15. Section 30-12-12 of the New Mexico Statutes grants district courts power and discretion to order the exhumation of remains at a grave site.

16. This Court's power and discretion should be exercised and the exhumation be allowed to proceed for purposes of examining the purported remains of Billy the Kid. And for the extraction of DNA samples from the same.

WHEREFORE, Petitioners request that this Court issue an order allowing the exhumation of William H. Bonney, and all such further relief as the Court deems just and proper.

Respectfully submitted this 24th day of February, 2004.

Heard, Robins, Cloud, Lubel & Greenwood L.L.P.
Bill Robins III, David Sandoval
Attorneys for Co-Petitioner BILLY the KID

**[AUTHOR'S NOTE: Do not miss that Bill Robins's *client* is still the dead Billy the Kid - requesting his own exhumation!]**

APPENDIX: 7. No Author. "Contact List for "William H. Bonney Case # 2003-274." No Date. **[AUTHOR'S NOTE: Omitted below are addresses and telephone numbers which were included with each listing]**

Contact List, William H. Bonney Case # 2003-274

"**Lincoln County Sheriff's Office & Investigators**": Tom Sullivan - Sheriff, Lincoln County Sheriff's Office, Carrizozo, New Mexico; Steven M. Sederwall - Deputy, Capitan, New Mexico; Dale Tunnell - Criminal Investigator, State of Arizona, Phoenix, Arizona; Doctor Rick Staub – DNA Expert, Orchid Cellmark, Dallas, Texas; Paul Andrew Hutton - Historian, University of New Mexico, Albuquerque, New Mexico;

"**New Mexico Governor's Office**": Bill Richardson, Governor of New Mexico, Capital [sic] Building, Santa Fe, New Mexico; Billy Sparks - Director of Communications, State Capitol Building, Santa Fe, New Mexico; Jon Hendry - Marketing Director State of New Mexico, New Mexico Department of Tourism; Santa Fe, New Mexico;

"**Attorney's**" [sic]: Bill Robins III - Attorney at Law, Heard, Robins, Cloud, Lubel & Greenwood, LLP, Santa Fe, New Mexico;

"**Other Numbers to Investigation:** DeAnn Kessler - Monument Manager, Lincoln New Court House [sic], Lincoln State Monument, Lincoln, New Mexico; Ron Pastore - Exhumed Jesse James, Wichita, Kansas; Robert L. Heart, Farm & Ranch Museum, Las Cruces, New Mexico; Ron Hadley - President of Billy the Kid Outlaw Gang, Santa Teresa, New Mexico;

"**Brushy Bill Roberts:** Dr. Jannay Valdez, Desoto, Texas;

"**Media**": Lee Arnone - Film Producer, Capitan, New Mexico; Mia Rue - Lost Pecos Productions, L/L/C., Santa Fe, New Mexico; Mike Janofsky - New York Times, cell phone number only; Roy Freddy Anderson VG Norway's Largest Daily Newspaper, New York, New York; Tim Hurley - Court TV, New York, New York; Scott Wilson, Medical Examiners Office

**[AUTHOR'S NOTE: The early date of this list, obtained in my open records litigation against the hoaxing lawmen, is indicated by the names of people later replaced – like Bill Kurtis Productions replacing Lee Arnone by 2004, and Michael Janofsky, who wrote the *New York Times* article announcing the hoax, as being a media contact. This "Contact List" was in Sheriff Rick Virden's file for Case No. 2003-274.]**

APPENDIX: 8. The authentic forensic report of Dr. Henry Lee. "Forensic Research & Training Center Forensic Examination Report." February 25, 2005. Page count was 25. It listed "Requested by as Lincoln County Sheriff's Office, New Mexico; Investigation History Program, Kurtis Production." Its "Local Case No." was "2003-274." [AUTHOR'S NOTE: The report was obtained on January 31, 2012 by my open records litigation.]

## Forensic Research & Training Center

### Forensic Examination Report

Date of Request: May 22, 2004
Requested By: Lincoln County Sheriff's Office, New Mexico
Investigation History Program, Kurtis Production
Local Case No. 2003-274
Date of Report: February 25, 2005
Report to: Steve Sederwell
Lincoln County Sheriff's Office, New Mexico

### Introduction

At the request of Steve Sederwell of Lincoln County Sheriff's Office, Lincoln County, Bill Kurtis and Jamie Schenk of Kurtis Production, Dr. Henry Lee went to New Mexico on July 31, 2004 to assist in the re-investigation of the case of Billy the Kid. The forensic investigation team participating in re-investigation consist the following individuals:

Dr. Henry Lee, Chief Emeritus of the Connecticut State Police Forensic Laboratory
Calvin Ostler, Forensic Consultant, Riverton, Utah
Kim Ostler, Crime Scene Assistant, Riverton, Utah
Tom Sullivan, Sheriff, Lincoln County, New Mexico
Steve Sederwall Deputy Sheriff, Lincoln County, New Mexico
David Turk, US Marshall, United States Marshall Service

In addition, Mike Haag, Firearm examiner from Albuquerque Police Department Crime Lab, also provided valuable technical assistance in the investigation.

The forensic investigation team arrived at the Mr. Manny Miller residence, located at 1503 Cleave Road, Albuquerque, New Mexico, at 18:20 hours on Saturday, July 31, 2004. Upon arrival we were presented with three pieces of evidence: a worktable, a washstand, and a headboard. The three pieces of evidence had been removed from a storage building at the rear of the residence by Sheriff Sullivan, Deputy Sederwall, and members of Bill Kurtis Productions. Each item was inspected visually and macroscopically. The following were found:

## Item # 1 Workbench

This Workbench is approximately 86 inches in length, 29 inches in width and is made entirely of wood. Figure 1 illustrates the approximate dimensions of the Workbench. The width of the workbench is not consistent throughout the length, and stands an average of approximately 31 inches in height, however each leg is a slightly different length (as shown in Figure 1).

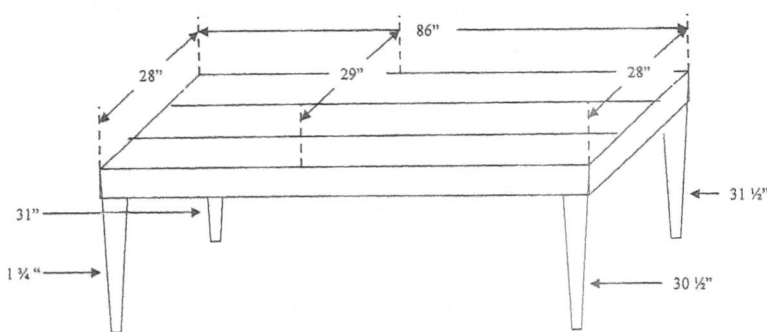

Figure 1

The wood comprising the Workbench is secured together with nails. At least four different types of nails were identified on the workbench. The top surface of the Workbench is comprised of three major planks which run longitudinally. Figure 2 shows the assembly of the planks on the surface of the workbench.

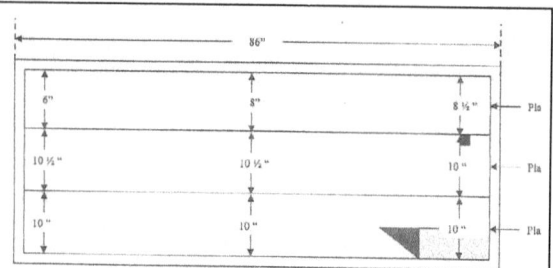

Figure 2 Top of Workbench with plank sizes

Photograph No 1 depicts an overall view of the workbench. There is a defective area on the lower right hand corner of Plank 1. This defective area is marked on the lower right hand corner of Figure 2. A piece of rectangular board has been nailed over the hole to cover this defective area as showing in photograph No. 1. The black triangle immediately to the left of the rectangle represents the end of the hole in Plank 1, which is the area that the board does not cover. The black square on the upper right hand edge of Plank 2 represents a hole in Plank 2.

Photo No. 1

Visual and macroscopical examinations reveal several brownish stains. Those areas were further examined under illumination of ALS light source. Some of the stains contain a variety of other colored crusty materials.

Three brown color stains were found on Plank 1. Following are observations of those stains on Plank 1:

- Area "1": Located approximately 4" to 11" from the right hand end of the Plank.
- Area "2": Located approximately 12" to 22" from the right hand end of the Plank and measuring 4" wide.
- Area "3": Located approximately 37" to 48" from the right hand end of the Plank and containing 10 separate spots.

Three stains were located on the top of Plank 2:

Area "1": Located approximately 2" to 19" from the right hand end of the Plank covering the full width of the Plank.
Area "2": Located approximately 29" to 32" from the right hand end of the Plank, one spot measuring approximately 3" in diameter.
Area "3": Located 43" to 50" from the right hand end of the Plank, one spot measuring approximately 2" in diameter.

Four stains were observed on the

Area "1": Located approx
of the Plank co
appearing to be
Area "2": Located appro
of the Plank a
Plank 2, cons
The white m
Area "3": Located 51
Plank, appr
weathered
Area "4": Located 7
brownish

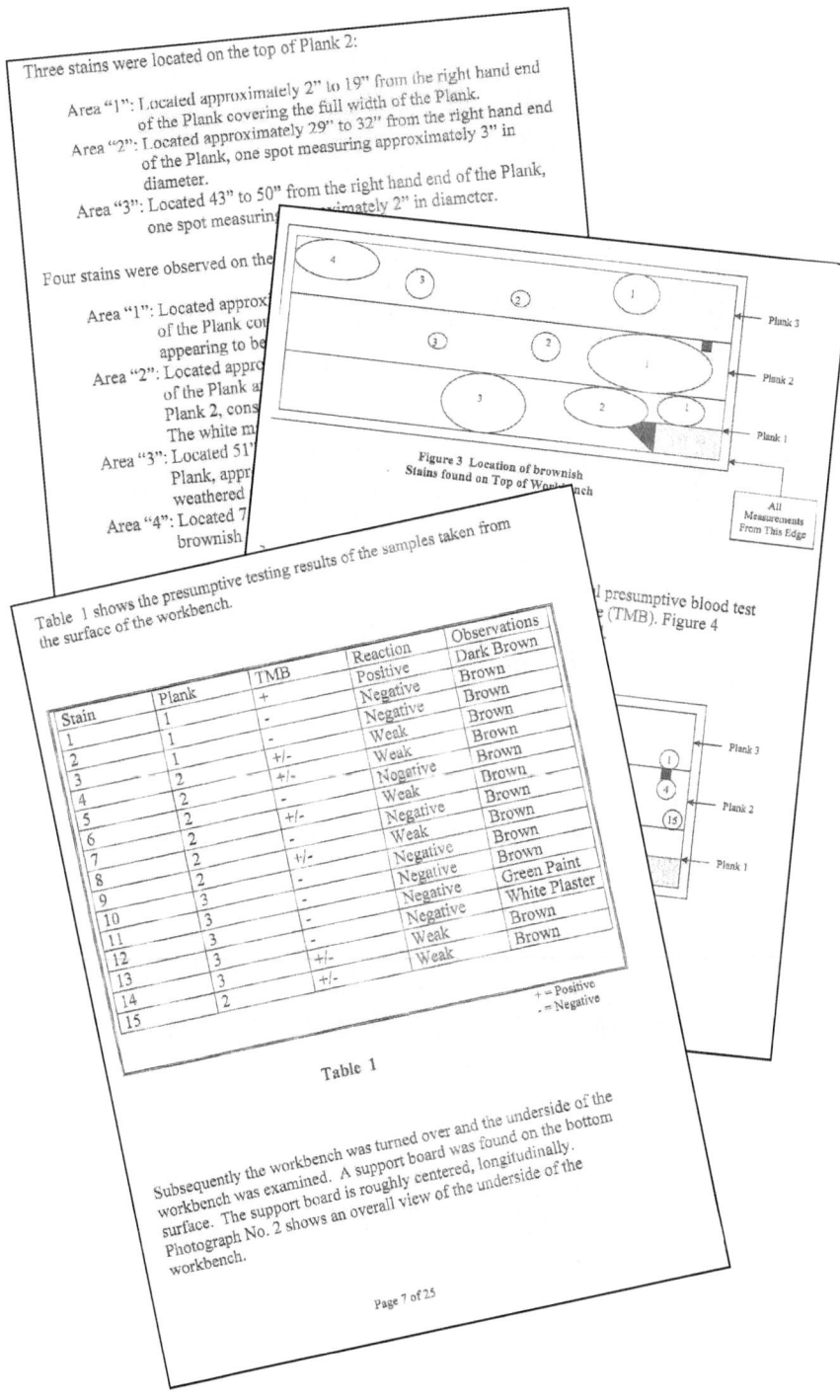

Figure 3 Location of brownish Stains found on Top of Workbench

All Measurements From This Edge

Table 1 shows the presumptive testing results of the samples taken from the surface of the workbench.

presumptive blood test (TMB). Figure 4

| Stain | Plank | TMB | Reaction | Observations |
|---|---|---|---|---|
| 1 | 1 | + | Positive | Dark Brown |
| 2 | 1 | - | Negative | Brown |
| 3 | 1 | - | Negative | Brown |
| 4 | 2 | +/- | Weak | Brown |
| 5 | 2 | +/- | Weak | Brown |
| 6 | 2 | - | Negative | Brown |
| 7 | 2 | +/- | Weak | Brown |
| 8 | 2 | +/- | Weak | Brown |
| 9 | 2 | - | Negative | Brown |
| 10 | 3 | - | Negative | Green Paint |
| 11 | 3 | - | Negative | White Plaster |
| 12 | 3 | - | Negative | Brown |
| 13 | 3 | +/- | Weak | Brown |
| 14 | 3 | +/- | Weak | Brown |
| 15 | 2 | | | |

+ = Positive
- = Negative

Table 1

Subsequently the workbench was turned over and the underside of the workbench was examined. A support board was found on the bottom surface. The support board is roughly centered, longitudinally. Photograph No. 2 shows an overall view of the underside of the workbench.

Photo No. 2

Various stained areas were noticed. Visual, ALS illumination and macroscopic examinations were conducted. Figure 5 is a drawing representing the areas in which brownish stains were located and samples taken for chemical presumptive blood tests.

Dividing, Support, Board, roughly centered

Figure 5, B

Table 2 shows the results of chemical presumptive tests for those brownish stains found on the underside of the workbench.

|    | Plank | TMB | Reaction |
|----|-------|-----|----------|
| 1  | 1     | +/- | Weak |
| 2  | 1     | +/- | Weak |
| 3  | 1     | +   | Positive |
| 4  | 1     | +++ | Strong Positive |
| 5  | 1     | -   | Negative |
| 6  | 3     | +/- | Weak |
| 7  | 3     | +/- | Weak |
| 8  | 3     | +   | Positive |
| 9  | 2/3   | +   | Positive |
| 10 | 3/1   | +   | Positive |
| 11 | 3     | +/- | Weak |

Table 2

Swab samples of area number "3" and area number "4" were collected for DNA testing. Two swabs were taken from each area and placed into two separate swab boxes, one box was labeled for area number "3" and one box was labeled for area number "4". **These two samples were transferred to Lincoln Sheriff Department. In addition, scraping samples were also taken from these two areas. These samples were placed into evidence envelopes and were transferred to Lincoln Sheriff Department.**

Luminol (a presumptive test reagent for blood) was then prepared and applied to the underside of the workbench. Luminol testing shows a positive indication in area "1" of the underside surface of the workbench and strong positive in areas "3" and "4" of the underside surface of the workbench. The Luminol test was positive on the top surface of the workbench in the general areas of number "2" on Plank 1 and general areas "2" and "3" on Plank 2.

**AUTHOR'S HIGHLIGHT** →

## Item # 2 Washstand

This Washstand measures approximately 28 ¾" long by 16" deep by 30" tall. Figure 6 is a sketch diagram of the washstand. This washstand is made of wood with a black color finish on it.

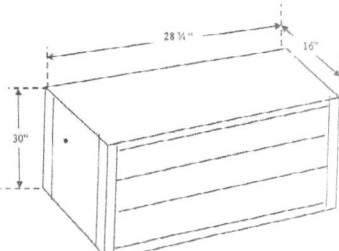

Figure 6, Washstand

Photograph # 3 shows the left side panel of the washstand and photograph # 4 depicts a view of the
Visual examination of the external s
holes, one single hole in each end of
examination of these holes indicates
bullet holes.

Photo No. 3    Photo No. 4

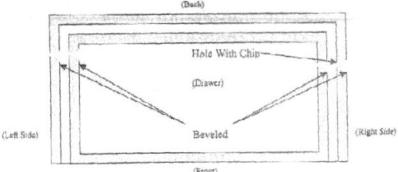

Figure 7, Washstand
Top, Cut Away View

Figure 7 is a cut away diagram of the washstand. This diagram depicts the relative locations of the two holes on the side panels of the washstand.

The hole on the left side panel is round and well defined. The hole on the right side panel is chipped and beveled. The left side panel hole is consistent with a bullet entrance hole.

The hole on the right side panel is slightly deformed and there is a chip of wood missing which is joining the hole and proceeds down approximately 1 ½" to 2". Figure 8 is a sketch diagram of this hole. The missing chip is approximately the width of the hole and approximately 1/8" deep. This hole is consistent with a bullet exit hole. Photograph 5 depicts a close-up view of this hole.

Sodium Rhodizonate test for lead was conducted with the assistance of Mike Haag. Four areas were tested for the presence of lead particles. Figure 9 is a diagram showing the surface areas tested. Surface 1, the exterior surface of the left side panel; Surface 2, interior surface of left side panel; Surface 3, the outside surface of the left side of the top drawer; Surface 4, inside surface of the right hand side panel of the Washstand.

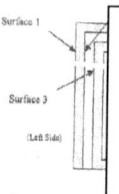

Subsequently, the top drawer of the Washstand was removed and a laser was set up to reconstruct the angle of the trajectory. The laser used in the ballistic angle reconstruction was a Cao Group, Inc. Prototype Diode Pumped Frequency Doubled Nd:YAG Laser. This laser has a maximum output of 200 milliwatts and produces 532 nanometer light. The laser was placed approximately 20 feet from the outside surface of the left side panel of the Washstand. The laser was then adjusted to project a beam through the entrance holes in the left side panel and to the exit hole in the right side panels of the Washstand. Figure 10 shows the reconstructed trajectory of the shot.

The general bullet path is from left to right with a slight downward and back to front angle. The horizontal trajectory angle was determined to be 5.22 degrees. The vertical angle was determined to be 4.47 degrees.

The results of tests are

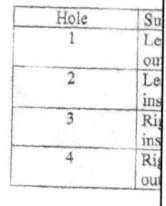

| Hole | Su |
|---|---|
| 1 | Le ou |
| 2 | Le ins |
| 3 | Ri ins |
| 4 | Ri ou |

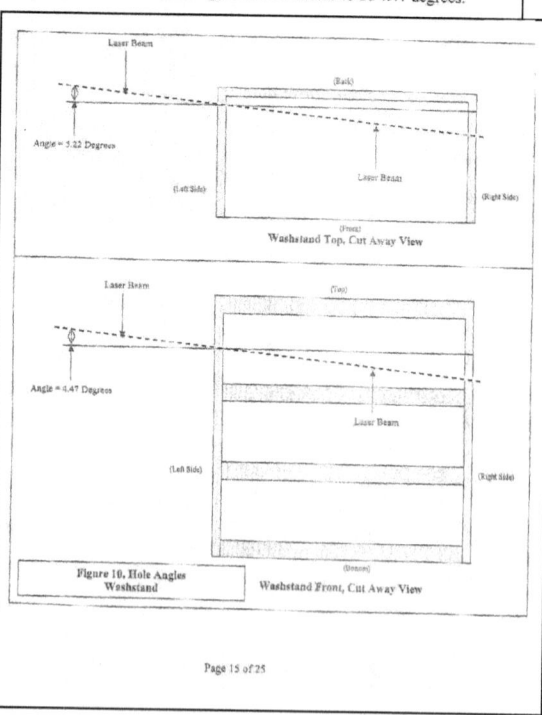

Figure 10. Hole Angles Washstand

Item #3 A piece of Headboard

A piece of Headboard was examined. No blood like stains were observed. No bullet hole was found. No evidence of extensive damage was noted.

## Examination of Lincoln County Court House

On Sunday, 8/1/04. the forensic investigation team examined the old Lincoln County Court House in Lincoln, New Mexico. Present at the scene were Sheriff Sullivan, Deputy Sederwall, Mr. Turk, Bill Kurtis, and Sheriff Gary Wayne Graves of De Baca County, New Mexico. The target area of examination is located on the top landing of the stairs of the old courtroom.

1. The staircase has been repainted several times over the years.
2. The $2^{nd}$ floor hallway floor was recovered with wooden floorboard. These floor boards were removed. The original floor was exposed. Photograph #6 shows an overall view of hall floor after the removal of new floor board.

Photo No. 6

3. Photograph #7 shows the target area which is at the top landing of the stairs where presumptive blood tests were done. The area measured approximately 28 7/8" deep by 43 ½ "wide.
4. Figure 11 is a sketch diagram shows the general dimensions of this staircase.

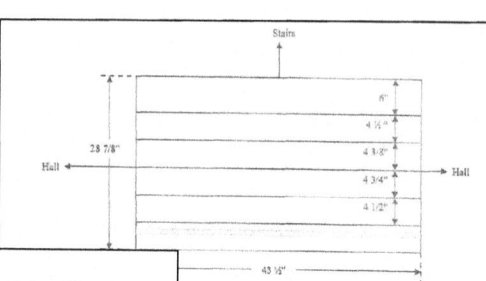

Figure 11, Stair Landing

depicts the location and condition of the floor
get area.

6. Visual examination of the Stair Landing reveals that different types of nails have been used to secure the floor boards. It appears that some of them are newer than others. The floorboards comprising the area also appear to be wood planks of different ages.

Photo No. 8

Photo No. 7

7. Macroscopic examination reveals a fragment of masking tape, grayish blue paint, hairs, fibers, soil and v
8. Tetramethylbenzideine (a chemical presu blood) was used to test the suspected stai depicts the area of the suspected stains wi blood test.

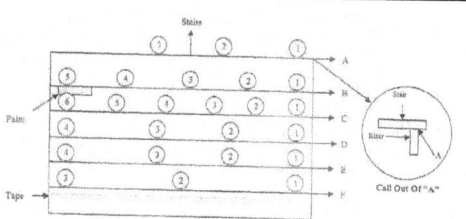

Figure 12, Stair Landing
Sample Location Map

9. The TMB chemical test results are showing in Table 4.

| Space | Sample | Results | Space | sample | Results |
|---|---|---|---|---|---|
| A | 1 | + | D | 1 | - |
|  | 2 | + |  | 2 | - |
|  | 3 | + |  | 3 | W+ |
| B | 1 | - |  | 4 | - |
|  | 2 | - | E | 1 | - |
|  | 3 | - |  | 2 | - |
|  | 4 | - |  | 3 | - |
| C | 1 | - |  | 4 | - |
|  | 2 | - | F | 1 | - |
|  | 3 | - |  | 2 | W+ |
|  | 4 | - |  | 3 | - |
|  | 5 | - | Controls |  | OK |

+ = Positive
- = Negative
W+ = Weak positive

Table 4

10. Subsequently, the underside of stairs case was examined. Photograph 9 depicts a view of the examination process.

Photo No. 9

11. Visual and macroscopic examinations of the underside of the floor landing area reveal a large number of stained areas where liquids have seeped down through the spaces. Photograph No. 10 shows some of these stained areas.

Photo No. 10

12. Figure 13 is a sketch diagram showing a visual map of the sampling areas for chemical presumptive test for blood.

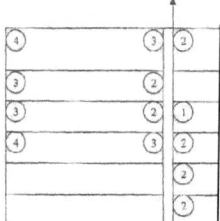

Figure 13, Un...
Sample I...

13. Photograph 11 is a close up view of the major stained area at the under side of the floor boards of the landing area.

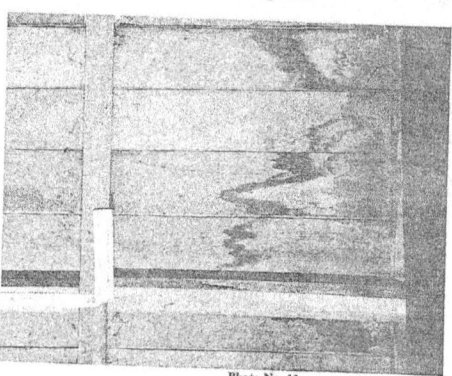

Photo No. 11

14. The suspected areas were tested with presumptive chemical reagent, TMB. Table 5 shows the test results.

| Space | Sample | Results | Space | Sample | Results |
|-------|--------|---------|-------|--------|---------|
| AU    | 1      | W+      | CU    | 3      | -       |
|       | 2      | W+      | DU    | 1      | -       |
|       | 3      | -       |       | 2      | W+      |
|       | 4      | -       |       | 3      | -       |
| BU    | 1      | W+      |       | 4      | W+      |
|       | 2      | W+      | EU    | 1      | +++     |
|       | 3      | -       |       | 2      | -       |
| CU    | 1      | +++     | FU    | 1      | +       |
|       | 2      | -       |       | 2      | -       |

+++ = Strong positive

Table No. 5

## Results and Conclusion

After a detail examination of the evidence and review of all the results of field testing, the following conclusion was reached.

1. Brownish dark stains were observed on different areas of the workbench. These areas were subjected to chemical presumptive blood tests. Some of those samples give a positive reaction. These results indicate the presence of Heme or Peroxidase like activity with those stains testing positive, which suggest that those stains could be bloodstains. Further DNA testing could reveal the nature and identity of these blood-like stains.

2. Two bullet holes were located on the side panels of the Washstand. The hole on the left side panel is consistent with a bullet entrance hole while the hole on the right side panel is consistent with a bullet exit hole. However, it is not possible to determine when those bullet holes were produced at this time. The angles produced in the examination tell us two things:

First, the bullet was fired from no more that 41" from the floor given the reported limitations of the room. The room is reported to be 20' by 20'; the maximum distance is assumed to be 20'. If the firearm was a maximum of 41" off of the floor it is unlikely that the shooter was standing. It is more likely the shooter was kneeling, squatting, or close to the floor.

Second, the horizontal angle is such that if the Washstand was positioned so that the back was against the wall, the shot could not have been fired from more that approximately 40 inches from the Washstand, because the wall would have been in the way. The angle of trajectory intersects the back plane of the Washstand at approximately 45 3/16", and no more than 46".

3. No bullet hole and no observable damage, no sign of bullet ricocheted type of defects were found on the Headboard. No blood or biological materials were observed on the Headboard.

4. The floor boards on the 2nd floor stair landing area of the court house have been repaired. Different types of wood and nails were used on this area.

5. Various stains were observed on the surface and the underside of the floor boards. Chemical tests for the presence of blood were positive with some of those stains. These results indicate the presence of Heme or Peroxidase like activity with those stains tested positive, which suggests that those stains could be bloodstains. Further DNA testing could reveal the nature and identity of those blood-like stains.

Dr. Henry C. Lee
Chief Emeritus, Connecticut State Forensic Laboratory
Distinguished Professor, University New Haven

Calvin D. Ostler
(Electronic signature)
Forensic Consultant
Crime Scene Investigator

APPENDIX: 9. Dr. Laura Fulginiti. "Re: Exhumation, Pioneer Home Cemetery, Prescott, Arizona for Dale L. Tunnell, Ph.D. [sic], Forensitec. June 2, 2005. **[AUTHOR'S NOTE: Report of moonlighting Maricopa County Office of the Medical Investigator's forensic anthropologist]**

## RE: EXHUMATION PIONEER HOME CEMETERY, PRESCOTT, ARIZONA FOR DALE L. TUNNELL, PhD, FORENSITEC. JUNE 2, 2005

On May 19, 2005 at approximately 1230 hours I am asked to assist in the exhumation of the remains of an individual known as Mr. John Miller by Dr. Dale Tunnell, President, Forensitec. The purpose of my involvement is to aid in the exhumation process as well as to assess any skeletal remains recovered. The exhumation takes place at the Arizona Pioneer [sic] Home Cemetery, Iron Springs Road in Prescott Arizona in the presence of Dr. Tunnell, several of his associates, members of the Arizona Pioneer Home staff and Kristen Harnett M.A., AMSU graduate student.

Dr. Tunnell located the alleged gravesite of Mr. Miller prior to our arrival on the scene. The gravesite was located using the line of headstones to the West of the target grave. A standard reference point was established as the headstone of Michael Clancy. At approximately 1400 hours, a backhoe began to remove the sod overlying the alleged grave, which was oriented in an East-West direction, with the head to the West. When fragments of wood began to be removed, the grave was excavated using a shovel. Once the top of the casket and a portion of femur were unearthed, the excavation relied on digging with trowels and by hand. The position of the femur indicated that the remains were supine, with the feet to the East and the skull to the West. The left femoral shaft, minus the head, was removed, examined, and packaged for DNA analysis.

**Dr. Tunnell, in consultation with the cemetery staff and his other associates determined that the adjacent grave to the North was likely that of Mr. Miller and excavation shifted to that gravesite.**

**[AUTHOR'S NOTE: This unmarked North Grave was not John Miller's, as Dr. Fulginiti later proved; and was that of random man, William Hudspeth. His exhumation was a multi-felony crime, later covered-up by the Maricopa County prosecutor.]**

The backhoe removed the overlying sod until fragments of wood began to be unearthed. The excavation shifted to shovels and the top of the casket was identified. Excavation proceeded using trowels and hand tools until various aspects of the skeleton were identified and cleared. The skeleton in this grave was also lying supine, head to the West and feet to the East.

The casket had collapsed onto the body at some point prior to the exhumation process. **A metal detector on loan from the Yavapai County Sheriff's Office and operated by Det. Mike Poling, YCSO, was used to locate metal items, including nails and casket fittings.** (These items were donated to the Arizona Pioneer Home for their museum).

**[AUTHOR'S NOTE: Poling was accidentally present to deliver specimens to Laura Fulginiti; but the hoaxers later lied that he was the lawman responsible for the exhumation.]**

Minimal historical artifacts, such as buttons, a possible rivet, portions of wood from the casket and casket fittings were identified as they were unearthed. Skeletal elements were measured for depth and location, removed from the grave and examined (see Forensitec report). Pathological conditions such as osteoarthritis, healed fractures and markers of occupation were noted as follows. The vertebrae exhibited signs of extreme osteoarthritis in the form of lipping of the vertebral bodies, collapse of some of the bodies and osteophytic activity. **There were extensive healed traumata on the right scapula**

**[AUTHOR'S NOTE: So the <u>damaged right scapula</u> was in North Grave of William Hudspeth, and was not a shot left scapula of John Miller as the hoaxers later lied.]**

and the left clavicle, a healed Colles' fracture of the right distal radius, a healed fracture of the second rib and a healed fracture of the left fourth metacarpal. The bone was dark brown in color, friable and dry. There was postmortem damage, both from the collapse of the lid of the casket onto the remains as well as from the removal process. The remains were photographed, samples were harvested for DNA (tooth and femur) and the remains were returned to the grave and reburied.

Anecdotal historical information suggested that Mr. John Miller had died from complications of a fractured hip while recuperating in the Arizona pioneer Home. The individual in the north grave, while having extensive pathological conditions, particularly in the upper body, did not have discernible pathology of the *os coxae*.

**[AUTHOR'S NOTE: Fulginiti saw that the North Grave's remains did not have John Miller's broken hip; so the scapula was not his. She therefore concluded that the South Grave is Miller's; and it had the broken hip.]**

At this point in the exhumation, a decision was made to exhume the *os coxae* of the individual in the south grave to confirm that we had indeed excavated the remains of Mr. John Miller from the north grave. The south grave was excavated by shovel to the point where the remnants of the casket lid were identified. Excavation resumed using trowels and hand tools until the left femoral head was identified.

The head of the femur was misshapen with bony remodeling, suggesting an antemortem [before death] injury. Additional excavation revealed the left innominate, which also had extensive remodeling of the acetabulum, ischium and pubis. The ischium tapered to a point with lack of union to the pubis, suggesting a healing fracture of the ischiopubic ramus. **This evidence led the team to believe that the individual in the south grave was, in fact, more consistent with the known facts regarding the Medical history of Mr. John Miller and additional DNA samples were recovered (femur, scalp?, matter from inside the braincase).**

**[AUTHOR'S NOTE: Confirmation of South Grave as John Miller's because of broken hip.]**

**The maxillae and mandible were recovered but were edentulous.** [author's boldface]

**[AUTHOR'S NOTE: Miller had NO TEETH AT ALL. The Hoaxers later lied that he had buck teeth like Billy the Kid's!]**

There was limited pathology of the vertebrae, ribcage, clavicles and scapulae of the individual from the south grave. Mild osteoarthritis of the vertebral bodies was the only pathology of note. Photographs of the cranium and mandible were taken and the remains were returned to the grave and reburied.

Biological profiles of the two individuals are similar. Both were adult males, consistent with individuals of European (White) descent, and of advancing years. The nasal apertures on both were tall and narrow, with a sharp nasal sill, the malars were retreating and the cranial shape, while fragmentary, was round. The pubic symphyses exhibited characteristics of Suchey-Brooks Phase IV (36-86 years, mean 61.2 years).The symphyseal faces were flat and eroded with marked ventral ligaments. The sternal ends of the ribs; while fragmentary, exhibited long bony extensions, consistent with an Iscan, Loth stage 8 (65 plus). **The individual in the south grave was edentulous.** [author's boldface]

**[AUTHOR'S NOTE: Repeated is that Miller had NO TEETH.]**

The scene was returned to a state approximating that prior to our arrival and was cleared shortly after sundown. Items of evidence collected were distributed to members of the Arizona Pioneer Home Cemetery staff and to Dr. Richard Staub (see Forensitec report).

Laura C. Fulginiti, Ph.D., D-ABFA
Forensic Anthropologist

**[AUTHOR'S NOTE: The "items of evidence" "distributed" to Arizona Pioneers' Home staff were supposedly parts of the smashed coffins of both desecrated graves.]**

**[AUTHOR'S NOTE: Fulginiti Report Summary.]**

1) As the fake expert, Dale Tunnell "located the alleged gravesite of Mr. Miller prior to our arrival on the scene."

2) Remains were taken from that South Grave. "**The left femoral shaft, minus the head, was removed, examined, and packaged for DNA analysis.**"

3) The North Grave was added by Tunnell and "associates," (presumably Sullivan and Sederwall). "**Dr. Tunnell, in consultation with the cemetery staff and his other associates determined that the adjacent grave to the North was likely that of Mr. Miller and excavation shifted to that gravesite.**"

4) The North Grave is excavated using a metal detector lent by a Yavapai County Detective, just delivering specimens from another case to Fulginiti. The hoaxers would later lie that the exhumation was done him. "**A metal detector on loan from the Yavapai County Sheriff's Office and operated by Det. Mike Poling, YCSO, was used to locate metal items, including nails and casket fittings.**"

5) The North Grave body has the <u>damaged right scapula and teeth</u>. "**There were extensive healed traumata on the right scapula and the left clavicle, a healed Colles' fracture of the right distal radius, a healed fracture of the second rib and a healed fracture of the left fourth metacarpal.**"

6) The North Grave is canceled out as Miller's. It is William Hudspeth's, and proved the wanton desecration and grave-robbing crimes. "**Anecdotal historical information suggested that Mr. John Miller had died from complications of a fractured hip while recuperating in the Arizona pioneer Home. The individual in the north grave, while having extensive pathological conditions, particularly in the upper body, did not have discernible pathology of the *os coxae*.**"

7) The South Grave is recognized as John Miller's. The hip injury is found with pelvic damage. And the jaws lack any teeth. "**The head of the femur was misshapen with bony remodeling, suggesting an antemortem injury ... The ischium tapered to a point with lack of union to the pubis, suggesting a healing fracture of the ischiopubic ramus. This evidence led the team to believe that the individual in the south grave was, in fact, more consistent with the known facts regarding the Medical history of Mr. John Miller and additional DNA samples were recovered ... The maxillae and mandible were recovered but were edentulous.**"

APPENDIX: 10. Deposition to Frank Warner Angel of Fort Stanton Assistant Post Surgeon Daniel M. Appel on his official autopsy on John H. Tunstall. July 1, 1878.

*Territory of New Mexico )*
*County of Lincoln        )*
Daniel M. Appel being duly sworn says that he is Assistant Surgeon U.S. Army and have been and am now stationed at Fort Stanton New Mexico.

That on or about the 21$^{st}$ day of February 1878 [sic- February 19, 1878] I made a postmortem examination of John H. Tunstall. I found that there were two wounds in his body, one in the shoulder passing through and fracturing the right clavicle near its centre coming out immediately over the superior border of the right scapula passing through in its course the right subclavian artery, this would have caused his death in a few minutes and would have been likely to have thrown him from his horse. It would not have produced immediate insensibility. The other wound entered the head about one inch to the right of the median line almost on a line with the occipital protuberance and passed out immediately above the border of the left orbit. There was a fracture of the skull extending around the whole circumference from the entrance to the exit of the ball – and a transverse fracture across the middle portion of the base of the skull extending from the line of fracture on one side to that of the other. In my opinion the skull both on account of its being very thin and from evidences of venereal disease was very likely to be extensively fractured from such a would and the fractures in this case resulted entirely from said wound. A wound of this kind would cause instantaneous death passing as it did through the most vital portion of the brain. There were no marks of violence on the body except the two above wounds – nor was the body or skull mutilated, The cap of the skull was not at all fractured.

It is my opinion that both of the wounds could be caused at one and the same time – and if made at the same time were made by different persons from different directions and were both most likely made while Tunstall was on horseback in as much as the direction of the wounds were slightly upwards.

There being no powder marks on the body to indicate that the wounds were made at a short distance – and the further fact that the edges of the wounds of exit were not very ragged I am of the opinion that they were both made by rifles.

Powder marks would be shown on the body of the gun or pistol was fired within about six feet of the body.

 D.M. Appel, Asst. Surgeon U.S. Army

APPENDIX: 11. U.S. Attorney Thomas Benton Catron's federal indictment of Regulators as "Case No. 411, United States vs. Charles Bowdry [Bowdre], Doc Scurlock, Henry Brown, Henry Antrim - alias Kid - John Middleton, Stephen Stevens, John Scroggins, George Coe and Frederick Waite." June 21, 1878.

The United States of America )
Territory of New Mexico )
Third Judicial District )

In the United States District Court for the Third Judicial District of the June Term of 1878.

The Grand Jury of the United States of America from the body of the good and lawful men of the Third Judicial District aforesaid – duly empanneled sworn and charged to the Term of aforesaid to inquire in and for the body of the Third Judicial District aforesaid upon their oaths do present that Charles Bowdry [sic - Bowdre throughout], Doc Scurlock, Henry Brown, **Henry Antrim – alias Kid** – John Middleton, Stephen Stevens, John Scroggins, George Coe and Frederick Waite, late of the Third Judicial District in the Territory of New Mexico on the fifth [sic - fourth] day of April in the year of our Lord Eighteen hundred and Seventy-eight **at and in this reservation of the Mescalero Apache Indians in the Said Third Judicial District, Said Reservation then and there being a part of the Indian country,** with force and armed in and upon one Andrew Roberts then and there being in the Said Reservation feloniously, willfully, unlawfully of this malice aforethought and from a premeditated design to effect the death of the Said Andrew Roberts, did make an assault, and that the Said Charles Bowdry, Doc Scurlock, Henry Brown, **Henry Antrim – alias Kid** – John Middleton, Stephen Stevens, John Scroggins, George Coe and Frederick Waite certain guns then and there loaded and charged with gunpowder and divers leaden bullets, which said guns the Said Charles Bowdry, Doc Scurlock, Henry Brown, **Henry Antrim (alias Kid)** John Middleton, Stephen Stevens, John Scroggins, George Coe and Frederick Waite in their hands then and there had and held to, against and upon the Said Andrew Roberts there and then within the Said Reservation feloniously, willfully, unlawfully of this malice aforethought and from a premeditated design to effect the death of the Said Andrew Roberts – did shoot and discharge, and that the Said Charles Bowdry, Doc Scurlock, Henry Brown, **Henry Antrim – alias Kid** – John Middleton, Stephen Stevens, John Scroggins, George Coe and Frederick Waite, with the leaden Bullets aforesaid, out of the guns aforesaid, then and there by force of the gunpowder that discharged *and sent forth as aforesaid and on Roberts in and upon the right side of the belly of him the Said Andrew Roberts then and there within the Said Reservation feloniously, willfully, unlawfully of this malice aforethought and from a premeditated design to effect the death of the Said Andrew Roberts, did strike, penetrate and wound, giving to the said Andrew Roberts then and there and within the said Reservation and with the leaden Bullets aforesaid, that discharged and sent forth out of the guns aforesaid by the said Andrew [Charles] Bowdry, Doc Scurlock, Henry Brown,* **Henry Antrim – alias Kid** *– John Middleton, Stephen Stevens, John Scroggins, George Coe and Frederick Waite in and upon the right side of the belly of him the said Andrew Roberts one mortal wound of the depth of ten inches and of breadth of one half of an inch of which said mortal wound the Said Andrew Roberts then and there at the said Reservation instantly died and so the Jury aforesaid upon their oaths as aforesaid do say that the Said Charles Bowdry, Doc Scurlock, Henry Brown,* **Henry Antrim – alias Kid** *– John Middleton, Stephen Stevens, John Scroggins, George Coe and Frederick Waite the Said Andrew Roberts in manner and form aforesaid feloniously, willfully, unlawfully of this malice aforethought and from a premeditated design to effect the death of the Said Andrew Roberts, did kill and murder against the form of the Statute in such case made and provided against the Peace & dignity of the United States. And the Jurors aforesaid upon their oaths aforesaid do further present that Charles Bowdry late of the Third Judicial District in the Territory of New Mexico on the fifth day of April in the year AD Eighteen hundred and Seventy-eight at and within the Reservation of the Mescalero Apache Indians said Reservation being then and there situate in the Third Judicial District aforesaid and then and there being Indian Country in and upon Andrew Roberts then and there being in the Said Reservation in the Said District, feloniously, willfully, unlawfully of his malice aforethought and from a premeditated design to effect the death of the Said Andrew Roberts did make an assault and that the Said Charles Bowdry a certain gun then and there loaded and charged with gunpowder and one leaden Bullet which gun he the Said Charles Bowdry in his right hand then and there had and held to at against and upon the Said Andrew Roberts then and there within the Said Reservation feloniously, willfully, unlawfully of his malice aforethought and from a premeditated design to effect the death of the Said Andrew Roberts, did shoot and discharge and that the Said Charles Bowdry with the leaden Bullet aforesaid out of the gun aforesaid then and there by force of the gunpowder aforesaid shot and sent forth as aforesaid the Said Andrew Roberts in and from the right side of the belly of him the Said Andrew Roberts then and there and in the Said Reservation* *feloniously, willfully, unlawfully of his malice aforethought and from a premeditated design to effect the death of the Said Andrew Roberts, did strike, penetrate and wound, giving to the Said Andrew Roberts then and there with the leaden Bullet aforesaid so as aforesaid that discharged and sent forth out of the gun aforesaid by the Said Charles Bowdry in and upon the right side of the belly of the Said Andrew Roberts one mortal wound of ten inches and of breadth of one half of an inch of which said mortal wound the Said Andrew Roberts then and there at the said Reservation instantly died and the Jury aforesaid upon their oaths aforesaid do further present that Doc Scurlock, Henry Brown,* **Henry Antrim – alias Kid** *– John Middleton, Stephen Stevens, John Scroggins, George Coe and Frederick Waite of the Third Judicial District aforesaid and on the day and year aforesaid with force and arms at the Said Reservation in the Said District aforesaid* **feloniously was present aiding and abetting and assisting the [Said] Charles Bowdry the felony and murder aforesaid to do and commit against the form of the Statute in such case made and provided against the Peace & dignity of the United States and the Jurors aforesaid upon their oaths aforesaid do say that the Said Charles Bowdry Doc Scurlock, Henry Brown, Henry Antrim – alias Kid – John Middleton, Stephen Stevens, John Scroggins, George Coe and Frederick Waite in manner and form aforesaid feloniously, willfully, unlawfully of his malice aforethought and from a premeditated design to effect the death of him the Said Andrew Roberts, him the Said Roberts did kill and murder against the form of the Statute in such case made and provided and against the peace and dignity of the United States.**

*Thomas B. Catron*
*United States Attorney*
*for New Mexico*

<u>411</u>...

*C.P. Crawford*
*Foreman of the Grand Jury*

*Witnesses*
*Aurelius Wilson, John Patten, John Watts, J.H. Blazer, Sam F. Mills, [missing first name] Howe, William Gentry*

*Filed in my Office*
*the 21 day of June 1878*
  *John S. Crouch, Clerk*

APPENDIX: 12. December 22, 1880 *New York Sun* article titled "Outlaws of New Mexico, The Exploits of a Band Headed by a New York Youth, The Mountain Fastness of the Kid and His Followers, War Against a Gang of Cattle Thieves and Murderers, The Frontier Confederates of Brockway, the Counterfeiter."

[AUTHOR'S NOTE: Santa Fe Ring outlaw myth propaganda against Billy Bonney as Billy the Kid.]

## OUTLAWS OF NEW MEXICO.
### THE EXPLOITS OF A BAND HEADED BY A NEW YORK YOUTH.

**The Mountain fastness of the Kid and his Followers— War against a Gang of Cattle Thieves and Murderers — The Frontier Confederates of Brockway, the Counterfeiter.**

LAS VEGAS, New Mexico, Dec. 20.—One hundred and twenty-seven miles southeast of Las Vegas, New Mexico, is Fort Sumner, once the base of operations against the Indians who committed depredations against the stockmen. The fort was abandoned some ten or twelve years ago, owing to the removal of troops further south, toward the border of Mexico. The property was condemned and sold to Pete Maxwell, a well-known ranchman of the section. Since then it has been a depot of supplies for stockmen and a stage station on the postal route to the Pecos Valley and Panhandle, Texas.

Until recently, on almost any fair day, there might have been seen lounging about the store or engaged in target practice four men, all of them young, neatly dressed, and of good appearance. A stranger riding in the little hamlet would have taken them to be a party of Eastern gentlemen who had come into that sparsely settled region in search of sport. Many who have gone into that country have struck up an acquaintance with these men and found them agreeable fellows. These men are the worst desperadoes in the West, and large parties of armed men are now scouring the country in pursuit of them.

For a number of years the people of eastern New Mexico and Panhandle, Texas, have been harassed by a gang who have run off stock, burned ranches, and committed acts of violence and murder. It was only recently that the leaders and organization of the band were discovered. The leaders are Billy the Kid, so called from his youth; Dave Rudabaugh, Billy Wilson, and Tom O'Phallier, the four loungers about Fort Sumner. The Kid is the captain of the gang. Their fastness is about thirty-five miles nearly due east from Fort

Sumner, on the edge of the great Staked Plain. In that region there is a small lake called Las Portales. It is surrounded by steep hills, from which flow numerous streams that feed the little lake. This place the robbers selected for their resort partly on account of its hiding places, but mainly on account of the opportunities it afforded them for stock thieving. No matter from what direction the storm came, it drove to the lake the herds of cattle which roam at large in the rich grazing country. There the band built for themselves one of those rude dugouts so common on the Western frontier, two sides formed by the side of the hill, the other two constructed of sod and dirt plastered together, and the whole covered by a thatched roof. Stockades or corrals were built near by in which to put stolen stock. During pleasant weather the members of the gang lounged about Fort Sumner or other stations in that section. When the storm sent cattle scudding over the plains to the haven afforded by the hill-protected lake basin, the gang would hurry to their rendezvous and cut out from the herds the best cattle, driving them into their corral, whence they were later sent to market. Their booty was large, for they had a vast stock to select from, the whole country for a distance of one hundred and fifty miles either way being a rich, continuous pasture. Besides the active members of the band, there were many who had apparently some settled occupation and made themselves useful in disposing of the stolen cattle. In every town of any size within a radius of 150 miles there were butchers who dealt regularly in this stolen stock. When supplies from roving herds ran short the desperadoes would make a raid on herds that were guarded, attacking ranches and killing or diving off the inmates. Besides their station at Las Portales, they had one at Bosque Grande, fifty miles to the southwest, and another at Greathouse's rancho, fifty miles to the north. Whenever they were pursued when running of stock, they had the choice of three places to which to resort.

The people of the surrounding country finally found the existence of this band unendurable. After repeated searches, which failed, owing to the smallness of the pursuing parties, it was resolved to organize several bands, who should cooperate in a campaign, which should end only when the outlaws were driven out of the country, or their capture, dead or alive, was effected. The authorities of the several counties which bordered on the country ranged over by **the Kid's gang** had been repeatedly petitioned to send out a posse of men to hunt them down, but, as Las Portales was on disputed territory, the authorities were never able to settle upon any plan of action. At last the ranchmen took the matter into their own hands, and the first party they sent out succeeded in getting on the track of a detachment of the gang who were hauling material to Las Portales, where they were building large stock yards. Although the party was not successful in capturing the outlaws, they made the outlaws flit about the country in a more lively manner than had been their wont. This showed that nothing could be done by a small force. A guard was always kept out on the numerous peaks about Las Portales, from which outlook; the country for twenty miles either way could be scanned by the outlaws, so that they could easily elude a small party!

The Panhandle Transportation Company, an association of stockmen of western Texas, banded together for mutual protection, commissioned their superintendent, Frank Stewart, a brave fellow, who was just the man for such work, to organize an expedition against the outlaws. The White Oaks, a flourishing mining camp, organized a band of rangers. Still another party of picked men, under the lead of Sheriff Pat Garrett of Lincoln County, who is considered one of the bravest and coolest men in the whole region, joined in the campaign. In the latter part of November Garrett, with a force of fourteen men, made a dash for Bosque Grande, riding all night, and there succeeded in capturing five of the outlaws. One of them was a condemned murderer who had escaped from jail; another of them was a murderer for whose arrest $1,500 had been offered. These are the sort of men who reinforce the band. Las Portales has long been an asylum for fugitives from justice. Bosque Grande (Great Forest) is situated in one of the most fertile regions of the West, and as the rich lands bordering on the Pecos River are the objective point of many who intend to settle in the Territory, it was thought best to rid that region of the outlaws first, in order that none might be deterred from settling there. Precautions have been taken which will prevent this refuge of the band from ever sheltering them again.

It was expected that the two other parties would work with Garrett's band, but the Panhandle party were delayed, owing to scarcity of feed, and the White Oaks Rangers had their hands full in another quarter. The latter party had a brush with the Kid, Rudabaugh, Wilson, and several others at Coyote Spring, near the Oaks camp, and the outlaws succeeded in escaping, although two had their horses shot from under them. The rangers started back for reinforcements and supplies, and then pressed on after the outlaws, coming upon them at their other station at Greathouse's ranch. It was night when the rangers reached the ranch. They threw up earthworks a few hundred yards from the stockade of the ranch, and when the outlaws rose up in the morning they found themselves hemmed in.

The rangers sent a messenger to Jim Greathouse, the owner of this ranch, demanding the surrender of the outlaws. Greathouse replied in person. He came out to the camp of the rangers and stoutly asserted that the outlaws had taken possession of his ranch and that he had no power over them nor anything to do with them. It was considered best to hold Greathouse as a hostage, while Jim Carlyle, the leader of the rangers, heeded to the Kid's request for a conference. A long time elapsed and Carlyle did not return. His men began to feel uneasy about him, and dispatched a note to the renegade chief saying that unless Carlyle was given up in less than five minutes they would kill Greathouse. No reply was received. Soon after the rangers saw Carlyle leap from the window and dash down the hill toward their entrenchments. He had not gone far, however, when they saw the Kid throw half his body through the window, and, taking deliberate aim, brought down poor Carlyle, killing him instantly. A sharp fight followed, but the outlaws succeeded in making their escape, Greathouse also getting away during the confusion. Before leaving for home with the dead body of their leader, the rangers fired everything about the place, and Greathouse concealed some miles away, saw the smoke of his burning property.

The three parties are now engaged in scouting the country, and will not give up the chase till the country is rid of every one of the outlaws. Money and outfits have been freely offered by men who have large interests in that section. **Government officials are now interested in the campaign, for, in addition to their other crimes, the outlaws have put in circulation a large quantity of the counterfeit money manufactured by William Brockway, the forger. The bills were obtained by one of the gang named Doyle who formerly operated in Chicago, and counterfeit $100 bills in large numbers have been put in circulation among the stockmen and merchants in all that region.**

[AUTHOR'S NOTE: This was the fake news that possibly inspired Steve Sederwall's his hoax that Billy Bonney was a counterfeiter in cahoots with the Brockway gang; with James Doyle being a real Brockway gang member]

The information that enabled the Government officers to discover the handling of counterfeit money by the Kid's gang came from a freighter named Smith. Soon afterward, while Smith was on his way from Las Vegas to Fort Sumner with a load of freight, he was waylaid and murdered by some of the gang.

[AUTHOR'S NOTE: This was the fake news lifted by

Steve Sederwall to make-up that freighter Sam Smith had reported Billy to Secret Service Operative Azariah Wild as a counterfeiter; and that Billy had murdered Smith in revenge. In fact, Smith had no connection to Billy, and was killed by Apaches.]

William Bonney, alias the Kid, the leader of the band, is scarcely over 20 years of age. **He is handsome and dresses well. He has a fair complexion, smooth face, blue eyes, and light brown hair. He is about six feet tall and deceptively handsome.** A beautiful bay mare, that he has carefully trained, is all that he seems to care for, unless he reserves some affection for his brace of six-shooters and Winchester rifle, which have helped him out of many a tight place. His care of the beautiful mare is well deserved, for many a time has her fleetness which surpasses that of any other horse in the Territory, saved his life. The Kid is an admirable rider, and as he is always expected to be obliged to take flight, he usually rides another horse, leading his pet behind, in order to make the best time possible on a fresh horse. He is considered a dead shot and much of his time is spent in target practice. He was born in New York State, but his parents removed to Indiana when he was quite small, and thence to Arizona. There in the Tombstone District the Kid killed his first man when he was only 17 years old, and was obliged to leave the country. He came to New Mexico, where he has since lived.

About three years ago a difficulty arose in Lincoln County, New Mexico, between the stockmen and the Indian agent on the reservation. The trouble arose in regard to some cattle that had been purchased for the Indians. Nearly every man in the county was under arms, and the troops were called out by Gov. Wallace to quell the disturbance. The Kid was mixed up in the affair, and had some narrow escapes. On one occasion he was hotly pursued and was obliged to take refuge in a house in Lincoln, which was surrounded by sixty solders. To the demand to surrender, he only laughed and shot down a soldier just to show that he was game. The house was set on fire, when the Kid, after loading up his Winchester Rifle, leaped from the burning building and made a dash for liberty. All the while he was running he kept firing from his Winchester, bringing down a number of his pursuers. Bullets whistled over his head, but he made his escape, and leaping on a horse was soon laughing at his pursuers. There is no telling how many men he has killed. He sets no value on human life, and has never hesitated at murder when it would serve his purpose. Gov. Wallace a few days ago offered a reward of $500 for his capture, and prominent citizens would make up a handsome purse in addition.

Billy Wilson is much the same sort of good looking fellow as his chief. He is about the same build, with dark hair and a slight moustache. He left the Ohio home where his people, who are all highly esteemed, still reside, several years ago. After being engaged in the cattle business in Texas for some time, he came to New Mexico. When the excitement broke out over the new camp at White Oaks, he went there and was engaged in the butchering business. He was always considered a smart, energetic fellow, and was well thought of. In some way the Kid persuaded him to join his party, and it was by him that much of the forged paper was put into circulation.

Tom O'Phallier is a Texan and is also a man of good appearance. He has a ruddy, face, and can be an exceedingly agreeable companion. He has been with the band from the first, and has committed many crimes.

Dave Rudabaugh is 36 years old, and was born in New York city, where he lived until about eight years ago. He has raided over southern Kansas, the Indian nations, Texas, southern Colorado, and New Mexico. It would not be difficult to establish charges of murder against him in any or all of those States and Territories. In Colorado, a few years ago he ran off some Government stock, and, while pursued by a detachment of soldiers, he killed a Sergeant and two privates. He once headed an attack on the Las Vegas jail, in order to liberate one of his friends, and shot down a guard who interfered. He is a thorough desperado in look, word, and action, ready at all times for a fight. He thinks no more of putting a bullet through a human brain than through the bull's eyes of the target before which he is continually practicing. He is 5 feet 8 inches tall, and weighs about 180 pounds. He has a swarthy complexion, black hair and beard, and hazel eyes, whose cruel, defiant expression has often been noted.

**The career of the band is about run, for they are hotly pursued, and the chances are that before long they will be killed or captured. It is not expected that the Kid or Rudabaugh will be taken alive, as they will fight to the last.**

# ANNOTATED BIBLIOGRAPHY

## RELEVANT 19th CENTURY HISTORY

### COMPREHENSIVE REFERENCES

Nolan, Frederick. *The War: A Documentary History*. Norman: University of Oklahoma Press. **1992**.
_____. *The West of Billy the Kid*. Norman: University of Oklahoma Press. **1998**.

### HISTORICAL ORGANIZATIONS (PERIOD)

#### SANTA FE RING, 19th CENTURY

***MODERN SOURCES***

Brown, Richard Maxwell. *Strain of Violence: Historical Studies of American Violence and Vigilantism*. New York: Oxford University Press. 1975. (**New Mexico unique for assassination as part of political system**)

Caffey, David L. *Chasing the Santa Fe Ring: Power and Privilege in Territorial New Mexico*. Albuquerque, New Mexico: University of New Mexico Press. 2014.
_____. *Frank Springer and New Mexico: From the Colfax County War to the Emergence of Modern Santa Fe*. Texas A and M. University Press. 2007.

Cleaveland, Agnes Morley. *No Life for a Lady*. Boston: Houghton Mifflin. 1941.
_____. *Satan's Paradise: From Lucien Maxwell to Fred Lambert*. Boston: Houghton Mifflin Company. 1952.

Cleaveland, Norman, *Colfax County's Chronic Murder Mystery*. Santa Fe: New Mexico. The Rydel Press. 1977.
_____. *A Synopsis of the Great New Mexico Cover-up*. Self-printed. 1989.
_____. *Some Comments Norman Cleveland May Make to the Huntington Westerners on Sept. 19, 1987*. Unpublished.
_____. *Some Highlights of William R. Morley's Contribution to the Pioneer Development of the Southwest*. Self-printed. No Date.
_____. *The Great Santa Fe Cover-up*. Based on a Talk given Before the Santa Fe Historical Society on November 1, 1978. Self-printed. 1982.

Cleaveland, Norman and George Fitzpatrick. *The Morleys - Young Upstarts on the Southwest Frontier*. Albuquerque, New Mexico: Calvin Horn Publisher, Inc. 1971.

Cooper, Gale. *The Santa Fe Ring Versus Billy the Kid: The Making of An American Monster*. Albuquerque, New Mexico: Gelcour Books. 2018.

Klasner, Lilly. Eve Ball. Ed. *My Girlhood Among Outlaws*. Tucson, Arizona: The University of Arizona Press. 1972. Klasner, Lilly. Eve Ball. Ed. *My Girlhood Among Outlaws*. Tucson, Arizona: The University of Arizona Press. 1972. (**John Chisum's in jail write-up about Santa Fe Ring injustices to himself**)

Lamar, Howard Robert N. *The Far Southwest 1846 – 1912: A Territorial History*. New Haven and London: Yale University Press. 1966. (**Chapter 6 covers the Santa Fe Ring**))

Meinig, D. W. *The Shaping of America. A Geographical Perspective on 500 Years of History. Vol. 3. Transcontinental America 1850 - 1915*. New Haven and London: Yale University Press. 1998. (**Pages 127 and 132 are on the Santa Fe Ring.**)

Montoya, María E. *Translating Property. The Maxwell Land Grant and the Conflict Over Land in the American West, 1840-1900*. Berkeley and Los Angeles: University of California Press. 2002.

Naegle, Conrad Keeler. *The History of Silver City, New Mexico 1870-1886*. University of New Mexico Bachelor of Arts thesis. Pages 30-60. Unpublished. 1943. Collection of the Silver City Museum, Silver City, New Mexico. (**Grant County rebellion**)

_____. "The Rebellion of Grant County, New Mexico in 1876." *Arizona and the West: A Quarterly Journal of History*. Autumn, 1968. Volume 10. Number 3. Tucson, Arizona: The University of Arizona Press. 1968. Pages 225-240. (**Grant County rebellion against Santa Fe Ring**)

Newman, Simeon Harrison III. "The Santa Fe Ring." *Arizona and the West*. Volume 12. Autumn 1970. Pages 269-288.

Otero, Miguel A. *My Life on the Frontier, 1882-1897: Incidents and Characters of the period when Kansas, Colorado, and New Mexico were Passing Through the Last of their Wild and Romantic Years*. New York: The Press of the Pioneers. 1935. Pages 232-233. (Quoted by Victor Westphall, *Thomas Benton Catron and His Era*. Page 188) (**Quote: "the 'Santa Fe Ring,' the real machine controlling the political situation in New Mexico."**)

Pearson, Jim Berry. *The Maxwell Land Grant*. Norman: University of Oklahoma Press. 1961.

Taylor, Morris F. *O.P. McMains and the Maxwell Land Grant Conflict*. Tucson, Arizona: The University of Arizona Press. 1979. (**Traces origins of the Santa Fe Ring**)

Theisen, Lee Scott. "Frank Warner Angel's Notes on New Mexico Territory, 1878." *Arizona and the West: A Quarterly Journal of History*. Winter 1976. Volume 18. Number 4. Pages 333-370. (**About the Angel notebook given to Lew Wallace and listing names of Santa Fe Ring members**)

Westphall, Victor. *Thomas Benton Catron and His Era*. Tucson, Arizona: University of Arizona Press. 1973. (**Ring-denier, who cites sources exposing the Ring**)

## *CONTEMPORARY SOURCES (CHRONOLOGICAL)*

A.C.L. Editorial. "New Mexico, A Sorry Showing for a Would-be State, Tweed's Disciples Preying on the Populace, How the Territorial Ring is Run, Why the Territory Should Not Be Made a State. **March 13, 1876.** *The Boston Daily Globe*. Volume IX, Number 62. Newspaperarchive.com.

No Author. "A Contemplated Political Change." Grant County *Herald*. **September 16, 1876.** Quoted by Conrad Keeler Naegle in *The History of Silver City, New Mexico 1870-1886* doctoral thesis. Pages 39-40. (**Listing reasons to escape the Ring by annexing to Arizona Territory**)

Wallace, Lew. "Our mutual friend, M. Hinds, who will hand you this ..." Letter to A.H. Markland. **November 14, 1878.** Indiana Historical Society. Lew Wallace Collection. M0292. Box 3. Folder 17. (**Ring tries to remove him as governor**)

Leonard, Ira E. "When you left here I promised to write you concerning events transpiring here ..." Letter to Lew Wallace. **May 20, 1878 [sic - 79]**. Indiana Historical Society. Lew Wallace Collection. M0292. Box 4. Folder 10. (**Quote: "Santa Fe ring ... so long an incubus on the government."**)

Wallace, Lew. "I have the honor to inform you that the Legislature of this Territory adjourned ..." **February 16, 1880.** Letter to Carl Schurz. Indiana Historical Society. Lew Wallace Collection. M0292. Box 4. Folder 14. (**Key documentation of Catron as head of the Santa Fe Ring, and Wallace's Ring opposition**)

No Author. "White Cap's Proclamation." *Las Vegas Optic*. March 12, 1880. (**Manifesto against land-grabbing Catron and the Ring**)

No Author. "The Santa Fe Ring is the most corrupt combination that ever cursed any country or community." Las Cruces *Thirty-Four Newspaper*. **October 27, 1880.** From Victor Westphall, *Thomas Benton Catron and His Era*. Page 186. (**Article on Santa Fe Ring abuses urging voters to oppose Ring candidates**)

No Author. "The Ring must soon discover that the time has passed in New Mexico when men can be herded like so many sheep ..." *Albuquerque Daily Democrat*.

March 4, 1884. (Quoted by Victor Westphall, *Thomas Benton Catron and His Era*. Page 191.) (**About Santa Fe Ring control of appointments to legislature**)

No Author. *Santa Fe Weekly New Mexican Review*. **March 13, 1884.** *Santa Fe Weekly New Mexican Review*. (**Accusation of Catron and the Ring of controlling grand juries and** bribery)

No Author. *Albuquerque Daily Democrat*. **March 15, 1884.** (**Oscar P. McMains "Memorial" against land-grabbing Ring**)

Valdez, Jose and Enrique Mares. "Scorching Letter, The Knights of Labor Send a Communication to Powderly! Politicians Arraigned! The Boldest Document Ever Issued in the Territory." **August 18, 1890.** *Las Vegas Democrat*. Volume 1. Center for Southwest Studies. Thomas B. Catron Papers, MSS 29, Series 102, Box 8, Folder 4. (**Gives history of Santa Fe Ring with T.B. Catron as head**)

No Author. *Los Angeles Times*. **1899.** Undated clipping, Laughlin Papers, State Records Center, Santa Fe, New Mexico. Quoted by Victor Westphall, *Thomas Benton Catron and His Era*. Page 285. (**Joking article about the Santa Fe Ring**)

## EXPOSÉS Of (CONTEMPORARY)

## COMPLAINT ABOUT TO PRESIDENT RUTHERFORD B. HAYES

Matchett, W.B. and Mary E. McPherson. " W.B. Matchett and Mary E. McPherson 'Make certain charges against the U.S. Officials in the Territory of New Mexico.' " Letter to President Rutherford B. Hayes. Received and filed **May 1, 1877.** Interior Department Papers 1850-1907; Appointments Division and Subsequent Actions. Microfilm File Case Number 44-4-8-3. Record Group 48. Microfilm No. M750. Roll 1. National Archives and Records Administration. U. S. Department of Justice. Washington, D.C. (**Sent to President Rutherford B. Hayes and Secretary of the Interior Carl Schurz.**)

McPherson, Mary and W.B. Matchett. "To the President. Please make the enclosed a part of the evidence in the case of "Charges Against New Mexican Officials" Letter to President Rutherford B. Hayes. **May 3, 1877.** McPherson, Mary E. Letters and Petitions to President Rutherford B. Hayes re: Removal Governor Axtell and the Santa Fe Ring. Interior Department Papers 1850-1907; Appointments Division and Subsequent Actions. Microfilm File Case Number 44-4-8-3. Record Group 48. Microfilm Roll M750. National Archives and Records Administration. U.S. Department of Justice. Washington, D.C. (**Addendum to their May, 1877 "Certain Charges Against U.S. Officials in New Mexico Territory."**)

_____. "The Secretary of the Interior, Sir – Accompanying please find <u>copy</u> of charges, &c., against S.B. Axtell, Governor, and Other New Mexican Officials ..." "Charges Against New Mexican Officials." Letter to Secretary of the Interior Carl Schurz. **May 5, 1877.** McPherson, Mary E. Letters and Petitions to President Rutherford B. Hayes re: Removal Governor Axtell and the Santa Fe Ring. Interior Department Papers 1850-1907; Appointments Division and Subsequent Actions. Microfilm File Case Number 44-4-8-3. Record Group 48. Microfilm Roll M750. National Archives and Records Administration. U.S. Department of Justice. Washington, D. C.

_____."In the Matter of Charges vs. Gov. S.B. Axtell and Other New Mexico Officials. Submitted to the Departments of the Interior and Justice. **August, 1877.** Printed as a 31 page booklet. No publisher listed. Indiana Historical Society. Lew Wallace Collection. M0292. Box 3. Folder 20. (**About the Santa Fe Ring, Catron, and Elkins; in Lew Wallace's personal possession**)

McPherson, Mary. "Please place before the Attorney General ..." Letter to President Rutherford B. Hayes. **August 23, 1877.** Interior Department Papers 1850-1907; Appointments Division and Subsequent Actions. Microfilm File Case Number 44-4-8-3. Record Group 48. Microfilm No. M750. Roll 1. National Archives and Records Administration. U. S. Department of Justice. Washington, D.C.

Springer, Frank. Deposition to Investigator Frank Warner Angel for the Departments of Justice and the Interior. **August 9, 1878**. Frank Warner Angel report titled *In the Matter of the Investigation of the Charges Against S.B. Axtell Governor of New Mexico*. October 3, 1878. Interior Department Papers 1850-1907; Appointments Division and Subsequent Actions. Microfilm Case File No. 44-4-8-3. Record Group 48. Microfilm Roll M750. National Archives and Records Administration. U.S. Department of Interior. Washington, D.C.

(SEE: Thomas Benton Catron; Frank Warner Angel, Legislature Revolt, Grant County Rebellion, Colfax County War, Lincoln County War)

## NORTH CAROLINA REGULATORS, 18th CENTURY

Hudson, Arthur Palmer. "Songs of the Carolina Regulators." *William and Mary Quarterly*. 4. No. 4 (1947): Page 146.
Kars, Marjoline. *Breaking Loose Together: The Regulator Rebellion in Pre-Revolutionary North Carolina*. Chapel Hill and London: The University of North Carolina Press. 2002.
Maier, Pauline. *From Resistance to Revolution: Colonial radicals and the development of American opposition to Britain, 1765-1776*. New York and London: W.W. Norton & Company. 1991.

## LINCOLN COUNTY REGULATORS, 19th CENTURY

Lody, William F. "Gold Bullet Sport; The Knights of the Overland". *Beadle's Dime New York Library*. 7(83). New York: Beadle & Adams, Publishers. December 17, 1874.
Cooms, Oll. "The Boy Ranger: or, The Heiress of the Golden Horn." *Pocket Series. No. 11*. New York: Beadle & Adams, Publishers. 1874.
Wheeler, Edward L. *The Deadwood Dick Library*. "A Tale of the Regulators and Road-Agents of the Black Hills. The Double Daggers; or, Deadwood Dick's Defiance." Beadles Half Dime Library. No. 20. Cleveland, Ohio: Arthur Westbrook Co. 1877.
_____. "Deadwood Dick, The Prince of the Road: or The Black Rider of the Black Hills". *The Deadwood Dick Library. 1(1)*. Cleveland, Ohio: The Arthur Westbrook Co. 1877.
No Author. "The Rover of the Forest." *Munro's Ten Cent Novels*. No. 42. New York: George Munro & Co. 1864.

## LINCOLN COUNTY REGULATOR MANIFESTO (BY BILLY BONNEY)

Regulator. "Mr. Walz. Sir ..." Letter to Edgar Walz. July 13, 1878. Adjutant General's Office. File 1405 AGO 1878. (Quoted in Maurice Garland Fulton, *History of the Lincoln County War*. Tucson: University of Arizona Press. 1975. pages 246-247, and Frederick Nolan, *The Lincoln County War: A Documentary History*, page 310.)

## SECRET SERVICE, 19th CENTURY (CHRONOLOGICAL)

Bowen, Walter S. and Harry Edward Neal. *The United States Secret Service*. Philadelphia and New York: Chilton Company Publishers. **1960**.
Brooks, James J. *1877 Report on Secret Service Operatives*. (**September 26, 1877**). "On Azariah Wild." Page 392. Department of the Treasury. United States Secret Service. Washington, D.C.
Johnson, David R. *Illegal Tender. Counterfeiting and the Secret Service in Nineteenth Century America*. Washington and London: Smithsonian Institution Press. **1995**.

## OPERATIVE ANDREW L. DRUMMOND

Drummond, Arthur L. "Daily Reports of U. S. Secret Service Agents, 1875-1937. Record Group 87. ." Microfilm T-915. Rolls: 91, 92. (January 1, 1880 – September 30, 1880). 92 (October 1, 1880 - June 30, 1881)). National Archives and Records Department. Department of the Treasury. Secret Service Division. Washington, D.C. (**Reports in *Cold Case Billy the Kid's* counterfeiting hoax against Billy Bonney: September 14, 1880, November 30, 1880) (Additional reports for debunking *Cold Case Billy the Kid* hoaxers: September 18, 1880, December 2, 1880, (Pages 660-661) June 10, 1881, June 29, 1881)**

## OPERATIVE WALLACE W. HALL

Hall, Wallace W. "Daily Reports of U. S. Secret Service Agents, 1875-1937." Microfilm T-915. Record Group 87. Microfilm Rolls: 153 (January 1, 1879 – December 31, 1880), 154 (January 1, 1881 - December 31, 1881; February 24, 1881), 155: (January 1, 1882 – July 31, 1883; January–June 1882, July 1, 1882). National Archives and Records Department. Department of the Treasury. Secret Service Division. Washington, D.C. (**Reports cited in *Cold Case Billy the Kid's* fake counterfeiting claim against Billy Bonney: May 19, 1880, August 4, 1880, February 24, 1881, February 26, 1881, October 11, 1881, May 9, 1882, May 19, 1882, May 27, 1882; though they have no link to Billy Bonney) (Additional reports for debunking *Cold Case Billy the Kid* hoaxers: August 3, 1880, August 24, 1880, October 10, 1880, January 24, 1881, January 27, 1881, February 27, 1881, October 10, 1881, October 11, 1881, May 19, 1882, June 6, 1882, June 17, 1882, July 1, 1882, September 1, 1882, October 7, 1882, July 10, 1885)**

Dye, John S. *Government Counterfeiter Detector.* **March, 1881.** Volume XXIX. Number 10. From Secret Service Library, Counterfeit Division via Archivist Michael Sampson. (**Applies to Wallace Hall's report of January 24, 1881 about counterfeit currency in Moundville, Missouri**)

## OPERATIVE PATRICK D. TYRRELL

Tyrell, Patrick D. "Daily Reports of U. S. Secret Service Agents, 1875-1937." Record Group 87. Microfilm T-915. Roll 285. National Archives and Records Department. Department of the Treasury. Secret Service Division. Washington, D.C. (**Report cited in *Cold Case Billy the Kid's* fake counterfeiting claim against Billy Bonney: July 8, 1881**)

## OPERATIVE AZARIAH F. WILD

### *BIOGRAPHICAL SOURCE*

Nolan, Frederick. "Biography of Azariah Wild." Unpublished and personal communications, June 11, 2005 and October 9, 2005.

### *CONTEMPORARY SOURCES (CHRONOLOGICAL)*

Brooks, James J. *1877 Report on Secret Service Operatives.* "On Azariah Wild." **September 26, 1877.** Page 392. Department of the Treasury. United States Secret Service. Washington, D.C.

Wild, Azariah F. "Daily Reports of U. S. Secret Service Agents, 1875-1937." Record Group 87. Microfilm T-915. Microfilm Rolls 306 (June 15, 1877 - December 31, 1877), 307 (January 1,1878 - June 30, 1879), 308 (July 1, 1879 - June 30, 1881; October 4, 1880, Pages 330-333; October 5, 1880, Pages 336-339; November 11, 1880, Pages 484-488), 309 (July 1, 1881 - September 30, 1883), 310 (October 1, 1883 - July 31, 1886). National Archives and Records Department. Department of the Treasury. Secret Service Division. Washington, D.C. (**Cited in *Cold Case**

*Billy the Kid* Bibliography for counterfeiting claim against Billy Bonney: June 11, 1880, June 12, 1880, October 28, 1880, November 10, 1880, November 30, 1880, January 3, 1881, October 4, 1881, October 6, 1881, October 16, 1881) (Other reports relevant to *Cold Case Billy the Kid's* counterfeiting claim against Billy Bonney: May 1, 1880-July 31, 1880; October 4, 1880, October 5, 1880, November 11, 1880, November 21, 1880, November 28, 1880)

Wild, Azariah. Telegraph on counterfeit bills. **January 4, 1881.** Herman B. Weisner Papers, ca. 1957-1992. New Mexico State University Library at Las Cruces. Archives and Special Collections Department. Accession No. Ms 0249. Box 11. Folder O-1. Folder Name: "Olinger, Robert and James W. Bell."

# NEW MEXICO TERRITORY REBELLIONS AGAINST THE SANTA FE RING (CHRONOLOGICAL)

## LEGISLATURE REVOLT (1872)

No Author. *Journal of the House of Representatives of the Territory of New Mexico, Session of 1871-1872*. Santa Fe: A.P. Sullivan. **1872.** Pages 144-154. (**Confirms troops used by Ring to suppress the Legislature Revolt of 1872** )

No Author. "Our Own Dear Steve, How Elkins Made His Influence Felt in New Mexico – The Ring in Which a Judge Figured – Politics in 1870. *Las Vegas Daily Optic*. **September 2, 1884.** (Reprinted from the *Omaha Herald*) Front Page. Volume V, Number 258, Column 4. Newspaperarchive.com. (**Exposing the Ring in the 1872 Legislature Revolt with Catron's and Elkins's corrupt alliance with Judge Joseph Palen** )

## GRANT COUNTY REBELLION (1876)

### *MODERN SOURCES*

Naegle, Conrad Keeler. *The History of Silver City, New Mexico 1870-1886*. University of New Mexico Bachelor of Arts thesis. Pages 30-60. Unpublished. 1943. Collection of the Silver City Museum, Silver City, New Mexico.

_____. "The Rebellion of Grant County, New Mexico in 1876." *Arizona and the West: A Quarterly Journal of History*. Autumn, 1968. Volume 10. Number 3. Tucson, Arizona: The University of Arizona Press. 1968. Pages 225-240. (**Rebellion against Santa Fe Ring**)

### *CONTEMPORARY SOURCES (CHRONOLOGICAL)*

No Author. "Diario del Consejo der Territorio de Neuvo Mejico, Session de 1871-1872." *Santa Fe New Mexican*. **January 8, 1872.** Santa Fe: A.P. Sullivan. 1872. Pages 144-154. New Mexico Supreme Court Library. Santa Fe, New Mexico. (**A Ring expurgated document, with a copy found in 1942 by Conrad Naegle; confirming troops used by Ring to suppress Territorial legislature**)

No Author. "Diario del Consejo der Territorio de Neuvo Mejico, Session de 1871-1872. Las Cruces *Borderer*. **January 24, 1872.** Pages 110-113. (**Don Diego Archuleta, President of the Council, gives speech objecting to troops in legislature**)

No Author. "Ring influence [in the Territorial legislature is] being actively used against every measure that tends to do justice" [in Grant and Doña Ana Counties]." *Grant County Herald*. **August 8, 1875.** Quoted by Conrad Keeler Naegle in *The History of Silver City, New Mexico 1870-1886*, doctoral thesis. Page 39.

No Author. "A Contemplated Political Change." Grant County *Herald*. **September 16, 1876**. Quoted by Conrad Keeler Naegle in *The History of Silver City, New Mexico*

*1870-1886* doctoral thesis. Pages 39-40. (**Listing reasons to escape the Ring by annexing to Arizona Territory**)

No Author. [Grant County should not] "sort o' wait and hear from Santa Fe ... before taking action." Tucson *Arizona Citizen*. **September 23, 1876.** Quoted by Conrad Keeler Naegle in *The History of Silver City, New Mexico 1870-1886* doctoral thesis. Page 41. (**Arizona encourages escape from Santa Fe Ring**)

No Author. Grant County *Herald*. **September 23, 1876.** (**Need for school system stressed.**)

No Author. Grant County *Herald*. **September 30, 1876.** (**"Annexation Meeting" announced**)

No Author. "Proceedings of Grant County Annexation Meeting." Grant County *Herald*. **Saturday October 7, 1876.** Page 2. Columns 1 and 2. Collection of the Silver City, New Mexico, Museum. (**Anti-Santa Fe Ring "Grant County Declaration of Independence" published**)

No Author. Grant County *Herald*. " 'Petition to Remove Judge Bristol. We the undersigned citizens of the Third Judicial District of the Territory of New Mexico, without regard to party, would respectfully request and petition for the removal of Judge Warren Bristol ...' " No date. **1876 or 1877.**(Quoted in "W.B. Matchett and Mary E. McPherson 'Make certain charges against the U.S. Officials in the Territory of New Mexico.' " Letter to President Rutherford B. Hayes. Received and filed May 1, 1877. Interior Department Papers 1850-1907; Appointments Division and Subsequent Actions. Microfilm File Case Number 44-4-8-3. Record Group 48. Microfilm No. M750. Roll 1. National Archives and Records Administration. U.S. Department of Justice. Washington, D.C.) (**Anti-Santa Fe Ring article**)

(SEE: Santa Fe Ring; Thomas Benton Catron; Stephen Benton Elkins)

## COLFAX COUNTY WAR (1877)

### *MODERN SOURCES*

Caffey, David L. *Frank Springer and New Mexico: From the Colfax County War to the Emergence of Modern Santa Fe.* Texas A and M. University Press. 2007.

Cleaveland, Norman. *The Morleys - Young Upstarts on the Southwest Frontier.* Albuquerque, New Mexico: Calvin Horn Publisher, Inc. 1971.

Dunham, Harold H. "New Mexican Land Grants with Special Reference to the Title Papers of the Maxwell Grant." *New Mexico Historical Review.* (January 1955) Vol. 30, No. 1. pp. 1 - 23.

Keleher, William A. *The Maxwell Land Grant. A New Mexico Item.* Albuquerque, New Mexico: University of New Mexico Press. 1964.

Lamar, Howard Roberts. *The Far Southwest 1846 - 1912. A Territorial History.* New Haven and London: Yale University Press. 1966.

Montoya, María E. *Translating Property. The Maxwell Land Grant and the Conflict Over Land in the American West, 1840-1900.* Berkeley and Los Angeles, California: University of California Press. 2002.

Murphy, Lawrence R. *Lucien Bonaparte Maxwell. Napoleon of the Southwest.* Norman: University of Oklahoma Press. 1983.

Pearson, Jim Berry. *The Maxwell Land Grant.* Norman: University of Oklahoma Press. 1961.

Poe, Sophie. *Buckboard Days.* Albuquerque, New Mexico: University of New Mexico Press. 1964.

Taylor, Morris F. *O.P. McMains and the Maxwell Land Grant Conflict.* Tucson, Arizona: The University of Arizona Press. 1979.

## CONTEMPORARY SOURCES (CHRONOLOGICAL)

No author. "Anarchy at Cimarron." *Santa Fe Weekly New Mexican.* **November 16, 1875. (Ringite backing of Axtell's use of troops in the Colfax County War)**

Dawson, Will. Editorial. *Cimarron News and Press.* **December 31, 1875. (Ring-biased editorial by temporary editor blaming citizens for unrest)**

No Author. Report on murder trial for Franklin Tolby. Pueblo, *Colorado Chieftain.* **May 25, 1876.** Quoting *Daily New Mexican,* May 1, 1876. From Morris F. Taylor. *O.P. McMains and the Maxwell Land Grant Conflict.* Tucson, Arizona: The University of Arizona Press. 1979. Page 49. **(Ring-biased jury instructions by Judge Henry Waldo to protect Ring murderers of Tolby)**

No Author. "Rejoicing at Cimarron," "Axtell's Head Falls at Last," "General Lew. Wallace Appointed Governor." *Cimarron News and Press.* **September 6, 1878.**

No Author. *Santa Fe Weekly New Mexican.* **September 21, 1878 and October 19, 1878. (Ring-biased accolades for removed Gov. Axtell)**

(SEE: Regulators, Santa Fe Ring; Thomas Benton Catron; Stephen Benton Elkins, Colfax County War, Lincoln County War)

## LINCOLN COUNTY WAR (1878)

### MODERN SOURCES

Cramer, T. Dudley. *The Pecos Ranchers in the Lincoln County War.* Orinda, California: Branding Iron Press. 1996.

Fulton, Maurice Garland. Robert N. Mullin. Ed. *History of the Lincoln County War.* Tucson, Arizona: The University of Arizona Press. 1997.

Jacobsen, Joel. *Such Men as Billy the Kid: The Lincoln County War Reconsidered.* Lincoln and London: University of Nebraska Press. 1994.

Keleher, William A. *The Fabulous Frontier: Twelve New Mexico Items.* Albuquerque, New Mexico: The University of New Mexico Press. 1962.

_____. *County 1869-1881.* Albuquerque, New Mexico: University of New Mexico Press. 1957.

Mullin, Robert N. Re: Frank Warner Angel Meeting with President Hayes. August, 1878. Binder RNM, VI, M. Midland, Texas: Nita Stewart Haley Memorial Library and J. Evetts Haley History Center. (Unpublished).

Nolan, Frederick W. *The Life and Death of John Henry Tunstall.* Albuquerque, New Mexico: The University of New Mexico Press. 1965.

_____. *The Lincoln County War: A Documentary History.* Norman: University of Oklahoma Press. 1992.

_____. *The West of Billy the Kid.* Norman: University of Oklahoma Press. 1998.

Rasch, Philip J. *Gunsmoke in Lincoln County.* Laramie, Wyoming: National Association for Outlaw and Lawmen History, Inc. with University of Wyoming. 1997.

_____. Robert K. DeArment. Ed. *Warriors of Lincoln County.* Laramie: National Association for Outlaw and Lawmen History, Inc. with University of Wyoming. 1998.

Utley, Robert M. *High Noon in Lincoln. Violence on the Western Frontier.* Albuquerque, New Mexico: University of New Mexico Press. 1987.

Wilson, John P. *Merchants, Guns, and Money: The Story of Lincoln County and Its Wars.* Santa Fe, New Mexico: Museum of New Mexico Press. 1987.

No Author. "Disturbances in the Territories, 1878 - 1894. Lawlessness in New Mexico." Senate Documents. 67th Congress. 2nd Session. December 5, 1921 - September 22, 1922. pp. 176 - 187. Washington, D.C.: Government Printing Office. 1922.

## CONTEMPORARY SOURCES (CHRONOLOGICAL)

No Author. "Brady Inventory McSween Property." **February, 1878.** Herman B. Weisner Papers, ca. 1957-1992. New Mexico State University Library at Las Cruses. Rio Grande Historical Collections. Accession No. Weisner Ms 0249. Box 10. Folder M15. Folder Name. "Will and Testament A. McSween."

No Author. "Amnesty for Matthews and Long in the Third Judicial Court April Term 1879." **April, 1879.** Herman B. Weisner Papers, ca. 1957-1992. New Mexico State University Library at Las Cruces. Rio Grande Historical Collections. Accession No. Ms 0249. Box 1. Folder 4. Folder Name. "Amnesty."

No Author. "Charges against Jessie Evans and John Kinney." Doña Ana County Civil and Criminal Docket Book. **August 18, 1875 to November 7, 1878.** Herman B. Weisner Papers, ca. 1957-1992. New Mexico State University Library at Las Cruces. Rio Grande Historical Collections. Accession No. Ms 0249. Box 13. Folder V 3. Folder Name. "Venue, Change Of."

No Author. "Dismissal of Cases Against Dolan, Matthews, Peppin, October 1879 District Court." **October, 1879.** Herman B. Weisner Papers, ca. 1957-1992. New Mexico State University Library at Las Cruces. Rio Grande Historical Collections. Accession No. Ms 0249. Box 13. Folder V3. Folder Name: "Venue, Change Of."

No Author. "Killers of Tunstall. February 18, 1879." Herman B. Weisner Papers, ca. 1957-1992. New Mexico State University Library at Las Cruces. Rio Grande Historical Collections. Accession No. Ms 0249. Box 12. Folder T1. Folder Name: "Tunstall, John H."

No Author. "Lincoln County Indictments July 1872 - 1881." Herman B. Weisner Papers, ca. 1957-1992. New Mexico State University Library at Las Cruces. Rio Grande Historical Collections. Accession No. Ms 0249. Box 8. Folder L11. Folder Name. "Lincoln Co. Indictments."

(SEE: William H. Bonney, John Henry Tunstall, Alexander McSween, Samuel Beach Axtell, Frank Warner Angel, Nathan Augustus Monroe Dudley)

# HISTORY OF WILLIAM HENRY BONNEY (WILLIAM HENRY McCARTY, HENRY ANTRIM, AKA BILLY THE KID)

## BIOGRAPHICAL SOURCES

Abbott, E.C. ("Teddy Blue") and Helena Huntington Smith. *We Pointed Them North: Recollections of a Cowpuncher.* Norman, Oklahoma: University of Oklahoma Press. 1955. (**Billy the Kid's multi-culturalism, Page 47.**)

Anaya, Paco. *I Buried Billy.* College Station, Texas: Creative Publishing Company. 1991.

Ball, Eve. *Ma'am Jones of the Pecos.* Tucson, Arizona: The University of Arizona Press. 1969.

Bell, Bob Boze. *The Illustrated Life and Times of Billy the Kid.* Cave Creek, Arizona: Boze Books. 1992. (Frank Coe quote about the Kid's cartridge use, Page 45.)

Bell, Bob Boze. *The Illustrated Life and Times of Billy the Kid.* Second Edition. Phoenix, Arizona: Tri Star-Boze Publications, Inc. 1996.

Burns, Walter Noble. *The Saga of Billy the Kid.* Stamford, Connecticut: Longmeadow Press. 1992. (Original printing: 1926, Doubleday.)

_____. *"I also know that the Kid and Paulita were sweethearts."* Unpublished letter to Jim East. June 3, 1926. Robert N. Mullin Collection. File RNM, IV, NM, 116-117. Nita Stewart Haley Memorial Museum, Haley Library. Midland, Texas.

Coe, George with Doyce B. Nunis, Jr. Ed. *Frontier Fighter. The Autobiography of George Coe Who Fought and Rode With Billy the Kid.* Chicago: R. R. Donnelley and Sons Company. 1984.

Cooper, Gale. *Billy the Kid's Writings, Words, and Wit.* Gelcour Books: Albuquerque: New Mexico. 2012.

_____. *Billy and Paulita: The Saga of Billy the Kid, Paulita Maxwell, and the Santa Fe Ring.* Gelcour Books: Albuquerque: New Mexico. 2012.

_____. *The Lost Pardon of Billy the Kid: An Analysis Factoring in the Santa Fe Ring, Governor Lew Wallace's Dilemma, and a Territory in Rebellion.* Gelcour Books: Albuquerque: New Mexico. 2017.

_____. *The Santa Fe Ring Versus Billy the Kid: The Making of an American Monster.* Gelcour Books: Albuquerque: New Mexico. 2018.

Garrett, Pat F. *The Authentic Life of Billy the Kid The Noted Desperado of the Southwest, Whose Deeds of Daring and Blood Made His Name a Terror in New Mexico, Arizona, and Northern Mexico.* Santa Fe, New Mexico: New Mexico Printing and Publishing Co. 1882. (Edition used: Edited by Maurice Garland Fulton. New York: The Macmillan Company. 1927)

Hendron, J. W. *The Story of Billy the Kid. New Mexico's Number One Desperado.* New York: Indian Head Books. 1994.

Hoyt, Henry. *A Frontier Doctor.* Boston and New York: Houghton Mifflin Company. 1929. **(Describes Billy's superior abilities. Pages 93-94, including fluency in Spanish.)**

Jacobsen, Joel. *Such Men as Billy the Kid: The Lincoln County War Reconsidered.* Lincoln and London: University of Nebraska Press. 1994.

Kadlec, Robert F. *They "Knew" Billy the Kid. Interviews with Old-Time New Mexicans.* Santa Fe, New Mexico: Ancient City Press. 1987.

Keleher, William A. *The Fabulous Frontier: Twelve New Mexico Items.* Albuquerque, New Mexico: The University of New Mexico Press. 1962.

_____.*Violence in Lincoln County 1869-1881.* Albuquerque, New Mexico: University of New Mexico Press. 1957.

McFarland, David F. Reverend. *Ledger: Session Records 1867-1874. Marriages in Santa Fe New Mexico.* "Mr. William H. Antrim and Mrs. Catherine McCarty." *March 1, 1873.* (Unpublished). Santa Fe, New Mexico: First Presbyterian Church of Santa Fe.

Meadows, John P. "Billy the Kid to John P. Meadows on the Peñasco, May 1-2, 1881." *Roswell Daily Record.* February 16, 1931. Page 6.

_____. Ed. John P. Wilson. *Pat Garrett and Billy the Kid as I Knew Them: Reminiscences of John P. Meadows.* Albuquerque: University of New Mexico Press. 2004.

Mullin, Robert N. *The Boyhood of Billy the Kid.* Monograph 17, Southwestern Studies 5(1). El Paso, Texas: Texas Western Press. University of Texas at El Paso. 1967.

Poe, John W. *The Death of Billy the Kid.* (Introduction by Maurice Garland Fulton). Boston and New York: Houghton Mifflin Company. 1933.

_____. "The Killing of Billy the Kid." (a personal letter written at Roswell, New Mexico to Mr. Charles Goodnight, Goodnight P.C., Texas) July 10, 1917. Earle Vandale Collection. 1813-946. No. 2H475. Center for American History. University of Texas at Austin.

Rakocy, Bill. *Billy the Kid.* El Paso, Texas: Bravo Press. 1985.

Rasch, Phillip J. *Trailing Billy the Kid.* Laramie, Wyoming: National Association for Outlaw and Lawman History, Inc. with University of Wyoming. 1995.

Russell, Randy. *Billy the Kid. The Story - The Trial.* Lincoln, New Mexico: The Crystal Press. 1994.

Scanland, John M. (Foreword) using Patrick F. Garrett, Patrick F. *Billy the Kid: The Outlaw. Authentic Story of Billy the Kid by Pat F. Garrett. Greatest Sheriff of the Old Southwest.* New York: Atomic Books Inc. **1946**. Oberlin College Library Special Collections, Pop Culture. Walter F. Tunks Collection. Number 2344. **(Pirated edition of Pat Garrett's *Authentic Life of Billy the Kid* featuring apocryphal outlawry of Billy the Kid)**

Siringo, Charles A. *The History of Billy the Kid.* Santa Fe: New Mexico. Privately Printed. 1920.
Tuska, Jon. *Billy the Kid. His Life and Legend.* Westport, Connecticut: Greenwood Press. 1983.
Utley, Robert M. *High Noon in Lincoln. Violence on the Western Frontier.* Albuquerque, New Mexico: University of New Mexico Press. 1987.
_____. *Billy the Kid. A Short and Violent Life.* Lincoln and London: University of Nebraska Press. 1989.
Weddle, Jerry. *Antrim is My Stepfather's Name. The Boyhood of Billy the Kid.* Monograph 9, Globe, Arizona: Arizona Historical Society. 1993.
No Author. "The Prisoners Who Saw the Kid Kill Olinger." April 28, 1881. Herman B. Weisner Papers, ca. 1957-1992. New Mexico State University Library at Las Cruces. Rio Grande Historical Collections. Accession No. Ms 0249. Box 30 T. Folder 8.

## *WORDS OF (CHRONOLOGICAL)*

### SPENCERIAN PENMANSHIP

Spencer, Platt Rogers. *Spencerian Penmanship.* New York: Ivison, Phinney, Blakemont Co. **1857.**
_____. *Spencerian System of Practical Penmanship.* New York: Ivison, Phinney, Blakemont Co. **1864.** (Reprinted by Milford, Michigan: Mott Media, Inc. 1985.)
Spencer, H.C. (Prepared for the "Spencerian Authors) *Spencerian Key to Practical Penmanship.* New York: Ivison, Phinney, Blakemont, Taylor & Co. **1874.**
_____. (Prepared for the "Spencerian Authors) *Theory of Spencerian Penmanship for Schools and Private Learners Developed by Questions and Answers with Practical Illustrations: Designed to Be Used by Pupils in Connection With the Use of Spencerian Copybooks.* New York: Ivison, Phinney, Blakemont, Taylor & Co. **1874.**
Spencerian Authors. *Theory of Spencerian Penmanship for Schools and Private Learners Developed by Questions and Answers with Practical Illustrations: Designed to Be Used by Pupils in Connection With the Use of Spencerian Copybooks.* (New York: Ivison, Phinney, Blakemont, Taylor & Co. 1874.) Reprinted and modified by Milford, Michigan: Mott Media, Inc. **1985.** (**Page 30 describes forming "the capital stem;" pages 2-7 describe "position" and "hand-arm movements;" and page 45 describes the pen and "shading;" all used by Billy Bonney**)
Sull, Michael, *Spencerian Script and Ornamental Penmanship.* Prairie Village: Kansas. (Unpublished, undated, modern manual).
Cooper, Gale. *Billy the Kid's Writings, Words, and Wit.* Albuquerque, New Mexico: Gelcour Books. **2012.**

### HOYT BILL OF SALE

Bonney, W H. "Know all persons by these presents ..." Thursday, **October 24, 1878.** Collection of Panhandle-Plains Historical Museum, Canyon, Texas. Item No. X1974-98/1. (**Hoyt Bill of Sale**)

### LETTERS TO LEW WALLACE

Bonney, W H. "I have heard you will give one thousand $ dollars for my body which as I see it means alive ..." **March 13(?), 1879.** Fray Angélico Chávez Historical Library, Santa Fe, New Mexico. Lincoln County Heritage Trust Collection. (AC481).
_____. "I will keep the keep the appointment ..." **March 20, 1879.** Indiana Historical Society. M0292.

_____. "... on the Pecos." ("Billie" letter fragment). **March 24(?), 1879.** Indiana Historical Society. Lew Wallace Collection. M0292. Box 4. Folder 7.

_____. "I noticed in the *Las Vegas* Gazette a piece which stated that 'Billy the Kid' ..." **December 12, 1880.** Indiana Historical Society. Lew Wallace Collection. M0292.

_____. "I would like to see you ..." **January 1, 1881.** Indiana Historical Society. Lew Wallace Collection. M0292.

_____. "I wish you would come down to the jail and see me ..." **March 2, 1881.** Fray Angélico Chávez Historical Library, Santa Fe, New Mexico. Lincoln County Heritage Trust Collection. (AC481).

_____. "I wrote you a little note day before yesterday ..." **March 4, 1881.** Indiana Historical Society. Lew Wallace Collection. M0292.

_____. "For the last time I ask ..." **March 27, 1881.** Indiana Historical Society. Lew Wallace Collection. M0292.

(SEE: Lew Wallace response letters to)

### LETTER TO SQUIRE WILSON

Bonney, W H. "Friend Wilson ..." **March 18, 1879.** Indiana Historical Society. Lew Wallace Collection. M0292. (**For pardon negotiation with Lew Wallace**)

### LETTER TO EDGAR CAYPLESS

Bonney, W H. "I would have written before ..." **April 15, 1881.** Copy in William Kelleher's *Violence in Lincoln County;* originally reproduced in Griggs *History of the Mesilla Valley.* (**Original lost**)

### REGULATOR MANIFESTO LETTER

Regulator. "Mr. Walz. Sir ..." Letter to Edgar Walz. **July 13, 1878.** Adjutant General's Office. File 1405 AGO 1878. (Quoted in Maurice Garland Fulton, *History of the Lincoln County War.* Tucson: University of Arizona Press. 1975. Pages 246-247.)

### DEPOSITION OF

Bonney, William Henry. Deposition to Frank Warner Angel. **June 8, 1878.** Frank Warner Angel report, Pages 314-319 from *In the Matter of the Examination of the Causes and Circumstances of the Death of John H. Tunstall a British Subject.* Report filed October 4, 1878. Angel Report. Records of the Justice Department. Record Group 60. Class 44 Litigation Files. Container 21. National Archives and Records Administration. U.S. Department of Justice. Washington, D.C. or Angel Report in Interior Department Papers 1850-1907; Appointments Division and Subsequent Actions. Microfilm File Case Number 44-4-8-3. Record Group 48. Microfilm No. M750. Roll 1. National Archives and Records Administration. U.S. Department of Justice. Washington, D.C.

### COURT TESTIMONY OF

Rynerson, William. "The Grand Jurors for the Territory of New Mexico taken from the body of the good and lawful men of the County of Lincoln ..." Indictments of the April, Lincoln County Grand Jury. **April 28, 1879.** Herman B. Weisner Papers, ca. 1957-1992. New Mexico State University Library at Las Cruces. Rio Grande Historical Collection. Accession No. Ms 0249. Box 4/39. Folder E-Z. Folder Name: "Jessie Evans Accessory to Murder." (**Billy's testimony for pardon bargain**)

Bonney, William Henry. Testimony in Court of Inquiry for N.A.M. Dudley. **May 28-29, 1879.** *Proceedings of a Court of Inquiry in the Case of Lt. Col. N.A.M. Dudley (May 2,1879 – July 5, 1879).* File No. QQ1284. (Boxes 3304, 3305, 3305A); Court Martial Files 1809-1894. Records of the Office of the Judge Advocate General -

Army. Record Group 153. Old Military and Civil Branch. National Archives and Records Administration. Washington, D. C.

Waldo, Henry. "Then was brought forward William Bonney, alias "Antrim," alias "the Kid," a known criminal of the worst type ..." Closing argument on Billy Bonney's testimony in Court of Inquiry for N.A.M. Dudley. **July 5, 1879**. *Proceedings of a Court of Inquiry in the Case of Lt. Col. N.A.M. Dudley (May 2,1879 – July 5, 1879)*. File No. QQ1284. (Boxes 3304, 3305, 3305A); Court Martial Files 1809-1894. Records of the Office of the Judge Advocate General – Army. Record Group 153. Old Military and Civil Branch. National Archives and Records Administration. Washington, D. C.

## INTERVIEW WITH LEW WALLACE OF

Wallace, Lew. "Statements by Kid, made Sunday night **March 23, 1879**." (Cover sheet reads: "Fort Stanton, March 20, 1879. William Bonney ("Kid") relative to arrangement with him." Indiana Historical Society. Lew Wallace Collection. M0292. Box 4. Folder 6.

## NEWSPAPER INTERVIEWS BY

Wilcox, Lucius "Lute" M. (city editor, owner, J.H. Koogler). "The Kid. Interview with Billy Bonney The Best Known Man in New Mexico." *Las Vegas Gazette*. **December 27, 1880.**

_____. Interview, at train depot. *Las Vegas Gazette*. **December 28, 1880**. (**Has Billy Bonney's "adios" quote**.)

No Author. "Something About the Kid." *Santa Fe Daily New Mexican*. **April 3, 1881**. (**With quotes Billy Bonney's "this is the man" and "two hundred men have been killed ... he did not kill all of them."**)

No Author. "I got a rough deal ..." *Mesilla News*. **April 15, 1881**.

Newman, Simon N. Ed. Interview with "The Kid." *Newman's Semi-Weekly*. **April 15, 1881**.

_____. Departure from Mesilla. *Newman's Semi-Weekly*. **April 15, 1881**.

No Author. "Advise persons never to engage in killing." *Mesilla News*. **April 16, 1881**. (**Billy Bonney's quote**)

## *FEDERAL INDICTMENT OF*

Catron, Thomas Benton. "Case No. 411. The United States vs. Charles Bowdry [Bowdre], Doc Scurlock, Henry Brown, Henry Antrim alias "Kid," John Middleton, Stephen Stevens, John Scroggins, George Coe and Frederick Waite." **June 21, 1878**. Herman B. Weisner Papers, ca. 1957-1992. New Mexico State University Library at Las Cruces. Rio Grande Historical Collections. Accession No. Ms 0249. Box 1. B-Folder 4. Name: Andrew Roberts Indictment.

## *GENERAL LETTERS ABOUT*

Kimbrell, George. "I have the honor to request that you will furnish me a posse ..." Letter to Lieutenant Millard Filmore Goodwin. **February 20, 1879**. Indiana Historical Society. Lew Wallace Collection. Box 4, Folder 3. (**For pursuit of William Bonney and Yginio Salazar**)

Goodwin, Millard Filmore. ""I have the honor to submit the following report regarding my duties performed ..." Letter to Fort Stanton Post Adjutant John Loud. **February 23, 1879**. Indiana Historical Society. Lew Wallace Collection. Box 4. Folder 3. (**Assisting pursuit of William Bonney and Yginio Salazar**)

Dudley, Nathan Augustus Monroe. "I enclose herewith report of 2[nd] Lieut. M.F. Goodwin ..." Letter to Acting Assistant Adjutant General at Headquarters. **February 24, 1879**. Indiana Historical Society. Lew Wallace Collection. M0292. Box 4, Folder 3. (**Documents military pursuit of William Bonney**)

Leonard, Ira. "The air is filled tonight with 'rumors of wars ... Letter to Lew Wallace. **April 20, 1879.** Indiana Historical Society. Lew Wallace Collection. M0292. Box 4. Folder 9. (**About DA Rynerson: "He is bent on going for the Kid"**)

Hoyt, Henry F. "This time it is me who is apologizing for the long delay in answering ..." (Letter to Lew Wallace Jr.) **April 27, 1927.** Indiana Historical Society. Lew Wallace Collection. M0292. Box 14, Folder 11.

—————. "Copy of a bill of sale written by W$^m$ H. Bonney ..." Letter to Lew Wallace Jr. **April 27, 1927.** Indiana Historical Society. Lew Wallace Collection. M0292. Box 14, Folder 11. (**Calls Billy Bonney "a natural leader of men"**)

## SECRET SERVICE REPORTS ABOUT

Wild, Azariah F. "Daily Reports of U. S. Secret Service Agents, Azariah F. Wild." Microfilm T-915. Record Group 87. Rolls 308 (July 1, 1879 - June 30, 1881) National Archives and Records Department. Department of the Treasury. United States Secret Service. Washington, D. C.

## LEW WALLACE WRITINGS TO AND ABOUT

### WALLACE'S LETTERS TO (CHRONOLOGICAL)

Wallace, Lew. "Come to the house of Squire Wilson ..." Letter to W H. Bonney. **March 15, 1879.** Indiana Historical Society. Lew Wallace Collection. M0292. Box 4. Folder 6.

—————. "The escape makes no difference in arrangements ..." Letter to W.H. Bonney. **March 20, 1879.** Indiana Historical Society. Lew Wallace Collection. M0292. Box 4. Folder 6.

### WALLACE'S LETTERS ABOUT (CHRONOLOGICAL)

Wallace, Lew. "I have just ascertained that 'The Kid' is at a place called Las Tablas ..." Letter to Edward Hatch. **March 6, 1879.** Indiana Historical Society. Lew Wallace Collection. Box 9, Folder 10. (**Written on dead John Tunstall's stationery**)

—————. "I beg to submit to you a list of persons whom it is necessary, in my judgment, to arrest ..." Letter to Henry Carroll. **March 11, 1879.** Indiana Historical Society. Lew Wallace Collection. M0292. Box 4. Folder 5. (**Sherman outlaw list with "The Kid" – William Bonney**)

—————. "I enclose a note for Bonney." Letter to John "Squire" Wilson. **March 20, 1879.** Indiana Historical Society. Lew Wallace Collection. M0292. Box 4. Folder 6.

—————. "My time has been so constantly occupied in getting my work into operation ..." Letter to Carl Schurz. **March 21, 1879.** Indiana Historical Society. Lew Wallace Collection. M0292. Box 4. Folder 7. (**Progress report with multiple enclosures; one listing "The Kid -William Bonney in anti-outlaw campaign of "taking the head off the evil."**)

—————. "To day I forwarded a telegram to you, with another to the President ..." Letter to Carl Schurz. **March 31, 1879.** Indiana Historical Society. Lew Wallace Collection. M0292. Box 4. Folder 7. (**Mention of "precious specimen nicknamed 'The Kid' "**)

### REWARD NOTICES FOR

Wallace, Lew. "Be good enough to prepare a draft of proclamation of reward $500 for the capture and delivery of William Bonney, alias the Kid ..." Letter to Territorial Secretary William Ritch. **December 13, 1880.** Herman B. Weisner Papers, ca. 1957-1992. New Mexico State University Library at Las Cruces. Rio Grande Historical Collections. Accession No. Ms 0249. Box W3. Folder 13. Folder Name: "Wallace, Gov. N.M." From Lew Wallace Papers. New Mexico State Records Center. Santa Fe, New Mexico. (**Wallace's first reward for Billy the Kid**)

_____. "Billy the Kid: $500 Reward." *Las Vegas Gazette*. **December 22, 1880**.
_____. "Billy the Kid. $500 Reward." **May 3, 1881**. *Daily New Mexican*. Vol. X, No. 33. Page 1, C 3.

## REWARD POSTERS FOR

Greene, Chas. W. "To the New Mexican Printing and Publishing Company." **May 20, 1881**. Indiana Historical Society. Lew Wallace Collection. M0292. Box 4, Folder 17. (**Printer's bill to Lew Wallace for Reward posters for "Kid"**)

_____. "I enclose a bill ..." Letter to Lew Wallace for "Kid" wanted posters. **June 2, 1881**. Indiana Historical Society. Lew Wallace Collection. M0292. Box 4, Folder 18.

## DEATH WARRANT FOR

Wallace, Lew. "To the Sheriff of Lincoln County, Greeting ..." **April 30, 1881**. Indiana Historical Society. Lew Wallace Collection. M0292. Box 9, Folder 11.

### *CORONER'S JURY REPORT FOR*

Rudulph, Milnor, Pedro Lucero, Jose Silba, Sabal Gutierrez, Lorenso Jaramillo. Coroner's Jury Report for William Bonney alias "Kid." **July 15, 1881**. Original in Spanish. Indiana Historical Society. Lew Wallace Collection. M0292. Box 9. Folder 11. (**Certified photocopy donated by Maurice Garland Fulton in 1951 of Spanish Coroner's Jury Report, July 15, 1881 - matches photo in William Kelleher's** *Violence in Lincoln County*, **Pages 306-307**)

Rudulph, Milnor, Pedro Lucero, Jose Silba, Sabal Gutierrez, Lorenso Jaramillo. Coroner's Jury Report for William Bonney alias "Kid." **July 15, 1881**. English translation. The Mullin Collection, RNM, VI, J - Legal Papers and Documents. Midland, Texas: Nita Stewart Haley Memorial Library and J. Evetts Haley History Center.

Rudulph, Milnor, Pedro Lucero, Jose Silba, Sabal Gutierrez, Lorenso Jaramillo. Coroner's Jury Report for William Bonney alias "Kid." **July 15, 1881**. English translation. William A. Keleher. *Violence in Lincoln County 1869-1881*. Pages 343-344.

Ritch, William G. "In the matter of the application by Patrick F. Garrett for a reward claimed to have been offered May-1881 for the capture of Wm Bonney alias "the Kid." *Executive Record Book Number 2*. July 25, 1867-November 8, 1882. **July 21, 1881**. Pages 533-535. New Mexico Secretary of State Records. Collection 1971-001, Series 1; Records of the Secretary of the Territory. (Accessed from Albuquerque Public Library Microfilm, Territorial Archives of New Mexico, Roll 21.) (**Presentation of Garret's bill for the reward and demonstrating that Acting-Governor Ritch agreed with the reward, and citing the Coroner's Jury Report's identification of William Bonney**)

No Author. *Executive Record Book Number 2*. July 25, 1867-November 8, 1882. **July 21, 1881**. Pages 533-535. New Mexico State Records Center and Archives, Santa Fe. New Mexico Secretary of the State Records Series 1. Records of the Secretary of the Territory. (**About granting Garrett's reward, citing copy of Coroner's Jury Report**)

No Author. "Kid the Killer Killed, Wm. Bonney alias Antrim, alias Billy the Kid, Fatally Meets Pat Garrett, the Lincoln County Sheriff." Las Cruces *Rio Grande Republican*. **July 23, 1881**. Page 2. Volume 1, Number 10. NewspaperArchive.com. (**Copy of Pat Garrett's letter to Acting Governor William Ritch confirming that the original Coroner's Jury Report was sent to District Attorney of the First Judicial District, and copy of it was included in this letter to the Governor**)

King, Frank M. *Wranglin' the Past: Reminiscences of Frank M. King*. "Chapter xix, The Kid's Exit." Pasadena, California: Trail's End Publishing Company. **1935 and**

1946. (Describes recent location of Pat Garrett's report to the Governor about the killing of Billy the Kid, with confirmation of Coroner's Jury Report, Page 171)

Keleher, William A. *Violence in Lincoln County 1869-1881.* Albuquerque, New Mexico: University of New Mexico Press. **1957. (Photocopy of Spanish Coroner's Jury Report, July 15, 1881. Pages 306-308; Kelleher's English translation, Pages 343-344.)**

## *OUTLAW MYTH ARTICLES ABOUT (CHRONOLOGICAL)*
## GENERAL ARTICLES (CHRONOLOGICAL)

No Author. Grant County *Herald.* **May 10, 1879.** Results of the Lincoln County Grand Jury. **(Also published in the Mesilla** *Thirty Four.* **Confirmation of the William Bonney testimony and James Dolan and Billy Campbell murder indictments, from Page 224 of William Kelleher,** *Violence in Lincoln County.***)**

Koogler, John H. Editorial. "Desperadoe's Stronghold, An Organized Gang Assisted by Nature and Defiantly Reckless, Who Terrorize the Country to the East of Us." *Las Vegas Morning Gazette.* **December 3, 1880.** Volume 2, Number 120. https://chroniclingamerica.loc.gov. **(Calling Billy Bonney an outlaw leader; motivating his denial letter of December 12, 1880 to Governor Lew Wallace.)**

No Author. "Outlaws of New Mexico, The Exploits of a Band Headed by a New York Youth, The Mountain Fastness of the Kid and His Followers - War Against a Gang of Cattle Thieves and Murderers - The Frontier Confederates of Brockway, the Counterfeiter." *The Sun.* New York. **December 22, 1880.** Vol. XLVIII, No. 118, Page 3, Columns 1-2.

No Author. "A Big Haul! Billy Kid, Dave Rudabaugh, Billy Wilson and Tom Pickett in the Clutches of the Law." *The Las Vegas Daily Optic.* Monday, **December 27, 1880.** Volume 2, Number. 45. Page 4, Column 2. chroniclingamerica.loc.gov.

No Author. "A Bay-Mare. Everyone who has heard of Billy 'the kid' has heard of his beautiful bay mare." *Las Vegas Morning Gazette.* Tuesday, **January 4, 1881.**

No Author. "The Kid. Billy 'the Kid' and Billy Wilson were on Monday taken to Mesilla for Trial." *Las Vegas Morning Gazette.* Tuesday, **March 15, 1881.**

Newman, Simon. "In the Name of Justice! In the Case of Billy Kid." *Newman's Semi-Weekly.* Saturday, **April 2, 1881.**

No Author. "Billy the Kid. Seems to be having a stormy journey on his trip Southward." *Las Vegas Morning Gazette.* Tuesday, **April 5, 1881.**

No Author. "The Kid." *Santa Fe Daily New Mexican.* **May 1, 1881.** Volume X, Number 32, Page 1, Column 2.

No Author. "Billy Bonney. Advices from Lincoln bring the intelligence of the escape of 'Billy the Kid.'" *Las Vegas Daily Optic.* Monday, **May 2, 1881.**

No Author. "The Kid's Escape." *Santa Fe Daily New Mexican.* Tuesday Morning, **May 3, 1881.** Volume X, Number 33, Page 1, Column 2.

No Author. "The above is the record of as bold a deed ..." *Santa Fe Daily New Mexican.* **May 4, 1881. (About Billy's great escape jailbreak)**

No Author. "Dare Devil Desperado. Pursuit of 'Billy the Kid' has been abandoned." *Las Vegas Daily Optic.* **May 4, 1881.**

No Author. "More Killing by Kid, When But a Short Distance From Lincoln, He Meets one of His Old Enemies, and Kills Him and His Companion. Two More Victims." Editorial. *Santa Fe Daily New Mexican.* **May 4, 1881.** Volume X, No. 34, Page 1, Column 2. Newspaperarchive.com. **(Claims Kid killed Billy Matthews)**

No Author. No headline. "Anything that the imagination can concoct ..." *Santa Fe Daily New Mexican.* **May 5, 1881.** Volume X. Page 4, Column 1. Newspaperarchive.com. **(Claims Kid was in Albuquerque)**

No Author. No headline. Mr. Richard Dunham says ..." *Santa Fe Daily New Mexican*, **May 5, 1881**, Volume X. Page 4, Column 3. Newspaperarchive.com. (**Claims Kid was in Stinking Springs**)

No Author. "Richard Dunham's May 2, 1881 encounter with Billy the Kid.", *Santa Fe Daily New Mexican*, **May 5, 1881**, Page 4, Column 3. (private collection)

No Author. "The question if how to deal with desperados who commit murder has but one solution - kill them." *Las Vegas Daily Optic*. Tuesday, **May 10, 1881**.

No Author. "Billy 'the Kid.' " *Las Vegas Gazette*. Thursday, **May 12, 1881**.

No Author. "The Kid was in Chloride City ..." *Santa Fe Daily New Mexican*. **May 13, 1881**. Page 4, Column 3.

No Author. "Billy 'the Kid' is in the vicinity of Sumner." *Las Vegas Gazette*. Sunday, **May 15, 1881**.

No Author. "The Kid is believed to be in the Black Range ..." *Santa Fe Daily New Mexican*. **May 19, 1881**. Page 4, Column 1.

No Author. "Billy the Kid was last seen in Lincoln County ..." *Santa Fe Daily New Mexican*. **May 19, 1881**. Page 4, Column 1.

No Author. (O.L. Houghton's Conversation with Lew Wallace, before May 26, 1881), *The Las Vegas Daily Optic*, **May 26, 1881**, p.4, c.4. Indiana Historical Society. Lew Wallace Collection. M0292.

No Author. " 'Billy the Kid' has been heard from again." *Las Vegas Daily Optic*. Friday, **June 10, 1881**.

No Author. " 'Billy the Kid,' He is Reported to Have Been Seen on Our Streets Saturday Night." *Las Vegas Daily Optic*. Monday Evening, **June 13, 1881**. Vol. 2, No. 188, Page 4, Column 2.

Wilcox, Lute, Ed. "Billy the Kid would make an ideal newspaper-man in that he always endeavors to 'get even' with his enemies." *Las Vegas Daily Optic*. Monday Evening, **June 13, 1881**. Volume 2, Number 188, Page 4, Column 1.

No Author. "Land of the Petulant Pistol, "Scenes" where Life and Land are Cheap ... 'Billy the Kid' as a Killer." *Las Vegas Daily Optic*. Wednesday Evening, **June 15, 1881**. Front Page. 1, Volume 2, Number 190, Columns 1-2. (Possibly contributed to by Lew Wallace, who published with a similar title in the Crawfordsville *Saturday Evening Journal* on June 18, 1881)

No Author. "Barney Mason at Fort Sumner states the 'Kid' is in Local Sheep Camps." *Las Vegas Morning Gazette*. **June 16, 1881**.

No Author. "The Kid." *Santa Fe Daily New Mexican*. **June 16, 1881**. Volume X, Number 90, Page 4, Column 2.

No Author. "Billy the Kid." *Las Vegas Daily Optic*. Thursday, June 28, 1881.

No Author. " 'The Kid' Killed." *Las Vegas Daily Optic*. July 18. 1881.

No Author. No title. **Thursday, July 28, 1881**. Pueblo, Colorado, *Colorado Chieftain*. www.coloradohistoricnewspapers.org. (**Quoting from the New York *Tribune* on killing of "Tiger in human form known as "Billy the Kid"**)

Gauss, Gottfried. Interview with *Lincoln County Leader*. **November 21, 1889**. (About Billy Bonney's Lincoln jailbreak)

## LEW WALLACE'S ARTICLES

Koogler, John H. "Interview with Governor Lew Wallace on 'The Kid.'" *Las Vegas Gazette*. **April 28, 1881**.

No Author. "The Thug's Territory. Stage Robbers and Cut-Throats Have Things Their Own Way in New Mexico. Gen. Lew Wallace Anxious to Punish the Crime That is So Prevalent – A Chapter About 'Billy the Kid' – The Governor has a Narrow Escape From Being Spanked." *St. Louis Daily Globe-Democrat*. Monday Morning, **May 16, 1881**. Page 2, Columns 5 and 6. (private collection)

No Author. (Lew Wallace interview) "Billy the Kid. General Wallace Tells Why the Young Desperado of New Mexico Wanted to Kill Him, A Dashing and Daring Career in the Land of the Petulant Pistol." (Lew Wallace interviewed on June 13,

1881), Crawfordsville *Saturday Evening Journal,* **June 18, 1881**. Indiana Historical Society. The Papers of Lew and Susan Wallace. Microfilm Edition. Indianapolis, Indiana: Indiana Historical Society Press. 2008.

No Author. (Lew Wallace interview) "Lew Wallace's Foe. Threatened by 'Billy the Kid.' The Writing of 'Ben Hur' Interrupted. An Incident of the Soldier-Author's Career in New Mexico. *San Francisco Chronicle.* December 10, 1893. Indiana Historical Society. Lew Wallace Collection. M0292. Box 14. Folder 11. (Lew Wallace creating outlaw myth of outlaw Billy the Kid")

No Author. "Street Pickings," Weekly *Crawfordsville Review - Saturday Edition,* **January 6, 1894.** Indiana Historical Society. The Papers of Lew and Susan Wallace. Microfilm Edition. Series I. Reel 27. Indianapolis, Indiana: Indiana Historical Society Press. 2008.

No Author. "An Old Incident Recalled." Crawfordsville *Weekly News-Review.* **December 20, 1901.** Indiana Historical Society. The Papers of Lew and Susan Wallace. Microfilm Edition. Series I. Reel 27. Indianapolis, Indiana: Indiana Historical Society Press. 2008.

Lewis, E.I. "Gen. Wallace's Feud with Billy the Kid, When the General Was Governor of New Mexico and Billy Bonne Was the Most Dangerous Western Outlaw. He Was a Waif and Was Reared in Indiana. *The Indianapolis Press.* Saturday, **June 23, 1900.** Page 7. Lew Wallace Collection. Indiana Historical Society. M0292. Box 14. Folder 11. (photocopy) (Original article is in OMB 23, Box 1. Folder 5) **(Creating self-serving myth of outlaw Billy the Kid")**

Wallace, Lew. "General Lew Wallace Writes a Romance of 'Billy the Kid' Most Famous Bandit of the Plains: Thrilling Story of the Midnight Meeting Between Gen Wallace, Then Governor of New Mexico, and the Notorious Outlaw, in a Lonesome Hut in Santa Fe." *New York World Magazine.* Sunday, **June 8, 1902.** Lew Wallace Collection. Indiana Historical Society. M0292. . Box 14. Folder 11.

# OTHER HISTORICAL FIGURES (PERIOD)

## ANGEL, FRANK WARNER

### *PRESIDENT HAYES MEETING BY*

Mullin, Robert N. Re: Frank Warner Angel Meeting With President Hayes August, 1878. Binder RNM, VI, M. (Unpublished). Midland, Texas: Nita Stewart Haley Memorial Library and J. Evetts Haley History Center. (Undated).

### *LETTERS BY*

Angel, Frank Warner. "I am in receipt of your favor of the 12th ..." Letter to Samuel Beach Axtell. **August 13, 1878.** Interior Department Papers 1850-1907; Appointments Division and Subsequent Actions. Microfilm Roll M750. National Archives and Records Administration Record Group 48. Microfilm Case Number 44-4-8-3. U.S. Department of Interior. Washington D.C.

_____. "I enclose copies of letters received by me from Gov Axtell ..." Letter to Secretary of the Interior Carl Schurz. **August 24, 1878.** (Enclosing copy of letter to him from Governor S.B. Axtell of August 12, 1878; and Angel's response to Axtell of August 13, 1878.) Microfilm File Case Number 44-4-8-3. Record Group 48. Microfilm No. M750. Roll 1. National Archives and Records Administration. U.S. Department of Justice. Washington, D.C.

_____. "I have just been favored by a call from W.L. Rynerson ..." Letter to Secretary of Interior Carl Schurz. **September 6, 1878.** Microfilm File Case Number 44-4-8-3. Record Group 48. Microfilm No. M750. Roll 1. National Archives and Records Administration. U.S. Department of Justice. Washington, D.C.

## REPORTS BY

Angel, Frank Warner. *Examination of charges against F. C. Godfroy, Indian Agent, Mescalero, N. M.* **October 2, 1878.** (Report 1981, Inspector E.C. Watkins; Cited as Watkins Report). M319-20 and L147, 44-4-8. Record Group 075. National Archives and Records Administration. U.S. Department of Justice. Washington, D. C.

_____. *In the Matter of the Investigation of the Charges Against S.B. Axtell Governor of New Mexico. Report and Testimony.* **October 3, 1878.** Angel Report. Interior Department Papers 1850-1907; Appointments Division and Subsequent Actions. Microfilm Case File No. 44-4-8-3. Record Group 48. Microfilm Roll M750. National Archives and Records Administration. U.S. Department of Interior. Washington, D.C. (**Mentions Santa Fe Ring**)

_____. *In the Matter of the Examination of the Causes and Circumstances of the Death of John H. Tunstall a British Subject.* Report filed **October 4, 1878.** Angel Report. Interior Department Papers 1850-1907; Appointments Division and Subsequent Actions. Microfilm File Case Number 44-4-8-3. Record Group 48. Microfilm No. M750. Roll 1. National Archives and Records Administration. U.S. Department of Justice. Washington, D.C.

_____. *In the Matter of the Lincoln County Troubles. To the Honorable Charles Devens, Attorney General.* **October 4, 1878.** Angel Report. Microfilm Case File No. 44-4-8-3. Record Group 48. Microfilm Roll M750. National Archives and Records Administration. U.S. Department of Justice. Washington, D.C.

## NOTEBOOK ON SANTA FE RING MEMBERS BY

Angel, Frank Warner. "To Gov. Lew Wallace / Santa Fe, N. M., 1878." Notebook. **1878.** Indiana Historical Society. Lew Wallace Collection. M0292. Microfilm No. F372. (**Original missing, copy on microfilm; Notebook prepared for Lew Wallace listing names of Santa Fe Ring members**)

Theisen, Lee Scott. "Frank Warner Angel's Notes on New Mexico Territory, 1878." *Arizona and the West: A Quarterly Journal of History.* Winter 1976. Volume 18. Number 4. Pages 333-370. (**About the Angel notebook**)

## AXTELL, SAMUEL BEACH

### CONTEMPORARY SOURCES (CHRONOLOGICAL)

No author. "Anarchy at Cimarron." *Santa Fe Weekly New Mexico.* **November 16, 1875.** (**Ring-biased article justifying Governor S.B. Axtell calling in troops in the Colfax County War after murder of Reverend Franklin Tolby**)

Axtell, Samuel B. "The Legislature to Assess Property. *Message of Gov. Samuel B. Axtell to the Legislative Assembly of New Mexico, Twenty-second Session.* Page 4. Manderfield & Tucker, Public Printers: Santa Fe, New Mexico. **1875 or 1876.** Interior Department Papers 1850-1907; Appointments Division and Subsequent Actions. Microfilm File Case Number 44-4-8-3. Record Group 48. Microfilm No. M750. Roll 1. National Archives and Records Administration. U.S. Department of Justice. Washington, D.C.

Elkins, Stephen B. "I trouble you to say a word in behalf of Gov. Axtell ..." Letter to President Rutherford B. Hayes. **June 11, 1877.** Interior Department Papers 1850-1907; Appointments Division and Subsequent Actions. Microfilm Roll M750. National Archives and Records Administration Record Group 48. Microfilm Case Number 44-4-8-3. U. S. Department of Interior. Washington D. C. (**Trying to prevent Axtell's removal as governor**)

Axtell, Samuel B. "I have today mailed to you a reply to the charges on file in your Dept against me." Letter to Secretary of the Interior Carl Schurz. **June 15, 1877.** Interior Department Papers 1850-1907; Appointments Division and Subsequent

Actions. Microfilm Roll M750. National Archives and Records Administration Record Group 48. Microfilm Case Number 44-4-8-3 U.S. Department of Interior. Washington D.C. (**Refuting charges made in Colfax County**).

Isaacs, I. and G.N. Coe. "Charges Against S.B. Axtell, Governor of New Mexico." **June 22, 1878**. Interior Department Papers 1850-1907; Appointments Division and Subsequent Actions. Microfilm File Case Number 44-4-8-3. Microfilm No. M750. Roll 1. National Archives and Records Administration. Record Group 48. U.S. Department of Justice. Washington, D.C.

Routt, John C. "I am here on a visit to my daughter and have more by accident than otherwise heard statements ..." Letter to President Rutherford B. Hayes. **August 29, 1878**. Interior Department Papers 1850-1907; Appointments Division and Subsequent Actions. Microfilm File Case Number 44-4-8-3. Microfilm No. M750. Roll 1. National Archives and Records Administration. U.S. Department of Justice. Washington, D.C. (**Ringite letter opposing removal of Governor Axtell and U.S. Attorney Catron.**)

Schurz, Carl. "I transmit herewith an order from the President ..." **September 4, 1878**. Letter to Lew Wallace. Indiana Historical Society. Lew Wallace Collection. M0292. Box 3. Folder 14. (**Suspension of Governor S.B. Axtell and Wallace's appointment as new Governor**)

Elkins, Stephen Benton. "To the President. Referring to a conversation had with you last week ..." Letter to President James Abram Garfield. **March 17, 1881**. (Received Executive Mansion April 6, 1881). Interior Department Papers 1850-1907; Appointments Division and Subsequent Actions. Microfilm Roll M750. National Archives and Records Administration Microfilm Roll M750. National Archives and Records Administration Record Group 48. Microfilm Case Number 44-4-8-3. U.S. Department of Interior. Washington D.C. Microfilm Case Number 44-4-8-3. U.S. Department of Interior. Washington D.C. (**Request for re-appointment of Axtell as Territorial New Mexico Governor**)

Bradstreet, George P. "Referring to the nomination of Sam'l B. Axtell of Ohio to be Chief Justice of the Supreme Court of New Mexico ... he is alleged to have been removed by President Hayes ..." Letter to Judiciary Committee of the U.S. Senate. **June 22, 1882**. Interior Department Papers 1850-1907; Appointments Division and Subsequent Actions. Microfilm Roll M750. National Archives and Records Administration Microfilm Roll M750. National Archives and Records Administration Record Group 48. Microfilm Case Number 44-4-8-3. U.S. Department of Interior. Washington D.C.

No Author. " 'Chief Justice Axtell' is a bitter pill for the Raton *News and Press*." *Santa Fe New Mexican*. **July 18, 1882**. (**Santa Fe Ring instatement of S.B. Axtell as Chief Justice**)

## BACA, SATURNINO

### *BIOGRAPHICAL SOURCES*

Charles, Tom. (Edited by Mrs. Tom Charles) "The Father of Lincoln County." *More Tales of Tularosa*. 1961. (unpublished manuscript)

Jonathan (no last name given). "About Saturnino Baca." July 23, 2001. http://www.genealogy.com/forum/surnames/topics/baca/509/

Nolan, Frederick. "New and Updated Biographies." *The Lincoln County War: A Documentary History. Revised Edition*. .Santa Fe: Sunstone Press. 2009.

### *LETTERS FROM AND ABOUT (CHRONOLOGICAL)*

Baca, Saturnino. "When I sent in my bid for the hay contract ..." Letter to Quartermaster Captain A.J. McGonigle. **July 19, 1871**. University of New Mexico Library. Center for Southwest Studies. Thomas B. Catron Papers, MSS 29, Series 803, Box 1, Folder 25. (**About hay contract to Fort Stanton**)

Kantz, August V. "I learn from Col. Fritz that you are under the impression ..." Letter to Quartermaster Captain A.J. McGonigle. **July 20, 1871.** University of New Mexico Library. Center for Southwest Studies. Thomas B. Catron Papers, MSS 29, Series 803, Box 1, Folder 25. **(Emil Fritz pressures Fort Stanton to take bottom hay - which would make contract for Baca fillable - and Kantz warns that Fritz and Murphy will get hay monopoly)**

Carey, A.B. "Letter of Saturnino Baca, dated Fort Stanton ..." Letter to Quartermaster Captain A.J. McGonigle. **July 20, 1871.** University of New Mexico Library. Center for Southwest Studies. Thomas B. Catron Papers, MSS 29, Series 803, Box 1, Folder 25. **(Baca declines his contract to supply grama hay)**

McGonigle, A.J.M. "I have the honor to forward enclosed herewith ..." Letter to Quartermaster General M.C. Meigs. **September 24, 1871.** University of New Mexico Library. Center for Southwest Studies. Thomas B. Catron Papers, MSS 29, Series 803, Box 1, Folder 25. **(Wants Baca barred from hay contracts)**

## BONNEY, WILLIAM HENRY
(See History of William Henry Bonney)

## BOWDRE, CHARLES

### *CONTEMPORARY SOURCES (CHRONOLOGICAL)*

Wallace, Lew. "Please select ten of your Rangers ..." Letter to Juan Patrón. **March 3, 1879.** Indiana Historical Society. Lew Wallace Collection. M0292. Box 4. Folder 4. **(To arrest "Scurlock and Bowdre")**

_____. Lew. "I have reliable information that J.G. Scurlock and Charles Bowdre are now at a ranch called Taiban ..." Letter to Edward Hatch. **March 6, 1879.** Indiana Historical Society. Lew Wallace Collection. Box 4, Folder 4.

## BRADY, WILLIAM

### *BIOGRAPHICAL SOURCE*

Lavash, Donald R. *Sheriff William Brady. Tragic Hero of the Lincoln County War.* Santa Fe, New Mexico: Sunstone Press. 1986.

### *CONTEMPORARY SOURCES (CHRONOLOGICAL)*

Brady, William. Affidavit of **July 2, 1876** concerning appointment as Administrator for the Emil Fritz Estate. Copied from the original District Court Record. (private collection)

_____. Affidavit of **August 22, 1876** documenting business debts to L. G. Murphy and Co. pertaining to the Emil Fritz Estate. Copied from the original District Court Record. (private collection)

_____. Affidavit of **July \_, 1876** of Resignation as Emil Fritz Estate Administrator. Copied from the original District Court Record. (private collection.)

_____. Affidavit of **August 22, 1876** confirming giving Alexander McSween the books of the L.G. Murphy Company for the purpose of making business debt collections. Copied from the original District Court Record. (private collection)

Tunstall, John Henry. "A Taxpayer's Complaint ... January 18, 1878." Mesilla *Independent.* **January 26, 1878.** **(Exposé of William Brady embezzling tax money to buy cattle for "The House;" and Catron then paid that bill)**

Dolan, James J. "Answer to A Taxpayer's Complaint." Mesilla *Independent.* **January 29, 1878. (Response to J.H. Tunstall's exposé)**

Bristol, Warren. "Action of Assumpsit to command Sheriff Brady of Lincoln County to attach goods of Alexander A. McSween." **February 7, 1878.** District Court Record. (private collection).

_____. Preprinted form for "Writ of Attachment" (Printed and sold at the office of the Mesilla News) filled out to command the Sheriff of Lincoln County to attach goods of Alexander McSween for a suit of damages for ten thousand dollars. **February 7, 1878.** District Court Record. (private collection).

Brady, William. "List of Articles Inventoried by Wm Brady sheriff in the suit of Charles Fritz & Emilie Scholand vs A.A. McSween now in the dwelling house belonging to A.A. McSween." (undated, but in **February of 1878**) (private collection)

## BRISTOL, WARREN HENRY
### *CONTEMPORARY SOURCES (CHRONOLOGICAL)*

Bristol Warren. "From sources of information that I deem perfectly reliable I am satisfied that there are public disorders in Lincoln County …" Letter to Governor Marsh Giddings. **January 10, 1874.** Herman B. Weisner Papers, ca. 1957-1992. New Mexico State University Library at Las Cruces. Rio Grande Historical Collections. Accession No. Weisner Ms 0249. Box 4/39. Folder D-4. Folder Name: "Judge Bristol's letter." (**Creating Ring's outlaw myth and proposing military intervention**)

_____. "Writ of Embezzlement." **December 21, 1877.** Herman B. Weisner Papers, ca. 1957-1992. New Mexico State University Library at Las Cruces. Rio Grande Historical Collections. Accession No. Ms 0249. Box 10. Folder M-13. Folder Name. "Will and Testament A. McSween." (**Emilie Fritz Scholand's sworn complaint against Alexander McSween**)

_____. "Action of Assumpsit to command Sheriff Brady of Lincoln County to attach goods of Alexander A. McSween." **February 7, 1878.** District Court Record. (private collection).

_____. Preprinted form for "Writ of Attachment" (Printed and sold at the office of the Mesilla News) filled out to command the Sheriff of Lincoln County to attach goods of Alexander McSween for a suit of damages for ten thousand dollars. **February 7, 1878.** District Court Record. (private collection).

_____. "My reasons for not holding October term of Court …" Telegram to U.S. Marshal John Sherman. **October 4, 1878.** Indiana Historical Society. Lew Wallace Collection. M0292. Box 3. Folder 15.

_____. *Instructions to the Jury.* District Court 3rd Judicial. District Doña Ana. Filed **April 9, 1881.** Writ of Embezzlement. New Mexico State University Library at Las Cruces. Rio Grande Historical Collection. Accession No. Ms 0249. Box 1. Folder 14C. Folder Name: "Billy the Kid Legal Documents."

## CATRON, THOMAS BENTON
### *BIBLIOGRAPHICAL SOURCES*

Cleaveland, Norman, *A Synopsis of the Great New Mexico Cover-up.* Self-printed. 1989.

_____. *The Great Santa Fe Cover-up. Based on a Talk given Before the Santa Fe Historical Society on November 1, 1978.* Self-printed. 1982.

_____. *The Morleys - Young Upstarts on the Southwest Frontier.* Albuquerque, New Mexico: Calvin Horn Publisher, Inc. 1971. (**Page 93 gives Catron's vindictive indictment of Cleaveland's grandmother, Ada Morley, for mail theft as revenge denying him use of a Maxwell Land Grant buggy.**

Dodge, Andrew R., and Betty K. Koed, eds. *Biographical Directory of the United States Congress 1774-2005.* Washington, D.C.: United States Government Printing Office. 2005

Dunham, Harold H. "New Mexican Land Grants with Special Reference to the Title Papers of the Maxwell Grant." *New Mexico Historical Review.* (January, 1955) Vol. 70. No. 1. pp. 1 - 23.

Hefferan, Vioalle Clark. *Thomas Benton Catron.* Albuquerque, New Mexico: University of New Mexico. Zimmerman Library. Unpublished Thesis for the Degree of Master of Arts. 1940. .(**In praise of Catron; includes railroad involvement, Page 35; First National Bank stockholder from 1871 to 1907, Page 28**)

Keleher, William A. *The Maxwell Land Grant. A New Mexico Item.* Albuquerque, New Mexico: University of New Mexico Press. 1964.

Klasner, Lilly. Eve Ball. Ed. *My Girlhood Among Outlaws.* Tucson, Arizona: The University of Arizona Press. 1972.

Lamar, Howard Robert N. *The Far Southwest 1846 - 1912: A Territorial History.* New Haven and London: Yale University Press. 1966. (**Chapter 6 covers the Santa Fe Ring**))

Montoya, María E. *Translating Property. The Maxwell Land Grant and the Conflict Over Land in the American West, 1840-1900.* Berkeley and Los Angeles: University of California Press. 2002.

Mullin, Robert N. "A Specimen of Catron's Dirty Work. Sworn Affidavit of Samuel Davis." October 1, 1878. Binder RNM IV, EE. (Unpublished). Midland, Texas: Nita Stewart Haley Memorial Library and J. Evetts Haley Historical Center.

_____. "Catron Embarrassed Throughout His Life by an Affliction." (Date Unknown). Binder RNM, IV, M. (Unpublished). Midland, Texas: Nita Stewart Haley Memorial Library and J. Evetts Haley Historical Center. Robert Mullin Papers. Binder RNM IV, EE (Unpublished).

_____. "Prior to Lincoln County War Catron Had Defended Colonel Dudley." (No Date). Notes from "Lincoln County War Cast of Characters." Midland, Texas: Nita Stewart Haley Memorial Library and J. Evetts Haley Historical Center.

Murphy, Lawrence R. *Lucien Bonaparte Maxwell. Napoleon of the Southwest.* Norman: University of Oklahoma Press. 1983.

Otero, Miguel A. *My Life on the Frontier, 1882-1897: Incidents and Characters of the period when Kansas, Colorado, and New Mexico were passing through the last of their Wild and Romantic Years.* New York: The Press of the Pioneers. 1935. Pages 232-233. (Quoted by Victor Westphall, *Thomas Benton Catron and His Era.* Page 188) (**Quote: "the 'Santa Fe Ring,' the real machine controlling the political situation in New Mexico."**)

Pearson, Jim Berry. *The Maxwell Land Grant.* Norman: University of Oklahoma Press. 1961.

Sluga, Mary Elizabeth. *Political Life of Thomas Benton Catron 1896-1912.* Albuquerque, New Mexico: University of New Mexico. Zimmerman Library. Unpublished Thesis for the Degree of Master of Arts. 1941. (**Thesis in praise of Catron for an M.A.**)

Taylor, Morris F. *O.P. McMains and the Maxwell Land Grant Conflict.* Tucson, Arizona: The University of Arizona Press. 1979. (**Traces origins of the Santa Fe Ring with T.B. Catron and S.B. Elkins**)

Westphall, Victor. *Thomas Benton Catron and His Era.* Tucson, Arizona: University of Arizona Press. 1973.

_____. "Fraud and Implications of Fraud in the Land Grants of New Mexico." *New Mexico Historical Review.* 1974. Vol. XLIX, No. 3. 189 - 218.

Wooden, John Paul. *Thomas Benton Catron and New Mexico Politics 1866-1921.* Albuquerque, New Mexico: University of New Mexico. Zimmerman Library. Unpublished Thesis for the Degree of Master of Arts. 1959. (**M.A. thesis praising Catron**)

## *GENERAL CONTEMPORARY EXPOSÉS OF(CHRONOLOGICAL)*

Middaugh, Asa F. Deposition. **March 31, 1876.** "Exhibit B" in the August 9, 1878 deposition of Frank Springer to Investigator Frank Warner Angel. Frank Warner Angel report titled *In the Matter of the Investigation of the Charges Against S.B. Axtell Governor of New Mexico.* October 3, 1878. Interior Department Papers

1850-1907; Appointments Division and Subsequent Actions. Microfilm Case File No. 44-4-8-3. Record Group 48. Microfilm Roll M750. National Archives and Records Administration. U.S. Department of Interior. Washington, D.C. (**About Catron's malicious prosecution of Ada McPherson Morley**)

Springer, Frank. Deposition to Investigator Frank Warner Angel. **August 9, 1878.** Frank Warner Angel report titled *In the Matter of the Investigation of the Charges Against S.B. Axtell Governor of New Mexico.* October 3, 1878. Interior Department Papers 1850-1907; Appointments Division and Subsequent Actions. Microfilm Case File No. 44-4-8-3. Record Group 48. Microfilm Roll M750. National Archives and Records Administration. U.S. Department of Interior. Washington, D.C. (**Mentions Catron, Elkins, and the Santa Fe Ring, and provided Exhibits of letters exposing Catron's evil.**)

No Author. "The Santa Fe Ring is the most corrupt combination that ever cursed any country or community." Las Cruces *Thirty-Four Newspaper.* **October 27, 1880.** From Victor Westphall, *Thomas Benton Catron and His Era.* Page 186. (**Article summarizing Ring abuses in urging voters to oppose Ring candidates**)

No Author. "The Ring must soon discover that the time has passed in New Mexico when men can be herded like so many sheep ..." *Albuquerque Daily Democrat.* **March 4, 1884.** Quoted by Victor Westphall, *Thomas Benton Catron and His Era.* Page 191. (**About Santa Fe Ring control of appointments to legislature**)

Valdez, Jose and Enrique Mares. "Scorching Letter, The Knights of Labor Send a Communication to Powderly! Politicians Arraigned! The Boldest Document Ever Issued in the Territory." **August 18, 1890.** *Las Vegas Democrat.* Volume 1. Center for Southwest Studies. Thomas B. Catron Papers, MSS 29, Series 102, Box 8, Folder 4. (**Gives history of Santa Fe Ring with T.B. Catron as head**)

No Author. "Catron and the Laboring Men." Unknown newspaper. **1892?** University of New Mexico Library. Center for Southwest Studies. Thomas B. Catron Papers, MSS 29, Series 401, Box 1, Folder 3. (**Opposition to Catron as Delegate to Congress as "the biggest corporation man in New Mexico"**)

Victory, John P. "No Consistent Democrat Should Vote for T.B. Catron, John P. Victory in Forcible and Cogent Language Gives Answerable Reasons." **No month, 1895.** Printed broadside. University of New Mexico Library. Center for Southwest Studies. Thomas B. Catron Papers, MSS 29, Series 409, Box 1, Folder 3.

Wallace, Lew. "I have your several letters, including the last one of the 3rd inst." Letter to Eugene Fiske. **November 6, 1897.** Indiana Historical Society. Lew Wallace Collection. AC233. Box 1. Folder 7. (part of 1981 addition) (**About Catron's control over New Mexicans**)

Cutting, Bronson. "Catron was the boss of the Territory ..." Letter to James Roger Addison. **December 11, 1911.** Cited by Victor Westphall in *Thomas Benton Catron and His Era* from his citation: Lincoln County Manuscripts Division. Box 12. Courtesy of David Stratton. (**Catron as head of the Santa Fe Ring**)

Johnson, E. Dana. "[H]e ruled with a rod of iron ..." Editorial. *Santa Fe New Mexican.* **May 16, 1921.** Catron Papers 801, Box 1. Quoted by Victor Westphall, *Thomas Benton Catron and His Era.* Pages 394-395. (**Tactics of "boss" Catron without using the words Santa Fe Ring**)

(SEE: Santa Fe Ring; Frank Warner Angel)

## *FEDERAL INDICTMENT OF REGULATORS BY*

Catron, Thomas Benton. "Case No. 411. The United States vs. Charles Bowdry [Bowdre], Doc Scurlock, Henry Brown, Henry Antrim alias "Kid," John Middleton, Stephen Stevens, John Scroggins, George Coe and Frederick Waite." **June 21, 1878.** Herman B. Weisner Papers, ca. 1957-1992. New Mexico State University Library at Las Cruces. Rio Grande Historical Collections. Accession No. Ms 0249. Box 1. Folder B-4. Folder Name: Andrew Roberts Indictment.

## RESIGNATION AS TERRITORIAL U.S. ATTORNEY BY

Elkins, Stephen Benton. "Elkins – Telegraph Cipher, Cipher with Catron." Sent to T.B. Catron. ___ 1878? University of New Mexico Library. Center for Southwest Studies. Thomas B. Catron Papers, MSS 29, Series 108, Box 1, Folder 4. (**Ring code-cipher key about T.B. Catron's resignation as U.S. Attorney**)

_____. "Asking delay of action upon charges against U.S. Atty. Catron ..." **September 24, 1878**. Angel Report. Microfilm File Case No. 44-4-8-3. Record Group 48. National Records and Archives Administration. Microfilm No. M750. Roll 1. U.S. Department of Justice. Washington, D. C.

_____. "Regarding Attorney General's decision on T.B. Catron." Letter. **September___, 1878**. Angel Report. Microfilm File Case No. 44-4-8-3. Record Group 48. National Records and Archives Administration. Microfilm No. M750. Roll 1. U.S. Department of Justice. Washington, D.C.

Catron, Thomas Benton. "In accordance with a purpose long entertained ...." Letter to Charles Devens. **October 10, 1878**. Angel Report. Microfilm File Case No. 44-4-8-3. Record Group 48. National Records and Archives Administration. Microfilm No. M750. Roll 1. U.S. Department of Justice. Washington, D.C. (**Resignation as U.S. Attorney**)

Devens, Charles. "Your resignation of the office of United States Attorney ..." Letter to T.B. Catron. **October 19, 1878**. Angel Report. Microfilm File Case No. 44-4-8-3. Record Group 48. National Records and Archives Administration. Microfilm No. M750. Roll 1. U.S. Department of Justice. Washington, D. C.

Catron, Thomas Benton. "Please change my resignation ...." **November 4, 1878**. Telegram to Charles Devens. Angel Report. Microfilm File Case No. 44-4-8-3. Record Group 48. National Records and Archives Administration. Microfilm No. M750. Roll 1. U.S. Department of Justice. Washington, D. C. (**Resignation as U.S. Attorney**)

Devens, Charles. "Your resignation of the office of United States Attorney ..." Letter to T.B. Catron. **November 12, 1878**. Angel Report. Microfilm File Case No. 44-4-8-3. Record Group 48. National Records and Archives Administration. Microfilm No. M750. Roll 1. U.S. Department of Justice. Washington, D.C.

Elkins, Stephen Benton. "Relative to resignation of T. B. Catron U. S. Attorney." Letter to Charles Devens. **November 10, 1878**. Angel Report. Microfilm File Case No. 44-4-8-3. Record Group 48. National Records and Archives Administration. Microfilm No. M750. Roll 1. U.S. Department of Justice. Washington, D.C.

Devens, Charles. "To honorable S. B. Elkins re. T. B. Catron continuing to act as U.S. Attorney ..." Letter to Stephen B. Elkins. **November 12, 1878**. Angel Report. Microfilm File Case No. 44-4-8-3. Record Group 48. National Records and Archives Administration. Microfilm No. M750. Roll 1. U.S. Department of Justice. Washington, D.C.

Barnes, Sidney M.. "I Sidney M. Barnes do solemnly swear ..." Swearing in as U.S. Attorney. **January 20, 1879**. Angel Report. Microfilm File Case No. 44-4-8-3. Record Group 48. National Records and Archives Administration. Microfilm No. M750. Roll 1. U.S. Department of Justice. Washington, D.C. (**Catron replaced by Ringite attorney Sidney Barnes**)

Elkins, Stephen Benton. "I have waited some time to reply to your lengthy letter ..." Letter to T.B. Catron. **August 15, 1879**. West Virginia & Regional History Center. West Virginia University Libraries, Morgantown, W. Va. Stephen B. Elkins Papers (A&M 53). Box 1. Folder 1. (**Reveals he prevented Catron's dismissal and indictment from Angel's report**)

Clancy, Frank W. "From something I have heard ..." Letter to T.B. Catron. **September 20, 1892**. University of New Mexico Library. Center for Southwest Studies. Thomas B. Catron Papers, MSS 29, Series 102, Box 16, Folder 2. (**Warning Catron that opponents are seeking the Angel Report to use against his campaign for Delegate, but Elkins is making obstacles**)

———. "I am much surprised at what you say in your letter ..." Letter to T.B. Catron. **December 2, 1896.** University of New Mexico Library. Center for Southwest Studies. Thomas B. Catron Papers, MSS 29, Series 106, Box 1, Folder 6. **(Surprise that Catron now wants to be U.S. Attorney again)**

## *PECOS RIVER COW CAMP OF (CHRONOLOGICAL)*

Riley, John H. Letter to N.A.M. Dudley. **May 19, 1878.** **(Fabricated Regulator theft of Catron's cattle from the Dolan Pecos Cow Camp)** Cited by Victor Westphall, Page 87.

Catron, Thomas Benton. Catron letter to Governor S. B. Axtell to intervene in Lincoln County. **May 30, 1878.** Midland, Texas: Nita Stewart Haley Memorial Library and J. Evetts Haley Historical Center. Robert Mullin Papers. Binder RNM IV, EE (Unpublished). **(Fabricated attack of Regulators on his cow camp workers)** Cited by Victor Westphall, Page 89-90.

## *OWNERSHIP FILING ON CARRIZOZO CATTLE COMPANY BY*

Catron, Thomas Benton.. Statement of Sole ownership of Carrizozo Ranch in Tax Dispute Case. No date. Herman B. Weisner Papers, ca. 1957-1992. New Mexico State University Library at Las Cruces. Rio Grande Historical Collections. Accession No. Ms 0249. Box. 2. Folder C-8. Folder Name "T.B. Catron Tax Troubles." **(One of Catron's Lincoln County holdings)**

## CHAPMAN, HUSTON INGRAM

## *CONTEMPORARY SOURCES (CHRONOLOGICAL)*

Wallace, Lew. "I enclose you a copy of a letter from Las Vegas ..." Letter to Edward Hatch. **October 28, 1878.** Indiana Historical Society. Lew Wallace Collection. M0292. Box 3. Folder 16. **(Forwards Chapman's letter to Hatch)**

———. "In a communication, dated October 28. inst., I requested, for reasons stated, a safe-guard for Mrs. McSween ..." Letter to Edward Hatch. **November 9, 1878.** Indiana Historical Society. Lew Wallace Collection. M0292. Box 3. Folder 17.

No Author. (signed E.). "Death of Chapman." *Las Vegas Gazette.* **March 1, 1879.** From *Proceedings of a Court of Inquiry in the Case of Lt. Col. N.A.M. Dudley (May 2,1879 – July 5, 1879).* File No. QQ1284. (Boxes 3304, 3305, 3305A); Court Martial Files 1809-1894. Records of the Office of the Judge Advocate General – Army. Record Group 153. Old Military and Civil Branch. National Archives and Records Administration. Washington, D. C.

No Author. "Wallace and Lincoln County." Grant County *Herald.* **March 1, 1879.** Indiana Historical Society. The Papers of Lew and Susan Wallace. Microfilm Edition. Indianapolis, Indiana: Indiana Historical Society Press. 2008. **(Ridicule about Huston Chapman's murder)**

Chapman, W.W. "Yours of the 1st inst. came ..." Letter to Ira E. Leonard. **March 20, 1879.** Indiana Historical Society. Lew Wallace Collection. M0292. Box 4. Folder 6.

Rynerson, William. "The Grand Jurors for the Territory of New Mexico taken from the body of the good and lawful men of the County of Lincoln ..." Indictments of the April, Lincoln County Grand Jury. **April 28, 1879.** Herman B. Weisner Papers, ca. 1957-1992. New Mexico State University Library at Las Cruces. Rio Grande Historical Collection. Accession No. Ms 0249. Box 4/39. Folder E-Z. Folder Name: "Jessie Evans Accessory to Murder." **(Billy's testimony indicts J.J. Dolan, Billy Campbell, and Jessie Evans fulfilling his pardon bargain)**

Chapman, W.W. "Since receiving yours of the 1st March ..." Letter to Ira Leonard. **May 8, 1879.** Indiana Historical Society. Lew Wallace Collection. M0292. Box 4. Folder 10.

## LETTERS BY

Chapman, Huston I. "You will please pardon me for presuming so much upon your kindness ..." Letter to Lew Wallace. **October 24, 1878.** Indiana Historical Society. Lew Wallace Collection. M0292. Box 3. Folder 16. (**Makes clear N.A.M. Dudley's danger to Susan McSween**)

_____. 'You attach much importance to the awe-inspiring influence of the military ..." Letter to Lew Wallace. **November 25, 1878.** From Frederick Nolan, *The Lincoln County War*, p. 359.

_____. "You must pardon me for so often presuming upon your kindness ..." Letter to Lew Wallace. **November 29, 1878.** Indiana Historical Society. Lew Wallace Collection. M0292. Box 3. Folder 18.

## CHISUM, JOHN SIMPSON

Hinton, Harwood P., Jr. "John Simpson Chisum, 1877-84." *New Mexico Historical Review* 31(3) (July 1956): 177 - 205; 31(4) (October 1956): 310 - 337; 32(1) (January 1957): 53 - 65.

Klasner, Lilly. Eve Ball. Ed. *My Girlhood Among Outlaws*. Tucson, Arizona: The University of Arizona Press. 1972. (**Contains John Chisum's in jail write-up about Santa Fe Ring injustices to himself**)

## COE FAMILY

### BIOGRAPHICAL SOURCES

Coe, George. Doyce B. Nunis, Jr. Ed. *Frontier Fighter. The Autobiography of George Coe Who Fought and Rode With Billy the Kid*. Chicago: R. R. Donnelley and Sons Company. 1984.

Coe, Wilbur. *Ranch on the Ruidoso. The Story of a Pioneer Family in New Mexico, 1871 - 1968*. New York: Alfred A. Knopf. 1968.

## DEDRICK BROTHERS

### BIOGRAPHICAL SOURCES

Upham, Elizabeth. (Related by marriage to Daniel Dedrick). Personal interviews. 1998.
Upham, Marquita. (Relative by marriage to Daniel Dedrick). Personal interview. 1998.

### CONTEMPORARY SOURCES (CHRONOLOGICAL)

Dedrick, Dan. "I have been under an arrest for six days ..." **April 5, 1879.** Letter to Lew Wallace. Indiana Historical Society. Lew Wallace Collection. M0292. Box 4. Folder 8. (**Says he was not told his arrest charges**)

No Author. "Arrests of Dedricks. Legal Documents." Herman B. Weisner Papers, ca. 1957-1992. New Mexico State University Library at Las Cruces. Rio Grande Historical Collections. Accession No. Ms 0249. Box 1. Folder B-8. Folder Name: "Lincoln County Bonds."

## DOLAN, JAMES JOSEPH

### BIOGRAPHICAL SOURCE

Slates, Thomas. "The James J. Dolan House, Lincoln New Mexico." *New Mexico Architecture* 11. 8/9 (1969). pp. 17-20.(**With Dolan biography**)

### CONTEMPORARY SOURCES BY AND ABOUT (CHRONOLOGICAL)

Tunstall, John Henry. "A Tax-payer's Complaint, Office of John H. Tunstall, Lincoln, Lincoln Co., N.M., January 18, 1878, 'The Present Sheriff of Lincoln County Has

Paid Nothing During His Present Term of Office.' Governor's Message for 1878." Mesilla *Independent.* **January 26, 1878.** Volume 1, Number 32. NewspaperArchive.com. **(Exposé of William Brady and John Riley for embezzling tax money to buy cattle; T.B. Catron then paid that bill)**

Dolan, James J. "Answer to A Taxpayer's Complaint." Mesilla *Independent.* **January 29, 1878. (Response to J.H. Tunstall's exposé of embezzlement of tax money to buy cattle)**

McSween, Alexander. "It looks as though the agent were the property of J.J. Dolan & J.H. Riley, known here as Dolan & Co." Letter to Secretary of Interior Carl Schurz. **February 11, 1878.** From Frederick Nolan. *The Life and Death of John Henry Tunstall.* Albuquerque, New Mexico: The University of New Mexico Press. 1965. Page 266.

Rynerson, William. "Friends Riley & Dolan, Lincoln N.M. I have just received letters from you mailed 10th inst." **February 14, 1878.** Letter to James Dolan and John Riley. Copy as Exhibit B in June 6, 1878 deposition of Alexander McSween. Frank Warner Angel report. *In the Matter of the Examination of the Causes and Circumstances of the Death of John H. Tunstall a British Subject.* Report filed October 4, 1878. Frank Warner Angel report. Interior Department Papers 1850-1907; Appointments Division and Subsequent Actions. Microfilm File Case Number 44-4-8-3. Record Group 48. Microfilm No. M750. Roll 1. National Archives and Records Administration. U.S. Department of Justice. Washington, D.C. (James J. Dolan Deposition. June 20, 1878. Pages 235-247.) **(Implying planned killing of J.H. Tunstall)**

Wilson, John, George B. Barker, Robert M. Gilbert, John Newcomb, Samuel Smith, Benjamin Ellis. "We the undersigned Justice of the Peace and Coroners Jury who sat upon the inquest held this 19th day of February 1878 on the body of John H. Tunstall ..." Coroner's Jury Report for John Tunstall. **February 19, 1878. (Naming as murderers, among others, James Dolan, Frank Baker, Jessie Evans, William Morton, and George Hindman)**

Rynerson, William. "The Grand Jurors for the Territory of New Mexico taken from the body of the good and lawful men of the County of Lincoln ..." Indictments of the April, Lincoln County Grand Jury. **April 28, 1879.** Herman B. Weisner Papers, ca. 1957-1992. New Mexico State University Library at Las Cruces. Rio Grande Historical Collection. Accession No. Weisner MS 249. Box 4/39. Folder E-Z. Folder Name: "Jessie Evans Accessory to Murder." **(Billy Bonney's testimony indicts J.J. Dolan, Billy Campbell, and Jessie Evans for pardon bargain)**

Purington, George Augustus. "The District Court adjourned on Thursday ..." **May 3, 1879.** Indiana Historical Society. Lew Wallace Collection. M0292. Box 4. Folder 10. **(Letter to Adjutant General on Grand Jury indictments of the Murphy-Dolans - including Dolan for the H.I. Chapman murder - and N.A.M. Dudley; copy sent to Lew Wallace)**

Wild, Azariah F. "Daily Reports of U. S. Secret Service Agents, Azariah F. Wild." Microfilm T-915. Record Group 87. Rolls 307 (January 1,1878 - June 30, 1879) and 308 **(July 1, 1879 - June 30, 1881).** National Archives and Records Department. Department of the Treasury. United States Secret Service. Washington, D. C. **(Dolan as an informer against "the Kid gang")**

## DUDLEY, NATHAN AUGUSTUS MONROE

### *BIOGRAPHICAL SOURCES*

Heitman, Francis B. *Historical Register and Dictionary of the United States Army, From Its Organization, September 29, 1789, to March 2, 1903.* (Entry for Galusha Pennypacker, Pages 782-7830.) Washington, D.C.: Government Printing Office. 1903.

Kaye, E. Donald. *Nathan Augustus Monroe Dudley: Rogue, Hero, or Both?* Parker, Colorado: Outskirts Press, Inc. 2007.

Oliva, Leo E., *Fort Union and the Frontier Army in the Southwest*. Southwest Cultural Resource Center, Professional Papers No. 41, National Park Service, 1993, Pages 488-489, 550, 574, 624-626, 656-659 are on Dudley. **(Quoted to E. Donald Kaye from the now-lost letter of Amos Kimball: "I guess you heard that Dudley made Colonel. The army bureaucracy is like a giant cesspool, where the biggest chunks rise to the top.")**

## *MILITARY COURT OF INQUIRY FOR*

Leonard, Ira E. *"Charges and specifications against Lieutenant Colonel N.A.M. Dudley, Commander at Fort Stanton, New Mexico."* **March 4, 1879**. Letter to Secretary of War George McCrary. *Proceedings of a Court of Inquiry in the Case of Lt. Col. N.A.M. Dudley (May 2,1879 - July 5, 1879)*. File No. QQ1284. (Boxes 3304, 3305, 3305A); Court Martial Files 1809-1894. Records of the Office of the Judge Advocate General - Army. Record Group 153. Old Military and Civil Branch. National Archives and Records Administration. Washington, D. C. **(Charges against Dudley for murders of A.A. McSween and H.I. Chapman and arson of McSween's house)**

No Author. *Proceedings of a Court of Inquiry in the Case of Lt. Col. N.A.M. Dudley (May 2,1879 - July 5, 1879)*. File No. QQ1284. (Boxes 3304, 3305, 3305A); Court Martial Files 1809-1894. Records of the Office of the Judge Advocate General - Army. Record Group 153. Old Military and Civil Branch. National Archives and Records Administration. Washington, D. C.

## *OTHER CONTEMPORARY SOURCES FOR (CHRONOLOGICAL)*

Dudley, Nathan Augustus Monroe. "I am in receipt of a copy of letter written by one H.I. Chapman, calling himself the Attorney ..." **November 9, 1878**. Letter to Lew Wallace. From *Proceedings of a Court of Inquiry in the Case of Lt. Col. N.A.M. Dudley (May 2,1879 - July 5, 1879)*. File No. QQ1284. (Boxes 3304, 3305, 3305A); Court Martial Files 1809-1894. Records of the Office of the Judge Advocate General – Army. Record Group 153. Old Military and Civil Branch. National Archives and Records Administration. Washington, D.C. **(Forwarding the Susan McSween affidavits in answer to the charges made by Chapman)**

Wallace, Lew. "I am in receipt of Col. Dudley's reply to the charges against him ..." Letter to Edward Hatch. **November 14, 1878**. Indiana Historical Society. Lew Wallace Collection. M0292. Box 3. Folder 17. **(Has quote: "the "reply is perfectly satisfactory")**

_____. "I am constrained to request that Lieut Col. N.A.M. Dudley, Commanding at Fort Stanton, be relieved ..." Letter to Edward Hatch. **December 7, 1878**. Indiana Historical Society. Lew Wallace Collection. M0292. Box 3. Folder 18. **(Removal of Dudley requested)**

Dudley, Nathan Augustus Monroe. "An Open Letter, By Lieut. Col. N.A.M. Dudley, 9[th] Cavalry, to His Excellency Governor Lew Wallace." Letter to Lew Wallace. Santa Fe *Weekly New Mexican*. **December 14, 1878**. Reprinted in *Mesilla News*. December 21, 1878. As Exhibit 13 from *Proceedings of a Court of Inquiry in the Case of Lt. Col. N.A.M. Dudley (May 2,1879 - July 5, 1879)*. File No. QQ1284. (Boxes 3304, 3305, 3305A); Court Martial Files 1809-1894. Records of the Office of the Judge Advocate General – Army. Record Group 153. Old Military and Civil Branch. National Archives and Records Administration. Washington, D.C. **(Attacks Wallace's Amnesty Proclamation as applying to the military)**

_____. "I have the honor to repeat the request made on a former occasion that Lt. Col. N.A.M. Dudley be relieved of the command ..." Letter to Edward Hatch. **March 7, 1879**. Indiana Historical Society. Lew Wallace Collection. M0292. Box 4, Folder 4.

Hatch, Edward. "Lieutenant Colonel N.A.M. Dudley is hereby relieved from command and duty ..." Special Field Order 2. **March 8, 1879.** Indiana Historical Society. Lew Wallace Collection. M0292. Box 4, Folder 4. (**Wallace succeeds in removing Dudley**)

Wallace, Lew. "I have official information that a court of inquiry for Col. Dudley has been ordered ..." Letter to Carl Schurz. **April 4, 1879.** Indiana Historical Society. Lew Wallace Collection. M0292. Box 4. Folder 8.

Purington, George Augustus. "The District Court adjourned on Thursday ..." **May 3, 1879.** Indiana Historical Society. Lew Wallace Collection. M0292. Box 4. Folder 10. (**Letter to Adjutant General on Grand Jury indictments of the Murphy-Dolans and N.A.M. Dudley; copy sent to Lew Wallace**)

No Author. Verdict on Civil Cause 298 for arson of Susan McSween's house. *Mesilla News.* **December 6, 1879.** Unpublished. personal communication from Frederick Nolan. July 29, 2005. (**Dudley exonerated**)

## ELKINS, STEPHEN BENTON

### *BIOGRAPHICAL SOURCES (CHRONOLOGICAL)*

Lambert, Oscar Doane. *Stephen Benton Elkins. American Foursquare.* Pittsburgh, Pennsylvania: University of Pittsburg Press. **1955.**

Cleaveland, Norman, *The Morleys - Young Upstarts on the Southwest Frontier.* Albuquerque, New Mexico: Calvin Horn Publisher, Inc. **1971.**

Westphall, Victor. *Thomas Benton Catron and His Era.* Tucson, Arizona: University of Arizona Press. **1973.**

Taylor, Morris F. *O.P. McMains and the Maxwell Land Grant Conflict.* Tucson, Arizona: The University of Arizona Press. **1979.** (**Traces origins of the Santa Fe Ring with T.B. Catron and S.B. Elkins**)

Cleaveland, Norman. *The Great Santa Fe Cover-up. Based on a Talk given Before the Santa Fe Historical Society on November 1, 1978.* Self-printed. **1982.**

_____. *A Synopsis of the Great New Mexico Cover-up.* Self-printed. **1989.**

### *ARTICLE ABOUT*

No Author. " 'The Territory of Elkins.' Assassination of Supposed Sun Correspondent. The Murder of the Rev. F.J. Tolby in New Mexico. A Probate Judge Accused of Complicity in the Crime. Indignation Meeting." *New York Weekly Sun.* **December 22, 1875.** Interior Department Papers 1850-1907; Appointments Division and Subsequent Actions. Microfilm Roll M750. National Archives and Records Administration. Record Group 48. Microfilm Case File Number 44-4-8-3. U. S. Department of Interior. Washington, D.C. (**In May 1, 1877 complaint to President Hayes as "Mary E. McPherson and W.B. Matchett 'Make certain charges**

(SEE: Santa Fe Ring, Thomas Benton Catron)

## ELLIS, ISAAC

Ellis, Isaac. "We are two residents of Lincoln County ..." Letter written with George Coe to President Rutherford B. Hayes. **June 22, 1878.** In Angel Report papers. Microfilm File Case Number 44-4-8-3. Record Group 48. Microfilm No. M750. Roll 1. National Archives and Records Administration. U.S. Department of Justice. Washington, D.C.

_____. Affidavit of Isaac Ellis. **March ?, 1879.** Indiana Historical Society. Lew Wallace Collection. M0292. Box 4, Folder 7.

## EVANS, JESSIE

### BIOGRAPHICAL SOURCE

McCright, Grady E. and James H. Powell. *Jessie Evans: Lincoln County Badman.* College Station, Texas: Creative Publishing Company. 1983.

### CONTEMPORARY SOURCES (CHRONOLOGICAL)

Wilson, John, George B. Barker, Robert M. Gilbert, John Newcomb, Samuel Smith, Benjamin Ellis. "We the undersigned Justice of the Peace and Coroners Jury who sat upon the inquest held this 19th day of February 1878 on the body of John H. Tunstall ..." Coroner's Jury Report for John Tunstall. **February 19, 1878.** (**Naming as murderers, among others, James Dolan, Frank Baker, Jessie Evans, William Morton, and George Hindman**)

Wallace, Lew. "I have information that William Campbell, J.B. Matthews, and Jesse Evans were of the party engaged in the killing ..." Letter to Edward Hatch. **March 5, 1879.** Indiana Historical Society. Lew Wallace Collection. M0292. Box 4, Folder 4. (**Murder of Huston Chapman**)

Rynerson, William. "Indictments of the April, Lincoln County Grand Jury." **April 28, 1879.** Herman B. Weisner Papers, ca. 1957-1992. New Mexico State University Library at Las Cruces. Rio Grande Historical Society Collection. Accession No. Ms 0249. Box 4/39. Folder E-Z. Folder Name: "Jessie Evans Accessory to Murder." (**Billy's testimony indicts Dolan, Campbell, and Evans for his pardon**)

Purington, George Augustus. "The District Court adjourned on Thursday ..." **May 3, 1879.** Indiana Historical Society. Lew Wallace Collection. M0292. Box 4. Folder 10. (**Letter to Adjutant General on Grand Jury indictments of the Murphy-Dolans - including Evans for the H.I. Chapman murder - and N.A.M. Dudley; copy sent to Lew Wallace**)

## FOUNTAIN, ALBERT JENNINGS

### BIBLIOGRAPHICAL SOURCE

Gibson, A. M. *The Life and Death of Colonel Albert Jennings Fountain.* Norman: University of Oklahoma Press. 1965.

### CONTEMPORARY SOURCE

Fountain, Albert Jennings, Attorney and J.D. Bail. "Instructions Asked for by Defendants Counsel. April 9, 1881. Herman B. Weisner Papers, ca. 1957-1992. New Mexico State University Library at Las Cruces. Rio Grande Historical Society Collection. Accession No. Ms 0249. Box 1. Folder 14-D. Folder Name: "Billy the Kid Legal Documents."

## FRITZ FAMILY (EMIL AND CHARLES FRITZ AND EMILIE FRITZ SCHOLAND)

Fritz, Charles. Affidavit of **September 18, 1876** claiming that Emil Fritz had a will. Probate Court Record. (private collection)

_____. Affidavit of **September 26, 1876** Authorizing Alexander McSween to Receive Payments for the Emil Fritz Estate. Probate Court Record. (private collection)

Scholand, Emilie and Charles Fritz. Affidavit of **September 26, 1876** appointing McSween to collect debts for the Emil Fritz Estate. Copied from the original District Court Record. (private collection)

Fritz, Charles. Affidavit of **December 7, 1877** to order Alexander McSween to pay the Emil Fritz insurance policy money. Probate Court Record. (private collection)

Scholand, Emilie. Affidavit of **December 21, 1877** Accusing Alexander McSween of Embezzlement. Copied from the original District Court Record. (private collection)

Bristol Warren. "Writ of Embezzlement." **December 21, 1877.** Herman B. Weisner Papers, ca. 1957-1992. New Mexico State University Library at Las Cruces. Rio Grande Historical Collections. Accession No. Ms 0249. Box 10. Folder M-13. Folder Name. "Will and Testament A. McSween." **(Emilie Fritz Scholand's sworn complaint against Alexander McSween)**

Fritz, Charles. Affidavit sworn before John Crouch, Clerk of Doña Ana District Court, for Writ of Attachment issued against property of Alexander A. McSween. Probate Court Record. **February 6, 1878.** (private collection)

_____ and Emilie Scholand. Attachment Bond sworn before John Crouch, Clerk of Doña Ana District Court, against Alexander A. McSween for indebtedness to them. **February 6, 1878.** (private collection)

No Author. Diagram showing parcels of land to each of the heirs of Emil Fritz. Herman B. Weisner Papers, ca. 1957-1992. New Mexico State University Library at Las Cruces. Rio Grande Historical Collections. Accession No. Ms 0249. Box P1. Folder 11. Folder Name. "Charles Fritz Estate."

## GARRETT, PATRICK FLOYD

### *BIBLIOGRAPHICAL SOURCES*

Metz, Leon C. *Pat Garrett. The Story of a Western Lawman.* Norman: University of Oklahoma Press. 1974.

Mullin, Robert N. "Killing of Joe Briscoe." Letter to Eve Ball. January 31, 1964. (Unpublished). Binder RNM, VI, H. Nita Stewart Haley Memorial Museum. Haley Library. Midland, Texas.

_____. "Pat Garrett. Two Forgotten Killings." *Password.* X(2) (Summer 1965). pp. 57 - 65.

_____. "Skelton Glen's Manuscript Entitled 'Pat Garrett As I Knew Him on the Buffalo Ranges.'" (1890, Unpublished). Binder RNM, III B, 20. Nita Stewart Haley Memorial Museum. Haley Library. Midland, Texas. **(The killing of Joe Briscoe is recounted)**

### *AUTOBIOGRAPHICAL SOURCES*

Garrett, Pat F. *The Authentic Life of Billy the Kid The Noted Desperado of the Southwest, Whose Deeds of Daring and Blood Made His Name a Terror in New Mexico, Arizona, and Northern Mexico.* Santa Fe, New Mexico: New Mexico Printing and Publishing Co. 1882. (Edition used: Edited by Maurice Garland Fulton. New York: The Macmillan Company. 1927)

### *REWARD FOR KILLING BILLY THE KID*

No Author. No title. *Santa Fe Daily New Mexican.* **July 21, 1881.** Volume X, Number 120, Page 4. Column 1. NewspaperArchive.com. **(Pat Garrett's meeting with Acting Governor Ritch about the Billy the Kid reward.)**

Ritch, William G. "In the matter of the application by Patrick F. Garrett for a reward claimed to have been offered May-1881 for the capture of Wm Bonney alias "the Kid." *Executive Record Book Number 2.* July 25, 1867- November 8, 1882. **July 21, 1881.** Pages 533-535. New Mexico Secretary of State Records. Collection 1971-001, Series 1; Records of the Secretary of the Territory. (Accessed from Albuquerque Public Library Microfilm, Territorial Archives of New Mexico, Roll 21.) **(Presentation of Garret's bill for the reward, showing that Acting-Governor Ritch agreed with the reward, but legal opinion from Attorney General William Breeden necessitated getting a legislative act to convert Wallace's private reward to Territorial)**

No Author. "Kid the Killer Killed, Wm. Bonney alias Antrim, alias Billy the Kid, Fatally Meets Pat Garrett, the Lincoln County Sheriff." Las Cruces *Rio Grande Republican.* **July 23, 1881.** Page 2. Volume 1, Number 10. NewspaperArchive.com. (**Copy of Pat Garrett's letter to Acting Governor William Ritch confirming that the original Coroner's Jury Report was sent to District Attorney of the First Judicial District, and copy of it was included in this letter to the Governor**)

Sheldon, Lionel. "In the Matter of the Claim of Sheriff Pat Garrett." Letter to the Legislature. **February 14, 1882.** Territorial Archives of New Mexico. Microfilm Roll 5, Frame 765. (**As Governor, approving Garrett's reward and stating he would have granted it outright had it not already been sent to the Legislature by Acting-Governor Ritch for an act**)

No Author. "An Act for the Relief of Pat. Garrett." *1882 Acts of the Legislative Assembly of the Territory of New Mexico, Twenty-Fifth Session. Convened at the Capitol, at the City of Santa Fe, on Monday, the 2d day of January, 1882, and adjourned on Thursday, the 2d day of March, 1882.* **February 18, 1882.** Chapter 101. Page 191. (**Granting Pat Garrett's reward for Billy the Kid, confirming it had been withheld on a technicality**)

Fulton, Maurice Garland. "I think I have solved the puzzle of the reward offers ..." October 28, 1951. Letter to Robert N. Mullin. Nita Stewart Haley Memorial Library and J. Evetts Haley History Center, Midland, Texas. Mullin Collection. Series RNM, VI, J, Legal Papers and Documents. "William Bonney, Reward for Death, Lincoln Notes." (**Confirming Attorney General's opinion to Acting Governor William Ritch about conversion of reward by legislative act**)

_____. "The rewards for the Kid give a clue to Catron's participation ..." **November 26, 1951.** Letter to Robert N. Mullin. Nita Stewart Haley Memorial Library and J. Evetts Haley History Center, Midland, Texas. Mullin Collection. Series RNM, VI, J, Legal Papers and Documents. "William Bonney, Rewards." (**Contemplating Catron's participation for the reward**)

_____. "Ritch was governor for the time-being ..." **March 15, 1953.** Letter to Robert N. Mullin. Nita Stewart Haley Memorial Library and J. Evetts Haley History Center, Midland, Texas. Mullin Collection. Series RNM, VI, J, Legal Papers and Documents. "William Bonney, Rewards." (**Confirming Attorney General's opinion to Acting Governor William Ritch about conversion of reward by legislative act**)

## *OTHER CONTEMPORARY SOURCES (CHRONOLOGICAL)*

No Author. "Garrett Exonerates Maxwell." *Santa Fe Daily New Mexican.* **July 21, 1881.** Volume X, Number 120. NewspaperArchive.com. (**Confirming Pat Garrett's killing of Billy the Kid**)

Wild, Azariah F. "Daily Reports of U. S. Secret Service Agents, Azariah F. Wild." Microfilm T-915. Record Group 87. Roll 308 (**July 1, 1879 - June 30, 1881**). National Archives and Records Administration. Department of the Treasury. United States Secret Service. Washington, D. C. (**Using Garrett to capture Billy Bonney**)

## GAUSS, GOTTFRIED

Gauss, Gottfried. Interview with *Lincoln County Leader.* **November 21, 1889.** (**About Billy Bonney's Lincoln jailbreak**)

## HOYT, HENRY F.

### *AUTOBIOGRAPHICAL SOURCE*

Hoyt, Henry. *A Frontier Doctor.* Boston and New York: Houghton Mifflin Company. 1929. (**Describes Billy Bonney's superior abilities, pp. 93-94.**)

***CONTEMPORARY SOURCES (CHRONOLOGICAL)***

Bonney, William H. Bill of Sale to Henry Hoyt. **October 24, 1878**. Collection of Panhandle-Plains Historical Museum. Canyon, Texas. (Item No. X1974-98/1)

Hoyt, Henry F. "This time it is me who is apologizing ..." Letter to Lew Wallace Jr. (Lew Wallace's grandson) **April 27, 1927**. Indiana Historical Society. Lew Wallace Collection. M0292. Box 14, Folder 11.

_____. "Copy of a bill of sale written by W$^m$ H. Bonney ..." Letter to Lew Wallace Jr. **April 27, 1927**. Indiana Historical Society. Lew Wallace Collection. M0292. Box 14, Folder 11.

## KINNEY, JOHN

***BIOGRAPHICAL SOURCE***

Mullin, Robert N. "Here Lies John Kinney." *Journal of Arizona History*. 14 (Autumn 1973). Pages 223 - 242.

***CONTEMPORARY SOURCES (CHRONOLOGICAL)***

No Author. "Charges against Jessie Evans and John Kinney." Doña Ana County Criminal Docket Book. **August 18, 1875 to November 7, 1878**. Herman Weisner Collection. New Mexico State University Library at Las Cruces. Rio Grande Historical Collections. Accession No. Ms 0249. Box 13. Folder V-3. Folder Name: "Venue, Change of."

No Author. "Obituary of John Kinney." *Prescott Courier*. **August 30, 1919**. Obituary Section.

No Author. Obituary. "Over the Range Goes Another Pioneer." *Journal Miner*. Tuesday Morning, **August 26, 1919**.

No Author. "Captain Kinney Dead." *The Daily Arizona Silver Belt*. August 29, 1919. Page 2. NewspaperArchive.com.

## LEONARD, IRA E.

***BIOGRAPHICAL SOURCE***

Nolan, Frederick. Biography and photograph of Ira Leonard. Unpublished. personal communication. July 29, 2005.

***COURT OF INQUIRY OF N.A.M. DUDLEY BY*** (SEE: Nathan Augustus Monroe Dudley Court of Inquiry)

***LETTERS TO AND FROM***

### LEW WALLACE TO AND FROM

Leonard, Ira E. "Dear Gov. You have undoubtedly learned ere this of the assassination ..." Letter to Lew Wallace. **February 24, 1879**. Indiana Historical Society. Lew Wallace Collection. M0292. Box 4. Folder 3. (**On Chapman murder.**)

Wallace, Lew. "It is important to take steps to protect the coming court ..." Letter to Ira Leonard. **April 6, 1879**. Indiana Historical Society. Lew Wallace Collection. M0292. Box 4. Folder 8.

Leonard, Ira. "The air is filled tonight with 'rumors of wars ... Letter to Lew Wallace. **April 20, 1879**. Indiana Historical Society. Lew Wallace Collection. M0292. Box 4. Folder 9. (**About District Attorney Rynerson: "He is bent on going for the Kid"**)

_____. "When you left here I promised to write you concerning events transpiring here ..." Letter to Lew Wallace. **May 20, 1878 [sic - 79]**. Indiana Historical Society. Lew Wallace Collection. M0292. Box 4. Folder 10. (**Has quote on the**

Murphy-Dolan party as: "part and parcel of the Santa Fe ring that has been so long an incubus on the government of this territory.")

_____. "I write to you with pencil because I am laboring for breath ..." Letter to Lew Wallace. **May 23, 1879**. Indiana Historical Society. Lew Wallace Collection. M0292. Box 4. Folder 11. (**With quote "we are pouring the 'hot shot' into Dudley." (With enclosed letter of May 20, 1879)**

_____. "Dudley commenced on the defense Thursday afternoon ..." Letter to Wallace. **June 6, 1879**, Indiana Historical Society. Lew Wallace Collection. M0292. Box 4. Folder 11. (**About disgust at corrupt Court.**")

_____. "Yours of the 7th inst reached me ..." Letter to Lew Wallace. **June 13, 1879**. Indiana Historical Society. Lew Wallace Collection. M0292. Box 4. Folder 11. (**about Court of Inquiry corruption**)

## MATTHEWS, JACOB BASIL "BILLY"

### BIOGRAPHICAL SOURCE

Fleming, Elvis E. *J.B. Matthews. Biography of a Lincoln County Deputy*. Las Cruces, New Mexico: Yucca Tree Press. 1999.

## MAXWELL, DELUVINA

Maxwell, Deluvina. "I came here after Lucien Maxwell was already here...." Letter to J. Evetts Haley. June 24, 1927. Nita Stewart Haley Memorial Library and J. Evetts Haley History Center, Midland, Texas. J. Evetts Haley Collection, JEH, J-I – Maxwell, Deluvina. (**Debunking "Billy the Kid Case" hoax and *Cold Case Billy the Kid* claims that Peter Maxwell's bedroom had no door to the outside, and that Pat Garrett did not kill Billy the Kid**)

## MAXWELL FAMILY

Cleaveland, Agnes Morley. *No Life for a Lady*. Boston: Houghton Mifflin. 1941.

_____. *Satan's Paradise: From Lucien Maxwell to Fred Lambert*. Boston: Houghton Mifflin Company. 1952.

Cleaveland, Norman. *The Morleys - Young Upstarts on the Southwest Frontier*. Albuquerque, New Mexico: Calvin Horn Publisher, Inc. 1971.

Dunham, Harold H. "New Mexican Land Grants with Special Reference to the Title Papers of the Maxwell Grant." *New Mexico Historical Review*. (January 1955) Vol. 30, No. 1. pp. 1 - 23.

Freiberger, Harriet. *Lucien Maxwell: Villain or Visionary*. Santa Fe, New Mexico: Sunstone Press. 1999.

Keleher, William A. *The Maxwell Land Grant. A New Mexico Item*. Albuquerque, New Mexico: University of New Mexico Press. 1964.

Lamar, Howard Roberts. *The Far Southwest 1846 - 1912. A Territorial History*. New Haven and London: Yale University Press. 1966.

Miller, Kenny. Descendant of Lucien Bonaparte Maxwell. Personal communication. 2011 to 2012.

Montoya, María E. *Translating Property. The Maxwell Land Grant and the Conflict Over Land in the American West, 1840-1900*. Berkeley and Los Angeles, California: University of California Press. 2002.

Murphy, Lawrence R. *Lucien Bonaparte Maxwell. Napoleon of the Southwest*. Norman: University of Oklahoma Press. 1983.

Pearson, Jim Berry. *The Maxwell Land Grant*. Norman: University of Oklahoma Press. 1961.

Poe, Sophie. *Buckboard Days*. Albuquerque, New Mexico: University of New Mexico Press. 1964.

Taylor, Morris F. *O. P. McMains and the Maxwell Land Grant Conflict*. Tucson, Arizona: The University of Arizona Press. 1979. (**Origins of Santa Fe Ring**)

No Author. "Mrs. Paula M. Jaramillo, 65 Died Here Tuesday." *The Fort Sumner Leader*. Official Newspaper County of De Baca. December 20, 1929. No. 1158, Page 1, Column 1. (**Billy Bonney's sweetheart, Paulita Maxwell**)

### COMMANDING OFFICER'S QUARTERS BEFORE MAXWELL FAMILY CONVERSION

Diagram. "Commanding Officer's Quarters Fort Sumner, New Mexico Territory." National Archives, Microfilm RG 98, Consolidated Files Quartermaster General; with copy in Fort Sumner, New Mexico, State Monument. (**Faked in** *Cold Case Billy the Kid* **as being the Maxwell house itself**)

### MAXWELL FAMILY HOUSE IN FORT SUMNER

Drawing. "As per Burns account." Maxwell family house, and diagram of Peter Maxwell's bedroom with external door. Nita Stewart Haley Memorial Library and J. Evetts Haley History Center, Midland, Texas. Mullin Collection. Series RNM, IV, Y, Notebook: Places and Events, A-O. (**Debunking** *Cold Case Billy the Kid* **hoax that Peter Maxwell's bedroom had no door to the outside**)

Photograph. "Pete Maxwell's House Fort Sumner." Annotated on back by Robert N. Mullin. **Undated.** Nita Stewart Haley Memorial Library and J. Evetts Haley History Center, Midland, Texas. Mullin Collection. Series RNM, IV, A, 161.0. (**Maxwell family house showing external door in Peter Maxwell's bedroom debunking** *Cold Case Billy the Kid* **that the Maxwell house was one story and that Maxwell's bedroom had no door to the outside**)

Mullin, Robert N. "Pete Maxwell's House Fort Sumner, Prior to Erection of New Home 2 ½ Mi. S.E.[after sale of town]; Originally 1 Story Flat Roof, Officers Quarters. 2nd Floor Added By Maxwell." Annotation on back of photograph of Maxwell house. **Undated.** . Nita Stewart Haley Memorial Library and J. Evetts Haley History Center, Midland, Texas. Mullin Collection. Series RNM, IV, A, 161.0. (**Making clear the distinction between the Officer's Quarters and the later Maxwell house**)

### PETER MAXWELL'S HOUSE OUTSIDE OF FORT SUMNER

Photograph. "Peter Maxwell's home near Fort Sumner, post Lincoln County War, presented to Robert N. Mullin by Maurice Garland Fulton, who obtained it from Mrs. Susan McSween Barber. Nita Stewart Haley Memorial Library and J. Evetts Haley History Center, Midland, Texas. Mullin Collection. Series RNM, IV, A-161. (**For debunking** *Cold Case Billy the Kid* **hoax that Peter Maxwell lived as a cook in a San Andres Mountain cow camp because he moved from Fort Sumner**)

No Author. "Las Vegas." Death Notice of Peter Maxwell. **June 28, 1898.** *The Albuquerque Citizen*. Page 2, Column 3. NewspaperArchive.com. (**Peter Maxwell death notice about Fort Sumner area residence and death**)

### MAXWELL FAMILY FURNITURE

Blythe, Dee. "Billy the Kid Landmarks Fast Vanishing: Historic Spots Hard to Find; Markers Needed." *Clovis, New Mexico Evening News-Journal*. **May 31, 1937** Volume 9. Number 2. Section E. Monday,. (**Photo and article about Maxwell family furniture**)

Weddle, Jerry. "The Kid at Old Fort Sumner." *The Outlaw Gazette: Billy the Kid Outlaw Gang New Mexico*. **December, 1992.** (**Louisa Beaubien Barrett, Luz Maxwell's niece, error-filled history as recorded by her daughter Marian Barrett, including the claim that Pat Garrett's second shot went through a washstand; later used in the "Billy the Kid Case" hoax**)

_____. Statement that he interviewed Stella Abreu Maxwell in Albuquerque in her old age, and she stated she got the carpenter's bench from a man in Fort Sumner for her 1925 Billy the Kid Museum. Author's interview. February 5, 2018. **(The bench had not been kept by the family )**

## McSWEEN, ALEXANDER

Bristol Warren. "Writ of Embezzlement." December 21, 1877. Writ of Embezzlement. New Mexico State University Library at Las Cruces. Rio Grande Historical Collections. Lincoln County Papers. New Mexico State University Library at Las Cruces. Rio Grande Historical Collections. Accession No. Ms 0249. Box No. 10. Folder M-13. "Will and Testament A. McSween." **(Emilie Fritz Scholand's sworn complaint against Alexander McSween)**

Fritz, Charles. Affidavit sworn before John Crouch, Clerk of Doña Ana District Court, for Writ of Attachment issued against property of Alexander A. McSween. Probate Court Record. **February 6, 1878.** (private collection).

Bristol, Warren. Action of Assumpsit to command Sheriff of Lincoln County to attach goods of Alexander A. McSween. **February 7, 1878.** District Court Record. (private collection).

_____. Preprinted form in his name for "Writ of Attachment" (Printed and sold at the office of the Mesilla News) filled out to command the Sheriff of Lincoln County to attach goods of Alexander McSween for a suit of damages for ten thousand dollars. **February 7, 1878.** (private collection).

McSween, Alexander. "It looks as though the agent were the property of J.J. Dolan & J.H. Riley, known here as Dolan & Co." Letter to Secretary of Interior Carl Schurz. **February 11, 1878.** From Frederick Nolan. *The Life and Death of John Henry Tunstall.* Albuquerque, New Mexico: The University of New Mexico Press. 1965. Page 266.

_____. "Will and Testament A. McSween." **February 25, 1878.** Herman B. Weisner Papers, ca. 1957-1992. New Mexico State University Library at Las Cruces. Rio Grande Historical Collections. Accession No. Ms 0249. Box 10. Folder M15. Folder Name. "Will and Testament A. McSween."

_____. and B.H. Ellis. Secretaries. "The undersigned have the Honor of transmitting you, as requested, a copy of the proceedings of a meeting held by the citizens of Lincoln County ..." Letter to President Rutherford B. Hayes; with attached proceedings of the April 1878 Lincoln Grand Jury. **April 26, 1878.** Microfilm File Case Number 44-4-8-3. Record Group 48. Microfilm No. M750. Roll 1. National Archives and Records Administration. U.S. Department of Justice. Washington, D.C.

_____. Deposition to Frank Warner Angel. **June 6, 1878.** Pages 5-183 of Frank Warner Angel report *In the Matter of the Examination of the Causes and Circumstances of the Death of John H. Tunstall a British Subject.* Report filed **October 4, 1878.** Angel Report. Microfilm File Case Number 44-4-8-3. Record Group 48. Microfilm No. M750. Roll 1. National Archives and Records Administration. U.S. Department of Justice. Washington, D.C. **(Reports secret**

Angel, Frank Warner. *In the Matter of the Lincoln County Troubles. To the Honorable Charles Devens, Attorney General.* **October 4, 1878.** Angel Report. Microfilm File Case Number 44-4-8-3. Record Group 48. Microfilm No. M750. Roll 1. National Archives and Records Administration. U.S. Department of Justice. Washington, D.C.

## McSWEEN, SUSAN

### *BIOGRAPHICAL SOURCE FOR*

Chamberlain, Kathleen P. *In the Shadow of Billy the Kid: Susan McSween and the Lincoln County War.* Albuquerque: University of New Mexico Press. 2013.

## *CONTEMPORARY SOURCES ABOUT (CHRONOLOGICAL)*

Dudley, Nathan Augustus Monroe. "I am in receipt of a copy of letter written by one H.I. Chapman, calling himself the Attorney ..." **November 9, 1878**. Letter to Lew Wallace. From *Proceedings of a Court of Inquiry in the Case of Lt. Col. N.A.M. Dudley (May 2,1879 – July 5, 1879)*. File No. QQ1284. (Boxes 3304, 3305, 3305A); Court Martial Files 1809-1894. Records of the Office of the Judge Advocate General - Army. Record Group 153. Old Military and Civil Branch. National Archives and Records Administration. Washington, D.C. (**Answer to charges, with attached defamatory affidavits against Susan McSween**)

McSween, Susan. Testimony in Court of Inquiry for Lieutenant Colonel N.A.M. Dudley. **May 23-24, 26, 1879**. *Proceedings of a Court of Inquiry in the Case of Lt. Col. N.A.M. Dudley (May 2,1879 – July 5, 1879)*. File No. QQ1284. (Boxes 3304, 3305, 3305A); Court Martial Files 1809-1894. Records of the Office of the Judge Advocate General – Army. Record Group 153. Old Military and Civil Branch. National Archives and Records Administration. Washington, D.C.

No Author. Verdict on Civil Cause 298 for arson of Susan McSween's house. *Mesilla News*. **December 6, 1879**. Unpublished. personal communication from Frederick Nolan. July 29, 2005. (**Dudley exonerated**)

## MEADOWS, JOHN P.

Meadows, John P. "Billy the Kid to John P. Meadows on the Peñasco, May 1-2, 1881." *Roswell Daily Record*. February 16, 1931. Page 6.

Meadows, John P. Ed. John P. Wilson. *Pat Garrett and Billy the Kid as I Knew Them: Reminiscences of John P. Meadows*. Albuquerque: University of New Mexico Press. 2004.

## MURPHY, LAWRENCE GUSTAV

Murphy, Lawrence G. "Will of Lawrence G. Murphy." Herman B. Weisner Papers, ca. 1957-1992. New Mexico State University Library at Las Cruces. Rio Grande Historical Collections. Accession No. Ms 0249. Box 11. Folder P15. Folder Name: "Murphy, Lawrence G."

## O'FOLLIARD, THOMAS "TOM"

### *GENEALOGY SEARCHES (NO CERTAIN MATCH TO HISTORICAL TOM O'FOLLIARD, OR TO PROOF OF KIN RELATIONSHIP WITH THOMAS "KIP" McKINNEY)*

Kendall, F.A. "U.S. Census Record 1870. Year: 1870. Census place Zavalla County, Uvalde, Texas." **September 26, 1870**. United States Federal Census. Roll 593_1597, Page 551 B, Family History Library Film 553096. Ancestry.com. 1870 United States Federal Census. Provo, Utah. (**With O'Folliard misspelled as Folliard, but claimed by hoaxers as discovering it as his real name**)

Find A Grave, database and images (https://www.findagrave.com: accessed 27 January 2019), memorial page for Elizabeth Jane "Eliza" McKinney Cook (1829–1901), Find A Grave Memorial no. 100551036, citing Marathon Cemetery, Marathon, Brewster County, Texas, USA ; Maintained by Jim McKinney.

"Mississippi Marriages, 1800-1911," database, FamilySearch (https://familysearch.org/ark:/61903/1:1:V28W-VB6: 10 February 2018), David Cook and Eliza Jane Mc Kinney, 24 Sep 1846; citing Monroe, Mississippi; FHL microfilm 866,906.

Find A Grave, database and images (https://www.findagrave.com: accessed 17 February 2019), memorial page for Collin "Cullen" McKinney (1795–1845), Find A Grave Memorial no. 70869601, citing Old Stand Cemetery, Franklin County, Alabama, USA ; Maintained by Jim McKinney (contributor 47510435).

Find A Grave, database and images (https://www.findagrave.com: accessed 17 February 2019), memorial page for Thalis Newton McKinney, Sr (1 Mar 1817–12 Nov 1886), Find A Grave Memorial no. 67306306, citing Uvalde Cemetery, Uvalde, Uvalde County, Texas, USA ; Maintained by Jim McKinney (contributor 47510435).

Thomas C. McKinney is listed in the 1870 U.S. Census for Uvalde as the son of Thalis McKinney: Source Citation: Year: 1870; Census Place: Uvalde, Texas; Roll: M593_1597; Page: 541B; Family History Library Film: 553096. Source Information: Ancestry.com. 1870 United States Federal Census [database on-line]. Provo, UT, USA: Ancestry.com Operations, Inc., 2009. Images reproduced by FamilySearch.

"Texas, County Marriage Index, 1837-1977," database, FamilySearch (https://familysearch.org/ark:/61903/1:1:QK8B-F35P : 22 December 2016), Stephen Folliard and Sarah Rop Cook, 06 May 1859; citing Uvalde, Texas, United States, county courthouses, Texas; FHL microfilm 1,017,584. https://www.wikitree.com/wiki/Folliard-1.

## PATRÓN, JUAN

Wallace, Lew. "Be good enough to send word to all your men to turn out soon as possible ..." Letter to Juan Patrón. **March 19, 1879**. Indiana Historical Society. Lew Wallace Collection. M0292. Box 4. Folder 6. (**Reports escape of Jessie Evans and Billy Campbell from Fort Stanton**)

Patrón, Juan. First letter to Lew Wallace on **March 29, 1879**. Indiana Historical Society. Lew Wallace Collection. M0292. Box 4, Folder 7.

_____. Second letter to Lew Wallace on **March 29, 1879**. Indiana Historical Society. Lew Wallace Collection. M0292. Box 4, Folder 7.

## PEPPIN, GEORGE

No Author. "Old Citizen Gone." *Capitan News*. **September 23, 1904.** Volume 5. Number 29. Page 4. Center for Southwest Research. Microfilm AN2.L52a.

## POE, JOHN WILLIAM

Poe, John W. "The Killing of Billy the Kid." (a personal letter written at Roswell, New Mexico to Mr. Charles Goodnight, Goodnight P.C., Texas) July 10, 1917.

_____. *The Death of Billy the Kid*. (Introduction by Maurice Garland Fulton). Boston and New York: Houghton Mifflin Company. 1933.

Poe, Sophie. *Buckboard Days*. Albuquerque, New Mexico: University of New Mexico Press. 1964.

## RILEY, JOHN HENRY

### *CONTEMPORARY SOURCES ABOUT*

Tunstall, John Henry. "A Tax-payer's Complaint, Office of John H. Tunstall, Lincoln, Lincoln Co., N.M., January 18, 1878, 'The Present Sheriff of Lincoln County Has Paid Nothing During His Present Term of Office.' Governor's Message for 1878." Mesilla *Independent*. **January 26, 1878**. Volume 1, Number 32. NewspaperArchive.com. (**Exposé of William Brady and John Riley for embezzling tax money to buy cattle; and T.B. Catron then paid that bill**)

Dolan, James J. "Answer to A Taxpayer's Complaint." Mesilla *Independent*. **January 29, 1878**. (**Response to J.H. Tunstall's exposé**)

McSween, Alexander. "It looks as though the [Indian] agent were the property of J.J. Dolan & J.H. Riley, known here as Dolan & Co." Letter to Secretary of Interior Carl Schurz. **February 11, 1878**. From Frederick Nolan. *The Life and Death of John Henry Tunstall*. Albuquerque, New Mexico: The University of New Mexico Press. 1965. Page 266.

## RUDULPH, MILNOR

Keleher, William A. *Violence in Lincoln County 1869-1881.* Pages 350-351. Albuquerque, New Mexico: University of New Mexico Press. 1957.

## RYNERSON, WILLIAM LOGAN

### *BIOGRAPHICAL SOURCES*

Miller, Darlis A. "William Logan Rynerson in New Mexico. 1862-1893." *New Mexico Historical Review* 48 (April 1973) pp. 101-131.

No Author. "A Brief History of the Rynerson House." Las Cruces: Del Valle Design & Imaging. No copyright. https://delvalleprintinglc.com/rynerson-house/.

### *CONTEMPORARY SOURCES BY AND ABOUT (CHRONOLOGICAL)*

Rynerson, William L "Indictments of the April, Lincoln County Grand Jury." **April 28, 1879.** Herman B. Weisner Papers, ca. 1957-1992. New Mexico State University Library at Las Cruces. Rio Grande Historical Society Collection. Accession No. Ms 0249. Box 4/39. Folder E-Z. Folder Name: "Jessie Evans Accessory to Murder." **(Indictments of Dolan, Campbell, and Evans)**

_____. "Friends Riley & Dolan, Lincoln N.M. I have just received letters from you mailed 10th inst." Letter to James Dolan and John Riley. **February 14, 1878.** Copy as Exhibit B in June 6, 1878 deposition of Alexander McSween. Frank Warner Angel report. *In the Matter of the Examination of the Causes and Circumstances of the Death of John H. Tunstall a British Subject.* Report filed October 4, 1878. Interior Department Papers 1850-1907; Appointments Division and Subsequent Actions. Microfilm File Case Number 44-4-8-3. Microfilm No. M750. Roll 1. National Archives and Records Administration. U.S. Department of Justice. Washington, D.C. (James J. Dolan Deposition. June 20, 1878. Pages 235-247.) **(Planned killing of J.H. Tunstall)**

Angel, Frank Warner. "I have just been favored by a call from W.L. Rynerson ..." Letter to Secretary of Interior Carl Schurz. **September 6, 1878.** Microfilm File Case Number 44-4-8-3. Record Group 48. Microfilm No. M750. Roll 1. National Archives and Records Administration. U. S. Department of Justice. Washington, D.C.

Rynerson, William. Venue Change. **April 21, 1879.** Herman B. Weisner Papers, ca. 1957-1992. New Mexico State University Library at Las Cruces. Rio Grande Historical Collection. Accession No. Ms 0249. Box 1. Folder 14-D. Folder Name: "Billy the Kid Legal Documents." **(Change of Billy Bonney's trial venue from Lincoln County to Doña Ana County to insure a hanging trial by prevent Lincoln County citizens knowledgeable about the War being jurors)**

## SALAZAR, YGINIO

Wallace, Lew. "I beg to submit to you a list of persons ... to arrest ..." Letter to Henry Carroll. **March 11, 1879.** Indiana Historical Society. Lew Wallace Collection. M0292. Box 4. Folder 5. **(Lists Ygenio Salazar and "the Kid)**

Salazar, Joe. (Grandson of Yginio Salazar). Personal Interviews 1999-2001. **(My interviews about Ygenio)**

## SHERMAN, JOHN

Sherman, John. Letter to Governor Lew Wallace. **October 6, 1878.** Indiana Historical Society. Lew Wallace Collection. M0292. Box 3, Folder 15. **(First reference of "outlaw," Billy Bonney, to Governor Wallace.)**

## TUNSTALL, JOHN HENRY

### BIOGRAPHICAL SOURCES

Nolan, Frederick W. *The Life and Death of John Henry Tunstall.* Albuquerque, New Mexico: The University of New Mexico Press. 1965.

### CONTEMPORARY SOURCES (CHRONOLOGICAL)

Tunstall, John Henry. "A Tax-payer's Complaint, Office of John H. Tunstall, Lincoln, Lincoln Co., N.M., January 18, 1878, 'The Present Sheriff of Lincoln County Has Paid Nothing During His Present Term of Office.' Governor's Message for 1878." Mesilla *Independent.* **January 26, 1878.** Volume 1, Number 32. NewspaperArchive.com. (**Exposé of William Brady and John Riley for embezzling tax money to buy cattle; and T.B. Catron then paid that bill**)

Dolan, James J. "Answer to A Taxpayer's Complaint." Mesilla *Independent.* **January 29, 1878.** (**Response to J.H. Tunstall's exposé of embezzlement of tax money to buy cattle**)

Rynerson, William. "Friends Riley & Dolan, Lincoln N.M. I have just received letters from you mailed 10th inst." Letter to James Dolan and John Riley. **February 14, 1878.** Copy as Exhibit B in June 6, 1878 deposition of Alexander McSween. Frank Warner Angel report. *In the Matter of the Examination of the Causes and Circumstances of the Death of John H. Tunstall a British Subject.* Report filed October 4, 1878. Interior Department Papers 1850-1907; Appointments Division and Subsequent Actions. Microfilm File Case Number 44-4-8-3. Record Group 48. Microfilm No. M750. Roll 1. National Archives and Records Administration. U. S. Department of Justice. Washington, D.C. (James J. Dolan Deposition. June 20, 1878. pp. 235-247.) (**Planned killing of J.H. Tunstall**)

Wilson, John, George B. Barker, Robert M. Gilbert, John Newcomb, Samuel Smith, Benjamin Ellis. "We the undersigned Justice of the Peace and Coroners Jury who sat upon the inquest held this 19th day of February 1878 on the body of John H. Tunstall ..." Coroner's Jury Report for John Tunstall. **February 19, 1878.** (**Naming Tunstall's murderers**)

Springer, Frank. "I hope you have received a full account of the Troubles in Lincoln County from your nephew ..." Letter to Senator Rush Clark. **April 9, 1878.** Herman B. Weisner Papers, ca. 1957-1992. New Mexico State University Library at Las Cruces. Rio Grande Historical Collections. Accession No. Ms 0249. Box 4/39. Folder D-6. Folder Name "Frank Springer Letter to Rush Clark." (**Links Santa Fe Ring to murder of J.H. Tunstall**)

(SEE: Frank Warner Angel)

## TWITCHELL, RALPH EMERSON

### BOOKS BY

Twitchell, Ralph Emerson. *The Leading Facts of New Mexico History.* Vol. I-II. Santa Fe: Sunstone Press. 2007. (Reprinted from a 1912 edition) (**Ring cover-up historian**)

## WALLACE, LEW

### AUTOBIOGRAPHICAL AND BIOGRAPHICAL SOURCES

Governor of Territorial New Mexico. 1878-81." *New Mexico Historical Review.* 59(1) (January, 1984).

Morsberger, Robert E. and Katherine M. Morsberger. *Lew Wallace: Militant Romantic.* New York: McGraw-Hill Book Company. 1980.

Wallace, Lew. *An Autobiography. Vol. I.* New York and London: Harper and Brothers Publishers. 1997.

———. *An Autobiography. Vol. II.* New York and London: Harper and Brothers Publishers. 1997.

## COLLECTED PAPERS OF

Wallace, Lew. Collected Papers. Microfilm Project Sponsored by the National Historical Publications Commission. Microfilm Roll No. 99. Santa Fe, New Mexico: State of New Mexico Records Center and Archives. 1974.

———. Lew and Susan Wallace Collection. Indiana Historical Society. M0292.

———. Collected Papers. Lilly Library. Bloomington, Indiana.

## SECRET ANGEL NOTEBOOK ON SANTA FE RING FOR

Angel, Frank Warner. "To Gov. Lew Wallace, Santa Fe, N. M., 1878." Notebook. **1878**. Indiana Historical Society. Lew Wallace Collection. M0292. Microfilm No. F372. (**Original missing, copy on microfilm; secret notebook prepared for Lew Wallace listing names for Lincoln County and the Santa Fe Ring**)

Theisen, Lee Scott. "Frank Warner Angel's Notes on New Mexico Territory, 1878." *Arizona and the West: A Quarterly Journal of History*. Winter 1976. Volume 18. Number 4. Pages 333-370. (**About the Angel notebook**)

## AMNESTY PROCLAMATION OF

Wallace, Lew. "Proclamation by the Governor." **November 13, 1878**. Indiana Historical Society. Lew Wallace Collection. M0292. Box 3. Folder 17. (**Amnesty Proclamation for Lincoln County War fighters, but excluding those already indicted, like Billy Bonney**)

## DUDLEY COURT OF INQUIRY TESTIMONY BY

Wallace, Lew. Testimony in Court of Inquiry for Lieutenant Colonel N.A.M. Dudley. **May 12-15, 1879.** *Proceedings of a Court of Inquiry in the Case of Lt. Col. N.A.M. Dudley (May 2,1879 – July 5, 1879)*. File No. QQ1284. (Boxes 3304, 3305, 3305A); Court Martial Files 1809-1894. Records of the Office of the Judge Advocate General – Army. Record Group 153. Old Military and Civil Branch. National Archives and Records Administration. Washington, D.C.

## INTERVIEW NOTES ON BILLY BONNEY BY (SEE: William H. Bonney)

## REWARD NOTICES AND POSTERS FOR WILLIAM BONNEY BY
(SEE: William H. Bonney)

## LETTERS BY AND TO

### TO AND FROM WILLIAM BONNEY
(SEE: History of William H. Bonney)

### TO SHERIFF PATRICK F. GARRETT

Wallace, Lew. "To the Sheriff of Lincoln County, New Mexico, Greeting ..." **April 30, 1881**. Indiana Historical Society. Lew Wallace Collection. M0292. Box 9. Folder 11. (**Death Warrant for William Bonney after his Mesilla trial and before his Lincoln jailbreak**)

### TO AND FROM IRA E. LEONARD (SEE: Ira Leonard)

## TO AND FROM JUSTICE OF THE PEACE JOHN B. WILSON

Wallace, Lew. "I hasten to acknowledge receipt of your favor of the 11th Jan. ult. ..." **January 18, 1879**. Indiana Historical Society. Lew Wallace Collection. M0292. Box 4. Folder 1. (**Lincoln County as carrying on a revolution**)

Wallace, Lew. "I enclose a note for Bonney." Letter to John "Squire" Wilson. **March 20, 1879**. Indiana Historical Society. Lew Wallace Collection. M0292. Box 4. Folder 6. (**The pardon negotiation for Billy Bonney**)

Wilson, John B. Signed JBW. **April 8, 1879**. Indiana Historical Society, Lew Wallace Collection. M0292. Box 4, Folder 8. (**Notes on rustling**)

_____. Letter to Lew Wallace. **May 18, 1879**. Indiana Historical Society. Lew Wallace Collection. M0292. Box 4, Folder 5.

## *ARTICLES ABOUT WILLIAM BONNEY BY* (SEE: William H. Bonney)

## WALZ, EDGAR A.

No Author. *The American Book of Biography: Men of 1912*. Chicago: American Publishers Association. 1913. Page 614.

No Author. "Edgar A. Walz Dead: Expert on credit, Founder of The Travelers Hotel Credit Corporation – Managed New Mexico Ranch in Youth." *The New York Times*. **April 5, 1935**. Volume LXXXIV, Number 28,195. Page 24.

## WILD, AZARIAH (SEE: Secret Service)

## WILSON, JOHN B. "SQUIRE"

### *CORONER'S JURY REPORT FOR JOHN H. TUNSTALL BY*

Wilson, John, George B. Barker, Robert M. Gilbert, John Newcomb, Samuel Smith, Benjamin Ellis. "We the undersigned Justice of the Peace and Coroners Jury who sat upon the inquest held this 19th day of February 1878 on the body of John H. Tunstall ..." Coroner's Jury Report for John Tunstall. **February 19, 1878**. (**Naming as murderers, among others, James Dolan, Frank Baker, Jessie Evans, William Morton, and George Hindman**)

### *LETTERS FROM*

Wilson, John B. Letter to Lew Wallace. Unsigned but noted as from "Sqr. Wilson by Wallace. Undated, but likely **March, 1879**. Indiana Historical Society. Lew Wallace Collection. M0292. Box 4, Folder 7. (**On Lady Liberty stationery**)

_____. Affidavit of John Wilson. **March ?, 1879**. Indiana Historical Society. Lew Wallace Collection. M0292. Box 4, Folder 7.

_____. Signed JBW. **April 8, 1879**. Indiana Historical Society, Lew Wallace Collection. M0292. Box 4, Folder 8. (**Notes on rustling**)

_____. Letter to Lew Wallace. **May 18, 1879**. Indiana Historical Society. Lew Wallace Collection. M0292. Box 4, Folder 5.

### *LETTERS TO*

Bonney, W H. "Friend Wilson ..." **March 18, 1879**. Indiana Historical Society. Lew Wallace Collection. M0292. (**For mediating his pardon negotiation with Lew Wallace**)

Wallace, Lew. "I enclose a note for Bonney." Letter to John "Squire" Wilson. **March 20, 1879**. Indiana Historical Society. Lew Wallace Collection. M0292. Box 4. Folder 6. (**The pardon negotiation for Billy Bonney**)

# OLIVER "BRUSHY BILL" ROBERTS BILLY THE KID IMPOSTER HOAX

## SOURCES TO DEBUNK CLAIMS IN "BRUSHY BILL" HOAX, IN ADDITION TO CITED SOURCES FOR WILLIAM BONNEY'S REAL HISTORY (CHRONOLOGICAL)

No Author. Roberts family members. Federal Census for Arkansas, Sebastian County, Bates Township. **June 1, 1880.** Lines 27-33. (Cited in Don Cline's *Brushy Bill Roberts: I Wasn't Billy the Kid* to show "Brushy" was 10 months old at the census – 20 years too young to be Billy Bonney)

Wilcox, Lucius "Lute" M. (city editor, owner, J.H. Koogler). "The Kid. Interview with Billy Bonney The Best Known Man in New Mexico." *Las Vegas Gazette*. **December 27, 1880.** (Mentions that Billy Bonney has squirrel-like incisors; that contradicts "Brushy's" tusk-like extracted canine teeth)

Rudulph, Milnor. Coroner's Jury Report for William Bonney alias "Kid." **July 15, 1881.** Indiana Historical Society. Lew Wallace Collection. M0292. Box 9. Folder 11. Accession Number 1951.0104 from Maurice G. Fulton. (**Photostatic copy of original Spanish Coroner's Jury Report, certified on January 18, 1951, donated by Maurice Garland Fulton - matches photo in William Kelleher's *Violence in Lincoln County* copy; identifying body of Billy Bonney**)

Ritch, William G. "In the matter of the application by Patrick F. Garrett for a reward claimed to have been offered May-1881 for the capture of Wm Bonney alias "the Kid." *Executive Record Book Number 2*. July 25, 1867- November 8, 1882. **July 21, 1881.** Pages 533-535. New Mexico Secretary of State Records. Collection 1971-001, Series 1; Records of the Secretary of the Territory. (Accessed from Albuquerque Public Library Microfilm, Territorial Archives of New Mexico, Roll 21.) (**Presentation of Garret's bill for the reward and demonstrating that Acting-Governor Ritch agreed with the reward, but legal opinion from Attorney General William Breeden necessitated getting a Legislative act to convert Wallace's private reward to Territorial; also shows that Charles Greene was the printer of the reward notice, not Garrett's attorney as C.L. Sonnichsen wrongly claimed**)

No Author. "Kid the Killer Killed, Wm. Bonney alias Antrim, alias Billy the Kid, Fatally Meets Pat Garrett, the Lincoln County Sheriff." Las Cruces *Rio Grande Republican*. **July 23, 1881.** Page 2. Volume 1, Number 10. NewspaperArchive.com. (**Copy of Pat Garrett's letter to Acting Governor William Ritch confirming that the original Coroner's Jury Report was sent to District Attorney of the First Judicial District, and copy of it was included in this letter to the Governor**)

No Author. " 'The Kid' Killed! He Meets His Death at the Hands of Sheriff Pat Garrett, of Lincoln County. The Particulars of the Affair as Poured into the Ears of Eager Reporters. *The Las Vegas Daily Optic*. **July 18, 1881.** Volume 2, Number 217. Newspaperarchives.com. (**Confirming Pat Garrett's killing of Billy the Kid**)

No Author. *Executive Record Book Number 2*. July 25, 1867-November 8, 1882. **July 21, 1881.** Pages 533-535. New Mexico State Records Center and Archives, Santa Fe. New Mexico Secretary of the State Records Series 1. Records of the Secretary of the Territory. (**About granting Garrett's reward; source used by Sonnichsen to fabricate irregularity**)

No Author. "Garrett Exonerates Maxwell." *Santa Fe Daily New Mexican*. **July 21, 1881.** Volume X, Number 120. Newspaperarchives.com. (**Confirming Pat Garrett's killing of Billy the Kid**)

No Author. No title. *Santa Fe Daily New Mexican.* **July 21, 1881.** Volume X, Number 120, Page 4. Column 1. (**Pat Garrett's presentation to Acting Governor Ritch of his reward request, with Ritch willing to pay but needed to go through procedures.**)

No Author. "Words of Commendation and Encouragement." *Las Vegas Daily Gazette.* **July 22, 1881.** Volume 3. Number 15. Newspapers.com. (**Confirming Pat Garrett's killing of Billy the Kid**)

Ashenfelter, Singleton M. "Exit 'The Kid', The Fugitive Murderer Hunted Down and Killed by Sheriff Garrett." *The New Southwest, And Grant County Herald.* **July 23, 1881.** Number 30. University of New Mexico. Zimmerman Library. Microfilm AN2 G71. (**Ashenfelter's apocryphal description of Billy the Kid's body, but confirmation of the killing**)

No Author. "The Life of Billy the Kid. His Name Was Billy McCarthy, and He was Born in New York." *The New York Sun.* (From *The St. Louis Globe-Democrat*) **August 10, 1881.** Volume XLIII, Number 314. Newspapers.com. (**Confirming Pat Garrett's killing of Billy the Kid**)

Glen, Skelton. "Pat Garrett As I Knew Him on the Buffalo Ranges." (1890, Unpublished). Binder RNM, III B, 20. Nita Stewart Haley Memorial Museum. Haley Library. Midland, Texas. (**The killing of Joe Briscoe is recounted, but was unknown to "Brushy" who garbles it from a John Meadows article**)

No Author. "Death of T.C. McKinney." *The Carlsbad Current.* **September 24, 1915.** Front page. Column 5. ChroniclingAmerica.loc.gov/. (**With no claim that Kip McKinney and Tom O'Folliard were cousins**)

Taeger, Mary Nell. "Severo Gallegos Tells His Story and of His Family's Friend, 'Billy the Kid.' " *Ruidoso News.* **July 30, 1948.** Front page, Page 6. Volume II, Number 11. NewspaperArchive.com. (**A Billy the Kid history confabulator, used by Morrison as a prompt for "Brushy's" jailbreak tale. Gallegos was then used give a fake affidavit that "Brushy" was Billy**)

_____. No Author. "Severo Gallegos Tells His Story and of His Family's Friend, 'Billy the Kid.' " (continued) *Ruidoso News.* **August 6, 1948.** Page 3. Volume II, Number 12. NewspaperArchive.com. (**A Billy the Kid history confabulator, with this part 2 article used by Morrison as a prompt for "Brushy's" jailbreak tale. Gallegos was then used give a fake affidavit that "Brushy" was Billy**)

Roberts, Oliver Pleasant. ("Brushy" writing as O.L. Roberts) "Dear Uncle Kit Carson, We got here O.K. ..." Letter to Oran Ardious Woodman. **April 1, 1949.** From Roy L. Haws, *Brushy Bill: Proof His Claim to Be Billy the Kid Was a Hoax.* 2015. (Pages 113-117) (**"Brushy Bill's" possibly modeling himself as Billy the Kid based on this Kit Carson imposter**)

No Author. "Cornering Jesse James." *Hico News Review.* **February 3, 1950.** Front Page. Volume LXIV, Number 38. Texas Tech University Library. Southwest Collections/Special Collections Library. Microfilm H626 Hico (Texas) News Review 1929-1974 Reel 8. (**"Brushy" claiming to identify J. Frank Dalton as Jesse James**)

Holford, Carolyn. " 'Brushy Bill' Is Back From Gotham." *Hico News Review.* **February 20, 1950.** Front Page. Volume LXIV, Number 36. Texas Tech University Library. Southwest Collections/Special Collections Library. Microfilm H626 Hico (Texas) News Review 1929-1974 Reel 8. (**Reporting on Morrison-backed radio show on January 3, 1950 with J. Frank Dalton as Jesse James and "Brushy" backing him and having "wild west" tales**)

No Author. "Fort Sumner Jury Thought the Kid Had Been Killed." *Alamogordo News.* **November 30, 1950.** Volume 53, Number 48. .NewspaperArchive.com. (**Finding the Coroner's Jury Report; ignored in *Alias Billy the Kid***)

No Author. "Will A. Keleher, History Student, Sure Kid Was Shot." *Albuquerque Journal.* **December 1, 1950.** Volume illegible, Number 61. Newspaperarchive.com. (**Debunking "Brushy's" claim to be Billy the Kid**)

No Author. "Notorious Character is Buried." *Hico News Review.* **January 5, 1951.** Front Page. Volume LXV, Number 34. Texas Tech University Library. Southwest Collections/Special Collections Library. Microfilm H626 Hico (Texas) News Review 1929-1974 Reel 8. **(Obituary of "Brushy Bill" Roberts)**

Morrison, William V. Letter to Carl Breihan. **March 17, 1954. (Cited in Don Cline's** *Brushy Bill Roberts: I Wasn't Billy the Kid* **to show Morrison's attempt to sell "Brushy's" story for movies or TV)**

_____. Letter to Philip Rasch. **April 12, 1954.** Rio Grande Historical Collections./Hobson Huntslinger University Archives. New Mexico State University, Las Cruces. **(Lying that he was being backed for "Brushy" by many people, including William Keleher)**

Sonnichsen, C.L. and William V. Morrison. *Alias Billy the Kid.* Albuquerque, New Mexico: University of New Mexico Press. **1955. (Backing Roberts as Billy the Kid)**

Keleher, William A. *Violence in Lincoln County 1869-1881.* Albuquerque, New Mexico: University of New Mexico Press. **1957. (Photocopy of Spanish Coroner's Jury Report, July 15, 1881. Pages 306-308; Kelleher's English translation, Pages 343-344.)**

Walker, Dale L. *C.L. Sonnichsen: Grassroots Historian.* El Paso: Texas Western Press. **1972. (About co-author of Roberts in the Billy the Kid hoax)**

Pittmon, Geneva Roberts. "Dear Sir: the reason you are not finding my family ..." **December 16, 1987.** Letter to Joe Bowlin. In collection of Old Fort Sumner Museum, Fort Sumner, New Mexico. **(Roberts's niece using family Bible to prove Roberts was not Billy the Kid)**

_____. "I don't know of any job he held ..." Letter to Don Cline. **April 27, 1988. (Cited in Don Cline's** *Brushy Bill Roberts: I Wasn't Billy the Kid* **to show "Brushy" was a mentally disabled farm hand in his real life.)**

Sonnichsen, C.L. "I believe, without evidence, that Bill Morrison had a law degree ..." Letter to Don Cline. **June 30, 1988. (About believing that Morrison was a lawyer)**

Metz, Leon. "I met William V. Morrison in the early 1970's ..." Letter to Don Cline. **July 2, 1988. (Cited in Don Cline's** *Brushy Bill Roberts: I Wasn't Billy the Kid* **to show that Morrison denied being a lawyer)**

Tunstill, William A. *Billy the Kid and Me Were the Same: A Documentary on the Life of Billy the Kid.* Roswell, New Mexico: Western History Research Center. **1988. ("Brushy"-backer faking a genealogy using duped Eulaine Emerson Haws's approval, and debunked by "Brushy's" relative Roy L. Haws, Eulaine Emerson Haws's son, in his 2015** *Brushy Bill: Proof That His Claim to Be Billy the Kid Was a Hoax***)**

Cline, Don. *Brushy Bill Roberts: I Wasn't Billy the Kid.* **Undated [1988 or 1989?].** Unpublished manuscript. New Mexico Commission of Public Records. State Records Center and Archives. Santa Fe. MS Donald Cline Collection. Subseries 5.2, Folder 138. Box 10421. Serial No. 9560 Santa Fe NMSRCA. **(Debunking "Brushy's" Billy the Kid claims)**

_____. Interview with "Brushy's" brother, Tom's daughter, Mary June Roberts. **January 28, 1988. (Denying "Brushy's" genealogical claims)**

Anaya, Paco. *I Buried Billy.* College Station, Texas: Creative Publishing Company. **1991. (Eye-witness claim of burying Billy Bonney)**

Jameson, W.C. and Frederic Bean. *The Return of the Outlaw Billy the Kid.* Plano, Texas: Republic of Texas Press. **1998. (Backing Roberts as Billy the Kid)**

Walker, Dale L. *Legends and Lies: Great Mysteries of the American West.* New York: A Tom Doherty Associates Book. **1997. (Backing Roberts as Billy the Kid)**

Nolan, Frederick. *The West of Billy the Kid.* Norman: University of Oklahoma Press. **1998. (See Page 7 for quote on the Eugene Cunningham hoaxed photo of Catherine Antrim, which "Brushy" confabulated as his aunt, Kathleen Bonney)**

Johnson, Jim. *Billy the Kid: His Real Name Was ...*" Denver, Colorado: Outskirts Press, Inc. **2006. (Debunking Roberts as Billy the Kid)**
Haws, Roy L. *Brushy Bill: Proof That His Claim to Be Billy the Kid Was a Hoax.* Santa Fe: Sunstone Press. **2015. (Roberts relative debunking him as Billy the Kid)**
Jameson, W.C. *Cold Case Billy the Kid: Investigating History's Mysteries.* Guilford, Connecticut: Twodot. **2018. (Recycling the "Billy the Kid Case" hoax to argue for Roberts as Billy the Kid)**
No Author. "Memorials." *El Paso Post-Herald.* **September 9, 1977.** Volume XCVII, Number 216. Page 24, Column 5. Newspaperarchive.com **(Obituary for William V. Morrison, showing he was not an attorney)**
Caperton, Thomas J. *Historic Structure Report. Lincoln State Monument. Lincoln New Mexico.* Santa Fe, New Mexico: Office of Cultural Affairs, Department of Finance and Administration, Historic Preservation Division. **1983. (With floor plan of the Lincoln court-house proving "Brushy's" faked armory location)**
Nolan, Frederick. *The West of Billy the Kid.* Norman: University of Oklahoma Press. **1998. (Seven Rivers boy's tintype with Marion Turner identified by Eve Ball, but claimed to be himself at 17 as Billy the Kid by Brushy Bill;" Page 157)**
Salazar, Joe. (Grandson of Yginio Salazar). Interviews **1999-2001. (My interviews about Ygenio Salazar, cited by the hoaxers as believing Billy had survived the Garrett shooting)**
Cox, Jim. *The Great Radio Soap Operas.* Jefferson, North Carolina: McFarland & Company, Inc. Publishers. **1999. (About "We the People" radio show, in which "Brushy" appeared to vouch for J. Frank Dalton as Jesse James)**
No Author. "We the People." https://www.otrcat.com/p/we-the-people. **2019. (About "We the People" radio show, in which "Brushy" appeared to vouch for J. Frank Dalton as Jesse James)**

(See William H. Bonney's Coroner's Jury Report)

## *ARTICLES ON REJECTED PARDON (CHRONOLOGICAL)*

Humphreys, Sexton. "Pardon Me, I'm Alive," Says Billy the Kid." *Indianapolis News.* **November 25, 1950.** Page 9. Indiana Historical Society. Lew Wallace Collection. M0292. Box 14. Folder 12.
Morgan, Art. "Billy the Kid Only a Phony It Turns Out." *Santa Fe New Mexican.* **November 30, 1950.** Issue 6. Front page, Page 3. NewspaperArchive.com.
No Author. "Mabry Terms "Billy" Outright Imposter." *Clovis News Journal.* **November 30, 1950.** Volume 22, Number 208. Newspaperarchive.com. **(Thursday, when interview was held)**
Smylie, Vernon. "Billy the Kid Flunks in Talk With Governor." *El Paso Herald Post.* **November 30, 1950.** Volume LXX, Number 285. Front Page, Page 13. Newspaperarchive.com. **(Thursday, when interview was held)**
United Press. "Pardon Mt 6-Shooters. Billy the Kid? Governor to Decide." *The Indianapolis News.* **November 30, 1950.** Indiana Historical Society. Lew Wallace Collection. M0292. Box 14. Folder 12.
No Author. " 'Billy the Kid' Bubble Bursts as Gov. Mabry Rejects Oldster's Claim." *Albuquerque Journal.* **December 1, 1950.** Volume [illegible], Number 61. Front Page, Page 4. Newspapers.com.
No Author. "Will A. Keleher, History Student, Sure Kid Was Shot." *Albuquerque Journal.* **December 1, 1950.** Volume [illegible], Number 61. Front Page. Newspaperarchive.com. **(Supports Governor Mabry calling "Brushy Bill" a Billy the Kid imposter)**
No Author. "Billy the Kid is Called Imposter by New Mexico Chief." *Lubbock Morning Avalanche.* **December 30, 1950.** Page 12. Newspaperarchive.com.

## WILLIAM V. MORRISON'S PROMPTING RESEARCH FOR PARROTING BY "BRUSHY" FOR INTERVIEW TAPING AND FOR THE PARDON INTERVIEW (CHRONOLOGICAL)

### BILLY THE KID'S WRITINGS FROM LEW WALLACE COLLECTION AT THE INDIANA HISTORICAL SOCIETY

Morrison, William V. "Urgent need of photostatic copies correspondence ..." **October 6, 1950.** Telegram to Indiana Historical Society, The William Henry Smith Memorial Library. Indiana Historical Society. Collection Number RG6. Box 17, Folder 11.

Dunn, Caroline. "We have microfilm of Bonney-Wallace correspondence ..." Letter to William V. Morrison. **October 7, 1950.** Letter to William V. Morrison. Indiana Historical Society, The William Henry Smith Memorial Library. Collection Number RG6. Box 17, Folder 11.

Morrison, William V. "Upon my return from Lincoln, N.M., today I have your telegram ..." **October 9, 1950. Letter** to The William Henry Smith Memorial Library. Collection Number RG6. Box 17, Folder 11.

Dunn, Caroline. "Your letter of the 9th received ..." **October 13, 1950.** Letter to William V. Morrison. Indiana Historical Society. Collection Number RG6. Box 17, Folder 11.

Morrison, William V. "Your letter of the 13th received ..." **October 17, 1950.** Letter to Caroline Dunn of The William Henry Smith Memorial Library. Indiana Historical Society. Collection Number RG6. Box 17, Folder 11.

No Author. Bill for $9.78 for "17 sheets photostats, Lew Wallace Collection. **October 25, 1950.** Telegram to Indiana Historical Society Memorial Library. Indiana Historical Society. Collection Number RG6. Box 17, Folder 11.

Dunn, Caroline. "Enclosed are the photostats of the documents in the Lew Wallace collection, with certification ..." **October 25, 1950.** Letter to William V. Morrison. Indiana Historical Society. Collection Number RG6. Box 17, Folder 11.

Morrison, William V. "This will serve to acknowledge receipt ..." **October 28, 1950.** Letter to Caroline Dunn of The William Henry Smith Memorial Library. Indiana Historical Society. Collection Number RG6. Box 17, Folder 11.

No Author. Bill for $2.61 for "6 Pstat neg." **October 30, 1950.** Telegram to Indiana Historical Society Memorial Library. Indiana Historical Society. Collection Number RG6. Box 17, Folder 11.

Wallace, Lew Jr. "A photostatic copy is being prepared of the letter in my possession from William H. Bonney ..." **October 30, 1950 .** Letter to William V. Morrison. Indiana Historical Society. Lew Wallace Collection. M0292. Box 8. Folder 3. **(Received a copy of actual Billy Bonney pardon plea letter of March 13, 1879)**

_____. "Your letter of November 2 confuses me ..." **November 10, 1950.** Letter to William V. Morrison. Indiana Historical Society. Lew Wallace Collection. M0292. Box 8. Folder 3. **(Expressing suspicion about a Billy the Kid imposter)**

Unnamed Archivist. "Copy of transcript sent by Wm V. Morrison ..." **November 10, 1950.** Indiana Historical Society. Lew Wallace Collection. M0292. Box 8. Folder 3. **(Seeking a copy of original of Billy Bonney's first pardon request letter)**

Dunn, Caroline. "In my letter to you of November 5 I said I was returning the transcripts ..." **November 14, 1950.** Letter to William V. Morrison. Indiana Historical Society. Collection Number RG6. Box 17, Folder 11.

## LINCOLN COUNTY WAR HISTORY
## FROM BLAZER FAMILY PAPERS 1864-1965
## AT NEW MEXICO STATE UNIVERSITY, LAS CRUCES

Morrison, William V. "Regarding Billy the Kid." Correspondence. **October 28, 1949-August 4, 1955.** New Mexico State University Library, Archives and Special Collections Department. Blazer Family Papers, 1864-1965. MS 0110, 15:12 and MS 0110, 15:13, William Vincent Morrison Correspondence, Billy the Kid, regarding and General, August 18, 1952-April 24, 1956, March 31, 1962. **(Using the historical papers of the Joseph Blazer family)**

### *WILLIAM VINCENT MORRISON CORRESPONDENCE, BILLY THE KID, MS 0110, 15:12*

Morrison, William V. "I certainly enjoyed talking with you ..." Letter to Paul A. Blazer. **August 18, 1952. (Getting information on Billy being ambidextrous and using single action pistols)**

_____. "First, I want to thank you for taking me through the cemetery ..." Letter to Paul A. Blazer. **April 27, 1953. (Getting information on the graves of "Buckshot" Roberts and Dick Brewer.)**

_____. "I wish to thank you for your time ..." Letter to Paul A. Blazer. **June 26, 1953. (Trying to convince people that Garrett did not kill the Kid)**

_____. "Your winter issue, 1953, Volume 1, No. 3, was handed to me ..." Letter to Fred Gipson. **April 17, 1954. (Informing editor of *True West* magazine that Garrett did not kill the Kid)**

_____. "Your letter of the first arrived here ..." Letter to Paul A. Blazer. **April 6, 1955. (Announcing publication of *Alias Billy the Kid*)**

### *WILLIAM VINCENT MORRISON CORRESPONDENCE, BILLY THE KID, MS 0110, 15:13*

Olyanova, Nadya. "I have your letter of May 13th in which you throw out the challenge ..." Letter to William V. Morrison. **May 18, 1953. (Contact with a handwriting analyst about a Billy the Kid letter)**

Morrison, William V. "I have your letter of the 13th ..." Letter to Carl W. Breihan. **March 17, 1954. (About J. Frank Dalton being Jesse James, that historians, like William Keleher, accepted that "Brushy" was Billy the Kid, that he sought movie and television rights for his work, and that he had sought exhumations)**

_____. "Your comment in the March issue with reference to Corle's 'Billy the Kid' ..." Letter to Raymond Carlson. **March 17, 1954. (Boasting to *Arizona Highway* editor, Carlson, that he knew that Ira Leonard did not represent Billy in Mesilla – even though Leonard did – revealing where "Brushy" got that error from coaching Morrison)**

Autry, Gene. "Your letter of March 23rd regarding information on Billy the Kid ..." Letter to William V. Morrison. **March 31, 1954. (Trying to sell his "Brushy" tale to Gene Autry)**

Morrison, William V. "I have your letter of March 24, and wish to thank you ..." Letter to Carl W. Breihan. **April 3, 1954. (Faking reasons for why "Brushy" lost the Governor Mabry pardon)**

_____. "Thanks for your most interesting letter ..." Letter to Philip J. Rasch. **April 19, 1954. (Trying to convince Rasch that "Brushy" matched Billy physically, and the Mabry hearing was affected by the Santa Fe Ring)**

_____. "Thanks for your letter of the first ..." Letter to Philip J. Rasch. **May 7, 1954. (Comparing C.L. Sonnichsen with Billy the Kid historians, trying to convince Rasch that "Brushy" was Billy because the Santa Fe Ring made up the Coroner's Jury Report)**

Truman, Harry S. "I can't tell you how very much I appreciate the Number 1 copy ..." Letter to William V. Morrison. **May 19, 1955. (Past President Truman as duped by *Alias Billy the Kid*)**

Morrison, William V. "I am very grateful for your kind letter ..."Letter to William Waters. **June 29, 1955. (About wanting to exhume Billy the Kid')**

_____. "I have a letter from Doc. Sonnichsen ..." Letter to Robert N. Mullin. **(Claiming "Brushy" could not read)**

## WILLIAM VINCENT MORRISON ROTARY CLUB LECTURE, CORRESPONDENCE BILLY THE KID, MS 0110, 15:12

Morrison, William V. "Billy the Kid." Talk to the El Paso, Texas, Rotary Club. **December 3, 1953.** Text of talk sent to Paul A. Blazer. **(Presenting the full-blown "Brushy Bill" hoax, with introduction by C.L. Sonnichsen)**

## *ALIAS BILLY THE KID'S PROMPT FOOTNOTES'* RESEARCH BY WILLIAM V. MORRISON AND C.L. SONNICHSEN (CHRONOLOGICAL)

### BOOKS

Walter Noble Burns's 1926 *The Saga of Billy the Kid*. **(fictionalized account using Pat Garrett's 1882 edition of *The Authentic Life of Billy the Kid*)**

Garrett, Pat F. *The Authentic Life of Billy the Kid The Noted Desperado of the Southwest, Whose Deeds of Daring and Blood Made His Name a Terror in New Mexico, Arizona, and Northern Mexico.* Santa Fe, New Mexico: New Mexico Printing and Publishing Co. 1882. (Edition used: Edited by Maurice Garland Fulton. New York: The Macmillan Company. 1927)

Coe, George with Doyce B. Nunis, Jr. Ed. *Frontier Fighter. The Autobiography of George Coe Who Fought and Rode With Billy the Kid.* Chicago: R. R. Donnelley and Sons Company. 1934. **(multiple references)**

Siringo, Charles A. *History of Billy the Kid.* Printed by Charles A. Siringo. 1920. Page 32. **(largely fictionalized, using Garrett's *The Authentic Life of Billy the Kid*, by a Garrett posseman not involved in capturing Billy, for claim that Billy worked for Murphy and Dolan. Also, it contained the Jim East letter used by "Brushy" to confabulate a story about giving an "Indian girl" the Billy the Kid tintype)**

Poe, John W. *The Death of Billy the Kid.* Boston and New York: Houghton Mifflin Company. 1933. Page 21. [sic- Page 31 in *Alias Billy the Kid*]. **(cited by Sonnichsen for fake argument that Fort Sumner residents would have hidden Billy's survival of the Garrett shooting)**

Miguel Otero. *The Real Billy the Kid.* Rufus Rockwell Wilson, Inc. 1936. Page 37. **(for Pat Garrett's statement that Billy tried to shoot Billy Matthews at Sheriff Brady's ambush, then repeated verbatim by "Brushy")**

Hudson, Bell. Ed. Mary Hudson Brothers. *Billy the Kid.* Farmington, New Mexico: The Hustler Press. 1949. Page 47. **(for Billy staying in sheep camps near Fort Sumner and a scene of encountering Barney Mason in one )**

### LETTERS

Jim East. "At the time of the capture of Billy, the Maxwell family were living at Fort Sumner ..." Letter to W.H. Burgess. **May 20, 1926. (source for the Jim East name, but its key mention of Paulita Maxwell as Billy's love was missed; identified as copy from Burgess supplied by Sonnichsen, who also had a copy of Walter Noble Burns's June 3, 1926 reply to Burgess that Paulita was Billy's "sweetheart")** (Page 38)

Roberts, Oliver P. "Brushy Bill." "She said she had three affidavits that people knew me in 1887 ..." **May 24, 1949**. Letter to William V. Morrison. Footnote in *Alias Billy the Kid*. (Page 59)

## JOURNAL/MAGAZINE ARTICLES (CHRONOLOGICAL)

Adams, Ramon F. "Billy the Kid's Lost Years: Cyclone Denton Tells of Bonney's Life as a Cowboy in Arizona." *The Texas Monthly*. 4.2. (**August-December, 1929**). Pages 205-211. (Scan courtesy of Cornette Library at West Texas A&M. (**source for claiming falsely that Billy worked at the Gila Ranch in Arizona**)

Smith, Wilbur. Interview. "The Amigo of 'Billy the Kid': The Man Who Fought Side by Side With Lincoln County's Outlaw Character Tells About the Days of 'Judge Colt's Rule.'" *New Mexico Magazine* article interview of **April, 1933**. Pages 26-49. University of New Mexico, Albuquerque. Zimmerman Library. Center for Southwest Research Anderson. Call Number F 791 N45. (**gives names of people hoping that Billy was alive, including Ygenio) Salazar**)

Traylor, Leslie. "Facts Regarding the Escape of Billy the Kid." *Frontier Times*. **July, 1936**. Pages 506-513 (on Page 509). FrontierTimesMagazine.com. (**About Billy the Kid's jailbreak being aided by Sam Corbett placing a gun in the latrine, based on a hearsay interview by Traylor in Lincoln in 1933 and 1935; also in article are his Jesus Silva interview on identifying Billy's body and his confirming the erroneous identification of Billy's gravesite in the Fort Sumner cemetery in 1935**)

Ball, Eve. "Billy Strikes the Pecos." *New Mexico Folklore Record*, IV. **1949-50**. Pages 7-10. University of New Mexico, Albuquerque. Zimmerman Library. Call Number GR 1 N 47 Vol 4. (**source for Billy Bonney's crossing the Guadalupe Mountains on foot to the Seven Rivers Jones family**)

Fulton, Maurice Garland. "Billy the Kid in Life and Books." *The New Mexico Folklore Record*. Volume IV, **1949-1950**. Pages 1-6. University of New Mexico, Albuquerque. Zimmerman Library. Call Number GR 1 N 47 Vol 4. (**source for the Greathouse shooting of Jim Carlyle, for the Mesilla trial being unjust to Billy, for a photo claimed to be Billy's mother, and for her name being "Mrs. Antrim"**)

## NEWSPAPER ARTICLES

*Hunter's Frontier Times Magazine*. "A Story of 'Billy the Kid.'" July, 1943, Pages 217-218. (quoting *Laredo Times* for **August 10, 1881**). frontiertimesmagazine.com/. (**source for claiming falsely Billy's demanding $5 per day payment from John Chisum**)

No Author. *Las Vegas Gazette* December 24, 1880, and the *Santa Fe New Mexican* of May 7, 1881. (**straw man argument for no reward made by Sonnichsen by citing editions with wrong dates for Lew Wallace's Billy the Kid reward notices**)

Wallace, Lew. *New York World Magazine*. "General Lew Wallace Writes a Romance of 'Billy the Kid' Most Famous Bandit of the Plains: Thrilling Story of the Midnight Meeting Between Gen Wallace, Then Governor of New Mexico, and the Notorious Outlaw, in a Lonesome Hut in Santa Fe." **June 8, 1902**. Lew Wallace Collection. Indiana Historical Society. M0292. . Box 14. Folder 11.(**"Brushy's" source for pardon bargain misinformation and for "pardon in your pocket" quote**) Cited by Sonnichsen, but identified as from the Indiana Historical Society, meaning Morrison's research.

No Author. "Billy the Kid, Alive Is Ridiculed by Oldtimers." El Paso *Herald*. **June 23, 1926**. Page 7. Newspapers.com. (**contradicting hearsay reports that Garrett had not killed the Kid, but used by hoax to quote those hearsay reports**)

John Meadows "John Meadows Tells of His Association With Pat Garrett." [sic - "My Association With Pat Garrett, Peace Officer of New Mexico."] *Alamogordo News*, **March 8, 1936**. Pages 1, 4. University of New Mexico, Albuquerque.

Zimmerman Library. Zimmerman New Mexico Microfilm AN2, A46. (**source of error for Garrett killing his buffalo hunter partner, when he actually killed Joe Briscoe**)

No Author. "Frontiersmen Track Reports 'Kid' Is Alive." El Paso *Herald-Post*. **June 22, 1938.** newspaperarchive.com. and El Paso *Times*. **November 10, 1937.** (**article about Pawnee Bill's planned to search for Billy the Kid as being alive as dishonestly misstated by Morrison and Sonnichsen to mean Pawnee Bill was searching for "Brushy"**)

## COURT, MILITARY, AND LEGISLATIVE RECORDS

U.S. District Court Minute Book B, Third Judicial District, Indictment 411 for killing "Buckshot" Roberts [**1878,**], Page 76, quashed.

Lincoln County Grand Jury Minute Book B for **April, 1879**, for Indictments 243, 244; Pages 92-93, 298-299 (**misread and confused with Billy's 1880 Mesilla hanging trial**) (Page 34)

Adjutant General's files from the State Library in Austin, Texas, about Jessie Evans's **July 7, 1880** capture near Fort Stockton, Texas. (**about Jessie Evan's 1880 capture in Texas**)

Doña Ana County Court Minutes, "Instructions to the Jury," Cause No. 532. Pages 100-103; (**indictment for Brady ?**)

Doña Ana County Court Minute Book D for Cause No. 532 (verdict and sentence), killing of William Brady. [**1881**] Page 406. (**listing attorney as Simon B. Newcomb**)

No Author. *Executive Record Book Number 2*. July 25, 1867-November 8, 1882. **July 21, 1881.** Pages 533-535. New Mexico State Records Center and Archives, Santa Fe. New Mexico Secretary of the State Records. Records of the Secretary of the Territory. (**About granting Garrett's reward; used by Sonnichsen to fabricate irregularity**)

## INTERVIEWS

Mullin, Robert N. cited as having copies of reminiscences of Louis Abraham about Silver City and Billy. No date. (**noted by Sonnichsen as showing the murder at 12 as fictitious, but rest of information was ignored**) (Page 77)

Anaya, A.P. "Paco." Interview given to a George Fitzpatrick. Undated. (**Used to claim that he claimed two coroner's jury reports, but not knowing that he also claimed in a manuscript, published in 1991, that he buried Billy Bonney**)

Sonnichsen, C.L. Interview With Jack Fountain. April 15, 1944. (**A.J. Fountain's fake hearsay account of Garrett telling him he killed Billy to get a $10,000 reward, and that the side of beef was beside Maxwell's bedroom**)

Morrison, William V. Interviews with Oliver "Brushy Bill" Roberts. 1949-1950. (Unpublished)

Morrison, William V. Miscellaneous hearsay interviews of non-historical people for claims of Garrett not killing Billy, or identifying "Brushy" as Billy.

## APPARENT SOURCES FOR ALIAS BILLY THE KID NOT CITED (CHRONOLOGICAL)

No Author. *Proceedings of a Court of Inquiry in the Case of Lt. Col. N.A.M. Dudley* (***May 2, 1879 – July 5, 1879***). File No. QQ1284. (Boxes 3304, 3305, 3305A); Court Martial Files 1809-1894. Records of the Office of the Judge Advocate General - Army. Record Group 153. Old Military and Civil Branch. National Archives and Records Administration. Washington, D. C. (**A page of Billy Bonney's testimony about escaping the burning McSween house, with a quote**)

Newman, Simon. No title. *Newman's Semi-Weekly*. **April 20, 1881.** Pages 1, 3. InfowebNewsBank.com, America's Historical Newspapers.

Lewis, E.I. "Gen. Wallace's Feud with Billy the Kid, When the General Was Governor of New Mexico and Billy Bonne Was the Most Dangerous Western Outlaw. He Was a Waif and Was Reared in Indiana. *The Indianapolis Press.* Saturday, **June 23, 1900.** Page 7. Lew Wallace Collection. Indiana Historical Society. M0292. Box 14. Folder 11. (**available to Morrison**)

Roberts, Dan W. *Rangers and Sovereignty.* San Antonio: Wood Publishing & Engraving Co. **1914. (Referenced by Don Cline in *Brushy Bill Roberts: I Wasn't Billy the Kid* to show source of his "grandfather" Dan Roberts fabrication)**

Twitchell, Ralph Emerson. *The Leading Facts of New Mexico History.* Vol. I-II. Santa Fe: Sunstone Press. 2007. (Reprinted from a **1912** edition) (**misstates the Lincoln County War as a cattle feud**)

Hoyt, Henry F. "This time it is me who is apologizing for the long delay in answering ..." (Letter to Lew Wallace Jr.) **April 27, 1927.** Indiana Historical Society. Lew Wallace Collection. M0292. Box 14, Folder 11.

_____. "Copy of a bill of sale written by W$^m$ H. Bonney ..." Letter to Lew Wallace Jr. **April 27, 1927.** Indiana Historical Society. Lew Wallace Collection. M0292. Box 14, Folder 11. (**Provided a copy of the Bill of Sale of October 24, 1878**)

King, Frank M. *Wranglin' the Past: Reminiscences of Frank M. King.* "Chapter xix, The Kid's Exit." Pasadena, California: Trail's End Publishing Company. **1935 and 1946. (Claims: Tom O'Folliard and Kip McKinney were cousins, Page 173; Billy had unfair trial, Page 169; shackle-slipping, Page 170**)

Taeger, Mary Nell. "Severo Gallegos Tells His Story and of His Family's Friend, 'Billy the Kid.' " *Ruidoso News.* **July 30, 1948.** Front page, Page 6. Volume II, Number 11. NewspaperArchive.com. (**A Billy the Kid history confabulator, used by Morrison as a prompt for "Brushy's" jailbreak tale. Gallegos was then used give a fake affidavit that "Brushy" was Billy**)

_____. No Author. "Severo Gallegos Tells His Story and of His Family's Friend, 'Billy the Kid.' " (continued) *Ruidoso News.* **August 6, 1948.** Page 3. Volume II, Number 12. NewspaperArchive.com. (**A Billy the Kid history confabulator, with this part 2 article used by Morrison as a prompt for "Brushy's" jailbreak tale. Gallegos was then used give a fake affidavit that "Brushy" was Billy**)

## *ADDITIONAL SOURCES CITED IN THE RETURN OF THE OUTLAW BILLY THE KID (CHRONOLOGICAL)*

Ashenfelter, Singleton M. "Exit 'The Kid', The Fugitive Murderer Hunted Down and Killed by Sheriff Garrett." *The New Southwest, And Grant County Herald.* **July 23, 1881.** Number 30. University of New Mexico. Zimmerman Library. Microfilm AN2 G71. (**Ashenfelter's apocryphal description of Billy the Kid's body as dark and bearded**)

Morrison, William V. Letter to Robert N. Mullin. **July 12, 1955.** (**Claiming "Brushy" could not read, so could not have studied sources**)

Branch, Louis Leon. From manuscript of Charles Frederick Rudulph. *"Los Billitos": The Story of "Billy the Kid" and His Gang: As Told by Charles Frederick Rudulph – a Member of Garrett's Historical Posse.* New York: Carleton Press. **1980.** (**Hearsay claim that the body of Billy the Kid was left in the Maxwell bedroom overnight for the coroner's Jury**)

Haws, Eulaine Emerson. Genealogical papers provided to Martha Vada Roberts Heath. Tyler, Texas. No date. Unpublished. (**Fake "Brushy Bill" genealogy debunked by Eulaine Roberts's son, Roy L. Haws** )

Tunstill, William A. *Billy the Kid and Me Were the Same: A Documentary on the Life of Billy the Kid.* Roswell, New Mexico: Western History Research Center. 1988. (**"Brushy"-backer faking a genealogy using duped Robert's family member and debunked by Roy L. Haws in his 2015 *Brushy Bill: Proof That His Claim to Be Billy the Kid Was a Hoax*)**

Acton, Scott. Unpublished results of computerized pattern recognition system comparing facial images of William Henry Roberts and Billy the Kid. **1990**. (**Fake photo-matching of "Brushy Bill" and Billy Bonney**)

Kyle, Thomas G. "Computers, Billy the Kid, and Brushy Bill: The Verdict Is In." *True West.* **July, 1990.** Pages 16-19. (**No "Brushy" photo-match**)

Sonnichsen, Charles Leland. Interview. Oklahoma City, Oklahoma. **1991**. (**With Sonnichsen's unrepentant claim that there was not a "shred of evidence" that "Brushy" was not Billy Bonney**)

## JOHN MILLER
## BILLY THE KID IMPOSTER HOAX

No Author. Obituary of John Miller. *Prescott Courier.* **November 8, 1937.** (**Gives date of birth as December, 1850**)

Huff, J. Wesley. "Did Pat Garrett Kill Billy the Kid? Herman Tecklenburg Says No; Billy Lived on Ranch at Ramah 35 Years Ago and Visited Him. *The Gallup Independent.* **August 9, 1944.** Volume 55, Number 185. Newspapers.com. (**Tecklenburg's Billy the Kid confabulations**)

Airy, Helen L. *Whatever Happened to Billy the Kid?* Santa Fe, New Mexico: Sunstone Press. **1993**. (**John Miller as Billy the Kid**)

Johnson, Jim. *Billy the Kid: His Real Name Was …* Denver, Colorado: Outskirts Press, Inc. **2006**. (**Debunking evidence for John Miller as Billy the Kid, and providing his dates of arrival and death at the Arizona Pioneers' home cemetery, and his obituary**)

Sams, Dale. Arizona Pioneers' Home and Cemetery Administrator. Personal communication. January 12, 2010. (**Confirmed that records list John Miller's DOB as December – 1850; and birthplace as Fort Sill, Texas**)

## "BILLY THE KID CASE" HOAX
## LINCOLN COUNTY SHERIFF'S DEPARTMENT
## CASE NO. 2003-274

### RELEVANT BOOKS

Althouse, Bill. *Frozen Lightening: Bill Richardson's Strike on the Political Landscape of New Mexico.* Buckman, New Mexico: Thinking Out Loud Press. **2006.**

Bugliosi, Vincent. *Outrage: The Five Reasons Why O.J. Simpson Got Away With Murder.* New York and London: W.W. Norton & Company. **1996**. (**Exposé of Dr. Henry Lee faking forensics in legal cases, Pages 47-49**)

Cline, Donald. *Alias Billy the Kid: The Man Behind the Legend.* Santa Fe: New Mexico: Sunstone Press. **1986**. (**Historian cited by the hoaxers as backing them; apparently unaware of his 1988 manuscript:** *Brushy Bill Roberts: I Wasn't Billy the Kid* )

Cooper, Gale. *Billy the Kid's Pretenders: Brushy Bill and John Miller.* Albuquerque, New Mexico: Gelcour Books. **2012.**

_____. *Billy the Kid's Writings, Words, and Wit.* Albuquerque, New Mexico: Gelcour Books. **2012.**

_____. *MegaHoax: The Strange Plot to Exhume Billy the Kid and Become President.* Albuquerque, New Mexico: Gelcour Books. **2012.**

_____. *Cracking the Billy the Kid Case Hoax: The Strange Plot to Exhume Billy the Kid, Convict Sheriff Pat Garrett of Murder, and Become President of the United States.* Albuquerque, New Mexico: Gelcour Books. **2014**.
_____. *The Billy the Kid Imposter Hoax of Brushy Bill Roberts.* Albuquerque, New Mexico: Gelcour Books. **2019**.
_____. *Billy the Kid's Pretender John Miller.* Albuquerque, New Mexico: Gelcour Books. **2019**.
_____. *The Famous Coroner's Jury Report of Billy the Kid: An Inquest That Made History.* Albuquerque, New Mexico: Gelcour Books. **2019**.
Garcia, Elbert A. *Billy the Kid's Kid 1875-1964, The Hispanic Connection.* Santa Rosa, New Mexico: Los Products Press. **1999**. (**Early participant in "Billy the Kid Case" as unsubstantiated kin of Billy the Kid**)
Garrett, Pat F. *The Authentic Life of Billy the Kid The Noted Desperado of the Southwest, Whose Deeds of Daring and Blood Made His Name a Terror in New Mexico, Arizona, and Northern Mexico.* Santa Fe, New Mexico: New Mexico Printing and Publishing Co. **1882**. (Edition used: Edited by Maurice Garland Fulton. New York: The Macmillan Company. 1927)
Metz, Leon C. *Pat Garrett. The Story of a Western Lawman.* Norman: University of Oklahoma Press. **1974**.
Nolan, Frederick. *The West of Billy the Kid.* Norman: University of Oklahoma Press. **1998**. (**Page 7 for quote on the Eugene Cunningham hoaxed photo of Catherine Antrim**)
Palast, Greg. *Armed Madhouse.* New York: Penguin Group USA. **2007**. (**Bill Richardson exposé**)
Poe, John W. *The Death of Billy the Kid.* (Introduction by Maurice Garland Fulton). Boston and New York: Houghton Mifflin Company. **1933**. (**Pages 22 and 25-26 have Milnor Rudulph quote with the part omitted by hoaxers' from their Probable Cause Statement**)
Richardson, Bill, with Michael Ruby. *Between Worlds: The Making of an American Life.* New York: G.P. Putnam's Sons. **2005**. (**Bill Richardson autobiography**)
Siringo, Charles. *The History of Billy the Kid.* Santa Fe: New Mexico. Privately Printed. **1920**. (**Reproduces the Jim East letter on pages 96-107**)

(SEE: William H. Bonney; Oliver "Brushy Bill" Roberts Billy the Kid Imposter Hoax; John Miller Billy the Kid Imposter Hoax; *Cold Case Billy the Kid* Megahoax

## *CORONER'S JURY REPORT FOR WILLIAM H. BONNEY (SEE WILLIAM H. BONNEY)*

## *PAT GARRETT'S PROSECUTION IMMUNITY "BILLY THE KID CASE" BY STATUTE OF LIMITATIONS*

No Author. "An Act to Provide the Limitation of Criminal Actions." *Acts of the Legislative Assembly of the Territory of New Mexico, Twenty-Second Session, Convened at the Capitol. at the City of Santa Fe on Monday the 6th Day of December, 1875, and Adjourned on Friday the 14 th day of January, 1876.* Santa Fe, New Mexico: Manderfield & Tucker, Public Printers. **1876**. Hathitrust Digital Library. (**Providing for a 10 year statute of limitations on murder; so Garrett could not be prosecuted in 2003 for the 1881 killing of Billy Bonney, since that expired in 1891**)
No Author. Ed. L. Bradford Prince. *The General Laws of New Mexico.* "Limitations of Criminal Actions. "Limitation of Criminal Actions, Acts of the Legislative Assembly of the Territory of New Mexico, Twenty-Second Session, Convened at the Capitol, at the City of Santa Fe on Monday the 6th day of December, 1875, and Adjourned on Friday the 14th day of January, 1876." Chapter 13, Section 1. **1882**. (**Providing for a 10 year statute of limitations on murder; so Garrett could not be prosecuted in 2003 for the 1881 killing of Billy Bonney**)

## PAMPHLETS FOR (CHRONOLOGICAL)

Turk, David S. Historian U.S. Marshals Service. "Research Report: The U.S. Marshals Service and Billy the Kid. To Be Added in its Present Entirety, with Exhibits, to Lincoln County, New Mexico Case # 2003-274." U.S. Marshals Service Executive Services Division." **December, 2003.** (**a major hoax document by "Billy the Kid Case" participant as an addendum to the "Probable Cause Statement"**)

Madrid, Patricia A. Attorney General. *Inspection of Public Records Act Compliance Guide. Fourth Edition. The "Inspection of Public Records Act" NMSA 1978, Chapter 14, Article 2: A Compliance Guide for New Mexico Public Officials and Citizens.* Santa Fe: Office of the Attorney General. **January, 2004.** (**For open records compliance and litigation**)

## PRESS RELEASE FOR (GOVERNOR BILL RICHARDSON)

Richardson, Bill. "Governor Bill Richardson Announces State Support of Billy the Kid Investigation." **June 10, 2003.** (**Announcement at State Capitol of state backing of case # 2003-274 and listing of the participants: Tom Sullivan, Steve Sederwall, Gary Graves, Sherry Tippett, and Paul Hutton**)

_____. "Gov. Bill Richardson Appoints Criminal Defense Lawyer to NM Supreme Court." **November 2, 2007.** (**Corrupt Charles Daniels, husband of Richardson's attorney Randi McGinn**)

_____. "Governor Bill Richardson to Consider Billy the Kid Pardon Petition." Press release. **December 16, 2010.** (**The Randi McGinn pardon petition for "Billy the Kid"**)

_____. "Governor Richardson to Announce his decision on Billy the Kid Pardon Request Tomorrow." Press release. **December 30, 2010.**

## PAST ARRESTS OF "BILLY THE KID CASE" HOAXERS FOR OTHER MATTERS

### LIONEL W. LIPPMAN

Texas Department of Public Safety Conviction Records Database. Dates of arrests for Lionel Whitby Lippman: **June 11, 1973** (San Antonio, Bexar County, forgery and passing), **July 7, 1970** (San Antonio, Bexar County, assault with intent to commit rape), and **February 17, 1970** (San Antonio, Bexar County, vehicular theft), (**Photographer of Sederwall holding John Miller's (or William Hudspeth's) skull for the press after illegal exhumation**)

Obituary information. "Born on January 2, 1941 and passed away on Thursday, **November 22, 2007.** http://www.tributes.com.

### STEVEN M. SEDERWALL

Kirkland, Ray. "State of Oklahoma vs A.B. McReynolds, Jr., John (Nick) Moore and Steve Sederwall. Case No. CRM-83-55." **February 9, 1983.** (**Affidavit accusing Steve Sederwall and others with assault and battery of a Darryl Gene Williams; claimed by him to be another "Sederwall"**)

Warrant of Arrest. "State of Oklahoma, County of LeFlore, vs. Steve Sederwall. Filed **February 10, 1983.** (**Sederwall accused of assault and battery in Case No. CRM-83-55; he claimed it was another "Sederwall"**)

No Author. "5 Charged in Beatings." *The Daily Oklahoma.* **February 17, 1983.** Page 55. (**"Steve Sederwall," age "30," accused of assault and battery; claimed by Sederwall to be another "Sederwall"**)

No Author. "Order of Dismissal of State of Oklahoma vs. A.B. McReynolds, Jr., John (Nick) Moore and Steve Sederwall." **March 17, 1983.** (**Claimed by Sederwall to be another "Sederwall"**)

Concerned Citizens of Lincoln County. "Should Lincoln County Have Grave Concerns Over A Person Like Steve Sederwall Running for Sheriff? *Lincoln County News.* **October 16, 2008.** Volume 103, Number 42, Page 6. **(Providing a tell-tale resume and his alleged 1983 assault case; with DOB corresponding to assault suspect Sederwall's age)**

## *LETTERS ABOUT*

Kurtis, Bill. "This letter is provided as official verification ..." Letter to Steve Sederwall. **October 4, 2010.** Entered by Sederwall's Defense Attorney as Exhibit A in Sandoval District Court Case No. D-1329-CV-2007-1364 Hearing on January 17, 2012. **(Paying for Dr. Henry Lee's forensics)**

## *E-MAILS ABOUT*

Saar, Meghan. To Gale Cooper. "BTK Hoax Article." E-Mail To Gale Cooper. **January 31, 2006.** **(Hoax-backing *True West* magazine rejecting my article proposal to expose the "Billy the Kid Case" hoax)**

Ford, Simon. "Subj. Questions regarding Orchid-Cellmark." E-mail to Gale Cooper. **January 31, 2011. (Consultation on mixed DNA samples and DNA separation costs)**

Miller, Kenny. Personal communication to author about family history and showing Maxwell family objects - including the carpenter's bench, bedstead, and wash stand - and providing photos of them to author. **2011 to 2012. (Information from Maxwell family descendant)**

## *BLOGS ABOUT*

No author. "Fraud Alleged at Cellmark, DNA Testing Firm. TalkLeft: The Politics of Crime. http://www.talkleft.com./new_archives/008809.html. **November 18, 2004.**

Boze Bell, Bob. "The Wild is back in the West." BBB's Blog. **April 24, 2006.** **(Announcement of invitation of Sullivan and Sederwall to Cannes Film Festival.)** http://www.truewestmagazine.com/weblog/blogger1.htm

## *WEBSITE FOR:*

Sederwall, Steve. "billythekidcase.com" Website. From **October (?) 2010 to 2012(?)**. **(For $25.00 membership selling Case 2003-274 records)**

## *TELEVISION DOCUMENTARIES PERPETRATING*

History Channel. "Investigating History: Billy the Kid." Week **of April 24, 2004 and May 2, 2004.(Co-Producer, writer, narrator was "Billy the Kid Case" hoaxer Paul Hutton)**

National Geographic International Discovery ID Channel. "History Mysteries." **2010. (Sederwall presenting the fake Dr. Lee Deputy James Bell top-of-the-stairs murder "investigation")**

## *ARTICLES ABOUT (CHRONOLOGICAL)*

Humphreys, Sexson. "Pardon My 6-Shooters: Billy the Kid? Governor to Decide; 'Pardon Me, I'm Alive,' Says Billy the Kid." *The Indianapolis News.* Thursday, **November 30, 1950.** Indiana Historical Society. Lew Wallace Collection (M292). Box 14. Folder 12.

Hutton, Paul Andrew. "Dreamscape Desperado." *New Mexico Magazine.* Volume 68. Number 6. Pages 44-58. **June, 1990.**

Janofsky, Michael. "122 Years Later, the Lawmen Are Still Chasing Billy the Kid." *The New York Times.* **June 5, 2003.** Vol. CLII, No. 52,505. Pages 1 and A31. **(First national announcement of Billy the Kid Case)**

No Author. "Lincoln County deputy sheriff sends his own letter to governor." *Silver City Daily Press.* **June 25, 2003.** Pages 1, 13.

DellaFlora, Anthony. "State Not Kidding Around: Governor won't mind if probe of the notorious 19th century N.M. outlaw boosts tourism." *Albuquerque Journal.* **June 11, 2003.** No. 162. Pages 1 and A1. **(First big New Mexico announcement of Billy the Kid Case)**

Bommersbach, Jana. "Digging Up Billy: If Pat Garrett didn't kill the Kid, who's buried in his grave?" *True West.* **August/September 2003.** Volume 50. Issue 7. P. 42-45.

No Author. AP. "Authorities call for exhumation of Billy the Kid's mother to solve mystery." *Silver City Sun News.* **October 11, 2003.**

Bommersbach, Jana. "From Shovels to DNA: The inside story of digging up Billy." *True West.* **October/November, 2003.** Volume 50. Issue 7. Pages 42-45.

Jameson, W.C. and Leon Metz. "Was Brushy Bill Really Billy the Kid? Experts face off over new evidence," *True West.* **November/December, 2003.** Volume 50. Issue 10. Pages 32-33.

Murphy, Mary Alice. "Billy the Kid 'Hires' a Lawyer." *Silver City Daily Press Internet Edition.* http://www.thedailypress.com/NewsFolder/11.17.2.html. **November 17, 2003.**

Boyle, Alan. "Billy the Kid gets a lawyer: 122 years after shootout, attorney to gather information for a pardon." msnbc.com. **November 18, 2003.**

Fecteau, Louie. "No Kidding: Governor Taps Lawyer For Billy." *Albuquerque Journal.* Page 1, A6. **November 19, 2003.**

No Author. AP. "Lawyer Appointed to Represent Dead Outlaw." *Silver City Sun News.* http://www.krqe.com/expanded.asp?RECORD_KEY%5bContent. **November 19, 2003. (Bill Robins III's appointment by Richardson)**

No Author. "Lawmakers Consider Posthumous Pardon for Billy the Kid." *abqtrib.com News.* **November 21, 2003.**

Boyle, Alan. "Billy the Kid's DNA Sparks Legal Showdown: Sheriffs and mayors face off over digging up remains from the Old West." *msnbc.com.* **November 21, 2003.**

Romo, Rene. "Kid's Mom May Stay Buried: Silver City wins round to block exhumation for outlaw's DNA." *Albuquerque Journal.* **December 9, 2003.** Section D3.

Janna Bommersbach. "Breaking Out More Shovels: Fort Sumner's Sheriff Gary Graves commits to digging up Billy the Kid's Grave." *True West.* **January/February, 2004.** Volume 51. Issue 1. Pages 46-47. **(Hoax-backing article)**

Benke, Richard. AP. "N.M. Re-Opens Case of Billy the Kid." Yahoo! News. **January 13, 2004.**

_____. "Billy the Kid's Life and Death May Be Put to DNA Test: Officials want to examine the body of the outlaw's mother to test a Texas man's claim that he was Bonney. If so, Pat Garrett didn't kill the Kid." *The Nation.* **January 18, 2004. (Uses fake Overton Affidavit given by Attorney Sherry Tippett)**

No Author. AP. "Billy the Kid hearing delayed for months: Sheriffs need more time to prepare arguments for exhuming remains of outlaw's mother." **January 23, 2004.**

Miller, Jay. "Digging Up the Latest on Billy the Kid." *Las Cruces Sun-News.* **February 3, 2004.**

Gonzales. Carolyn. "Hutton writes wild frontier stories for History Channel." *University of New Mexico Campus News.* **February 16, 2004.** Volume 39. No. 12. **(Hoaxer Hutton's TV program announced)**

Miller, Jay. "The Billy the Kid Code." *Las Cruces Sun-News.* **March 29, 2004.**

Nathanson, Rick. "Grave Doubts: 'Investigating History' series tries to clear up the mysteries surrounding Billy the Kid." *Albuquerque Journal Weekly TV Guide: Entertainer.* **April 24, 2004.** Pages 3, 5.

Garrett, Wm. F. "Letters to the Editor." *De Baca County News.* Page 4. **May 6, 2004. (Garrett family member objects to hoax)**

Murphy, Mary Alice and Melissa St. Aude. "Sederwall, Sullivan uninvited to ball." *Silver City Daily Press Internet Edition.* **June 10, 2004.**

Hill, Levi. "Billy the Kid Stirring Up Dust in Silver City." *Las Cruces Sun-News.* **June 12, 2004.** Section 5A. Pages 1, A2.

No Author. "Attorney Refuses Judge's statements concerning exhumation." *thedailypress.com.* **June 15, 2004. (Attorney Tippett lies about the OMI)**

Richardson, Bill. "Verbatim: I have to decide whether to pardon him. But not right away – after the investigation, after the state gets more publicity." *Time.* **June 21, 2004.** Vol. 163. No. 25. Page 17.

Romo, Rene. "Back off on Billy, Gov. Asked: Silver City says inquiry into death of Kid would harm state tourism. *Albuquerque Journal.* **June 23, 2004.** Section B-1, B-5.

No Author. "Lincoln county deputy sheriff sends his own letter to governor." *Silver City Daily Press.* **June 25, 2004.** Pages 1, 13. **(Letter from Steve Sederwall)**

No Author. "Editorials: New Racing Schedule Tramples Horseman." *Albuquerque Journal.* **June 26, 2004.**

Miller, Jay. "Inside the Capitol. Bizarre case of Billy the Kid." *Roswell Daily Record.* **July 2, 2004.** Page A4.

Romo, Rene. "Forensic Expert on Billy's Case: Questions Remain on Outlaw's Fate." *Albuquerque Journal.* **August 2, 2004.** Page 1. **(Falsely claims blood on bench; says "trace blood")**

No Author. "Forensic expert joins Billy the Kid inquiry in New Mexico." *AP SignOnSanDiego.com.* **August 2, 2004. (Announcing Dr. Henry Lee)**

Miller, Jay. "Inside the Capitol. Sheriffs slippery on Billy the Kid Case." *Roswell Daily Record.* **August 9, 2004.** Page A4.

Cherry, Doris. "Forensics 101 for 'Billy'." *Lincoln County News.* **August 12, 2004.** Pages 2, 10. **(Quotes Sullivan's lie: "a lot" of blood on bench)**

Miller, Jay. "Inside the Capitol. Expert questions Kid probe." *Roswell Daily Record.* **August 20, 2004.** Page A4.

_____. "Inside the Capitol. Hat dance on probe funding." *Roswell Daily Record.* **September 1, 2004.** Page A4.

_____. "Inside the Capitol. Three sheriffs push Kid Case." *Roswell Daily Record.* **September 5, 2004.** Page A4.

_____. "Inside the Capitol. Sheriffs hoax is world-class." *Roswell Daily Record.* **September 8, 2004.** Page A4.

_____. "Inside the Capitol. Kid gets day in court Sept. 27." *Roswell Daily Record.* **September 12, 2004.** Page A4.

_____. "Inside the Capitol. Kid probe making us think." *Roswell Daily Record.* **September 13, 2004.** Page A4.

Stinnett, Scot. "De Baca County Citizens' Committee Files Petition for Recall of Sheriff Gary Graves." *De Baca County News.* **September 14, 2004.**

Miller, Jay. "Inside the Capitol. Who is Attorney Bill Robins?" *Roswell Daily Record.* **September 15, 2004.** Page A4.

Green, Keith. "Mountain Asides: Billy's restless bones are stirred up once again. *RuidosoNews.com.* **September 16, 2004.**

Miller, Jay. "Inside the Capitol. Kid Case: David fights Goliath." *Roswell Daily Record.* **September 17, 2004.** Page A4.

_____. "Inside the Capitol. Many reasons to dig up Kid." *Roswell Daily Record.* **September 19, 2004.** Page A4.

_____. "Inside the Capitol. Nothing to worry about." *Roswell Daily Record.* **September 20, 2004.** Page A4.

Stallings, Dianne. "Showdown in the County Seat." *RuidosoNews.com* **September 21, 2004. (Commissioner Leo Martinez's meeting threatening recall of Sheriff Sullivan for perpetrating a hoax)**

Miller, Jay. "Inside the Capitol. Who speaks for Pat Garrett?" *Roswell Daily Record.* **September 22, 2004.** Page A4.

Stallings, Dianne. "Showdown in the County Seat: shouting match erupts at County Commissioners meeting Tuesday over investigation of Billy the Kid." *Ruidoso News.* **September 22, 2004.**

Cherry, Doris. "Lincoln County 'War' Heats Up Over 'Billy: Capitan Mayor Tracks His Kind of '---' To County Commission Meeting. Tells Jay Miller where to go: wonders why commissioner has his panties in a wad." *Lincoln County News.* **September 23, 2003.** Vol. 99. No. 38. Pages 1-3. (**Commissioner Martinez stops the hoaxers' exhuming Billy the Kid**)

Miller, Jay. "Inside the Capitol. Is there a new Santa Fe Ring?" *Roswell Daily Record.* **September 24, 2004.** Page A4.

Stinnett, Scott. "Rest in Peace, Billy! Exhumation case dismissed." *De Baca County News.* **September 30, 2004.** Vol. 104. No. 2. Pages 1, 5, 6.

Miller, Jay. "Inside the Capitol. Fort Sumner celebrates win." *Roswell Daily Record.* **October 1, 2004.** Page A4.

No author. "Fraud Alleged at Cellmark, DNA Testing Firm. TalkLeft: The Politics of Crime. http://www.talkleft.com./new_archives/008809.html. **November 18, 2004.** (**Dr. Henry Lee's lab commits DNA faking**)

Jana Bommersbach. "Kid Exhumation Nixed: Billy and his mom to rest in peace. *True West.* **January/February 2005.** Volume 52. Issue 1. Pages 68-69.

Massey, Barry. "Casinos, contracting lawyers fund Madrid." The New Mexican. http://www.freenewmexican.com/news/13746.html **May 14, 2005.**

Stinnett, Scott. "Judge rules Graves recall can proceed: Parker finds probable cause after two-day hearing." *De Baca County News.* **August 25, 2005.** Vol. 104. No. 49. Pages 1, 4, 10. (**The Recall Hearing of Sheriff Gary Graves**)

_____. "Testimony paints Graves as 'above the law': Recall probable cause hearing emotional, contentious." *De Baca County News.* **September 1, 2005.** Vol. 104. No. 50. Pages 1, 5, 6, 8, 9, 10.

Carter, Julie. "Follow the Blood: In the Billy the Kid Case, Miller Exhumed." *RuidosoNews.com.* **October 6, 2005.** (**Sederwall lies about blood on bench; gives "dead men don't bleed" quote; has the Lonnie Lippman photo of him holding John Miller/William Hudspeth skull**)

Sullivan, Tom. "Letters: Your Opinion." *RuidosoNews.com.* **October 21, 2005.** (**Sullivan letter to the editor: "Why are they so afraid of the truth?"**)

Carter, Julie. "Billy the Kid in Prescott? *New Mexico Stockman.* **November, 2005.** Pages 38, 39, 76.

Romo, Rene. "Billy the Kid Probe May Yield New Twist. *Albuquerque Journal. ABQ Journal.com.* **November 6, 2005.** (**Claims Sullivan and Sederwall have John Miller's DNA**)

Struckman, Robert. "Bitterroot man hopes to uncover truth about Billy the Kid." http://www.helenair.com/articles/2006/03/13/montana/a05031306_01.txt (Missoulian) **March 13, 2006.** (**Hoaxer Dale Tunnell backing John Miller as Billy the Kid**)

Dodder, Joanna. "Officials could face charges for digging up alleged Billy the Kid." *The Daily Courier of Prescott Arizona.* **April 12, 2006.** (**Sullivan claims DNA in "two months," and fakes Hudspeth skeleton as John Miller's and makes up a left scapula bullet wound**)

Banks, Leo W. "The New Billy the Kid? The mad search for the bones of an American outlaw icon has come to Arizona." *Tucson Weekly.* http://www.tucsonweekly.com/gbase/Currents/Content?oid=oid:81013 **April 13, 2006.** (**Sullivan lies that bench is "saturated with blood; Dr. Rick Staub says DNA extracted from William Hudspeth not John Miller**)

Carter, Julie. "Digging up bones, Arizona may protest Miller exhumation." jcarter@tularosa.net. **April 19, 2006.**

Dodder, Joanna. "Officials could face charges for digging up alleged Billy the Kid." *The Daily Courier of Prescott Arizona.* **April 12, 2006.** (**Sullivan claims DNA in "two months," and fakes Hudspeth skeleton as John Miller's with buck teeth and a left scapula bullet wound**)

Banks, Leo W. "The New Billy the Kid? The mad search for the bones of an American outlaw icon has come to Arizona." *Tucson Weekly.*

http://www.tucsonweekly.com/gbase/Currents/Content?oid=oid:81013

**April 13, 2006. (Sullivan lies that bench is "saturated with blood; Dr. Rick Staub says DNA extracted from William Hudspeth not John Miller)**

Carter, Julie. "Digging up bones, Arizona may protest Miller exhumation." jcarter@tularosa.net. **April 19, 2006.**

Carter, Julie. "Culture Shock: The cowboys and the Kid go to France." jcarter@tulerosa.net. **May 5, 2006. (Sullivan worked on movie 9 months)**

Shafer, Mark. "N.M. pair may face charges in grave case." **May 13, 2006.** markshafer @ArizonaRepublic.com.
http://www.azcentral.com/arizonarepublic/local/articles/0513billythekid0513.html

Myers, Amanda Lee. "New Mexicans Dig Up Trouble in Arizona." *Albuquerque Journal, New Mexico and the West.* **May 14, 2006.** Page B4. **(Also in gulfnews.com; states Dallas lab" is doing DNA comparisons)**

_____."Billy the Kid Still 'Wanted.' " **May 16, 2006.** gulfnews.com. http://archive.gulfnews.com/articles/06/05/16/10040234.html.

No author. "Festival de Cannes, **May 17-28, 2006.** Requiem for Billy the Kid." http://www.festival-cannes.fr/films/fiche_film.php?langue=4355535.
**(Cannes Film Festival synopsis)**

No author. "Out of Competition/Cannes Classics: Requiem for Billy the Kid. Festival de Cannes May 17-28, 2006." http://www.festival-cannes.fr/films/fiche_film.php?langue=4355535. **May 20, 2006. (Sullivan and Sederwall called two sheriffs)**

McCarthy, Todd. "Requiem for Billy the Kid." **May 21, 2006.** Variety.com. http://www.variety.com/review/VE1117930570?categoryid=2220&cs=1&nid=2562.

McCoy, Dave. "L 'Ouest Américain." **May 25, 2006.** MSN Movies. http://movies.msn.com/movies/canneso6/dispatch8.

Bennett, Ray. "Requiem for Billy the Kid." TheHollywoodReporter.com. **May 26, 2006. (Demonstration of hoax damage to history)**

Carter, Julie. "The cowboys are back in town, film in six months." jcarter@tulerosa.net. **June 9, 2006. (Describes plans for more programs)**

Valdez, Jannay. "Digging Up the Truth About Billy." *RuidosoNews.com.* http://ruidosonews.com/apps/pbcs.dll./article?AID=/2006069/OPINION03/6060903 51/101 **June 9, 2006.**

Dodder, Joanna. "Back at Rest: Bones of Billy the Kid return to Prescott." *The Daily Courier.* **July 9, 2006.** http://prescottdailycourier.com/print.asp?ArticleID=40353&Section ID=1&SubSectionID=1

No Author. AP. "Prescott, Ariz. - Prosecutors won't seek charges against two men who exhumed the remains of a man who claimed to be the outlaw Billy the Kid." AOL News. **October 23, 2006.**

_____. AP. "Billy the Kid Case Dropped." *Albuquerque Journal. Metro.* D3. **October 24, 2006.**

_____. AP. "Men Who Exhumed Billy the Kid Won't Be Charged." **October 24, 2006.** *New York Sun.* http://www.nysun.com/article/42176. **(Claims Sullivan and Sederwall did Arizona exhumation, have Miller DNA, and sent to Orchid for matchings to bench DNA)**

_____. AP. "Arizona: No Charges Sought for Exhuming Remains." *New York Times.* A-26. **October 24, 2006.** http://www.nytimes.com/2006/10/24/us/24brfs-002.html?r=1&oref=slogin. **(Cover-up of illegal John Miller/William Hudspeth exhumations)**

Martínez, Tony and Alison. "Better Days Ahead for New Mexico Highlands University?" *The Hispanic Outlook in Higher Education.* **December 4, 2006.**

Turk, David S. "Billy the Kid and the U.S. Marshals Service." *Wild West.* **February, 2007.** Volume 19. Number 5. Pages 34 – 41. **(Turk's expurgated "U.S. Marshals Service and Billy the Kid")**

Jason Strykowski. "A Tale of Two Governors ... And one Kid." *True West*. **May, 2007.** Vol. 54. Issue 5. Page 64.

No Author. AP. "Billy the Kid Exhumation a Possibility." *Roswell Daily Record*. **May 2, 2007. From Stephenville, Texas AP on "Brushy Bill" exhumation attempt; Sederwall claims has John Miller's DNA)**

Carter, Julie. "Brushy Bill targeted for DNA testing; Billy the Kid workbench goes on display." *Ruidoso News*. **May 3, 2007.**

_____. AP. "Manhunt for Real Billy the Kid Goes On: Deputy hopes DNA will finally reveal outlaw's true identity." *Albuquerque Journal*. **May 4, 2007.** B3.

Zorosec, Thomas. "DNA could solve mystery of Billy the Kid." Chron.com - Houston Chronicle. **May 5, 2007. (From Hamilton, Texas; "Brushy Bill" exhumation attempt )**

Carter, Julie. AP. "Texas town denies request to exhume Billy the Kid claimant." *Houston Chronicle*. **May 11, 2007.**

_____. "Evidence Hidden in Spector Trial." BBC Internet News. May 24, 2007. **(Dr. Henry Lee alleged as destroying evidence)**

_____. AP. "Famed experts credibility takes a hit at Spector trial." CNN.com law center. **May 25, 2007. (Dr. Henry Lee allegedly destroyed evidence)**

Stallings, Dianne. "Billy the Kid case straps county for insurance." *RuidosoNews.com*. **August 13, 2008.**

Carter, Julie. "Lincoln County deputies resign commissions for Kid case." *Ruidosonews.com*. **August 16, 2007. (Start of ploy calling Case 2003-274 a "hobby")**

Romo, Rene. "Seeking the Kid, Minus Badges. Deputies Resign to Hunt for Billy." *Albuquerque Journal*. **August 18, 2007.** No. 230. pp. 1-2.

Concerned Citizens of Lincoln County. "Should Lincoln County Have Grave Concerns Over A Person Like Steve Sederwall Running for Sheriff? *Lincoln County News*. **October 16, 2008.** Page 6.

Miller, Jay. "Kid's Pardon a Publicity Stunt." "Inside the Capitol" syndicated column "Inside the Capitol" and blog, insidethecapitol.blogspot.com. **June 23, 2010.**

Stinnett, Scot. "Billy the Kid historian says pardon all part of the hoax." *De Baca County News*. Pages 3, 9. **June 24, 2010. (Reprint of my Jay Miller article without commentary)**

No Author. "Billy the Kid 'to be pardoned.' " *Press Trust of India* (*Hindustan Times*) and Pakistan *Daily Express*. **July 11, 2010. (Pardon for "Brushy Bill")**

Romo, Rene. "Gov. Weighs Pardon for Billy the Kid." *Albuquerque Journal*. Saturday, No. 205. Front page, and A6. **July 24, 2010.**

Licón, Adriana Gómez. "Pardon form New Mexico governor unlikely for Billy the Kid." *El Paso Times*. **July 29, 2010.**

Massey, Barry. Associated Press. Santa Fe. "Billy the Kid To Be Pardoned, 130 Years Later? Lawman's Grandchildren Outraged; 'Would You Issue A Pardon For Someone Who Made His Living As A Thief?' National, international, and internet publications. **July 30, 2010.**

Gardner, David. Los Angeles. "Pat Garrett's family plan showdown over plans to finally pardon Billy the Kid." London's *Daily Mail Online*. **July 31, 2010.**

Boardman, Mark. "The Lunacy of Billy the Kid." *True West*. **August, 2010.** Volume 57. Issue 8. Pages 42-47. **(Defamatory article about me)**

Massey, Barry. Associated Press. Santa Fe. "NM gov meets with lawman Pat Garrett's descendants." **August 4, 2010.** www.wthr.com/global/story.asp?s=12926188.

Vaughn, Chris. "Texas Town seeks New Mexico pardon for Billy the Kid." *Fort Worth Star-Telegram*. **August 14, 2010. (Bid for "Brushy Bill" Roberts pardon.)**

Lacey, Marc. "Old West Showdown Is Revived. *New York Times*. **August 15, 2010. (Richardson shape-shifted to "amateur historian.")**

No Author. "A Tale of Two Billys." *New English Review: The Iconoclast*. (Internet). **August 15, 2010.**

Gordon, Bea. "Examining Legend: The Pardoning of Billy the Kid.. New Mexico Gov. Bill Richardson's talking about exonerating the state's most famous outlaw. But at what cost?" www.newwest.net/topic/article/29850/C37/L37/ **August 17, 2010.**

Massey, Barry. Associated Press. Santa Fe. " 'Billy the Kid' pardon effort draws Wild West showdown." Wilkes-Barre, Pennsylvania. *The Times Leader.* **August 21, 2010. (Introduction of William N. Wallace and Indiana Historical Society opposition. In starpress.com of east central Indiana as "Should Billy the Kid Be Pardoned?")**

Miller, Jay. "When is a promise not a promise?" *Inside the Capitol.* **August 30, 2010.** (Sides, Hampton. "Not-So-Charming Billy." *NY Times Opinion Section Op-Ed Contributor.* September 6, 2010.

Richardson, Bill. "Governor Bill Richardson to Consider Billy the Kid Pardon Petition." Press release. **December 16, 2010. (Floating the Randi McGinn petition)**

Martinez, Edecio. "Billy the Kid to be Pardoned 130 Years Later." CBSNEWS.com. **December 27, 2010.**

Guarino, Mark. "Outgoing New Mexico Gov. Bill Richardson is considering a pardon for celebrated outlaw Billy the Kid. An informal e-mail poll shows support. But time is running out." Associated Press. **December 29, 2010.**

Levy, Glen. "Will Billy the Kid Be Pardoned? Governor Has Until Friday." TIME NewsFeed.com. **December 29, 2010.**

Richardson, Bill. "Governor Richardson to Announce his decision on Billy the Kid Pardon Request Tomorrow." Press release. **December 30, 2010.**

Burke, Kelly David. "Billy the Kid Pardon?" FoxNews.com. **December 30, 2010.**

Hopper, Jessica. "Gov. Bill Richardson: 'I've Decided Not to Pardon Billy the Kid.' " ABCNEWS.com. **December 31, 2010.**

Rojas, Rick. "No Pardon for Billy the Kid. New Mexico Gov. Bill Richardson says, 'The Romanticism appealed to me ... but the facts and evidence did not support it." *Los Angeles Times.* **December 31, 2010.**

Watson, Kathryn. "Alas, no pardon for Billy the Kid: New Mexico's Richardson says close call." washingtontimes.com. **December 31, 2010.**

No Author. "Richardson Declines to Pardon Outlaw Billy the Kid." FoxNews.com. **December 31, 2010.**

Lacey, Marc. "For 2nd Time in 131 Years, Billy the Kid is Denied Pardon." *New York Times.* Page A10. **January 1, 2011.**

Todd, Jeff. "Trial seeks truth in Billy the Kid case." KRQE. **February 17, 2011.**

Romo, Rene. "Fight Won, Questions Remain: Billy the Kid DNA Report Released." *Albuquerque Journal.* Front Page and Page B1. **April 29, 2012.**

Sandlin, Scott. "Billy the Kid case costs taxpayers nearly $200K: Billy the Kid lives on in battle of public records." *Albuquerque Journal.* Front Page, Page A2, Page A8. No. 162. **June 11, 2013. (Fakes blood on carpenter's bench)**

Cherry, Doris. "Modern Billy the Kid 'Cases' Cost Public Plenty: County Shells Out Bucks for Failing to Release Information." *Lincoln County News.* **June 27, 2013.** Volume 109. Number 6. Front Page and Pages 7-8. **(Based on my June 18, 2013 letter to the Lincoln County Commissioners)**

Stallings, Dianne. "Former Lincoln County sheriff dies in Texas: Tom Sullivan died Saturday in Texas." **October 22, 2013.** ruidosonews.com.

## "BILLY THE KID CASE" LEGAL DOCUMENTS (BY LOCATION)

### CAPITAN, NEW MEXICO
### (FIRST ANNOUNCEMENT OF CASE NO. 2003-274)

Sederwall, Steve, "Mayor's Report, **May 5, 2003.**" *Village of Capitan: Capitan Village Hall News.* Capitan, New Mexico. **(Announces filed Case 2003-274)**

## ALBUQUERQUE, NEW MEXICO
## (OPPOSITION OF THE OMI TO EXHUMATIONS)

Zumwalt, Ross E. "Affidavit of Ross E. Zumwalt, MD. In the Matter of Catherine Antrim. Case No. MS 2003-11 Sixth Judicial Court, County of Grant, State of New Mexico. **January 9, 2004**. **(Exhumation refused based on invalid DNA)**

Komar, Debra. "Affidavit of Debra Komar, PhD. In the Matter of Catherine Antrim. Case No. MS 2003-11 Sixth Judicial Court, County of Grant, State of New Mexico. **January 9, 2004**. **(Exhumation refused based on invalid DNA)**

Snead, William E. Attorney for Office of Medical Investigator." "In the Matter of Catherine Antrim: Response of Office of Medical Investigator to Petition to Exhume Remains of Catherine Antrim." Case No. MS 2003-11. Sixth Judicial Court, Grant County. **January 13, 2004**. **(Opposition of OMI to exhumation)**

Komar, Debra. "Deposition of Debra Komar, Ph.D. In the Matter of Catherine Antrim. Case No. MS 2003-11." Sixth Judicial Court, County of Grant, State of New Mexico. Taken by Adam S. Baker, Attorney for Town of Silver City. Signed: Debra Komar, Ph.D. **January 20, 2004**. **(Exhumation refused based on invalid DNA in Billy the Kid's and mother's graves)**

## LINCOLN COUNTY, NEW MEXICO
## (LINCOLN COUNTY SHERIFF'S DEPARTMENT CASE NO. 2003-274, "BILLY THE KID CASE")

Virden, R.E. Lincoln County Undersheriff report. "I participated in the investigative reconstruction ..." **April 28, 2003**. **(Participation in Case # 2003-274.)**

Sullivan, Tom. Lincoln County Sheriff. "Lincoln County Sheriff's Department is currently conducting an investigation ..." Letter to Charles Ryan, Director Arizona Department of Corrections. **April 30, 2003**. **(Describes Garrett as murderer and planned exhumations of John Miller and "Brushy Bill" Roberts)**

_____. "Denial Letter." Pre-printed form to my attorney, Randall M. Harris. **October 8, 2003**. **(Open records denial for the Probable Cause Statement using exception of ongoing law enforcement investigation.)**

Sullivan, Tom. Sheriff, Lincoln County Sheriff's Office, and Steven M. Sederwall. Deputy Sheriff, Lincoln County Sheriff's Office. "Lincoln County Sheriff's Office, Lincoln County, New Mexico, Case: William H. Bonney, a.k.a. William Antrim, a.k.a. The Kid, a.k.a. Billy the Kid: An Investigation into the events of April 28, 1881 through July 14, 1881 – seventy-seven days of doubt." **No Date**. **(Rejected Probable Cause Statement for Case No. 2003-274. In Lincoln County Sheriff's Department case file for 2003-274.)**

_____. "Lincoln County Sheriff's Department Case #2003-274 Probable Cause Statement." Filed in Lincoln County Sheriff's Department. Carrizozo, New Mexico. **December 31, 2003**. **(Became publicly available as "Plaintiff Exhibit 1 in Petitioner's Attorney Sherry Tippett's Silver City "Brief in Chief in Support of the Exhumation of Catherine Antrim." Case No. MS 03-011." Sixth Judicial Court, County of Grant, State of New Mexico." January 5, 2004)**

Overton, Homer D. aka Homer D. Kinsworthy. "Affidavit for Lincoln County Sheriff's Department Case #2003-274 Probable Cause Statement." **December 22, 2003**. **(Fake swearing that Garrett's widow –dead in 1936 - told him in 1940 that Garrett did not kill the Kid. Became publicly available as "Plaintiff Exhibit 1 in Petitioner's Attorney Sherry Tippett's Silver City "Brief in Chief in Support of the Exhumation of Catherine Antrim." Case No. MS 03-011." Sixth Judicial Court, County of Grant, State of New Mexico." January 5, 2004)**

No Author. "Contact List, William H. Bonney Case # 2003-274, Lincoln County Sheriff's Office & Investigators." No Date. **Probably 2003. (In Lincoln County Sheriff's Department Case file for 2003-274)**

Virden, Rick, Lincoln County Sheriff. "Deputy Sheriff Commission [Card] to Tom Sullivan." **January 1, 2005.**

_____. "Deputy Sheriff Commission [Card] to Steven Sederwall." **February 25, 2005.**

Sederwall, Steven M., Lincoln County Sheriff's Deputy Investigator. "Lincoln County Sheriff's Department Supplemental Report, Case #2003-274. Subject: Exhumation of John Miller. Location: Arizona Pioneers' Cemetery, Prescott, Arizona." **May 19, 2005. (Arizona exhumations John Miller and William Hudspeth)**

Virden, R.E. Lincoln County Sheriff. letter to Jay Miller. "We are interested in the truth surrounding Billy the Kid and are continuing the investigation ..." **November 28, 2005. (Virden confirms continuing Billy the Kid case and deputizing Sullivan and Sederwall for it.)**

Virden, R.E. Lincoln County Sheriff. To Hamilton, Texas, Mayor Roy Ramsey [sic]. "This letter will inform you that Tom Sullivan and Steve Sederwall are both commissioned deputies ..." **No date, but around May 2007. (Virden's attempt to exhume "Brushy" with Sullivan and Sederwall as the Deputies)**

Lee, Henry, Dr. Letter to Jay Miller. "In response to your letter dated March 27, 2006 ..." **May 1, 2006. (Lee confirms sending his carpenter's bench and floorboard report to Lincoln County Sheriff's Department.)**

"Jordan, Wilma" aka Gale Cooper. To David Turk, Historian U.S. Marshals Service. "Looking for the truth is good ..." **June 15, 2006. (Attempt to get the Turk's "U.S. Marshal's Service and Billy the Kid " pamphlet for Case 2003-274.)**

Turk, David. Historian U.S. Marshals Service. To "Wilma Jordan." "Thank you for your thoughtful and thorough letter ..." **July 3, 2006. (Tracked "Wilma's" address; refuses to give his "U.S. Marshal's Service and Billy the Kid "pamphlet.)**

Sederwall, Steve. "billythekidcase.com." Sederwall's pay for view website with Case 2003-274 records. **October, 2010. (Selling public records online.**

## SILVER CITY, NEW MEXICO
## (EXHUMATION ATTEMPT ON CATHERINE ANTRIM)

Tippett, Sherry. Attorney. To Richard Gay, Assistant to the Chief of Staff, Governor Richardson's Office. "Memorandum, RE: Exhumation of Catherine Antrim." **July 11, 2003. (Tippett's lie of OMI backing exhumation.)**

Tippett, Sherry. Attorney for Petitioners Sullivan, Sederwall, and Graves. "In the Matter of Catherine Antrim: Petition to Exhume Remains." Case No. MS 03-011. Sixth Judicial Court, County of Grant, State of New Mexico. **October 3, 2003. (Start of exhumation attempts; perjury about permission from OMI)**

Kennedy, Paul J., Adam S. Baker, Thomas F. Stewart, Robert L. Scavron, Attorneys for Mayor Terry Fortenberry on Behalf of the Town of Silver City. "In the Matter of Catherine Antrim: Motion to Intervene." Case No. MS 03-011. Sixth Judicial Court, County of Grant, State of New Mexico. **October 31, 2003. (Start of my exhumation opposition)**

_____. "In the Matter of Catherine Antrim: Response in Opposition to the Petition to Exhume Remains." Case No. MS 03-011. Sixth Judicial Court, County of Grant, State of New Mexico. **October 31, 2003.**

Tippett, Sherry J. Attorney for Petitioners. "State of New Mexico, County of Grant, Sixth Judicial District Court, In the Matter of Catherine Antrim, No. MS. 2003-11. Petitioner's Response in Opposition to the Town of Silver City's Motion to Intervene." (Unfiled) **No Date.**

Baker, Adam S. Attorneys for Mayor Terry Fortenberry on Behalf of Silver City. "In the Matter of Catherine Antrim: Request for Hearing." Case No. MS 03-011. Sixth Judicial Court, County of Grant, State of New Mexico. **November 4, 2003.**

Foy, Jim, District Judge. "In the Matter of Catherine Antrim: Notice of Recusal." Case No. MS 03-011. Sixth Judicial Court, County of Grant, State of New Mexico. **November 14, 2003. (Honest Judge Foy removes himself)**

Miranda, Velia C., District Court Clerk. "In the Matter of Catherine Antrim: Notice of Assignment/Designation of District Judge H.R. Quintero." Case No. MS 03-011. Sixth Judicial Court, County of Grant, State of New Mexico. **November 14, 2003. (Entry of Richardson appointee judge)**

Tippett, Sherry J. Attorney for Petitioners Sullivan, Sederwall and Graves. "In the Matter of Catherine Antrim: Petitioner's Response in Opposition to the Town of Silver City's Motion to Intervene." No. MS. 2003-11. State of New Mexico, County of Grant, Sixth Judicial District Court. (Unfiled) **No Date.**

Robins, Bill III and David Sandoval, Attorneys for Billy the Kid. "In the Matter of Catherine Antrim: Billy the Kid's Unopposed Motion for Intervention and Request for Expedited Disposition." Case No. MS 2003-11. Sixth Judicial Court, County of Grant, State of New Mexico. **November 26, 2003. (First petition with dead Billy the Kid as co-Petitioner to Sullivan, Sederwall, and Graves.)**

Amos-Staats, Joani. "In the Matter of Catherine Antrim: Joani Amos-Staats' [sic] Response in Opposition to the Petition to Exhume." Case No. MS 2003-11. Sixth Judicial Court, County of Grant, State of New Mexico. **December 5, 2003. (Adjacent grave opposition based on disturbing remains)**

_____. "In the Matter of Catherine Antrim: Joani Amos-Staats' [sic] Motion to Intervene and Request for Expedited Hearing." Case No. MS 2003-11. Sixth Judicial Court, County of Grant, State of New Mexico. **December 8, 2003.**

_____. "In the Matter of Catherine Antrim: Joani Amos-Staats' [sic] Response in Opposition to the Petition to Exhume Remains." Case No. MS 2003-11. Sixth Judicial Court, County of Grant, State of New Mexico. **December 8, 2003.**

Kennedy, Paul J., Adam S. Baker, Thomas F. Stewart, Robert L. Scavron, Attorneys for Mayor Terry Fortenberry on Behalf of the Town of Silver City. "In the Matter of Catherine Antrim: Reply in Support of the Town of Silver City's Motion to Intervene." Case No. MS 2003-11. Sixth Judicial Court, County of Grant, State of New Mexico. **December 8, 2003. (Justifying need to protect Antrim grave)**

Tippett, Sherry J. Attorney for Petitioners Sullivan, Sederwall and Graves. "In the Matter of Catherine Antrim: Petitioners Response in Opposition to the Town of Silver City's Motion to Intervene." Case No. MS 2003-11. Sixth Judicial Court, County of Grant, State of New Mexico. **December 8, 2003. (Tippett lies by saying town has no "legal interest" to intervene)**

Quintero, H.R. District Judge. "In the Matter of Catherine Antrim: Order." Case No. MS 03-011. Sixth Judicial Court, County of Grant, State of New Mexico. **December 9, 2003. (Rescheduling hearing from January 6, 2004 to January 27, 2004.)**

Baker, Adam S. Attorneys for Mayor Terry Fortenberry on Behalf of the Town of Silver City. "In the Matter of Catherine Antrim: Intervenor Town of Silver City's Brief on Petition to Exhume." Case No. MS 03-011. Sixth Judicial Court, County of Grant, State of New Mexico. **January 5, 2004. (Arguing 1962 precedent case of Lois Telfer blocking exhumation)**

Tippett, Sherry J. Attorney. To Mayor Steve Sederwall, Sheriff Tom Sullivan, Sheriff Gary Graves. "In the Matter of Catherine Antrim: Petitioners Brief in Chief in Support of Exhumation." Case No. MS 2003-11. Sixth Judicial Court, County of Grant, State of New Mexico. **January 5, 2004. (Using Probable Cause Statement and Homer Overton Affidavit as Plaintiff exhibits)**

Robins, Bill III and David Sandoval. Attorneys for Billy the Kid. "In the Matter of Catherine Antrim: Billy the Kid's Pre-Hearing Brief." Case No. MS 2003-11. Sixth Judicial Court, Grant County. **January 5, 2004. (Linking exhumation and pardon with "Brushy Bill" Roberts as Billy – CRACKED THE HOAX as a "Brushy Bill" scam by using "Brushy's" dark night for July 14, 1881)**

Tippett, Sherry. Attorney for law enforcement Petitioners Tom Sullivan, Steve Sederwall, Gary Graves. "In the Matter of Catherine Antrim: Petitioner's [sic] Brief in Chief in Support of Exhumation." Case No. MS 2003-11. Sixth Judicial Court, Grant County. **January 5, 2004.**

Amos-Staats, Joani. "In the Matter of Catherine Antrim: Intervenor Joani Amos-Staats' [sic] Brief on Petition to Exhume." Case No. MS 2003-11. Sixth Judicial Court, County of Grant, State of New Mexico. **January 6, 2004.**

Kennedy, Paul J., Adam S. Baker, Thomas F. Stewart, Robert L. Scavron, Attorneys for Mayor Terry Fortenberry on Behalf of the Town of Silver City. "In the Matter of Catherine Antrim: Response in Opposition to Petitioners' Brief in Chief." Case No. MS 2003-11. Sixth Judicial Court, County of Grant, State of New Mexico. **January 21, 2004.**

_____. "In the Matter of Catherine Antrim: Silver City's Response in Opposition to Petitioners' Motion for Continuance." Case No. MS 2003-11. Sixth Judicial Court, County of Grant, State of New Mexico. **January 21, 2004.**

Tippett, Sherry J. Attorney. To Mayor Steve Sederwall, Sheriff Tom Sullivan, Sheriff Gary Graves. "Attached is a copy of Judge Quintero's Order of December 9, 2003, ruling on our Hearing ..." **December 17, 2003. (States that they will win on January 27, 2004; urges completing the Probable Cause Statement)**

Quintero, H.R. District Judge, Division 1. "Order of Continuance. In the Matter of Catherine Antrim. Case No. MS 03-011." Filed **January 23, 2004.** Sixth Judicial Court, County of Grant, State of New Mexico. Filed January 23, 2004. **(Tippett sanctioned to pay airfare for witness, Frederick Nolan for changing the hearing date on short notice)**

Robins, Bill III and David Sandoval. Attorneys for Billy the Kid. "In the Matter of Catherine Antrim: Billy the Kid's Brief on the Question of Ripeness." Case No. MS 2003-11. Sixth Judicial Court, Grant County. **February 24, 2004. (Setting up Quintero's sending the exhumation to Fort Sumner)**

Acúna, Mark Anthony and Sherry J. Tippett. Attorneys for Petitioners Sullivan, Sederwall and Graves. "In the Matter of Catherine Antrim: Petitioners' Brief on the Question of Ripeness." Case No. MS 2003-11. Sixth Judicial Court, Grant County. **February 24, 2004.**

Baker, Adam S. and Thomas F. Stewart, Robert L. Scavron, Attorneys for Silver City and Joani Amos-Staats. "In the Matter of Catherine Antrim: Silver City's and Joani Amos-Staats' [sic] Joint Motion to Dismiss on Grounds of Ripeness." Case No. MS 2003-11. Sixth Judicial Court, County of Grant, State of New Mexico. **February 24, 2004.**

Acúna, Mark Anthony. Attorney for Petitioners Sullivan, Sederwall and Graves. "In the Matter of Catherine Antrim: Entry of Appearance." Case No. MS 03-011. Sixth Judicial Court, County of Grant, State of New Mexico. **February 26, 2004. (Replacing Tippett for law enforcement Petitioners)**

Robins, Bill III and David Sandoval. Attorneys for Billy the Kid. "In the Matter of Catherine Antrim: Response to Motion to Dismiss." Case No. MS 2003-11. Sixth Judicial Court, Grant County. **March 10, 2004.**

Quintero, Henry R. "In the Matter of Catherine Antrim: Decision and Order." Case No. MS 03-011." Sixth Judicial Court, County of Grant, State of New Mexico. **April 2, 2004. (Stipulation that case is not ripe, and requires DNA from Fort Sumner Billy the Kid grave first before trying to exhume Catherine Antrim)**

Fortenberry, Terry D, Mayor; Thomas A. Nupp Councilor District 2; Steve May, Councilor District 4; Gary Clauss, Councilor District 3; Judy Ward, Councilor District 1; Alex Brown, Town Manager; Cissy McAndrew, Executive Director Chamber of Commerce; Frank Milan, Director Silver City Mainstreet Project; Susan Berry, Director Silver City Museum. "Open Letter to Governor Bill Richardson." **June 21, 2004. (Request to cease "Billy the Kid Case" exhumations)**

Kemper, Lisa. Kennedy Han, PC. Controller, (via fax). To Gale Cooper. "*In the Matter of Catherine Antrim, 6th Judicial Dist. Ct. Case No. MS 2003-001*, 'This is to confirm our receipt of payment ...'" Baker, Adam. Confirmation of payment of Attorney Sherry Tippett's Judge Henry Quintero sanction by Attorney Bill Robins III. **September 1, 2004.** (See "Order of Continuance. In the Matter of Catherine Antrim. Case No. MS 03-011.") Filed January 23, 2004. Sixth Judicial Court, County of Grant, State of New Mexico. Signed: H.R. Quintero, District Judge, Division 1." April 28, 2004, (**Court sanctions Tippett, and secret donor to case, Bill Robins III pays her sanction.**)

## FORT SUMNER, NEW MEXICO
## (EXHUMATION ATTEMPT ON WILLIAM H. BONNEY)

De Baca County Commissioners Special Meeting." Minutes. (Powhatan Carter III, Chairman; Joe Steele; Tommy Roybal; Nancy Sparks, County Clerk. To whom it may concern. "The De Baca County Commissioners are in full support of Village of Fort Sumner's stand against exhuming the body of Billy the Kid." **September 25, 2003. (Voted against exhumation of Billy the Kid)**

Robins, Bill III and David Sandoval, Mark Acuña, Attorneys for Co-Petitioner Billy the Kid and Sheriff-Petitioners. "In the Matter of William H. Bonney, aka 'Billy the Kid': Petition for the Exhumation of Billy the Kid's Remains." Case No. CV-04-00005. Tenth Judicial District, County of De Baca, State of New Mexico. **February 26, 2004. (Robins joins Acuña to exhume the Kid)**

Robins, Bill III and David Sandoval, Attorneys for Co-Petitioner Billy the Kid. "In the Matter of William H. Bonney, aka 'Billy the Kid': Notice of Excusal." Case No. CV-2004 [sic]-00005. Tenth Judicial District, County of De Baca, State of New Mexico. **March 5, 2004. (Petitioners' removal of honest Judge Ricky Purcell from hearing the case.)**

Jimenez Maes, Petra, Chief Justice. "In the Matter of William H. Bonney, aka 'Billy the Kid': Order Designating Judge." Case No. CV-2004-00005. Tenth Judicial District, County of De Baca, State of New Mexico. **April 1, 2004. (Richardson's corrupt judge appointee, Ted Hartley, is appointed to case)**

Baker, Adam S. and Herb Marsh, Jr., Attorneys for the Village of Fort Sumner. "In the Matter of William H. Bonney, aka 'Billy the Kid': Village of Fort Sumner's Unopposed Motion to Intervene." Case No. CV-04-00005. Tenth Judicial District, County of De Baca, State of New Mexico. **April 12, 2004.**

_____. "In the Matter of William H. Bonney, aka 'Billy the Kid': Response in Opposition to the Petitioners for the Exhumation of Billy the Kid's Remains. In the Matter of William H. Bonney, aka 'Billy the Kid.' " Case No. CV-04-00005. Tenth Judicial District, County of De Baca, State of New Mexico. **April 12, 2004.**

Hartley, Teddy L. "In the Matter of William H. Bonney, aka 'Billy the Kid': Order." Case No. CV-04-00005. Tenth Judicial District, County of De Baca, State of New Mexico. **April 20, 2004. (Intervention of Village of Fort Sumner granted)**

Baker, Adam S. and Herb Marsh, Jr., Attorneys for the Village of Fort Sumner. "In the Matter of William H. Bonney, aka 'Billy the Kid': Response in Opposition to the Petition for the Exhumation of Billy the Kid's Remains." Case No. CV-04-00005. Tenth Judicial District, County of De Baca, State of New Mexico. **May 6, 2004.**

_____. "In the Matter of William H. Bonney, aka 'Billy the Kid': Village of Fort Sumner's Motion For Proof of Attorneys' Authority To Act On Behalf Of William H. Bonney." Case No. CV-04-00005. Tenth Judicial District, County of De Baca, State of New Mexico. **June 24, 2004. (Confronting Attorney Bill Robins III's fakery of representing Billy the Kid based on dead Billy not being real so he cannot have a lawyer)**

_____. "In the Matter of William H. Bonney, aka 'Billy the Kid': Village of Fort Sumner's Motion to Dismiss Against Petitioners Sullivan, Sederwall, and Graves for Lack of Standing." Case No. CV-04-00005. Tenth Judicial District, County of

De Baca, State of New Mexico. **June 24, 2004.** (**Invalid murder case because Pat Garrett properly killed Billy the Kid**)

Hartley, Teddy L. District Judge. "Notice of Hearing. "In the Matter of William H. Bonney, aka 'Billy the Kid': Notice of Hearing." Case No. CV-04-00005. Tenth Judicial District, County of De Baca, State of New Mexico. **July 6, 2004.** (**Hearing set for September 27, 2004**)

Acuña, Mark Anthony, Attorney for the Petitioners Sullivan, Sederwall and Graves. "In the Matter of William H. Bonney, aka 'Billy the Kid': Petitioner's Response to the Village of Ft. Sumner's Motion to Dismiss." Case No. CV-04-00005." Tenth Judicial District, State of New Mexico, County of De Baca. **July 29, 2004.**( **Acuña argues Sheriff-petitioners' Sullivan, Graves, and Sederwall's standing based on law enforcement as Sheriffs and Deputy Sheriff; later Sullivan and Sederwall would lie that they had done the case as private hobbyists to avoid the open records act for public officials to hide their fake DNA documents**)

Robins, Bill III and David Sandoval; Attorneys for the Billy the Kid; and Adam S. Baker and Herb Marsh, Jr., Attorneys for the Village of Fort Sumner. "In the Matter of William H. Bonney, aka 'Billy the Kid': Stipulation of Dismissal." Case No. CV-04-00005. Tenth Judicial District, County of   De Baca, State of New Mexico. **August 23, 2004.** (**Fake dead Billy the Kid petition dismissed with prejudice**)

"In the Matter of De Baca County Sheriff Gary Graves. Petition for Order Allowing Recall Vote." Case No. CV-04-00019. Tenth Judicial District Court, State of New Mexico, County of De Baca. **September 13, 2004.** (**Recall starts against Sheriff Gary Graves, separate from the exhumation case.**)

Acuña, Mark Anthony and Adam S. Baker, Attorneys for Petitioners Graves, Sullivan and Sederwall; and the Village of Fort Sumner. "In the Matter of William H. Bonney, aka 'Billy the Kid': Stipulation of Dismissal With Prejudice." Case No. CV-04-00005. Tenth Judicial District, County of De Baca, State of New Mexico. **September 24, 2004.** (**Petitioners withdraw with prejudice at Fort Sumner. Definitive victory against Billy the Kid exhumation.**)

## ARIZONA: YAVAPAI (PRESCOTT) AND MARICOPA COUNTIES (EXHUMATIONS OF JOHN MILLER AND WILLIAM HUDSPETH)

Sederwall, Steven M., Lincoln County Sheriff's Deputy Investigator. "Lincoln County Sheriff's Department Supplemental Report, Case #2003-274. Subject: Exhumation of John Miller. Location: Arizona Pioneers' Cemetery, Prescott, Arizona." **May 19, 2005.** (**Arizona exhumations John Miller and William Hudspeth**)

Cahall, Anna, Detective Prescott Police Department. "CASE REPORT 0600012767." **April 5, 2006.** (**Concerning the John Miller exhumation**)

Tunnell, Dale. To Jeanine Dike. "Subject: RE: Disinterment of Wm Bonney." **May 3, 2005.**

Dike, Jeanine. To Dale Tunnell. "Subject: Disinterment of Wm Bonney." **May 3, 2005.**

_____. To Dale Sams. "Subject: FW: Disinterment Wm Bonney." **May 3, 2005.**

_____. To Dale Sams. "Subject: FW: Disinterment Wm Bonney." **May 4, 2005.**

Sams, Dale. To George Thompson. "Subject: Disinterment." **May 4, 2005.** (**Confirms Sams has no idea where the Miller grave is located.**)

Sederwall, Steven M., Lincoln County Sheriff's Deputy Investigator. "Lincoln County Sheriff's Department Supplemental Report, Case #2003-274. Subject: Exhumation of John Miller. Location: Arizona Pioneers' Cemetery, Prescott, Arizona." **May 19, 2005.** (**Arizona exhumations John Miller and William Hudspeth**)

Fulginiti, Laura C. Ph.D., D-ABFA. Forensic Anthropologist. To Dale L. Tunnell, Ph.D. "RE: Exhumation, Pioneer Home Cemetery, Prescott, Arizona." **June 2, 2005.** (**Report of the Miller-Hudspeth exhumations revealing fake hoaxer claims of buck teeth and bullet wound to left scapula of John Miller.**)

Sederwall, Steven. To Misty Rodarte. "Subject: Billy the Kid." **July 6, 2005.**

Winter, Anne. "To: Tim Nelson; Alan Stephens. Subject: Pioneer Home, Grave, Billy the Kid and DNA." **August 18, 2005. (Has attachment of Pioneers' Home Supervisor Gary Olson's cover-up letter to her and implied internal cover-up. Also states that Sullivan paid for the exhumation.)**

_____. "To: Tim Nelson; Alan Stephens. Subject: Billy the Kid." **September 8, 2005. ("80% DNA match" with Miller claimed)**

Olson, Gary. Superintendent Arizona Pioneers' Home. To David Snell. "You recently asked the Arizona Pioneers' Home if a body in its cemetery had been exhumed ..." October 3, 2005. **(Confirms original cover-up of John Miller exhumation.)**

Winter, Anne. "To Gary Olson. Subject: RE: the kid." **October 17, 2005. (Requesting any DNA results yet to him.)**

Olson, Gary. "To Anne Winter. Subject: RE: the kid." **October 17, 2005. (Reporting on no DNA results yet to him.)**

Winter, Anne. "To: Jeanine L'Ecuyer. Subject: FW: the kid." **October 17, 2005. (Reporting on no DNA results yet to Olson.)**

Olson, Gary. "To: Anne Winter. Subject: FW: re. John Miller." **October 20, 2005. (Cover-up `planned for Romo. "I thought you and the Governor may want to know about this request.")**

Winter, Anne. "To: Tim Nelson; Alan Stephens. Subject: FW: re. John Miller. **October 20, 2005. (Cover-up plan for Romo presentation: "Remember there was the legal issue that they dug up two bodies.")**

_____. "To: Jeanine L'Ecuyer. Subject: FW: re. John Miller." **October 25, 2005. (Planning cover-up for media requests.)**

Sederwall, Steven. "To: Barbara J. Miller; Steve McGregor; Rick Staub; Misty Rodarte; Emily Smith; Bob Boze Bell. Subject: in the Albuquerque Journal." **November 6, 2005. (Copy Romo article.)**

Olson, Gary. "To Anne Winter, Mark Wilson. Subject: FW: in the Albuquerque Journal." **November 7, 2005. (Copy Romo article.)**

Winter, Anne. "To: Jeanine L'Ecuyer; Tim Nelson; Alan Stephens. Subject: Billy the Kid. **November 7, 2005. (About Gary Olson's cover-up in KPNX interview.)**

Snell, David. To Shiela Polk. Yavapai County Attorney. "I feel it is my duty to report to you that graverobbers are plying their trade ..." **March 11, 2006. (Arizona citizen starting criminal investigation of Miller/Hudspeth exhumations.)**

Jacobson, Marcia. "To Anne Winter, Policy Advisor for Health, Office of the Governor, and Chief Randy Oaks, Prescott Police Department. Re: Disinterment of bodies at Arizona Pioneer's [sic] Home Cemetery." **March 30, 2006. (Attempted cover-up of John Miller and William Hudspeth exhumations.)**

Cahall, Anna, Detective Prescott Police Department. "CASE REPORT 0600012767." **April 5, 2006. (Concerning the John Miller exhumation; interviews with Sullivan, Sederwall, Tunnell)**

Savona, Glenn A. Prescott City Prosecutor. To Shiela Sullivan Polk, Yavapai County Attorney. "Re: Police Department DR# 2006-12767 Arizona Pioneers' Home Cemetery." **April 13, 2006. (Calls exhumations potential felonies)**

Cooper, Gale. To Detective Anna Cahall. Prescott Police Department. "Re: Exhumation of John Miller and adjacent grave for pursuing the New Mexico Billy the Kid Case." **April 13, 2006.**

_____. To Detective Anna Cahall. Prescott Police Department. "Re: Pertinent articles regarding exhumation of John Miller and remains from adjacent grave for alleged promulgation of the New Mexico Billy the Kid Case, a murder investigation." **April 17, 2006.**

_____. To Deputy County Attorney Steve Jaynes and County Attorney Dennis McGrane. (via fax) "Re: Information on the New Mexico Billy the Kid Case pertinent to the Arizona John Miller exhumations." **May 2, 2006.**

Sederwall, Steve. To confidential recipient. "Well we have the governor reaching out to the Arizona to stop this investigation." **May 16, 2006.**

Cooper, Gale. To Attorney Jonell Lucca (via fax). "Re: Case # CA20006020516. Follow-up to our telephone conversation of June 9, 2006, to address the issue of Permit for the exhumations of John Miller and the remains from an adjacent grave for promulgation of the New Mexico Billy the Kid Case, a murder investigation." **June 12, 2006**.

_____. To Attorney Jonell Lucca (via fax). "Re: Case # CA20006020516. Follow-up to my fax of June 12, 2006, to address additional issues pertinent to the exhumations of John Miller and William Hudspeth, done for promulgation of the New Mexico Billy the Kid Case, an alleged murder investigation." July 11, 2006.

Sams, Dale. Arizona Pioneers' Home Administrator. To Gale Cooper. Confirming approximate date of John Miller's birth as 1850. **August 8, 2006**.

Cooper, Gale. To Attorney Jonell Lucca (via fax). "Re: Case # CA20006020516. Follow-up to my fax of July 11, 2006, to address issues pertinent to the promulgators of the New Mexico Billy the Kid Case (which resulted in the exhumations of John Miller and William Hudspeth); with added focus on its alleged forensic experts and co-participants." **August 11, 2006**.

_____. To Attorney Jonell Lucca. "Re: Enclosed reference copy of Freedom of Information Act (FOIA) to Governor Janet Napolitano regarding her possible participation in the Prescott, Arizona exhumations of John Miller and William Hudspeth, and their legal issues related to Maricopa County Prosecutor's Office Case # CA20006020516." **September 22, 2006**.

_____. To Attorney Jonell Lucca. "Re: Information pertaining to Case # CA20006020516 (exhumations of John Miller and William Hudspeth) - American Academy of Forensic Science Ethics and Conduct Complaint against Dr. Henry Lee." **October 2, 2006**.

Lucca, Jonell L. To Dr. Gale Cooper. "This letter is to inform you that the Maricopa County Attorney's Office has declined to file charges ..." **October 17, 2006**. **(Corrupt claim that the only suspects were Jeanine Dike and Dale Tunnell to shield Sullivan and Sederwall)**

Cooper, Gale. To Attorney Jonell Lucca. "Re: Maricopa County Case # CA20006020516." **October 30, 2006**. **(Confirmation of getting her case termination letter, and asking why she changed suspects. Never answered.)**

Cooper, Gale. To Detective Anna. Prescott Police Department. "Re: Freedom of Information Act Request for Records of Prescott Police Department Case No. 06-12767. **September 11, 2008**. **(No response)**

## HAMILTON, TEXAS
## (EXHUMATION ATTEMPT ON "BRUSHY BILL" ROBERTS)

Cooper, Gale. "Billy the Kid Case in a Nutshell." Faxed letter to Hamilton, Texas, Mayor Roy Rumsey. **May 3, 2007**. **(About hoax to dig up "Brushy Bill")**

Virden, R.E. Lincoln County Sheriff. To Hamilton, Texas, Mayor Roy Ramsey [sic]. "This letter will inform you that Tom Sullivan and Steve Sederwall are both commissioned deputies ..." **No date, but around May 2007**. **(Virden's attempt to exhume "Brushy Bill" Roberts.)**

Cooper, Gale. "RE: Lincoln County Sheriff's Department's 2007 attempt to exhume Oliver "Brushy Bill" Roberts. Faxed letter to Hamilton, Texas, Mayor Roy Rumsey. **September 11, 2008**.

Rumsey, Roy. Hamilton Mayor. "RE: Lincoln County Sheriff's Department's 2007 attempt to exhume Oliver Roberts." Faxed letter to Gale Cooper. **September 12, 2008**. **(Confirmation that the case is closed)**

## PAST ATTEMPT TO EXHUME WILLIAM H. BONNEY

"Motion to Intervene. In Re Application of Lois Telfer, Petitioner for the Removal of the Body of William H. Bonney, Deceased, From the Ft. Sumner Cemetery in Which

He is Interred for Reinterment in the Lincoln, New Mexico, Cemetery. Case No. 3255." **December 5, 1961.** In the District Court of the Tenth Judicial District Within and For the County of De Baca. Signed: Victor C. Breen and John Humphrey, Jr., Attorneys for Louis A Bowdre. **(Louis Bowdre was the relative of Charles Bowdre whose grave is contiguous to William Bonney's.)**

Breen, Victor C. and John Humphrey, Jr., Attorneys for Louis A Bowdre. "Motion to Intervene. In Re Application of Lois Telfer, Petitioner for the Removal of the Body of William H. Bonney, Deceased, From the Ft. Sumner Cemetery in Which He is Interred for Reinterment in the Lincoln, New Mexico, Cemetery." Case No. 3255. In the District Court of the Tenth Judicial District, County of De Baca. **December 5, 1961. (Louis Bowdre was the relative of Charles Bowdre whose grave is contiguous to William Bonney's.)**

Kinsley, E.T. District Judge. "Decree. In Re Application of Lois Telfer, Petitioner for the Removal of the Body of William H. Bonney, Deceased, From the Ft. Sumner Cemetery in Which He is Interred for Reinterment in the Lincoln, New Mexico, Cemetery." Case No. 3255." In the District Court of the Tenth Judicial District Within and For the County of De Baca. **April 6, 1962. (Petition for exhumation Billy the Kid denied on basis that his grave could not be located and the search would disturb Bowdre's remains. That precedent was ignored by the current Petitioners and their attorneys.)**

## MY OPEN RECORDS REQUESTS (CHRONOLOGICAL)

### *RECORDS REQUESTS BY JAY MILLER AS MY PROXY*

Miller, Jay. To Steve Sederwall, Mayor of Capitan and Deputy Sheriff of Lincoln County. "FOIA/IPRA." **May 13, 2004.**

_____. To Village of Capitan Records Custodian. "I would like to inspect and copy the following documents of Steve Sederwall ..." **May 13, 2004.**

_____. To County Clerk of Lincoln County/Records Custodian, Lincoln County Courthouse. "Re: I would like to inspect the following documents of Tom Sullivan, elected Sheriff of Lincoln County." **May 13, 2004.**

_____. To County Clerk of DeBaca County/Records Custodian. "Freedom of Information Act Request: Inspect and copy records pertaining to Gary Graves, elected sheriff ..." **May 13, 2004.**

Morel, Alan P. Lincoln County Attorney. To Jay Miller. "RE: Freedom of Information Act Request dated May 13, 2004." **May 19, 2004.**

Grassie, Anna Gail. (For Village of Capitan and Mayor Steve Sederwall). To Jay Miller. "Reference: Freedom of Information Request from Jay Miller dated May 13, 2004." **May 25, 2004.**

Miller, Jay. To Michael Cerletti, Secretary, Department Tourism. "RE: FOIA/IPRA on Billy the Kid Case promulgators and Department of Tourism." **May, 28, 2004.**

_____. To Attorney Alan P. Morel. "Re: Response to your letter dated May 19, 2004 on behalf of the County Clerk of Lincoln County and Lincoln County Sheriff Tom Sullivan." **June 1, 2004.**

_____. To Mayor Steve Sederwall. "FOIA/IPRA on Steve Sederwall as Mayor of Capitan and Deputy Sheriff of Lincoln County." **June 1, 2004.**

Morel, Alan P. Lincoln County Attorney. To Jay Miller. "RE: Response to your letter dated May 19, 2004 on behalf of the County Clerk of Lincoln County and Lincoln County Sheriff Tom Sullivan. **June 1, 2004.**

Sederwall, Steven: Mayor. To Jay Miller. "I am in receipt of your letter dated June 1, 2004." **June 3, 2004.**

Morel, Alan P. Lincoln County Attorney. To Jay Miller. "RE: Freedom of Information Act Request June 1, 2004." **June 4, 2004.**

Cerletti, Mike.. To Jay Miller. "Reply to your freedom of information request." **June 7, 2004. (Denied participation of Tourism Department in Billy the Kid Case)**

Miller, Jay. To Lincoln County Attorney Alan Morel. "Copy all documents relevant to David Turk, historian for the U.S. Marshals Service ..." **June 9, 2004**.

_____. To Mayor of Capitan and Deputy Sheriff of Lincoln County Steve Sederwall. "Evade response by claiming that you were being addresses solely in your capacity as Mayor ..." **June 9, 2004**.

_____. To Sheriff Gary Graves and Nancy Sparks, De Baca County Clerk. "Freedom of Information Act Request: I would like to inspect any and all documents relevant to David Turk ..." **June 9, 2004**.

Sederwall, Steven M. To Jay Miller. "This office has no records ..." **June 10, 2004**.

Miller, Jay. To Mayor Steve Sederwall. "FOIA/IPRA on Steve Sederwall as Mayor of Capitan and Deputy Sheriff of Lincoln County." **June 10, 2004**.

_____. To Attorney General Patricia Madrid. "Re: Follow-up on FOIA/IPRA Request to Lincoln County Sheriff Tom Sullivan." **June 14, 2004**. (**This was stonewalled. No response ever came.**)

Sparks Nancy. (Clerk for Sheriff Gary Graves). To Jay Miller. "Re: FOIA/IPRA request for records of De Baca County Sheriff Gary Graves." **June 14, 2004**.

Miller, Jay. To Mayor of Capitan and Deputy Sheriff of Lincoln County Steve Sederwall. "Thank you for your prompt response to my letter of June 1, 2004 ... " **June 21, 2004**.

_____. To Attorney General Patricia Madrid. RE: Follow-up on FOIA/IPRA Requests to Steve Sederwall, Mayor of Capitan and Deputy Sheriff of Lincoln County." **June 21, 2004**.

_____. To Lincoln County Attorney Alan Morel. "I would like to inspect and copy any and all documents relevant to your client Tom Sullivan, Sheriff of Lincoln County with regard to a statement made by his attorney Sherry Tippett ..." **June 23, 2004**.

_____. To Mayor of Capitan and Deputy Sheriff of Lincoln County Steve Sederwall. "To inspect and copy all records relevant to your attorney, Sherry Tippett's, claims ..." **June 23, 2004**.

_____. To Michael Cerletti, Secretary Tourism. "Thanks for your response ..." **June 23, 2004**.

Lama, Albert J. Assistant Attorney General. To Jay Miller. "Concerning an alleged violation of the Inspection of Public Records Act by the Lincoln County, De Baca County, and Village of Capitan." **June 24, 2004**. (**This was sent to corrupt Assistant AG Mary Smith, who later covered-up for Sederwall.**)

Miller, Jay. To Attorney General Patricia Madrid. "Re: Follow-up on FOIA/IPRA Requests to Steve Sederwall, Mayor of Capitan and Deputy Sheriff of Lincoln County." **June 21, 2004**. (**Instead of answering, they closed the case**)

Graves, Gary W. De Baca County Sheriff. To Jay Miller. "I am writing in response to your request ..." **June 22, 2004**. (**Denies information on David Turk**)

Miller, Jay. To Sheriff Gary Graves. "Freedom of Information Act Request: Inspect and copy all records relevant to your attorney, Sherry Tippett ..." **June 23, 2004**.

_____. To Sheriff Gary Graves and Nancy Sparks. "Re: FOIA/IPRA request for records." **June 25, 2004**.

Graves, Gary W. De Baca County Sheriff. To Jay Miller. "I do not maintain requests for travel reimbursements ..." **June 29, 2004**. (**His clerk did send records!**)

_____. To Jay Miller. "As per your FOIA/IPRA Request on **June 23, 2004** ..." June 29, 2004. (**Denies records on Attorney Sherry Tippett.**)

_____. To Jay Miller. "I do not maintain or have any records in reference to Sherry Tippett ..." **June 29, 2004**.

Miller, Jay. To Attorney Alan Morel. "Re: Deputizing of Capitan Mayor Steve Sederwall as referenced in your letter dated June 4, 2004 on behalf of Lincoln County Sheriff Tom Sullivan." **July 1, 2004**.

Morel, Alan P. Attorney for Lincoln County. To Jay Miller. "Re: Deputizing of Capitan Mayor Steve Sederwall as referenced in your letter dated June 4, 2004 on behalf of Lincoln County Sheriff Tom Sullivan." **July 1, 2004**.

_____. To Jay Miller. "RE: Freedom of Information Act/Inspection of Public Records Act Request dated June 23, 2004." **July 2, 2004.**

Sparks, Nancy. De Baca County Clerk. "I have sent you everything I have on Sheriff Graves ..." July 2, 2004.

Prelo, Marc. Attorney for Village of Capitan. To Jay Miller. "RE: Village of Capitan/Freedom of Information Act - Inspection of Public Records Request. **July 5, 2004. (Response for Sederwall to Jay Miller)**

Miller, Jay. To Assistant AG Mary Smith. "Re: Response to your letter of June 24, 2004." **July 8, 2004.**

_____. To Sheriff Gary Graves. "Re: Follow-up on your responses to my prior FOIA/IPRA requests." **July 8, 2004.**

Morel, Alan P. Lincoln County Attorney. To Jay Miller. "RE: Freedom of Information Act Request dated July 1, 2004." **July 9, 2004. (Statutes justifying deputizing Sederwall)**

Smith, Mary H., Assistant Attorney General. To Jay Miller. "Re: Determination of Inspection of Public Records Act Complaint v Village of Capitan." **August 3, 2004. (Corrupt rejection of open records complaint.)**

_____. To Jay Miller. "Re: Determination of Inspection of Public Records Act complaint v De Baca County." **August 3, 2004. (Corrupt rejection of open records complaint.)**

Miller, Jay. To Sheriff Tom Sullivan. "Re: David Turk, Historian for the U.S. Marshals Service." **August 5, 2004.**

_____. To Office of General Counsel - FOIA REQUEST, Attn. Arleta Cunningham, U.S. Marshal's Service. "Re. David Turk, historian for U.S. Marshal's Service, FOIA on Sederwall/Sullivan/Graves/ Billy the Kid Case." **August 5, 2004.**

_____. To Assistant AG Mary Smith. "Re. Response to your letter of August 3, 2004 about determination of my IPRA complaint v Mayor of Capitan Steve Sederwall, who also represents himself as Deputy Sheriff of Lincoln County; and the Village of Capitan." **August, 10, 2004.**

Sullivan, Tom, Lincoln County Sheriff. "In response to your 'Inspection of Public Records Act" request dated August 5, 2004." **August 18, 2004. (Denies open records request on David Turk based on ongoing criminal investigation)**

Morel, Alan P. Lincoln County Attorney. To Jay Miller. "In response to your "Information Act Request dated August 5, 2004." **August 18, 2004.**

Miller, Jay. To Deputy Attorney General Stuart Bluestone. "Re: Complaint and appeal for assistance with regard to non-compliance with FOIA/IPRA requests made to Capitan Mayor Steve Sederwall, who represents himself as Deputy Sheriff of Lincoln County and the Village Clerk of Capitan." **August 28, 2004. (No response)**

_____. To Deputy Attorney General Stuart Bluestone. "Re: Complaint and appeal for assistance with regard to non-compliance with FOIA/IPRA requests made to Lincoln County Sheriff Tom Sullivan and Lincoln County Clerk." **September 4, 2004. (No response)**

Utley, Robert M. "Billy Again." **September 16, 2004. (Sent to Jay Miller and forwarded to me regarding Paul Hutton in Billy the Kid Case.)**

Smith Mary. Assistant Attorney General. To Jay Miller. "Re: Inspection of Public Records Act complaint v Steve Sederwall, Mayor of Capitan and Lincoln County Deputy Sheriff." **May 17, 2005. (Nine months later: Rejection of complaint)**

Bordley, William E. To Jay Miller. "Freedom of Information/Privacy Act Request No. 2004USMS7634, Subject: David Turk, Historian U.S. Marshals Service, FOIA on Sederwall/Sullivan/Graves/Billy the Kid Case." June 22, 2005.

Miller, Jay. To William E. Bordley, Associate General Counsel/FOIPA Officer, U.S. Marshal's Service. "Follow-up on your response titled Freedom of Information Act Request No. 2004USMS7634 Subject: David Turk, Historian U.S. Marshal's Service, FOIA on Sederwall/Sullivan/Graves/Billy the Kid Case." **July 25, 2005.**

DeZulovich, Mavis. FOI/PA Liaison, Office of Public Affairs. To Jay Miller. "This letter is in response to your Freedom of Information/Privacy Act Request No. 2004USMS7634 in reference to David Turk. **August 24, 2005. (States Turk is not Probable Cause Statement author, but references his pamphlet.)**

Virden, R.E. Lincoln County Sheriff. Letter to Jay Miller. "We are interested in the truth surrounding Billy the Kid and are continuing the investigation ..." **November 28, 2005. (Confirms deputizing Sullivan and Sederwall for "Billy the Kid Case")**

Miller, Jay. To Paul Hutton. "As a journalist following the Billy the Kid Case ..." **February 6, 2006.**

_____. To Attorney General Patricia Madrid. "Re: Follow-up on non-response by Attorney General to my September 4, 2004 Complaint and Appeal for assistance with regard to non-compliance by past Lincoln County Sheriff Tom Sullivan with my FOIA/IPRA Requests." **March 20, 2006.**

_____. To Paul Hutton. "Repeat of one sent to you on February 6, 2006, because I received no response to it." **March 20, 2006.**

_____. To Sheriff Rick Virden. "Inspection of Public Records Act/Freedom of Information Act request." **March 27, 2006.**

_____. To Attorney Marc Prelo. "Re: Follow-up on Freedom of Information Request response dated July 5, 2004." **March 27, 2006. (Requests information on taxpayer money for Sederwall's Billy the Kid Case participation)**

Prelo, Marc Attorney. To Jay Miller. "RE: Village of Capitan/Freedom of Information Act – Inspection of Public Records Request." **Match 31, 2006. (Confirms his use of taxpayer money for Sederwall's Billy the Kid Case participation)**

Morel, Alan P. Lincoln County Attorney. To Jay Miller. "RE: Freedom of Information Act/Inspection of Public Records Act request dated March 27, 2006, to Lincoln County Sheriff Rick Virden. **April 3, 2006.**

_____. To Jay Miller. "Re: Follow-up on Freedom of Information Act Request Responses Dated May 19, 2004 and June 4, 2004." **April 17, 2006. (Confirms his use of taxpayer money for Sullivan's Billy the Kid Case participation)**

Miller, Jay. To Attorney General Patricia Madrid. "Re: Follow-up on FOIA/IPRA Request to Lincoln County Sheriff Tom Sullivan." **May 6, 2006. (No response )**

_____. To Assistant Attorney General Mary Smith. "Re. Response to your letter of May 17, 2005 rejecting my IPRA complaint against then Mayor of Capitan Steve Sederwall, who also represented himself as Deputy Sheriff of Lincoln County." **May 6, 2006. (No response.)**

Miller, Jay. To Assistant Attorney General Mary Smith. "Re. Response to your letter of May 17, 2005 rejecting my IPRA complaint against then Mayor of Capitan Steve Sederwall, who also represented himself as Deputy Sheriff of Lincoln County." **June 13, 2006. (Repeat complaint with new information. No response.)**

_____. To Paul Hutton. "Re. Clarification of my letter to you dated March 20, 2006, and reframing of it as a FOIA/IPRA Request." **June 13, 2006.**

_____. To Attorney Mark Acuña. "Re. Follow-up on your legal participation in the New Mexico Billy the Kid Case and participation of the Jaffe Law Firm in the New Mexico Billy the Kid Case." **June 22, 2006. (No response.)**

_____. To Attorney General Patricia Madrid. "Re. FOIA/IPRA Request with regard to your relationship with Attorney Bill Robins III and/or his law firm Heard, Robins, Cloud, Lubel & Greenwood LLP." **August 8, 2006.**

_____. To Attorney Mark Acuña.. "Re. Follow-up on my unanswered letter of June 22, 2006 with regard to your legal participation in the New Mexico Billy the Kid Case and the participation of your Jaffe Law Firm in the New Mexico Billy the Kid Case." **August 8, 2006. (No response).**

_____. To Mavis DeZulovich. FOIA/PA Liaison U.S. Department of Justice. "Re: Follow-up to your August 24, 2005 response to my Freedom of Information Act request No. 2004USMS7634 in reference to David Turk, Historian for the U.S. Marshals Service." **August 8, 2006. (Request for Turk's pamphlet)**

Hutton, Paul "I was never the 'state historian' ..." . Letter to Jay Miller. **June 20, 2006**. (**Central "Billy the Kid Case" hoaxer lies about his role**)

Miller, Jay. To Attorney Mark Acuña. "Re. Follow-up on your legal participation in the New Mexico Billy the Kid Case and participation of the Jaffe Law Firm in the New Mexico Billy the Kid Case." June 22, 2006. (**No response.**)

_____. To Attorney General Patricia Madrid. "Re. FOIA/IPRA Request with regard to your relationship with Attorney Bill Robins III and/or his law firm Heard, Robins, Cloud, Lubel & Greenwood LLP." **August 8, 2006**.

_____. To Attorney Mark Acuña.. "Re. Follow-up on my unanswered letter of June 22, 2006 with regard to your legal participation in the New Mexico Billy the Kid Case and the participation of your Jaffe Law Firm in the New Mexico Billy the Kid Case." **August 8, 2006**. (**No response**).

_____. To Mavis DeZulovich. FOIA/PA Liaison U.S. Department of Justice. "Re: Follow-up to your August 24, 2005 response to my Freedom of Information Act request No. 2004USMS7634 in reference to David Turk, Historian for the U.S. Marshals Service." **August 8, 2006**. (**Requesting copy of David Turk's pamphlet on Billy the Kid and U.S. Marshals Service**)

_____. To Dr. Rick Staub, Director Orchid Cellmark Lab. "Re: The participation by you and Orchid Cellmark in the New Mexico Billy the Kid Case." **August 8, 2006**. (**No response.**)

Kupfer, Elizabeth, Records Custodian. To Jay Miller. "Need additional time ..." **August 14, 2006**.

Miller, Jay. To Attorney General Patricia Madrid. "RE: FOIA/IPRA request regarding Attorney Bill Robins III and/or his law firm Heard, Robins, Cloud, Lubel, and Greenwood." **August 24, 2006**.

Cedrick, Nikki. FOIA/PA Liaison U.S. Department of Justice. "Per your FOI request No. 2004USMS7634." **August 31, 2006**. (**Refuses to send copy of David Turk's pamphlet on Billy the Kid**)

Miller, Jay. To Attorney General Patricia Madrid. "Re: Second FOIA/IPRA Request with regard to documentation of financial relationship of Attorney General Patricia Madrid and/or her Office, and Attorney Bill Robins III and/or his law firm Heard, Robins, Cloud, Lubel, and Greenwood LLP." **September 1, 2006**.

_____. To Assistant Attorney General Mary Smith. "Re. Response to your letter of May 17, 2005 rejecting my IPRA complaint against then Mayor of Capitan Steve Sederwall, who also represented himself as Deputy Sheriff of Lincoln County." **September 1, 2006**. (**No response**)

_____. To Deputy Attorney General Stuart Bluestone. "Re: Follow-up on your recent telephone call to me about my current, repeated, FOIA/IPRA non-compliance complaints to Attorney General Patricia Madrid with regard to Tom Sullivan's and Steve Sederwall's participation in the Billy the Kid Case in their capacities as public officials." **September 1, 2006**. (**No response**)

Bordley, William E. Associate General Counsel/FOIPA Officer for U.S. Department of Justice. To Jay Miller. "Re: Freedom of Information/Privacy Act Request No. 2006USMS9782 Subject: Copy of Report Entitled *The U.S. Marshals Service and Billy the Kid.*" **September 5, 2006**. (**Refuses to send copy of David Turk's pamphlet on Billy the Kid**)

Kupfer, Elizabeth, Records Custodian. To Jay Miller. "Need additional time ..." **September 6, 2006**.

Miller, Jay. To Nikki Cedrick, FOIA/PA Liaison U.S. Department of Justice. "Re: Follow-up to your August 31, 2006 response to my Freedom of Information Act request No. 2004USMS7634 in Reference to David Turk, Historian for the U.S. Marshals Service; and request for clarification." **September 11, 2006**.

Smith, Glenn R., Deputy Attorney General and Elizabeth Kupfer, Custodian of Public Records. (For Attorney General Patricia Madrid). To Jay Miller." RE: Inspection of Public Records Request." **September 20, 2006**.

Bordley, William E. Associate General Counsel/FOIPA Officer for U.S. Department of Justice. To Jay Miller. "Re: Freedom of Information/Privacy Act Request No. 2006USMS9782 Subject: Copy of Report Entitled *The U.S. Marshals Service and Billy the Kid*." **September 5, 2006.** (**Refuses copy of David Turk's pamphlet on Billy the Kid.**)

Kupfer, Elizabeth, Records Custodian. To Jay Miller. "Need additional time ..." **September 6, 2006.**

Miller, Jay. To Nikki Cedrick, FOIA/PA Liaison U.S. Department of Justice. "Re: Follow-up to your August 31, 2006 response to my Freedom of Information Act request No. 2004USMS7634 in Reference to David Turk, Historian for the U.S. Marshals Service; and request for clarification." **September 11, 2006.**

Smith, Glenn R., Deputy Attorney General and Elizabeth Kupfer, Custodian of Public Records. (For Attorney General Patricia Madrid). To Jay Miller." RE: Inspection of Public Records Request." **September 20, 2006.**

## *RECORDS REQUESTS BY GALE COOPER*

"Jordan, Wilma" aka Gale Cooper. To David Turk, Historian U.S. Marshals Service. "Looking for the truth is good ..." **June 15, 2006.** (**Attempt to get the Turk's "U.S. Marshal's Service and Billy the Kid " pamphlet for Case 2003-274.**)

Turk, David. Historian U.S. Marshals Service. To "Wilma Jordan." "Thank you for your thoughtful and thorough letter ..." **July 3, 2006.** (**Creepy Turk traced a "Wilma Jordan's" address; refused to send his Billy the Kid pamphlet**)

Cooper, Gale. To Governor Bill Richardson and Records Custodian for FOIA/IPRA Requests. "Re: Freedom of Information Act (FOIA)/Inspection of Public Records Act (IPRA) request concerning participation of Governor Bill Richardson in the New Mexico Billy the Kid Case and related issues." **September 22, 2006.**

_____. To Governor Janet Napolitano. "Re: Freedom of Information Act (FOIA) request pertaining to the Prescott, Arizona exhumations of John Miller and William Hudspeth at the Arizona Pioneers' Home Cemetery on May 19, 2005." **September 22, 2006.**

_____. To Sheriff Rick Virden. "Re: Freedom of Information Act (FOIA)/New Mexico Inspection of Public Records Act (IPRA) request pertaining to Lincoln County Sheriff's Department Case # 2003-274 ("Billy the Kid Case") and to its May 19, 2005 Prescott Arizona exhumations of John Miller and William Hudspeth." **September 22, 2006.**

Morel, Alan P. Lincoln County Attorney. To Gale Cooper. "Re: Freedom of Information Act/Inspection of Public Records Act Request dated September 22, 2006, to Lincoln County Sheriff Rick Virden." **September 29, 2006.**

Sullivan, Tom and Steve Sederwall. To Lincoln County Attorney Alan Morel. "The Dried Bean. 'You Believin' Us or Them Lyin' Whores.' " **September 30, 2006.** (**Exhibit 4 in IPRA response to me of October 11, 2006 from Sheriff Rick Virden through Lincoln County Attorney Alan Morel.**)

Maestas, Marcie. Records Custodian for Governor Bill Richardson. To Gale Cooper, M.D. "Received your request to inspect certain records ..." **October 3, 2006.**

Morel, Alan P. Lincoln County Attorney. To Gale Cooper. "RE: Freedom of Information Act (FOIA)/New Mexico Inspection of Public Records Act (IPRA) to Lincoln County Sheriff Ricky [sic] Virden and the Lincoln County Records Custodian, dated September 22, 2006." **October 11, 2006.**

Maestas, Marcie. Records Custodian for Governor Bill Richardson. To Gale Cooper, M.D. "Response to your Inspection of Public Records request received by our office on September 28, 2006 ..." **October 13, 2006.** (**Denial of each item, but miscellaneous documents provided**)

Michael R. Haener. Deputy Chief of Staff to Governor Janet Napolitano. "Enclosed records responsive to your request ..." **November 13, 2006.**

Cooper, Gale. To Governor Janet Napolitano. "Re: Repeated Freedom of Information Act (FOIA) request pertaining to the Prescott, Arizona exhumations of John Miller and William Hudspeth at the Arizona Pioneers' Home Cemetery on May 19, 2005." **March 20, 2007. (Repeated because of no response)**

_____. To Governor Janet Napolitano's Records Custodian. "Re: Repeat submission of incompletely answered Freedom of Information Act request dated September 22, 2006. **March 21, 2007.**

Shilo Mitchell, Deputy Press Secretary for Governor Janet Napolitano. To Gale Cooper, M.D. ""We have no responsive documents from your last request ..." **August 2, 2007.**

Cooper, Gale. To January Contreras, Policy Advisor for Health for Governor Janet Napolitano. "Re: Non- response to my Freedom of Information Act request dated June 29, 2007." **August 10, 2007.**

_____. "Re: Freedom of Information Act request pertaining to New Mexico Governor Bill Richardson's Grand Jury investigation(s) concerning CDR Financial Products, Inc." To Attorney General Eric Holder. **May 25, 2010.**

_____. "Re: Freedom of Information Act request pertaining to New Mexico Governor Bill Richardson's Grand Jury investigation(s) concerning CDR Financial Products, Inc." To President Barak Obama. **May 25, 2010.**

_____. "Re: Freedom of Information Act request pertaining to New Mexico Governor Bill Richardson's Grand Jury investigation(s) concerning CDR Financial Products, Inc." To New Mexico U.S. Attorney Greg Fouratt Obama. **May 25, 2010.**

Hardy, David M. Section Chief, Record/Information Dissemination Section. "Subject: Bill Richardson, January 2008 – Present, FOIPA Request No.: 1149852-000." To Gale Cooper. U.S. Department of Justice, Federal Bureau of Investigation. **June 28, 2010. (Refused records as being on a "third party")**

Stewart, William G. II. Assistant Director. "Subject of Request: Gov. Bill Richardson (grand jury investigation), Request Number 2010-2058." To Gale Cooper. U.S. Department of Justice. **July 14, 2010. (Refused based on "personal privacy")**

_____. "Subject of Request: Gov. Bill Richardson (grand jury investigation), Request Number 2010-2045." To Gale Cooper. U.S. Department of Justice. **July 28, 2010. (Refused information based on "personal privacy")**

## INVESTIGATIONS OF DR. HENRY LEE AND ORCHID CELLMARK LAB (CHRONOLOGICAL)

### *BACKGROUND*

Bugliosi, Vincent. *Outrage: The Five Reasons Why O.J. Simpson Got Away With Murder.* New York and London: W.W. Norton & Company. **1996. (Exposé of Dr. Henry Lee forensic scams, Pages 47-49.)**

No author. "Fraud Alleged at Cellmark, DNA Testing Firm." TalkLeft: The Politics of Crime. http://www.talkleft.com./new_archives/008809.html. **November 18, 2004.**

Bailey, James A. and Margaret B. Bailey. "Billy the Kid Death Scene: Reviewing Ballistic Evidence. *Wild West History Association.* **September, 2016.** Volume 9, Number 3, Pages 30-46. **(Using Lee's forensic fakery of the washstand to create a death scene; also traces is furniture 's provenance (Pages 31-32)**

Shen, Maxine. "CBS and the brother of JonBenet Ramsey settle their $750m defamation lawsuit to the 'satisfaction of both parties' after he claimed their documentary implied he killed his sister." January 5, 2019. DailyMailOnline.com. **(Defamation case involving Dr. Henry Lee's forensics)**

### *RECORDS REQUESTS BY JAY MILLER AS MY PROXY*

Miller, Jay. To Dr. Henry Lee. "Re: Forensic consultation in the New Mexico Billy the Kid Case." **March 27, 2006. (Included all the articles with Lee's forensic claims)**

Lee, Henry, Dr. To Jay Miller. "In response to your letter dated March 27, 2006 ..." **May 1, 2006. (Says sent his single forensic report for Case No. 2003-274 to the Lincoln County Sheriff's Department directly)**

Miller, Jay. To Dr. Henry Lee. "Re: Follow-up on your letter of May 1, 2006 responding to my request of March 27, 2006 for information on your forensic consultation in the New Mexico Billy the Kid Case." **June 15, 2006.**

_____. To Dr. Henry Lee. "Re: Follow-up to my letter of June 15, 2006 with regard to your forensic consultation in the New Mexico Billy the Kid Case." **August 8, 2006.**

_____. To Dr. Rick Staub. "Re: The participation by you and Orchid Cellmark in the New Mexico Billy the Kid Case." **August 8, 2006. (No response)**

## *ETHICS COMPLAINT AGAINST*

Cooper, Gale. To Haskell Pitluck, AAFS Ethics Committee Chairman and members of the AAFS Ethics Committee. "Re: Formal Ethics Complaint against Dr. Henry Lee for his work as a forensic expert in Lincoln County, New Mexico, Sheriff's Department Case # 2003-274 ('the Billy the Kid Case')." **October 2, 2006.**

Cooper, Gale. To Haskell Pitluck, AAFS Ethics Committee Chairman. "Re: Follow-up on my October 2, 2006 complaint on Dr. Henry Lee to the Ethics Committee of the American Academy of Forensic Sciences." **March 5, 2007.**

_____. To Dr. Bruce Goldberger. President AAFS. "Re: Informing of non-action to date on my American Academy of Forensic Sciences Ethics Committee complaint filed October 2, 2006 against Dr. Henry Lee." **April 10, 2007.**

Goldberger, Bruce. Dr. and President AAFS. To Gale Cooper. (via fax) "I have received the complaint today ..." **April 12,, 2007.**

_____. To Gale Cooper. (via fax) "You should receive a letter from Mr. Pitluck in the coming week or two ..." **May 4, 2007.**

Pitluck, Haskell M. AAFS Ethics Committee Chairman. To Gale Cooper, M.D. "Ethics Committee has completed its investigation ..." **May 9, 2007. (Corrupt denial)**

Cooper, Gale. To Haskell Pitluck, AAFS Ethics Committee Chairman. "Re: Follow-up on the May 9, 2007 AAFS response to my October 2, 2006 Ethics Complaint on Dr. Henry Lee. **May 30, 2007.**

_____. To Dr. Bruce Goldberger. President AAFS. "Re: Need for clarification in the May 9, 2007 AAFS Ethics Committee response to my AAFS Ethics and Conduct Complaint of October 2, 2006 against Dr. Henry Lee." **May 30, 2007.**

Pitluck, Haskell M. AAFS Ethics Committee Chairman. To Gale Cooper, M.D. "Ethics Committee has completed its investigation ..." **June 2, 2007. (Denial of any responsibility by Dr. Lee for "actions or statements of others.")**

Cooper, Gale. To Rene Romo. *Albuquerque Journal*. "Re: Attributions made by you in your August 2, 2004 *Albuquerque Journal* article titled 'Forensic Expert on Billy's Case: Questions Remain on Outlaws Fate.'" **June 19, 2007.**

_____. To Haskell Pitluck, AAFS Ethics Committee Chairman. "Re: Requested clarification of your responses of May 9, 2007 and June 2, 2007 to my October 2, 2006 AAFS Ethics Complaint against Dr. Henry Lee." **June 19, 2007.**

_____. To Den Slaney. Albuquerque Museum of Art and History. "Re: Information request for Dreamscape Desperado exhibit." **June 29, 2007. (Using fake carpenter's bench blood claim)**

Pitluck, Haskell M. AAFS Ethics Committee Chairman. To Gale Cooper, M.D. "Ethics Committee has completed its investigation ..." **July 6, 2007.**

Cooper, Gale. To Albuquerque Museum of Art and History Director Cathy Wright. "Re: Information request concerning past Dreamscape Desperado exhibit." **July 30, 2007. (Concerning their labeling of the carpenter's bench as having blood according to Dr. Henry Lee)**

Slaney, Deborah. Curator of History at the Albuquerque Museum of Art and History. To Gale Cooper. "Re: Information request concerning past Dreamscape Desperado exhibit." **August 6, 2007. (Claim Paul Hutton verified bench blood)**

Walz, Kent. Editor-in-Chief *Albuquerque Journal*. To Gale Cooper. "Response to your letter concerning Rene Romo's story of August 2, 2004." **August 13, 2007. (Stated Lee never denied the claims attributed to him)**

## RICO CASE AGAINST PARTICIPANTS

Cooper, Gale. To New Mexico U.S. Attorney David Iglesias. "Re: Enclosed reference copy of Freedom of Information Act (FOIA)/New Mexico Inspection of Public Records Act (IPRA) request concerning participation of Governor Bill Richardson in the New Mexico Billy the Kid Case and related issues." **September 22, 2006.**

_____. To New Mexico U.S. Attorney David Iglesias. "Re: Enclosed reference copy of Freedom of Information Act (FOIA)/New Mexico Inspection of Public Records Act (IPRA) request to Lincoln County Sheriff Rick Virden regarding his conducting the New Mexico Billy the Kid Case (Lincoln County Sheriff's Department Case # 2003-274) and its issues related to Maricopa County, Arizona Case # CA 2006020516 (pertaining to the Prescott, Arizona exhumations of John Miller and William Hudspeth.) **September 22, 2006.**

_____. To FBI Squad 5. "Re: RICO Complaint against New Mexico and Arizona public officials promulgating together Lincoln County Sheriff's Department Case # 2003-274 and De Baca County Sheriff's Department Case # 03-06-136-01 ('The Billy the Kid Case'). **October 10, 2006.**

_____. To FBI Special Agent Mark Humphrey. "RE: Additional evidence for my RICO complaint sent to you on October 10, 2006." **October 30, 2006.**

_____. To FBI Special Agent Mark Humphrey. "RE: Personal threats from Lincoln County Attorney Alan Morel, Lincoln County Sheriff Ricky Virden, alleged Lincoln County Deputy Tom Sullivan, and alleged Lincoln County Deputy Steve Sederwall.." **October 30, 2006.**

_____. To FBI Supervisor of White Collar Crime Attorney Mary Higgins. "RE: Copy of documentation of RICO complaint filed with Special Agent Mark Humphrey on October 10, 2006 with addendum of October 30, 2006. **October 30, 2006.**

Iglesias, David, U.S. Attorney and Mary L. Higgins, Assistant U.S. Attorney. Letter to Gale Cooper, M.D. "Re: Copy of RICO Complaint Concerning the 'Billy the Kid Case.'" **November 16, 2006. (Rejection of complaint.)**

_____. To New Mexico GOP Chairman Allen Weh. "RE: RICO Case." March 14, 2007.

Cooper, Gale. To FBI Special Agent Mark Humphrey. "Re: RICO Complaint against Governor Bill Richardson and other, New Mexico, public officials." **January 29, 2008. (Second complaint.)**

Humphrey, Mark D. To Gale Cooper. "We are in receipt of your complaint ..." **February 5, 2008. (Rejection of second complaint.)**

## STATE BAR COMPLAINTS AGAINST

Cooper, Gale. To State Bar of New Mexico, The Disciplinary Board. "RE: State Bar of New Mexico Disciplinary Board Ref. # 26036: Professional Misconduct Complaint against New Mexico Attorney Alan P. Morel." **November 13, 2006.**

Long, Christine E., Special Assistant Disciplinary Counsel. To Dr. Gale Cooper. "Re: Complaint filed against Alan P. Morel, Esq." **December 11, 2006. (Rejection of complaint.)**

Cooper, Gale. To State Bar of Arizona A/CAP Division. "RE: Inquiry Complaint to Arizona State Bar Concerning Allegations of Legal Misconduct Against Maricopa County Prosecutor's Office's Deputy Attorney Jonell Lucca." **January 5, 2007.**

Worth, Ariel I. Staff Bar Counsel, State Bar of Arizona. To Gale Cooper. "Re: File No. 07-0060 Jonell L. Lucca Respondent." Letter to me. **February 27, 2006**. **(Rejection of complaint.)**

Cooper, Gale. To Worth, Ariel I. Staff Bar Counsel, State Bar of Arizona. "Re: Response to letter titled 'Re: File No. 07-0060 Jonell L. Lucca Respondent.'" **March 21, 2007**.

Worth, Ariel. Staff Bar Counsel, State Bar of Arizona. To Gale Cooper. "RE: File No: 07-0060. Jonell L. Lucca, Respondent." Letter to me. **November 2, 2007**. **(Second rejection of my Bar complaint.)**

## RICHARDSON'S PARDON THRUST AND OPPOSITION TO

Cooper, Gale. "Re: Referred by Bob McCubbin." E-mail to Susannah Garrett. **June 13, 2010**.

Miller, Jay. "Kid's Pardon a Publicity Stunt." "Inside the Capitol" syndicated column and blog, insidethecapitol.blogspot.com. **June 23, 2010**. **(Papers refused to print; on blog only)**

Stinnett, Scot. "Billy the Kid historian says pardon all part of the hoax." *De Baca County News*. Pages 3, 9. **June 24, 2010**. **(Reprint of my Jay Miller article without commentary)**

Garrett, Jarvis Patrick "JP." "RE: Meeting" "... I would like el pinto." E-mail to Gale Cooper. **June 29, 2010**. **(Meeting with JP in which he suggested a meeting with Richardson)**

Cooper, Gale. "Lunch with Tourism Secretary." E-mail to JP and Susannah Garrett. **July 9, 2010**. **(I set up lunch with Mike Cerletti, Jay Miller, and the Garretts at La Fonda)**

_____. "Subj: Listing of Garrett Damages." E-mail to JP Garrett. July 10, 2010.

No Author. "Billy the Kid 'to be pardoned.'" *Press Trust of India* (*Hindustan Times*) and Pakistan *Daily Express*. **July 11, 2010**. **(Richardson's pardon publicity move - with "Brushy" as Billy.)**

Cooper, Gale. "Re: More Thoughts on Pardon Write-Up." "... the key is that Richardson has no other way of justifying a pardon – except by making 'Brushy' a possibility. Richardson has to be stopped." E-mail to Susannah Garrett. **July 15, 2010**.

_____. "Re: Friday Meeting." "... I'll meet you at La Plazuela at noon." E-mail to Susannah Garrett. **July 15, 2010**.

Garrett, Jarvis Patrick "JP." "Petition in Opposition to Pardon of Billy the Kid." **July 20, 2010**. **(Made for signings at the Ruidoso Wild West Round-up)**

Romo, Rene. "Gov. Weighs Pardon for Billy the Kid." *Albuquerque Journal*. Saturday, No. 205. Front page, lead story, cont. A6. **July 24, 2010**.

Garrett, Jarvis Patrick "JP," Susan Floyd Garrett, and Pauline Garrett Tillinghast. "Representatives of the Garrett Family." "As grandchildren of Pat Garrett, we have watched with outrage and sadness ..." Letter to Governor Richardson. **July 25, 2010**. **(Prepared with my input)**

Licón, Adriana Gómez. "Pardon form New Mexico governor unlikely for Billy the Kid." *El Paso Times*. **July 29, 2010**.

Sharpe, Tom. "English kin trace path of 'Billy the Kid's' ex-boss: Tunstall's murder sparked Lincoln County War." *The New Mexican*. **July 29, 2010**.

Massey, Barry. AP. "Billy the Kid To Be Pardoned, 130 Years Later? Lawman's Grandchildren Outraged; 'Would You Issue A Pardon For Someone Who Made His Living As A Thief?' National, international, and internet publications. **July 30, 2010**.

Cooper, Gale. Re: Old West Royalty." "Don't forget that you are all Old West royalty." E-mail to Garrett family. **July 31, 2010**.

Gardner, David. Los Angeles. "Pat Garrett's family plan showdown over plans to finally pardon Billy the Kid." London's *Daily Mail Online*. **July 31, 2010**.

Garrett, Jarvis Patrick "JP," Susan Floyd Garrett, and Pauline Garrett Tillinghast. "Representatives of the Garrett Family. "Re. August 2, 2010 meeting with you concerning your possible pardon of Billy the Kid ..." Letter to Governor Richardson. **August 2, 2010.**

Cooper, Gale. "Garrett Family Statement to Governor Bill Richardson." **August 4, 2010.**

Massey, Barry. Associated Press. Santa Fe. "NM gov meets with lawman Pat Garrett's descendants." **August 4, 2010.** www.wthr.com/global/story.asp?s=12926188.

Cooper, Gale. "Re: Thanks." "I want to thank you and your children for the tremendous effort and grace that went into the Richardson meeting." E-mail to Garrett family. **August 5, 2010.**

Garrett, Susannah. "Re: Thanks." "Thanks for all your valuable and supportive presence through all this." E-mail to Gale Cooper. **August 5, 2010.**

Richardson, Bill. "Dear Garrett Family, Thank you for meeting with me ..." Letter to the Garretts. **August 9, 2010. (Follow-up to the August 4, 2010 meeting)**

Cooper, Gale. "Subj: Sample Wallace Family Statement." E-mail to William N. Wallace. **August 10, 2010.**

Wallace, William N. "Re: Sample Wallace Family Statement." ... "I have sent Governor Richardson by e-mail a modified version of the proposed 'Wallace Family' letter. E-mail to Gale Cooper. **August 10, 2010. (Lew Wallace's great-grandson)**

Cooper, Gale. "Re: Copy of *MegaHoax*." Letter to William N. Wallace. **August 11, 2010.**

_____. "Re: More on 1900, 1902 Wallace Articles." E-mail to Barry Massey. **August 12, 2010.**

_____. "Subj: More on Pardon Issue" "... [Y]ou are my best and last hope for ending Governor Bill Richardson's seven year hoaxing of Billy the Kid history ..." E-mail to William N. Wallace. **August 13, 2010.**

Nolan, Frederick." Re: Pardon Question." "... To the best of my knowledge no contemporary of the Kid's ever mentioned his 'deal' with Wallace ..." E-mail to Gale Cooper. **August 13, 2010.**

Cooper, Gale. "Re: Talking Points on Pardon Issue." E-mail to William N. Wallace. **August 14, 2010.**

Brady, Nicole. "Re: More on Past Brady Opposition." "... I don't imagine much of a role for myself ..." E-mail to Gale Cooper. **August 30, 2010. (Refusal of KOB reporter and Sheriff William Brady granddaughter to help)**

Vaughn, Chris. "Texas Town seeks New Mexico pardon for Billy the Kid." *Fort Worth Star-Telegram.* **August 14, 2010. (Bid for "Brushy Bill" Roberts pardon.)**

Lacey, Marc. "Old West Showdown Is Revived. *New York Times.* **August 15, 2010. (Richardson shape-shifted to "amateur historian.")**

No Author. "A Tale of Two Billys." *New English Review: The Iconoclast.* (Internet). **August 15, 2010.**

Gordon, Bea. "Examining Legend: The Pardoning of Billy the Kid.. New Mexico Gov. Bill Richardson's talking about exonerating the state's most famous outlaw. But at what cost?" www.newwest.net/topic/article/29850/C37/L37/ **August 17, 2010.**

Massey, Barry. Associated Press. Santa Fe. " 'Billy the Kid' pardon effort draws Wild West showdown." Wilkes-Barre, Pennsylvania. *The Times Leader.* **August 21, 2010. (Introduction of William N. Wallace opposition)**

Sides, Hampton. "Not-So-Charming Billy." *NY Times Opinion Section Op-Ed Contributor.* **September 6, 2010.**

Wallace, William N. . "Re: Reply wnwallace: "Barry Massey of the AP has ready from me a reaction quote should Gov. Richardson go ahead with the pardon. E-mail to Gale Cooper. **September 16, 2010.**

Cooper, Gale. "Re: Reply wnwallace: 'That powerful stance of yours gives me hope that it can deter Governor Richardson's pardon publicity stunt." E-Mail to William N. Wallace. **September 16, 2010.**

McGinn, Randi. "RE: Application for Pardon for Henry McCarty, AKA William Bonney or Billy the Kid." Letter to Shammara Henderson, Legal Counsel Governor Richardson. **December 14, 2010. (Secret Richardson attorney for a lost payto play Grand Jury case; wife of Charlie Daniels, appointed by Richardson in 2007 as Chief Justice of the state Supreme Court; with both major Richardson donors )**

Richardson, Bill. "Governor Bill Richardson to Consider Billy the Kid Pardon Petition." Press release. **December 16, 2010. (Floating the Randi McGinn petition)**

Garrett, Jarvis Patrick "JP." "No Subject." "... the petitioner for the pardon is Randi McGinn, so what's her link to Richardson ..." E-mail to Gale Cooper. **December 16, 2010.**

Garrett, Susannah. "RE; The Pardon Draft to Eric." "... I think a panel of historians should debate ..." E-mail to Eric Witt. **December 18, 2010. (To Richardson's Deputy Chief of Staff)**

Wallace, William N. "Governor Richardson - Your imminent action ..." Letter to Bill Richardson. **December 21, 2010. (Opposition to Billy the Kid pardon)**

_____. "Subject: BtK/WnWallace." ... Ms. Cooper: I have sent the following to governor ..." E-mail to Gale Cooper. **December 21, 2010. (Copy of opposition letter)**

Garrett, Jarvis Patrick, JP. "Subj: Wallace draft." "I'm just sending you my thoughts ..." E-mail to William N. Wallace. **December 26, 2010. (I put the Garretts and Wallace together)**

Martinez, Edecio. "Billy the Kid to be Pardoned 130 Years Later." CBSNEWS.com. **December 27, 2010.**

Guarino, Mark. "Outgoing New Mexico Gov. Bill Richardson is considering a pardon for celebrated outlaw Billy the Kid. An informal e-mail poll shows support. But time is running out." Associated Press. **December 29, 2010.**

Levy, Glen. "Will Billy the Kid Be Pardoned? Governor Has Until Friday." TIME NewsFeed.com. December 29, 2010.

Garrett, Jarvis Patrick, JP. "RE: CNN Comment ... press letter revised." E-mail to Gale Cooper. **December 30, 2010.**

Ray, Alarie. "Subj: FW: Governor Bill Richardson to Announce Decision on Billy the Kid Pardon Request Tomorrow." E-mail forwarded to Gale Cooper. **December 30, 2013.**

Richardson, Bill. "Governor Richardson to Announce his decision on Billy the Kid Pardon Request Tomorrow." Press release. **December 30, 2010.**

Burke, Kelly David. "Billy the Kid Pardon?" FoxNews.com. **December 30, 2010.**

Garrett, Jarvis Patrick "JP." "No Subject" "yea!!! no pardon!!! =" E-mail to Gale Cooper. **December 31, 2010.**

Hopper, Jessica. "Gov. Bill Richardson: 'I've Decided Not to Pardon Billy the Kid.' " ABCNEWS.com. **December 31, 2010.**

Rojas, Rick. "No Pardon for Billy the Kid. New Mexico Gov. Bill Richardson says, 'The Romanticism appealed to me ... but the facts and evidence did not support it." *Los Angeles Times*. **December 31, 2010.**

Watson, Kathryn. "Alas, no pardon for Billy the Kid: New Mexico's Richardson says close call." washingtontimes.com. **December 31, 2010. (With "waste time" quote by Governor Susana Martinez)**

No Author. "Richardson Declines to Pardon Outlaw Billy the Kid." FoxNews.com. **December 31, 2010.**

Wallace, William N. "Your persistence ... enabled common sense." E-mail To Gale Cooper. **December 31, 2010.**

Lacey, Marc. "For 2$^{nd}$ Time in 131 Years, Billy the Kid is Denied Pardon." *New York Times*. Page A10. **January 1, 2011.**

## OPEN RECORDS VIOLATION CASE:

Sandoval County District Cause No. D-1329-CV-2007-1364, Gale Cooper and De Baca County News, a New Mexico Corporation, PLAINTIFFS, vs. Rick Virden, Lincoln County Sheriff and Custodian of Records; and Steven M. Sederwall, Former Lincoln County Deputy Sheriff; and Thomas T. Sullivan, Former Lincoln County Sheriff and Former Lincoln County Deputy Sheriff, DEFENDANTS. **(CHRONOLOGICAL)**

### *INSPECTION OF PUBLIC RECORDS ACT STATUTE*

Madrid, Patricia A. Attorney General. *Inspection of Public Records Act Compliance Guide. Fourth Edition. The "Inspection of Public Records Act" NMSA 1978, Chapter 14, Article 2: A Compliance Guide for New Mexico Public Officials and Citizens.* Santa Fe: Office of the Attorney General. **January, 2004**.

King, Gary, Attorney General. "IPRA Guide: The Inspection of Public Records Act NMSA 1978, Chapter 14, Article 2; A Compliance Guide for New Mexico Public Officials and Citizens. Seventh Edition. **2012**.

### *RECORDS REQUEST PHASE*

Cheves, Philip W. Barnett Law Firm. To Sheriff Rick Virden. "Re: Request for Inspection of Public Records." **April 24, 2007**. **(Start of my records requesting for the Dr. Henry Lee and Orchid Cellmark forensic DNA records)**

Morel, Alan P., Lincoln County Attorney. To Barnett Law Firm. "Re: Freedom of Information Act/Inspection of Public Records Act Request Dated April 24, 2007." **April 27, 2007. (Fakes Case 2003-274 as only deputy murder investigation.)**

Cheves, Philip W. Barnett Law Firm. To Sheriff Rick Virden. "Re: Request for Inspection of Public Records." **May 9, 2007**.

_____. To Alan P. Morel, Esquire. "Re: Request for Inspection of Public Records." **May 9, 2007**.

Morel, Alan P., Lincoln County Attorney. To Barnett Law Firm. "RE: Freedom of Information Act/Inspection of Public Records Act Request to Sheriff Rick Virden Dated May 9, 2007." **May 11, 2007. (Lies that Lincoln County have no Case 2003-274 records "whatsoever")**

_____. To Barnett Law Firm. "RE: Freedom of Information Act/Inspection of Public Records Act Request to Alan P. Morel, Esq., Dated May 9, 2007." **May 14, 2007. (Fakes "deputies too records" excuse)**

Cheves, Philip W., Barnett Law Firm. To Alan P. Morel, Esquire. "Re: Request for Inspection of Public Records." **June 8, 2007**.

Cheves, Philip W., Barnett Law Firm. "Re: Request for Inspection of Public Records" to Tom Sullivan. **June 14, 2007**.

_____. "Re: Request for Inspection of Public Records" to Steve Sederwall. **June 14, 2007**.

Morel, Alan P., Lincoln County Attorney. Thomas Stewart, Lincoln County Manager, and Rick Virden, Lincoln County Sheriff. To Tom Sullivan and Steve Sederwall. "Re: Request for Inspection of Public Records." **June 21, 2007. (This was attached to Morel's letter of June 22, 2007 as feigned records recovery attempt from Sullivan and Sederwall.)**

Sederwall, Steven M. and Thomas T. Sullivan. To Rick Virden, Lincoln County Sheriff. "Memorandum. Subject: Billy the Kid Investigation." **June 21, 2007. (Key hoax document attached to the Morel letter of June 22, 2007, blames Richardson and Robins for case, attaches $6,500 in "bribery" checks to Sullivan, and quitting as deputies)**

Morel, Alan P. Lincoln County Attorney. To Barnett Law Firm. "RE: Freedom of Information Act/Inspection of Public Records Act Request to Alan Morel, Esq.,

Cooper, Gale. To Governor Janet Napolitano. "Re: Repeated Freedom of Information Act (FOIA) request pertaining to the Prescott, Arizona exhumations of John Miller and William Hudspeth at the Arizona Pioneers' Home Cemetery on May 19, 2005." **March 20, 2007. (Repeated because of no response)**

_____. To Governor Janet Napolitano's Records Custodian. "Re: Repeat submission of incompletely answered Freedom of Information Act request dated September 22, 2006. **March 21, 2007.**

Shilo Mitchell, Deputy Press Secretary for Governor Janet Napolitano. To Gale Cooper, M.D. ""We have no responsive documents from your last request ..." **August 2, 2007.**

Cooper, Gale. To January Contreras, Policy Advisor for Health for Governor Janet Napolitano. "Re: Non- response to my Freedom of Information Act request dated June 29, 2007." **August 10, 2007.**

_____. "Re: Freedom of Information Act request pertaining to New Mexico Governor Bill Richardson's Grand Jury investigation(s) concerning CDR Financial Products, Inc." To Attorney General Eric Holder. **May 25, 2010.**

_____. "Re: Freedom of Information Act request pertaining to New Mexico Governor Bill Richardson's Grand Jury investigation(s) concerning CDR Financial Products, Inc." To President Barak Obama. **May 25, 2010.**

_____. "Re: Freedom of Information Act request pertaining to New Mexico Governor Bill Richardson's Grand Jury investigation(s) concerning CDR Financial Products, Inc." To New Mexico U.S. Attorney Greg Fouratt Obama. **May 25, 2010.**

Hardy, David M. Section Chief, Record/Information Dissemination Section. "Subject: Bill Richardson, January 2008 – Present, FOIPA Request No.: 1149852-000." To Gale Cooper. U.S. Department of Justice, Federal Bureau of Investigation. **June 28, 2010. (Refused records as being on a "third party")**

Stewart, William G. II. Assistant Director. "Subject of Request: Gov. Bill Richardson (grand jury investigation), Request Number 2010-2058." To Gale Cooper. U.S. Department of Justice. **July 14, 2010. (Refused based on "personal privacy")**

_____. "Subject of Request: Gov. Bill Richardson (grand jury investigation), Request Number 2010-2045." To Gale Cooper. U.S. Department of Justice. **July 28, 2010. (Refused information based on "personal privacy")**

## INVESTIGATIONS OF DR. HENRY LEE AND ORCHID CELLMARK LAB (CHRONOLOGICAL)

### BACKGROUND

Bugliosi, Vincent. *Outrage: The Five Reasons Why O.J. Simpson Got Away With Murder.* New York and London: W.W. Norton & Company. **1996. (Exposé of Dr. Henry Lee forensic scams, Pages 47-49.)**

No author. "Fraud Alleged at Cellmark, DNA Testing Firm." TalkLeft: The Politics of Crime. http://www.talkleft.com./new_archives/008809.html. **November 18, 2004.**

Bailey, James A. and Margaret B. Bailey. "Billy the Kid Death Scene: Reviewing Ballistic Evidence. *Wild West History Association.* **September, 2016.** Volume 9, Number 3, Pages 30-46. **(Using Lee's forensic fakery of the washstand to create a death scene; also traces is furniture 's provenance (Pages 31-32))**

Shen, Maxine. "CBS and the brother of JonBenet Ramsey settle their $750m defamation lawsuit to the 'satisfaction of both parties' after he claimed their documentary implied he killed his sister." **January 5, 2019.** DailyMailOnline.com. **(Defamation case involving Dr. Henry Lee's forensics)**

### RECORDS REQUESTS BY JAY MILLER AS MY PROXY

Miller, Jay. To Dr. Henry Lee. "Re: Forensic consultation in the New Mexico Billy the Kid Case." **March 27, 2006. (Included all the articles with Lee's forensic claims)**

tecum of Sheriff's Department file for Case # 2003-274 – minus any forensic documents; calls case criminal investigation)

Virden, Rick. Case 2003-274 file Turn-over. **September 3, 2008. (By subpoena duces tecum; 193 pages)**

Rogers, Patrick J. Attorney. "Docs for editing. To: Mickey Barnett; David A. Garcia." (via e-mail). Monday, **September 22, 2008**. (Forwarded to Gale Cooper on September 25, 2008.) **(Threat FOG to pressure for dismissing Virden)**

Cooper, Gale. From Attorney David Garcia. (via e-mail). "Re: FW: Docs for editing." **September 25, 2008.**

_____. "Subj. IPRA Case Communication for Review. To Attorneys Barnett and Garcia and Scot Stinnett." (via e-mail). **September 28, 2008. (Case overview, our legal relationship, and responses to the Rogers e-mail.)**

_____. To Attorney Leonard DeLayo. "Fwd: Response regarding IPRA Case." **September 29, 2008. (Case overview for Barnett of September 28, 2008 with responses to the Rogers e-mail.)**

Rogers, Patrick. Forwarded from Scot Stinnett. (via e-mail). "No Subject." **September 30, 2008. (A copy of an e-mail from corrupt Attorney Rogers to Attorney DeLayo pushing falsely for Sederwall as Records Custodian.)**

_____. "Re: Second Response To Your FOG Proposal." To Gale Cooper. (via e-mail) **October 1, 2008** 4:40:27 AM.. **(Attorney Rogers tries to coerce me by Sederwall as Records Custodian or he will withdraw FOG )**

Barnett, Mickey D. Attorney. "Re: Sullivan Sederwall Depositions. To Gale Cooper." (via e-mail). **October 1, 2008.**

Brown, Kevin M. Attorney. "Re: Cooper v. Lincoln County, et al. No. D-1329-CV-07-1364. To Patrick J. Rogers." **October 16, 2008.**

Cooper, Gale. To Attorney Pat Rogers. "Re: Response documents forwarded to me by e-mail on October 20, 2008 concerning NMFOG's actions in relation to my IPRA case No. D-1329-CV-1364." **October 27, 2008.**

Rogers, Patrick J. Attorney. Letter of withdrawal as the FOG attorney pertaining to my IPRA case. **November 10, 2008. (Corruptly trying to throw my case)**

Cooper, Gale. "Re: My response to your letter of October 16, 2008 to Attorney Pat Rogers, and my dissociation from the referenced Foundation For Open Government communications." Letter to Brown. **November 17, 2008.**

Threet, Martin E. Attorney and Attorney A. Blair Dunn." Plaintiffs' Motion for Summary Judgment. Gale Cooper and De Baca County News, a New Mexico Corporation, Plaintiffs, vs. Lincoln County and Rick Virden, Lincoln County Sheriff and Custodian of Records; and Steven M. Sederwall, Former Lincoln County Deputy Sheriff; and Thomas T. Sullivan, Former Lincoln County Sheriff and Former Lincoln County Deputy Sheriff, Defendants. No. D-1329-CV-07-1364." County of Sandoval , Thirteenth Judicial District Court. **July 31, 2009.**

Werkmeister, H. Nicole. Attorney. Defendant Rick Virden's Response to Plaintiff's [sic] Motion for Summary Judgment and Cross-Motion for Summary Judgment. Gale Cooper and De Baca County News, a New Mexico Corporation, Plaintiffs, vs. Lincoln County and Rick Virden, Lincoln County Sheriff and Custodian of Records; and Steven M. Sederwall, Former Lincoln County Deputy Sheriff; and Thomas T. Sullivan, Former Lincoln County Sheriff and Former Lincoln County Deputy Sheriff, Defendants. No. D-1329-CV-07-1364." County of Sandoval , Thirteenth Judicial District Court. **August 29, 2009.**

Brown, Kevin. Attorney. "Defendants Sederwall and Sullivan's Response to Motion for Summary Judgment. Gale Cooper and De Baca County News, a New Mexico Corporation, Plaintiffs, vs. Lincoln County and Rick Virden, Lincoln County Sheriff and Custodian of Records; and Steven M. Sederwall, Former Lincoln County Deputy Sheriff; and Thomas T. Sullivan, Former Lincoln County Sheriff and Former Lincoln County Deputy Sheriff, Defendants. No. D-1329-CV-07-1364." County of Sandoval , Thirteenth Judicial District Court. **September 2, 2009.**

Threet, Martin E. Attorney and Attorney A. Blair Dunn. "Plaintiffs' Reply and Motion to Exceed Page Limit For Exhibits. Gale Cooper and De Baca County News, a New Mexico Corporation, Plaintiffs, vs. Lincoln County and Rick Virden, Lincoln County Sheriff and Custodian of Records; and Steven M. Sederwall, Former Lincoln County Deputy Sheriff; and Thomas T. Sullivan, Former Lincoln County Sheriff and Former Lincoln County Deputy Sheriff, Defendants. No. D-1329-CV-07-1364." County of Sandoval, Thirteenth Judicial District Court. **September 29, 2009. (Attempt to enter my extensive evidence into court record)**

_____. Motion for Summary Judgment. **January, 2010.**

Eichwald, George P. Hearing for "Plaintiffs' Motion for Summary Judgment." Transcript. **November 20, 2009. (Plaintiffs' Motion for Summary Judgment Granted.)**

_____. "Summary Judgment" granted for Plaintiffs. January, 2010.

Brown, Kevin. "I am enclosing the document Mr. Sederwall received from Dr. Lee ..." Letter. **February 18, 2010. (Unrequested Lee floorboard report)**

Lee, Henry and Calvin Ostler. "Forensic Research and Training Center Forensic Examination Report: "Examination of Lincoln County Court House." **February 25, 2005. (Given to Plaintiffs on February 18, 2010 by Brown and on April 6, 2010 by Werkmeister as a requested Lee report – but was the fake Version I (9 pages) of an unrequested floorboard report )**

Threet, Martin E. "I am returning the Lee report ..." Letter to Brown. (Rejecting and returning the Lee floorboard report) **February 25, 2010.**

"Presentment Hearing." Transcript. **March 9, 2010. (Defendants give unrequested Lee floorboard report as fulfilling records turn-over; and lying that it is only the record in Sederwall's possession)**

Eichwald, George P., District Judge. "Order Granting Plaintiff's Motion for Summary Judgment and Denying Defendant Virden's Cross Motion for Summary Judgment and Order Granting Leave to File Interlocutory Appeal" **March 12, 2010. (Grants evidentiary hearing.)**

Werkmeister, Nicole. "Attached is the Forensic Examination Report From Dr. Henry Lee ..." Fax cover letter. **April 6, 2010. (Copy faxed of same unrequested (fake) Lee floorboard report from Brown was enclosed)**

Eichwald. George P., District Judge. "Order Granting Plaintiffs' Motion for Summary Judgment and Denying Defendant Virden's Cross-Motion for Summary Judgment and Order Granting Leave to File Interlocutory Appeal." **March 12, 2010. (Major Plaintiff victory)**

Threet, Martin E. "Take a look at this letter ..." Fax cover letter to me. **April 13, 2010. (Werkmeister sending fake floorboard Lee report to us)**

Threet, Martin E. "The time for interlocutory appeal having passed ..." Letter to Werkmeister and Brown. **May 3, 2010.**

Hearing for "Mandatory Order of Disclosure and Production Hearing." Transcript. **September 9, 2010.**

Threet, Martin E. "Re: Billy the Kid. "Henry Narvaez has again repeated his assurance to me that if we will agree to dismiss Virden ..." Fax to me. **September 14, 2010. (Threet's attempt to trick me into dismissing Virden)**

_____. "Re: Plaintiff's response to letter from Sheriff Rick Virden. It is the position of my clients ..." Letter. **September 27, 2010.**

Virden, Rick. "It is my understanding that on May 22, 2004, Steve Sederwall ..." Letter to Henry Lee. **October 26, 2010. (sham recovery attempt to Dr. Henry Lee)**

_____. "It is my understanding that in the spring or summer of 2004, Steve Sederwall sent a blood sample(s) to Orchid Cellmark ..." Letter "To Whom It May Concern." **October 26, 2010. (Sham recovery attempt to Orchid Cellmark)**

Narvaez Law Firm. Billing to New Mexico County Insurance Authority. **October 31, 2010. (Listing secret meetings with Attorney Threet to dismiss Virden)**

Gulliksen, Joan., Orchid Cellmark Customer Liaison, Forensics. "Orchid Cellmark is in receipt of your letter requesting DNA documents ..." Letter to Virden.

November 2, 2010. (**Orchid Cellmark response requesting client name to release records; Virden did not get the records**)

———. "Orchid Cellmark, this is Joan ..." Transcript of telephone call from Virden. **November 2, 2010. (Virden did no follow-up**)

———. "Orchid Cellmark, this is Joan ..." E-mail to Virden. **November 2, 2010. (Virden did no follow-up**)

Brown, Kevin. "Enclosed please find a copy of another report dated February 25, 2005 which deals with the examination of furniture by Dr. Lee." Letter to Threet. **November 10, 2010. (Sending Lee's forged bench report; different font than the first forged floorboard report**)

Lee, Henry and Calvin Ostler. "Forensic Research and Training Center Forensic Examination Report: "Examination of furniture from Pete Maxwell's of July 15, 1881." February 25, 2005. (**Given to Plaintiffs on November 10, 2010 as Lee bench report (16 pages) – but was its forged Version I** )

Werkmeister, Nicole. Letter to Threet. **November 4, 2010. (Shaming Virden recovery of Orchid Cellmark records; saying Lee did not respond**)

Lee, Henry. "This letter is in response to your letter ..." Letter to Virden. **November 12, 2010. (Lee confirms report; Virden never asked for it!**)

Werkmeister, Nicole. Letter to Threet. **November 22, 2010. (copies of Virden's sham Lee and Orchid Cellmark requests sent to Threet**)

Robins, Bill III. Deposition taken by Attorney Martin E. Threet. **January 6, 2011.**

"Evidentiary Hearing on Plaintiff's Motion for Mandatory Order of Disclosure and Production." Transcript. **January 21, 2011. (Defendants gave forged Lee Floorboard report (9 pages) Version II entered as Exhibit F; forged Lee bench report (16 pages) Version I entered as Exhibit E**)

Lee, Henry and Calvin Ostler. "Forensic Research and Training Center Forensic Examination Report: "Examination of furniture from Pete Maxwell's of July 15, 1881." February 25, 2005. (**Given to Court on January 21, 2011 as Lee bench report (16 pages), Exhibit E – but was its fake Version 1** )

Lee, Henry and Calvin Ostler. "Forensic Research and Training Center Forensic Examination Report: "Examination of Lincoln County Court House." February 25, 2005. (**Given to Court on January 21, 2011 as Lee floorboard report (9 pages), Exhibit F – but was its forged Version II** )

Brown, Kevin. "I represent Steve Sederwall ..." Letter to Dr. Staub. **February 3, 2011. (Sederwall's court-ordered bogus Orchid Cellmark recovery attempt**)

Cooper, Gale. "Re: Termination of legal services for Gale Cooper and the *De Baca County News* vs Lincoln County Sheriff Rick Virden et al case." Letter to Attorney Martin E. Threet. **February 12, 2011. (Termination of Threet**)

———. "Subj: Change of Legal Representation for Virden et al." E-mail to Attorney Blair Dunn. **April 13, 2011. (Termination of Dunn**)

Brown, Kevin. Letter. **June 7, 2011. (Follow-up to Sederwall's court-ordered Dr. Lee report turn-over**)

"Presentment Hearing." Transcript. **September 23, 2011. (Plaintiffs presenting discrepancies in the Lee reports**)

Eichwald, George P., District Judge. "Order on Hearing of January 21, 2011." **September 28, 2011. (Joined the deputy killings and Kid killing investigations; calling them and records public**)

Riordan, William and Patrick Griebel. "Plaintiffs' Requested Findings of Fact and Conclusions of Law." **November 4, 2011.**

Cooper, Gale. "Re: Immediate termination of services for Sandoval District Court Cause No. D-1329-CV-07-1364." Letter to Attorney Griebel. **November 21, 2011.**

Griebel, Patrick and Jeremy Theoret. "Plaintiff's Motion for Payment of Damages, Costs and Fees." **December 12, 2011.**

———. "Plaintiff's Reply in Support of Motion for Payment of Damages, Costs and Fees." **January 13, 2012.**

Hearing on "Plaintiffs' Motion to Supplement the Record and a Request for Sanctions, and Co-Plaintiff's Motion For Attorney Fees." **January 17, 2012. (Lee reports presented for sanctions as forged; and co-plaintiff Stinnett requests fees for past attorneys. Judge grants 100% fees)**

Brown, Kevin. Court-ordered turn-over of 25 page, "original" Lee report. **January 31, 2012. (Turn-over of the authentic, 25 page, Lee report)**

Eichwald, George P., District Judge. "Order on Plaintiffs Motion to Supplement the Record and Request for Award of Sanctions against Defendants." **February 23, 2012. (Ordered Sederwall to produce original Lee report)**

Lee, Henry and Calvin Ostler. "Forensic Research and Training Center Forensic Examination Report." February 25, 2005. **(Court-ordered turn-over to Plaintiffs on January 31, 2012 as "original" Lee report (25 pages) combining bench, floorboards, and wash stand)**

Griebel, Patrick J. Attorney for Scot Stinnett. "Subpoena for Production or Inspection to Laboratory Corporation of America." **March 29, 2012. (Non-IPRA subpoena of records from Orchid Cellmark parent company)**

_____. "Reply in Support of Plaintiff's Motion for Order to Show Cause." **April 11, 2012. (Co-Plaintiff's attempt to get Sullivan and Sederwall "Private Donor Fund" checking account information))**

Hearing on "Plaintiffs' Second Motion to Supplement the Record and a Request for Sanctions." **May 31, 2012 (Forged Lee reports for sanctions)**

Brown, Kevin. Court-ordered turn-over of another 25 page, "original" Lee report. **June 7, 2012. (CD of same report as given on January 31, 2012, but with color photos and no signatures)**

Sederwall, Steven. Deposition. **June 26, 2012. (Admitted forgery as "massaging!")**

Virden, Rick. Deposition. **June 27, 2012.**

"Status Conference." Transcript. **September 21, 2012.**

Eichwald, George P., District Judge. "Order." For Status Conference of **September 21, 2012. (Court-ordered mediation and Evidentiary hearing)**

Eichwald, George P., District Judge. "Order." For Settlement Conference of **March 27, 2013. (Court-ordered mediation and Evidentiary hearing)**

## THE FORGED DR. HENRY LEE REPORTS

Brown, Kevin. "I am enclosing the document Mr. Sederwall received from Dr. Lee ..." Letter. **February 18, 2010. (Unrequested Lee floorboard report which was a forgery)**

Lee, Henry and Calvin Ostler. "Forensic Research and Training Center Forensic Examination Report: "Examination of Lincoln County Court House." February 25, 2005. **(Given to me on February 18, 2010 by Kevin Brown and on April 6, 2010 by Nicole Werkmeister as a requested Lee report – but was Version I (9 pages) of an unrequested and forged floorboard report )**

Threet, Martin E. "I am returning the Lee report ..." Letter to Brown. (Rejecting and returning the Lee floorboard report) **February 25, 2010. (Not knowing it was a forgery, I returned it merely as unrequested)**

"Presentment Hearing." Transcript. **March 9, 2010. (Defendants gave the judge the unrequested (forged) Lee floorboard report as fulfilling records turn-over; and lied that was the only record in Sederwall's possession)**

Werkmeister, Nicole. "Attached is the Forensic Examination Report From Dr. Henry Lee ..." Fax cover letter. **April 6, 2010. (Copy faxed of same unrequested (forged) Lee floorboard report from Brown)**

Brown, Kevin. "Enclosed please find a copy of another report dated February 25, 2005 which deals with the examination of furniture by Dr. Lee." Letter to Threet. **November 10, 2010. (Sending Lee's (forged) bench report; different font than the (forged) floorboard report)**

Lee, Henry and Calvin Ostler. "Forensic Research and Training Center Forensic Examination Report: "Examination of furniture from Pete Maxwell's of July 15, 1881." February 25, 2005. **(Given to me on November 10, 2010 as Lee bench report (16 pages) – but was forged)**

"Evidentiary Hearing on Plaintiff's Motion for Mandatory Order of Disclosure and Production." Transcript. **January 21, 2011. (Defendants gave forged Lee Floorboard report (9 pages) Version II as Exhibit F; and forged Lee bench report (16 pages) as Exhibit E)**

Lee, Henry and Calvin Ostler. "Forensic Research and Training Center Forensic Examination Report: "Examination of furniture from Pete Maxwell's of July 15, 1881." February 25, 2005. **(Given to Court on January 21, 2011 as Lee bench report (16 pages), Exhibit E – but was a forgery)**

Lee, Henry and Calvin Ostler. "Forensic Research and Training Center Forensic Examination Report: "Examination of Lincoln County Court House." February 25, 2005. **(Given to Court on January 21, 2011 as Lee floorboard report (9 pages), Exhibit F – but was its forged Version II )**

"Presentment Hearing." Transcript. September 23, 2011. **(I realized forgery was taking place and presented discrepancies in the Lee reports)**

Hearing on "Plaintiffs' Motion to Supplement the Record and a Request for Sanctions, and Co-Plaintiff's Motion For Attorney Fees." January 17, 2012 **(Sanctions against Defendants requested for forged reports; and co-plaintiff requested fees for past attorneys. Judge granted 100% fees)**

Eichwald, George P., District Judge. "Order on Plaintiffs Motion to Supplement the Record and Request for Award of Sanctions against Defendants." February 23, 2012. **(Ordered Sederwall to produce authentic Lee report)**

Lee, Henry and Calvin Ostler. "Forensic Research and Training Center Forensic Examination Report." February 25, 2005. **(Court-ordered turn-over to Plaintiffs on January 31, 2012 as "original," authentic, sole Lee report (25 pages) combining bench, floorboards, and wash stand)**

Hearing on "Plaintiffs' Second Motion to Supplement the Record and a Request for Sanctions." **May 31, 2012 (Sanctions requested for forged Lee reports)**

## ORCHID CELLMARK RECORDS SUBPOENAED (RECEIVED 133 PAGES ON APRIL 20, 2012)

Griebel, Patrick J. Attorney for Scot Stinnett. "Subpoena for Production or Inspection to Laboratory Corporation of America." **March 29, 2012. (Non-IPRA subpoena of records from Orchid Cellmark parent company; got 133 pages of results of Lee's floorboards and bench, and Arizona exhumations; missing DNA matching results of bench to remains)**

### *SELECT RECORDS*

Evidence Bag Photo. Chain of Custody Label: "Case No. 2003-274, Underside Bench 4. Date: 07,31,04." Below is written Orchid Cellmark Case and Specimen No. 4444-002B. **July 31, 2004. (Case 2003-274 was made Orchid Cellmark Case No. 4444)**

Ostler, Calvin D. "FedEx Mailing Envelope and tracking information to "Rick Staub, Orchid Cellmark." **August 3, 2004. (Specimens delivered August 4, 2004)**

"Orchid Cellmark Evidence Evaluation Worksheet Case No. 4444 A and B." **August 16, 2004. (Identifying Calvin Ostler as client; listing Lee's floorboard and bench specimens)**

"Orchid Cellmark Evidence Evaluation Worksheet Case No. 4444." **April 13, 2006. (Listing specimens from John Miller-William Hudspeth exhumations.**

"Orchid Cellmark Chain of Custody for Case No. 4444." **May 19, 2005. (On date of John Miller exhumation and signed by Orchid Cellmark Director Rick Staub with the south and north grave specimens he collected listed)**

"Orchid Cellmark Laboratory Report - Forensic Identity - Mitochondrial Analysis for 4444." **January 26, 2009. (Listing specimens for reports requested by me: Lee's from bench and Orchid Cellmark's from the Arizona graves.)**

## *GALE COOPER AS PRO SE*

Cooper, Gale. "Plaintiff Gale Cooper's Court Ordered Request for Evidentiary Hearing Already Scheduled for December 18, 2012." **November 1, 2012.**

Cooper, Gale. "Plaintiff Gale Cooper's Entry of Pro Se Appearance." **November 13, 2012.**

_____. "Plaintiff Gale Cooper's Pre-Evidentiary Hearing Brief." **November 14, 2012.**

_____. "Plaintiff Gale Cooper's Pre-Evidentiary Hearing Brief." **November 14, 2012.**

Narvaez, Henry, Attorney for Virden. "It is our position that those deposition [sic] and exhibits are not relevant to the subject matter of the hearing..." Letter to Gale Cooper. **November 20, 2012. (Trying to keep out June 26-27, 2012 incriminating depositions of Sullivan and Sederwall)**

Cooper, Gale. "Plaintiff Gale Cooper's Witness List for Evidentiary Hearing on December 18, 2012." **December 10, 2012.**

"Evidentiary Hearing." Transcript. **December 18, 2012. (Virden testifies)**

Cooper, Gale. "Plaintiff Gale Cooper's Motion to Compel Defendants' Production of the Requested Forensic DNA Records of Lincoln County Sheriff's Department Case No. 2003-274." **January 3, 2013.**

_____. "Plaintiff Gale Cooper's Motion for Expedited Hearing on Her Filed Motions for the February 4, 2013 Evidentiary Hearing." **January 14, 2013.**

"Evidentiary Hearing." Transcript. February 4, 2013. **(Sederwall and Morel testify)**

Cooper, Gale. "Notice of Filing of Attached Plaintiff Gale Cooper's Proposed Findings of Fact and Conclusions of Law." **February 27, 2013.**

_____. "Plaintiff Gale Cooper's Proposed Findings of Fact and Conclusions of Law." **February 27, 2013.**

Cooper, Gale. "Plaintiff Gale Cooper's Motion to Request Award of Her Costs and Damages From Defendants and to Request Award of Sanctions Against Defendants." **May 23, 2013.**

_____. "Affidavit of Gale Cooper." **May 22, 2013. (Sworn costs)**

_____. "Plaintiff Gale Cooper's Request for Hearing." **May 23, 2013.**

Cooper, Gale. "Re: Open letter to Lincoln County Commissioners about Lincoln County Sheriff's Department **Case No. 2003-274** and Sandoval County District Court **Cause No. D-1329-CV-1364**, Gale Cooper and De Baca County News vs. Rick Virden, Lincoln County Sheriff and Custodian of the Records of the Lincoln County Sheriff's Office; and Steven M. Sederwall, Former Lincoln County Deputy Sheriff; and Thomas T. Sullivan, Former Lincoln County Sheriff and Former Lincoln County Deputy Sheriff." **June 18, 2013. (Summary of "Billy the Kid Case" hoax, its litigation, and its costs; no response)**

_____. "Plaintiff Gale Cooper's Notice of Briefing Completion with Repeated Request for Hearing." **July 1, 2013.**

_____. "Addendum to Plaintiff Gale Cooper's Motion to Request Award of Her Costs and Damages From Defendants and to Request Award of Sanctions Against Defendants." **July 1, 2013.**

_____.Hearing for Plaintiff Gale Cooper's Motion to Request Award of Her Costs and Damages From Defendants and to Request Award of Sanctions Against Defendants." Transcript. December 18, 2013. **(I won!)**

Eichwald, George P. Judge. "Findings of Fact and Conclusions of Law and Order of the Court." **May 15, 2014. (Plaintiff Gale Cooper prevailed)**

_____ "Final Judgment." **March 8, 2017. (Plaintiff Gale Cooper prevailed)**

# COLD CASE BILLY THE KID MEGAHOAX OF W.C. JAMESON'S 21st CENTURY BOOKS

## THE JAMESON BOOKS (CHRONOLOGICAL)

Jameson, W.C. *Billy the Kid: Beyond the Grave*. Boulder, Lanham, Maryland: Taylor Trade Publishing. **2005. (A repeat of the "Brushy Bill" imposter hoax)**

_____. *Billy the Kid: The Lost Interviews*. Clearwater, Florida: Garlic Press Publishing. **2012.** (Reprint 2017). **(Forged rewriting of the 1949 Morrison transcript of "Brushy" to fake dialogue to update the hoax)**

_____. *Pat Garrett: The Man Behind the Badge*. Boulder, Colorado: Taylor Trade Publishing. **2016. (Defamation of Pat Garrett, "Brushy Bill" as a quoted authority, and "Billy the Kid Case" hoaxing as evidence to claim Garrett murdered an innocent victim instead of Billy the Kid)**

_____. *Cold Case Billy the Kid: Investigating History's Mysteries*. Guilford, Connecticut: Twodot. **2018. (Fusing the "Brushy" hoax and "Billy the Kid Case" hoax to argue for "Brushy" as Billy the Kid)**

## SOURCES FOR DEBUNKING CLAIMS (CHRONOLOGICAL)

(SEE: sources debunking "Brushy Bill" Roberts; see "Billy the Kid Case" hoax)

### RELEVANT TO DENYING WILLIAM H. BONNEY'S CORONER'S JURY REPORT'S EXISTENCE

(SEE: William H. Bonney, Coroner's Jury Report; and Patrick F. Garrett, Reward)

### RELEVANT TO FAKING BILLY THE KID'S LETTERS AS WRITTEN BY OTHERS

Cooper, Gale. *Billy the Kid's Writings, Words, and Wit*. Gelcour Books: Albuquerque: New Mexico. **2012. (Analysis of Billy Bonney's handwriting which refutes the W.C. Jameson claim in his 2005 *Billy the Kid: Beyond the Grave* that the writings were by different "law clerks" by showing the letters were by same person)**

### RELEVANT TO FAKING "INVESTIGATION" OF JOHN TUNSTALL'S MURDER

Gonzales, Florencio. Deposition to Frank Warner Angel. **June 8, 1878**. Frank Warner Angel report, Pages 314-319 from *In the Matter of the Examination of the Causes and Circumstances of the Death of John H. Tunstall a British Subject*. Report filed October 4, 1878. Angel Report. Records of the Justice Department. Record Group 60. Class 44 Litigation Files. Container 21. National Archives and Records Administration. U.S. Department of Justice. Washington, D.C. or Angel Report in Interior Department Papers 1850-1907; Appointments Division and Subsequent Actions. Microfilm File Case Number 44-4-8-3. Record Group 48. Microfilm No. M750. Roll 1. National Archives and Records Administration. U.S. Department of Justice. Washington, D.C. **(Showing that Steve Sederwall's claim that Gonzales was involved in a cover-up of Tunstall's murder was wrong)**

Appel, Daniel M. Deposition to Frank Warner Angel. **July 1, 1878**. Frank Warner Angel report, Pages 314-319 from *In the Matter of the Examination of the Causes and Circumstances of the Death of John H. Tunstall a British Subject*. Report filed October 4, 1878. Angel Report. Records of the Justice Department. Record Group 60. Class 44 Litigation Files. Container 21. National Archives and Records Administration. U.S. Department of Justice. Washington, D.C. or Angel Report in Interior Department Papers 1850-1907; Appointments Division and Subsequent Actions. Microfilm File Case Number 44-4-8-3. Record Group 48. Microfilm No. M750. Roll 1. National Archives and Records Administration. U.S. Department of Justice. Washington, D.C. (**Contradicting Steve Sederwall's description of Appel's autopsy report on John Tunstall**)

Nolan, Frederick W. *The Life and Death of John Henry Tunstall*. Albuquerque, New Mexico: The University of New Mexico Press. **1965**. (**With Tunstall's Coroner's Jury Report, page 285; and Daniel Appel's autopsy report, pages 286-287; and with Dr Taylor Ealy's; to counter hoaxer claims about their "investigation" of Tunstall's murder**)

## RELEVANT TO FAKING "BUCKSHOT" ROBERTS KILLING

Catron, Thomas Benton. "Case No. 411. The United States vs. Charles Bowdry [Bowdre], Doc Scurlock, Henry Brown, Henry Antrim alias "Kid," John Middleton, Stephen Stevens, John Scroggins, George Coe and Frederick Waite." **June 21, 1878**. Herman B. Weisner Papers, ca. 1957-1992. New Mexico State University Library at Las Cruces. Rio Grande Historical Collections. Accession No. Ms 0249. Box 1. B-Folder 4. Name: Andrew Roberts Indictment. (**Describes the "Buckshot" Roberts killing and his single fatal would, contradicting the fabrication used of A.N. Blazer**)

## RELEVANT TO FRAMING BILLY BONNEY AS A BROCKWAY GANG COUNTERFEITER

(See Historical Organizations: Secret Service, Operatives)

No Author. "Outlaws of New Mexico, The Exploits of a Band Headed by a New York Youth, The Mountain Fastness of the Kid and His Followers - War Against a Gang of Cattle Thieves and Murderers - The Frontier Confederates of Brockway, the Counterfeiter." *The Sun*. New York. **December 22, 1880**. Vol. XLVIII, No. 118, Page 3, Columns 1-2. (**Apparent inspiration for faking a counterfeiting connection between Billy Bonney and William Brockway**)

Carter, Julie. "Counterfeit Bank Note Rewrites Chapter of Billy the Kid." **July 16, 2010**. *Ruidoso News*. Pages 1A, 9A. http://archives.lincolncountynm.gov/. (**Steve Sederwall linking Billy the Kid to national counterfeiting; then recycled in *Cold Case Billy the Kid* without this reference**)

Sederwall, Steve. "Billy Bonney's Bad Bucks: Did the Kid Travel the Counterfeit Trail?" **June, 2015**. *True West*. Volume 62. Number 6. Page 29. (**Sederwall's repeat of his 2010 counterfeiting claim to "Billy the Kid Case" hoax-backing *True West*; later in *Cold Case Billy the Kid* without this reference**)

## *BROCKWAY SOURCES CITED BY HOAXERS*

No Author. "Old Counterfeiters Caught, Brockway and Two Others Arrested as J.B. Doyle's Accomplices." **October 24, 1880**. *New York Times*. Volume XXX, Number 9087. Page 5. National Archives. Secret Service Library, Counterfeit Division, via Archivist Michael Sampson.

No Author. "Brockway's Forged Bonds: The Counterfeiter Telling How Doyle Got the Bonds – Curious Statements in Court." **May 6, 1882**. *New York Times*. Volume XXXI, Number 9567. Column 2, Page 5. ProQuest.

Drummond, A.L. "True Detective Stories: A Genius Who Went Wrong." **December 20, 1908.** *New York Herald.* Page 7. National Archives. Secret Service Library, Counterfeit Division, via Archivist Michael Sampson.

## *OTHER BROCKWAY COUNTERFEITING REFERENCES*

Dye, John S. *Dye's Government Counterfeiter Detector.* "The Boss of the Boodle and King of the 'Outside Men.'" **March, 1881.** Volume XXIX. Number 10, Pages 4-6. National Archives, Secret Service Library, Counterfeit Division via Archivist Michael Sampson. **(On James Brace Doyle as passing Brockway's counterfeit $100 bills nationally; case of Operative Andrew L. Drummond)**

_____. *Dye's Government Counterfeiter Detector.* "Quotations From the Record." **March, 1881.** Volume XXIX. Number 10, Pages 2-3. National Archives, Secret Service Library, Counterfeit Division via Archivist Michael Sampson. **(On finding some Brockway counterfeit bills in the Moundville, Missouri, haystack of John Hays; case of Operative Wallace W. Hall)**

Brooks, James J. "Annual Report of the Secret Service Division of the United States Treasury Department." **June 30, 1881.** *Government Counterfeiter Detector.* National Archives, Secret Service Library, Counterfeit Division, via Archivist Michael Sampson. **(About apprehension of Brockway gang)**

No Author. *Secret Service Currency Reference Information: 1860's-1880's.* Pages 160-165. National Archives, Secret Service Library, Counterfeit Division, via Archivist Michael Sampson. **(Banks used for Brockway's counterfeits)**

Dye, John S. "The Smith Plates." *Government Counterfeiter Detector.* **February, 1882.** Volume XXX. Number 9. National Archives, Secret Service Library, Counterfeit Division, via Archivist Michael Sampson. **(Description of Charles Smith's plates for William Brockway)**

_____. *Government Counterfeiter Detector.* **November, 1882.** Volume XXXI. Number 6. National Archives, Secret Service Library, Counterfeit Division, via Archivist Michael Sampson. **(General description of how counterfeit currency and skeleton plates are made)**

No Author. "Notes." The American Law Review (1866-1906) Volume 38. **1904.** Pages 576-577. Proquest. **(Biography of William Brockway)**

## *FAKING A COUNTERFEIT BILL AS FROM BILLY THE KID*

Sampson, Michael. Interviews and Consultation with Gale Cooper. **February and March of 2019.** National Archives at College Park. Secret Service Library, Counterfeit Division. 8601 Adelphi Road, College Park, Maryland. **(Statement that National Archives counterfeit bank note provided to Steve Sederwall was random, and not connected to Azariah Wild, Billy Bonney or documented as by William Brockway as claimed by Sederwall)**

## *FAKING RUSTLING AS COUNTERFEIT MONEY-LAUNDERING*

Haley, J. Evetts. *The XIT Ranch of Texas and the Early Days of the Llano Estacado.* Chicago: Lakeside Press. **1929. (Confirming James Cook as a liar in his** *Lane of the Llano***, used as an "eye witness" source by Sederwall)**

Cook, James L. *Lane of the Llano: Being the Story of Jim (Lane) Cook as Told to T.M. Pearce.* Pages 91-92 Boston: Little Brown & Company. **1936.** (Old-timer malarkey about selling Billy the Kid's cattle rustled from John Chisum; faked by Steve Sederwall as an "eye witness" source for Billy's rustling-counterfeit money-laundering scheme)

Dobie, J. Frank. "Son-of-a-Gun Stew." Review. *Southwest Review.* **July, 1936.** Volume 21, Number 4. Pages 444-445. jstor.org. **(Calling Jim Cook's** *Lane of the Llano* **"puerile invention")**

Haley, J. Evetts. "Jim Cook: On the Frontiers of Fantasy." *The Shamrock.* Spring, 1964. Pages 4-7. (**Stating Cook wrote in "fantasy"**)

No Author. *Deaf Smith County: The Land and its People.* Hereford, Texas: Deaf Smith County Historical Society. **1982. (Cook as liar in his** *Lane of the Llano*)

No Author. Biography of James L. Cook. Texas State Historical Association. https://tshaonline.org/handbook/online/articles/fco49. (**Cook as liar in his** *Lane of the Llano*)

## *FAKING COUNTERFEITING CONSPIRACY WITH JESSE JAMES*

Hoyt, Henry. *A Frontier Doctor.* Boston and New York: Houghton Mifflin Company. **1929. (Billy Bonney eating a meal with Jesse James (Pages 110-113) used to claim counterfeiting partnership.)**

Settle, William A. *Jesse James Was His Name.* Columbia, Missouri: University of Missouri Press. **1966. (No mention of Jesse James as a counterfeiter)**

Ross, James R. *I, Jesse James.* Dragon Publishing Corp. **1988. (Great-grandson of Jesse James as author. No mention of counterfeiting, William Brockway, or Billy Bonney)**

Pennington, William. "Roster of Quantrill's, Anderson's and Todd's Guerrillas and Other 'Missouri Jewels.' " **1998.** pennington.tripod.com/roster.htm . (**Showing times of service of Joseph Lea, and Frank and Jesse James, and that they did not serve together with Quantrill; also with John Hays with no dates**)

Stiles, T.J. *Jesse James: Last Rebel of the Civil War.* New York: Vintage Books. **2003. (No mention of counterfeiting, William Brockway, or Billy Bonney)**

James, Eric F. *Jesse James Soul Liberty: Behind the Family Wall of Stigma and Silence.* Danville, Kentucky: Cashel Cadence House. **2012. (No mention of counterfeiting, William Brockway, or Billy Bonney)**

Sederwall, Steve. "Billy Bonney's Bad Buck's: Did the Kid Travel the Counterfeiting Trail." *True West.* **June, 2015.** Volume 62. Number 6. Page 29. (**Contention that Billy the Kid and Jesse James were in cahoots in counterfeiting**)

Sampson, Michael. Interviews and Consultation with Gale Cooper. **February and March of 2019.** National Archives at College Park. Secret Service Library, Counterfeit Division. 8601 Adelphi Road, College Park, Maryland. (**Confirming no Secret Service investigation of Jesse James as a counterfeiter**)

## *FAKING JAMES DOLAN AS A COUNTERFEITER (FAKING WITNESS MISS N.M. FERGUSON)*

Hall, Wallace W. "Daily Reports of U. S. Secret Service Agents, 1875-1937." Microfilm T-915. Record Group 87. Microfilm Rolls: 153 (January 1, 1879 – December 31, 1880); 155: (January 1, 1882 – July 31, 1883; January–June 1882, July 1, 1882). National Archives and Records Department. Department of the Treasury. Secret Service Division. Washington, D.C. (**Reports misstated as being letters by an N.M. Ferguson reporting a counterfeit bill concerning Will Dowlin, not James Dolan: for August 3, 1880, completed August 4, 1880 (questioning Ferguson about if she got a response from J.C. Delaney about getting a counterfeit bill); for August 24, 1880 completed August 30, 1880 (refers to undated cover note from Ferguson with two enclosed letters: one dated August 8, 1880 from Fort Stanton, which she got from J.C. Delaney; one dated August 5, 1880 from Tularosa, which was from M.J. Dowlin to Will Dowlin & Co.); for October 10, 1880, completed October 11, 1880 (reminding Chief Brooks about his Ferguson reporting); and for July 1, 1882, completed July 7, 1882, reporting that he had sent Chief Brooks the letters on the Ferguson case, but Brooks had not returned them. So Hall's reports have no actual Ferguson letters**)

No Author. National Archives and Records Administration, College Park, Maryland. RG 87, Records of the Secret Service, Entry A1-9 Register of letters received,

1863-1903, Volume 5. (**No actual letters referenced by Wallace Hall on the N.M. Ferguson case are present'**)

No Author. National Archives and Records Administration, College Park, Maryland. RG 87, Records of the Secret Service, Entry A1-7 Register of letters received, 1863-1903, Volume 9. (**No actual letters referenced by Wallace Hall on the N.M. Ferguson case are present**)

## *FAKING PAT GARRETT'S CONNECTION TO COUNTERFEITING*

Metz, Leon C. *Pat Garrett. The Story of a Western Lawman.* Norman: University of Oklahoma Press. **1974**. (**Contradicts Steve Sederwall's fakery that that Frank Lea was connected to counterfeiting and was Garrett's friend, giving instead a Captain Joseph C. Lea, his brother, as Garrett's friend**)

## *FAKING FREIGHTER SAM SMITH'S KILLING AS CONNECTED TO BILLY THE KID AND COUNTERFEITING*

Secretary of War. "Samuel Smith, killed by Mescaleros at Pato Spring, April 15, 1880. *Annual Report of the Secretary of War for the Year 1880*. Volume 1. Washington: Government Printing Office. **1880**. Page 106. Google books. (**Listing Sam Smith as killed by Mescaleros; contradicting hoaxers' tale that Smith was killed by Billy the Kid gang in revenge for revealing their counterfeiting**)

No Author. "The Indian News." **April 27, 1880**. *Las Vegas Daily Gazette.* chroniclingamerica.loc.gov. (**Confirming Smith was killed by Victorio's band, contradicting hoaxers' claim that he was killed by Billy the Kid gang in revenge for revealing their counterfeiting**)

No Author. "Indian Depredations in Colorado and Dakota." **May 4, 1880**. *Sacramento Daily Record-Union.* Front page. Volume XLIX, Number 477, Column 6. chroniclingamerica.loc.gov. (**Confirming Smith was killed by Mescalero Apaches, contradicting hoaxers' claim that he was killed by Billy the Kid gang in revenge for revealing their counterfeiting**)

No Author. "Mescalero Marauders." *Santa Fe Daily New Mexican.* **May 21, 1880**. Page 4, Column 1. NewspaperArchives.com. (**Confirming Smith was killed by Mescalero Apaches, contradicting hoaxers' claim that he was killed by Billy the Kid gang in revenge for revealing their counterfeiting**)

No Author. "Outlaws of New Mexico, The Exploits of a Band Headed by a New York Youth, The Mountain Fastness of the Kid and His Followers - War Against a Gang of Cattle Thieves and Murderers - The Frontier Confederates of Brockway, the Counterfeiter." *The Sun.* New York. **December 22, 1880**. Vol. XLVIII, No. 118, Page 3, Columns 1-2. (**Actual source of quote by Steve Sederwall, wrongly attributed to the May 21, 1880 *Santa Fe New Mexican*, with this Santa Fe Ring outlaw myth press accusing Billy Bonney of counterfeiting with William Brockway and murdering freighter Sam Smith**)

(SEE: Historical Organizations: Secret Service, Operatives: Azariah F. Wild, A.L. Drummond, Wallace Hall, Patrick Tyrell,)

## *FAKING MAIL CONTRACTOR MIKE COSGROVE IN A MAIL THEFT-COUNTERFEITING CONSPIRACY WITH BILLY*

Wilcox, Lucius "Lute" M. (city editor, owner, J.H. Koogler). "The Kid. Interview with Billy Bonney The Best Known Man in New Mexico." *Las Vegas Gazette.* **December 27, 1880**. (**Source of misread "mail contractor" as "mail carrier" to fabricate Billy in a conspiracy with carrier to read Wild's mail**)

No Author. "Cosgrave's Contract." *The Las Vegas Daily Optic.* **October 19, 1881**. Volume 2, Number 206, Page 4. www.newspaperarchive.com (**Mike Cosgrove as a mail contractor**)

No Author. *Official Register of the United States Containing a List of the Officers and Employees in the Civil, Military, and Naval Service on the First of July, 1881, Volume II.* The Post-Office Department and Postal Service. Washington: Government Printing Office. **1881**. Page 209. Google books. (**Listing Mike Cosgrove's Star Route contract**)

No Author. "Optical Oracles." *The Las Vegas Daily Optic.* **April 26, 1882.** Volume IIL, Number 147, Page 4. www.newspaperarchive.com. (**Mike Cosgrove as a mail contractor having a man named "Dutch" as a mail carrier**)

Michael, W.H. (Clerk). *Miscellaneous Documents of the Senate of the United States for the First Session of the Fiftieth Congress. Volume II.* Washington: Government Printing Office. **1888.** Page 190. Google books. (**About mail contractors**)

## *FAKING STINKING SPRINGS'S ROCK HOUSE AS CONNECTED TO COUNTERFEITING*

Anaya, Paco. *I Buried Billy.* College Station, Texas: Creative Publishing Company. **1991.** (**Using his malarkey about Billy having "spurious" money**)

Rasch, Philip J. *Trailing Billy the Kid.* National Association for Outlaw and Lawman History, Inc. **1995.** Page 108. (**Used for misstating Tom Pickett's malarkey about failure to get *counterfeit money* hidden by Billy in the Stinking Springs rock cabin; when Rasch wrote that it was *real money*; Page 108**)

## RELEVANT TO FAKING PAT GARRETT AS A NON-LEGITIMATE DEPUTY U.S. MARSHAL

Wild, Azariah F. "Daily Reports of U. S. Secret Service Agents, 1875-1937." Microfilm T-915. Record Group 87. Microfilm Roll 308 (July 1, 1879 - June 30, 1881; October 13, 1880; October 21, 1880; October 29, 1880; January 3, 1881 (replacing his name with crossed-out John Hurley); January 25, 1881 (letter praising Garrett's service). National Archives and Records Department. Department of the Treasury. Secret Service Division. Washington, D.C. (**Showing legal appointment**)

## RELEVANT TO FAKING TOM O'FOLLIARD'S NAME AND GENEALOGY

No Author. "Death of T.C. McKinney." *The Carlsbad Current.* **September 24, 1915.** Page 1. Column 5. ChroniclingAmerica.loc.gov/. (**With no claim that Kip McKinney and Tom O'Folliard were cousins**)

Shipman, Jack. "Brief Career of Tom O'Folliard, Billy the Kid's Partner." No Author. *Voice of the Mexican Border.* Volume 1, Number 5. **January, 1934.** Pages 216-219. (**Gives unsubstantiated genealogy of Tom O'Folliard (Page 216) with no mention that he and Kip McKinney were cousins**)

King, Frank M. *Wranglin' the Past: Reminiscences of Frank M. King.* "Chapter xix, The Kid's Exit." Pasadena, California: Trail's End Publishing Company. **1935 and 1946.** (**False claim that Tom O'Folliard and Kip McKinney were cousins, Page 173**)

Rasch, Philip J. *Trailing Billy the Kid.* National Association for Outlaw and Lawman History, Inc. **1995.** Page 108. (**Used as source for Tom O'Folliard's false genealogy; Page 77**)

Clifford, Frank. Ed. Frederick Nolan. *Deep Trails in the Old West: A Frontier Memoir.* Norman: University of Oklahoma Press. **2011.** Page 276. (**From original unpublished manuscript written in 1940) (Explaining "cousin" error linking Tom O'Folliard to Kip McKinney as a marriage of a McKinney *cousin* into the O'Folliard family; which does not make Tom and Kip cousins; and stating Tom O'Folliard's genealogy is uncertain**)

## RELEVANT TO FAKING THE LOCATION OF THE COURTHOUSE-JAIL'S ARMORY

Caperton, Thomas J. *Historic Structure Report. Lincoln State Monument. Lincoln New Mexico*. Santa Fe, New Mexico: Office of Cultural Affairs, Historic Preservation Division. **1983**. **(Its Lincoln courthouse's second floor diagram (Page 252) is used as a fix-up to place the armory correctly, instead of "Brushy's" confabulated location opposite Garrett's office)**

## RELEVANT TO FAKING PETER MAXWELL'S EXTERNAL BEDROOM DOOR AS ABSENT

Armstrong, Mel and John McCarty. "Kid Dobbs Interviews: An Interview with Garrett H. 'Kid' Dobbs at Farmington, New Mexico," on September 12, 1942, with Mel Armstrong and John McCarty [with] Garrett H. Kid Dobbs in his Home in Farmington, New Mexico, Thursday Morning, October 22, 1942, In the Presence of Mrs. Dobbs and Pat Flynn. J.D. White, Amarillo, Heard Part of the Final Statements of this Interview Re. Billy the Kid's Death." **October 22, 1942**. John L. McCarty Papers. Amarillo Public Library. **(Old-timer malarkey claiming no outside door in Maxwell bedroom used as a source)**

Author Unknown. (Falsely attributed to Gregory Scott Smith). "The Death of Billy the Kid: A New Scenario?" Using "Kid Dobbs Interviews: An Interview with Garrett H. 'Kid' Dobbs at Farmington, New Mexico," on September 12, 1942, with Mel Armstrong and John McCarty" with undated commentary attributed incorrectly to Gregory Scott Smith, Monument Manager at the Fort Sumner State Monument, and using mislabeled diagram of Fort Sumner Commanding Officer's Quarters as the Maxwell house. Fort Sumner, New Mexico, State Monument files. **(Article using Kid Dobbs's fakery with added mislabeled diagram of Fort Sumner's Commanding Officer's Quarters as being the Maxwell house, to fabricate no outside door to the Maxwell bedroom )**

Boze Bell, Bob. (With Steve Sederwall) "Caught With His Pants Down? Billy the Kid Vs Pat Garrett. One Door Closes." **August, 2010**. *True West*. Volume 57. **(Using wrongly alleged author, Gregory Scott Smith's, "Death of Billy the Kid" article to claim no outside door, plus Sederwall hoaxing "CSI" proof of it by Dr. Henry Lee's fake washstand investigation. It was recycled by Sederwall in W.C. Jameson's *Cold Case Billy the Kid*)**

## RELEVANT TO FAKING FACE DOWN CORPSE

Traylor, Leslie. "Facts Regarding the Escape of Billy the Kid." *Frontier Times*. **July, 1936**. Pages 506-513 (on Page 509). FrontierTimesMagazine.com. **(About his Jesus Silva interview on identifying Billy's body)**

Otero, Miguel, *The Real Billy the Kid*. New York: Rufus Rockwell Wilson. **1936**. **(Claim that Jesus Silva saw shot Billy Bonney face down.)**

## RELEVANT TO FAKING OLD PETER MAXWELL AS A COOK DENYING GARRETT SHOT BILLY

Avant, Bundy. (Told to Arthur Clements). "The Bundy Avant Story: New Mexico in the days when a thin population was intent on bettering itself and each man could devise his own method for 'getting' while getting' was good.' " (Part One) *True West*. **May-June, 1978**, Volume 25, Number 5. **(Old-timer malarkey about a "Peter Maxwell" in the San Andres Mountains telling Avant that Garrett did not kill Billy the Kid)**

No Author. "Las Vegas." *The Albuquerque Citizen*. **June 28, 1898**. Page 2, Column 3. NewspaperArchive.com. **(Peter Maxwell death notice about Fort Sumner area residence and death)**

## *KEY SOURCES CITED BY HOAXERS (CHRONOLOGICAL)*
(SEE: "Brushy Bill" Robert's hoax sources; Secret Service Operatives in Historical Organizations; and counterfeiting framing of Billy Bonney)

Bonney, William Henry. Deposition to Frank Warner Angel. **June 8, 1878.** Depositions, Pages 314-319. National Archives and Records Administration. Records of the Justice Department. Record Group 60. Class 44 Litigation Files. Container 21. Washington, D.C. (**A quote was used, but the deposition was hidden, since "Brushy" was unaware of it**)

Garrett, Pat F. *The Authentic Life of Billy the Kid.* Santa Fe, New Mexico: New Mexico Printing and Publishing Co. **1882.** (Edition used by me: Edited by Maurice Garland Fulton. New York: The Macmillan Company. 1927)

Hoyt, Henry F. "Copy of a bill of sale written by W$^m$ H. Bonney ..." Letter to Lew Wallace Jr. **April 27, 1927.** Indiana Historical Society. Lew Wallace Collection. M0292. Box 14, Folder 11. (**Provided a copy of the Bill of Sale of October 24, 1878**)

Poe, John W. *The Death of Billy the Kid.* (Introduction by Maurice Garland Fulton). Boston and New York: Houghton Mifflin Company. **1933.**

Otero, Miguel, *The Real Billy the Kid.* New York: Rufus Rockwell Wilson. **1936.** (**Claim that Jesus Silva for shot Billy Bonney face down. But Otero had no first-hand knowledge, and the book was 55 years after the event.**)

Poe, Sophie. *Buckboard Days.* Albuquerque, New Mexico: University of New Mexico Press. **1964.**

Klasner, Lilly. Eve Ball. Ed. *My Girlhood Among Outlaws.* Tucson, Arizona: The University of Arizona Press. **1972.**

Avant, Bundy. (Told to Arthur Clements). "The Bundy Avant Story: New Mexico in the days when a thin population was intent on bettering itself and each man could devise his own method for 'getting' while getting' was good.' " (Part One) *True West.* **May-June, 1978**, Volume 25, Number 5. (**Old-timer malarkey about a "Peter Maxwell" in the San Andres Mountains telling Avant that Garrett did not kill Billy the Kid; plus other apocryphal Billy the Kid tales**)

Caperton, Thomas J. *Historic Structure Report. Lincoln State Monument. Lincoln New Mexico.* Santa Fe, New Mexico: Office of Cultural Affairs, Historic Preservation Division. **1983.** (**Used to fix-up "Brushy's" faked armory location in the Lincoln courthouse by adding a diagram faked from Caperton's Report to minimize "Brushy's" fatal error**)

Tunstill, William A. *Billy the Kid and Me Were the Same: A Documentary on the Life of Billy the Kid.* Roswell, New Mexico: Western History Research Center. **1988.** (**"Brushy"-backer faking a genealogy; debunked by Roy L. Haws, Eulaine Emerson Haws's son, in his 2015 *Brushy Bill: Proof That His Claim to Be Billy the Kid Was a Hoax*)

Anaya, Paco. *I Buried Billy.* College Station, Texas: Creative Publishing Company. **1991**.(**Cited as claiming counterfeiting for Billy**)

Rasch, Philip J. *Trailing Billy the Kid.* National Association for Outlaw and Lawman History, Inc. **1995.** Page 108. (**Used as source about Tom O'Folliard false genealogy; Page 77; misstated 1932 tale by Tom Pickett of failing to get *counterfeit money* hidden in the Stinking Springs rock cabin; when Rasch wrote that it was *real money*; Page 108**)

Lee, Henry and Calvin Ostler. "Forensic Research and Training Center Forensic Examination Report: "Examination of Lincoln County Court House." February 25, 2005. (**Apparently the forged "Billy the Kid Case's floorboard report** )

Lee, Henry. "Forensic Examination Report (Examination of Furniture From Pete Maxwell's of July 15, 1881) 22 May 2004." From W.C. Jameson, *Cold Case Billy the Kid.* Page 187. (**Apparently the forged "Billy the Kid Case's" carpenter's bench, washstand, and headboard report**)

# INDEX

Abbott, E.C. "Teddy Blue" – 55, 274
Abbott, George – 15
Abbott, Harold – 15, 700
"ABC Good Morning America" – 463
Able, John – 199, 535
Able, Martile – 119, 199, 535
Abraham, Louis – 203
Abreu, Manuel – 341, 403, 702
Abreu, Odelia – 403, 702
Abreu, Stella – 341-342, 402-403, 410, 412-415, 702; **Billy the Kid Museum with alleged Peter Maxwell furniture of:** 193, 299, 341-342, 402-403, 410, 412-414, 501, 511, 574-575, 702-704
Acton, Scott – 252-254, 274, 299, 525, 539, 707
Acuña, Mark Anthony – 374, 385, 387, 422, 475, 713, 744
Adams, Ramon F. - 159
adobe wall (Tunstall corral William Brady ambush) – 149, 167, 239, 595
Agler, Don – 355
Airy, Helen – 271-282, 287, 259-260, 425-426, 435; *Whatever Happened to Billy the Kid?* by: 271, 359, 425-426
Alamogordo, New Mexico – 15, 196, 290, 610
*Alamogordo News* – 15, 55, 116, 175, 205-206, 261
*Albuquerque Journal* – 116-117, 124, 127, 296, 322, 360, 389, 406-407, 411, 413, 417, 434-435, 444, 446, 475, 706-707
Albuquerque Museum of Art and History – 404, 415
Albuquerque, New Mexico – 116-117, 123, 127, 134, 282, 341, 360, 388, 393-394, 402-403, 448, 463, 469, 502, 506, 679, 702, 727, 730, 747

Allison, Bill – 232, 235, 363, 525, 530, 539-541
Amarillo, Texas – 689
ambidextrousness – 125, 137, 150, 334, 531
American Academy of Forensic Sciences Ethics Committee complaint (See Dr. Henry Lee)
Amos, Donna Jenice – 308
Aamos-Staats, Joani – 308
Amnesty Proclamation (see Lew Wallace)
Analla, Pablo – 79, 610
Anaya, A.P. "Paco" – 25, 56, 206-207, 261, 343-344, 575, 652, 661-663, 666, 700; *I Buried Billy* by: 56, 207, 261, 344, 652, 661-663, 700
Anaya, Louis – 343, 661
Anaya, Sam – 661
Anderson, Carl – 577
Andress, Lipscomb, and Petticolas Law Firm – 122, 147
Andress, Ted – 118, 147
Angel, Frank Warner – 20-21, 24, 37, 39-40, 52, 59, 60, 142, 165, 167, 197, 216, 232, 238, 308, 317, 324, 332, 463, 530, 569, 586-590, 593, 601, 611, 765
Anti-Horse Thief Association – 117, 122, 248, 533, 541
Anton Chico, New Mexico Territory – 610
Antrim, Catherine McCarty – 32, 154, 264, 271, 274, 291, 294-295, 305, 307-311, 329, 346, 374, 378-379, 381-382, 387, 422, 436, 440, 446, 468, 475, 487, 491, 496, 541, 712-713, 726-733, 739-744; **fake photograph of:** 195; **exhumation attempt on:** 291, 294-295, 305, 307-311, 329, 346, 378-379, 381-382, 387, 422, 436, 440, 446, 468, 475, 487, 491, 712-713, 726-733,

739-744 (See "Billy the Kid Case" hoax)
Antrim, Henry - (see William H. Bonney)
Antrim, William Henry (see William H. Bonney)
Antrim, Joseph "Josie" – 19, 32, 227, 234; **added to "Brushy" in fake Jameson fix-up:** 234
Antrim, William Henry Harrison – 32, 160, 234; **added to "Brushy" in fake Jameson fix-up:** 234
Appel, Daniel – 587-588, 602, 604; **Tunstall autopsy deposition by:** 587-588, 765
Argentina – 192-193
Arizona Pioneers' Home – 272, 277, 296, 300, 423, 425, 434, 763
*Arizona Highway* – 179
Arizona Pioneers' Home Cemetery – 272, 277, 282, 296, 300, 359, 423, 425, 427-428, 434, 437, 484, 761, 763
armory (see Lincoln County courthouse-jail)
Armstrong, Mel – 689
Ashenfelter, Singleton M. – 258, 262, 538, 555, 569, 575-576, 667
Autry, Gene – 97, 135
Avant, Bundy – 573, 696-698, 702
Awly, J. – 59
Axtell, Samuel Beach – 20, 36, 38-39, 60, 216, 229, 450-451, 589, 593-595, 602, 675, 677
Baca, Bonificio – 184
Baca, Saturnino – 39, 86, 184, 602-604
Bailey, David – 487, 716
Bailey, James – 415
Bailey, Margaret – 415
Bailey, Todd – 578
Baker, Frank – 36, 44, 48, 58-61, 70-71, 160, 589, 595
Ball, Eve – 161, 194
Banks, Leo W. – 407-408, 430, 432, 436-437
Barber, George B. – 588

Baxter, Carl – 281
Barlow Billy – 116-117, 120-123, 126, 134, 205, 216, 231, 247, 258, 262, 266, 286, 290, 297, 305, 320-321, 349, 363, 365-366, 368-369, 371, 420, 525-527, 532, 538, 553-556, 558, 573, 576, 675, 678, 681, 693, 703, 708; **as Billy B. Barlow:** 134
Barnes, Sidney – 23, 397, 401, 622, 648, 654
Barrow-Rutledge Funeral Chapel – 129
Barnum, P.T. – 129, 135
Barrier, Adolph – 24, 35-36, 596
bay mare – 82, 85, 177, 773
Bean, Frederick – 99, 135, 140, 143, 225-227, 231-236, 238, 240, 244-255, 257-264, 266, 268, 287, 294, 298, 349, 363, 525, 530, 533, 537, 539-542, 554, 583, 708-709; *The Return of the Outlaw Billy the Kid* **by:** 99, 140-141, 225-264, 268, 294, 363, 520, 523-524, 526-527, 530, 534-535, 537-540, 442-543, 554-555, 562, 564, 583, 585, 608, 660, 668, 707-709; **locating and transcribing Morrison's "Brushy" tapes by:** 135, 143, 225, 232, 235, 537, 540-542; **alternate claim that transcribing Morrison's tapes was by Bill Allison:** 232, 363; **possible involvement in hoaxed Roberts family Bible by:** 235, 525, 530, 540 (See Oliver Pleasant "Brushy Bill" Roberts, William V. Morrison, C.L. Sonnichsen)
Beaver Bank Hat Company – 317
Beaver Smith's Saloon – 42
Beckwith family – 71
Beckwith, Henry – 71
Beckwith, John – 71

Beckwith, Robert W. "Bob" – 59, 74-75, 170, 250, 546-547, 564, 608, 662

Bell, James W. – 32, 47-48, 53-54, 93, 124-125, 142, 149, 184-185, 188, 199, 230, 233, 250, 276, 291, 293, 298, 320-321, 323, 325, 327-328, 352-355, 366-368, 371-372, 394, 399-400, 416-420, 424, 450, 455, 468-469, 472, 474, 478, 481, 485, 493, 497, 499, 508, 552, 570-572, 664, 668-674; **Dr. Henry Lee's fake forensics for shooting of**: 417-420, 499, 508, 669-674; **"Probable Cause Statement" sub-investigation for**: 320, 323, 327-328, 416, 468-469, 481, 485, 497, 508, 514, 572, 668, 670 (See "Billy the Kid Case" hoax)

Bennett, Ray – 442

Bernstein, Morris – 203

Berryman, Clifford – 577

"Big Casino" – 42

Bill Kurtis Productions (See Bill Kurtis)

Billy-Dolan peace meeting (see William H. Bonney)

Billy the Kid (see William H. Bonney)

BillytheKidCase.com website (See Steve Sederwall)

"Billy the Kid Case" (see "Billy the Kid Case" hoax)

"Billy the Kid Case" hoax (Lincoln County Sheriff's Department Case No. 2003-274, De Baca County Sheriff's Department Case No. 03-06-136-01) – 6, 16-88, 137, 145-146, 148, 152, 176, 192, 226, 262-263, 265-266, 268, 271-272, 285-440, 443-444, 465-520, 553, 558, 560-566, 568, 570-572, 574-576, 579-580, 583-584, 606, 618-619, 621, 652, 666-669, 674-675, 678, 681, 691, 693, 698-699, 701-702, 707-710, 714, 717-719, 723, 726-746; **summary of**: 295-304; **Statute of Limitations on murder blockade of Garrett "prosecution" by**: 16, 148, 286, 291, 294-295, 321-322, 372; **Statute of Limitations on murder removing pardon need for Billy the Kid for 1878 murders**: 147; blockade of OMI exhumation permit refusals for: 306-313, 726-732; Lois Telfer case blockade of: 16, 148, 226, 306, 725-726; historical blockade of: 17-88; *New York Times* announcement of: 288-291; **HOAXERS AND HOAX DOCUMENTS FOR**: 307-308, 314, 320, 322-346, 349-372; 374-377, 379-387, 393-401, 407, 410-411, 416, 424, 468-469, 474, 481, 485, 489, 497, 508, 514, 523, 572, 587, 595, 668-670, 682, 698-699, 732-746, (<u>"Probable Cause Statement" for Pat Garrett as a murderer for</u>: 314, 322-346, 393-394, 401, 407, 410-411, 416, 424, 468-469, 474, 485, 489, 523, 587, 595, 669-670, 682, 698-699; <u>Deputy Bell killing sub-investigation for</u>: 320, 323, 327-328, 416, 468-469, 481, 485, 497, 508, 514, 572, 668, 670; <u>Overton Affidavit for</u>: 323, 349-372; <u>David Turk "Probable Case Statement Addendum U.S. Marshals Service and Billy the Kid" for</u>: 396-401; "<u>Seventy-Seven Days of Doubt Document</u>" for: 323, 349-372, 527, 542; <u>exhumation petitions for Catherine Antrim and William Bonney for</u>: 307-308, 374-377, 379-387, 732-746 (See Catherine Antrim, William H. Bonney); **FAKE FORENSICS FOR**: 297-298, 300-301, 328,

331, 340-341. 393-394, 401-420, 431-432, 436-437, 466, 473-474, 498, 505-506, 512, 670, 681, 691, 693, 702, 704, (for carpenter's workbench: 297-298, 300-301, 331, 340-341. 393-394, 401-409, 466, 473, 505-506, 512, 681, 702 (with hiding no "reference DNA" of Billy the Kid for comparison: 298, 407, 409, 420) (for courthouse floorboards for Deputy Bell killing: 301, 328, 416-419, 474, 466, 473, 498, 505-506, 571-572, 668-674 (with hiding having no "reference DNA" of Deputy Bell for comparison: 417, 420, 670) (for washstand: 410-416, 473, 505-506, 512, 681, 691, 693) (for "crime scene" reconstruction against Pat Garrett using washstand: 411, 415, 691, 693, 704) (for headboard: 413-414, 505-506, 512, 703-704 (See Henry Lee, Steve Sederwall); **illegal exhumations of John Miller and William Hudspeth for:** 423-440 (See Laura Fulginiti); **exhumation attempt on "Brushy Bill" Roberts for:** 443-444; **fake Billy the Kid pardon for:** 285, 287-290, 292-293, 295, 302-303, 321, 361, 378-383, 386, 388-390, 392, 423, 444-464; **open records case against:** 465-520; **HIDDEN DNA ORCHID CELLMARK LAB RESULTS REVEALED FOR:** no existing reference DNA of Billy the Kid for: 298, 407, 409, 420; no existing reference DNA of Deputy James Bell for: 417, 420, 670; no blood on carpenter's bench: 409, 419; no DNA on carpenter's bench: 419; useless mixed DNA on Bell killing courthouse floorboards: 420, 474; no DNA from John Miller: 436-437; DNA from John Miller: 432; DNA from William Hudspeth: 432
(See hoaxers: Bill Richardson, Bill Robins III, Paul Hutton, Henry Lee, Tom Sullivan, Gary Graves, Steve Sederwall, David Turk, Alan Morel, Sherry Tippett, Henry Quintero, Ted Hartley, Rick Staub, Randi McGinn) (See Orchid Cellmark Laboratory)

Billy the Kid Museum in Canton, Texas – 288, 290

Billy the Kid Outlaw Gang – 155, 343, 661, 714, 747

Black Hills of South Dakota – 102, 159

Blakely's Mills, Colorado – 616

Blandano, Manuel – 186

Blazer, A.N. – 599-600

Blazer, Joseph – 99, 103-104, 137, 179, 599

Blazer, Paul – 99, 103-104, 131-135, 137, 140, 180, 224, 285, 531

Blazer's Mill – 37, 47, 137, 145, 168, 229, 569, 599-600, 603

"blood" of Billy the Kid (see "Billy the Kid Case" hoax)

Bonita, Arizona – 19, 33, 159-161

Bonito River – 170

Bonney, William H. "Billy" (William Henry McCarty, Henry Antrim, Billy Bonney, Billy the Kid) – 3-5, 7-26, 29, 31-88, 113-114, 121, 124-127, 148-151, 153, 162, 168, 171-175, 177-178, 180, 182, 185, 187-188, 194, 197, 202-210, 212-217, 220-223, 225, 228-230, 238, 242, 244, 249-250, 252-254, 256-257, 260-264, 267-268, 274-276, 287, 293-296, 297-298, 305-306, 309-312, 314, 319, 322-323, 329, 337-339, 344, 349, 355-356, 372-379, 378,

385-387, 391-392, 398-399, 401, 454-455, 487, 490-492, 526, 529-531, 539, 561, 568-570, 572, 575, 586-587, 589-590, 593, 598, 602, 610, 613, 622, 627, 640, 642, 647-648, 650, 665, 667-668, 679, 691-692, 694-695, 699, 710, 715-717, 723, 725-726; **outlaw myth of:** 4, 91, 147, 149, 152, 169, 172, 203, 272, 276, 369, 594, 623, 642, 769; **"Billy the Kid" moniker for:** 4, 57, 73, 147, 272, 656; **tintype of :** 17, 29, 37, 44, 125, 148-150, 162, 177-178, 194, 225, 249, 252-254, 263, 274, 531, 539; **history of:** 31-49; **writings and words of:** 57-88; **contemporary champions of:** 50-56; **Peñasco River Ranch of:** 33, 40, 60, 165, 223, 229; **deputizing of:** 36, 50, 58-59; **Lincoln pit jailing of:** 36, 59, 197; **Paulita Maxwell as sweetheart of:** 25, 31-32, 43, 48, 127, 178, 187-188, 223, 244, 287, 349, 355-356, 572, 593, 610, 640, 665, 679, 691-692; **deposition to Frank Warner Angel by:** 20, 24, 37, 52, 57, 223, 229, 238, 569, 586-587, 589-590; **as bi-cultural anti-Santa Fe Ring Freedom fighter:** 3-4, 24, 32, 46, 55, 185, 223, 264, 267, 274, 287, 297 (See John Tunstall, Lincoln County War and Battle); **"Regulator Manifesto" by:** 26, 38, 40, 54, 64-65, 168, 598, 602, 609; **Hoyt Bill of Sale by:** 65; **pardon bargain with Lew Wallace:** 4, 18, 21, 25, 41, 46, 51, 57, 67, 72, 77, 81, 113, 153, 168, 172-174, 197, 203, 223, 230, 275, 529, 627 (pardon bargain letters and interview by: 65-71, 77-82); **Dudley Court of Inquiry testimony by:** 18, 21-22, 42, 57, 72-77, 114, 151, 171, 174, 250; **pardon bargain with Secret Service by:** 21, 23-24, 45, 78, 175, 223, 613, 622, 647-648; **capture of:** 32, 46-47, 78, 82-83, 177, 180, 222, 230, 244, 263, 276, 392, 454-455, 568, 672, 650; **replevin case of:** 47, 82, 180; **Santa Fe jailing of:** 46, 79-81, 178, 202, 230, 242, 276, 392, 526, 529-530, 569, 667-668; **Mesilla trial of:** 21, 25, 46-47, 51, 79, 81, 83, 174, 179, 198, 222, 230, 249, 569, 596-597, 667; "Buckshot" Roberts hearing in: 46-47, 174, 179, 230, 569; Brady trial and hanging sentence for: 47, 83, 242; correct defense for:404, 596; **Lincoln courthouse jailing and escape of:** 29, 47-48, 668; **Wallace rewards for:** 14, 46, 126, 208, 212-217; Wallace reward posters for: 217; **July 14, 1881 killing of:** 5, 7, 16, 19, 31, 42-43, 121, 124; **Coroner's Jury Report of:** 7-15, 19, 49, 127, 202, 204-210, 215-216, 220, 2222-223, 256-257, 260, 268, 329, 337-339, 344, 561, 570, 575, 694-695, 699, 723; **Fort Sumner townspeople's death vigil for:** 25, 49, 207, 221, 228, 256-257, 261-262, 391, 401, 561, 695, 699; **1961-1962 exhumation attempt on:** 294, 305-306, 378, 387-388, 475, 492, 716, 725-726; **2003-2004 exhumation attempt on:** 293, 295-296, 298, 305-306, 309-312, 314, 319, 322-323, 372-379, 385-387, 398-399, 487, 490-491, 710, 715-717 (hiding no existing "reference DNA" of Billy the Kid for comparison: 298, 407, 409, 420)

Boomersbach, Jana – 373-374

Bordley, William – 394
Borrego Pass, Arizona – 277
Bosque Grande – 40, 161-162, 566-567, 610-611, 617, 627-629, 651, 770-771
Bosque Redondo – 42, 161-162, 236, 686
Bowdre, Charles "Charlie" – 32, 36-37, 40, 43-44, 46, 48, 54, 64, 78-79, 85, 168, 177, 188-189, 230, 239, 244-245, 265, 274, 281, 294, 306, 310, 312, 327, 370, 387, 550, 568, 599, 600, 610, 612-613, 627, 648, 656, 662, 664, 716-717, 725-726, 766; **killed as mistaken for Billy Bonney**: 230, 244, 550-551, 662; **exhumation involvement in** (See Lois Telfer case, Louis Bowdre)
Bowdre, Louis – 295, 306, 387, 725
Bowdre, Manuela – 40, 188, 274, 281, 370, 610
Bowlin, Joe – 155, 343, 661
Bowlin, Marlyn – 155, 661, 714, 716
Boyd, Linda – 319
Boyle, Andrew "Andy" – 607
Boze Bell, Bob – 134, 296, 299, 318, 389-391, 621, 691
Brady, Arcadio – 116-123
Brady, William – 24-25, 34-40, 44, 47-48, 52-54, 58-59, 63, 65-66, 82, 86, 99, 116-118, 120-121, 123, 149-150, 165-166, 168, 173, 180-181, 194, 197, 200, 203-205, 227-230, 237-239, 242-243, 245, 274, 276, 282, 289, 316, 324, 351, 360, 380, 382, 391-392, 441, 449-452, 455-456, 538, 544-545, 550-552, 564, 569, 587-589, 591, 594-598, 603, 608-609, 621, 664, 677, 737
Bradford, Illinois – 613, 616, 626, 646
Branch, Louis Leon – 257
Branch, Tom – 292
Brazel, Wayne – 134, 577-578

Breeden, William – 7, 13, 208
Breihan, Carl W. – 97, 103, 131, 134, 180
Brewer, Richard "Dick" – 36-37, 48, 51-52, 58-59, 61-63, 137, 168, 228, 545, 599-601, 613
Brininstool, E.A. – 332
Briscoe, Joe – 42, 175-175, 423, 565
Bristol, Warren H. – 35, 41-42, 46-47, 82, 181, 203, 275, 351, 551, 586, 596
British Ambassador – 37
British Royal Society – 435
Brockway's bills banks (See William E. Brockway)
Brockway, William E. "Long Bill" alias Edward W. Spencer – 609, 611, 613-621, 623-627, 629-631, 634-636, 638, 641, 643, 645-647, 652, 769, 772; **counterfeit bill banks of:** 615
Brooklyn, New York – 577, 614, 625
Brooks, James J. – 22, 44-45, 327, 611, 613, 615, 622, 630, 638, 645, 654-655 (See Secret Service, Azariah Wild)
Brothers, Mary Hudson – 188
Brown, "Hank" – 180
Brown, Henry Newton – 46, 53, 61, 450, 600, 612, 766-768
Brown, Kevin – 468, 471-472, 478, 498-501, 503, 505
Brownsville, Texas – 192
Brunswick, M. – 211
"Brushy Bill" hoax (See Oliver Pleasant Roberts, William V. Morrison, C.L. Sonnichsen, W.C. Jameson, Frederick Bean)
"Brushy Bill" Roberts - (see Oliver Pleasant Roberts)
Budd, William (See William H. West)
Buffalo Gap, Texas – 102, 121-122, 125, 128, 130, 152-154, 156, 233, 578

Bugliosi, Vincent – 405; *The Five Reasons Way O.J. Simpson Got Away With Murder* by: 405
Burgess, W.H. – 177-178
Burnam, George P. – 614; *American Counterfeiters* by: 614
Burns, Walter Noble – 18, 25, 114, 127, 136, 138, 142, 153, 158-159, 164-165, 167, 169-170, 172-174, 177-178, 180, 185-187, 191, 222, 251, 278; *The Saga of Billy the Kid* by: 18, 114, 136, 138, 142, 153, 158-159, 164-165, 167, 169-170, 174, 177-178, 185-188, 191, 198, 222, 251, 278
Burt, Billy – 54, 187, 198, 363, 667, 675
Cahill, Frank "Windy" – 33, 36-37, 44, 48, 161, 277, 350
Camp, Ralph – 666
Campbell, Billy – 41, 68, 72, 172, 230, 240, 391, 452-454, 548, 642
Cannes Film Festival – 301, 441
Canton, Texas – 288, 290
Capitan Mountains – 48, 69, 166, 187, 200, 238, 592
Capitan, New Mexico – 289, 292, 296, 314-317, 390, 398, 422, 434, 468, 494, 501, 504, 696, 710, 747
"Capitan Village Hall News" – 320
Caplan, Sara – 405
Cardon, Bill – 96, 535; **Cardon Real Estate Company of:** 97; **Dautrich Reality Company of:** 535
Carlson, Raymond – 179
Carlyle, Jim – 45, 48, 78-79, 152, 175-176, 203, 243, 251, 253, 550, 567, 772
carpenter's bench (See "Billy the Kid Case" hoax, Cold Case Billy the Kid megahoax, Henry Lee fake forensics on, Steve Sederwall forgery of forensic report on)

carpenter's shop vigil for Billy the Kid's body (See William H. Bonney)
Carson, Kit – 93, 141
Carter, Julie – 320, 404, 408, 415, 430, 435, 440, 618
Carter, Powhatan – 373
Casey, Robert – 34
Catron, Thomas Benton – 26, 32, 34-35, 37-44, 46-47, 54-55, 64-65, 133, 139-140, 163-164, 179, 181, 211, 237, 273, 275, 277, 548, 551, 577, 593, 598, 600, 602-603, 605-606, 609, 611-612, 646, 648-649, 651, 665; **Carrizozo Land and Cattle Company of:** 26, 34, 38, 44, 54, 65, 140, 598, 609, 611, 651; **Federal indictment No. 411 of Regulators by:** 21, 25, 46, 66, 179, 612, 665, 766-768
Caypless, Edgar – 18, 47, 82, 107, 109, 145, 178-180, 249, 251, 455, 569
"CBS News" – 462
Cedric, Nikki – 396, 404
Chandler, Howard – 529
Chapman, Huston – 21, 40-42, 66-67, 72, 162, 171-174, 181, 222, 230, 240-242, 275, 326, 391, 451-452, 454, 548-549, 551, 564-565, 613, 642
Charles Fritz Ranch – 598, 608
Chávez, Florencio – 38
Chávez y Chávez, José – 38, 73, 76-77
Cherry, Doris – 315-316, 403, 406, 408-409, 418, 422
Chisum, John Simpson – 35-37, 71, 79, 85, 93, 117, 126, 138-139, 142, 161-164, 169-170, 175, 187-189, 201, 236-237, 241, 266, 281, 451, 586, 596, 610, 612, 617, 621-623, 626-627, 631-635, 639, 652, 686
Christ's Forty Acres – 316
Cisneros, Ben – 119
Cisneros house – 149, 167, 239
Claiborne Parish, Louisiana – 42

Clarkson, Lana – 405
Cleaveland, Norman – 27
Cleaver, Dennis – 319
Clifford, Frank – 658, 660
Cline, Donald – 92-97, 101, 130. 147-148, 154-157, 159, 192-193, 199-200, 253, 483, 533, 535; ***Brushy Bill Roberts: I Wasn't Billy the Kid* by:** 92-93, 95, 101, 147, 154-157, 159, 192, 199-200, 253, 533
Cody, Buffalo Bill – 102, 195; **Buffalo Bill Cody Wild West Show of:** 93
Coe, Frank – 36-37, 50-51, 116, 127, 236, 360, 588, 602
Coe, George – 37, 46, 50-51, 114, 127, 136, 163, 168, 196, 198, 282, 599-600, 696, 766-768; ***Frontier Fighter* by:** 51, 136, 163
Coe, Wilbur – 116
Coghlan, Pat – 40, 610
Cold Case Billy the Kid megahoax – 6, 268, 271, 287, 295, 304, 312-313, 318, 320, 327, 334-335, 339, 341, 344, 394, 406, 480, 520, 523-524, 534 545, 560-562, 564, 567, 570-575, 580, 583-719, 723 (See "Brushy Bill" hoax, "Billy the Kid Case" hoax)
Coles, Ed – 666
Colfax County War – 4, 27, 594
Colorado Springs, Colorado – 616
Comanche mother (See John Miller)
confabulation – 92
Conley, Joe – 281
Cook, David – 657-660
Cook, Eliza Jane (See Eliza Jane McKinney Cook)
Cook, Eliza Jane McKinney – 657, 660
Cook, Jim (Lane) – 622, 631-632, 635-636, 660; ***Lane of the Llano: Being the Story of Jim (Lane) Cook as Told to T.M. Pearce* by:** 622, 632

Cook, John (author) – 632
Cook, John – 657-658
Cook, John Enoch – 660
Cook, Margaret Jane – 658
Cook, Sarah – 657
Cook, Thalis – 658
Cooper, Thomas "Tom" – 44, 611, 614, 617, 652
Copeland, John – 37-38, 602-603, 675
Corbett, Sam – 69, 184-185, 250, 571-572, 674
Corn, Robert – 675
Coroner's Jury Report (see William H. Bonney)
Cosgrove, Cornelius – 650
Cosgrove, Michael "Mike" – 83, 622-623, 647, 649-650
counterfeiting-rustling hoax (See Steven M. Sederwall)
Court of Inquiry for Colonel Dudley (see Nathan Augustus Monroe Dudley)
Coyote Spring – 45, 175, 771
Crawford, Charles "Charlie" – 605
Crawfordsville, Indiana – 169, 642
Creasy, Frank Burrard "Burt" – 278-279, 281
Crockett, Bill – 279
Cuba – 192-193, 533
Cunningham, Eugene – 193; ***Triggernometry* by:** 193
Court of Inquiry (see Nathan Augustus Monroe Dudley)
Dalton gang – 192
Dalton, J. Frank – 101-103, 147, 201, 231, 524; **as Jesse James:** 101-103, 147, 201, 231, 524; **as a "Missourian":** 101, 231, 524; **as a "Texan":** 524
Daniels, Charles "Charlie" – 303, 448, 467
dark night for death scene - (see Oliver P. Roberts)
Davidson, Morrey – 101
Davis, George – 58-59, 71, 567
Darwin, Charles – 435
Dawson, Charles – 435

De Baca County, New Mexico – 296, 307, 319, 373, 375, 379, 385, 422, 468, 475, 713, 744

*De Baca County News* – 319

De Baca County Sheriff's Department Case No. 03-06-136-01 (See "Billy the Kid Case" hoax)

Dedrick brothers livery – 40, 44-45, 567, 610, 628, 651

Dedrick, Dan – 40, 44, 162, 178, 566, 610-612, 619, 627, 629, 635, 643, 648, 651-652; **counterfeit money cattle deal of:** 619, 635; **fled to California:** 652

Dedrick, Mose – 610

Dedrick, Sam – 629

Deer Trail, Colorado – 616, 625, 631-632, 634-635

Deherra, Toby Jr. – 430

Delaney, John C. – 617, 644, 647 (See Dowlin & Delaney)

Denton, Cyclone – 159

Department of Electrical and Computer Engineering and the Laboratory for Vision Systems and Advanced Graphic Laboratory at the University of Texas – 252

Devours, James – 611-612, 651-652

DeZulovich, Marvis – 395

Diaz, Porfiro – 192

Dike, Jeanine – 427-428, 434, 439-440

Dillon, Matt – 288

Dills, Lucius – 592

DNA (see Billy the Kid Case hoax)

"DNA of Billy the Kid" (see Billy the Kid Case hoax)

Dobbs, Garrett H. "Kid" – 689-691

Dobe, J. Frank – 632

Dodge City, Kansas – 159, 194

Doerr, Steve – 319

Dolan, James – 26, 34, 36, 38, 42, 44, 47, 58-59, 61, 66, 68, 71-72, 86, 162, 164, 171-172, 180, 228, 230, 237-238, 240, 325, 391, 450-454, 548-549, 551, 589-590, 592-595, 602-603, 605-606, 611-612, 617, 648; **faked as a counterfeiter:** 619-620, 622-623, 644-647

Dolan man (outfit, faction) – 21, 71, 139, 162, 241, 325

Donaldson, Sam – 264

Doña Ana County, New Mexico – 41, 85-86, 181, 183, 351, 577

Donica, Riley – 317

Donnell and Lawson law firm – 228

Dowlin, M. J. – 622, 645-646

Dowlin, William "Will" – 617, 620, 645-647 (See Dowlin & Delaney)

Dowlin & Delaney – 617

Doyle, Frank W. – 614-617, 626-627, 629-630, 634, 636, 638, 644, 646; **aka "Kibby":** 614, 636-638; **aka "Duncan":** 566-567, 614, 628

Doyle, James Brace – 613-617, 620, 624-626, 630, 634-636, 646-647, 772

Doyle, William "young Doyle" – 616, 626

Drummond, Arthur L. – 611, 615, 625

Dudley, Nathan Augustus Monroe – 21-22, 38, 40, 602; **Court of Inquiry for:** 17-18, 21-22, 41-42, 57, 114, 151, 171, 174, 250, 549, 601, 606-607, 656; **past Court Martials of:** 41 (See William H. Bonney prosecution testimony)

"Duncan" (See Frank Doyle)

Ealy, Taylor – 167, 588, 605-606

*Eanthropus dawsoni* – 435 (See Piltdown Man hoax)

Earl, James H. – 342, 355

Earp, Wyatt – 288, 446

East, Jim – 25, 114, 177-178, 222, 244, 598

Easton, David – 603-604

Eichwald, George – 501

Ellis, Benjamin J. "Ben" – 588, 605
Ellis, Isaac – 86, 150, 181; **Mesilla trial subpoena for:** 150
*El Paso Herald* – 195-196
*El Paso Herald Post* – 116, 122, 360
El Paso Rotary Club – 132, 138, 171, 173, 179, 202
El Paso, Texas – 15, 70, 96-97, 105-106, 111, 117, 119, 122, 124, 128, 130, 135, 147, 191, 199-200, 280, 342, 365, 535, 566, 577, 617, 653
*El Paso Times* – 50, 282, 360, 675
embezzlement case and trial (see Alexander McSween)
Emerson, Joseph – 157
Emerson, Paul – 157-158, 585
Emil Fritz life insurance policy - (see Emil Fritz)
Enst, Clara – 430
Evans, Jessie – 33, 35-36, 40-41, 58-61, 70-72, 93, 101, 147, 160, 162, 172, 195, 222, 228, 230-231, 236, 240, 324, 362, 391, 450, 452-454, 524, 548, 567, 589, 604, 642
*Executive Record Book* – 136, 207, 210-211, 214-215
fanning a gun – 150
Farmington, New Mexico Territory – 50, 689
Feinsilber, Anne – 441-442; **"Requiem for Billy the Kid" by:** 441-442
Feliz River (Rio) – 34, 60, 69, 165, 229, 236, 449
Feliz River Ranch (See John H. Tunstall)
Ferguson, N.M. – 620, 622, 625-626, 644-647
Ferguson, Sara Elizabeth (See Henry Oliver Roberts wife)
Fidler, Larry Paul – 405
Fisher, Linda – 430
First Presbyterian Church of Santa Fe – 19

Fitzpatrick, George – 206
floorboards (See "Billy the Kid Case" hoax, Cold Case Billy the Kid megahoax, Henry Lee fake forensics on, Steve Sederwall forgery of forensic report on)
Flynn, Pat – 689
"Folliard," Tom (See Tom O'Folliard)
Forensitec – 427-428, 437, 761-763
Fortenberry, Terry – 401
Fort Grant, Arizona – 33, 160-161
Fort Sill, Texas – 272, 425
Fort Smith, Arkansas – 192, 248
Fort Stanton, New Mexico Territory – 18, 21, 23, 34, 38, 67-70, 72, 98, 151, 182-183, 222, 230, 242, 250, 275, 350, 453, 551, 587, 596, 602, 605-606, 611, 644-646, 649, 765
Fort Sumner, New Mexico Territory – 5, 7-8, 12-13, 15, 18, 25, 29, 31-32, 40, 42-46, 48-49, 56, 78-79, 95, 116, 119-121, 123-124, 127, 129, 131, 140, 143-144, 152, 155, 162, 174, 176-177, 184, 187-190, 194, 196-197, 204-206, 208-208, 212, 216-218, 221, 226, 230-231, 236, 245-247, 252, 257, 262-265, 272-274, 276-282, 286, 290-291, 293-295, 297-298, 305-306, 311-315, 319-320, 323, 326-330, 332-360, 363-368, 370-375, 377-379, 384-387, 389-390, 392, 401-404, 411-412, 414, 416, 422, 426, 433-434, 440, 442, 444-445, 447, 449, 454-455, 460, 468, 475, 485-493, 495-497, 520, 526-527, 536, 538, 550, 553, 555-556, 561, 566-568, 572-574, 576, 579, 610, 612, 620, 627-628, 634, 640, 648, 653, 662, 665-666, 670, 678-679, 681-683, 685-686, 689-690, 695, 697-698, 700-701, 708, 711-717, 725-726, 733, 739-741, 745-746, 769-770, 772

Fort Sumner State Monument – 685-686, 689
Foster, Nathan B. "Nate" – 614, 617, 625-626, 629-632, 634-636, 643-644, 646
Fountain, Albert Jennings – 47, 82, 174, 179-180, 190, 242, 258, 455, 549, 551, 556, 563, 569, 576-578, 696
Fountain, Henry – 696
Fountain, Jack – 190, 258, 556, 573
FoxNews.com – 462-463
French, Jim "Frenchie" – 36, 38, 150, 167, 194, 450, 594, 602, 612, 656
Fritz, Charles "Charlie" – 228, 598, 602, 609
Fritz, Emil – 24, 34, 164, 227-228, 237-238, 586, 590; **life insurance policy of:** 24, 34, 164, 228, 327-238, 544
Fritz heirs – 391, 586
Fulginiti, Laura – 301, 429-431, 434, 436-439, 706, 761-764; **"Hip Man" by:** 436-437, 439; **"Scapula Man" by:** 436-437, 439; **denial of John Miller buck teeth by:** 438-439, 706; **denial John Miller's scapula wound by:** 439, 706; **description William Hudspeth exhumation by:** 436, 438-439, 761-762, 764; **forensic report of:** 437, 761-764
Fulton, Maurice Garland – 18, 52, 64, 99, 105, 107-109, 114, 139-140, 145, 163-164, 175, 180, 193, 206, 216, 275, 353, 402, 404, 483, 492, 497, 599, 699, 687
Fusco, John – 265-266, 441; **"Young Guns II" by:** 265-266, 268, 285, 301, 441
Gallegos, Pantaleon – 58
Gallegos, Severo – 183, 185-187, 197-200, 245, 250, 571, 661, 676, 698; **Affidavit for**

"Brushy Bill" of: 197-199
Garcia, Alarie Ray – 462
Garland, Texas – 317
Garrett, Apolinaria (see Apolinaria Gutierrez)
Garrett, Juanita (see Juanita Gutierrez)
Garrett, Jarvis – 116, 121, 123, 125, 290, 302
Garrett, Jarvis Patrick "J.P." – 302, 445
Garrett, Oscar – 116, 121, 123, 125-126
Garrett, Patrick Floyd "Pat" – 4-8, 12-16, 18-19, 23, 25, 29-30, 32, 42-49, 55, 78-79, 82, 92, 96, 101, 114-116, 118-121, 123-129, 131-134, 136, 139, 141-143, 145-147, 149, 151-153, 156, 158-170, 172, 174-180, 182-184, 187-192, 194-196, 198, 200, 202-212, 215-223, 226-227, 230-232, 243, 245-246, 250-252, 255-268, 271-282, 286-295, 297-299, 302, 304-305, 307, 313-314, 321-338, 340-349, 351-377, 380, 382, 384-385, 388-393, 395-403, 407, 410-411, 413, 415-416, 418, 425-426, 434-436, 441-442, 445-448, 450, 454-460, 462-463, 465, 467-469, 475-476, 482, 484, 486-490, 492, 508, 514, 520, 524-529, 531-532, 534, 538, 543, 550, 552-570, 572-579, 583-585, 591-594, 598-599, 601, 608-610, 612-613, 620, 623, 626-627, 629-630, 632, 635, 639, 642, 644, 650-658, 660-666, 668-686, 689-696, 698-701, 703-704, 706-707, 709-711, 717-718, 723, 727-728, 730, 737-738, 741, 743-746, 771; *The Authentic Life of Billy the Kid* **by:** 18, 29, 114, 139-142,145, 149, 153, 158-170, 172, 174, 177, 179, 183-184, 206, 216, 255, 259, 275, 278, 325, 333, 354, 358, 369, 416, 456, 482, 489, 572, 576, 585,

593, 599, 610, 627, 629, 635, 644, 651, 656, 660, 663-664, 668, 671 679-680, 682; **working with Secret service as Deputy U.S. Marshal:** 23, 45, 203, 399, 612, 653-656; **collecting the Billy the Kid reward by:** 12, 14, 210-220, 259-260, 391, 525, 528, 559, 570, 632, 678, 694, 773; **Statute of Limitations for murder applicable to** – 16, 148, 286, 291, 294-295, 321-322, 372 (See Coroner's Jury Report for William H. Bonney, Tom O'Folliard, Charles Bowdre, Statute of Limitations on murder, William Ritch, William Breeden, "Brushy Bill" hoax, "Billy the Kid Case" hoax, Cold Case Billy the Kid megahoax)

Gates, Susan – 605

Gatling gun – 39, 170, 250, 564, 606

Gauss, Gottfried – 47-48, 52-53, 61-62, 185, 187, 198-199, 245, 325, 352, 354, 367-368, 416, 552, 570-571, 662, 667-668, 672-673, 676-677

Gay, Richard – 307

George Hervey Real Estate Company – 97

Gila Ranch – 159, 236

Gila River – 236

Gilbert, Robert M. – 588

Gilliland, Jim – 577

Gipson, Fred – 134

Gladewater, Texas – 94, 200, 533, 541

Glen, Willis Skelton – 176

Godfroy, Frederick – 20, 137, 587, 617

Goff, D.L. – 157

Gomber, Drew – 456

Gomber, Elise – 456

Gonzales, Florencio – 228, 586, 589-590

Gonzales, Ignacio – 38

Grand Saline, Texas – 191

*Grant County Herald* – 72

Grant County, New Mexico – 262, 292, 296, 379, 538, 667, 712-713

Grant County Rebellion of 1876 – 4

Grant, Joe – 44, 48, 174, 223, 230

Graves, Arthur – 96

Graves, Gary Wayne – 292, 296, 307, 314, 319, 373-375, 385, 387, 398, 422, 426, 475, 487-488, 495, 407, 571, 583, 713-714, 716, 744; **De Baca County Case No. 03-06-136-01 for exhumation of Billy the Kid by:** 314, 373, 375, 468, 744; **DeBaca County Detention Center used by:** 319; **DeBaca County Case No. CV-04-00019, In the Matter of DeBaca County Sheriff Gary Graves, Petition for Order Allowing Recall Vote:** 319; **as only recalled New Mexico Sheriff:** 319, 387, 422 (See "Billy the Kid Case" hoax, Cold Case Billy the Kid Megahoax)

Greathouse, Jim "Whiskey Jim" – 45, 78-79, 772; **Greathouse ranch of:** 152, 175, 230, 243, 543, 550, 567, 770-772

Greene, Charles W. – 133, 212, 215, 217; **affidavit about printing reward notices:** 212; **printer of *Santa Fe Daily New Mexican*:** 215; **faked as Pat Garrett's lawyer in "Brushy Bill" hoax:** 217

Green, T. – 59

Greenham, Walter B. – 613-614, 630, 636-638

Gricus, Greg – 430

Griffin, Willie E. – 312, 716

Griggs, George – 193

Grzelachowski, Alexander – 610, 627, 635

Guadalupe Mountains – 70, 161, 236
Guarino, Mark – 462
Gulliksen, Joan – 477
Gutierrez, Apolinaria – 43-44, 189, 347, 557, 565
Gutierrez, Celsa – 43, 49, 121, 178, 188-191, 231, 245-247, 258, 330, 356, 365, 526, 528, 557-558, 561, 572, 679
Gutierrez, Juanita – 43, 189, 565
Gutierrez, Saval (Sabal) – 7-8, 43, 49, 188-190, 245, 247, 337, 344, 363, 526-527, 557, 699
Haag, Mike – 502, 506, 575
Hadley, Russ – 430
Haley, A.J. – 319
Haley, J. Evetts – 331, 441, 632
Hall, Levi – 315
Hall, Wallace W. – 611, 615-616, 620, 625, 630, 632, 634-635, 641, 644, 647
Hamilton, Texas – 94, 101, 125, 130, 147, 222, 231, 291, 295, 300, 312, 361-362, 372, 378, 435, 443-444, 446, 472, 493, 495-498, 708
Hargrove's Saloon – 42-43, 174
Harnett, Kristen – 437, 761
Harris, David – 306
Harris, Randall – 471
Hart, Bob – 263
Hartley, Ted – 296, 313, 379, 386, 422
Haws, Eulaine Faye Goff – 157, 233, 235, 525, 531; **duped to fake a Roberts family genealogy:** 233, 531 (See William A. Tunstill)
Haws, Leonard – 157, 233
Haws, Roy L. – 92-93, 101, 141, 155-158, 189, 193-195, 233-235, 525, 531, 540, 585; *Brushy Bill: Proof That His Claim to Be Billy the Kid Was a Hoax* by: 92-93, 101, 141, 155-156, 158, 189, 193-195, 525, 531
Hayes, Rutherford B. – 4, 20, 37, 39, 593

Hays, John W. – 615-617, 621-622, 625-626, 629-632, 634-636, 638-639, 641, 644, 646-647; **Moundville, Missouri, farm haystack of: 616,** 625-626, 630, 632, 635, 646
headboard (See "Billy the Kid Case" hoax, Cold Case Billy the Kid megahoax, Henry Lee fake forensics on, Steve Sederwall forgery of forensic report on)
Heard, Robins, Cloud, Lubel & Greenwood LLP  - 377-378, 380, 385, 732, 743, 746-747
Heath, Cora – 158, 585
Heath, Dudley – 157, 233
Heath, Martha Vada Roberts – 57, 157-158, 233-235, 539-540
Heath, Vada Bell Roberts – 157, 233
Hendron, J.W. – 116, 125
Herrera, Fernando - 605
*Hico News Review* – 102-103, 129, 153, 157
Hico, Texas – 93-94, 96, 102-103, 130-131, 144, 153, 157, 251, 290-291, 378, 385, 707, 746
Hill, Thomas "Tom" – 59-61, 71, 342
Hindman, George – 25, 36, 40, 44, 47-48, 58-59, 60, 66, 167, 173, 176, 230, 243, 450-451, 589, 594, 597, 664
Hines, Jim – 101, 147, 524
"Hip Man"(See John Miller, Laura Fulginiti)
History Channel – 296, 299, 388-389, 393, 406, 462
Holguin, Raul – 314
Honobia, Oklahoma – 316
Hooker Ranch – 160
Hopper, Jessica – 463
Hotel de Luna – 160
Howard, George J. – 65, 530, 598
howitzer cannon – 39, 170, 250, 604, 606
Hoyt, Henry F. – 40, 54, 57, 65, 141, 274, 530, 532, 569, 597-598, 609, 639-641; **W.H.**

Bonney bill of sale to: 40, 54, 57, 65, 530, 569, 597-598; *A Frontier Doctor* by: 141, 274, 532, 639; **sighting of Jesse James by**: 639-640 (See Cold Case Billy the Kid megahoax)
Hudson, Bell – 188; *Billy the Kid* by: 188
Hudspeth, William – 271, 300-302, 314, 420, 423-425, 429-440, 466, 480, 494, 514, 536, 580, 584, 705-706, 761-762, 764; **illegal exhumation of**: 423-425, 429-440 (See "Billy the Kid Case" hoax, Laura Fulginiti)
Huff, J. Wesley – 277
Hunter and Evans – 162
Hurley, John – 60, 62, 74, 327, 567, 653, 655
Hurley, Johnnie – 198
Hutton, Paul – 292-293, 296, 299, 388-392, 402, 404-405, 407, 462, 523, 575, 711, 747; **official historian for "Billy the Kid Case" as**: 292-293, 296, 299, 388, 393 (confirmed by Robert Utley), 405, 407, 523, 747; **"Investigating History: Billy the Kid" History Channel TV by**: 299, 388-392, 462, 523, 718; **fake carpenter's bench authentication by**: 402; **backing Bill Richardson's fake "Billy the Kid" pardon by**: 462 (See "Billy the Kid Case" hoax)
Iglesias, David – 301
Ideal Toy Company – 577
Ingle, Debra L. – 317-318, 480; **Lincoln County Solid Waste Authority in**: 317; **defamed by Steve Sederwall as a "cocaine whore"**: 317, 480, 536; **Twelfth Judicial District Court Ingle vs. Sederwall (and Village of Capitan) No. D-1226-CV-200400142** – 317-318

innocent victim (See "Brushy Bill" hoax, and "Billy the Kid Case" hoax)
Jackson, Calvin – 637
Jackson, Georgie – 281
Jacobsen, Joel – 19, 456, 656; *Such Men as Billy the Kid: The Lincoln County War Revisited* by: 19, 456, 656
Jaffe Law Firm – 375, 377
James, Frank – 192, 267, 641
James, Jesse – 54, 93-94, 97, 101-103, 147, 201, 231, 236, 524, 567, 609, 621, 623, 638-642, 742, 747
Jameson, William Carl "W.C." – 6, 99-100, 135, 140, 143-144, 225-227, 231-236, 238, 240, 242, 244-255, 257-264, 266, 268, 271, 285, 287, 294-296, 298-299, 304-305, 312-313, 320, 327, 334-335, 339, 341, 344, 349, 362-363, 389-390, 394, 478, 490, 520, 523-545, 547-580, 583-586, 591-594, 599, 601-602, 608-609, 623, 647, 652-653, 656-657, 661-662, 667-670, 672, 674-678, 680-681, 693-695, 698-701, 705-710, 717-718, 723; **participating in History Channel "Investigating History: Billy the Kid**: 296, 299, 390; *The Return of the Outlaw Billy the Kid* by: 99, 140-141, 225-264, 268, 294, 363, 520, 523-524, 526-527, 530, 534-535, 537-540, 442-543, 554-555, 562, 564, 583, 585, 608, 660, 668, 707-709; *Billy the Kid: Beyond the Grave* by: 523-536, 538-540, 561, 583, 668; *Billy the Kid: The Lost Interviews* by: 537-562, 564, 573, 579, 583, 668; *Pat Garrett: The Man Behind the Badge* by: 563-580, 583, 678, 685; *Cold Case Billy the Kid: Investigating History's*

*Mysteries* **by:** 6, 268, 271, 287, 295, 304, 312-313, 318, 320, 327, 334-335, 339, 341, 344, 394, 406, 478, 490, 520, 523-524, 534, 545, 547, 560, 562, 564, 567, 570-575, 580, 583-719 (See Frederick Bean, Steve Sederwall, "Billy the Kid Case" hoax, Cold Case Billy the Kid megahoax)

Janofsky, Michael – 288, 291-292, 747

Jaramillo, Lorenzo – 7-8, 13, 337, 669

Jennings, Al – 103

J.J. Vance Microfilm Service – 96

*John S. Dye's Government Counterfeit Detector* – 615

Johnson, Jim – 274-275, 278, 425, 532; *Billy the Kid: His Real Name Was ...* **by:** 275, 278, 425, 532

Jones, Bill – 194, 201

Jones, Elis – 319

Jones, Heiskell – 161

Jones, Jim – 70, 161, 201, 236

Jones, John – 70, 74, 76, 161, 236, 547

Jones, John Paul – 742

Jones, Sam – 194, 201

Jones, Tom – 71

Kahn, A. – 638

Kansas City, Missouri – 191, 614, 622, 631-632, 634-635

Kearny Code – 203

Keleher, William – 19, 116, 127, 134, 179, 206, 261, 700; *Violence in Lincoln County 1869-1881* **by:** 19, 127, 206, 261, 700

Kennedy Han Law Firm – 308, 310, 313, 378, 386, 401, 491, 714-715

Kerry, John –377

Kibby (See Frank Doyle)

Kimbrell, George – 40, 45, 68, 454, 526, 549, 567, 653

King, Frank M. – 14, 149, 176, 181, 660; *Wranglin' the Past:*

*Reminiscences of Frank M. King*: 14, 149, 176, 181, 660

Kinney, John – 26, 38, 64, 88, 182-183, 547, 552, 602, 604, 610, 612; **gang of:** 168, 602, 604; **San Patricio massacre by:** 26, 38, 602; **Murphy-Kinney party of:** 26, 64, 598, 609; **made Deputy U.S. Marshal:** 612

Kirkland, Ray – 316

Kistler, Russ – 149

Klasner, Lilly – 678; *My Girlhood Among Outlaws* **by:** 678

Komar, Debra – 306-313, 485, 487, 490-491, 714-716, 727, 730-732; **Affidavit opposing exhumations of:** 309-310, 730-732; **Deposition opposing exhumations of:** 310-313, 715; **testimony of faked by Steve Sederwall:** 487, 490-491, 714-716 (See "Billy the Kid Case" hoax, Cold Case Billy the Kid megahoax)

Kristopherson, Cris – 301

Kurtis, Bill – 300-301, 388, 405-407, 417, 419, 423, 508, 571, 707; **funding Dr. Henry Lee by:** 406, 419; **Bill Kurtis Productions of:** 299, 388, 406, 408, 410, 415, 417, 419, 423, 429-430, 499, 501-502, 504, 506, 747-748

Kyle, Thomas G. – 253-254, 535

Lacey, Marc – 464

Lake of Ozarks, Missouri – 317

Lalire, Greg – 318

LaRue, Lash – 92; **"Son of Billy the Kid" movie in:** 92

Las Cruces, New Mexico – 12, 70, 86, 123, 137, 252, 347, 394, 517, 578, 650, 694, 747

*Las Cruces Sun* – 315

*Las Vegas Daily Gazette* – 14, 46, 83, 204, 208, 533, 623, 649-650, 694

Billy's return. The Olinger killing and Billy's use of a pickax to break the leg chains is given. (Page 25) Billy's destination of Fort Sumner has town owner, Peter Maxwell, betraying him to Garrett because of "the outlaw's affections for his servant girls!" (Pages 25-26) **[This is made-up.]**

For a July 14, 1881, Maxwell bedroom shooting of Billy, (Page 26), Billy starts in Celsa Gutierrez's house; though she is called one of Maxwell's "servant girls." Billy goes to the side of beef on the porch where deputies Thomas McKinney and John Poe, are "**lurking in the dark.**" Then he enters the bedroom.

REVEALING ERRORS: This is not "accepted" history. It is "Brushy's" parroting of Sonnichsen's fake construct that the side of beef was beside Maxwell's door; which Sonnichsen then wrongly placed at the "back porch." That is why "Brushy" made-up that Billy Barlow was shot on the back porch. (See pages 189-190 above)

Noteworthy too is "Brushy's" error about "the dark." Here, Jameson's and Bean's ignorance will be a boon for hoaxbusting: they are unaware of the bright moonlight! So when it comes to "Brushy's" own quotes, they will not do fix-ups if he sticks to "the dark!!!"

## INTRODUCING THEIR MAN "BRUSHY"

Jameson and Bean rely on the original "Brushy" hoax, calling him William Henry Roberts (the name he made up). They state that others had claimed to survive Garrett's shooting, but only he had "intimate and confounding Lincoln County War connections" (Page 27); and he had other old-timers who believed he was Billy the Kid. (Page 28)

Morrison enters as a probate attorney; a Missouri Historical Society member; a descendant of Ferdinand Maxwell (brother of Lucien Maxwell, and uncle of Peter Maxwell); and expert on Billy the Kid history. He meets a Joe Hines, who was Jessie Evans, who tells him Billy the Kid was living in Texas. He meets another unnamed old-timer in Missouri (his being J. Frank Dalton as Jesse James from the original hoax is omitted, likely because real Jesse was proved to be in his Kearney, Missouri, grave by DNA testing in 1995, ending Dalton's imposter scam). This Missourian knew Billy the Kid was O.L. Roberts of Hamilton, Texas. So in June of 1949, Morrison went there to meet him. (Pages 28-29)

Lincoln County courthouse-jail – 29, 47, 52, 114, 116-117, 120, 125, 135, 146, 182-184, 194, 198-199, 215, 230, 249-250, 263, 278, 289, 293, 298, 351, 366, 392, 394, 417-418, 446, 450, 455, 460, 470, 477, 499, 505, 509, 526, 528, 551, 556, 569, 571, 667-638, 646, 669-670, 672; **outhouse (privy, latrine) of**: 47, 184, 207, 230, 276, 290, 354-355, 366-368, 392, 454, 570-572, 668, 673-674, 676-677; **armory of:** 184, 187, 198, 250, 254, 366, 528-259, 570, 668, 671, 674

Lincoln County Grand Jury – **of 1878**: 24, 35-37, 60, 168, 228-229, 238-239, 450, 595-595, 603, 766; **of 1879**: 21, 41, 72, 173-174, 197, 242, 326, 391, 451-452, 454, 549, 551

Lincoln County Heritage Trust – 194, 253, 263, 535, 539

Lincoln County Justice of the Peace (see John "Squire" Wilson)

*Lincoln County Leader* – 53

Lincoln County, New Mexico – 14, 20, 22-23, 26, 37, 39-45, 47, 55, 58-60, 67, 83, 86, 114, 123, 127, 138, 146, 161, 170, 183, 186, 197, 200, 204-205, 208, 212, 214, 218-219, 227, 236, 264, 274-275, 279-281, 288-289, 294, 299, 307, 314-318, 320, 323, 349-351, 362-363, 370, 372, 375, 387, 397-398, 408, 417, 421, 423-424, 427, 440, 444, 447, 449, 451, 455, 506, 508, 525, 566, 588, 603, 609, 618, 623-624, 639, 642-643, 653-654, 664, 677, 679, 714, 744, 765, 771, 773

Lincoln County Sheriff (see Pat Garrett, William Brady, Tom Sullivan, Rick Virden)

Lincoln County Sheriff's Department Case No. 2003-274 (see "Billy the Kid Case" hoax)

Lincoln County Sheriff's Department Supplemental Report for Case No. 2003-274 (See John Miller)

Lincoln County War – 5, 22, 24-25, 30-32, 34, 36, 38, 41, 43, 45-48, 50-52, 60, 64-66, 68, 71, 93, 99, 101, 103, 116-117, 120, 123-126, 128, 133, 137-139, 142-143, 147-148, 152, 160, 163, 166, 172, 176, 181, 185, 198, 223, 229, 231, 236, 264, 267, 275, 279, 282, 287, 289, 297, 324, 326, 351, 360, 362, 392, 396-399, 445-446, 450-451, 457, 459-461, 525, 538, 545, 553, 564, 586, 593-594, 611-612, 621, 623-624, 626, 633, 640, 741, 745; **Battle in:** 3-4, 18, 21, 26, 38, 40, 47, 51-52, 54, 64, 72, 99, 141, 151, 168-171, 196, 240, 250, 252, 275, 391, 526, 598, 601-609, 612, 662-664, 677, 689; **white possemen on south hills:** 151; **white soldiers firing a volley in (reported by Billy Bonney):** 22, 39, 42, 72, 76-77, 170-171, 250, 608

Lincoln jail (See Lincoln pit jail; Lincoln County courthouse-jail)

Lincoln Museum – 18, 105, 107-108, 145, 151-152, 206-207, 263

Lincoln, New Mexico – 18, 21, 24, 29, 32, 34-36, 38-41, 44, 47-48, 51-53, 58-63, 66, 68, 72-73, 78-79, 82, 85-88, 91, 105-108, 114, 116, 120, 123, 135, 138-139, 144, 149-150, 163-166, 168-174, 181, 183-186, 194, 196-198, 200, 203-204, 214, 228-229, 237-240, 242, 245, 249, 253, 262, 265, 279, 281, 288-290, 293, 298, 306, 321, 323, 325-327, 345, 350-352, 355-356, 360, 366-368, 371-372, 391,

394, 399-400, 407, 417, 450, 452, 454-455, 460-461, 256, 530, 545, 548, 551-553, 570, 586, 588, 595-596, 599, 601, 603-606, 612, 624-625, 627, 633, 642, 646, 649, 655, 662, 664-665, 671, 676, 679, 695, 717, 725, 747, 773
Lincoln pit jail – 36, 59, 197
Lincoln State Monument – 747
Lippman, Lionel Whitby "Lonnie" – 320, 430, 583, 706
"Little Casino" – 42
Lobato, Frank – 528, 561
Long, Jack – 74, 603-604
Longino, Andrew H. – 577
"Long Rail Brand" – 696
"Long S Brand" – 696
Longview, Texas – 200
Lopez, Raymond – 315, 401, 487-488, 492, 495, 497, 711-712, 714
Los Alamos Laboratory – 253, 293
*Los Angeles Times* – 463
"L'Ouest American" – 442
Lovorn, Lynita – 319
Lucca, Jonnell – 439-440, 480
Lucero, Pedro Antonio – 7-8, 13, 337, 699
Luminol – 408, 417, 502
Luna, Miguel – 186
Mabry, Thomas Jewett – 105, 115-129, 131-132, 147-148, 184, 189, 192, 196, 199, 205, 220, 222, 226, 245, 248, 263, 285, 302, 378, 445, 524, 529, 531-532, 535, 538-539, 578, 583, 709, 723, 737, 745; **biography of: 115; pardon rejection of "Brushy Bill" by:** 116-128, 524, 529, 723
Mackie, John – 33, 160-161
MacNab, Frank – 36, 38, 48, 161, 450, 592, 602, 613
mail contractor – 83, 622, 647, 650
mail deliverer – 650
Markland, Absalom – 26
Maricopa County District Attorney's Office – 301-302, 426
Martin, Billie – 430

Martinez, Atanacio – 36, 59, 239, 545
Martinez, Edecio – 462
Martinez, Leo – 315-316, 387, 421-422, 492-493, 714
Martz, Martin "Dutch" – 53, 61-62
Mason, Barney – 43, 177, 187-188, 245, 566-568, 612, 617, 619, 627-629, 635, 637-638, 651-652, 654, 660; **as Secret Service spy:** 43, 48, 566, 612, 617, 654; **as exposing Dedrick counterfeiting-cattle deal:** 566-567, 612, 619, 627-629, 635, 637-638, 651-652
Massey, Barry – 448, 458-459, 461
Master Bank of Kansas City – 634-635
Masterson, Bat – 288
Mastin Bank of Kansas City – 631-632, 634-635
Matthews, Jacob Basil "Billy" – 37, 42, 59-62, 86, 149, 165, 167-168, 182, 239, 245, 274, 450, 454, 552, 594, 603, 679
Maxwell bedroom (Peter Maxwell) (See Maxwell house)
Maxwell cemetery – 43, 115, 262, 306, 312, 332, 342, 345, 492, 576, 708, 714-717, 725-726, 740, 745
Maxwell, Deluvina – 31, 256-257, 262-263, 331, 341-343, 403, 411, 528, 532, 558, 561, 695
Maxwell family – 18, 31-32, 298-299, 340, 403-404, 610
Maxwell, Ferdinand (See William V. Morrison)
Maxwell house (mansion) – 116, 120-121, 123, 126, 177-178, 189, 244, 246, 251, 256, 258, 280, 299, 339, 341, 359, 364, 373, 390, 410, 416, 455, 527, 553-556, 573-574, 679-680, 686-697, 699, 701; **floor plan of:** 687-688; **hoaxers' faked floor plan of:** 685-686, 689-691; **Peter Maxwell's bedroom in:**

31, 49, 189-190, 226, 231, 247, 255-256, 258-259, 272, 299, 340-343, 369, 396, 402, 415, 476, 524, 526-527, 532-533, 539, 553, 556-557, 573-578, 589, 682-683, 685-694, 704, 710 (hoaxers faking no outside door of : 534, 573-574, 685-691) (hoaxers faking location of as back porch: 189-190, 231, 247, 256, 258, 364, 527, 553, 555-556, 681) (alleged furniture from: See "Billy the Kid Case" hoax, Stella Abreu Museum); **sale of:** 298, 340, 402, 701 (See "Brushy Bill" hoax, "Billy the Kid Case" hoax, Cold Case Billy the Kid megahoax)

Maxwell Land Grant – 25, 32, 43, 95, 524, 593, 697

Maxwell, Lucien Bonaparte – 25, 31-32, 43, 95, 101, 147, 162, 231, 236, 257, 341, 361, 402-403, 411, 524, 573, 686, 690-691, 697, 717

Maxwell, Luz Trotier de Beaubien – 8, 43, 244, 257, 337, 339, 341, 402, 691, 697, 699

Maxwell, Paulita – 25, 31-32, 43, 48, 127, 178, 187-188, 223, 244, 287, 349, 355-356, 372, 593, 610, 640, 665, 679, 691-692; **hoaxers' Paulita as Peter Maxwell's sister error:** 355-356, 679

Maxwell, Peter "Pete" – 8, 31, 43, 49, 127, 189, 191, 204, 231, 236, 246-247, 256-257, 262, 273, 282, 290, 299, 321, 330-331, 336-337, 341, 345, 349, 356-357, 360-361, 365, 370-371, 390-391, 400, 402-403, 413, 415-416, 532, 534, 554, 557, 566, 573-575, 679, 683, 686-691, 693, 695-698, 700, 702, 710, 717, 769; **as witness to William Bonney's killing:** 8, 337, 415-416, 693; **as hoaxed**

**pseudo-Pete Maxwell:** 695-698, 702 (See "Brushy Bill" hoax, "Billy the Kid Case" hoax, Cold Case Billy the Kid megahoax)

McCarthy, Todd – 442

McCarty, Catherine (see Catherine Antrim)

McCarty, John L. – 689

McCarty, Joseph "Josie" – 19, 32

McCarty, Michael – 234

McCarty, William Henry (see William H. Bonney)

McCloskey, William – 592

McCoy, Dave – 442

McDaniels, Jim – 70, 160-162

McFarland, David F. "Ledger: Session Records 1867-1874. Marriages in Santa Fe New Mexico. Mr. William H. Antrim and Mrs. Catherine McCarty" – 19

McGinn, Carpenter, Montoya & Love P.A. – 448-449

McGinn, Randi – 303, 448-458, 462-463, 467; **Pardon Petition by:** 449-456 (See Charles Daniels)

McIntosh, Jim – 689

McKinney, Collin – 660

McKinney, Cliff – 116, 121, 123

McKinney, Elizabeth Francis – 660

McKinney, Thomas Christopher "Kip" – 116, 123, 127, 176, 244, 335, 550, 657, 660

McKnight, Cotton – 424

McKnight, Judy – 424

McMasters, James E. – 65, 530, 598

McNatt, C.C. – 196-197

McReynolds, A.B. – 316-317

McSween, Alexander – 22, 24-26, 34-41, 48, 61, 65, 69, 71-72, 74-77, 98, 139, 149, 151, 163-164, 166, 168, 170-171, 204, 228-230, 237-240, 275, 350, 391, 544-545, 547-548, 564, 586-588, 593-596, 601-611, 613, 633,

662, 677; **malicious prosecution embezzlement case of**: 24, 34-36, 165, 168, 237-238, 391, 595-596, 611; **arson burning of house of**: 21-22, 40, 69, 72, 77, 170-171, 240, 250, 275, 564, 601, 607-608, 624, 772-773; **murder of**: 21, 39-40, 596, 611, 613, 677

McSweens (followers) – 38-39, 77, 151, 391, 564, 605

McSween, Susan – 21-22, 40, 42, 170-171, 230, 240, 281, 451-452, 548, 564-565, 606-607, 656

Meadows, John – 48, 55, 175, 665

Meinig, D.W. – 27

Memory Lane Cemetery – 307, 309-310, 727-728, 730-731

Mescalero Indian Reservation – 34, 37, 68, 137, 179, 203, 237, 587, 599

Mesilla, New Mexico Territory – 21, 25, 35, 38, 42, 46-47, 51, 72, 79, 81, 83, 86-87, 160, 174, 178-179, 182-183, 198, 203, 222, 230, 237, 242, 244, 249, 276, 293, 351, 367, 397, 401, 464, 544, 549, 551-552, 569, 596, 604 667

*Mesilla News* – 86, 367, 464

Metz, Leon – 19, 96-97, 262, 299, 564, 639, 654; *Pat Garrett: The Story of a Western Lawman* by: 19, 262, 639, 654

Michtom, Morris –577

Michtom, Rose –577

Middleton, John – 36-37, 46, 52, 58, 61-63, 168, 450, 599-600, 766-768

Miller, Isadora – 273-274, 281, 356, 426

Miller, James – 577

Miller, Jay – 316, 393-396, 404, 418, 421-422, 424, 446, 465-467, 472-473, 475, 479-485, 484-495, 498, 506

Miller, John – 5-6, 29, 253, 271-282, 287-288, 291, 296, 300-301, 313-314, 320, 349, 356, 359-360, 382-383, 386-387, 401, 420, 423-441, 447, 466-467, 472, 477, 480, 483, 514, 536, 580, 584, 705-707, 712-716, 723, 746, 761-764; **birthdate of**: 272, 425, 723; **Comanche mother of**: 272; **Indian friend victim for**: 279; **faking Billy the Kid physical resemblance for**: 274; **Lincoln County Sheriff's Department Supplemental Report for exhumation of**: 429-430; **illegal exhumation of**: 423-440, 472, 705-707, 761-764; **exhumation of filmed by Bill Kurtis Productions**: 432; **Piltdown Man-style hoax with**: 301, 435-437 (See Helen Airy, "Billy the Kid Case" hoax, Laura Fulginiti, Cold Case Billy the Kid megahoax)

Miller, Kenneth "Kenny" – 403, 414, 702

Miller, Manuel "Mannie" – 341, 343, 402-404, 502, 702

Miller, Max – 272, 279

Miller, Stella Abreu (See Stella Abreu)

Mills, A.H. – 58-59

miner's pick – 48, 185, 668

Monclova, Coahuila, Mexico – 657

Montaño, José – 68, 453, 453, 597, 606, 617

moon (dark night) error (See Oliver Pleasant "Brushy Bill" Roberts)

Moore, John (Nick) – 316

Moore Scott – 82, 180

Moore's Hotsprings Hotel – 639-640

Moore, Tex – 195

Morel, Alan –296, 301, 318, 320, 421-422, 466, 468-471, 475, 479-482, 484-485, 494 (See "Billy the Kid Case" hoax)

Morgan, Art – 120

Morrison, William Vincent "Bill" – 5, 91-93, 95-227, 231-232, 235-236, 238, 240-241, 244-246, 248-250, 254, 258, 261, 265-267, 285-286, 296, 299, 304, 320-321, 347, 349, 361-363, 369-370, 523-524, 527-528, 530-532, 534-544, 551, 553-556, 559, 562, 564, 571, 573, 578, 580, 583, 585, 591-592, 598-599, 601, 674, 707, 709, 718; **background of:** 95-97; **impersonating a lawyer by:** 5, 96-98, 117, 119, 122, 147, 199, 226-227, 266, 321, 361, 534-535, 538; **impersonating Ferdinand Maxwell by:** 95, 147, 231, 361-362, 369-370, 524; **promotion of J. Frank Dalton as Jesse James by:** 101-103; **research and touring for "Brushy Bill" hoax by:** 104-114, 135, 143-144, 166, 183-184, 200, 223, 238, 249-250, 674; **rehearsal tapes for "Brushy" by:** 97, 135-136, 143-144, 225-226, 232, 235-236, 241, 523, 528, 537, 539-542, 554, 579; **seeking pardon for "Brushy" as Billy the Kid:** 115-128; *Alias Billy the Kid* **by:** 128-224; **letter from Harry S, Truman to:** 224 (See Oliver Pleasant Roberts, C.L. Sonnichsen, T.J. Mabry, W.C. Jameson, Frederick Bean)

Morton, William "Buck" – 36, 44, 48, 58-59, 160, 162, 165-166, 238, 324, 589, 591-592, 595

"MSN Movies" – 442

Moundville, Missouri – 616, 625-626, 641

Mule Shoe, Texas – 134

Mullin, Robert N. – 18, 99, 114, 140, 144, 203, 402, 492, 497, 657, 686-688, 697, 702

Murphy-Dolan House (see "The House")

Murphy-Dolan(s) – 38, 138, 230, 237

Murphy-Kinney party – 26, 64, 598, 609

Murphy, Lawrence G. – 26, 34, 138-139, 163-165, 227-228, 237, 350-351, 544-545, 564, 586-587, 593, 603, 607; **L.G. Murphy & Co. of:** 350, 590, 646

Murphy, Mary Alice – 315

Napolitano, Janet – 296, 300, 302, 427-428, 432, 434, 439

Narvaez, Henry – 470

Narvaez Law Firm – 478, 500-501, 504

National Cemetery of Santa Fe – 312, 708, 716

National Frontiersmen's Association – 195

Nation, Arleigh – 360

Nevada, Missouri – 616, 631, 641, 644

Newcomb, John – 586, 588

Newman, Simon – 203

*Newman's Semi-Weekly* – 87, 182

*New Mexico Magazine* – 196, 203, 206, 544

New York Children's Aid Society – 277

*New York Sun* – 44, 204, 276, 370, 622-623, 648, 769

*New York Times* – 288, 303, 369, 377, 441, 444, 458-460, 464, 486, 625, 718, 747

*New York World Magazine* – 149, 172, 177, 276, 452, 642

Nicholi, Bill – 345

Nolan, Frederick – 19-20, 26, 165, 193-194, 354, 378, 387, 389, 456, 461, 476, 480, 482, 489-490, 493, 537, 589, 658, 660, 692, 709, 711, 714; *The Life and Death of John Henry Tunstall* **by:** 19, 26; *The Lincoln County War: A Documentary History* **by:** 19, 537, 692; *The West of Billy the Kid* **by:** 19, 193-194, 456

Oakley, Kenneth – 436

Office of the Medical Investigator (OMI), Albuquerque, New Mexico – 295, 297, 305-313, 378, 386-387, 392, 407, 475, 485, 487-488, 490-491, 497, 710, 714-716, 726-732; **exhumation permits refused by:** 306-313; **response by:** 726-727 (See Ross Zumwalt, Debra Komar)

O'Folliard, Tom – 32, 38, 40-41, 43-46, 54, 78, 176-177, 230, 243-244, 265, 310, 312, 327, 547, 550, 568, 610, 612-613, 622, 627, 648, 657-660, 663, 689, 716-717; **killed by Pat Garrett:** 46, 78, 176-177, 230, 243, 265, 327, 550, 568, 613; **hoaxed name of "Folliard" for:** 547, 657-660; **hoaxed as "Kip" McKinney's cousin:** 176-177, 243-244, 622; **hoaxed as Jim (Lane) Cook's cousin:** 622, 631, 633; **hoaxed as doing counterfeiting:** 631, 633

O'Keffe, Tom – 160-161

Oklahoma Indian Territory – 141, 159

Olinger, Robert "Bob" – 32, 47-48, 53-54, 71, 88, 124-125, 182-186, 198, 231, 276, 291, 293, 323, 325, 328, 352-355, 366, 368, 372, 398-400, 424, 450, 455, 468-469, 472, 474, 478, 485, 493, 497, 514, 570-572, 656, 664, 668, 671, 673-674, 678; **Whitney double barrel shotgun of:** 48, 198, 355, 572, 678

Olsen, Gary – 428

Orchid Cellmark Laboratory – 302, 409-410, 418-419, 423, 428-429, 430-432, 456-437, 444, 466-467, 469, 471, 473-474, 476-478, 494, 503, 513-519, 672, 702, 708, 747; **DNA faking scandal of:** 410

Ostler, Calvin – 407-408, 411, 413, 415, 417, 469-470, 474, 477, 499, 501-503, 505-506, 513, 515-516, 519, 571, 575

Ostler, Kim – 415, 506

Otero, Miguel – 127, 167, 245, 552, 640-641, 695; *The Real Billy the Kid* **by:** 167, 245, 695

Ortho-tolidine (O-tolidine) – 417, 499, 502, 671, 702

Overton, Homer D. aka Homer D. Kinsworthy – 347-348, 698; **Affidavit by:** 347-348, 698 (See "Billy the Kid Case" hoax)

Owens, Jasper – 625

*Pakistan Daily Express* – 445

parade ground (see Fort Sumner)

Parker, Isaac C. "hanging judge" – 192, 248

Parker, Joe – 319

Patrón, Juan – 34, 41, 68, 173, 181, 242, 452, 454, 530, 565, 627

Paul, Jay – 319

"Pawnee Bill" (See Gorden W. Lillie)

Pawnee Bill's Wild West Show (See Gorden W. Lillie)

Peckinpah, Sam – 441-442

Pecos River – 34, 42, 161, 229, 294, 650, 708, 771

Peñasco River – 33, 42, 60, 165, 223, 229, 240

Peñasco River Ranch (See William H. Bonney)

Pennington, William – 639, 641

Peppin, George – 26, 38-40, 69, 71-73, 75, 151, 168-171, 186, 229, 230, 275, 546, 552, 564, 601-605, 607, 612, 656, 662, 675 (See San Patricio massacre, Lincoln County War Battle)

Phenophthlien – 502

Picacho, New Mexico – 30, 38, 602

Pickett, Tom – 45-46, 83, 163, 195, 610, 617, 620, 643, 651, 663, 666

Piltdown Man hoax – 435-437, 536, 706

pit jail (see Lincoln pit jail)
Pittmon, Geneva Roberts – 94-95, 155, 157-158, 233, 235, 525, 537, 585
Poe, Frank – 689
Poe, John William – 12, 42, 49, 86, 127, 136, 191, 209, 221-222, 226, 231, 255-257, 260, 262, 273, 276, 329-342, 345-346, 356, 358, 369, 390-391, 400, 410, 413, 415, 527-528, 531-532, 534, 557, 561, 565, 572-574, 585, 673, 679-684, 686, 689, 691-694, 696, 698, 703-704; *The Death of Billy the Kid* by: 136, 191, 221, 255, 273, 329, 331-332, 336, 410, 527, 557, 572, 585, 682
Poe, Sophie – 571, 672-673 *Buckboard Days* by: 672
Poling, Mike – 430, 439, 762, 764
Pope, Rex – 319
Posse Comitatus Act – 38-39, 42, 72, 171, 604, 606
Powers, Tom – 577
Prescott, Arizona – 272, 277, 282, 291, 296, 359-360, 423, 429, 433, 437, 481, 484, 705-706, 761
Prescott, Arizona Pioneers' Home Cemetery (see Arizona Pioneers' Home Cemetery)
*Prescott Courier* – 275
Prescott Police Department – 426-427, 429, 434, 437
*Press Trust of India Hindustan Times* – 445
"Prime Time Live" – 264
Prince, L. Bradford – 16
Purcell, Ricky D. – 379; **Notice of Excusal of. March 4, 2004:** 379
Purington, George – 605
Quantrill, William – 154, 638-639, 641
Quintero, Henry – 296, 307, 313, 378-379, 384, 386-387, 422, 440, 444, 491, 712-713, 733, 736, 744

Raffe, Jerry – 348
Ralston, William – 641
Ramath, Arizona – 277-278
Ramsey, JonBenet – 405
Ramsey, Burke – 405
Rasch, Philip J. – 19, 99, 131-133, 148, 329, 331, 658, 666; *Trailing Billy the Kid by*: 19, 332, 658, 666
Regulators – 22, 24-25, 36-41, 47-48, 50, 54, 60, 65, 82, 149, 166-169, 197, 204, 223, 226, 228-230, 237-240, 244, 250, 264, 266, 274-275, 391, 450, 545, 564-565, 591-596, 599-603, 610-612, 614, 621, 643, 648, 677, 766
replevin case – 47, 82, 180 (See William H. Bonney, Edgar Caypless, Frank Stewart)
reward for capture of Billy the Kid (see William H. Bonney; Patrick F. Garrett)
Richardson, William Blaine III "Bill" – 6, 115, 263, 285-289, 291-292, 294-297, 299, 301-303, 306-308, 313-315, 377-382, 384, 386, 388-390, 392-393, 407, 423, 427-428, 434, 439-441, 443-448, 456-464, 467-468, 485-486, 488, 494, 497, 520, 583, 711-712, 714-715, 717-718, 723; **press release for "Billy the Kid Case" hoax by:** 292; **press release for hoax pardon by:** 456-457; **pay-to-play for "Billy the Kid Case"** by: 285, 314, 378, 392, 488 (See "Billy the Kid Case" hoax)
RICO – 301
Riley, John – 34, 68, 71, 593, 606
*Rio Grande Republican* – 7, 12, 208, 694
Ritch, William – 7, 12-14, 207, 210-217, 219, 259, 483, 694, 700
Rivers, Frank – 450
Roberts, Andrew "Buckshot" – 21, 25, 37, 44, 46-48, 59, 66, 137, 168, 179, 203, 229, 230, 239,

244, 276, 451, 551, 569, 599-601, 612; **Blazer's Mill killing of:** 37, 47, 137, 145, 168, 229, 569, 599-600, 603, 656, 664; **hoaxing grave of:** 600-601 (See T.B. Catron's federal indictment for killing)
Roberts, Caroline Dunn (See wife of Henry Oliver Roberts)
Roberts, Cordelia – 156
Roberts, Dan W. – 154;*Rangers and Sovereignty* by: 154
Roberts, Henry Oliver "H.O." – 155-157, 233-234, 239; **children of marriage to Caroline Dunn:** Samantha Belle Roberts, 157; Martha Vada Roberts, 157; **children of marriage to Sara Elizabeth Ferguson:** Andrew Berry Roberts, 157; Mary C. Roberts, 157; Oliver Pleasant "Brushy Bill" Roberts, 157; John W. Roberts, 157; Lonnie V. Roberts, 157; Thomas Ulce Roberts (father Geneva Pittmon), 157; Nora Roberts, 157, Joseph Irvin Roberts, 157
Roberts, Joseph – 156
Roberts, Mary June – 156
Roberts, Oliver L. "Ollie" " Brushy Bill" (see Oliver Pleasant Roberts)
Martha Vada Roberts (See Martha Vada Roberts Heath)
Roberts, Oliver Pleasant "Brushy Bill" – 5-6, 15, 22, 29, 91-268, 441-463, 523-566, 568-574, 576, 578-580, 583-585, 589, 591-595, 597-599, 601-602, 606-609, 647, 652-653, 656, 660-661, 665-670, 674-679, 681, 683, 693, 695, 698, 700-701, 703-705, 707-709, 712-713, 716-717, 723, 729, 732, 737-738, 742, 745-747; **background of:** 92-95; **birthday of:** 152, 156, 233, 267 530, 723; **age faking by:** 91-92, 95, 140, 148, 153-154, 157, 531, 585; **Social Security benefits fraud as "Oliver L. Roberts" by:** 92, 153-154, 157, 267 (name changed to Oliver L. for: 92); **other aliases by:** "William Henry" Roberts: 100, 118, 153-154, 156, 225, 231, 234, 246, 252, 258, 361, 525-526, 531, 543, 563-564, 567-568, 571, 573, 668, 712; "Kid Roberts": 93, 154; "Texas Kid": 93, 151, 159, 191-192, 236; "Rattlesnake Bill": 93, 151; "Hugo Kid": 93, 151, 192; **FAKED GENEALOGY BY AND FOR:** Ben Roberts as grandfather: 153; James Henry "J.H. "Wild Bill" "Two Gun" Roberts as father:154, 234; Mary Adeline Dunn as mother: 154, 156, 194, 234, 540; Elizabeth Ferguson as stepmother (real mother's name): 154; Aunt Katherine Ann Bonney (as half-sister of Mary Adeline Dunn): 154, 193, 540 (Jameson-Bean fix-up as Catherine: 234); cousin Ollie Roberts (actually himself): 154; 157, 195; William Dunn (Mary Adeline Dunn's father): 234; Martha Vada Roberts Heath (Jameson-Bean fix-up addition; actually daughter of H.O. Robert's first wife, Caroline Dunn): 234-235 (See Martha Vada Roberts Heath); **fake Roberts family Bible for:** 233-235, 525, 530-531, 539-541 (See William A. Tunstill); **DEBUNKING BY ROBERTS FAMILY OF:** real genealogy of: 93-95, 155-157, 194, 233-234; Geneva Roberts Pittmon: 93-95, 155, 157-158, 233, 525, 530, 537, 585; Roy L. Haws: 92-93, 101, 141, 155-158, 189, 193-

195, 233-235, 525, 531, 540, 585; Paul Emerson: 158, 585; Cora Heath: 158, 585; **Roberts family Bible for:** 155, 235, 525, 537; **wives of:** Anna Lee Roberts, 158; Mollie Brown Roberts, 158; Luticia Ballard Roberts, 158; Malinda F. Allison Roberts, 158; **earlier faking being Frank James by:** 267; 891; **fake illiterate claim for:** 18, 91, 98, 104, 107, 136, 140-141, 145, 151, 153, 191, 195, 222, 227, 232, 241, 267, 299, 530, 538, 569, 579; **fake semi-literate claim:** 232; **not-reading-things-printed trick for:** 91, 136, 249: **non-Spanish-speaking of:** 96, 141, 199, 223, 232, 525, 532; **things-not-printed trick for:** 91, 104, 136, 142-143, 147-150, 225, 251, 266, 525, 538, 542, 562, 579, 591, 707; **FAKING PHYSICAL RESEMBLANCE TO BILLY THE KID FOR:** 117, 119, 148-150, 232, 248-249, 525, (fake Acton photo-comparison for: 252-254, 274, 299, 525, 539, 707; no match in Lincoln County Heritage Trust tintype photo-comparison: 253-254, 263, 535), abnormal eye-teeth (canines) of: 200-201, 249, 533, 541; **PARDON ATTEMPTS FOR:** Governor Mabry pardon failure for: 5, 15, 18, 115-128; Governor Richardson fake pardon attempt for: 285, 287-290, 292-293, 295, 302-303, 321, 361, 378-383, 386, 388-390, 392, 423, 444-464; **KEY HOAXBUSTING ERRORS BY:** shooting "nigger" soldiers by: 98, 148, 151, 170-171, 226, 240, 250, 264, 525-526, 545-547, 608, (dishonest Sonnichsen racism fix-up of: 98, 148, 151; dishonest Jameson racism fix-up of: 525-526, 545-547); Celsa-Saval Gutierrez as siblings error by: 126, 188-189, 245, 247, 557, 679 (Jameson's fake fix-up of: 526); moon (dark night) error for July 14, 1881: 189, 191, 231, 246, 255, 264, 349, 363, 379, 386, 390, 526-528, 553-555, 558, 562, 723, 745 (fake fix-up by Morrison/Sonnichsen of: 189, 191, 349, 562; fake fix-up by Jameson of: 526-528, 553-555, 564); **faking no William Bonney Coroner's Jury Report to claim survival:** 131, 133, 202, 205-207, 210-216, 220, 259, 261, 273, 344, 388-390, 525, 561, 570, 575, 632, 700; **FILMS FOR:** "Investigating History: Billy the Kid" History Channel TV: 299, 388-392, 406, 462, 501, 506, 520, 523, 718; "Young Guns III about: 265-266, 268, 285, 301, 441; "Requiem for Billy the Kid" about: 441-442, 520; **attempted exhumation of:** 443-444; **FAKE FIX-UPS OF "BRUSHY" FOR:** from original Pardon "Brushy": 22, 115-129, 143-144, 189, 226, 264, 520; for *Alias Billy the Kid* "Brushy": 129-224; for *The Return of the Outlaw* "Brushy": 225-264; for *Beyond the Grave* "Brushy": 523-536; for *Lost Interviews* "Brushy": 537-562 (as transcript forgeries for: 541, 553, 555, 562) (as planted evidence for: 541); for *Cold Case* "Brushy": 583, 585-586, 591, 594, 601, 606, 667-668, 679, 707 (See William V. Morrison, C.L. Sonnichsen, W.C. Jameson, Frederick Bean, "Billy the Kid Case" hoax)

Roberts, Vada Bell (See Vada Bell Roberts Heath)
Roberts, William Henry (see Oliver Pleasant Roberts)
Robins, Bill III – 286, 288, 295-296, 299, 306, 310-314, 319, 322, 349, 362, 377-387, 389-390, 392, 444, 448, 463, 485, 490-493, 497, 711-713, 715, 732-746 (see "Billy the Kid Case" hoax)
Robinson, Berry – 39, 603, 605
Robinson, Deborah – 274
Robinson, Will – 116, 123, 126
Rodarte, Anthony – 430
Rodarte, Misty – 428-430
Rojas, Rick – 463
Romero, Vincente – 38-39, 41, 72-73, 608, 613
Romney, Pearl Tenney – 430
Romo, Rene – 406-407, 411, 413, 417, 434-435, 446, 475, 706-707
Roosevelt, Theodore – 577; **Rough Riders of:** 93, 192-193, 532; **Teddy Bear for:** 576-577
R.R. Roberts Accounting and Law Firm – 127
Rose, Noah H. – 103, 193
*Roswell Daily Record* – 55, 444
Roswell, New Mexico Territory – 44, 55, 70, 127, 155, 161-162, 204, 638-639, 650, 696, 698
Roybal, Tommy – 373
Rudabaugh, Dave "Dirty Dave" – 44-46, 83, 163, 177, 236, 244, 643, 663, 679, 771, 774
Rudulph, Charles "Charlie" – 247, 573; *Los Billitos: The Story of Billy the Kid and His Gang* **by:** 257, 573
Rudulph, Milnor – 7-8, 49, 257, 260, 329, 333, 337, 561, 699 (see Legislature Revolt, Coroner's Jury Report for William H. Bonney)
Ruidoso, New Mexico – 119, 197-198, 228-229, 394, 446
*Ruidoso News* – 186, 197, 199, 315, 421-422, 435, 440, 490, 618

RuidosoNews.com – 320, 404, 430, 476, 709
Ruidoso River – 51, 63, 236, 646
Rumsey, Roy – 443-444, 472
Rynerson, William – 21, 35, 41-42, 203, 230, 325, 454, 565
Salazar, Francisco – 184
Salazar, Yginio – 52, 187, 196, 245, 552-553, 675
Sampson, Michael – 618-619, 625, 643
Sams, Dale – 427-428, 430
San Andres Mountains – 577, 696-697, 702
Sanches, Arley – 360
Sandia Laboratory – 293, 448
Sandoval, David – 379-380, 385, 713, 732, 743-744, 746
San Miguel County, New Mexico Territory – 7, 13, 15 45, 83, 133, 202, 205-206, 216-217, 261, 279, 370, 559, 653, 700
San Patricio massacre (See San Patricio)
San Patricio, New Mexico Territory – 26, 30, 36, 38, 64, 67-68, 107, 168-169, 198, 223, 239, 453, 547, 590, 602, 612; **massacre at:** 26, 38, 64, 168-169, 223, 298, 602, 612 (See George Peppin, John Kinney)
*Santa Fe Daily New Mexican* – 14, 83, 86, 204, 210, 330, 649, 679
Santa Fe jail – 46, 79-81, 178, 202, 230, 242, 244, 276, 392, 526, 529, 530, 551, 569
Santa Fe, New Mexico – 4, 15, 19, 81, 84-85, 116, 122, 124-125, 177-128, 131, 138-139, 154, 163, 173, 201, 206, 214, 127-128, 131, 138-139, 154, 163, 201, 206, 214, 127-128, 131, 138-139, 154, 163, 173, 201, 206, 214, 219, 234, 236, 261, 263, 292, 294, 316, 351, 394, 422, 446-448, 453-454, 457, 459, 461, 495, 548, 561, 606, 613, 622, 625-626, 638, 646, 653, 700, 710, 747

Santa Fe Ring (the Ring) – 3-4, 17, 19-21, 24, 26-27, 29-38, 40-46, 49-50, 52, 55, 57, 64, 68, 72-73, 86, 91, 132-133, 138-140, 142, 163-164, 168, 176, 197, 203, 216-217, 220-221, 223, 227-229, 237, 260, 273, 277, 282, 286-287, 297, 304, 350, 391, 440, 456, 464, 467, 520, 551, 586, 588, 590, 592-594, 598, 601-602, 604, 606, 610-614, 633, 677-678, 769

Sapatori, Joel – 430

Savona, Glen – 434

"Scapula Man" (See William Hudspeth, Laura Fulginiti)

Scholand, Emilie Fritz – 228

Scurlock, Josiah "Doc" – 37-38, 41, 46, 600, 610, 612, 627, 648, 766-768

Secret Service – 17, 21-22, 24, 44, 78, 175-176, 205, 223, 230, 243, 391, 394, 566, 609-611, 614-615, 618-620, 625, 629, 631-632, 634-635, 642-645, 647, 664 (See Azariah F. Wild, Wallace W. Hall, Arthur L. Drummond, Patrick D. Tyrrell)

*Secret Service Currency Reference Information: 1860's-1880's* – 615

Sederwall, Steven M. "Steve" – 288-292, 296-297, 300-303, 307, 314-318, 320-346, 349-372, 374-377, 380-381, 385, 388-390, 394-396, 398, 401-408, 411, 415, 417-418, 420-424, 426-430, 433-444, 466-470, 472-478, 480-516, 518-519, 523, 527, 536-538, 547-556, 560, 562-563, 566-567, 570-579, 583-666, 669-691, 693-707, 710-719, 744, 747, 764, 772-773; **alleged physical assault by:** 316-317, 535; **defamation of political rival by:** 317-318, 536 (See Debra Ingle); **as Mayor of Capitan:** 289, 292, 296, 314-317, 320-322, 390, 398, 422, 434, 468, 483, 490, 710; **"Mayor's Report" of:** 320-322; **commissioned Deputy for Case No. 2003-274 of:** 296, 301, 314, 398, 408, 423-424, 468, 472, 481, 514, 518; **Deputy commission card of:** 472, 481; **authorship of "Case 2003-274 Probable Cause Statement" claimed by:** 322-346, 394, 469, 536, 670; **listed as co-signer for unused "Seventy-Seven Days of Doubt Document" Case 2003-274 probable cause statement:** 323, 349-372; **exhumation petitions as a Deputy Sheriff for Catherine Antrim and William Bonney by:** 307-308, 374-377, 385, 744-746; **in History Channel "Investigating History: Billy the Kid":** 388-390; **in illegal exhumations of John Miller and William Hudspeth for Case 2003-274:** 426-430, 433-437, 536; **in Lincoln County Sheriff's Department Supplemental Report for Case 2003-274 exhumation of John Miller:** 429-430; **press photo holding Miller's (or Hudspeth's) skull of:** 300; **exposed in press for exhumations:** 433-435; **Piltdown Man-style hoax for John Miller by:** 435-439, 536; **exposed in forensic report of Laura Fulginiti:** 759-764 (See Laura Fulginiti); **criminal investigation for exhumations on:** 439-440; **Cannes Film Festival for "Requiem of Billy the Kid" with:** 301, 441; **BillytheKidCase.com website of:** 406, 519, 621; **OPEN RECORDS**

VIOLATION CASE AGAINST: 303, 420, 422, 467, 469-470, 472-477, 479, 485-513, 515-516, 518-519; with co-authoring of "The Dried Bean: You Believin' Us or Them Lyin' Whores for: 315, 480-484, 536; with co-authoring of "Memorandum: The Billy the Kid Investigation" for: 471, 484-498, 536 (faking Debra Komar Deposition in: 485, 487, 490-491); **lying about not being a Deputy for Case 2003-274 (hobbyist claim):** 466-467, 469-470, 472-477, 515, 519, 536; **forging Dr. Henry Lee reports for the Court by:** 472, 498-519, 536 (and repeated for *Cold Case Billy the Kid*: 702-704); **faking that a mixed DNA sample came from the carpenter's bench, when no DNA was extracted:** 419 (and repeated for *Cold Case Billy the Kid*: 702-703); **faking that a mixed sample costs $50,000 to separate:** 420, 474;

ADDITIONAL HOAXES BY: faking Billy the Kid's escape horse as Pat Garrett's by: 570-571; faking Dr. Lee's fake Deputy Bell killing forensics as for him: 571-572; faking Dr. Lee's fake washstand forensics as for him: 574-575, 704; faking Dr. Lee's fake headboard forensics as for him: 703-704; faking Dr. Lee's fake carpenter's bench forensics as for him: 701-703; faking claims of the "Billy the Kid Case's" John Miler exhumation and calling it his own investigation: 705-707; faking the block to the "Brushy Bill" exhumation by: 708; faking no outside door in Peter Maxwell's bedroom by: 534, 572-574, 684-691; faking history of the Teddy Bear (!) by: 576-577; faking investigation of John Tunstall's murder by: 586-591; faking Morton and Baker killing by: 592; faking Sheriff Brady killing by: 594-598; faking "Buckshot" Roberts killing by: 599 (with faking Roberts grave by: 600-601); faking Lincoln County War Battle by: 601-608; faking Billy the Kid as a counterfeiter by: 567, 609-644, 650-652 (with faked partnership with Jesse James by: ; with faking the Kid's murder of an informer by: 647-650; with faking the Kid's witness intimidation to hide counterfeiting by: 651-652; with faking the Kid's hiding counterfeit money in the Stinking Springs cabin by: 661-666); faking James Dolan as a counterfeiter by: 644-647; faking Pat Garrett as not a legitimate Deputy U.S. Marshal by: 653-656; faking discovery of "Billy the Kid" moniker by: 656; faking Tom O'Folliard's name as "Folliard" by: 547, 657-660; faking the fake "Billy the Kid Case" forensics of the Deputy Bell killing as his own investigation: 669-674; faking the fake "Billy the Kid Case" claim of Garrett as the escape accomplice as his own investigation: 674-677; faking death scene discrepancies by: 681, 693-695; faking a pseudo-Peter Maxwell by: 695-698; faking no Coroner's Jury Report

by: 699-700; **faking a conspiracy against himself by:** 710-718 (with repeat faking of Dr. Debra Komar's Deposition by: 690-691, 710, 714-716) (See "Billy the Kid Case" hoax, Cold Case Billy the Kid Megahoax)
Segura, Alejandro – 7-9, 11, 206, 257, 261, 331, 337-338, 344, 699
Segura, Melquiadez "Mel" – 160
Selman, John – 70, 195
Seven Rivers boys (rustlers) – 38, 48, 65, 194, 201, 602-604, 607
Seven Rivers, New Mexico Territory – 68-71, 162, 196, 236, 610
"Seven Rivers Warriors" – 604
Sexual Maturity Ratings – 262, 667, 693
Shen, Maxine – 405
Shenefield, Diane – 430
Shenefield, Jesse – 430
Sherman, John – 81, 202, 327, 455, 653-655
Sherman, Texas – 613-614, 626, 630, 636-638
Shetland Islands – 192-193
Shield, David – 606
Shield, Elizabeth – 606
Shield family – 605-606
Shipman, Jack – 658
Shipman, O.L. – 657
side of beef (on Maxwell porch) – 31, 189-190, 231, 247, 256, 258, 279, 555-556, 691 (See Maxwell house)
Sides, Hampton – 461
Silva, Jesus – 189, 247, 263, 332, 363-364, 527, 559, 695, 716
*Silver City Daily Press* – 315
*Silver City Independent* – 203
Silver City, New Mexico Territory – 19, 32-33, 69-70, 121, 153-154, 158-160, 193, 203, 227, 235-236, 252, 275, 286, 291, 293-295, 297, 305, 307-308, 310, 313-315, 371, 378-379, 383-384, 386, 392, 394, 401, 440, 446-447, 449, 485, 487-489, 491-493, 495-496, 525, 529, 537, 539-540, 544, 576, 712, 715, 728, 730, 733-734, 738-739, 741, 744
Simpson, Nicole – 405
Simpson, O.J. – 297, 405
Siringo, Charles "Charlie" – 114, 127, 162, 568; *History of Billy the Kid* **by:** 162
"slipping from shackles" (Billy the Kid myth) – 29, 148-149, 185, 200, 232, 249-250, 274, 538, 571-572, 668
"small hands" (of Billy the Kid myth) – 29, 119, 148-149, 274
Smith, Charles H. – 614, 618-620, 625
Smith, Gregory Scott – 689
Smith, Henry Street – 360
Smith, Sam – 623, 647-649, 651-652, 773; **as killed by Apaches:** 648-649
Smith, Wilbur – 196
Smylie, Vernon – 122
Snead, William – 308-309, 313, 726
Snow, Clyde – 253, 263, 535
Sonnichsen, Charles Leland – 91-92, 96-100, 128-224, 132-133, 136, 138, 140-141, 143-148, 151, 153, 161, 169, 174, 177-178, 183, 190, 193, 195-197, 201-207, 210-211, 215-218, 220-223, 225-226, 231-232, 235-237, 240-241, 244-247, 254, 256, 258-261, 265-268, 286, 298, 349, 523, 525, 527-528, 532, 535-537, 339-540, 542, 544, 548, 551-556, 559, 561-562, 564, 570-571, 573, 575, 578, 580, 583-585, 591-592, 609, 632, 677, 693, 700, 707, 709, 718; **background of:** 97-100; *Alias Billy the Kid* **by:** 91-92, 95-101, 104, 129-227, 232, 235-236, 238, 240-246, 248-250, 252-253, 258-260, 268, 285, 323, 347, 349, 361-362, 389-

390, 525, 527-533, 535, 537-562, 575, 578, 583, 592, 595, 598-599, 641, 660, 674, 693-695, 707, 718 (See Oliver Pleasant "Brushy Bill" Roberts, William V. Morrison)
South Spring River Ranch – 162, 188
Sparks, Allen – 319
Sparks, Billy – 288, 292, 392, 486, 492, 497, 711, 713-714, 747
Sparks, Nancy – 373
Spector, Phil – 406
Speer, Lucas – 497
Spencer, Edward W. (See William E. Brockway)
Spencerian handwriting – 32, 41, 249, 529, 598
Spitz, Werner – 406
Stallings, Diane – 315, 421-422
Star Route scandals – 650
Starr, Bell aka Myra Belle Shirley Reed – 93, 159
State Land Office, Santa Fe, New Mexico – 15
Statute of Limitations for murder in New Mexico Territory – 16, 148, 286, 291, 294-295, 321-322, 372
Staub, Rick – 300, 410, 428-432, 436-437, 444, 466, 474, 476-478, 484, 583, 747, 763
St. Aude, Melissa - 315
Steele, Joe – 373
Steiff Toy Company – 577
Stephanville, Texas – 444
Stewart, Frank – 47, 83, 180, 568, 771 (See William H. Bonney replevin case)
Stinking Springs – 25, 32, 46-47, 78, 82083, 126, 177, 180, 198, 222, 230, 244, 263, 265, 276, 326, 351, 392, 454-455, 543, 568, 623, 642, 650, 661-666
*St. Louis Globe-Democrat* – 204
Stockton, Ike – 597
Stolorow, Mark – 409-410, 419
Sullivan, Pat – 430

Sullivan, Thomas T. "Tom" – 288-292, 296, 300-303, 307, 314-316, 318, 320-324, 346-347, 349, 372, 375-378, 380-381, 385, 387-390, 392, 395, 398, 401, 406, 408-409, 411, 417-418, 421-426, 428, 430, 433-437, 440-443, 466-472, 474-477, 479-482, 484-486, 490-492, 494-499, 502-503, 668, 698, 709-710, 713-714, 735, 744, 747, 764; **fake Overton Affidavit "Probable Cause Statement" made to:** 347-348 (See "Billy the Kid Case" hoax)
Struckman, Robert – 425-427
Sunnyside, New Mexico – 49, 206, 260, 329, 332-333, 338, 679, 699
Taeger, Mary Nell – 186, 197
TalkLeft.com – 410, 432
Tascosa, Texas – 40, 54, 65, 177, 597-598, 640
Taylor, Daniel – 340
Taylor, Manuel – 196
Tecklenburg, Herman – 277-278, 280
Teddy Bear invention – 576-577
Telfer, Lois – 306, 378, 387, 492, 716, 725-726; **denied Billy the Kid exhumation petition of:** 725-726
Texas Ranger Museum (Hall of Fame) – 355
"The House" – 24, 34, 162, 164, 237, 451, 455, 528, 587, 590, 603, 646, 676
*The Albuquerque Citizen* – 697
*The Hollywood Reporter* – 442
*The Indianapolis Press* – 276, 642
*The New Mexico Folklore Record* – 161, 175, 180, 193
*The New Southwest* – 258, 262
Thievin' Vaqueros Ht Company – 317
Thomas, Andrew – 439
Thompson, George – 428
Thunderer (Colt .41) – 559
Tietjen, Emma – 280
Tietjen, Earnest – 280

TimeNewsFeed.com – 462
Tippett, Sherry – 292, 307-308, 310, 312-313, 378, 468, 475, 740
Totty, Frances E. – 345, 397
Traylor, Leslie – 184, 695, 717
Travis, Dewitt – 130, 200-201, 533; **Affidavit for "Brushy Bill" of:** 200-201
Trinidad, Colorado – 154
*True West* magazine – 134, 252, 266, 296, 299, 318, 373, 389-390, 393, 396, 573, 621, 631, 647, 649-650, 691, 696
Trujillo, Francisco – 400, 595
Truman, Harry S. – 97, 224, 285; **duped letter to William V. Morrison by:** 224
Tucson, Arizona – 98
*Tucson Weekly* – 407-408, 430, 432, 436
Tularosa Ditch War – 184, 571, 676
Tularosa, New Mexico Territory – 622, 645-646
Tunnell, Dale – 296, 300, 425-431, 433-434, 436-440, 583, 747, 761, 764
Tunstall, John Henry – 20, 24-26, 33-37, 41, 47, 50-53, 58, 60-63, 138-139, 162-165, 167, 185, 197, 227-229, 237-238, 272, 275, 350-351, 359, 367, 391, 449-451, 455, 545, 547, 586-589, 592-593, 596, 610, 611, 626, 662, 674, 676-677, 696; **Lincoln store (building) of:** 24, 35-36, 42, 72-73, 75-76, 165, 167, 171, 237, 544, 586, 595, 602, 607, 677; **Feliz River Ranch of:** – 35, 52, 165, 197, 229, 236, 544-545, 676; **murder of:** 20, 24-25, 39-40, 42, 48, 50, 52, 58-60, 142, 150, 165-167, 171, 197, 229, 237-239, 275, 324, 351, 391, 451, 564-565, 586-587, **funeral of:** 165-166, 238, 545; **hoaxers' autopsy of:** 587; **Daniel Appel autopsy report to Frank Warner Angel of:** 587-588, 765; **Coroner's Jury Report of:** 588-589
Tunstall, John Partridge – 26
Tunstill, William A. – 95, 155, 158, 226, 233-235, 248, 525, 530-531, 540-541; *Billy the Kid and Me Were the Same* **by:** 226, 233, 525, 530, 540
Turk, David S. – 296, 302, 318, 320, 322, 326, 345, 349, 391-402, 407-408, 417, 421, 479, 484, 499, 502, 506, 571, 575, 585, 587, 607; **input for "Probable Cause Statement by:** 326, 345; **"The U.S. Marshals Service and Billy the Kid" by:** 391-392, 397-401; **vouching for Dr. Henry Lee by:** 407; **fake authentication of carpenter's bench by:** 402, 404, 619; **fake authentication of counterfeit bill by:** 618-619, 622 (See "Billy the Kid Case" hoax, counterfeiting-rustling hoax)
Turner, Marion F. – 70, 194, 201
Tyrrell, Patrick D. – 641
University of Texas at El Paso, College of Mines and Metallurgy – 96, 98
Upson, Ashmun "Ash" – 44, 127, 153, 166, 325, 370, 489
Utley, Robert M. – 19, 325, 393, 476, 489, 595, 710; *Billy the Kid: A Short and Violent Life*: 19, 489; **exposing Paul Hutton as "Billy the Kid Case" official historian by:** 393
Valdez, Jannay P. – 288, 290-291, 441, 444, 718, 747
*Variety* magazine – 442
Villa, Pancho – 93, 97, 192, 444
Virden, Rick E. – 296, 300-303, 314, 320, 396, 421, 423-425, 429-430, 443-444, 466-471, 474, 476-482, 484-485, 500-501, 514-519, 584, 621, 747; **alleged**

theft of railroad ties by: 320; deputizing Tom Sullivan and Steve Sederwall by: 301, 424, 474-476, 514, 518, 710; **exhumations of John Miller/William Hudspeth under:** 300, 314, 423-425, 429-430; **attempted exhumation of "Brushy Bill" Roberts by:** 314, 443-444; **open records violation case against:** 302-303, 320, 396, 421, 466, 476-482, 484-485, 500-501, 514-519 (See "Billy the Kid Case" hoax)

Waggoner, Tom – 195

Waite, Fred Tecumseh – 33, 37, 46, 53, 59-60, 62-63, 150, 165, 167, 194, 229, 239, 450, 545, 564, 586, 600, 766-768

Waldo, Henry – 42

Walker, Charlie – 359

Walker, Dale L. – 97, 99, 115, 140, 294, 584; *C.L. Sonnichsen: Grassroots Historian* by: 97, 140; *Legends and Lies: Great Mysteries of the American West* by: 99, 115, 294, 584

Wallace, Lew – 4, 9, 14, 18, 20-21, 26, 32, 40-42, 45-46, 51, 57, 65-68, 71-72, 77, 78-81, 87, 100, 105-114, 118, 126, 147, 149-153, 169-169, 172-173, 177, 188-189, 197, 202-203, 206, 208, 211-212, 214, 216-217, 222-223, 230, 232, 240, 243, 251, 259, 273, 276, 288-289, 293-294, 303, 326, 380, 382, 391, 445-446, 448, 451-452, 456459, 462, 529, 568-569, 594, 610, 613, 620, 627, 642, 648, 656, 694, 737; **Amnesty Proclamation of:** 40, 66, 222, 391, 451; **pardon bargain with Billy Bonney of:** 4, 18, 21, 25, 41, 46, 51, 57, 67, 72, 77, 81, 113, 147, 149, 153, 168, 172, 175, 197, 203, 223, 230, 241, 275, 529, 549, 551, 627

Wallace, Lew Jr. – 18, 65, 107-108, 110-114, 457, 530, 598

Wallace, William N. – 303, 457-459, 461, 463

Walz, Edgar – 26, 44, 54, 64, 140, 598, 602, 611-612, 648, 651-652

Walz, Kent – 296

*Washington Post* – 577

*Washington Times* – 55, 463

washstand (See "Billy the Kid Case" hoax, Cold Case Billy the Kid megahoax, Henry Lee fake forensics on, Steve Sederwall forgery of forensic report on)

Waters, William – 104, 134, 285, 532

Watson, Kathryn – 463

Weddle, Jerry (Richard) – 19, 158, 402, 537, 585; *Antrim is my Stepfather's Name* by: 19, 158, 537, 585; **consultation on carpenter's bench by:** 402

West, William H. aka William Budd – 643-644, 651

"We the People" radio – 101-102

Whipple, Arizona Veterans' Hospital – 196

White, J.D. – 689

Whitehill, Harvey – 33, 544

White Oaks livery – 40, 44-45, 567, 610, 628, 651

White Oaks, New Mexico – 47, 49, 88, 127, 368, 550, 566, 611, 613-614, 606, 625, 628, 638, 643-644, 646, 648-649, 671, 676

White Oaks posse – 45, 48, 78, 175, 230, 243

"White Oaks Rangers" – 771

Widenmann, Robert – 53, 58, 60-63, 450

Wilcox-Brazil Ranch – 661

Wilcox, Lucius "Lute" – 83, 533, 623, 650

Wild, Azariah F. – 22-24, 44-48, 175, 327, 369, 394, 397, 399, 611, 613-614, 617, 619, 622-623, 625, 627-630, 636-638, 641-642, 651-656, 658, 664, 773; **Sherman, Texas, investigation of Brockway bill distributors by:** 613-614,

626, 630, 636-638; **Barney Mason as spy in New Mexico counterfeit-cattle deal for:** 617, 627-628; **pardon bargain for Billy the Kid by:** 45, 647-648; **appointment Pat Garrett as Deputy U.S. Marshal by:** 653-656; **hoaxers' fake link to Jesse James as counterfeiter of:** 641-642

*Wild World Magazine* – 332

Wilkes-Barre, Pennsylvania – 459

Will Dowlin & Company – 645-646

William Henry Smith Memorial Library – 105, 110

Williams, Darryl Gene – 316

Wilson & Kid Gang – 612, 619, 658

Wilson, Gorgonio – 675

Wilson, John B. "Squire" – 39, 41, 59, 63, 173, 229, 452-453, 530, 545, 569, 588, 591, 596

Wilson, William "Billy" – 44-46, 83, 86, 567, 610, 612, 620, 622-623, 629, 643-644, 651-652, 769, 774

Winchester '73 carbine – 36-37, 58-59, 85, 150, 166-167, 239, 392, 545

Wood, Miles – 350

Woodman, Oran Ardious "Uncle Kit Carson, Father of Billy the Kid" – 93, 103, 141

Wortley Hotel – 47, 75, 321, 352-353

Yaqui Indians – 122, 191

Yavapi County, Arizona – 430, 433-434, 439, 762, 764

Yerby Ranch – 79, 189, 245, 247, 363, 567, 610, 627

Yerby, Thomas – 189, 567, 610

"Young Guns II" (See John Fusco)

Zamora, Francisco – 38-39, 41, 72-73, 608, 613

Zimitski, Wayne – 316

Zuber, Hugo – 79, 610

Zumwalt, Ross – 306, 308, 310, 386; **Affidavit of:** 309-310, 386, 727-729

www.ingramcontent.com/pod-product-compliance
Lightning Source LLC
Chambersburg PA
CBHW060356230426

43663CB00008B/1290